# A Shakespearean Genealogy

This chart reflects Shakespeare's history plays and is thus not historically accurate. Many descendants of Henry II and Edward III are omitted. On occasion, Shakespeare combined or simply invented historical figures. These deviations from fact are explained in the notes.

In the chart, the names of Kings and Queens are printed in capitals, and the dates of their reigns are printed in bold. The names of characters appearing in the plays are underlined.

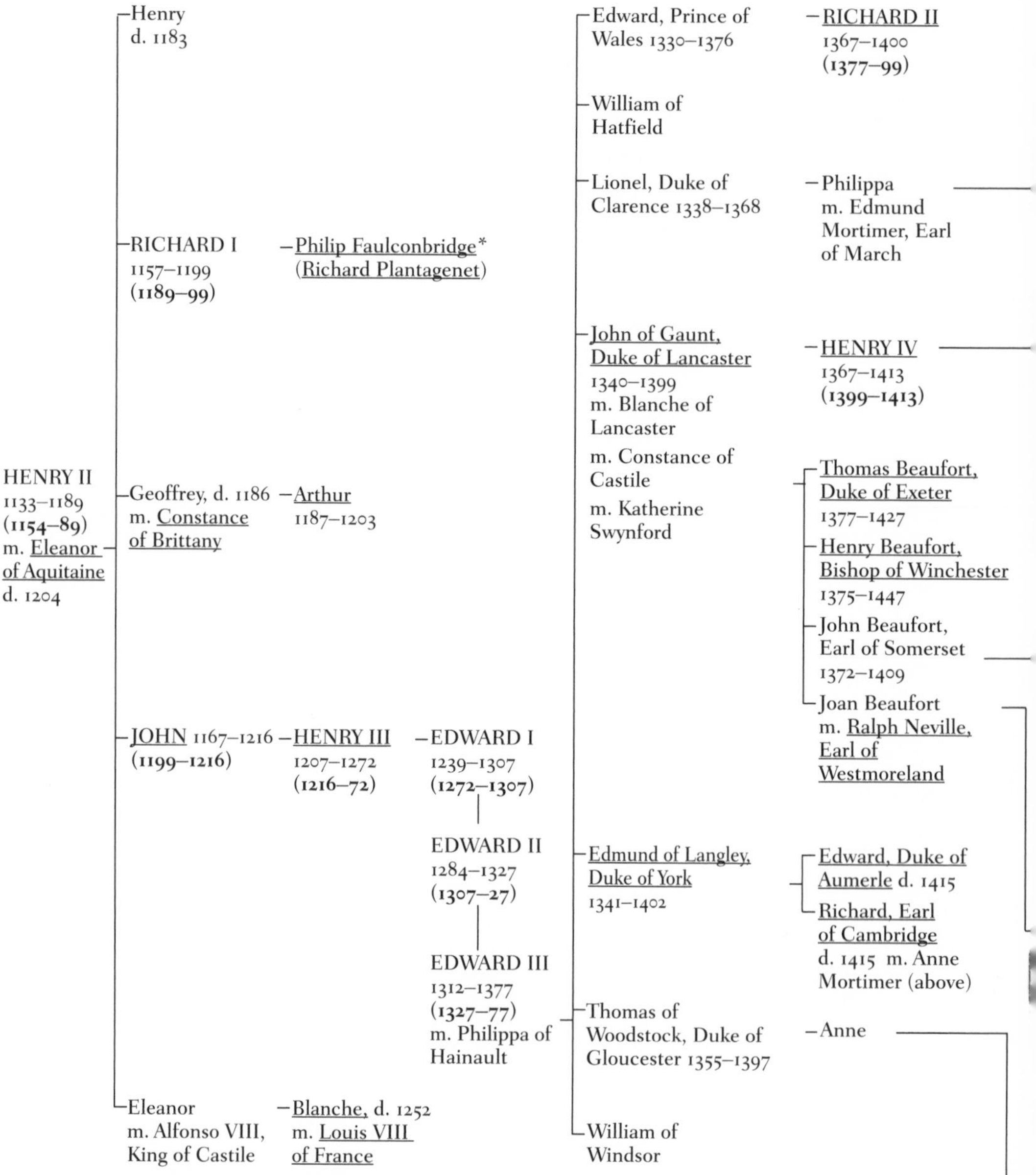


*Philip Faulconbridge, the bastard son of Richard I, had no historical existence. Such a character appears in the play *The Life and Death of King John* and is referred to in passing in Holinshed's *Chronicles*.

† In the character of Edmund Mortimer, Shakespeare combines two historical figures. The Edmund Mortimer who married Catrin, daughter of Owain Glyndŵr, was the grandson of Lionel, Duke of Clarence, and the younger brother of Roger, Earl of March. He died in 1409. Shakespeare combines him with his nephew, the Edmund Mortimer recognized by Richard II as his heir (d. 1424). This second Edmund was the brother of Anne Mortimer and the uncle of Richard Plantagenet.

‡ The character of the Duke of Somerset combines Henry Beaufort with his younger brother Edmund (d. 1471), who succeeded him as Duke.

Elizabeth Mortimer ("Kate") m. Henry Percy ("Hotspur") 1364–1403

Edmund Mortimer†

Anne Mortimer m. Richard, Earl of Cambridge (below)

HENRY V 1387–1422 (1413–22) m. Catherine 1401–1437

Thomas, Duke of Clarence d. 1421

John of Lancaster, Duke of Bedford 1389–1435

Humphrey, Duke of Gloucester 1391–1447 m. Eleanor Cobham d. 1454

John Beaufort, Duke of Somerset 1403–1444

Edmund Beaufort, Duke of Somerset 1406–1455

Richard Neville, Earl of Salisbury 1400–1460

Cicely Neville m. Richard Plantagenet, Duke of York (above)

Humphrey, Duke of Buckingham 1402–1460

---

Henry, Earl of Northumberland 1394–1455

Richard Plantagenet, Duke of York 1411–1460 m. Cicely Neville (below)

HENRY VI 1421–1471 (1422–61) m. Margaret of Anjou d. 1482

Margaret Beaufort m. Edmund Tudor, Earl of Richmond

Henry Beaufort, Duke of Somerset 1436–1464‡

Richard Neville, Earl of Warwick 1428–1471

John Neville, Marquess of Montague d. 1471

Humphrey Stafford d. 1455

---

EDWARD IV 1442–1483 (1461–83) m. Elizabeth Woodville d. 1492

Edmund, Earl of Rutland 1443–1460

George, Duke of Clarence 1449–1478 m. Isabel Neville (below)

RICHARD III 1452–1485 (1483–85) m. Anne Neville (below)

Edward, Prince of Wales 1453–1471 m. Anne Neville (below)

HENRY VII 1457–1509 (1485–1509) m. Elizabeth of York (above)

Isabel Neville d. 1476 m. George, Duke of Clarence (above)

Anne Neville d. 1485 m. Edward, Prince of Wales (above) m. RICHARD III (above)

Henry, Duke of Buckingham 1454?–1483

---

EDWARD V 1470–1483 (1483)

Richard, Duke of York 1472–1483

Elizabeth of York 1465–1503 m. HENRY VII (below)

Edward, Prince of Wales

Arthur m. Catherine of Aragon (below)

Margaret m. James IV of Scotland

HENRY VIII 1491–1547 (1509–47) m. Catherine of Aragon m. Anne Boleyn m. Jane Seymour m. Anne of Cleves m. Katherine Howard m. Katherine Parr

Mary m. Charles Brandon

Edward, Duke of Buckingham 1478–1521

---

James V of Scotland

Mary, Queen of Scots

JAMES I 1566–1625 (1603–25)

MARY I 1516–1558 (1553–58) m. Philip of Spain

ELIZABETH I 1533–1603 (1558–1603)

EDWARD VI 1537–1553 (1547–53)

Frances

Jane Grey 1537–1554

# The Kings and Queens of England

## 1377–1625

Richard II, 1377–99 Richard was the eldest son of Edward the Black Prince, himself the eldest son of King Edward III, who ruled England from 1327 to 1377. When the Black Prince died in battle in France in 1376, Richard became the legitimate heir to the throne. He ruled from Edward's death in 1377 until he was deposed in 1399 by Henry Bolingbroke, the eldest son of John of Gaunt, Duke of Lancaster. Because he was the fourth son of Edward III, Gaunt and his Lancastrian descendants had weaker hereditary claims to the throne than did Richard. When deposed, Richard had no children to succeed him, but he recognized Edmund Mortimer, Fifth Earl of March, as his heir presumptive. This Mortimer was descended from Lionel, Duke of Clarence, the third son of Edward III, and therefore also had stronger hereditary claims to the throne than did Bolingbroke. Shakespeare combined this Mortimer with his uncle Edmund Mortimer, who married Owain Glyndŵr's daughter.

Henry IV, 1399–1413 Henry Bolingbroke, eldest son of John of Gaunt, seized the throne from Richard II in 1399. When Henry died in 1413, he was succeeded by his eldest son, Prince Hal, who became Henry V.

Henry V, 1413–22 Henry V became king in 1413 and reigned until his death in 1422. He was succeeded by his son, Henry VI.

Henry VI, 1422–61 Henry VI was less than one year old when he succeeded his father, Henry V. In the young king's minority, his uncle Humphrey, Duke of Gloucester, was named Lord Protector, and the kingdom was ruled by an aristocratic council. Henry VI assumed personal authority in 1437. He was deposed in 1461 by his third cousin, who was crowned Edward IV. Henry was murdered in 1471.

Edward IV, 1461–83 Edward, the eldest son of Richard, Duke of York, seized the throne from Henry VI in 1461. His Yorkist claim to the throne derived from his grandmother, Anne Mortimer, who was descended from Lionel, third son of Edward III, and was sister to that Edmund Mortimer recognized by Richard II as his heir presumptive; Edward IV's grandfather, Richard, Earl of Cambridge, was the son of Edmund of Langley, fifth son of Edward III. Edward IV reigned until his death in 1483. His heir was his eldest son (Edward), but the throne was usurped by his brother Richard, Duke of Gloucester.

Richard III, 1483–85 Richard III was the youngeer brother of Edward IV. After the death of Edward IV in 1483, Richard prevented the coronation of Edward V with a claim of illegitimacy and succeeded to the throne himself. Edward and his younger brother, Richard, Duke of York, were murdered in the Tower of London. Richard III was killed at the Battle of Bosworth Field in 1485, and the kingdom fell to the victor, Henry Tudor, Earl of Richmond.

Henry VII, 1485–1509 Henry Tudor seized the throne from Richard III in 1485. He was descended from John of Gaunt by John's third marriage, with Catherine Swynford. He married Elizabeth, daughter of Edward IV, uniting the houses of Lancaster and York. He died in 1509 and was succeeded by his son, Henry VIII.

Henry VIII, 1509–47 Henry was the second son of Henry VII. His older brother, Arthur, died in 1502. Henry VIII's first wife was Catherine of Aragon, who bore his daughter Mary. His second wife, Anne Boleyn, was the mother of Elizabeth. His third wife, Jane Seymour, bore him a son, who succeeded to the throne as Edward VI after Henry VIII died in 1547.

Edward VI, 1547–53 Edward VI was nine years old when he became king. From 1547 to 1549, the realm was governed by a Lord Protector, the Duke of Somerset; power then passed to John Dudley, Duke of Northumberland. When Edward VI died in 1553, Northumberland attempted unsuccessfully to prevent the succession of Mary Tudor by installing as queen his daughter-in-law, Lady Jane Grey, a great-granddaughter of Henry VII.

Mary I, 1553–58 Mary, daughter of Henry VIII and his first wife, Catherine of Aragon, came to the throne in 1553. She married King Philip of Spain but died childless. She was succeeded by her half sister, Elizabeth.

Elizabeth I, 1558–1603 Elizabeth, the daughter of Henry VIII and his second wife, Anne Boleyn, became queen after the death of her half sister, Mary, in 1558. She ruled until her death in 1603. She was succeeded by her cousin James.

James I, 1603–1625 James VI of Scotland became James I of England in 1603. His claim to the throne of England derived from his great-grandmother, Margaret Tudor, a daughter of Henry VII who married James IV of Scotland. James ruled England and Scotland until his death in 1625; he was succeeded by his son, Charles I.

# THE NORTON SHAKESPEARE

THIRD EDITION

*Romances and Poems*

## TEXTUAL EDITORS

**DAVID M. BERGERON,** University of Kansas, *The Winter's Tale*

**PATRICK CHENEY,** Pennsylvania State University, *Venus and Adonis, The Rape of Lucrece, The Passionate Pilgrim, The Phoenix and Turtle,* and *Attributed Poems*

**HANNAH CRAWFORTH,** King's College London, *The Two Noble Kinsmen*

**LYNNE MAGNUSSON,** University of Toronto, *The Sonnets* and *A Lover's Complaint*

**LOIS POTTER,** University of Delaware, *Pericles*

**WILLIAM H. SHERMAN,** University of York, *The Tempest*

**ANN THOMPSON,** King's College London, *Cymbeline*

---

*The Theater of Shakespeare's Time,* **HOLGER SCHOTT SYME,** University of Toronto

*Performance Notes,* **BRETT GAMBOA,** Dartmouth College

# THE NORTON SHAKESPEARE

## THIRD EDITION

*Romances and Poems*

Stephen Greenblatt, *General Editor*
HARVARD UNIVERSITY

Walter Cohen
UNIVERSITY OF MICHIGAN

Suzanne Gossett, *General Textual Editor*
LOYOLA UNIVERSITY CHICAGO (EMERITA)

Jean E. Howard
COLUMBIA UNIVERSITY

Katharine Eisaman Maus
UNIVERSITY OF VIRGINIA

Gordon McMullan, *General Textual Editor*
KING'S COLLEGE LONDON

W · W · NORTON & COMPANY · NEW YORK · LONDON

W. W. Norton & Company has been independent since its founding in 1923, when William Warder Norton and Mary D. Herter Norton first published lectures delivered at the People's Institute, the adult education division of New York City's Cooper Union. The firm soon expanded its program beyond the Institute, publishing books by celebrated academics from America and abroad. By mid-century, the two major pillars of Norton's publishing program—trade books and college texts—were firmly established. In the 1950s, the Norton family transferred control of the company to its employees, and today—with a staff of 400 and a comparable number of trade, college, and professional titles published each year—W. W. Norton & Company stands as the largest and oldest publishing house owned wholly by its employees.


Printed in the United States of America.

*Editor:* Julia Reidhead
*Managing Editor, College:* Marian Johnson
*Associate Editor:* Emily Stuart
*Manuscript Editors:* Harry Haskell, Alice Vigliani
*Media Editor:* Carly Fraser Doria
*Media Project Editor:* Kristin Sheerin
*Production Manager:* Eric Pier-Hocking
*Digital Production:* Mateus Texeira, Colleen Caffrey
*Marketing Manager, Literature:* Kim Bowers
*Photo Editor:* Trish Marx
*Composition:* Westchester Book Company
*Manufacturing:* RR Donnelley

**The Library of Congress has catalogued the full edition as follows:**
Shakespeare, William, 1564–1616.
The Norton Shakespeare / Stephen Greenblatt, General Editor, Harvard University; Walter Cohen, University of Michigan; Suzanne Gossett, General Textual Editor, Loyola University Chicago (Emerita); Jean E. Howard, Columbia University; Katharine Eisaman Maus, University of Virginia; Gordon McMullan, General Textual Editor, King's College London.—Third edition.
pages cm
Includes bibliographical references and index.
**ISBN 978-0-393-93499-1 (hardcover)**
I. Greenblatt, Stephen, 1943– editor. II. Cohen, Walter, 1949– editor. III. Gossett, Suzanne, editor. IV. Howard, Jean E. (Jean Elizabeth), 1948– editor. V. Maus, Katharine Eisaman, 1955– editor. VI. McMullan, Gordon, 1962– editor. VII. Title.
PR2754.G74 2015
822.3'3—dc23

2015018869

**This edition: ISBN 978-0-393-93862-3**

W. W. Norton & Company, Inc., 500 Fifth Avenue, New York, NY 10110-0017
wwnorton.com

W. W. Norton & Company Ltd., Castle House, 75/76 Wells Street, London W1T 3QT

# Contents

Additional works, media, contextual materials, and bibliographies are available in the Digital Edition

## Appendices

# Illustrations

# Preface

This Third Edition of *The Norton Shakespeare* is both a continuation and a new beginning. Readers who have already found the format of the printed book and its editorial apparatus to their liking will get what they are looking for. The emphasis continues to be on the pleasure of reading, with a particular attention to undergraduates who may be encountering Shakespeare for the first time. "If then you do not like him," wrote Shakespeare's first editors almost four hundred years ago, "surely you are in some manifest danger not to understand him." We have from the start made every effort, through the glosses, notes, introductions, and other materials, to facilitate understanding and hence to enhance liking. We are careful not to overburden Shakespeare's words with explication or to crowd the page with distracting commentary. The clear, uncluttered, single-column format is designed to encourage absorption. But we try to offer enough help to allow the beauty and the luminous intelligence of these stupendous works to shine.

We have in this edition carefully revised each of our introductions (including the long General Introduction) and reviewed every one of our notes and glosses, altering and adding where appropriate. Our goal has been to hold onto what our readers have told us works well, but also to update the introductions, bibliographies, filmographies, and other materials to reflect current scholarship, shifting emphases, and newly released films. An entirely new feature of this edition is an illuminating Performance Note, by Brett Gamboa (Dartmouth College), that accompanies each of the plays. These notes describe the particular and recurrent theatrical challenges with which actors and directors have grappled in mounting any given work. The strategies devised over the centuries in response to these challenges are a fascinating point of entry into critical issues of interpretation. The notes are also an invaluable guide to what audiences should look for when they attend a new production.

From its inception, *The Norton Shakespeare* has paid exceptionally close attention to the accuracy as well as the accessibility of the texts and, in particular, to the challenge posed by those plays that exist in multiple substantive versions. For the Third Edition, all of Shakespeare's plays and poems have been newly edited, from scratch, by an international team of leading textual scholars. This hugely ambitious and complex undertaking has been based on the principle of single-text editing—that is, where more than one early authoritative text of a given play has survived, rather than merging them into one (as has been traditionally done), we have edited each text in its own right. We thereby offer the reader texts as close as possible to the original versions as read by Shakespeare's contemporaries. A lively and accessible new General Textual Introduction fully articulates this principle, explores the nature of the documents that have come down to us from Shakespeare's own time, and explains in detail the editorial practices on which this new text of the complete works is meticulously based.

Approximately half of Shakespeare's plays appeared both in small-format versions (quartos), printed in the playwright's own lifetime, and in the large-format First Folio (1623), published seven years after his death. As early as the eighteenth century, careful readers began to notice that there were differences, sometimes minor and sometimes quite significant, between these printings of the same plays. Starting with the landmark Shakespeare editions of Alexander Pope (1723) and Lewis Theobald (1733), editors initiated the practice of blending the different versions together, picking and choosing as their taste dictated or as they imagined that Shakespeare would have done, had he himself produced a definitive text. Hence, for example, the two distinct texts of *King Lear* were routinely fashioned into a single text, with editors combining lines that appear only in one or the other early version and choosing among hundreds of variant readings.

From its inception, *The Norton Shakespeare* rejected this editorial method (known as "conflation"). We have continued in the current print edition our hallmark practice of offering, on facing pages, the 1608 Quarto text of *King Lear* and the substantial revision of the play as printed in the First Folio (1623). While each version may be read independently—we have provided glosses and footnotes for each—the significant points of difference between the two are immediately apparent and available for comparison. It is thus possible to watch in extraordinarily sharp focus changes in the early modern text of one of Shakespeare's greatest plays. We recognize at the same time that a combined text, in one form or another, has long served as the *King Lear* upon which innumerable performances of the play have been based and on which a huge body of literary criticism has been written. Hence in addition to providing the Quarto and Folio texts, we wanted to offer readers a version of this great tragedy that combines the two without entirely erasing their differences. The solution that we provide in these pages is what in the first two editions of *The Norton Shakespeare* we used in the comparable case of *Hamlet*. We print the Folio text of *King Lear*, but we have moved the lines that are solely in the Quarto into the body of the play. In doing so, however, we did not want simply to produce a conflated version. We have therefore indented the Q-only passages, printed them in a slightly different typeface, and numbered them in such a way as to make clear their provenance. We call this a "scars-and-stitches" solution, since, though still eminently readable and enjoyable, it clearly marks the points of insertion and difference.

*The Norton Shakespeare*, then, includes three separate texts of *King Lear*. The reader can compare them, analyze the role of editors in constructing the texts we now call Shakespeare's, explore in detail the kinds of decisions that playwrights, editors, and printers make and remake, witness firsthand the historical transformation of what might at first glance seem fixed and unchanging. We offer extraordinary access to this supremely brilliant, difficult, compelling play.

*Hamlet*, the other great tragedy at the very center of Shakespeare's achievement, similarly exists in multiple versions: the 1604 Second Quarto (Q2), the longest of the early editions; the 1623 Folio text (F), which lacks some 200 lines found in Q2 but includes more than 70 lines not found there; and, casting a fascinating light on the more familiar version of the tragedy, the drastically different First Quarto (Q1, the so-called Bad Quarto). As in the case of *Lear*, editors for centuries have routinely conflated the Q2 and F *Hamlets*.

The realities of bookbinding—not to mention our recognition of the limited time in the typical undergraduate syllabus—preclude our offering in the print edition four *Hamlets* (Q1, Q2, F, and combined) to parallel the three *Lears*. What we have provided in these pages instead is a new incarnation of the solution we came up with in the first two editions of *The Norton Shakespeare*. While basing our *Hamlet* on the Q2 text, we have moved the Folio passages, among which are some of the tragedy's most famous lines, into the body of the play. But, as with the "scars-and-stitches" *Lear*, we have made it possible for readers who are interested to see what has been added.

The growing interest in the possibility of teaching the First Quarto of *Hamlet* has also led us to add that strange text, in fully glossed and annotated form, alongside the more familiar version of Shakespeare's most famous tragedy. Readers can wonder at a *Hamlet* in which the hero muses "To be, or not to be—ay, there's the point," and they can see how drastically one theater troupe in Shakespeare's own time probably cut the play for performance.

These and other changes all serve to keep *The Norton Shakespeare* fresh and current. But this Third Edition, as I have already suggested, is much more than a careful revision and updating. It is a thoroughgoing rethinking both of the entire Shakespeare corpus and of the whole way in which Shakespeare is experienced by contemporary readers. For the purposes of this preface, a single feature of the newly edited text should be emphasized: it was created not only for the print edition, but also for a new and exciting Digital Edition. From its inception the print edition featured both the Quarto and the Folio texts of *King Lear,* and we have now added the First Quarto of *Hamlet.* Our Digital Edition makes available fully glossed and annotated Quarto and Folio versions of the plays—fifteen in all—for which more than one early authoritative text exists, thereby offering the reader access to these plays as they were first experienced by Shakespeare's contemporaries. This means not only the two versions of *Lear,* which can be viewed in side-by-side scrolling format for comparison as well as individually, and not only the three versions of *Hamlet.* It also means multiple versions, with fascinating variants, of such beloved, centrally important plays as *Romeo and Juliet, Othello, Richard II, Richard III, Henry V, Love's Labor's Lost,* and *A Midsummer Night's Dream.* There are Quarto and Folio versions as well of 2 and 3 *Henry VI, Titus Andronicus,* 2 *Henry IV, The Merry Wives of Windsor,* and *Troilus and Cressida.* The Digital Edition also offers an appendix of selected scenes from a number of multiple-version plays, presented side-by-side so that they can easily be compared for teaching purposes. For anyone interested in Shakespeare's practices of composition and revision and in the fascinating process through which his plays, passing through the printing house, have managed to reach us, the digital *Norton Shakespeare* is an unprecedented resource.

Links to the widely respected *Norton Facsimile of the First Folio of Shakespeare,* edited by Charlton Hinman, and to quarto facsimile pages make it possible for readers to see for themselves the original materials with which the editors have been working to create this new text of the complete works.

In the digital *Norton Shakespeare* we also include for the first time an edition of the full text of *Sir Thomas More,* a multi-authored play, unpublished in the period, whose manuscript includes a section in Shakespeare's own hand, the only surviving one of its kind. We also include an edition of *Edward III,* another play of which Shakespeare appears to have been part-author. Both texts are interesting as examples of the collaborative nature of much Elizabethan and Jacobean theater, a collaboration reflected as well in the late plays *Pericles, Henry VIII, The Two Noble Kinsmen,* the lost *Cardenio,* and—more debatably—such works as *1 Henry VI, Titus Andronicus,* and *Timon of Athens.*

This extraordinary wealth of texts, all complete with introductions, notes, and glosses, has been made possible by the vastness of the digital space. That space has allowed us to supplement the useful aids in the print edition—including maps, genealogies, a glossary, a short bibliography, a timeline, and a selection of key documents—with further resources. For the Digital Edition, the volume editors have created expanded bibliographies for the study of Shakespeare's works, and Misha Teramura (Harvard University), who edited and glossed the documents in the print text, has assembled and edited a larger archive of Tudor and Stuart documents relevant to Shakespeare and his theater world.

The remarkable expansion of texts is only the beginning. The resources of the Digital Edition have made possible innovations that were, until very recently, only a teacher's idle daydreams. Shakespeare scholars have long understood that the decisions editors make—for example, choosing one variant over another, or adding stage directions, or making consistent the multiple speech prefixes often used for a single character—can affect the meaning of the plays. But on the printed page it has been difficult to call attention to the significance of these decisions without interrupting the flow of the reading experience, while the long lists of textual variants printed at the ends of plays are so much raw data, rarely consulted or understood by anyone but experts. Now, by clicking a marginal icon, readers can summon illuminating Textual Comments for each play, written by the textual editor, that focus on textual-editing decision points influencing interpretation. It is possible for all interested readers now to understand textual cruxes and to see—and, for that matter, to call into question—key editorial choices.

Similarly, a crucially important dimension of Shakespeare's texts, as everyone grasps, is that they were originally intended for performance. Hence the brief discussion in the General Introduction of the theatrical scene Shakespeare encountered and helped to transform is now greatly enriched in "The Theater of Shakespeare's Time," a lively and original essay by Holger Schott Syme (University of Toronto). Syme conjures up a fiercely competitive world of multiple theater companies and rival venues, all scrambling for plays that will survive the attention of the government censor and lure crowds of spectators to part with their pennies.

Performance is obviously not only a matter of historical interest. It remains, for most of us and certainly for our students, central to the full experience of the plays. But, without overfreighting the page, it has been difficult to highlight this dimension in the printed book. Descriptions of famous performances, from Garrick to the present, rarely capture the significance of key interpretive choices by actors or directors. Now clicking on marginal icons keyed to particular moments in the texts allows one to read incisive and insightful Performance Comments that supplement the Performance Note preceding each play. These comments, by Brett Gamboa, highlight passages that are particularly famous challenges in performance and explore how a director or actor's interpretive choices affect meaning. Taken individually, the Performance Comments call attention to specific decisions that must be made in the realization of a play; taken together, they constitute a brilliant exploration of the performative dimensions of Shakespeare's art.

The performative dimension is enhanced by two further features of the Digital Edition. First, there are recordings of all of the songs—66 of them—in the plays, from the award-winning *Shakespeare's Songbook* audio companion by Ross Duffin. It is now possible for readers to take in fully the pervasive presence of music in Shakespeare's plays, something that the printed stage direction "*Music*" cannot hope to do. Second, there are over eight hours of spoken-word audio of key passages and scenes and those that pose particular challenges to readers. These have been specially recorded for the Digital Edition by the highly regarded company, Actors from the London Stage. With a simple click it is now possible for readers to hear the words on the page come alive in the voices of gifted actors.

The digital *Norton Shakespeare* brings together in one place an unparalleled array of resources for understanding and enjoying Shakespeare. These resources are not the primitive accumulation of materials, of dubious utility or reliability, which often makes the web an untrustworthy guide. Rather, each of the texts and other material has received the same careful scholarly and pedagogical attention that has made the print edition a success. But we are aware that different readers will have different interests and needs, often varying from time to time. The reading experience of the Digital Edition, including the visibility of icons, line numbers, glosses, and notes, can be easily customized, so that with a click readers can either "quiet" the page or access Norton's abundant reading help. The Digital Edition platform provides customizable highlighting, annotating, and comment-sharing tools that facilitate active reading.

The publisher also provides instructors with a wealth of free resources beyond the Digital Edition. An Instructor Resource Disc created for the new edition features the more than eight hours of spoken-word audio recorded by Actors from the London Stage, 150 songs, and over 100 images from the book in both JPEG and PowerPoint for easy classroom presentation. The images are available for download on the publisher's instructor resource page, wwnorton.com/instructors. In addition, the Norton Shakespeare YouTube channel brings together a carefully curated and regularly updated collection of the best of the web's Shakespeare video resources, allowing instructors to easily show clips from stage and film in class.

The extraordinary labor of love that has led to this new and revised edition of *The Norton Shakespeare* has involved a large number of collaborators. The volume editors owe a substantial debt of thanks to the readers of the earlier editions. Our readers have formed a large, engaged community, and their endorsements, observations, and suggestions for revision and expansion have proved invaluable. We have also profited from the highly detailed reviews of each individual feature of the edition commissioned by the publisher and performed with exemplary seriousness by many of our most esteemed professional colleagues.

At the very center of the Third Edition is the newly edited text of the Complete Works, an enormous, exhaustive, and exhausting enterprise. We wish to acknowledge with deepest gratitude the extraordinary labors of our gifted team of textual editors, listed on the title-page spread, led with an exemplary blend of discipline, patience, intellectual seriousness, and scholarly rigor by Gordon McMullan and Suzanne Gossett.

The *Norton Shakespeare* editors have had the valuable—indeed, indispensable—support of our publisher and a host of undergraduate and graduate research assistants, colleagues, friends, and family, whose names we gratefully note in the Acknowledgments that follow. All of these companions have helped us find in this long collective enterprise what the "Dedicatorie Epistle" to the First Folio promises to its readers: delight. We make the same promise to the readers of our edition and invite them to continue the great Shakespearean collaboration.

Stephen Greenblatt
Cambridge, Massachusetts

# Volume Editors' Acknowledgments

The creation of this edition has drawn heavily on the resources, experience, and skill of its remarkable publisher, W. W. Norton. Norton's record of success in academic publishing has sometimes made it seem like a giant, akin to the multinational corporations that dominate the publishing world, but it is in fact the only major publishing house that is employee-owned. Our principal guide has been our brilliant editor Julia Reidhead, whose calm intelligence, common sense, and steady focus have been essential in enabling us to reach our goal. With this Third Edition, we were blessed once again with the indispensable judgment and project-editorial expertise of Marian Johnson, managing editor, college department, as well as scrupulous manuscript editing by Alice Vigliani and Harry Haskell. Carly Fraser Doria, literature media editor, skillfully guided us through the new waters of the Digital Edition, following Cliff Landesman's innovative lead. Assistant editor Emily Stuart managed with remarkable skill and graciousness the complexities of manuscript preparation and review. Kim Yi, managing editor, digital media, and Kristin Sheerin, digital project editor, oversaw the monumental checking and proofing of files. In addition, we are deeply grateful to Cara Folkman, media assistant editor; JoAnn Simony and Elizabeth Audley, digital file coordinators; Eric Pier-Hocking, production manager; and Debra Morton Hoyt, corporate art director, who, along with designer Timothy Hsu, created our Ortelius-inspired cover design. Thanks also to Mary Jo Mecca for design and construction of the jester hat. For invaluable help in creating the Digital Edition, we would like to thank Jane Chu and Colleen Caffrey, digital designers, and Mateus Teixiera and Kristian Sanford, digital production.

The editors have, in addition, had the valuable—indeed, indispensable—support of a host of undergraduate and graduate research assistants, colleagues, friends, and family. Even a partial listing of those to whom we owe our heartfelt thanks is very long, but we are all fortunate enough to live in congenial and supportive environments, and the edition has been part of our lives for a long time. We owe special thanks for sustained dedication and learning to our colleagues, friends, and principal assistants:

Stephen Greenblatt wishes to thank his talented research assistants at Harvard, including Maria Devlin, Seth Herbst, Rhema Hokama, David Nee, Elizabeth Weckhurst, Benjamin Woodring, Catherine Woodring, and, above all, Misha Teramura. In addition, he is grateful for valuable assistance from Rebecca Cook and Aubrey Everett, along with advice and counsel from many friends, colleagues, and students. Thanks also go to C. Edward McGee (University of Waterloo), Barbara D. Palmer (late of the University of Mary Washington), Sylvia Thomas (the Yorkshire Archaeological Society), and John M. Wasson (late of Washington State University). He acknowledges a special and enduring debt to Ramie Targoff (Brandeis University).

Walter Cohen wishes to thank Marjorie Levinson (University of Michigan).

Jean Howard would like to acknowledge the help of each of her excellent research assistants at Columbia University: Bryan Lowrance, John Kuhn, Alexander Paulsson Lash, Chris McKeen, and especially Emily Shortslef, whose scholarly contributions have been indispensable and impeccable and whose good cheer is astonishingly unflagging.

We gratefully acknowledge the reviewers who provided thoughtful critiques for particular plays or of the project as a whole: Bernadette Andrea (University of Texas at San Antonio), John M. Archer (New York University), Oliver Arnold (University of California–Berkeley), Amanda Bailey (University of Connecticut), JoAnn D. Barbour

(Texas Woman's University), Catherine Belsey (Swansea University), Barbara Bono (University at Buffalo), Michael D. Bristol (McGill University), Karen Britland (University of Wisconsin–Madison), James C. Bulman (Allegheny College), William C. Carroll (Boston University), Kent Cartwright (University of Maryland, College Park), Joseph Cerami (Texas A&M University), Julie Crawford (Columbia University), Jonathan Crewe (Dartmouth College), Stephen Deng (Michigan State University), Christy Desmet (University of Georgia), Donald R. Dickson (Texas A&M University), Mario DiGangi (Graduate Center of the City University of New York), Tobias Doering (University of Munich), Frances Dolan (University of California–Davis), John Drakakis (University of Stirling), Heather Dubrow (Fordham University), Holly Dugan (George Washington University), Amy E. Earhart (Texas A&M University), Katherine E. Eggert (University of Colorado–Boulder), Lars D. Engle (University of Tulsa), Christopher John Fitter (Rutgers University), Mary Floyd-Wilson (University of North Carolina–Chapel Hill), Susan Caroline Frye (University of Wyoming), Brett Gamboa (Dartmouth College), Evelyn Gajowski (University of Nevada, Las Vegas), Hugh Hartridge Grady, Jr. (Arcadia University), Kenneth Gross (University of Rochester), Elizabeth Hanson (Queen's University), Jonathan Gil Harris (George Washington University), Michael Hattaway (New York University), Diana Henderson (Massachusetts Institute of Technology), Terence Allan Hoagwood (Texas A&M University), Lucia Kristina Hodgson (Texas A&M University), Peter Holbrook (The University of Queensland), Peter Holland (University of Notre Dame), John W. Huntington (University of Illinois at Chicago), Lorna Hutson (University of St. Andrews), Coppélia Kahn (Brown University), Jeffrey Knapp (University of California–Berkeley), Yu Jin Ko (Wellesley College), Paul A. Kottman (The New School), Bryon Lew (Trent University), Genevieve Love (Colorado College), Julia R. Lupton (University of California–Irvine), Ellen MacKay (Indiana University), Cristina Malcolmson (Bates College), Lawrence G. Manley (Yale University), Steven Mentz (St. John's University), Erin Minear (College of William and Mary), Arash Moradi (Shiraz University), Ian Moulton (Arizona State University), Steven Mullaney (University of Michigan), Cyrus Mulready (State University of New York–New Paltz), Karen Newman (Brown University), Mary A. O'Farrell (Texas A&M University), Laurie E. Osborne (Colby College), Simon Palfrey (Oxford University), Garry Partridge (Texas A&M University), Thomas Pendleton (Iona College), Peter G. Platt (Barnard College), Christopher Pye (Williams College), Phyllis R. Rackin (University of Pennsylvania), Sally Robinson (Texas A&M University), Mary Beth Rose (University of Illinois at Chicago), Suparna Roychoudhury (Mount Holyoke College), Elizabeth D. Samet (United States Military Academy at West Point), Melissa E. Sanchez (University of Pennsylvania), Michael Schoenfeldt (University of Michigan), Laurie J. Shannon (Northwestern University), Jyotsna Singh (Michigan State University), Elizabeth Spiller (Florida State University), Tiffany Stern (Oxford University), Richard Strier (University of Chicago), Ayanna Thompson (George Washington University), Douglas Trevor (University of Michigan), Henry S. Turner (Rutgers University), Brian Walsh (Yale University), Tiffany Jo Werth (Simon Fraser University), Adam Zucker (University of Massachusetts).

# General Textual Editors' Acknowledgments

First and foremost, we are grateful to Stephen Greenblatt for inviting us to imagine, and then to create, a wholly new text of Shakespeare for the Third Edition of *The Norton Shakespeare*; to the volume editors—Jean Howard, Katharine Maus, and Walter Cohen—for working closely with us and for supporting the single text–editing principle we adopted; and to Julia Reidhead, the edition's publisher, for her gracious engagement and direction at every stage. And of course we are hugely grateful to the remarkable team of editors with whom we have worked, all of whom, without exception, accepted the invitation with alacrity, edited superbly, completed their work in timely fashion, and tolerated the necessary processes stemming from the need to ensure that each individual play functions both in its own right and as part of the edition as a whole. We want to thank and acknowledge them all. We also wish to thank Lacey Conley, who provided invaluable research assistance at crucial moments in the creation of the text. None of this would have been possible without the indefatigable work of the team at Norton. Marian Johnson, managing editor, college, provided invaluable wisdom and care for the newly edited text. Cliff Landesman's enthusiasm for the project and his willingness to explore—and help us understand—the digital possibilities were invaluable. Carly Fraser Doria and Emily Stuart responded with remarkable generosity, patience, and professionalism to our requests and anxieties. And we are particularly grateful to Norton's copy editors, Alice Vigliani and Harry Haskell, for their wonderfully precise work on the texts of the plays.

Editors tend to fight like cats in a sack over the choices they make when editing Shakespeare—they did this in the eighteenth century, and they try their best to keep up the tradition today—yet they also know that they are in fact highly mutually dependent, and it matters a great deal to us to note that we have had a second set of collaborators in the creation of this new text, none of whom has had actual direct involvement in *The Norton Shakespeare*, Third Edition—due in some cases to working on equivalent editions for other presses—but without whose textual and critical work we could not have acquired the knowledge we needed to create this edition. These include David Bevington, Peter Blayney, A. R. Braunmuller, R. A. Foakes, John Jowett, David Scott Kastan, Laurie Maguire, Sonia Massai, Eric Rasmussen, Tiffany Stern, Gary Taylor, Stanley Wells, and Martin Wiggins. And we would like in particular to acknowledge our considerable debt to Richard Proudfoot, who mentored us both in the fine art of editing and whose knowledge of the Shakespearean text and generosity with that knowledge are unsurpassed. We should acknowledge too certain key resources without which our editorial work would have been, practically speaking, impossible: these include the British Library's remarkable Shakespeare in Quarto website and the online text and facsimiles provided by the Internet Shakespeare Edition (a remarkable enterprise led by the generous and endlessly energetic Michael Best).

Finally, we should also note that any edition of Shakespeare is merely one in a very long line, and all modern Shakespearean editors are indebted to the extraordinary work of the earliest toilers in the field—from Shakespeare's friends Heminges and Condell assembling the First Folio and thus providing the crucial basis for all subsequent work on the Shakespeare canon, to the anonymous editors of the Second, Third, and Fourth Folios, to the crucial work of Rowe, Capell, Pope, Johnson, Theobald, and their successors in the eighteenth, nineteenth, and twentieth centuries. How they did any of it without word-processing software and the resources of the Internet we cannot for the life of us figure out.

Gordon McMullan and Suzanne Gossett

# General Introduction

## STEPHEN GREENBLATT

"He was not of an age, but for all time!"

There are writers whose greatness is recognized only long after they have vanished from the earth. There are writers championed by a coterie of devoted followers who tend the flame of admiration against the cold world's indifference. There are writers beloved in their native land but despised abroad, and others neglected at home yet celebrated on distant shores. Shakespeare is none of these. His genius was recognized almost immediately. The famous words with which we have begun were written by his friend and rival Ben Jonson. They have been echoed innumerable times, across the centuries, across national and linguistic boundaries, across the demarcation lines of race and class, religion and ideology. Shakespeare belongs not simply to a particular culture—English culture of the late sixteenth and early seventeenth centuries—but to world culture, the dense network of constraints and entitlements, dreams and practices that help to make us fully human. Indeed, so absolute is Shakespeare's achievement that he has himself come to seem like great creating nature. His works embody the imagination's power to transcend time-bound beliefs and assumptions, particular historical circumstances, and specific artistic conventions. If we should ever be asked as a species to bring forward one artist who has most fully expressed the human condition, we could with confidence elect Shakespeare to speak for us. As it is, when we do ask ourselves the most fundamental questions about life—about love and hatred, ambition, desire, and fear, the demand for justice and the longing for a second chance—we repeatedly turn to Shakespeare for the words we wish to hear.

The near-worship Shakespeare inspires is one of the salient facts about his art. But we must at the same time acknowledge that this art is the product of peculiar historical circumstances and specific conventions, four centuries distant from our own. The acknowledgment is important because Shakespeare the working dramatist did not typically lay claim to the transcendent, visionary truths attributed to him by his most fervent admirers; his characters more modestly say, in the words of the magician Prospero, that their project was "to please" (*The Tempest,* Epilogue, line 13). The starting point, and perhaps the ending point as well, in any encounter with Shakespeare is simply to enjoy him, to savor his imaginative richness, to take pleasure in his infinite delight in language.

"If then you do not like him," Shakespeare's first editors wrote in 1623, "surely you are in some manifest danger not to understand him." Over the years, accommodations have been devised to make liking Shakespeare easier for everyone. When aspects of his language began to seem difficult, texts were published with notes and glosses. When the historical events he depicted receded into obscurity, explanatory introductions were written. When the stage sank to melodrama and light opera, Shakespeare made his appearance in suitably revised dress. When the populace had a craving for hippodrama, plays performed entirely on horseback, *Hamlet* was dutifully rewritten and mounted. When audiences went mad for realism, live frogs croaked in productions of *A Midsummer Night's Dream.* When the stage was stripped bare and given over to stark exhibitions of sadistic cruelty, Shakespeare was our contemporary. And when the theater ceded some of its cultural centrality to radio, film, and television, Shakespeare moved effortlessly to Hollywood and the sound stages of the BBC.

This virtually universal appeal is one of the most astonishing features of the Shakespeare phenomenon: plays that were performed before glittering courts thrive in junior high school auditoriums; enemies set on destroying one another laugh at the same jokes and weep at the same catastrophes; some of the richest and most complex English verse ever written migrates with spectacular success into German and Italian, Hindi, Swahili, and Japanese. Is there a single, stable, continuous object that underlies all of these migrations and metamorphoses? Certainly not. The global diffusion and long life of Shakespeare's works depend on their extraordinary malleability, their protean capacity to elude definition and escape secure possession. His art is the supreme manifestation of the mobility of culture. At the same time, this art is not without identifiable shared features: across centuries and continents, family resemblances link many of the wildly diverse manifestations of plays such as *Romeo and Juliet, Hamlet,* and *Twelfth Night.* Moreover, if there is no clear limit or end point, there is a reasonably clear beginning, the England of the late sixteenth and early seventeenth centuries, when the plays and poems collected in *The Norton Shakespeare* made their first appearance.

An art virtually without end or limit but with an identifiable, localized, historical origin: Shakespeare's achievement defies the facile opposition between transcendent and time-bound. It is not necessary to choose between an account of Shakespeare as the scion of a particular culture and an account of him as a universal genius who created works that continually renew themselves across national and generational boundaries. On the contrary: crucial clues to understanding his art's remarkable power to soar beyond the time and place of its origin lie in the very soil from which that art sprang.

## Shakespeare's World

### *Life and Death*

Life expectancy at birth in early modern England was exceedingly low by our standards: under thirty years, compared with over seventy today. Infant mortality rates were extraordinarily high, and it is estimated that in the poorer parishes of London only about half the children survived to the age of fifteen, while the children of aristocrats fared only a little better. In such circumstances, some parents must have developed a certain detachment—one of Shakespeare's contemporaries writes of losing "some three or four children"—but there are many expressions of intense grief, so that we cannot assume that the frequency of death hardened people to loss or made it routine.

Still, the spectacle of death, along with that other great threshold experience, birth, must have been far more familiar to Shakespeare and his contemporaries than to ourselves. There was no equivalent in early modern England to our hospitals, and most births and deaths occurred at home. Physical means for the alleviation of pain and suffering were extremely limited—alcohol might dull the terror, but it was hardly an effective anesthetic—and medical treatment was generally both expensive and worthless, more likely to intensify suffering than to lead to a cure. This was a world without a concept of antiseptics, with little actual understanding of disease, with few effective ways of treating earaches or venereal disease, let alone the more terrible instances of what Shakespeare calls "the thousand natural shocks that flesh is heir to."

The worst of these shocks was the bubonic plague, which repeatedly ravaged England, and particularly English towns, until the third quarter of the seventeenth

1609.
From the 24 Augusto
to the 31. there
died in London, the Liberties,
the out parishes, & the pesthouse } 364
whereof of the Plague——177
Christned in all those places——123
Parishes clear 73 parishes infec. 48

Bill recording plague deaths in London, 1609.

century. The plague was terrifyingly sudden in its onset, rapid in its spread, and almost invariably lethal. Physicians were helpless in the face of the epidemic, though they prescribed amulets, preservatives, and sweet-smelling substances (on the theory that the plague was carried by noxious vapors). In the plague-ridden year of 1564, the year of Shakespeare's birth, some 254 people died in his native Stratford-upon-Avon, out of a total population of 800. The year before, some 20,000 Londoners are thought to have died; in 1593, almost 15,000; in 1603, 36,000, or over a sixth of the city's inhabitants. The social effects of these horrible visitations were severe: looting, violence, and despair, along with an intensification of the age's perennial poverty, unemployment, and food shortages. The London plague regulations of 1583, reissued with modifications in later epidemics, ordered that the infected and their households should be locked in their homes for a month; that the streets should be kept clean; that vagrants should be expelled; and that funerals and plays (as occasions in which large numbers of people gathered and infection could be spread) should be restricted or banned entirely. Comparable restrictions were not placed on gatherings for religious observance, since it was hoped that God would heed the desperate prayers of his suffering people.

The plague, then, had a direct and immediate impact on Shakespeare's own profession. City officials kept records of the weekly number of plague deaths; when these surpassed a certain number, the theaters were peremptorily closed. The basic idea was not only to prevent contagion but also to avoid making an angry God still angrier with the spectacle of idleness. While restricting public assemblies may in fact have slowed the epidemic, other public policies in times of plague, such as killing the cats and dogs, may have made matters worse (since the disease was spread not by these animals but by the fleas that bred on the black rats that infested the poorer neighborhoods). Moreover, the playing companies, driven out of London by the closing of the theaters, may have carried plague to the provincial towns.

Even in good times, when the plague was dormant and the weather favorable for farming, the food supply in England was precarious. A few successive bad harvests, such as occurred in the mid-1590s, could cause serious hardship, even starvation. Not surprisingly, the poor bore the brunt of the burden: inflation, low wages, and rent increases left large numbers of people with very little cushion against disaster. Further, at its best, the diet of most people seems to have been seriously deficient. The lower classes then, as throughout most of history, subsisted on one or two foodstuffs, usually low in protein. The upper classes disdained green vegetables and milk and gorged themselves on meat. Illnesses that we now trace to vitamin deficiencies were rampant. Some but not much relief from pain was provided by the beer that Elizabethans, including children, drank almost incessantly. (Home brewing aside, enough beer was sold in England for every man, woman, and child to have consumed forty gallons a year.)

### *Wealth*

Despite rampant disease, the population of England in Shakespeare's lifetime grew steadily, from approximately 3,060,000 in 1564 to 4,060,000 in 1600 and 4,510,000 in 1616. Though the death rate was more than twice what it is in England today, the birthrate was almost three times the current figure. London's population in particular soared, from 60,000 in 1520 to 120,000 in 1550, 200,000 in 1600, and 375,000 a half-century later, making it the largest and fastest-growing city not only in England but in all of Europe. Every year in the first half of the seventeenth century, about 10,000 people migrated to London from other parts of England—wages in London tended to be around 50 percent higher than in the rest of the country—and it is estimated that one in eight English people lived in London at some point in their lives. The economic viability of Shakespeare's profession was closely linked to this extraordinary demographic boom: between 1567 and 1642, theater historians have estimated, the London playhouses were paid anywhere between 50 and 75 million visits.

As these visits to the theater indicate, in the capital city and elsewhere a substantial number of English men and women, despite hardships that were never very distant, had money to spend. After the disorder and dynastic wars of the fifteenth century, England in the sixteenth and early seventeenth centuries was for the most part a nation at peace, and with peace came a measure of enterprise and prosperity: the landowning classes busied themselves building great houses, planting orchards and hop gardens, draining marshlands, bringing untilled acreage under cultivation. The artisans and laborers who actually accomplished these tasks, though they were generally paid very little, often managed to accumulate something, as did the small freeholding farmers, the yeomen, who are repeatedly celebrated in the period as the backbone of English national independence and well-being. William Harrison's *Description of Britain* (1577) lovingly itemizes the yeoman's precious possessions: "fair garnish of pewter on his cupboard, with so much more odd vessel going about the house, three or four featherbeds, so many coverlets and carpets of tapestry, a silver salt [cellar], a bowl for wine (if not a whole nest) and a dozen of spoons." There are comparable accounts of the hard-earned acquisitions of the city dwellers—masters and apprentices in small workshops, shipbuilders, wool merchants, cloth makers, chandlers, tradesmen, shopkeepers, along with lawyers, apothecaries, schoolteachers, scriveners, and the like—whose pennies from time to time enriched the coffers of the players.

The chief source of England's wealth in the sixteenth century was its textile industry, an industry that depended on a steady supply of wool. The market for English textiles was not only domestic. In 1565, woolen cloth alone made up more than three-fourths of England's exports. (The remainder consisted mostly of other textiles and raw wool, with some trade in lead, tin, grain, and skins.) The Company of Merchant Adventurers carried cloth not only to nearby countries like France, Holland, and Germany but also to distant ports on the Baltic and Mediterranean, establishing links with Russia and Morocco (each took about 2 percent of London's cloth in 1597–98). English lead and tin, as well as fabrics, were sold in Tuscany and Turkey, and merchants found a market for Newcastle coal on the island of Malta. In the latter half of the century, London, which handled more than 85 percent of all exports, regularly shipped abroad more than 100,000 woolen cloths a year, at a value of at least £750,000. This figure does not include the increasingly important and profitable trade in so-called New Draperies, including textiles that went by such exotic names as bombazines, callamancoes, damazellas, damizes, mockadoes, and virgenatoes. When the Earl of Kent in *King Lear* insults Oswald as a "filthy, worsted-stocking knave" (2.2.14–15) or when the aristocratic Biron in *Love's Labor's Lost* declares that he will give up "taffeta phrases, silken terms precise, / Three-piled hyperboles" and woo henceforth "in russet 'yeas,' and honest kersey 'noes'" (5.2.407–08, 414), Shakespeare is assuming that a substantial portion of his audience will be alert to the social significance of fabric.

There is amusing confirmation of this alertness from an unexpected source: the report of a visit made to the Fortune playhouse in London in 1614 by a foreigner, Father Orazio Busino, the chaplain of the Venetian embassy. Father Busino neglected to mention the name of the play he saw, but like many foreigners, he was powerfully struck by the presence of gorgeously dressed women in the audience. In Venice, there was a special gallery for courtesans, but socially respectable women would not have been permitted to attend plays, as they could in England. In London, not only could middle- and upper-class women go to the theater, but they could also wear masks and mingle freely with male spectators and women of ill repute. The bemused cleric was uncertain about the ambiguous social situation in which he found himself:

> These theaters are frequented by a number of respectable and handsome ladies, who come freely and seat themselves among the men without the slightest hesitation. On the evening in question his Excellency and the Secretary were pleased to play me a trick by placing me amongst a bevy of young women. Scarcely was I seated ere a very elegant dame, but in a mask, came and placed herself beside me. . . . She asked me for my address both in French and English; and, on my turning a deaf ear, she determined to honor me by showing me some fine diamonds on her fingers, repeatedly taking off not fewer than three gloves, which were worn one over the other. . . . This lady's bodice was of yellow satin richly embroidered, her petticoat of gold tissue with stripes, her robe of red velvet with a raised pile, lined with yellow muslin with broad stripes of pure gold. She wore an apron of point lace of various patterns: her head-tire was highly perfumed, and the collar of white satin beneath the delicately-wrought ruff struck me as extremely pretty.

Father Busino may have turned a deaf ear on this "elegant dame" but not a blind eye: his description of her dress is worthy of a fashion designer and conveys something of the virtual clothes cult that prevailed in England in the late sixteenth and early seventeenth centuries, a cult whose major shrine, outside the royal court, was the theater.

### *Imports, Patents, and Monopolies*

England produced some luxury goods, but the clothing on the backs of the most fashionable theatergoers was likely to have come from abroad. By the late sixteenth century, the English were importing substantial quantities of silks, satins, velvets, embroidery, gold and silver lace, and other costly items to satisfy the extravagant tastes of the elite and of those who aspired to dress like the elite. The government tried to put a check on the sartorial ambitions of the upwardly mobile by passing sumptuary laws—that is, laws restricting to the ranks of the aristocracy the right to wear certain of the most precious fabrics. But the very existence of these laws, in practice almost impossible to enforce, only reveals the scope and significance of the perceived problem.

Sumptuary laws were in part a conservative attempt to protect the existing social order from upstarts. Social mobility was not widely viewed as a positive virtue, and moralists repeatedly urged people to stay in their place. Conspicuous consumption that was tolerated, even admired, in the aristocratic elite was denounced as sinful and monstrous in less exalted social circles. English authorities were also deeply concerned throughout the period about the effects of a taste for luxury goods on the balance of trade. One of the principal English imports was wine: the "sherris" whose virtues Falstaff extols in 2 *Henry IV* came from Xeres in Spain; the malmsey in which poor Clarence is drowned in *Richard III* was probably made in Greece or in the Canary Islands (from whence came Sir Toby Belch's "cup of canary" in *Twelfth Night*); and the "flagon of rhenish" that Yorick in *Hamlet* had once poured on the Gravedigger's head came from the Rhine region of Germany. Other imports included canvas, linen, fish, olive oil, sugar, molasses, dates, oranges and lemons, figs, raisins, almonds, capers, indigo, ostrich feathers, and that increasingly popular drug tobacco.

Joint stock companies were established to import goods for the burgeoning English market. The Merchant Venturers of the City of Bristol (established in 1552) handled great shipments of Spanish sack, the light, dry wine that largely displaced the vintages of Bordeaux and Burgundy when trade with France was disrupted by war. The Muscovy Company (established in 1555) traded English cloth and manufactured goods for Russian furs, oil, and beeswax. The Venice Company and the Turkey Company—uniting in 1593 to form the wealthy Levant Company—brought silk and spices home from Aleppo and carpets from Constantinople. The East India Company (founded in 1600), with its agent at Bantam in Java, brought pepper, cloves, nutmeg, and other spices from East Asia, along with indigo, cotton textiles, sugar, and saltpeter from India. English privateers "imported" American products, especially sugar, fish, and hides, in huge quantities, along with more precious cargoes. In 1592, a privateering expedition principally funded by Sir Walter Ralegh captured a huge Portuguese carrack (sailing ship), the *Madre de Dios*, in the Azores and brought it back to Dartmouth. The ship, the largest that had ever entered any English port, held 536 tons of pepper, cloves, cinnamon, cochineal, mace, civet, musk, ambergris, and nutmeg, as well as jewels, gold, ebony, carpets, and silks. Before order could be established, the English seamen began to pillage this immensely rich prize, and witnesses said they could smell the spices on all the streets around the harbor. Such piratical expeditions were rarely officially sanctioned by the state, but the Queen had in fact privately invested £1,800, for which she received about £80,000.

In the years of war with Spain, 1586–1604, the goods captured by the privateers annually amounted to 10–15 percent of the total value of England's imports. But organized theft alone could not solve England's balance-of-trade problems. Statesmen were particularly worried that the nation's natural wealth was slipping away in exchange for unnecessary things. In his *Discourse of the Commonweal* (1549), the prominent humanist Sir Thomas Smith exclaims against the importation of such trifles as mirrors, paper, laces, gloves, pins, inkhorns, tennis balls, puppets, and playing cards. And more than a century later, the same fear that England was trading its riches for trifles and wasting away in idleness was expressed by the Bristol merchant John Cary. The solution, Cary argues in "An Essay on the State of England in Relation to Its Trade" (1695), is to expand productive domestic employment. "People are or may be the Wealth of a Nation," he writes, "yet it must be where you find Employment for them, else they are a Burden to it, as the Idle Drone is maintained by the Industry of the laborious Bee, so are all those who live by their Dependence on others, as Players, Ale-House Keepers, Common Fiddlers, and such like, but more particularly Beggars, who never set themselves to work."

Forging a magnet, 1600. The metal on the anvil is aligned North/South (Septentrio/Auster). From *De Magnete* by William Gilbert.

Stage players, all too typically associated here with vagabonds and other idle drones, could have replied in their defense that they not only labored in their vocation but also exported their skills abroad: English actors routinely performed on the Continent. But their labor was not regarded as a productive contribution to the national wealth, and plays were in truth no solution to the trade imbalances that worried authorities.

The government attempted to stem the flow of gold overseas by establishing a patent system initially designed to encourage skilled foreigners to settle in England by granting them exclusive rights to produce particular wares by a patented method. Patents were granted for such things as the making of hard white soap (1561), ovens and furnaces (1563), window glass (1567), sailcloths (1574), drinking glasses (1574), sulfur, brimstone, and oil (1577), armor and horse harness (1587), starch (1588), white writing paper made from rags (1589), aqua vitae and vinegar (1594), playing cards (1598), and mathematical instruments (1598).

By the early seventeenth century, English men and women were working in a variety of new industries like soap making, pin making, knife making, and the brewing of alegar and beeregar (ale- and beer-based vinegar). But although the ostensible purpose of the government's economic policy was to increase the wealth of England, encourage technical innovation, and provide employment for the poor, the effect of patents was often the enrichment of a few and the hounding of poor competitors by wealthy monopolists, a group that soon extended well beyond foreign-born entrepreneurs to the favorites of the monarch who vied for the huge profits to be made. "If I had a monopoly out" on folly, the Fool in *King Lear* protests, glancing at the "lords and great men" around him, "they would have part in't." The passage appears only in the Quarto version of the play (*History of King Lear* 4.140–41); it may have been cut for political reasons from the Folio. For the issue of monopolies provoked bitter criticism and parliamentary debate for decades. In 1601, Elizabeth was prevailed upon to revoke a number of the most hated monopolies, including aqua vitae and vinegar, bottles, brushes, fish livers, the coarse sailcloth known as poldavis and mildernix, pots, salt, and starch. The whole system was revoked during the reign of James I by an act of Parliament.

## *Haves and Have-Nots*

When in the 1560s Elizabeth's ambassador to France, Sir Thomas Smith, wrote a description of England, he saw the commonwealth as divided into four sorts of people: "gentlemen, citizens, yeomen artificers, and laborers." At the forefront of the class of gentlemen was the monarch, followed by a very small group of nobles—dukes, marquesses, earls, viscounts, and barons—who either inherited their exalted titles, as the eldest male heirs of their families, or were granted them by the monarch. Under Elizabeth, this aristocratic peerage numbered between 50 and 60 individuals; James's promotions increased the number to nearer 130. Strictly speaking, Smith notes, the younger sons of the nobility were only entitled to be called "esquires," but in common speech they were also called "lords."

Below this tiny cadre of aristocrats in the social hierarchy of gentry were the knights, a title of honor conferred by the monarch, and below them were the "simple gentlemen." Who was a gentleman? According to Smith, "whoever studieth the laws of the realm, who studieth in the universities, who professeth liberal sciences, and to be short, who can live idly and without manual labor, and will bear the port, charge and countenance of a gentleman, he shall be called master . . . and shall be taken for a gentleman." To "live idly and without manual labor": where in Spain, for example, the crucial mark of a gentleman was "blood," in England it was "idleness," in the sense of sufficient income to afford an education and to maintain a social position without having to work with one's hands.

For Smith, the class of gentlemen was far and away the most important in the kingdom. Below were two groups that had at least some social standing and claim to authority: the citizens, or burgesses, those who held positions of importance and responsibility in their cities, and yeomen, farmers with land and a measure of economic independence. At the bottom of the social order was what Smith calls "the fourth sort of men which do not rule." The great mass of ordinary people have, Smith writes, "no voice nor authority in our commonwealth, and no account is made of them but only to be ruled." Still, even they can bear some responsibility, he notes, since they serve on juries and are named to such positions as churchwarden and constable.

In everyday practice, as modern social historians have observed, the English tended to divide the population not into four distinct classes but into two: a very small empowered group—the "richer" or "wiser" or "better" sort—and all the rest who were without much social standing or power, the "poorer" or "ruder" or "meaner" sort. References to the "middle sort of people" remain relatively rare until after Shakespeare's lifetime; these people are absorbed into the rulers or the ruled, depending on speaker and context.

The source of wealth for most of the ruling class, and the essential measure of social status, was land ownership, and changes to the social structure in the sixteenth and seventeenth centuries were largely driven by the land market. The property that passed into private hands as the Tudors and early Stuarts sold off confiscated monastic estates and then their own crown lands for ready cash amounted to nearly a quarter of all the land in England. At the same time, the buying and selling of private estates was on the rise throughout the period. Land was bought up not only by established landowners seeking to enlarge their estates but also by successful merchants, manufacturers, and urban professionals; even if the taint of vulgar moneymaking lingered around such figures, their heirs would be taken for true gentlemen. The rate of turnover in land ownership was great; in many counties, well over half the gentle families in 1640 had appeared since the end of the fifteenth century. The class that Smith called "simple gentlemen" was expanding rapidly: in the fifteenth century, they had held no more than a quarter of the land in the country, but by the later seventeenth, they controlled almost half. Over the same period, the land held by the great aristocratic magnates held steady at 15–20 percent of the total.

### *Riot and Disorder*

London was a violent place in the first half of Shakespeare's career. There were thirty-five riots in the city in the years 1581–1602, twelve of them in the volatile month of June 1595. These included protests against the deeply unpopular Lord Mayor Sir John Spencer, attempts to release prisoners, anti-alien riots, and incidents of "popular market regulation." There is an unforgettable depiction of a popular uprising in *Coriolanus,* along with many other glimpses in Shakespeare's works, including Jack Cade's grotesque rebellion in *2 Henry VI,* the plebeian violence in *Julius Caesar,* and Laertes' "riotous head" in *Hamlet.*

The London rioters were mostly drawn from the large mass of poor and discontented apprentices who typically chose as their scapegoats foreigners, prostitutes, and gentlemen's servingmen. Theaters were very often the site of the social confrontations that sparked disorder. For two days running in June 1584, disputes between apprentices and gentlemen triggered riots outside the Curtain Theater involving up to a thousand participants. On one occasion, a gentleman was said to have exclaimed that "the apprentice was but a rascal, and some there were little better than rogues that took upon them the name of gentlemen, and said the prentices were but the scum of the world." These occasions culminated in attacks by the apprentices on London's law schools, the Inns of Court.

The most notorious and predictable incidents of disorder came on Shrove Tuesday (the Tuesday before the beginning of Lent), a traditional day of misrule when apprentices ran riot. Shrove Tuesday disturbances involved attacks by mobs of young men on the brothels of the South Bank, in the vicinity of the Globe and other public theaters. The city authorities took precautions to keep these disturbances from getting completely out of control, but evidently did not regard them as serious threats to public order.

Of much greater concern throughout the Tudor and early Stuart years were the frequent incidents of rural rioting. Though in *The Winter's Tale* Shakespeare provides a richly comic portrayal of a rural sheepshearing festival, the increasingly intensive production of wool had its grim side. When a character in Thomas More's *Utopia* (1516) complains that "the sheep are eating the people," he is referring to the practice of enclosure: throughout the sixteenth and early seventeenth centuries, many acres of croplands once farmed in common by rural communities were fenced in by wealthy landowners and turned into pasturage. The ensuing misery, displacement, and food shortages led to repeated protests, some of them violent and bloody, along with a series of government proclamations, but the process of enclosure was not reversed. The protests were at their height during Shakespeare's career: in the years 1590–1610, the frequency of anti-enclosure rioting doubled from what it had been earlier in Elizabeth's reign.

Although they often became violent, anti-enclosure riots were usually directed not against individuals but against property. Villagers—sometimes several hundred, often fewer than a dozen—gathered to tear down newly planted hedges. The event often took place in a carnival atmosphere, with songs and drinking, that did not prevent the participants from acting with a good deal of political canniness and forethought. Especially in the Jacobean period, it was common for participants to establish a fund for legal defense before commencing their assault on the hedges. Women were frequently involved, and on a number of occasions wives alone participated in the destruction of the enclosure, since there was a widespread, though erroneous, belief that married women acting without the knowledge of their husbands were immune from prosecution. In fact, the powerful Court of Star Chamber consistently ruled that both the wives and their husbands should be punished.

Although Stratford was never the scene of serious rioting, enclosure controversies turned violent more than once in Shakespeare's lifetime. In January 1601, Shakespeare's friend Richard Quiney and others leveled the hedges of Sir Edward Greville, lord of Stratford manor. Quiney was elected bailiff of Stratford in September of that year but did not live to enjoy the office for long. He died from a blow to the head struck by one of Greville's men in a tavern brawl. Greville, responsible for the administration of justice, neglected to punish the murderer.

There was further violence in January 1615, when William Combe's men threw to the ground two local aldermen who were filling in a ditch by which Combe was enclosing common fields near Stratford. The task of filling in the offending ditch was completed the next day by the women and children of Stratford. Combe's enclosure scheme was eventually stopped in the courts. Though he owned land whose value would have been affected by this controversy, Shakespeare took no active role in it, since he had previously come to a private settlement with the enclosers insuring him against personal loss.

The Peddler. From Jost Amman, *The Book of Trades* (1568).

Most incidents of rural rioting were small, localized affairs, and with good reason: when confined to the village community, riot was a misdemeanor; when it spread outward to include multiple communities, it became treason, punishable by death. The greatest of the anti-enclosure riots, those in which hundreds of individuals from a large area participated, commonly took place on the eve of full-scale regional rebellions. The largest of these disturbances, Kett's Rebellion, involved some 16,000 peasants, artisans, and townspeople who rose up in 1549 under the leadership of a Norfolk tanner and landowner, Robert Kett, to protest economic exploitation. The agrarian revolts in Shakespeare's lifetime were on a much smaller scale. In the abortive Oxfordshire Rebellion of 1596, a carpenter named Bartholomew Steer attempted to organize a rising against the hated enclosures. The optimistic Steer allegedly promised his followers that "it was but a month's work to overrun England" and informed them "that the commons long since in Spain did rise and kill all gentlemen . . . and since that time have lived merrily there." Steer expected several hundred men to join him on Enslow Hill on November 21, 1596, for the start of the rising; no more than twenty showed up. They were captured, imprisoned, and tortured. Several were executed, but Steer apparently cheated the hangman by dying in prison.

Rebellions, most often triggered by hunger and oppression, continued into the reign of James I. The Midland Revolt of 1607, which may be reflected in *Coriolanus*, consisted of a string of agrarian risings in the counties of Northamptonshire, Warwickshire, and Leicestershire, involving assemblies of up to five thousand rebels in various places. The best known of their leaders was John Reynolds, called "Captain Powch" because of the pouch he wore, whose magical contents were supposed to defend the rebels from harm. (According to the chronicler Edmund Howes, when Reynolds was captured and the pouch opened, it contained "only a piece of green cheese.") The rebels, who were called by themselves and others both "Levelers" and "Diggers," insisted that they had no quarrel with the King but only sought an end to injurious enclosures. But Robert Wilkinson, who preached a sermon against the leaders at their trial, credited them with the intention to "level all states as they leveled banks and ditches." Most of the rebels got off relatively lightly, but, along with other ringleaders, Captain Powch was executed.

### *The Legal Status of Women*

English women were not under the full range of crushing constraints that afflicted women in some countries in Europe. Foreign visitors were struck by their relative freedom, as shown, for example, by the fact that respectable women could venture unchaperoned into the streets and attend the theater. Yet while England was ruled for over forty years by a powerful woman, the great majority of women in the kingdom had very restricted social, economic, and legal standing. To be sure, a tiny number of influential aristocratic women, such as the formidable Countess of Shrewsbury, Bess of Hardwick, wielded considerable power. But, these rare exceptions aside, women were denied any rightful claim to institutional authority or personal autonomy. When Sir Thomas Smith thinks of how he should describe his country's social order, he declares that "we do reject women, as those whom nature hath made to keep home and to nourish their family and children, and not to meddle with matters abroad, nor to bear office in a city or commonwealth." Then, with a kind of glance over his shoulder, he makes an exception of those few for whom "the blood is respected, not the age nor the sex": for example, the Queen.

Single women, whether widowed or unmarried, could, if they were of full age, inherit and administer land, make a will, sign a contract, possess property, sue and be sued, without a male guardian or proxy. But married women had no such rights under English common law, the system of law based on court decisions rather than on codified written laws. Early modern writings about women and the family constantly return to a political model of domination and submission, in which the husband and father justly rules over wife and children as the monarch rules over the state. The husband's dominance in the family was the justification for the common-law rule that prohibited married women from possessing property, administering land, signing contracts, or bringing lawsuits in their own names: married women were described as legally "covered" by their husbands. Yet this conception of a woman's role conveniently ignores the fact that a *majority* of the adult women at any time in Shakespeare's England were not married. They were either widows or spinsters (a term that was not yet pejorative), and thus for the most part managed their own affairs. Even within marriage, women typically had more control over certain spheres than moralizing writers on the family cared to admit. For example, village wives oversaw the production of eggs, cheese, and beer, and sold these goods in the market. As seamstresses, pawnbrokers, second-hand clothing dealers, peddlers and the like—activities not controlled by the all-male craft guilds–women managed to acquire some economic power of their own, and, of course, they participated as well in the unregulated, black-market economy of the age and in the underworld of thievery and prostitution.

Women were not in practice as bereft of property as, according to English common law, they should have been. Demographic studies indicate that the inheritance system called primogeniture, the orderly transmission of property from father to eldest male heir, was more often an unfulfilled wish than a reality. Some 40 percent of marriages failed to produce a son, and in such circumstances fathers often left their land to their daughters, rather than to brothers, nephews, or male cousins. In many families, the father died before his male heir was old enough to inherit property, leaving the land, at least temporarily, in the hands of the mother. And while they were less likely than their brothers to inherit land ("real property"), daughters normally inherited a substantial share of their parents' personal property (cash and movables).

In fact, the legal restrictions upon women, though severe in Shakespeare's time, actually worsened in subsequent decades. English common law was significantly less egalitarian in its approach to wives and daughters than were alternative legal codes (manorial, civil, and ecclesiastical) still in place in the late sixteenth century. The eventual triumph of common law stripped women of many traditional rights, slowly driving them out of economically productive trades and businesses.

Limited though it was, the economic freedom of Elizabethan and Jacobean women far exceeded their political and social freedom—the opportunity to receive a grammar school or university education, to hold office in church or state, to have a voice in public debates, or even simply to speak their mind fully and openly in ordinary conversation. Women who asserted their views too vigorously risked being perceived as shrewish and labeled "scolds." Both urban and rural communities had a horror of scolds. In the Elizabethan period, such women came to be regarded as a threat to public order, to be dealt with by the local authorities. The preferred methods of correction included public humiliation—of the sort Katherina endures in *The Taming of the Shrew*—and such physical abuse as slapping, bridling with a bit or muzzle, and half-drowning by means of a contraption called the "cucking stool" (or "ducking stool"). This latter punishment originated in the Middle Ages, but its use spread in the sixteenth century, when it became almost exclusively a punishment for women. From 1560 onward, cucking stools were built or renovated in many English provincial towns; between 1560 and 1600, the contraptions were installed by rivers or ponds in Norwich, Bridport, Shrewsbury, Kingston-upon-Thames, Marlborough, Devizes, Clitheroe, Thornbury, and Great Yarmouth.

Such punishment was usually intensified by a procession through the town to the sound of "rough music," the banging together of pots and pans. The same cruel festivity accompanied the "carting" or "riding" of those accused of being whores. In some parts of the country, villagers also took the law into their own hands, publicly shaming women who married men much younger than themselves or who beat or otherwise domineered over their husbands. One characteristic form of these charivaris, or rituals of shaming, was known in the West Country as the Skimmington Ride. Villagers would rouse the offending couple from bed with rough music and stage a raucous pageant in which a man, holding a distaff, would ride backward on a donkey, while his "wife" (another man dressed as a woman) struck him with a ladle. In these cases, the collective ridicule and indignation were evidently directed at least as much at the henpecked husband as at his transgressive wife.

### *Women and Print*

Books published for a female audience surged in popularity in the late sixteenth century, reflecting an increase in female literacy. (It is striking how many of Shakespeare's women are shown reading.) This increase is probably linked to a Protestant longing for direct access to the Scriptures, and the new books marketed specifically for women included devotional manuals and works of religious instruction. But there were also practical guides to such subjects as female education (for example, Giovanni Bruto's *Necessary, Fit, and Convenient Education of a Young Gentlewoman,* 1598), midwifery (James Guillemeau's *Child-birth; or, the Happy Delivery of Women,* 1612), needlework (Federico di Vinciolo's *New and Singular Patterns and Works of Linen,* 1591), cooking (Thomas Dawson's *The Good Housewife's Jewel,* 1587), gardening (Pierre Erondelle's *The French Garden,* 1605), and married life (Patrick Hanney's *A Happy Husband; or, Directions for a Maid to Choose Her Mate,* 1619). As the authors' names suggest, many of these works were translations, and almost all were written by men.

Starting in the 1570s, writers and their publishers increasingly addressed works of recreational literature (romance, fiction, and poetry) partially or even exclusively to women. Some books, such as Robert Greene's *Mamillia, a Mirror or Looking-Glass for the Ladies of England* (1583), directly specified in the title their desired audience. Others, such as Sir Philip Sidney's influential and popular romance *Arcadia* (1590–93), solicited female readership in their dedicatory epistles. The ranks of Sidney's followers eventually included his own niece, Mary Wroth, whose romance *Urania* was published in 1621.

In the literature of Shakespeare's time, women readers were not only wooed but also frequently railed at, in a continuation of a popular polemical genre that had long inspired heated charges and countercharges. Both sides in the polemic generally agreed that it was the duty of women to be chaste, dutiful, and modest in demeanor; the argument was whether women fulfilled or fell short of this proper role. Ironically, then, a modern reader is more likely to find inspiring accounts of courageous women not in the books written in defense of female virtue but in attacks on those who refused to be silent and obedient.

The most famous English skirmish in this controversy took place in a rash of pamphlets at the end of Shakespeare's life. Joseph Swetnam's crude *Arraignment of Lewd, Idle, Froward, and Unconstant Women* (1615) provoked three fierce responses attributed to women: Rachel Speght's *A Muzzle for Melastomus,* Esther Sowernam's *Esther Hath Hang'd Haman,* and Constantia Munda's *Worming of a Mad Dog,* all in 1617. There was also an anonymous play, *Swetnam the Woman-Hater Arraigned by Women* (first performed around 1618), in which Swetnam, depicted as a braggart and a lecher, is put on trial by women and made to recant his misogynistic lies.

Prior to the Swetnam controversy, only one English woman, writing under the pseudonym "Jane Anger," had published a defense of women (*Jane Anger Her Protection for Women,* 1589). Learned women writers in the sixteenth century tended not to become involved in public debate but rather to undertake a project to which it was difficult for even obdurately chauvinistic males to object: the translation of devotional literature into English. Thomas More's daughter Margaret More Roper translated Erasmus (*A Devout Treatise upon the Pater Noster,* 1524); Francis Bacon's mother, Anne Cooke Bacon, translated Bishop John Jewel (*An Apology or Answer in Defence of the Church of England,* 1564); Anne Locke Prowse, a friend of John Knox, translated the *Sermons of John Calvin* in 1560; and Mary Sidney, the Countess of Pembroke, completed the metrical version of the Psalms that her brother Sir Philip

Sidney had begun. Elizabeth Tudor (the future queen) herself translated, at the age of eleven, Marguerite de Navarre's *Le Miroir de l'âme pécheresse* (*The Glass of the Sinful Soul,* 1544). The translation was dedicated to her stepmother, Katherine Parr, herself the author of a frequently reprinted book of prayers.

There was in the sixteenth and early seventeenth centuries a social stigma attached to print. Far from celebrating publication, authors, and particularly female authors, often apologized for exposing themselves to the public gaze. Nonetheless, a number of women ventured in print beyond pious translations. Some, including Elizabeth Tyrwhitt, Anne Dowriche, Isabella Whitney, Mary Sidney, and Aemilia Lanyer, composed and published their own poems. Aemilia Lanyer's *Salve Deus Rex Judaeorum,* published in 1611, is a poem in praise of virtuous women, from Eve and the Virgin Mary to her noble patron, the Countess of Cumberland. "A Description of Cookeham," appended to the poem, is one of the first English country house poems, a celebration in verse of an aristocrat's rural estate.

The first Tudor woman to translate a play was the learned Jane Lumley, who composed an English version of Euripides' *Iphigenia at Aulis* (ca. 1550). The first known original play in English by a woman was by Elizabeth Cary, Viscountess Falkland, whose *Tragedy of Mariam, the Fair Queen of Jewry* was published in 1613. This remarkable play, which was not intended to be performed, includes speeches in defense of women's equality, though the most powerful of these is spoken by the villainous Salome, who schemes to divorce her husband and marry her lover. Cary, who bore

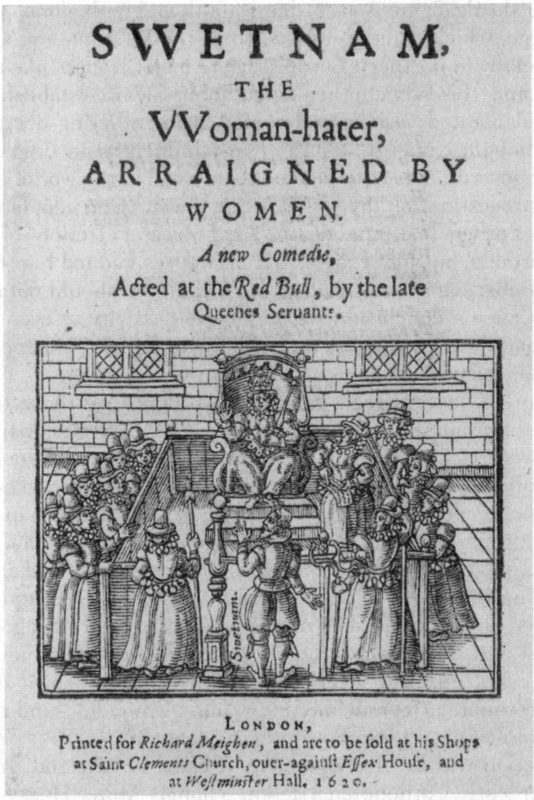
SWETNAM, THE VVoman-hater, ARRAIGNED BY WOMEN. *A new Comedie,* Acted at the *Red Bull,* by the late Queenes Seruants.



LONDON, Printed for *Richard Meighen*, and are to be sold at his Shops at Saint *Clements* Church, ouer-against *Essex* House, and at *Westminster* Hall. 1620.

Title page of *Swetnam the Woman-Hater, Arraigned by Women* (1620), a play written in response to Joseph Swetnam's *The Arraignment of Lewd, Idle, Forward, and Unconstant Women* (1615); the woodcut depicts the trial of Swetnam in act 4.

eleven children, herself had a deeply troubled marriage, which effectively came to an end in 1625 when, defying her husband's staunchly Protestant family, she openly converted to Catholicism. Her biography was written by one of her four daughters, all of whom became nuns.

### *Henry VIII and the English Reformation*

There had long been serious ideological and institutional tensions in the religious life of England, but officially, at least, England in the early sixteenth century had a single religion, Catholicism, whose acknowledged head was the pope in Rome. In 1517, drawing upon long-standing currents of dissent, Martin Luther, an Augustinian monk and professor of theology at the University of Wittenberg, challenged the authority of the pope and attacked several key doctrines of the Catholic Church. According to Luther, the Church, with its elaborate hierarchical structure centered in Rome, its rich monasteries and convents, and its enormous political influence, had become hopelessly corrupt, a conspiracy of venal priests who manipulated popular superstitions to enrich themselves and amass worldly power. Luther began by vehemently attacking the sale of indulgences—certificates promising the remission of punishments to be suffered in the afterlife by souls sent to purgatory to expiate their sins. These indulgences were a fraud, he argued; purgatory itself had no foundation in the Bible, which in his view was the only legitimate source of religious truth. Christians would be saved not by scrupulously following the ritual practices fostered by the Catholic Church—observing fast days, reciting the ancient Latin prayers, endowing chantries to say prayers for the dead, and so on—but by faith and faith alone.

This challenge, which came to be known as the Reformation, spread and gathered force, especially in northern Europe, where major leaders like the Swiss pastor Ulrich Zwingli and the French theologian John Calvin established institutional structures and elaborated various and sometimes conflicting doctrinal principles. Calvin, whose thought came to be particularly influential in England, emphasized the obligation of governments to implement God's will in the world. He advanced too the doctrine of predestination, by which, as he put it, "God adopts some to hope of life and sentences others to eternal death." God's "secret election" of the saved made Calvin uncomfortable, but his study of the Scriptures had led him to conclude that "only a small number, out of an incalculable multitude, should obtain salvation." It might seem that such a conclusion would lead to passivity or even despair, but for Calvin predestination was a mystery bound up with faith, confidence, and an active engagement in the fashioning of a Christian community.

The Reformation had a direct and powerful impact on those territories, especially in northern Europe, where it gained control. Monasteries, many of them fabulously wealthy, were sacked, their possessions and extensive landholdings seized by princes or sold off to the highest bidder; the monks and nuns, expelled from their cloisters, were encouraged to break their vows of chastity and find spouses, as Luther and his wife, a former nun, had done. In the great cathedrals and in hundreds of smaller churches and chapels, the elaborate altarpieces, bejeweled crucifixes, crystal reliquaries holding the bones of saints, and venerated statues and paintings were attacked as "idols" and often defaced or destroyed. Protestant congregations continued, for the most part, to celebrate the most sacred Christian ritual, the Eucharist, or Lord's Supper, but they did so in a profoundly different spirit from that of the Catholic Church—more as commemoration than as miracle—and they now prayed not in the ancient liturgical Latin but in the vernacular.

The Reformation was at first vigorously resisted in England. Indeed, with the support of his ardently Catholic chancellor, Thomas More, Henry VIII personally wrote (or at least lent his name to) a vehement, often scatological attack on Luther's character and views, an attack for which the pope granted him the honorific title "Defender of the Faith." Protestant writings, including translations of the Scriptures into English, were seized by officials of the church and state and burned. Protestants who made their views known were persecuted, driven to flee the country, or arrested, put on trial, and burned at the stake. But the situation changed drastically and decisively when in 1527 Henry decided to seek an annulment from his first wife, Catherine of Aragon, in order to marry Anne Boleyn.

Catherine had given birth to six children, but since only a daughter, Mary, survived infancy, Henry did not have the son he craved. Then as now, the Catholic Church did not ordinarily grant divorce, but Henry's lawyers argued on technical grounds that the marriage was invalid (and therefore, by extension, that Mary was illegitimate and hence unable to inherit the throne). Matters of this kind were far less doctrinal than diplomatic: Catherine, the daughter of Ferdinand of Aragon and Isabella of Castile, had powerful allies in Rome, and the pope ruled against Henry's petition. A series of momentous events followed, as England lurched away from the Church of Rome. In 1531, Henry charged the entire clergy of England with having usurped royal authority in the administration of canon law (the ecclesiastical law that governed faith, discipline, and morals, including such matters as divorce). Under extreme pressure, including the threat of mass confiscations and imprisonment, the Convocation of the Clergy begged for pardon, made a donation to the royal coffers of over £100,000, and admitted that the King was "supreme head of the English Church and clergy" (modified by the rider "as far as the law of Christ allows"). On May 15 of the next year, the convocation submitted to the demand that the King be the final arbiter of canon law; on the next day, Thomas More resigned his post.

In 1533, Henry's marriage to Catherine was officially declared null and void, and on June 1 Anne Boleyn was crowned queen (a coronation Shakespeare depicts in his late play *Henry VIII*). The King was promptly excommunicated by Pope Clement VII. In the following year, the parliamentary Act of Succession confirmed the effects of the annulment and required an oath from all adult male subjects confirming the new dynastic settlement. Thomas More and John Fisher, the Bishop of Rochester, were among the small number who refused. The Act of Supremacy, passed later in the year, formally declared the King to be "Supreme Head of the Church in England" and again required an oath to this effect. In 1535 and 1536, further acts made it treasonous to refuse the oath of royal supremacy or, as More had tried to do, to remain silent. The first victims were three Carthusian monks who rejected the oath—"How could the King, a layman," said one of them, "be Head of the Church of

The Pope as Antichrist riding the Beast of the Apocalypse. From *Fiery Trial of God's Saints* (1611; author unknown).

England?"—and in May 1535, they were duly hanged, drawn, and quartered. A few weeks later, Fisher and More were convicted and beheaded. Between 1536 and 1539, the monasteries were suppressed and their vast wealth seized by the crown.

Royal defiance of the authority of Rome was a key element in the Reformation but did not by itself constitute the establishment of Protestantism in England. On the contrary, in the same year that Fisher and More were martyred for their adherence to Roman Catholicism, twenty-five Protestants, members of a sect known as Anabaptists, were burned for heresy on a single day. Through most of his reign, Henry remained an equal-opportunity persecutor, ruthless to Catholics loyal to Rome but also hostile to some of those who espoused Reformation ideas, though many of these ideas gradually established themselves on English soil.

Even when Henry was eager to do so, it proved impossible to eradicate Protestantism, as it would later prove impossible for his successors to eradicate Catholicism. In large part this tenacity arose from the passionate, often suicidal heroism of men and women who felt that their souls' salvation depended on the precise character of their Christianity. It arose too from a mid-fifteenth-century technological innovation that made it almost impossible to suppress unwelcome ideas: the printing press. Early Protestants quickly grasped that with a few clandestine presses they could defy the Catholic authorities and flood the country with their texts. "How many printing presses there be in the world," wrote the Protestant polemicist John Foxe, "so many blockhouses there be against the high castle" of the pope in Rome, "so that either the pope must abolish knowledge and printing or printing at length will root him out." By the century's end, it was the Catholics who were using the clandestine press to propagate their beliefs in the face of Protestant persecution.

The greatest insurrection of the Tudor age was not over food, taxation, or land but over religion. On Sunday, October 1, 1536, stirred up by their vicar, the traditionalist parishioners of Louth in Lincolnshire, in the north of England, rose up in defiance of the ecclesiastical delegation sent to enforce royal supremacy. The rapidly spreading rebellion, which became known as the Pilgrimage of Grace, was led by the lawyer Robert Aske. The city of Lincoln fell to the rebels on October 6, and though it was soon retaken by royal forces, the rebels seized cities and fortifications throughout Yorkshire, Durham, Northumberland, Cumberland, Westmoreland, and northern Lancashire. Carlisle, Newcastle, and a few castles were all that were left to the King in the north. The Pilgrims soon numbered 40,000, led by some of the region's most prominent noblemen. The Duke of Norfolk, representing the crown, was forced to negotiate a truce, with a promise to support the rebels' demands that the King restore the monasteries, shore up the regional economy, suppress heresy, and dismiss his evil advisers. The Pilgrims kept the peace for the rest of 1536, on the naive assumption that their demands would be met. But Henry moved suddenly early in 1537 to impose order and capture the ringleaders; 130 people, including lords, knights, heads of religious houses, and, of course, Robert Aske, were executed.

In 1549, two years after the death of Henry VIII, the west and north of England were the sites of further unsuccessful risings for the restoration of Catholicism. The Western Rising is striking for its blend of Catholic universalism and intense regionalism among people who did not yet regard themselves as English. One of the rebels' articles, protesting against the imposition of the English Bible and religious service, declares, "We the Cornish men (whereof certain of us understand no English) utterly refuse this new English." The rebels besieged but failed to take the city of Exeter. As with almost all Tudor rebellions, the number of those executed in the aftermath of the failed rising was far greater than those killed in actual hostilities.

### *The Children of Henry VIII: Edward, Mary, and Elizabeth*

Upon Henry's death in 1547, his ten-year-old son, Edward VI, came to the throne, with his maternal uncle Edward Seymour named as Duke of Somerset and Lord

Protector (regent while the King was still a minor). Both Edward and his uncle were staunch Protestants, and reformers hastened to transform the English church accordingly. During Edward's reign, Archbishop Thomas Cranmer formulated the forty-two articles of religion that became the core of Anglican orthodoxy and wrote the first Book of Common Prayer, which was officially adopted in 1549 as the basis of English worship services.

Somerset fell from power in 1549 and was replaced as Lord Protector by John Dudley, later Duke of Northumberland. When Edward fell seriously ill, probably of tuberculosis, Northumberland persuaded him to sign a will depriving his half-sisters Mary (the daughter of Catherine of Aragon) and Elizabeth (the daughter of Anne Boleyn) of their claim to royal succession. The Lord Protector was scheming to have his daughter-in-law, the Protestant Lady Jane Grey, a great-granddaughter of Henry VII, ascend to the throne. But when Edward died in 1553, Mary marshaled support, quickly secured the crown from Lady Jane (who had been titular queen for nine days), and had Lady Jane executed, along with her husband and Northumberland.

Queen Mary immediately took steps to return her kingdom to Roman Catholicism. Though she was unable to get Parliament to agree to return church lands seized under Henry VIII, she restored the Catholic Mass, once again affirmed the authority of the pope, and put down a rebellion that sought to depose her. Seconded by her ardently Catholic husband, Philip II, King of Spain, she initiated a series of religious persecutions that earned her (from her enemies) the name "Bloody Mary." Hundreds of Protestants took refuge abroad in cities such as Calvin's Geneva; almost three hundred less fortunate Protestants were condemned as heretics and burned at the stake.

Mary died childless in 1558, and her younger half-sister Elizabeth became queen. Elizabeth's succession had been by no means assured. For if Protestants regarded the marriage of Henry VIII to Catherine as invalid and hence deemed Mary illegitimate, so Catholics regarded his marriage to Anne Boleyn as invalid and deemed Elizabeth illegitimate. Henry VIII himself seemed to support both views, since only

*The Family of Henry VIII: An Allegory of the Tudor Succession*, by Lucas de Heere (ca. 1572). Henry, in the middle, is flanked by Mary to his right, and Edward and Elizabeth to his left.

three years after divorcing Catherine, he beheaded Anne Boleyn on charges of treason and adultery and urged Parliament to invalidate the marriage. Moreover, though during her sister's reign Elizabeth outwardly complied with the official Catholic religious observance, Mary and her advisers were deeply suspicious, and the young princess's life was in grave danger. Poised and circumspect, Elizabeth warily evaded the traps that were set for her. As she ascended the throne, her actions were scrutinized for some indication of the country's future course. During her coronation procession, when a girl in an allegorical pageant presented her with a Bible in English translation—banned under Mary's reign—Elizabeth kissed the book, held it up reverently, and laid it to her breast; when the abbot and monks of Westminster Abbey came to greet her in broad daylight with candles (a symbol of Catholic devotion) in their hands, she briskly dismissed them with the telling words "Away with those torches! We can see well enough." England had returned to the Reformation.

Many English men and women, of all classes, remained inwardly loyal to the old Catholic faith; Shakespeare's father and mother may well have been among these. But English authorities under Elizabeth moved steadily, if cautiously, toward ensuring at least an outward conformity to the official Protestant settlement. Recusants, those who refused to attend regular Sunday services in their parish churches, were fined heavily. Anyone who wished to receive a university degree, to be ordained as a priest in the Church of England, or to be named as an officer of the state had to swear an oath to the royal supremacy. Commissioners were sent throughout the land to confirm that religious services were following the officially approved liturgy and to investigate any reported backsliding into Catholic practice or, alternatively, any attempts to introduce more radical reforms than the Queen and her bishops had chosen to embrace. For many of the Protestant exiles who streamed back to England were eager not only to undo the damage Mary had done but to carry the Reformation much further. They sought to dismantle the church hierarchy, to purge the calendar of folk customs deemed pagan and the church service of ritual practices deemed superstitious, to dress the clergy in simple garb, and, at the extreme edge, to smash "idolatrous" statues, crucifixes, and altarpieces. Pressing for a stricter code of life and a simplified system of worship, the religious radicals came to be called Puritans. Throughout her long reign, however, Elizabeth herself remained cautiously conservative and determined to hold in check what she regarded as the religious zealotry of Catholics, on the one side, and Puritans, on the other.

Shakespeare's plays tap into the ongoing confessional tensions: "sometimes," Maria in *Twelfth Night* says of the sober, festivity-hating steward Malvolio, "he is a kind of puritan" (2.3.129). But the plays tend to avoid the risks of direct engagement: "The devil a puritan that he is, or anything constantly," Maria adds a moment later, "but a time-pleaser" (2.3.135–36). *The Winter's Tale* features a statue that comes to life—exactly the kind of magical image that Protestant polemicists excoriated as Catholic superstition and idolatry—but the play is set in the pre-Christian world of the Delphic Oracle. And as if this careful distancing might not be enough, the play's ruler goes out of his way to pronounce the wonder legitimate: "If this be magic, let it be an art / Lawful as eating" (5.3.110–11).

In the space of a single lifetime, England had gone officially from Roman Catholicism, to Catholicism under the supreme headship of the English king, to a guarded Protestantism, to a more radical Protestantism, to a renewed and aggressive Roman Catholicism, and finally to Protestantism again. Each of these shifts was accompanied by danger, persecution, and death. It was enough to make some people wary. Or skeptical. Or extremely agile.

## *The English Bible*

Luther had undertaken a fundamental critique of the Catholic Church's sacramental system, a critique founded on the twin principles of salvation by faith alone *(sola fide)* and the absolute primacy of the Bible *(sola scriptura)*. *Sola fide* contrasted faith with "works," by which was meant primarily the whole elaborate system of rituals sanctified, conducted, or directed by the priests. Protestants proposed to modify or reinterpret many of these rituals or, as with the rituals associated with purgatory, to abolish them altogether. *Sola scriptura* required direct lay access to the Bible, which meant in practice the widespread availability of vernacular translations. The Roman Catholic Church had not always and everywhere opposed such translations, but it generally preferred that the populace encounter the Scriptures through the interpretations of the priests, trained to read the Latin translation known as the Vulgate. In times of great conflict, this preference for clerical mediation hardened into outright prohibition of vernacular translation and into persecution and book burning.

Zealous Protestants set out, in the teeth of fierce opposition, to put the Bible into the hands of the laity. A remarkable translation of the New Testament, by an English Lutheran named William Tyndale, was printed on the Continent and smuggled into England in 1525; Tyndale's translation of the Pentateuch, the first five books of the Hebrew Bible, followed in 1530. Many copies of these translations were seized and burned, as was the translator himself, but the printing press made it extremely difficult for authorities to eradicate books for which there was a passionate demand. The English Bible was a force that could not be suppressed, and it became, in its various forms, the single most important book of the sixteenth century.

Tyndale's translation was completed by an associate, Miles Coverdale, whose rendering of the Psalms proved to be particularly influential. Their joint labor was the basis for the Great Bible (1539), the first authorized version of the Bible in English, a copy of which was ordered to be placed in every church in the kingdom. With the accession of Edward VI, many editions of the Bible followed, but the process was sharply reversed when Mary came to the throne in 1553. Along with people condemned as heretics, English Bibles were burned in great bonfires.

Marian persecution was indirectly responsible for what would become the most popular as well as most scholarly English Bible, the translation known as the Geneva Bible (1560), prepared, with extensive, learned, and often fiercely polemical marginal notes, by English exiles in Calvin's Geneva and widely diffused in England after Elizabeth came to the throne. In addition, Elizabethan church authorities ordered a careful revision of the Great Bible, and this version, known as the Bishops' Bible (1568), was the one read in the churches. The success of the Geneva Bible in particular prompted those Elizabethan Catholics who now in turn found themselves in exile to bring out a vernacular translation of their own in order to counter the Protestant readings and glosses. This Catholic translation, the so-called Rheims Bible (1582), may have been known to Shakespeare, but he seems to have been far better acquainted with the Geneva Bible, and he would also have repeatedly heard the Bishops' Bible read aloud. Scholars have identified over three hundred references to the Bible in Shakespeare's work; in one version or another, the Scriptures had a powerful impact on his imagination.

## *A Female Monarch in a Male World*

In the last year of Mary's reign, 1558, the Scottish Calvinist minister John Knox thundered against what he called "the monstrous regiment of women." When the Protestant Elizabeth came to the throne the following year, Knox and his religious brethren were less inclined to denounce female rulers, but in England as elsewhere in Europe there remained a widespread conviction that women were unsuited to wield power over men. Many men seem to have regarded the capacity for rational thought as exclusively male; women, they assumed, were led only by their passions. While gentlemen mastered the arts of rhetoric and warfare, gentlewomen were expected to display the virtues of silence and good housekeeping. Among upper-class males, the will to dominate others was acceptable and indeed admired; the same will in women was condemned as a grotesque and dangerous aberration.

The Armada portrait: note Elizabeth's hand on the globe.

Apologists for the Queen countered these prejudices by appealing to historical precedent and legal theory. History offered inspiring examples of just female rulers, notably Deborah, the biblical prophetess who judged Israel. In the legal sphere, crown lawyers advanced the theory of "the king's two bodies." As England's crowned head, Elizabeth's person was mystically divided between her mortal "body natural" and the immortal "body politic." While the queen's natural body was inevitably subject to the failings of human flesh, the body politic was timeless and perfect. In political terms, therefore, Elizabeth's sex was a matter of no consequence, a thing indifferent.

Elizabeth, who had received a fine humanist education and an extended, dangerous lesson in the art of survival, made it immediately clear that she intended to rule in more than name only. She assembled a group of trustworthy advisers, foremost among them William Cecil (later named Lord Burghley), but she insisted on making many of the crucial decisions herself. Like many Renaissance monarchs, Elizabeth was drawn to the idea of royal absolutism, the theory that ultimate power was properly concentrated in her person and indeed that God had appointed her to be his deputy in the kingdom. Opposition to her rule, in this view, was not only a political act but also a kind of impiety, a blasphemous grudging against the will of God. Apologists for absolutism contended that God commands obedience even to manifestly wicked rulers whom he has sent to punish the sinfulness of humankind. Such arguments were routinely made in speeches and political tracts and from the pulpits of churches, where they were incorporated into the Book of Homilies, which clergymen were required to read out to their congregations.

In reality, Elizabeth's power was not absolute. The government had a network of spies, informers, and agents provocateurs, but it lacked a standing army, a national police force, an efficient system of communication, and an extensive bureaucracy. Above all, the Queen had limited financial resources and needed to turn periodically to an independent and often recalcitrant Parliament, which by long tradition had the sole right to levy taxes and to grant subsidies. Members of the House of Commons were elected from their boroughs, not appointed by the monarch, and though the Queen had considerable influence over their decisions, she could by no means dictate policy. Under these constraints, Elizabeth ruled through a combination of adroit political maneuvering and imperious command, all the while enhancing her authority in the eyes of both court and country by means of an extraordinary cult of love.

"We all loved her," Elizabeth's godson Sir John Harington wrote, with just a touch of irony, a few years after the Queen's death, "for she said she loved us." Ambassadors, courtiers, and parliamentarians all submitted to Elizabeth's cult of love, in which the Queen's gender was transformed from a potential liability into a significant asset. Those who approached her generally did so on their knees and were expected to address her with extravagant compliments fashioned from the period's most passionate love poetry; she in turn spoke, when it suited her to do so, in the language of love poetry. The court moved in an atmosphere of romance, with music, dancing, plays, and the elaborate, fancy-dress entertainments called masques. The Queen adorned herself in gorgeous clothes and rich jewels. When she went on one of her summer "progresses," ceremonial journeys through her land, she looked like an exotic, sacred image in a religious cult of love, and her noble hosts virtually bankrupted themselves to lavish upon her the costliest pleasures. England's leading artists, such as the poet Edmund Spenser and the painter Nicholas Hilliard, enlisted themselves in the celebration of Elizabeth's mystery, likening her to the goddesses of classical mythology: Diana, Astraea, Phoebe, Flora. Her cult drew its power from cultural discourses that ranged from the secular (her courtiers could pine for her as a chaste, unattainable maiden) to the sacred (the veneration that under Catholicism had been due to the Virgin Mary could now be directed toward England's semidivine queen).

There was a sober, even grim aspect to these poetical fantasies: Elizabeth was brilliant at playing one dangerous faction off against another, now turning her gracious smiles on one favorite, now honoring his hated rival, now suddenly looking elsewhere and raising an obscure upstart to royal favor. And when she was disobeyed or when she felt that her prerogatives had been challenged, she was capable of an anger that, as Harington put it, "left no doubtings whose daughter she was." Thus when Sir Walter Ralegh, one of the Queen's glittering favorites, married without her knowledge or consent, he found himself promptly imprisoned in the Tower of London. And when the Protestant polemicist John Stubbs ventured to publish a pamphlet stridently denouncing the Queen's proposed marriage to the French Catholic Duke of Alençon, Stubbs and his publisher were arrested and had their right hands chopped off. (After receiving the blow, the now prudent Stubbs lifted his hat with his remaining hand and cried, "God save the Queen!")

The Queen's marriage negotiations were a particularly fraught issue. When she came to the throne at twenty-five years old, speculation about a suitable match, already widespread, intensified and remained for decades at a fever pitch, for the stakes were high. If Elizabeth died childless, the Tudor line would come to an end. The nearest heir was her cousin Mary, Queen of Scots, a Catholic whose claim was supported by France and by the papacy and whose penchant for sexual and political intrigue confirmed the worst fears of English Protestants. The obvious way to avert the nightmare was for Elizabeth to marry and produce an heir, and the pressure upon her to do so was intense.

More than the royal succession hinged on the question of the Queen's marriage; Elizabeth's perceived eligibility was a vital factor in the complex machinations of international diplomacy. A dynastic marriage between the Queen of England and a foreign ruler would forge an alliance powerful enough to alter the balance of power in Europe. The English court hosted a steady stream of ambassadors from kings and princes eager to win the hand of the royal maiden, and Elizabeth, who prided herself on speaking fluent French and Italian (and on reading Latin and Greek), played her romantic part with exemplary skill, sighing and spinning the negotiations out for months and even years. Most probably, she never meant to marry any of her numerous foreign (and domestic) suitors. Such a decisive act would have meant the end of her independence, as well as the end of the marriage game by which she played one power off against another. One day she would seem to be on the verge of accepting a proposal; the next, she would vow never to forsake her virginity. "She is a princess," the French ambassador remarked, "who can act any part she pleases."

## *The Kingdom in Danger*

Beset by Catholic and Protestant extremists, Elizabeth contrived to forge a moderate compromise that enabled her realm to avert the massacres and civil wars that poisoned France and other countries on the Continent. But menace was never far off, and there were constant fears of conspiracy, rebellion, and assassination. Many of the fears swirled around Mary, Queen of Scots, who had been driven from her own kingdom in 1568 by a powerful faction of rebellious nobles and had taken refuge in England. Her presence, under a kind of house arrest, was a source of intense anxiety and helped generate continual rumors of plots. Some of these plots were real enough, others imaginary, still others traps set in motion by the secret agents of the government's intelligence service under the direction of Sir Francis Walsingham. The situation worsened greatly after Spanish imperial armies invaded the Netherlands in order to stamp out Protestant rebels (1567), after the St. Bartholomew's Day Massacre of Protestants (Huguenots) in France (1572), and after the assassination there of Europe's other major Protestant leader, William of Orange (1584).

The Queen's life seemed to be in even greater danger after the proclamation of Pope Gregory XIII in 1580 that the assassination of the great heretic Elizabeth (who had been excommunicated a decade before) would not constitute a mortal sin. The immediate effect of the proclamation was to make existence more difficult for English Catholics, most of whom were loyal to the Queen but who fell under grave suspicion. Suspicion was intensified by the clandestine presence of English Jesuits, trained at seminaries abroad and smuggled back into England to serve the Roman Catholic cause. When Elizabeth's spymaster Walsingham unearthed an assassination plot in the correspondence between the Queen of Scots and the Catholic Anthony Babington, the wretched Mary's fate was sealed. After vacillating, a very reluctant Elizabeth signed the death warrant in February 1587, and her cousin was beheaded.

The long-anticipated military confrontation with Catholic Spain was now unavoidable. Elizabeth learned that Philip II, her former brother-in-law and onetime suitor, was preparing to send an enormous fleet against her island realm. It was to sail to the Netherlands, where a Spanish army would be waiting to embark and invade England. Barring its way was England's small fleet of well-armed and highly maneuverable fighting vessels, backed up by ships from the merchant navy. The Invincible Armada reached English waters in July 1588, only to be routed in one of the most famous and decisive naval battles in European history. Then, in what many viewed as an act of God on behalf of Protestant England, the Spanish fleet was dispersed and all but destroyed by violent storms.

As England braced itself to withstand the invasion that never came, Elizabeth appeared in person to review a detachment of soldiers assembled at Tilbury. Dressed in a white gown and a silver breastplate, she declared that though some among her councillors had urged her not to appear before a large crowd of armed men, she would never fail to trust the loyalty of her faithful and loving subjects. Nor did she fear the Spanish armies. "I know I have the body of a weak and feeble woman," Elizabeth declared, "but I have the heart and stomach of a king, and of England too." In this celebrated speech, Elizabeth displayed many of her most memorable qualities: her self-consciously histrionic command of grand public occasion, her subtle blending of magniloquent rhetoric and the language of love, her strategic appropriation of traditionally masculine qualities, and her great personal courage. "We princes," she once remarked, "are set on stages in the sight and view of all the world."

### *The English and Otherness*

Shakespeare's London had a large population of resident aliens, mainly artisans and merchants and their families, from Portugal, Italy, Spain, Germany, and above all France and the Netherlands. Many of these people were Protestant refugees, and they were accorded some legal and economic protection by the government. But they were not always welcomed by the local populace. Throughout the sixteenth century, London was the site of repeated demonstrations and, on occasion, bloody riots against the communities of foreign artisans, who were accused of taking jobs away from Englishmen. There was widespread hostility as well toward the Welsh, the Scots, and especially the Irish, whom the English had for centuries been struggling unsuccessfully to subdue. The kings of England claimed to be rulers of Ireland, but in reality they effectively controlled only a small area known as the Pale, extending north from Dublin. The great majority of the Irish people remained stubbornly Catholic and, despite endlessly reiterated English repression, burning of villages, destruction of crops, and massacres, incorrigibly independent.

Shakespeare's *Henry V* (1598–99) seems to invite the audience to celebrate the conjoined heroism of English, Welsh, Scots, and Irish soldiers all fighting together as a "band of brothers" against the French. But such a way of imagining the national community must be set against the tensions and conflicting interests that often set these brothers at each other's throats. As Shakespeare's King Henry realizes, a feared or hated foreign enemy helps at least to mask these tensions, and indeed, in the face of the Spanish Armada, even the bitter gulf between Catholic and Protestant Englishmen seemed to narrow significantly. But the patriotic alliance was only temporary.

Another way of partially masking the sharp differences in language, belief, and custom among the peoples of the British Isles was to group these people together in contrast to the Jews. Medieval England's Jewish population, the recurrent object of persecution, extortion, and massacre, had been officially expelled by King Edward I in 1290. Therefore few if any of Shakespeare's contemporaries would have encountered on English soil Jews who openly practiced their religion. Elizabethan England probably did, however, harbor a small number of so-called Marranos, Spanish or Portuguese Jews who had officially converted to Christianity but secretly continued to observe Jewish practices. One of those suspected to be Marranos was Elizabeth's own physician, Roderigo Lopez, who was tried in 1594 for an alleged plot to poison the Queen. Convicted and condemned to the hideous execution reserved for traitors, Lopez went to his death, in the words of the Elizabethan historian

A Jewish man depicted poisoning a well. From Pierre Boaistuau, *Certain Secret Wonders of Nature* (1569).

William Camden, "affirming that he loved the Queen as well as he loved Jesus Christ; which coming from a man of the Jewish profession moved no small laughter in the standers-by." It is difficult to gauge the meaning here of the phrase "the Jewish profession," used to describe a man who never as far as we know professed Judaism, just as it is difficult to gauge the meaning of the crowd's cruel laughter.

Elizabethans appear to have been fascinated by Jews and Judaism but quite uncertain whether the terms referred to a people, a foreign nation, a set of strange practices, a living faith, a defunct religion, a villainous conspiracy, or a messianic inheritance. Protestant reformers brooded deeply on the Hebraic origins of Christianity; government officials ordered the arrest of those "suspected to be Jews"; villagers paid pennies to itinerant fortune-tellers who claimed to be descended from Abraham or masters of cabalistic mysteries; and London playgoers, perhaps including some who laughed at Lopez on the scaffold, enjoyed the spectacle of the downfall of the wicked Barabas in Christopher Marlowe's *Jew of Malta* (ca. 1589) and the forced conversion of Shylock in Shakespeare's *Merchant of Venice* (1596–97). Jews were not officially permitted to resettle in England until the middle of the seventeenth century, and even then their legal status was ambiguous.

Shakespeare's England also had a small African population whose skin color was the subject of pseudo-scientific speculation and theological debate. Some Elizabethans believed that Africans' blackness resulted from the climate of the regions in which they lived, where, as one traveler put it, they were "so scorched and vexed with the heat of the sun, that in many places they curse it when it riseth." Others held that blackness was a curse inherited from their forefather Chus, the son of Ham, who had, according to Genesis, wickedly exposed the nakedness of the drunken Noah. George Best, a proponent of this theory of inherited skin color, reported that "I myself have seen an Ethiopian as black as coal brought into England, who taking a fair English woman to wife, begat a son in all respects as black as the father was, although England were his native country, and an English woman his mother: whereby it seemeth this blackness proceedeth rather of some natural infection of that man."

Man with head beneath his shoulders. From a Spanish edition of Mandeville's *Travels*. See *Othello* 1.3.144–45: "and men whose heads / Grew beneath their shoulders." Such men were frequently reported by medieval travelers to the East.

As the word "infection" suggests, Elizabethans frequently regarded blackness as a physical defect, though the blacks who lived in England and Scotland throughout the sixteenth century were also treated as exotic curiosities. At his marriage to Anne of Denmark, James I entertained his bride and her family by commanding four naked black youths to dance before him in the snow. (The youths died of exposure shortly afterward.) In 1594, in the festivities celebrating the baptism of James's son, a "Black-Moor" entered pulling an elaborately decorated chariot that was, in the original plan, supposed to be drawn in by a lion. There was a black trumpeter in the courts of Henry VII and Henry VIII, while Elizabeth had at least two black servants, one an entertainer and the other a page. Africans became increasingly popular as servants in aristocratic and gentle households in the last decades of the sixteenth century.

Some of these Africans were almost certainly slaves, though the legal status of slavery in England was ambiguous. In Cartwright's Case (1569), the court ruled "that England was too Pure an Air for Slaves to breathe in," but there is evidence that black slaves were owned in Elizabethan and Jacobean England. Moreover, by the mid-sixteenth century, the English had become involved in the profitable trade that carried African slaves to the New World. In 1562, John Hawkins embarked on his first slaving voyage, transporting some three hundred blacks from the Guinea coast to Hispaniola, where they were sold for £10,000. Elizabeth is reported to have said of this venture that it was "detestable, and would call down the Vengeance of Heaven upon the Undertakers." Nevertheless, she invested in Hawkins's subsequent voyages and loaned him ships.

English men and women of the sixteenth century experienced an unprecedented increase in knowledge of the world beyond their island, for a number of reasons. Religious persecution compelled both Catholics and Protestants to live abroad; wealthy gentlemen (and, in at least a few cases, ladies) traveled in France and Italy to view the famous cultural monuments; merchants published accounts of distant lands such as Turkey, Morocco, and Russia; and military and trading ventures took English ships to still more distant shores. In 1496, a Venetian tradesman living in Bristol, John Cabot, was granted a license by Henry VII to sail on a voyage of exploration; with his son Sebastian, he discovered Newfoundland and Nova Scotia. Remarkable feats of seamanship and reconnaissance soon followed: on his ship the *Golden Hind,* Sir Francis Drake circumnavigated the globe in 1579 and laid claim to California on behalf of the Queen; a few years later, a ship commanded by Thomas Cavendish also completed a circumnavigation. Sir Martin Frobisher explored bleak Baffin Island in search of a Northwest Passage to the Orient; Sir John Davis explored the west coast of Greenland and discovered the Falkland Islands off the coast of Argentina; Sir Walter Ralegh ventured up the Orinoco Delta, in what is now Venezuela, in search of the mythical land of El Dorado. Accounts of these and other exploits were collected by a clergyman and promoter of empire, Richard Hakluyt, and published as *The Principal Navigations* (1589; expanded edition 1599).

"To seek new worlds for gold, for praise, for glory," as Ralegh characterized such enterprises, was not for the faint of heart: Drake, Cavendish, Frobisher, and Hawkins all died at sea, as did huge numbers of those who sailed under their command. Elizabethans sensible enough to stay at home could do more than read written accounts of their fellow countrymen's far-reaching voyages. Expeditions brought back native plants (including, most famously, tobacco), animals, cultural artifacts, and, on occasion, samples of the native peoples themselves, most often seized against their will. There were exhibitions in London of a kidnapped Eskimo with his kayak and of Native Virginians with their canoes. Most of these miserable captives, violently uprooted and vulnerable to European diseases, quickly perished, but even in death they were evidently valuable property: when the English will not give one small coin "to relieve a lame beggar," one of the characters in *The Tempest* wryly remarks, "they will lay out ten to see a dead Indian" (2.2.30–31).

Perhaps most nations learn to define what they are by defining what they are not. This negative self-definition is, in any case, what Elizabethans seemed constantly to be doing, in travel books, sermons, political speeches, civic pageants, public exhibitions, and theatrical spectacles of otherness. The extraordinary variety of these exercises (which include public executions and urban riots, as well as more benign forms of curiosity) suggests that the boundaries of national identity were by no means clear and unequivocal. Even peoples whom English writers routinely, viciously stigmatize

An Indian dance. From Thomas Hariot, *A Brief and True Report of the New Found Land of Virginia* (1590).

as irreducibly alien—Italians, Indians, Turks, and Jews—have a surprising instability in the Elizabethan imagination and may appear for brief, intense moments as powerful models to be admired and emulated before they resume their place as emblems of despised otherness.

### *James I and the Union of the Crowns*

Though under great pressure to do so, the aging Elizabeth steadfastly refused to name her successor. It became increasingly apparent, however, that it would be James Stuart, the son of Mary, Queen of Scots, and by the time Elizabeth's health began to fail, several of her principal advisers, including her chief minister, Robert Cecil, had been for several years in secret correspondence with him in Edinburgh. Crowned King James VI of Scotland in 1567 when he was but one year old, Mary's son had been raised as a Protestant by his powerful guardians, and in 1589 he married a Protestant princess, Anne of Denmark. When Elizabeth died on March 24, 1603, English officials reported that on her deathbed the Queen had named James to succeed her.

Upon his accession, James—now styled James VI of Scotland and James I of England—made plain his intention to unite his two kingdoms. As he told Parliament in 1604, "What God hath conjoined then, let no man separate. I am the husband, and all of the whole isle is my lawful wife; I am the head and it is my body; I am the

Funeral procession of Queen Elizabeth. From a watercolor sketch by an unknown artist (1603).

shepherd and it is my flock." But the flock was less perfectly united than James optimistically envisioned: English and Scottish were sharply distinct identities, as were Welsh and Cornish and other peoples who were incorporated, with varying degrees of willingness, into the realm.

Fearing that to change the name of the kingdom would invalidate all laws and institutions established under the name of England, a fear that was partly real and partly a cover for anti-Scots prejudice, Parliament balked at James's desire to be called "King of Great Britain" and resisted the unionist legislation that would have made Great Britain a legal reality. Though the English initially rejoiced at the peaceful transition from Elizabeth to her successor, there was a rising tide of resentment against James's advancement of Scots friends and his creation of new knighthoods. Lower down the social ladder, English and Scots occasionally clashed violently on the streets: in July 1603, James issued a proclamation against Scottish "insolencies," and in April 1604, he ordered the arrest of "swaggerers" waylaying Scots in London. The ensuing years did not bring the amity and docile obedience for which James hoped, and, though the navy now flew the Union Jack, combining the Scottish cross of St. Andrew and the English cross of St. George, the unification of the kingdoms remained throughout his reign an unfulfilled ambition.

Unfulfilled as well were James's lifelong dreams of ruling as an absolute monarch. Crown lawyers throughout Europe had long argued that a king, by virtue of his power to make law, must necessarily be above law. But in England sovereignty was identified not with the king alone or with the people alone but with the "King in Parliament." Against his absolutist ambitions, James faced the crucial power to raise taxes that was vested not in the monarch but in the elected members of the Parliament. He faced as well a theory of republicanism that traced its roots back to ancient Rome and that prided itself on its steadfast and, if necessary, violent resistance to tyranny. Shakespeare's fascination with monarchy is apparent throughout his work, but in his Roman plays in particular, as well as in his long poem *The Rape of Lucrece*, he manifests an intense imaginative interest in the idea of a republic.

## *The Jacobean Court*

With James as with Elizabeth, the royal court was the center of diplomacy, ambition, intrigue, and an intense jockeying for social position. As always in monarchies, proximity to the king's person was a central mark of favor, so that access to the royal bedchamber was one of the highest aims of the powerful, scheming lords who followed James from his sprawling London palace at Whitehall to the hunting lodges and country estates to which he loved to retreat. A coveted office, in the Jacobean as in the Tudor court, was the Groom of the Stool, the person who supervised the disposal of the king's wastes. The officeholder was close to the king at one of his most exposed and vulnerable moments and enjoyed the further privilege of sleeping on a pallet at the foot of the royal bed and assisting the monarch in putting on the royal undershirt. Another, slightly less privileged official, the Gentleman of the Robes, dressed the king in his doublet and outer garments.

The royal lifestyle was increasingly expensive. Unlike Elizabeth, James had to maintain separate households for his queen and for the heir apparent, Prince Henry. (Upon Henry's death at the age of eighteen in 1612, his younger brother, Prince Charles, became heir, eventually succeeding his father in 1625.) James was also extremely generous to his friends, amassing his own huge debts in the course of paying off theirs. As early as 1605, he told his principal adviser that "it is a horror to me to think of the height of my place, the greatness of my debts, and the smallness of my means." This smallness notwithstanding, James continued to lavish gifts upon handsome favorites such as the Earl of Somerset, Robert Carr, and the Duke of Buckingham, George Villiers.

The attachment James formed for these favorites was highly romantic. "God so love me," the King wrote to Buckingham, "as I desire only to live in the world for your sake, and that I had rather live banished in any part of the earth with you than live a sorrowful widow's life without you." Such sentiments, not surprisingly, gave rise to widespread rumors of homosexual activities at court. The rumors are certainly plausible, though the surviving evidence of same-sex relationships, at court or elsewhere, is extremely difficult to interpret. A statute of 1533 made "the detestable and abominable vice of buggery committed with mankind or beast" a felony punishable by death. (English law declined to recognize or criminalize lesbian acts.) The effect of the draconian laws against sodomy seems to have been to reduce actual prosecutions to the barest minimum: for the next hundred years, there are no known cases of trials resulting in a death sentence for homosexual activity alone. If the legal record is therefore unreliable as an index of the extent of homosexual relations, the literary record (including, most famously, the majority of Shakespeare's sonnets) is equally opaque. Any poetic avowal of male-male love may simply be a formal expression of affection based on classical models, or, alternatively, it may be an expression of passionate physical and spiritual love. The interpretive difficulty is compounded by the absence in the period of any clear reference to a homosexual "identity," though there are many references to same-sex acts and feelings. What is clear is that male friendships at the court of James and elsewhere were suffused with eroticism, at once exciting and threatening, that subsequent periods policed more anxiously.

James I. Attributed to John De Critz the Elder (ca. 1606).

In addition to the extravagant expenditures on his favorites, James

*Two Young Men.* By Crispin van den Broeck.

was also the patron of ever more elaborate feasts and masques. Shakespeare's work provides a small glimpse of these in *The Tempest,* with its exotic banquet and its "majestic vision" of mythological goddesses and dancing nymphs and reapers. The actual Jacobean court masques, designed by the great architect, painter, and engineer Inigo Jones, were spectacular, fantastic, technically ingenious, and staggeringly costly celebrations of regal magnificence. With their exquisite costumes and their elegant blend of music, dancing, and poetry, the masques, generally performed by the noble lords and ladies of the court, were deliberately ephemeral exercises in conspicuous expenditure and consumption: by tradition, at the end of the performance, the private audience would rush forward and tear to pieces the gorgeous scenery. And though masques were enormously sophisticated entertainments, often on rather esoteric allegorical themes, they could on occasion collapse into grotesque excess. In a letter of 1606, Sir John Harington describes a masque in honor of the visiting Danish king in which the participants, no doubt toasting their royal majesties, had had too much to drink. A lady playing the part of the Queen of Sheba attempted to present precious gifts, "but, forgetting the steps arising to the canopy, overset her caskets into his Danish Majesty's lap. . . . His Majesty then got up and would dance with the Queen of Sheba; but he fell down and humbled himself before her, and was carried to an inner chamber and laid on a bed." Meanwhile, Harington writes, the masque continued with a pageant of Faith, Hope, and Charity, but Charity could barely keep her balance, while Hope and Faith "were both sick and spewing in the lower hall." This was, we can hope, not a typical occasion.

While the English seem initially to have welcomed James's free-spending ways as a change from the parsimoniousness of Queen Elizabeth, they were dismayed by its consequences. Elizabeth had died owing £400,000. In 1608, the royal debt had risen to £1,400,000 and was increasing by £140,000 a year. The money to pay off this debt, or at least to keep it under control, was raised by various means. These included customs farming (leasing the right to collect customs duties to private individuals); the highly unpopular impositions (duties on the import of nonnecessities, such as spices, silks, and currants); the sale of crown lands; the sale of baronetcies; and appeals to an increasingly grudging and recalcitrant Parliament. In 1614, Parliament demanded an end to impositions before it would relieve the King and was angrily dissolved without completing its business.

### *James's Religious Policy and the Persecution of Witches*

Before his accession to the English throne, the King had made known his view of Puritans, the general name for a variety of Protestant sects that were agitating for a radical reform of the church, the overthrow of its conservative hierarchy of bishops, and the rejection of a large number of traditional rituals and practices. In a book he wrote, *Basilikon Doron* (1599), James denounced "brainsick and heady preachers" who were prepared "to let King, people, law and all be trod underfoot." Yet he was not entirely unwilling to consider religious reforms. In religion, as in foreign policy, he was above all concerned to maintain peace.

On his way south to claim the throne of England in 1603, James was presented with the Millenary Petition (signed by one thousand ministers), which urged him as "our physician" to heal the disease of lingering "popish" ceremonies. He responded by calling a conference on the ceremonies of the Church of England, which duly took place at Hampton Court Palace in January 1604. The delegates who spoke for reform were moderates, and there was little in the outcome to satisfy Puritans. Nevertheless, while the Church of England continued to cling to such remnants of the Catholic past as wedding rings, square caps, bishops, and Christmas, the conference did produce some reform in the area of ecclesiastical discipline. It also authorized a new English translation of the Bible, known as the King James Bible, which was printed in 1611, too late to have been extensively used by Shakespeare. Along with Shakespeare's works, the King James Bible has probably had the profoundest influence on the subsequent history of English literature.

Having arranged this compromise, James saw his main task as ensuring conformity. He promulgated the 1604 Canons (the first definitive code of canon law since the Reformation), which required all ministers to subscribe to three articles. The first affirmed royal supremacy; the second confirmed that there was nothing in the Book of Common Prayer "contrary to the Word of God" and required ministers to use only the authorized services; the third asserted that the central tenets of the Church of England

The "swimming" of a suspected witch.

were "agreeable to the Word of God." There were strong objections to the second and third articles from those of Puritan leanings inside and outside the House of Commons. In the end, many ministers refused to conform or subscribe to the articles, but only about ninety of them, or 1 percent of the clergy, were deprived of their livings. In its theology and composition, the Church of England was little changed from what it had been under Elizabeth. In hindsight, what is most striking are the ominous signs of growing religious divisions that would by the 1640s burst forth in civil war and the execution of James's son Charles.

James seems to have taken seriously the official claims to the sacredness of kingship, and he certainly took seriously his own theories of religion and politics, which he had printed for the edification of his people. He was convinced that Satan, perpetually warring against God and His representatives on earth, was continually plotting against him. James thought moreover that he possessed special insight into Satan's wicked agents, the witches, and in 1597, while King of Scotland, he published his *Demonology,* a learned exposition of their malign threat to his godly rule. Hundreds of witches, he believed, were involved in a 1589 conspiracy to kill him by raising storms at sea when he was sailing home from Denmark with his new bride.

In the 1590s, Scotland embarked on a virulent witch craze of the kind that had since the fifteenth century repeatedly afflicted France, Switzerland, and Germany, where many thousands of women (and a much smaller number of men) were caught in a nightmarish web of wild accusations. Tortured into making lurid confessions of infant cannibalism, night flying, and sexual intercourse with the devil at huge, orgiastic "witches' Sabbaths," the victims had little chance to defend themselves and were routinely burned at the stake.

In England too there were witchcraft prosecutions, though on a much smaller scale and with significant differences in the nature of the accusations and the judicial procedures. Witch trials began in England in the 1540s; statutes against witchcraft were enacted in 1542, 1563, and 1604. English law did not allow judicial torture, stipulated lesser punishments in cases of "white magic," and mandated jury trials. Juries acquitted more than half of the defendants in witchcraft trials; in Essex, where the judicial records are particularly extensive, some 24 percent of those accused were executed, while the remainder of those convicted were pilloried and imprisoned or sentenced and reprieved. The accused were generally charged with *maleficium,* an evil deed—usually harming neighbors, causing destructive storms, or killing farm animals—but not with worshipping Satan.

After 1603, when James came to the English throne, he somewhat moderated his enthusiasm for the judicial murder of witches, for the most part defenseless, poor women resented by their neighbors. Though he did nothing to mitigate the ferocity of the ongoing witch hunts in his native Scotland, he did not try to institute Scottish-style persecutions and trials in his new realm. This relative waning of persecutorial eagerness principally reflects the differences between England and Scotland, but it may also bespeak some small, nascent skepticism on James's part about the quality of evidence brought against the accused and about the reliability of the "confessions" extracted from them. It is sobering to reflect that plays like Shakespeare's *Macbeth* (1606), Thomas Middleton's *Witch* (before 1616), and Thomas Dekker, John Ford, and William Rowley's *Witch of Edmonton* (1621) seem to be less the allies of skepticism than the exploiters of fear.

## The Playing Field

### *Cosmic Spectacles*

The first permanent, freestanding public theaters in England date only from Shakespeare's own lifetime: a London playhouse, the Red Lion, is mentioned in 1567, and

James Burbage's playhouse, The Theatre, was built in 1576. (The innovative use of these new stages, crucial to a full understanding of Shakespeare's achievement, is discussed in a separate essay in this volume, by the theater historian Holger Schott Syme.) But it is quite misleading to identify English drama exclusively with these specially constructed playhouses, for in fact there was a rich and vital theatrical tradition in England stretching back for centuries. Many towns in late medieval England were the sites of annual festivals that mounted elaborate cycles of plays depicting the great biblical stories, from the creation of the world to Christ's Passion and its miraculous aftermath. Most of these plays have been lost, but the surviving cycles, such as those from York, are magnificent and complex works of art. They are sometimes called "mystery plays," either because they were performed by the guilds of various crafts (known as "mysteries") or, more likely, because they represented the mysteries of the faith. The cycles were most often performed on the annual feast day instituted in the early fourteenth century in honor of the Corpus Christi, the sacrament of the Lord's Supper, which is perhaps the greatest of these religious mysteries.

The Feast of Corpus Christi, celebrated on the Thursday following Trinity Sunday, helped give the play cycles their extraordinary cultural resonance, but it also contributed to their downfall. For along with the specifically liturgical plays traditionally performed by religious confraternities and the "saints' plays," which depicted miraculous events in the lives of individual holy men and women, the mystery cycles were closely identified with the Catholic Church. Protestant authorities in the sixteenth century, eager to eradicate all remnants of popular Catholic piety, moved to suppress the annual procession of the Host, with its gorgeous banners, pageant carts, and cycle of visionary plays. In 1548, the Feast of Corpus Christi was abolished. Towns that continued to perform the mysteries were under increasing pressure to abandon them. It is sometimes said that the cycles were already dying out from neglect, but recent research has shown that many towns and their guilds were extremely reluctant to give them up. Desperate offers to strip away any traces of Catholic doctrine and to submit the play scripts to the authorities for their approval met with unbending opposition from the government. In 1576, the courts gave York permission to perform its cycle but only if

> in the said play no pageant be used or set forth wherein the Majesty of God the Father, God the Son, or God the Holy Ghost or the administration of either the Sacraments of baptism or of the Lord's Supper be counterfeited or represented, or anything played which tend to the maintenance of superstition and idolatry or which be contrary to the laws of God . . . or of the realm.

Such "permission" was tantamount to an outright ban. The local officials in the city of Norwich, proud of their St. George and the Dragon play, asked if they could at least parade the dragon costume through the streets, but even this modest request was refused. It is likely that as a young man Shakespeare had seen some of these plays: when Hamlet says of a noisy, strutting theatrical performance that it "out-Herods Herod," he is alluding to the famously bombastic role of Herod of Jewry in the mystery plays. But by the century's end, the cycles were no longer performed by live actors in great civic celebrations. They survived, if at all, in the debased form of puppet shows.

Early English theater was by no means restricted to these civic and religious festivals. Payments to professional and amateur performers appear in early records of towns and aristocratic households, though the Latin terms—*ministralli, histriones, mimi, lusores*, and so forth—are not used with great consistency and make it difficult to distinguish among minstrels, jugglers, stage players, and other entertainers. Performers acted in town halls and the halls of guilds and aristocratic mansions, on scaffolds erected in town squares and marketplaces, on pageant wagons in the streets, and in inn yards. By the fifteenth century, and probably earlier, there were organized companies of players traveling under noble patronage. Such companies earned a living providing amusement, while enhancing the prestige of the patron.

Panorama of London, showing two theaters, both round and both flying flags: a flying flag indicated that a performance was in progress. The Globe is in the foreground, and the Hope, or Beargarden, is to the left.

A description of a provincial performance in the late sixteenth century, written by one R. Willis, provides a glimpse of what seems to have been the usual procedure:

> In the City of Gloucester the manner is (as I think it is in other like corporations) that when the Players of Interludes come to town, they first attend the Mayor to inform him what nobleman's servant they are, and so to get license for their public playing; and if the Mayor like the Actors, or would show respect to their Lord and Master, he appoints them to play their first play before himself and the Aldermen and common Council of the City and that is called the Mayor's play, where everyone that will come in without money, the Mayor giving the players a reward as he thinks fit to show respect unto them.

In addition to their take from this "first play," the players would almost certainly have supplemented their income by performing in halls and inn yards, where they could on some occasions charge an admission fee. It was no doubt a precarious existence.

The "Interludes" mentioned in Willis's description of the Gloucester performances are likely plays that were, in effect, staged dialogues on religious, moral, and political themes. Such works could, like the mysteries, be associated with Catholicism, but they were also used in the sixteenth century to convey polemical Protestant messages, and they reached outside the religious sphere to address secular concerns as well. Henry Medwall's *Fulgens and Lucrece* (ca. 1490–1501), for example, pits a wealthy but dissolute nobleman against a virtuous public servant of humble origins, while John Heywood's *Play of the Weather* (ca. 1525–33) stages a debate among social rivals, including a gentleman, a merchant, a forest ranger, and two millers. The structure of such plays reflects the training in argumentation that students received in Tudor schools and, in particular, the sustained practice in examining all sides of a difficult question. Some of Shakespeare's amazing ability to look at critical issues from multiple perspectives may be traced back to this practice and the dramatic interludes it helped to inspire.

Another major form of theater that flourished in England in the fifteenth century and continued on into the sixteenth was the morality play. Like the mysteries, moralities addressed questions of the ultimate fate of the soul. They did so, however, not by rehearsing scriptural stories but by dramatizing allegories of spiritual struggle. Typically, a person named Human or Mankind or Youth is faced with a choice between a pious life in the company of such associates as Mercy, Discretion, and Good Deeds and a dissolute life among riotous companions like Lust or Mischief. Plays like *Mankind* (ca. 1465–70) and *Everyman* (ca. 1495) show how powerful these unpromising-sounding dramas could be, in part because of the extraordinary comic vitality of the evil character, or the Vice, and in part because of the poignancy and terror of an individual's encounter with death. Shakespeare clearly grasped this power. The hunchbacked Duke of Gloucester in *Richard III* gleefully likens himself to "the formal Vice, Iniquity." And when Othello wavers between Desdemona and Iago (himself a Vice figure), his anguished dilemma echoes the fateful choice repeatedly faced by the troubled, vulnerable protagonists of the moralities.

If such plays sound a bit like sermons, it is because they were. Clerics and actors shared some of the same rhetorical skills. It would be misleading to regard churchgoing and playgoing as comparable entertainments, but in attacking the stage, ministers often seemed to regard the professional players as dangerous rivals. "To leave a Sermon to go to a Play," warned the preacher John Stoughton, "is to forsake the Church of God; to betake oneself to the Synagogue of Satan, to fall from Heaven to Hell." The players themselves were generally too discreet to rise to the challenge; it would have been foolhardy to present the theater as the church's direct competitor. Yet in its moral intensity and its command of impassioned language, the stage frequently emulates and outdoes the pulpit.

### *Music and Dance*

Playacting took its place alongside other forms of public expression and entertainment as well. Perhaps the most important, from the perspective of the theater, were music and dance, since these were directly and repeatedly incorporated into plays. Many plays, comedies and tragedies alike, include occasions that call upon the characters to dance: hence Beatrice and Benedict join the other masked guests at the dance in *Much Ado About Nothing;* in *Twelfth Night,* the befuddled Sir Andrew, at the instigation of the drunken Sir Toby Belch, displays his skill, such as it is, in capering; Romeo and Juliet first see each other at the Capulet ball; the witches dance in a ring around the hideous caldron and perform an "antic round" to cheer Macbeth's spirits; and, in one of Shakespeare's strangest and most wonderful scenes, the drunken Antony in *Antony and Cleopatra* joins hands with Caesar, Enobarbus, Pompey, and others to dance "the Egyptian Bacchanals."

Moreover, virtually all plays in the period, including Shakespeare's, apparently ended with a dance. Brushing off the theatrical gore and changing their expressions from woe to pleasure, the actors in plays like *Romeo and Juliet* and *Julius Caesar* would presumably have received the audience's applause and then bid for a second round of applause by performing a stately pavane or a lively jig. The vogue may have begun to wane in the early seventeenth century, but only to give way to other post-play entertainments, such as the improvisation game known as "themes" where someone in the audience would shout out a theme or question (for example, "Why barks that dog?") and the actor would come up with an extempore response. (The clown Robert Armin, who played the Fool in *King Lear,* was apparently an expert at this game.) Jigs, with their comical leaping dance steps often accompanied by scurrilous ballads, remained popular enough to draw not only large crowds but also official disapproval. A court order of 1612 complained about the "cut-purses and other lewd and ill-disposed persons" who flocked to the theater at the end of every play to be entertained by "lewd jigs, songs, and dances." The players were warned to suppress these disreputable entertainments on pain of imprisonment.

The displays of dancing onstage clearly reflected a widespread popular interest in dancing outside the walls of the playhouse as well. Renaissance intellectuals conjured up visions of the universe as a great cosmic dance, poets figured relations between men and women in terms of popular dance steps, stern moralists denounced dancing as an incitement to filthy lewdness, and, perhaps as significant, men of all classes evidently spent a great deal of time worrying about how shapely their legs looked in tights and how gracefully they could leap. Shakespeare assumes that his audience will be quite familiar with a variety of dances. "For, hear me, Hero," Beatrice tells her friend, "wooing, wedding, and repenting is as a Scotch jig, a measure, and a cinquepace" (*Much Ado About Nothing* 2.1.61–62). Her speech dwells on the comparison a bit, teasing out its implications, but it still does not make much sense if you do not already know something about the dances and perhaps occasionally venture to perform them yourself.

Closely linked to dancing and even more central to the stage was music, both instrumental and vocal. In the early sixteenth century, the Reformation had been disastrous for sacred music: many church organs were destroyed, choir schools were closed, the glorious polyphonic liturgies sung in the monasteries were suppressed. But by the latter part of the century, new perspectives were reinvigorating English music. Latin Masses were reset in English, and tunes were written for newly translated, metrical psalms. More important for the theater, styles of secular music were developed that emphasized music's link to humanist eloquence, its ability to heighten and to rival rhetorically powerful texts.

This link is particularly evident in vocal music, at which Elizabethan composers excelled. Renowned composers William Byrd, Thomas Morley, John Dowland, and others wrote a rich profusion of madrigals (part songs for two to eight voices unaccompanied) and ayres (songs for solo voice, generally accompanied by the lute). These works, along with hymns, popular ballads, rounds, catches, and other forms of song, enjoyed immense popularity, not only in the royal court, where musical skill was regarded as an important accomplishment, and in aristocratic households, where professional musicians were employed as entertainers, but also in less exalted social circles. In his *Plain and Easy Introduction to Practical Music* (1597), Morley tells a

Frans Hals, *The Clown with the Lute* (1625).

story of social humiliation at a failure to perform that suggests that a well-educated Elizabethan was expected to be able to sing at sight. Even if this is an exaggeration in the interest of book sales, there is evidence of impressively widespread musical literacy, reflected in a splendid array of music for the lute, viol, recorder, harp, and virginal, as well as the marvelous vocal music.

Whether it is the aristocratic Orsino luxuriating in the dying fall of an exquisite melody or bully Bottom craving "the tongs and the bones," Shakespeare's characters frequently call for music. They also repeatedly give voice to the age's conviction that there was a deep relation between musical harmony and the harmonies of the well-ordered individual and state. "The man that hath no music in himself," warns Lorenzo in *The Merchant of Venice,* "nor is not moved with concord of sweet sounds, / Is fit for treasons, stratagems, and spoils" (5.1.83–85). This conviction in turn reflects a still deeper link between musical harmony and the divinely created harmony of the cosmos. When Ulysses in *Troilus and Cressida* wishes to convey the image of universal chaos, he speaks of the untuning of a string (1.3.108–09).

The playing companies must have regularly employed trained musicians, and many actors (like the actor who in playing Pandarus in *Troilus and Cressida* is supposed to accompany himself on the lute) must have possessed musical skill. When Shakespeare's company began to use an indoor theater, the Blackfriars, as a second venue, it became famous for its orchestra, and, among other composers, the King's Musician, Robert Johnson, seems to have written songs for the actors to sing. Unfortunately, we possess the original settings for very few of Shakespeare's songs, possibly because many of them may have been set to popular tunes of the time that everyone knew and no one bothered to write down.

### *Alternative Entertainments*

Plays, music, and dancing were by no means the only shows in town. There were jousts, tournaments, royal entries, religious processions, pageants in honor of newly installed civic officials or ambassadors arriving from abroad; wedding masques, court masques, and costumed entertainments known as "disguisings" or "mummings"; juggling acts, fortune-tellers, exhibitions of swordsmanship, mountebanks, folk healers, storytellers, magic shows; bearbaiting, bullbaiting, cockfighting, and other blood sports; folk festivals such as Maying, the Feast of Fools, Carnival, and Whitsun Ales. For several years, Elizabethan Londoners were delighted by a trained animal—Banks's Horse—that performed elaborate dance steps and could, it was thought, do arithmetic and answer questions. And there was always the grim but compelling spectacle of public shaming, mutilation, and execution.

Most English towns had stocks and whipping posts. Drunks, fraudulent merchants, adulterers, and quarrelers could be placed in carts or mounted backward on asses and paraded through the streets for crowds to jeer and throw refuse at. Women accused of being scolds, as we have already remarked, could be publicly muzzled by an iron device called a "brank" or tied to a cucking stool and dunked in the river. Convicted criminals could have their ears cut off, their noses slit, their foreheads branded. Public beheadings (generally reserved for the elite) and hangings were common. Those convicted of treason were sentenced to be "hanged by the neck, and being alive cut down, and your privy members to be cut off, and your bowels to be taken out of your belly and there burned, you being alive."

Shakespeare occasionally takes note of these alternative entertainments: at the end of *Macbeth,* for example, with his enemies closing in on him, the doomed tyrant declares, "They have tied me to a stake. I cannot fly, / But bearlike I must fight the course" (5.7.1–2). The audience is reminded then that it is witnessing the human equivalent of a popular spectacle—a bear chained to a stake and attacked by fierce dogs—that they could have paid to watch at an arena near the Globe. And when, a few moments later, Macduff enters carrying Macbeth's head, the audience is seeing the theatrical equiva-

An Elizabethan hanging.

lent of the execution of criminals and traitors that they could have also watched in the flesh, as it were, nearby. In a different key, the audiences who paid to see *A Midsummer Night's Dream* or *The Winter's Tale* got to enjoy the comic spectacle of a Maying and a Whitsun Pastoral, while the spectators of *The Tempest* could gawk at what the Folio list of characters calls a "savage and deformed slave" and to enjoy an aristocratic magician's wedding masque in honor of his daughter.

## *The Enemies of the Stage*

In 1624, a touring company of players arrived in Norwich and requested permission to perform. Permission was denied, but the municipal authorities, "in regard of the honorable respect which this City beareth to the right honorable the Lord Chamberlain," gave the players twenty shillings to get out of town. Throughout the sixteenth and early seventeenth centuries, there are many similar records of civic officials prohibiting performances and then, to appease a powerful patron, paying the actors to take their skills elsewhere. As early as the 1570s, there is evidence that the London authorities, while mindful of the players' influential protectors, were energetically trying to drive the theater out of the city.

Why should what we now regard as one of the undisputed glories of the age have aroused so much hostility? One answer, curiously enough, is traffic: plays drew large audiences—the public theaters could accommodate thousands—and residents objected to the crowds, the noise, and the crush of carriages. Other, more serious concerns were public health and crime. It was thought that numerous diseases, including the dreaded bubonic plague, were spread by noxious odors, and the packed playhouses were obvious breeding grounds for infection. (Patrons often tried to protect themselves by sniffing nosegays or stuffing cloves into their nostrils.) The large crowds drew pickpockets, cutpurses, and other scoundrels. On more than one occasion, if Shakespeare's fellow actor Will Kemp may be believed, pickpockets, caught in the act during a performance, were tied to a post onstage "for all people to wonder at." The theater was, moreover, a well-known haunt of prostitutes and, it was alleged, a place where innocent

Syphilis victim in tub. Frontispiece to the play *Cornelianum Dolium* (1638), possibly written by Thomas Randolph. The tub inscription translates as "I sit on the throne of love, I suffer in the tub"; and the banner as "Farewell, O sexual pleasures and lusts."

maids were seduced and respectable matrons corrupted. It was darkly rumored that "chambers and secret places" adjoined the theater galleries, and in any case, taverns, disreputable inns, and whorehouses were close at hand.

There were other charges as well. Plays in the public, outdoor amphitheaters were performed in the afternoon and therefore drew people, especially the young, away from their work. They were schools of idleness, luring apprentices from their trades, law students from their studies, housewives from their kitchens, and potentially pious souls from the sober meditations to which they might otherwise devote themselves. Wasting their time and money on disreputable shows, citizens exposed themselves to sexual provocation and outright political sedition. Even when the content of plays was morally exemplary—and, of course, few plays were so gratifyingly high-minded—the theater itself, in the eyes of most mayors and aldermen, was inherently disorderly.

The attack on the stage by civic officials was echoed and intensified by many of the age's moralists and religious leaders, especially those associated with Puritanism. While English Protestants earlier in the sixteenth century had attempted to counter the Catholic mystery cycles and saints' plays by mounting their own doctrinally correct dramas, by the century's end a fairly widespread consensus, even among those mildly sympathetic toward the theater, held that the stage and the pulpit were in tension with one another. After 1591, a ban on Sunday performances was strictly enforced, and in 1606, Parliament passed an act imposing a hefty fine of £10 on any person who shall "in any stage-play, interlude, show, May-game, or pageant, jestingly or profanely speak or use the holy name of God, or of Christ Jesus, or of the Holy Ghost, or of the Trinity (which are not to be spoken but with fear and reverence)." If changes in the printed texts are a reliable indication, the players seem to have complied at least to some degree with the ruling. The Folio (1623) text of *Richard III,* for example, omits the Quarto's (1597) four uses of "zounds" (for "God's wounds"), along with a mention of "Christ's dear blood shed for our grievous sins"; "God's my judge" in *The Merchant of Venice* becomes "well I know"; "By Jesu" in *Henry V* becomes a very proper "I say"; and in all the plays, "God" is from time to time metamorphosed to "Jove."

But for some of the theater's more extreme critics, these modest expurgations were tiny bandages on a gaping wound. In his huge book *Histriomastix* (1633), William Prynne regurgitates a half-century of frenzied attacks on the "sinful, heathenish, lewd, ungodly Spectacles." In the eyes of Prynne and his fellow antitheatricalists, stage plays were part of a demonic tangle of obscene practices proliferating like a cancer in the body of society. It is "manifest to all men's judgments," he writes, that

> effeminate mixed dancing, dicing, stage-plays, lascivious pictures, wanton fashions, face-painting, health-drinking, long hair, love-locks, periwigs, women's curling, powdering and cutting of their hair, bonfires, New-year's gifts, May-games, amorous pastorals, lascivious effeminate music, excessive laughter, luxurious disorderly Christmas-keeping, mummeries . . . [are] wicked, unchristian pastimes.

Given the anxious emphasis on effeminacy, it is not surprising that denunciations of this kind obsessively focused on the use of boy actors to play the female parts. The enemies of the stage charged that theatrical transvestism excited illicit sexual desires, both heterosexual and homosexual.

Since cross-dressing violated a biblical prohibition (Deuteronomy 22:5), religious antitheatricalists attacked it as wicked regardless of its erotic charge; indeed, they often seemed to consider any act of impersonation as inherently wicked. In their view, the theater itself was Satan's domain. Thus a Cambridge scholar, John Greene, reports the sad fate of "a Christian woman" who went to the theater to see a play: "She entered in well and sound, but she returned and came forth possessed of the devil. Whereupon certain godly brethren demanded Satan how he durst be so bold, as to enter into her a Christian. Whereto he answered, that *he found her in his own house,* and therefore took possession of her as his own" (italics in original). When the "godly brethren" came to power in the mid-seventeenth century, with the overthrow of Charles I, they saw to it that the playhouses, shut down in 1642 at the onset of the Civil War, remained closed. Public theater did not resume until the restoration of the monarchy in 1660.

Faced with enemies among civic officials and religious leaders, Elizabethan and Jacobean playing companies relied on the protection of their powerful patrons. As the liveried servants of aristocrats or of the monarch, the players could refute the charge that they were mere vagabonds, and they claimed, as a convenient legal fiction, that their public performances were necessary rehearsals in anticipation of those occasions when they would be called upon to entertain their noble masters. But harassment by the mayor and aldermen of the City of London—an area roughly one mile square, defined by the old Roman walls—continued unabated, and the players were forced to build their theaters outside the immediate jurisdiction of these authorities, either in the suburbs or in the areas known as the "liberties." A liberty was a piece of land within the City of London itself that was not directly subject to the authority of the Lord Mayor. The most significant liberty from the point of view of the theater was the area near St. Paul's Cathedral called "the Blackfriars," where, until the dissolution of the monasteries in 1538, there had been a Dominican priory. It was here that in 1608 Shakespeare's company, then called the King's Men, took over an indoor playhouse in which they performed during the winter months, reserving the open-air Globe in the suburb of Southwark for the warmer months.

## *Censorship and Regulation*

In addition to those authorities who campaigned to shut down the theater, there were others whose task was to oversee, regulate, and censor it. Given the outright hostility of the former, the latter may have seemed to the London players equivocal allies rather than enemies. After all, plays that passed the censor were at least licensed to be performed and hence conceded to have some limited legitimacy. In April 1559, at the very start of her reign, Queen Elizabeth drafted a proposal that for the first time envisaged a system for the prior review and regulation of plays throughout her kingdom:

> The Queen's Majesty doth straightly forbid all manner interludes to be played either openly or privately, except the same be notified beforehand, and licensed within any city or town corporate, by the mayor or other chief officers of the same, and within any shire, by such as shall be lieutenants for the Queen's Majesty in

> the same shire, or by two of the Justices of Peace inhabiting within that part of the shire where any shall be played. . . . And for instruction to every of the said officers, her Majesty doth likewise charge every of them, as they will answer: that they permit none to be played wherein either matters of religion or of the governance of the estate of the commonweal shall be handled or treated upon, but by men of authority, learning and wisdom, nor to be handled before any audience, but of grave and discreet persons.

This proposal, which may not have been formally enacted, makes an important distinction between those who are entitled to address sensitive issues of religion and politics—authors "of authority, learning and wisdom" addressing audiences "of grave and discreet persons"—and those who are forbidden to do so.

The London public theater, with its playwrights who were the sons of glovers, shoemakers, and bricklayers and its audiences in which the privileged classes mingled with rowdy apprentices, masked women, and servants, was clearly not a place to which the government wished to grant freedom of expression. In 1581, the Master of the Revels, an official in the Lord Chamberlain's department whose role had hitherto been to provide entertainment at court, was given an expanded commission. Sir Edmund Tilney, the functionary who held the office, was authorized

> to warn, command, and appoint in all places within this our Realm of England, as well within franchises and liberties as without, all and every player or players with their playmakers, either belonging to any nobleman or otherwise . . . to appear before him with all such plays, tragedies, comedies, or shows as they shall in readiness or mean to set forth, and them to recite before our said Servant or his sufficient deputy, whom we ordain, appoint, and authorize by these presents of all such shows, plays, players, and playmakers, together with their playing places, to order and reform, authorize and put down, as shall be thought meet or unmeet unto himself or his said deputy in that behalf.

What emerged from this commission was in effect a national system of regulation and censorship. One of its consequences was to restrict virtually all licensed theater to the handful of authorized London-based playing companies. These companies would have to submit their plays for official scrutiny, but in return they received implicit, and on occasion explicit, protection against the continued fierce opposition of the local authorities. Plays reviewed and allowed by the Master of the Revels had been deemed fit to be performed before the monarch; how could mere aldermen legitimately claim that such plays should be banned as seditious?

The key question, of course, is how carefully the Master of the Revels scrutinized the plays brought before him either to hear or, more often from the 1590s onward, to peruse. What was Tilney, who served in the office until his death in 1610, or his successor, Sir George Buc, who served from 1610 to 1621, looking for? What did they insist be cut before they would release what was known as the "allowed copy," the only version licensed for performance? Unfortunately, the office books of the Master of the Revels in Shakespeare's time have been lost; what survives is a handful of scripts on which Tilney, Buc, and their assistants jotted their instructions. These suggest that the readings were rather painstaking, with careful attention paid to possible religious, political, and diplomatic repercussions. References, direct or strongly implied, to any living Christian prince or any important English nobleman, gentleman, or government official were particularly sensitive and likely to be struck. Renaissance political life was highly personalized; people in power were exceptionally alert to insult and zealously patrolled the boundaries of their prestige and reputation.

Moreover, the censors knew that audiences and readers were quite adept at applying theatrical representations distanced in time and space to their own world. At a time of riots against resident foreigners, Tilney read *Sir Thomas More,* a play in which Shakespeare probably had a hand, and instructed the players to cut scenes that, though set in

1517, might have had an uncomfortable contemporary resonance. "Leave out the insurrection wholly," Tilney's note reads, "and the cause thereof and begin with Sir Thomas More at the Mayor's sessions, with a report afterwards of his good service done being sheriff of London upon a mutiny against the Lombards only by a short report and not otherwise at your own perils. E. Tilney." Of course, as Tilney knew perfectly well, most plays succeed precisely by mirroring, if only obliquely, their own times, but this particular reflection evidently seemed to him too dangerous or provocative.

The topical significance of a play depends in large measure on the particular moment in which it is performed, and on certain features of the performance—for example, a striking resemblance between one of the characters and a well-known public figure—that the script itself will not necessarily disclose to us at this great distance, or even disclosed to the censor at the time. Hence the Master of the Revels noted angrily of one play performed in 1632 that "there were diverse personated so naturally, both of lords and others of the court, that I took it ill." Hence too a play that was deemed allowable when it was first written and performed could return, like a nightmare, to disturb a different place and time. The most famous instance of such a return involves Shakespeare, for on the day before the Earl of Essex's attempted coup against Queen Elizabeth in 1601, someone paid the Lord Chamberlain's Men (Shakespeare's company at the time) forty shillings to revive their old play about the deposition and murder of Richard II. "I am Richard II," the Queen declared. "Know ye not that?" However distressed she was by this performance, the Queen significantly did not take out her wrath on the players: neither the playwright nor his company was punished, nor was the Master of the Revels criticized for allowing the play in the first place. It was Essex and several of his key supporters, including the man who commissioned the performance, who lost their heads.

Evidence suggests that the Master of the Revels often regarded himself not as the strict censor of the theater but as its friendly guardian, charged with averting catastrophes. He was a bureaucrat concerned less with subversive ideas per se than with potential trouble. That is, there is no record of a dramatist being called to account for his heterodox beliefs; rather, plays were censored if they risked offending influential people, including important foreign allies, or if they threatened to cause public disorder by exacerbating religious or other controversies. The distinction is not a stable one, but it helps to explain the intellectual boldness, power, and freedom of a censored theater in a society in which the perceived enemies of the state were treated mercilessly. Shakespeare could have Lear articulate a searing indictment of social injustice—

> Robes and furred gowns hide all. Plate sins with gold,
> And the strong lance of justice hurtless breaks.
> Arm it in rags, a pigmy's straw does pierce it.
> (4.5.159–61)

—and evidently neither the Master of the Revels nor the courtiers in their robes and furred gowns protested. But when the Spanish ambassador complained about Thomas Middleton's anti-Spanish allegory *A Game at Chess,* performed at the Globe in 1624, the whole theater was shut down, the players were arrested, and the King professed to be furious at his official for licensing the play in the first place and allowing it to be performed for nine consecutive days.

In addition to the system for the licensing of plays for performance, there was a system for the licensing of plays for publication. At the start of Shakespeare's career, such press licensing was the responsibility of the Court of High Commission, headed by the Archbishop of Canterbury and the Bishop of London. Their deputies, a panel of junior clerics, were supposed to review the manuscripts, granting licenses to those worthy of publication and rejecting any they deemed "heretical, seditious, or unseemly for Christian ears." Without a license, the Stationers' Company, the guild of the book trade, was not supposed to register a manuscript for publication. In practice, as various complaints and attempts to close loopholes attest, some playbooks were printed without a license. In 1607, the system was significantly revised when Sir George Buc began to license plays for the press. When Buc succeeded to the post of Master of the Revels in 1610, the powers to license plays for the stage and the page were vested in one man.

## *Theatrical Innovations*

The theater continued to flourish under this system of regulation after Shakespeare's death in 1616; by the 1630s, as many as five playhouses were operating daily in London. When the theater reemerged in 1660 after the eighteen-year hiatus imposed by Puritan rule, it quickly resumed its cultural importance, but not without a number of significant changes. Major innovations in staging resulted principally from continental influences on the English artists who accompanied the court of Charles II into exile in France, where they supplied it with masques and other theatrical entertainments.

The institutional conditions and business practices of the two companies chartered by Charles after the Restoration in 1660 also differed from those of Shakespeare's theater. In place of the more collective practice of Shakespeare's company, the Restoration theaters were controlled by celebrated actor-managers who not only assigned themselves starring roles, in both comedy and tragedy, but also assumed sole responsibility for many business decisions, including the setting of their colleagues' salaries. At the same time, the power of the actor-manager, great as it was, was limited by the new importance of outside capital. No longer was the theater, with all of its properties from script to costumes, owned by the "sharers," that is, by those actors who held shares in the joint stock company. Instead, entrepreneurs would raise capital for increasingly fantastic sets and stage machinery that could cost as much as £3,000, an astronomical sum, for a single production. This investment in turn not only influenced the kinds of new plays written for the theater but helped to transform old plays that were revived, including Shakespeare's.

In his diary entry for August 24, 1661, Samuel Pepys notes that he has been "to the Opera, and there saw Hamlet, Prince of Denmark, done with scenes very well, but above all, Betterton did the prince's part beyond imagination." This is Thomas Betterton's first review, as it were, and it is typical of the enthusiasm he would inspire throughout his fifty-year career on the London stage. Pepys's brief and scattered remarks on the plays he voraciously attended in the 1660s are precious because they are among the few records from the period of concrete and immediate responses to theatrical performances. Modern readers might miss the significance of Pepys's phrase "done with scenes": this production of *Hamlet* was only the third play to use the movable sets first introduced to England by its producer, William Davenant. The central historical fact that makes the productions of this period so exciting is that public theater had been banned altogether for eighteen years until the Restoration of Charles II.

A brief discussion of theatrical developments in the Restoration period will enable us at least to glance longingly at a vast subject that lies outside the scope of this introduction: the rich performance history that extends from Shakespeare's time to our own, involving tens of thousands of productions and adaptations for theater, opera, dance, Broadway musicals, and of course films. The scale of this history is vast in space as well as time: already in the late sixteenth and early seventeenth centuries, troupes of English actors performed as far afield as Poland and Bohemia.

While producing masques at the court of Charles I, the poet William Davenant had become an expert on stage scenery, and when the theaters reopened, he set to work on converting an indoor tennis court into a new kind of theater. He designed a broad open platform like that of the Elizabethan stage, but at the back of this platform he added or expanded a space, framed by a proscenium arch, in which scenes could be displayed. These elaborately painted scenes could be moved on and off, using grooves on the floor. The perspectival effect for a spectator of one central painted panel with two "wings" on either side was that of three sides of a room. This effect anticipated that of the familiar "picture frame" stage, developed fully in the nineteenth century, and began a subtle shift in theater away from the elaborate verbal descriptions that are so central to Shakespeare and toward the evocative visual poetry of the set designer's art.

Another convention of Shakespeare's stage, the use of boy actors for female roles, gave way to the more complete illusion of women playing women's parts. The King issued a decree in 1662 forcefully permitting, if not requiring, the use of actresses. The royal decree is couched in the language of social and moral reform: the introduction of actresses will require the "reformation" of scurrilous and profane passages in plays, and this in turn will help forestall some of the objections that shut the theaters down in 1642. In reality, male theater audiences, composed of a narrower range of courtiers and aristocrats than in Shakespeare's time, met this intended reform with the assumption that the new actresses were fair game sexually; most actresses (with the partial exception of those who married male members of their troupes) were regarded as, or actually became, whores. But despite the social stigma, and the fact that their salaries were predictably lower than those of their male counterparts, the stage saw some formidable female stars by the 1680s.

The first recorded appearance of an actress was that of a Desdemona in December 1660. Betterton's Ophelia in 1661 was Mary Saunderson (ca. 1637–1712), who became Mrs. Betterton a year later. The most famous Ophelia of the period was Susanna Mountfort, who appeared in that role for the first time at the age of fifteen in 1705. The performance by Mountfort that became legendary occurred in 1720, after a disappointment in love, or so it was said, had driven her mad. Hearing that *Hamlet* was being performed, Mountfort escaped from her keepers and reached the theater, where she concealed herself until the scene in which Ophelia enters in her state of insanity. At this point, Mountfort rushed onto the stage and, in the words of a contemporary, "was in truth Ophelia herself, to the amazement of the performers and the astonishment of the audience."

David Garrick and George Anne Bellamy in a celebrated production of *Romeo and Juliet* at Drury Lane, London. Engraving after a painting by Benjamin Wilson (1753).

That the character Ophelia became increasingly and decisively identified with the mad scene owes something to this occurrence, but it is also a consequence of the text used for Restoration performances of *Hamlet.* Having received the performance rights to a good number of Shakespeare's plays, Davenant altered them for the stage in the 1660s, and many of these acting versions remained in use for generations. In the case of *Hamlet,* neither Davenant nor his successors did what they so often did with other plays by Shakespeare, that is, alter the plot radically and interpolate other material. But many of the lines were cut or "improved." The cuts included most of Ophelia's sane speeches, such as her spirited retort to Laertes' moralizing; what remained made her part almost entirely an emblem of "female love melancholy."

Thomas Betterton (1635–1710), the prototype of the actor-manager, who would be the dominant figure in Shakespeare interpretation and in the English theater generally through the nineteenth century, made Hamlet his premier role. A contemporary who saw his last performance in the part (at the age of seventy-four, a rather old Prince of Denmark) wrote that to *read* Shakespeare's play was to encounter "dry, incoherent, & broken sentences," but that to see Betterton was to "prove" that the play was written "correctly." Spectators especially admired his reaction to the Ghost's appearance in the Queen's bedchamber: "his Countenance . . . thro' the violent and sudden Emotions of Amazement and Horror, turn[ed] instantly on the Sight of his fathers Spirit, as pale as his Neckcloath, when every Article of his Body seem's affected with a Tremor inexpressible." A piece of stage business in this scene, Betterton's upsetting his chair on the Ghost's entrance, became so thoroughly identified with the part that later productions were censured if the actor left it out. This business could very well have been handed down from Richard Burbage, the star of Shakespeare's original production, for Davenant, who had coached Betterton in the role, had known the performances of Joseph Taylor, who had succeeded Burbage in it. It is strangely gratifying to notice that Hamlets on stage and screen still occasionally upset their chairs.

## Shakespeare's Life and Art

Playwrights, even hugely successful playwrights, were not ordinarily the objects of popular curiosity in early modern England. Many plays in this period were issued without the name of the author—there was no equivalent to our copyright system, and publishers were not required to specify on their title pages who wrote the texts they printed. Only occasionally were there significant exceptions, motivated by the pursuit of profit. Though by 1597 seven of Shakespeare's plays had been printed, the title pages did not identify him as the author. Beginning in 1598 Shakespeare's name, spelled in various ways, began to appear, and indeed several plays almost certainly not written by him were printed with his name. His name—Shakespeare, Shake-speare, Shakspeare, Shaxberd, Shakespere, and the like—had evidently begun to sell plays. During his lifetime more published plays were attributed to Shakespeare than to any other contemporary dramatist.

But this marketplace interest did not extend to the details of his life. It is both revealing and frustrating that the First Folio editors, John Heminges and Henry Condell—who knew Shakespeare well—were virtually silent about their friend's personal history. Though they included the author's picture, they did not bother to include his birth and death dates, his marital status, the names of his surviving children, his intellectual and social affiliations, his endearing or annoying quirks of character, let alone anything more psychologically revealing, such as the "table talk" carefully recorded by followers of Martin Luther. Shakespeare may have been a very private man, but, as he was dead when the edition was produced, it is unlikely to have been his own wishes that dictated the omissions. The editors evidently assumed that the potential buyers of the book—and this was an expensive commercial venture—would not be particularly interested in what we would now regard as essential biographical details.

Such presumed indifference is, in all likelihood, chiefly a reflection of Shakespeare's modest origins. He flew below the radar of ordinary Elizabethan and Jacobean social curiosity. In the wake of the death of the poet Sir Philip Sidney, Fulke Greville wrote a fascinating biography of his friend, but Sidney was a dashing aristocrat, linked by birth and marriage to the great families of the realm, and he died tragically of a wound he received on the battlefield. Writers of a less exalted station did not excite the same interest, unless, like Ben Jonson, they cultivated an extravagant public persona, or, like another of Shakespeare's contemporaries, Christopher Marlowe, they ran afoul of the authorities and got themselves murdered. The fact that there are no police reports, Privy Council orders, indictments, or postmortem inquests about Shakespeare, as there are about Marlowe, tells us something significant about Shakespeare's life—he possessed a gift for staying out of trouble—but it is not the kind of detail on which biographers thrive.

Yet Elizabethan England was a record-keeping society, and centuries of archival labor have turned up a substantial number of traces of its greatest playwright and his family. By themselves the traces would have relatively little interest, but in the light of Shakespeare's plays and poems, they have come to seem like precious relics and manage to achieve a considerable resonance.

## *Shakespeare's Family*

William Shakespeare's grandfather, Richard, farmed land by the village of Snitterfield, near the small, pleasant market town of Stratford-upon-Avon, about ninety-six miles northwest of London. The playwright's father, John, moved in the mid-sixteenth century to Stratford, where he became a successful glover, landowner, moneylender, and dealer in wool and other agricultural goods. In or about 1557, he married Mary Arden, the daughter of a prosperous and well-connected farmer from the same area, Robert Arden of Wilmcote.

John Shakespeare was evidently highly esteemed by his fellow townspeople, for he held a series of important posts in local government. In 1556, he was appointed ale taster, an office reserved for "able persons and discreet," in 1558 was sworn in as a constable, and in 1561 was elected as one of the town's fourteen burgesses. As burgess, John served as one of the two chamberlains, responsible for administering borough property and revenues. In 1567, he was elected bailiff, Stratford's highest elective office and the equivalent of mayor. Though John Shakespeare signed all official documents with a cross or other sign, it is likely, though not certain, that he knew how to read and write. Mary, who also signed documents only with her mark, is less likely to have been literate.

According to the parish registers, which recorded baptisms and burials, the Shakespeares had eight children, four daughters and four sons, beginning with a daughter, Joan, born in 1558. A second daughter, Margaret, was born in December 1562 and died a few months later. William Shakespeare ("Gulielmus, filius Johannes Shakespeare"), their first son, was baptized on April 26, 1564. Since there was usually a few days' lapse between birth and baptism, it is conventional to celebrate Shakespeare's birthday on April 23, which happens to coincide with the Feast of St. George, England's patron saint, and with the day of Shakespeare's death fifty-two years later.

William Shakespeare had three younger brothers, Gilbert, Richard, and Edmund, and two younger sisters, Joan and Anne. (It was often the custom to recycle a name, so the first-born Joan must have died before the birth in 1569 of another daughter christened Joan, the only one of the girls to survive childhood.) Gilbert, who died in his forty-fifth year in 1612, is described in legal records as a Stratford haberdasher; Edmund followed William to London and became a professional actor, though evidently of no

Southeast prospect of Stratford-upon-Avon, 1746. From *Gentleman's Magazine* (December 1792).

particular repute. He was only twenty-eight when he died in 1607 and was given an expensive funeral, perhaps paid for by his successful older brother.

At the high point of his public career, John Shakespeare, the father of this substantial family, applied to the Herald's College for a coat of arms, which would have marked his (and his family's) elevation from the ranks of substantial middle-class citizenry to that of the gentry. But the application went nowhere, for soon after he initiated what would have been a costly petitioning process, John apparently fell on hard times. The decline must have begun when William was still living at home, a boy of twelve or thirteen. From 1576 onward, John Shakespeare stopped attending council meetings. He became caught up in costly lawsuits, started mortgaging his land, and incurred substantial debts. In 1586, he was finally replaced on the council; in 1592, he was one of nine Stratford men listed as absenting themselves from church out of fear of being arrested for debt.

The reason for the reversal in John Shakespeare's fortunes is unknown. Some have speculated that it may have stemmed from adherence to Catholicism, since those who remained loyal to the old faith were subject to increasingly vigorous and costly discrimination. But if John Shakespeare was a Catholic, as seems possible, it would not necessarily explain his decline, since other Catholics (and Puritans) in Elizabethan Stratford and elsewhere managed to hold on to their offices. In any case, his fall from prosperity and local power, whatever its cause, was not absolute. In 1601, the last year of his life, his name was included among those qualified to speak on behalf of Stratford's rights. And he was by that time entitled to bear a coat of arms, for in 1596, some twenty years after the application to the Herald's office had been initiated, it was successfully renewed. There is no record of who paid for the bureaucratic procedures that made the grant possible, but it is likely to have been John's oldest son, William, by that time a highly successful London playwright. By elevating his father, he would have made himself a gentleman as well.

## *Education*

Stratford was a small provincial town, but it had long been the site of an excellent free school, originally established by the church in the thirteenth century. The main purpose of such schools in the Middle Ages had been to train prospective clerics; since many aristocrats could neither read nor write, literacy by itself conferred no special distinction and was not routinely viewed as desirable. But the situation began to change markedly in the sixteenth century. Protestantism placed a far greater emphasis upon lay literacy: for the sake of salvation, it was crucially important to be intimately acquainted with the Holy Book, and printing made that book readily available. Schools became less strictly bound up with training for the church and more linked to the general acquisition of "literature," in the sense both of literacy and of cultural knowledge. In keeping with this new emphasis on reading and with humanist educational reform, the school was reorganized during the reign of Edward VI (1547–53). School records from the period have not survived, but it is almost certain that William Shakespeare attended the King's New School, as it was renamed in Edward's honor.

Scholars have painstakingly reconstructed the curriculum of schools of this kind and have even turned up the names and rather impressive credentials of the schoolmasters who taught at the King's New School when Shakespeare was of school age. (The principal teacher at that time was Thomas Jenkins, an Oxford graduate, who received £20 a year and a rent-free house.) A child's education in Elizabethan England began at age four or five with two years at what was called the "petty school," attached to the main grammar school. The little scholars carried a "hornbook," a sheet of paper or parchment framed in wood and covered, for protection, with a transparent layer of horn. On the paper was written the alphabet and the Lord's Prayer, which were reproduced as well in the slightly more advanced *ABC with the Catechism,* a combination primer and rudimentary religious guide.

After students demonstrated some ability to read, education for most girls came to a halt, but boys could go on, at about age seven, to the grammar school. Shakespeare's images of the experience are not particularly cheerful. In his famous account of the Seven Ages of Man, Jaques in *As You Like It* describes

> the whining schoolboy with his satchel
> And shining morning face, creeping like snail
> Unwillingly to school.
> (2.7.145–47)

The schoolboy would have crept quite early: the day began at 6:00 A.M. in summer and 7:00 A.M. in winter and continued until 5:00 P.M., with very few breaks or holidays.

At the core of the curriculum was the study of Latin, the mastery of which was in effect a prolonged male puberty rite involving much discipline and pain as well as pleasure. A late sixteenth-century Dutchman (whose name fittingly was Batty)

*The Cholmondeley Ladies* (ca. 1600–1610). Artist unknown. This striking image brings to mind Shakespeare's fascination with twinship, both identical (notably in *The Comedy of Errors*) and fraternal (in *Twelfth Night*).

proposed that God had created the human buttocks so that they could be severely beaten without risking permanent injury. Such thoughts dominated the pedagogy of the age, so that even an able young scholar, as we might imagine Shakespeare to have been, could scarcely have escaped recurrent flogging.

Shakespeare evidently reaped some rewards for the miseries he probably endured: his works are laced with echoes of many of the great Latin texts taught in grammar schools. One of his earliest comedies, *The Comedy of Errors,* is a brilliant variation on a theme by the Roman playwright Plautus, whom Elizabethan schoolchildren often performed as well as read; and one of his earliest tragedies, *Titus Andronicus,* is heavily indebted to Seneca. These are among the most visible of the classical influences that are often more subtly and pervasively interfused in Shakespeare's works. He seems to have had a particular fondness for *Aesop's Fables,* Apuleius's *Golden Ass,* and above all Ovid's *Metamorphoses.* His learned contemporary Ben Jonson remarked that Shakespeare had "small Latin and less Greek," but from this distance what is striking is not the limits of Shakespeare's learning but rather the unpretentious ease, intelligence, and gusto with which he draws upon what he must have first encountered as laborious study.

## *Traces of a Life*

In November 1582, William Shakespeare, at the age of eighteen, married twenty-six-year-old Anne Hathaway, who came from the village of Shottery near Stratford. Their first daughter, Susanna, was baptized six months later. This circumstance, along with the fact that Anne was eight years Will's senior, has given rise to a mountain of speculation, all the more lurid precisely because there is no further evidence. Shakespeare depicts in several plays situations in which marriage is precipitated by a pregnancy, but he also registers, in *Measure for Measure* (1.2.133ff), the Elizabethan belief that a "true contract" of marriage could be legitimately made and then consummated simply by the mutual vows of the couple in the presence of witnesses.

On February 2, 1585, the twins Hamnet and Judith Shakespeare were baptized in Stratford. Hamnet died at the age of eleven, when his father was already living for much of the year in London as a successful playwright. These are Shakespeare's only known children, though in the mid-seventeenth century the playwright and impresario William Davenant hinted that he was Shakespeare's bastard son. Since people did not ordinarily advertise their illegitimacy, the claim, though impossible to verify, at least suggests the unusual strength of Shakespeare's posthumous reputation.

William Shakespeare's father, John, died in 1601; his mother died seven years later. They would have had the satisfaction of witnessing their eldest son's prosperity, and not only from a distance, for in 1597 William purchased New Place, the second-largest house in Stratford. In 1607, the playwright's daughter Susanna married a successful and well-known physician, John Hall. The next year, the Halls had a daughter, Elizabeth, Shakespeare's first grandchild. In 1616, the year of Shakespeare's death, his daughter Judith married a vintner, Thomas Quiney, with whom she had three children. Shakespeare's widow, Anne, died in 1623, at the age of sixty-seven. His first-born, Susanna, died at the age of sixty-six in 1649, the year that King Charles I was beheaded by the parliamentary army. Judith lived through Cromwell's Protectorate and on to the Restoration of the monarchy; she died in February 1662, at the age of seventy-seven. By the end of the century, the line of Shakespeare's direct heirs was extinct.

Patient digging in the archives has turned up other traces of Shakespeare's life as a family man and a man of means: assessments, small fines, real estate deeds, minor actions in court to collect debts. In addition to his fine Stratford house and a large garden and cottage facing it, Shakespeare bought substantial parcels of land in the vicinity. When in *The Tempest* the wedding celebration conjures up a vision of "barns and garners never empty," Shakespeare could have been glancing at what the legal documents record as his own "tithes of corn, grain, blade, and hay" in the fields near

Stratford. At some point after 1610, Shakespeare seems to have begun to shift his attention from the London stage to his Stratford properties, though the term "retirement" implies a more decisive and definitive break than appears to have been the case. By 1613, when the Globe Theater burned down during a performance of Shakespeare and Fletcher's *Henry VIII,* Shakespeare was probably residing for the most part in Stratford, but he retained his financial interest in the rebuilt playhouse and probably continued to have some links to his theatrical colleagues. Still, by this point, his career as a playwright was substantially over. Legal documents from his last years show him concerned to protect his real estate interests in Stratford.

A half-century after Shakespeare's death, a Stratford vicar and physician, John Ward, noted in his diary that Shakespeare and his fellow poets Michael Drayton and Ben Jonson "had a merry meeting, and it seems drank too hard, for Shakespeare died of a fever there contracted." It is not inconceivable that Shakespeare's last illness was somehow linked, if only coincidentally, to the festivities on the occasion of the wedding in February 1616 of his daughter Judith (who was still alive when Ward made his diary entry). In any case, on March 25, 1616, Shakespeare revised his will, and on April 23 he died. Two days later, he was buried in the chancel of Holy Trinity Church beneath a stone bearing an epitaph he is said to have devised:

> Good friend for Jesus' sake forbear,
> To dig the dust enclosed here:
> Blest be the man that spares these stones,
> And curst be he that moves my bones.

The verses are hardly among Shakespeare's finest, but they seem to have been effective: though bones were routinely dug up to make room for others—a fate imagined with unforgettable intensity in the graveyard scene in *Hamlet*—his own remains were undisturbed. Like other vestiges of sixteenth- and early seventeenth-century Stratford, Shakespeare's grave has for centuries now been the object of a tourist industry that borders on a religious cult.

Shakespeare's will has been examined with an intensity befitting this cult; every provision and formulaic phrase, no matter how minor or conventional, has borne a heavy weight of interpretation, none more so than the sole bequest to his wife, Anne, of "my second-best bed." Scholars have pointed out that Anne would in any case have been provided for by custom and that the terms are not necessarily a deliberate slight, but the absence of the customary words "my loving wife" or "my well-beloved wife" is difficult to ignore.

## *Portrait of the Playwright as Young Provincial*

The great problem with the surviving traces of Shakespeare's life is not that they are few but that they are unspectacular. Christopher Marlowe was a double or triple agent, accused of brawling, sodomy, and atheism. Ben Jonson, who somehow clambered up from bricklayer's apprentice to classical scholar, served in the army in Flanders, killed a fellow actor in a duel, converted to Catholicism in prison in 1598, and returned to the Church of England in 1610. Provincial real estate investments and the second-best bed cannot compete with such adventurous lives. Indeed, the relative ordinariness of Shakespeare's social background and life has contributed to a persistent current of speculation that the glover's son from Stratford-upon-Avon was not in fact the author of the plays attributed to him.

The anti-Stratfordians, as those who deny Shakespeare's authorship are sometimes called, almost always propose as the real author someone who came from a higher social class and received a more prestigious education. Francis Bacon, the Earl of Oxford, the Earl of Southampton, even Queen Elizabeth, have been advanced, among many others, as glamorous candidates for the role of clandestine playwright. Several famous people, including Mark Twain and Sigmund Freud, have espoused these theories, though very few scholars have joined them. Since Shakespeare was quite well known in his own time as the author of the plays that bear his name, there would need to have been an extraordinary conspiracy to conceal the identity of the real master who (the theory goes) disdained to appear in the vulgarity of print or on the public stage. Like many conspiracy theories, the extreme implausibility of this one seems only to increase the fervent conviction of its advocates.

To the charge that a middle-class author from a small town could not have imagined the lives of kings and nobles, one can respond by citing the exceptional qualities that Ben Jonson praised in Shakespeare: "excellent *Phantsie;* brave notions, and gentle expressions." Even in ordinary mortals, the human imagination is a strange faculty; in Shakespeare, it seems to have been uncannily powerful, working its mysterious, transforming effects on everything it touched. His imagination was intensely engaged by what he found in books. He seems throughout his life to have been an intense, voracious reader, and it is fascinating to witness his creative encounters with Raphael Holinshed's *Chronicles of England, Scotland, and Ireland*, Plutarch's *Lives of the Noble Grecians and Romans*, Ovid's *Metamorphoses*, Montaigne's *Essays*, and the Bible, to name only some of his favorite books. But books were clearly not the only objects of Shakespeare's attention; like most artists, he drew upon the whole range of his life experiences.

To those accustomed to instant telecommunication, photography, film, and digital media, that range might seem narrowly circumscribed, but in fact something like the opposite was the case. Though we inhabit a vast virtual world, our experiential world is deliberately reduced, carefully screened, and tightly delimited. Most of us are born, sicken, and die in special institutions set apart from everyday life. We have invented means to quiet toothaches, heal wounds, and put us to sleep through painful surgeries. Those we condemn as criminals are penned up and punished behind high, windowless walls. We scarcely ever see our political representatives in person, and when we vote, we enter small, private booths. We take our entertainments most often in the dark or in the privacy of our homes, and those homes are generally walled off from the homes of others. Our meat bears little or no visible relation to the animal from which it comes; the slaughtering and butchering is discretely done out of sight. Our wastes disappear down drains; our rubbish is collected and disposed of; we live and move about in a well-lit, heavily policed, massively controlled environment.

None of this was the case in Shakespeare's world. Virtually anyone who grew up in the late sixteenth century would have had occasion to hear the sharp cries of childbirth and the groans of dying. There were a small number of hospitals and lazar houses (for lepers), but for the most part the sick, the maimed, and the mad mingled with everyone else in the crowded, muddy streets. The sufferings attendant on ordinary life were inescapable, and very few palliatives were available. (There were limits to the oblivion that the strongest ale could bring.) Malefactors, as we have seen, were most often punished in public, often hideously. There was nothing remotely equivalent to our taste for privacy. Servants were ubiquitous, and it was a rare person who had the privilege or perhaps the inclination to escape into solitude. Guests at an inn would often find themselves sharing a room or even a bed with a complete stranger. Smells and tastes—in a world without flush toilets and refrigeration—were intense, and so too were colors, for Elizabethans of any means favored vividly dyed and elaborately worked clothing. There were no streetlights, and the days faded into nights that were pitch dark and often dangerous.

Nothing here is particular to Shakespeare's biography; these were the conditions in this period of everyone's life. And what would astonish or appall us, if we were suddenly carried back into the past, would simply have been taken for granted as the way things are by most of those born into that world. But Shakespeare seems precisely not to have taken anything for granted: he seems to have carefully noted everything, from the carter who urinates in the chimney and complains of his fleabites (*1 Henry IV* 2.1.19–20) to the mad beggar who sticks sprigs of rosemary into his numbed arms (*King Lear* 2.2.177–79) to the merchant who keeps his money locked up in a desk that is covered with a Turkish tapestry (*Comedy of Errors* 4.1.103–04).

Shakespeare may have begun this practice of noting quite early in his life. When he was a very young boy—not quite four years old—his father was chosen by the Stratford council as the town bailiff. The bailiff of an Elizabethan town was a significant position; he served the borough as a justice of the peace and performed a variety of other functions, including coroner and clerk of the market. He dealt routinely with an unusually wide spectrum of local society, for on the one hand he distributed alms and on the other he negotiated with the lord of the manor. More to the point, for our purposes, the office was attended with considerable ceremony. The bailiff and his deputy were entitled to appear in public in furred gowns, attended by sergeants bearing maces before them. On Rogation Days (three days of prayer for the harvest, before Ascension Day), they would solemnly pace out the parish boundaries, and they would similarly walk in processions on market and fair days. On Sundays, the sergeants would accompany the bailiff to church, where he would sit with his wife in a front pew, and he would have a comparable seat of honor at sermons in the Guild Chapel. On special occasions, there would also be plays in the Guildhall, at which the bailiff would be seated in the front row.

On a precocious child (or even, for that matter, on an ordinary child), this ceremony must have had a significant impact. It would have conveyed irresistibly the power of clothes (the ceremonial gown of office) and of symbols (the mace) to transform identity as if by magic. It would have invested the official in question—Shakespeare's own father—with immense power, distinction, and importance, awakening what we may call a lifelong dream of high station. And perhaps, pulling slightly against this dream, it would have provoked an odd feeling that the father's clothes do not fit, a perception that the office is not the same as the man, and an intimate, firsthand knowledge that when the robes are put off, their wearer is inevitably glimpsed in a far different, less exalted light.

The honoring of the bailiff was only one of the political rituals that Shakespeare could easily have witnessed as a young man growing up in the provinces. As we have seen, Queen Elizabeth was fond of going on what were known as "progresses," triumphant ceremonial journeys around her kingdom. In 1574—when Shakespeare was ten years old—one of these progresses took her to Warwick, near Stratford-upon-Avon. The crowds that gathered to watch were participating in an elaborate celebration of charismatic power: the courtiers in their gorgeous clothes, the nervous local officials bedecked in velvets and silks, and at the center, carried in a special litter like a bejeweled icon, the virgin queen. The Queen cultivated this charisma, taking over in effect some of the iconography associated with the worship of the Virgin Mary, but she was also paradoxically fond of calling attention to the fact that she was after all quite human. For example, on this occasion at Warwick, after the trembling Recorder, presumably a local civil official of high standing, had made his official welcoming speech, Elizabeth offered her hand to him to be kissed: "Come hither, little Recorder," she said. "It was told me that you would be afraid to look upon me or to speak boldly; but you were not so afraid of me as I was of you; and I now thank you for putting me in mind of my duty." Of course, the charm of this royal "confession" of nervousness depends on its manifest implausibility: it is, in effect, a theatrical performance of humility by someone with immense confidence in her own histrionic power.

A royal progress was not the only form of spectacular political activity that Shakespeare might well have seen in the 1570s; it is still more likely that he would have witnessed parliamentary elections, particularly since his father was qualified to vote. In 1571, 1572, 1575, and 1578, there were shire elections conducted in Warwick, elections that would certainly have attracted well over a thousand voters. These were often memorable events: large crowds came together; there was usually heavy drinking and carnivalesque festivity; and at the same time, there was enacted, in a very different register from that of the monarchy, a ritual of empowerment. The people, those entitled to vote by virtue of meeting the property and residence requirements, chose their own representatives by giving their votes—their voices—to candidates for office. Here, legislative sovereignty was conferred not by God but by the consent of the community, a consent marked by shouts and applause.

Recent cultural historians have been so fascinated by the evident links between the spectacles of the absolutist monarchy and the theater that they have largely ignored the significance of this alternative public arena, one that generated intense excitement throughout the country. A child who was a spectator at a parliamentary election in the 1570s might well have found the occasion enormously compelling. It is striking, in any case, how often the adult Shakespeare returns to scenes of mass consent, and striking too how much the theater depends on assembling crowds and soliciting popular acclamation.

The most frequent occasions for the gathering together of crowds were neither elections nor theatrical performances, but rather the religious services that all Elizabethans were expected to attend at least once a week. (Recurrent absences were noted and investigated.) Protestant spokesmen routinely condemned the Catholic Mass as a form of perverse theatrical performance: a "play of sacred miracles," a "wonderful pageant," a "devil Theater." The Catholic Mass, as it had been celebrated for centuries, was outlawed, and with it a range of other Catholic rites. On occasion those rites were still practiced in secret, at considerable danger, and it is possible that Shakespeare could have been among those present. He was certainly present at the services of the English Church, whose ceremonies led by berobed priests, guided by the resonant prose of the Book of Common Prayer, and held in settings whose magnificence continues to astonish us, had their own intense histrionic power.

The young Shakespeare, whether true believer or skeptic or something in between ("So have I heard, and do in part believe it," says Hamlet's friend Horatio [1.1.164]), might have carried away from such ceremonies several impressions: an intimation of immense, cosmic forces that may impinge upon human life; a heightened understanding of the power of language to form and exalt the spirit; an awareness of intense, even murderous competition and rivalry among competing rituals; and perhaps a sense of the longing to believe that may be awakened and shaped in large crowds.

I have placed Shakespeare himself in each of these scenes—which together sketch the root conditions of the Elizabethan theater—because some people have found it difficult to conceive how this one man, with his provincial origins and his restricted range of experience, could have so rapidly and completely mastered the central imaginative themes of his times. Moreover, it is sometimes difficult to grasp how seeming abstractions such as market society, monarchical state, and theological doctrine were actually experienced directly by distinct individuals. Shakespeare's plays were social and collective events, but they also bore the stamp of a particular artist, one endowed with a remarkable capacity to craft lifelike illusions, a daring willingness to articulate an original vision, and a loving command, at once precise and generous, of language. These plays are stitched together from shared cultural experiences, inherited dramatic devices, and the pungent vernacular of the day, but we should not lose sight of the extent to which they articulate an intensely personal vision, a bold shaping of the available materials. Four centuries of feverish biographical speculation, much of it foolish, bear witness to a basic intuition: the richness of these plays, their inexhaustible openness, is the consequence not only of the auspicious collective conditions of the culture but also of someone's exceptional skill, inventiveness, and courage at taking those conditions and making of them something rich and strange.

## *The Theater of the Nation*

What precisely were the collective conditions disclosed by the spectacles that Shakespeare would likely have witnessed? First, the growth of Stratford-upon-Avon, the bustling market town of which John Shakespeare was bailiff, is a small version of a momentous sixteenth-century development that made Shakespeare's career possible: the making of an urban "public." That development obviously depended on adequate numbers; the period experienced a rapid and still unexplained growth in population. With it came an expansion and elaboration of market relations: markets became less periodic, more continuous, and more abstract—centered, that is, not on the familiar materiality of goods but on the liquidity of capital and goods. In practical terms, this meant that it was possible to conceive of the theater not only as festive entertainment for special events—Lord Mayor's pageants, visiting princes, seasonal festivals, and the like—but as a permanent, year-round business venture. The venture relied on revenues from admission—it was an innovation of this period to have money advanced in the expectation of pleasure rather than offered to servants afterward as a reward—and counted on habitual playgoing, with a concomitant demand for new plays from competing theater companies: "But that's all one, our play is done," sings the Clown at the end of *Twelfth Night* and adds a glance toward the next afternoon's proceeds: "And we'll strive to please you every day" (5.1.393–94).

Second, the royal progress is an instance of what the anthropologist Clifford Geertz has called the Theater State, a state that manifests its power and meaning in exemplary public performances. Professional companies of players, like the one Shakespeare belonged to, understood well that they existed in relation to this Theater State and would, if they were fortunate, be called upon to serve it. Unlike Ben Jonson, Shakespeare did not, as far as we know, write royal entertainments on commission, but his plays were frequently performed before Queen Elizabeth and then before King James and Queen Anne, along with their courtiers and privileged guests. There are many fascinating glimpses of these performances, including a letter from Walter Cope to Robert Cecil, early in James's reign. "Burbage is come," Cope writes, referring to the leading actor of Shakespeare's company, "and says there is no new play that the Queen hath not seen, but they have revived an old one, called *Love's Labor's Lost,* which for wit and mirth he says will please her exceedingly. And this is appointed to be played tomorrow night at my Lord of Southampton's." Not only would such theatrical performances have given great pleasure—evidently, the Queen had already exhausted the company's new offerings—but they conferred prestige upon those who commanded them and those in whose honor they were mounted.

Monarchical power in the period was deeply allied to spectacular manifestations of the ruler's glory and disciplinary authority. The symbology of power depended on regal magnificence, reward, punishment, and pardon, all of which were heavily theatricalized. Indeed, the conspicuous public display does not simply serve the interests of power; on many occasions in the period, power seemed to exist in order to make pageantry possible, as if the nation's identity were only fully realized in theatrical performance. It would be easy to exaggerate this perception: the subjects of Queen Elizabeth and King James were acutely aware of the distinction between shadow and substance. But they were fascinated by the political magic through which shadows could be taken for substantial realities, and the ruling elite was largely complicit in the formation and celebration of a charismatic absolutism. At the same time, the claims of the monarch who professes herself or himself to be not the representative of the nation but its embodiment were set against the counterclaims of the House of Commons. And this institution too, as we have glimpsed, had its own theatrical rituals, centered on the crowd whose shouts of approval, in heavily stage-managed elections, chose the individuals who would stand for the polity and participate in deliberations held in a hall whose resemblance to a theater did not escape contemporary notice.

Third, in outlawing the Catholic Mass and banning the medieval mystery plays, along with pilgrimages and other rituals associated with holy shrines and sacred images, English Protestant authorities hoped to hold a monopoly on religious observances. But they inevitably left some people, perhaps substantial numbers of them, mourning what they had lost. Playing companies could satisfy at least some of the popular longings and appropriate aspects of the social energy no longer allowed a theological outlet. That is, official attacks on certain Catholic practices made it more possible for the public theater to appropriate and exploit their allure. Hence, for example, the plays that celebrated the solemn miracle of the Catholic Mass were banned, along with the most elaborate church vestments, but in *The Winter's Tale* Dion can speak in awe of what he witnessed at Apollo's temple:

> I shall report,
> For most it caught me, the celestial habits—
> Methinks I so should term them—and the reverence
> Of the grave wearers. Oh, the sacrifice!
> How ceremonious, solemn, and unearthly
> It was i'th' off'ring!
>
> (3.1.3–8)

And at the play's end, the statue of the innocent mother breathes, comes to life, and embraces her child.

The theater in Shakespeare's time, then, is intimately bound up with all three crucial cultural formations: market society, the Theater State, and the church. But it is important to note that the institution is not *identified* with any of them. The theater may be a market phenomenon, but it is repeatedly and bitterly attacked as the enemy of diligent, sober, productive economic activity. Civic authorities generally regarded the theater as a pestilential nuisance, a parasite on the body of the commonwealth, a temptation to students, apprentices, housewives, even respectable merchants to leave their serious business and lapse into idleness and waste. That waste, it might be argued, could be partially recuperated if it went for the glorification of a guild or the entertainment of an important dignitary, but the only group regularly profiting from the theater were the players and their disreputable associates.

For his part, Shakespeare made a handsome profit from the commodification of theatrical entertainment, but he seems never to have written "city comedy"—plays set in London and more or less explicitly concerned with market relations—and his characters express deep reservations about the power of money and commerce: "That smooth-faced gentleman, tickling commodity," Philip the Bastard observes in *King John,* "wins of all, / Of kings, of beggars, old men, young men, maids" (2.1.569–73). We could argue that the smooth-faced gentleman is none other than Shakespeare himself, for his drama famously mingles kings and clowns, princesses and panderers. But the mingling is set against a romantic current of social conservatism: in *Twelfth Night,* the aristocratic heiress Olivia falls in love with someone who appears far beneath her in wealth and social station, but it is revealed that he (and his sister Viola) are of noble blood; in *The Winter's Tale,* Leontes' daughter Perdita is raised as a shepherdess, but her noble nature shines through her humble upbringing, and she marries the Prince of Bohemia; the strange island maiden with whom Ferdinand, son of the King of Naples, falls madly in love in *The Tempest* turns out to be the daughter of the rightful Duke of Milan. Shakespeare pushes against this conservative logic in *All's Well That Ends Well,* but the noble young Bertram violently resists the unequal match thrust upon him by the King, and the play's mood is notoriously uneasy.

Similarly, Shakespeare's theater may have been patronized and protected by the monarchy—after 1603, his company received a royal patent and was known as the King's Men—but the two institutions were by no means identical in their interests or their ethos. To be sure, *Richard III* and *Macbeth* incorporate aspects of royal propaganda, but given the realities of censorship, Shakespeare's plays, and the period's drama as a whole, are surprisingly independent and complex in their political vision. There is, in any case, a certain inherent tension between kings and player kings: Elizabeth and James may both have likened themselves to actors onstage, but they were loath to admit their dependence on the applause and money, freely given or freely withheld, of the audience. The charismatic monarch insists that the sacredness of authority resides in the body of the ruler, not in a costume that may be worn and then discarded by an actor. Kings are not *representations* of power—or do not admit that they are—but claim to be the thing itself. The government institution that was actually based on the idea of representation, Parliament, had theatrical elements, as we have seen, but it significantly excluded any audience from its deliberations. And Shakespeare's oblique portraits of parliamentary representatives, the ancient Roman tribunes Sicinius Velutus and Junius Brutus in *Coriolanus,* are anything but flattering.

Finally, the theater drew significant energy from the liturgy and rituals of the late medieval church, but as Shakespeare's contemporaries widely remarked, the playhouse and the church were scarcely natural allies. Not only did the theater represent a potential competitor to worship services, and not only did ministers rail against prostitution and other vices associated with playgoing, but theatrical representation itself, even when ostensibly pious, seemed to many to empty out whatever it presented, turning substance into mere show. The theater could and did use the period's deep currents of religious feeling, but it had to do so carefully and with an awareness of conflicting interests.

## *Shakespeare Comes to London*

How did Shakespeare decide to turn his prodigious talents to the stage? When did he make his way to London? How did he get his start? Concerning these and similar questions we have a mountain of speculation but no secure answers. There is not a single surviving record of Shakespeare's existence from 1585, when his twins were baptized in Stratford church, until 1592, when a rival London playwright made an envious remark about him. In the late seventeenth century, the delightfully eccentric collector of gossip John Aubrey was informed that prior to moving to London the young Shakespeare had been a schoolteacher in the country. Aubrey also recorded a story that Shakespeare had been a rather unusual apprentice butcher: "When he killed a calf, he would do it in a high style, and make a speech."

These and other legends, including one that has Shakespeare whipped for poaching game, fill the void until the unmistakable reference in Robert Greene's *Groatsworth of Wit Bought with a Million of Repentance* (1592). An inspired hack writer with a university education, a penchant for self-dramatization, a taste for wild living, and a strong streak of resentment, Greene, in his early thirties, was dying in poverty when he penned his last farewell, piously urging his fellow dramatists Christopher Marlowe, Thomas Nashe, and George Peele to abandon the wicked stage before they were brought low, as he had been, by a new arrival: "For there is an upstart crow, beautified with our feathers, that with his 'Tiger's heart wrapped in player's hide' supposes he is as well able to bombast out a blank verse as the best of you, and, being an absolute *Johannes Factotum,* is in his own conceit the only Shake-scene in a country." If "Shake-scene" is not enough to identify the object of his attack, Greene parodies a line from Shakespeare's early play 3 *Henry VI*: "O tiger's heart wrapped in a woman's hide" (1.4.137). Greene is accusing Shakespeare of being an upstart, a plagiarist, an egomaniacal jack-of-all-trades—and, above all perhaps, a popular success.

By 1592, then, Shakespeare had already arrived on the highly competitive London theatrical scene. He was successful enough to be attacked by Greene and, a few months later, defended by Henry Chettle, another hack writer who had seen Greene's manuscript through the press (or, some scholars speculate, had written the attack himself and passed it off as the dying Greene's). Chettle expresses his regret that he did not suppress Greene's diatribe and spare Shakespeare "because myself have seen his demeanor no less civil than he excellent in the quality he professes." Besides, Chettle adds, "divers of worship have reported his uprightness of dealing, which argues his honesty and his facetious [polished] grace in writing that approves his art." "Divers of worship": not only was Shakespeare established as an accomplished writer and actor, but he evidently had aroused the attention and the approbation of several socially prominent people. In Elizabethan England, aristocratic patronage, with the money, protection, and prestige it alone could provide, was probably a professional writer's most important asset.

This patronage, or at least Shakespeare's quest for it, is most visible in the dedications in 1593 and 1594 of his narrative poems *Venus and Adonis* and *The Rape of Lucrece* to the young nobleman Henry Wriothesley, Earl of Southampton. It may be glimpsed as well, perhaps, in the sonnets, with their extraordinary adoration of the fair youth, though the identity of that youth has never been determined. What return Shakespeare got for his exquisite offerings is likewise unknown. We do know that among wits and gallants, the narrative poems won Shakespeare a fine reputation as an immensely stylish and accomplished poet. An amateur play performed at Cambridge University at the end of the sixteenth century, *The Return from Parnassus,* makes fun of this vogue, as a foolish character effusively declares, "I'll worship sweet Mr. Shakespeare, and to honor him will lay his *Venus and Adonis* under my pillow." Many readers at the time may have done so: the poem went through sixteen editions before 1640, more than any other work by Shakespeare.

Patronage was crucially important not only for individual artists but also for the actors, playwrights, and investors who pooled their resources to form professional theater companies. The public playhouses had enemies, especially among civic and religious authorities, who wished greatly to curb performances or to ban them altogether. An Act of Parliament of 1572 included players among those classified as vagabonds, threatening them therefore with the horrible punishments meted out to those regarded as economic parasites. The players' escape route was to be nominally enrolled as apprentices in guilds, as if they were learning to be goldsmiths or grocers rather than actors. Alternatively, as we have noted, they could be officially listed as the servants of high-ranking noblemen.

When Shakespeare came to London, presumably in the late 1580s, there were more than a half-dozen of these companies operating under the patronage of various aristocrats. We do not know for which of these companies, several of which had toured in Stratford, he originally worked, nor whether he began, as legend has it, by holding gentlemen's horses outside the theater or by serving as a prompter's assistant and then graduated to acting and playwriting. Shakespeare is listed among the actors in Ben Jonson's *Every Man in His Humor* (performed in 1598) and *Sejanus* (performed in 1603), but we do not know for certain what roles he played, nor are there records of any of his other performances. Tradition has it that he played Adam in *As You Like It* and the Ghost in *Hamlet,* but he was clearly not one of the leading actors of the day.

Shakespeare may initially have been associated with the company of Ferdinando Stanley, Lord Strange; that company included actors with whom Shakespeare was later linked. Or he may have belonged to the Earl of Pembroke's Men, since there is evidence that they performed *The Taming of a Shrew* and a version of *3 Henry VI.* At any event, by 1594, Shakespeare was a member of the Chamberlain's Men, for his name, along with those of Will Kemp and Richard Burbage, appears on a record of those "servants to the Lord Chamberlain" paid for performance at the royal palace at Greenwich on December 26 and 28. Shakespeare stayed with this company, which during the reign of King James received royal patronage and became the King's Men, for the rest of his career.

Many playwrights in Shakespeare's time worked freelance, moving from company to company as opportunities arose, collaborating on projects, adding scenes to old plays, scrambling from one enterprise to another. But certain playwrights, among them the most successful, wrote for a single company, often agreeing contractually to give that company exclusive rights to their theatrical works. Shakespeare seems to have followed such a pattern. For the Chamberlain's Men, later the King's Men, he wrote an average of two plays per year. His company initially performed in The Theatre, a playhouse built in 1576 by an entrepreneurial actor and trained craftsman, James Burbage, the father of the actor Richard, who was to perform many of Shakespeare's greatest roles. When in 1597 their lease on this playhouse expired, the Chamberlain's Men passed through a difficult time, but they formed a joint stock company, raising sufficient capital to lease a site and put up a splendid new playhouse in the suburb of Southwark, on the south bank of the Thames. This playhouse, the Globe, opened in 1599. Shakespeare is listed in the legal agreement as one of the principal investors, and when the company began to use Blackfriars as their indoor playhouse around 1610, he was a major shareholder in that theater as well. The Chamberlain's Men dominated the theater scene, and the shares were quite valuable. Then as now, the theater was an extremely risky enterprise—most of those who wrote plays and performed in them made pathetically little money—but Shakespeare was a notable exception. The fine house in Stratford and the coat of arms he succeeded in acquiring were among the fruits of his multiple mastery, as actor, playwright, and investor of the London stage.

Edward Alleyn. Artist unknown. Alleyn was the great tragic actor of the Admiral's Men (the principal rival to Shakespeare's company). He was famous especially for playing the major characters of Christopher Marlowe.

## *The Shakespearean Trajectory*

Though Shakespeare's England was in many ways a record-keeping society, no reliable record survives that details the performances, year by year, in the London theaters. Every play had to be licensed by the Master of the Revels, but the records kept by the relevant government officials from 1579 to 1621 have not survived. A major theatrical entrepreneur, Philip Henslowe, kept a careful account of his expenditures, including what he paid for the scripts he commissioned, but unfortunately Henslowe's main business was with the Rose and the Fortune theaters and not with the playhouses at which Shakespeare's company performed. A comparable ledger must have been kept by the shareholders of the Chamberlain's Men, but it has not survived. Shakespeare himself apparently did not undertake to preserve all his writings for posterity, let alone to clarify the chronology of his works or to specify which plays he wrote alone and which with collaborators.

The principal source for Shakespeare's works is the 1623 Folio volume of *Mr. William Shakespeares Comedies, Histories, & Tragedies*. The world owes this work,

IF YOV KNOW NOT ME,
You know no body.
OR,
The troubles of Queene Elizabeth.
London.
Printed by B.A. and T.F. for Nathanaell Butter. 1632.


Title page of *If You Know Not Me, You Know Nobody; or, the Troubles of Queen Elizabeth* (1632).

lovingly edited after his death by two of the playwright's friends, an incalculable debt: without it, nearly half of Shakespeare's plays, including many of his greatest masterpieces, would have been lost forever. The edition does not, however, include any of Shakespeare's nondramatic poems, and it omits four plays in which Shakespeare is now thought to have had a significant hand, *Edward III, Pericles, Cardenio,* and *The Two Noble Kinsmen,* along with his probable contribution to the multiauthored *Sir Thomas More.* (A number of other plays were attributed to Shakespeare, both before and after his death, but scholars have not generally accepted any of these into the established canon.) Moreover, the Folio edition does not print the plays in chronological order, nor does it attempt to establish a chronology. We do not know how much time would normally have elapsed between the writing of a play and its first performance, nor, with a few exceptions, do we know with any certainty the month or even the year of the first performance of any of Shakespeare's plays. The quarto editions of those plays that were published during Shakespeare's lifetime obviously establish a date by which we know a given play had been written, but they give us little more than an end point, because there was likely to be a substantial though indeterminate gap between the first performance of a play and its publication.

With enormous patience and ingenuity, however, scholars have gradually assembled a considerable archive of evidence, both external and internal, for dating the composition of the plays. Besides actual publication, the external evidence includes explicit reference to a play, a record of its performance, or (as in the case of Greene's attack on the "upstart crow") the quoting of a line, though all of these can be maddeningly ambiguous. The most important single piece of external evidence appears in 1598 in *Palladis Tamia,* a long book of jumbled reflections by the churchman Francis Meres that includes a survey of the contemporary literary scene. Meres finds that "the sweet, witty soul of Ovid lives in mellifluous and honey-tongued Shakespeare, witness his *Venus and Adonis,* his *Lucrece,* his sugared Sonnets among his private friends, etc." Meres goes on to list Shakespeare's accomplishments as a playwright as well:

> As Plautus and Seneca are accounted the best for Comedy and Tragedy among the Latins: so Shakespeare among the English is the most excellent in both kinds for the stage; for Comedy, witness his *Gentlemen of Verona,* his *Errors,* his *Love labors lost,* his *Love labors won,* his *Midsummers night dream,* & his *Merchant of Venice:* for Tragedy his *Richard the 2, Richard the 3, Henry the 4, King John, Titus Andronicus* and his *Romeo and Juliet.*

Meres thus provides a date by which twelve of Shakespeare's plays had definitely appeared (including one, *Love's Labor's Won,* that appears either to have been lost or to be known to us by a different title). Unfortunately, Meres provides no clues about the order of appearance of these plays, and there are no other comparable lists.

Faced with the limitations of the external evidence, scholars have turned to a bewildering array of internal evidence, ranging from datable sources and topical allusions on the one hand to evolving stylistic features (ratio of verse to prose, percentage of rhyme to blank verse, colloquialisms, use of extended similes, and the like) on the other. Thus, for example, a cluster of plays with a high percentage of rhymed verse may follow closely upon Shakespeare's writing of the rhymed poems *Venus and Adonis* and *The Rape of Lucrece* and therefore be datable to 1594–95. Similarly, vocabulary overlap probably indicates proximity in composition, so if four or five plays share relatively "rare" vocabulary, it is likely that they were written in roughly the same period. Again, there seems to be a pattern in Shakespeare's use of colloquialisms, with a steady increase from *As You Like It* (1599–1600) to *Coriolanus* (1608), followed in the late romances by a retreat from the colloquial.

Ongoing computer analysis should provide further guidance in the future, though the precise order of the plays, still very much in dispute, is never likely to be settled to universal satisfaction. Still, certain broad patterns are now widely accepted. These patterns can be readily grasped in *The Norton Shakespeare,* which presents the plays according to our best estimate of their chronological order.

Shakespeare began his career, probably in the early 1590s, by writing both comedies and history plays. The attack by Greene suggests that he made his mark with the series of theatrically vital, occasionally brilliant, and often crude plays based on the foreign and domestic broils that erupted during the unhappy reign of the Lancastrian Henry VI. Modern readers and audiences are more likely to find the first sustained evidence of unusual power in *Richard III* (ca. 1592), a play that combines a richly imagined central character, a dazzling command of histrionic rhetoric, and an overarching moral vision of English history.

At virtually the same time that he was setting his stamp on the genre of the history play, Shakespeare was writing his first—or first surviving—comedies. Here, there are even fewer signs than in the histories of an apprenticeship. *The Comedy of Errors,* one of his early works in this genre, already displays a rare command of the resources of comedy: mistaken identity, madcap confusion, and the threat of disaster, giving way in the end to reconciliation, recovery, and love. Shakespeare's other comedies from the first half of the 1590s, *The Two Gentlemen of Verona, The Taming of the Shrew,* and *Love's Labor's Lost,* are no less remarkable for their sophisticated variations on familiar comic themes, their inexhaustible rhetorical inventiveness, and their poignant intimation, in the midst of festive celebration, of loss.

Successful as are these early histories and comedies, and indicative of an extraordinary theatrical talent, Shakespeare's achievement in the later 1590s would still have been all but impossible to foresee. Starting with *A Midsummer Night's Dream* (1595–96), Shakespeare wrote an unprecedented series of romantic comedies—*The Merchant of Venice, Much Ado About Nothing, The Merry Wives of Windsor, As You Like It,* and *Twelfth Night* (1600–1601)—whose poetic richness and emotional complexity remain unmatched. In the same period, he wrote a sequence of profoundly searching and ambitious history plays—*Richard II, 1* and *2 Henry IV,* and *Henry V*—which together explore the death throes of feudal England and the birth of the modern nation-state ruled by a charismatic monarch. Both the comedies and histories of this period are marked by their capaciousness, their ability to absorb characters who press up against the outermost boundaries of the genre: the comedy *The Merchant of Venice* somehow contains the figure, at once nightmarish and poignant, of Shylock, while the *Henry IV* plays, with their somber vision of crisis in the family and the state, bring to the stage one of England's greatest comic characters, Falstaff.

If in the mid- to late 1590s Shakespeare reached the summit of his art in two major genres, he also manifested a lively interest in a third. As early as 1592–93, he wrote the crudely violent tragedy *Titus Andronicus,* the first of several plays on themes from Roman history, and a few years later, in *Richard II,* he created in the protagonist a figure who achieves by the play's close the stature of a tragic hero. In the same year that Shakespeare wrote the wonderfully farcical "Pyramus and Thisbe" scene in *A Midsummer Night's Dream,* he probably also wrote the deeply tragic realization of the same story in *Romeo and Juliet.* But once again, the lyric anguish of *Romeo and Juliet* and the tormented self-revelation of *Richard II,* extraordinary as they are, could not have led anyone to predict the next phase of Shakespeare's career, the great tragic dramas that poured forth in the early years of the seventeenth century: *Hamlet, Othello, King Lear, Macbeth, Antony and Cleopatra,* and *Coriolanus.* These plays, written between 1600 and 1608, seem to mark a major shift in sensibility, an existential and metaphysical darkening that many readers think must have drawn upon a deep personal anguish, perhaps caused by the decline and death of Shakespeare's father, John, in 1601.

Whatever the truth of these speculations—and we have no direct, personal testimony either to support or to undermine them—there appears to have occurred in the same period a shift as well in Shakespeare's comic sensibility. The comedies written between 1601 and 1607, *Troilus and Cressida, Measure for Measure,* and *All's Well That Ends Well,* are sufficiently different from the earlier comedies—more biting in tone, more uneasy with comic conventions, more ruthlessly questioning of the values of the characters and the resolutions of the plots—that they led many twentieth-century scholars to classify them as "problem plays" or "dark comedies." This category has recently begun to fall out of favor, since Shakespeare criticism is perfectly happy to demonstrate that *all* of the plays are "problem plays." But there is another group of plays, among the last Shakespeare wrote, that continue to constitute a distinct category. *Pericles, Cymbeline, The Winter's Tale,* and *The Tempest*—written between 1607 and 1611, when the playwright had developed a remarkably fluid, dreamlike sense of plot and a poetic style that could veer, apparently effortlessly, from the tortured to the ineffably sweet—have been known since the late nineteenth century as the "romances." These plays share an interest in the moral and emotional life less of the adolescents who dominate the earlier comedies than of their parents. The romances are deeply concerned with patterns of loss and recovery, suffering and redemption, despair and renewal. They have seemed to many critics to constitute a deliberate conclusion to a career that began in histories and comedies and passed through the dark and tormented tragedies.

One effect of the practice of printing Shakespeare's plays in a reconstructed chronological order, as this edition does, is to produce a kind of authorial plot, a progress from youthful exuberance and a heroic grappling with history, through psychological anguish and radical doubt, to a mature serenity built upon an understanding of loss. The ordering of Shakespeare's "complete works" in this way reconstitutes the figure of the author as the beloved hero of his own, lived romance. There are numerous reasons to treat this romance with considerable skepticism: the precise order of the plays remains in dispute, the obsessions of the earliest plays crisscross with those of the last, the drama is a collaborative art form, and the relation between authorial consciousness and theatrical representation is murky. Yet a longing to identify Shakespeare's personal trajectory, to chart his psychic and spiritual as well as professional progress, is all but irresistible.

## *The Fetishism of Dress*

Whatever the personal resonance of Shakespeare's own life, his art is deeply enmeshed in the collective hopes, fears, and fantasies of his time. For example, throughout his plays, Shakespeare draws heavily upon his culture's investment in costume, symbols of authority, visible signs of status—the fetishism of dress he must have witnessed from early childhood. Disguise in his drama is often assumed to be incredibly effective: when Henry V borrows a cloak, when Portia dresses in a jurist's robes, when Viola puts on a young man's suit, it is as if each has become unrecognizable, as if identity resided in clothing. At the end of *Twelfth Night,* even though Viola's true identity has been disclosed, Orsino continues to call her Cesario; he will do so, he says, until she resumes her maid's garments, for only then will she be transformed into a woman:

> Cesario, come—
> For so you shall be while you are a man—
> But when in other habits you are seen,
> Orsino's mistress and his fancy's queen.
> (5.1.371–74)

The pinnacle of this fetishism of costume is the royal crown, for whose identity-conferring power men are willing to die, but the principle is everywhere, from the filthy blanket that transforms Edgar into Poor Tom to the coxcomb that is the badge of the licensed fool. Antonio, wishing to express his utter contempt, spits on Shylock's "Jewish gaberdine," as if the clothing were the essence of the man; Kent, pouring insults on the loathsome Oswald, calls him a "filthy worsted-stocking knave"; and innocent Imogen, learning that her husband has ordered her murder, thinks of herself as an expensive cast-off dress, destined to be ripped at the seams:

> Poor I am stale, a garment out of fashion,
> And for I am richer than to hang by th' walls,
> I must be ripped: to pieces with me.
> (*Cymbeline* 3.4.50–52)

What can be said, thought, felt in this culture seems deeply dependent on the clothes one wears—clothes that one is, in effect, *permitted* or *compelled* to wear, since there is little freedom in dress. Shakespearean drama occasionally represents something like such freedom: after all, Viola in *Twelfth Night* chooses to put off her "maiden weeds," as does Rosalind, who declares, "We'll have a swashing and a martial outside" (*As You Like It* 1.3.116). But these choices are characteristically made under the pressure of desperate circumstances, here shipwreck and exile. Part of the charm of Shakespeare's heroines is their ability to transform distress into an opportunity for self-fashioning, but the plays often suggest that there is less autonomy than meets the eye. What looks like an escape from cultural determinism may be only a deeper form of constraint. We may take, as an allegorical emblem of this constraint, the transformation of the beggar Christopher Sly in the playful Induction to *The Taming of the Shrew* into a nobleman. The transformation seems to suggest that you are free to make of yourself whatever you choose to be—the play begins with the drunken Sly claiming the dignity of his pedigree ("Look in the Chronicles" [Induction 1.3–4])—but in fact he is only the subject of the mischievous lord's experiment, designed to demonstrate the interwovenness of clothing and identity. "What think you," the lord asks his huntsman,

> if he were conveyed to bed,
> Wrapped in sweet clothes, rings put upon his fingers,
> A most delicious banquet by his bed,
> And brave attendants near him when he wakes—
> Would not the beggar then forget himself?

To which the huntsman replies, in words that underscore the powerlessness of the drunken beggar, "Believe me, lord, I think he cannot choose" (Induction 1.33–38).

Petruccio's taming of Katherina is similarly constructed around an imposition of identity, an imposition closely bound up with the right to wear certain articles of clothing. When the haberdasher arrives with a fashionable lady's hat, Petruccio refuses it over his wife's vehement objections: "This doth fit the time, / And gentlewomen wear such caps as these." "When you are gentle," Petruccio replies, "you shall have one, too, /

And not till then" (4.3.70–73). At the play's close, Petruccio demonstrates his authority by commanding his tamed wife to throw down her cap: "Off with that bauble; throw it underfoot" (5.2.122). Here as elsewhere in Shakespeare, acts of robing and disrobing are intensely charged, a charge that culminates in the trappings of monarchy. When Richard II, in a scene that was probably censored during the reign of Elizabeth from the stage as well as the printed text, is divested of his crown and scepter, he experiences the loss as the eradication of his name, the symbolic melting away of his identity:

> Alack the heavy day,
> That I have worn so many winters out
> And know not now what name to call myself.
> Oh, that I were a mockery king of snow,
> Standing before the sun of Bolingbroke
> To melt myself away in water-drops.
> (4.1.250–55)

When Lear tears off his regal "lendings" in order to reduce himself to the nakedness of the Bedlam beggar, he is expressing not only his radical loss of social identity but the breakdown of his psychic order as well, expressing therefore his reduction to the condition of the "poor bare forked animal" that is the primal form of undifferentiated existence. And when Cleopatra determines to kill herself in order to escape public humiliation in Rome, she magnificently affirms her essential being by arraying herself as she had once done to encounter Antony:

> Show me, my women, like a queen. Go, fetch
> My best attires. I am again for Cydnus
> To meet Mark Antony.
> (5.2.226–28)

Such scenes are a remarkable intensification of the everyday symbolic practice of Renaissance English culture, its characteristically deep and knowing commitment to illusion: "I know perfectly well that the woman in her crown and jewels and gorgeous gown is an aging, irascible, and fallible mortal—she herself virtually admits as much—yet I profess that she is the virgin queen, timelessly beautiful, wise, and just." Shakespeare understood how close this willed illusion was to the spirit of the theater, to the actors' ability to work on what the chorus in *Henry V* calls the "imaginary forces" of the audience. But there is throughout Shakespeare's works a counterintuition that, while it does not exactly overturn this illusion, renders it poignant, vulnerable, fraught. The "masculine usurp'd attire" that is donned by Viola, Rosalind, Portia, Jessica, and other Shakespeare heroines alters what they can say and do, reveals important aspects of their character, and changes their destiny, but it is, all the same, not theirs and not all of who they are. They have, the plays insist, natures that are neither transformed nor altogether concealed by their dress: "Pray God defend me," exclaims the frightened Viola. "A little thing would make me tell them how much I lack of a man" (*Twelfth Night* 3.4.271–72).

### *The Paradoxes of Identity*

The gap between costume and identity is not simply a matter of what women supposedly lack; virtually all of Shakespeare's major characters, men and women, convey the sense of both a *self-division* and an *inward expansion.* The belief in a complex inward realm beyond costumes and status is a striking inversion of the clothes cult: we know perfectly well that the characters have no inner lives apart from what we see on the stage, and yet we believe that they continue to exist when we do not see them, that they exist apart from their represented words and actions, that they have hidden dimensions. How is this conviction aroused and sustained? In part, it is the effect of what the characters themselves say: "My grief lies all within," Richard II tells Bolingbroke,

> And these external manner of laments
> Are merely shadows to the unseen grief
> That swells with silence in the tortured soul.
> (4.1.288–91)

Similarly, Hamlet, dismissing the significance of his outward garments, declares, "I have that within which passes show— / These but the trappings and the suits of woe" (1.2.85–86). And the distinction between inward and outward is reinforced throughout this play and elsewhere by an unprecedented use of the aside and the soliloquy.

The soliloquy is a continual reminder in Shakespeare that the inner life is by no means transparent to one's surrounding world. Prince Hal seems open and easy with his mates in Eastcheap, but he has a hidden reservoir of disgust:

> I know you all, and will a while uphold
> The unyoked humor of your idleness.
> Yet herein will I imitate the sun,
> Who doth permit the base contagious clouds
> To smother up his beauty from the world,
> That, when he please again to be himself,
> Being wanted he may be more wondered at
> By breaking through the foul and ugly mists
> Of vapors that did seem to strangle him.
> (*I Henry IV* 1.2.170–78)

"When he please again to be himself": the line implies that identity is a matter of free choice—you decide how much of yourself you wish to disclose—but Shakespeare employs other devices that suggest more elusive and intractable layers of inwardness. There is a peculiar, recurrent lack of fit between costume and character, in fools as in princes, that is not simply a matter of disguise and disclosure. If Hal's true identity is partially "smothered" in the tavern, it is not completely revealed either in his soldier's armor or in his royal robes, nor do his asides reach the bedrock of unimpeachable self-understanding.

Identity in Shakespeare repeatedly slips away from the characters themselves, as it does from Richard II after the deposition scene and from Lear after he has given away his land and from Macbeth after he has gained the crown. The slippage does not mean that they retreat into silence; rather, they embark on an experimental, difficult fashioning of themselves and the world, most often through role-playing. "I cannot do it," says the deposed and imprisoned Richard II. "Yet I'll hammer't out" (5.5.5). This could serve as the motto for many Shakespearean characters: Viola becomes Cesario, Rosalind calls herself Ganymede, Kent becomes Caius, Edgar presents himself as Poor Tom, Hamlet plays the madman that he has partly become, Hal pretends that he is his father and a highwayman and Hotspur and even himself. Even in comedy, these ventures into alternate identities are rarely matters of choice; in tragedy, they are always undertaken under pressure and compulsion. And often enough it is not a matter of role-playing at all, but of a drastic transformation whose extreme emblem is the harrowing madness of Lear and of Leontes.

There is a moment in *Richard II* in which the deposed king asks for a mirror and then, after musing on his reflection, throws it to the ground. The shattering of the glass serves to remind us not only of the fragility of identity in Shakespeare but of its characteristic appearance in fragmentary mirror images. The plays continually generate alternative reflections, identities that intersect with, underscore, echo, or otherwise set off that of the principal character. Hence, Desdemona and Iago are not only important figures in Othello's world—they also seem to embody partially realized aspects of himself; Falstaff and Hotspur play a comparable role in relation to Prince Hal, Fortinbras and Horatio in relation to Hamlet, Gloucester and the Fool in relation to Lear, and so forth. In many of these plays, the complementary and contrasting characters figure in subplots, subtly interwoven with the play's main plot and illuminating its concerns. The note so conspicuously sounded by Fortinbras at the close of *Hamlet*—what the hero might have been, "had he been put on"—is heard repeatedly in Shakespeare and contributes to the overwhelming intensity, poignancy, and complexity of the characters. This is a world in which outward appearance is everything and nothing, in which individuation is at once sharply etched and continually blurred, in which the victims of fate are haunted by the ghosts of the possible, in which everything is simultaneously as it must be and as it need not have been.

Are these alternatives signs of a struggle between contradictory and irreconcilable perspectives in Shakespeare? In certain plays—notably, *Measure for Measure, All's Well That Ends Well, Coriolanus,* and *Troilus and Cressida*—the tension seems both high and entirely unresolved. But Shakespearean contradictions are more often reminiscent of the capacious spirit of Montaigne, who refused any systematic order that would betray his sense of reality. Thus, individual characters are immensely important in Shakespeare—he is justly celebrated for his unmatched skill in the invention of particular dramatic identities, marked with distinct speech patterns, manifested in social status, and confirmed by costume and gesture—but the principle of individuation is not the rock on which his theatrical art is founded. After the masks are stripped away, the pretenses exposed, the claims of the ego shattered, there is a mysterious remainder; as the shamed but irrepressible Paroles declares in *All's Well That Ends Well,* "Simply the thing I am / Shall make me live" (4.3.316–17). Again and again the audience is made to sense a deeper energy, a source of power that at once discharges itself in individual characters and seems to sweep right through them.

## *The Poet of Nature*

In *The Birth of Tragedy,* Nietzsche called a comparable source of energy that he found in Greek tragedy "Dionysos." But the god's name, conjuring up Bacchic frenzy, does not seem appropriate to Shakespeare. In the late seventeenth and eighteenth centuries, it was more plausibly called Nature: "The world must be peopled," says the delightful Benedict in *Much Ado About Nothing* (2.3.213), and there are frequent invocations elsewhere of the happy, generative power that brings couples together—

> Jack shall have Jill,
> Naught shall go ill,
> The man shall have his mare again, and all shall be well.
> (*A Midsummer Night's Dream* 3.2.461–63)

—and the melancholy, destructive power that brings all living things to the grave: "Golden lads and girls all must, / As chimney-sweepers, come to dust" (*Cymbeline* 4.2.261–62).

But the celebration of Shakespeare as a poet of nature—often coupled with an inane celebration of his supposedly "natural" (that is, untutored) genius—has its distinct limitations. For Shakespearean art brilliantly interrogates the "natural," refusing to take for granted precisely what the celebrants think is most secure. His comedies are endlessly inventive in showing that love is not simply natural: the playful hint of bestiality in the line quoted above, "the man shall have his mare again" (from a play in which the Queen of the Fairies falls in love with an ass-headed laborer), lightly unsettles the boundaries between the natural and the perverse. These boundaries are called into question throughout Shakespeare's work, from the cross-dressing and erotic crosscurrents that deliciously complicate the lives of the characters in *Twelfth Night* and *As You Like It* to the terrifying violence that wells up from the heart of the family in *King Lear* or from the sweet intimacy of sexual desire in *Othello.* Even the boundary between life and death is not secure, as the ghosts in *Julius Caesar, Hamlet,* and *Macbeth* attest, while the principle of natural death (given its most eloquent articulation by old Hamlet's murderer, Claudius!) is repeatedly tainted and disrupted.

Disrupted too is the idea of order that constantly makes its claim, most insistently in the history plays. Scholars have observed the presence in Shakespeare's works of the so-called Tudor myth—the ideological justification of the ruling dynasty as a restoration of national order after a cycle of tragic violence. The violence, Tudor apologists claimed, was divine punishment unleashed after the deposition of the anointed king, Richard II, for God will not tolerate violations of the sanctified order. Traces of this propaganda certainly exist in the histories—Shakespeare may, for all we know, have personally subscribed to its premises—but a closer scrutiny of his plays has disclosed so many ironic reservations and qualifications and subversions as to call into question any straightforward adherence to a political line. The plays manifest a profound fascination with the monarchy and with the ambitions of the aristocracy, but the fascination is never simply endorsement. There is always at least the hint of a slippage between the great figures, whether admirable or monstrous, who stand at the pinnacle of authority and the vast, miscellaneous mass of soldiers, scriveners, ostlers, poets, whores, gardeners, thieves, weavers, shepherds, country gentlemen, sturdy beggars, and the like who make up the commonwealth. And the idea of order, though eloquently articulated (most memorably by Ulysses in *Troilus and Cressida*), is always shadowed by a relentless spirit of irony.

## *The Play of Language*

If neither the individual nor nature nor order will serve, can we find a single comprehensive name for the underlying force in Shakespeare's work? Certainly not. The work is too protean and capacious. But much of the energy that surges through this astonishing body of plays and poems is closely linked to the power of language. Shakespeare was the supreme product of a rhetorical culture, a culture steeped in the arts of persuasion and verbal expressiveness. In 1512, the great Dutch humanist Erasmus published a work called *De copia* that taught its readers how to cultivate "copiousness," verbal richness, in discourse. (Erasmus obligingly provides, as a sample, a list of 144 different ways of saying "Thank you for your letter.") Recommended modes of variation include putting the subject of an argument into fictional form, as well as the use of synonym, substitution, paraphrase, metaphor, metonymy, synecdoche, hyperbole, diminution, and a host of other figures of speech. To change emotional tone, he suggests trying *ironia, interrogatio, admiratio, dubitatio, abominatio*—the possibilities seem infinite.

In Renaissance England, certain syntactic forms or patterns of words known as "figures" (also called "schemes") were shaped and repeated in order to confer beauty or heighten expressive power. Figures were usually known by their Greek and Latin names, though in an Elizabethan rhetorical manual, *The Art of English Poesy,* George Puttenham made a valiant if short-lived attempt to give them English equivalents, such as "*Hyperbole,* or the Overreacher," "*Ironia,* or the Dry Mock," and "*Ploce,* or the Doubler." Those who received a grammar school education throughout Europe at almost any point between the Roman Empire and the eighteenth century probably knew by heart the names of up to one hundred such figures, just as they knew by heart their multiplication tables. According to one scholar's count, Shakespeare knew and made use of about two hundred.

As certain grotesquely inflated Renaissance texts attest, lessons from *De copia* and similar rhetorical guides could encourage mere prolixity and verbal self-display. But though he shared his culture's delight in rhetorical complexity, Shakespeare always understood how to swoop from baroque sophistication to breathtaking simplicity. Moreover, he grasped early in his career how to use figures of speech, tone, and rhythm not only to provide emphasis and elegant variety but also to articulate the inner lives of his characters. Take, for example, these lines from *Othello,* where, as scholars have noted, Shakespeare deftly combines four common rhetorical figures—*anaphora, parison, isocolon,* and *epistrophe*—to depict with painful vividness Othello's psychological torment:

By the world,
I think my wife be honest, and think she is not;
I think that thou art just, and think thou art not.
I'll have some proof.
(3.3.380–83)

*Anaphora* is simply the repetition of a word at the beginning of a sequence of sentences or clauses ("I/I"). *Parison* is the correspondence of word to word within adjacent sentences or clauses, either by direct repetition ("think/think") or by the matching of noun with noun, verb with verb ("wife/thou"; "be/art"). *Isocolon* gives exactly the same length to corresponding clauses ("and think she is not/and think thou art not"), and *epistrophe* is the mirror image of *anaphora,* in that it is the repetition of a word at the end of a sequence of sentences or clauses ("not/not"). Do we need to know the Greek names for these figures in order to grasp the effectiveness of Othello's lines? Of course not. But Shakespeare and his contemporaries, convinced that rhetoric provided the most natural and powerful means by which feelings could be conveyed to readers and listeners, were trained in an analytical language that helped at once to promote and to account for this effectiveness. In his 1593 edition of *The Garden of Eloquence,* Henry Peacham remarks that *epistrophe* "serveth to leave a word of importance in the end of a sentence, that it may the longer hold the sound in the mind of the hearer," and in *Directions for Speech and Style* (ca. 1599), John Hoskins notes that *anaphora* "beats upon one thing to cause the quicker feeling in the audience."

Shakespeare also shared with his contemporaries a keen understanding of the ways that rhetorical devices could be used not only to express powerful feelings but to hide them: after all, the artist who created Othello also created Iago, Richard III, and Lady Macbeth. He could deftly skewer the rhetorical affectations of Polonius in *Hamlet* or the pedant Holofernes in *Love's Labor's Lost.* He could deploy stylistic variations to mark the boundaries not of different individuals but of different social realms; in *A Midsummer Night's Dream,* for example, the blank verse of Duke Theseus is played off against the rhymed couplets of the well-born young lovers, and both in turn contrast with the prose spoken by the artisans. At the same time that he thus marks boundaries between both individuals and groups, Shakespeare shows a remarkable ability to establish unifying patterns of imagery that knit together the diverse strands of his plot and suggest subtle links among characters who may be scarcely aware of how much they share with one another.

One of the hidden links in Shakespeare's own works is the frequent use he makes of a somewhat unusual rhetorical figure called *hendiadys.* An example from the Roman poet Virgil is the phrase *pateris libamus et auro,* "we drink from cups and gold" (*Georgics* 2.192). Rather than serving as an adjective or a dependent noun, as in "golden cups" or "cups of gold," the word "gold" serves as a substantive joined to another substantive, "cups," by a conjunction, "and." Shakespeare uses the figure over three hundred times in all, and since it does not appear in ancient or medieval lists of tropes and schemes and is treated only briefly by English rhetoricians, he may have come upon it directly in Virgil. *Hendiadys* literally means "one through two," though Shakespeare's versions often make us quickly, perhaps only subliminally, aware of the complexity of what ordinarily passes for straightforward perceptions. When Othello, in his suicide speech, invokes the memory of "a malignant and a turbaned Turk," the figure of speech at once associates enmity with cultural difference and keeps them slightly apart. And when Macbeth speaks of his "strange and self-abuse," the *hendiadys* seems briefly to hold both "strange" and "self" up for scrutiny. It would be foolish to make too much of any single feature in Shakespeare's varied and diverse creative achievement, and yet this curious rhetorical scheme has something of the quality of a fingerprint.

But all of his immense rhetorical gifts, though rich, beautiful, and supremely useful, do not adequately convey Shakespeare's relation to language, which is less strictly functional than a total immersion in the arts of persuasion may imply. An Erasmian admiration for copiousness cannot fully explain Shakespeare's astonishing vocabulary of some 25,000 words. (His closest rival among the great English poets of the period was John Milton, with about 12,000 words, and most major writers, let alone ordinary people, have much smaller vocabularies.) This immense word hoard, it is worth noting, was not the result of scanning a dictionary; in the late sixteenth century, there were no large-scale English dictionaries of the kind to which we are now accustomed. Shakespeare seems to have absorbed new words from virtually every discursive realm he ever encountered, and he experimented boldly and tirelessly with them. These experiments were facilitated by a flexibility in grammar, orthography, and diction that the more orderly, regularized English of the later seventeenth and eighteenth centuries suppressed.

Owing in part to the number of dialects in London, pronunciation was variable, and there were many opportunities for phonetic association between words: the words "bear," "barn," "bier," "bourn" "born," and "barne" could all sound like one another. Homonyms were given greater scope by the fact that the same word could be spelled so many different ways—Christopher Marlowe's name appears in the records as Marlowe, Marloe, Marlen, Marlyne, Merlin, Marley, Marlye, Morley, and Morle—and by the fact that a word's grammatical function could easily shift, from noun to verb, verb to adjective, and so forth. Since grammar and punctuation did not insist on relations of coordination and subordination, loose, nonsyntactic sentences were common, and etymologies were used to forge surprising or playful relations between distant words.

It would seem inherently risky for a popular playwright to employ a vocabulary so far in excess of what most mortals could possibly possess, but Shakespeare evidently counted on his audience's linguistic curiosity and adventurousness, just as he counted on its general and broad-based rhetorical competence. He was also usually careful to provide a context that in effect explained or translated his more arcane terms. For example, when Macbeth reflects with horror on his murderous hands, he shudderingly imagines that even the sea could not wash away the blood; on the contrary, his bloodstained hand, he says, "will rather / The multitudinous seas incarnadine." The meaning of the unfamiliar word "incarnadine" is explained by the next line: "Making the green one red" (2.2.64–66).

What is most striking is not the abstruseness or novelty of Shakespeare's language but its extraordinary vitality, a quality that the playwright seemed to pursue with a kind of passionate recklessness. Perhaps Samuel Johnson was looking in the right direction when he complained that the "quibble," or pun, was "the fatal Cleopatra for which [Shakespeare] lost the world, and was content to lose it." For the power that continually discharges itself throughout the plays, at once constituting and unsettling everything it touches, is the polymorphous power of language, language that seems both costume and that which lies beneath the costume, personal identity and that which challenges the merely personal, nature and that which enables us to name nature and thereby distance ourselves from it.

Shakespeare's language has an overpowering exuberance and generosity that often resembles the experience of love. Consider, for example, Oberon's description in *A Midsummer Night's Dream* of the moment when he saw Cupid shoot his arrow at the fair vestal: "Thou rememberest," he asks Puck,

> Since once I sat upon a promontory
> And heard a mermaid on a dolphin's back
> Uttering such dulcet and harmonious breath
> That the rude sea grew civil at her song

And certain stars shot madly from their spheres
To hear the sea-maid's music?
(2.1.148–54)

Here, Oberon's composition of place, lightly alluding to a classical emblem, is infused with a fantastically lush verbal brilliance. This brilliance, the result of masterful alliterative and rhythmical technique, seems gratuitous; that is, it does not advance the plot, but rather exhibits a capacity for display and self-delight that extends from the fairies to the playwright who has created them. The rich music of Oberon's words imitates the "dulcet and harmonious breath" he is intent on recalling, breath that has, in his account, an oddly contradictory effect: it is at once a principle of order, so that the rude sea is becalmed like a lower-class mob made civil by a skilled orator, and a principle of disorder, so that celestial bodies in their fixed spheres are thrown into mad confusion. And this contradictory effect, so intimately bound up with an inexplicable, supererogatory, and intensely erotic verbal magic, is a key to *A Midsummer Night's Dream,* with its exquisite blend of confusion and discipline, lunacy and hierarchical ceremony.

The fairies in this comedy seem to embody a pervasive sense found throughout Shakespeare's work that there is something uncanny about language, something that is not quite human, at least in the conventional and circumscribed sense of the human that dominates waking experience. In the comedies, this intuition is alarming but ultimately benign: Oberon and his followers trip through the great house at the play's close, blessing the bride-beds and warding off the nightmares that lurk in marriage and parenthood. But there is in Shakespeare an alternative, darker vision of the uncanniness of language, a vision also embodied in creatures that test the limits of the human—not the fairies of *A Midsummer Night's Dream* but the weird sisters of *Macbeth.* When in the tragedy's opening scene the witches chant, "Fair is foul, and foul is fair," they unsettle through the simplest and most radical act of linguistic equation (*x* is *y*) the fundamental distinctions through which a moral order is established. And when Macbeth appears onstage a few minutes later, his first words unconsciously echo what we have just heard from the witches' mouths: "So foul and fair a day I have not seen" (1.3.39). What is the meaning of this linguistic "unconscious"? On the face of things, Macbeth presumably means only that the day of fair victory is also a day of foul weather, but the fact that he echoes the witches (something that we hear but that he cannot know) intimates an occult link between them, even before their direct encounter. It is difficult, perhaps impossible, to specify exactly what this link signifies—generations of emboldened critics have tried without notable success—but we can at least affirm that its secret lair is in the play's language, like a half-buried pun whose full articulation will entail the murder of Duncan, the ravaging of his kingdom, and Macbeth's own destruction.

*Macbeth* is haunted by half-buried puns, equivocations, and ambiguous grammatical constructions known as amphibologies. They manifest themselves most obviously in the words of the witches, from the opening exchanges to the fraudulent assurances that deceive Macbeth at the close, but they are also present in his most intimate and private reflections, as in his tortured broodings about his proposed act of treason:

If it were done when 'tis done, then 'twere well
It were done quickly. If th'assassination
Could trammel up the consequence and catch
With his surcease success—that but this blow
Might be the be-all and the end-all!—here,
But here, upon this bank and shoal of time,
We'd jump the life to come.
(1.7.1–7)

The dream is to reach a secure and decisive end, to catch as in a net (hence "trammel up") all of the slippery, unforeseen, and uncontrollable consequences of regicide, to hobble time as one might hobble a horse (another sense of "trammel up"), to stop the flow ("success") of events, to be, as Macbeth later puts it, "settled." But Macbeth's words themselves slip away from the closure he seeks; they slide into one another, trip over themselves, twist and double back and swerve into precisely the sickening uncertainties their speaker most wishes to avoid. And if we sense a barely discernible note of comedy in Macbeth's tortured language, a discordant playing with the senses of the word "done" and the hint of a childish tongue twister in the phrase "catch / With his surcease success," we are in touch with a dark pleasure to which Shakespeare was all his life addicted.

Look again at the couplet from *Cymbeline:* "Golden lads and girls all must, / As chimney-sweepers, come to dust." The playwright who insinuated a pun into the solemn dirge is the same playwright whose tragic heroine in *Antony and Cleopatra,* pulling the bleeding body of her dying lover into the pyramid, says, "Our strength is all gone into heaviness" (4.15.34). He is the playwright whose Juliet, finding herself alone on the stage, says, "My dismal scene I needs must act alone" (*Romeo and Juliet* 4.3.19), and the playwright who can follow the long, wrenching periodic sentence that Othello speaks, just before he stabs himself, with the remark "O bloody period!" (5.2.349). The point is not merely the presence of puns in the midst of tragedy (as there are stabs of pain in the midst of Shakespearean comedy); it is rather the streak of wildness that they so deliberately disclose, the sublimely indecorous linguistic energy of which Shakespeare was at once the towering master and the most obedient, worshipful servant.

### *From Page to Stage: Shakespeare at Work*

Shakespeare's extraordinary imaginative and linguistic power left its mark, like a personal signature, on everything he wrote. But his plays became the property of the theatrical company in which he was a shareholder. The company could choose to sell its plays to printers who might hope to profit if the public was eager to read as well as to watch a popular hit. But relatively few plays excited that level of public interest. Moreover, playing companies did not always think it was in their interest to have their scripts circulating in print, at least while the plays were actively in repertory: players evidently feared competition from rival companies and thought that reading might dampen playgoing. Plays were on occasion printed quickly, in order to take advantage of their popularity, but they were most often sold to the printers when the theaters were temporarily closed by plague, or when the company was in need of capital (four of Shakespeare's plays were published in 1600, presumably to raise money to pay the debts incurred in building the new Globe), or when a play had grown too old to revive profitably. There is no conclusive evidence that Shakespeare disagreed with this professional caution. There was clearly a market for his plays in print as well as onstage, and he himself may have taken pride in what he wrote as suitable for reading as well as viewing. But unlike Jonson, who took the radical step of rewriting his own plays for publication in the 1616 folio of his *Works,* Shakespeare evidently never undertook to constitute his plays as a canon. If in the sonnets he imagines his verse achieving a symbolic immortality, this dream apparently did not extend to his plays, at least through the medium of print.

Moreover, there is no evidence that Shakespeare had an interest in asserting authorial rights over his scripts, or that he or any other working English playwright had a public "standing," legal or otherwise, from which to do so. (Jonson was ridiculed for his presumption.) There is no indication whatever that he could, for example, veto changes in his scripts or block interpolated scenes or withdraw a play from production if a particular interpretation, addition, or revision did not please him. To be sure, in his advice to the players, Hamlet urges that those who play the clowns "speak no more than is set down for them," but—apart from the question of whether the prince speaks for the playwright—the play-within-the-play in *Hamlet* is precisely an instance of a script altered to suit a particular occasion. It seems likely that Shakespeare would have routinely accepted the possibility of such alterations. Moreover, he would of necessity have routinely accepted the possibility, and in certain cases the virtual inevitability, of cuts in order to stage his plays in the two to two and one-half hours that was the normal performing time. There is an imaginative generosity in many of Shakespeare's scripts, as if he were deliberately offering his fellow actors more than they could use on any one occasion and hence giving them abundant materials with which to reconceive and revivify each play again and again, as they or their audiences liked it. The Elizabethan theater, like most theater in our own time, was a collaborative enterprise, and the collaboration almost certainly extended to decisions about selection, trimming, shifts of emphasis, and minor or major revision.

Writing for the theater for Shakespeare was never simply a matter of sitting alone at his desk and putting words on paper; it was a social process as well as individual act. We do not know the extent to which this process frustrated him; in Sonnet 66 he writes of "art made tongue-tied by authority." Shakespeare may have been forced on occasion to cut lines and even whole scenes to which he was attached; shifting political circumstances may have occasioned rewriting, possibly against his will; or his fellow players may have insisted that they could not successfully perform what he had written, compelling him to make changes he did not welcome. But compromise and collaboration are part of what it means to be in the theater, and Shakespeare was, supremely, a man of the theater.

As a man of the theater, Shakespeare understood that whatever he set down on paper was not the end of the story. It would inevitably be shaped by the words he spoke to his fellow actors and by their own ideas concerning emphasis, stage business, tone, pacing, possible cuts, and so forth. It could be modified too by the intervention of the government censor or by intimations that some powerful figure might take offense at something in the script. To the extent that the agreed-upon alterations were ever written down, they were recorded in the promptbook used for a particular performance, and that promptbook could in turn be modified for a subsequent performance in a different setting.

For many years, it was thought that Shakespeare himself did little or no revising. Some recent editors have argued persuasively that there are many signs of authorial revision, even wholesale rewriting. But there is no sign that Shakespeare sought through such revision to bring each of his plays to its "perfect," "final" form. On the contrary, many of the revisions seem to indicate that the scripts remained open texts that the playwright and his company expected to add to, cut, and rewrite as the occasion demanded.

Ralph Waldo Emerson once compared Shakespeare and his contemporary Francis Bacon in terms of the relative "finish" of their work. All of Bacon's work, wrote Emerson, "lies along the ground, a vast unfinished city." Each of Shakespeare's dramas, by contrast, "is perfect, hath an immortal integrity. To make Bacon's work complete, he must live to the end of the world." Recent scholarship suggests that Shakespeare was more like Bacon than Emerson thought. Neither the Folio nor the quarto texts of Shakespeare's plays bear the seal of final authorial intention, the mark of decisive closure that has served, at least ideally, as the guarantee of textual authenticity. We want to believe, as we read the text, "This is the play as Shakespeare himself wanted it read," but there is no license for such a reassuring sentiment. To be "not of an age, but for all time" means in Shakespeare's case not that the plays have achieved a static perfection, but that they are creatively, inexhaustibly unfinished.

### *The Status of the Artist*

That we have been so eager to link certain admired scripts to a single known playwright is closely related to changes in the status of artists in the Renaissance, changes that led to a heightened interest in the hand of the individual creator. Like medieval painting, medieval drama gives us few clues as to the particular individuals who fashioned the objects we admire. We know something about the places in which these objects were made, the circumstances that enabled their creation, the spaces in which they were placed, but relatively little about the particular artists themselves. It is easy to imagine a wealthy patron or a civic authority in the late Middle Ages commissioning a play on a particular subject (appropriate, for example, to a seasonal ritual, a religious observance, or a political festivity) and specifying the date, place, and length of the performance, the number of actors, even the costumes to be used, but it is more difficult to imagine him specifying a particular playwright and still less insisting that the entire play be written by this dramatist alone. Only with the Renaissance do we find a growing insistence on the name of the maker, the signature that heightens the value and even the meaning of the work by implying that it is the emanation of a single, distinct shaping consciousness.

In the case of Renaissance painting, we know that this signature does not necessarily mean that every stroke was made by the master. Some of the work, possibly the greater part of it, may have been done by assistants, with only the faces and a few finishing touches from the hand of the illustrious artist to whom the work is confidently attributed. As the skill of individual masters became more explicitly valued, contracts began to specify how much was to come from the brush of the principal painter. Consider, for example, the Italian painter Luca Signorelli's contract of 1499 for frescoes in Orvieto Cathedral:

> The said master Luca is bound and promises to paint [1] all the figures to be done on the said vault, and [2] especially the faces and all the parts of the figures from the middle of each figure upwards, and [3] that no painting should be done on it without Luca himself being present. . . . And it is agreed [4] that all the mixing of colors should be done by the said master Luca himself.

Such a contract at once reflects a serious cash interest in the characteristic achievement of a particular artist and a conviction that this achievement is compatible with the presence of other hands, provided those hands are subordinate, in the finished work. For paintings on a smaller scale, it was more possible to commission an exclusive performance. Thus the contract for a small altarpiece by Signorelli's great teacher, Piero della Francesca, specifies that "no painter may put his hand to the brush other than Piero himself."

There is no record of any comparable concern for exclusivity in the English theater. Unfortunately, the contracts that Shakespeare and his fellow dramatists almost certainly signed have not, with one significant exception, survived. But plays written for the professional theater are by their nature an even more explicitly collective art form than paintings; they depend for their full realization on the collaboration of others, and that collaboration may well extend to the fashioning of the script. It seems that some authors may simply have been responsible for providing plots that others then dramatized; still others were hired to "mend" old plays or to supply prologues, epilogues, or songs. A particular playwright's name came to be attached to a certain identifiable style—a characteristic set of plot devices, a marked rhetorical range, a tonality of character—but this name may refer in effect more to a certain product associated with a particular playing company than to the individual artist who may or may not have written most of the script. The one contract whose details do survive, that entered into by Richard Brome and the actors and owners of the Salisbury Court Theater in 1635, does not stipulate that Brome's plays must be written by him alone or even that he must be responsible for a certain specifiable proportion of each script. Rather, it specifies that the playwright "should not nor would write any play or any part of a play to any other players or playhouse, but apply all his study and endeavors therein for the benefit of the said company of the said playhouse." The Salisbury Court players want rights to everything Brome writes for the stage; the issue is not that the plays associated with his name be exclusively *his* but rather that he be exclusively *theirs.*

Recent textual scholarship, then, has been moving steadily away from a conception of Shakespeare's plays as direct, unmediated emanations from the mind of the author and toward a conception of them as working scripts, composed and continually reshaped as part of a collaborative commercial enterprise in competition with other, similar enterprises. One consequence has been the progressive weakening of the idea of the solitary, inspired genius, in the sense fashioned by Romanticism and figured splendidly in the statue of Shakespeare in the public gardens in Germany's Weimar, the city of Goethe and Schiller: the poet, with his sensitive, expressive face and high domed forehead sitting alone and brooding, a skull at his feet, a long-stemmed rose in his crotch. In place of this projection of German Romanticism, we have now a playwright and sometime actor who is also (to his considerable financial advantage) a major shareholder in the company—the Chamberlain's Men, later the King's Men—to which he loyally supplies for most of his career an average of two plays per year.

As a shareholder Shakespeare had to concern himself with such matters as economic cycles, lists of plague deaths, the cost of costumes, government censorship, city ordinances, the hiring and firing of personnel, and innumerable other factors that affected his enterprise. Practical considerations did not merely affect the context of his writing for the stage; they also shaped the form of what he wrote. His plays were not monuments, fixed in every detail and immobilized forever. They were like living beings, destined to change as a condition for their very survival.

One of the very first biographical mentions of Shakespeare, in the Reverend Thomas Fuller's *History of the Worthies of England* (1662), seems to have grasped this principle of mobility. Fuller reports—or imagines—the "wit-combats" that Shakespeare and Jonson had at the Mermaid Tavern:

> which two I behold like a Spanish great galleon and an English man of war; Master Jonson (like the former) was built far higher in learning, solid but slow in his performances. Shakespeare, with the English man of war, lesser in bulk, but lighter in sailing, could turn with all tides, tack about, and take advantage of all winds by the quickness of his wit and invention.

The encounters Fuller describes may be apocryphal, but to "turn with all tides, tack about, and take advantage of all winds" is a canny description of the highly mobile texts that Shakespeare fashioned and bequeathed to posterity.

## *Conjuring Shakespeare*

The Elizabethan and Jacobean public had an interest in reading plays as well as seeing them. There was a lively market in such texts, often rushed into print to catch public excitement, and there is even evidence that at certain performances it was possible for audiences at the playhouse to purchase a copy of the very play they were watching.

Shakespeare's attitude to this market is unclear. Unlike Ben Jonson, he never personally edited and oversaw the publication of his plays, either individually or as a collection, but he may, for all we know, have imagined some day doing so. Perhaps death simply overtook him before he reached that goal. Certainly the Folio editors, though they were themselves fellow actors, thought of his plays as literary works. In 1623, seven years after the playwright's death, Heminges and Condell believed they could sell copies of their expensive collection of Shakespeare's plays—"What euer you do," they urge their readers, "buy"—by insisting that their texts were "as he conceiued them."

"As he conceived them": potential readers in the early seventeenth century then were already interested in access to Shakespeare's "conceits"—his "wit," his imagination, and his creative power—and were willing to assign a high value to the products of his particular, identifiable skill, one distinguishable from that of his company and of his rival playwrights. After all, Jonson's dedicatory poem in the Folio praises Shakespeare not as the playwright of the incomparable King's Men but as the equal of Aeschylus, Sophocles, and Euripides. And if we now see Shakespeare's dramaturgy in the context of his contemporaries and of a collective artistic practice, readers continue to have little difficulty recognizing that most of the plays attached to his name tower over those of his rivals.

The First Folio included an engraving purporting to show what Shakespeare looked like, but in the little poem that accompanied this image Jonson urged the reader to "look / Not on his Picture, but his Book." The words on the page then should conjure up the author himself; they should ideally give the reader unmediated access to the astonishing forge of imaginative power that was the mind of the dramatist. Such is the vision—at its core closely related to the preservation of the divinely inspired text in the great scriptural religions—that has driven many of the great editors who have for centuries produced successive editions of Shakespeare's works. The vision was not yet fully formed in the First Folio, for Heminges and Condell still felt obliged to apologize to their noble patrons for dedicating to them a collection of mere "trifles." But by the eighteenth century, there were no longer any ritual apologies for Shakespeare; instead, there was growing recognition of the supreme artistic importance of his works.

At the same time, from the eighteenth century onward, there was growing recognition of the uncertain, conflicting, and in some cases corrupt state of the surviving texts. Every conceivable step, it was thought, must be undertaken to correct mistakes, strip away corruptions, and return the texts to their pure and unsullied form. Noticing that there were multiple texts of fully half of the plays and noticing too that these texts often contain significant variants, editors routinely conflated the distinct versions into a single text in an attempt to reconstruct the ideal, definitive, complete, and perfect copy that they imagined Shakespeare must have aspired to and eventually reached for each of his plays. In doing so they succeeded in producing something that Shakespeare himself never wrote.

Heminges and Condell, who knew the author and had access to at least some of his manuscripts, lamented the fact that Shakespeare did not live "to have set forth and overseen his own writings." But even had he done so—or, alternatively, even if a cache of his manuscripts were discovered in a Warwickshire attic tomorrow—all of the editorial problems would not be solved, though the textual landscape would change, nor would all of the levels of mediation be swept away. The written word has strange powers: it seems to hold onto something of the very life of the person who has written it, but it also seems to pry that life loose from the writer, exposing it to vagaries of history and chance quite independent of those to which the writer was personally subject. Moreover, with the passing of centuries, the language itself and the whole frame of reference within which language and symbols are understood have decisively changed. The most learned modern scholar still lives at a huge experiential remove from Shakespeare's world and, even holding a precious copy of the First Folio in hand, cannot escape having to read across a vast chasm of time what is, after all, an edited text. The rest of us cannot so much as indulge in the fantasy of direct access: our eyes inevitably wander to the glosses and the explanatory notes.

Abandoning the dream of direct access to Shakespeare's final and definitive intentions is not a cause for despair, nor should it lead us to throw our hands up and declare that one text is as good as another. What it does is to encourage us to be actively interested in the editorial principles that underlie the particular edition that we are using. It is said that the great artist Brueghel once told an inquisitive connoisseur who had come to his studio, "Keep your nose out of my paintings; the smell of the paint will poison you." In the case of Shakespeare, it is increasingly important to bring one's nose close to the page, as it were, and sniff the ink. More precisely, it is important to understand the rationale for the choices that the editors have made.

The rationale behind *The Norton Shakespeare* is described at length in the Textual Introduction to this volume. What should be stressed here is the fact that

Shakespeare was the master of the unfinished, the perpetually open. The notion of finding a perfectly fixed text of one of his plays, the copy that he directly handed over to the printer as his "final" version, goes against everything we know about his personal practice and about Elizabethan and Jacobean theater. Shakespeare wrote his plays to be performed by professional players in a range of different settings, at different times, and before different publics. The project required considerable flexibility. As a working playwright, he seems to have thought about the creation of "parts" or roles, often with specific actors in mind though always with the understanding that the personnel might change. Taken all together, of course, the parts made up a whole, but both the individual pieces and the larger structure they formed were and have remained open. The editors of *The Norton Shakespeare* have tried to record and preserve this openness.

Speaking only for myself, I will confess a further ambition: I would like to meet Shakespeare in person. I think that throughout his career Shakespeare produced in effect detachable parts of himself, parts that derived from his personhood (his social relationships, his acquired knowledge, his temperament, his memories, his inner life, and so forth) but that moved independently in the world. He created out of himself hundreds of secondary agents, his characters, some of whom seem even to float free of the particular narrative structures in which they perform their given roles and to take on an agency we ordinarily reserve for biological persons. As an artist he literally gave his life to these agents, transferring his personal energies to them.

I do not mean that Shakespeare's characters are all self-portraits in the sense of referring back to his individual existence (though some of them almost certainly do). I mean rather that Shakespeare's life is, in an unusually intense and vivid way, in his works. And therefore when I open the printed book or scroll through the Digital Edition, I feel his eerie presence and want to call out, with the words Ben Jonson wrote in his dedicatory poem to the First Folio, "My Shakespeare, rise!"

# General Textual Introduction

GORDON McMULLAN AND SUZANNE GOSSETT

Most people read an edition of Shakespeare's plays and poems because they want to read the plays and poems, not because they wish to dwell on the material origins of the texts they are reading—where the texts came from, how the manuscripts looked, who printed them, for whom they were printed, how the publishing practices of the English Renaissance made them what they are. Yet attention to the text itself is, we believe, an integral part of understanding the meaning of Shakespeare's works, considerably enhancing the pleasure of the reading experience. Seeing Shakespeare in the theater, reading Shakespeare on the page: both can offer extraordinary, multiply layered experiences of entertainment and intellectual uplift, a sense of unparalleled access to the past, and often simply a great deal of fun. We have edited the text of Shakespeare with these pleasures, and the reader's choices, in mind, and we wish to share with you a sense of the further levels of engagement that close attention to the origins of the text itself can bring.

For us, first and foremost, the *textual* is inseparable from the *critical*. That is, the "themes" we locate in Shakespeare, the sense of the place of the plays and poems in Shakespeare's world and in our own, the ways in which these remarkable writings require us to reflect on being human, on being gendered, on living in community, on having an ethnicity and a class status, all have their foundation in the words we read—and if we don't know whether the words we are reading are the "right" ones, or if we don't have the tools to reflect on the challenges presented by the very idea of "right" words, then we may miss out on key aspects of the Shakespearean experience. The fantasies of the "anti-Stratfordians" (people who claim Shakespeare's works were written by one or another equally implausible candidate) serve to remind us of the obsession of our age with Shakespearean *authenticity*, with the urge to ensure that the Shakespeare we see performed, or that we read or study, is the *real* Shakespeare, the *authentic* Shakespeare. The primary question we address in our textual introduction is central to this debate—"How authentic is the text I am reading?"—and in order to do this we need to reflect on two things: on the nature of the Shakespearean text and on the complex idea of "authenticity." Once we have done that, we can begin to explain some of the decisions we made in editing the texts that together form *The Norton Shakespeare*.

## The "Authentic" Shakespeare

For centuries, playgoers and readers had two questions answered for them in advance: which plays and poems to read as "Shakespeare's" (the reader logically assumed that if a play or poem was in the "complete works," then it was Shakespeare's, and if not, not), and, beyond that, which *text* of a given Shakespeare play or poem to read. This second question might seem odd. Surely there is only one *Hamlet* and that is the *Hamlet* Shakespeare wrote? Yet not only does more than one authoritative text of certain plays (above all, as it happens, of *Hamlet*) exist, some of which are very different from each other, but the word "authoritative" raises a third question—notably, "On what grounds do we decide that a printed text is close to what Shakespeare actually wrote?" Moreover, the first of these questions is itself not straightforward. The boundaries of the Shakespeare canon—those texts accepted as being written in whole or in part by Shakespeare—have always been porous. Neither *Pericles* nor *The Two Noble Kinsmen,* for instance, was included in the First Folio, yet both have long been attributed to Shakespeare (in each case, as it happens, to Shakespeare working jointly with another playwright, as pretty much all his fellow Elizabethan and Jacobean playwrights did), and both are now invariably included in "Complete Works" editions. Some plays have been considered part of the Shakespeare canon for far less time. *Edward III,* for instance, now appears in editions as a "Shakespeare and others" play, where a couple of decades ago it did not. Times change, evidence surfaces, and methods of attributing authorship develop. As a result, other plays continue to hover at the edges of the canon. At the time of writing, the newest contender for inclusion is a celebrated play by Thomas Kyd called *The Spanish Tragedy,* for which, it is suggested, Shakespeare supplied extra scenes, capitalizing on the play's success. *The Spanish Tragedy* does not appear in the present edition of *The Norton Shakespeare,* but if in due course we are sufficiently convinced by the arguments for its inclusion, then in it will come. What the French thinker Jacques Derrida called "the logic of the supplement" operates here: each time you add something to a volume called "Complete" you make it *more* complete, but the fact that you needed to add something to complete a volume already claiming to be "complete" has the effect of undermining the very possibility of completeness. For editors of Shakespeare, this is unavoidable—and to be celebrated, not resented.

It is not only the *external* borders of the Shakespeare canon that are fluid; the *internal* borders too—the choice of words within a given play or poem—have never, to the surprise of many readers, been firmly fixed. Shakespeare lovers are aware, perhaps, that Hamlet's flesh is too "solid," "sullied," or "sallied," depending on which version of the play one reads; they may also have wondered which of two "others"—"the base Judean" or "the base Indian"—is the one to which Othello really means to compare himself just before his suicide; but they may not realize that these celebrated instances of Shakespearean textual choice are part of a much broader canvas of instabilities, uncertainties, and options. This means that not only the choice of play, but the choice of *text* of that play, affects the reader's experience of Shakespeare.

The key question arising here is that of the "right" reading, the "authentic" reading, a status usually taken to require a direct relationship to the author. The mental adjustment needed is to accept that, quite often, there may be either *no* "right" reading or *more than one.* We cannot ever know exactly what Shakespeare wrote because (with one limited, debated exception) we do not have the holograph manuscript (a manuscript in his own handwriting) of any of his plays or poems. Shakespeare's own manuscripts of the plays in the First Folio or in the various quartos that predate the Folio have not survived, and so editors are unable to do the one thing they would most like to be able to do, which is to compare what Shakespeare actually wrote with what was printed. The apparent exception is the lines in the surviving manuscript of *Sir Thomas More* that are largely accepted as being in Shakespeare's hand—but, maddeningly, this is the one play in the Shakespeare canon as currently constituted that never found its way into print in the late sixteenth or early seventeenth century. So, even in the case of the one brief section of extant manuscript generally thought to be in Shakespeare's hand, we cannot make a direct comparison between what was written and what was printed.

It was long believed that Shakespeare never revised his texts (a myth prompted by the prefatory material to the First Folio) and therefore that there must have been one, and only one, lost master original from which all subsequent texts derive. But further complicating the notion of the "authentic Shakespeare" is the existence of short, variant quarto texts of several plays. Because certain of these are noticeably inferior to the Folio (or, sometimes, to a fuller quarto) text of the same play, they were traditionally referred to as "bad quartos." In recent years, scholars have sought to replace the unhelpful connotations of "bad" with neutral descriptive terms such as "short quartos," but the point of origin of these texts remains unclear. Are they "authentic"? One long-standing argument has it that they are "reported" texts, the product of "pirate" printers who sat a handful of actors down and persuaded them to recall not only their own lines but the entire play—this, it is claimed, explains the discrepancy in quality between the lines of certain characters in these quartos (e.g., Mercutio in the First Quarto of *Romeo and Juliet*, whose lines are nearly identical to those in the much fuller Second Quarto) and those of others. These quartos vary considerably, from the brief, highly problematic quarto of *The Merry Wives of Windsor* to the much more independent and interpretively convincing First Quarto of *Hamlet*. It has sometimes been proposed that these quartos may represent Shakespeare's early drafts. A further possibility, championed recently as a development of increasing editorial openness to the possibility that Shakespeare did occasionally revise his own work, is that the short quartos represent "theatrical" versions of the plays, whereas the lengthy Folio texts represent more overtly "literary" versions designed with readers in mind. It may be that we will never fully understand how these quartos came to be so different from the fuller, ostensibly more authoritative versions in the First Folio and elsewhere, but it seems essential to present them in all their intriguing difference. Our editorial principles and the technology we adopt in this edition allow us to include fully edited versions of all these quartos, so that the reader may understand the complexity of deciding what constitutes "authentic" Shakespeare.

## The Text in the Print House

One reason it is hard to know what Shakespeare actually wrote is that all early modern printed texts include interpretations, adjustments, and misreadings of the manuscripts on which they are based (which may have been the author's own or a neater scribal copy), as well as mechanical errors made by the compositors in the process of setting the type for printing. Moreover, workers in the Renaissance print house did not simply transfer the words passively from writer to reader; they actively intervened in what they printed. There was no fixed way to spell words in Shakespeare's day—Shakespeare himself spelled his own name differently at different times when signing documents—and compositors made the most of this irregularity to even out or "justify" the line they were setting (for example, by adding or removing a final "e" on an individual word). Similarly, there was no sense that the printer's duty was to print exactly what he found in the manuscript with which he was working. On the contrary, since early modern play manuscripts typically included little or no punctuation, it was the job of the compositor setting the type to add punctuation so as to enable and enhance the reader's experience. One of the most misleading of Shakespearean myths, one prevalent among actors even today, is the claim that the punctuation in the First Folio expresses "Shakespeare's instructions to actors": those theater professionals who have carefully timed their pauses and breaths according to the arrangement of commas and semicolons in the First Folio may be sad to learn that they are almost certainly basing their practice on the habits of Compositor A or Compositor J (since we almost never know the names of the workers in the print houses, compositors are usually referred to by letter).

To understand how the printing process affected the texts we read, it helps to know how the two principal formats in which Shakespeare's plays were printed—folio and quarto—were put together. A folio is made up of standard-sized sheets of paper printed with two pages on each side, then folded in half and assembled with several other such folded sheets inserted inside each other to form a "gathering" or "quire"; these gatherings are then stitched together to form the book. A quarto is made of the same standard-sized sheets of paper but is printed with four pages on each side and then folded twice (so that it is a quarter the size of the original sheet and half the size of a folio); each set of four leaves is either stitched together with other sets or inserted into a number of others to form a gathering as with a folio; the gatherings are then sewn through the central fold to form a book (which is why, very occasionally, you might come across a book where some of the pages need cutting apart if the print is to be read; the folding of the sheet to form eight pages will always require two edges to be cut after binding). Try folding a sheet of paper and you will see how this works. If you write the page numbers from one to eight on the folded sheet and then unfold it again, you will see that pages 1, 4, 5, and 8 (the "outer forme") are on one side and 2, 3, 6, and 7 (the "inner forme") are on the other, and that only some pages on each side are printed consecutively. (Scholars in fact tend to specify locations in early printed texts not by page numbers, which are notoriously unreliable in books from Shakespeare's day, but by what are called "signatures," which express the physical construction of the book—that is, the number of leaves collected together as a gathering and the number of gatherings that make up the book. Thus B2, or B2r, signifies the front side—recto—of the second sheet in gathering B, while C3v means the reverse side—verso—of the third sheet in gathering C.) A compositor setting either an inner or an outer form was thus not setting the type in the order of the plot, and you can imagine the loss of understanding this might produce at moments of complication in the text, even in an experienced professional. And then of course there is the Elizabethan equivalent of the coffee break to consider: one compositor would at times take over from another and carry on setting the type, and you can see where this has happened because the new compositor has different habits—his own preferences for abbreviating speech prefixes, say—and in a context where there are two characters with similar names he might misunderstand the speech prefix for the one and set it as the other, thus attributing a speech to the wrong speaker—all of which makes it that much harder to determine the nature of the manuscript from which the compositors were working.

If you look at the illustration on the next page, you can see a visual summary of the print workers' tasks. In the right foreground a boy is examining a forme (the frame into which the type is locked for printing) that has been set with type; he seems to be doing a last check against the manuscript while waiting for the forme to be placed in the press. To the far left, a pair of compositors is setting type from typecases, with the manuscript copy from which they are working stuck to the wall in front of them; behind them, a worker is replacing used type into a typecase arranged alphabetically and vertically ("upper-case" letters, i.e., capitals, at the top, "lower-case" below); to his right, a bespectacled proofreader checks an as-yet-uncorrected sheet against copy; in the background, a figure who is just possibly a woman (there is evidence that women worked in, and sometimes even, as printers' widows, owned, print houses) is using absorbent, wool-stuffed leather balls to apply ink to the forme before it is placed on the bed of the press; and, finally, the pressman pulls the bar across to lower the central weight of the press onto the conjunction of inked type and blank paper and thus imprint the sheet.

The first sheet pulled would be handed to the proofreader for checking, and he would mark errors for correction; when he finished, the press would be stopped, the (now very inky) type adjusted to make the corrections, and the process would then continue. The pressman would, however, keep printing sheets during the twenty minutes it might take the proofreader to work through the proof, and those uncorrected sheets (a hundred or so) would be stacked together indiscriminately with the corrected ones in the overall print run (which was 1,200 or so copies in the case of the First Folio), not separated or discarded. The result is that early printed books are a blend of uncorrected and corrected sheets, and no individual copy of a book such

Unknown engraver, after Stradanus (Jan van der Straet), *Invention of Book Printing,* from *Nova reperta* (New inventions and discoveries of modern times; ca. 1599–1603).

as the Folio is likely to be exactly the same as any other, given the random distribution of uncorrected sheets. If you look closely at the list of textual variants to this edition, you will see that editors sometimes note when they have selected a corrected reading from a copy of the base text other than the primary one from which they are working.

One printing-house factor likely to affect the text was the need for print workers to "cast off," that is, to work out how many lines of a given manuscript would fit on a printed page, and to make pencil annotations in the manuscript to mark where page breaks would fall in print. Occasionally mistakes would be made, and you can see in the printed text where either a compositor has realized that he still has a lot of words to set but little space to play with, and so keeps everything tight, or where he is, by contrast, running out of words yet still has a fair amount of page to fill, and so deploys white space, printers' ornaments, and the like. For examples of these composition strategies, see pages 80 and 81.

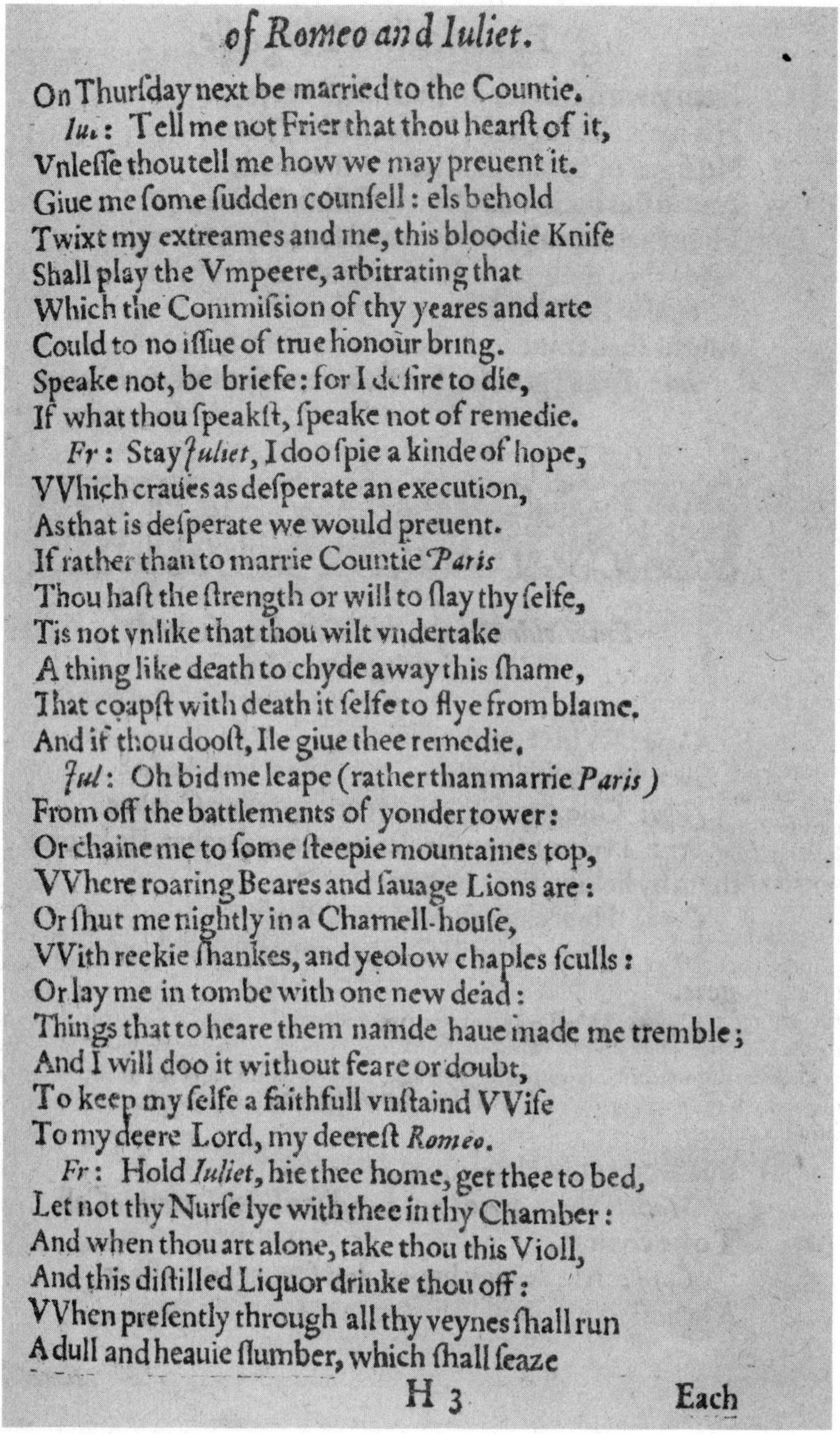

of *Romeo and Iuliet.*

On Thurſday next be married to the Countie.
*Iu.*: Tell me not Frier that thou hearſt of it,
Vnleſſe thou tell me how we may preuent it.
Giue me ſome ſudden counſell: els behold
Twixt my extreames and me, this bloodie Knife
Shall play the Vmpeere, arbitrating that
Which the Commiſsion of thy yeares and arte
Could to no iſſue of true honour bring.
Speake not, be briefe: for I deſire to die,
If what thou ſpeakſt, ſpeake not of remedie.
*Fr*: Stay *Iuliet*, I doo ſpie a kinde of hope,
VVhich craues as deſperate an execution,
As that is deſperate we would preuent.
If rather than to marrie Countie *Paris*
Thou haſt the ſtrength or will to ſlay thy ſelfe,
Tis not vnlike that thou wilt vndertake
A thing like death to chyde away this ſhame,
That coapſt with death it ſelfe to flye from blame.
And if thou dooſt, Ile giue thee remedie.
*Iul*: Oh bid me leape (rather than marrie *Paris*)
From off the battlements of yonder tower:
Or chaine me to ſome ſteepie mountaines top,
VVhere roaring Beares and ſauage Lions are:
Or ſhut me nightly in a Charnell-houſe,
VVith reekie ſhankes, and yeolow chaples ſculls:
Or lay me in tombe with one new dead:
Things that to heare them namde haue made me tremble;
And I will doo it without feare or doubt,
To keep my ſelfe a faithfull vnſtaind VVife
To my deere Lord, my deereſt *Romeo*.
*Fr*: Hold *Iuliet*, hie thee home, get thee to bed,
Let not thy Nurſe lye with thee in thy Chamber:
And when thou art alone, take thou this Violl,
And this diſtilled Liquor drinke thou off:
VVhen preſently through all thy veynes ſhall run
A dull and heauie ſlumber, which ſhall ſeaze

H 3 Each

Q1 *Romeo and Juliet,* H3r. An example of a "tight" page where the casting-off seems to have been efficient.

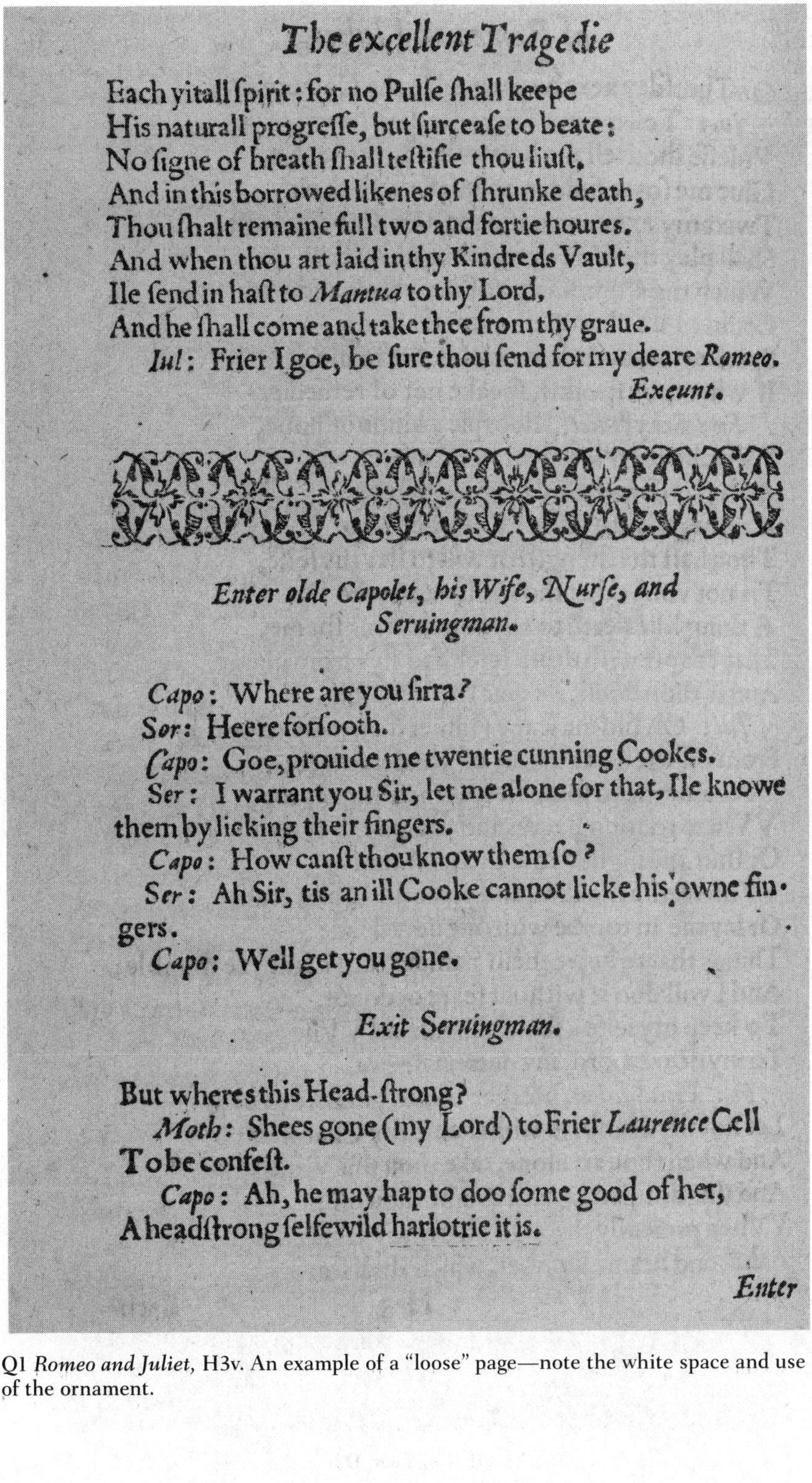

The excellent Tragedie

Each yitall ſpirit : for no Pulſe ſhall keepe
His naturall progreſſe, but ſurceaſe to beate :
No ſigne of breath ſhall teſtifie thou liuſt.
And in this borrowed likenes of ſhrunke death,
Thou ſhalt remaine full two and fortie houres.
And when thou art laid in thy Kindreds Vault,
Ile ſend in haſt to *Mantua* to thy Lord,
And he ſhall come and take thee from thy graue.
*Iul* : Frier I goe, be ſure thou ſend for my deare *Romeo.*
*Exeunt.*

*Enter olde Capolet, his Wife, Nurſe, and Seruingman.*

*Capo* : Where are you ſirra?
*Ser* : Heere forſooth.
*Capo* : Goe, prouide me twentie cunning Cookes.
*Ser* : I warrant you Sir, let me alone for that, Ile knowe them by licking their fingers.
*Capo* : How canſt thou know them ſo?
*Ser* : Ah Sir, tis an ill Cooke cannot licke his owne fingers.
*Capo* : Well get you gone.

*Exit Seruingman.*

But wheres this Head-ſtrong?
*Moth* : Shees gone (my Lord) to Frier *Laurence* Cell
To be confeſt.
*Capo* : Ah, he may hap to doo ſome good of her,
A headſtrong ſelfewild harlotrie it is.

*Enter*

Q1 *Romeo and Juliet,* H3v. An example of a "loose" page—note the white space and use of the ornament.

These moments of professional adjustment necessarily affect the texts we have inherited, and a close look at the early printed page may explain why lines that seem metrically regular have been set as prose, say, or as fragmented verse lines. Here from the First Quarto of *King Lear* is an example of verse lines that have been squeezed into prose in order to save space:

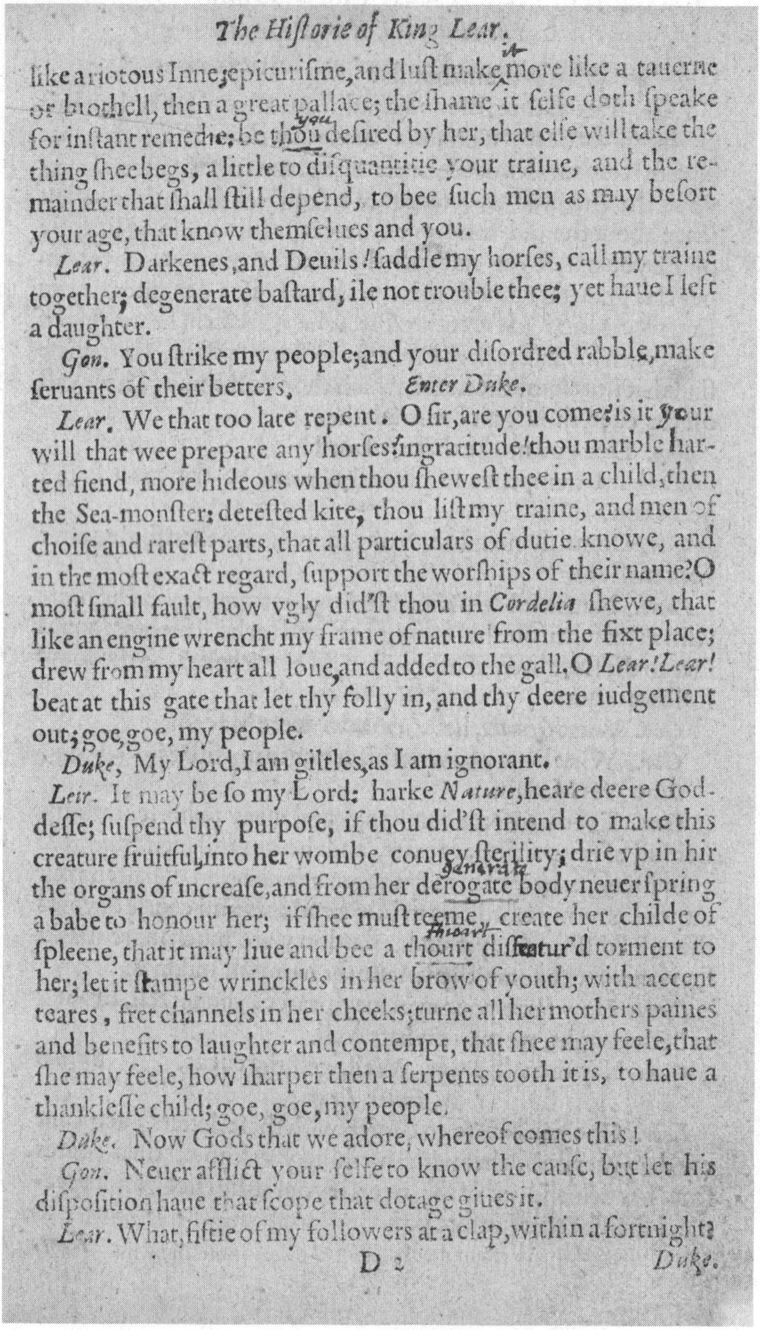

*The Hiſtorie of King Lear.*

like a riotous Inne, epicuriſme, and luſt make more like a tauerne or brothell, then a great pallace; the ſhame it ſelfe doth ſpeake for inſtant remedie; be thou deſired by her, that elſe will take the thing ſhee begs, a little to diſquantitie your traine, and the remainder that ſhall ſtill depend, to bee ſuch men as may beſort your age, that know themſelues and you.

*Lear.* Darkenes, and Deuils! ſaddle my horſes, call my traine together; degenerate baſtard, ile not trouble thee; yet haue I left a daughter.

*Gon.* You ſtrike my people; and your diſordred rabble, make ſeruants of their betters, *Enter Duke.*

*Lear.* We that too late repent. O ſir, are you come? is it your will that wee prepare any horſes? ingratitude! thou marble harted fiend, more hideous when thou ſheweſt thee in a child, then the Sea-monſter: deteſted kite, thou liſt my traine, and men of choiſe and rareſt parts, that all particulars of dutie knowe, and in the moſt exact regard, ſupport the worſhips of their name? O moſt ſmall fault, how vgly did'ſt thou in *Cordelia* ſhewe, that like an engine wrencht my frame of nature from the fixt place; drew from my heart all loue, and added to the gall. O *Lear! Lear!* beat at this gate that let thy folly in, and thy deere iudgement out; goe, goe, my people.

*Duke,* My Lord, I am giltles, as I am ignorant.

*Leir.* It may be ſo my Lord: harke *Nature*, heare deere Goddeſſe; ſuſpend thy purpoſe, if thou did'ſt intend to make this creature fruitful, into her wombe conuey ſterility; drie vp in hir the organs of increaſe, and from her derogate body neuer ſpring a babe to honour her; if ſhee muſt teeme, create her childe of ſpleene, that it may liue and bee a thourt diſfeatur'd torment to her; let it ſtampe wrinckles in her brow of youth; with accent teares, fret channels in her cheeks; turne all her mothers paines and benefits to laughter and contempt, that ſhee may feele, that ſhe may feele, how ſharper then a ſerpents tooth it is, to haue a thankleſſe child; goe, goe, my people.

*Duke.* Now Gods that we adore, whereof comes this!

*Gon.* Neuer afflict your ſelfe to know the cauſe, but let his diſpoſition haue that ſcope that dotage giues it.

*Lear.* What, fiftie of my followers at a clap, within a fortnight?

D 2 *Duke.*

Q1 *King Lear*, D2r

And here from the First Quarto of *Henry V* is an example of prose that has been set as rough verse (notice how the first word of each line of Fluellen's speeches is capitalized) in order to stretch it out to fill the available space:

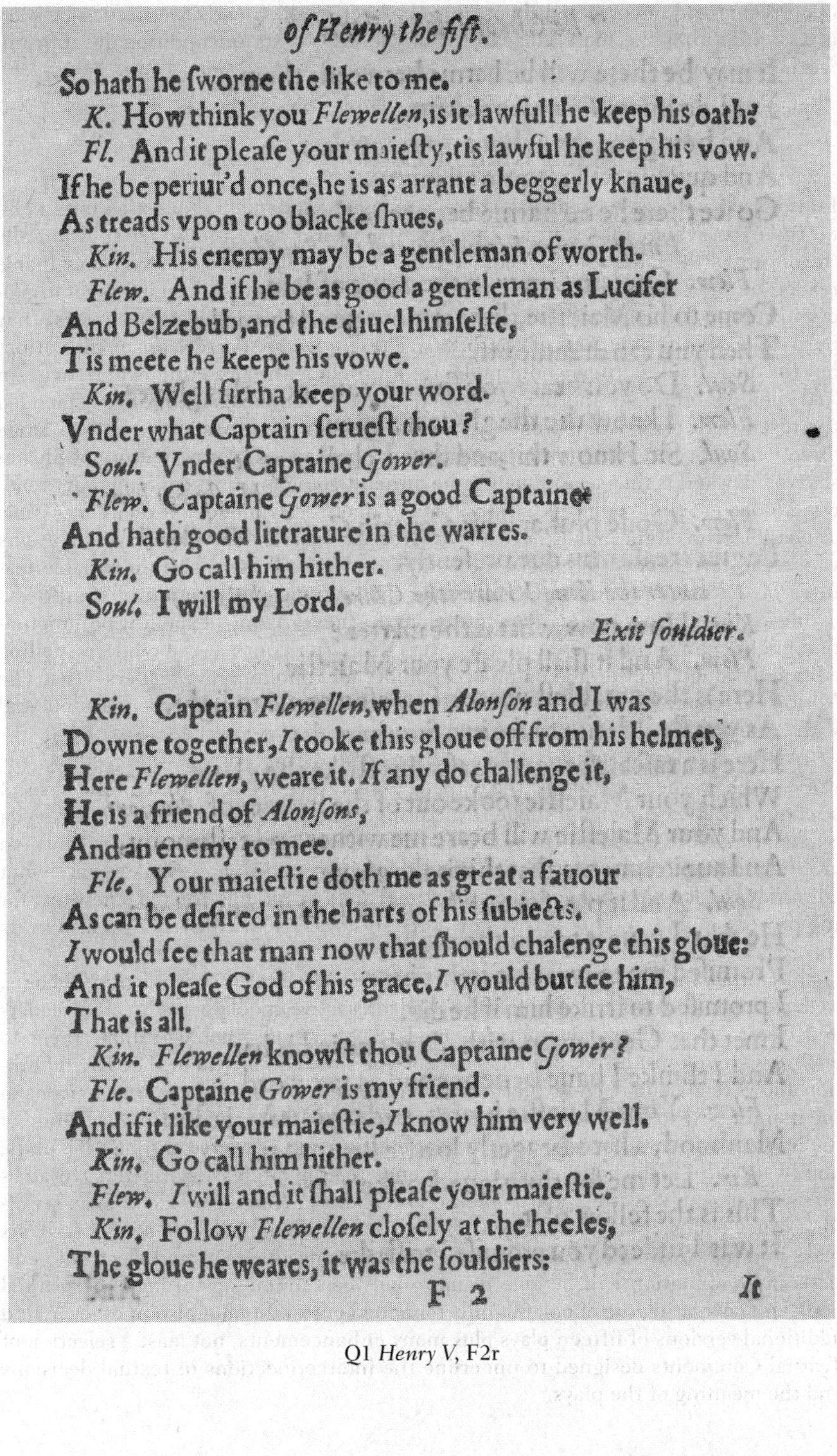

*of Henry the fift.*

So hath he ſworne the like to me.
*K.* How think you *Flewellen*,is it lawfull he keep his oath?
*Fl.* And it pleaſe your maieſty,tis lawful he keep his vow.
If he be periur'd once,he is as arrant a beggerly knaue,
As treads vpon too blacke ſhues.
*Kin.* His enemy may be a gentleman of worth.
*Flew.* And if he be as good a gentleman as Lucifer
And Belzebub,and the diuel himſelfe,
Tis meete he keepe his vowe.
*Kin.* Well ſirrha keep your word.
Vnder what Captain ſerueſt thou?
*Soul.* Vnder Captaine *Gower*.
*Flew.* Captaine *Gower* is a good Captaine
And hath good littrature in the warres.
*Kin.* Go call him hither.
*Soul.* I will my Lord.
*Exit ſouldier.*

*Kin.* Captain *Flewellen*,when *Alonſon* and I was
Downe together,*I* tooke this gloue off from his helmet,
Here *Flewellen*, weare it. *If* any do challenge it,
He is a friend of *Alonſons*,
And an enemy to mee.
*Fle.* Your maieſtie doth me as great a fauour
As can be deſired in the harts of his ſubiects.
*I* would ſee that man now that ſhould chalenge this gloue:
And it pleaſe God of his grace,*I* would but ſee him,
That is all.
*Kin.* *Flewellen* knowſt thou Captaine *Gower*?
*Fle.* Captaine *Gower* is my friend.
And if it like your maieſtie,*I* know him very well.
*Kin.* Go call him hither.
*Flew.* *I* will and it ſhall pleaſe your maieſtie.
*Kin.* Follow *Flewellen* cloſely at the heeles,
The gloue he weares, it was the ſouldiers:
F 2 *It*

Q1 *Henry V*, F2r

Understanding these print-house procedures clarifies how at each stage of the printing process error and variety may be introduced: at the stage of "casting off," at the stage of setting the type from manuscript (especially if the writer had difficult handwriting), at the stages of proofreading and press correction, and in the assembly of corrected and uncorrected sheets into the book itself. Clearly, we need to be wary of assuming that the material features of the early texts unconditionally transmit "authorial intention."

## What Kind of Edition Is This?

Editions always exist for readers. There is no more fundamental question for an editor than "For whom am I editing?" because the answer determines very substantially the nature of the edition produced. No edition can be designed for every imaginable reader; on the contrary, specific kinds of editing are done with specific sets of readers in mind. "Diplomatic" editions, for instance, are designed for scholars: they reproduce all the features of the original text without correction or alteration, but for most readers they would make for an unappealing reading experience. An "old-spelling" edition is another possibility: it is edited (that is, an editor has emended the text where error is apparent and included other aids to reading, such as stage directions), but it remains in the spelling (and, perhaps, the punctuation) of Shakespeare's day and is thus again likely to be difficult going for most contemporary readers. Modern-spelling editions are designed to make early modern texts as accessible as possible: the editor makes necessary corrections to the text, adds stage directions where they are needed to clarify the action, makes consistent certain variable features of the original, and modernizes the spelling and punctuation of those texts (while keeping a close eye on moments when the modernizing of spelling or punctuation might change the actual meaning). It is this latter course—the modern-spelling edition designed to offer maximum accessibility for contemporary readers—that *The Norton Shakespeare* adopts, but with certain developments and enhancements and with a specific set of principles for editorial choice.

We—the team of editors who together created this edition—have edited the works of Shakespeare—that is, the existing early texts—from scratch on the basis of a set of principles known as "single-text editing." The first two editions of *The Norton Shakespeare* were based on the text created in 1986 for Oxford University Press—a groundbreaking edition that transformed the modern editing of Shakespeare—but editorial practice has changed since that time, and Norton has created a new text for the present moment. This text is new both in its physical construction and in its theoretical underpinnings.

First, this, the Third Edition of *The Norton Shakespeare,* is "born digital." That is, we have taken the opportunity offered by the interactive ebook format to offer readers and classroom teachers an unprecedented set of options that will allow them to engage with, not just be passive recipients of, the words before them. The Digital Edition allows readers to open textual and performance comments by clicking on icons in the margin next to the line they are reading; to toggle from the text to a facsimile of the original printed folio or quarto; to hear all the songs scattered through the plays; and to listen to eight hours of selected scenes read by professional actors. In addition, readers can view the Quarto and Folio versions of *King Lear* side by side, scrolling as they choose; side-by-side viewing is also available for selected scenes from six plays and for two versions of a sonnet. Readers using the print and electronic editions in combination will be able to move between thumbing through the printed book and navigating the ebook not only for added portability but also in order to find additional versions of fifteen plays plus many enhancements, not least a selection of Textual Comments designed to underline the interconnections of textual decisions and the meaning of the plays.

Second, this edition adopts a new approach to the Shakespearean text, one made possible in part by the opportunities offered by the digital platform. Our underlying editorial principle has been, at its simplest, to edit the *text,* not the *work.* Let us explain what we mean by this with reference in particular to the plays (though there are similar issues with the sonnets). Shakespeare's plays exist in imperfect ways—none of them ideal, none of them perfectly representing what Shakespeare wrote or what his first audiences heard. Editors have always recognized that these surviving printed texts vary in their origins, though all must bear in some way "traces" of the original literary works that Shakespeare wrote out with quill and paper. Lying behind the surviving texts are, variously, authorial drafts, "fair" or scribal copies, theatrical promptbooks, and occasionally unfinished materials—often a mixture of more than one of these. One older editorial tradition sought to address the imperfections present in the texts as a result of this variable provenance by reconstructing, to a greater or lesser extent, an imagined original, creating an edition that—drawing on their professional knowledge of the writing habits of Shakespeare and his contemporaries, of Elizabethan handwriting, and of the printing process—the editors believed to be nearer to what Shakespeare and his audiences would have known or wanted than the actual surviving text with its flaws and imperfections. Of course editors need to correct many of those flaws and imperfections: to give readers a comprehensible reading experience, you must address errors and other distractions. But we believe it is not necessary or even desirable to try to reconstruct a "perfect" work that may never have existed in this form. Consequently, we have made the decision not to do what editors have normally done for centuries, which is to emend at will by merging the differing elements of distinct early texts of a given play, but rather to provide carefully considered editions of each of the early authoritative texts of works for which more than one such text survives. Similarly, in dealing with plays for which only one text survives, we have stayed as close as possible to that text when sense can be made of it, not adopting a traditional emendation if it appears to us to be the product of editorial preference rather than necessary for sense. In other words, we have chosen to edit the *texts* we actually have, not the *play* or the *poem* we do not, to accept uncertainty, and to exercise a certain skepticism toward earlier claims that sometimes made the editor seem a substitute for Shakespeare.

As we have noted, this edition was "born digital"—that is, we set out to invert the prior hierarchy of page and screen by creating an edition that would reach its fullest potential in digital form. Both the print and the digital editions are, in different ways, "complete works." The print volume includes all the poems, some of which exist in various manuscripts and others in print; there is usually only one form of each of these, though we include the entire *Passionate Pilgrim,* which was falsely ascribed to Shakespeare alone but does include some of his poems in variant forms. It—the print volume—includes all the plays too, providing one text for each play (except for *Hamlet,* for which we offer two editions, the First Quarto and a text merging the Second Quarto with materials from the Folio, and *King Lear,* for which we offer editions of the Quarto and the Folio, plus a merged text including all materials in both: for an account of the inclusion of these merged editions, or "conflations," in an edition based on single-text editing principles, see page 87, below. In deciding which of several texts to include in the bound volume we have used a pragmatic and flexible measure. Rather than (as has been done in the past) claiming to be able to determine and present the text that was Shakespeare's "original" version—or his "final" version, or the one that the company probably performed—we have in the case of plays that exist in significantly different texts printed the text that is most complete and apparently most finished. This often means the text in the First Folio, where about half the plays appear for the first time in the only text we have. But when—as, for example, in the case of *Romeo and Juliet* or of *1 Henry IV*—the Folio text is itself derived from a good quarto, we choose that earlier quarto as the base text from which our print edition is created.

We encourage readers to work with both versions, digital and print, to gain the most possible from *The Norton Shakespeare*. Editing Shakespeare digitally enables us to offer readers the opportunity to read, compare, and contrast the two (or, in the case of *Hamlet*, three) early texts of each of the plays for which multiple texts exist. Whether the plays exist in one substantive text or several, we have taken the same approach to the editing—modernizing spelling and punctuation on principles that are consistent across the edition, providing additional stage directions where they are required to clarify the action, and trusting the original text wherever possible, emending only where absolutely necessary and not "reconstructing" material in addition to that provided by the surviving texts.

The primary impact of these choices is, naturally, on those plays for which more than one early substantive text exists. For instance, we provide (in the Digital Edition) edited texts of Quarto *Othello* and Folio *Othello*—two different texts representing, we believe, two subtly different plays. Even when two separate early texts are nearly identical, the differences can be fascinating. Thus, in *Othello*, the female protagonist, Desdemona, infuriates her father by marrying an older man who is both black and a convert from Islam. Her father, who initially voices a series of racist reasons for assuming that Othello had brainwashed his daughter into eloping with him, sees her as shy and almost worryingly asexual (she has shown no interest in the eligible men he has introduced her to), but Othello's narrative of the process by which he wooed her suggests that she is more actively aware of her sexuality than her father believes: "My story being done, / She gave me for my pains a world of sighs. / [. . .] She thanked me / And bade me, if I had a friend that loved her, / I should but teach him how to tell my story, / And that would woo her" (Q 1.3.145–46, 150–53).

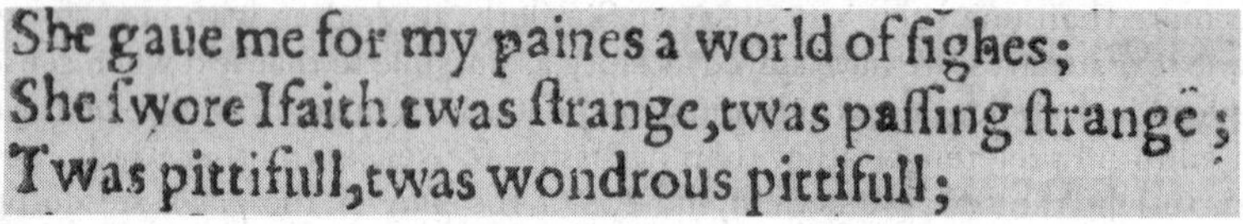
She gaue me for my paines a world of ſighes;
She ſwore Ifaith twas ſtrange,twas paſſing ſtrange;
Twas pittifull,twas wondrous pittifull;

Q1 *Othello*, C3v

So the Quarto. The slightly later Folio version of the play alters one key word: "My story being done, / She gave me for my pains a world of kisses" (F 1.3.158–59).

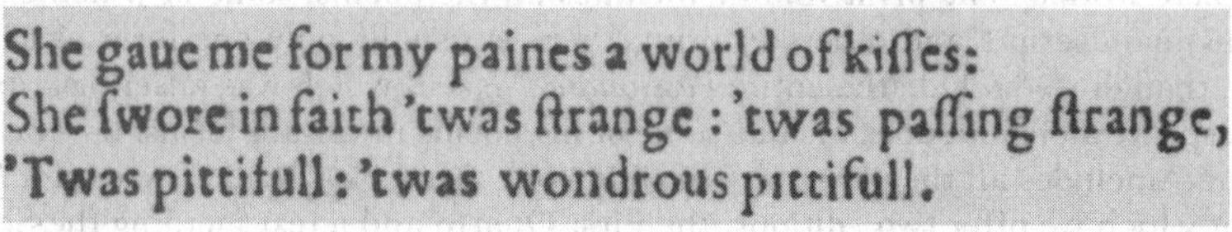
She gaue me for my paines a world of kiſſes:
She ſwore in faith 'twas ſtrange: 'twas paſſing ſtrange,
'Twas pittifull: 'twas wondrous pittifull.

F *Othello*, ss5v

Thus there are two equally coherent versions of the same line, different in one small but significant way. By providing editions of both texts, we avoid the necessity of preferring the one reading over the other (male editors have typically preferred "sighs," just as the editorial tradition seems generally to assume, in the phrasing of inserted stage directions, that men kiss women, not that women and men kiss each other), and we open up for our readers a degree of choice—to read the Quarto with its sighing Desdemona or the Folio with its more ardent, kissing Desdemona—and their decision about which version to read will impact the way they see the tragedy unfolding and thus their interpretation of the play. In this way, the study of the material features of the text and of the meaning of the play are inseparable.

This tiny difference between Quarto *Othello* and Folio *Othello* may represent revised authorial intention or some incidental external influence; we cannot know for certain. But there is a category of difference between Quarto and Folio that reminds us that when we read Shakespeare's plays we are dealing with the substantially collaborative process that is theatrical production—and thus with texts that have in various ways gone through the performance process. The severe reduction in Emilia's and Desdemona's parts in act 4 of Quarto *Othello*—the cutting, for instance, of the "Willow Song" that Desdemona sings before she goes to bed for the last time or of Emilia's wry lines about husbands—may be due not to authorial choice, a decision on Shakespeare's part to reduce the prominence of the women at this late stage of the play, but to theatrical necessity, that is, the presumed absence from the King's Men at one point of boy actors with sufficient singing ability or stamina. Often we can only guess at the reasons for such changes, but the point is that they are very often material and environmental, not intentional in the sense of being deliberate changes made for artistic reasons by the author. Yet they cannot be dismissed simply as "inauthentic," not only because we do not know Shakespeare's role at such moments but also because all staged plays are necessarily constructed through collaborative engagement between text and actor. Furthermore, for readers and playgoers across subsequent centuries, these renegotiated texts, offering evidence of multiple inputs for a range of practical reasons, were the "real" Shakespeare. Knowing about the practical processes of playwriting, performance, and printing enables the reader to gain a fuller understanding of the nature of the Shakespearean text as an expression of the highly socialized process of dramatic creativity.

We have noted in passing that, across the centuries, the borders of the Shakespeare canon have been fluid. For a century and a half, the *King Lear* that audiences saw in the theater was not Shakespeare's *King Lear* as we know it, but an adaptation of the play created by Irish poet and playwright Nahum Tate in the late seventeenth century that radically cut and altered the original, even providing a happy ending that suited the theatrical expectations of the day but looks to us bewilderingly inappropriate. Once the popularity of the Tate version had faded, the *King Lear* that audiences began to see reverted to "Shakespeare's *King Lear*"—or, rather, to a particular version of that play, one that editors (and directors) assembled from the two markedly different early texts, Quarto and Folio, by including as many of the different lines as possible from each and merging or "conflating" them into a play a few hundred lines longer than either of the early texts. The paradox is obvious—in the process of trying to present the reader with a "Shakespearean" text, editors produced a text different from either of the ones for which Shakespeare was responsible—yet for readers from the mid-nineteenth to the late twentieth centuries, this elongated version of *King Lear* was the one they read and grew to know and love as "Shakespeare's" play.

This history underpins the decision of *The Norton Shakespeare* to include, alongside editions of the early texts of *Hamlet* and *King Lear*, a further, "scars and stitches" conflated edition of each—that is, an edition of each play that, by way of indentation and a distinctive yet quiet difference in font, makes the process of conflation visible without intruding excessively on the pleasure of the reading experience. We provide these multiple options because they will enable readers to see how these texts changed, developed, and were remade across time. In the case of *King Lear*, it is very possible that Shakespeare was involved in reworking his tragedy a couple of years after he had first written it and it had gone into regular production, and readers can reflect on that dynamic process by comparing the two early versions; equally, they can choose to read the "scars and stitches" edition, which both replicates the experience of nineteenth- and twentieth-century readers who came to know the play through traditional conflated editions and makes visible the process through which that conflation was achieved. Thus in the Digital Edition we offer three versions of *King Lear*—and four of *Hamlet*—so as to enable readers to witness the dynamic and contingent processes that go into the bringing-into-the-present of Shakespeare's plays.

## "Single-Text Editing" and the Treatment of Error

*The Norton Shakespeare* seeks to minimize intervention by the editor, but there are nonetheless occasions when the editor must assist the reader in making sense of the text and where it is not immediately obvious how to do so. In order to explain our decision making at such moments, we will offer some examples. Readers will see that for all texts in this edition, both print and digital, we offer in the Digital Edition a set of Textual Variants, compressed notes in which editors mark each moment where the edited version is in some way different from the "base text," that is, from the original quarto or folio text from which the edition is formed, specifying where the preferred word or other feature originates—from another early text, or from the editorial tradition, or from our own choice. No edition of a Shakespeare play can simply present the exact words of its base text, because no early text is free from error or complication. How many times, after all, reading a modern printed book, have you spotted errors, omissions, or typos? Even with the vast technological transformations since Shakespeare's death, the printing process remains flawed; so you would expect that any text printed in (or somewhat after) Shakespeare's day—created on a manually operated press using fiddly metal type set by hand in wooden frames, in often cramped conditions, using toxic ink, and always under pressure to speed up the process to keep the business afloat—would include a fair number of such errors. As we have noted, the print-house workers were actively involved in the creation of the Shakespearean text, an involvement that is by no means limited to error—but human error is inevitable and pervasive.

Consequently, editors working on the basis of single-text editing must always balance their commitment to the text against the possibility of error. Our basic premise is that the editor should not attempt to alter or "improve"—by following a different text, the editorial tradition, or her own informed invention—any reading that can make sense, even if that meaning seems a little strained. While such difficulties may arise from print-house errors, they may instead be signs of the semantic or syntactical differences between our current version of the English language and that of the late sixteenth and early seventeenth centuries. Single-text editing compels editors—and their readers—to make an effort to understand the given text, rather than to slide into something apparently more familiar. This is known as the principle of the "harder reading" (in Latin, *lectio difficilior*), and it expresses our urge not to risk obliterating the powerful specificity and difference of Shakespeare's works, even as it remains the editor's task to address error when it is undoubtedly present.

The multiplicity of early authoritative texts sometimes confronts the editor adhering to single-text-editing principles with difficult decisions. For example, at one point in the Folio text of *Troilus and Cressida,* Thersites is abusing Patroclus: "Let thy bloud be thy direction till thy death," he sneers, "then, if she that laies thee out sayes thou art a fair coarse [i.e., corpse], I'll be sworne and sworne upon't, she never shrowded any but Lazars." The earlier Quarto reads the central section as follows: "if she that layes thee out sayes thou art not a fair course," and it seems clear that the Folio corrects the Quarto reading, since the "not" makes nonsense of the meaning ("You'll be so ugly by the time you die that if the person laying out your corpse says you're beautiful then the only possible conclusion would be that the dead bodies she usually buries must all be lepers"). The editor therefore emends by removing the "not" from her Quarto edition on the grounds that while single-text editing normally requires her to maintain differences between cognate texts—that is, between texts of the same play that have reached us through different processes of transmission—she must not do this at the expense of sense.

By contrast, the two texts of *King Lear* provide a fine instance of the presence or absence of a word—again, as it happens, "not"—offering equal sense in two cognate texts. At the very end of the long first scene in the Folio, Lear's daughters Goneril and Regan talk together about their aging father's increasingly erratic behavior, and

Goneril notes that "the obseruation we haue made of it hath beene little"—an expression of regret for not taking notice of these mood swings before they led to the current crisis:

> *Gon.* You ſee how full of changes his age is, the ob-ſeruation we haue made of it hath beene little: he alwaies lou'd our Siſter moſt, and with what poore iudgement he hath now caſt her off, appeares too groſſely.

F *King Lear*, qq3r

In the Quarto, however, Goneril notes that "the obseruation we haue made of it hath *not* bin little" (our italics)—that is, that the sisters have in fact been aware of the problem for quite a while:

> *Gon.* You ſee how full of changes his age is the obſeruation we haue made of it hath not bin little; hee alwaies loued our ſiſter moſt, and with what poore iudgement hee hath now caſt her off, appeares too groſſe.

Q1 *King Lear*, C1r

It is this earlier version that is invariably chosen by conflating editors and is thus the reading that those who already know *King Lear* will recognize. Yet it is not the only meaningful option. Both readings make sense, even if one is less familiar, and the advantage of single-text editing is that the editor is not forced to choose one option and thus to dilute the possibilities for meaning on both page and stage.

We briefly mentioned earlier one of the best-known cruxes in *Othello,* the moment at which the protagonist, just prior to his suicide, compares himself to a racial other who also failed to recognize the extraordinary value of what he had until he lost it. In the Quarto, the lines read "one whose hand, / Like the base *Indian*, threw a pearle away, / Richer then all his Tribe"; this has, marginally, been the version preferred by editors across time:

> Perplext in the extreame; of one whoſe hand,
> Like the baſe *Indian*, threw a pearle away,
> Richer then all his Tribe: of one whoſe ſubdued eyes,

Q1 *Othello*, N2r

In the Folio, the lines read "one, whose hand / (Like the base Iudean) threw a Pearle away / Richer then all his Tribe"—the "Judean" here probably being associated with Christ's betrayer, Judas Iscariot, and thus, for Shakespeare's audiences, with Jews in general:

> Perplexed in the extreame: Of one, whoſe hand
> (Like the baſe Iudean) threw a Pearle away
> Richer then all his Tribe: Of one, whoſe ſubdu'd Eyes,

F *Othello*, vv5v

Note two elements here. First, the punctuation differs; neither version can be said to be either *better* or *more authorial* than the other in this regard (the parentheses in the Folio, for instance, are probably the preference of the King's company scribe, Ralph Crane, who transcribed several plays for inclusion in the Folio). Second, the difference between "*Indian*" and "Iudean" could be attributed to two kinds of easy error: a misreading of a scratchy secretary-hand "i" for "e" (or vice versa)—

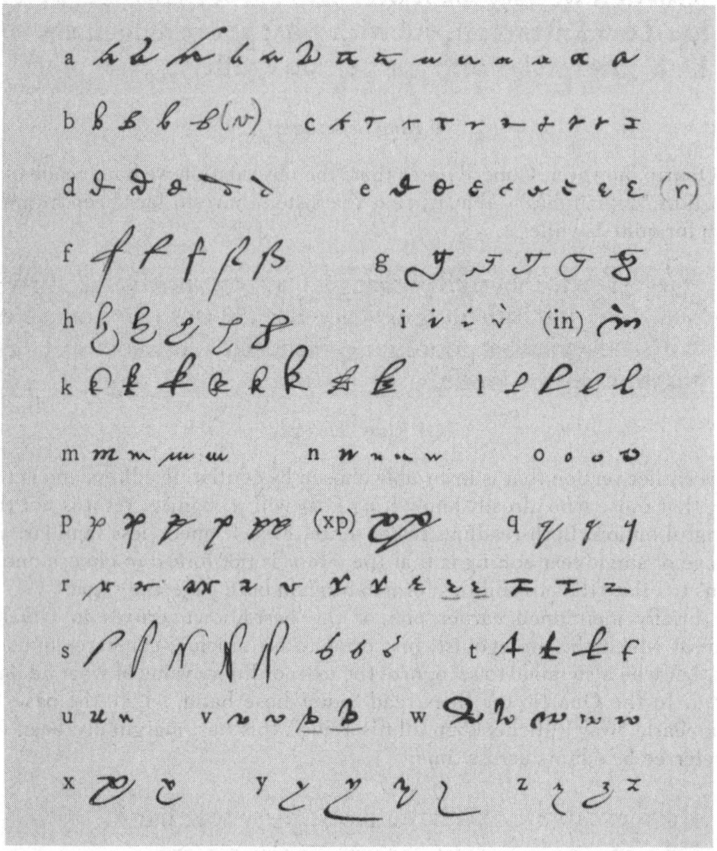


Sample minuscules in secretary hand from Ronald B. McKerrow, *An Introduction to Bibliography for Literary Students*, Oxford 1927.

—and an accidental inversion of the individual type "n" for "u" (or vice versa) by the compositor. The vice versas underline the impossibility of deciding which is "correct," and the presence in *The Norton Shakespeare* of editions of both early texts removes the need for the imposition of editorial preference.

Single-text editing thus seeks to minimize editorial intervention while remaining aware of the needs of the reader and offering clarification (e.g., in the form of expanded or inserted stage directions, which we mark with square brackets) of action, speaker, or other elements of the original that may delay the reader's progress through the play. For these pragmatic reasons, we have chosen to maintain certain traditional overarching elements that could be considered to run counter to the theory of single-text editing. An instance is our division of almost all play texts into acts and scenes, an editorial practice that dates back to the eighteenth century. Such neat divisions are by no means always present in the base texts—either in the Folio, which is not always consistent or precise in its divisions (*Love's Labor's Lost,* for instance, has two different acts marked "*Actus Quartus*"; Folio *Hamlet* stops marking act divisions after act 2), or in the various quartos, many of which either mark scene divisions only or offer no divisions or numbers at all. Act divisions only became fully formalized with the development of indoor playhouses, where the necessity of trimming the candles every half-hour or so required breaks in the action; they thus apply far less to Elizabethan plays than to Jacobean. Our working premise for this edition, however, is that many of our readers will wish to locate scholarly discussions of these plays by critics who, almost without exception, cite speeches by act and scene number; thus, we offer act and scene numbers for all main texts and reserve scene divisions only for a handful of quartos that do not fall into the usual divisions.

The single-text editor's task is not necessarily more straightforward when she is dealing with plays with only one early authoritative text. One of the key questions anyone editing on single-text-editing principles has to ask is when to emend and when to leave alone. An instance comes in *All's Well That Ends Well,* which opens (in our modernized version) with this stage direction:

> *Enter young* BERTRAM, *Count of Roussillon, his mother* [*the Dowager* COUNTESS], *and* HELEN, *Lord* LAFEU, *all in black.*

The "*and*" seems to be in an odd place here; that is, you might expect it to be positioned between "HELEN" and "*Lord,*" completing the list. Yet it comes instead between "*Mother*" and "HELEN." Is this simply a mistake by the compositor? It could easily be. Often, editors simply move the "*and*" to what seems to be the logical place between "HELEN" and "*Lord.*" But what if there is a different logic to its positioning? It might be that Shakespeare is using the conjunction to separate two pairs: to connect Bertram and his mother on the one hand, and Helen and Lafeu on the other. Equally, the "*and*" might serve to connect the Countess and Helen, a connection that proves particularly resilient in the action to follow. Rather than limit the possibilities, we leave the stage direction as it is in the Folio, simply modernizing and standardizing the names and clarifying (with "dowager") that the Countess is the widow of Bertram's father. A theater director might wish to think about the staging options this stage direction offers.

All of these editorial challenges inevitably require the creation of something hybrid, something impure, despite the earnest intentions of the regularizing editor. Editing is always negotiation, and it is always compromise. This does not mean it is slapdash or arbitrary; on the contrary, it must be exceptionally precise, requiring a level of patience and concentration that is not everyone's forte. The paradox for editors is that the outcome of good work—words or lines or stage directions that took a great deal of experience, research, and agonizing to establish—will be simply, and rightly, invisible to the reader. In this, the editor's lot is not so very different—structurally, if not creatively—from that of the collaborating playwright. Effective collaboration is about effacing the joins between the work of different contributors—we presume that Shakespeare and Fletcher, composing *Henry VIII* and *The Two Noble Kinsmen* together, would not have wanted audience members to register when the writing of a given scene switched from the one to the other—and the quiet collaboration across time that is the work of the editor ought by definition to be hidden, at least in the case of editions created for the general reader and the advanced student who do not want or need the intrusion of the mediator.

## Shakespeare and the Multiplication of Meaning

Most people, reading a Shakespeare poem or play, have in mind the question "What did Shakespeare mean here?" as they reflect on the words, especially if the words are not easy to make sense of. Despite the profound ways in which the Romantic construction of authorship as a process of untrammeled, transcendent individual inspiration has been questioned and deconstructed over the last half-century, the general understanding of the processes of writing, as of all forms of creativity, remains firmly bound up with ideas of intention, of textual "ownership," of the creative artist as "author"— that is, as the sole source of "authority" in respect of the form and meaning of a given text. We have tried in this introduction to suggest that the meanings of Shakespeare's plays and poems have a wider range of starting points, emerge from a more complex, varied, and fascinating creative base, than simply what the poet himself "meant"—in other words, that Shakespearean "authenticity" is a multivalent concept, one that includes at its core what the author meant but also a range of other, contiguous collaborations, negotiations, and origins for meaning. The Shakespearean text is fluid and multiple, and the nature of the engagement of both editor and reader with that text should, we believe, follow suit. We have much to gain by being open to the increased possibilities this transformed understanding can bring. The very words themselves are, in so many ways, unfixed in their meanings; the ways through which they came into the public domain in Shakespeare's own day—in manuscript, on the stage, in the various print formats available to those seeking to profit from publication—are also multiple; and the ways in which the plays and poems have been presented and re-presented in subsequent centuries make "multiple" seem a gross understatement. Shakespeare seems to have re-thought and re-imagined his own writings; his colleagues in the King's Men negotiated and adapted his work to suit conditions; publishers printed it in a range of ways, official and unofficial, working with Shakespeare himself on the poems if not on the plays (we have no evidence that Shakespeare—unlike his friend and rival Ben Jonson—oversaw the printing of his plays, whereas he clearly did pay attention to the publication of his poems), and his former colleagues gathered most, though not all, of the plays into a single, rather grandiose Folio in 1623, initiating the long tradition of editing the works to make them available for the "great variety of readers." *The Norton Shakespeare* offers its readers a set of options for reading and understanding Shakespeare that makes the most both of the digital technologies and of the editorial practices of the present, giving the reader choices—of text, of taxonomy, of glossarial support—and in the process providing the means for a new generation actively to discover, engage with, learn from, and—above all—be thrilled and moved by these astonishing works in all their fabulous multiplicity.

# The Theater of Shakespeare's Time

HOLGER SCHOTT SYME

Early modern London was a theatrical city like no other, as the travel writer Fynes Moryson proudly proclaimed: "as there be, in my opinion, more plays in London than in all parts of the world I have seen, so do these players or comedians excel all others in the world." Moryson wrote just after Shakespeare's death, around 1619, but the world of playacting he described had thrived in and around England's capital long before Shakespeare arrived there. The decades between 1567, when the first theater built in England since the Romans opened its doors, and 1642, when playacting was prohibited by Parliament, saw an unprecedented and still unparalleled flourishing of theatrical artistry. Moryson's account emphasizes not just the quality of London's actors, but also the sheer quantity of plays on offer: as far as he was concerned, there was more theater in the city than anywhere else in the world. The historical record bears out his impression. English acting companies, driven by a constant hunger for new work, kept dozens of dramatists busy writing a staggering number of plays—more than 2,500 works, of which just over 500 survive. Theaters sprang up all around London in the 1570s. Throughout Shakespeare's career, there were never fewer than four acting venues in operation; some years, up to nine theaters were competing for audiences. Different spaces and different companies catered to different tastes and income brackets: the tiny indoor location of the Boys of St. Paul's, an acting company of youths, could accommodate fewer than 100 of the wealthy courtiers and law students who were their typical spectators; the Swan Theater, on the other hand, the largest of the open-air venues that were the most common type of theater in Shakespeare's London, had room for over 3,000 people from all social backgrounds. The theater was rich and varied, an engine of artistic experiment and a place where traditions flourished; it was an art form both elite and popular; it provided entertainment for kings and queens even as their governments worried that it was difficult to control, attracting large and boisterous crowds and posing a threat to public health during plague outbreaks.

In London, theater was everywhere. But *what* was it? Who performed it, where, under what circumstances, using what methods and techniques, and for whom?

## History

Before we can approach these questions, a few words about historical evidence are in order. Theater is a transitory art, not designed to leave behind lasting records or traces; it is, as Shakespeare never tired of noting, a kind of dream. In Shakespeare's time, it was a pursuit about which the government cared only intermittently, and was therefore rarely the subject of official recordkeeping. Much of what we know about playhouses and acting companies derives from squabbles over money and the lawsuits that followed. What information survives is just enough to make theater historians realize how much has been lost. For instance, with few exceptions, we do not know who performed which roles. We cannot name a single character Shakespeare played. Even for the most famous actors of the age, we can list at most a handful of parts. Nor do we know how popular most of Shakespeare's plays were. His history plays, more than his tragedies or comedies, sold well as books—but did they do as well on stage? We would like to think so, but without attendance records, we cannot know for sure. *Much Ado About Nothing* was never reprinted on its own after its initial publication in 1600. Does that mean it was a theatrical flop too? Probably not—else why print it at all? But we cannot be certain.

One extant document contains a tremendous amount of information: Philip Henslowe's business record, known as his *Diary*. Henslowe was a financier who owned three theaters and served as a financial manager of sorts for the acting companies that rented his venues. The *Diary* includes performance records from 1592 through 1597, mostly for the Lord Admiral's Men. It allows us to get a sense of this company's business practices, its repertory of plays, its inventory of props and costumes, and its dealings with playwrights and artisans. And the *Diary* makes us realize just how many plays have disappeared: it mentions about 280 titles, of which at most 31 survive.

This may all sound rather depressing, as if the story of Shakespeare's theater were ultimately irretrievable. But it is not. We can interpret archaeological discoveries; extrapolate from extant records such as Henslowe's or the accounts of court officials; trace contemporary responses to the theater in letters, diaries, satires, and polemics; and study plays and their stage directions to understand what features playwrights expected in playhouses and how they intended to use them. We can make the most of what survives to construct a tentative and careful, but not baseless, narrative of what this world may have been like.

## Playhouses

Theater in Shakespeare's London was predominantly an outdoor activity. Most playhouses were open-air spaces much larger than the few indoor venues. The building simply called The Theatre, in the suburb of Shoreditch, north of the City of London, created a model in 1576 that many playhouses would follow for the next forty years. It was a fourteen-sided polygonal structure, nearly round, with an external diameter of about seventy-two feet; audiences stood in the open yard or sat in one of three galleries. There was probably a permanent stage, which thrust out into the yard, with the galleries behind it serving as a balcony over the performance area and, where they were walled off, providing a backstage area (the "tiring house" in early modern terminology). The Theatre may not have had a roof over its stage. The Rose Theater in Southwark, across the Thames from the City of London, was built without such a roof in 1587; one was added during renovations in 1592. The shape of the stage also changed over time: archaeological excavations have shown that the Rose's original stage was relatively shallow, not extending far into the yard. In 1592, the space was redesigned to allow the stage to thrust out farther, creating a deeper playing area surrounded by standing spectators on three sides. This model would be followed in later playhouses, but whereas the Rose's stage (and probably those of other early theaters as well) tapered toward the front, later ones were rectangular and thus quite large. Judging from the erosion around the stage area in the excavated Rose, audiences responded with enthusiasm to the new configuration, pressing as close to the action as possible.

This first generation of playhouses also included The Theatre's close neighbor in Shoreditch, the Curtain, built in 1577 and named not after a stage curtain, which these theaters did not have, but after its location, the "Curtain Estate." The Theatre, the Curtain, and the Rose resembled one another in size and shape and had room for 2,000–2,500 spectators. The next generation of theaters did not depart from the earlier model in shape, but anticipated larger crowds. The Swan (1595), the Globe (1599), and the last outdoor theater erected in London, the Hope (1613), had a capacity of about 3,000. They were impressive buildings not just because of their size but

This view of London's northern suburbs shows the Curtain playhouse (the three-story polygonal structure with the flag on the left). It aptly illustrates the almost rural location of these early theaters: the Curtain stands adjacent to farmhouses and windmills.

also because they were beautifully decorated, as foreign visitors reported. Johannes de Witt, a Dutchman, described the Swan in 1596 as an "amphitheater of obvious beauty," admiring its wooden columns painted to look like marble.

Although some of the later playhouses modified the formula set by The Theatre, all the open-air venues shared a common spatial and social logic. They all separated their audience into those standing in the yard (the "groundlings" or "understanders"), who paid a penny to enter the theater, and those who sat in one of the galleries, paying two pennies for the lower level or three for the upper levels, where the benches had cushions. The most exclusive seats, at sixpence, were in the "lords' rooms," probably located in the sections of the galleries closest to the stage, and possibly in the balcony over the stage. Fashionable gallants and wealthy show-offs could also sit on the stage itself, paying an additional sixpence for a stool. Neither the "lords' rooms" nor the stools onstage gave the best view of the play, but they provided unparalleled opportunities to put fancy clothes on display: these were seats for being seen. Stage-sitting was often satirized as a vain and foolish habit, and the groundlings evidently objected to the rich fops blocking their view. As Shakespeare's contemporary Thomas Dekker describes the scene at one of the outdoor theaters, the "scarecrows in the yard hoot at you, hiss at you, spit at you, yea, throw dirt even in your teeth: 'tis most Gentlemanlike patience to endure all this, and to laugh at the silly animals."

The theaters, though hierarchically structured, were unusually inclusive: audience members from all social spheres could gain admission and enjoy the same spectacles. Social hierarchies became dangerously porous in this shared space, as Dekker's stage-sitters experienced firsthand: the commoners in the yard could hurl abuse and even dirt at the gentle and noble audience members onstage. Lords had to suffer close proximity with their social inferiors. However, the playhouses' inclusiveness had limits, too: the poor and royalty were unlikely to enter a theater. Neither Queen Elizabeth I nor King James I ever did.

Purpose-built theaters were not the only places where plays were performed. From the mid-1570s on, four inns also regularly hosted acting companies: the Bell, the Bull, the Cross Keys, and the Bell Savage. Only one of them, the Bell, seems to have had an indoor hall for play performances; the others had yards in which a stage could be erected. These yards had open galleries to give guests access to rooms on the upper floors, so that the overall structure of the auditorium was similar to the theaters: an open yard surrounded by galleries, at least some of which would have had benches. Unlike the theaters, however, which stood in the suburbs surrounding London, the inns were within or just outside the city walls. This location made them favored acting sites in the winter, when the roads were unpredictable and the days

A Victorian photograph of the Elizabethan galleried yard of the White Hart Inn in Southwark, similar to the layout of the inns used for performing plays.

were short, making it difficult for audience members to return to the City before the gates were shut at nightfall. But the inns irked London authorities. No venues other than churches allowed for the assembly of as many people as inn yards did, and play performances could attract particularly unruly crowds. For the authorities, these places created a threat of public disorder right in the heart of the City, and for over two decades, Lord Mayors and aldermen made intermittent attempts to shut down acting at the inns. It seems they succeeded by 1596, since references to regular performances in those venues cease after that year.

No adult acting company regularly performed in an indoor space in London between 1576 and 1610. There were a number of such venues, though, notably a very small theater near St. Paul's Cathedral, with room for only a select few, and a somewhat larger space inside the former Blackfriars friary. Both were active in the 1570s and 1580s, when two children's companies used them—acting troupes made up of choirboys from the royal chapels and St. Paul's Cathedral. By the time Shakespeare arrived in London, however, the old Blackfriars had closed, and neither space was used during the 1590s. But the boys' companies started performing again around the turn of the century, acting exclusively indoors.

This reemergence lies behind the conversation between Rosencrantz and Hamlet about the "eyrie of children" that produce plays mocking "the common stages." Although the boys' companies could not seriously jeopardize the adult troupes' economic success, their reappearance around 1600 apparently made their grown-up competitors look unfashionable among the trendiest patrons. Exclusivity was the hallmark of these companies and their indoor theaters, which were referred to as "private" playhouses; unlike the "common" theaters, these venues kept the wider world out both architecturally and socially. Entrance fees were much higher, probably starting at sixpence (the price of the costliest seats in the open-air theaters) and going up to over two shillings.

The boys also performed less frequently than the adult companies. They made the most of their elite status, thriving on satirical plays and a willingness to court controversy that sometimes landed them in hot water with persons of influence. Their financial situation was as unstable as their favor with the authorities. When King James, in March 1608, shut down the children's company that was using a recently constructed theater inside the former Blackfriars monastery, he unwittingly made theater history. Soon thereafter, the decades-old division between outdoor adult and indoor boys' companies came to an end. In 1610, near the end of Shakespeare's career, the King's Men adopted the Blackfriars as a second venue. Even after that, however, most audiences would still have experienced plays in the outdoor playhouses that remained the most popular, accessible, and visible acting venues in and around London.

## Companies and Repertories

What was an acting company in Shakespeare's time? Formally, a group of players serving a noble patron. A law of 1572 had forced performers to find official sponsors to avoid legal prosecution as "vagrants" and "masterless men." That is why the troupe with which Shakespeare was associated for most of his documented career was first known as the Lord Chamberlain's Servants, and after 1603 as the King's Servants: these actors were officially servants of the Lord Chamberlain (the member of the Privy Council in charge of the royal household), and later of King James I. (Modern scholars generally refer to these companies as the Lord Chamberlain's Men and the King's Men.) All companies resident in London for at least part of the year were associated with high-ranking noblemen. After 1603, most of these troupes came under royal patronage, formally serving the King, the Queen, or a member of their family.

In all likelihood, the connection between patrons and companies was fairly loose, although the players technically formed part of their patrons' households. Take the example of James's son-in-law, the Count Palatine: his troupe, the Palsgrave's Men, operated under that name from 1613 to 1632, although their supposed patron only lived in England for a few months from 1612 to 1613. Links may have been closer where companies were sponsored by nobles of lower rank, as was common throughout the kingdom. Dozens of these groups appear in contemporary records. They toured the towns, cities, and stately homes surrounding their lords' seats, returning at Christmas to entertain families and guests. Whether they visited London is unclear, as is the question of what plays they performed; but some of them were so active on the road that they probably traveled to the country's biggest city as well.

What most defined a company were its leading members: the actors who would typically take on all major roles and who jointly owned the troupe's stock of costumes, props, and, crucially, play scripts. There were between six and a dozen of these "sharers." They not only formed the heart of any acting company, but also had an immediate financial interest in its success, as they divided the weekly profits among themselves. But there was more to a troupe of actors than its sharers. When the King's Men received their royal patent, or license, in 1603, the document not only identified the nine sharers (Shakespeare among them) as "servants" of James I, but also recognized that those servants required further "associates" to stage plays. These hired actors could in some cases be as closely associated with a company as the sharers. John Sincklo, for example, was a member of the Chamberlain's Men for most of their existence and is mentioned by name in the stage directions to three of Shakespeare's plays. He was apparently an extraordinarily thin man and is often linked with very skinny characters—in *1 Henry IV* he played the Beadle whom Doll Tearsheet calls a "thin man in a censer." Sincklo was a fixture of Chamberlain's Men productions for playwrights and audiences alike, and an integral part of their identity. Yet despite this status,

Sincklo continued to be an employee rather than an owner of the company for the rest of his recorded life.

The theatrical power of one other set of actors likewise outstripped their institutional power within the company: the male youths who played all female roles. These "boys"—in reality, adolescents who would not have started acting before they were twelve or thirteen and sometimes continued into their early twenties—were associated with the companies as sharers' apprentices. In effect, therefore, none of the actors who played Shakespeare's great female roles, from Tamora to Lady Macbeth to Hermione, were officially members of an acting troupe; rather, they belonged to a sharer's household. Each boy was contracted to serve his master for at least seven years, in return for instruction, room, and board. But officially, they would not have been in training as actors, since there was no guild for actors (and thus no official training available). Instead, they formally became apprentices in the trade governed by the guild to which their master belonged. For example, John Heminges, one of the leading sharers in Shakespeare's troupe, was a member of the Company of Grocers, the guild that oversaw that trade. Over thirty years, he had about ten apprentices. Since Heminges did not actually work as a grocer, these youths were probably boy actors, being trained as stage performers. If they completed their term, though, they could pay a fee and become "freemen" of the Company of Grocers and citizens of London—positions that came with many legal advantages and privileges. Although many boy actors did not become leading men, the social status they gained by formally completing an apprenticeship left them free to make their way in life after their careers as players had ended.

Although increasingly integrated into London's social life over the course of Shakespeare's career, most acting companies also spent part of the year touring market towns and stately homes. Acting was frowned upon if not strictly forbidden in London during Lent, the forty days or so before Easter, and companies had to go elsewhere to secure an income then; there was also a long-standing custom of traveling during the summer, when days were longer and roads more reliable (see the map of touring routes in the map appendix, below). Many companies only knew this itinerant existence, and it was their work that the young Shakespeare may have seen in Stratford. But around the time he began working as a theater professional some companies had started to regard London as their home. By the 1590s, that group included Lord Strange's Men, the Admiral's Men, and the Earl of Pembroke's Men. They established long-term relationships with the owners of playhouses where they performed more or less permanently. The Admiral's Men became associated with the Rose and later the Fortune, both theaters belonging to Philip Henslowe. The Chamberlain's Men, founded in 1594, started at The Theatre, owned by James Burbage (whose son Richard would soon emerge as the troupe's young star). Pembroke's Men may have been the resident company at the Swan once that playhouse opened in 1595. A further troupe probably occupied the Curtain. By 1599 yet another company, the Earl of Derby's Men, took up residence at the Boar's Head. In fact, so many acting troupes

Money was collected in small, round earthenware containers that had to be smashed after a performance. Many fragments of these were found during the excavation of the Rose playhouse.

performed in London that there were never fewer than four venues in operation during Shakespeare's career, and in some years the city sustained nine theaters.

The proprietors of most of those playhouses rented their buildings to the actors for a share of the revenues: half the takings from the galleries belonged to the landlord, while the sharers in the company retained all income from the yard and the other half of the takings from the galleries. Troupes and theater owners thus divided profits as well as risk: if a play flopped, the landlord also lost income, just as he gained from popular offerings. Some owners, Henslowe in particular, acted as the company's financial manager, keeping stock of belongings and conducting transactions on the actors' behalf.

Despite the great variety of playhouses and acting companies, or perhaps because of it, some venues developed specific profiles. This happened surprisingly early in the history of London theater. Writing in 1579, the antitheatrical polemicist Stephen Gosson excluded some plays from his general criticism, praising two "shown at the Bull"; two others "usually brought into the Theater"; and especially "the two prose books played at the Bell Savage, where you shall find never a word without wit, never a line without pith, never a letter placed in vain." Within a few years of opening, then, two of the inns and The Theatre were already known for specific plays one could expect to see there—whereas the four venues Gosson does not mention may have staged precisely the kinds of plays of which he disapproved.

All the same, few playhouses or acting companies were famous exclusively for a handful of titles or a particular kind of drama. The repertories of most troupes, including the Chamberlain's Men and King's Men, were inclusive in their approach to themes and genres and combined old favorites with new and potentially challenging material. The King's Men's 1603 patent describes them as performing not only "comedies, tragedies, histories"—the kinds of plays we might expect from Shakespeare's company—but also "interludes, morals, pastorals." Shakespeare's works do not represent all these categories, and they likely do not represent the full range of shows his troupe staged. If Henslowe's *Diary* is a reliable model, companies commissioned ten to twenty plays each year, and new plays dominated their repertory. If a play failed to draw crowds, it disappeared quickly. If it had staying power, it would remain in circulation for a while, but few became recognized classics destined to be revived every couple of years. In general, it seems that audiences enjoyed periodically reencountering older scripts, but had a more voracious appetite for fresh material—although old stories might frequently return in novel versions. Companies would produce their own take on plays from competing repertories: the Admiral's Men paid Ben Jonson in 1602 for a script about Richard III, for instance; and the Chamberlain's Men bought Jonson's *Every Man in His Humor* in 1598, probably hoping to capitalize on a 1597 hit at the Rose, George Chapman's *Comedy of Humors*. Even a single troupe's repertory might feature multiple plays drawn from the same stories or materials. The King's Men owned another *Richard II* play, which they staged at the Globe in April 1611—within weeks of performances of *Macbeth*, *Cymbeline*, and *The Winter's Tale*. Of those three Shakespearean offerings, the latter two were then still quite new; but *Macbeth* would have been a revival, an indication that it was a success when first performed.

The repertory system required daily turnover. Staging the same play for days at a time, let alone for weeks, was practically unheard of. The nine consecutive performances of Thomas Middleton's *A Game at Chess* at the Globe in 1624 were described as extraordinary at the time—nowadays, of course, a run of nine nights would be notable for its brevity. We can get a glimpse of what a typical selection of shows would have looked like in Shakespeare's company from Henslowe's *Diary*, which contains the only surviving sample of the Chamberlain's Men's repertory (staged in collaboration with the Admiral's Men in June 1594):

| | |
|---|---|
| MON 3 June | *Hesther and Ahasuerus* |
| TUE 4 June | *The Jew of Malta* |
| WED 5 June | *Titus Andronicus* |

| | |
|---|---|
| THU 6 June | *Cutlack* |
| SAT 8 June | *Belin Dun* |
| SUN 9 June | *Hamlet* |
| MON 10 June | *Hesther and Ahasuerus* |
| TUE 11 June | *The Taming of a Shrew* |
| WED 12 June | *Titus Andronicus* |
| THU 13 June | *The Jew of Malta* |

The two companies performed seven different plays in ten days. Of those, two were tragedies based on fictional plots (*The Jew of Malta* and *Titus Andronicus*), two were tragedies set in the distant northern European past (*Cutlack* and *Hamlet*—the latter not Shakespeare's version), one was a biblical drama (*Hesther and Ahasuerus*), one was a history or tragedy drawn from the English chronicles (*Belin Dun*, about a highwayman hanged by King Henry I), and one was a comedy (*The Taming of a Shrew*—again, not Shakespeare's). One play was brand-new (*Belin Dun*); one recent (*Titus Andronicus*, first performed in January 1594); two quite old (*The Jew of Malta* and *The Taming of a Shrew* were probably written before 1590); and we know nothing about the others.

The two companies' combined offerings constitute a representative mixture of old and new; of different geographical settings and historical periods; of tragic, heroic, moral, and comedic entertainments. Variety was a predictable feature of any company's stock of plays. Predictability, however, was not. For theatergoers keen to see a performance of *Titus* after its successful June 5 outing, finding out when the play was going to be mounted next was neither easy nor straightforward (we now know that their next chance would have come on June 12). They may have relied on word of mouth, as the actors commonly announced the next day's play at the end of a show; they might have encountered the players marching through the City in the morning hours, advertising that day's performance; or they may have read the news on one of the playbills posted daily all over the City to inform audiences what was being staged where. But would-be spectators had to keep their eyes peeled: while repertories responded to popular demand, they did not follow an easily foreseeable schedule. Since *Titus* did well, it would certainly be back onstage soon. But exactly when was uncertain.

## Why Shakespeare's Company Was Different

The playhouse in which the Chamberlain's Men and the King's Men performed after 1599, the Globe, was a unique building project. In 1597 James Burbage's lease for the land on which The Theatre stood ran out, and a year later the Chamberlain's Men were forced to vacate the premises and move to the neighboring Curtain. The building itself, however, still belonged to Burbage, and after his death in 1597, to his sons Cuthbert and Richard, the latter Shakespeare's fellow sharer. The Burbages therefore took the extraordinary step of having a carpenter dismantle the structure and use the salvaged timber to build a new playhouse. This would be erected on a plot of land on the other side of London, south of the river and across the street from Henslowe's Rose Theater. This new theater, the Globe, would be significantly bigger than its predecessor. As archaeological digs have revealed, it was probably a sixteen-sided polygon with a diameter of about eighty-five feet, nearly fourteen feet more than The Theatre's. It was operational by September 1599, when the Swiss traveler Thomas Platter saw a performance of *Julius Caesar* at what he called "the straw-thatched house"—almost certainly the Globe, which had a thatched roof over the galleries and stage.

Opening a new playhouse right next to the small and aging Rose might look like an aggressive gesture on the Burbages' part, bringing the Chamberlain's Men into direct competition with the Admiral's Men. In such a turf-war narrative, Burbage and company look like history's winners: Henslowe and his son-in-law Edward Alleyn almost immediately started building a new playhouse elsewhere. The Admiral's Men abandoned the Rose in 1600 and moved into their new home, the Fortune, in Clerkenwell, northwest of the City and far away from the Globe. But there is no reason to think that a desire to ramp up competition motivated the Burbages' decision. For one thing, this kind of thinking would have been out of step with the general atmosphere of mutual respect among London's acting companies. For another, the very speed with which Henslowe and Alleyn acted supports a different story. In fact, the Burbages may have chosen the Southwark location because they knew that Henslowe had started to look for a suitable site for a new playhouse and that the Admiral's Men would soon leave their old home.

What made the Globe a remarkable project was neither its builders' allegedly aggressive approach to the theatrical marketplace nor its size or design, which were no more impressive than the Swan's. The Globe was unique for the way it was financed: it belonged not to a separate landlord, but to members of the acting company itself.

How did this come about? It may be that when the Burbages decided to move their playhouse in 1598, they did not have sufficient funds for that enterprise. In 1596, their father had spent the very large sum of £600 to transform a medieval hall inside the former Blackfriars monastery into a theater. The purpose of this investment is uncertain: the doomed lease negotiations for The Theatre had not yet begun, so James Burbage might have been trying to expand his activities as a theater owner rather than replace his old playhouse. He had only been his son's company's landlord for a little over a year when he bought the Blackfriars, and may very well have had another company in mind for the new space. Whatever the case, the new venue was the largest indoor performance space in London, and probably the first hall theater designed for an adult company. But the undertaking failed. Almost instantly, a group of wealthy inhabitants of the Blackfriars precinct successfully protested against the plan. The composition of that group is enlightening: it contained Lord Hunsdon, the patron of Shakespeare's company; and Hunsdon's recently deceased father had tried to buy part of the same property Burbage was after the year before. If the new playhouse was meant for the Chamberlain's Men, it is certainly strange that both these patrons of the company attempted to prevent its construction.

In any event, the property was not a viable alternative when Richard Burbage and his fellows lost The Theatre. Whether for financial reasons or because neither Cuthbert nor Richard Burbage wanted to play the role of theater owner and landlord, the brothers devised a solution that would for the first time put a venue mostly in actors' hands. Half the enterprise belonged to the Burbages (since they contributed the timber from The Theatre), but the remaining 50 percent was divided equally among five of the seven or eight remaining sharers in the Chamberlain's Men: John Heminges, William Kemp, Augustine Phillips, Thomas Pope, and William Shakespeare. At Christmas 1598, this consortium signed the lease for the plot of land in Southwark. They subsequently covered the construction costs of £700, exactly what The Theatre had cost to build in 1576.

Having a playhouse owned by the majority of the sharers in an acting company was a unique business model. These sharers now were responsible for the upkeep of the building, but they also, as landlords, received a portion of the entire revenue from every show (the Globe used the same rental agreement as the Rose, splitting performance income between landlords and actors). Beyond economics, the agreement created an unparalleled strong bond between these actors and their venue. It practically ensured that the Globe became their default home, and that its joint owners would remain members of the same acting company. The Globe was made for the Chamberlain's Men—but the Chamberlain's Men, in a sense, were also made by the Globe.

What happened to the Blackfriars property in the meantime? It stood empty for three years; and then, in 1600, it became an active theater after all. That year, Richard Burbage, clearly unwilling to adopt his father's or Henslowe's business model, leased

This section of Wenceslaus Hollar's 1647 "Long View" of London, drawn from Southwark, shows the Globe in its rebuilt state. The Globe is the round building in the middle, misidentified as a "Beere bayting" arena. The round building to its right, mislabeled "The Globe," is in fact the Hope playhouse, which by the 1620s was used exclusively as a bearbaiting venue.

the Blackfriars venue outright to the manager of a boys' acting company—for a flat annual fee of £40, and for twenty-one years. No revenue sharing, no managerial services: Burbage washed his hands of his father's failed endeavor. (The boys' company did not face the same opposition as the 1596 venture, perhaps because it performed as rarely as once a week, or because it represented a more up-market kind of playing.)

Eventually, the Blackfriars would become the King's Men's second venue: they probably started performing plays there sometime in 1610, at the very end of Shakespeare's career. But neither the company nor the Burbages were in any rush to move indoors. In 1604, the boys' company's manager tried to return the building to them and cut the twenty-one-year lease short, but the Burbages were uninterested. Only after the King forced out the children's troupe in 1608 did they agree to terminate the lease. The brothers owned the property and certainly had no financial incentive to search for investors. And yet the Burbages immediately turned the Blackfriars into another shared venture, splitting costs and revenues equally among themselves, one outsider, and four King's Men's sharers, including Shakespeare. The idea here was evidently not to maximize personal gain, but to enhance the company's profile—and its leaders' fortunes.

Within a decade, the Blackfriars turned into *the* place for new, fashionable plays. But during Shakespeare's lifetime, it never outshone the older outdoor space. For the first years of the new theater's existence, references to King's Men plays mention only the Globe; prominent audience members, including foreign princes, still visited the open-air venue; and in 1613, the company emphatically reaffirmed its commitment to its traditional playhouse. That year, the building's cost-effective thatched roof caught

A different section of Hollar's panorama shows the Blackfriars precinct across the river from the Globe and Hope theaters. Just to the left of the center, next to the spire of St. Bride's Church, the long roof with two tall chimneys marks the probable location of the Blackfriars theater.

fire during the first performance of Shakespeare and Fletcher's *Henry VIII*. The Globe burned down, leaving the King's Men with only an indoor theater at their disposal. However, instead of redefining themselves as the Blackfriars company, they extended their lease on the Southwark plot, invested the enormous sum of £1,400, and rebuilt their playhouse—with decorations that made it, in the words of an eyewitness, "the fairest that ever was in England." This time, the galleries and stage had tiled roofs.

If the Chamberlain's/King's Men were unique in forming such a strong interconnection between actors and theaters, they also benefited from the unusual privilege of having an in-house playwright. No other company in the 1590s seems to have had a sharer who could also provide, on average, two plays a year. In addition, Shakespeare apparently performed other tasks for his company that would normally have been farmed out to hired dramatists, which included writing new scenes for old plays. The sheets in the *Sir Thomas More* manuscript that are probably in Shakespeare's handwriting are one example: there, he provided a long scene for a collaboratively authored text that needed major patching to be stageable. There is also evidence that additions to Thomas Kyd's *Spanish Tragedy* first printed in 1602 are by Shakespeare; if so, he wrote them for a Chamberlain's Men revival of this early classic (originally staged around 1587). The role of Hieronimo in the play was one of Richard Burbage's star turns, so we know the script found its way into the company's repertory at some point in the late 1590s or early 1600s.

Although the Chamberlain's Men were unusually fortunate to have Shakespeare as a sharer, we should not overestimate his place in their repertory. He was no Thomas Dekker, the dramatist who between 1597 and 1603 wrote or coauthored 41 new plays for a range of companies. Nor was Shakespeare as productive as Thomas Heywood, who claimed to have authored or cowritten more than 220 plays in a career spanning forty years. Given a need for at least ten fresh scripts a year, Shakespeare's contributions to his company's repertory were valuable, even indispensable—but they could never make up more than a fraction of the new material commissioned every year. Even if demand for new plays slowed in the 1620s, after the King's Men had accumulated a stock of reliably popular offerings, those of Shakespeare's works that had proved their lasting appeal would always be part of a much larger set of scripts. And the company treated Shakespeare's plays much like other authors' works, hiring playwrights to spruce up the old texts and make them newly exciting for audiences; in Shakespeare's case, it was Thomas Middleton who revised *Measure for Measure*, *Macbeth*, and possibly others.

## At Court

Thinking of theater as a commercial enterprise taking place in venues accessible to all who paid the price of admission means leaving out one important aspect of early modern theater: private performances for aristocratic audiences. Companies were occasionally paid to stage their plays inside the London houses of noble clients, but such interactions with the highest social ranks were intermittent and unpredictable. The court, on the other hand, annually required actors to provide entertainments during lengthy revels between Christmas and Twelfth Night, and usually at Shrovetide (the three days before Ash Wednesday). Under Elizabeth I, there was only one court, her own, and theatrical activities were limited to those two holiday periods. With the ascension of James I, however, the number of royal courts multiplied—besides the King's own, Queen Anne, Prince Henry, and later Prince Charles also maintained courts with their own occasions for entertainment—and playing was no longer limited to holidays. The records show that the royally sponsored adult companies could be summoned to one of the palaces at any time. Officially, the courts' desire for theater justified the actors' need to play all year round in public venues, despite the City authorities' concerns: companies constantly had to rehearse and try out plays in front of live audiences so they could be ready to perform whenever a royal patron needed them.

The person in charge of organizing royal entertainments was the Master of the Revels, an officer who worked for the Lord Chamberlain. Under Elizabeth, the office was held by Sir Edmund Tilney. His job was not an easy one: he was responsible for choosing the appropriate companies and plays from the multitude available in London. In his early years, Tilney's approach seemed scattershot, with up to seven different troupes playing at court per season. The sheer complexity of keeping that many companies organized may have led to the foundation of an elite troupe under Elizabeth's own patronage, the Queen's Men, who dominated court entertainments for a few years after 1583. In 1594, the Master of the Revels apparently undertook a second effort to streamline holiday performances, this time relying not on a single troupe, but on a pair—and his superior, the Lord Chamberlain, adopted one of those companies as his own. For five years thereafter, Tilney could draw on two consistently excellent groups of actors, the Chamberlain's Men and the Admiral's Men.

As in 1583, though, this approach gave the Queen's revels a rather different complexion from the popular theaters. The Queen's Men were the leading company for about ten years after their creation, but other troupes eventually reappeared in the court season. Similarly, Shakespeare's company and their colleagues at the Rose were prominent but far from alone in London, and their competitors also turned up on Tilney's payroll again before long. Derby's Men, Worcester's Men, Hertford's Men, and the boys' companies all performed at court within a few years of the establishment of the Lord Chamberlain's troupe in 1594. Tilney's tenure as Master of the Revels was marked by repeated, ultimately futile efforts to limit actors' access to courtly employment—efforts seemingly designed to shut out the unrestrained variety of the public theatrical marketplace.

Under James I, the Lord Chamberlain's office finally acknowledged the size and diversity of London's theater world. Abandoning the model of a separate set of privileged companies with access to the court, the crown instead brought all major London companies gradually under royal patronage. By 1615, five adult troupes were being officially sponsored by members of James's family. Only those companies were asked to perform at court, but they were probably also the only acting outfits remaining in London: there were not enough playhouses to accommodate more than five permanent adult companies.

Even if the diversity of companies performing at court came to reflect the situation in the public playhouses over the course of Shakespeare's career, the repertory the actors drew on for their courtly performances remained distinct in surprising ways. We might expect that kings and queens, princes, ambassadors, and wealthy courtiers would have made for the most discerning and demanding audience imaginable, but the records tell a different story. Often, the plays staged at court were already several years old; by the 1610s, Revels playlists begin to feel like compilations of the classics that had their place in every company's repertory but could not normally compete with the appeal of new material. The court's, or the Master of the Revels', taste was broadly on the conservative side.

Though the records list almost no specific play titles from Elizabeth's reign, those surviving from James's time suggest that the King and his inner circle liked their Shakespeare well aged. In 1604, there were *A Midsummer Night's Dream*, nine years old; *The Merry Wives of Windsor*, seven years old; and *The Comedy of Errors*, over ten years old. The next year, we have recorded performances of *Henry V*, six or seven years after its first staging; and of *The Merchant of Venice*, at least seven years old, but performed twice within three days in James's presence in February 1605. These were the typical Shakespearean offerings. Exceptions occurred, including the still-new *Tempest* and *Winter's Tale* in November 1611, but for the most part, the Master of the Revels assembled an unadventurous repertory in which certain favorites often reappear. *Twelfth Night*, *The Winter's Tale*, *Othello*, and *1 Henry IV* show up every few years, as do some of Ben Jonson's plays (*Volpone* and *The Alchemist* in particular) and titles whose continued popularity at court now seems puzzling (such as the anonymous *Greene's Tu Quoque* and *The Merry Devil of Edmonton*). A company that performed for the royal households as often as did the King's Men must have adjusted to their courtly audience's expectations to some degree, and may therefore have been less quick to follow the latest artistic fashions than a company less in demand at court. But even so, Shakespeare and his fellows probably saw acting for their royal patrons as quite a different challenge from playing for London audiences. And in spite of the unquestionable importance of their connection to the royal household, the fact that they performed publicly far more frequently and depended on the income from those performances probably meant that their day-to-day activities were less influenced by the preferences of the court than we might imagine.

## The Regulation of Playing and Its Failures

Organizing court entertainments was the most important aspect of the Master of the Revels' job, but he had another major responsibility: the licensing of new plays. Every script had to be submitted to him for approval, and only manuscripts bearing his license and signature were allowed to be performed. In their censorship activities, Tilney and his successors concentrated mainly on three concerns: no actual persons could be slandered or attacked; plays had to steer clear of incendiary topics and language; and, after a law banning profanity onstage had been passed in 1606, actors were no longer allowed to utter oaths using the name of God in any form. In the main, though, the Master of the Revels was not the acting companies' antagonist. For instance, Tilney did not simply reject *Sir Thomas More*, although he found the play objectionable on a number of counts; instead, he suggested changes that would enable him to give the players his license.

That relatively benign mode of control could quickly shift into an aggressive register when the players crossed a line. Companies that staged plays without first having them licensed, if discovered, were severely reprimanded. Stricter actions followed whenever a performance offended a person of high rank and influence. Playhouses were sometimes shut down as a consequence, and actors and playwrights found themselves in prison while under investigation. When these perceived transgressions happened (and they happened infrequently), the state was typically unable to explain what had gone wrong, especially if the play had been licensed. Playwrights would routinely offer the likeliest theory: the actors had ad-libbed, adding content the Master of the Revels had not seen and the author(s) had not written. There was certainly a kernel of truth to those defenses. Live performance is invariably different from the script on which it is based. But although that insight was not unknown to Shakespeare's contemporaries, it never seemed to affect the official system of licensing, which continued to operate unchanged throughout the early modern period.

Beyond the licensing requirements, there are few signs that the state took any sustained interest in regulating the theatrical marketplace, in London or elsewhere in the country. Nor were such efforts especially effective when they did occur. One of the most significant interventions took place in July 1597, apparently in response to a now-lost play, *The Isle of Dogs*, performed by Pembroke's Men at the Swan. This performance caused a massive scandal, landed some actors and the playwright Ben Jonson in jail under investigation for sedition, shut down all the theaters, and ruined Pembroke's Men financially. We do not know what made the play so offensive, but it must have been a serious trespass. The Privy Council's reaction to what it regarded as the players' "lewd and mutinous behaviour" was unprecedentedly severe; an order went out to stop all performances and have all playhouses demolished within three months. As telling as this order, though, is what happened next: almost nothing. The company was broken up, but no theaters were destroyed. Henslowe's *Diary* shows no signs that he was concerned about loss of income, and before long a new London-based company established itself in a new theater, the Boar's Head. For the next few years, the Privy Council attempted to control the number of troupes and playhouses in London, but every one of its annual letters to the local authorities expresses frustration about the inefficient implementation of the previous set of orders. No letters on the subject written after 1602 survive.

The Privy Council's general indifference to tightly regulating the theaters and its relatively hands-off attitude, even in the brief period when it adopted restrictive policies, did not align well with the wishes of the Lord Mayor and aldermen of the City, for whom the theaters posed a perennial challenge to public order. However, even the City authorities were not consistent in their opposition: they habitually relied on actors and playwrights for the annual civic entertainments, especially the Lord Mayor's pageants. Some aldermen befriended players, and actors participated in parish-level government (Shakespeare's colleagues Henry Condell and John Heminges were church wardens; Edward Alleyn and Philip Henslowe served as members of the vestry, or parish council, of St. Saviour's Church in Southwark). And although opposition to regular performances at the inns in the City was fairly consistent over twenty years, this policy may not have been the reason that all the large playhouses were built in the suburbs. Rather, high property prices and the scarcity of plots of land large enough for an amphitheater-style structure inside the densely packed City probably forced theater-builders to look beyond the city walls. Having large gathering places close to their gates but beyond their control vexed London authorities, but their anger may have been fueled by more than a simple desire to prohibit playacting: the theaters made a lot of money, and none of that income could be taxed by the City—despite the fact that the vast majority of playgoers would have been Londoners. The Mayor and his aldermen thus had many reasons for feeling aggrieved. Not only did they have to suffer the threat of riots and public disturbances sparked at the theaters, but they could not even collect fees and taxes in return.

The one cause that brought the interests of City and Privy Council together was also the single biggest economic threat to the acting companies, and the most frequent reason for playhouse closures: the plague. While the transmission of diseases was not well understood in early modern England, the authorities knew that crowds spread illness. Hence the government would order the theaters to shut whenever plague deaths reached a certain level (these figures had to be recorded and reported parish by parish every week). Sometimes, such closures were a precaution and did not last long. But on a number of occasions during Shakespeare's career, the theaters were closed for many months, with disastrous consequences for the London-based companies. A plague outbreak in 1593 halted performances for almost the entire year, forced all companies to tour, and caused a major reorganization of the theatrical landscape—out of which the Chamberlain's Men emerged as a new troupe formed from the fragments of its disbanded predecessors. At least as devastating was the horrific eruption of plague that shut down all playing in London from March 1603 to September 1604, and the less severe but longer episode that kept the theaters closed from August 1608 to the end of 1610. The first decade of James's reign was an especially chaotic and challenging time for the London companies, as there were lengthy plague closures even in the years when the playhouses were periodically open. If the world of London theater changed fundamentally after Shakespeare's retirement in 1613, the great watershed may not have been the introduction of multiple royal patrons or of new indoor performance venues, but instead the comparative stability offered by an extended period without plague outbreaks. In any case, it seems clear that the greatest threat to an acting company's fortunes was not the Privy Council, the censor, or local authorities, but a mysterious, unpredictable, and lethal disease.

## Casting

We have already glimpsed some of the details of how an early modern acting company was put together: at its core were the sharers, the actors who jointly owned the troupe's assets; then there were a number of male youths, usually apprenticed to the sharers, who played women and children; and then there was a group of hired men, who had no financial stake in the group's success, as they were paid a set salary, although some (such as John Sincklo) stayed loyally with the same troupe. Beyond those actors, most London companies employed someone who functioned like a modern stage manager, the book-holder. That person was responsible for maintaining play scripts and organizing the backstage action during performances; he likely also acted as a prompter. Finally, there were employees who collected admission fees, cleaned the theater, and probably doubled as stagehands. Some of these workers were women, a female presence in an otherwise entirely male business.

Senior actors developed a degree of professional specialization. The most obvious experts were the clowns or fools, often among the most prominent members of any company. Richard Tarlton was the first of the great and famous Elizabethan clowns, and he was the Queen's Men's undisputed star until his death in 1588. Will Kemp, a sharer in the Chamberlain's Men as well as, for a short while, in the Globe, took over Tarlton's crown as the funniest man on English stages. After Kemp left the company in 1599, Robert Armin inherited his role as clown. The styles of these comedic performers differed, with Tarlton famed as an improviser and singer, Kemp known for his athleticism, and Armin for his subtler verbal wit, but they all had one thing in common: their responsibilities included the comic entertainments performed after plays

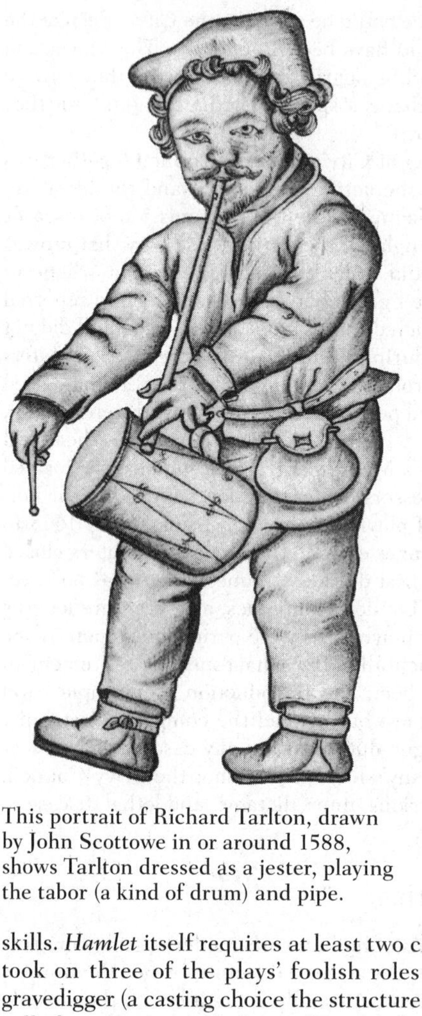
This portrait of Richard Tarlton, drawn by John Scottowe in or around 1588, shows Tarlton dressed as a jester, playing the tabor (a kind of drum) and pipe.

were done. Hence, they regularly appeared before audiences as themselves or as recognizable stage personae. They were certainly among the most readily identifiable faces of the company.

Unlike other roles, the clowns' parts in plays were often not fully scripted, and allowed for improvisation—the excessive use of which Hamlet criticizes when he tells the players to "let those that play your clowns speak no more than is set down for them." It is thus no coincidence that even as playwriting became a profession separate from acting, famous clowns still continued to be known as dramatists as well: Tarlton, Kemp, and Armin all wrote, as did John Shank, John Singer, and William Rowley. The line between the play and its performance, between the playwright's text and what the actors said and did, was particularly blurred in these performers' roles—and we should not assume that authors (or anyone else) found this especially troubling. It would be an error to read Hamlet's views as Shakespeare's, let alone the audience's: by all accounts, including Hamlet's, theatergoers enjoyed the clowns' ad-libbing and did not mind if such riffing delayed the progress of the play. We should, however, take seriously Hamlet's use of the plural "clowns." The company's specialist clown would never have been the only actor with comedic skills. *Hamlet* itself requires at least two clowns, the two gravediggers, even if Armin took on three of the plays' foolish roles and acted Polonius, Osric, and the first gravedigger (a casting choice the structure of the play allows). *Twelfth Night*, similarly, calls for a designated clown, but also needs another comically gifted actor as Sir Andrew Aguecheek. Shakespeare's company included a number of such performers. Thomas Pope, one of its founding sharers, had a reputation as a comedian, as did Richard Cowley, a hired man with the Chamberlain's Men who became a sharer in the King's Men.

If not all comic parts always went to the same performer, the same is true of dramatic leads. Two great tragic actors dominate all narratives of Shakespeare's stage: Edward Alleyn, the Admiral's Men's star, and Richard Burbage, the Chamberlain's and King's Men's leading player. Both rose to prominence in the 1590s. Alleyn, Burbage's senior by three years, gained fame first. However, although he led the longer life (Burbage died in 1619, Alleyn in 1626), his career as an actor lasted nowhere near as long as his colleague's: sometime before 1606, Alleyn retired from the stage to devote his attention to even more profitable ventures, whereas Burbage continued acting until his death. But even these two titans of the stage would not have taken the lead in every play: that is not how ensembles work. Alleyn certainly performed the title characters in Christopher Marlowe's *Tamburlaine* and *Doctor Faustus* and Barabas in *The Jew of Malta*, though he may not have originated those roles; beyond these, we know of five other parts in which he acted, four of them from lost plays. Burbage's list is not much longer. An elegy written shortly after his death laments that with him died characters that

A contemporary portrait of Richard Burbage. Burbage sometimes worked as a visual artist, and some scholars believe this painting to be a self-portrait.

no other actor could bring to life as powerfully: "No more young Hamlet, old Hieronimo, / Kind Lear, the grievèd Moor." He was closely associated, then, with three of Shakespeare's plays and Kyd's *Spanish Tragedy*; notably, those works were at least ten years old when he died.

We might expect that Burbage, at the height of his fame, played all the largest parts, but the elegy suggests otherwise: Othello is a smaller role than Iago. What is more, when the Chamberlain's Men were established in 1594, Burbage was only twenty-five, the youngest sharer, and had not yet risen to the level of prominence he would later attain; and the company included other well-known actors: George Bryan, John Heminges, Augustine Phillips, and William Sly. Initially, Burbage's name would not have been the most recognizable among these, and even when his reputation ultimately eclipsed the others', he would—and could—not have been the only choice for leads. Think of Shakespeare's plays from the mid-1590s: Burbage probably played Romeo, but what about *Richard II*? Would Burbage have been a better fit for the king or for the usurper Bolingbroke? In *The Merchant of Venice*, Shylock is the star turn nowadays, but Bassanio may have been the likelier role for Burbage, with older actors, like Bryan or Phillips, taking the roles of the other two male leads, Antonio and Shylock—or Thomas Pope, if Shylock was considered a comic part. Or take, as a final example, *Titus Andronicus*. Titus is the largest role, but Burbage may well have been a better fit for Aaron, a younger and more agile character.

Matching actors' ages to those of their characters, though, is a complicated business, and a casting consideration that was treated differently in Shakespeare's time from now. Burbage played Lear when he was no older than thirty-seven; and he was famous in the role of Hieronimo—an elderly father figure—by 1601, when he was just thirty-two. The same actor, then, might have acted the aged King Lear, "old Hieronimo," and "young Hamlet" within the span of a few days. And yet, despite this apparent disregard for verisimilitude, it was the supposedly lifelike quality of his acting that made Burbage famous. A writer in the 1660s reported on his ability to "wholly transfor[m] himself into his part, putting off himself with his clothes, as he never assumed himself again until the play was done." Part of Burbage's power was that he could seemingly become another person, even if that meant aging by decades. If the effect was a kind of make-believe, however, the means were an orator's, not those of modern psychological realism. What contemporary witnesses praise is Burbage's facility with speech, with finding the right vocal affect and the right quality of voice to express his character. As important was his aptitude at suiting his physical movement to the role, finding what were called the right "actions." That term probably referred to an elaborate arsenal of gestures and body positions that was systematic enough that audiences could read and make sense of actors' movements: putting a hand on the heart, holding one's face in one's hands, making a fist, and so on. Even if Burbage seemed able to go beyond conventions and give his actions an unusually personal or individual quality, though, it is clear that what seemed lifelike in Shakespeare's theater had little to do with a modern understanding of stage realism.

Burbage's specific talent may have been self-transformation; Alleyn, on the other hand, was known and remembered for his extraordinary stage presence. But both actors used a similar technical arsenal. Alleyn, like Burbage, was praised for his "excellent action"—as Thomas Nashe wrote in 1592, not even the greatest Roman actors "could ever perform more in action than famous Ned Alleyn." If Burbage disappeared into his roles, Alleyn was celebrated for the awe-inspiring quality he himself lent the characters he played. We do not know what his acting would have looked like onstage, but its outsized effect was not universally popular. Hamlet's criticism of players that "so strutted and bellowed" that "they imitated humanity so abominably" may refer to actors of Alleyn's ilk, perhaps an implicit statement that the Chamberlain's Men favored a different approach to performance. After Alleyn's death, in the reign of Charles I, the larger-than-life style associated with him was frowned upon by some writers and by spectators at some theaters. But there is no evidence that Burbage's brand of acting displaced Alleyn's within Shakespeare's lifetime. More probably, the two actors' particular aptitudes represented the pinnacles of two different but not incompatible acting techniques that in other players' work appeared in mixed forms. Both of these men were exceptional figures, after all. The Admiral's Men were not a company of many Alleyns, nor were the Chamberlain's Men a troupe of Burbages. What most performers and audiences probably understood "acting" (or "playing") to mean is captured vividly in these lines from *Richard III*:

> Come, cousin, canst thou quake, and change thy color,
> Murder thy breath in middle of a word,
> And then begin again, and stop again,
> As if thou wert distraught and mad with terror?
>
> (3.5.1–4)

What Richard is asking Buckingham here is whether he can act—and Buckingham replies that he can indeed "counterfeit the deep tragedian," in part because he can use the appropriate actions (looks, trembling, starts, smiles). Both characters describe a kind of performance that is highly codified, quite predictable, and not exactly lifelike; but both share the confidence that a talented actor can turn hackneyed gestures and tics into a convincing impression of reality.

If actors were capable of creating something like reality out of obvious fictions, and if those fictions could stretch to having an actor in his thirties play an old king one day and a young prince the next, then it cannot have been difficult for performers and audiences to come to terms with the widespread practice of doubling. All but the actors cast in the largest roles routinely played multiple characters, often leaving the stage as one person only to return shortly thereafter, wearing a new hat or a different cloak, as an entirely different character. Doubling meant that most early modern plays, although they may feature thirty or more characters, could be staged by around fourteen actors. In *The Merchant of Venice*, for example, the same player could take the parts of Old Gobbo, Tubal, the Jailer, and the Duke; or Morocco, Arragon, and the Duke—in either case, characters ranging widely in age and social status.

Like doubling, the casting of male youths in all female parts was a firmly established theatrical convention, though one that had less to do with pragmatic considerations than with a strong moral rationale. The idea of women putting their bodies on public display, even if fully clothed, was widely regarded as immoral and likened to prostitution. All-male casts were so deeply ingrained in English theatergoers' expectations that seeing actual women play female roles startled those who traveled abroad, where female actors were common. Some expressed their surprise that women could in fact act; others compared the Continental female performers critically to English boy players, whom they considered preferable not on moral but on artistic grounds. The women, these witnesses argued, played their characters too close to life, not artfully enough. A degree of artifice was as desirable in the boy actors' performances as in those delivered by the men. But as with the adult players, that artfulness did not diminish the potential impact of the show, as a famous account of a 1610 staging of *Othello* in Oxford attests. There, the scholar Henry Jackson recalls how Desdemona's death affected him: "although she always acted her whole part supremely well, yet when she was killed she was even more moving, for when she fell back upon the bed she implored the pity of the spectators by her very face." The boy player disappears behind the female pronouns, as if the artifice of the performance had become invisible. At the same time, Jackson registers that the body onstage, female or not, is not quite like a real corpse either; it responds to, and demands a response from, "the spectators." Yet, despite his recognition that the actor, or the character, is manipulating the audience's emotions, Jackson still responds emotionally and is in fact moved. The convention of using male youths for female parts, then, was of a piece with the broader understanding of acting in Shakespeare's time as an art that deployed heightened artifice in order to create an affectively powerful semblance of real life.

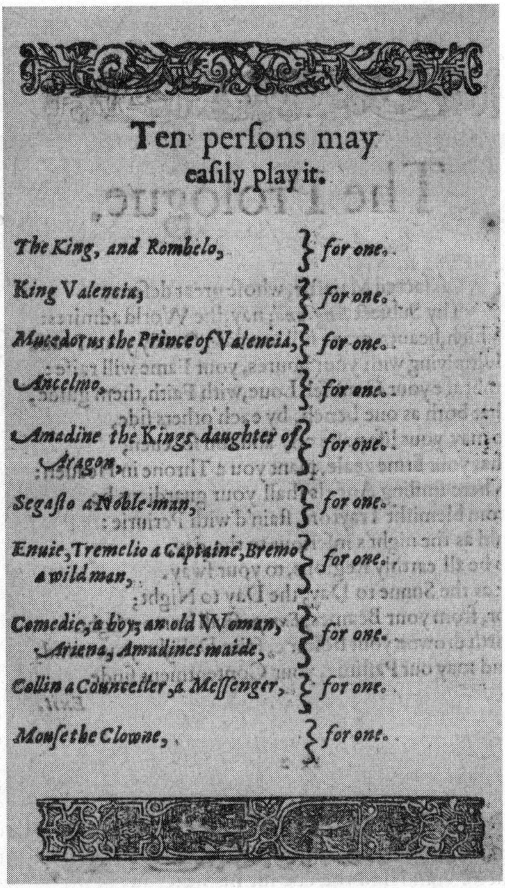
Ten perſons may
eaſily play it.

| | |
|---|---|
| The King, and Rombelo, | for one. |
| King Valencia, | for one. |
| Mucedorus the Prince of Valencia, | for one. |
| Ancelmo, | for one. |
| Amadine the Kings daughter of Aragon, | for one. |
| Segaſto a Noble-man, | for one. |
| Enuie, Tremelio a Captaine, Bremo a wild man, | for one. |
| Comedie, a boy, an old Woman, Ariena, Amadines maide, | for one. |
| Collin a Counceller, a Meſſenger, | for one. |
| Mouſe the Clowne, | for one. |

A chart from the second edition of the very popular anonymous play *Mucedorus* (1606), showing which actors can play more than one part.

## Staging and Its Meanings

The staging of a new play in Shakespeare's time did not begin in a rehearsal room or in a theater, but in an actor's home. One of the first tasks of the company book-holder in readying a new script for performance was the preparation of the players' individual parts: each actor received only his own lines, along with the cues to which he was to respond and a handful of stage directions. Initially, then, most actors did not know who else was onstage with them, how many lines those other characters had, how much time passed between the scenes in which they appeared, or even who would give them their cues—nor what those characters said before the two or three words that made up the cue. Since companies performed together almost every day and actors often lived close to each other, informal discussions must have taken place to clarify relationships between characters, but any performer's primary duty would have been to learn

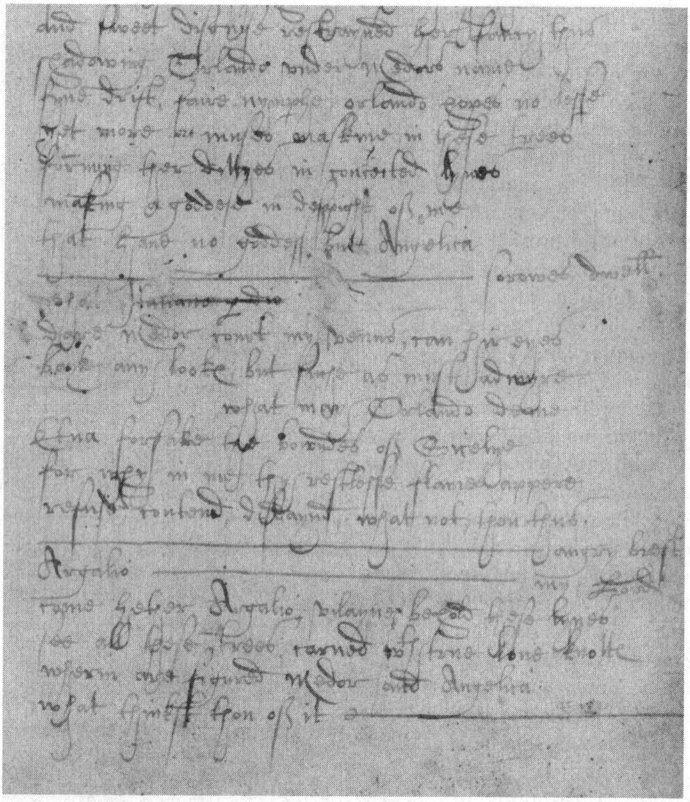

A section of Edward Alleyn's part for the role of Orlando in Robert Greene's *Orlando Furioso*. The long lines across the page mark breaks in Orlando's speech; at their end, the actor could find the cue for his next line.

his part in relative isolation, finding appropriate actions and intonations for his lines and memorizing cues. For leads, this was a formidable responsibility. Parts were written on strips of paper that were glued together to form a roll—which is why the terms "role" and "part" are synonymous. The scrolls for leads could reach remarkable length and heft. The one extant early modern part, Alleyn's copy of Orlando in Robert Greene's *Orlando Furioso*, is six inches wide and an impressive thirteen feet long, but its 530 lines probably did not overly tax an actor who had mastered more than 1,100 lines in *The Jew of Malta* and nearly 900 lines in the second part of *Tamburlaine*.

By Shakespeare's time, the solitary actor preparing his role could have predicted how the play would be staged with some certainty. The setup illustrated in the 1596 drawing of the Swan Theater is broadly representative of what a performer could expect in any venue: a rectangular, flat, largely empty stage; no sets in the modern sense, and few large furniture items; two pillars, probably set back from the edges of the stage by a few feet; at least two stage doors, and possibly a third in the center; and a balcony where scenes described as taking place "aloft" or "above" would be staged, though sections of it may also have offered additional audience seating, and part of it may have been used as a "music room." Even if there was no central stage door, there would have been an area between the two entrances that lay concealed behind an arras or a curtain that could be drawn to reveal pre-set tableaux, such as Hermione's statue in *The Winter's Tale*, Ferdinand and Miranda's chess game in *The Tempest*, or the caskets in *The Merchant of Venice*. There was also a trapdoor giving access to the space underneath the stage (sometimes called hell)—the place from which the ghost of Hamlet's father calls out to his son and his friends. In some theaters,

The interior of the Swan Theater, a sixteenth-century copy of a drawing by the Dutch traveler Johannes de Witt.

there was a pulley system that allowed objects, such as the figure of Jupiter in *Cymbeline*, to be lowered to the stage from the roof above it. That roof was often called the heavens, so that the stage as a whole represented a Christian microcosm, with hell, earth, and heaven enclosed in a round—*Hamlet*'s "distracted globe" or *Henry V*'s "wooden O."

This fairly stable, symbolically rich staging setup lent itself to an emblematic

The modern Globe on London's South Bank. This 1997 reconstruction is significantly larger than the original, but it captures the general idea of what an early modern theater may have looked like.

approach to performance. Figures appearing in the balcony are not always more powerful than those on the stage itself, but their position above could be dramatically exploited that way. When Tamora appears "aloft" alongside Saturninus in *Titus Andronicus*, for example, the staging suggests her elevation from prisoner of war to empress—a shift that officially does not take place until twenty lines later. The appearance of a prisoner and a foreigner in the location symbolically associated with supreme national power, however, also instantly signals how much of a topsy-turvy world Saturninus's Rome is about to become. This kind of visual logic of power returns in many plays that deal with the subjects of governance or rule: the descent of Richard II from the balcony to the stage when he surrenders to Bolingbroke is a particularly rich example. However, the emblematic use of the stage (where "above" means "powerful") could always be layered onto other modes of representation. In *Richard II*, the balcony also stands for an actual space "above," the battlements of Flint Castle; as the stage direction has it, Richard and his allies "enter on the walls." The stage to which he descends likewise is not simply "below" but also the "base court," the castle's lower court where Bolingbroke is waiting. From the perspective of the actor working with his part, the scene and its stage directions would have carried these various representational meanings—the text informed him both of Richard's movement from sun-like power to debasement before his enemy, and of the fact that the scene is taking place in two different locations in a castle. But the directions also had additional pragmatic value, as "on the walls" told the actor that he would have to enter on the balcony.

Stage directions such as these are explicit. Far more common are "internal" stage directions: textual references to actions characters perform. Often, these are straightforward: for instance, Bolingbroke's "there I throw my gage" in *Richard II*. But they can also be quite opaque. In *Hamlet*, when Polonius says, "Take this from this if this be otherwise," the line only tells the actor to perform some kind of gesture—he needs to indicate what "this" should be taken from what other "this" if Polonius is wrong. The most common interpretation is "my head from my shoulders" (indicated with appropriate gestures), but he may also be talking about his staff of office and his hand, or

A performance at the modern Globe.

his chain of office and his neck, or something else. The line requires actions to complete it, but it does not prescribe those actions.

Explicit and implicit stage directions allowed for a very short rehearsal period: they made it possible for the actor to conceive much of his performance alone. The text may not always tell him what to do, but it will often tell him when he needs to do *something*. However, there are also many cases where Shakespeare's plays seem to presuppose a good deal of back and forth between actors. For example, when Hamlet tells his mother to "leave wringing of your hands" in 3.4, the youth playing Gertrude would have needed to know to perform that action before Hamlet tells him to stop it—but there may have been no indication of this in his part. So while the part system allowed players to prepare for much, and while the established shape and features of playhouses by the 1590s made it possible for actors to anticipate many staging decisions before ever rehearsing a play, Shakespeare's texts also contain many instances where a successful performance depends on the players going beyond their individual parts.

Even if rehearsal periods were short, it is hard to imagine that the elaborate dumbshows, masques, and battle scenes featured in some plays were not carefully prepared. But rehearsal in the modern sense did not exist, mainly because the modern idea of character work did not exist. Renaissance actors did not spend long hours developing ideas about their characters' biographies, inner lives, or hidden feelings. Acting was primarily a physical and oratorical art and, in its conventionality, quite predetermined. What made any individual performance surprising and unpredictable were the specific effects achieved by bringing together a particular text with a conventionalized physical and vocal arsenal. But rehearsal also did not have to address many of the technological challenges that only came into being in the modern theater. In an outdoor venue without artificial lighting, actors do not need to hit their "marks"; an expansive stage lit only by sunlight allows for greater freedom of movement than one illuminated by an elaborate lighting design. Lastly, staging was determined in part by the architecture of the playhouses. Certain spots on stage worked especially well for certain set pieces. Soliloquies, for instance, were at their most powerful not when delivered front and center, but instead from a position farther away from the audience, off-center, and underneath the stage roof, which provided the greatest sense of acoustic intimacy. Therefore, an actor preparing a speech could predict with some certainty where onstage he would deliver it.

Of course there is more to staging a play than speaking lines and finding positions. Nowadays, sets are of paramount importance. In Shakespeare's time, they were all but nonexistent, except for some big-impact items: the Rose Theater owned a hell-mouth, probably covering the trapdoor, for devils to enter and exit in plays such as Marlowe's *Doctor Faustus*. Tombs, caves, and cages also appear in Henslowe's inventory, as do magical trees and severed heads. One other cost factor of modern productions, however, loomed similarly large in Shakespeare's time: costumes. Dresses in particular could be more expensive to commission than new plays, and companies maintained a rich stock of costumes; in 1598, the Admiral's Men owned at least eighty complete men's outfits. Most of these were generic items, but some were character-specific: "Harry the Fifth's velvet gown," "Longshanks' suit," or "Merlin's gown and cape."

What the actors wore was the most noteworthy visual aspect of staging. On a basic level, costumes identified characters. If the actor playing Tubal in *The Merchant of Venice* also played the jailor and the Duke, his three characters would have been distinguished initially and immediately by different garments. But costumes did more than facilitate identification. Dress signified social rank. It instantly allowed audiences to place characters, without having heard them speak or knowing anything else about them. More important, dress could set the scene: a nightgown signaled where and when an action took place; a forester's outfit told the audience to imagine a woodland setting; an innkeeper's costume moved the scene to a tavern. And dress denoted historical periods—as can be seen in Henry Peacham's famous illustration of *Titus Andronicus*. In this 1590s drawing, Titus's garments—Roman armor and a toga accessorized with a laurel wreath—immediately inform the viewer that this is a classical figure, and that the play is set in ancient Rome.

Yet Peacham's picture also shows that costume functioned in multiple registers on Shakespeare's stage. Titus wears Roman dress, and the short tunics of the three figures on the right also suggest quasiclassical costumes. But Tamora, on her knees in a flowing, embroidered gown and wearing a nonclassical crown, signifies less an ancient figure (Goth or Roman) than royalty. Her garments, unlike those of the characters beside her, are designed to situate her not in history, but in a particular social sphere. The outfits of the two leftmost characters follow a different logic yet again: they are Elizabethan soldiers, with breeches, halberds, and contemporary helmets. Their costume has no historical function; its sole purpose is to identify them as having a particular occupation. Dress, then, could signify in multiple, mutually contradictory ways at the same time on Shakespeare's stage. What Peacham's image

Henry Peacham's illustration of a scene from *Titus Andronicus* (ca. 1595).

suggests visually is that *Titus Andronicus*, while set in Rome, is also concerned with general questions of monarchic power and soldierly virtue. All three of those aspects of the play could be communicated through costume. If the picture portrays a kind of theater capable of sustaining anachronistic and logical contradictions in the pursuit of its thematic goals, it is representative of the broader, and pervasive, anachronism of Shakespearean drama, in which church bells ring and books rather than scrolls are read in *Julius Caesar*'s Rome, while the title character wears that most Elizabethan of male garments, a doublet. No matter how far back in historical time these plays were set, they also always took place in the present moment.

Audience members seem to have consumed a wide range of foods at the theater. Archaeologists found oyster shells, remnants of crab, and a large quantity of nutshells and fruit seeds at the Rose Theater site.

Impressive and expensive as the actors' costumes could be, their visual impact would necessarily have been lessened by the daylight playing conditions: performers were not isolated in space and light as they can be in modern theaters, but always competed for attention with the audience itself, with the equally splendid figures in the lords' rooms and on stage stools, and with whatever distracting things spectators chose to do while the play was in progress: play cards, smoke tobacco, solicit prostitutes (or johns). Aurally, too, Shakespeare's stage was not as insulated as a modern theater. Spectators were rowdier and more audibly present than audiences now. But the sounds of the city would also have infiltrated the open-air space: church bells, the noise of bears and hounds from the nearby bearbaiting arenas, the cries of street vendors, and perhaps even the sound of performances at neighboring playhouses might all have been heard. Going to a play in early modern London was never exclusively about the action and words onstage; it was always also about the theater itself, its temporary inhabitants, and the places where the theaters stood. Visually and aurally, the stage was in competition with the world, but it also found ways of integrating that world into its fictions.

Although the early modern theatrical experience was shaped by a host of immediate sensory perceptions, it equally depended on the audience's ability to refashion those impressions in their minds—even as plays insisted on drawing attention to the material reality of the stage. The Prologue to *Henry V* illustrates this condition perfectly. On the one hand, it mocks the apparent inadequacy of the theater, an "unworthy scaffold," a "cockpit" laughably ill suited to representing the "vasty fields of France"; it mercilessly reminds the audience where they are. At the same time, the Prologue also encourages the listeners to ignore all these carefully catalogued shortcomings and allow the play to work "on your imaginary forces," pleading with them to "piece out our imperfections with your thoughts." The Prologue seems to indulge in a risky game: it explains in detail why the theater should fail even as it dares the audience to make it work. But this risk lay at the heart of Shakespeare's theatrical art. We can detect it in the use of boy actors as much as in contradictory costuming choices and willful anachronisms. It found its most daring expression in the frequent use of narrative, seemingly the least theatrical form of writing. Antonio's tearful farewell to Bassanio in *The Merchant of Venice*; the deaths of the Dukes of Suffolk and York in *Henry V*; the reunion of Perdita and Leontes in *The Winter's Tale*; most remarkably, the death of as charismatic a character as Falstaff, in *Henry V*: again and again, Shakespeare chose to have events such as these reported by other characters rather than staging them before his spectators' eyes. In these scenes, the words and their demands on the audience's imagination do not just compete with what is visible, as they always did in the early modern playhouse. These narrations do more than that: they celebrate and rely on the power of words to take audiences out of the theater altogether, to transport them, without any visual aid whatsoever, to places and encounters that even the characters in the play itself only imagine.

And yet, despite placing such trust in language's capacity to transform reality, both the scenes and their author depended on their actors' ability to make audiences believe those words. If language's appeal to the imagination was meant to pull theatergoers out of their immediate sensory experience and into an engagement with a world of fiction, that goal could be achieved only by virtue of the very bodies, costumes, and props whose specific presence audiences were encouraged to transform into representations of an alternative reality. If a play worked, it enabled its viewers almost to forget the theaters whose splendor impressed so many visitors; allowed them to imagine for a moment that the words they heard did not come from a scroll of paper, that they had not been preapproved and licensed by a government official, purchased by a profit-hungry company, and written by a commercial playwright. Ultimately, then, in spite of the theater's undeniably powerful architectural, social, cultural, and visual presence in the lives of Shakespeare's contemporaries, its success in creating alternative, fictional worlds depended on an audience capable of understanding that all this splendor was not an end in itself. That is the marvelous paradox of Shakespeare's theater: it invested a great deal of goods, money, and physical labor in an effort to persuade people not to ignore those material realities altogether, but to use them as a means of accessing greater, still more wondrous, and wholly imaginary worlds beyond.

# ROMANCES

# Shakespearean Romance

*by*

WALTER COHEN

What is a romance? Renaissance playwrights inherited two main genres from classical antiquity: comedy and tragedy. Shakespearean drama, however, has never been parceled out into just these two groups. The first relatively complete edition of Shakespeare's plays was published in 1623, seven years after the dramatist's death. John Heminges and Henry Condell, two of Shakespeare's colleagues in the King's Men, the theater company to which he belonged, collected and printed the plays in a single large volume that became known as the First Folio. While the Folio adopted the classical categories of comedy and tragedy, it also added a third division: history. Under "Histories," the editors included Shakespeare's works on English history that take place from the thirteenth to the sixteenth centuries. The Folio's three resulting rubrics—"Comedies," "Tragedies," "Histories"—have considerable value, but they make for a certain conceptual messiness. A Shakespearean history designates a narrowly defined subject matter that may be comic or tragic or neither. Shakespearean comedy and tragedy suggest both a prevailing tone (light or somber) and a likely outcome (happy or sad). None of these designations, however, fits particularly well with the plays included here under the heading of "Romance"—plays that do not concern medieval English history and that often combine a somber feel with a happy ending. The First Folio deals with these plays in three ways. *The Tempest* (1611) opens and *The Winter's Tale* (1611) closes the comedies, *Cymbeline* (1610) appears last among the tragedies, and *Pericles* (1607–08) and *The Two Noble Kinsmen* (1613) are excluded entirely—presumably because they are coauthored pieces. This essay, however, brings together these five works while also drawing on two other collaborative Shakespearean productions: the lost *Cardenio* (1612) and the English history play *Henry VIII* (1613). After briefly reviewing their relationship to earlier European literature and theater, we will consider them from the three main perspectives that have emerged in modern scholarship. The late plays may accordingly be viewed as the culmination of Shakespearean comedy, as members of the distinct genre of romance, or as two different versions of tragicomedy.

Although Heminges and Condell did not employ the term, the notion of romance was well established by the Renaissance. Based on the word "Rome," romance was used originally as the collective name for the everyday speech derived from Latin and now called the Romance languages. The books written in those languages came to be known as romances. Beginning in the twelfth century, romance was deployed to indicate a literary genre, although the genre so indicated differed among the countries—primarily present-day Italy, France, Spain, and Portugal—where Romance languages were spoken. The most influential variation of the romance as a literary form occurred in Old French, where *roman* originally meant a courtly, or chivalric, narrative. Medieval French romance spread across Europe, inspiring both learned and popular emulation. For their collaborative work *The Two Noble Kinsmen,* Shakespeare and John Fletcher looked to the late fourteenth century and one of Geoffrey Chaucer's *Canterbury Tales,* "The Knight's Tale," itself an adaptation of Giovanni Boccaccio's Italian original from a few decades before. Such narratives, in prose as well as verse, continued to be composed in the sixteenth century: Ludovico Ariosto's *Orlando Furioso,* Torquato Tasso's *Jerusalem Liberated,* Sir Philip Sidney's *Arcadia,* and Edmund Spenser's *Faerie Queene* are among the most influential contributions to the genre. Like their medieval predecessors, these chivalric romances and many others invited dramatic adaptation.

A second narrative form that had an impact on Shakespearean romance is late classical Greek and, to a lesser extent, Latin prose fiction. A number of these works were translated into English in the late sixteenth century—Heliodorus's *Aethiopica,* the anonymous *Daphnis and Chloe,* and Achilles Tatius's *Clitophon and Leucippe*—and were exploited by Sidney as well as various playwrights. In such tales, faithful lovers are separated and often driven back and forth across the Mediterranean by bad people, bad weather, and bad luck. Ultimately, however, the virtuous couple earns a triumphant reunion that sometimes expands to include the restoration of the relationship between parent and child as well. In *Pericles,* Shakespeare and George Wilkins turned to Chaucer's contemporary John Gower for a story in his *Confessio Amantis* that is taken from an earlier Latin version that, in turn, goes back to a lost fifth- or sixth-century Greek original. In *The Winter's Tale,* Shakespeare borrowed from *Pandosto* (1588), a romance by his contemporary Robert Greene that is generally inspired by Greek fiction.

In addition to drawing on classical and medieval sources, Shakespeare's final plays were influenced by important predecessors in English drama. Although few texts survive, we often know their titles. The romantic plays of the 1570s and 1580s seem to have combined a certain naïveté with theatrically effective plot twists and concluding scenes of recognition and reconciliation. In the anonymous *Rare Triumphs of Love and Fortune* (1580s), the Olympian gods intervene to set human affairs right. Shakespeare may have turned to this play in both *Cymbeline* and *The Tempest.* A second legacy from the English theater is the saint's life, a dramatic form that dates from the late medieval period through the 1560s, after which it was suppressed by Protestant authorities. The anonymous work *Mary Magdalene,* preserved in a fifteenth-century manuscript, anticipates *Pericles* in sending a queen to her death at sea, only to save her, along with her child, through the prayers of the titular character.

Late sixteenth-century Italian pastoral tragicomedy provided yet another dramatic model for Shakespearean romance. Tasso's *Aminta* (1573) is probably the best-known specimen of the genre. Of central importance here is Battista Guarini's *Pastor Fido* (*The Faithful Shepherd*, 1590). Unlike either narrative or dramatic romance, *Il Pastor Fido* directly engages both Aristotle's *Poetics* (fourth century B.C.E.), the profoundly influential work of theatrical theory, and Sophocles' tragedy *Oedipus Rex* (fifth century B.C.E.). One of Guarini's innovations was to subvert Sophocles' tragic plot at the very last moment, thereby allowing his protagonist to avoid incest and its catastrophic consequences. Shakespeare may have learned of Guarini through Fletcher's unsuccessful adaptation, *The Faithful Shepherdess* (1608–09). Although Shakespeare never borrows as directly as Fletcher did and is more circumspect than his Italian predecessors in finding a providential design in human affairs, most of his romances are indebted either to Guarini or to Italian pastoral tragicomedy in general for their overall shape, settings, and much more.

The most traditional approach to Shakespearean romance approximates the logic of the First Folio's editors in treating all the playwright's romantic comedies, "problem plays" (*Troilus and Cressida, Measure for Measure, All's Well That Ends Well*), and romances as variations on a comic movement from disorder to harmony. Beginning in 1875, when the critic Edward Dowden first applied the term "romance" to *Pericles* and the final three solely authored plays (*Cymbeline*, *The Winter's Tale*, and *The Tempest*), this first view has gradually been eclipsed by a second, now-dominant paradigm—that the romances differ from the comedies and, indeed, constitute a distinct form within Shakespeare's dramatic oeuvre. That form is marked by its vertical, historical perspective, by a retrospective view that nonetheless leaves room for the future. Separation and long suffering of families, perilous sea journeys beset by storms that form part of a symbolic geography, near-death experiences followed by spiritual rebirths, the cultivation of patience, the healing power of time, the eventual reunion of royal families whose children (primarily daughters) have been separated from their parents (primarily fathers) at birth, the power of those daughters to redeem their fathers—all these are recurrent motifs. Plot complications are unraveled in ultimate scenes of recognition and reconciliation, where music and visionary spectacle herald the appearance of Greco-Roman gods, who perhaps stand in for a mysterious Christian providence that guides human beings through the labyrinth of life. A third view of the late plays, developed by scholars in recent decades, gives new weight to the three heterogeneous tragicomic works—*Cardenio, Henry VIII,* and *The Two Noble Kinsmen*—on which Shakespeare collaborated with John Fletcher. *The Two Noble Kinsmen* is the only romance extant from this collaboration. *Henry VIII* is a national history play that treats some of the key events and personalities from the monarchy of King Henry VIII (reigned 1509–47). But it draws on the tone and many of the motifs of romance, with the presumed fictiveness of the standard romance story replaced by a narrative in which "all is true" (the play's original title). And in the lost *Cardenio,* abandoned lovers are reduced to despair before heaven brings about a romance-style reunion. The two playwrights apparently extracted the plot from an interpolated tale in Miguel de Cervantes' *Don Quixote,* Part 1 (1605; English translation by Thomas Shelton, 1612). In general, the heterogeneous tragicomic, coauthored plays seem to constitute a more pessimistic corrective to the core romances.

Each of these three views of the plays is worth considering in greater detail. Like the romantic comedies, the romances have their roots in seasonal festivities, emblematized in some of the titles: *The Winter's Tale* recalls *A Midsummer Night's Dream* and *Twelfth Night.* In all these plays, the seasonal cycle underlies a movement toward regeneration that is celebrated in the resolution of the plot. Shakespearean romantic comedy is indebted to classical New Comedy, a form invented in ancient Greece whose main surviving examples are the plays of the ancient Roman dramatists Plautus and Terence. With plots confined to the private lives of well-to-do citizens, New Comedy features a series of stock situations (hidden identity) and stock characters (young lovers, restrictive fathers, clever servants, braggart soldiers). The comic action turns on the young man's pursuit of the apparently unsuitable young woman, in the course of which various obstacles must be—and are—overcome. The legacy of Plautus and Terence was revised and elaborated upon in sixteenth-century Italian drama, which introduced to it elements of the Italian novella, or short story, beginning with Boccaccio's *Decameron* in the mid-fourteenth century. Nearly all of Shakespeare's romantic comedies, problem comedies, and romances are indebted to Italian narrative or drama, either directly or via French, Spanish, and English translation. Among the romances, *Cymbeline* borrows from the *Decameron, The Winter's Tale* exploits Sicily's association with literary pastoral in its setting, *The Tempest* resembles some of the scenarios from Italian popular theater (the commedia dell'arte), *Cardenio* presumably adapts a Cervantine novella that is itself influenced by Boccaccio and his successors, and, as we have seen, *The Two Noble Kinsmen* also goes back to Boccaccio's narrative poetry.

But Shakespearean comedy and romance depart from classical and Renaissance models in important ways that also sharply distinguish the plays from the classically minded satiric comedy of Shakespeare's contemporary Ben Jonson. Shakespeare replaces the prosperous private citizens of earlier comedy with aristocrats and rulers, thereby blurring the traditional division between the private concerns of comedy and the public affairs of tragedy. Special attention is accorded to the fate of virtuous young women, whose marriages are crucial to the happy resolution of the plot. That resolution is complicated by a feature common to comedy and romance alike—a paternal or political decree that initially thwarts the romantic aspirations of the young lovers. Such a decree figures in the comedies from *The Two Gentlemen of Verona* through *Love's Labor's Lost* to *Measure for Measure,* and in the late plays from *Pericles* through *The Tempest* to *Henry VIII.* To avoid its force, the characters flee the society of sanctioned public power for a world of disorder, license, and confused sexual identity. Geographically, this is the pastoral or green world that represents a physical and symbolic alternative to the city or, more often, the court. It is the setting for most of *As You Like It,* for the concluding resolution of both plots of *The Merry Wives of Windsor,* and, indeed, for much else in the romantic comedies. It is also a recurrent locale in the romances, above all in *The Tempest* but to some extent in each of them. The pastoral world is marked by a series of motifs shared by comedy and romance alike. The dreamlike madness of *The Comedy of Errors* and *A Midsummer Night's Dream* is echoed by *The Tempest, Cardenio,* and *The Two Noble Kinsmen.* The male disguise adopted by numerous women in the romantic comedies is also donned by Imogen in *Cymbeline* and, ineffectually, by Dorotea/Violante in *Cardenio* (where the first name, Dorotea, comes from Shelton's translation of Cervantes, while the second, Violante, is from the imitation of *Cardenio* by Lewis Theobald in his tragicomedy *Double Falsehood; or, The Distrest Lovers,* 1728). A lower-class theatrical performance honors the Athenian wedding of Theseus and Hippolyta in both *A Midsummer Night's Dream* and *The Two Noble Kinsmen.*

Both the comedies and the romances also erect barriers to young love very different from the initial prohibition. First, lovers create problems for themselves through their own defects. Katherine's shrewishness in *The Taming of the Shrew* is one example, but more frequently the difficulty is the failings of men. Proteus comes close to raping Silvia in *The Two Gentlemen of Verona.* Similarly, in *Cardenio,* Ferdinando/Theobald promises his love to Dorotea/Violante, rapes her, abandons her for Luscinda/Leonora, and later abducts Luscinda/Leonora from a nunnery. Just as Claudio doesn't question the slanderous attack on Hero's sexual virtue in *Much Ado About Nothing,* so Posthumus believes the worst of Imogen in *Cymbeline*—outdoing Claudio, however, by ordering his wife's death. In *The Winter's Tale,* King Leontes does not need to be deceived: for no reason he becomes convinced that his wife, Hermione, has been unfaithful. A second barrier is very different, however. The triumph of heterosexual love entails the loss of something valuable, intimacy with another member of one's own sex. In *The Merchant of Venice,* Bassanio must learn to choose Portia over Antonio. In *The Winter's Tale,* Polixenes nostalgically recalls the innocence of his youthful friendship with Leontes. And in *The Two Noble Kinsmen,* the mere sight of Emilia tears apart the kinsmen, Palamon and Arcite, while Emilia herself sadly recalls her childhood love for Flavina, who died when the two girls were eleven.

Nonetheless, the pastoral experience usually leads to festivity and forgiveness, transforms character, and restores community. The concluding reconciliation enables some of the characters to get more than they deserve. Just as Proteus is allowed to marry Julia in *The Two Gentlemen of Verona,* Fernando/Henriquez is paired off with Dorotea/Violante in *Cardenio.* Claudio wins Hero in *Much Ado About Nothing,* Posthumus regains Imogen in *Cymbeline,* and Leontes recovers Hermione in *The Winter's Tale.* While the plot mechanisms of the concluding resolutions tend to strain credulity, the happy outcome reveals the power of timely human intervention—whether of Portia in *The Merchant of Venice,* Duke Vincentio in *Measure for Measure,* Prospero in *The Tempest,* or Henry VIII in the play of the same name. What are we to make of this? Should emphasis fall on the unruly process or the sometimes hastily arranged harmonious conclusion? Such is the unresolved tension of this group of plays.

If comedy and romance share so many characteristics, where are the distinctive qualities of romance to be found? One answer lies in the intervening experience of

*Le Naufrage* (*The Shipwreck*). Etching by Claude Lorrain (1600–1682).

tragedy. During the 1590s, Shakespeare wrote the majority of his romantic comedies. For most of the next decade, he focused on tragedy. The romances depart from the romantic comedies in their incorporation of a tragic perspective, which in most instances is ultimately transcended. Both the storms and the redemptive reconciliation of father and daughter in *Pericles* hark back to *King Lear,* a work that is itself based on a dramatic romance and that seems headed in the same direction until catastrophe intervenes. The jealousy of Posthumus in *Cymbeline* and of Leontes in *The Winter's Tale* reprises the fatal behavior of Othello. *Henry VIII* seems to have raided *Macbeth* for its Porter at the christening of the baby Elizabeth in act 5. *The Tempest* echoes *Richard II, Julius Caesar, Hamlet,* and *Macbeth* in its concern with usurpation, *Hamlet* in its recourse to a play within a play, *Othello* in its setting on a Mediterranean island located between Christianity and Islam, and *Othello* and *King Lear* in its dramatization of a father's difficulty in letting go of his daughter. In *The Two Noble Kinsmen,* both Emilia's comparison of pictures and the Jailer's Daughter's madness go back to *Hamlet*, the Daughter's willow song is borrowed from Desdemona in *Othello,* and the Doctor's effort to cure her and the enigmatic prophecies that provide false comfort to the protagonists come from *Macbeth*.

Shakespeare's incorporation of tragic elements in the romances often represents less a break with comedy than a shift in relative weight. Thus, the storm and shipwreck that wash Viola up on the coast of Illyria in *Twelfth Night* anticipate similar scenes not just in *Pericles* but also in *The Winter's Tale* and *The Tempest.* Similarly, the threat of rape that Silvia faces in *The Two Gentlemen of Verona* returns not only for Dorotea/Violante in *Cardenio* but also for Marina in *Pericles,* Imogen in *Cymbeline*, and Miranda in *The Tempest*.

But sometimes in the romances tragedy is felt more strongly—as a rupture rather than a shift. This is true in the case of mortality—rare in the comedies, routine in the romances. The incestuous Antiochus and his Daughter, like Cleon and his murderous wife Dionyza, are spectacularly dispatched in *Pericles*. In *Cymbeline,* death comes to both the murderous Queen and her sexually predatory son, Cloten. In *The Winter's Tale,* Leontes' jealousy costs him both his son and Antigonus, the courtier who saves Leontes' daughter Perdita from death only at the expense of his own life. In *Cardenio,* a hearse comes by at a crucial moment. *Henry VIII* chronicles the decline and death of the possibly treasonous Duke of Buckingham, the virtuous Catharine of Aragon, and the corrupt Cardinal Wolsey. It celebrates the corresponding rise of Cromwell, More, Cranmer, and Anne Boleyn, all of whom, however—as at least some of the audience would have known—went on to meet violent deaths as a result of the bloody controversy between Protestants and Catholics in sixteenth-century England. And in *The Two Noble Kinsmen,* only one of the kinsmen can survive: Arcite, the apparent victor over Palamon in a struggle to the death, is fatally injured when thrown from his horse.

The mechanism for defeating death is, paradoxically, time—despite its often being thought of as the enemy of life, by both other writers and Shakespeare himself. While some romance characters die, others experience a quasi-ritualistic symbolic or metaphorical death. This is the fate of Thaisa and Marina in *Pericles;* Imogen in *Cymbeline;* Perdita and Hermione in *The Winter's Tale;* Prospero, Miranda, and Ferdinand in *The Tempest;* Cardenio/Julio in *Cardenio;* and Palamon in *The Two Noble Kinsmen.* The characteristic romance movement from symbolic death to spiritual rebirth is hardly automatic, however. The passage of the years is necessary if the tragic dimension of life is to be overcome. In general, the romances operate across far greater temporal spans than the romantic comedies. In *Pericles* and *The Winter's Tale,* events stretch out over the better part of a generation. *Cymbeline* and *The Tempest* conjure up crucial experiences in the past from the perspective of the present. Reversing the strategy of these two plays, *Henry VIII* anticipates the supposed triumphs of the audience's present (the play's future) from the perspective of the audience's past (the play's present).

Emphasis on the workings of time is tied to a shift in the portrayal of virtuous young women. Shakespeare's romance heroines are less involved in getting their men than are their predecessors in the comedies, and their prospective or reconstituted marriages are less crucial to the restoration of the community. More generally, compared to the comedies, the romances arguably feature fewer multiple-plot narratives and certainly stage fewer multiple-marriage conclusions. Both the reduced activity of these women and the reduced significance of their marriages may seem paradoxical, since the redemptive role of the romance heroines tends to exceed that of their predecessors in romantic comedy and is a far cry from the sometimes misogynistic view of women in the immediately preceding tragedies. But whatever their intentions, that role is directed less toward marriage than toward intergenerational restoration, and usually in particular toward the repair of their parents' suffering or misdeeds. An older man may recover both wife and daughter (Pericles, Leontes in *The Winter's Tale*), a daughter and two sons (*Cymbeline*), or a son (Alonso in *The Tempest*). Although Marina delivers her father Pericles from his misery, that moment of deliverance is just a prelude to the actual climax, in which Pericles is reunited with his wife Thaisa while Marina stands mutely by. Similarly, *The Winter's Tale* seems headed toward Perdita's return to the court of her father Leontes, but the anticipated occasion is narrated rather than dramatized so that the stage can be reserved for the miraculous revival of the statue of her mother Hermione, and hence for the reconciliation of father and mother, of husband and wife, while Perdita characteristically remains silent. In *Cymbeline,* Imogen's reconciliation with husband and father alike after comparatively brief separations is followed by Cymbeline's recovery of his long-lost sons Guiderius and Arviragus. In *The Tempest,* however important the dynastic implications of Miranda's upcoming marriage to Ferdinand may be, the work's conclusion is devoted primarily to her father Prospero's settling of accounts with men of his own age. Finally, rather than displacing the young woman's impact back to the previous generation, *Henry VIII* projects it forward to the next one. Anne Boleyn matters only as the mother of the future Queen Elizabeth, whose reign unfolds long after the end of the play.

This temporal, intergenerational logic may be understood structurally. *The Winter's Tale* perhaps represents the paradigmatic case. Although in Shakespeare's career comedy precedes tragedy, in this play it is the other way around. The first three acts revive *Othello,* the fourth *As You Like It.* A generation passes between these two movements of the plot. In other words, courtly tragedy is ultimately set in the past, so that its crimes and errors can be redeemed by pastoral comedy, peopled with the rural lower classes, located in the present. The rebirth, recognition, and reconciliation of act 5 are made possible by the preceding sequence. One kind of variation on this pattern appears in both *Cymbeline* and *The Tempest.* The represented action is confined to the present, but part of what happens in *Cymbeline* and all of what happens in *The Tempest* depends on events as remote as those of the opening acts of *The Winter's Tale.* In all three instances, the potentially tragic moment is located at the birth or during the very early childhood of the youths who, now on the verge of adulthood, will prove crucial to the transcendence of tragedy. In still another variation on the paradigm of *The Winter's Tale*, *Pericles* and *Henry VIII* present a sequence of minitragedies. In *Pericles,* these concern both the protagonist and his victimizers, the crucial difference being that Pericles' suffering can be overcome after a generation, whereas the others simply meet their deserved fate. The multiple tragedies of *Henry VIII* dramatize the fall of one illustrious personage after another from a position of eminence, with the jump forward in time relegated to a concluding prophecy inspired by the birth of the future Queen Elizabeth. Finally, *The Two Noble Kinsmen,* like *The Winter's Tale,* combines a relatively tragic work with a comic one. Like *Troilus and Cressida,* it draws on Chaucer for an account of violently destructive sexuality. Like *A Midsummer Night's Dream,* as we have seen, it offers a popular theatrical performance in the context of Theseus and Hippolyta's wedding. Here, however, the order seems to replicate, not reverse, that of Shakespeare's career. Rather than *A Midsummer Night's Dream* lightening the experience of *Troilus and Cressida,* the latter play seems to darken the outlook of the former.

As these examples suggest, the recapitulation characteristic of the romances places enormous structural pressure on the dramatic narrative. This seems like a deliberate strategy on Shakespeare's part, an aesthetic self-consciousness that takes pleasure in the rejection of reigning theoretical norms. In the 1580s, Sidney's *Apology for Poetry* criticized English tragicomedy for its violation of morally appropriate emotional effects in its indifference to the classical separation of styles—of comedy from tragedy.

> But besides these gross absurdities, how all their plays be neither right tragedies, nor right comedies, mingling kings and clowns, not because the matter so carrieth it, but thrust in clowns by head and shoulders, to play a part in majestical matters, with neither decency nor discretion, so as neither the admiration and commiseration, nor the right sportfulness, is by their mongrel tragicomedy obtained.

This criticism sounds as if it were anticipatorily directed toward Shakespearean drama in general. Sidney also disparages dramatic romance for its violation of probability in its indifference to the classical unities of time (a play should last no more than a day) and place (it should take place in a single location).

> You shall have Asia of the one side, and Afric of the other . . . the player, when he cometh in, must ever begin with telling where he is, or else the tale will not be conceived. . . . By and by we hear news of shipwreck. . . . Upon the back of that comes out a hideous monster, . . . and then the miserable beholders are bound to take it for a cave. While in the meantime two armies fly in, represented with four swords and bucklers, and then what hard heart will not receive it for a pitched field? . . . [T]wo young princes fall in love. After many traverses, she is got with child, delivered of a fair boy; he is lost, groweth a man, falls in love, and is ready to get another child; and all this in two hours' space.

Here, it is as if Sidney were attacking Shakespeare's late plays in particular—Asia and Africa in *Antony and Cleopatra* (1606–07) and *Pericles;* shipwreck in *Pericles* and *The Tempest;* the hideous monster also in *The Tempest;* the cave in *Cymbeline* and *The Tempest;* the armies in *Antony and Cleopatra, Coriolanus* (1608), and *Cymbeline;* the love affairs followed by children lost for a generation in *Pericles, Cymbeline,* and *The Winter's Tale.*

A generation later Ben Jonson actually did attack Shakespeare's romances on similar grounds. (See the introductions to *Pericles* and *The Winter's Tale.*) It is easy to see why. Shakespeare goes out of his way to flaunt the primitivism of his materials and methods. Beyond employing Gower as narrator, *Pericles* repeatedly resorts to the outmoded dramatic device of the dumb show. *The Winter's Tale* ostentatiously rings out the old by having Antigonus, savior of Perdita, "*Exit, pursued by a bear*" (3.3.57 SD). It brings in the new by sending Time onstage as a Chorus to apologize for the sixteen-year gap in the action. *Cymbeline* passes well beyond the normal bounds of Shakespearean anachronism by combining ancient Britain, classical Rome, and Renaissance Italy. In the long final recognition scene, the playwright delays the improbable revelations to such an extent that the audience, although more in the know than the characters, sympathizes with Cymbeline's impatience:

> I had rather thou shouldst live while nature will
> Than die ere I hear more. Strive, man, and speak.
> (5.5.151–52)

> I stand on fire.
> Come to the matter.
> (5.5.168–69)

> Nay, nay, to th' purpose.
> (5.5.178)

In *The Tempest,* where adherence to the unities of time and place requires Prospero to narrate the back story to his daughter Miranda, the conventionality of the device is again laid bare, as Prospero repeatedly accuses Miranda of not listening: "Dost thou attend me?" "Thou attend'st not!" "Dost thou hear?" (1.2.78, 87, 106). And earlier in the same scene, the audience learns that the play's opening storm is nothing more than a trick of the magician's art—nothing more, that is, than a trick of the dramatist's art.

In other words, much of the sophistication of the romances consists in Shakespeare's deliberate recourse to a threadbare stagecraft, in his undermining of the illusion of reality that is so important in many of the immediately preceding plays. He wants the audience to see and hear the creaking stage machinery, to recognize the dissonance that results from incorporating incompatible experiences, and nonetheless to find something moving and new. A similar project seems to shape Shakespeare's style. It is marked by the elision of sounds and words that would earlier have been present, the suppression of connectives between clauses, the recourse to complicated and occasionally impenetrable syntax, a penchant for parenthetical interruption of the flow of thought, and the addition of elaborating—but not necessarily essential—phrases that prolong the sentence. In the same vein, the extended metaphors characteristic of the tragedies are replaced in the romances by briefer comparisons that often follow quickly upon one other. The blank verse is less regular than before: some lines have fewer than ten syllables; many have more. And enjambment is common—which is to say that the meter goes one way and the syntax another. All of this is both destabilizing and ostentatious. The language calls attention to itself, thereby providing less of the naturalistic illusion of unmediated access to a character's mind than is often the case in the plays of the preceding decade.

On the other hand, the style of the romances also includes far more repetition, in sound, word, phrase, and rhythm. This tendency might be seen as a countervailing principle of order. The logic here, as in the discontinuous plots, seems to be that of an art that for all its artificiality also cooperates with the natural world. But the character of the cooperation between art and nature remains unclear. In act 4 of *The Winter's Tale,* Perdita speaks against the improvement of nature by art in the cultivation of flowers. King Polixenes disagrees, arguing that

> we marry
> A gentler scion to the wildest stock
> And make conceive a bark of baser kind
> By bud of nobler race.
> (4.4.92–95)

But when he discovers that his son is in love with Perdita, whom he believes to be a shepherdess, he violently opposes the marriage of a "gentler scion to the wildest stock" that he has just advocated.

The conflict between Polixenes and Perdita points away from impersonal structures. In the romances, regeneration depends on more than time and artful dramaturgy. It requires a patience often accompanied by suffering, and sometimes by repentance. Wronged aristocrats—Belarius in *Cymbeline,* Prospero in *The Tempest*—must spend the better part of a generation in distant rural exile from the court. Pericles is separated from his daughter for a similar period of time, during the last part of which he also grieves over her, believing her dead. The time of mourning lasts an entire generation for Leontes, who justly holds himself responsible for the real death of his son, the supposed death of his daughter, and the apparent death of his wife in *The Winter's Tale*. In *Cymbeline,* Posthumus has to confront his guilt for what he believes is the murder of his wife. And much the same goes for Fernando/Henriquez in *Cardenio.*

The complement of remorse is a self-mastery on the part of the wronged characters that issues in forgiveness far more difficult to offer than in the romantic comedies because there is so much more to forgive. This is the forgiveness Wolsey receives from his enemies at the moment of his fall in *Henry VIII.* Such forgiveness is linked to the acceptance of social responsibility near the end of *The Tempest,* when, in a gesture at once appalling, enigmatic, and moving, Prospero says of the semihuman Caliban, native of the island, would-be rapist of Prospero's daughter and murderer of Prospero himself, "this thing of darkness I / Acknowledge mine" (5.1.278–79). The acknowledgment here seems connected to Prospero's concluding renunciation of magic, emphasis on his own weakness, and consequent humility in the Epilogue he delivers, where the standard appeal for the audience's benevolence takes a sudden religious turn:

> And my ending is despair,
> Unless I be relieved by prayer,
> Which pierces so that it assaults
> Mercy itself and frees all faults.
> As you from crimes would pardoned be,
> Let your indulgence set me free.
> (lines 15–20)

The moment is significant because Prospero is more in control of his own destiny than is any other character in Shakespeare. But in the end, even he must depend on others.

The terms of that dependence, moreover, only underscore the infirmity of mortal creatures. Far more than the romantic comedies, the romances reduce the efficacy of human agency. Their virtuous, redemptive young women are less activist than emblematic. They are part of the pattern rather than its creator. Their symbolic names, derived from Latin, tell the story: in *Pericles,* Marina means "of the sea"; in *The Winter's Tale,* Perdita signifies "lost"; and in *The Tempest,* Miranda indicates "someone or something to be wondered at." The plays accordingly pay more cursory attention to the women's psychological complexity, to their inner lives, than one finds in many of the romantic comedies. But the same reduced interest in characterization holds for the men, especially if they are compared to the tragic protagonists of the preceding years. There is less depth to Posthumus in *Cymbeline* or Leontes in *The Winter's Tale* than there is to Othello—a point that can be extended even to Prospero in *The Tempest* when juxtaposed with Hamlet or Lear. Not surprisingly, then, the romances offer not the distinctive, highly individualized verbal styles of the leading men and women of the tragedies, but, more uniformly, the distinctive late verbal style of the playwright himself.

Most of the salient features of the romances—violence and literal or metaphorical death, the passage of time, an intergenerational orientation, suffering and repentance, forgiveness and the acceptance of human frailty—result in encompassing final reconciliations. This inclusive spirit is possible because in the romances' conclusions the natural world with which art cooperates seems connected with an invisible supernatural reality. Like the incorporation of tragedy and the long temporal perspective, the providential guidance of mortal affairs is a signature of Shakespearean romance. The plays opt for resolutions that are rationally inexplicable (*The Winter's Tale, The Tempest*), accessible only through inspired Christian prophecy (*Henry VIII*), produced by luck but retrospectively coded as Christian providence (*Cardenio*), or manifestly generated by divine intervention that is classical in nomenclature (Diana in *Pericles;* Jupiter in *Cymbeline;* Mars, Venus, and Diana in *The Two Noble Kinsmen*) but Christian in nature (except, perhaps, in *The Two Noble Kinsmen*). The characters wander in a spiritual labyrinth, often stumbling as they go. But the fall is usually a fortunate one, a *felix culpa* (Latin, literally, for "happy fault") that replicates the foundational failure of Adam and Eve, opening the way to earthly redemption and a fleeting glimpse of eternal reality. This vision, often in the form of a dream, is granted only to a character who strives to be worthy of it. Yet the plays suggest that these efforts alone may not be enough. It is the intertwining of divine and human agency that leads to the comic resolution.

Jupiter. From the Chapel of the Planets (Rimini, Italy; fifteenth century), by Agostino di Duccio. The classical deities play crucial roles in the resolutions of *Pericles, Cymbeline,* and *The Two Noble Kinsmen.*

Behind this outlook lies the dramaturgy of late sixteenth-century Italy, based in the religious movement known as the Catholic Counter-Reformation. That dramaturgy also drew on a philosophical tradition known today as Renaissance Neoplatonism for a mystical belief in the unity of opposites, the cosmic harmony that gives meaning to the apparently random vicissitudes of earthly existence. This does not necessarily imply that the romances are Catholic in outlook. It does mean that "the music of the spheres" (*Pericles* 5.1.217), indication of divine harmony, is audible to

*Venus of Urbino* (1538). By Titian (ca. 1488/90–1576).

the privileged. It is heard by Pericles ("I hear most heavenly music," 5.1.220). Cardenio/Julio believes he detects it in the singing of Dorotea/Violante. The revival of Hermione at the end of *The Winter's Tale* is accompanied by music. So, too, are Posthumus's vision of his family in *Cymbeline* and the appearance of the classical deities in *The Tempest*. "Some heavenly music" brings the shipwrecked nobility to their senses in Prospero's charmed circle toward the end of the same play (5.1.52). And music is also heard at the altars of Venus and Diana in act 5 of *The Two Noble Kinsmen*.

There is less of this in the romantic comedies. In those earlier plays, one or two characters often remain unincorporated at the end, less because they are cast out than because they find the terms of inclusion unpalatable. Shakespeare thereby signals the incomplete character of his festive endings, the continuing presence of melancholy, critique, skepticism, or isolation. In the romances, the sense that the resolution is partial and provisional is created by the previous losses, including, of course, death itself. Hence, all survivors are included regardless of their prior behavior and regardless of whether they have undergone a long period of repentance (Leontes in *The Winter's Tale*), only belatedly confessed their sins (Giacomo, slanderer of Imogen in *Cymbeline*), or not reformed at all (Antonio and Sebastian, murderous usurpers in *The Tempest*; arguably Gardiner, the overly zealous Catholic bishop of *Henry VIII*). In other words, the potential conflict between process and outcome noted earlier in the romantic comedies is ratcheted up in the romances. The more inclusive endings leave more open the threat of future tragedy—a tragedy lived out by the characters extra-theatrically, as we have seen, in *Henry VIII*.

In all these respects, the romances represent a logical development of Shakespeare's earlier dramatic practice, and arguably the culmination of his career in the theater. They are also part of a more general movement on the English stage, although it is possible that Shakespeare himself initiated that movement. The romances seem to respond to a series of additional developments, however. One is institutional. In

1608, Shakespeare's company began performing during the winter at the Blackfriars, an indoor, "private" theater that catered to a more uniformly upscale audience than the patrons of the outdoor, "public" Globe, where the King's Men had been playing since 1599. The Blackfriars provided more elaborate theatrical machinery than was available in an open-air theater, and some of the romances take advantage of these resources. For instance, *The Tempest* and *Henry VIII* adapt the masque, a newly fashionable court theatrical genre that demanded complex special effects. The shift toward the Blackfriars may be seen as part of an elitist turn in Shakespeare's late plays, also noticeable in the declining role of the clown, a characteristic figure in the romantic comedies often integral to a subplot that comments on the central action. Yet members of the lower classes continue to be prominent in the romances. Such figures include the fishermen and the managers of the house of prostitution in *Pericles;* the Old Shepherd, the Clown, and Autolycus in *The Winter's Tale;* the Boatswain, Caliban, Stefano, and Trinculo in *The Tempest;* the Citizens, the shepherds, and their vicious but witty Master in *Cardenio;* the Porter and unruly citizens in *Henry VIII;* and the Jailer's Daughter, in addition to the country actors, in *The Two Noble Kinsmen.* Equally important, *Pericles,* the earliest of the romances, predates the King's Men's lease of the Blackfriars. The company continued to use the Globe in the warmer months, and it is certain that *The Winter's Tale* was performed there in 1611 and *Henry VIII* in 1613. In short, it is easy to make too much of the distinction between playhouses and probably best to view romance as an institutionally transitional form, with one foot in the "public" theater and the other in the "private."

A second motive behind the romances may be biographical. In 1607, Shakespeare's daughter Susanna got married. The next year she had a daughter, Elizabeth, and Shakespeare's own mother died. Thus, the romances coincide with a generational shift in the dramatist's family. The emphasis in the plays on daughters who both marry and help redeem their aging fathers seems compatible with this moment. So, too, does the celebration of the birth of a baby Elizabeth at the end of *Henry VIII.*

Political changes may also have influenced the romances. Upon assuming the throne in 1603, King James placed each of London's professional acting troupes under the patronage of a member of his immediate family. As the most successful of these troupes, Shakespeare's company, the Lord Chamberlain's Men, became the King's Men. The late plays seem to register this increased proximity to the crown. Just as the romantic comedies shift the focus from the middle class of New Comedy to the aristocracy, so the romances further elevate the social status of the protagonists by concerning themselves with royalty—Pericles, Prince (that is, ruler) of Tyre; Cymbeline, King of Britain; Leontes, King of Sicilia, in *The Winter's Tale;* Prospero, Duke of Milan, in *The Tempest;* Henry VIII, King of England; Theseus, Duke of Athens, in *The Two Noble Kinsmen;* and, more ambiguously, Duke Angelo and his elder son, Roderick, in *Cardenio.* The attention to the younger generation in relation to the older may also respond to the cult that grew up around James's children. The Welsh setting of the cave of Guiderius and Arviragus, Cymbeline's lost sons, may glance at the 1610 investiture of James's first son, Henry, as Prince of Wales. *Henry VIII* enthusiastically alludes to the marriage of James's daughter Elizabeth in 1613. Perhaps the same event lies behind the far more somber concluding union of Emilia and Palamon in *The Two Noble Kinsmen;* in this case, however, Arcite's apparently meaningless fatal fall parallels the death the previous year of Elizabeth's brother Henry, symbol of the revival of chivalry and martial valor that the play nostalgically evokes. It is unclear if these allusions are flattering to the royal family. And, of course, the point is not to ascertain whether the romances are secretly allegories of that family—they are not—but to understand that the family's prominence, following the long rule of the unmarried and childless Queen Elizabeth, could have helped turn Shakespeare's imagination in a new direction.

Finally, the romances seem to meditate upon imperial expansion. English merchant ships had aggressively entered the Mediterranean in the 1570s, trading directly

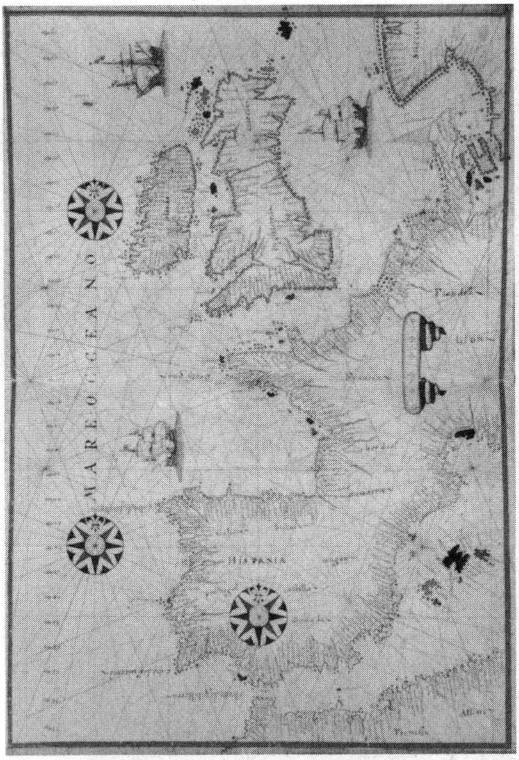

The Mediterranean, western Europe, and the northwest coast of Africa. By Joan Oliva (fl. 1580–1615).

with the Ottoman Empire and thereby cutting into Venice's traditional economic dominance in the region. Although many of Shakespeare's plays throughout his career are set in and around the Mediterranean, beginning with *Antony and Cleopatra* all of them with the exception of *Henry VIII* are partly or wholly located there. Western European extracontinental voyages—around Africa to India, across the Atlantic to America, and soon around the world—had begun in the late fifteenth century, and references to distant lands, peoples, and products are dotted throughout Shakespeare's oeuvre. Yet the foundation of England's first permanent colony in the New World at Jamestown in 1607 apparently sharpened the playwright's interest in the topic. Accordingly, the romances' Mediterranean voyages sometimes feel as if they were also American ones. Unmistakable allusions are rare, however. *Henry VIII* overtly refers to the New World. The island of *The Tempest,* although clearly located in the Mediterranean, is also connected with Bermuda, and in Caliban it possesses a character whose name is a near anagram of cannibal. Shakespeare would have made the link to America from reading Michel de Montaigne's essay "Of Cannibals" (1580). Prospero colonizes the island and effectively enslaves Caliban, its native, but leaves it behind at the end of the play. Critics have accordingly debated the work's relationship to colonialism. One perspective on this issue is suggested by Thomas More's *Utopia* (1516), which was itself inspired by the European encounter with America and its peoples. In *The Tempest,* the goodhearted, loyal Gonzalo, cast upon the island, presents a utopian vision that is effectively ridiculed by the most treacherous characters in the play. But the redemptive structure of *The Tempest* and the other romances, the providential triumph over adversity following a long period of suffering, is itself a utopian scenario. This scenario distinguishes the late plays from their comic precursors. If America significantly influences the romances, it does so not through incidental references but at the level of conceptual and dramatic structure.

Most discussions of the romances concentrate on *Pericles, Cymbeline, The Winter's Tale,* and *The Tempest*—and with good reason. Of Shakespeare's three subsequent plays, one is lost (*Cardenio*), another is a history play (*Henry VIII*), and the third seems very different from the four standard romances (*The Two Noble Kinsmen*). Yet in one obvious respect, the three plays belong together: as already noted, all are collaborations with Fletcher. English Renaissance playwrights routinely coauthored plays, and early and late in his career Shakespeare was no exception. By 1595, he had probably collaborated on at least *1 Henry VI, Titus Andronicus,* and *Edward III;* after

Mapping the New World. From *Americae sive quartae orbis partis nova et exactissima desciptio*, engraved by Hieronymous Cock (1562).

1603, he jointly wrote *Sir Thomas More, Timon of Athens,* and, as we have seen, *Pericles, Cardenio, Henry VIII,* and *The Two Noble Kinsmen.* Coauthored works arguably have a less uniformly "Shakespearean" quality than the plays that Shakespeare composed by himself. One effect of attending to the final three plays, then, is to loosen the definition of the romances, to align them with the more general interest in romantic tragicomedy on the English stage at the time, and to underscore the uniquenesss of each of the late plays, the extent to which each deviates from the norms of even such capacious generic categories as romance or tragicomedy.

The Fletcherian collaborations might also be seen as a second stage of Shakespearean romance. Although these last plays share with the earlier romances the assertion of a providential plan, they transmute or eliminate the long temporal vistas previously necessary to the transcendence of tragedy. The final three works thus reduce the thematic depth of divine guidance—the sense that redemption is granted for effort, patience, and suffering, that though the bad may not always be punished, the good are always rewarded. The *Cardenio* story urges patience and the need to trust in time, but the assertions are metaphorical: things are quickly tidied up. *The Two Noble Kinsmen* offers a world of timeless serenity when Palamon and Arcite are first imprisoned, but the ordinary world of time means suffering without redemption. The two works lack the vertical perspective of the preceding romances, instead reverting to the horizontal structure of the still earlier problem plays. *Henry VIII* seems different. The passage of the years is instrumental in delivering the happy ending, as in the first four romances. But the role of time is less emphasized. And for whom is the ending happy? Not for anyone who has suffered along the way, with the limited and temporary exception of Archbishop Cranmer. Certainly not for Henry VIII, who always gets what he wants, who both does and does not seem responsible for what goes wrong, and whose tortured conscience over his marriage to Catharine is treated with amused skepticism. In other words, *Henry VIII* is a romance on the model of the earlier plays only if its protagonist is England itself. This plausible conclusion implies, however, the workings of a more austerely impersonal providence than is found in *Pericles, Cymbeline, The Winter's Tale,* and *The Tempest.*

What is true of time also holds for space. The problematic providentialism and foreshortened temporality of the final three plays may be connected to a geographical narrowing of the plot. Each of these works is confined to a single country. Gone, except metaphorically, are the perilous sea journeys of the immediately preceding years. Spatial breadth thus goes the way of temporal depth. The characters' problems are as grave as those in the previous romances, but both human and providential action seems constricted. These landlocked plays may suggest that the initial enthusiasm over the Virginia colony proved difficult to sustain. In retrospect, *The Tempest* appears both to justify and repudiate colonialism. Prospero's decision to leave the island parallels his rejection of magic: both acknowledge limits. Thereafter, although the colonial enterprise may be celebrated, as it is in *Henry VIII,* it is no longer represented. *Cardenio, Henry VIII,* and *The Two Noble Kinsmen* accordingly constitute a second movement within Shakespearean romance that reconfigures the entire sequence of plays that begins with *Pericles.*

The same point can be made of characterization. In *The Tempest,* Prospero, despite his failings, is clearly associated with providence. In the succeeding plays, he is replaced by far weaker providential figures—Duke Angelo in *Cardenio,* Henry VIII, Duke Theseus in *The Two Noble Kinsmen.* Similarly, daughters lose their redemptive role. Their marriages fail to connote the projection forward, much less the dynastic projection forward, of the family in time. In *Cardenio,* although the fathers are gladdened by the return of their children, the emotional force of the resolution arises overwhelmingly from the pairing off of the young lovers. In *The Two Noble Kinsmen,* Emilia becomes an object of contention and hence a source of destruction rather than reconciliation. Even Elizabeth doesn't save Henry in *Henry VIII.* He doesn't need saving, and in any case she's a mere babe at the end of the play and never marries. *Henry VIII* instead proceeds by homonyms, celebrating the marriage of King James's daughter Elizabeth as a substitute for actual familial continuity.

Symptomatically, the actual weddings are transformed from festive into tearful affairs. The hearse in *Cardenio* arrives just before the lovers' reunion. Henry's marriage to Anne in *Henry VIII* entails the rejection of Catharine and in the event her death. *The Two Noble Kinsmen* opens with the interruption of Theseus and Hippolyta's nuptials by the lamentations of the three widowed queens, is followed by the appearance of Palamon and Arcite on "*two hearses*" (biers, 1.4.0 SD), and ends by echoing its beginning, as the marriage of Palamon and Emilia competes with the mourning for Arcite. The scaling back of the young women's symbolic significance also accords with a casual attitude toward premarital sex. If *Cardenio* follows Cervantes, Dorotea consents to intercourse because she believes the false promises of a cad; if it corresponds to Theobald, she is raped. Either way, she loses her virginity. In the subplot of *The Two Noble Kinsmen,* the Doctor cures the Jailer's Daughter of madness by sending her to bed with someone she mistakenly believes to be Palamon. And in *Henry VIII,* Anne Boleyn's sexual modesty is treated with irreverence by the Old Lady who waits on her—an irreverence the audience is invited to share.

The last three plays also offer a darker view of violence and death than the previous romances. In *The Tempest,* no one dies. The same is true of *Cardenio.* But the near rape of Miranda by Caliban is replaced by the real rape of Dorotea/Violante by Fernando/Henriquez—a rape for which the perpetrator suffers mild pangs of conscience, fleeting public embarrassment, and the felicity of familial approval and wedded bliss. In *Pericles* and *Cymbeline,* although all who are vicious do not necessarily die, all who die are necessarily vicious. In *The Winter's Tale,* Leontes' son perishes because Leontes must be punished, and Antigonus dies because he has nobly risked everything to save Leontes' daughter, Perdita. Here too, then, death is part of an ethical calculus. In *Henry VIII,* however, morality and mortality are randomly related. Buckingham, Wolsey, and Catharine must be removed so that Elizabeth can come to power. Catharine is the finest person in the play, but her death represents neither a voluntary sacrifice for the benefit of England nor a punishment of Henry for his misdeeds. And in *The Two Noble Kinsmen,* Palamon and Arcite seem morally equivalent. Hence, Arcite's death feels at best random, at worst a cruel trick played by providence on shell-shocked mortals. Theseus's assertion of divine wisdom accordingly seems desperate and unconvincing.

In short, the final three plays reveal a growing pessimism, a bleaker outlook, a grimmer universe, a declining belief in the possibility of transcending tragedy. It is unclear how this development relates to the apparently greater tolerance for Catholicism suggested by the Spanish setting of *Cardenio,* unique in Shakespeare's oeuvre, and the admiring treatment of Catharine of Aragon in *Henry VIII*. Perhaps the point is that "all is true," that everyone is right. Both Catharine and Anne are celebrated. But Anne's victory comes in this world, Catharine's only in the next. In other words, this is merely a disguised form of the either-or logic characteristic of all three of the final plays: either Anne or Catharine, either Palamon or Arcite, either Protestants or Catholics. And in an additional sign of the reduced capaciousness of these works, their inability to integrate all the virtuous characters and more, the losers must die.

Finally, the successive views presented here of Shakespearean romance—as a continuation of the comedies, as a distinct and coherent category, and as an internally divided one—are by no means incompatible. They merely provide different ways into the subject. And even these three models are hardly exhaustive. In recent criticism, one finds signs of a rethinking of romance that goes beyond the juxtaposition of the four sole-authored plays with the three collaborative ones. The move here is chronological: the object of inquiry becomes the common features of the plays Shakespeare composed in the last part of his career, regardless of genre. Several more works then enter the picture. First, *All's Well That Ends Well,* long seen as a problem play or tragicomedy, comes into the orbit of the romances thanks to a growing scholarly consensus that dates it to 1606–07 and hence places it closer to *Pericles* than to either of the two earlier problem plays. Second, *Coriolanus* (1608), actually composed after *Pericles*, provides evidence of overlap with the standard romances. Third, the plausible conjecture that the First Folio prints a version of *King Lear* that Shakespeare himself revised around 1610 opens the possibility of seeing the changes from the earlier quarto text (composed 1605) as indicative of a shift in the playwright's outlook, again toward romance. Similarly, the distance *Antony and Cleopatra* travels from the earlier tragedies may be a sign of a transition from one dramatic genre to the next. So far, these are merely straws in the wind. In time, they could acquire greater significance. But at the very least, they indicate that a broad approach to the romances should be open to all of these perspectives—and more.

## SELECTED BIBLIOGRAPHY


Alexander, Catherine M. S., ed. *Shakespeare's Last Plays.* Cambridge: Cambridge UP, 2009. Discusses various contexts—artistic, historical—for understanding the final six romances and tragicomedies, while also providing accounts of the later fortunes of these plays.

Cooper, Helen. *The English Romance in Time: Transforming Motifs from Geoffrey of Monmouth to the Death of Shakespeare.* Oxford: Oxford UP, 2004. Explores the changing use in medieval and Renaissance English literature of standard romance tropes—quests, providence and the sea, magic, fairy monarchs, eroticism and misogyny, foundling heirs, and the threat of tragedy.

Leggatt, Alexander, ed. *The Cambridge Companion to Shakespearean Comedy.* Cambridge: Cambridge UP, 2002. Includes essays on Italian backgrounds of romantic comedy and romance and on the innovations of romance.

McDonald, Russ. *Shakespeare's Late Style.* Cambridge: Cambridge UP, 2006. Finds in the distinctive features of "Shakespeare's late style"—ellipsis, suppressed logical connectives, convoluted syntax, parenthetical interruption, repetition, irregular blank verse, rapidly shifting metaphors—parallels to the generic innovations of the plays.

McMullan, Gordon. *Shakespeare and the Idea of Late Writing.* Cambridge: Cambridge UP, 2007. Provides a skeptical account of the critical construction over the past two centuries of the transhistorical category of an artist's late style, in Shakespeare and beyond, arguing that the notion is incompatible with the conditions of early modern theatrical production.

Palfrey, Simon. *Late Shakespeare: A New World of Words.* Oxford: Clarendon P, 1997. Argues against conventional readings that stress the providentialism, elitism, and royalism of the four main romances in favor of emphasis on verbal, generic, and political complexity and dissonance.

Power, Andrew J., and Rory Loughnane, eds. *Late Shakespeare, 1608-1613.* Cambridge: Cambridge UP, 2013. Offers essays on the final seven extant plays—including, notably, *Coriolanus*—as well as on broader topics: performance and publication, language, actors, cities, King James, religion, and magic and gender.

Richards, Jennifer, and James Knowles, eds. *Shakespeare's Late Plays: New Readings.* Edinburgh: Edinburgh UP, 1999. Helps establish a new direction for scholarship by grouping the four standard romances with the three collaborations with Fletcher—*The Two Noble Kinsmen, Henry VIII,* and *Cardenio.*

Ryan, Kiernan, ed. *Shakespeare: The Last Plays.* London: Longman, 1999. Collects leading essays from 1980 to the mid-1990s on the four main romances from various theoretical perspectives.

Smith, Stephen W., and Travis Curtright, eds. *Shakespeare's Last Plays: Essays in Literature and Politics.* Lanham, MD: Lexington Books, 2002. Explores the four romances and *Henry VIII* from a variety of vantage points, including political theory, philosophy, theology, and classical literature.

# Pericles

*Pericles, Prince of Tyre* (1607–08) was one of the most popular plays of its time and has proven effective in modern productions as well. Coherent and innovative, it brought a new dramatic genre—romance—into Shakespeare's work and, arguably, onto the English stage in general. As a written text, however, *Pericles* has proven problematic. It is not clear whether the difficulty is intrinsic to the play or results from a tendency to interpret it in light of Shakespeare's earlier works and thus to make unwarranted assumptions about plot, characterization, morality, dramaturgy, and style. Does the romance pattern succeed in mastering the play's messy materials? Does the play raise but not resolve social, political, and sexual anxieties, despite its structural and thematic unity? Are these even the right questions to ask?

Shakespeare's younger contemporary Ben Jonson spoke for many subsequent critics in disparaging *Pericles* as "a mouldy tale . . . and stale" and in attributing its success on the stage to its use of "scraps out of every dish." It is easy to see why. In *Pericles,* a king adorns his palace walls with his victims' skulls. A princess commits incest with her father. Another princess is kidnapped by pirates and sold to a brothel. Famine brings a city to its knees. An entire crew is lost in a storm. Two royal families are sent to fiery destruction. And Pericles is almost deposed by members of his restless nobility.

From the perspective of genre, *Pericles* enacts a transition from one kind of romance to another. Pericles first looks like a knight-errant risking death to win the beautiful maiden. But this standard medieval romance plot quickly gives way to late antique Greek romance narrative, in which faithful, virtuous lovers suffer separation and misfortune before their triumphant reunion. Pericles, then, does not act; he is acted upon. Bad things (as well as good) just happen to him. Every member of his family narrowly escapes death: two evade assassins sent by murderous monarchs, and the third survives burial at sea. Each is reported dead, only to experience apparently miraculous rebirth. The play eschews the probing of the protagonist's psyche that marks Shakespeare's immediately preceding tragic period in favor of clear-cut moral oppositions and emphatic poetic justice. By its end, the good are rewarded and the bad annihilated, but generally not owing to the protagonist's efforts.

Indeed, Pericles does not even get to act out significant portions of his destiny. Much of the story is told by Gower, the onstage presence of the fourteenth-century writer John Gower, whose major work, *Confessio Amantis,* is the most important direct source of *Pericles.* The eighth book of this verse narrative is devoted primarily to the tale of Apollonius of Tyre, which, via medieval intermediaries dating back to a fifth- or sixth-century Latin text, derives from a now-lost late classical Latin or, more probably, Greek romance influenced by *The Odyssey.* A different route through the medieval sources, this time incorporating the lives of early Christian saints who suffered persecution in brothels, leads to the other proximate source of the play, Laurence Twine's *Pattern of Painful Adventures* (written by 1576; published 1594?). *Pericles* is the first dramatization of these lengthy traditions. The shift in the protagonist's name from "Apollonius" to "Pericles" may derive from still other strains in the Apollonius tradition; from Sir Philip Sidney's *Arcadia* (1590), one of whose protagonists is named Pyrocles; or from one of Shakespeare's favorite sources, Plutarch's *Lives,* which perhaps provides still other characters' names. In addition to praising the renowned fifth-century B.C.E. Athenian statesman Pericles—head of the most famous of ancient city-states and

The true Hiſtory of the Play of Pericles, as it was lately preſented by the worthy and an-cient Poet John Gower.
John
Gower.

Woodcut of John Gower, from the title page of *The Painful Adventures of Pericles Prince of Tyre,* by George Wilkins (1608).

hence appropriate to the play's world of city-states—it harshly judges his rival and successor, Cleon, as well as the fourth-century B.C.E. general Lysimachus, all names of characters in the play.

*Pericles* follows its sources more faithfully than do many of Shakespeare's works—for instance, by retaining an episodic plot. More striking still is the appearance of Gower himself as a character. His role as Chorus is broadly anticipated in *Henry V* (1599), but Gower also gives a specifically (pseudo-) medieval feel to the action—a feel connected to the antiquarian efforts of the time to recover the distant origins of England. Although Gower eventually reverts to standard pentameter lines, he starts out primarily in the rhymed tetrameter couplets in which *Confessio Amantis* is written: "To sing a song that old was sung / From ashes ancient Gower is come" (1.0.1–2). In addition, the theatrical Gower's diction often echoes the medieval poet's, extending even to antiquated language ("iwis" for "certainly," for example, at 2.0.2). His moralizing speeches are frequently graced by an unrealistic theatrical device—the dumb show. Further, Gower recounts much of the action in his eight monologues, as if to emphasize that poet's authorship of what sometimes feels like narrative, rather than dramatic, material. These metatheatrical strategies undermine the naturalistic illusion of the play, encouraging the audience to view events from a distance, to grasp the larger pattern rather than becoming emotionally engaged. Yet *Pericles* ultimately elicits that emotional engagement as well.

Gower's monologues structure the play more effectively than does the division into five acts introduced by later editors. The scene often shifts within each of the seven main groupings, but there is always a central focus. Gower introduces Antioch and incest (1.0), Pentapolis and Pericles' wooing of Thaisa (2.0), Ephesus and the saving of Thaisa (3.0), Tarsus and the attempted murder of Marina (4.0), Mytilene and Marina's virtuous life in the brothel (4.4), Mytilene again and Marina's reunion with Pericles (5.0), and Ephesus and the reunion with Thaisa (5.2), before providing the brief, concluding Epilogue.

The problematic authorship of *Pericles* is treated in the Textual Introduction. In brief, George Wilkins probably wrote at least the first two acts and Shakespeare most of the remaining three. The stylistic differences between the two parts of the play have long been recognized. Wilkins's dialogue is closer to Gower's language than is Shakespeare's. He also uses far more end-stopped rhyming couplets than does Shakespeare. By contrast, Shakespeare's predilection for blank-verse enjambment, in which the phrase or idea does not conclude at the end of the line, produces a tension between syntax and verse form.

Thus, Wilkins's Pericles decorously repudiates the incestuous Daughter of Antiochus:

> Fair glass of light, I loved you, and could still,
> Were not this glorious casket stored with ill.

. . . . . . . . . . . . . . . . . . . . . . . . . . . . . . . . . . . . . .
For he's no man on whom perfections wait
That, knowing sin within, will touch the gate.
. . . . . . . . . . . . . . . . . . . . . . . . . . . . . . . . . . . . . .
But being played upon before your time,
Hell only danceth at so harsh a chime.
(1.1.77–86)

Shakespeare's Pericles reacts to a storm in more complex but also more colloquial verse:

Oh, still
Thy deafening dreadful thunders; gently quench
Thy nimble sulphurous flashes! . . .
. . . . . . . . . . . . . . . . . . . . . . . . . . . . . . . . . . . . . .
. . . The seaman's whistle
Is as a whisper in the ears of death,
Unheard. —Lychorida! —Lucina, O
Divinest patroness and midwife gentle
To those that cry by night, convey thy deity
Aboard our dancing boat, make swift the pangs
Of my queen's travails! —Now, Lychorida!
(3.1.4–14)

As a result, Shakespeare's section of the play is theatrically livelier, the contrast with Gower's increasingly frequent monologues sharper. Pericles' meeting with the Fishermen is Wilkins's only episode of a piece with such later parts of the play as the second tempest; the revival of Pericles' wife, Thaisa; the two brothel scenes; and the first recognition scene. And structurally, *Pericles* breaks neatly in two: in the first two acts, Pericles moves from felicity to misfortune and back to felicity; in the remaining three, he repeats this pattern more intensely.

Yet such distinctions are misleading. Many Renaissance plays were written by more than one dramatist; Shakespeare collaborated on about a fifth of his plays, mostly near the beginning and end of his career. Especially in performance, such works do not necessarily seem any less unified than single-author pieces. Even though its "feel" shifts, *Pericles*' motifs remain consistent—Pericles as noble tree, his jewel-like family, destructive eating, providential storms, divine music.

Its episodes also echo one another, within and across the play's two parts. The deadly skulls at Antiochus's palace are answered by the harmless jousting at Simonides' court; the bad potential marriage to Antiochus's Daughter is echoed by the good real one to Simonides'. The incestuous relationship between Antiochus and his Daughter is contrasted with the lovingly innocent one between Pericles and Marina. Thaliard's foiled attempt to assassinate Pericles at Antiochus's behest anticipates Leonine's failed effort to murder Marina at Dionyza's. Cleon calls down the "curse of heaven and men" (1.4.103) should his family prove ungrateful to Pericles, and when his family does so prove, "him and his they [his subjects] in his palace burn" (Epilogue 14). The storm that costs Pericles his men but leads him to Thaisa is paralleled by the later tempest that apparently disposes of Thaisa. The vigorous popular culture of the Fishermen is set against the degraded popular culture of the brothel. The vow of chastity that Simonides attributes to Thaisa to dismiss all her suitors except Pericles is fulfilled in her vow of chastity when she thinks Pericles is gone forever and in Marina's successful defense of her chastity in the brothel. The apparent burial of Thaisa is duplicated in the apparent interment of her daughter. And the excessive love of Antiochus for his daughter and, in a different way, of Dionyza for hers contrasts with the defective love of Cleon for his daughter and, arguably, of Pericles for Marina—until the end of the play, when Pericles demonstrates the appropriate love of father for daughter.

Throughout, the play insists that the miseries inflicted on Pericles and his family ultimately lead to higher felicity. As noted earlier, this is the structure of tragicomic romance, the genre of nearly all of Shakespeare's final plays. Typically, *Pericles* recapitulates Shakespeare's previous work while reversing its chronology: the tragic mood of the early seventeenth century precedes the comic tone of the 1590s. The play echoes *King Lear* in its storm scenes and its reunion of ravaged father and redemptive daughter, who gives "another life / To Pericles thy father" (5.1.196–97); it then duplicates *The Comedy of Errors,* which draws on the same sources as *Pericles* in its concluding retrieval of the missing wife-turned-priestess from Diana's temple at Ephesus.

Gower emphasizes this larger pattern—"I'll show you those in troubles reign, / Losing a mite, a mountain gain" (2.0.7–8)—which becomes especially prominent in Shakespeare's scenes owing to Diana's presiding benevolence. She is first mentioned when, according to Simonides, Thaisa opts for continued virginity (2.5.10). Thaisa invokes her upon awakening in an opened coffin (3.2.102–03), as does Pericles when he vows not to cut his hair until his baby, Marina, is married (3.3.28–30). Thaisa becomes Diana's priestess (3.4.12, 4.0.4), and Marina places her virginity in the goddess's protection (4.2.136). Finally, after Pericles is reunited with Marina, Diana appears to him in a dream, promising him happiness only if he goes to her temple in Ephesus and publicly recounts his loss of Thaisa (5.1.226–36). This supernatural moment recalls Thaisa's quasi-magical preservation by Cerimon (of whom Pericles says, "The gods can have no mortal officer / More like a god than you," 5.3.62–63), anticipates Pericles' actual meeting with Thaisa in the final scene (where Diana is repeatedly mentioned), and follows hard upon Pericles' perhaps unique ability to hear "the music of the spheres" (5.1.217)—a heavenly harmony that extends to human affairs below. Sensitivity to music has marked Pericles' family throughout.

The Temple of Diana at Ephesus (from the series The Eight Wonders of the World) after Maarten van Heemskerck, 1572. Found in the collection of the Museum Boijmans Van Beuningen, Rotterdam.

Pericles is "music's master," Thaisa awakens to "rough and woeful music," and, most telling, Marina "sings like one immortal" (2.5.30, 3.2.86, 5.0.3).

These signs of a divine providence guiding the destiny of Pericles' family are pagan in form but Christian in content. They draw on Catholic traditions, only partially reworked along Protestant lines. Tragicomedy's movement from tribulation to triumph is modeled on the *felix culpa,* Adam and Eve's fortunate fall that led to the redemptive coming of Christ. Antioch recalls Eden's sinister side: Pericles will "taste the fruit of yon celestial tree / Or die in th'adventure"; Antiochus praises the "golden fruit, but dangerous to be touched" and later warns, "touch not, upon thy life" (1.1.22–23, 29, 88). *Pericles*' eastern Mediterranean of late Greek antiquity also evokes Judaism and early Christianity. Tyre, connected with the reigns of David and Solomon, was later captured by the Christians in the First Crusade and was seen during the Renaissance as the home of Britain's first colonizers. Antioch recalls the Maccabee rebellion; in addition, Peter and Paul preached there. Paul was born in Tarsus and had a ministry in Ephesus. The Fishermen of Pentapolis are literally, like St. Peter, fishers of men. Amid talk of devouring whales (2.1.28–42), they fish out Pericles, whom "the sea hath cast upon [their] coast" (2.1.55) in a manner that recalls the biblical Jonah, understood in Christian allegory to prefigure Christ's resurrection. Thaisa later undergoes a similar resurrection; and at Mytilene, the Pander laments, "Neither is our profession any . . . calling" (4.2.35)—where "calling" has religious reverberations.

In a final, typically moralistic speech, Gower tells the audience:

> In Pericles, his queen, and daughter seen,
> Although assailed with fortune fierce and keen,
> Virtue preserved from fell destruction's blast,
> Led on by heaven and crowned with joy at last.
> (Epilogue 3–6)

Although there is no ambiguity here, the play as a whole leaves room for doubts. Despite the triumph over a pagan "fortune" by an implicitly Christian "heaven," Pericles' sufferings feel arbitrary. It is hard to understand, except by fairy-tale logic, why his predecessors cannot solve Antiochus's riddle or why the King advertises the very secret he wants to preserve. Similarly, the play does not explain why Pericles leaves his daughter at Tarsus or why Dionyza, eager to be rid of Marina, does not consider sending her home instead of murdering her. More important, the misfortunes in *Pericles* seem unrelenting, unconnected, and unrelated to the behavior of their victims. Yet this disjunction fails to inspire any Job-like reflections on injustice. In short, divine providence is not fully integrated with secular misfortune. Perhaps the play reveals a contingent relationship between human vicissitude and redemptive transcendence, thereby unsettling its own ostensible program.

Second, *Pericles* bears a complicated relationship to its social and political material. Popular culture provides some of the play's most engaging scenes without, however, linking up to the larger movement of the plot. The initial storm leaves Pericles "[be]reft of ships and men" (2.3.81). The Fishermen who help him receive his praise:

> FIRST FISHERMAN . . . I can compare our rich misers to nothing so fitly as to a whale; 'a plays and tumbles, driving the poor fry before him, and at last devours them all at a mouthful. . . .
> PERICLES [*aside*] A pretty moral. (2.1.29–35)

This account, which may echo the language of the 1607 Midlands Uprising against landlord enclosures of the common lands, leads to a rebuke of the monarch: "if the good King Simonides were of my mind . . . We would purge the land of these drones that rob the bee of her honey" (2.1.42–46). But the complaint quickly disappears, leaving only the positive image of Pericles' future father-in-law. Similarly, although

Pericles promises the fishermen "if that ever my low fortune's better, / I'll pay your bounties; till then, rest your debtor" (2.1.140–41), the debt, which is usually honored in previous tales of Apollonius (including Twine's), is not recalled when Pericles' fortunes quickly improve.

The anticommercial outlook implicit in the Fisherman's denunciation of "rich misers" also informs the brothel scenes, which, like Pericles' encounter with the Fishermen, peoples the Greek Mediterranean setting with English characters. Prostitution is the only market-driven activity depicted in the play. The Bawd advises Marina in economic terms: "You have fortunes coming upon you. Mark me: you must seem to do that fearfully which you commit willingly, despise profit where you have most gain. To weep that you live as ye do makes pity in your lovers. Seldom but that pity begets you a good opinion, and that opinion a mere profit" (4.2.105–10). Marina is thus urged to perform like an actor in London's professional theaters. With commerce almost reduced to the oldest profession, a profession practiced in the neighborhoods around the theaters, the play implicitly links itself to the very activity that it depicts Marina nobly resisting.

Further, despite exploiting popular culture for theatrical effect, *Pericles* excludes that culture from the final reconciliation, concluding with a purely aristocratic and royal circle. This ending is tacitly anticipated by the linguistic divisions of the popular scenes: the Fishermen and brothel-keepers speak prose, whereas Pericles and Marina favor blank verse. Nevertheless, *Pericles* is the only Shakespearean romance written before the King's Men began performing during the winter at Blackfriars, a "private," elite, commercial theater. It was acted at the Globe, the preeminent "public" theater, and its success in the early seventeenth century attests to the at least partly popular appeal of its traditional romance plot.

*Pericles* also seems critical of absolute monarchy. This makes sense: the value of such leadership is questionable. Antioch has been ruled by an incestuous murderer, with no indication of his successor. The Governor of Tarsus lets his city slip into famine; his wife is an attempted murderer. Although the inhabitants eventually kill the couple, their own earlier behavior does not inspire confidence: "All poverty was scorned, and pride so great, / The name of help grew odious to repeat" (1.4.30–31). Under duress, they are even worse:

> Those mothers who to nuzzle up their babes
> Thought naught too curious are ready now
> To eat those little darlings whom they loved.
> (1.4.42–44)

The passage echoes in reverse the riddle's equation of cannibalism with incest—"I feed / On mother's flesh" (1.1.65–66)—while also recalling other moments where "to eat" is to devour. The Fishermen express dissatisfaction with the state of things, which their good King does nothing to remedy. Ephesus's future remains unspecified: Lord Cerimon acts as a private figure. Lysimachus, the Governor of Mytilene, frequents a brothel until Marina converts him; at the play's end, the brothel remains, while Lysimachus, betrothed to Marina, leaves Mytilene in uncertain hands and goes off to rule Tyre. In so doing, does he bring syphilis into Pericles' family? The verbal juxtapositions upon his initial entry allow for this possibility: "there's no way to be rid on't [Marina's virginity] but by the way to the pox [syphilis]. Here comes the Lord Lysimachus disguised" (4.6.13–14).

Earlier, Pericles' departure from Tyre inspires aristocratic "mutiny" (3.0.29) and begins the practice of absentee landlordism that reaches its climax near the end when his deputy, Helicanus, appoints Escanes as *his* deputy and sets out with Pericles. Shortly thereafter, Pericles and Thaisa accede to the throne of Pentapolis, a society whose defects the Fishermen have dissected. The death of Thaisa's father, "the good Simonides," is not an occasion for grief but an opportunity to dole out kingdoms and divide a family only just reunited. This outcome may parallel the isolation of James I's family members, an isolation emblematized by James's failure to come to the deathbeds of two of his children. Pericles' absenteeism could also reflect on James's style of governing. Alternatively, it might simply recognize the necessity of intergenerational separation for dynastic continuity, just as Marina's redemptive role may reflect upon Shakespeare's relationship with his own daughter.

Here, *Pericles* also raises sexual doubts. Although the protagonists are subjected to debased sexuality only to demonstrate their Diana-like purity, perhaps they do not escape unpolluted. In Gower's *Confessio Amantis,* Pericles' daughter is not Marina but Thaisa. From an extradramatic perspective, then, sexual relations with Thaisa, which in Gower would have been incest, become appropriate marital intimacy. It is as if the name change allowed Pericles to have the experience castigated in Antioch under the protection of the marriage bond. When the catatonic Pericles reaches Mytilene, Lysimachus agrees that Marina might be the cure:

> She questionless, with her sweet harmony
> And other choice attractions, would allure
> And make a batt'ry through his deafened ports.
> (5.1.37–39)

Hence, Lysimachus, ignorant of Marina's parentage, suggests through "choice attractions" and "allure" an unfamilial relationship between father and daughter. So, too, does Pericles. He addresses Marina as "Thou that begett'st him that did thee beget" (5.1.185)—a line that expresses gratitude but that also recalls the generational reversals of Antiochus's incestuous riddle: "He's father, son, and husband mild; / I, mother, wife, and yet his child" (1.1.69–70).

Tragicomic romance often provides a nontragic resolution to the tale of Oedipus, Pericles' predecessor in solving murderous riddles. Do Pericles' words to Marina reverse or repeat Antiochus's riddle? Ambiguities such as this one trouble the providential pattern. By name, Pericles recalls an Athenian virtue at odds with the quasi-allegorical landscape through which he travels, a landscape of Asiatic luxury and decadence, of an incest associated with tyranny whose primary alternative seems to be anarchy. In other words, the various social, political, and sexual ambiguities of *Pericles* bear less on the psychology or morality of the protagonist than on the overall import of the play.

Modern performances of *Pericles* embrace the challenge posed by this pattern. Although some productions attempt naturalistic settings and complex characters, most respect *Pericles*' indifference to such matters by exploiting what's unrealistic about the play and Renaissance theater generally. The doubling of parts has led to the same actress playing Antiochus's Daughter and Marina, Marina and Thaisa, or Thaisa and Dionyza. This procedure can accentuate the differences between the paired characters; more often, however, it generates overtones of incest. Relatedly, when one actor plays all the Mediterranean kings, the stage captures the similarity, the repetitiousness, of Pericles' adventures and, hence, the ritualistic quality of the work. Second, although Gower can establish intimacy between audience and action, the tendency has been to follow the German dramatist Bertolt Brecht in resisting empathy and identification. Gower's role thus underscores the play's theatricality: it has been sung, treated as a voice-over, and played by a street performer. The dramatized action itself has been represented as street theater, as the work of a traveling troupe, as Chinese opera, as an African American boatswain's sea chantey to his fellow sailors aboard ship, as a child's picture book, as events in an asylum, as the floor show in a gay brothel. Sometimes the result is an ironic, farcical approach to the plot's absurdities. The price, however, is the failure of the climactic recognition scenes, which thrive on psychological nuance. Similar problems may arise with overtly political interpretations, though a feminist or multiethnic perspective can be suggestive. Perhaps the solution is to refuse to level the unevenness of the play, remaining faithful to its various registers.

WALTER COHEN

## SELECTED BIBLIOGRAPHY

Frye, Susan. "Incest and Authority in *Pericles, Prince of Tyre.*" *Incest and the Literary Imagination.* Ed. Elizabeth Barnes. Gainesville: UP of Florida, 2002. 39–58. Focuses on three key scenes (incest, tournament, reunion) to argue that incest—understood physically, politically, and psychologically—is tied to questions of the royal family's legitimacy.

Gossett, Suzanne. "'You not your child well loving': Text and Family Structure in *Pericles.*" *A Companion to Shakespeare's Works.* Vol. 4: *Poems, Problem Comedies, Late Plays.* Ed. Richard Dutton and Jean E. Howard. Malden, MA: Blackwell, 2003. 348–64. Treats the play as an exploration of the proper love between parent and daughter (neither excessive nor deficient), perhaps rooted in Shakespeare's own family experience.

Halpern, Richard. *Shakespeare among the Moderns.* Ithaca, NY: Cornell UP, 1997. 140–58. Explores the weak internal causal logic of the plot combined with the transcendent romance plan as a symptomatic response to the decaying older social order.

Healy, Margaret. "*Pericles* and the Pox." *Shakespeare's Late Plays: New Readings.* Ed. Jennifer Richards and James Knowles. Edinburgh: Edinburgh UP, 1999. 92–107. Argues that the original audience, recognizing that Lysimachus carried venereal disease, would have been horrified by the marriage of Marina to pox-ridden Lysimachus.

Hiscock, Andrew. "*Pericles, Prince of Tyre* and the Appetite for Narrative." *Late Shakespeare, 1608–1613.* Ed. Andrew J. Power and Rory Loughnane. Cambridge: Cambridge UP, 2013. 16–36. Considers the importance of narrative at the expense of character, with Gower and, later, Marina as the key narrators among many.

Orkin, Martin. *Local Shakespeares: Proximations and Power.* London: Routledge, 2005. 63–81. Describes *Pericles* as a meditation on male unruliness, in this way providing a partial critique of its own patriarchal romance resolution.

Roebuck, Thomas, and Laurie Maguire. "*Pericles* and the Language of National Origins." *This England, That Shakespeare: New Angles on Englishness and the Bard.* Ed. Willy Maley and Margaret Tudeau-Clayton. Farnham, Surrey: Ashgate, 2010. 23–48. Examines the play's pattern of loss and recovery as a means of constructing national identity through, for instance, Gower's link with Welsh and Catholic heritages, or Phoenicians as the original settlers of Britain.

Skeele, David, ed. *"Pericles": Critical Essays.* New York: Garland, 2000. A collection of criticism beginning with Ben Jonson in the early seventeenth century and of theatrical reviews beginning in the mid-nineteenth. Modern critics include Knight, Felperin, Barber and Wheeler, Kahn, Mullaney, Adelman, and Novy, among others.

Tanner, Tony. *Prefaces to Shakespeare.* Cambridge: Harvard UP, 2010. 695–721. Presents a general interpretation of the play focusing on the relationship between father and daughter and drawing on religion (saints' lives, pagan gods) and ritual (incest and cannibalism taboos).

Werth, Tiffany Jo. *The Fabulous Dark Cloister: Romance in England after the Reformation.* Baltimore, MD: Johns Hopkins UP, 2011. 80–96. Explores *Pericles* as a romance drawing on the tradition of saints' miracles, treated in Catholic terms in Thaisa's resurrection, in Protestant terms in Marina's behavior, and ambiguously in the conclusion at Diana's temple.

### Film

*Pericles, Prince of Tyre.* 1984. Dir. David Hugh Jones. UK. 177 min. Generally praised BBC production, naturalistic by TV-studio standards but not by those of big-budget movies.

## TEXTUAL INTRODUCTION

Since *Pericles* was not printed in the Folio of 1623, the basis for all editions is the quarto published by Henry Gosson in 1609 (Q1). This was the work of two printing houses and three different compositors, which speeded up the process and helped spread employment but seems to have led to a poor printing job, perhaps because Gosson's workmen had never printed a play before. The mixture of verse and prose made it hard to estimate how many lines to allocate to each sheet, and verse is sometimes set as prose to save space. Speech prefixes and stage directions seem to have been written in italics, and the compositors could not always tell the one from the other, sometimes omitting speech prefixes altogether. But while some of the textual problems may result from compositor error, others are consistent across the work of all three compositors and probably originated with complex manuscript copy.

Differences in literary quality between the first two acts and the rest led the play's earliest editors to suggest that the play might be collaborative. Recent studies, particularly those of MacDonald P. Jackson, argue that at least the first two acts are by George Wilkins, a minor writer. His part of *Pericles* shares mannerisms with his other writings, not least a tendency to omit relative pronouns for the sake of meter (e.g., the implied "what" in "Since I have here my father gave in his will" [2.1.132]).

The King's Men had originally registered the play with the Stationers' Company in 1608, the same year that Wilkins published a prose novel called *The Painful Adventures of Pericles Prince of Tyre, Being the True History of the Play of Pericles, as it was lately presented by the worthy and ancient Poet John Gower,* which begins, like a play, with a cast of characters and presents itself as "the book of the play" successfully performed "by the Kings Majesties Players." It may be that the publication of a pamphlet claiming a direct connection made it difficult for the company to proceed with publication of their play, and scholars believe that the manuscript Gosson used was not the official playbook.

One view is that the manuscript was based on what "reporters" could remember about the play in performance. Actors in Shakespeare's theaters received only their own "parts," consisting of lines and cues; the authors may have retained only the sections of the play they themselves had written. Judging by the lines apparently best remembered, Gary Taylor has suggested that the main "reporter" was a boy actor playing Lychorida, Marina, and the Third Fisherman. If this boy were apprenticed to the actor playing Gower, this might explain why the choruses seem mostly accurate. However, this theory assumes that the boy actor was "fired" when his voice broke or because of the frequent plague closures of the public theaters between 1604 and 1611. The King's Men continued to play privately, however, and a boy good enough to play leading female roles might have tried to sustain his career. The evidence is not clear-cut. The boy's absence from the scenes at Tyre could explain their incoherence, but not the apparent discrepancy at 4.6, where Lysimachus first behaves like a familiar visitor to the brothel and then rapidly backtracks.

The culprit may be Wilkins. That he had already published with Gosson raises suspicions: *The Painful Adventures* may be an attempt to make money out of a play that had been a huge financial success for the King's Men while earning its co-writer only a flat fee. However, certain misreadings do seem to be the result of mishearing and are less likely to come from Wilkins than from someone taking down the lines in shorthand. And it remains possible that the manuscript behind Gosson's edition came from the King's Men themselves. If they could not print the play without Gosson lodging a complaint against them for harming sales of the Wilkins novel, they may have decided to cut their losses by selling the play to him. If so, then the manuscript might have been copied quickly and carelessly, and there may also have been censorship, particularly in the scenes at Tyre that suggest a threat of mutiny among Pericles' subjects. The scene between Lysimachus and Marina might have been revised to avoid showing a man in high office visiting a brothel.

The main question for an editor is how much—or *how*—to use the Wilkins novel. Directors have often drawn on it to supplement the text in performance; some editors have printed passages from it in footnotes or appendices, and the Oxford edition "reconstructed" the play by importing material from the novel into both dialogue and stage directions. The first part of *The Painful Adventures* can help clarify the first two acts of the play, which are often verbally close to it (the novel even falls into blank verse at times). Unlike the play, the novel gives full details about the five princes who compete with Pericles in the tournament. Some editions and productions transfer this information to the speeches of Thaisa and Simonides, assuming that the ritual presentation remains consistent throughout, yet it is possible that the scene was deliberately truncated to avoid repetition. Additions based on Wilkins may make the play more attractive to modern tastes—for instance, by giving Thaisa and Marina more dialogue—but have no textual justification.

*The Norton Shakespeare* takes the view that, for students of Shakespeare, it is better to acknowledge rather than conceal textual problems. We correct obvious printers' errors and print as verse passages that have a basic blank verse rhythm, while recognizing that there can be no certainty about lineation and that it is hard to distinguish between errors and bad or hasty writing. We insert minimal stage directions, but we do not attempt to direct the play. *Pericles* works well in the theater precisely because it leaves so much to the imagination.

LOIS POTTER

## TEXTUAL BIBLIOGRAPHY

Gossett, Suzanne. "'To foster is not always to preserve': Feminist Inflections in Editing *Pericles*." *In Arden: Editing Shakespeare*. Ed. Ann Thompson and Gordon McMullan. London: Thompson Learning, 2003: 65–80.

Jackson, Macdonald P. *Defining Shakespeare:* Pericles *as Test Case*. Oxford: Oxford UP, 2003.

Taylor, Gary. "The Transmission of *Pericles*." *Publications of the Bibliographical Society of America* 80 (1986): 193–217.

## PERFORMANCE NOTE

Forty-six of *Pericles'* fifty-four speaking roles are limited to one act or scene, so a foremost concern for directors is how to redeploy actors throughout its many episodes. Doubling roles can lend coherence to the play's distinct halves and complement its pronounced artificiality, while reinforcing (or destabilizing) initial archetypes and hierarchies. Productions can easily reprise kings and courtiers at each new setting; additionally, the murderers Thaliard and Leonine can be played by one actor, the fishermen can return as sailors and pirates, and Dionyza, doubled as the Bawd, can continue harassing Marina. Doubling can also enhance the quality of the play's resolution, if, for example, the incestuous Antiochus and his Daughter progress to the more acceptably coupled Lysimachus and Marina. Gower, too, can assume minor roles within scenes, or his role can be divided among several performers, as indeed can Pericles', productions sometimes working through two or three substitutions to literalize the length of the protagonist's suffering.

Directors must also determine how to portray Gower and how to build psychological depth in Pericles: dramaturgical challenges that are, in fact, closely intertwined. Gower can appear well integrated into the play's Mediterranean world in costume and presentational manner; or he can stand apart from the action, presenting a calm naturalism against the artifice otherwise prevalent. A blatant performer, increasing the audience's sense of spectacle, may help Pericles seem comparatively human and sympathetic, while an unaffected Gower can earn support for Pericles through plain, credible accounts of his misfortunes. Productions can also "deepen" Pericles by lingering over his brief soliloquies, or making his and Marina's tormentors less cartoonish, though some exploit his two-dimensionality to increase audience surprise at his moving recognition scene with Marina. Productions also must decide how complicit Antiochus's Daughter is; whether Bolt and the brothel keepers are comic pragmatists or genuine threats; whether Marina's innocence is genuine or cleverly affected. They also must determine the nature and audibility of the "music of the spheres" (see Digital Edition PC 1) and resolve the staging for Simonides' tournament, Thaisa's burial at sea, and the appearance of Diana.

Brett Gamboa

# The Play of Pericles, Prince of Tyre

[THE PERSONS OF THE PLAY

John GOWER, Presenter and Chorus

PERICLES, Prince of Tyre
MARINA, daughter to Pericles and Thaisa

*In Antioch:*
ANTIOCHUS, King of Antioch
DAUGHTER to Antiochus
THALIARD, attendant to Antiochus

*In Tyre:*
HELICANUS, counselor in Tyre
ESCANES, counselor in Tyre
Three LORDS of Tyre

*In Tarsus:*
CLEON, Governor of Tarsus
DIONYZA, wife to Cleon
LORD of Tarsus
LEONINE, servant to Cleon and Dionyza
Three PIRATES

*In Pentapolis:*
Three FISHERMEN
SIMONIDES, King of Pentapolis
THAISA, daughter to Simonides
FIRST KNIGHT, of Sparta
SECOND KNIGHT, of Macedon
THIRD KNIGHT, of Antioch
FOURTH KNIGHT
FIFTH KNIGHT
MARSHALL
LYCHORIDA, a nurse
Five Squires

MASTER of a ship
SAILORS

*In Ephesus:*
CERIMON, a gentleman of Ephesus
PHILEMON, his servant
Two VISITING SERVANTS
SERVANTS to Cerimon
Two GENTLEMEN of Ephesus

*In Mytilene:*
PANDER
BAWD, wife to Pander

BOLT, servant in the brothel
Two GENTLEMEN of Mytilene
LYSIMACHUS, Governor of Mytilene
LORD of Mytilene
Maid, companion to Marina

DIANA, Goddess of chastity

Lords, Ladies, Attendants, Messengers, Sailors, Pages, Priestesses of Diana, Worshippers at the Temple of Diana]

## 1.0

*Enter* GOWER [*as Chorus*].[1]

GOWER[2] To sing a song that old° was sung — *of old*
From ashes ancient Gower is come,[3]
Assuming man's infirmities° — *Donning mortal flesh*
To glad your ear and please your eyes.
It hath been sung at festivals,
On ember eves and holy ales,[4]
And lords and ladies in their lives
Have read it for restoratives.° — *as a medicine*
The purchase° is to make men glorious, — *benefit*
*Et bonum quo antiquius eo melius*.[5]
If you, born in these latter times
When wit's more ripe,° accept my rhymes, — *poetry's more advanced*
And that° to hear an old man sing — *And if*
May to your wishes pleasure bring,
I life would wish, and that I might
Waste it° for you like taper° light. — *Use it up / candle*
[*He indicates the stage setting.*]
This° Antioch, then. Antiochus the great[6] — *This is*
Built up this city for his chiefest seat,° — *capital*
The fairest in all Syria.
I tell you what mine authors° say. — *sources*
This king unto him took a fere° — *mate*
Who died and left a female heir
So buxom,° blithe, and full of face° — *lively / attractive (?)*
As° heaven had lent her all his° grace, — *As if / its*
With whom the father liking took
And her to incest did provoke.
Bad child, worse father, to entice his own
To evil should° be done by none. — *that should*
By custom what they did begin
Was with long use accounted no sin.[7]
The beauty of this sinful dame
Made many princes thither frame° — *go*
To seek her as a bedfellow,
In marriage pleasures playfellow.
Which to prevent, he made a law

1.0
1. TEXTUAL COMMENT For the role of Gower and the division of the play into acts and scenes, see Digital Edition TC 1.
2. Gower's story of Apollonius of Tyre is an important source of the play. See the Introduction.
3. Like most of Gower's choruses in the play, this one is mainly in rhyming tetrameter couplets.
4. *ember eves:* evenings before periods of religious fasting. *holy ales:* country festivals.
5. And the older something good is, the better (Latin).
6. *Antioch . . . Antiochus:* Recalling the Maccabee rebellion and the missions of Peter and Paul.
7. *By . . . sin:* When what they started (incest) became a habit, they no longer experienced it as a sin.

To keep her still,° and men in awe, *always*
That whoso asked her for his wife,
His riddle told not,[8] lost his life.
So for her many a wight° did die— *fellow*
[*He indicates a display of severed heads.*]
As yon grim looks do testify.
What now ensues, to the judgment of your eye
I give my cause who best can justify.[9] *Exit.*

## 1.1

*Enter* ANTIOCHUS, *Prince* PERICLES,[1] *and followers.*

ANTIOCHUS Young Prince of Tyre,[2] you have at large received° *fully understood*
The danger of the task you undertake.
PERICLES I have, Antiochus, and with a soul
Emboldened with the glory of her praise
Think death no hazard in this enterprise.
ANTIOCHUS Music!
[*Music plays.*][3]
Bring in our daughter, clothèd like a bride
For the embracements even of Jove himself,
At whose conception, till Lucina reigned,
Nature this dowry gave: to glad her presence,[4]
The senate house of planets all did sit
To knit in her their best perfections.[5]
*Enter Antiochus'* DAUGHTER.
PERICLES See where she comes, appareled like the spring,
Graces her subjects[6] and her thoughts the king
Of every virtue gives[7] renown to men;
Her face the book of praises[8] where is read
Nothing but curious° pleasures, as° from thence *delicate / as if*
Sorrow were ever razed, and testy wrath
Could never be her mild° companion. *(modifies "her")*
You gods that made me man, and sway° in love, *hold sway*
That have enflamed desire in my breast
To taste the fruit of yon celestial tree
Or die in th'adventure, be my helps,
As I am son and servant to your will,
To compass° such a boundless happiness. *attain*
ANTIOCHUS Prince Pericles—
PERICLES That would be son to great Antiochus—
ANTIOCHUS Before thee stands this fair Hesperides
With golden fruit, but dangerous to be touched,
For deathlike dragons here affright thee hard.[9]

8. If he failed to explain Antiochus's riddle.
9. *to . . . justify:* I present my case ("cause") to your judgment—you who can best legally excuse me of lying (or perceive the truth of my story).
1.1 Location: The palace at Antioch.
1. *Pericles:* Named after Pericles, the fifth-century B.C.E. Athenian leader, from Plutarch's *Lives,* or Pyrocles, a protagonist in Sidney's *Arcadia* (1590).
2. *Tyre:* Associated with David and Solomon; captured by a Christian army in the First Crusade.
3. TEXTUAL COMMENT On the role of music in the play, in relationship to both textual and performance issues, see Digital Edition TC 2.
4. *At . . . presence:* From my daughter's conception until she was born (Lucina was the Roman goddess of childbirth, often equated with Diana), nature gave her this dowry: to make her presence welcome (or to make her happy).
5. *The . . . perfections:* Astrological forces arranged to give her every perfection.
6. With mastery of all human graces.
7. *virtue gives:* virtue that gives. Shakespeare's coauthor, Wilkins, who likely wrote this part of the play, often omits "that," "which," or "who" in such phrases.
8. The anthology of all that is commendable.
9. *Before . . . hard:* The Hesperides (here representing Antiochus's Daughter) were daughters of Hesperus inhabiting a garden where golden apples grew, whose entrance was patrolled by a dragon. The "golden fruit, but dangerous to be touched," like "the fruit of yon celestial tree" (line 22), also evokes Eden.

Her face like heaven enticeth thee to view
Her countless° glory, which desert must gain, *(like the stars)*
And which without desert, because thine eye
Presumes to reach, all the whole heap° must die. *your whole body*
[*He indicates the severed heads.*]
Yon sometimes° famous princes, like thyself *at one time*
Drawn by report, adventurous by° desire, *taking a risk out of*
Tell thee with speechless tongues and semblance° pale *appearances*
That, without covering save yon field of stars,
Here they stand martyrs slain in Cupid's wars,
And with dead cheeks advise thee to desist
From going on° death's net whom none resist. *into*

PERICLES Antiochus, I thank thee, who hath taught
My frail mortality to know itself
And by those fearful objects to prepare
This body, like to them, to what I must.° *to die*
For death remembered should be like a mirror
Who tells us life's but breath, to trust it, error.
I'll make my will then, and, as sick men do
Who know the world, see heaven, but, feeling woe,
Grip not at earthly joys as erst° they did. *previously*
So I bequeath a happy peace to you
And all good men, as every prince should do;
My riches to the earth, from whence they came;
[*to* DAUGHTER] But my unspotted fire of love to you.
Thus ready for the way of life or death,
I wait the sharpest blow, Antiochus.

ANTIOCHUS Scorning advice, read the conclusion,° then. *riddle*
[*He gives* PERICLES *the riddle.*]
Which read and not expounded, 'tis decreed,
As these before thee, thou thyself shalt bleed.

DAUGHTER Of all 'sayed° yet, mayst thou prove prosperous. *who have tried ("assayed")*
Of all 'sayed yet, I wish thee happiness.

PERICLES Like a bold champion I assume the lists,° *enter combat*
Nor ask advice of any other thought
But faithfulness and courage.
[*He reads*] *the riddle.*
"I am no viper, yet I feed
On mother's flesh which did me breed.[1]
I sought a husband, in which labor
I found that kindness° in a father. *kinship; affection*
He's father, son, and husband mild;
I, mother, wife, and yet his child.
How they may be, and yet in two,° *only two people*
As you will live resolve it you."
Sharp physic° is the last!° [*aside*] But, O you powers *Harsh medicine / (threat)*
That gives heaven countless eyes° to view men's acts! *(the stars)*
Why cloud they not their sights perpetually,
If this be true, which makes me pale to read it?
Fair glass° of light,° I loved you, and could still, *image / (the Daughter)*
Were not this glorious casket stored with ill.[2]

1. Vipers were thought to eat their way out of their mother's body at birth.
2. If your beautiful body did not contain a sinful soul.

But I must tell you, now my thoughts revolt.
For he's no man on whom perfections wait° *(as servants)*
That, knowing sin within, will touch the gate.
You are a fair viol, and your sense° the strings *senses*
Who,° fingered to make man his lawful music, *(strings; daughter)*
Would draw heaven down, and all the gods to hearken.
But being played upon before your time,
Hell only danceth at so harsh a chime.
Good sooth,° I care not for you. *Truly*
[*He approaches the* DAUGHTER.]

ANTIOCHUS Prince Pericles, touch not,[3] upon thy life,
For that's an article within our law
As dangerous as the rest. Your time's expired.
Either expound now or receive your sentence.

PERICLES Great King,
Few love to hear the sins they love to act.
'Twould 'braid° yourself too near° for me to tell it. *upbraid / plainly*
Who° has a book of all that monarchs do, *Whoever*
He's more secure to keep it shut than shown.
For vice repeated is like the wand'ring wind
Blows dust in others' eyes to spread itself.
And yet the end of all is bought thus dear:
The breath is gone and the sore eyes see clear
To stop the air would hurt them.[4] The blind mole casts
Copped° hills towards heaven, to tell° the earth is thronged *Peaked / tell that*
By man's oppression, and the poor worm doth die for't.[5]
Kings are earth's gods; in vice, their law's their will,
And, if Jove stray, who dares say Jove doth ill?
It is enough you know,° and it is fit, *(that I know)*
What being more known grows worse,[6] to smother° it. *conceal*
All love the womb that their first being bred[7]—
Then give my tongue like leave to love my head.

ANTIOCHUS [*aside*] Heaven, that I had thy head! He has found
the meaning.
But I will gloze° with him. —Young prince of Tyre, *dissemble*
Though by the tenor of our strict edict,
Your exposition misinterpreting,° *since you misinterpreted*
We might proceed to cancel° of your days, *to the termination*
Yet hope, succeeding from so fair a tree[8]
As your fair self, doth tune° us otherwise. *move*
Forty days longer we do respite you,
If by which time our secret be undone,
This mercy shows we'll joy in such a son.
And until then your entertain° shall be *entertainment*
As doth befit our honor and your worth.

3. Perhaps Pericles makes some movement that Antiochus misinterprets (further Edenic overtones).
4. *For vice . . . them:* For with the breath used to speak word of others' sins, one blows irritating dust in the eyes of the offenders. But the consequence is merely the speaker's death, since the offenders nevertheless see well enough to stop the news-spreading breath.
5. *The blind . . . for't:* When we blindly protest against the injustice of our superiors, we die (with "mole" meaning "worm"), or, less likely, innocent creatures suffer (here, the "mole" is different from the "worm" and may even destroy it).
6. Since bad deeds become worse for being known.
7. All love the daughter they raised when young (hence, hinting at incest). The obvious meaning is: all love their mother's womb.
8. Hope of a correct answer (an heir), with the successful answer (succession) coming from such a fine specimen (Pericles' regal lineage).

[*Exeunt* ANTIOCHUS *and his* DAUGHTER.]
PERICLES *remains alone.*

PERICLES How courtesy would seem° to cover sin, *lie*
When what is done is like an hypocrite,
The which is good in nothing but in sight!° *appearance*
If it be true that I interpret false,
Then were it certain you were not so bad
As with foul incest to abuse your soul.
Where now you're both a father and a son
By your untimely claspings with your child—
Which pleasures fits a husband, not a father—
And she an eater of her mother's flesh
By the defiling of her parents' bed,
And both like serpents are, who, though they feed
On sweetest flowers, yet they poison breed.
Antioch, farewell, for wisdom sees those men° *men who*
Blush not in actions blacker than the night
Will shun no course° to keep them from the light. *means*
One sin, I know, another doth provoke:
Murder's as near to lust as flame to smoke.
Poison and treason are the hands of sin—
Ay, and the targets° to put off the shame. *shields*
Then, lest my life be cropped to keep you clear,° *(of blame)*
By flight I'll shun the danger which I fear. *Exit.*

*Enter* ANTIOCHUS.

ANTIOCHUS He hath found the meaning—for which we mean
To have his head.
He must not live to trumpet forth my infamy
Nor tell the world Antiochus doth sin
In such a loathèd manner.
And therefore instantly this prince must die,
For by his fall my honor must keep high.
—Who attends us there?

*Enter* THALIARD.

THALIARD Doth your highness call?
ANTIOCHUS Thaliard!
You are of our chamber,° Thaliard, and our mind *my chamberlain*
Partakes° her° private actions to your secrecy, *Imparts / its*
And for your faithfulness we will advance you.
Thaliard, behold:
Here's poison, and here's gold.
We hate the prince of Tyre, and thou must kill him.
It fits° thee not to ask the reason why. *befits*
Because we bid it.
Say, is it done?
THALIARD My lord, 'tis done.

*Enter a* MESSENGER.

ANTIOCHUS Enough.
[*to* MESSENGER] Let your breath cool yourself, telling your haste.[9]
MESSENGER My lord,
Prince Pericles is fled. [*Exit* MESSENGER.]
ANTIOCHUS [*to* THALIARD] As thou wilt live,

9. Use your rapid breathing to cool yourself by explaining the reason for your haste.

Fly after, and, like an arrow shot
From a well experienced archer hits the mark
His eye doth level° at, so thou—never return *aim*
Unless thou say, "Prince Pericles is dead."

THALIARD My lord, if I can get him within my pistol's[1] length,° *range*
I'll make him sure° enough. So farewell to your highness. *unthreatening (dead)*

ANTIOCHUS Thaliard, adieu. [*Exit* THALIARD.]
Till Pericles be dead,
My heart can lend no succor to my head. [*Exit.*]

## 1.2

*Enter* PERICLES *with his* LORDS[, HELICANUS *among them*].[1]

PERICLES Let none disturb us.
[LORDS *wait at a distance.*]
Why should this change of thoughts,° *changed state of mind*
The sad companion, dull-eyed melancholy,
Be my so used° a guest as not an hour *accustomed*
In the day's glorious walk or peaceful night—
The tomb where grief should sleep—can breed me quiet?
Here pleasures court mine eyes, and mine eyes shun them,
And danger, which I feared, is at Antioch,
Whose arm seems far too short to hit me here.
Yet neither pleasure's art can joy my spirits
Nor yet the other's° distance comfort me. *(danger's)*
Then it is thus: the passions of the mind,° *obsessions*
That have their first conception by misdread,° *fear*
Have after-nourishment and life by care,° *worry*
And what was first but fear what might be done,
Grows elder now and cares it be not done.[2]
And so with me. The great Antiochus,
'Gainst whom I am too little to contend,
Since he's so great can° make his will his act, *that he can*
Will think me speaking though I swear to silence.
Nor boots it° me to say I honor him, *does it help*
If he suspect I may dishonor him.
And what may make him blush in being known,
He'll stop the course by which it might be known.
With hostile forces he'll o'erspread the land,
And with the ostent° of war will look so huge *display*
Amazement° shall drive courage from the state, *Terror*
Our men be vanquished ere they do resist,
And subjects punished that ne'er thought offense—
Which care of them, not pity of myself,
Who am no more but as the tops of trees
Which fence° the roots they grow by and defend them, *shield*
Makes both my body pine and soul to languish,
And punish that° before that he would punish.[3] *(myself)*
*All the* LORDS *come forward.*

FIRST LORD Joy and all comfort in your sacred breast!

1. Anachronism: assassination by pistol is a sixteenth-century development, depicted in many plays of the period.
1.2 Location: The palace at Tyre.
1. TEXTUAL COMMENT For the problematic relationship between these Lords and the ones at line 33, see Digital Edition TC 3.
2. *And what . . . done:* And what starts out as simple fear matures into a more rational concern for safety.
3. *before . . . punish:* before he punishes me ("that").

SECOND LORD And keep your mind, till you return to us,
Peaceful and comfortable!
HELICANUS Peace, peace, and give experience tongue!
They do abuse the King that flatter him.
For flattery is the bellows blows up° sin— *that blows up*
The thing the which° is flattered but° a spark *which / is but*
To which that wind gives heat and stronger glowing,
Whereas reproof, obedient and in order,
Fits kings as they are men, for they may err.
When Signor Sooth[4] here does proclaim "peace,"
He flatters you, makes war upon your life.
[*He kneels.*] Prince, pardon me, or strike me if you please—
I cannot be much lower than my knees.
PERICLES [*to the other* LORDS] All leave us else°—but let your cares o'erlook *except Helicanus*
What shipping and what lading's[5] in our haven,
And then return to us. [*Exeunt* LORDS.]
Helicanus, thou
Hast movèd us. What seest thou in our looks?
HELICANUS An angry brow, dread lord.
PERICLES If there be such a dart° in princes' frowns, *danger*
How durst thy tongue move anger to our face?
HELICANUS How dares the plants look up to heaven from whence
They have their nourishment?
PERICLES Thou knowest I have power
To take thy life from thee.
HELICANUS I have ground the ax myself;
Do but you strike the blow.
PERICLES Rise! Prithee, rise. [*He raises* HELICANUS.] Sit down.
Thou art no flatterer.
I thank thee for't, and heaven forbid
That kings should let their ears hear their faults hid.
Fit counselor and servant for a prince,
Who by thy wisdom makes a prince thy servant,
What wouldst thou have me do?
HELICANUS To bear with patience such griefs
As you yourself do lay upon yourself.
PERICLES Thou speak'st like a physician, Helicanus,
That ministers a potion unto me
That thou wouldst tremble to receive thyself.
Attend me° then: I went to Antioch, *Listen to me*
Where, as thou know'st, against the face of death
I sought the purchase° of a glorious beauty *acquisition*
From whence an issue I might propagate,
Are arms° to princes, and bring joys to subjects. *Which are weapons*
Her face was to mine eye beyond all wonder,
The rest—hark in thine ear—as black as incest.
Which by my knowledge found, the sinful father
Seemed not to strike but smooth,° but thou know'st this: *smooth over*
'Tis time to fear when tyrants seem to kiss.
Which fear so grew in me, I hither fled—

4. Mock name for a flatterer, a soother of egos.
5. *let . . . lading's:* look carefully to find out what vessels are coming and going and what their cargo is.

Under the covering of a careful night
Who seemed my good protector—and, being here,
Bethought me what was past, what might succeed.° *happen next*
I knew him tyrannous, and tyrants' fears
Decrease not but grow faster than the years,
And should he doubt,° as doubt no doubt he doth, *suspect*
That I should open° to the listening air *declare*
How many worthy princes' bloods were shed
To keep his bed of blackness unlaid ope,
To lop that doubt, he'll fill this land with arms
And make pretense of wrong that I have done him,
When all for mine—if I may call—offense
Must feel war's blow, who° spares not innocence. *which*
Which love to all of which thyself art one,
Who now reproved'st me for't—
HELICANUS Alas, sir—
PERICLES Drew sleep out of mine eyes, blood from my cheeks,
Musings into my mind, with thousand doubts
How I might stop this tempest ere it came,
And finding little comfort to relieve them,° *(his subjects; his doubts)*
I thought it princely charity to grieve them.° *grieve (for) my subjects*
HELICANUS Well, my lord, since you have given me leave to speak,
Freely will I speak. Antiochus you fear,
And justly too, I think, you fear the tyrant
Either by public war or private treason
Will take away your life.
Therefore, my lord, go travel for a while,
Till that his rage and anger be forgot, or till
The destinies do cut his thread of life.[6]
Your rule direct° to any. If to me, *assign*
Day serves not light more faithful than I'll be.
PERICLES I do not doubt thy faith.
But, should he wrong my liberties° in my absence? *attack my country*
HELICANUS We'll mingle our bloods together in the earth
From whence we had our being and our birth.
PERICLES Tyre, I now look from thee then, and to Tarsus° *(St. Paul's birthplace)*
Intend° my travel, where I'll hear from thee, *Direct*
And by whose letters I'll dispose myself.
The care I had and have of subjects' good
On thee I lay, whose wisdom's strength can bear it.
I'll take thy word for faith, not ask thine oath—
Who° shuns not to break one, will sure crack both. *He who*
But in our orbs° we'll live so round° and safe, *places / prudently*
That time of both this truth shall ne'er convince:° *refute*
Thou showed'st a subject's shine,° I a true prince.° *Exeunt.* *radiance / prince's*

## 1.3

*Enter* THALIARD.

THALIARD So this is Tyre, and this the court. Here must I kill King Pericles, and if I do it not I am sure to be hanged at home: 'tis dangerous. Well, I perceive he was a wise fellow and had good discretion that, being bid to ask what he would

6. In Greek mythology, a person died when the three Fates "cut his thread of life."

1.3 Location: Scene continues.

of the king, desired he might know none of his secrets.[1] Now do I see he had some reason for't, for if a king bid a man be a villain, he's bound by the indenture° of his oath to be one. *servant's contract*
Hush, here comes the lords of Tyre.

*[He stands aside.] Enter* HELICANUS, ESCANES, *with other* LORDS.

HELICANUS You shall not need, my fellow peers of Tyre,
Further to question me of your king's departure.
His sealed° commission, left in trust with me, *(with royal wax)*
Does speak sufficiently: he's gone to travel.

THALIARD *[aside]* How? The King gone?

HELICANUS If further yet you will be satisfied
Why, as it were, unlicensed of your loves,° *without your approval*
He would depart, I'll give some light unto you.
Being at Antioch—

THALIARD *[aside]* What from Antioch?

HELICANUS Royal Antiochus, on what cause I know not,
Took some displeasure at him—at least he judged so—
And, doubting lest° he had erred or sinned, *And fearing*
To show his sorrow he'd correct° himself. *he wished to punish*
So puts himself unto the shipman's toil,
With° whom each minute threatens life or death. *For*

THALIARD *[aside]* Well, I perceive
I shall not be hanged now, although I would.[2]
But since he's gone, the King's ears it must please:
He 'scaped° the land to perish on the seas. *escaped*
I'll present myself. —Peace to the lords of Tyre.

*[He gives a letter.]*[3]

HELICANUS *[after looking at the letter]*[4] Lord Thaliard from Antiochus is welcome.

THALIARD From him I come
With message unto princely Pericles,
But since my landing I have understood
Your lord has betook himself to unknown travels.
Now message must return from whence it came.

HELICANUS We have no reason to desire it,
Commended° to our master, not to us. *Directed*

*[He returns the letter.]*

Yet ere you shall depart, this we desire:
As friends to Antioch we may feast° in Tyre. *Exeunt.* *prepare a feast for you*

## 1.4

*Enter* CLEON, *the Governor of Tarsus, with his wife[,* DIONYZA,*] and others.*

CLEON My Dionyza, shall we rest us here
And by relating tales of others' griefs
See if 'twill teach us to forget our own?

DIONYZA That were to blow at fire in hope to quench it.
For who digs hills because they do aspire

1. According to Plutarch's *Lives* and Barnabe Riche in *Soldiers Wish to Briton's Welfare* (1604), the poet Philippides made this request of King Lysimachus of Thrace.
2. Even if I return home (?); even if that's what I wanted.
3. Persumably Thaliard's way of getting Pericles "within my pistol's length" (1.1.169).
4. The stage direction is added to explain how Helicanus knows who Thaliard is.
1.4 Location: Tarsus.

Throws down one mountain to cast up a higher.[1]
O my distressed lord, even such our griefs are.
Here they are but felt and seen with mischief's° eyes, *the sufferer's*
But, like to groves, being topped° they higher rise. *pruned*
CLEON O Dionyza,
Who wanteth food and will not say he wants it,
Or can conceal his hunger till he famish?
Let's teach our tongues and sorrows to sound° deep *proclaim; plumb*
Our woes into the air, our eyes to weep,
Till lungs fetch breath that may proclaim them louder,
That if heavens slumber while their° creatures want, *(heavens')*
They° may awake their° helps to comfort them. *(creatures) / (heavens')*
I'll then discourse our woes felt several years,
And, wanting° breath to speak, help me with tears. *when I'm out of*
DIONYZA I'll do my best, sir.
CLEON This Tarsus o'er which I have the government,
A city on whom plenty held full hand°— *generously presided*
For riches strewed herself even in her streets—
Whose towers bore heads so high they kissed the clouds,
And strangers ne'er beheld but wondered at;° *without admiring*
Whose men and dames so jetted° and adorned° *strutted / (themselves)*
Like one another's glass to trim them[2] by;
Their tables were stored full to glad the sight,
And not so much to feed on as delight.
All poverty was scorned, and pride so great,
The name of help grew odious to repeat—
DIONYZA Oh, 'tis too true.
CLEON But see what heaven can do by this our change:
These mouths who but of late° earth, sea, and air *just recently*
Were all too little to content and please,
Although they° gave their creatures in abundance— *("earth, sea, and air")*
As houses are defiled for want° of use, *by lack*
They are now starved for want of exercise.
Those palates who, not yet two summers younger,
Must have inventions° to delight the taste, *Demanded novel foods*
Would now be glad of bread and beg for it.
Those mothers who to nuzzle up° their babes *raise*
Thought naught too curious° are ready now *exquisite*
To eat those little darlings whom they loved.
So sharp are hunger's teeth that man and wife
Draw lots who first shall die to lengthen life.[3]
Here stands a lord and there a lady weeping;
Here many sink, yet those which see them fall
Have scarce strength left to give them burial.
Is not this true?
DIONYZA Our cheeks and hollow eyes do witness it.
CLEON Oh, let those cities that of plenty's cup
And her prosperities so largely taste
With their superfluous riots° hear these tears: *excessive indulgence*
The misery of Tarsus may be theirs.

1. *For . . . higher:* Digging up hills because "they" (the hills) "aspire" (rise up) results only in new hills; or, "they" who "aspire" dig up "hills" (attempt to undermine the eminent)—again, unsuccessfully.
2. Mirror to dress themselves. (Everyone was a model of fashion.)
3. *lengthen life:* (of the other, through cannibalism).

*Enter a* LORD.

LORD Where's the Lord Governor?

CLEON Here.
Speak out the sorrows which thou bring'st in haste,
For comfort is too far for us to expect.

LORD We have descried upon our neighboring shore
A portly sail° of ships make hitherward. *stately fleet*

CLEON I thought as much.
One sorrow never comes but brings an heir
That may succeed as his inheritor.
And so in ours: some neighboring nation,
Taking advantage of our misery,
Hath stuffed the hollow vessels with their power° *soldiers*
To beat us down, the which are down already,
And make a conquest of unhappy men,
Whereas no glory's got to overcome.[4]

LORD That's the least fear,° for by the semblance *not to be feared*
Of their white flags displayed, they bring us peace
And come to us as favorers, not as foes.

CLEON Thou speak'st like him's untutored to repeat:[5]
Who makes the fairest show means most deceit.
But, bring they° what they will and what they can, *let them bring*
What need we fear?
Our grave's the lowest,° and we are halfway there. *lowest we can go*
Go tell their general we attend° him here *await*
To know for what he comes, and whence he comes,
And what he craves.

LORD I go, my lord. [*Exit.*]

CLEON Welcome is peace, if he on peace consist.° *resolves*
If wars, we are unable to resist.

*Enter* PERICLES *with Attendants.*

PERICLES Lord Governor—for so we hear you are—
Let not our ships and number of our men
Be like a beacon fired t'amaze° your eyes. *to terrify*
We have heard your miseries as far as Tyre
And seen the desolation of your streets,
Nor come we to add sorrow to your hearts
But to relieve them of their heavy load.
And these our ships, you happily° may think *which you perhaps*
Are like the Trojan horse was stuffed within
With bloody veins expecting overthrow,[6]
Are stored with corn to make your needy bread,
And give them life whom hunger starved half dead.

ALL TARSIANS [*kneeling*] The gods of Greece protect you,
And we'll pray for you.

PERICLES Arise, I pray you, rise.
We do not look for reverence but for love
And harborage for ourself, our ships, and men.

CLEON The which when any shall not gratify,
Or pay you with unthankfulness in thought,
Be it our wives, our children, or ourselves,

4. Where there's no glory in winning.
5. Like him who hasn't learned (the following lesson) by heart.
6. *was . . . overthrow:* that was laden with Greek soldiers ("bloody veins") who (correctly) expected to sack Troy.

The curse of heaven and men succeed° their evils! *follow from*
Till when—the which, I hope, shall ne'er be seen—
Your grace is welcome to our town and us.

PERICLES Which welcome we'll accept, feast here a while,
Until our stars that frown lend us a smile. *Exeunt.*

## 2.0

*Enter* GOWER.

GOWER Here have you seen a mighty king
His child, iwis,° to incest bring; *certainly*
A better prince° and benign lord *(Pericles)*
That will prove awful° both in deed and word. *worthy of respect*
Be quiet then, as men should be,
Till he hath passed necessity.[1]
I'll show you those° in troubles reign, *those who*
Losing a mite, a mountain gain.
The good in conversation,[2]
To whom I give my benison,° *blessing*
Is still at Tarsus, where each man
Thinks all is writ he speken can,[3]
And to remember what he does
Build his statue to make him glorious.
But tidings to the contrary° *news of calamities*
Are brought your eyes; what need speak I?

*Dumb show.*[4]

*Enter at one door* PERICLES *talking with* CLEON, *all the train with them. Enter at another door a Gentleman with a letter to* PERICLES. PERICLES *shows the letter to* CLEON. PERICLES *gives the [Gentleman] a reward and knights him:*

*Exeunt [with their trains]* PERICLES *at one door and* CLEON *at another.*

Good Helicane that stayed at home,
Not to eat honey like a drone
From others' labors, for that he° strive *but rather to*
To killen bad, keep good alive,
And to fulfil his prince' desire,
Sends word of all that haps in Tyre:
How Thaliard came full bent with° sin *intent on*
And hid intent to murder him,
And that in Tarsus was not best
Longer for him to make his rest.[5]
He, doing so, put forth to seas,
Where when men been° there's seldom ease. *are*
For now the wind begins to blow:
Thunder above and deeps below
Makes such unquiet that the ship
Should° house him safe is wrecked and split, *Which should*
And he, good prince, having all lost,
By waves from coast to coast is tossed.

2.0
1. *necessity:* the suffering that is his lot.
2. The good man (Pericles) in conduct.
3. Archaic (as is often the case in Gower's speeches): Thinks all Pericles says is holy scripture ("writ").
4. In Renaissance drama, a brief pantomime performance used to advance the plot.
5. It is not clear how Helicanus knows this.

All perishen, of man, of pelf,° *goods*
Ne aught escapen° but himself, *Nothing escaping*
Till Fortune, tired with doing bad,
Threw him ashore to give him glad.° *joy*
And here he comes. What shall be next
Pardon old Gower: this 'longs the text.[6] [*Exit*.]

## 2.1

*Enter* PERICLES *wet*.

PERICLES Yet cease your ire, you angry stars of heaven!
Wind, rain, and thunder, remember earthly man
Is but a substance that must yield to you,
And I, as fits my nature, do obey you.
Alas, the seas hath cast me on the rocks,
Washed me from shore to shore, and left me breath° *life*
Nothing° to think on but ensuing death. *With nothing*
Let it suffice the greatness of your powers
To have bereft a prince of all his fortunes,
And, having thrown him from your wat'ry grave,
Here to have death in peace is all he'll crave.

*Enter three* FISHERMEN. [PERICLES *stands aside*.]

FIRST FISHERMAN What ho, Pelch![1]

SECOND FISHERMAN Ha, come and bring away the nets.

FIRST FISHERMAN What, Patch-breech,° I say! *(a nickname)*

THIRD FISHERMAN What say you, master?

FIRST FISHERMAN Look how thou stirr'st now! Come away or I'll fetch thee with a wanion.[2]

THIRD FISHERMAN Faith, master, I am thinking of the poor men that were cast away before us° even now. *in our sight*

FIRST FISHERMAN Alas, poor souls! It grieved my heart to hear what pitiful cries they made to us to help them, when—welladay!°—we could scarce help ourselves. *alas*

THIRD FISHERMAN Nay, master, said not I as much when I saw the porpoise, how he bounced and tumbled?° They say they're half fish, half flesh. A plague on them! They ne'er come but I look to be washed.° Master, I marvel how the fishes live in the sea. *(predictive of storms)* *(by a storm)*

FIRST FISHERMAN Why, as men do a-land:° the great ones eat up the little ones. I can compare our rich misers to nothing so fitly as to a whale; 'a° plays and tumbles, driving the poor fry before him, and at last devours them all at a mouthful. Such whales have I heard on° o'th' land, who never leave gaping° till they swallowed the whole parish, church, steeple, bells, and all. *on land* *he* *of* *close their mouths*

PERICLES [*aside*] A pretty moral.

THIRD FISHERMAN But, master, if I had been the sexton,° I would have been that day in the belfry.° *church bellringer* *bell tower*

SECOND FISHERMAN Why, man?

6. *'longs the text:* belongs to the original story (don't blame me for Pericles' sufferings).

2.1 Location: The seashore at Pentapolis, which was the coastal area of Cyrenaica, in the northeastern corner of what is now Libya. This scene locates it in Greece, however (line 63).

1. Nickname derived from a rustic leather garment. The nicknames, homely references, and social critiques in this scene have a distinctively English feel.

2. *Look . . . wanion:* Look how quick you are (ironic). Hurry along, or I'll beat you with a vengeance.

THIRD FISHERMAN Because he should have swallowed me too, and when I had been in his belly, I would have kept such a jangling of the bells that he should never have left till he cast° bells, steeple, church, and parish up again. But if the good King Simonides were of my mind— *vomited*

PERICLES [*aside*] Simonides?

THIRD FISHERMAN —We would purge the land of these drones that rob the bee of her honey.

PERICLES [*aside*] How from the finny subjects° of the sea[3] *citizens*
These fishers tell the infirmities of men
And from their wat'ry empire recollect° *gather*
All that may men approve or men detect!° *expose*
[*He comes forward.*]
Peace be at your labor, honest fishermen!

SECOND FISHERMAN "Honest," good fellow—what's that? If it be a day fits you, search out the calender, and nobody look after it![4]

PERICLES May° see the sea hath cast upon your coast— *You may*

SECOND FISHERMAN What a drunken knave was the sea to cast thee in our way![5]

PERICLES A man, whom both the waters and the wind
In that vast tennis-court hath made the ball
For them to play upon,° entreats you pity him. *with*
He asks of you that never used to beg.

FIRST FISHERMAN No, friend, cannot you beg? Here's them° in our country of Greece gets° more with begging than we can do with working. *There are those* / *who get*

SECOND FISHERMAN Canst thou catch any fishes, then?

PERICLES I never practiced it.

SECOND FISHERMAN Nay, then thou wilt starve, sure, for here's nothing to be got nowadays unless thou canst fish for't.° *get it by deception*

PERICLES What I have been, I have forgot to know;
But what I am, want teaches me to think on:
A man thronged up° with cold. My veins are chill, *overwhelmed*
And have no more of life than may suffice
To give my tongue that heat to ask your help—
Which if you shall refuse, when I am dead,
For that° I am a man, pray see me burièd. *Because*

FIRST FISHERMAN Die, quotha?° Now, gods forbid't, an° I have a gown here. Come, put it on, keep thee warm. *says he / if*
[PERICLES *puts on the First Fisherman's gown.*]
Now, afore me,° a handsome fellow! Come, thou shalt go home, and we'll have flesh for holidays, fish for fasting days and more°—or puddings° and flapjacks—and thou shalt be welcome. *on my word* / *also other days / sausages*

PERICLES I thank you, sir.

SECOND FISHERMAN Hark you, my friend. You said you could not beg?

3. Although the Fishermen speak in prose, Pericles uses verse.
4. *If . . . after it:* Perhaps: If honesty is a day in the calendar that suits you, you could remove it without anyone noticing or challenging you for it—honesty being so rare.
5. Like St. Peter, the Fishermen are literally fishers of men, who help save Pericles from the sea. Their discussion of whales also evokes the tale of Jonah. The scene is full of biblical echoes. *cast:* pun on "vomit."

PERICLES I did but crave.

SECOND FISHERMAN But crave? Then I'll turn craver too, and so I shall 'scape whipping.° *(for begging)*

PERICLES Why, are your beggars whipped, then?

SECOND FISHERMAN Oh, not all, my friend, not all, for if all your° beggars were whipped, I would wish no better office than to be beadle.[6] But, master, I'll go draw up the net. *the*

[*Exeunt* SECOND *and* THIRD FISHERMEN.]

PERICLES [*aside*] How well this honest mirth becomes their labor!

FIRST FISHERMAN Hark you, sir; do you know where ye are?

PERICLES Not well.

FIRST FISHERMAN Why, I'll tell you. This is called Pentapolis, and our king, the good Simonides.

PERICLES "The good Simonides," do you call him?

FIRST FISHERMAN Ay, sir, and he deserves so to be called for his peaceable reign and good government.

PERICLES He is a happy king, since he gains from his subjects the name of "good" by his government. How far is his court distant from this shore?

FIRST FISHERMAN Marry,° sir, half a day's journey. And I'll tell you, he hath a fair daughter, and tomorrow is her birthday, and there are princes and knights come from all parts of the world to joust and tourney for her love. *To be sure*

PERICLES Were my fortunes equal to my desires, I could wish to make one° there. *be one of the princes*

FIRST FISHERMAN O sir, things must be as they may: and what a man cannot get, he may lawfully deal for with his wife's soul.[7]

*Enter* [SECOND *and* THIRD] FISHERMEN, *drawing up a net.*

SECOND FISHERMAN Help, master, help! Here's a fish hangs in the net like a poor man's right in the law: 'twill hardly come out.

[*All three* FISHERMEN *haul in the net, which contains a piece of armor.*]

Ha! Bots on't,° 'tis come at last, and 'tis turned to a rusty armor. *A pox (plague) on it*

PERICLES An armor, friends? I pray you, let me see it.
[*aside*] Thanks, Fortune, yet, that after all thy crosses° *hardships*
Thou givest me somewhat to repair myself!
It was mine own, part of my heritage,
Which my dead father did bequeath to me
With this strict charge, even as he left his life:
"Keep it, my Pericles; it hath been a shield
Twixt me and death"—and pointed to this brace.° *arm armor*
"For that° it saved me, keep it. In like necessity, *Because*
From which the gods protect thee, may't defend thee."
It kept° where I kept, I so dearly loved it, *remained*
Till the rough seas that spares not any man

6. Minor parish official who administered corporal punishment.

7. *what . . . soul:* probably ironic: when a man can no longer "get" (make a living; have children), he can legitimately do so by persuading his "wife's soul" (her conscience; also, "his wife's hole") to trade (prostitute) herself (with men who will "get"—beget—children with her).

Took it in rage, though, calmed, have given't again.
I thank thee for't—my shipwreck now's no ill,
Since I have here my° father gave in his will. *what my*

FIRST FISHERMAN What mean you, sir?

PERICLES [*to* FISHERMEN] To beg of you, kind friends, this coat of worth,
For it was sometime target° to a king. *once a shield*
I know it by this mark. He loved me dearly,
And for his sake I wish the having of it,
And that you'd guide me to your sovereign's court,
Where, with it, I may appear a gentleman,
And if that ever my low fortune's better,
I'll pay your bounties;° till then, rest your debtor. *repay your generosity*

FIRST FISHERMAN Why, wilt thou tourney for the lady?

PERICLES I'll show the virtue I have borne in arms.

FIRST FISHERMAN Why, d'ye take it, and the gods give thee good on't!

SECOND FISHERMAN Ay, but, hark you, my friend, 'twas we that made up° this garment through the rough seams of the waters. There are certain condolements,[8] certain vails°—I hope, sir, if you thrive, you'll remember from whence you had them. *raised; sewed (pun)* *tips; leftover cloth*

PERICLES Believe't, I will.
By your furtherance I am clothed in steel,
And, spite of all the rapture° of the sea, *plundering*
This jewel holds his building° on my arm. *its place*
Unto thy° value I will mount myself *(the jewel's)*
Upon a courser,° whose delightful steps *a horse*
Shall make the gazer joy to see him tread.
Only, my friend, I yet am unprovided of a pair of bases.[9]

SECOND FISHERMAN We'll sure provide. Thou shalt have my best gown to make thee a pair, and I'll bring thee to the court myself.

PERICLES Then, honor, be but equal to my will!
This day I'll rise, or else add ill to ill. [*Exeunt.*]

## 2.2

*Enter King* SIMONIDES, THAISA, *and* [THREE LORDS, *with*] *Attendants.*

SIMONIDES Are the knights ready to begin the triumph?° *tournament*

FIRST LORD They are, my liege,
And stay° your coming to present themselves. *await*

SIMONIDES Return° them, we are ready, and our daughter, *Answer*
In honor of whose birth these triumphs are,
Sits here like Beauty's child, whom Nature gat° *conceived*
For men to see and, seeing, wonder at. [*Exit* FIRST LORD.]

THAISA It pleaseth you, my royal father, to express
My commendations great, whose merit's less.

SIMONIDES It's fit it should be so, for princes° are *rulers*
A model which heaven makes like to itself.
As jewels lose their glory if neglected,

8. Blunder for "doles."
9. Skirts for armored knights on horseback.

2.2 Location: Pentapolis, area near the tournament arena, including a reviewing stand.

So princes their renowns if not respected.
'Tis now your honor, daughter, to entertain° *review*
The labor of each knight in his device.[1]

THAISA Which, to preserve mine honor, I'll perform.

*[Enter] the* FIRST KNIGHT. *[He] passes by [and his Squire presents a shield to* THAISA*].*

SIMONIDES Who is the first that doth prefer° himself? *present*

THAISA A knight of Sparta, my renownèd father,
And the device he bears upon his shield
Is a black Ethiop reaching at the sun:
The word: *Lux tua vita mihi.*[2]

SIMONIDES He loves you well, that holds his life of° you. *receives his life from*

*The* SECOND KNIGHT *[and Squire pass by, as before].*

Who is the second that presents himself?

THAISA A prince of Macedon, my royal father,
And the device he bears upon his shield
Is an armed knight that's conquered by a lady:
The motto thus, in Spanish: *Più per dolcezza che per forza.*[3]

*[The* THIRD KNIGHT *and Squire pass by.]*

SIMONIDES And what's the third?

THAISA The third of Antioch,
And his device a wreath of chivalry,[4]
The word: *Me pompae provexit apex.*[5]

*[The* FOURTH KNIGHT *and Squire pass by.]*

SIMONIDES What is the fourth?

THAISA A burning torch that's turnèd upside down;
The word: *Qui me alit me extinguit.*[6]

SIMONIDES Which shows that beauty hath his power and will,
Which can as well enflame as it can kill.

*[The* FIFTH KNIGHT *and Squire pass by.]*

THAISA The fifth, an hand environèd with clouds,
Holding out gold that's by the touchstone[7] tried.
The motto thus: *Sic spectanda fides.*[8]

*[The* SIXTH KNIGHT *(*PERICLES*), in rusty armor and without a squire, presents his shield to* THAISA *and passes by.]*

SIMONIDES And what's the sixth and last, the which the knight
Himself with such a graceful courtesy° delivered? *bow*

THAISA He seems to be a stranger, but his present° is *presented object*
A withered branch that's only green at top,
The motto: *In hac spe vivo.*° *I live in this hope*

SIMONIDES A pretty moral!
From the dejected state wherein he is,
He hopes by you his fortunes yet may flourish.

FIRST LORD He had need mean° better than his outward show *must intend something*
Can any way speak in his just commend,° *on his behalf*

1. An emblem in heraldry, consisting of an image and a motto, or "word" (line 21), usually in a foreign language, and displayed on banners, shields, and elsewhere.
2. Your light is my life (Latin).
3. Garbled Italian for: more by gentleness than by force; *in Spanish:* a mishearing or a joke.
4. (Heraldic term): twisted band that joins the crest and the knight's helmet.
5. The summit of glory has led me on (Latin).
6. Who nourishes me extinguishes me (Latin).
7. Black stone used to check the purity of gold and silver; symbol of fidelity.
8. Thus is faith to be examined (Latin).

For by his rusty outside he appears
To have practiced more the whipstock than the lance.[9]
SECOND LORD He well may be a stranger,° for he comes *foreigner*
To an honored triumph strangely furnishèd.° *bizarrely equipped*
THIRD LORD And on set purpose let his armor rust
Until this day—to scour it in the dust.[1]
SIMONIDES Opinion's but a fool that makes us scan
The outward habit° for the inward man. *costume*
But stay, the knights are coming.
We will withdraw into the gallery.
[*Exeunt King* SIMONIDES, THAISA, *and* LORDS.]
[*A banquet table is brought in.*] *Great shouts* [*offstage*], *and all cry, "The mean° knight!"*[2] *impoverished*

## 2.3

*Enter King* [SIMONIDES, THAISA, MARSHALL, LORDS, *Ladies,*] *and* KNIGHTS[, *including* PERICLES, *in their armor,*] *from tilting.*

SIMONIDES Knights, to say you're welcome were superfluous.
To place upon the volume of your deeds,
As in a title page,[1] your worth in arms,
Were more than you expect, or more than's fit,
Since every worth in show° commends itself. *in practice*
Prepare for mirth, for mirth becomes a feast.
You are princes and my guests.
THAISA [*to* PERICLES] But you, my knight and guest,
To whom this wreath of victory I give,
And crown you king of this day's happiness.
[PERICLES *kneels.* THAISA *crowns him.*]
PERICLES 'Tis more by fortune, lady, than my merit.
SIMONIDES Call it by what you will, the day is yours,
And here, I hope, is none that envies it.
In framing° artists, art hath thus decreed, *making*
To make some good, but others to exceed,
And you are her labored scholar.[2] [*to* THAISA] Come, queen o'th' feast—
For, daughter, so you are—here take your place.
[THAISA *sits beside King* SIMONIDES.]
[*to* MARSHALL] Marshall the rest as they deserve their grace.[3]
[MARSHALL *leads guests to their places.*]
KNIGHTS We are honored much by good Simonides.
SIMONIDES Your presence glads our days. Honor we love,
For who hates honor, hates the gods above.
MARSHALL [*to* PERICLES] Sir, yonder is your place.
PERICLES Some other is more fit.
FIRST KNIGHT Contend not, sir, for we are gentlemen
Have° neither in our hearts nor outward eyes *Who've*
Envied the great, nor shall the low despise.

9. *he appears . . . lance:* he looks more like a manual laborer (a "whipstock" was the handle of a whip used to drive workhorses) than a knight.
1. To polish it in the dust (when he is unhorsed).
2. TEXTUAL COMMENT For the staging of the combat, see Digital Edition TC 4.

2.3 Location: The palace at Pentapolis.
1. Renaissance publishers often advertised the contents on the title page of a book ("volume").
2. Art (creative power) worked hard to make you.
3. Arrange the others according to the honor they deserve.

PERICLES You are right courteous knights.
SIMONIDES Sit, sir, sit.
[*aside*] By Jove I wonder, that is king of thoughts,[4]
These cates resist me, he but thought upon.[5]
THAISA [*aside*] By Juno, that is queen of marriage,
All viands that I eat do seem unsavory,
Wishing him my meat. [*to* SIMONIDES] Sure, he's a gallant gentleman.
SIMONIDES He's but a country gentleman.
He's done no more than other knights have done—
He's broken a staff° or so. So let it pass. *an opponent's lance*
THAISA To me he seems like diamond to glass.
PERICLES [*aside*] Yon king's to me like to my father's picture,
Which tells me in that glory once he was:
Had princes sit like stars about his throne,
And he the sun for them to reverence.
None that beheld him but, like lesser lights,
Did vail° their crowns to his supremacy; *lower*
Where now his son's a glowworm in the night,
The which hath fire in darkness, none in light.
Whereby I see that Time's the king of men:
He's both their parent and he is their grave,
And gives them what he will, not what they crave.
SIMONIDES What, are you merry, knights?
KNIGHTS Who can be other in this royal presence?
SIMONIDES Here, with a cup that's stored unto the brim,
As you do love, fill[6] to your mistress' lips!
We drink this health to you.
[*He drinks.*]
KNIGHTS We thank your grace.
SIMONIDES Yet pause awhile. [*He indicates* PERICLES.] Yon knight doth sit too melancholy,
As if the entertainment in our court
Had not a show might countervail° his worth. *that might equal*
Note it not you, Thaisa?
THAISA What is't to me, my father?
SIMONIDES Oh, attend, my daughter. Princes in this
Should live like gods above, who freely give
To everyone that come to honor them,
And princes not doing so are like to gnats
Which make a sound but, killed, are wondered at.[7]
Therefore, to make his entertain° more sweet, *entertainment*
Here, say we drink this standing bowl° of wine to him. *bowl on a pedestal*
[*He drinks.*]
THAISA Alas, my father, it befits not me
Unto a stranger knight to be so bold.
He may my proffer take for an offense,
Since men take women's gifts for impudence.

4. TEXTUAL COMMENT Here, as elsewhere, the line might be an aside or might be addressed to another character. See Digital Edition TC 5.
5. *These . . . upon:* (I'm so taken with him that, merely) thinking of him, I lose my appetite for delicacies.
6. If you are in love, drink up.
7. Which, when dead, appear surprisingly small for all the noise they made alive.

SIMONIDES How? Do as I bid you, or you'll move° me else. *anger*
THAISA [*aside*] Now, by the gods, he could not please me better!
SIMONIDES And further tell him we desire to know
Of whence he is, his name, and parentage.
[THAISA *takes the bowl of wine to* PERICLES.]
THAISA The King my father, sir, has drunk to you—
PERICLES I thank him—
THAISA Wishing it so much blood unto your life.
PERICLES I thank both him and you, and pledge° him freely. *drink to*
[*He drinks.*]
THAISA And, further, he desires to know of you
Of whence you are, your name and parentage.
PERICLES A gentleman of Tyre, my name Pericles,
My education been in arts° and arms, *liberal arts*
Who, looking for adventures in the world,
Was by the rough seas reft° of ships and men, *bereft*
And, after shipwreck, driven upon this shore.
[THAISA *returns to* SIMONIDES.]
THAISA [*to* SIMONIDES] He thanks your grace; names himself Pericles,
A gentleman of Tyre,
Who only by misfortune of the seas,
Bereft of ships and men, cast on this shore.
SIMONIDES Now by the gods, I pity his misfortune
And will awake him from his melancholy.
—Come, gentlemen, we sit° too long on trifles *dwell*
And waste the time which looks for other revels.
Even in your armors, as you are addressed,° *dressed*
Will well become a soldiers' dance.
I will not have excuse with saying this:
"Loud music° is too harsh for ladies' heads," *The sound of armor*
Since they love men in arms as well as beds.
[*The* KNIGHTS] *dance.*° *(without the ladies)*
So, this was well asked, 'twas so well performed.
[*to* PERICLES, *indicating* THAISA] Come, sir, here's a lady that wants breathing° too, *exercise*
And I have heard you knights of Tyre
Are excellent in making ladies trip° *dance; go astray sexually*
And that their measures° are as excellent. *dances; sexual means*
PERICLES In those that practice them they are, my lord.
SIMONIDES Oh, that's as much as you would be denied
Of your fair courtesy.[8] Unclasp, unclasp![9]
[PERICLES *and* THAISA] *dance* [*with the other* KNIGHTS *and Ladies.*]
—Thanks, gentlemen, to all. All have done well,
[*to* PERICLES] But you the best. —Pages and lights, to conduct
These knights unto their several° lodgings! *separate*
[*to* PERICLES] Yours, sir, we have given order be next our own.

8. *that's . . . courtesy:* that's just what your modesty about your dancing ability dictates you should say.
9. Remove your armor, and dance with the ladies.

PERICLES I am at your grace's pleasure.
SIMONIDES Princes, it is too late to talk of love,
And that's the mark I know you level° at. *aim*
Therefore each one betake him to his rest.
Tomorrow all for speeding do their best.[1] [*Exeunt.*]

## 2.4

*Enter* HELICANUS *and* ESCANES.

HELICANUS No, Escanes! Know this of me:
Antiochus from incest lived not free,
For which, the most high gods, not minding° longer *wishing*
To withhold the vengeance that they had in store
Due to this heinous capital offense,
Even in the height and pride of all his glory,
When he was seated in a chariot
Of an inestimable value, and
His daughter with him, a fire from heaven came
And shriveled up their bodies even to loathing—
For they so stunk
That all those eyes adored° them ere their fall *that adored*
Scorn now their° hands should give them burial. *that their*
ESCANES 'Twas very strange.
HELICANUS And yet but justice. For
Though this king were great, his greatness was no guard
To bar heaven's shaft, but sin had his° reward. *its*
ESCANES 'Tis very true.

*Enter three* LORDS. [*They speak apart.*][1]

FIRST LORD See, not a man in private conference
Or council has respect° with him but he.° *influence / (Escanes)*
SECOND LORD It shall no longer grieve° without reproof. *cause us grief*
THIRD LORD And cursed be he that will not second it.
FIRST LORD Follow me, then. —Lord Helicane, a word.
HELICANUS With me? And welcome. Happy day, my lords!
FIRST LORD Know that our griefs° are risen to the top, *grievances*
And now at length they overflow their banks.
HELICANUS Your griefs—for what? Wrong not your prince you love.
FIRST LORD Wrong not yourself, then, noble Helicane.
But, if the prince do live, let us salute him
Or know what ground's made happy by his breath.
If in the world he live, we'll seek him out;
If in his grave he rest, we'll find him there
And be resolved:° he lives to govern us *know one way or the other*
Or, dead, gives cause to mourn his funeral
And leaves us to our free election.
SECOND LORD Whose death's indeed the strongest° in our *(likelihood)*
censure.° *judgment*
And knowing this: kingdoms without a head,
Like goodly buildings left without a roof,
Soon fall to ruin—your noble self,
That best know how to rule and how to reign,

1. Each one do his best to succeed (in wooing the princess).
**2.4** Location: Tyre, the Governor's house.

1. TEXTUAL COMMENT For the possible inconsistencies in this scene involving Escanes and the Lords' motives, see Digital Edition TC 6.

We thus submit unto: our sovereign!
ALL LORDS Live, noble Helicane!
HELICANUS For honor's cause, forbear your suffrages!° *voting (for me)*
If that you love Prince Pericles, forbear!
[*aside*] Take I° your wish, I leap into the seas, *If I accept*
Where's° hourly trouble for a minute's ease. *Where there is*
—A twelvemonth longer let me entreat you
To further bear the absence of your king;
If in which time expired he not return,
I shall with aged patience bear your yoke.
But if I cannot win you to this love,° *(of Pericles)*
Go search like nobles, like noble subjects,
And in your search, spend your adventurous worth,
Whom° if you find and win unto° return, *(Pericles) / persuade to*
You shall like diamonds sit about his crown.
FIRST LORD To wisdom he's a fool that will not yield.
And since Lord Helicane enjoineth us,
We with our travels will endeavor.
HELICANUS Then you love us, we you, and we'll clasp hands:
When peers thus knit, a kingdom ever stands. [*Exeunt.*]

## 2.5

*Enter the King* [SIMONIDES] *reading of a letter at one door; the* KNIGHTS *meet him* [*from another door*].
FIRST KNIGHT Good morrow to the good Simonides.
SIMONIDES Knights, from my daughter this I let you know:
That for this twelvemonth she'll not undertake
A married life.
Her reason to herself is only known,
Which from her by no means can I get.
SECOND KNIGHT May we not get access to her, my lord?
SIMONIDES Faith, by no means. She hath so strictly tied
Her to her chamber that 'tis impossible.
One twelve moons more she'll wear Diana's livery.[1]
This by the eye of Cynthia[2] hath she vowed,
And on her virgin honor will not break it.
THIRD KNIGHT Loath to bid farewell, we take our leaves.
[*Exeunt* KNIGHTS.]
SIMONIDES So, they are well dispatched!
Now to my daughter's letter.
She tells me here she'll wed the stranger knight
Or never more to view nor° day nor light. *neither*
'Tis well, mistress: your choice agrees with mine.
I like that well. Nay, how absolute she's in't,
Not minding whether I dislike or no!
Well, I do commend her choice
And will no longer have it be delayed.
Soft, here he comes. I must dissemble it.
*Enter* PERICLES.
PERICLES All fortune to the good Simonides.
SIMONIDES To you as much. Sir, I am beholden to you

**2.5** Location: The palace at Pentapolis.
1. She'll serve Diana, goddess of chastity.
2. Another name for Diana, as goddess of the moon.

For your sweet music this last night. I do
Protest, my ears were never better fed
With such delightful pleasing harmony.
PERICLES It is your grace's pleasure to commend,
Not my desert.
SIMONIDES Sir, you are music's master.
PERICLES The worst of all her scholars,° my good lord. *students*
SIMONIDES Let me ask you one thing:
What do you think of my daughter, sir?
PERICLES A most virtuous princess.
SIMONIDES And she is fair too, is she not?
PERICLES As a fair day in summer, wondrous fair.
SIMONIDES Sir, my daughter thinks very well of you—
Ay, so well that you must be her master
And she will be your scholar. Therefore look to it.° *be prepared*
PERICLES I am unworthy for° her schoolmaster. *to be*
SIMONIDES She thinks not so. Peruse this writing else.° *if you doubt me*
[*He gives* PERICLES *Thaisa's letter.*]
PERICLES [*aside, after reading*] What's here, a letter that she loves the knight of Tyre?
'Tis the King's subtlety to have my life.
—Oh, seek not to entrap me, gracious lord:
A stranger and distressèd gentleman
That never aimed so high to° love your daughter *as to*
But bent all offices[3] to honor her.
SIMONIDES Thou hast bewitched my daughter, and thou art
A villain.
PERICLES By the gods, I have not!
Never did thought of mine levy° offense; *give*
Nor never did my actions yet commence
A deed might° gain her love or your displeasure. *that might*
SIMONIDES Traitor, thou liest!
PERICLES Traitor?
SIMONIDES Ay, traitor.
PERICLES Even in his throat, unless it be the King
That calls me traitor, I return the lie.° *(with my sword)*
SIMONIDES [*aside*] Now, by the gods, I do applaud his courage!
PERICLES My actions are as noble as my thoughts
That never relished of° a base descent. *gave a hint of*
I came unto your court for honor's cause
And not to be a rebel to her state,
And he that otherwise accounts of me,
This sword shall prove he's honor's enemy.
SIMONIDES No? Here comes my daughter; she can witness it.
*Enter* THAISA.
PERICLES [*to* THAISA] Then, as you are as virtuous as fair,
Resolve° your angry father if my tongue *Inform*
Did ere solicit or my hand subscribe
To any syllable that made love to you.
THAISA Why, sir, say if you had—
Who takes offense at that° would make me glad? *what*

3. *bent all offices:* performed all services.

SIMONIDES Yea, mistress, are you so peremptory?° *determined*
(*aside*) I am glad on't with all my heart.
—I'll tame you; I'll bring you in subjection.
Will you, not having my consent,
Bestow your love and your affections,
Upon a stranger? (*aside*) —who, for aught I know,
May be, nor can I think the contrary,
As great in blood as I myself.
Therefore, [*to* THAISA] hear you, mistress: either frame° *mold*
Your will to mine —[*to* PERICLES] and you, sir, hear you:
Either be ruled by me, or I'll make you—
Man and wife!
Nay, come, your hands and lips must seal it too.
[*He joins their hands.* PERICLES *and* THAISA *kiss.*]
And, being joined, I'll thus your hopes destroy!
[*He separates them.*]
And, for further grief [*joining them again*] —God give you joy!
What, are you both pleased?
THAISA Yes [*to* PERICLES] —if you love me, sir?
PERICLES Even as my life° my blood that fosters it. *as my life loves*
SIMONIDES What, are you both agreed?
THAISA *and* PERICLES Yes, if't please your majesty.
SIMONIDES It pleaseth me so well that I will see you wed,
And then, with what haste you can, get you to bed.
*Exeunt.*

## 3.0

*Enter* GOWER.
GOWER Now sleep y-slackèd hath the rouse:[1]
No din but snores about the house,
Made louder by the o'erfed breast° *stomach*
Of this most pompous° marriage feast. *lavish*
The cat with eyne° of burning coal *eyes*
Now couches fore° the mouse's hole; *before*
And crickets sing° at the oven's mouth *that sing*
Are the blither for their drouth.[2]
Hymen° hath brought the bride to bed, *god of marriage*
Where by the loss of maidenhead
A babe is molded. Be attent,° *attentive*
And time that is so briefly spent° *spent onstage*
With your fine fancies quaintly eche.° *skillfully fill out*
What's dumb in show, I'll plain° with speech. *clarify*
[*Dumb show.*]
*Enter* PERICLES *and King* SIMONIDES *at one door with Attendants. A Messenger meets them, kneels, and gives* PERICLES *a letter.* PERICLES *shows it* SIMONIDES. *The* LORDS *kneel to* [PERICLES]. *Then enter* THAISA *with child, with* LYCHORIDA, *a nurse. The King shows* [THAISA] *the letter. She rejoices. She and* PERICLES *take leave of her father, and depart* [*with* LYCHORIDA. *Then exeunt* SIMONIDES *and his court*].

**3.0**
1. Sleep has rendered everyone inactive. *rouse:* drinking party.
2. As if happier for being dry.

By many a dern° and painful perch° *wild / patch of land*
Of Pericles the careful search,
By the four opposing coigns° *corners*
Which the world together joins,
Is made with all due diligence
That horse and sail and high expense
Can stead° the quest. At last from Tyre, *sustain in*
Fame° answering the most strange enquire,° *Rumor / distant queries*
To th' court of King Simonides
Are letters brought, the tenor these:
Antiochus and his daughter dead,
The men of Tyrus on the head
Of Helicanus would set on
The crown of Tyre, but he will° none. *desires*
The mutiny he there hastes t'appease,
Says to 'em, if King Pericles
Come not home in twice six moons,
He, obedient to their dooms,° *judgments*
Will take the crown. The sum of this
Brought hither to Pentapolis
Y-ravishèd° the regions round, *Enraptured*
And every one with claps can° sound, *started to*
"Our heir apparent is a king!
Who dreamt, who thought of such a thing?"
Brief,° he must hence depart to Tyre. *In short; quickly*
His queen, with child, makes her desire—
Which who shall cross?—along to go.
Omit we all their dole and woe.
Lychorida her nurse she takes.
And so to sea. Their vessel shakes
On Neptunè's billow. Half the flood° *sea*
Hath their keel cut, but Fortune's mood
Varies again: the grizzled° North *grisly*
Disgorges such a tempest forth
That, as a duck for life that dives,
So up and down the poor ship drives.
The lady shrieks and, well-a-near,° *alas*
Does fall in travail° with her fear. *Goes into labor*
And what ensues in this fell° storm *cruel*
Shall for itself itself perform.
I nill° relate; action may *will not*
Conveniently the rest convey,
Which might not what by me is told.[3]
In your imagination hold° *think*
This stage the ship, upon whose deck
The seas-tossed Pericles appears to speak. [*Exit.*]

3. Which could not easily "convey" what I've related so far.

## 3.1

[*Thunder and lightning.*] *Enter* PERICLES *on shipboard.*

PERICLES Thou god of this great vast,° rebuke these surges *vast sea*
Which wash both heaven and hell! And thou that hast
Upon the winds command, bind them in brass,
Having called them from the deep. Oh, still° *quiet*
Thy deafening dreadful thunders; gently quench
Thy nimble sulphurous flashes! Oh! —[*He calls offstage.*]
How, Lychorida!
How does my queen? —Thou storm'st venomously;
Wilt thou spit all thyself? The seaman's whistle
Is as a whisper in the ears of death,° *of a dead person*
Unheard. —Lychorida! —Lucina,° O *goddess of childbirth*
Divinest patroness and midwife gentle
To those that cry by night, convey thy deity
Aboard our dancing boat, make swift the pangs
Of my queen's travails! —Now, Lychorida!

*Enter* LYCHORIDA [*carrying a newborn child*].

LYCHORIDA Here is a thing too young for such a place,
Who if it had conceit° would die, as I *understanding*
Am like° to do. Take in your arms this piece *likely*
Of your dead queen.

PERICLES How? How, Lychorida?

LYCHORIDA Patience, good sir. Do not assist the
storm.° *(by ranting and shedding tears)*
Here's all that is left living of your queen,
A little daughter. For the sake of it,
Be manly, and take comfort.

PERICLES O you gods!
Why do you make us love your goodly gifts,
And snatch them straight away? We here below
Recall° not what we give, and therein may *Demand back*
Vie honor with you.[1]

LYCHORIDA Patience, good sir,
Even for this charge.[2]

PERICLES [*to the child*] Now, mild may be thy life,
For a more blusterous birth had never babe;
Quiet and gentle thy conditions,° for *circumstances*
Thou art the rudeliest welcome to this world
That ever was prince's child; happy° what follows. *let be happy*
Thou hast as chiding° a nativity *upsetting*
As fire, air, water, earth, and heaven can make
To herald thee from the womb.
Even at the first, thy loss is more than can
Thy portage quit, with all thou canst find here.[3]
Now the good gods throw their best eyes° upon't! *look favorably*

*Enter* [*the* MASTER *and a* SAILOR].

3.1 Location: At sea.
1. *therein . . . you:* in this respect may compete with you in honor.
2. For the sake of this child.
3. *thy . . . here:* Perhaps: your loss of your mother is more than can be repaid you through your birth, even along with everything you find in this life.

MASTER What courage, sir? God save you.
PERICLES Courage enough. I do not fear the flaw°— *squall*
It hath done to me the worst—yet for the love
Of this poor infant, this fresh new seafarer,
I would it would be quiet.
MASTER [*calls*] Slack the bow-lines there!
—Thou° wilt not, wilt thou? Blow and split thyself! *(the storm)*
SAILOR But sea-room![4] An° the brine and cloudy billow *If*
Kiss the moon, I care not!
MASTER [*to* PERICLES] Sir, your queen must overboard. The sea works° high, the wind is loud, and will not lie° till the ship be cleared of the dead. *surges / lie still*
PERICLES That's your superstition.
MASTER Pardon us, sir;
With us at sea it hath been still° observed, *always*
And we are strong in custom. Therefore briefly° yield'er, *quickly*
For she must overboard straight.
PERICLES As you think meet.
Most wretched queen!
LYCHORIDA [*reveals Thaisa's body*] Here she lies, sir.
PERICLES A terrible childbed hast thou had, my dear:
No light, no fire; th'unfriendly elements
Forgot thee utterly. Nor have I time
To give thee hallowed to thy grave, but straight
Must cast thee, scarcely coffined, in the ooze,° *seabed*
Where for° a monument upon thy bones *in place of*
The e'er-remaining° lamps,[5] the belching whale, *ever-burning*
And humming water must o'erwhelm thy corpse,
Lying with simple shells. —O Lychorida,
Bid Nestor bring me spices, ink, and paper,
My casket, and my jewels; and bid Nicander
Bring me the satin coffer. Lay the babe
Upon the pillow. Hie° thee, whiles I say *Hurry*
A priestly farewell to her. Suddenly,° woman! *Immediately*
[*Exit* LYCHORIDA.]
SAILOR Sir, we have a chest beneath the hatches, caulked and bitumed° ready. *sealed with pitch*
PERICLES I thank thee. —Mariner, say, what coast is this?
MASTER We are near Tarsus.
PERICLES Thither, gentle mariner,
Alter thy course for° Tyre. When canst thou reach it? *that was for*
MASTER By break of day, if the wind cease.
PERICLES Oh, make for Tarsus.
There will I visit Cleon, for the babe
Cannot hold out to Tyre. There I'll leave it
At careful nursing. Go thy ways,° good mariner. *Get to it*
I'll bring the body presently.
*Exeunt* [MASTER *and* SAILOR, *followed by* PERICLES].[6]

4. As long as we're at sea (safe from the rocks).
5. Either funeral lamps, which, like "a monument" (line 60), will be absent; or the stars as lamps, which, like the "whale" and "water" (lines 61–62), replace the "monument."
6. TEXTUAL COMMENT For the staging of this scene and the handling of Thaisa and the baby, see Digital Edition TC 7.

## 3.2

*Enter Lord* CERIMON *with* [*two* VISITING SERVANTS].[1]

CERIMON Philemon, ho!

*Enter* PHILEMON.

PHILEMON Doth my lord call?

CERIMON Get fire and meat for these poor men.° *the servants or men offstage*
'T has been a turbulent and stormy night.

[*Exit* PHILEMON.]

FIRST VISITING SERVANT I have been in many, but such a night as this
Till now I ne'er endured.

CERIMON [*to him*] Your master will be dead ere you return;
There's nothing can be ministered to nature
That can recover him. [*to* SECOND VISITING SERVANT] Give this to the 'pothecary,° *druggist*
And tell me how it works.

[*Exeunt* FIRST *and* SECOND VISITING SERVANTS.]

*Enter two* GENTLEMEN.

FIRST GENTLEMAN Good morrow.

SECOND GENTLEMAN Good morrow to your lordship,

CERIMON Gentlemen!
Why do you stir so early?

FIRST GENTLEMAN Sir,
Our lodgings, standing bleak upon° the sea, *exposed to*
Shook as° the earth did quake. *as if*
The very principals° did seem to rend *principal rafters*
And all to topple. Pure surprise and fear
Made me to quit the house.

SECOND GENTLEMAN That is the cause we trouble you so early.
'Tis not our husbandry.° *good work habits*

CERIMON Oh, you say well!

FIRST GENTLEMAN But I much marvel that your lordship, having
Rich tire° about you, should at these early hours *bed furniture*
Shake off the golden slumber of repose.
'Tis most strange
Nature should be so conversant with pain,[2]
Being thereto not compelled.

CERIMON I held it ever,° *always believed*
Virtue and cunning° were endowments greater *knowledge*
Than nobleness and riches. Careless heirs
May the two latter darken and expend,
But immortality attends the former,
Making a man a god. 'Tis known I ever° *always*
Have studied physic,° through which secret art, *medicine*
By turning o'er authorities,° I have, *reading learned texts*
Together with my practice, made familiar
To me and to my aid° the blest infusions *benefit*
That dwells in vegetives,[3] in metals, stones.
And I can speak of the disturbances

3.2 Location: Cerimon's house in Ephesus.
1. TEXTUAL COMMENT For the roles of servants in this scene, see Digital Edition TC 8.
2. That your nature should be so accustomed to labor.
3. Beneficial substances in plants.

That Nature works and of her cures, which doth
Give more content in course of true delight
Than to be thirsty after tottering° honor *unstable*
Or tie my pleasure up in silken bags,° *(of money)*
To please the fool and Death.[4]
SECOND GENTLEMAN Your honor has
Through Ephesus poured forth your charity,
And hundreds call themselves your creatures[5] who
By you have been restored. And not your knowledge,
Your personal pain,° but even your purse still° open, *labor / always*
Hath built Lord Cerimon such strong renown
As time shall never—
*Enter* [PHILEMON *and two* SERVANTS] *with a chest.*
FIRST SERVANT So, lift there.
CERIMON What's that?
FIRST SERVANT Sir, even now
Did the sea toss upon our shore this chest.
'Tis of some wreck.
CERIMON Set't down. Let's look upon't.
SECOND GENTLEMAN 'Tis like a coffin, sir.
CERIMON Whate'er it be,
'Tis wondrous heavy. [*to* SERVANTS] Wrench it open straight.[6]
[SERVANTS *get implements.*]
If the sea's stomach be o'ercharged with gold,
'Tis a good constraint of Fortune it belches[7] upon us.
SECOND GENTLEMAN 'Tis so, my lord.
CERIMON How close° 'tis caulked and bitumed! *tightly*
Did the sea cast it up?
FIRST SERVANT I never saw so huge a billow, sir,
As tossed it upon shore.
CERIMON Wrench it open. —Soft!° *But wait*
It smells most sweetly in my sense!
SECOND GENTLEMAN A delicate odor!
CERIMON As ever hit my nostril.
So, up with it.
[SERVANTS *raise the lid.*]
O you most potent gods!
What's here?
A corpse?
SECOND GENTLEMAN Most strange!
CERIMON Shrouded in cloth of state,° *royal fabric*
Balmed and entreasured with full bags of spices.
[*He finds a paper.*]
A passport° too! Apollo, perfect me *An identification paper*
In the characters.[8]
[*Reads.*] "Here I give to understand,
If ere this coffin drives a-land,
I, King Pericles, have lost
This queen worth all our mundane cost.° *earthly wealth*

4. To gladden the fool who trusts in wealth, which death inherits.
5. *call . . . creatures:* owe their lives to you.
6. TEXTUAL COMMENT On the elaborate stage business of this scene, see Digital Edition TC 9.
7. It is good that fortune forces the sea to belch.
8. Apollo (patron of both scholars and physicians) help me read the writing correctly.

Who° finds her, give her burying: — *Whoever*
She was the daughter of a king.
Besides this treasure for a fee,
The° gods requite his charity." — *May the*
If thou livest, Pericles, thou hast a heart
That ever cracks for woe! —This chanced tonight.° — *occurred last night*

SECOND GENTLEMAN Most likely, sir.

CERIMON Nay, certainly tonight—
For look how fresh she looks! They were too rough
That threw her in the sea. [*to* SERVANTS] Make a fire within.
Fetch hither all my boxes in my closet. [*Exeunt* SERVANTS.]
Death may usurp on nature many hours,
And yet the fire of life kindle again
The o'er-pressed° spirits. I heard of an Egyptian — *overcome*
That had nine hours lain dead,
Who was by good appliance° recovered. — *medical treatment*

*Enter* [SERVANTS] *with* [*boxes,*] *napkins and fire.*

Well said, well said; the fire and cloths.
[*to* FIRST GENTLEMAN] The rough° and woeful music that we have, — *harsh; unrefined*
Cause it to sound, beseech you.
[*to a* SERVANT] The vial° once more. How thou stirr'st,[9] thou block! — *(of medicine)*
The music there! [*Music sounds.*] I pray you, give her air.
Gentlemen, this queen will live. Nature awakes.
A warmth breathes out of her. She hath not been entranced° — *unconscious*
Above five hours. See how she 'gins to blow° — *bloom*
Into life's flower again.

FIRST GENTLEMAN The heavens, through you,
Increase our wonder, and sets up your fame
Forever.

CERIMON She is alive. Behold,
Her eyelids, cases to those heavenly jewels
Which Pericles hath lost, begin to part
Their fringes of bright gold. The diamonds
Of a most praised water° doth appear. — *luster*
[*to* THAISA] To make the world twice rich,[1] live,
And make us weep to hear your fate, fair creature,
Rare° as you seem to be. — *Exquisite*

*She moves.*

THAISA O dear Diana,
Where am I? Where's my lord? What world is this?

SECOND GENTLEMAN Is not this strange?

FIRST GENTLEMAN Most rare.

CERIMON Hush, my gentle neighbors.
Lend me your hands. To the next chamber bear her.
Get linen. Now this matter must be looked to,
For her relapse is mortal.° Come, come; — *would be fatal*
And Aesculapius° guide us! — *god of healing*

*They carry* [THAISA] *away. Exeunt.*

9. How lively you are (ironic).
1. Once by the precious gold of her eyelids and again by the jewels they conceal.

## 3.3

*Enter* PERICLES *at Tarsus with* CLEON, DIONYZA[, *and* LYCHORIDA *with the child*].

PERICLES Most honored Cleon, I must needs be gone.
My twelve months are expired,[1] and Tyrus stands
In a litigious° peace. You and your lady — *conflict-ridden*
Take from my heart all thankfulness. The gods
Make up the rest upon you.[2]
CLEON Your shafts of fortune,
Though they hurt you mortally, yet glance
Full woundingly on us.
DIONYZA Oh, your sweet queen!
That the strict fates had pleased you had brought[3] her hither
To have blessed mine eyes with her!
PERICLES We cannot but obey
The powers above us. Could° I rage and roar — *Even if*
As doth the sea she lies in, yet the end
Must be as 'tis. My gentle babe Marina,
Whom for° she was born at sea I have named so, — *because*
Here I charge° your charity withal,° — *request; burden / with*
Leaving her the infant of your care,
Beseeching you to give her princely training,
That she may be mannered° as she is born. — *brought up*
CLEON Fear not, my lord, but think
Your grace, that fed my country with your corn,
For which the people's prayers still fall upon you,
Must in your child be thought on. If neglection
Should therein make me vile, the common body,° — *the people*
By you relieved, would force me to my duty.
But if to that° my nature need a spur, — *that duty*
The gods revenge it upon me and mine
To the end of generation!
PERICLES I believe you.
Your honor and your goodness teach me to't° — *to do so*
Without your vows. Till she be married, madam,
By bright Diana whom we honor, all
Unscissored shall this hair of mine remain,
Though I show ill° in't. So I take my leave. — *look bad*
Good madam, make me blessèd in your care
In bringing up my child.
DIONYZA I have one myself,
Who shall not be more dear to my respect° — *attention*
Than yours, my lord.
PERICLES Madam, my thanks and prayers.
CLEON We'll bring your grace e'en to the edge o'th' shore,
Then give you up to the masked Neptune° and — *calm (or treacherous) sea*
The gentlest winds of heaven.
PERICLES I will embrace your offer.
—Come, dearest madam. —Oh, no tears, Lychorida, no tears.
Look to your little mistress, on whose grace° — *favor*
You may depend hereafter. —Come, my lord. [*Exeunt*.]

3.3 Location: The governor's house in Tarsus.
1. See 3.0.25–33.
2. Give you the rest of what you deserve.
3. *That . . . brought*: I wish it had pleased the "strict fates" to have allowed you to bring.

## 3.4

*Enter* CERIMON *and* THAISA.

CERIMON Madam, this letter and some certain jewels
Lay with you in your coffer, which are at your command:
Know you the character?° *handwriting*

THAISA It is my lord's.
That I was shipped° at sea I well remember, *on a ship*
Even on my groaning° time, but whether there delivered, *birthing*
By the holy gods I cannot rightly say.
But since King Pericles, my wedded lord,
I ne'er shall see again,
A vestal livery[1] will I take me to
And never more have joy.

CERIMON Madam, if this you purpose° as ye speak, *intend*
Diana's temple is not distant far,
Where you may abide till your date expire.° *life ends*
Moreover, if you please, a niece of mine
Shall there attend you.

THAISA My recompense is thanks; that's all.
Yet my good will is great, though the gift small. *Exeunt.*

## 4.0

*Enter* GOWER.

GOWER Imagine Pericles arrived at Tyre,
Welcomed and settled to his own desire.
His woeful queen we leave at Ephesus,
Unto Diana there as votaress.° *devotee*
Now to Marina bend your mind,
Whom our fast-growing scene must find
At Tarsus, and by Cleon trained
In music, letters, who hath gained
Of education all the grace,
Which makes her both the heart and place° *focal point*
Of general wonder. But, alack,
That monster envy, oft the wrack° *ruin*
Of earnèd praise, Marina's life
Seeks to take off by treason's knife.
And in this kind:° our Cleon hath *way*
One daughter and a full-grown wench
Even ripe for marriage rite. This maid
Hight° Philoten, and it is said *Was called*
For certain in our story, she
Would ever° with Marina be. *always*
Be't when they weaved the sleided° silk, *divided into filaments*
With fingers long, small, white as milk,
Or when she would with sharp needle wound
The cambric° which she made more sound *fine linen*
By hurting it, or when to th' lute
She sung, and made the night bird° mute *nightingale*
That still records° with moan, or when *always sings*

**3.4** Location: Cerimon's house in Ephesus.
1. Vestal virgin's (metaphorical) uniform of religious chastity.

She would with rich and constant pen,
Vail° to her mistress Dian—still — *Inscribe praises*
This Philoten contends in skill
With absolute° Marina. So — *perfect*
With dove of Paphos might the crow
Vie feathers white.[1] Marina gets
All praises, which are paid as debts
And not as given.[2] This so darks° — *darkens*
In Philoten all graceful marks
That Cleon's wife with envy rare° — *extreme*
A present murder does prepare
For good Marina, that her daughter
Might stand peerless by° this slaughter. — *by means of*
The sooner her vile thoughts to stead,° — *help*
Lychorida, our nurse, is dead,
And cursèd Dionyza hath
The pregnant instrument of wrath
Pressed for this blow.[3] The unborn event,° — *outcome*
I do commend to your content.° — *(viewing) pleasure*
Only I carry wingèd Time,
Post° on the lame feet of my rhyme, — *Quickly*
Which never could I so convey,
Unless your thoughts went on my way.
Dionyza does appear,
With Leonine, a murderer. *Exit.*

## 4.1

*Enter* DIONYZA *with* LEONINE.

DIONYZA Thy oath remember—thou hast sworn to do't.
'Tis but a blow which never shall be known.
Thou canst not do a thing in the world so soon° — *quickly*
To yield thee so much profit. Let not conscience,
Which is but cold, enflaming thy low° bosom, — *base*
Enflame too nicely;° nor let pity, which — *scrupulously*
Even women have cast off, melt thee, but be
A soldier to thy purpose.

LEONINE I will do't.
But yet she is a goodly creature.

DIONYZA The fitter then the gods should have her.
Here she comes, weeping for her nurse's death.
Thou art resolved?

LEONINE I am resolved.

*Enter* MARINA *with a basket of flowers.*

MARINA No, I will rob Tellus of her weed° — *earth of its garment*
To strew thy green with flowers: the yellows, blues,
The purple violets, and marigolds
Shall as a carpet hang upon thy grave,
While summer days doth last. Ay me, poor maid,
Born in a tempest when my mother died,

**4.0**

1. *So . . . white:* So might the crow try to be whiter than the dove. Paphos was a city sacred to Venus.
2. *Marina . . . given:* Marina's gifts compel others to praise her, willingly or not.
3. Has enlisted a ready means to carry out her anger.

**4.1** Location: Tarsus, near the seashore.

This world to me is a lasting storm
Whirring° me from my friends. *Hurrying*
DIONYZA How now, Marina? Why do you keep alone?
How chance° my daughter is not with you? *Why is it*
Do not consume your blood with sorrowing.[1]
Have you a nurse of me![2] Lord, how your favor's° *appearance is*
Changèd with this unprofitable woe!
Come, give me your flowers. O'er the sea margin° *seashore*
Walk with Leonine. The air is quick° there *refreshing*
And it pierces and sharpens the stomach.° *appetite*
Come, Leonine,
Take her by the arm, walk with her.
MARINA No, I pray you.
I'll not bereave you of your servant.
DIONYZA Come, come,
I love the King your father and yourself
With more than foreign heart.° We every day *As if we were kin*
Expect him here. When he shall come and find
Our paragon to all reports thus blasted,[3]
He will repent the breadth of his great voyage,
Blame both my lord and me, that we have taken
No care to your best courses.° Go, I pray you. *courses of action*
Walk and be cheerful once again; reserve° *preserve*
That excellent complexion which did steal
The eyes of young and old. Care not for me—
I can go home alone.
MARINA Well, I will go,
But yet I have no desire to it.
DIONYZA Come, come,
I know 'tis good for you. —Walk half an hour,
Leonine, at the least. Remember what I have said.
LEONINE I warrant° you, madam. *guarantee*
DIONYZA I'll leave you, my sweet lady, for a while.
Pray, walk softly; do not heat your blood.
What! I must have care of you!
MARINA My thanks, sweet madam.
[*Exit* DIONYZA.]
Is this wind westerly that blows?
LEONINE Southwest.
MARINA When I was born the wind was north.
LEONINE Was't so?
MARINA My father, as nurse says, did never fear,
But cried, "Good seamen," to the sailors,
Galling° his kingly hands hauling° ropes, *Irritating / pulling*
And, clasping to the mast, endured a sea
That almost burst the deck.
LEONINE When was this?
MARINA When I was born.

1. Sighs were thought to consume one's blood.
2. Let me be your nurse.
3. Our universally admired paragon of beauty so blighted.

Never was waves nor wind more violent,
And from the ladder tackle° washes off — *climbing rope; rope-ladder*
A canvas-climber.° "Ha," says one, "wolt out?"[4] — *sailor in the rigging*
And with a dropping° industry they skip — *dripping-wet*
From stem to stern. The boatswain° whistles, and — *senior crew member*
The master calls, and trebles their confusion—

LEONINE Come, say your prayers.

MARINA What mean you?

LEONINE If you require a little space for prayer,
I grant it. Pray, but be not tedious,° for — *drawn out*
The gods are quick of ear, and I am sworn
To do my work with haste.

MARINA Why will you kill me?

LEONINE To satisfy my lady.

MARINA Why would she have me killed?
Now, as I can remember, by my troth,° — *faith*
I never did her hurt in all my life,
I never spake bad word, nor did ill turn
To any living creature: Believe me, la,° — *(exclamation)*
I never killed a mouse nor hurt a fly.
I trod upon a worm against my will,
But I wept for't. How have I offended
Wherein my death might yield her any profit, or
My life imply her any danger?

LEONINE My commission
Is not to reason of the deed, but do't.

MARINA You will not do't for all the world, I hope.
You are well favored, and your looks foreshow
You have a gentle heart. I saw you lately
When you caught° hurt in parting two that fought: — *got*
Good sooth,° it showed well in you. Do so now: — *Truly*
Your lady seeks my life; come you between,° — *(Dionyza and me)*
And save poor me, the weaker.

LEONINE I am sworn and will dispatch.

*[He draws his sword.] Enter [three]* PIRATES.

FIRST PIRATE Hold, villain!

[LEONINE *runs off and hides.]*

SECOND PIRATE A prize,° a prize! — *Booty (Marina)*

THIRD PIRATE Half part,° mates, half part. Come, let's have — *To be shared*
her aboard suddenly.° *Exeunt [carrying off* MARINA]. — *quickly*

LEONINE *[comes forward.]*

LEONINE These roguing° thieves serve the great pirate Valdes,[5] — *law-breaking*
And they have seized Marina. Let her go.
There's no hope she will return; I'll swear she's dead
And thrown into the sea.—But I'll see further:
Perhaps they will but please themselves upon her,° — *will only rape her*
Not carry her aboard. If she remain,
Whom they have ravished must by me be slain. *Exit.*

4. So you want to get off ship? (a cruel joke)

5. Probably named after an admiral in the Spanish Armada.

## 4.2

*Enter* [PANDER, BAWD (*his wife*), *and* BOLT].[1]

PANDER Bolt!

BOLT Sir?

PANDER Search the market narrowly.° Mytilene is full of gal- — *carefully*
lants. We lost too much money this mart° by being too — *market time*
wenchless.

BAWD We were never so much out of creatures.° We have but — *prostitutes*
poor three,° and they can do no more than they can do, and — *only three*
they with continual action are even as good as rotten.° — *have venereal disease*

PANDER Therefore let's have fresh ones, whate'er we pay for
them. If there be not a conscience to be used[2] in every trade,
we shall never prosper.

BAWD Thou say'st true. 'Tis not our bringing up of poor
bastards°—as I think I have brought up some eleven— — *(that enriches us)*

BOLT Ay, to eleven, and brought them down again.[3]—But
shall I search the market?

BAWD What else, man? The stuff we have, a strong wind will
blow it to pieces, they are so pitifully sodden.[4]

PANDER Thou sayest true. They're too unwholesome,
o'conscience.° The poor Transylvanian is dead that lay with — *on my conscience*
the little baggage.° — *prostitute*

BOLT Ay, she quickly pooped° him; she made him roast meat — *overcame (by disease)*
for worms—but I'll go search the market. *Exit.*

PANDER Three or four thousand chequins° were as pretty a — *gold coins*
proportion° to live quietly and so give over°— — *sum / retire*

BAWD Why "to give over," I pray you? Is it a shame to get° — *earn*
when we are old?

PANDER Oh, our credit comes not in like the commodity, nor
the commodity wages not with the danger.[5] Therefore if in
our youths we could pick up some pretty estate, 'twere not
amiss to keep our door hatched.° Besides, the sore terms we — *closed for business*
stand upon with the gods[6] will be strong° with us for giving — *a strong argument*
o'er.

BAWD Come, other sorts offend as well as we.

PANDER As well as we? Ay, and better, too. We offend worse.
Neither is our profession any trade. It's no calling°—but — *(religious) vocation*
here comes Bolt.

*Enter* BOLT *with the* PIRATES *and* MARINA.

BOLT [*to the* PIRATES] Come your ways,° my masters.° You say — *Come along / gentlemen*
she's a virgin?

FIRST PIRATE O sir, we doubt it not.

BOLT Master, I have gone through° for this piece° you see. If — *bargained / (of flesh)*
you like her, so.° If not, I have lost my earnest.° — *fine / deposit*

BAWD Bolt, has she any qualities?° — *accomplishments*

**4.2** Location: Mytilene, on the island of Lesbos; before a brothel.

1. *Pander:* sexual go-between, after Pandarus in Chaucer's poem, *Troilus and Criseyde. Bawd:* supplier of prostitutes. The name "Bolt" may have phallic connotations.
2. We need undiseased prostitutes for both economic and ethical reasons.
3. And prostituted them when they turned eleven.
4. Overboiled in the sweating tub as treatment for venereal disease.
5. Our reputation doesn't accumulate like our profit, nor does the profit justify the danger (with extended economic wordplay: "credit," "commodity," "wages").
6. The Pander's admission here, indicating his ambivalence, is part of the religious undercurrent of the scene.

BOLT She has a good face, speaks well, and has excellent good clothes. There's no farther necessity of qualities can° make her be refused. *whose absence can*

BAWD What's her price, Bolt?

BOLT I cannot be bated one doit of[7] a thousand pieces.

PANDER [*to the* PIRATES] Well, follow me, my masters; you shall have your money presently.° —Wife, take her in; instruct her what she has to do, that she may not be raw in her entertainment.[8] [*Exeunt* PANDER *and the* PIRATES.] *immediately*

BAWD Bolt, take you the marks of her—the color of her hair, complexion, height, her age—with warrant of her virginity, and cry, "He that will give most shall have her first." Such a maidenhead were no cheap thing if men were as they have been. Get this done as I command you.

BOLT Performance shall follow. *Exit.*

MARINA Alack that Leonine was so slack, so slow—
He should have struck, not spoke!—or that° these pirates, *if only*
Not enough barbarous, had but o'erboard thrown me
For to seek my mother!

BAWD Why lament you, pretty one?

MARINA That I am pretty.

BAWD Come, the gods have done their part in you.

MARINA I accuse them not.

BAWD You are light° into my hands, where you are like° to live. *arrived / likely*

MARINA The more my fault,° *misfortune*
To scape his hands where I was like to die.

BAWD Ay, and you shall live in pleasure.

MARINA No.

BAWD Yes, indeed shall you, and taste gentlemen of all fashions. You shall fare well, you shall have the difference of all complexions[9]—what? Do you stop your ears?

MARINA Are you a woman?

BAWD What would you have me be, an° I be not a woman? *if*

MARINA An honest° woman or not a woman. *A chaste*

BAWD Marry, whip the gosling! I think I shall have something to do° with you. Come, you're a young foolish sapling and must be bowed as I would have you. *some trouble*

MARINA The gods defend me!

BAWD If it please the gods to defend you by men, then men must comfort you, men must feed you, men stir you up.

[*Enter* BOLT.]

Bolt's returned. —Now, sir, hast thou cried° her through the market? *advertised*

BOLT I have cried her almost to° the number of her hairs, I have drawn her picture with my voice. *down to*

BAWD And I prithee tell me, how dost thou find the inclination of the people, especially of the younger sort?

7. I cannot get the price reduced a penny (*doit:* small coin) from.
8. May not be unprepared to entertain customers.
9. The variety of appearances (temperaments; ethnicities).

BOLT Faith, they listened to me as they would have harkened to their father's testament.° There was a Spaniard's mouth watered, and he went to bed to her very description.

*will*

BAWD We shall have him here tomorrow with his best ruff° on.

*collar; (sexual?)*

BOLT Tonight, tonight! But, mistress, do you know the French knight that cowers i'the hams?[1]

BAWD Who, Monsieur Veroles?°

*Mr. Pox*

BOLT Ay, he. He offered to cut a caper[2] at the proclamation, but he made a groan at it and swore he would see her tomorrow.

BAWD Well, well, as for him, he brought his disease hither;[3] here he does but repair° it. I know he will come in our shadow, to scatter his crowns in the sun.[4]

*renew*

BOLT Well, if we had of every nation a traveler we should lodge them with this sign.[5]

BAWD [*to* MARINA] Pray you, come hither a while. You have fortunes coming upon you.[6] Mark me: you must seem to do that fearfully which you commit willlingly, despise profit where you have most gain. To weep that you live as ye do° makes pity in your lovers. Seldom but that pity begets you a good opinion, and that opinion a mere° profit.

*(by prostitution)*
*clear*

MARINA I understand you not.

BOLT Oh, take her home,° mistress, take her home. These blushes of hers must be quenched with some present practice.

*inside; to task*

BAWD Thou sayest true i'faith, so they must, for your° bride goes to that with shame which is her way to go with warrant.[7]

*even a*

BOLT Faith, some do and some do not. But, mistress, if I have bargained for the joint°—

*cut of meat*

BAWD Thou mayst cut a morsel off the spit.°

*have a taste yourself*

BOLT I may so.

BAWD Who should deny it? [*to* MARINA] Come, young one. I like the manner of your garments well.

BOLT Ay, by my faith, they shall not be changed yet.[8]

BAWD [*gives him money*] Bolt, spend thou that in the town. Report what a sojourner we have. You'll lose nothing by custom.[9] When Nature framed this piece,° she meant thee a good turn. Therefore, say what a paragon she is, and thou hast the harvest out of thine own report.

*(of work; of flesh)*

BOLT I warrant you, mistress. Thunder shall not so awake the beds of eels[1] as my giving out her beauty stirs up the lewdly inclined. I'll bring home some tonight. [*Exit.*]

1. Who crouches (from venereal disease).
2. He tried to leap up and clap his heels together.
3. Englishmen called syphilis "the French disease." This allusion, as well as the equally anachronistic references to "a Spaniard's mouth" (line 91) and "the French knight" (lines 94–95), is one indication of the contemporary, distinctively English feel of the scene; see also act 2, scene 1.
4. He will come inside our house to spend his French crowns; to lose his hair (on the crown of his head) from syphilis. With a play on "shadow" and "sun."
5. This description would draw them like the painted sign of an inn.
6. You have prosperity (wealthy men) about to come to (have an orgasm on top of) you.
7. Even a bride, who has a legal right to sexual enjoyment, is shy, because, like Marina, she is a virgin.
8. Exchanged or sold (for a prostitute's wardrobe), since they proclaim her virginity and social status.
9. You'll gain in tips if we get more customers.
1. Eels were supposedly roused by thunder.

BAWD [*to* MARINA] Come your ways, follow me.
MARINA If fires be hot, knives sharp, or waters deep,
Untried I still my virgin knot will keep.[2]
Diana,° aid my purpose! *goddess of chastity*
BAWD What have we to do with Diana? Pray you, will you go with us? *Exeunt.*

## 4.3

*Enter* CLEON *and* DIONYZA.

DIONYZA Why, are you foolish? Can it be undone?
CLEON O Dionyza, such a piece of slaughter
The sun and moon ne'er looked upon.
DIONYZA I think you'll turn a child again.
CLEON Were I chief lord of all this spacious world,
I'd give it to undo the deed. A lady° *(Marina)*
Much less in blood than virtue, yet a princess
To equal any single crown o'th' earth
I'th' justice of compare!° O villain Leonine! *In a fair comparison*
—Whom thou hast poisoned too!
If thou hadst drunk to him 't had been a kindness
Becoming well thy fact![1] What canst thou say
When noble Pericles shall demand his child?
DIONYZA That she is dead. Nurses are not the Fates.
To foster is not ever° to preserve. *always*
She died at night—I'll say so; who can cross° it? *deny*
Unless you play the pious innocent
And for an honest attribute,° cry out, *reputation*
"She died by foul play."
CLEON Oh, go to!° Well, well, *(contemptuous)*
Of all the faults beneath the heavens the gods
Do like this worst.
DIONYZA Be one of those that thinks
The petty wrens of Tarsus will fly hence
And open° this to Pericles. I do shame *disclose*
To think of what a noble strain° you are, *bloodline*
And of how coward a spirit.
CLEON To such proceeding
Whoever but° his approbation added, *only*
Though not his prime° consent, he did not flow *prior*
From honorable sources.
DIONYZA Be it so then,
Yet none does know but you how she came dead,
Nor none can know, Leonine being gone.
She did distain° my child and stood between *stain (by comparison)*
Her and her fortunes: none would look on her,
But cast their gazes on Marina's face
Whilst ours was blurted at° and held a malkin° *scorned / dirty peasant*
Not worth the time of day. It pierced me through.
And though you call my course unnatural,
You not your child well loving,[2] yet I find

2. *Untried . . . keep:* I will still remain a virgin. Q reads "Untied," which, with the pun of "knot" and "not," means not untied—hence, the same thing.
**4.3** Location: The governor's house in Tarsus.

1. *If . . . fact:* If you had drunk to his health (from the same poison), the self-punishment would have fit the crime.
2. Since you don't love your child very much.

It greets° me as an enterprise of kindness — *strikes*
Performed to your sole daughter.
CLEON — Heavens forgive it!
DIONYZA — And as for Pericles, what should he say?
We wept after her hearse, and yet° we mourn. — *still*
Her monument is almost finished, and her epitaphs
In glitt'ring golden characters express
A general praise to her and care in us
At whose expense 'tis done.
CLEON — Thou art like the harpy[3]
Which, to betray, dost with thine angel's face
Seize[4] with thine eagle's talons.
DIONYZA — You're like one that superstitiously
Do swear to th' gods that winter kills the flies.[5]
But yet I know you'll do as I advise. — [*Exeunt.*]

## 4.4

[*Enter* GOWER.]

GOWER — Thus time we waste,° and long leagues make short,[1] — *pass quickly*
Sail seas in cockles,° have and wish but for't,[2] — *seashells*
Making to take° our imagination — *Proceeding by*
From bourn° to bourn, region to region. — *border*
By you being pardoned, we commit no crime
To use one language in each several clime° — *separate region*
Where our scene seems to live. I do beseech you
To learn of me who stand i'th' gaps° to teach you — *(between scenes)*
The stages of our story. Pericles
Is now again thwarting° the wayward seas, — *crossing*
Attended on by many a lord and knight,
To see his daughter, all his life's delight.
Old Helicanus goes along. Behind
Is left to govern, if you bear in mind,
Old Escanes, whom Helicanus late° — *recently*
Advanced in Tyre to great and high estate.° — *rank*
Well-sailing ships and bounteous winds have brought
This king to Tarsus—think his pilot thought;[3]
So with his steerage shall your thoughts go on—
To fetch his daughter home, who first° is gone. — *already*
Like motes and shadows[4] see them move a while.
Your ears unto your eyes I'll reconcile.

[*Dumb show.*]

*Enter* PERICLES *at one door with all his train,* CLEON *and* DIONYZA *at the other.* CLEON *shows* PERICLES *the tomb, whereat* PERICLES *makes lamentation, puts on sackcloth,° and in a mighty passion° departs* [*with his train. Exeunt* CLEON *and* DIONYZA *separately*]. — *mourning clothes / sorrow*

3. Monstrous creature with a woman's face and an eagle's talons.
4. *Which . . . Seize:* Who deceives with your "angel's face" and then "Seize[s]."
5. *You're . . . flies:* Perhaps: You're so afraid of the gods that you'd disclaim responsibility even for petty things like killing flies.

4.4 Location: Before Marina's tomb in Tarsus.
1. Here, Gower speaks in pentameter couplets.
2. Get something merely by wishing for it.
3. Think that his pilot is swiftly traveling thought.
4. Like specks of dust in a sunbeam and like (theatrical) illusions.

See how belief may suffer by foul show:° *false appearances*
This borrowed passion stands for true-owed woe,[5]
And Pericles, in sorrow all devoured,
With sighs shot through and biggest tears o'ershowered,
Leaves Tarsus and again embarks. He swears
Never to wash his face nor cut his hairs.
He puts on sackcloth, and to sea he bears
A tempest which his mortal vessel tears,[6]
And yet he rides it out. Now please you wit° *know*
The epitaph is° for Marina writ *that is*
By wicked Dionyza:
[*He reads the inscription on the tomb.*]
"The fairest, sweetest, and best lies here,
Who withered in her spring of year:° *early in life*
She was of Tyrus the King's° daughter *the King of Tyre's*
On whom foul death hath made this slaughter.
Marina was she called, and at her birth
Thetis,[7] being proud, swallowed° some part o'th' earth. *flooded*
Therefore the earth, fearing to be o'erflowed,
Hath Thetis' birth-child on the heavens bestowed,
Wherefore she° does, and swears she'll never stint, *(Thetis)*
Make raging battery upon shores of flint."° *rocky shores*
No visor does become black villainy
So well as soft and tender flattery.
Let Pericles believe his daughter's dead,
And bear his courses to be orderèd[8]
By Lady Fortune, while our stage must play
His daughter's woe and heavy welladay° *lamentation*
In her unholy service. Patience, then,
And think you now are all in Mytilene. *Exit.*

## 4.5

*Enter two* GENTLEMEN.

FIRST GENTLEMAN Did you ever hear the like?

SECOND GENTLEMAN No, nor never shall do in such a place as this, she being once gone.

FIRST GENTLEMAN But to have divinity preached there—did you ever dream of such a thing?

SECOND GENTLEMAN No, no. Come, I am for no more bawdy houses. Shall's go hear the vestals sing?[1]

FIRST GENTLEMAN I'll do anything now that is virtuous, but I am out of the road of rutting° forever. *Exeunt.* *fornication*

5. Cleon and Dionyza's "woe" is "borrowed," not "true-owed" (owned); perhaps also a self-referential comment on the sorrow simulated by the actor playing Pericles.

6. *he bears . . . tears:* His suffering assaults his body. (Note the internalization of the earlier storms.)

7. A sea nymph here confused with Tethys, wife of Oceanus (in Greek mythology, the ruler of a river that encircled the earth). The image in this passage is of the ocean (because of Thetis/Tethys) surging happily in response to Marina's birth during the storm of act 3, scene 1, and angrily in response to her death.

8. And allow his fate to be arranged.

**4.5** Location: The brothel in Mytilene.

1. Shall we go hear the vestal virgins (religious devotees) sing?

## 4.6

*Enter* [PANDER, BAWD, *and* BOLT].

PANDER Well, I had rather than twice the worth of her she had ne'er come here.

BAWD Fie, fie upon her, she's able to freeze the god Priapus and undo a whole generation.[1] We must either get her ravished or be rid of her. When she should do for clients her fitment,° and do me the kindness of our profession,[2] she has° me her quirks, her reasons, her master reasons, her prayers, her knees,° that she would make a puritan of the devil if he should cheapen° a kiss of her.

*duty* / *gives* / *(kneeling to plead)* / *bargain for*

BOLT Faith, I must ravish her, or she'll disfurnish us of all our *cavalleria*° and make our swearers[3] priests.

*gentlemen customers*

PANDER Now the pox upon her greensickness,[4] for me!

BAWD Faith, there's no way to be rid on't but by the way to the pox.° Here comes the Lord Lysimachus disguised.

*venereal disease*

BOLT We should have both lord and loon° if the peevish baggage° would but give way to customers.

*lowborn* / *worthless woman*

*Enter* LYSIMACHUS [*masked*].

LYSIMACHUS How now, how° a dozen of virginities?

*how much for*

BAWD Now the gods to-bless your honor!

BOLT I am glad to see your honor in good health.

LYSIMACHUS You may so: 'tis the better for you that your resorters° stand upon sound legs.[5] How now? Wholesome iniquity° have you, that a man may deal withal° and defy the surgeon?°

*visitors* / *Healthy whore / with* / *avoid the doctor*

BAWD We have here one, sir, if she would—but there never came her like in Mytilene.

LYSIMACHUS If she'd do the deeds of darkness, thou wouldst say.

BAWD Your honor knows what 'tis to say° well enough.

*what I mean*

LYSIMACHUS Well, call forth, call forth. [*Exit* PANDER.]

BOLT For flesh and blood, sir, white and red, you shall see a rose. And she were a rose indeed, if she had but—[6]

LYSIMACHUS What, prithee?

BOLT O sir, I can be modest.

LYSIMACHUS That dignifies the renown of a bawd, no less than it gives a good report to a number to be chaste.[7]

[*Re-enter* PANDER *with* MARINA.]

BAWD Here comes that which grows to° the stalk: never plucked yet, I can assure you. Is she not a fair creature?

*is affixed to*

LYSIMACHUS Faith, she would serve after a long voyage at sea. Well, there's for you. [*He gives the* BAWD *money*.] Leave us.

BAWD I beseech your honor, give me leave a word, and I'll have done presently.°

*be done soon*

**4.6** Location: Scene continues.

1. Able to stop the "whole" (hole) work of breeding. Priapus was the god of procreation, especially of male virility and lechery.
2. Enable me to profit from her profession of prostitution. "Do me" and "has me" (line 7) are here colloquial expressions of annoyance.
3. Make our customers sincerely worship the gods they usually invoke blasphemously.
4. Moody stubbornness, supposedly caused by anemia in young women; queasiness from lack of experience.
5. Rather than upon legs bent from venereal disease.
6. If she had but a thorn; if she were sexually experienced (implied pun on "prick").
7. Than it gives many (whores? wives?) a (falsely) good reputation for chastity.

LYSIMACHUS I beseech you, do.

[BAWD *speaks privately with* MARINA.]

BAWD First, I would have you note, this is an honorable man.

MARINA I desire to find him so, that I may worthily note him.

BAWD Next, he's the governor of this country and a man whom I am bound to.

MARINA If he govern the country you are bound to him indeed, but how honorable he is in that, I know not.

BAWD Pray you, without any more virginal fencing, will you use him kindly? He will line your apron with gold.

MARINA What he will do graciously, I will thankfully receive.

LYSIMACHUS Ha' you done?

BAWD My lord, she's not paced° yet; you must take some pains to work her to your manage.[8] —Come, we will leave his honor and her together. —Go thy ways.° *trained (like a horse)* / *Come along*

[*Exeunt* BAWD, PANDER, *and* BOLT.]

LYSIMACHUS Now, pretty one, how long have you been at this trade?

MARINA What trade, sir?

LYSIMACHUS Why, I cannot name it but I shall offend.

MARINA I cannot be offended with my trade; please you to name it.

LYSIMACHUS How long have you been of this profession?

MARINA E'er since I can remember.

LYSIMACHUS Did you go to't° so young? Were you a gamester° at five, or at seven? *copulate / loose woman*

MARINA Earlier, too, sir, if now I be one.

LYSIMACHUS Why, the house you dwell in proclaims you to be a creature of sale.

MARINA Do you know this house to be a place of such resort,° and will come into't? I hear say you're of honorable parts and are the governor of this place. *purpose*

LYSIMACHUS Why, hath your principal° made known unto you who I am? *employer*

MARINA Who is my principal?

LYSIMACHUS Why, your herb-woman, she that sets seeds and roots of shame and iniquity.—Oh, you have heard something of my power and so stand aloof for more serious wooing, but I protest to thee, pretty one, my authority shall not see thee, or else look friendly upon thee.[9] Come, bring me to some private place. Come, come.

MARINA If you were born to honor,° show it now. *high status; virtue*
If put upon you,[1] make the judgment good
That thought you worthy of it.

LYSIMACHUS [*aside*] How's this? How's this? Some more. Be sage.

MARINA For me
That am a maid, though most ungentle Fortune
Have placed me in this sty, where, since I came,
Diseases have been sold dearer than physic—[2]
That the gods

8. To bring her under your control (from horsemanship).
9. *my authority . . . upon thee:* Lysimachus won't use his power to punish prostitution, or he will patronize her (personally, financially).
1. If you were granted rank not by birth but by merit.
2. Sold at a higher price than medical treatment.

Would set me free from this unhallowed place,
Though they did change me to the meanest° bird *(humblest)*
That flies i'th' purer air!

LYSIMACHUS I did not think
Thou couldst have spoke so well, ne'er dreamt thou couldst.
Had I brought hither a corrupted mind,
Thy speech had altered it. Hold, here's gold for thee.
Persevere in that clear way thou goest
And the gods strengthen thee.

MARINA The good gods preserve you!

LYSIMACHUS For me, be you bethoughten that I came
With no ill intent, for to me the very doors
And windows savor vilely. Fare thee well.
Thou art a piece of virtue, and I doubt not
But thy training hath been noble.
Hold, here's more gold for thee.
A curse upon him, die he° like a thief, *(may he die)*
That robs thee of thy goodness! If thou dost
Hear from me it shall be for thy good.

[*He opens the door to leave. Enter* BOLT.]

BOLT I beseech your honor, one piece for me.

LYSIMACHUS Avaunt,° thou damnèd doorkeeper! *(Begone)*
Your house, but for this virgin that doth prop it,
Would sink and overwhelm you. Away! [*Exit.*]

BOLT How's this? We must take another course with you! If your peevish chastity, which is not worth a breakfast in the cheapest country under the cope,° shall undo a whole household, let me be gelded like a spaniel. Come your ways. *(sky)*

MARINA Whither would you have me?

BOLT I must have your maidenhead taken off, or the common hangman shall execute it.[3] Come your ways, we'll have no more gentlemen driven away. Come your ways, I say.

*Enter* [BAWD *and* PANDER].

BAWD How now, what's the matter?

BOLT Worse and worse, mistress; she has here spoken holy words to the Lord Lysimachus.

BAWD Oh, abominable!

BOLT He makes our profession as it were to stink afore the face of the gods.

BAWD Marry,° hang her up forever. *((expresses irritation))*

BOLT The nobleman would have dealt with her like a nobleman,[4] and she sent him away as cold as a snowball, saying his prayers too.

BAWD Bolt, take her away, use her at thy pleasure. Crack the glass of her virginity, and make the rest malleable.

BOLT An if° she were a thornier piece of ground than she is, she shall be plowed. *(Even if)*

MARINA Hark, hark, you gods!

3. By cutting off the maidenhead (virginity), as an executioner cuts off heads.

4. Would have used her and rewarded her well.

BAWD She conjures°—away with her! Would she had never come within my doors. —Marry, hang you! —She's born to undo us. —Will you not go the way of womenkind? Marry come up, my dish of chastity with rosemary and bays.[5] — *calls on the gods*

[*Exeunt* BAWD *and* PANDER.]

BOLT Come, mistress, come your ways with me.

MARINA Whither wilt thou have me?

BOLT To take from you the jewel you hold so dear.

MARINA Prithee, tell me one thing first.

BOLT Come now, your one thing?

MARINA What canst thou wish thine enemy to be?[6]

BOLT Why, I could wish him to be° my master, or rather, my mistress. — *(as bad as)*

MARINA Neither of these are so bad as thou art,
Since they do better thee in their command.[7]
Thou hold'st a place for which the painedest° fiend — *most tortured*
Of hell would not in reputation change.
Thou art the damnèd doorkeeper to every
Coistrel° that comes enquiring for his Tib.° — *Base fellow / loose woman*
To the choleric fisting of every rogue
Thy ear is liable;[8] thy food is such
As hath been belched on by infected lungs.

BOLT What would you have me do? Go to the wars, would you—where a man may serve seven years for the loss of° a leg, and have not money enough in the end to buy him a wooden one? — *only to lose*

MARINA Do anything but this thou dost. Empty
Old receptacles, or common shores,° of filth, — *(where waste was placed)*
Serve by indenture° to the common hangman— — *as apprentice*
Any of these ways are yet better than this.
For what thou professest, a baboon, could he speak,
Would own a name too dear.° —Oh, that the gods — *consider beneath him*
Would safely deliver me from this place!
—Here, here's gold for thee.
[*She gives him the money.*]
If that thy master would gain by me,
Proclaim that I can sing, weave, sew, and dance,
With other virtues° which I'll keep from boast, — *accomplishments*
And will undertake all these to teach.
I doubt not but this populous city will
Yield many scholars.° — *pupils*

BOLT But can you teach all this you speak of?

MARINA Prove° that I cannot, take me home again — *If you prove*
And prostitute me to the basest groom° — *lowest servant*
That doth frequent your house.

BOLT Well, I will see what I can do for thee. If I can place thee, I will.

MARINA But amongst honest women.

5. The Bawd chides Marina for thinking herself too exquisite a dish (for making too much of her chastity).

6. What is the worst thing you could wish on your enemy?

7. Since they at least can command you to do what they want.

8. *To . . . liable*: Even the lowest rogue would box your ear if angry.

BOLT Faith, my acquaintance lies little amongst them. But since my master and mistress hath bought you, there's no going but by their consent; therefore I will make them acquainted with your purpose, and I doubt not but I shall find them tractable enough. Come, I'll do for thee what I can. Come your ways. *Exeunt.*

## 5.0

*Enter* GOWER.

GOWER Marina thus the brothel scapes, and chances[1]
Into an honest house, our story says.
She sings like one immortal, and she dances
As goddess-like to her admirèd lays.° *songs*
Deep clerks she dumbs[2] and with her nee'le° composes *needle*
Nature's own shape of bud, bird, branch, or berry,
That even her art sisters° the natural roses; *equals*
Her inkle,° silk, twin with the rubied cherry— *linen thread*
That° pupils lacks she none of noble race *So that*
Who pour their bounty on her, and her gain
She gives the cursèd bawd. Here we her place,
And to her father turn our thoughts again.
We left him on the sea; we there him lost,
Where, driven before the winds, he is arrived
Here where his daughter dwells, and on this coast
Suppose him now at anchor. The city strived° *endeavored*
God Neptune's annual feast to keep, from whence
Lysimachus our Tyrian ship espies—
His° banners sable,° trimmed with rich expense— *Its / black*
And to him° in his barge with fervor hies. *it*
In your supposing° once more put your sight *imagination*
Of heavy° Pericles; think this his bark,° *sad / ship*
Where what is done in action, more if might,
Shall be discovered.[3] Please you sit and hark. *Exit.*

## 5.1

*Enter two* SAILORS[, *the* FIRST *from Tyre and the* SECOND *from Mytilene*].

FIRST SAILOR Where is Lord Helicanus? [*to* SECOND SAILOR]
He can resolve° you. *answer*
[*Enter* HELICANUS.]
Oh, here he is.
—Sir, there is a barge put off from Mytilene
And in it is Lysimachus, the Governor,
Who craves to come aboard. What is your will?

HELICANUS That he have his. [*Exit* SECOND SAILOR.]
Call up some gentlemen.

FIRST SAILOR Ho, gentlemen, my lord calls!

5.0
1. Unlike Gower's other prologues, which are in tetrameter or, less often, pentameter rhyming couplets, this one rhymes alternate pentameter lines.
2. Her wisdom reduces learned men to silence.
3. *Where . . . discovered:* Where the stage action, which would show more if it could, will reveal what happens.
5.1 Location: Pericles' ship, off Mytilene.

*Enter two or three* GENTLEMEN.

FIRST GENTLEMAN Doth your lordship call?
HELICANUS Gentlemen, there is some of worth° — *some noble visitor*
Would come aboard. I pray, greet him fairly.

*Enter* LYSIMACHUS [*with* SECOND SAILOR *and* LORDS].

SECOND SAILOR [*to* LYSIMACHUS] Sir, this is the man that can
In aught you would resolve° you. — *Answer anything for*
LYSIMACHUS [*to* HELICANUS] Hail, reverend sir!
The gods preserve you.
HELICANUS And you, to outlive the age I am
And die as I would do.
LYSIMACHUS You wish me well.
Being on shore, honoring of Neptune's triumphs,° — *festival*
Seeing this goodly vessel ride before us,
I made to it, to know of whence you are.
HELICANUS First, what is your place?
LYSIMACHUS I am the governor of this place you lie before.
HELICANUS Sir, our vessel is of Tyre, in it the King,
A man who for this three months hath not spoken
To anyone, nor taken sustenance
But to prorogue° his grief. — *extend*
LYSIMACHUS Upon what ground is his distemperature?° — *emotional disturbance*
HELICANUS 'Twould be too tedious to repeat,
But the main grief springs from the loss
Of a beloved daughter and a wife.
LYSIMACHUS May we not see him?
HELICANUS You may,
But bootless° is your sight. He will not speak — *pointless*
To any.
LYSIMACHUS Yet let me obtain my wish.
HELICANUS Behold him.

[PERICLES *is revealed.*]

This was a goodly person,
Till the disaster that one mortal° night — *fatal*
Drove him to this.
LYSIMACHUS Sir King, all hail! The gods preserve you! Hail,
royal sir!
HELICANUS It is in vain; he will not speak to you.
FIRST LORD Sir, we have a maid in Mytilene, I durst wager
Would win some words of him.
LYSIMACHUS 'Tis well bethought.
She questionless, with her sweet harmony
And other choice attractions, would allure
And make a batt'ry through his deafened ports,
Which now are midway stopped.° She is all happy,° — *half closed / skillful*
And the fairest of all her fellow maids—
[*to* FIRST LORD] Now upon the leafy shelter that abuts
Against the island's side. [*Exit* FIRST LORD.]
HELICANUS Sure, all effectless.
Yet nothing we'll omit
That bears recovery's name.° But since your kindness — *That might cure him*
We have stretched thus far, let us beseech you
That for our gold we may provision have,
Wherein we are not destitute for want,
But weary for the staleness.

LYSIMACHUS O sir, a courtesy
Which if we should deny, the most just gods
For every graft° would send a caterpillar *cultivated plant*
And so inflict° our province. Yet once more *afflict (with famine)*
Let me entreat to know at large° the cause *in detail*
Of your king's sorrow.

HELICANUS Sit, sir; I will
Recount it to you—

[*Re-enter* FIRST LORD with MARINA *and another Maid.*]

but see, I am prevented.

LYSIMACHUS Oh, here's the lady that I sent for.
Welcome, fair one. —Is't not a goodly presence?° *Isn't she attractive*

HELICANUS She's a gallant° lady. *fine*

LYSIMACHUS She's such a one that, were I well assured
Came of a gentle kind° and noble stock, *a gentry family*
I'd wish no better choice, and think me rarely° to wed. *superbly*
[*to* MARINA] Fair one, all goodness that consists in bounty
Expect even here, where is a kingly patient.
If that thy prosperous and artificial feat° *artful skill*
Can draw him but to answer thee in aught,
Thy sacred physic° shall receive such pay *treatment*
As thy desires can wish.

MARINA Sir, I will use
My utmost skill in his recovery,° provided *cure*
That none but I and my companion maid
Be suffered° to come near him. *permitted*

LYSIMACHUS Come, let us leave her,
And the gods make her prosperous.

[*Exeunt all except* MARINA, *the Maid, and* PERICLES.]

*The Song.*

[MARINA *and the other Maid sing and play to* PERICLES, *who does not respond. Re-enter* LYSIMACHUS *and* HELICANUS.]

LYSIMACHUS Marked° he your music? *Noticed*

MARINA No, nor looked on us.

LYSIMACHUS [*to* HELICANUS] See, she will speak to him.

[LYSIMACHUS, HELICANUS, *and the Maid withdraw.*]

MARINA Hail, sir! My lord, lend ear!

PERICLES Hmm? Ha!

[*He pushes her back.*]

MARINA I am a maid, my lord,
That ne'er before invited eyes, but have
Been gazed on like a comet.° She speaks, *in awe*
My lord, that maybe hath endured a grief
Might° equal yours, if both were justly weighed. *That might*
Though wayward fortune did malign my state,° *reduce my status*
My derivation was from ancestors
Who stood equivalent with mighty kings.
But time hath rooted out[1] my parentage,
And to the world and awkward casualties° *adverse events*
Bound me in servitude. [*aside*] I will desist.
But there is something glows upon my cheek

1. Uprooted me from; obscured; killed.

And whispers in mine ear, "Go not till he speak."
PERICLES My fortunes, parentage—good parentage,
To equal mine—was it not thus? What say you?
MARINA I said, my lord, if you did know my parentage,
You would not do me violence.
PERICLES I do think so.
Pray you, turn your eyes upon me.
You're like something that—What countrywoman?° *What nationality*
Here, of these shores?
MARINA No, nor of any shores.
Yet I was mortally[2] brought forth, and am
No other than I appear.
PERICLES [*aside*] I am great° with woe, and shall deliver *pregnant*
weeping.
My dearest wife was like this maid, and such a one
My daughter might have been: my queen's square brows,
Her stature to an inch, as wand-like straight,
As silver-voiced, her eyes as jewel-like
And cased as richly, in pace° another Juno; *stride*
Who starves the ears she feeds and makes them hungry
The more she gives them speech. —Where do you live?
MARINA Where I am but a stranger.° From the deck *foreigner*
You may discern the place.
PERICLES Where were you bred?
And how achieved you these endowments which
You make more rich to owe?° *by your owning them*
MARINA If I should tell
My history, it would seem like lies
Disdained in the reporting.° *as soon as told*
PERICLES Prithee, speak.
Falseness cannot come from thee, for thou lookest
Modest as justice, and thou seemest a palace
For the crowned Truth to dwell in. I will believe thee
And make sense credit thy relation° *trust your story*
To° points that seem impossible, for thou lookest *Even to*
Like one I loved indeed. What were thy friends?° *kin*
Didst thou not say when I did push thee back—
Which was when I perceived thee—that thou cam'st
From good descending?
MARINA So indeed I did.
PERICLES Report thy parentage. I think thou said'st
Thou hadst been tossed from wrong to injury,
And that thou thought'st thy griefs might equal mine,
If both were opened.° *revealed*
MARINA Some such thing I said,
And said no more but what my thoughts
Did warrant° me was likely. *assure*
PERICLES Tell thy story.
If thine considered° prove the thousandth part *yours, when considered,*
Of my endurance,° thou art a man, and I *suffering*
Have suffered like a girl. Yet thou dost look

2. Normally, not supernaturally, despite not being born on "any shores"; perhaps also fatally—to her mother.

Like Patience gazing on kings' graves and smiling
Extremity out of act.[3] What were thy friends?
How lost thou them? Thy name, my most kind[4] virgin?
Recount, I do beseech thee. Come, sit by me.

MARINA [*sitting*] My name is Marina.

PERICLES Oh, I am mocked,
And thou by some incensèd god sent hither
To make the world to laugh at me.

MARINA Patience, good sir,
Or here I'll cease.

PERICLES Nay, I'll be patient.
Thou little know'st how thou dost startle me
To call thyself Marina.

MARINA The name
Was given me by one that had some power:
My father, and a king.

PERICLES How? A king's daughter
And called Marina?

MARINA You said you would believe me.
But not to be a troubler of your peace,
I will end here.

PERICLES But are you flesh and blood?
Have you a working pulse, and are no fairy?
Motion° as well? Speak on. Where were you born? *(of life)*
And wherefore called Marina?

MARINA Called Marina
For I was born at sea.

PERICLES At sea—what mother?

MARINA My mother was the daughter of a king,
Who died the minute I was born, as my good nurse
Lychorida hath oft delivered weeping.

PERICLES Oh, stop there a little! [*aside*] This is the rarest dream
That e'er dulled sleep did mock sad fools withal!° *with*
This cannot be my daughter, buriėd.
—Well, where were you bred?
I'll hear you more, to th' bottom° of your story, *the end*
And never interrupt you.

MARINA You scarce believe me; 'twere best I did give o'er.° *stop*

PERICLES I will believe you by the syllable
Of what you shall deliver. Yet give me leave:° *(to ask)*
How came you in these parts? Where were you bred?

MARINA The King my father did in Tarsus leave me,
Till cruel Cleon with his wicked wife
Did seek to murder me and wooed a villain
To attempt it, who having drawn to do't,
A crew of pirates came and rescued me,
Brought me to Mytilene. But, good sir, whither
Will you have me? Why do you weep? It may be
You think me an impostor. No, good faith.

3. *Yet . . . act:* Yet you resemble a statue of Patience on a royal tomb, facing down the worst extremities with a smile.

4. Sympathetic; related by blood ("kind" also meant "kin").

I am the daughter to King Pericles,
If good King Pericles be.° *live*
PERICLES Ho, Helicanus?
[HELICANUS *and* LYSIMACHUS *come forward.*]
HELICANUS Calls my lord?
PERICLES Thou art a grave and noble counselor,
Most wise in general. Tell me, if thou canst,
What this maid is, or what is like° to be, *likely*
That thus hath made me weep.
HELICANUS I know not,
But here's the regent, sir, of Mytilene,
Lysimachus, speaks° nobly of her. *who speaks*
LYSIMACHUS She never
Would tell her parentage. Being demanded that,
She would sit still and weep.
PERICLES O Helicanus, strike me, honored sir,
Give me a gash, put me to present° pain, *immediate*
Lest this great sea of joys rushing upon me
O'erbear° the shores of my mortality *Overflow*
And drown me with their sweetness. [*to* MARINA] Oh, come
hither,
Thou that begett'st him that did thee beget,[5]
Thou that wast born at sea, buried at Tarsus,
And found at sea again. —O Helicanus,
Down on thy knees, thank the holy gods as loud
As thunder threatens us! This is Marina.
—What was thy mother's name? Tell me but that,
For truth can never be confirmed enough,
Though doubts did ever sleep.[6]
MARINA First, sir, I pray,[7]
What is your title?
PERICLES I am Pericles of Tyre.
But tell me now my drowned queen's name, as in
The rest foresaid thou hast been godlike perfect°— *have been omniscient*
The heir of kingdoms, and another life
To Pericles thy father.
MARINA Is it no more to be your daughter than
To say my mother's name was Thaisa?
Thaisa was my mother, who did end
The minute I began.
[*She kneels. He blesses her.*]
PERICLES Now blessing on thee. Rise, thou'rt my child.
[*She rises. He calls to Attendants.*]
—Give me fresh garments! —Mine own Helicanus,
She is not dead at Tarsus, as she should have been[8]
By savage Cleon. She shall tell thee all
When thou shalt kneel and justify in knowledge° *satisfy yourself that*

5. The possible sexual complications here, including incest, can be highlighted in performance by doubling the part of Marina with that of Thaisa or Antiochus's Daughter.
6. Even in the absence of doubts.
7. TEXTUAL COMMENT For problems of lineation and decisions about whether to set certain lines as verse or prose, see Digital Edition TC 10.
8. As she was believed (intended) to be.

She is thy very princess.
[*Attendants enter with robes.* LYSIMACHUS *approaches* PERICLES.]
Who is this?
HELICANUS Sir, 'tis the Governor of Mytilene,
Who, hearing of your melancholy state,
Did come to see you.
PERICLES [*to* LYSIMACHUS] I embrace you, sir.
[*to Attendants*] Give me my robes. —I am wild in my beholding.[9]
O heavens, bless my girl! —But hark, what music!
—Tell Helicanus, my Marina, tell him
O'er point by point, for yet he seems to doubt,
How sure you are my daughter. —But what music?
HELICANUS My lord, I hear none.
PERICLES None?
The music of the spheres![1] —List,° my Marina. *Listen*
LYSIMACHUS [*aside to the others*] It is not good to cross him; give him way.
PERICLES Rarest sounds—do ye not hear?
LYSIMACHUS Music, my lord? I hear.
PERICLES Most heavenly music.
It nips° me unto listening, and thick slumber *compels*
Hangs upon mine eyes. Let me rest.
[*He sleeps.*]
LYSIMACHUS A pillow for his head. —So, leave him all.
Well, my companion friends, if this but answer to
My just belief, I'll well remember° you. *reward; recall*
[*Exeunt, leaving* PERICLES *asleep.*]
DIANA [*descends*].
DIANA [*to* PERICLES] My temple stands in Ephesus; hie thee thither
And do upon mine altar sacrifice.
There when my maiden priests are met together,
[
]² Before the people all
Reveal how thou at sea didst lose thy wife;
To mourn thy crosses° with thy daughter's, call,° *losses / call out loudly*
And give them repetition to the life.° *an accurate accounting*
Perform my bidding or thou livest in woe.
Do't and be happy, by my silver bow.[3]
Awake, and tell thy dream. [*She ascends.*]
PERICLES [*awakening*] Celestial Dian, goddess argentine,° *silvery (like the moon)*
I will obey thee. —Helicanus!
[*Enter* HELICANUS, MARINA, *and* LYSIMACHUS.]
HELICANUS Sir?
PERICLES My purpose was for Tarsus, there to strike
The inhospitable Cleon, but I am
For other service first. Toward Ephesus

9. I am too ecstatic to see correctly.
1. PERFORMANCE COMMENT "The music of the spheres" is a sign of celestial harmony, brought about by the proper movement of the heavenly bodies around earth (hence a sign of divine order). For possible ways of performing this music, see Digital Edition PC 1.
2. The break in the rhyme scheme of Diana's speech (no rhyme for "sacrifice") plus the shortness of line 230 suggest that one-and-a-half lines are missing.
3. A crescent moon. Diana was goddess of the moon and a renowned hunter.

Turn our blown° sails. Eftsoons° I'll tell thee why. *inflated / Later*
[*to* LYSIMACHUS] Shall we refresh us, sir, upon your shore,
And give you gold for such provision
As our intents will need?

LYSIMACHUS Sir, with all my heart,
And when you come ashore,
I have another suit.

PERICLES You shall prevail,
Were it to woo my daughter, for it seems
You have been noble towards her.

LYSIMACHUS Sir, lend me your arm.

PERICLES Come, my Marina.

*Exeunt.*

## 5.2

[*Enter* GOWER.]

GOWER Now our sands are almost run.
More a little, and then dumb.° *silent*
This my last boon give me,
For such kindness must relieve me:
That you aptly will suppose° *readily will imagine*
What pageantry, what feats, what shows,
What minstrelsy and pretty din
The regent° made in Mytilene *(Lysimachus)*
To greet the king. So he° thrived *So well (Lysimachus)*
That he is promised to be wived
To fair Marina, but in no wise° *way*
Till he° had done his sacrifice *(Pericles)*
As Dian bade, whereto being bound,
The interim, pray you all, confound.° *skip*
In feathered° briefness sails are filled *winged*
And wishes fall out as they're willed.
At Ephesus the temple see
Our king, and all his company.
That he can hither come so soon,
Is by your fancy's thankful doom.[1] [*Exit.*]

## 5.3

[*Enter the Priestesses of Diana, among them* THAISA, *and Worshippers, including* CERIMON. *To them, enter* PERICLES, MARINA, HELICANUS, LYSIMACHUS, *and Attendants.*]

PERICLES Hail, Dian! To perform thy just° command, *precise*
I here confess myself the King of Tyre
Who, frighted from my country, did
Wed at Pentapolis the fair Thaisa.
At sea in childbed died she, but brought forth
A maid° child called Marina who, O goddess, *girl*
Wears yet thy silver livery.[1] She at Tarsus
Was nursed with° Cleon, who at fourteen years *by*

5.2
1. Thanks to your imaginations' agreement.

5.3 Location: The temple of Diana in Ephesus.
1. Still wears your uniform (remains a virgin).

He sought to murder, but her better stars
Brought her to Mytilene, 'gainst whose shore riding,° *where we anchored*
Her fortunes brought the maid aboard us, where
By her own most clear remembrance, she
Made known herself my daughter.

THAISA Voice and favor°— *appearance*
You are—you are—O royal Pericles!
[*She faints.*]

PERICLES What means the nun? She dies! Help, gentlemen!
[CERIMON *and others go to* THAISA.]

CERIMON Noble sir,
If you have told Diana's altar true,
This is your wife.

PERICLES Reverend appearer,° no. *Reverend-looking man*
I threw her overboard with these very arms.

CERIMON Upon this coast, I warrant you.

PERICLES 'Tis most certain.

CERIMON Look to the lady. Oh, she's but overjoyed.
Early one blustering morn this lady was
Thrown upon this shore. I oped the coffin,
Found there rich jewels, recovered° her, and placed her *revived*
Here in Diana's temple.

PERICLES May we see them?

CERIMON Great sir, they shall be brought you to° my house, *at*
Whither I invite you. Look, Thaisa is
Recoverèd.

THAISA [*rising*] Oh, let me look!
If he be none of mine, my sanctity
Will to my sense bend no licentious ear,
But curb it, spite of seeing.[2] —O my lord,
Are you not Pericles? Like him you spake,
Like him you are. Did you not name a tempest,
A birth, and death?

PERICLES The voice of dead Thaisa!

THAISA That Thaisa am I, supposèd dead
And drowned.

PERICLES Immortal Dian!

THAISA Now I know you better.
When we with tears parted° Pentapolis, *departed*
The King my father gave you such a ring.

PERICLES This, this! No more, you gods, your present kindness
Makes my past miseries sports.° You shall do well *trifles (by comparison)*
That° on the touching of her lips I may *If*
Melt and no more be seen. —Oh, come, be buried
A second time within these arms.
[PERICLES *and* THAISA *embrace.*]

MARINA [*kneeling to* THAISA] My heart
Leaps to be gone into my mother's bosom.

PERICLES Look who kneels here—flesh of thy flesh, Thaisa,
Thy burden at the sea, and called Marina,
For she was yielded° there. *Because she was born*

2. *my sanctity . . . seeing:* my religious vows will forbid my sense to feel desire, in spite of what I see.

THAISA [*kissing* MARINA] Blest, and mine own!
HELICANUS [*kneeling to* THAISA] Hail, madam, and my queen!
THAISA I know you not.
PERICLES You have heard me say when I did fly from Tyre,
I left behind an ancient substitute.
Can you remember what I called the man?
I have named him oft.
THAISA 'Twas Helicanus, then.
PERICLES Still confirmation!
Embrace him, dear Thaisa. This is he.
Now do I long to hear how you were found,
How possibly preserved, and who to thank,
Besides the gods, for this great miracle.
THAISA Lord Cerimon, my lord; this man
Through whom the gods have shown their power, that can
From first to last resolve° you. *answer everything for*
PERICLES [*to* CERIMON] Reverend sir,
The gods can have no mortal officer
More like a god than you. Will you deliver° *explain*
How this dead queen relives?
CERIMON I will, my lord.
Beseech you first, go with me to my house,
Where shall be shown you all was° found with her, *that was*
How she came° placed here in the temple, *came to be*
No needful thing omitted.
PERICLES Pure Dian,
I bless thee for thy vision,° and will offer *(in act 5, scene 1)*
Night oblations° to thee. —Thaisa, *offerings*
This prince, the fair betrothèd of your daughter,
Shall marry her at Pentapolis.
[*to* MARINA] And now this ornament° *this hair that*
Makes me look dismal will I clip to form,
And what this fourteen years no razor touched
To grace thy marriage day I'll beautify.
THAISA Lord Cerimon hath letters of good credit,° sir, *trustworthiness*
My father's dead.
PERICLES Heavens make a star of him!
Yet there, my queen,
We'll celebrate their nuptials, and ourselves
Will in that kingdom spend our following days.
Our son and daughter shall in Tyrus reign.
Lord Cerimon, we do our longing stay° *delay our desire*
To hear the rest untold. Sir, lead's the way. [*Exeunt*.]

## Epilogue

[*Enter* GOWER.]

GOWER In Antiochus and his daughter you have heard[1]
Of monstrous lust the due and just reward;
In Pericles, his queen, and daughter seen,° *you have seen*
Although assailed with fortune fierce and keen,

**Epilogue**
1. The second of Gower's speeches in pentameter couplets.

Virtue preserved from fell° destruction's blast, *cruel*
Led on by heaven and crowned with joy at last.
In Helicanus may you well descry
A figure of truth, of faith, of loyalty.
In reverend Cerimon there well appears
The worth that learnèd charity aye° wears. *always*
For wicked Cleon and his wife, when fame° *rumor*
Had spread his cursèd deed to° the honored name *against*
Of Pericles, to rage the city turn,° *turned*
That° him and his they in his palace burn. *So that*
The gods for murder seemèd so content
To punish—although not done, but meant.
So, on your patience evermore attending,
New joy wait on you. Here our play has ending. [*Exit.*]

# Cymbeline

Toward the end of *Cymbeline,* one of the chief characters, Posthumus Leonatus, awakens from a dream vision to find a tablet on his chest, left there by Jupiter, king of the gods. In the dream, Jupiter had promised that the tablet would explain Posthumus's future fortunes. But when Posthumus reads the writing on the tablet, it is incomprehensible to him:

> 'Tis still a dream, or else such stuff as madmen
> Tongue . . .
> Or senseless speaking, or a speaking such
> As sense cannot untie.

Yet he concludes: "Be what it is, / The action of my life is like it" (5.4.115–19). By his own estimation, Posthumus's life is a senseless riddle. His immediate circumstances perhaps warrant such a conclusion. When Jupiter appears to him, Posthumus, a Briton crucial to his country's recent defeat of Rome, has subsequently disguised himself as a Roman and been put in a British prison. He deliberately sought his own capture and death because he was overwhelmed by guilt for having ordered the death of his wife, Imogen, the British king's daughter, falsely accused of sexual infidelity. Unbeknownst to him, however, Imogen, not dead but disguised as a Roman boy named Fidele, is likewise among those held captive by the Britons. Posthumus's own name, moreover, is something of a riddle. It literally means "after the death," signifying that Posthumus was born after the death of his father, Leonatus; but it also suggests a more fundamental disordering of expectations in a play in which (1) not only is a son born after his father's death, but other sons are stolen from fathers and wives severed from husbands, and (2) the temporal setting of the play seems simultaneously to be first-century C.E. Britain and seventeenth-century Italy.

Plot complexities abound in *Cymbeline*, leading not only Posthumus but also theatergoers to find it challenging to interpret. An inordinate number of characters assume disguises, have more than one name, don't know who their "real" parents are, or find themselves unable to decipher the complicated events around them. In one of the play's most famous (or infamous) scenes, Imogen, traveling in a page's disguise to find Posthumus, wakes up from a drug-induced sleep to find herself lying beside the body of a headless man dressed in her husband's clothing. The man is really Cloten, Posthumus's rival for Imogen's hand and the wicked son of Imogen's evil stepmother. Seeing the headless body, Imogen breaks into a lament for the man she believes to be her husband. Her grief is genuine and affecting, but it is prompted by a profound misreading of the corpse before her.

The improbabilities and complexities of *Cymbeline*'s plot have given some critics pause, as has the freedom with which times and places are handled. Ostensibly set in Roman Britain at the time of Christ's birth (which, according to early modern chronicles, occurred during the reign of Cymbeline), the play also contains scenes that appear to take place in contemporary Italy. It is in this modern Italy, for example, that Posthumus is tricked into believing that Imogen is sexually unfaithful to him. Reacting to the play's unusual features, the eighteenth-century critic Samuel Johnson complained:

> This play has many just sentiments, some natural dialogues, and some pleasing scenes, but they are obtained at the expense of much incongruity. To remark the folly of the fiction, the absurdity of the conduct, the confusion of the

> names, and manners of different times, and the impossibility of the events in any system of life, were to waste criticism upon unresisting imbecility, upon faults too evident for detection, and too gross for aggravation.

This response, however, may say more about Johnson's neoclassical tastes than about the ultimate value of Shakespeare's play. In *Cymbeline,* the complexity of the action seems deliberate rather than inadvertent or unskillful. It creates in the audience both a longing for clarity and control and an anxiety that the play may afford neither. The conclusion of the final act, therefore, comes as a relief when—after a dizzying whirl of events, reversals, revelations, and disguises—peace descends, all identities are revealed, and all riddles are expounded. The sense of wonder produced by this miraculous untangling of complicated events is one of the distinguishing features of Shakespeare's late plays, but *Cymbeline* never quite dispels the sense that the world of the play is fundamentally chaotic and mysterious and the plot's happy ending is a precarious bit of artifice.

This is probably one reason why in the First Folio of 1623 the play appeared as the last of Shakespeare's tragedies and was called *The Tragedy of Cymbeline*, a title retained in this edition in keeping with the emphasis on reproducing as far as possible the features of the text that serves as the basis for *The Norton Shakespeare*'s edition of a given play. In the early modern period, *Cymbeline* might have been classified as a tragedy both because, like *King Lear,* it dramatizes serious historical matter taken from the reign of an early Briton king, and also because of the dark and confusing atmosphere of much of the action and the deaths of Cloten and the Queen in the play's final acts. Modern critics, however, have usually preferred to call the play a tragicomedy or a romance, arguing that, like *The Winter's Tale, Pericles,* and *The Tempest, Cymbeline* does not end with the death of the protagonists but, rather, restores families and transforms suffering to joy. While verging on tragedy, *Cymbeline* does arguably move to a bittersweet conclusion in which shattered families are reconstituted and plot complexities untangled—but at a cost. In all the late plays, mistakes often have tragic consequences: some sons die; years are lost in exile and wandering; women suffer from unjust slander. If, in the end, good fortune returns to the sufferers, it does not cancel their former pain but provides a miraculous contrast to it. It is fitting, therefore, that ambiguity haunts *Cymbeline*'s generic categorization. Whether we call it tragedy, tragicomedy, or romance, the play blends catastrophe with hope in ways that have both confused and delighted audiences.

The date of *Cymbeline* is uncertain, although it is usually given as 1609 or 1610. Scholars differ as to whether it preceded or followed *The Winter's Tale.* We know that it was in performance by 1611 because Simon Forman, a London doctor and astrologer, wrote about seeing it, probably between April 20 and April 30 of that year. It is not clear whether he saw the play at the Globe, the outdoor theater that Shakespeare's company used after 1599, or at Blackfriars, the indoor theater that the company acquired in 1608. The spectacular scenic effects possible in staging this play, such as the descent of Jupiter on the back of an eagle in act 5, suggest that it was designed with the more elaborate technical capacities of the Blackfriars venue in mind. Some critics have tried to date the play by relating it to the investiture of Henry, King James's oldest son, as Prince of Wales in 1610, since a number of key scenes of the play take place in Wales. We have no record of a court performance until 1634, however, when it was played before King Charles, who liked it. Other critics have tried to determine the play's relationship to Beaumont and Fletcher's popular tragicomedy *Philaster,* usually dated 1609, to which *Cymbeline* bears some resemblance, but it is not clear which play influenced the other.

Regardless of its exact date, *Cymbeline* belongs to Shakespeare's late period, and it enabled him to address his long-standing interests in both British and Roman history. The play intertwines three plot lines, the main one involving Imogen, the daughter and apparently the only living heir of Cymbeline, King of Britain, and her thwarted attempts to live with her chosen husband, Posthumus. Angry that Imogen loves a man of lesser social rank than herself and that she has not married Cloten, his second wife's son, Cymbeline banishes Posthumus from Britain. The exiled husband travels to Italy, where he wagers on his wife's chastity with the villain Giacomo, who ultimately makes Posthumus believe that Imogen is unfaithful. Whether the love of Imogen and Posthumus can be restored is one of the key questions of this plot. This wager story draws on two sources: Boccaccio's *Decameron,* a series of prose tales first translated into English in 1620 but available in a French translation in the sixteenth century, and *Frederick of Jennen,* an English translation of a German version of the same story.

A second plot strand deals with Britain's relationship with Rome, especially Rome's demand that Britons pay the tribute pledged to Julius Caesar when he conquered the island. For these events, Shakespeare drew primarily on the brief account of Cymbeline's reign in Raphael Holinshed's *Chronicles of England, Scotland, and Ireland* (2nd ed., 1587). Cymbeline was king when the Roman emperor Augustus Caesar ushered in the famous period of peace known as the Pax Romana. In most of the sources, it was Cymbeline's son Guiderius who refused to pay Rome tribute. Shakespeare modified the story, however, so that Cymbeline, urged on by his Queen and her son, is the one who withholds the tribute and provokes a Roman invasion.

The third plot line has to do with two sons of Cymbeline, stolen from their nursery by a wrongly defamed courtier, Belarius, who raises them in the mountains of Wales. By chance, their sister Imogen, disguised as a boy, stumbles upon their mountain cave on her flight from her father's court in pursuit of Posthumus. Near this cave, Cloten, wearing Posthumus's clothes, is killed by one of these sons; also near this cave, Imogen awakes from her sleep to find herself beside his headless body. For the play to reach its resolution, Cymbeline's sons must be reunited with their father. This reunion occurs, but only after the sons play a decisive role in the final battle against the Roman invaders. Their heroic actions in this battle are modeled on another part of Holinshed, *The History of Scotland,* which recounts the story of a farmer named Hay and his two sons, who routed Danish invaders at the Battle of Luncarty in about 976 C.E.

From these complex and diverse materials, Shakespeare wove a play whose rich allusiveness has invited many kinds of topical interpretations. One line of criticism has focused on *Cymbeline*'s relationship to events and ideas connected to the reign of King James I. James was interested in linking imperial Rome to modern Britain and to his own kingship. He had himself painted crowned with laurel leaves, in the Roman manner, and had coins stamped with his laurel-crowned profile. Like Augustus Caesar, James presented himself as a great peacemaker after Elizabeth's reluctant involvement in wars in Ireland and in defending the Protestant countries of the Continent against Catholic powers. Moreover, just as Augustus ruled over a vast empire, James aspired to unite Scotland and England (along with the already incorporated Wales) into a single entity with one church and one set of laws. His project failed, but he exerted much effort in promoting this union during the first years of his reign. *Cymbeline* uncannily echoes some of James's preoccupations. Sometimes called Shakespeare's last Roman play, *Cymbeline* dramatizes ancient Britain's attempts to come to terms with imperial Rome. Names of Roman gods—particularly Diana, Apollo, and Jupiter—abound (Jupiter alone is mentioned over thirty times); and figures from Roman mythology and history, such as Tarquin, Philomela, and Aeneas, are often evoked. The play's title character, like James, is a British monarch respectful of Rome, even when asserting his independence in the matter of the tribute. The final word of the play, spoken by the King, is "peace." The analogies between the play and the Stuart court, however, have their limits. Cymbeline is also a king duped by his wicked queen and her doltish son—hardly a compliment to James and the royal family if events in the play are seen literally to mirror their circumstances.

Other allusions expand the play's possible range of meanings. For example, Milford Haven, the port in southern Wales where the Romans come ashore for their invasion of England, was also the place where Henry Tudor, Earl of Richmond, landed

James I liked to present himself as heir to Roman greatness. In this 1613 engraving, Crispin van de Passe portrays him crowned with the laurel wreath worn by Roman emperors.

in 1485 to begin his campaign against Richard III. Having defeated Richard, Henry was crowned Henry VII, first of the Tudor kings; Henry's daughter Margaret married James IV of Scotland, grandfather to the James who assumed the English throne in 1603. When the Romans land at Milford Haven in Shakespeare's play, they in effect precipitate a transformation of the kingdom, much as Henry Tudor was to do 1,500 years later. At the time of their arrival, Cymbeline believes his two sons to be dead, and his daughter and Cloten have both fled the court. Britain is without an heir. But through the battle with the Romans, the lost sons of Cymbeline are discovered and the kingdom renewed. So, too, James fancied himself an agent of renewal, a second Henry VII arriving from Scotland to unite the whole island under his rule.

Wales itself is an important symbolic location in this play. Although officially incorporated into England in the 1530s, Wales remained distinct, often stigmatized as rude and uncivilized. (In *1 Henry IV*, it is the home of the dangerous rebel Glyndŵr.) The Welsh language, banned from use in public contexts, was taken to symbolize the barbarity of this borderland region. However, in some narratives Wales was also the place from which sprang the legitimate rulers of England. The mythical King Arthur was given a Welsh origin, and traditionally the eldest son of the British monarch was (and still is) given the title Prince of Wales. In *Cymbeline,* Wales is imagined as a harsh pastoral landscape in which Belarius and the King's sons live in a cave, hunt the food they eat, and have little contact with other human beings. While these sons, Guiderius and Arviragus, frequently complain that they know nothing of the world and its customs and manners, Wales shelters them from the vices of court life. In fact, as is traditional in pastoral literature, the Welsh scenes contain a good deal of anticourt satire. In the play's spatial and symbolic economies, Wales is the place where true British manhood is preserved. *Cymbeline* thus works with material imbued with a new kind of significance under the reign of James.

Yet it may be a mistake to tie the play too closely to the royal family or to particular events that we retrospectively marshall to make sense of its mysteries. The play doesn't just reflect the world around it; it transforms the materials from that world into a powerful and challenging imaginative structure. In the largest sense, *Cymbeline* works to define both Britain and proper British manhood by constructing a complex narrative about national origins. The wager plot, with its story of sexual slander and threatened rape, is central to that narrative, not only because Imogen often seems to stand for Britain itself (she is several times addressed as "Britain," and her name resembles that of Innogen, the wife of Brute, the legendary ancient king of Britain), but also because the realignment of gender relations plays a crucial role in the renewal of Britain and in the play's turn from tragedy to comedy.

Strikingly, this play about Britain's past never mentions the word "England." In the history plays written in the 1590s, the reverse tends to be true: "Britain" is seldom employed, but "England" is invoked with great frequency. There are several reasons for Shakespeare's choice in this later play. He is, of course, deliberately evoking the world of the ancient Britons, the early inhabitants of the island who provide the starting point for his creation of a fictive national past. At the same time, he is to some extent reflecting, and helping to create, the Stuart monarch's sense of the entity over which he ruled. James, after all, was not an "Englander" in the same way Elizabeth had been. He was a Scotsman who spoke with an accent and aspired to bring the entire island into a new political alignment under the name Britannia or Great Britain.

Setting the play during the reign of Cymbeline enabled Shakespeare to imagine a primitive Britain that was also the cosmopolitan heir to the westward movement of empire. The treatment of Rome is particularly interesting in *Cymbeline*. Partly, the Romans are figured as an invading force, threatening the island. Yet the British characters most eager to repel the Romans and to treat them as an enemy are the evil Queen and her evil son. Cymbeline himself, while defending Britain's right to live free and under its own laws, is more disposed to come to terms with his great opponents and invariably treats them with respect. The play is marked by a pervasive tension between Britain's desire to defeat the Romans and to emulate them, to be insular and to be cosmopolitan. This tension is managed in part through the splitting of the Romans into the noble figure of Lucius and the devilish figure of Giacomo, who in his deceit and misogyny resembles the villainous Italians popular on the early modern stage.

When Giacomo comes to Britain to test Imogen's fidelity, he fails in his initial attempt to portray Posthumus as a philanderer upon whom Imogen should seek sexual revenge. He then proceeds more deviously, having himself conveyed in a trunk into her bedroom, from which he emerges in the dead of night to survey her sleeping body and the contents of her room. References to infamous acts of rape frame his incursion. As he steps from the trunk, Giacomo compares himself to Tarquin, the Roman tyrant who raped Lucrece (a story told in Shakespeare's lengthy poem *The Rape of Lucrece*, written in the 1590s). Furthermore, the book that Imogen had been reading when she fell asleep is opened to the story of Tereus, who raped Philomela and cut out her tongue. Although Giacomo does not literally rape Imogen, he violates the privacy of her body with his peering eyes and rapes her honor by lying successfully to Posthumus about her infidelity. At one level, this incident is about the unjust sufferings of a slandered woman. At another level, Imogen is Britain, itself, threatened by a skillful invader. Giacomo penetrates Imogen's bedchamber and later he penetrates and infects the ear of Posthumus with his poisonous slander.

In the play's denouement, the threat of foreign penetration is graphically repelled when Belarius and the sons of Cymbeline come from the Welsh mountains, joined by Posthumus disguised as a British peasant, and take a stand "in a narrow lane," putting

*Tarquin's Rape of Lucrece*. Sixteenth-century copy of an engraving by Agostino Veneziano.

the Romans to flight and instilling courage in the British. The vulnerable narrow lane is thus barricaded against outsiders by the sons of Cymbeline crying, "Stand, stand!" (5.3.28). The moment has gendered and sexual overtones. A vulnerable and feminized Britain is protected from invasion by the swords of virile young men whose cry, "Stand," means both to hold one's ground and to have an erection. This event proves pivotal, lending itself equally well to aphorism and to Posthumus's mocking rhyme: "Two boys, an old man twice a boy, a lane, / Preserved the Britons, was the Romans' bane" (5.3.57–58). In the play's symbolic economy, the threat of penetration initiated by Giacomo is thus repulsed by Imogen's long-lost brothers, and in the final scene Giacomo kneels to Posthumus, asking his forgiveness—the Italian subdued by the Briton.

Something quite different occurs with Lucius, the Roman military leader, who embodies the laudable virtues of ancient Rome rather than the hideous vices of early modern Italy. Even though the Roman army is defeated, Cymbeline decides to resume paying tribute, and in his final speech the King says: "Let / A Roman and a British ensign wave / Friendly together" (5.5.477–79). This rapprochement of warring powers is ratified by one of the play's several mysterious visions. Before the battle, a Roman soothsayer tells Lucius what the gods had revealed to him:

> I saw Jove's bird, the Roman eagle, winged
> From the spongy south to this part of the west,
> There vanished in the sunbeams; which portends,
> Unless my sins abuse my divination,
> Success to th' Roman host.
>
> (4.2.347–51)

In this play, not even soothsayers have perfect interpretive skills. The outcome of the battle requires some revisions in the exegesis of the vision. After the battle, the soothsayer says:

> For the Roman eagle,
> From south to west on wing soaring aloft,
> Lessened herself, and in the beams o'th' sun
> So vanished; which foreshowed our princely eagle,

> Th'imperial Caesar, should again unite
> His favor with the radiant Cymbeline,
> Which shines here in the west.
>
> (5.5.468–74)

Conquest has been transformed into concord as the Roman eagle and the British sun merge and as Cymbeline celebrates this peace within the temple of Jupiter.

In stressing the final union of Britain and Rome, the play's conclusion makes Britain the heir of Rome's imperial legacy even as Britain proclaims the integrity of its own land, laws, and customs. In the early modern period, the course of empire was thought to move westward. When Troy fell, the Trojan hero Aeneas bore his father on his back from the fires of the burning city and eventually fulfilled his destiny by establishing a new kingdom in Italy in what was to become the center of the Roman Empire. In the soothsayer's vision, the Roman eagle journeys even farther west, renewing itself, as eagles were believed to do, by enduring the burning fires of Britain's sun to purge away old feathers in preparation for the growth of new.

The play's culminating vision of a Britain separate unto itself but also the cosmopolitan heir of an imperial tradition is anticipated in the actions of Imogen and Posthumus. In the final act, both are partly Roman in their dress and sympathies. Posthumus Leonatus comes to Britain in the company of the Italian gentry, but then he dresses as a British peasant and fights with Belarius in the narrow lane before reassuming his Italian garb. Imogen is present at the battle as page to Lucius, the Roman general who had found her weeping over the headless corpse of Cloten. In the final moments of reconciliation, Cymbeline's daughter and her husband stand before the British King in foreign clothes. Imogen, moreover, earlier makes a telling speech about Britain's place in the world when discussing with a trusted servant where she would live after Posthumus has come to believe her unchaste. Her father's court, with Cloten present, she finds unthinkable. She then asks:

> Hath Britain all the sun that shines? Day, night,
> Are they not but in Britain? I'th' world's volume
> Our Britain seems as of it, but not in't:
> In a great pool a swan's nest.
>
> (3.4.136–39)

Imogen nicely captures the play's most complex view of Britain. Eschewing an insular patriotism associated with Cloten and the Queen, she recognizes a vast world beyond the shores of Britain. Punning on the double meaning of "volume" as "expanse" or "book," Imogen suggests Britain's partial separation from a larger entity. Britain is a little part of a bigger expanse, a page detached from a large book, or a swan's nest in a great pool. As the image of the swan's nest suggests, Britain remains the special seat of grace and beauty. But it is also connected to something larger than itself. There are other pages in the volume to which, even if detached, Britain belongs.

The play, then, seems to be negotiating a new vision of the nation suited for the Stuart moment—a vision resulting from the richly suggestive concatenation of discursive traditions that Shakespeare brought together in this play. Reaching back into the chronicle materials of ancient Britain, he provides a genealogy for modern Britain that (1) insists on the integrity and freedom of the island kingdom but (2) presents it as purged—largely through the efforts of the King's "Welsh" sons—of the corruptions of modern court life as embodied in figures such as Giacomo or Cloten, and (3) aligns Britain with the cosmopolitan values of Rome, positioning the island kingdom as the appropriate heir of Roman greatness: both warlike and peace-loving.

The renewed Britain has a fourth striking characteristic, and that is its decidedly masculine coloration. The wager plot makes plain the role of gender in configuring British national identity. Consider first the changing fortunes of Imogen. At the beginning of the play, she is a beloved and important figure in her father's court. Cymbeline's

The eagle, king of birds and emblem of the Roman god Jupiter. According to myth, it could stare at the sun without blinking and fly into the sun in order to burn off its old feathers. From Joachim Camerarius, *Symbolorum et Emblematum* (1605 ed.).

only living heir, the strong-willed and decisive princess chooses Posthumus for her husband even though he has little money and is not of royal birth. By the end of the play, Imogen has been displaced from the succession by her two rediscovered brothers; she has also been ordered killed by her husband, threatened with rape, knocked unconscious by a drug she believes to be medicine, and struck by her husband when, in her page's attire, she steps forward to reveal her identity to him in the last scene. Though cross-dressed for much of the second half of the play, she does not, like Portia in *The Merchant of Venice* and Rosalind in *As You Like It,* use that disguise aggressively to shape her own destiny. Rather, burdened by the knowledge that her husband unjustly and inexplicably desires her death, Imogen grows less powerful and more passive as the play progresses. Her decline can be summarized in the pun on "heir" and "air." Imogen begins as the former and ends as the latter. The mysterious tablet laid on Posthumus's breast contained a riddling prophecy:

> Whenas a lion's whelp shall, to himself unknown, without seeking find, and be embraced by a piece of tender air; and when from a stately cedar shall be lopped branches which, being dead many years, shall after revive, be jointed to the old stock, and freshly grow: then shall Posthumus end his miseries, Britain be fortunate and flourish in peace and plenty. (5.5.434–40)

When the soothsayer finally untangles this riddle, he declares Posthumus Leonatus to be the lion's offspring; Cymbeline the cedar tree; his lost sons the lopped branches; and Imogen the tender air, because "tender air" in Latin translates as *mollis aer,* which (by a stretch of the imagination) derives from *mulier,* Latin for "wife." When Posthumus is embraced by the "tender air" (no longer an "heir"), his miseries will cease. Now less important to the succession, Imogen is finally allowed to live with her chosen husband.

Nineteenth-century critics loved Imogen, idealizing her as a paragon of selfless and long-suffering womanhood. She never, for example, protests her demotion from the position of heir apparent; in fact, she considers finding her brothers worth the loss of the kingdom. To many contemporary critics, however, her role in the play's narrative of nation is a troubling one. Britain renews itself as women are disempowered or disappear. Cymbeline's Queen is an embodiment of hypocritical viciousness (Shakespeare does not even bother to give her a name), and her son, a figure whose father is never mentioned or seen, bears her taint. The play's happy resolution occurs only after all traces of this Queen and her offspring have been erased. When finally united with his children, Cymbeline articulates the fantasy of having himself given birth to all three: "Oh, what am I? / A mother to the birth of three? Ne'er mother / Rejoiced deliverance more" (5.5.367–69). This is the dream of androgenesis, reproduction without union with women.

Much earlier in the play, Posthumus, believing that Imogen has been sexually unfaithful to him, voices a similar wish: "Is there no way for men to be, but women / Must be half-workers?" (2.5.1–2). In one of the most deeply misogynist speeches in the Shakespeare canon, Posthumus then blames all the vices of the world on "The woman's part" (line 20)—on woman herself and on that part of woman lodged in man, the fallen Eve's mark upon the human race. This mistaken projection onto woman of responsibility for evil may partly explain Cymbeline's fantasy of androgenesis and also why, in the last scene, no persons appareled as women are to be seen (Imogen is still dressed as a page). The happy union of Britain and Rome and Wales is overwhelmingly a union of men.

The troubled status of marriage in the play further hints at its difficulties with "the woman's part" in establishing lineage and in forging the nation. Imogen's marriage initially is so slightly regarded by her father and stepmother, who remain intent on her marrying Cloten, that students often ask: is she really married? The answer is yes, but the marriage is never recognized as a proper dynastic union and is quickly further jeopardized by Posthumus's rash wager with Giacomo. The King's first wife is long dead, her role as mother to her male children usurped by Belarius and their nurse and her role as Imogen's mother assumed by Cymbeline's nightmarish second wife. At the end of the play, everyone is relieved when the stepmother abruptly dies, leaving Cymbeline to his happy fantasy of having given birth, alone, to his three children. Heterosexual union is fleeting, disastrous, or vulnerable to slander. By the end of act 5, only Posthumus and Imogen remain married—though in diminished circumstances that put them both firmly out of the line of succession.

To be sure, the play queries its most virulent forms of misogyny by punishing the slanderous Giacomo and highlighting Posthumus's gradual recovery of faith in Imogen. When Posthumus receives a bloody cloth signifying (falsely) that his order to murder Imogen has been fulfilled, he is overcome with remorse and berates husbands like himself for murdering their wives "For wrying but a little" (5.1.5). At this point, Posthumus still believes his wife to have been sexually unfaithful to him, yet he castigates himself for having ordered her punished. His words form a remarkable exception to the more usual patriarchal assumption that female chastity is the primary marker of a woman's value and virtue and that loss of chastity is an unforgivable crime. Critics differ as to how much weight to assign this speech. Posthumus delivers it when he believes Imogen to be dead; and generally it is easier to forgive the dead than the living. By the time he is finally reconciled to the living, breathing woman, Giacomo's lies have been exposed and Posthumus takes to himself a wife whose chastity is not in question.

The play, moreover, clearly punishes the evil Cloten, who had fantasized raping Imogen; and it punishes the misogynous lies of Giacomo, who submits to Posthumus in the final scene. Moreover, Posthumus, having suffered for his lack of faith in Imogen, emerges as the play's one proper husband, though he now assumes the dominant position in his marriage—a position once held by Imogen. Jupiter himself provides the warrant for this reversal. In prison, Posthumus has a dream that not only reconnects him to his familial origins but also provides an image of his own future family. As he sleeps, Posthumus's two warlike brothers and his warlike father appear to him. The father is described as "*leading in his hand an ancient matron (his wife, and mother to Posthumus)*" (stage direction following 5.4.29). After this dream, sent by Jupiter, Posthumus recovers his "true" identity as Imogen's husband and Britain's warrior hero. As he assumes his position in the honored line of Leonati men, the place marked for Imogen is that of Roman/British wife, "led in his hand." *Cymbeline* thus reproves the most virulent forms of misogyny while simultaneously removing women from public power, transforming them into chaste, domesticated wives, and reaffirming the dominance of husbands.

Samuel Johnson was right when he said that *Cymbeline* is a play with many incongruities of time, place, and circumstance. And yet it is not an incoherent play, but rather one that richly interweaves the history of the nation with the stories of the figures who take up their positions within it. What is eerie about *Cymbeline* is that its characters often understand so little about what is happening to them, and yet each appears to play out the part assigned to him or her by some higher power: Jupiter, destiny, time. In this regard, *Cymbeline* is of a piece with Shakespeare's other romances, plays in which a higher power often seems to steer all boats to shore and reunite long-severed families.

But fictions of inevitability can be deceiving. One should remember that the soothsayer had to revise his interpretation of his vision of the eagle and the sun to make his narrative square with events as they actually happened. And to decipher Posthumus's tablet, he could make the prophecy tally with the facts only by means of a tortuous transformation of "tender air" into "wife." This might suggest that in this play, at least, the higher powers determine less than they appear to do; rather, the forms taken by family, nation, and empire are in some measure the result of human efforts, interventions, and narratives. Shakespeare's play is one such narrative. The resolution of its complex plot may invite relieved assent to its culminating vision, but the very artifice of that resolution also reveals its contingency, suggesting that there is nothing either natural or inevitable about the familial and political arrangements that are repeatedly contested and reordered in this tragicomic play.

JEAN E. HOWARD

## SELECTED BIBLIOGRAPHY

Berry, Amanda. "desire vomit emptiness: *Cymbeline*'s Marriage Time." *Shakesqueer: A Queer Companion to the Complete Works of Shakespeare.* Ed. Madhavi Menon. Durham, NC: Duke UP, 2011. 89–96. Argues that the play queers heterosexual marriage by underscoring the problematic status and unfulfilled nature of such unions.

Cheney, Patrick. "Venting Rhyme for a Mockery: *Cymbeline* and National Romance," Chapter 8 of *Shakespeare's Literary Authorship.* Cambridge: Cambridge UP, 2008. 234–63. Argues that *Cymbeline* implicitly constructs Shakespeare as Britain's national poet by inserting him into the lineage of other poets whose works are alluded to by the play, by including many references to Shakespeare's earlier works, and by emphasizing the drama's lyricism and embedded songs and poems.

Escobedo, Andrew. "From Britannia to England: *Cymbeline* and the Beginning of Nations." *Shakespeare Quarterly* 59:1 (2008): 60–87. Suggests that the play explores two kinds of nationalism—one based on ancient British origins and embracing heterogeneity, the other drawing on Saxon precedent and stressing English purity.

Jones, Emrys. "Stuart *Cymbeline*." *Essays in Criticism* 11 (1961): 84–99. Takes a historical approach to the play by emphasizing its links to James I's dedication to peace and the role of Milford Haven in Tudor national mythology.

Kahn, Coppélia. "Postscript: *Cymbeline*: Paying Tribute to Rome." *Roman Shakespeare: Warriors, Wounds, and Women.* London: Routledge, 1997. 160–70. Argues that *Cymbeline* shares much with Shakespeare's other Roman plays, including a preoccupation with Roman *virtu* as the root of masculine identity—but an identity constantly made precarious by the woman's part in its formation.

Menon, Madhavi. "Facts: *Cymbeline* and the "Whore" of Historicism." Chapter 2 of *Unhistorical Shakespeare: Queer Theory in Shakespearean Literature and Film.* New York: Palgrave Macmillan, 2008. 51–71. Questions some historical criticism's uncritical embrace of "facts" and argues for a theoretical approach to *Cymbeline* that sees "facts" as fluidly open to retrospective interpretation; uses the play to show how evidence is treacherous and "facts" often lie, as with Giacomo's "proof" of Imogen's infidelity.

Mikalachki, Jodi. "Cymbeline and the Masculine Romance of Roman Britain." *The Legacy of Boadicea: Gender and Nation in Early Modern England.* London: Routledge, 1998. 96–114. From a feminist perspective, explores the respective roles of ancient British savagery and Roman civility in the forging of an all-male national community in *Cymbeline*.

Parker, Patricia. "Romance and Empire: Anachronistic *Cymbeline*." *Unfolded Tales: Essays on Renaissance Romance.* Ed. George M. Logan and Gordon Teskey. Ithaca, NY: Cornell UP, 1989. 189–207. Examines the pervasive allusions to *The Aeneid* in *Cymbeline*, arguing that the play intimates the passing of Rome's imperial greatness westward to Britain.

Warren, Roger. *Cymbeline*. Shakespeare in Performance series. Manchester: Manchester UP, 1989. Focuses on performances of the play, especially on striking stage and television versions from the second half of the twentieth century.

Wayne, Valerie. "The Woman's Parts of *Cymbeline*." *Staged Properties in Early Modern English Drama.* Ed. Jonathan Gil Harris and Natasha Korda. Cambridge: Cambridge UP, 2002. 288–315. Traces the history of three stage properties—manacle, ring, and bloody cloth—as they represent Imogen, and women more generally, in *Cymbeline*.

### FILM

*Cymbeline.* 1982. Dir. Elijah Moshinsky. UK. 175 min. This BBC production boasts such cast luminaries as Richard Johnson (the King), Claire Bloom (the Queen), and Helen Mirren (Imogen), among others.

## TEXTUAL INTRODUCTION

*Cymbeline* was never printed in Shakespeare's lifetime. The only authoritative text is that published in the First Folio of 1623 (F), where the play is included as the last of the tragedies. It was reprinted in the Second Folio of 1632 (F2) with some minor corrections. The relatively heavy punctuation of F, including the frequent use of parentheses, colons, hyphens, and apostrophes, seems to indicate that the text was prepared for publication by a professional scribe, probably Ralph Crane, who also prepared the manuscripts of *The Winter's Tale* and *The Tempest* for publication in F. By early seventeenth-century standards, the text is a good one, requiring little intervention by the editor apart from the correction of a few misprints and obvious minor errors. The lineation is mainly clear and accurate—although, as usual, F does not indicate where a line is divided between two speakers, merely printing such cases as two short lines. Stage directions, especially for the battle scenes in act 5, are relatively full, although they do not include some sound effects such as trumpet flourishes to mark the entrances of royalty, or "*alarums*" and other noises associated with battles. Modern editors routinely add clarification of whether characters are in disguise and whether lines are spoken "*aside*."

Punctuation is a major challenge for the editor of this text. This is not just a question of "translating" the heavy punctuation of the scribe into an acceptable modern format—by substituting dashes for some of the Folio's parentheses, for example—but of attempting to disentangle the complex syntax of very long sentences that can be, by modern standards, ungrammatical or even incoherent. Examples of such speeches are those made by Posthumus at 5.3.14–51 and by Giacomo at 5.5.153–209. Sometimes this style can be attributed to particular characters and situations, but it pervades the whole play. Shorter passages also present problems: the first four speeches made by the First Gentleman in the opening scene of the play contain examples of elliptical structure and frequent self-interruption. We can usually grasp the general meaning, but the actual words and the relations between them give us difficulty.

Another contentious issue is the naming of the characters. This edition reverts to the traditional name of "Imogen" for the heroine. This name is consistently used in the Folio text and in the editorial and critical tradition. The Oxford editors argued that "Imogen" is a misprint for "Innogen." However, their arguments are not entirely compelling. The name "Imogen," which they thought did not occur before the First Folio, can be found both in a fifteenth-century translation of Ralph Higden's *Polychronicon* (Pitcher, "Names in *Cymbeline*," 4) and in the "Second Table" or index to the first volume of the 1586 edition of Holinshed (King, *Constructions of Britain*, 72). In contrast, while the Folio also consistently uses "Iachimo" for the name of the villain, the name is here modernized to Giacomo according to the editorial principle of *The Norton Shakespeare* of using the standard modernizations of foreign names and words.

Finally, the Folio indicates act and scene numbers throughout, but editors disagree about how to divide the fifth act. The usual rule of thumb whereby a new scene begins when the stage is vacated, however briefly, is challenged by the desirability of rendering the battle from 5.2 to 5.4 fluidly as a continuous sequence, and the Folio's elaborate narrative stage directions (at 5.2.0, 5.2.10, 5.2.13, and 5.3.0) are a further complication. Two of these (at 5.2.10 and 5.2.13) prescribe actions that are subsequently described in detail by Posthumus (at 5.3.14–51). An important piece of action is rendered entirely through a stage direction, here given as 5.4.0 SD. In the Folio, this lengthy direction comes at the end of "*Scena Tertia*." It is followed by "*Scena Quarta*" and a new direction for the entrance for Posthumus and his Jailer. The scene changes from the battlefield to a prison—the Jailer tells Posthumus: "You have locks upon you"—although the Folio never directs that the stage be cleared of the large group of people present at the end of 5.3. In this edition, therefore, an *Exeunt* is added at the end of 5.3 and the stage direction moved to 5.4, even though for Posthumus and the Jailer it implies a violation of the "rule of re-entry," whereby characters normally do not exit and re-enter immediately.

ANN THOMPSON

### Textual Bibliography

Dessen, Alan C., and Leslie Thomson. *Dictionary of Stage Directions in Early Modern Drama*. Cambridge: Cambridge UP, 1999.
King, Ros. *"Cymbeline": Constructions of Britain*. Aldershot: Ashgate, 2005.
Knight, G. Wilson. *The Crown of Life*. London: Oxford UP, 1947.
Pitcher, John. "Names in *Cymbeline*." *Essays in Criticism* 43 (1993): 1–16.

## PERFORMANCE NOTE

Like other late Shakespeare plays, *Cymbeline* abounds with staging challenges. It mingles diverse settings, periods, and genres, and requires actors to portray ghosts, the Roman army, even Jupiter descended from heaven astride an eagle. Its final scene, among Shakespeare's longest and most populated, sustains a sense of climax through twenty-four discrete anagnorises (recognitions or discoveries). Although the play is capable of generating unequaled wonder and delight for audiences, its success nevertheless depends on unusually precise blocking and timing. Trickiest of all, productions must sustain both dramatic momentum and audience interest across the tangle of episodes preceding the climactic series of denouements. In short, *Cymbeline*'s long-absent protagonist, reliance on exposition, and repeated indulgence in lyricism at the expense of plot-advancing action all potentially consort to try the audience's resolve and undermine the god Jupiter's assertion that "the more delayed, [the more] delighted" (5.4.72).

Directors often respond to the play's length (only *Hamlet* is longer), structural unconventionality, and sometimes halting pace by cutting and by tipping the generic balance toward comedy by, for instance, laying exaggerated emphasis on Cloten's role or Imogen's cross-dressing. Some create lavish, fairy tale–inflected productions, seizing on archetypes to simplify the plot and push the play toward melodrama. Others exploit the play's emphasis on dreams to confer visual and tonal coherence on the whole. Still others foreground the plot's challenges to representation and complex characterization as prominent dramaturgical themes, double-casting actors and eliminating costumes, sets, and other conventional tools of representation.

Whatever their approach, directors make critical decisions respecting character and (by extension) genre. Cloten can seem pitiably foolish and inept or irredeemably arrogant and vile; Giacomo can be an attractive mischief-maker or a contemptible would-be rapist. Directors likewise must decide whether the Queen is a Snow White stereotype or a realistic villain; whether Cymbeline's episodes of rage and severely lapsed judgment bespeak insanity, dotage, or mere archetypal duty; and whether Posthumus's pursuit of Imogen's life proceeds from a distraction born of despair or from something profoundly evil within him.

Brett Gamboa

# The Tragedy of Cymbeline

[THE PERSONS OF THE PLAY

*In Cymbeline's Britain:*
CYMBELINE, King of Britain
QUEEN, second wife to Cymbeline
IMOGEN, daughter to Cymbeline by his first wife, later disguised as Fidele
POSTHUMUS Leonatus, husband to Imogen
CLOTEN, son to the Queen by a former husband
PISANIO, Posthumus' servant
CORNELIUS, a doctor
FIRST LORD } attending Cloten
SECOND LORD } attending Cloten
LORDS at Cymbeline's court
LADIES at Cymbeline's court
Two GENTLEMEN
Two British CAPTAINS
Two British JAILERS
MESSENGERS
MUSICIANS
Soldiers

*In Wales:*
BELARIUS, a banished lord, known as Morgan
GUIDERIUS, known as Polydore
ARVIRAGUS, known as Cadwal

*In Rome:*
PHILARIO, Posthumus' friend in Rome
GIACOMO, an Italian } friends of Philario
FRENCHMAN } friends of Philario
Dutchman } friends of Philario
Spaniard } friends of Philario
Two Roman SENATORS
Roman TRIBUNES

*Romans in Britain:*
CAIUS LUCIUS, Roman ambassador and general
Roman CAPTAINS
Philharmonus, a SOOTHSAYER
JUPITER
Ghost of SICILIUS Leonatus, father to Posthumus
Ghost of Posthumus' MOTHER, wife to Sicilius
Ghosts of Posthumus' two BROTHERS
Attendants]

## 1.1

*Enter two* GENTLEMEN.

FIRST GENTLEMAN You do not meet a man but frowns. Our bloods
No more obey the heavens than our courtiers
Still seem as does the King.[1]
SECOND GENTLEMAN But what's the matter?
FIRST GENTLEMAN His daughter, and the heir of 's° kingdom, whom *of his*
He purposed to° his wife's sole son (a widow *intended for*
That late° he married) hath referred° herself *recently / given*
Unto a poor but worthy gentleman. She's wedded,
Her husband banished, she imprisoned. All
Is outward sorrow, though I think the King
Be touched at very heart.
SECOND GENTLEMAN None but the King?
FIRST GENTLEMAN He° that hath lost her too; so is the Queen, *(the Queen's son)*
That most desired the match. But not a courtier,
Although they wear their faces to the bent
Of° the King's looks, hath a heart that is not *In accordance with*
Glad at the thing they scowl at.
SECOND GENTLEMAN And why so?
FIRST GENTLEMAN He that hath missed the Princess is a thing
Too bad for bad report; and he that hath her—
I mean that married her (alack, good man,
And therefore banished)—is a creature such
As to seek through the regions of the earth
For one his like, there would be something failing° *lacking*
In him that should compare.[2] I do not think
So fair an outward and such stuff° within *substance; fabric*
Endows a man but he.
SECOND GENTLEMAN You speak him far.° *praise him greatly*
FIRST GENTLEMAN I do extend him, sir, within himself,[3]
Crush him together, rather than unfold
His measure duly.[4]
SECOND GENTLEMAN What's his name and birth?
FIRST GENTLEMAN I cannot delve him to the root.[5] His father
Was called Sicilius, who did join his honor° *prowess (as a soldier)*
Against the Romans with Cassibelan,
But had his titles by Tenantius,[6] whom
He served with glory and admired success,
So gained the sur-addition, "Leonatus";[7]
And had, besides this gentleman in question,
Two other sons who in the wars o'th' time
Died with their swords in hand. For which their father,
Then old and fond of issue,° took such sorrow *of his offspring*
That he quit being, and his gentle lady,
Big of° this gentleman, our theme, deceased *Pregnant with*
As he was born. The King, he takes the babe

1.1 Location: Cymbeline's court, Britain.
1. *Our . . . King:* Our dispositions ("bloods") are not more subject to planetary influences than our courtiers' moods are determined by the King's. (The planets were believed to affect human actions and emotions.)
2. In any man selected for comparison.
3. I set forth his virtues, sir, within the boundaries of his own merit.
4. *rather . . . duly:* rather than reveal what he is really worth. The metaphor picks up on the sense of "stuff" as "fabric" in line 23. Fabric can be crushed together or unfolded and accurately measured.
5. I cannot completely account for his lineage.
6. Tenantius was Cymbeline's father and the brother of Cassibelan, who in 3.1.5 is described as Cymbeline's uncle.
7. The additional name "Leonatus" (born of a lion).

To his protection, calls him Posthumus[8] Leonatus,
Breeds him,° and makes him of his bedchamber,[9] — *Brings him up*
Puts to him° all the learnings that his time — *Offers him*
Could make him the receiver of, which he took
As we do air, fast as 'twas ministered,
And in 's° spring became a harvest; lived in court— — *in his*
Which rare it is to do—most praised, most loved;
A sample° to the youngest, to the more mature — *An example*
A glass that feated them,[1] and to the graver
A child that guided dotards.° To his mistress, — *foolish old men*
For whom he now is banished, her own price
Proclaims how she esteemed him; and his virtue[2]
By her election° may be truly read, — *choice (of him)*
What kind of man he is.

SECOND GENTLEMAN I honor him
Even out° of your report. But pray you tell me, — *Even beyond the limits*
Is she sole child to th' King?

FIRST GENTLEMAN His only child.
He had two sons—if this be worth your hearing,
Mark it—the eldest of them at three years old,
I'th' swathing° clothes the other, from their nursery — *swaddling*
Were stol'n, and to this hour, no guess in knowledge° — *no informed conjecture*
Which way they went.

SECOND GENTLEMAN How long is this ago?

FIRST GENTLEMAN Some twenty years.

SECOND GENTLEMAN That a king's children should be so conveyed,
So slackly guarded, and the search so slow
That could not trace them!

FIRST GENTLEMAN Howso'er 'tis strange,
Or that the negligence may well be laughed at,
Yet is it true, sir.

SECOND GENTLEMAN I do well believe you.

*Enter the* QUEEN, POSTHUMUS, *and* IMOGEN.[3]

We must forbear.° Here comes the gentleman, — *withdraw*
The Queen, and Princess. *Exeunt [the two* GENTLEMEN.*]*[4]

QUEEN No, be assured you shall not find me, daughter,
After the slander of[5] most stepmothers,
Evil-eyed unto you. You're my prisoner, but
Your jailer shall deliver you the keys
That lock up your restraint. For you, Posthumus,
So soon as I can win th'offended King,
I will be known your advocate. Marry,[6] yet
The fire of rage is in him, and 'twere good

8. In Latin, the word means "after death." As applied to a child, it means "one born after his or her father's death."
9. Makes him a personal servant.
1. A mirror that furnished ("feated") them with images of virtue or elegance.
2. *her . . . virtue:* the price she paid (for loving him) demonstrates how much she valued him and his virtue; her own worth ("price") shows the high esteem in which she held him and his virtues.
3. TEXTUAL COMMENT Although some scholars have suggested that the Folio's "Imogen" is a misprint for "Innogen," the name of the wife of the ancient English king Brute in Holinshed's *Chronicles*, this edition reverts to the more familiar "Imogen," since F is consistent in its use of this spelling. See Digital Edition TC 1.
4. F marks *Scena Secunda* (second scene) after the gentlemen exit. Then the Queen, Posthumus, and Imogen enter. There is, however, no change of time or place, and the Queen and the lovers are probably in view at line 68 when the Second Gentleman announces their entrance. Most editors do not indicate a new scene here.
5. In accordance with the slanderous things said about.
6. A mild oath, from the name of the Virgin Mary.

You leaned unto° his sentence with what patience — *You obeyed*
Your wisdom may inform° you. — *instill in*

POSTHUMUS
Please your highness,
I will from hence today.

QUEEN
You know the peril.
I'll fetch a turn° about the garden, pitying — *go for a walk*
The pangs of barred affections, though the King
Hath charged you should not speak together. *Exit.*

IMOGEN
Oh, dissembling courtesy! How fine this tyrant
Can tickle° where she wounds! My dearest husband, — *flatter*
I something° fear my father's wrath, but nothing— — *somewhat*
Always reserved my holy duty—what
His rage can do on me.[7] You must be gone,
And I shall here abide the hourly shot
Of angry eyes, not comforted to live
But that there is this jewel in the world
That I may see again.

POSTHUMUS
My queen, my mistress!
O lady, weep no more, lest I give cause
To be suspected of more tenderness
Than doth become a man. I will remain
The loyal'st husband that did e'er plight troth.° — *pledge marriage*
My residence in Rome at one Philario's,
Who to my father was a friend, to me
Known but by letter; thither write, my queen,
And with mine eyes I'll drink the words you send
Though ink be made of gall.° — *bile; bitter liquid*

*Enter* QUEEN.

QUEEN
Be brief, I pray you:
If the King come, I shall incur I know not
How much of his displeasure. [*aside*] Yet I'll move him
To walk this way. I never do him wrong,
But he does buy my injuries to be friends,[8]
Pays dear for my offenses. [*Exit.*]

POSTHUMUS
Should we be taking leave
As long a term° as yet we have to live, — *time*
The loathness° to depart would grow. Adieu. — *unwillingness*

IMOGEN
Nay, stay a little.
Were you but riding forth to air yourself
Such parting were too petty. Look here, love:
This diamond was my mother's. Take it, heart,
[*She gives him a ring.*]
But keep it till you woo another wife,
When Imogen is dead.

POSTHUMUS
How, how? Another?
You gentle gods, give me but this I have,
And sear up[9] my embracements from a next° — *another wife*
With bonds of death!
[*He puts on the ring.*]

7. *but . . . me:* an ambiguous phrase. My holy duty of obedience to my father excepted (a bond put in jeopardy by Cymbeline's act), I do not at all ("nothing") fear what Cymbeline's rage can do to me. Or: My holy duty to my husband excepted (which Cymbeline could disrupt by interfering with the marriage), I do not at all fear what Cymbeline's rage may do to me.

8. But he does endure the consequences of ("buy") my injuries in order to be friends.

9. And wrap up (in the cerecloth, or waxed linen, used in burial shrouds).

Remain, remain thou here,
While sense° can keep it on; and sweetest, fairest, — *the ability to feel*
As I my poor self did exchange for you
To your so infinite loss, so in our trifles° — *love tokens*
I still win of you.[1] For my sake wear this:
It is a manacle of love, I'll place it
Upon this fairest prisoner.
[*He puts a bracelet on her arm.*]

IMOGEN O the gods!
When shall we see again?
*Enter* CYMBELINE *and* LORDS.

POSTHUMUS Alack, the King!

CYMBELINE Thou basest° thing, avoid hence,° from my sight! — *most lowborn / be off*
If after this command thou fraught° the court — *burden*
With thy unworthiness, thou diest. Away,
Thou'rt poison to my blood.

POSTHUMUS The gods protect you,
And bless the good remainders of° the court! — *people remaining at*
I am gone. *Exit.*

IMOGEN There cannot be a pinch° in death — *pain*
More sharp than this is.

CYMBELINE O disloyal thing
That shouldst repair° my youth, thou heap'st — *restore*
A year's age on me.

IMOGEN I beseech you, sir,
Harm not yourself with your vexation.
I am senseless of° your wrath; a touch° more rare — *unable to feel / an emotion*
Subdues all pangs, all fears.

CYMBELINE Past grace?° Obedience? — *all sense of duty*

IMOGEN Past hope and in despair: that way past grace.[2]

CYMBELINE That mightst have had the sole son of my queen!

IMOGEN Oh, blest that I might not! I chose an eagle
And did avoid a puttock.[3]

CYMBELINE Thou took'st a beggar, wouldst have made my throne
A seat for baseness.

IMOGEN No, I rather added
A luster to it.

CYMBELINE O thou vile one!

IMOGEN Sir,
It is your fault that I have loved Posthumus:
You bred him as my playfellow, and he is
A man worth any woman, overbuys me
Almost the sum he pays.[4]

CYMBELINE What! Art thou mad?

IMOGEN Almost, sir. Heaven restore me! Would I were
A neatherd's° daughter, and my Leonatus — *cowherd's*
Our neighbor shepherd's son.
*Enter* QUEEN.

1. I still am enriched by you. Posthumus suggests that he is unequal in rank and wealth to Imogen. Correspondingly, his love token is of less value than hers.
2. Redemption. Alluding to the Christian belief that those who despair distrust God and are beyond the reach of grace.
3. A kite, or common predatory bird.
4. *overbuys . . . pays:* pays too much for me by almost the amount he gives for me. (Posthumus both gives himself to Imogen in marriage and also pays the price of banishment.) Imogen insists that Posthumus's worth equals her own and that their marriage consequently does not degrade her.

CYMBELINE Thou foolish thing!
[*to* QUEEN] They were again together; you have done
Not after° our command. [*to* LORDS] Away with her, *according to*
And pen her up.
QUEEN Beseech° your patience. —Peace, *I beseech*
Dear lady daughter, peace. —Sweet sovereign,
Leave us to ourselves, and make yourself some comfort
Out of your best advice.
CYMBELINE Nay, let her languish
A drop of blood a day[5] and, being aged,
Die of this folly. *Exit* [*with* LORDS].
QUEEN Fie, you must give way.

*Enter* PISANIO.

Here is your servant. —How now, sir? What news?
PISANIO My lord your son drew° on my master. *drew a sword*
QUEEN Ha?
No harm, I trust, is done?
PISANIO There might have been,
But that my master rather played than fought,
And had no help of anger. They were parted
By gentlemen at hand.
QUEEN I am very glad on't.
IMOGEN Your son's my father's friend; he takes his part
To draw upon an exile.° O brave sir! *(Posthumus)*
I would they were in Afric° both together, *Africa*
Myself by with a needle, that I might prick° *urge on*
The goer-back.° [*to* PISANIO] Why came you from your master? *swordsman who retreated*
PISANIO On his command. He would not suffer° me *allow*
To bring him to the haven; left these notes
Of what commands I should be subject to,
When't pleased you to employ me.
QUEEN This hath been
Your faithful servant. I dare lay mine honor
He will remain so.
PISANIO I humbly thank your highness.
QUEEN Pray walk a while.[6]
IMOGEN [*to* PISANIO] About some half hour hence, pray you speak with me.
You shall at least go see my lord aboard.
For this time leave me. *Exeunt.*

## 1.2

*Enter* CLOTEN *and two* LORDS.

FIRST LORD Sir, I would advise you to shift° a shirt;[1] the violence of action hath made you reek° as a sacrifice. Where air comes out, air comes in; there's none abroad so wholesome as that you vent.[2] *change* *emit vapors; stink*

5. Referring to the popular belief that one lost a drop of blood with each sigh.
6. F does not mark a separate exit for the Queen here, but Imogen appears to be speaking privately to Pisanio, and only Pisanio, in the following three lines.
1.2 Location: Scene continues.
1. PERFORMANCE COMMENT The roles of Cloten and Posthumus have successfully been doubled in performance, and other characters can be doubled as well. See Digital Edition PC 1.
2. The First Lord flatters Cloten by saying that the odorous vapors he is giving off are more healthful than the outside ("abroad") air that is being exchanged for them.

**CLOTEN** If my shirt were bloody, then to shift it.° Have I hurt him? *then I would change it*

**SECOND LORD** [*aside*] No, faith, not so much as his patience.

**FIRST LORD** Hurt him? His body's a passable° carcass if he be not hurt. It is a thoroughfare for steel if it be not hurt. *pretty good; penetrable*

**SECOND LORD** [*aside*] His steel was in debt: it went o'th' backside the town.[3]

**CLOTEN** The villain would not stand° me. *confront; stay still for*

**SECOND LORD** [*aside*] No, but he fled forward still,° toward your face. *always*

**FIRST LORD** Stand you? You have land enough of your own, but he added to your having, gave you some ground.° *fell back before you*

**SECOND LORD** [*aside*] As many inches as you have oceans.° Puppies! *(i.e., no inches)*

**CLOTEN** I would they had not come between us.

**SECOND LORD** [*aside*] So would I, till you had measured how long a fool you were upon the ground.

**CLOTEN** And that she should love this fellow and refuse me!

**SECOND LORD** [*aside*] If it be a sin to make a true election,[4] she is damned.

**FIRST LORD** Sir, as I told you always, her beauty and her brain go not together. She's a good sign,° but I have seen small reflection of her wit. *She looks good*

**SECOND LORD** [*aside*] She shines not upon fools lest the reflection should hurt her.

**CLOTEN** Come, I'll to my chamber. Would there had been some hurt done.

**SECOND LORD** [*aside*] I wish not so, unless it had been the fall of an ass, which is no great hurt.

**CLOTEN** You'll go with us?

**FIRST LORD** I'll attend your lordship.

**CLOTEN** Nay, come, let's go together.

**SECOND LORD** Well, my lord. *Exeunt.*

## 1.3

*Enter* IMOGEN *and* PISANIO.

**IMOGEN** I would thou grew'st unto the shores o'th' haven
And questioned'st every sail. If he should write
And I not have it, 'twere a paper lost
As offered mercy is.[1] What was the last
That he spake to thee?

**PISANIO** It was his queen, his queen!

**IMOGEN** Then waved his handkerchief?

**PISANIO** And kissed it, madam.

**IMOGEN** Senseless° linen, happier therein than I! *Unfeeling*
And that was all?

**PISANIO** No, madam. For so long
As he could make me with this eye or ear

3. Cloten's sword, like a debtor avoiding creditors, kept to the backstreets—that is, avoided the thoroughfare or main street of Posthumus's body (with a possible allusion to anal penetration).

4. A proper choice; with a pun on the Christian doctrine that certain souls are "elected," or predestined for salvation.

1.3 Location: Cymbeline's palace.

1. *'twere . . . is:* the lost letter would be a document written in vain, like an offer of mercy that is not accepted or received (for example, a judge's reprieve that comes too late or God's mercy to an unrepentant sinner).

Distinguish him from others, he did keep
The deck, with glove or hat or handkerchief
Still waving, as the fits and stirs of 's mind
Could best express how slow his soul sailed on,
How swift his ship.

IMOGEN Thou shouldst have made him
As little as a crow, or less, ere left
To after-eye him.[2]

PISANIO Madam, so I did.

IMOGEN I would have broke mine eyestrings,[3] cracked them, but
To look upon him, till the diminution
Of space had pointed him sharp as my needle;[4]
Nay, followed him till he had melted from
The smallness of a gnat to air, and then
Have turned mine eye and wept. But, good Pisanio,
When shall we hear from him?

PISANIO Be assured, madam,
With his next vantage.° *his first opportunity*

IMOGEN I did not take my leave of him, but had
Most pretty things to say. Ere I could tell him
How I would think on him at certain hours,
Such thoughts and such; or I could make him swear
The shes° of Italy should not betray *women*
Mine interest° and his honor; or have charged him *My entitlement (to him)*
At the sixth hour of morn, at noon, at midnight,
T'encounter me with orisons[5]—for then
I am in heaven for him—or ere I could
Give him that parting kiss which I had set
Betwixt two charming words,[6] comes in my father,
And, like the tyrannous breathing of the north,° *north wind*
Shakes all our buds from growing.

*Enter a* LADY.

LADY The Queen, madam,
Desires your highness' company.

IMOGEN [*to* PISANIO] Those things I bid you do, get them dispatched.
I will attend the Queen.

PISANIO Madam, I shall. *Exeunt.*

## 1.4

*Enter* PHILARIO, GIACOMO,[1] *a* FRENCHMAN, *a Dutchman, and a Spaniard.*

GIACOMO Believe it, sir, I have seen him in Britain. He was then of a crescent note,° expected to prove so worthy as since he hath been allowed the name of. But I could then have looked on him without the help of admiration,° though the catalogue of his endowments had been tabled° by his side, and I to peruse him by items.° *growing reputation* *wonder* *listed* *part by part*

2. *ere . . . him:* before ceasing to gaze after him.
3. The muscles of the eye, which were supposed to break at death or from overuse.
4. *till . . . needle:* until the distance between us had made him seem as small as the point on my needle.
5. To join me in prayers ("orisons"); to assail me (as an object of devotion) with prayers.
6. Between two words carrying a charm to ward off danger.
1.4 Location: Philario's house, Rome.
1. TEXTUAL COMMENT The character whose name is anglicized in this edition as "Giacomo" is called "Iachimo" in F. See Digital Edition TC 2.

PHILARIO You speak of him when he was less furnished than now he is with that which makes° him both without and within.

*constitutes*

FRENCHMAN I have seen him in France. We had very many there could behold the sun with as firm eyes as he.[2]

GIACOMO This matter of marrying his king's daughter, wherein he must be weighed rather by her value than his own, words him, I doubt not, a great deal from the matter.[3]

FRENCHMAN And then his banishment—

GIACOMO Ay, and the approbation of those that weep this lamentable divorce under her colors[4] are wonderfully to extend him,° be it but to fortify her judgment, which else an easy battery° might lay flat for taking a beggar without less quality.° But how comes it he is to sojourn with you? How creeps acquaintance?[5]

*exaggerate his worth*
*a slight assault*
*of no rank or merit*

PHILARIO His father and I were soldiers together, to whom I have been often bound for no less than my life.

*Enter* POSTHUMUS.

Here comes the Briton. Let him be so entertained amongst you as suits with gentlemen of your knowing° to a stranger° of his quality. I beseech you all, be better known to this gentleman, whom I commend to you as a noble friend of mine. How worthy he is I will leave to appear hereafter rather than story° him in his own hearing.

*knowledge / foreigner*
*give an account of*

FRENCHMAN Sir, we have known together° in Orléans.

*been acquainted*

POSTHUMUS Since when I have been debtor to you for courtesies which I will be ever to pay, and yet pay still.

FRENCHMAN Sir, you o'er-rate my poor kindness; I was glad I did atone° my countryman and you. It had been pity you should have been put together° with so mortal° a purpose as then each bore, upon importance° of so slight and trivial a nature.

*reconcile*
*(in a duel) / deadly*
*matters*

POSTHUMUS By your pardon, sir, I was then a young traveler, rather shunned to go even° with what I heard than[6] in my every action to be guided by others' experiences: but upon my mended° judgment—if I offend not to say it is mended—my quarrel was not altogether slight.

*refused to agree*
*improved*

FRENCHMAN Faith, yes, to be put to the arbitrement of swords,° and by such two that would by all likelihood have confounded° one the other, or have fallen both.

*settlement by duel*
*destroyed*

GIACOMO Can we with manners ask what was the difference?

FRENCHMAN Safely, I think; 'twas a contention in public, which may without contradiction suffer° the report. It was much like an argument that fell out last night, where each of us fell in praise of our country mistresses.[7] This gentleman, at that time vouching—and upon warrant of bloody affirmation°—his to be more fair, virtuous, wise, chaste, constant, qualified,° and less attemptable° than any the rarest of our ladies in France.

*permit*
*affirming it with blood*
*having notable qualities*
*open to seduction*

GIACOMO That lady is not now living, or this gentleman's opinion by this° worn out.

*now*

2. Alluding to the popular belief that only eagles could gaze directly on the sun. At 1.1.139, Imogen described Posthumus as an eagle.
3. *words . . . matter:* causes his reputation, I am sure, to be amplified beyond what is true.
4. That is, on Imogen's side (with a pun on "colors" as meaning both "a military banner" and "pretexts").
5. How does he claim a connection to you? Giacomo implies that Posthumus cunningly insinuated himself into Philario's friendship.
6. Than to appear.
7. The women of our country.

POSTHUMUS She holds her virtue still, and I my mind.

GIACOMO You must not so far prefer her fore ours of Italy.

POSTHUMUS Being so far provoked as I was in France, I would
abate her nothing,[8] though I profess myself her adorer, not
her friend.° *lover; spouse*

GIACOMO As fair and as good—a kind of hand in hand comparison[9]— had been something too fair and too good for any
lady in Britain. If she went before° others I have seen as that *surpassed*
diamond of yours outlusters many I have beheld, I could not
but believe she excelled many; but I have not seen the most
precious diamond that is, nor you the lady.

POSTHUMUS I praised her as I rated° her; so do I my stone. *valued*

GIACOMO What do you esteem it at?

POSTHUMUS More than the world enjoys.° *possesses*

GIACOMO Either your unparagoned° mistress is dead, or she's *matchless*
outprized° by a trifle. *exceeded in value*

POSTHUMUS You are mistaken: the one° may be sold or given, *(the ring)*
or if° there were wealth enough for the purchase, or merit *if either*
for the gift. The other° is not a thing for sale, and only the *(his mistress)*
gift of the gods.

GIACOMO Which the gods have given you?

POSTHUMUS Which by their graces I will keep.

GIACOMO You may wear her in title yours,[1] but you know
strange fowl light upon neighboring ponds.[2] Your ring[3] may
be stol'n too, so your brace of unprizable estimations,[4] the
one is but frail and the other casual.[5] A cunning thief or a
that-way-accomplished courtier[6] would hazard° the winning *venture*
both of first and last.

POSTHUMUS Your Italy contains none so accomplished a
courtier to convince° the honor of my mistress, if in the *overcome*
holding or loss of that you term her frail. I do nothing
doubt you have store° of thieves; notwithstanding, I fear *an abundance*
not° my ring. *am not worried about*

PHILARIO Let us leave° here, gentlemen. *stop the conversation*

POSTHUMUS Sir, with all my heart. This worthy signor, I
thank him, makes no stranger of me; we are familiar at first.

GIACOMO With five times so much conversation I should get
ground° of your fair mistress, make her go back,° even to the *advantage / relent*
yielding, had I admittance and opportunity to friend.° *to assist me*

POSTHUMUS No, no.

GIACOMO I dare thereupon pawn the moiety° of my estate to *one-half*
your ring, which in my opinion o'ervalues it something. But
I make my wager rather against your confidence than her reputation, and to bar your offense[7] herein too, I durst attempt it
against any lady in the world.

8. I would subtract nothing from my estimation of her.
9. A comparison claiming equality (not superiority).
1. You may claim her as your legal possession (with a pun on "wear" as meaning "enjoy her sexually").
2. *strange . . . ponds:* strangers may come upon your property (with a pun on "pond" as referring to female genitals).
3. Punning on "ring" as another slang term for female genitals.
4. So of the two ("brace of") objects you deem invaluable.
5. And the other subject to accident (referring to the ring).
6. A courtier skilled in that way (in the arts of seduction and theft).
7. To prevent you from feeling personally affronted.

POSTHUMUS You are a great deal abused in too bold a persuasion,[8] and I doubt not you sustain° what you're worthy of by your attempt.

*will receive*

GIACOMO What's that?

POSTHUMUS A repulse; though your attempt, as you call it, deserve more: a punishment too.

PHILARIO Gentlemen, enough of this. It came in too suddenly; let it die as it was born, and I pray you be better acquainted.

GIACOMO Would I had put my estate and my neighbor's on th'approbation° of what I have spoke.

*the proof*

POSTHUMUS What lady would you choose to assail?

GIACOMO Yours, whom in constancy you think stands so safe. I will lay° you ten thousand ducats to your ring that, commend me to the court where your lady is, with no more advantage than the opportunity of a second conference, and I will bring from thence that honor of hers, which you imagine so reserved.

*wager*

POSTHUMUS I will wage against your gold, gold to it.° My ring I hold dear as my finger, 'tis part of it.

*gold equal to it*

GIACOMO You are a friend, and therein the wiser.[9] If you buy ladies' flesh at a million a dram,[1] you cannot preserve it from tainting. But I see you have some religion in you, that° you fear.

*since*

POSTHUMUS This is but a custom in your tongue;[2] you bear a graver purpose, I hope.

GIACOMO I am the master of my speeches, and would undergo° what's spoken, I swear.

*undertake*

POSTHUMUS Will you? I shall but lend my diamond till your return. Let there be covenants° drawn between 's. My mistress exceeds in goodness the hugeness of your unworthy thinking. I dare you to this match: here's my ring.

*agreements*

PHILARIO I will have it no lay.°

*I will have no wager*

GIACOMO By the gods, it is one. If I bring you no sufficient testimony that I have enjoyed the dearest bodily part of your mistress, my ten thousand ducats are yours, so is your diamond too. If I come off and leave her in such honor as you have trust in, she your jewel, this your jewel, and my gold are yours—provided I have your commendation for my more free entertainment.[3]

POSTHUMUS I embrace these conditions; let us have articles betwixt us. Only thus far you shall answer: if you make your voyage upon her and give me directly° to understand you have prevailed, I am no further your enemy; she is not worth our debate. If she remain unseduced, you not making it appear otherwise, for your ill opinion, and th'assault you have made to her chastity, you shall answer me with your sword.

*plainly*

8. A great deal deceived in your too-bold belief.
9. Implying that Posthumus's intimacy with Imogen ("friend" means "lover" or "husband") makes him wise enough not to risk his ring in a wager on her chastity or wise enough to know the danger of this wager.
1. Even if you pay a large amount of money for a very small amount (a "dram") of female flesh.
2. This is merely a conventional way for you to speak.
3. Provided I have your introduction (to Imogen) to ensure a generous reception.

GIACOMO Your hand, a covenant. We will have these things set down by lawful counsel, and straight away° for Britain, lest the bargain should catch cold and starve.° I will fetch my gold, and have our two wagers recorded. *depart at once* / *die*

POSTHUMUS Agreed. [*Exeunt* POSTHUMUS *and* GIACOMO.]

FRENCHMAN Will this hold, think you?

PHILARIO Signor Giacomo will not from it. Pray, let us follow 'em. *Exeunt.*

## 1.5

*Enter* QUEEN, LADIES, *and* CORNELIUS.

QUEEN Whiles yet the dew's on ground, gather those flowers;
Make haste. Who has the note° of them? *list*

LADY I, madam.

QUEEN Dispatch.° *Exeunt* LADIES. *Make haste*
Now, master doctor, have you brought those drugs?

CORNELIUS Pleaseth° your highness, ay. Here they are, madam. *If it please*
[*He gives her a box.*]
But I beseech your grace, without offense—
My conscience bids me ask—wherefore° you have *why*
Commanded of me these most poisonous compounds,
Which are the movers of a languishing death,
But though slow, deadly.

QUEEN I wonder, doctor,
Thou ask'st me such a question. Have I not been
Thy pupil long? Hast thou not learned° me how *taught*
To make perfumes, distil, preserve?—yea, so
That our great King himself doth woo me oft
For my confections?° Having thus far proceeded— *medical compounds*
Unless thou think'st me devilish—is't not meet° *fitting*
That I did amplify my judgment in
Other conclusions?° I will try° the forces *experiments / test*
Of these thy compounds on such creatures as
We count not worth the hanging, but none human,
To try the vigor of them, and apply
Allayments° to their act,° and by them[1] gather *Antidotes / operation*
Their several virtues[2] and effects.

CORNELIUS Your highness
Shall from this practice but make hard your heart.
Besides, the seeing these effects will be
Both noisome° and infectious. *offensive*

QUEEN Oh, content thee.

*Enter* PISANIO.

[*aside*] Here comes a flattering rascal; upon him
Will I first work: he's factor° for his master *an agent*
And enemy to my son. —How now, Pisanio?
Doctor, your service for this time is ended;
Take your own way.

CORNELIUS [*aside*] I do suspect you, madam.
But you shall do no harm.

QUEEN [*to* PISANIO] Hark thee, a word.

1.5 Location: Cymbeline's court, Britain.
1. *them*: these experiments.
2. *gather . . . virtues*: determine the compounds' individual powers.

CORNELIUS [*aside*] I do not like her. She doth think she has
Strange ling'ring poisons. I do know her spirit,
And will not trust one of her malice with
A drug of such damned nature. Those she has
Will stupefy and dull the sense a while,
Which first, perchance, she'll prove° on cats and dogs, *test*
Then afterward up higher; but there is
No danger in what show of death it makes
More than the locking up the spirits a time,[3]
To be more fresh, reviving. She is fooled
With a most false effect, and I the truer° *more loyal*
So to be false with her.

QUEEN No further service, doctor,
Until I send for thee.

CORNELIUS I humbly take my leave. *Exit.*

QUEEN Weeps she still, say'st thou? Dost thou think in time
She will not quench,° and let instructions° enter *grow cool / good advice*
Where folly now possesses? Do thou work.
When thou shalt bring me word she loves my son,
I'll tell thee on the instant thou art then
As great as is thy master—greater, for
His fortunes all lie speechless, and his name° *reputation*
Is at last gasp. Return he cannot, nor
Continue where he is. To shift his being° *change his abode*
Is to exchange one misery with another,
And every day that comes comes to decay° *destroy*
A day's work in him. What shalt thou expect
To be depender on a thing that leans,[4]
Who cannot be new built, nor has no friends
So much as but to prop him?
[*She drops the box.* PISANIO *takes it up.*]
Thou tak'st up
Thou know'st not what; but take it for thy labor.
It is a thing I made, which hath the King
Five times redeemed from death. I do not know
What is more cordial.° Nay, I prithee, take it, *restorative*
It is an earnest° of a farther good *initial payment*
That I mean to thee. Tell thy mistress how
The case stands with her; do't as from thyself.
Think what a chance thou changest on,[5] but think
Thou hast thy mistress still; to boot,° my son, *in addition*
Who shall take notice of thee. I'll move the King
To any shape of thy preferment,° such *any kind of advancement*
As thou'lt desire; and then myself, I chiefly,
That set thee on to this desert,° am bound *action deserving reward*
To load thy merit richly. Call my women.
Think on my words. *Exit* PISANIO.
A sly and constant knave,
Not to be shaked; the agent for his master,

3. Other than the temporary suspension of the vital functions.
4. To be dependent on a thing that is about to fall.
5. Consider what opportunity you have to change your service (and become my servant).

And the remembrancer of her° to hold *he who reminds her*
The handfast° to her lord. I have given him that[6] *marriage contract*
Which, if he take, shall quite unpeople her
Of liegers for her sweet,[7] and which she after,
Except she bend her humor,[8] shall be assured
To taste of too.

*Enter* PISANIO *and* LADIES.

So, so; well done, well done.
The violets, cowslips, and the primroses
Bear to my closet.° Fare thee well, Pisanio. *private chamber*
Think on my words. *Exeunt* QUEEN *and* LADIES.

PISANIO And shall do.
But when to my good lord I prove untrue,
I'll choke myself—there's all I'll do for you. *Exit.*

## 1.6

*Enter* IMOGEN *alone.*

IMOGEN A father cruel and a stepdame false,
A foolish suitor to a wedded lady
That hath her husband banished.[1] Oh, that husband,
My supreme crown of grief, and those repeated[2]
Vexations of it. Had I been thief-stol'n,
As my two brothers, happy;[3] but most miserable
Is the desire that's glorious.[4] Blest be those,
How mean soe'er,[5] that have their honest wills,° *simple desires*
Which seasons comfort.[6]

*Enter* PISANIO *and* GIACOMO.

Who may this be? Fie!

PISANIO Madam, a noble gentleman of Rome
Comes from my lord with letters.

GIACOMO Change you,° madam? *Do you turn pale*
The worthy Leonatus is in safety,
And greets your highness dearly.
[*He gives her the letters.*]

IMOGEN Thanks, good sir,
You're kindly welcome.

GIACOMO [*aside*] All of her that is out of door,° most rich: *is visible*
If she be furnished with a mind so rare
She is alone th'Arabian bird,[7] and I
Have lost the wager. Boldness, be my friend;
Arm me, audacity, from head to foot,
Or, like the Parthian, I shall flying fight[8]—
Rather, directly fly.

6. The box supposedly containing poison.
7. Of ambassadors for her sweetheart.
8. Unless she changes her disposition.
1.6 Location: Scene continues.
1. Who has a banished husband.
2. Those already enumerated. Imogen has already complained of her father, stepmother, and foolish suitor.
3. *happy:* I would have been glad or fortunate.
4. But most wretched is the longing for what is exalted (in her case, a longing for Posthumus).
5. However low in status.
6. Which adds spice to their comfort.
7. The phoenix, only one of which existed at any given time. This mythical bird consumed itself in fire every five hundred years but then rose from its own ashes.
8. The mounted archers of Parthia were famous for their tactics in warfare, which included shooting arrows behind them as they retreated.

IMOGEN (*reads*) "He is one of the noblest note,° to whose kindnesses I am most infinitely tied. Reflect° upon him accordingly, as you value your trust. Leonatus." — *reputation* / *Bestow attention*

So far I read aloud,
But even the very middle of my heart
Is warmed by th' rest and takes it thankfully.
—You are as welcome, worthy sir, as I
Have words to bid you, and shall find it so
In all that I can do.

GIACOMO Thanks, fairest lady.
What, are men mad? Hath nature given them eyes
To see this vaulted arch° and the rich crop° — *the sky / harvest*
Of sea and land, which can distinguish twixt
The fiery orbs above and the twinned° stones — *identical*
Upon th'unnumbered beach,[9] and can we not
Partition make with spectacles[1] so precious
Twixt fair and foul?

IMOGEN What makes your admiration?° — *causes you to wonder*

GIACOMO It cannot be i'th' eye—for apes and monkeys,
Twixt two such shes,° would chatter this way[2] and — *women*
Contemn with mows° the other; nor i'th' judgment— — *Scorn with grimaces*
For idiots in this case of favor° would — *question of preference*
Be wisely definite; nor i'th' appetite—
Sluttery,° to such neat° excellence opposed, — *Sluttishness / elegant*
Should make desire vomit emptiness,
Not so allured to feed.[3]

IMOGEN What is the matter, trow?° — *in truth*

GIACOMO The cloyed will,° — *sated sexual desire*
That satiate° yet unsatisfied desire, that tub — *glutted*
Both filled and running,° ravening° first the lamb, — *emptying itself / devouring*
Longs after for the garbage.

IMOGEN What, dear sir,
Thus raps° you? Are you well? — *transports*

GIACOMO Thanks, madam, well.
[*to* PISANIO] Beseech° you, sir, — *I ask*
Desire° my man's abode where I did leave him: — *Seek out*
He's strange° and peevish.° — *a foreigner / irritable*

PISANIO I was going, sir,
To give him welcome. *Exit.*

IMOGEN Continues well my lord? His health, beseech you?

GIACOMO Well, madam.

IMOGEN Is he disposed to mirth? I hope he is.

GIACOMO Exceeding pleasant; none a stranger° there — *none of the foreigners*
So merry and so gamesome:[4] he is called
The Briton reveler.

IMOGEN When he was here
He did incline to sadness,° and ofttimes — *seriousness*
Not knowing why.

GIACOMO I never saw him sad.

9. Upon the beach whose grains of sand are uncounted.
1. Make distinction with organs of sight.
2. Would make their preference (for Imogen) clear.
3. *Should . . . feed:* Should destroy sexual desire, not arouse it (literally, should make desire vomit until it is empty, not tempt it to eat).
4. Sportive; sexually playful.

There is a Frenchman his companion, one
An eminent monsieur, that it seems much loves
A Gallian° girl at home. He furnaces[5] — *French*
The thick sighs from him, whiles the jolly° Briton— — *lively; lustful*
Your lord, I mean—laughs from 's free° lungs, cries "Oh, — *unconstrained*
Can my sides hold, to think that man, who knows
By history, report, or his own proof
What woman is, yea, what she cannot choose
But must be, will 's free hours languish° for — *pine away*
Assurèd bondage?"

IMOGEN Will my lord say so?

GIACOMO Ay, madam, with his eyes in flood with laughter.
It is a recreation to be by
And hear him mock the Frenchman. But heavens know
Some men are much to blame.

IMOGEN Not he, I hope.

GIACOMO Not he; but yet heaven's bounty towards him might
Be used more thankfully. In himself 'tis much;
In you, which I account his, beyond all talents.[6]
Whilst I am bound to wonder, I am bound
To pity too.

IMOGEN What do you pity, sir?

GIACOMO Two creatures heartily.

IMOGEN Am I one, sir?
You look on me: what wreck° discern you in me — *downfall*
Deserves your pity?

GIACOMO Lamentable! What,
To hide me from the radiant sun, and solace° — *take comfort*
I'th' dungeon by a snuff?° — *candle end*

IMOGEN I pray you, sir,
Deliver with more openness your answers
To my demands. Why do you pity me?

GIACOMO That others do—
I was about to say enjoy your—but
It is an office° of the gods to venge° it, — *a duty / avenge of it*
Not mine to speak on't.°

IMOGEN You do seem to know
Something of me, or what concerns me. Pray you,
Since doubting° things go ill often hurts more — *suspecting*
Than to be sure they do—for certainties
Either are past remedies or, timely knowing,
The remedy then born[7]—discover° to me — *reveal*
What both you spur and stop.[8]

GIACOMO Had I this cheek
To bathe my lips upon; this hand whose touch,
Whose every touch, would force the feeler's soul
To th'oath of loyalty; this object which
Takes prisoner the wild motion of mine eye,
Fixing it only here: should I, damned then,

5. He exhales sighs like a furnace.
6. *In himself . . . talents:* As regards his own qualities, heaven's generosity is considerable. In giving him you, whom I consider his, heaven's generosity surpasses all abundance.
7. *or . . . born:* or, they being known about in time, the remedy is then brought about.
8. What you both urge on and restrain (as one commands a horse).

Slaver with lips as common as the stairs
That mount the Capitol;[9] join gripes with hands
Made hard with hourly falsehood—falsehood as
With labor;[1] then by-peeping° in an eye *glancing coyly*
Base and illustrous° as the smoky light *lacking luster*
That's fed with stinking tallow[2]—it were fit
That all the plagues of hell should at one time
Encounter° such revolt.° *Confront / infidelity*

IMOGEN My lord, I fear,
Has forgot Britain.

GIACOMO And himself. Not I
Inclined to this intelligence pronounce
The beggary of his change,[3] but 'tis your graces
That from my mutest conscience° to my tongue *most quiet inner being*
Charms this report out.

IMOGEN Let me hear no more.

GIACOMO O dearest soul, your cause doth strike my heart
With pity that doth make me sick. A lady
So fair, and fastened to an empery° *empire*
Would make the great'st king double,° to be partnered *twice as great*
With tomboys hired with that self exhibition[4]
Which your own coffers yield; with diseased ventures° *prostitutes; vendors*
That play with all infirmities for gold,
Which rottenness can lend nature; such boiled stuff[5]
As well might poison poison! Be revenged,
Or she that bore you was no queen, and you
Recoil° from your great stock. *Degenerate*

IMOGEN Revenged?
How should I be revenged? If this be true—
As I have such a heart that both mine ears
Must not in haste abuse[6]—if it be true,
How should I be revenged?

GIACOMO Should he make me
Live like Diana's priest[7] betwixt cold sheets,
Whiles he is vaulting variable ramps[8]
In your despite, upon your purse[9]—revenge it.
I dedicate myself to your sweet pleasure,
More noble than that runagate° to your bed, *renegade*
And will continue fast° to your affection, *constant*
Still close as sure.[1]

IMOGEN What ho, Pisanio!

GIACOMO Let me my service tender on your lips—

IMOGEN Away, I do condemn mine ears that have
So long attended thee. If thou wert honorable

9. *Slaver . . . Capitol:* Offer drooling kisses to whores who, like the stairs to the Roman Capitol building, are available to everyone.
1. *join . . . labor:* clasp hands made as hard with hourly lies or sexual infidelities as they might have been made hard with work.
2. Animal fat used for making candles.
3. *Not . . . change:* It is not because I am disposed to give this information that I report the contemptible nature of his change.
4. With whores ("tomboys") hired with that same payment.
5. Such diseased prostitutes. Sweating, usually induced by the steam from boiling water, was a common treatment for syphilis.
6. *a heart . . . abuse:* a heart that my ears must not abuse by too hastily accepting what they hear.
7. That is, live chastely. Diana was the Roman goddess of the hunt known for her chastity and her circle of virgin followers.
8. While he is having sexual intercourse with whores ("ramps") of all kinds.
9. In contempt of you, with your money.
1. Always as secret as I am true.

Thou wouldst have told this tale for virtue, not
For such an end thou seek'st, as base as strange.
Thou wrong'st a gentleman who is as far
From thy report as thou from honor, and
Solicits here a lady that disdains
Thee and the devil alike. What ho, Pisanio!
The King my father shall be made acquainted
Of thy assault. If he shall think it fit
A saucy stranger in his court to mart° *do business*
As in a Romish stew,° and to expound *Roman brothel*
His beastly mind to us, he hath a court
He little cares for and a daughter who
He not respects at all. What ho, Pisanio!

GIACOMO O happy Leonatus! I may say
The credit° that thy lady hath of° thee *trust / in*
Deserves thy trust, and thy most perfect goodness
Her assured credit.[2] Blessèd live you long,
A lady to the worthiest sir that ever
Country called his;° and you his mistress, only *its own*
For the most worthiest fit. Give me your pardon;
I have spoke this to know if your affiance° *faith*
Were deeply rooted, and shall make your lord
That which he is new o'er;[3] and he is one
The truest mannered,[4] such a holy witch° *a charming person*
That he enchants societies into° him; *crowds of people to*
Half all men's hearts are his.

IMOGEN You make amends.

GIACOMO He sits 'mongst men like a descended god;
He hath a kind of honor sets him off
More than a mortal seeming.[5] Be not angry,
Most mighty Princess, that I have adventured° *dared*
To try° your taking of a false report, which hath *test*
Honored with confirmation your great judgment
In the election of a sir so rare,
Which° you know cannot err. The love I bear him *Whom*
Made me to fan[6] you thus, but the gods made you,
Unlike all others, chaffless.° Pray, your pardon. *without chaff; perfect*

IMOGEN All's well, sir. Take my power i'th' court for yours.

GIACOMO My humble thanks. I had almost forgot
T'entreat your grace but in a small request,
And yet of moment° too, for it concerns *importance*
Your lord; myself and other noble friends
Are partners in the business.

IMOGEN Pray, what is't?

GIACOMO Some dozen Romans of us, and your lord—
The best feather of our wing—have mingled sums
To buy a present for the Emperor,
Which I, the factor for the rest, have done

2. *and . . . credit:* and your most perfect goodness deserves her absolute trust.
3. *and . . . o'er:* and I (by this news of your fidelity) shall make your lord feel afresh what he already is (that is, your lord).
4. *he . . . mannered:* he is above all others the most perfect in conduct.
5. So that he appears more than mortal.
6. Winnow. When grain was harvested, wheat was winnowed from the chaff; metaphorically, the good was winnowed from the bad.

In France. 'Tis plate[7] of rare device, and jewels
Of rich and exquisite form; their value's great,
And I am something curious,° being strange, — *somewhat anxious*
To have them in safe stowage. May it please you
To take them in protection?

IMOGEN Willingly,
And pawn mine honor for their safety, since
My lord hath interest° in them. I will keep them — *a stake*
In my bedchamber.

GIACOMO They are in a trunk
Attended by my men. I will make bold
To send them to you, only for this night:
I must aboard tomorrow.

IMOGEN Oh, no, no!

GIACOMO Yes, I beseech, or I shall short° my word — *break*
By length'ning my return. From Gallia° — *France*
I crossed the seas on purpose and on promise
To see your grace.

IMOGEN I thank you for your pains;
But not away tomorrow!

GIACOMO Oh, I must, madam.
Therefore I shall beseech you, if you please
To greet your lord with writing, do't tonight.
I have outstood° my time, which is material — *overstayed*
To th' tender° of our present. — *the offering*

IMOGEN I will write.
Send your trunk to me: it shall safe be kept,
And truly yielded° you. You're very welcome. *Exeunt.* — *faithfully returned to*

## 2.1

*Enter* CLOTEN *and the two* LORDS.

CLOTEN Was there ever man had such luck? When I kissed the jack[1] upon an upcast,° to be hit away! I had a hundred pound on't; and then a whoreson jackanapes° must take me up[2] for swearing, as if I borrowed mine oaths of him and might not spend them at my pleasure. — *on a final throw*; *an idiotic bastard*

FIRST LORD What got he by that? You have broke his pate° with your bowl. — *head*

SECOND LORD [*aside*] If his wit had been like him that broke it, it would have run all out.

CLOTEN When a gentleman is disposed to swear, it is not for any standers-by to curtail[3] his oaths, ha?

SECOND LORD No, my lord [*aside*] —nor crop the ears of them.

CLOTEN Whoreson dog! I give him satisfaction? Would he had been one of my rank.[4]

SECOND LORD [*aside*] To have smelled like a fool.

7. Objects, often tableware, either made of precious metals or covered ("plated") with them.
2.1 Location: Cymbeline's court, Britain.
1. In the game of bowls, the jack is the target ball. To "kiss the jack" is to roll one's ball so that it touches the jack.
2. Challenge me; rebuke me.
3. Shorten, as one bobbed the tails (and sometimes the ears) of certain dogs. This leads the Second Lord to talk of cropping the ears of oaths in line 12.
4. Social position. Gentlemen were only supposed to fight ("give satisfaction" to) men of their own rank. The Second Lord puns on "rank" as meaning "strong smell."

CLOTEN I am not vexed more at anything in th'earth. A pox on't,[5] I had rather not be so noble as I am! They dare not fight with me because of the Queen my mother. Every jack-slave° hath his belly full of fighting, and I must go up and down like a cock that nobody can match.°

lowborn fellow / equal; fight with

SECOND LORD [*aside*] You are cock and capon too, an you crow cock with your comb on.[6]

CLOTEN Sayest thou?

SECOND LORD It is not fit your lordship should undertake° every companion° that you give offense to.

take on / fellow

CLOTEN No, I know that, but it is fit I should commit offense to[7] my inferiors.

SECOND LORD Ay, it is fit for your lordship only.

CLOTEN Why, so I say.

FIRST LORD Did you hear of a stranger that's come to court tonight?

CLOTEN A stranger, and I not know on't?°

of it

SECOND LORD [*aside*] He's a strange fellow himself, and knows it not.

FIRST LORD There's an Italian come, and 'tis thought, one of Leonatus' friends.

CLOTEN Leonatus? A banished rascal; and he's another, whatsoever he be. Who told you of this stranger?

FIRST LORD One of your lordship's pages.

CLOTEN Is it fit I went to look upon him? Is there no derogation° in't?

loss of dignity

SECOND LORD You cannot derogate,[8] my lord.

CLOTEN Not easily, I think.

SECOND LORD [*aside*] You are a fool granted;° therefore your issues° being foolish do not derogate.

an acknowledged fool / deeds

CLOTEN Come, I'll go see this Italian. What I have lost today at bowls I'll win tonight of him. Come, go.

SECOND LORD I'll attend your lordship.

*Exeunt* [CLOTEN *and* FIRST LORD].

That such a crafty devil as is his mother
Should yield the world this ass! A woman that
Bears all down° with her brain, and this her son  *Overcomes everyone*
Cannot take two from twenty, for his heart,°  *for the life of him*
And leave eighteen. Alas, poor Princess,
Thou divine Imogen, what thou endur'st,
Betwixt a father by thy stepdame governed,
A mother hourly coining plots, a wooer
More hateful than the foul expulsion is
Of thy dear husband, than that horrid act
Of the divorce he'd make! The heavens hold firm
The walls of thy dear honor, keep unshaked
That temple, thy fair mind, that thou mayst stand
T'enjoy thy banished lord and this great land. *Exit.*

5. A mild oath meaning "a plague on it."
6. And a castrated cock too if you brag ("crow") that you are a cock while wearing a fool's cap (coxcomb). There are puns here on "capon" and "cap on," on "cock's comb" and "coxcomb."
7. I should assault, with the perhaps unintended secondary meaning of "to defecate upon."
8. You cannot forfeit your dignity; you have no dignity to lose.

## 2.2

*[A trunk is brought on.] Enter* IMOGEN, *in her bed [reading], and a* LADY.[1]

IMOGEN Who's there? My woman Helen?
LADY Please you, madam.
IMOGEN What hour is it?
LADY Almost midnight, madam.
IMOGEN I have read three hours then; mine eyes are weak.
Fold down the leaf where I have left. To bed.
Take not away the taper; leave it burning,
And if thou canst awake by four o'th' clock,
I prithee call me. Sleep hath seized me wholly. *[Exit* LADY.]
To your protection I commend me, gods;
From fairies° and the tempters of the night *evil beings*
Guard me, beseech ye.° *I entreat you*
*[She] sleeps.* GIACOMO *[emerges] from the trunk.*
GIACOMO The crickets sing, and man's o'er-labored sense
Repairs itself by rest. Our Tarquin[2] thus
Did softly press the rushes[3] ere he wakened
The chastity he wounded. Cytherea,[4]
How bravely° thou becom'st thy bed. Fresh lily, *splendidly*
And whiter than the sheets! That I might touch,
But kiss, one kiss. Rubies unparagoned,
How dearly they do't.[5] 'Tis her breathing that
Perfumes the chamber thus. The flame o'th' taper
Bows toward her, and would underpeep her lids
To see th'enclosèd lights, now canopied
Under these windows,° white and azure laced *eyelids*
With blue of heaven's own tinct.° But my design[6]— *hue*
To note the chamber: I will write all down.
*[He starts taking notes.]*
Such and such pictures; there the window, such
Th'adornment of her bed; the arras, figures,
Why, such and such; and the contents o'th' story.[7]
Ah, but some natural notes° about her body *marks*
Above ten thousand meaner movables[8]
Would testify t'enrich mine inventory.
O sleep, thou ape° of death, lie dull° upon her, *mimic / heavy*
And be her sense but as a monument,[9]
Thus in a chapel lying. Come off, come off—
*[He takes the bracelet from her arm.]*

2.2 Location: Imogen's chambers.
1. TEXTUAL COMMENT F's stage direction reads *"Enter Imogen, in her Bed, and a Lady."* Imogen was probably revealed in a bed thrust out from a curtained space at the back of the stage. Other properties necessary for the scene, including the trunk containing Giacomo, would probably have been carried onstage by the actors. See Digital Edition TC 3.
2. The ancient Roman Sextus Tarquinius, whose rape of Lucrece (Lucretia) was the subject of a poem by Shakespeare.
3. Reeds commonly used as a floor covering.
4. A name for Aphrodite, or Venus, the goddess of beauty and love, who first set foot on the island of Cytherea after her birth from sea-foam.
5. How dearly do they (her ruby lips) kiss one another.
6. PERFORMANCE COMMENT The extent to which the actor playing Giacomo emphasizes the sexual menace of his actions in Imogen's bedroom will affect how the audience perceives the play's genre. See Digital Edition PC 2.
7. Possibly the design on the tapestry. In 2.4.67–91, Giacomo describes in more detail what he saw in Imogen's bedchamber: a tapestry depicting the story of Antony and Cleopatra and a chimneypiece carving of Diana bathing. He could here be referring to the "figures" and "contents" of either the tapestry or the chimneypiece.
8. Less important pieces of property, especially furniture or furnishings.
9. And let her senses be like those of an effigy on a tomb.

As slippery as the Gordian knot was hard.[1]
'Tis mine, and this will witness outwardly,
As strongly as the conscience does within,[2]
To th' madding° of her lord. On her left breast *maddening*
A mole cinque-spotted,° like the crimson drops *with five spots*
I'th' bottom of a cowslip. Here's a voucher,° *piece of evidence*
Stronger than ever law could make; this secret
Will force him think I have picked the lock and ta'en
The treasure of her honor.[3] No more. To what end?
Why should I write this down that's riveted,
Screwed to my memory? She hath been reading late
The tale of Tereus;[4] here the leaf's turned down
Where Philomel gave up. I have enough;
To th' trunk again, and shut the spring of it.
Swift, swift, you dragons of the night, that dawning
May bare the raven's eye.[5] I lodge in fear;
Though this a heavenly angel, hell is here.
*Clock strikes.*
One, two, three: time, time. *Exit [into the trunk].*

## 2.3

*Enter* CLOTEN *and [the two]* LORDS.

FIRST LORD Your lordship is the most patient man in loss, the most coldest° that ever turned up ace.[1] *least passionate*

CLOTEN It would make any man cold to lose.

FIRST LORD But not every man patient after° the noble temper of your lordship. You are most hot and furious when you win. *according to*

CLOTEN Winning will put any man into courage. If I could get this foolish Imogen I should have gold enough. It's almost morning, is't not?

FIRST LORD Day, my lord.

CLOTEN I would this music would come. I am advised to give her music o'mornings; they say it will penetrate.[2]

*Enter* MUSICIANS.

Come on, tune. If you can penetrate her with your fingering, so; we'll try with tongue too.[3] If none will do,° let her remain, but I'll never give o'er. First, a very excellent good-conceited° thing; after, a wonderful sweet air, with admirable rich words to it, and then let her consider. *suffice* *ingenious*

1. As easy to open as the Gordian knot was difficult to untie. Alluding to the myth of Gordius, King of Phrygia, who tied an impossibly intricate knot and declared that whoever untied it would reign over Asia; with a single thrust of his sword, Alexander the Great cut through it. Giacomo's unclasping of the bracelet has sexual implications. He is metaphorically violating Imogen's chastity and, by stealing Posthumus's love token, is interfering in the marriage bond that links Posthumus and Imogen.
2. As powerfully as does his (Posthumus's) inward consciousness.
3. Giacomo means his knowledge of the mole will make Posthumus believe he has slept with Imogen. To "pick the lock" is a euphemism for "to have sex."
4. In Greek mythology, Tereus, King of Thrace, raped his wife's sister Philomela and cut out her tongue so she could not reveal what had happened. Philomela later wove the story into a tapestry.
5. May cause the raven to wake. The bird supposedly slept facing east and awakened at dawn.

**2.3** Location: A room near Imogen's chambers.
1. *that . . . ace:* who ever threw the lowest score in a game of dice, with a pun on "ass."
2. Affect her emotions; arouse her sexually.
3. If your instrumental music can move her, that's good. We'll try to move her with song as well. These lines also carry an explicitly sexual secondary meaning: If you can insert your fingers inside her, that's good. We'll try oral sex as well. It is unclear if Cloten understands the bawdy import of his own words.

*Song.*

MUSICIAN [*sings*][4] Hark, hark, the lark at heaven's gate sings,
And Phoebus gins° arise,[5] — *Apollo (sun god) begins*
His steeds to water at those springs
On chaliced flowers[6] that lies,
And winking Mary-buds° begin to ope their golden eyes; — *closed marigold buds*
With everything that pretty is, my lady sweet, arise:
Arise, arise!

CLOTEN So, get you gone. If this penetrate, I will consider° your music the better; if it do not, it is a vice° in her ears which horsehairs, and calves' guts,[7] nor the voice of unpaved[8] eunuch to boot can never amend. [*Exeunt* MUSICIANS.] — *value* / *defect*

*Enter* CYMBELINE *and* QUEEN.

SECOND LORD Here comes the King.

CLOTEN I am glad I was up so late, for that's the reason I was up so early. He cannot choose but take this service I have done fatherly. —Good morrow to your majesty, and to my gracious mother.

CYMBELINE Attend you here the door of our stern daughter?
Will she not forth?

CLOTEN I have assailed her with musics, but she vouchsafes no notice.

CYMBELINE The exile of her minion° is too new; — *darling*
She hath not yet forgot him. Some more time
Must wear the print° of his remembrance out, — *imprint*
And then she's yours.

QUEEN [*to* CLOTEN] You are most bound to th' King,
Who lets go by no vantages° that may — *opportunities*
Prefer° you to his daughter. Frame° yourself — *Recommend / Prepare*
To° orderly solicits,° and be friended — *With / solicitations*
With aptness of the season.[9] Make denials
Increase your services; so seem as if
You were inspired to do those duties which
You tender to her; that you in all obey her,
Save when command to your dismission tends,
And therein you are senseless.[1]

CLOTEN Senseless? Not so.

[*Enter a* MESSENGER.]

MESSENGER [*to* CYMBELINE] So like you,° sir, ambassadors from Rome; — *If you please*
The one is Caius Lucius.

CYMBELINE A worthy fellow,
Albeit he comes on angry purpose now;
But that's no fault of his. We must receive him
According to the honor of his sender,

4. F does not attribute this song to a particular singer but simply introduces it as "song." It also appears in a seventeenth-century manuscript located in the Bodleian Library at Oxford.
5. These lines also echo Shakespeare's Sonnet 29, lines 10–12: "my state / Like to the lark at break of day arising / From sullen earth, sings hymns at heaven's gate."
6. Flowers with cuplike blossoms.
7. Both were used as strings for musical instruments.
8. Castrated (lacking stones).
9. And be assisted by appropriate timing.
1. *Save . . . senseless:* Except what pertains to your dismissal ("dismission"), which you are incapable of understanding. Cloten, however, takes "senseless" to mean "stupid."

And towards himself (his goodness forespent on us[2])
We must extend our notice. Our dear son,
When you have given good morning to your mistress,
Attend the Queen and us; we shall have need
T'employ you towards this Roman. Come, our Queen.
*Exeunt* [*all but* CLOTEN].

CLOTEN If she be up, I'll speak with her; if not
Let her lie still and dream. By your leave, ho!
[*He knocks.*]
I know her women are about her: what
If I do line° one of their hands? 'Tis gold — *fill (with gold)*
Which buys admittance—oft it doth—yea, and makes
Diana's rangers false° themselves, yield up — *gamekeepers turn false*
Their deer to th' stand o'th' stealer;[3] and 'tis gold
Which makes the true man killed and saves the thief,
Nay, sometime hangs both thief and true man. What
Can it not do and undo? I will make
One of her women lawyer to° me, for — *advocate for*
I yet not understand the case[4] myself.
—By your leave!
*He knocks* [*again*]. *Enter a* LADY.

LADY Who's there that knocks?
CLOTEN A gentleman.
LADY No more?
CLOTEN Yes, and a gentlewoman's son.
LADY That's more
Than some whose tailors are as dear° as yours — *expensive*
Can justly boast of. What's your lordship's pleasure?
CLOTEN Your lady's person. Is she ready?° — *dressed; prepared*
LADY Ay—
To keep her chamber.
CLOTEN There is gold for you:
Sell me your good report.
LADY How, my good name?° Or to report of you — *reputation*
What I shall think is good?
*Enter* IMOGEN.
The Princess. [*Exit.*]
CLOTEN Good morrow, fairest sister; your sweet hand.
IMOGEN Good morrow, sir; you lay out too much pains
For purchasing but trouble. The thanks I give,
Is telling you that I am poor of thanks
And scarce can spare them.
CLOTEN Still I swear I love you.
IMOGEN If you but said so, 'twere as deep° with me. — *solemn; binding*
If you swear still,° your recompense is still — *always*
That I regard it not.
CLOTEN This is no answer.
IMOGEN But° that you shall not say I yield being silent, — *Except*
I would not speak. I pray you spare me. Faith,
I shall unfold equal discourtesy[5]

2. *his . . . us:* in view of the virtue he has shown in previous dealings with us.
3. *yield . . . stealer:* surrender their deer to the place where the thief stands to shoot; surrender what is most dear or valuable (their chastity) to the thief's erect penis ("th' stand").
4. *for . . . case:* for I still do not know how to manage the matter (with wordplay on "stand under" as slang for "sexually penetrate" and on "case" as slang for "vagina").
5. I shall display discourtesy equal.

To your best kindness. One of your great knowing° *knowledge*
Should learn, being taught, forbearance.

CLOTEN To leave you in your madness, 'twere my sin;
I will not.

IMOGEN Fools cure not mad folks—

CLOTEN Do you call me fool?

IMOGEN As I am mad I do.
If you'll be patient, I'll no more be mad;
That cures us both. I am much sorry, sir,
You put me to forget a lady's manners
By being so verbal:[6] and learn now for all
That I, which know my heart, do here pronounce
By th' very truth of it: I care not for you,
And am so near the lack of charity
To accuse myself I hate you,[7] which I had rather
You felt than make't my boast.° *than I had to say it*

CLOTEN You sin against
Obedience, which you owe your father. For° *As for*
The contract you pretend° with that base wretch— *claim*
One bred of alms and fostered with cold dishes,
With scraps o'th' court—it is no contract, none.
And though it be allowed in meaner° parties *socially inferior*
(Yet who than he more mean?) to knit their souls,
On whom there is no more dependency
But brats and beggary,[8] in self-figured° knot, *self-contracted*
Yet you are curbed from that enlargement° by *freedom*
The consequence o'th' crown,[9] and must not foil° *defile*
The precious note° of it with a base slave, *reputation*
A hilding for a livery,[1] a squire's cloth,° *uniform*
A pantler°—not so eminent. *pantry servant*

IMOGEN Profane fellow!
Wert thou the son of Jupiter,° and no more *king of the gods*
But what thou art besides, thou wert too base
To be his° groom. Thou wert dignified enough[2] *(Posthumus's)*
Even to the point of envy, if 'twere made
Comparative for your virtues to be styled
The under-hangman[3] of his kingdom, and hated
For being preferred° so well. *advanced*

CLOTEN The south-fog[4] rot him!

IMOGEN He never can meet more mischance than come
To be but named of° thee. His meanest garment *by*
That ever hath but clipped° his body is dearer *encircled*
In my respect than all the hairs above thee,° *on your head*
Were they all made such men.

*Enter* PISANIO.

How now, Pisanio?

6. "Verbal" (talkative; plainspoken) may refer either to Cloten or to Imogen.
7. *And . . . you:* And I am so near uncharitableness that I can charge myself with hating you.
8. *On . . . beggary:* Upon whose marriage nothing depends but worthless children and extreme poverty.
9. *by . . . crown:* by the importance of the crown; by the consequences that flow from your inheritance of the crown.
1. A worthless person fit only to wear the uniform ("livery") of his master's household.
2. You were raised in status sufficiently.
3. *if 'twere . . . under-hangman:* if a comparison were made between your virtues and those of Posthumus and you were given the job of assistant hangman; if, in accordance with your virtues, you were given the job of assistant hangman.
4. A damp fog brought by the south wind and supposed to breed infections.

CLOTEN His garment? Now the devil—
IMOGEN [*to* PISANIO] To Dorothy my woman hie thee presently.° *at once*
CLOTEN His garment?
IMOGEN [*to* PISANIO] I am sprited with° a fool, *am haunted by*
Frighted, and angered worse. Go bid my woman
Search for a jewel that too casually
Hath left mine arm; it was thy master's. Shrew me° *Beshrew me (plague on me)*
If I would lose it for a revenue
Of any king's in Europe! I do think
I saw't this morning; confident I am
Last night 'twas on mine arm; I kissed it.
I hope it be not gone to tell my lord
That I kiss aught but he.
PISANIO 'Twill not be lost.
IMOGEN I hope so. Go and search. [*Exit* PISANIO.]
CLOTEN You have abused me:
"His meanest garment"?
IMOGEN Ay, I said so, sir.
If you will make't an action,° call witness to't. *a lawsuit*
CLOTEN I will inform your father.
IMOGEN Your mother too;
She's my good lady and will conceive,° I hope,° *think / expect*
But the worst of me. So I leave you, sir,
To th' worst of discontent. *Exit.*
CLOTEN I'll be revenged.
"His meanest garment"? Well! *Exit.*

## 2.4

*Enter* POSTHUMUS *and* PHILARIO.

POSTHUMUS Fear it not, sir. I would I were so sure
To win the King as I am bold her honor
Will remain hers.
PHILARIO What means° do you make to him? *intercessions*
POSTHUMUS Not any; but abide the change of time,
Quake in the present winter's state, and wish
That warmer days would come. In these feared° hopes *timid*
I barely gratify° your love; they failing, *repay*
I must die much your debtor.
PHILARIO Your very goodness and your company
O'erpays all I can do. By this° your king *By now*
Hath heard of great Augustus. Caius Lucius
Will do 's commission thoroughly. And I think
He'll grant the tribute, send th'arrearages,° *overdue payments*
Or look upon our Romans, whose remembrance° *the memory of whom*
Is yet fresh in their grief.[1]
POSTHUMUS I do believe,
Statist° though I am none, nor like to be, *Statesman*
That this will prove a war, and you shall hear
The legions now in Gallia sooner landed
In our not-fearing Britain than have tidings
Of any penny tribute paid. Our countrymen

2.4 Location: Philario's house, Rome.
1. The Britons' grief; the grief inflicted by the Romans.

Are men more ordered° than when Julius Caesar — *better disciplined*
Smiled at their lack of skill but found their courage
Worthy his frowning at. Their discipline,
Now mingled[2] with their courage, will make known
To their approvers° they are people such — *those who test them*
That mend upon the world.[3]

*Enter* GIACOMO.

PHILARIO See Giacomo.

POSTHUMUS The swiftest harts° have posted° you by land, — *deer / conveyed*
And winds of° all the corners° kissed your sails — *from / (of the globe)*
To make your vessel nimble.

PHILARIO Welcome, sir.

POSTHUMUS I hope the briefness of your answer made° — *caused*
The speediness of your return.

GIACOMO Your lady
Is one of the fairest that I have looked upon.

POSTHUMUS And therewithal the best, or let her beauty
Look through a casement[4] to allure false hearts,
And be false with them.

GIACOMO Here are letters for you.

POSTHUMUS Their tenor good, I trust.

GIACOMO 'Tis very like.

[POSTHUMUS *reads the letters.*]

PHILARIO Was Caius Lucius in the Briton court
When you were there?

GIACOMO He was expected then,
But not° approached. — *had not*

POSTHUMUS All is well yet.
Sparkles this stone as it was wont, or is't not
Too dull for your good wearing?

GIACOMO If I have lost it
I should have lost the worth of it in gold.
I'll make a journey twice as far t'enjoy
A second night of such sweet shortness which
Was mine in Britain—for the ring is won.

POSTHUMUS The stone's too hard to come by.

GIACOMO Not a whit,
Your lady being so easy.

POSTHUMUS Make not, sir,
Your loss your sport. I hope you know that we
Must not continue friends.

GIACOMO Good sir, we must,
If you keep covenant. Had I not brought
The knowledge° of your mistress home, I grant — *A sexual account*
We were to question° farther; but I now — *dispute*
Profess myself the winner of her honor,
Together with your ring, and not the wronger
Of her or you, having proceeded but
By both your wills.

2. Textual Comment F has "wing-led," which might suggest that the Britons are led with discipline on each flank (each "wing") of the army, or that their courage makes their discipline soar as if it had wings. This edition follows the Second Folio (F2, printed in 1632) in its use of "mingled." See Digital Edition TC 4.

3. *such . . . world:* who improve in the world's estimation.

4. Look out through a window (alluding to the manner in which prostitutes solicited customers).

POSTHUMUS If you can make't apparent
That you have tasted her in bed, my hand
And ring is yours. If not, the foul opinion
You had of her pure honor gains or loses
Your sword or mine,[5] or masterless leaves both° *both swords*
To who shall find them.

GIACOMO Sir, my circumstances,° *detailed evidence*
Being so near the truth as I will make them,
Must first induce you to believe; whose strength
I will confirm with oath, which I doubt not
You'll give me leave to spare° when you shall find *omit*
You need it not.

POSTHUMUS Proceed.

GIACOMO First, her bedchamber—
Where I confess I slept not, but profess
Had that was well worth watching°—it was hanged *staying awake for*
With tapestry of silk and silver; the story
Proud Cleopatra when she met her Roman,[6]
And Cydnus[7] swelled above the banks, or for° *either because of*
The press of boats or pride: a piece of work
So bravely° done, so rich, that it did strive *splendidly*
In workmanship and value,[8] which I wondered
Could be so rarely and exactly wrought,
Since the true life on't was—

POSTHUMUS This is true;
And this you might have heard of here by me,
Or by some other.

GIACOMO More particulars
Must justify° my knowledge. *confirm*

POSTHUMUS So they must,
Or do your honor injury.

GIACOMO The chimney° *fireplace*
Is south the chamber, and the chimneypiece[9]
Chaste Dian[1] bathing. Never saw I figures
So likely to report themselves;[2] the cutter
Was as another Nature, dumb; outwent her,
Motion and breath left out.[3]

POSTHUMUS This is a thing
Which you might from relation° likewise reap, *report*
Being, as it is, much spoke of.

GIACOMO The roof o'th' chamber
With golden cherubim is fretted.° Her andirons— *carved*
I had forgot them—were two winking Cupids[4]

5. *gains . . . mine:* makes one of us the winner, the other the loser, of his sword in a duel.
6. Alluding to a meeting, described also in Shakespeare's play *Antony and Cleopatra,* between the Egyptian Queen Cleopatra and Mark Antony, one of the Roman triumvirs, who was her lover.
7. A river in Cilicia (now Turkey).
8. *that . . . value:* that craftmanship and monetary worth both competed for preeminence.
9. Ornament above the fireplace.
1. Another reference to the goddess associated in classical mythology with hunting, childbirth, and chastity.
2. So lifelike that they could give an account of themselves.
3. *the cutter . . . out:* the sculptor ("cutter") was like a second nature in creative power. Speechless, the sculpture surpassed nature, apart from its lack of movement and breathing.
4. Two statues of Cupid, the god of love, with eyes shut. Cupid was often depicted as a beautiful boy with wings and a torch and wearing a blindfold to signify the blindness of love.

Of silver, each on one foot standing, nicely° *ingeniously*
Depending° on their brands.° *Leaning / torches*

POSTHUMUS This is her honor!
Let it be granted you have seen all this—and praise
Be given to your remembrance—the description
Of what is in her chamber nothing saves
The wager you have laid.

GIACOMO Then, if you can
Be pale,° I beg but leave to air this jewel: see! *Be unmoved*
[*He shows the bracelet.*]
And now 'tis up° again; it must be married *put away*
To that your diamond. I'll keep them.

POSTHUMUS Jove!° *king of the gods*
Once more let me behold it. Is it that
Which I left with her?

GIACOMO Sir, I thank her, that.
She stripped it from her arm—I see her yet—
Her pretty action did out-sell° her gift, *exceed in value*
And yet enriched it too. She gave it me,
And said she prized it once.

POSTHUMUS Maybe she plucked it off
To send it me.

GIACOMO She writes so to you, doth she?

POSTHUMUS Oh, no, no, no, 'tis true! Here, take this too.
[*He gives* GIACOMO *his ring.*]
It is a basilisk[5] unto mine eye,
Kills me to look on't. Let there be no honor
Where there is beauty, truth where semblance,° love *it's merely appearance*
Where there's another man. The vows° of women *Let the vows*
Of no more bondage be to where they are made
Than they are° to their virtues, which is nothing. *Than women are bound*
Oh, above measure false!

PHILARIO Have patience, sir,
And take your ring again; 'tis not yet won.
It may be probable she lost it, or
Who knows if one° her women, being corrupted, *one of*
Hath stol'n it from her?

POSTHUMUS Very true,
And so I hope he came by't. Back, my ring!
[*He takes his ring back.*]
Render to me some corporal° sign about her *bodily*
More evident° than this, for this was stol'n. *conclusive*

GIACOMO By Jupiter,[6] I had it from her arm.

POSTHUMUS Hark you, he swears; by Jupiter he swears.
'Tis true, nay, keep the ring, 'tis true. I am sure
She would not lose it. Her attendants are
All sworn° and honorable. They induced to steal it? *bound by oaths*
And by a stranger? No, he hath enjoyed her.
The cognizance° of her incontinency *token*
Is this: she hath bought the name of whore thus dearly.
[*He gives* GIACOMO *his ring again.*]

5. A mythical reptile able to kill with a glance those it gazed upon.

6. Another reference to the king of the gods. Only the most solemn vows would be made in his name.

There, take thy hire,° and all the fiends of hell *fee*
Divide themselves between you.

PHILARIO Sir, be patient.
This is not strong enough to be believed
Of one persuaded° well of. *thought*

POSTHUMUS Never talk on't;
She hath been colted° by him. *sexually enjoyed*

GIACOMO If you seek
For further satisfying, under her breast—
Worthy the pressing—lies a mole, right proud
Of that most delicate lodging. By my life
I kissed it, and it gave me present° hunger *immediate*
To feed again, though full. You do remember
This stain° upon her? *mark*

POSTHUMUS Ay, and it doth confirm
Another stain, as big as hell can hold,
Were there no more but it.

GIACOMO Will you hear more?

POSTHUMUS Spare your arithmetic, never count the turns.° *sexual acts*
Once, and a million![7]

GIACOMO I'll be sworn.

POSTHUMUS No swearing.
If you will swear you have not done't, you lie,
And I will kill thee if thou dost deny
Thou'st made me cuckold.

GIACOMO I'll deny nothing.

POSTHUMUS Oh, that I had her here, to tear her limb-meal!° *limb from limb*
I will go there and do't i'th' court, before
Her father. I'll do something— *Exit.*

PHILARIO Quite besides° *beyond*
The government° of patience! You have won. *control*
Let's follow him and pervert° the present wrath *turn aside*
He hath against himself.

GIACOMO With all my heart. *Exeunt.*

## 2.5

*Enter* POSTHUMUS.[1]

POSTHUMUS Is there no way for men to be,° but women *to exist*
Must be half-workers?° We are all bastards, *be partners*
And that most venerable man which I
Did call my father was I know not where
When I was stamped.[2] Some coiner with his tools[3]
Made me a counterfeit; yet my mother seemed
The Dian of that time; so doth my wife
The nonpareil° of this. Oh, vengeance, vengeance! *one who has no equal*
Me of my lawful pleasure[4] she restrained,
And prayed me oft forbearance;[5] did it with
A pudency° so rosy the sweet view on't° *modesty / of it*

7. That is, there is no difference between having been unfaithful once and having done it a million times.

2.5 Location: Scene continues.

1. In F, Posthumus's soliloquy is part of 2.4. He is making a reentry, however, after his departure at line 149, and most modern editions mark the soliloquy as a separate scene.

2. Conceived, as coins are stamped with images when they are made.

3. With pun on "tool" as meaning "penis."

4. The sexual pleasure to which marriage entitled him.

5. And often begged me to defer sexual pleasures.

Might well have warmed old Saturn[6]—that I thought her
As chaste as unsunned snow. Oh, all the devils!
This yellow° Giacomo in an hour—was't not?— *sallow*
Or less—at first?° Perchance he spoke not, but *instantly*
Like a full-acorned boar,[7] a German one,
Cried "Oh!" and mounted; found no opposition
But what he looked for should oppose[8] and she
Should from encounter guard. Could I find out
The woman's part in me—for there's no motion° *impulse*
That tends to vice in man but I affirm
It is the woman's part; be it lying, note it,
The woman's; flattering, hers; deceiving, hers;
Lust and rank thoughts, hers, hers; revenges, hers;
Ambitions, covetings, change of prides,° disdain, *varying extravagances*
Nice° longing, slanders, mutability, *Lustful*
All faults that may be named, nay, that hell knows, why hers
In part, or all, but rather all. For even to vice
They are not constant, but are changing still
One vice but of a minute old for one
Not half so old as that. I'll write against them,
Detest them, curse them; yet 'tis greater skill° *cleverness*
In a true hate, to pray they have their will:° *desire*
The very devils cannot plague them better. *Exit.*

## 3.1

*Enter in state* CYMBELINE, QUEEN, CLOTEN, *and* LORDS *at one door, and at another,* CAIUS LUCIUS *and Attendants.*

CYMBELINE Now say, what would Augustus Caesar with us?
LUCIUS When Julius Caesar—whose remembrance yet
Lives in men's eyes, and will to ears and tongues
Be theme and hearing ever—was in this Britain
And conquered it, Cassibelan, thine uncle,
Famous in Caesar's praises no whit less
Than in his feats deserving it, for him
And his succession° granted Rome a tribute, *heirs*
Yearly three thousand pounds, which by thee lately
Is left untendered.° *unpaid*
QUEEN And, to kill the marvel,[1]
Shall be so ever.
CLOTEN There be many Caesars
Ere such another Julius. Britain's a world
By itself, and we will nothing pay
For wearing our own noses.[2]
QUEEN That opportunity
Which then they had to take from 's, to resume° *take back*
We have again. Remember, sir, my liege,° *sovereign*

6. The Roman god of agriculture, usually characterized as cold and melancholy.
7. A boar fed full of acorns (with a pun on "boor" as meaning "a German or Dutch peasant").
8. *found . . . oppose:* found no opposition except the body parts he expected to encounter.
**3.1** Location: Cymbeline's court, Britain.
1. And, to put a stop to the amazement (which our nonpayment has caused).
2. Perhaps referring to contemporary theories of physiognomy that identified specific physical features, such as noses, with racial types. Roman noses were notoriously prominent.

The kings your ancestors, together with
The natural bravery° of your isle, which stands — *splendor*
As Neptune's park,[3] ribbed and paled in° — *enclosed and fenced in*
With oaks unscalable and roaring waters,
With sands that will not bear your enemies' boats
But suck them up to th' top-mast. A kind of conquest
Caesar made here, but made not here his brag
Of "came and saw and overcame."[4] With shame—
The first that ever touched him—he was carried
From off our coast, twice beaten; and his shipping,° — *ships*
Poor ignorant baubles,° on our terrible seas — *worthless toys*
Like eggshells moved upon their surges, cracked
As easily 'gainst our rocks. For joy whereof,
The famed Cassibelan, who was once at point°— — *ready*
O giglot° Fortune!—to master Caesar's sword, — *fickle; whorish*
Made Lud's Town[5] with rejoicing fires bright
And Britons strut with courage.

CLOTEN Come, there's no more tribute to be paid. Our kingdom is stronger than it was at that time, and, as I said, there is no more such Caesars. Other of them may have crooked noses, but to owe° such straight° arms, none. — *possess / powerful*

CYMBELINE Son, let your mother end.

CLOTEN We have yet many among us can gripe° as hard as Cassibelan. I do not say I am one, but I have a hand. Why tribute? Why should we pay tribute? If Caesar can hide the sun from us with a blanket, or put the moon in his pocket, we will pay him tribute for light; else, sir, no more tribute, pray you now. — *grasp (a sword)*

CYMBELINE You must know,
Till the injurious° Romans did extort — *insulting*
This tribute from us, we were free. Caesar's ambition,
Which swelled so much that it did almost stretch
The sides o'th' world, against all color[6] here
Did put the yoke upon 's, which to shake off
Becomes a warlike people, whom we reckon
Ourselves to be. We do say then to Caesar,
Our ancestor was that Mulmutius[7] which
Ordained our laws, whose use the sword of Caesar
Hath too much mangled, whose repair and franchise° — *free exercise*
Shall by the power we hold be our good deed,
Though Rome be therefore angry. Mulmutius made our laws,
Who was the first of Britain which did put
His brows within a golden crown and called
Himself a king.

LUCIUS I am sorry, Cymbeline,
That I am to pronounce Augustus Caesar—
Caesar, that hath more kings his servants than

3. As grounds owned by Neptune, Roman god of the sea.
4. When Julius Caesar, leading an army into Asia, defeated King Pharnaces and his allies, Plutarch reports that Caesar wrote three words to his friend Anitius in Rome: *veni, vidi, vici* ("I came, I saw, I overcame"). See Plutarch's *Life of Julius Caesar* in his *Lives of the Noble Grecians and Romanes* as translated by Thomas North (1579).
5. London. Contemporary texts such as Holinshed's *Chronicles* erroneously asserted that "London" was derived from "Lud," the name of the mythological British king who was Cymbeline's grandfather.
6. Without any pretense of justice.
7. According to Holinshed, the first king of Britain.

Thyself domestic officers—thine enemy.
Receive it from me then: war and confusion° *destruction*
In Caesar's name pronounce I 'gainst thee. Look
For fury not to be resisted. Thus defied,
I thank thee for myself.

CYMBELINE Thou art welcome, Caius.
Thy Caesar knighted me; my youth I spent
Much under him; of him I gathered honor,
Which he to seek of me again, perforce,
Behoves me keep at utterance.[8] I am perfect° *fully aware*
That the Pannonians and Dalmatians[9] for
Their liberties are now in arms, a precedent
Which not to read would show the Britons cold;° *lacking in spirit*
So Caesar shall not find them.

LUCIUS Let proof° speak. *the result*

CLOTEN His majesty bids you welcome. Make pastime with us a day or two or longer. If you seek us afterwards in other terms, you shall find us in our saltwater girdle.[1] If you beat us out of it, it is yours; if you fall in the adventure, our crows shall fare the better for you, and there's an end.

LUCIUS So, sir.

CYMBELINE I know your master's pleasure, and he mine.
All the remain° is "Welcome." *Exeunt.* *All that is left to say*

## 3.2

*Enter* PISANIO, *reading a letter.*

PISANIO How? Of adultery? Wherefore write you not
What monster's her accuser? Leonatus,
O master, what a strange infection
Is fall'n into thy ear? What false Italian,
As poisonous-tongued as handed,[1] hath prevailed
On thy too ready hearing? Disloyal? No.
She's punished for her truth,° and undergoes, *faithfulness*
More goddess-like than wife-like, such assaults
As would take in° some virtue. O my master, *overcome*
Thy mind to° hers is now as low as were *compared to*
Thy fortunes. How? That I should murder her,
Upon the love and truth and vows which I
Have made to thy command? I her? Her blood?
If it be so to do good service, never
Let me be counted serviceable. How look I,
That I should seem to lack humanity
So much as this fact° comes to? [*He reads.*] "Do't. The letter *action*
That I have sent her, by her own command
Shall give thee opportunity." O damned paper,[2]
Black as the ink that's on thee! Senseless bauble,
Art thou a fedary° for this act and look'st *an accomplice*
So virgin-like without?° Lo, here she comes. *on the outside*

8. *Which . . . utterance:* His seeking that honor of me again makes it necessary for me to defend ("keep") it to the death.
9. Inhabitants of Hungary and Dalmatia, a region on the Adriatic Sea.
1. In the sea that encircles us (as a girdle does the body).

3.2 Location: Scene continues.
1. Having as many poisons (lies) in his tongue as in his hands. Contemporary texts depicted Italians as infinitely skilled in making and administering poisons.
2. O hellish object (referring to the letter).

*Enter* IMOGEN.

I am ignorant in° what I am commanded. *will pretend ignorance of*

IMOGEN How now, Pisanio?

PISANIO Madam, here is a letter from my lord.

IMOGEN Who, thy lord that is my lord, Leonatus?
Oh, learned indeed were that astronomer° *astrologer*
That knew the stars as I his characters;° *handwriting*
He'd lay the future open. You good gods,
Let what is here contained relish° of love, *taste*
Of my lord's health, of his content—yet not
That we two are asunder; let that grieve him.
Some griefs are med'cinable;° that is one of them, *beneficial*
For it doth physic love[3]—of his content
All but in that. Good wax,° thy leave. Blest be *sealing wax*
You bees that make these locks of counsel.° Lovers *for private matters*
And men in dangerous bonds[4] pray not alike;
Though forfeiters you cast in prison,[5] yet
You clasp° young Cupid's tables.° Good news, gods! *lovingly embrace / tablets*
[*She reads.*] "Justice and your father's wrath, should he take me in his dominion, could not be so cruel to me as° you, O the dearest of creatures, would even renew me° with your eyes. Take notice that I am in Cambria,° at Milford Haven.[6] What your own love will out of this advise you, follow. So he wishes you all happiness, that remains loyal to his vow, and your increasing in love, *but that* / *revive me* / *Wales*

Leonatus Posthumus."

Oh, for a horse with wings! Hear'st thou, Pisanio?
He is at Milford Haven. Read, and tell me
How far 'tis thither. If one of mean affairs° *with unimportant business*
May plod it in a week, why may not I
Glide thither in a day? Then, true Pisanio,
Who long'st like me to see thy lord, who long'st—
Oh, let me bate°—but not like me, yet long'st *moderate my speech*
But in a fainter kind; oh, not like me:
For mine's beyond beyond. Say, and speak thick°— *quickly*
Love's counselor should fill the bores of hearing° *the ears*
To th' smothering of the sense[7]—how far it is
To this same blessed Milford. And by° th' way *on*
Tell me how Wales was made so happy as
T'inherit such a haven. But first of all,
How we may steal from hence; and for the gap
That we shall make in time from our hence-going
And our return, to excuse; but first, how get hence.
Why should excuse be born or ere begot?[8]
We'll talk of that hereafter. Prithee, speak,

3. For it nurtures love; for it keeps love in good health.
4. Men bound by agreements imposing penalties (which are sealed with wax). Imogen is contrasting the fear with which men in legal trouble greet sealed documents to the joy with which lovers receive a sealed love letter.
5. Although you cast those who default on agreements in prison (because sealed bonds lead to indictments).
6. A port in southern Wales that became important in later British history when Henry Tudor landed there in 1485. Defeating the army of Richard III, he was crowned Henry VII, bringing to an end the civil strife known as the Wars of the Roses.
7. Until the sense of hearing is overwhelmed.
8. Why should an excuse be born even before it is conceived—that is, be manufactured before it is needed?

How many score of° miles may we well ride *sets of twenty*
Twixt hour and hour?° *In an hour*
PISANIO One score twixt sun and sun,
Madam, 's enough for you, and too much, too.
IMOGEN Why, one that rode to 's execution, man,
Could never go so slow. I have heard of riding wagers
Where horses have been nimbler than the sands
That run i'th' clock's behalf.[9] But this is fool'ry.
Go, bid my woman feign a sickness, say
She'll home to her father; and provide me presently° *at once*
A riding suit no costlier than would fit° *suit*
A franklin's housewife.[1]
PISANIO Madam, you're best° consider— *you'd better*
IMOGEN I see before° me, man; not here, nor here, *straight ahead of*
Nor what ensues,[2] but have a fog in them
That I cannot look through. Away, I prithee,
Do as I bid thee. There's no more to say:
Accessible is none but Milford way. *Exeunt.*

## 3.3

[*A cave is discovered.*[1] *From it*] *enter* BELARIUS, GUIDERIUS, *and* ARVIRAGUS.

BELARIUS A goodly day not to keep house° with such *stay home*
Whose roof's as low as ours. Stoop, boys: this gate
Instructs you how t'adore the heavens, and bows you° *makes you bow down*
To a morning's holy office.° The gates of monarchs *a morning prayer*
Are arched so high that giants may jet° through *swagger*
And keep their impious turbans[2] on, without
Good morrow to the sun. Hail thou, fair heaven!
We house i'th' rock, yet use thee not so hardly° *badly*
As prouder livers° do. *those living more grandly*
GUIDERIUS Hail, heaven!
ARVIRAGUS Hail, heaven!
BELARIUS Now for our mountain sport: up to yond hill.
Your legs are young; I'll tread these flats.° Consider, *this plain*
When you above perceive me like a crow,
That it is place° which lessens and sets off,° *position / enhances*
And you may then revolve° what tales I have told you, *consider*
Of courts, of princes, of the tricks in war;
This service is not service, so being done,
But being so allowed.[3] To apprehend thus
Draws us a profit from all things we see,

9. *than . . . behalf:* than the sands that run through the hourglass.
1. The wife of a landowning farmer whose social status was lower than that of the gentry. Early modern English sumptuary codes prescribed specific fabrics and styles of dress for people of different ranks.
2. *not here . . . ensues:* Neither (what is) on this side, nor on that, nor what will happen (after Milford Haven is reached).
3.3 Location: The cave of Belarius, Wales.
1. In his account of a performance of the play in 1611, Simon Forman wrote of "the Cave in the woods" and of the "woods" where Imogen's supposedly dead body was laid. It is possible that some form of stage foliage surrounded the entrance to Belarius's cave.
2. The idea of giants wearing turbans may come from romances in which giants were often equated with Saracens, or followers of Islam, who wore turbans and were seen as impious enemies of Christians. See, for example, the Giant Disdain in Edmund Spenser's *Faerie Queene,* who "on his head a roll of linnen plight, / Like to the Mores of Malabar" (6.7.43.5–6).
3. *This service . . . allowed:* That acts of service are not acts of service simply by being done, but rather by being acknowledged as such (by superiors).

And often to our comfort shall we find
The sharded beetle[4] in a safer hold° *refuge*
Than is the full-winged eagle. Oh, this life
Is nobler than attending for a check,[5]
Richer than doing nothing for a bribe,
Prouder than rustling in unpaid-for silk;
Such gain the cap of him that makes him fine,
Yet keeps his book uncrossed.[6] No life to ours.

GUIDERIUS Out of your proof° you speak. We, poor unfledged,[7] *experience*
Have never winged from view o'th' nest, nor know not
What air's from° home. Haply° this life is best, *away from / Perhaps*
If quiet life be best; sweeter to you
That have a sharper known, well corresponding
With your stiff age; but unto us it is
A cell of ignorance, traveling abed,° *only while dreaming*
A prison, or a debtor that not dares
To stride a limit.[8]

ARVIRAGUS What should we speak of
When we are old as you? When we shall hear
The rain and wind beat dark December, how,
In this our pinching cave,[9] shall we discourse
The freezing hours away? We have seen nothing.
We are beastly:° subtle as the fox for prey, *like beasts*
Like° warlike as the wolf for what we eat. *As*
Our valor is to chase what flies; our cage
We make a choir, as doth the prisoned bird,
And sing our bondage freely.

BELARIUS How you speak!
Did you but know the city's usuries,[1]
And felt them knowingly; the art o'th' court,
As hard to leave as keep,° whose top to climb *dwell in*
Is certain falling, or so slipp'ry that
The fear's as bad as falling; the toil o'th' war,
A pain° that only seems to seek out danger *labor*
I'th' name of fame and honor, which dies i'th' search
And hath as oft a slanderous epitaph
As record of fair act—nay, many times
Doth ill deserve° by doing well; what's worse *earn ill treatment*
Must curtsy at the censure.[2] O boys, this story
The world may read in me: my body's marked
With Roman swords, and my report° was once *reputation*
First with the best of note.° Cymbeline loved me, *the most renowned*
And, when a soldier was the theme, my name
Was not far off. Then was I as a tree
Whose boughs did bend with fruit; but in one night
A storm or robbery—call it what you will—

4. The beetle who lives in dung. "Shard" means "patch of dung."
5. Than acting as a servant only to be rebuked.
6. *Such . . . uncrossed:* Such men win the deference (shown by removing "the cap") of the tailor who is the source of their grandeur, yet continue to have their debts standing ("uncrossed") in the tailor's account book.
7. Lacking the feathers necessary for flight (spoken of a young bird).
8. *that . . . limit:* who does not dare to leave a place of sanctuary (for fear of being arrested).
9. Our confining cave; our cave that pinches us with cold.
1. Financial practices whereby money was lent at excessive or illegal rates of interest.
2. Must defer to the person who finds fault.

Shook down my mellow hangings,° nay, my leaves, *ripe fruit*
And left me bare to weather.

GUIDERIUS Uncertain favor!

BELARIUS My fault being nothing, as I have told you oft,
But that two villains, whose false oaths prevailed
Before my perfect honor, swore to Cymbeline
I was confederate with the Romans. So
Followed my banishment, and this twenty years
This rock and these demesnes° have been my world, *regions*
Where I have lived at honest freedom, paid
More pious debts to heaven than in all
The fore-end° of my time. But up to th' mountains! *early days*
This is not hunters' language. He that strikes
The venison first shall be the lord o'th' feast,
To him the other two shall minister,
And we will fear no poison which attends° *is always present*
In place of greater state. I'll meet you in the valleys.

*Exeunt* [GUIDERIUS *and* ARVIRAGUS].

How hard it is to hide the sparks of nature!
These boys know little they are sons to th' King,
Nor Cymbeline dreams that they are alive.
They think they are mine, and, though trained up thus meanly° *in a humble style*
I'th' cave wherein they bow, their thoughts do hit
The roofs of palaces, and nature prompts them
In simple and low things to prince it° much *to act like princes*
Beyond the trick° of others. This Polydore, *custom*
The heir of Cymbeline and Britain, who
The King his father called Guiderius—Jove,
When on my three-foot stool I sit and tell
The warlike feats I have done, his spirits fly out
Into my story: say "Thus mine enemy fell,
And thus I set my foot on 's neck," even then
The princely blood flows in his cheek, he sweats,
Strains his young nerves,° and puts himself in posture *sinews*
That acts my words. The younger brother, Cadwal,
Once Arviragus, in as like a figure° *acting the part as well*
Strikes life into my speech, and shows much more
His own conceiving.° *imagination*

[*A hunting horn sounds.*]

Hark, the game is roused!
O Cymbeline, heaven and my conscience knows[3]
Thou didst unjustly banish me, whereon
At three and two years old I stole these babes,
Thinking to bar thee of succession, as
Thou reft'st° me of my lands. Euriphile, *deprived*
Thou wast their nurse; they took thee for their mother,
And every day do honor to her grave.
Myself, Belarius, that am Morgan called,
They take for natural father.

[*The horn sounds again.*]

The game is up.° *Exit.* *roused*

3. Editors have conjectured that lines 99–107 are either a non-Shakespearean addition or a section he added in revision. They stand apart from the rest of the speech, providing a hurried summary of information. Moreover, "the game is roused" (line 98) is repeated in "The game is up" (line 107).

## 3.4

*Enter* PISANIO *and* IMOGEN [*in a riding suit*].

IMOGEN Thou told'st me when we came from horse° the place — *we dismounted*
Was near at hand. Ne'er longed my mother so
To see me first as I have° now. Pisanio, man, — *do*
Where is Posthumus? What is in thy mind
That makes thee stare thus? Wherefore breaks that sigh
From th'inward of thee? One but painted thus
Would be interpreted a thing perplexed° — *bewildered*
Beyond self-explication. Put thyself
Into a havior of less fear,[1] ere wildness° — *madness*
Vanquish my staider senses. What's the matter?
[PISANIO *offers her a letter.*]
Why tender'st thou that paper to me with
A look untender? If't be summer news
Smile to't before; if winterly, thou need'st
But keep that count'nance still. My husband's hand?
That drug-damned Italy[2] hath out-craftied° him, — *outwitted*
And he's at some hard point.° Speak, man! Thy tongue — *in some crisis*
May take off some extremity° which to read — *reduce the horror*
Would be even mortal° to me. — *fatal*

PISANIO Please you read,
And you shall find me, wretched man, a thing
The most disdained of fortune.

IMOGEN (*reads*)
"Thy mistress, Pisanio, hath played the strumpet in my bed, the testimonies whereof lies bleeding in me. I speak not out of weak surmises but from proof as strong as my grief and as certain as I expect my revenge. That part thou, Pisanio, must act for me, if thy faith be not tainted with the breach of hers. Let thine own hands take away her life. I shall give thee opportunity at Milford Haven. She hath my letter for the purpose, where, if thou fear to strike and to make me certain it is done, thou art the pander° to her dishonor and equally to me disloyal." — *go-between; procurer*

PISANIO [*aside*] What shall I need to draw my sword? The paper
Hath cut her throat already. No, 'tis slander,
Whose edge is sharper than the sword, whose tongue
Out-venoms all the worms of Nile,[3] whose breath
Rides on the posting° winds and doth belie° — *speeding / deceive*
All corners of the world. Kings, queens, and states,
Maids, matrons, nay, the secrets of the grave
This viperous slander enters. —What cheer, madam?

IMOGEN False to his bed? What is it to be false?
To lie in watch° there and to think on him? — *wakefulness*
To weep twixt clock and clock?° If sleep charge° nature, — *continually / overcome*
To break it with a fearful dream of° him — *a dream fearful for*
And cry myself awake? That's false to 's bed, is it?

3.4 Location: Wales, near Milford Haven.
1. *Put . . . fear:* Adopt a less fearsome manner.
2. That country notorious for its poisons.
3. Alluding to the poisonous serpents associated with Egypt's Nile River. Slander was often personified as a woman with snakes issuing from her mouth. In early modern England, women frequently brought cases in the ecclesiastical courts against those who defamed or slandered them, usually by calling them unchaste. Pisanio rightly assumes that Imogen is the victim of just such slanderous accusations.

PISANIO Alas, good lady.
IMOGEN I false? Thy conscience witness, Giacomo,
Thou didst accuse him of incontinency.
Thou then look'dst like a villain; now, methinks
Thy favor's° good enough. Some jay° of Italy, *appearance is / strumpet*
Whose mother was her painting,[4] hath betrayed him.
Poor I am stale,° a garment out of fashion, *out of date; not new*
And for I am richer than to hang by th' walls,
I must be ripped:[5] to pieces with me. Oh,
Men's vows are women's traitors! All good seeming,° *appearance*
By thy revolt, O husband, shall be thought
Put on for° villainy; not born where't grows, *Worn to disguise*
But worn a bait for ladies.
PISANIO Good madam, hear me.
IMOGEN True honest men being heard like false Aeneas[6]
Were in his time thought false, and Sinon's[7] weeping
Did scandal° many a holy tear, took pity *discredit*
From most true wretchedness. So thou, Posthumus,
Wilt lay the leaven on all proper men:[8]
Goodly° and gallant shall be false and perjured *Admirable*
From thy great fail.° —Come, fellow, be thou honest; *failure*
Do thou thy master's bidding. When thou seest him,
A little witness° my obedience. Look: *Briefly attest to*
I draw the sword myself; take it, and hit
The innocent mansion of my love, my heart.
Fear not, 'tis empty of all things but grief.
Thy master is not there, who was indeed
The riches of it. Do his bidding: strike.
Thou mayst be valiant in a better cause;
But now thou seem'st a coward.
PISANIO Hence, vile instrument,
Thou shalt not damn my hand.
[*He puts the sword aside.*]
IMOGEN Why, I must die,
And if I do not by thy hand, thou art
No servant of thy master's. Against self-slaughter
There is a prohibition so divine
That cravens° my weak hand. Come, here's my heart. *makes cowardly*
Something's afore't. Soft,° soft, we'll no defense; *Gently*
Obedient as the scabbard. What is here?
[*She takes letters from her bosom.*]
The scriptures° of the loyal Leonatus, *writing; sacred texts*
All turned to heresy? Away, away,
Corrupters of my faith, you shall no more
Be stomachers[9] to my heart. Thus may poor fools
Believe false teachers; though those that are betrayed

4. Whose mother was entirely the product of her cosmetics—that is, who was false.
5. *And . . . ripped:* And because I am too valuable to be discarded (by being hung up and forgotten about), I must be torn apart (so that the material may be reused).
6. Being heard as though they were as false as the hero of Virgil's *Aeneid,* Aeneas, who deserted his love, Dido, the queen of Carthage.
7. Another deceitful character from the *Aeneid.* Sinon betrayed Troy to the Greeks by inducing the Trojans to let into the city a wooden horse in which Greek warriors were concealed.
8. Will corrupt the reputations of all faithful men (as a portion of inferior dough spoils the rest).
9. Ornamented chest coverings worn by women under their bodices.

Do feel the treason sharply, yet the traitor
Stands in worse case of woe.
And thou, Posthumus, that didst set up° *instigate*
My disobedience 'gainst the King my father,
And make me put into contempt the suits
Of princely fellows,° shalt hereafter find *those equal to my rank*
It is no act of common passage, but
A strain of rareness;[1] and I grieve myself
To think, when thou shalt be disedged° by her, *surfeited*
That now thou tirest on,[2] how thy memory
Will then be panged by° me. —Prithee, dispatch; *pierced by thoughts of*
The lamb entreats the butcher. Where's thy knife?
Thou art too slow to do thy master's bidding
When I desire it too.

PISANIO O gracious lady,
Since I received command to do this business
I have not slept one wink.

IMOGEN Do't, and to bed, then.

PISANIO I'll wake mine eyeballs out first.[3]

IMOGEN Wherefore, then,
Didst undertake it? Why hast thou abused
So many miles with a pretense? This place?
Mine action, and thine own? Our horses' labor,
The time inviting thee? The perturbed court
For my being absent, whereunto I never
Purpose° return? Why hast thou gone so far *Intend*
To be unbent[4] when thou hast ta'en thy stand,° *shooting position*
Th'elected° deer before thee? *The chosen*

PISANIO But to win time
To lose so bad employment, in the which
I have considered of a course. Good lady,
Hear me with patience.

IMOGEN Talk thy tongue weary, speak.
I have heard I am a strumpet, and mine ear,
Therein false struck, can take no greater wound,
Nor tent to bottom that.[5] But speak.

PISANIO Then, madam,
I thought you would not back° again. *go back (to court)*

IMOGEN Most like,
Bringing me here to kill me.

PISANIO Not so, neither.
But if I were as wise as honest, then
My purpose would prove well. It cannot be
But that my master is abused.° Some villain, *deceived*
Ay, and singular° in his art, hath done you both *unmatched*
This cursèd injury.

IMOGEN Some Roman courtesan.

PISANIO No, on my life.
I'll give but notice you are dead, and send him
Some bloody sign of it, for 'tis commanded

1. *It . . . rareness:* My choice was no commonplace action but the sign of exceptional qualities.
2. Whom now you feed on (in the manner of a bird of prey).
3. I'll stay awake until my eyes drop out before I'll do it.
4. To be with bow unready.
5. Nor probe ("tent") the depths of that wound.

I should do so. You shall be missed at court,
And that will well confirm it.

IMOGEN Why, good fellow,
What shall I do the while? Where bide? How live?
Or in my life what comfort, when I am
Dead to my husband?

PISANIO If you'll back° to th' court— *return*

IMOGEN No court, no father, nor no more ado
With that harsh, noble, simple nothing,
That Cloten, whose love-suit hath been to me
As fearful as a siege.

PISANIO If not at court,
Then not in Britain must you bide.

IMOGEN Where then?
Hath Britain all the sun that shines? Day, night,
Are they not but° in Britain? I'th' world's volume *Do they exist only*
Our Britain seems as of it, but not in't:[6]
In a great pool a swan's nest. Prithee, think
There's livers out of Britain.[7]

PISANIO I am most glad
You think of other place. Th'ambassador,
Lucius the Roman, comes to Milford Haven
Tomorrow. Now, if you could wear a mind
Dark° as your fortune is, and but disguise *Secret; dismal*
That which t'appear itself must not yet be
But by self-danger,[8] you should tread a course
Pretty and full of view;[9] yea, haply° near *perhaps*
The residence of Posthumus; so nigh, at least,
That though his actions were not visible, yet
Report should render° him hourly to your ear *describe*
As truly as he moves.

IMOGEN Oh, for such means,° *a method of access*
Though peril to my modesty, not death on't,° *of it*
I would adventure.° *take the risk*

PISANIO Well, then, here's the point:
You must forget to be a woman; change
Command[1] into obedience; fear and niceness°— *daintiness*
The handmaids of all women, or more truly
Woman it pretty self[2]—into a waggish° courage, *mischievous*
Ready in gibes, quick-answered, saucy, and
As quarrelous° as the weasel. Nay, you must *quarrelsome*
Forget that rarest treasure of your cheek,
Exposing it[3]—but oh, the harder heart![4]
Alack, no remedy—to the greedy touch
Of common-kissing Titan,[5] and forget

6. Seems part of the world, yet distinct. The metaphor is of the world as a book in which Britain is a page, but one not bound into the volume.
7. *Prithee . . . Britain:* I pray you, believe that there are people living outside Britain.
8. *and but . . . self-danger:* and simply disguise your appearance, which if it were now to show itself for what it is would put you in danger.
9. Advantageous and with good prospects.
1. The commanding ways of a princess.
2. *or . . . self:* or, more accurately, womanhood itself.
3. In early modern England, English women of the upper classes shielded themselves from the sun and cultivated pale complexions, the "treasure" of their cheeks.
4. The "harder heart" probably refers to Imogen, who must harden her heart even as she tans her skin. It may refer to Posthumus's cruelty to Imogen or to Pisanio's cruelty in forcing these harsh facts upon Imogen.
5. The sun god who shines on ("kisses") everyone alike.

Your laborsome and dainty trims° wherein — *apparel*
You made great Juno° angry. — *queen of the gods*

IMOGEN Nay, be brief.
I see into thy end,° and am almost — *purpose*
A man already.

PISANIO First, make yourself but like one.
Forethinking° this, I have already fit°— — *Anticipating / at hand*
'Tis in my cloak-bag—doublet, hat, hose, all
That answer to° them. Would you in their serving,[6] — *go with*
And with what imitation you can borrow
From youth of such a season,° fore° noble Lucius — *an age / before*
Present yourself, desire his service,° tell him — *to serve him*
Wherein you're happy[7]—which will make him know° — *convince him*
If that his head have ear in music—doubtless
With joy he will embrace you, for he's honorable
And, doubling that, most holy. Your means° abroad: — *As for your means of support*
You have me, rich, and I will never fail
Beginning nor supplyment.[8]

IMOGEN Thou art all the comfort
The gods will diet° me with. Prithee, away. — *feed*
There's more to be considered, but we'll even° — *keep pace with*
All that good time will give us. This attempt
I am soldier to,° and will abide it with — *committed to*
A prince's courage. Away, I prithee.

PISANIO Well, madam, we must take a short farewell,
Lest, being missed, I be suspected of
Your carriage° from the court. My noble mistress, — *removal*
Here is a box—I had it from the Queen—
What's in't is precious. If you are sick at sea,
Or stomach-qualmed° at land, a dram° of this — *nauseous / tiny portion*
Will drive away distemper. To some shade,
And fit you to your manhood.[9] May the gods
Direct you to the best.

IMOGEN Amen. I thank thee. *Exeunt.*

## 3.5

*Enter* CYMBELINE, QUEEN, CLOTEN, LUCIUS, LORDS[, *and a* MESSENGER].

CYMBELINE Thus far, and so farewell.

LUCIUS Thanks, royal sir.
My Emperor hath wrote I must from hence;
And am right sorry that I must report ye
My master's enemy.

CYMBELINE Our subjects, sir,
Will not endure his yoke, and for ourself
To show less sovereignty than they must needs
Appear unkinglike.

LUCIUS So, sir, I desire of you
A conduct° over land to Milford Haven. — *An escort*
Madam, all joy befall your grace, [*to* CLOTEN] and you.

6. If you would with their help.
7. In which things you are skilled.
8. In providing the initial amount nor in supplementing it.
9. Dress yourself in accordance with your (pretended) manhood.
3.5 Location: Cymbeline's court, Britain.

CYMBELINE My lords, you are appointed for that office:° *duty*
The due of honor in no point omit.
So farewell, noble Lucius.
LUCIUS Your hand, my lord.
CLOTEN Receive it friendly, but from this time forth
I wear it as your enemy.
LUCIUS Sir, the event° *outcome*
Is yet to name the winner. Fare you well.
CYMBELINE Leave not the worthy Lucius, good my lords,
Till he have crossed the Severn.[1] Happiness.
*Exeunt* LUCIUS [*and* LORDS].
QUEEN He goes hence frowning, but it honors us
That we have given him cause.
CLOTEN 'Tis all the better.
Your valiant Britons have their wishes in it.
CYMBELINE Lucius hath wrote already to the Emperor
How it goes here. It fits° us therefore ripely° *befits / quickly*
Our chariots and our horsemen be in readiness.
The powers° that he already hath in Gallia *military forces*
Will soon be drawn to head,[2] from whence he moves
His war for Britain.
QUEEN 'Tis not sleepy business,
But must be looked to speedily and strongly.
CYMBELINE Our expectation that it would be thus
Hath made us forward.° But, my gentle Queen, *well prepared*
Where is our daughter? She hath not appeared
Before the Roman, nor to us hath tendered
The duty of the day. She looks us° like *seems to us*
A thing more made of malice than of duty;
We have noted it. Call her before us, for
We have been too slight in sufferance.° [*Exit a* MESSENGER.] *mild in our tolerance*
QUEEN Royal sir,
Since the exile of Posthumus, most retired° *withdrawn*
Hath her life been; the cure whereof, my lord,
'Tis time must do. Beseech your majesty,
Forbear sharp speeches to her. She's a lady
So tender of° rebukes that words are strokes, *sensitive to*
And strokes death to her.
*Enter a* MESSENGER.
CYMBELINE Where is she, sir? How
Can her contempt be answered?
MESSENGER Please you, sir,
Her chambers are all locked, and there's no answer
That will be given to th' loud'st of noise we make.
QUEEN My lord, when last I went to visit her,
She prayed me to excuse her keeping close,° *staying confined*
Whereto, constrained by her infirmity,
She should that duty leave unpaid to you
Which daily she was bound to proffer. This
She wished me to make known, but our great court° *court business*
Made me too blame° in memory. *too faulty*
CYMBELINE Her doors locked?

1. River flowing between southern Wales and England.
2. Be gathered to their full strength.

Not seen of late? Grant heavens that which I fear
Prove false! *Exit.*

QUEEN Son, I say, follow the King.

CLOTEN That man of hers, Pisanio, her old servant,
I have not seen these two days.

QUEEN Go, look after. *Exit* [CLOTEN].
Pisanio, thou that stand'st so for° Posthumus! *sides so much with*
He hath a drug of mine; I pray his absence
Proceed by° swallowing that, for he believes *Results from*
It is a thing most precious. But for her,
Where is she gone? Haply° despair hath seized her, *Perhaps*
Or, winged with fervor of her love, she's flown
To her desired Posthumus. Gone she is
To death or to dishonor, and my end
Can make good use of either. She being down,
I have the placing of the British crown.

*Enter* CLOTEN.

How now, my son?

CLOTEN 'Tis certain she is fled.
Go in and cheer the King. He rages; none
Dare come about him.

QUEEN All the better. May
This night forestall him of the coming day.[3] *Exit.*

CLOTEN I love and hate her. For° she's fair and royal, *Because*
And that she hath all courtly parts° more exquisite *features*
Than lady, ladies, woman; from every one
The best she hath, and she, of all compounded,
Outsells° them all. I love her therefore, but *Exceeds in value*
Disdaining me and throwing favors on
The low Posthumus slanders° so her judgment *discredits*
That what's else° rare is choked; and in that point *otherwise*
I will conclude to hate her, nay, indeed,
To be revenged upon her. For, when fools
Shall—

*Enter* PISANIO.

Who is here? What, are you packing,° sirrah?[4] *scheming*
Come hither. Ah, you precious pander! Villain,
Where is thy lady? In a word, or else
Thou art straightway with the fiends.

PISANIO O good my lord!

CLOTEN Where is thy lady? Or, by Jupiter,
I will not ask again. Close° villain, *Secretive*
I'll have this secret from thy heart or rip
Thy heart to find it. Is she with Posthumus,
From whose so many weights° of baseness cannot *measures*
A dram of worth be drawn?

PISANIO Alas, my lord,
How can she be with him? When was she missed?
He is in Rome.

CLOTEN Where is she, sir? Come nearer.° *Be more precise*
No farther halting. Satisfy me home,° *completely*
What is become of her?

3. That is, kill him. *forestall:* deprive.
4. Fellow (a common form of address to a social inferior).

PISANIO O my all-worthy lord!
CLOTEN All-worthy villain,
Discover° where thy mistress is at once, *Reveal*
At the next word. No more of "worthy lord"!
Speak, or thy silence on the instant is
Thy condemnation and thy death.
PISANIO Then, sir,
This paper is the history of my knowledge
Touching her flight.
[*He gives* CLOTEN *a letter.*]
CLOTEN Let's see't. I will pursue her
Even to Augustus' throne.
PISANIO [*aside*] Or° this or perish. *Either*
She's far enough, and what he learns by this
May prove his travel,[5] not her danger.
CLOTEN Humph!
PISANIO [*aside*] I'll write to my lord she's dead. O Imogen,
Safe mayst thou wander, safe return again!
CLOTEN Sirrah, is this letter true?
PISANIO Sir, as I think.

CLOTEN It is Posthumus' hand; I know't. Sirrah, if thou wouldst not be a villain, but do me true service, undergo° those employments wherein I should have cause to use thee with a serious industry—that is, what villainy soe'er I bid thee do, to perform it directly and truly—I would think thee an honest man. Thou shouldst neither want° my means for thy relief, nor my voice° for thy preferment.° *undertake* *lack* *support / advancement*

PISANIO Well, my good lord.

CLOTEN Wilt thou serve me? For since patiently and constantly thou hast stuck to the bare fortune of that beggar Posthumus, thou canst not in the course of gratitude but be a diligent follower of mine. Wilt thou serve me?

PISANIO Sir, I will.

CLOTEN Give me thy hand; here's my purse. Hast any of thy late° master's garments in thy possession? *former*

PISANIO I have, my lord, at my lodging, the same suit he wore when he took leave of my lady and mistress.

CLOTEN The first service thou dost me, fetch that suit hither. Let it be thy first service, go.

PISANIO I shall, my lord. *Exit.*

CLOTEN Meet thee at Milford Haven! I forgot to ask him one thing;[6] I'll remember't anon. Even there, thou villain Posthumus, will I kill thee. I would these garments were come. She said upon a time—the bitterness of it I now belch from my heart—that she held the very garment of Posthumus in more respect than my noble and natural person, together with the adornment of my qualities. With that suit upon my back will I ravish her—first kill him, and in her eyes; there shall she see my valor, which will then be a torment to her contempt. He on the ground, my speech of insultment° ended on his dead body, and when my lust hath dined— *contemptuous triumph*

5. May turn out to be merely a long journey for him.
6. The "one thing" may be how much time has passed since Imogen set out for Milford Haven (see Cloten's question at line 143).

which, as I say, to vex her, I will execute in the clothes
that she so praised—to the court I'll knock° her back, *beat*
foot° her home again. She hath despised me rejoicingly, *kick*
and I'll be merry in my revenge.

*Enter* PISANIO [*with a suit of clothes*].

Be those the garments?

PISANIO Ay, my noble lord.

CLOTEN How long is't since she went to Milford Haven?

PISANIO She can scarce be there yet.

CLOTEN Bring this apparel to my chamber; that is the second
thing that I have commanded thee. The third is that thou
wilt be a voluntary mute to° my design. Be but duteous, and *be quiet about*
true preferment shall tender itself to thee. My revenge is
now at Milford; would I had wings to follow it. Come, and
be true. *Exit.*

PISANIO Thou bidd'st me to my loss:° for true to thee *damnation; ruin*
Were to prove false, which I will never be
To him that is most true. To Milford go,
And find not her whom thou pursuest. Flow, flow,
You heavenly blessings on her. This fool's speed
Be crossed° with slowness; labor be his meed.° *Exit.* *thwarted / reward*

## 3.6

*Enter* IMOGEN *alone* [*dressed as a man, before the cave*].

IMOGEN I see a man's life is a tedious one.
I have tired myself, and for two nights together
Have made the ground my bed. I should be sick,
But that my resolution helps me. Milford,
When from the mountaintop Pisanio showed thee,
Thou wast within a ken.° O Jove, I think *sight*
Foundations[1] fly the wretched—such I mean,
Where they should be relieved.[2] Two beggars told me
I could not miss my way. Will poor folks lie,
That have afflictions on them, knowing 'tis
A punishment or trial?[3] Yes; no wonder,
When rich ones scarce tell true. To lapse in fullness° *To do wrong when rich*
Is sorer° than to lie for need, and falsehood *worse*
Is worse in kings than beggars. My dear lord,
Thou art one o'th' false ones. Now I think on thee,
My hunger's gone, but even before° I was *just a moment ago*
At point° to sink for° food. But what is this? *Ready / for want of*
Here is a path to't. 'Tis some savage hold.° *refuge*
I were best not call; I dare not call; yet famine,
Ere clean° it o'erthrow nature, makes it valiant. *completely*
Plenty and peace breeds cowards; hardness° ever *hardship*
Of hardiness is mother. Ho! Who's here?
If anything that's civil, speak! If savage,
Take or lend.[4] Ho! No answer? Then I'll enter.

3.6 Location: Before the cave of Belarius, Wales.
1. Certainties; charitable institutions.
2. *such . . . relieved:* such certainties, I mean, as should give mental relief to the wretched; such charitable institutions as should give physical relief (food and rest) to the wretched.
3. *knowing . . . trial:* knowing that poverty is a punishment or a test of one's virtue.
4. Take everything I have, or help me.

Best draw my sword, and if mine enemy
But fear the sword like me, he'll scarcely look on't.
Such a foe, good heavens![5] *Exit [into the cave].*

*Enter* BELARIUS, GUIDERIUS, *and* ARVIRAGUS.[6]

BELARIUS You, Polydore, have proved best woodman° and — *hunter*
Are master of the feast. Cadwal and I
Will play the cook and servant; 'tis our match.° — *bargain*
The sweat of industry would dry and die
But for the end it works to. Come, our stomachs
Will make what's homely° savory. Weariness — *plain*
Can snore upon the flint when resty° sloth — *lazy*
Finds the down pillow hard. Now peace be here,
Poor house, that keep'st thyself.° [*Exit into the cave.*] — *goes untended*

GUIDERIUS I am thoroughly weary.

ARVIRAGUS I am weak with toil, yet strong in appetite.

GUIDERIUS There is cold meat i'th' cave; we'll browse° on that — *nibble*
Whilst what we have killed be cooked.

[*Enter* BELARIUS *from the cave.*]

BELARIUS Stay, come not in!
But° that it eats our victuals, I should think — *But for the fact*
Here were a fairy.

GUIDERIUS What's the matter, sir?

BELARIUS By Jupiter, an angel—or, if not,
An earthly paragon.° Behold divineness — *equal*
No elder than a boy.

*Enter* IMOGEN.

IMOGEN Good masters, harm me not.
Before I entered here I called, and thought° — *intended*
To have begged or bought what I have took. Good troth,
I have stol'n naught, nor would not, though I had found
Gold strewed i'th' floor. Here's money for my meat:
I would have left it on the board so° soon — *as*
As I had made my meal, and parted
With prayers for the provider.

GUIDERIUS Money, youth?

ARVIRAGUS All gold and silver rather turn to dirt,
As 'tis no better reckoned but of° those — *by*
Who worship dirty gods.

IMOGEN I see you're angry.
Know, if you kill me for my fault, I should
Have died had I not made it.

BELARIUS Whither bound?

IMOGEN To Milford Haven.

BELARIUS What's your name?

IMOGEN Fidele,[7] sir. I have a kinsman who
Is bound for Italy. He embarked at Milford,
To whom being going, almost spent with hunger,
I am fall'n in° this offense. — *into*

BELARIUS Prithee, fair youth,
Think us no churls,° nor measure our good minds — *base fellows*

5. May it please heaven I meet such a timid foe.
6. F marks a new scene at this point, but the action is continuous.
7. In French and Italian, the name means "faithful one."

By this rude° place we live in. Well encountered! *wild*
'Tis almost night; you shall have better cheer° *provisions*
Ere you depart, and thanks to° stay and eat it. *our gratitude if you*
Boys, bid him welcome.

**GUIDERIUS** Were you a woman, youth,
I should woo hard but be° your groom in honesty; *rather than fail to be*
Ay, bid for you as I'd buy.[8]

**ARVIRAGUS** I'll make't my comfort
He is a man; I'll love him as my brother,
[*to* IMOGEN] And such a welcome as I'd give to him,
After long absence, such is yours. Most welcome.
Be sprightly,° for you fall 'mongst friends. *cheerful*

**IMOGEN** 'Mongst friends,
If brothers.[9] [*aside*] Would it had been so—that they
Had been my father's sons. Then had my price° *worth*
Been less, and so more equal ballasting° *equal in weight*
To thee, Posthumus.

**BELARIUS** He wrings° at some distress. *twists in pain*

**GUIDERIUS** Would I could free't.° *remove it*

**ARVIRAGUS** Or I, whate'er it be,
What° pain it cost, what danger. Gods! *Whatever*

**BELARIUS** Hark, boys.

**IMOGEN** [*aside*] Great men
That had a court no bigger than this cave,
That did attend° themselves and had the virtue *wait on*
Which their own conscience sealed° them, laying by° *assured / disregarding*
That nothing-gift of differing multitudes,[1]
Could not outpeer° these twain. Pardon me, gods, *surpass*
I'd change my sex to be companion with them,
Since Leonatus false—

**BELARIUS** It shall be so.
Boys, we'll go dress our hunt.° Fair youth, come in. *game*
Discourse is heavy, fasting.[2] When we have supped
We'll mannerly demand thee of thy story,
So far as thou wilt speak it.

**GUIDERIUS** Pray draw near.

**ARVIRAGUS** The night to th'owl and morn to th' lark less welcome.

**IMOGEN** Thanks, sir.

**ARVIRAGUS** I pray draw near. *Exeunt* [*into the cave*].

## 3.7

*Enter two Roman* SENATORS, *and* TRIBUNES.

**FIRST SENATOR** This is the tenor of the Emperor's writ:
That since the common men are now in action
'Gainst the Pannonians and Dalmatians,
And that the legions now in Gallia are
Full weak° to undertake our wars against *Too weak*
The fall'n-off° Britons, that we do incite *rebelling*
The gentry to this business. He creates

8. Yes, make an offer for you with every intent to buy (that is, to marry you).
9. *'Mongst . . . brothers:* Yes, certainly I am among friends, if you claim me as a brother.
1. That worthless gift offered by a public that cannot agree on anything.
2. Conversation is difficult when one is without food.
3.7 Location: A public place, Rome.

Lucius proconsul,[1] and to you the tribunes,
For this immediate levy, he commends° — *entrusts*
His absolute commission.° Long live Caesar! — *authority*

TRIBUNE Is Lucius general of the forces?

SECOND SENATOR Ay.

TRIBUNE Remaining now in Gallia?

FIRST SENATOR With those legions
Which I have spoke of, whereunto your levy
Must be supplyant.° The words of your commission — *auxiliary*
Will tie you to° the numbers and the time — *indicate to you*
Of their dispatch.

TRIBUNE We will discharge our duty.

*Exeunt.*

## 4.1

*Enter* CLOTEN *alone [in Posthumus' clothes].*

CLOTEN I am near to th' place where they should meet, if Pisanio have mapped it truly. How fit° his garments serve me! Why should his mistress, who was made by him that made the tailor, not be fit° too? The rather—saving reverence of the word[1]—for 'tis said a woman's fitness comes by fits;[2] therein I must play the workman. I dare speak it to myself, for it is not vainglory for a man and his glass° to confer in his own chamber. I mean the lines of my body are as well drawn as his: no less young, more strong, not beneath him in fortunes, beyond him in the advantage of the time,[3] above him in birth, alike conversant in general services, and more remarkable in single oppositions;[4] yet this imperceiverant° thing loves him in my despite.° What mortality[5] is! Posthumus, thy head, which now is growing upon thy shoulders, shall within this hour be off, thy mistress enforced,° thy garments cut to pieces before her face; and all this done, spurn her home to her father, who may haply be a little angry for my so rough usage; but my mother, having power of° his testiness, shall turn all into my commendations. My horse is tied up safe. Out, sword, and to a sore purpose! Fortune, put them into my hand. This is the very description of their meeting-place, and the fellow dares not deceive me. *Exit.*

*fit: aptly* · *fit: apt; sexually compatible* · *glass: mirror* · *imperceiverant: stupid* · *in my despite: to spite me* · *enforced: raped* · *of: over*

## 4.2

*Enter* BELARIUS, GUIDERIUS, ARVIRAGUS, *and* IMOGEN *[dressed as a man] from the cave.*

BELARIUS [*to* IMOGEN] You are not well. Remain here in the cave,
We'll come to you after hunting.

ARVIRAGUS Brother, stay here.
Are we not brothers?

IMOGEN So man and man should be,
But clay and clay[1] differs in dignity,° — *social position*

1. One who acted as governor or military commander in a Roman province.

4.1 Location: Near the cave of Belarius, Wales.

1. With apologies for my punning.

2. For it is said that a woman's inclination for sexual intercourse comes intermittently.

3. In the favorable opportunities afforded by the times.

4. *alike . . . oppositions:* similarly acquainted with battle tactics, and superior in single combat or duels (with puns on "service" and "oppositions" as referring to sexual exploits).

5. Life; humankind.

4.2 Location: Before the cave of Belarius.

1. Yet two humans (alluding to the biblical notion that humans are formed out of clay).

Whose dust[2] is both alike. I am very sick—
GUIDERIUS [*to* BELARIUS *and* ARVIRAGUS] Go you to hunting,
I'll abide with him.
IMOGEN So sick I am not, yet I am not well;
But not so citizen a wanton as
To seem to die ere sick.[3] So please you, leave me.
Stick to your journal course:° the breach of custom *daily routine*
Is breach of all. I am ill, but your being by me
Cannot amend me. Society is no comfort
To one not sociable. I am not very sick,
Since I can reason of° it. Pray you, trust me here— *talk about*
I'll rob none but myself—and let me die
Stealing so poorly.[4]
GUIDERIUS I love thee: I have spoke it;
How much the quantity,° the weight as much, *As greatly*
As I do love my father.
BELARIUS What? How, how?
ARVIRAGUS If it be sin to say so, sir, I yoke me° *I share*
In my good brother's fault. I know not why
I love this youth, and I have heard you say
Love's reason's without reason. The bier[5] at door,
And a demand who is't shall die, I'd say
"My father, not this youth."
BELARIUS [*aside*] O noble strain!° *inherited character*
O worthiness of nature, breed of greatness!
Cowards father cowards, and base things sire base;
Nature hath meal and bran,° contempt and grace. *flour and husks*
I'm not their father, yet who this should be
Doth miracle itself, loved before me.[6]
—'Tis the ninth hour o'th' morn.[7]
ARVIRAGUS [*to* IMOGEN] Brother, farewell.
IMOGEN I wish ye sport.
ARVIRAGUS You health. —So please you, sir.
IMOGEN [*aside*] These are kind creatures. Gods, what lies I
have heard!
Our courtiers say all's savage but at court.
Experience, O thou disprov'st report.
Th'imperious° seas breeds monsters; for the dish, *imperial*
Poor tributary rivers as sweet fish.[8]
I am sick still, heartsick. Pisanio,
I'll now taste of thy drug.
[*She swallows the drug. The men speak apart.*]
GUIDERIUS I could not stir him.
He said he was gentle,° but unfortunate, *a gentleman by birth*
Dishonestly afflicted, but yet honest.

2. The substance to which all humans return at death.
3. *But . . . sick:* But I am not so city-bred a weakling ("wanton") as to think I am dying even before I am sick.
4. Stealing only from one so poor as myself.
5. The litter, or platform, on which a corpse was carried to the grave.
6. *yet . . . me*: yet who this may be who is loved more than me is a source of great wonder.
7. TEXTUAL COMMENT Guiderius and Arviragus don't hear the first six lines of Belarius's speech, indicated at line 24 by the phrase "*aside*." Some editions indicate that at line 4.2.29 he speaks "aloud," but this edition assumes a greater fluidity in stage practice. It was common on the early modern stage for some lines to be heard only by the audience and not by other characters, while succeeding lines would be heard by all. These switch points are determined by context or performers' choices and need not be marked by a stage direction. See Digital Edition TC 5.
8. *for . . . fish:* but when it comes to eating, small tributaries breed fish as sweet as does the sea.

ARVIRAGUS Thus did he answer me, yet said hereafter
I might know more.
BELARIUS To th' field, to th' field!
—We'll leave you for this time. Go in and rest.
ARVIRAGUS We'll not be long away.
BELARIUS Pray be not sick,
For you must be our housewife.
IMOGEN Well or ill,
I am bound° to you. *Exit [into the cave].* — *indebted*
BELARIUS And shalt be ever.
This youth, howe'er distressed, appears° he hath had — *apparently*
Good ancestors.
ARVIRAGUS How angel-like he sings!
GUIDERIUS But his neat° cookery! He cut our roots in characters,° — *dainty* / *alphabet shapes*
And sauced our broths as° Juno had been sick — *as if*
And he her dieter.° — *cook*
ARVIRAGUS Nobly he yokes
A smiling with a sigh, as if the sigh
Was that° it was for not being such a smile; — *Was what*
The smile mocking the sigh, that° it would fly — *because*
From so divine a temple to commix° — *join*
With winds that sailors rail at.
GUIDERIUS I do note
That grief and patience rooted in them both,° — *(both sighs and smiles)*
Mingle their spurs° together. — *roots*
ARVIRAGUS Grow patience,
And let the stinking elder,[9] grief, untwine
His perishing° root with° the increasing vine. — *deadly / from*
BELARIUS It is great morning.° Come away! Who's there? — *full daylight*
*Enter* CLOTEN *[in Posthumus' clothes].*
CLOTEN I cannot find those runagates;° that villain — *runaways; fugitives*
Hath mocked me. I am faint.
BELARIUS "Those runagates"?
Means he not us? I partly know him; 'tis
Cloten, the son o'th' Queen. I fear some ambush.
I saw him not these many years, and yet
I know 'tis he. We are held as outlaws. Hence!
GUIDERIUS He is but one. You and my brother search
What companies° are near. Pray you, away. — *companions*
Let me alone with him. *[Exeunt* BELARIUS *and* ARVIRAGUS.*]*
CLOTEN Soft, what are you
That fly me thus? Some villain mountaineers?° — *lowborn mountain people*
I have heard of such. What slave art thou?
GUIDERIUS A thing
More slavish did I ne'er than answering
A slave without a knock.° — *without striking him*
CLOTEN Thou art a robber,
A lawbreaker, a villain. Yield thee, thief.
GUIDERIUS To who? To thee? What art thou? Have not I
An arm as big as thine, a heart as big?
Thy words, I grant, are bigger, for I wear not

9. A tree with strong-smelling leaves and flowers on which Judas, the disciple who betrayed Jesus, is said to have hanged himself.

My dagger in my mouth.[1] Say what thou art,
Why I should yield to thee?

CLOTEN Thou villain base,
Know'st me not by my clothes?

GUIDERIUS No, nor thy tailor, rascal,
Who is thy grandfather. He made those clothes,
Which, as it seems, make thee.[2]

CLOTEN Thou precious varlet,° *absolute scoundrel*
My tailor made them not.

GUIDERIUS Hence, then, and thank
The man that gave them thee. Thou art some fool;
I am loath to beat thee.

CLOTEN Thou injurious° thief, *insulting*
Hear but my name and tremble.

GUIDERIUS What's thy name?

CLOTEN Cloten, thou villain.

GUIDERIUS Cloten, thou double villain, be thy name,
I cannot tremble at it. Were it Toad, or Adder, Spider,
'Twould move me sooner.

CLOTEN To thy further fear,
Nay, to thy mere confusion,° thou shalt know *absolute destruction*
I am son to th' Queen.

GUIDERIUS I am sorry for't, not seeming
So worthy as thy birth.

CLOTEN Art not afeard?

GUIDERIUS Those that I reverence, those I fear: the wise.
At fools I laugh, not fear them.

CLOTEN Die the death.
When I have slain thee with my proper° hand *own*
I'll follow those that even now fled hence
And on the gates of Lud's Town° set your heads.[3] *London*
Yield, rustic mountaineer. *Fight and exeunt.*

*Enter* BELARIUS *and* ARVIRAGUS.

BELARIUS No company's abroad?° *around*

ARVIRAGUS None in the world. You did mistake him sure.

BELARIUS I cannot tell. Long is it since I saw him,
But time hath nothing blurred those lines of favor° *facial features*
Which then he wore. The snatches° in his voice *hesitations*
And burst° of speaking were as his. I am absolute° *sudden rush / sure*
'Twas very Cloten.° *Cloten himself*

ARVIRAGUS In this place we left them.
I wish my brother make good time with° him, *is successful with*
You say he is so fell.° *fierce*

BELARIUS Being scarce made up,° *barely full-grown*
I mean to man, he had not apprehension° *had no consciousness*
Of roaring terrors; for defect of judgment
Is oft the cause of fear.[4]

*Enter* GUIDERIUS [*with Cloten's head*].

But see thy brother.

1. *for . . . mouth:* for I don't let words substitute for weapons.
2. Alluding to the proverb "The tailor makes the man."
3. The heads of criminals were frequently displayed on poles on London Bridge and other places throughout the city.
4. *for . . . fear:* an obscure passage. It may mean that Cloten's faulty judgment, which led him to know no fear, caused fear in others. A less likely meaning is that while defects in judgment cause fear, Cloten knew no fear because he had absolutely no judgment, being utterly witless.

GUIDERIUS This Cloten was a fool, an empty purse;
There was no money in't. Not Hercules[5]
Could have knocked out his brains, for he had none.
Yet I not doing this,° the fool had borne *had I not done this*
My head, as I do his.
BELARIUS What hast thou done?
GUIDERIUS I am perfect° what: cut off one Cloten's head, *certain*
Son to the Queen (after his own report)
Who called me traitor, mountaineer, and swore
With his own single hand he'd take us in,° *capture us*
Displace our heads where—thank the gods—they grow,
And set them on Lud's Town.
BELARIUS We are all undone.
GUIDERIUS Why, worthy father, what have we to lose
But that° he swore to take, our lives? The law *what*
Protects not us; then why should we be tender
To let[6] an arrogant piece of flesh threat us,
Play judge and executioner all himself,
For° we do fear the law? What company *Because*
Discover you abroad?[7]
BELARIUS No single soul
Can we set eye on, but in all safe reason
He must have some attendants. Though his humor° *disposition*
Was nothing but mutation,° ay, and that *changeableness*
From one bad thing to worse, not° frenzy, *neither*
Not° absolute madness, could so far have raved° *Nor / could have made him mad enough*
To bring him here alone. Although perhaps
It may be heard at court that such as we
Cave° here, hunt here, are outlaws, and in time *Live in a cave*
May make some stronger head,° the which he hearing— *raise a stronger force*
As it is like him—might break out and swear
He'd fetch us in, yet is't not probable
To come° alone, either he so undertaking, *That he would come*
Or they so suffering.[8] Then on good ground we fear,
If we do fear this body hath a tail° *rear end; followers*
More perilous than the head.
ARVIRAGUS Let ord'nance° *destiny*
Come as the gods foresay° it; howsoe'er, *predict*
My brother hath done well.
BELARIUS I had no mind
To hunt this day. The boy Fidele's sickness
Did make my way long forth.° *my journey tedious*
GUIDERIUS With his own sword,
Which he did wave against my throat, I have ta'en
His head from him. I'll throw't into the creek
Behind our rock, and let it to the sea
And tell the fishes he's the Queen's son, Cloten.
That's all I reck.° *Exit.* *care*
BELARIUS I fear 'twill be revenged.
Would, Polydore, thou hadst not done't, though valor
Becomes thee well enough.

5. Mythical hero of enormous strength.
6. *be tender / To let:* be so meek as to allow.
7. What companions (of Cloten) did you find hereabouts?
8. *either . . . suffering:* either that he would undertake it or that they would allow it.

ARVIRAGUS Would I had done't,
So the revenge alone pursued me.° Polydore, *only pursued me*
I love thee brotherly, but envy much
Thou hast robbed me of this deed. I would revenges
That possible strength might meet would seek us through
And put us to our answer.[9]
BELARIUS Well, 'tis done.
We'll hunt no more today, nor seek for danger
Where there's no profit. I prithee, to our rock.
You and Fidele play the cooks. I'll stay
Till hasty Polydore return, and bring him
To dinner presently.
ARVIRAGUS Poor sick Fidele!
I'll willingly to him. To gain° his color *restore*
I'd let a parish of such Clotens blood[1]
And praise myself for charity. *Exit [into the cave].*
BELARIUS O thou goddess,
Thou divine Nature, how thyself thou blazon'st[2]
In these two princely boys! They are as gentle
As zephyrs° blowing below the violet, *breezes from the west*
Not wagging his sweet head; and yet as rough,° *violent*
Their royal blood enchafed,° as the rud'st wind *inflamed*
That by the top doth take the mountain pine
And make him stoop to th' vale. 'Tis wonder
That an invisible instinct should frame° them *shape*
To royalty unlearned, honor untaught,
Civility not seen from other,° valor *not witnessed in others*
That wildly° grows in them, but yields a crop *without cultivation*
As if it had been sowed. Yet still it's strange
What Cloten's being here to us portends,
Or what his death will bring us.
*Enter* GUIDERIUS.
GUIDERIUS Where's my brother?
I have sent Cloten's clotpoll° down the stream *blockhead*
In embassy to his mother. His body's hostage
For his return.[3]
*Solemn music [plays].*
BELARIUS My ingenious° instrument! *artfully crafted*
Hark, Polydore, it sounds. But what occasion
Hath Cadwal now to give it motion? Hark!
GUIDERIUS Is he at home?
BELARIUS He went hence even now.
GUIDERIUS What does he mean? Since death of my dear'st mother
It did not speak before. All solemn things
Should answer° solemn accidents. The matter? *correspond to*
Triumphs for nothing and lamenting toys
Is jollity for apes and grief for boys.[4]
Is Cadwal mad?

9. *I would . . . answer:* I wish that revenges equal to all the power that we might muster would find us out and test our mettle.
1. I'd draw blood from a whole parish full of fools like Cloten.
2. How you proclaim yourself (as in a coat of arms).
3. *His body's . . . return:* I will hold his body hostage until his head returns (which will be never).
4. *Triumphs . . . boys:* Public celebrations for no reason and showing great grief for trivial matters are foolish and unmanly.

*Enter* ARVIRAGUS [*from the cave*] *with* IMOGEN [*seeming*] *dead, bearing her in his arms.*

BELARIUS Look, here he comes,
And brings the dire occasion in his arms
Of what we blame him for.

ARVIRAGUS The bird is dead
That we have made so much on.° I had rather — *of*
Have skipped from sixteen years of age to sixty,
To have turned my leaping time° into a crutch,° — *youth / (old age)*
Than have seen this.

GUIDERIUS O sweetest, fairest lily!
My brother wears thee not the one half so well
As when thou grew'st thyself.

BELARIUS O melancholy,
Whoever yet could sound thy bottom,° find — *measure your depths*
The ooze, to show what coast thy sluggish crare° — *small ship*
Might easiliest harbor in? Thou blessèd thing,
Jove knows what man thou mightst have made; but I,° — *I know*
Thou died'st a most rare boy, of melancholy.
How found you him?

ARVIRAGUS Stark,° as you see, — *Stiff*
Thus smiling, as° some fly had tickled slumber, — *as if*
Not as death's dart being laughed at;[5] his right cheek
Reposing on a cushion.

GUIDERIUS Where?

ARVIRAGUS O'th' floor,
His arms thus leagued.° I thought he slept, and put — *linked together*
My clouted brogues° from off my feet, whose rudeness — *hobnailed boots*
Answered° my steps too loud. — *Rendered*

GUIDERIUS Why, he but sleeps.
If he be gone, he'll make his grave a bed.
With female fairies will his tomb be haunted,
And worms will not come to thee.

ARVIRAGUS With fairest flowers
Whilst summer lasts and I live here, Fidele,
I'll sweeten thy sad grave. Thou shalt not lack
The flower that's like thy face, pale primrose, nor
The azured harebell,° like thy veins; no, nor — *blue hyacinth*
The leaf of eglantine,° whom not to slander, — *sweetbriar rose*
Out-sweetened not thy breath. The ruddock would
With charitable bill—O bill sore shaming
Those rich-left heirs, that let their fathers lie
Without a monument—bring thee all this,
Yea, and furred moss besides.[6] When flowers are none,
To winter-ground° thy corpse— — *protect for winter*

GUIDERIUS Prithee have done,
And do not play in wench-like words[7] with that
Which is so serious. Let us bury him,
And not protract with admiration° what — *wonder*
Is now due debt. To th' grave.

5. Not as if laughing at the approach of death. Death was often depicted carrying a spear ("dart").
6. *The ruddock . . . besides:* referring to the belief that the robins ("ruddocks") covered dead bodies with flowers and moss.
7. Words appropriate to women. In Shakespeare's plays, speeches about flowers are often delivered by female characters, perhaps most notably in *Hamlet* 4.4.165–74 and *The Winter's Tale* 4.4.73–134.

ARVIRAGUS Say, where shall 's° lay him? *ought we to*
GUIDERIUS By good Euriphile, our mother.
ARVIRAGUS Be't so,
And let us, Polydore, though now our voices
Have got the mannish crack, sing him to th' ground
As once to our mother; use like note° and words, *a similar tune*
Save that "Euriphile" must be "Fidele."
GUIDERIUS Cadwal,
I cannot sing. I'll weep, and word° it with thee; *speak*
For notes of sorrow out of tune are worse
Than priests and fanes° that lie. *temples*
ARVIRAGUS We'll speak it then.
BELARIUS Great griefs, I see, med'cine° the less, for Cloten *cure*
Is quite forgot. He was a queen's son, boys,
And though he came our enemy, remember
He was paid° for that. Though mean° and mighty rotting *punished / lowborn*
Together have one dust, yet reverence,
That angel of the world,[8] doth make distinction
Of place 'tween high and low. Our foe was princely,
And though you took his life as being our foe,
Yet bury him as a prince.
GUIDERIUS Pray you fetch him hither.
Thersites' body is as good as Ajax'[9]
When neither are alive.
ARVIRAGUS [*to* BELARIUS] If you'll go fetch him,
We'll say our song the whilst. [*Exit* BELARIUS.]
Brother, begin.
GUIDERIUS Nay, Cadwal, we must lay his head to th'east;[1]
My father hath a reason for't.
ARVIRAGUS 'Tis true.
GUIDERIUS Come on, then, and remove him.
ARVIRAGUS So, begin.[2]
[GUIDERIUS *and* ARVIRAGUS *sing the*] *song.*
GUIDERIUS Fear no more the heat o'th' sun,
Nor the furious winter's rages.
Thou thy worldly task hast done,
Home art gone and ta'en thy wages.
Golden lads and girls all must,
As° chimney-sweepers, come to dust. *Like*
ARVIRAGUS Fear no more the frown o'th' great,
Thou art past the tyrant's stroke.
Care no more to clothe and eat,
To thee the reed is as the oak.[3]
The scepter, learning, physic° must *medical knowledge*
All follow this and come to dust.

8. Reverence (respect for someone because of his or her social position) may here be called the "angel of the world" because social hierarchy was thought by some to imitate heavenly hierarchy.
9. Alluding to two Greeks present at the siege of Troy: Thersites, a scurrilous coward, and Ajax, a mighty hero. Both appear in Shakespeare's *Troilus and Cressida*.
1. An allusion to classical or Celtic burial practices. The English Christian custom was to lay the head to the west. This detail reinforces the pagan world of the play.
2. In F, the following duet is introduced as "song." Lines 239–41, in which the brothers say they cannot sing and must speak the words, may have been added because the particular actors who played Arviragus and Guiderius were not good singers.
3. Referring to traditional symbols of weakness and strength, respectively.

GUIDERIUS Fear no more the lightning flash,
ARVIRAGUS Nor th'all-dreaded thunder-stone.° *thunderbolt*
GUIDERIUS Fear not slander, censure rash.
ARVIRAGUS Thou hast finished joy and moan.
BOTH All lovers young, all lovers must
Consign to thee[4] and come to dust.
GUIDERIUS No exorciser° harm thee, *conjurer of spirits*
ARVIRAGUS Nor no witchcraft charm thee.
GUIDERIUS Ghost unlaid forbear thee.[5]
ARVIRAGUS Nothing ill come near thee.
BOTH Quiet consummation° have, *ending*
And renownèd be thy grave.

*Enter* BELARIUS *with the body of* CLOTEN.

GUIDERIUS We have done our obsequies. Come, lay him down.
BELARIUS Here's a few flowers, but 'bout midnight more;
The herbs that have on them cold dew o'th' night° *of the night*
Are strewings fitt'st for graves. Upon their faces.[6]
You were as flowers, now withered; even so
These herblets shall,° which we upon you strew. *shall wither*
Come on, away; apart upon our knees.[7]
The ground that gave them° first has them again. *gave them life*
Their pleasures here are past, so is their pain.

*Exeunt* [BELARIUS, GUIDERIUS, *and* ARVIRAGUS].

IMOGEN (*awakes*) Yes, sir, to Milford Haven. Which is the way?
I thank you. By yond bush? Pray, how far thither?
'Ods pittikins,° can it be six mile yet? *By God's pity (mild oath)*
I have gone° all night. Faith, I'll lie down and sleep. *walked*
[*She sees Cloten's body.*]
But soft,° no bedfellow! O gods and goddesses! *wait*
These flowers are like the pleasures of the world,
This bloody man the care on't.° I hope I dream, *the world's sorrow*
For so° I thought I was a cave-keeper, *For then*
And cook to honest creatures. But 'tis not so.
'Twas but a bolt° of nothing, shot at nothing, *an arrow*
Which the brain makes of fumes.[8] Our very eyes
Are sometimes like our judgments, blind. Good faith,
I tremble still with fear; but if there be
Yet left in heaven as small a drop of pity
As a wren's eye, feared gods, a part of it!
The dream's here still: even when I wake it is
Without me as within me; not imagined, felt.
A headless man? The garments of Posthumus?[9]
I know the shape of 's leg; this is his hand,
His foot Mercurial, his Martial[1] thigh,
The brawns° of Hercules; but his Jovial[2] face— *muscles*
Murder in heaven! How? 'Tis gone! Pisanio,

4. Submit to the same terms as you.
5. May spirits who have not been laid to rest leave you alone.
6. TEXTUAL COMMENT Although some editors have suggested that Belarius commands his sons to lay the bodies so that their faces are to the earth, this edition takes Belarius's words to mean that the boys should put the flowers on the front ("faces") of the bodies. See Digital Edition TC 6.
7. Some other place ("apart"), let us pray (be "upon our knees").
8. "Fumes" (vapors) were thought to rise from the stomach and cause dreams and distortions of the imagination.
9. PERFORMANCE COMMENT The overt theatricality of having the Cloten actor play his own dead body (as opposed to using a mannequin) can spur audience engagement. See Digital Edition PC 3.
1. Fashioned for battle, like that of Mars, the god of war. *Mercurial:* Like that of Mercury, the fleet-footed messenger of the gods.
2. Majestic like the face of Jove, king of the gods.

All curses madded Hecuba[3] gave the Greeks,
And mine to boot, be darted on thee! Thou,
Conspired° with that irregulous° devil, Cloten, *Conspiring / lawless*
Hath here cut off my lord. To write and read
Be henceforth treacherous. Damned Pisanio
Hath with his forgèd letters—damned Pisanio—
From this most bravest° vessel of the world *splendid*
Struck the main top!° O Posthumus, alas, *top mast; (his head)*
Where is thy head? Where's that? Ay me, where's that?
Pisanio might have killed thee at the heart
And left thy head on. How should this be? Pisanio?
'Tis he and Cloten: malice and lucre° in them *greed*
Have laid this woe here. Oh, 'tis pregnant,° pregnant! *clear*
The drug he gave me, which he said was precious
And cordial° to me, have I not found it *restorative*
Murd'rous to th' senses? That confirms it home:° *completely*
This is Pisanio's deed, and Cloten. Oh,
Give color to my pale cheek with thy blood,
That we the horrider° may seem to those *more terrifying*
Which chance to find us. O my lord, my lord!
[*She smears her face with blood and falls on the body.*]
*Enter* LUCIUS, CAPTAINS, *and a* SOOTHSAYER.

CAPTAIN To them,° the legions garrisoned in Gallia *In addition to them*
After your will[4] have crossed the sea, attending° *waiting for*
You here at Milford Haven with your ships:
They are here in readiness.

LUCIUS But what from Rome?

CAPTAIN The Senate hath stirred up the confiners° *inhabitants*
And gentlemen of Italy, most willing spirits
That promise noble service, and they come
Under the conduct of bold Giacomo,
Siena's° brother. *The Duke of Siena's*

LUCIUS When expect you them?

CAPTAIN With the next benefit o'th' wind.

LUCIUS This forwardness° *readiness*
Makes our hopes fair. Command our present numbers
Be mustered; bid the captains look to't. [*Exit a* CAPTAIN.]
[*to the* SOOTHSAYER] Now, sir,
What have you dreamed of late of this war's purpose?° *outcome*

SOOTHSAYER Last night the very gods showed me a vision—
I fast° and prayed for their intelligence°—thus: *fasted / information*
I saw Jove's bird, the Roman eagle, winged
From the spongy° south to this part of the west, *damp*
There vanished in the sunbeams; which portends,
Unless my sins abuse° my divination, *falsify*
Success to th' Roman host.

LUCIUS Dream often so,
And never false.° —Soft ho, what trunk is here *dream falsely*
Without his top? The ruin speaks that sometime° *once*
It was a worthy building. How, a page?
Or° dead or sleeping on him? But dead rather, *Either*
For nature doth abhor to make his bed

3. The queen of Troy, Priam's wife, whose desire for revenge against the Greeks made her insane ("madded").
4. According to your command.

With the defunct, or sleep upon the dead.
Let's see the boy's face.

CAPTAIN He's alive, my lord.

LUCIUS He'll then instruct us of this body. Young one,
Inform us of thy fortunes, for it seems
They crave to be demanded. Who is this
Thou mak'st thy bloody pillow? Or who was he
That, otherwise than noble nature did,[5]
Hath altered that good picture? What's thy interest
In this sad wreck?° How came't? Who is't? *ruin*
What art thou?

IMOGEN I am nothing; or if not,
Nothing to be were better.[6] This was my master,
A very valiant Briton and a good,
That here by mountaineers lies slain. Alas,
There is no more such masters. I may wander
From east to occident,° cry out for service, *west*
Try many, all good; serve truly, never
Find such another master.

LUCIUS 'Lack,° good youth, *Alas*
Thou mov'st no less with thy complaining than
Thy master in bleeding. Say his name, good friend.

IMOGEN Richard du Champ.[7] [*aside*] If I do lie and do
No harm by it, though the gods hear, I hope
They'll pardon it. —Say you, sir?

LUCIUS Thy name?

IMOGEN Fidele, sir.

LUCIUS Thou dost approve° thyself the very same: *show*
Thy name well fits thy faith,° thy faith thy name. *fidelity*
Wilt take thy chance with me? I will not say
Thou shalt be so well mastered, but be sure,
No less beloved. The Roman Emperor's letters,
Sent by a consul to me, should not sooner
Than thine own worth prefer° thee. Go with me. *recommend*

IMOGEN I'll follow, sir. But first, an't° please the gods, *if it*
I'll hide my master from the flies as deep
As these poor pickaxes° can dig; and when *(her hands)*
With wildwood leaves and weeds I ha' strewed his grave
And on it said a century of° prayers, *a hundred*
Such as I can, twice o'er, I'll weep and sigh,
And leaving so his service, follow you,
So please you entertain° me. *employ*

LUCIUS Ay, good youth,
And rather father thee than master thee. My friends,
The boy hath taught us manly duties. Let us
Find out the prettiest daisied plot we can,
And make him with our pikes and partisans[8]
A grave. Come, arm° him. Boy, he is preferred° *lift / recommended*

5. Who, in a manner different from nature's workings.
6. It were better to be nothing.
7. This French name translates as "Richard of the Field," perhaps an allusion to a well-known London printer named Richard Field, who was born in Stratford-upon-Avon and printed Shakespeare's *Rape of Lucrece* and *Venus and Adonis* in the 1590s.
8. With our spears and our halberds (long-handled weapons with ax-like blades).

By thee to us, and he shall be interred
As soldiers can. Be cheerful; wipe thine eyes.
Some falls are means the happier to arise.[9] *Exeunt.*

## 4.3

*Enter* CYMBELINE, LORDS, *and* PISANIO.

CYMBELINE Again, and bring me word how 'tis with her.
[*Exit a* LORD.]
A fever with° the absence of her son, *on account of*
A madness of which her life's in danger. Heavens,
How deeply you at once do touch° me! Imogen, *afflict*
The great part of my comfort, gone; my Queen
Upon a desperate bed,° and in a time *Extremely ill in bed*
When fearful wars point at me; her son gone,
So needful for this present!° It strikes me past *So needed now*
The hope of comfort. [*to* PISANIO] But for thee, fellow,
Who needs must know of her departure and
Dost seem so ignorant, we'll enforce it from thee
By a sharp torture.

PISANIO Sir, my life is yours;
I humbly set it at your will. But for my mistress,
I nothing know° where she remains, why gone, *know nothing about*
Nor when she purposes° return. Beseech° your highness, *intends to / I beseech*
Hold me° your loyal servant. *Regard me as*

LORD Good my liege,
The day that she was missing, he was here.
I dare be bound he's true, and shall perform
All parts of his subjection° loyally. For Cloten, *duty as a subject*
There wants° no diligence in seeking him, *is lacking*
And will° no doubt be found. *he will*

CYMBELINE The time is troublesome.° *dire*
[*to* PISANIO] We'll slip you° for a season, but our jealousy *let you go*
Does yet depend.[1]

LORD So please your majesty,
The Roman legions, all from Gallia drawn,
Are landed on your coast with a supply
Of Roman gentlemen by the Senate sent.

CYMBELINE Now for° the counsel of my son and Queen! *If only I now had*
I am amazed° with matter.° *overwhelmed / business*

LORD Good my liege,
Your preparation can affront no less
Than what you hear of.[2] Come more, for more you're ready.
The want° is but to put those powers in motion *The only thing needed*
That long to move.

CYMBELINE I thank you. Let's withdraw
And meet the time as it seeks us. We fear not
What can from Italy annoy° us, but *harm*
We grieve at chances° here. Away. *events*
*Exeunt* [CYMBELINE *and* LORDS].

PISANIO I heard no letter from my master since
I wrote him Imogen was slain. 'Tis strange.

9. Some falls are means by which good fortune arises.
4.3 Location: Cymbeline's court, Britain.
1. *but . . . depend:* but our suspicions still hold.
2. *Your . . . of:* Your forces can confront all those you have heard of.

Nor hear I from my mistress, who did promise
To yield me often tidings. Neither know I
What is betid° to Cloten, but remain — *has happened*
Perplexed in all. The heavens still must work.
Wherein I am false, I am honest; not true, to be true.
These present wars shall find I love my country,
Even to the note° o'th' King, or I'll fall in them. — *notice*
All other doubts, by time let them be cleared:
Fortune brings in some boats that are not steered. *Exit.*

## 4.4

*Enter* BELARIUS, GUIDERIUS, *and* ARVIRAGUS.

GUIDERIUS The noise is round about us.
BELARIUS Let us from it.
ARVIRAGUS What pleasure, sir, find we in life to lock it° — *shut it off*
From action and adventure?
GUIDERIUS Nay, what hope
Have we in hiding us? This way° the Romans — *By this action*
Must or° for Britons slay us, or receive us — *either*
For barbarous and unnatural revolts° — *rebels*
During their use,[1] and slay us after.
BELARIUS Sons,
We'll higher to the mountains; there secure us.
To the King's party there's no going. Newness
Of Cloten's death—we being not known, not mustered
Among the bands°—may drive us to a render° — *troops / an account*
Where we have lived, and so extort from 's that
Which we have done, whose answer would be death
Drawn on° with torture. — *Prolonged*
GUIDERIUS This is, sir, a doubt
In such a time nothing becoming you
Nor satisfying us.
ARVIRAGUS It is not likely
That when they hear the Roman horses neigh,
Behold their quartered fires,[2] have both their eyes
And ears so cloyed importantly[3] as now,
That they will waste their time upon our note,° — *in observing us*
To know from whence we are.
BELARIUS Oh, I am known
Of° many in the army. Many years, — *By*
Though Cloten then° but young, you see, not wore° him — *was then / have not worn*
From my remembrance. And besides, the King
Hath not deserved my service nor your loves,
Who find in my exile the want of breeding,
The certainty of this hard life;[4] aye hopeless
To have the courtesy your cradle promised,[5]
But to be still° hot summer's tanlings[6] and — *always*
The shrinking slaves of winter.

**4.4** Location: Before the cave of Belarius, Wales.
1. While they have need of us.
2. Fires set out in each quarter of the Roman encampment, indicating the orderly nature of the Roman forces.
3. So completely taken up with important matters.
4. *Who . . . life:* (You) who experience as a result of my exile a lack of proper education, the enduring fact of this hard life.
5. *aye . . . promised:* ever without hope to have the cultivated existence your noble birth promised.
6. People exposed to the sun. In England at this time, tanned skin denoted low social status.

GUIDERIUS Than be so,
Better to cease to be. Pray, sir, to th'army.
I and my brother are not known; yourself
So out of thought, and thereto° so o'ergrown,[7] *in addition*
Cannot be questioned.
ARVIRAGUS By this sun that shines,
I'll thither. What thing is't[8] that I never
Did see man die, scarce ever looked on blood
But that of coward hares, hot° goats, and venison, *lecherous*
Never bestrid a horse save one that had
A rider like myself, who ne'er wore rowel[9]
Nor iron on his heel! I am ashamed
To look upon the holy sun, to have
The benefit of his blest beams, remaining
So long a poor unknown.
GUIDERIUS By heavens, I'll go.
If you will bless me, sir, and give me leave,
I'll take the better care;° but if you will not, *be more careful*
The hazard therefore due[1] fall on me by
The hands of Romans.
ARVIRAGUS So say I, amen.
BELARIUS No reason I, since of your lives you set
So slight a valuation, should reserve
My cracked° one to more care. Have with you,° boys! *weakened / Come then*
If in your country° wars you chance to die, *country's*
That is my bed too, lads, and there I'll lie.
Lead, lead! [*aside*] The time seems long; their blood thinks
scorn° *disdains itself*
Till it fly out and show them princes born. *Exeunt.*

## 5.1

*Enter* POSTHUMUS *alone* [*dressed as a Roman, carrying a bloody cloth*].

POSTHUMUS Yea, bloody cloth, I'll keep thee, for I wished
Thou shouldst be colored thus. You married ones,
If each of you should take this course, how many
Must murder wives much better than themselves
For wrying° but a little? O Pisanio, *erring*
Every good servant does not all commands;
No bond but° to do just ones. Gods, if you *No obligation except*
Should have ta'en vengeance on my faults, I never
Had lived to put on this:° so had you saved *to undertake this deed*
The noble Imogen to repent, and struck
Me, wretch, more worth your vengeance. But alack,
You snatch some hence for little faults; that's love,
To have them fall no more.[1] You some permit
To second° ills with ills, each elder° worse, *reinforce / later fault*
And make them dread it, to the doers' thrift.[2]
But Imogen is your own; do your best wills,

7. So overgrown with hair or beard; so grown in years; so grown out of memory.
8. What a bad state of affairs it is.
9. Small rotating disk at the end of a spur. Wearing spurs was the privilege of gentlemen.
1. May the danger due to me (as a result of my disobedience).
5.1 Location: The Roman camp, Britain.
1. *that's . . . more:* that is a sign of love, to have them no longer sin.
2. And make them fear this escalation of sin, to their own benefit.

And make me blest to obey. I am brought hither
Among th'Italian gentry, and to fight
Against my lady's kingdom. 'Tis enough
That, Britain, I have killed thy mistress; peace,
I'll give no wound to thee. Therefore, good heavens,
Hear patiently my purpose: I'll disrobe me
Of these Italian weeds, and suit° myself — *dress*
As does a Briton peasant.
*[He changes his clothes.]*
So I'll fight
Against the part° I come with; so I'll die — *side*
For thee, O Imogen, even for whom my life
Is every breath a death; and thus unknown,
Pitied° nor hated, to the face of peril — *Neither pitied*
Myself I'll dedicate. Let me make men know
More valor in me than my habits° show. — *garments*
Gods, put the strength o'th' Leonati in me.
To shame the guise° o'th' world, I will begin — *customs; dress*
The fashion—less without and more within. *Exit.*

## 5.2[1]

*Enter* LUCIUS, GIACOMO, *and the Roman army at one door and the Briton army at another, Leonatus* POSTHUMUS *following[, dressed as] a poor soldier. They march over, and go out. Then enter again in skirmish* GIACOMO *and* POSTHUMUS: *he vanquisheth and disarmeth* GIACOMO, *and then leaves him.*

GIACOMO The heaviness and guilt within my bosom
Takes off° my manhood. I have belied° a lady, — *Destroys / slandered*
The princess of this country, and the air on't° — *of it*
Revengingly enfeebles me; or° could this carl,° — *otherwise / peasant*
A very drudge° of nature's, have subdued me — *slave*
In my profession? Knighthoods and honors borne
As I wear mine are titles but° of scorn. — *merely*
If that thy gentry, Britain, go before° — *surpass*
This lout as he exceeds our lords, the odds
Is that we scarce are men and you are gods. *Exit.*

*The battle continues; the Britons fly,* CYMBELINE *is taken. Then enter to his rescue* BELARIUS, GUIDERIUS, *and* ARVIRAGUS.

BELARIUS Stand, stand, we have th'advantage of the ground;
The lane is guarded. Nothing routs us but
The villainy of our fears.

GUIDERIUS *and* ARVIRAGUS Stand, stand, and fight.

*Enter* POSTHUMUS *[dressed as a poor soldier] and seconds the Britons. They rescue* CYMBELINE, *and exeunt. Then enter* LUCIUS, GIACOMO, *and* IMOGEN *[dressed as a man].*

5.2 Location: A field between the British and Roman camps, Britain.

1. TEXTUAL COMMENT Editors often disagree over how and where to divide the sequence of events represented from 5.2 to 5.4 in the present edition. This edition retains the divisions of the Folio, shifting only the stage direction at the end of F 5.3 to the beginning of 5.4 and adding an *Exeunt* to the end of 5.3. See Digital Edition TC 7.

LUCIUS Away, boy, from the troops, and save thyself!
For friends kill friends, and the disorder's such
As° war were hoodwinked.° *as if / blindfolded*
GIACOMO 'Tis their fresh supplies.
LUCIUS It is a day turned strangely. Or betimes
Let's reinforce, or fly.[2] *Exeunt.*

## 5.3

*Enter* POSTHUMUS *[dressed as a poor soldier], and a Briton* LORD.

LORD Cam'st thou from where they made the stand?
POSTHUMUS I did,
Though you, it seems, come from the fliers?
LORD Ay.
POSTHUMUS No blame be to you, sir, for all was lost,
But° that the heavens fought. The King himself *Had it not been*
Of his wings destitute,[1] the army broken,
And but° the backs of Britons seen, all flying *only*
Through a strait° lane; the enemy full-hearted,° *narrow / bold*
Lolling the tongue with slaught'ring,[2] having work
More plentiful than tools to do't, struck down
Some mortally, some slightly touched,° some falling *wounded*
Merely through fear, that the strait pass was dammed° *clogged*
With dead men hurt behind,[3] and cowards living
To die with length'ned shame.[4]
LORD Where was this lane?
POSTHUMUS Close by the battle, ditched, and walled with turf,
Which gave advantage to an ancient soldier,
An honest one, I warrant, who deserved
So long a breeding as his white beard came to,[5]
In doing this for 's country. Athwart° the lane, *Across*
He, with two striplings (lads more like° to run *likely*
The country base[6] than to commit such slaughter,
With faces fit for masks,[7] or rather fairer
Than those for preservation cased, or shame[8])
Made good° the passage, cried to those that fled: *Secured*
"Our Britain's harts° die flying, not our men; *deer*
To darkness fleet° souls that fly backwards. Stand, *rush*
Or we are Romans,[9] and will give you that° *(death)*
Like beasts which you shun beastly,° and may save *in cowardly fashion*
But to look back in frown.[1] Stand, stand!" These three,
Three thousand confident,[2] in act as many—
For three performers are the file,° when all *entire force*
The rest do nothing—with this word "Stand, stand!"

2. *Or betimes . . . fly:* Let us either promptly reinforce our troops or flee.
5.3 Location: Scene continues.
1. Deprived of his wings (that is, the troops to either side of the main division of the army).
2. With their tongues hanging out either from the labor of slaughter or from eagerness to commit the slaughter.
3. Hurt on their backs (as they were fleeing).
4. To die later after a life of prolonged shame.
5. *who . . . to:* who deserved to live so long again as his white beard indicated he had already lived.
6. *to run . . . base:* to play a children's game (prisoner's house) that involves running between two bases.
7. Gentlewomen wore masks to protect their complexions from the elements.
8. *fairer . . . shame:* more delicate than those covered with masks for protection ("preservation") or out of modesty.
9. Or we will behave like Romans.
1. *and may . . . frown:* and may prevent only by turning back upon the enemy with threatening face.
2. As confident as if they were three thousand.

Accommodated° by the place, more charming[3] — *Assisted*
With their own nobleness, which could have turned
A distaff to a lance,[4] gilded° pale looks; — *brought color to*
Part shame, part spirit renewed,[5] that some, turned coward
But by example[6]—Oh, a sin in war,
Damned in the first beginners[7]—'gan° to look — *began*
The way that they° did and to grin[8] like lions — *(the three)*
Upon the pikes o'th' hunters. Then began
A stop° i'th' chaser, a retire; anon° — *halt / soon*
A rout, confusion thick; forthwith they fly
Chickens, the way which they stooped eagles;[9] slaves,
The strides they victors made;[1] and now our cowards,
Like fragments° in hard voyages, became — *scraps of food*
The life o'th' need.[2] Having found the back door open
Of the unguarded hearts,[3] heavens, how they wound!
Some slain before,[4] some dying, some their friends
O'erborne° i'th' former wave, ten chased by one, — *Overwhelmed*
Are now each one the slaughterman of twenty.
Those that would die or ere° resist are grown — *before they would*
The mortal bugs° o'th' field. — *deadly terrors*

LORD This was strange chance:
A narrow lane, an old man, and two boys—

POSTHUMUS Nay, do not wonder at it. You are made
Rather to wonder at the things you hear
Than to work° any. Will you rhyme upon't, — *perform*
And vent it[5] for a mock'ry? Here is one:
"Two boys, an old man twice a boy,° a lane, — *in his second childhood*
Preserved the Britons, was the Romans' bane."

LORD Nay, be not angry, sir.

POSTHUMUS 'Lack,° to what end? — *Alas*
Who dares not stand° his foe, I'll be his friend; — *confront*
For if he'll do as he is made° to do, — *inclined*
I know he'll quickly fly my friendship too.
You have put° me into rhyme. — *forced*

LORD Farewell, you're angry. *Exit.*

POSTHUMUS Still going?° This is a lord! O noble misery,[6] — *Still running away*
To be i'th' field and ask "What news?" of me!
Today how many would have given their honors
To have saved their carcasses; took heel to do't
And yet died too.° I, in mine own woe charmed,[7] — *anyway*
Could not find Death where I did hear him groan,
Nor feel him where he struck. Being an ugly monster,
'Tis strange he hides him in fresh cups, soft beds,
Sweet words, or hath more ministers° than we — *other agents*
That draw his knives i'th' war. Well, I will find him;

3. *more charming:* casting a spell on others.
4. *could . . . lance:* that is, could have made women fight. The distaff, an instrument used in spinning wool, was a proverbial symbol of womanhood.
5. Shame inspired some, courage others.
6. Because of the example set by others.
7. In those who first set the example (of cowardly behavior).
8. To bare their teeth.
9. *forthwith . . . eagles:* straightway they (the Romans) fled like chickens along the passage down which they had just swooped like eagles.
1. *slaves . . . made:* like slaves, they retrace the steps they had made as victors.
2. Vital in the time of crisis.
3. *Having . . . hearts:* Having found unprotected the weak spot of these undefended souls (that is, the Romans).
4. Some that earlier were as good as dead.
5. And circulate ("vent") your rhymes.
6. What noble wretchedness.
7. In my despair preserved, as if by a charm.

[*He resumes his Roman clothes.*]
For being now a favorer to the Briton,[8]
No more° a Briton, I have resumed again — *I am no more*
The part° I came in. Fight I will no more, — *role*
But yield me to the veriest hind° that shall — *peasant*
Once touch my shoulder.° Great the slaughter is — *try to arrest me*
Here made by th' Roman; great the answer be° — *great the retaliation*
Britons must take. For me, my ransom's death:
On either side I come to spend my breath,
Which neither here I'll keep nor bear° again, — *carry away*
But end it by some means for Imogen.
*Enter two* [*Briton*] CAPTAINS, *and Soldiers.*
FIRST CAPTAIN Great Jupiter be praised, Lucius is taken.
'Tis thought the old man and his sons were angels.
SECOND CAPTAIN There was a fourth man, in a silly habit,° — *rustic garments*
That gave th'affront with them.
FIRST CAPTAIN So 'tis reported,
But none of 'em can be found. Stand, who's there?
POSTHUMUS A Roman,
Who had not now been drooping here, if seconds° — *supporters*
Had answered him.° — *followed him*
SECOND CAPTAIN Lay hands on him: a dog!
A leg of Rome shall not return to tell
What crows have pecked them here. He brags his service
As if he were of note:° bring him to th' King. [*Exeunt.*][9] — *high rank*

## 5.4

*Enter* CYMBELINE, BELARIUS, GUIDERIUS, ARVIRAGUS, PISANIO, *Roman captives*[, *and* JAILERS]. [*Enter*] *the* CAPTAINS [*who*] *present* POSTHUMUS [*dressed as a Roman*] *to* CYMBELINE, *who delivers him over to a* JAILER.
[*Exeunt all except*] POSTHUMUS *and* [*two*] JAILERS.
FIRST JAILER You shall not now be stol'n, you have locks upon you;
So graze as you find pasture.
SECOND JAILER Ay, or a stomach.
[*Exeunt* JAILERS.]
POSTHUMUS Most welcome bondage, for thou art a way,
I think, to liberty. Yet am I better
Than one that's sick o'th' gout, since he had rather
Groan so in perpetuity than be cured
By th' sure physician, death, who is the key
T'unbar these locks. My conscience, thou art fettered
More than my shanks° and wrists. You good gods, give me — *legs*
The penitent instrument to pick that bolt,
Then free for ever.[1] Is't enough I am sorry?
So children temporal fathers do appease;
Gods are more full of mercy. Must I repent,
I cannot do it better than in gyves,° — *shackles*

8. Since death is now looking kindly upon Britons.
9. TEXTUAL COMMENT F does not mark an exit here, but this edition adds an *Exeunt* in order to clear the stage of the large group of people present at the end of 5.3, and to mark the change of scene from the battlefield to a prison. See Digital Edition TC 7.

**5.4** Location: A prison.
1. *The . . . ever:* Give me penitence, the instrument to pick that lock (the lock on his conscience, which is fettered by guilt). Then (I am) free forever; then free me (by death).

Desired more than constrained.° To satisfy,° — *forced (upon me) / atone*
If of my freedom 'tis the main part,[2] take
No stricter render° of me than my all. — *repayment*
I know you are more clement° than vile men — *merciful*
Who of their broken° debtors take a third, — *bankrupt*
A sixth, a tenth, letting them thrive again
On their abatement;° that's not my desire. — *reduced amount*
For Imogen's dear life take mine, and though
'Tis not so dear,° yet 'tis a life; you coined it. — *valuable*
'Tween man and man they weigh not every stamp;
Though light, take pieces for the figure's sake,[3]
You rather mine, being yours.[4] And so, great powers,
If you will take this audit,° take this life, — *settle this account*
And cancel these cold bonds.[5] O Imogen,
I'll speak to thee in silence.

*[He sleeps.] Solemn music [plays]. Enter (as in an apparition)* SICILIUS *Leonatus (father to Posthumus, an old man, attired like a warrior), leading in his hand an ancient matron (his wife, and* MOTHER *to Posthumus), with music before them. Then, after other music, follow the two young Leonati (*BROTHERS *to Posthumus), with wounds as they died in the wars. They circle* POSTHUMUS *round as he lies sleeping.*[6]

SICILIUS No more, thou thunder-master,[7] show thy spite on mortal flies.° — *frail creatures*
With Mars° fall out, with Juno° chide, that° thy adulteries — *god of war / Jove's wife / who*
Rates° and revenges. — *Berates*
Hath my poor boy done aught but well, whose face I never saw?
I died whilst in the womb he stayed, attending nature's law.[8]
Whose father then—as men report, thou orphans' father art—
Thou shouldst have been, and shielded him from this earth-vexing smart.[9]

MOTHER Lucina° lent not me her aid, but took me in my throes, — *goddess of childbirth*
That from me was Posthumus ripped, came crying 'mongst his foes,
A thing of pity.

SICILIUS Great nature like his ancestry molded the stuff° so fair — *substance*
That he deserved the praise o'th' world as great Sicilius' heir.

FIRST BROTHER When once he was mature for man,° in Britain where was he — *had matured into manhood*
That could stand up his parallel, or fruitful° object be — *life-giving*
In eye of Imogen, that best could deem° his dignity?° — *judge / worth*

2. If it is the most important element in freeing me from guilt.
3. *'Tween . . . sake:* In business dealings between men, they do not weigh every coin ("stamp"). Even though some coins are deficient in weight ("light"), they accept them because of the image (of the King) stamped on them.
4. You should be more inclined to accept my coin (me), since your image is stamped on me. This line refers to the Christian belief that humans are made in the image of God.
5. These old legal agreements; these cruel links with life; these harsh fetters.
6. TEXTUAL COMMENT Before G. Wilson Knight argued for their authenticity in 1947, critics dismissed lines 29 SD–92 SD as un-Shakespearean, in part because of the archaic quality of the ghosts' speeches, which are preserved here in the iambic heptameter in which some of them appear in F. Iambic heptameters are very long poetic lines having fourteen syllables divided into seven poetic feet with the stress falling on the second syllable of each foot. See Digital Edition TC 8.
7. Jupiter, or Jove, the king of the gods, often made himself known to humans through thunder and lightning.
8. Awaiting the decree of nature (for his birth).
9. From this suffering that afflicts all humans.

MOTHER With marriage wherefore° was he mocked, to be exiled and thrown *why*
From Leonati seat, and cast from her, his dearest one,
Sweet Imogen?
SICILIUS Why did you suffer Giacomo, slight° thing of Italy, *worthless*
To taint his nobler heart and brain with needless jealousy,
And to become the geck° and scorn o'th' other's villainy? *dupe*
SECOND BROTHER For this, from stiller seats[1] we came, our parents and us twain,
That striking in our country's cause, fell bravely and were slain,
Our fealty and Tenantius'° right with honor to maintain. *(Cymbeline's father)*
FIRST BROTHER Like hardiment° Posthumus hath to Cymbeline performed: *Similar bold deeds*
Then Jupiter, thou king of gods, why hast thou thus adjourned° *deferred*
The graces for his merits due, being all to dolors° turned? *sorrows*
SICILIUS Thy crystal window ope,° look out, no longer exercise *open*
Upon a valiant race thy harsh and potent injuries.
MOTHER Since, Jupiter, our son is good, take off his miseries.
SICILIUS Peep through thy marble mansion, help, or we poor ghosts will cry
To th' shining synod° of the rest[2] against thy deity.° *assembly / godhead*
BROTHERS Help, Jupiter, or we appeal, and from thy justice fly.

JUPITER *descends in thunder and lightning, sitting upon an eagle. He throws a thunderbolt. The ghosts fall on their knees.*

JUPITER No more, you petty spirits of region low,
Offend our hearing. Hush! How dare you ghosts
Accuse the thunderer, whose bolt, you know,
Sky-planted,° batters all rebelling coasts? *Rooted in the heavens*
Poor shadows of Elysium, hence, and rest
Upon your never-withering banks of flowers.
Be not with mortal accidents° oppressed; *events*
No care of yours it is; you know 'tis ours.
Whom best I love, I cross,° to make my gift, *thwart*
The more delayed, delighted.° Be content: *the more pleasing*
Your low-laid son our godhead will uplift;
His comforts thrive, his trials well are spent.° *ended*
Our Jovial star° reigned at his birth, and in *The planet Jupiter*
Our temple was he married. Rise, and fade.
He shall be lord of Lady Imogen,
And happier much by his affliction made.
This tablet lay upon his breast, wherein
Our pleasure his full fortune doth confine.[3]

[*He gives the ghosts a tablet which they lay upon Posthumus' breast.*]

And so away. No farther with your din
Express impatience, lest you stir up mine.
Mount, eagle, to my palace crystalline. [*He*] *ascends.*
SICILIUS He came in thunder; his celestial breath
Was sulfurous to smell.[4] The holy eagle

1. From calmer regions (alluding to the Elysian Fields—in classical mythology the abode of the blessed after death).
2. The rest of the gods.
3. *wherein . . . confine:* wherein it is our pleasure his great fortune precisely to set forth.
4. Sulfur was popularly associated with thunder and lightning. As a constituent of gunpowder, its smell may have been detectable in the theater when gunpowder was used.

Stooped, as to foot us.[5] His ascension is
More sweet than our blest fields. His royal bird
Prunes the immortal wing and claws his beak,
As when his god is pleased.

ALL THE GHOSTS Thanks, Jupiter.

SICILIUS The marble pavement[6] closes; he is entered
His radiant roof. Away, and, to be blest,
Let us with care perform his great behest. [*The* GHOSTS] *vanish.*

POSTHUMUS [*awaking*] Sleep, thou hast been a grandsire and begot
A father to me; and thou hast created
A mother and two brothers. But oh, scorn,° — *bitter mockery*
Gone! They went hence so soon as they were born,
And so I am awake. Poor wretches that depend
On greatness' favor dream as I have done,
Wake, and find nothing. But, alas, I swerve.° — *go astray*
Many dream not to find, neither deserve,
And yet are steeped in favors; so am I,
That have this golden chance and know not why.
What fairies haunt this ground? A book? O rare one,
Be not, as is our fangled world,[7] a garment
Nobler than that it covers. Let thy effects
So follow to° be most unlike our courtiers, — *that they*
As good as promise.

(*Reads.*) "Whenas° a lion's whelp shall, to himself unknown, without seeking find, and be embraced by a piece of tender air; and when from a stately cedar shall be lopped branches which, being dead many years, shall after revive, be jointed to the old stock, and freshly grow; then shall Posthumus end his miseries, Britain be fortunate and flourish in peace and plenty." — *When*

'Tis still a dream, or else such stuff as madmen
Tongue° and brain° not; either both, or nothing, — *Speak / understand*
Or senseless speaking,° or a speaking such — *Either meaningless speech*
As sense° cannot untie. Be what it is, — *reason*
The action of my life is like it, which I'll keep,
If but for sympathy.[8]

*Enter* JAILER.

JAILER Come, sir, are you ready for death?

POSTHUMUS Over-roasted rather; ready long ago.

JAILER Hanging[9] is the word, sir. If you be ready for that, you are well cooked.

POSTHUMUS So if I prove a good repast to the spectators, the dish pays the shot.[1]

JAILER A heavy reckoning for you, sir. But the comfort is, you shall be called to no more payments, fear no more tavern bills, which are as often the sadness of parting as the procuring of mirth. You come in faint for want of meat, depart reeling with too much drink; sorry that you have paid too much, and sorry that you are paid too much;[2] purse and

5. Swooped as if to seize us in its talons.
6. Referring to the closing of the trapdoor in the ceiling above the stage, which represents the floor ("pavement") of the heavens.
7. Our world so obsessed with fashions.
8. If only because of the similarity.
9. Death by hanging, with a pun on "hanging" as referring to the practice of hanging up raw meat before cooking.
1. The food pays the reckoning; I am worth what it costs to hang me.
2. Subdued by too much drink.

brain, both empty; the brain the heavier for being too light,° *foolish*
the purse too light, being drawn of heaviness.[3] Oh, of this
contradiction you shall now be quit. Oh, the charity of a
penny cord! It sums up thousands in a trice.° You have no *an instant*
true debitor and creditor° but it: of what's past, is, and to come, *account book*
the discharge.° Your neck, sir, is pen, book, and counters;[4] *release from debt*
so the acquittance° follows. *deliverance*

POSTHUMUS I am merrier to die than thou art to live.

JAILER Indeed, sir, he that sleeps feels not the toothache; but
a man that were to° sleep your sleep, and a hangman to help *were about to*
him to bed, I think he would change places with his officer;° *(the hangman)*
for look you, sir, you know not which way you shall go.

POSTHUMUS Yes, indeed do I, fellow.

JAILER Your death has eyes in 's head then; I have not seen
him so pictured.[5] You must either be directed by some that
take upon them° to know, or take upon yourself that which I *some who profess*
am sure you do not know, or jump° the after-enquiry on your *risk*
own peril; and how you shall speed° in your journey's end I *succeed*
think you'll never return to tell one.

POSTHUMUS I tell thee, fellow, there are none want° eyes to *lacking*
direct them the way I am going, but such as wink° and will *shut their eyes*
not use them.

JAILER What an infinite mock is this, that a man should have
the best use of eyes to see the way of blindness!° I am sure *the way to death*
hanging's the way of winking.

*Enter a* MESSENGER.

MESSENGER Knock off his manacles: bring your prisoner to
the King.

POSTHUMUS Thou bring'st good news; I am called to be made
free.[6]

JAILER I'll be hanged then.

POSTHUMUS Thou shalt be then freer than a jailer; no bolts
for the dead.[7]

JAILER Unless a man would marry a gallows and beget young
gibbets, I never saw one so prone.° Yet, on my conscience, *eager*
there are verier knaves desire to live, for all° he be a Roman; *even though*
and there be some of them, too, that die against their wills;
so should I, if I were one. I would we were all of one mind,
and one mind good. Oh, there were desolation° of jailers and *the ruin*
gallowses! I speak against my present profit, but my wish
hath a preferment in't.[8] *Exeunt.*

## 5.5

*Enter* CYMBELINE, BELARIUS, GUIDERIUS, ARVIRAGUS, PISANIO, *and* LORDS.

CYMBELINE Stand by my side, you whom the gods have made
Preservers of my throne. Woe is my heart

3. Being emptied of the money that makes it heavy.
4. Metal tokens used for making calculations.
5. So depicted (referring to visual representations of death as a skeleton or skull with no eyes).
6. Posthumus means "set free by death." The Jailer thinks he means "set free from prison."
7. Most editions, following F2, have everyone leave the stage here except the Jailer. However, the Jailer himself has been ordered to bring the prisoner to the King, which would mean that he must not be separated from Posthumus.
8. Had a promotion in it (implying that a world without the need for jailers could offer him better employment).
**5.5** Location: The camp of Cymbeline, Britain.

That the poor soldier that so richly fought,
Whose rags shamed gilded arms, whose naked breast
Stepped before targes of proof,[1] cannot be found.
He shall be happy that can find him, if
Our grace can make him so.

BELARIUS I never saw
Such noble fury in so poor a thing,
Such precious deeds in one that promised naught
But beggary and poor looks.

CYMBELINE No tidings of him?

PISANIO He hath been searched° among the dead and living, *sought*
But no trace of him.

CYMBELINE To my grief, I am
The heir of his reward, which I will add
[*to* BELARIUS, GUIDERIUS, *and* ARVIRAGUS] To you, the liver, heart, and brain of Britain,
By whom I grant she lives. 'Tis now the time
To ask of whence you are. Report it.

BELARIUS Sir,
In Cambria° are we born, and gentlemen. *Wales*
Further to boast were neither true nor modest,
Unless I add we are honest.

CYMBELINE Bow your knees.
[*They kneel. He knights them.*]
Arise, my knights o'th' battle.[2] I create you
Companions to our person, and will fit° you *supply*
With dignities becoming your estates.° *(new) rank*

*Enter* CORNELIUS *and* LADIES.

There's business in these faces. Why so sadly
Greet you our victory? You look like Romans,
And not o'th' court of Britain.

CORNELIUS Hail, great King.
To sour your happiness, I must report
The Queen is dead.

CYMBELINE Who worse than a physician
Would this report become? But I consider,
By medicine life may be prolonged, yet death
Will seize the doctor too. How ended she?

CORNELIUS With horror, madly dying, like her life,
Which, being cruel to the world, concluded
Most cruel to herself. What she confessed
I will report, so please you. These her women
Can trip me° if I err, who with wet cheeks *correct me*
Were present when she finished.

CYMBELINE Prithee, say.

CORNELIUS First, she confessed she never loved you, only
Affected° greatness got by you, not you; *Desired*
Married your royalty, was wife to your place,° *position*
Abhorred your person.

CYMBELINE She alone knew this,
And but° she spoke it dying, I would not *except that*
Believe her lips in opening it. Proceed.

1. *targes of proof:* shields whose strength had been tested.

2. A special group of knights who won their titles for extraordinary bravery on the battlefield.

CORNELIUS Your daughter, whom she bore in hand° to love — *she pretended*
With such integrity, she did confess
Was as a scorpion to her sight, whose life,
But that her flight prevented it, she had
Ta'en off° by poison. — *Ended*
CYMBELINE O most delicate° fiend! — *subtle*
Who is't can read a woman? Is there more?
CORNELIUS More, sir, and worse. She did confess she had
For you a mortal mineral° which, being took, — *a deadly poison*
Should by the minute feed on life and, lingering,
By inches waste you. In which time she purposed
By watching,° weeping, tendance,[3] kissing, to — *staying awake*
O'ercome you with her show;° and in time, — *performance*
When she had fitted you with° her craft, to work — *shaped you by*
Her son into th'adoption of the crown;[4]
But failing of her end by his strange absence,
Grew shameless-desperate, opened,° in despite — *revealed*
Of heaven and men, her purposes, repented
The evils she hatched were not effected; so
Despairing, died.
CYMBELINE Heard you all this, her women?
LADIES We did, so please your highness.
CYMBELINE Mine eyes
Were not in fault, for she was beautiful;
Mine ears that heard her flattery, nor my heart
That thought her like her seeming.° It had been vicious° — *appearance / wrong*
To have mistrusted her. Yet, O my daughter,
That it was folly in me thou mayst say,
And prove it in thy feeling.[5] Heaven mend all!

*Enter* LUCIUS, GIACOMO, [*the* SOOTHSAYER,] *and other Roman prisoners* [*including*] POSTHUMUS *Leonatus* [*dressed as a Roman, following*] *behind, and* IMOGEN [*dressed as a man, all guarded by Soldiers*].

Thou com'st not, Caius, now for tribute: that
The Britons have razed out,° though with the loss — *erased*
Of many a bold one; whose kinsmen have made suit
That their good souls° may be appeased with slaughter — *(of the dead Britons)*
Of you their captives, which ourself have granted.
So think of your estate.° — *condition*
LUCIUS Consider, sir, the chance of war; the day
Was yours by accident. Had it gone with us,
We should not, when the blood was cool, have threatened
Our prisoners with the sword. But since the gods
Will have it thus, that nothing but our lives
May be called ransom, let it come. Sufficeth
A Roman with a Roman's heart can suffer—
Augustus lives to think on't[6]—and so much
For my peculiar care.° This one thing only — *concern for myself*
I will entreat: my boy, a Briton born,
Let him be ransomed. Never master had
A page so kind, so duteous, diligent,

3. Showing attention to you.
4. *to work . . . crown:* to work her son into the position of heir to the crown.
5. And find it true by your experience.
6. Augustus lives and can consider what to do.

So tender over his occasions,° true, *thoughtful of his needs*
So feat,° so nurse-like; let his virtue join *graceful*
With my request, which I'll make bold your highness
Cannot deny. He hath done no Briton harm,
Though he have served a Roman. Save him, sir,
And spare no blood beside.° *no one else*

CYMBELINE I have surely seen him;
His favor° is familiar to me. [*to* IMOGEN] Boy, *face*
Thou hast looked thyself into my grace,[7]
And art mine own. I know not why, wherefore,
To say, "Live, boy." Ne'er thank thy master. Live,
And ask of Cymbeline what boon° thou wilt, *reward*
Fitting my bounty and thy state;° I'll give it, *rank*
Yea, though thou do demand a prisoner
The noblest ta'en.

IMOGEN I humbly thank your highness.

LUCIUS I do not bid thee beg my life, good lad,
And yet I know thou wilt.

IMOGEN No, no; alack,
There's other work in hand. I see a thing[8]
Bitter to me as death. Your life, good master,
Must shuffle° for itself. *shift*

LUCIUS The boy disdains me;
He leaves me, scorns me. Briefly die their joys
That place them on the truth of girls and boys.[9]
Why stands he so perplexed?

CYMBELINE What wouldst thou, boy?
I love thee more and more. Think more and more
What's best to ask. Know'st him thou look'st on? Speak,
Wilt have him live? Is he thy kin, thy friend?

IMOGEN He is a Roman, no more kin to me
Than I to your highness, who, being born your vassal,
Am something nearer.

CYMBELINE Wherefore ey'st him so?

IMOGEN I'll tell you, sir, in private, if you please
To give me hearing.

CYMBELINE Ay, with all my heart,
And lend my best attention. What's thy name?

IMOGEN Fidele, sir.

CYMBELINE Thou'rt my good youth, my page,
I'll be thy master. Walk with me, speak freely.
[CYMBELINE *and* IMOGEN *speak apart.*]

BELARIUS [*aside to* GUIDERIUS *and* ARVIRAGUS] Is not this boy revived from death?

ARVIRAGUS One sand° another *One grain of sand*
Not more resembles that° sweet rosy lad *than he resembles that*
Who died and was Fidele. What think you?

GUIDERIUS The same dead thing alive.

BELARIUS Peace, peace, see further. He eyes us not; forbear.
Creatures may be alike. Were't he, I am sure
He would have spoke to us.

7. You have by your appearance gained my favor.
8. Referring to the ring that she gave to Posthumus and that is now on Giacomo's finger.
9. *Briefly . . . boys:* Quickly dies the happiness of those who depend on the fidelity of girls and boys.

GUIDERIUS But we see° him dead. *saw*
BELARIUS Be silent; let's see further.
PISANIO [*aside*] It is my mistress.
Since she is living, let the time run on
To good or bad.
CYMBELINE [*to* IMOGEN] Come, stand thou by our side;
Make thy demand aloud. [*to* GIACOMO] Sir, step you forth.
Give answer to this boy, and do it freely,
Or by our greatness and the grace of it,
Which is our honor, bitter torture shall
Winnow° the truth from falsehood. —On, speak to him. *Separate*
IMOGEN My boon is that this gentleman may render° *declare*
Of whom he had this ring.
POSTHUMUS [*aside*] What's that to him?
CYMBELINE That diamond upon your finger, say
How came it yours?
GIACOMO Thou'lt torture me to leave° unspoken that *for leaving*
Which to be spoke would torture thee.
CYMBELINE How? Me?
GIACOMO I am glad to be constrained to utter that
Which torments me to conceal. By villainy
I got this ring; 'twas Leonatus' jewel,
Whom thou didst banish; and, which more may grieve thee,
As it doth me, a nobler sir ne'er lived
Twixt sky and ground. Wilt thou hear more, my lord?
CYMBELINE All that belongs to this.
GIACOMO That paragon, thy daughter,
For whom my heart drops blood, and my false spirits
Quail to remember—give me leave, I faint.
CYMBELINE My daughter? What of her? Renew thy strength.
I had rather thou shouldst live while nature will° *as long as nature allows*
Than die ere I hear more. Strive, man, and speak.
GIACOMO Upon a time—unhappy was the clock[1]
That struck the hour; it was in Rome—accursed
The mansion where; 'twas at a feast—oh, would
Our viands had been poisoned (or at least
Those which I heaved to head°); the good Posthumus— *raised to my mouth*
What should I say? He was too good to be
Where ill men were, and was the best of all
Amongst the rar'st of good ones—sitting sadly,
Hearing us praise our loves of Italy
For beauty that made barren the swelled boast[2]
Of him that best could speak; for feature, laming
The shrine of Venus or straight-pight Minerva,[3]
Postures beyond brief nature;[4] for condition,° *character*
A shop of all the qualities that man
Loves woman for; besides that hook of wiving,° *bait for marriage*
Fairness which strikes the eye—

1. TEXTUAL COMMENT Some editions punctuate the first eight lines of Giacomo's speech with nine dashes, which may suggest that the speech's broken and ungrammatical syntax reflects its speaker's anguish. Such difficult syntax, found elsewhere in the play, may also suggest Shakespeare's experiments with the limits of English grammar. See Digital Edition TC 9.
2. For beauty so great that it rendered hollow even the exaggerated boasts.
3. *for . . . Minerva:* for looks rendering deficient even the body (shrine) of the goddess of love (Venus) or the magisterial goddess of the arts (Minerva). *straight-pight:* uprightly fixed; with erect posture.
4. Forms surpassing those of mere mortals.

CYMBELINE I stand on fire.
Come to the matter.
GIACOMO All too soon I shall,
Unless thou wouldst grieve quickly. This Posthumus,
Most like a noble lord in love, and one
That had a royal lover, took his hint,
And not dispraising whom we praised—therein
He was as calm as virtue—he began
His mistress' picture, which by his tongue being made,
And then a mind put in't, either our brags
Were cracked° of kitchen trulls, or his description — *uttered in defense*
Proved us unspeaking sots.° — *fools incapable of speech*
CYMBELINE Nay, nay, to th' purpose.
GIACOMO Your daughter's chastity—there it begins.
He spake of her as° Dian had hot° dreams — *as if / lustful*
And she alone were cold;° whereat I, wretch, — *chaste*
Made scruple of° his praise, and wagered with him — *Disputed*
Pieces of gold, 'gainst this which then he wore
Upon his honored finger, to attain
In suit° the place of 's bed and win this ring — *By urging my suit*
By hers and mine adultery. He, true knight,
No lesser of her honor confident
Than I did truly find her, stakes this ring—
And would so had it been a carbuncle
Of Phoebus' wheel,[5] and might so safely had it
Been all the worth of 's car.° Away to Britain — *worth the entire chariot*
Post° I in this design. Well may you, sir, — *Hasten*
Remember me at court, where I was taught
Of° your chaste daughter the wide difference — *By*
Twixt amorous and villainous. Being thus quenched
Of hope, not longing,° mine Italian brain — *though not of desire*
Gan° in your duller Britain[6] operate — *Began*
Most vilely—for my vantage,° excellent. — *profit*
And, to be brief, my practice° so prevailed — *deceit*
That I returned with simular° proof enough — *pretended; specious*
To make the noble Leonatus mad,
By wounding his belief in her renown° — *reputation*
With tokens thus and thus; averring° notes — *confirming*
Of chamber-hanging, pictures, this her bracelet
(Oh, cunning, how I got it!) nay, some marks
Of secret on her person, that he could not
But think her bond of chastity quite cracked,
I having ta'en the forfeit.[7] Whereupon—
Methinks I see him now—
POSTHUMUS [*coming forward*] Ay, so thou dost,
Italian fiend! Ay me, most credulous fool,
Egregious murderer, thief, anything
That's due[8] to all the villains past, in being,
To come! Oh, give me cord, or knife, or poison,
Some upright justicer!° Thou, King, send out — *judge*

5. *had . . . wheel:* even if it had been a precious stone from the wheel of the sun god's chariot.
6. Alluding to the belief that England's northern climate made its inhabitants sluggish and slow of wit.
7. Believing I had taken what she gave up (her chastity).
8. *anything / That's due:* any name that's owed.

For torturers ingenious: it is I
That all th'abhorred things o'th' earth amend[9]
By being worse than they. I am Posthumus,
That killed thy daughter—villain-like, I lie—
That caused a lesser villain than myself,
A sacrilegious thief, to do't. The temple
Of virtue was she; yea, and she herself.° *she was virtue herself*
Spit and throw stones, cast mire upon me, set
The dogs o'th' street to bay me. Every villain
Be called Posthumus Leonatus, and
Be villainy less than 'twas.[1] O Imogen!
My queen, my life, my wife, O Imogen,
Imogen, Imogen!

IMOGEN Peace, my lord, hear, hear—

POSTHUMUS Shall 's have a play of this? Thou scornful page,
There lie thy part![2]

[*He strikes her and she falls.*]

PISANIO O gentlemen, help!
Mine and your mistress! O my lord Posthumus,
You ne'er killed Imogen till now. Help, help!
Mine honored lady—

CYMBELINE Does the world go round?

POSTHUMUS How comes these staggers[3] on me?

PISANIO Wake, my mistress.

CYMBELINE If this be so, the gods do mean to strike me
To death with mortal° joy. *death-causing*

PISANIO How fares my mistress?

IMOGEN Oh, get thee from my sight!
Thou gav'st me poison. Dangerous fellow, hence!
Breathe not where princes are.

CYMBELINE The tune of Imogen!

PISANIO Lady, the gods throw stones of sulfur° on me if *thunderbolts*
That box I gave you was not thought by me
A precious thing; I had it from the Queen.

CYMBELINE New matter still.

IMOGEN It poisoned me.

CORNELIUS O gods!
I left out one thing which the Queen confessed,
Which must approve° thee honest. "If Pisanio *prove*
Have," said she, "given his mistress that confection° *compound*
Which I gave him for cordial, she is served
As I would serve a rat."

CYMBELINE What's this, Cornelius?

CORNELIUS The Queen, sir, very oft importuned me
To temper° poisons for her, still° pretending *mix / always*
The satisfaction of her knowledge only
In killing creatures vile, as cats and dogs
Of no esteem.° I, dreading that her purpose *value*
Was of more danger, did compound for her
A certain stuff which, being ta'en, would cease

9. Who makes all loathsome things seem better.
1. *Every . . . 'twas:* May the word "villainy" be less abhorrent than it was, since "Posthumus Leonatus" has replaced it.
2. Your part (in this play) is to lie there.
3. A disease, usually of horses, that causes an unsteady walk; dizziness.

The present power of life, but in short time
All offices of nature° should again — *All natural faculties*
Do their due functions. Have you ta'en of it?

IMOGEN Most like° I did, for I was dead. — *likely*

BELARIUS [*aside to* GUIDERIUS *and* ARVIRAGUS] My boys,
There was our error.

GUIDERIUS This is sure Fidele.

IMOGEN Why did you throw your wedded lady from you?
Think that you are upon a rock,[4] and now
Throw me again.

[*She embraces* POSTHUMUS.]

POSTHUMUS Hang there like fruit, my soul,
Till the tree die.

CYMBELINE How now, my flesh, my child?
What, mak'st thou me a dullard° in this act? — *sluggish performer*
Wilt thou not speak to me?

IMOGEN Your blessing, sir.

BELARIUS [*aside to* GUIDERIUS *and* ARVIRAGUS] Though you did love this youth, I blame ye not;
You had a motive° for't. — *reason*

CYMBELINE My tears that fall
Prove holy water on thee! Imogen,
Thy mother's dead.

IMOGEN I am sorry for't, my lord.

CYMBELINE Oh, she was naught,° and 'long° of her it was — *worthless / because*
That we meet here so strangely.° But her son — *like strangers*
Is gone, we know not how nor where.

PISANIO My lord,
Now fear is from me, I'll speak truth. Lord Cloten,
Upon my lady's missing,° came to me — *absence*
With his sword drawn, foamed at the mouth, and swore
If I discovered° not which way she was gone — *revealed*
It was my instant death. By accident° — *chance*
I had a feignèd letter of my master's[5]
Then in my pocket, which directed him
To seek her on the mountains near to Milford,
Where in a frenzy, in my master's garments,
Which he enforced from me, away he posts° — *hastens*
With unchaste purpose and with oath to violate
My lady's honor. What became of him,
I further know not.

GUIDERIUS Let me end the story:
I slew him there.

CYMBELINE Marry, the gods forfend!
I would not thy good deeds° should from my lips — *(on the battlefield)*
Pluck a hard sentence. Prithee, valiant youth,
Deny't again.° — *Take it back*

GUIDERIUS I have spoke it, and I did it.

CYMBELINE He was a prince.

GUIDERIUS A most incivil° one. The wrongs he did me — *barbarous*
Were nothing prince-like, for he did provoke me

4. This is a disputed passage; some editions emend to "lock," suggesting that Imogen is referring to a wrestling hold.

5. Referring to the letter written by Posthumus to mislead Imogen.

With language that would make me spurn the sea
If it could so roar to me. I cut off 's head,
And am right glad he is not standing here
To tell this tale of mine.[6]

CYMBELINE I am sorrow for thee.
By thine own tongue thou art condemned and must
Endure our law. Thou'rt dead.

IMOGEN That headless man
I thought had been my lord.

CYMBELINE [*to Soldiers*] Bind the offender,
And take him from our presence.

BELARIUS Stay, sir King.
This man is better than the man he slew,
As well descended as thyself, and hath
More of thee merited than a band of Clotens
Had ever scar for.[7] Let his arms alone;
They were not born for bondage.

CYMBELINE Why, old soldier,
Wilt thou undo the worth thou art unpaid for[8]
By tasting of our wrath? How of descent
As good as we?

ARVIRAGUS In that he spake too far.

CYMBELINE[9] And thou shalt die for't.

BELARIUS We will die all three,
But I will prove° that two on 's° are as good *Unless I prove / of us*
As I have given out him. My sons, I must
For mine own part unfold a dangerous speech,
Though haply° well for you. *perhaps*

ARVIRAGUS Your danger's ours.

GUIDERIUS And our good his.

BELARIUS Have at it, then. By leave,[1]
Thou hadst, great King, a subject, who
Was called Belarius.

CYMBELINE What of him?
He is a banished traitor.

BELARIUS He it is that hath
Assumed° this age. Indeed a banished man; *Reached*
I know not how a traitor.

CYMBELINE [*to Soldiers*] Take him hence.
The whole world shall not save him.

BELARIUS Not too hot.° *fast*
First pay me for the nursing of thy sons,
And let it° be confiscate all so soon *(the payment)*
As I have received it.

CYMBELINE Nursing of my sons?

BELARIUS I am too blunt and saucy. [*He kneels.*] Here's my knee.
Ere I arise I will prefer° my sons; *advance*
Then spare not the old father. Mighty sir,

6. To tell a tale of cutting off my head.
7. *than . . . for:* than an army of Clotens ever earned by their battle scars.
8. The merit you are not yet rewarded for.
9. It is unclear to whom—Arviragus or Belarius—Cymbeline speaks the next line. Arviragus has just addressed Cymbeline, and one might expect the King's reply to be directed to him. Belarius, however, made the offending remark about Guiderius being of as good birth as Cloten, and the threat of death probably applies to him.
1. Let's begin, then. With your permission.

These two young gentlemen that call me father
And think they are my sons are none of mine.
They are the issue° of your loins, my liege, *offspring*
And blood of your begetting.

CYMBELINE How? My issue?

BELARIUS So sure as you your father's. I, old Morgan,[2]
Am that Belarius whom you sometime° banished. *once*
Your pleasure was my mere offense,[3] my punishment
Itself, and all my treason; that I suffered
Was all the harm I did. These gentle princes,
For such and so they are, these twenty years
Have I trained up; those arts° they have, as I *accomplishments*
Could put into them. My breeding was, sir,
As your highness knows. Their nurse Euriphile,
Whom for the theft I wedded, stole these children
Upon my banishment. I moved° her to't, *persuaded*
Having received the punishment before
For that which I did then. Beaten° for loyalty *Having been beaten*
Excited me to treason. Their dear loss,
The more of you 'twas felt, the more it shaped° *suited*
Unto° my end° of stealing them. But, gracious sir, *With / purpose*
Here are your sons again, and I must lose
Two of the sweet'st companions in the world.
The benediction of these covering heavens
Fall on their heads like dew, for they are worthy
To inlay heaven with stars.° *To become constellations*

CYMBELINE Thou weep'st and speak'st.
The service that you three have done is more
Unlike° than this thou tell'st. I lost my children; *Improbable*
If these be they, I know not how to wish
A pair of worthier sons.

BELARIUS Be pleased awhile.
This gentleman, whom I call Polydore,
Most worthy prince, as yours is true Guiderius.
This gentleman, my Cadwal, Arviragus,
Your younger princely son. He, sir, was lapped° *wrapped*
In a most curious° mantle, wrought by th' hand *delicately fashioned*
Of his queen mother, which for more probation° *proof*
I can with ease produce.

CYMBELINE Guiderius had
Upon his neck a mole, a sanguine° star; *blood-red*
It was a mark of wonder.

BELARIUS This is he,
Who hath upon him still that natural stamp.
It was wise Nature's end in the donation° *purpose in giving it*
To be his evidence now.

CYMBELINE Oh, what am I?
A mother to the birth of three? Ne'er mother
Rejoiced deliverance more.[4] Blest pray you be,

2. Morgan was the Welsh name Belarius assumed during the years he spent in Wales.
3. What you pleased (to accuse me of) was my entire offense.
4. Never did giving birth cause a mother to rejoice more.

That, after this strange starting from your orbs,[5]
You may reign in them now! O Imogen,
Thou hast lost by this a kingdom.

IMOGEN No, my lord,
I have got two worlds by't. O my gentle brothers,
Have we thus met? Oh, never say hereafter
But I am truest speaker. You called me brother
When I was but your sister, I you brothers,
When we were so indeed.

CYMBELINE Did you e'er meet?

ARVIRAGUS Ay, my good lord.

GUIDERIUS And at first meeting loved,
Continued so until we thought he died.

CORNELIUS By the Queen's dram she swallowed.

CYMBELINE O rare instinct!
When shall I hear all through? This fierce° abridgment *drastic*
Hath to it circumstantial branches which
Distinction should be rich in.[6] Where? How lived you?
And when came you to serve our Roman captive?
How parted with your brothers? How first met them?
Why fled you from the court, and whither? These,
And your three motives° to the battle, with *the motives of you three*
I know not how much more should be demanded,
And all the other by-dependences,° *circumstances*
From chance° to chance. But nor° the time nor place *occurrence / neither*
Will serve our long interrogatories.° See, *lengthy questioning*
Posthumus anchors upon Imogen,
And she, like harmless lightning, throws her eye
On him, her brothers, me, her master, hitting
Each object with a joy: the counterchange
Is severally in all.[7] Let's quit this ground,
And smoke° the temple with our sacrifices. *fill with smoke*
[*to* BELARIUS] Thou art my brother; so we'll hold thee ever.

IMOGEN [*to* BELARIUS] You are my father too, and did relieve° me *save*
To see this gracious season.

CYMBELINE All o'erjoyed,
Save these in bonds. Let them be joyful too,
For they shall taste our comfort.

IMOGEN My good master,
I will yet do you service.

LUCIUS Happy be you!

CYMBELINE The forlorn° soldier that so nobly fought, *wretched*
He would have well becomed this place, and graced
The thankings of a king.

POSTHUMUS I am, sir,
The soldier that did company these three
In poor beseeming.° 'Twas a fitment[8] for *appearance*
The purpose I then followed. That I was he,
Speak, Giacomo: I had you down, and might
Have made you finish.° *die*

5. After this unnatural displacement from your rightful positions. Referring to astrological theories that each heavenly body moved in its proper orb, or circle, around the earth. For a planet to move outside its orb caused disturbances in the heavens.

6. *circumstantial . . . in:* many ramifications that will provide particulars in rich abundance.

7. *the . . . all:* the exchange (of glances) passes from each to each.

8. A suitable disguise.

GIACOMO [*kneels*] I am down again,
But now my heavy conscience sinks my knee,
As then your force did. Take that life, beseech you,
Which I so often owe;° but your ring first, *owe so many times over*
And here the bracelet of the truest princess
That ever swore her faith.
POSTHUMUS Kneel not to me.
The power that I have on you is to spare you;
The malice towards you to forgive you. Live,
And deal with others better.
CYMBELINE Nobly doomed!° *sentenced*
We'll learn our freeness of a son-in-law:
Pardon's the word to all.
ARVIRAGUS You holp° us, sir, *helped*
As° you did mean indeed to be our brother; *As if*
Joyed are we that you are.
POSTHUMUS Your servant, princes. [*to* LUCIUS] Good my lord of Rome,
Call forth your soothsayer. As I slept, methought
Great Jupiter, upon his eagle backed,° *riding on his eagle*
Appeared to me with other spritely shows° *ghostly apparitions*
Of mine own kindred. When I waked, I found
This label° on my bosom, whose containing° *tablet / contents*
Is so from sense in hardness that I can
Make no collection of it.[9] Let him° show *(the soothsayer)*
His skill in the construction.° *interpretation*
LUCIUS Philharmonus!
SOOTHSAYER Here, my good lord.
LUCIUS Read, and declare the meaning.
SOOTHSAYER (*reads*) "Whenas a lion's whelp shall, to himself unknown, without seeking find, and be embraced by a piece of tender air; and when from a stately cedar shall be lopped branches which, being dead many years, shall after revive, be jointed to the old stock, and freshly grow: then shall Posthumus end his miseries, Britain be fortunate and flourish in peace and plenty."
Thou, Leonatus, art the lion's whelp:
The fit and apt construction of thy name,
Being *leo-natus*,° doth import so much. *lion-born*
The piece of tender air, thy virtuous daughter,
Which we call *mollis aer*,[1] and *mollis aer*
We term it *mulier*, which *mulier* I divine
Is this most constant wife, who even now
Answering the letter of the oracle,[2]
Unknown to you, unsought, were clipped about° *embraced*
With this most tender air.
CYMBELINE This hath some seeming.
SOOTHSAYER The lofty cedar, royal Cymbeline,
Personates° thee, and thy lopped branches point *Stands for*
Thy two sons forth, who, by Belarius stol'n,

9. *Is . . . it:* Is so difficult to make sense of that I can draw no conclusion from it.
1. Latin for "gentle air." An ancient (and erroneous) etymology for *mulier*, Latin for "woman" or "wife."
2. Fulfilling the exact terms of the oracle.

For many years thought dead, are now revived,
To the majestic cedar joined, whose issue
Promises Britain peace and plenty.

CYMBELINE Well,
My peace we will begin; and, Caius Lucius,
Although the victor, we submit to Caesar
And to the Roman empire, promising
To pay our wonted tribute, from the which
We were dissuaded by our wicked Queen,
Whom° heavens in justice both on her and hers *On whom*
Have laid most heavy hand.

SOOTHSAYER The fingers of the powers above do tune
The harmony of this peace. The vision
Which I made known to Lucius ere the stroke
Of this yet scarce-cold battle,[3] at this instant
Is full° accomplished. For the Roman eagle, *entirely*
From south to west on wing soaring aloft,
Lessened herself,[4] and in the beams o'th' sun
So vanished; which foreshowed our princely eagle,
Th'imperial Caesar, should again unite
His favor with the radiant Cymbeline,
Which shines here in the west.

CYMBELINE Laud we the gods,
And let our crookèd° smokes climb to their nostrils *curling*
From our blest altars. Publish° we this peace *Proclaim*
To all our subjects. Set we forward.° Let *Let us go forth*
A Roman and a British ensign° wave *banner*
Friendly together. So through Lud's Town march,
And in the temple of great Jupiter
Our peace we'll ratify, seal it with feasts.
Set on there.° Never was a war did cease, *March forth*
Ere bloody hands were washed, with such a peace. *Exeunt.*

3. *ere . . . battle:* before the action of this battle, which has only just ceased.

4. Made herself small (by flying into the distance).

# The Winter's Tale

Ben Jonson, a playwright and Shakespeare's contemporary, had harsh things to say about plays like *The Winter's Tale.* He claimed that they "make Nature afraid," by which he meant that, eschewing realism, they staged fantastic and improbable events that defied the laws of nature. For example, in *The Winter's Tale,* after a sixteen-year span a lost child is miraculously found, a seemingly dead woman comes alive, and a figure named Time has a speaking part. Jonson himself was a classicist. He wrote plays whose action, usually occurring in one place in the span of one day, aspired to present life in a realistic fashion that spurned the supernatural and the fantastic. But Jonson did not speak for everyone. The romance plays he scorned were wildly popular in the early modern period, and they made for extraordinary theater full of spectacular stage effects, swift reversals of fortune, and fast-paced action. Moreover, rather than make nature afraid, these plays, then and now, invite the audience to ask whether the fantastic and the miraculous may not be as much a part of human experience as sober realism.

Modern editors often group the plays to which Jonson directs his scorn (such as *The Winter's Tale, Pericles, The Tempest,* and *Cymbeline)* together under the label "romances." This is not, however, a category used in the First Folio (1623). There Shakespeare's plays are divided into comedies, tragedies, and histories. *Pericles* is not included in the Folio; *Cymbeline* is placed at the end of the tragedies; *The Tempest* appears as the first of the comedies and *The Winter's Tale* (1610) as the last. These placements are suggestive of the mixed tragicomic nature of these particular dramas. Neither purely comic nor tragic, they exist in a fluid space between. Like Shakespeare's earlier comedies, they usually have mutedly happy endings with some family members reunited and marriages in prospect. But these plays are also marked by deep suffering. They not only depict tyranny, incest, shipwrecks, and the death of children, but they typically give us protagonists whose folly or egotism causes much of the terrible suffering the plays portray. What is distinctive about the romances, however, is how frequently they offer their protagonists second chances—an opportunity to make amends for former wrongdoing or to experience the miracle of forgiveness. Some of the wonder that the endings of these plays evoke stems from the sense that occasionally, for some fortunate characters, the harsh law of punishment and retribution gives way before the healing power of love and generosity.

The title of *The Winter's Tale* signals its affiliations with popular storytelling. In act 2, Mamillius, the King of Sicilia's young son, informs his mother that "A sad tale's best for winter" and offers to tell her one "Of sprites and goblins" (2.1.26–27). The only sprites and goblins in Shakespeare's play turn out to be the internal demons of jealousy and suspicion that erupt in the mind of its protagonist, King Leontes, but *The Winter's Tale* is permeated by sadness, even during its festive conclusion. Trouble starts with King Leontes' sudden certainty that his wife, Hermione, is pregnant not with his own child, but with that of his childhood friend, King Polixenes of Bohemia, a visitor at Leontes' Sicilian court. Warned of Leontes' jealousy, Polixenes flees back to Bohemia, leaving the King to vent his wrath on Hermione. Thrust into prison, Hermione gives birth there to a daughter, Perdita, whom Leontes orders to be abandoned in the countryside far from Sicilia. Even when the oracle of Apollo subsequently declares Hermione innocent, Leontes continues to insist on her guilt. As he does, the death of

In the early modern period, Time was often depicted with wings and an hourglass, both symbolizing how swiftly Time passes, and with a scythe, indicating Time's destructive power. At the beginning of act 4 of *The Winter's Tale,* Time describes himself as having wings and a glass. In this seventeenth-century Dutch painting, a genial Time displays all three: wings, hourglass, and scythe.

Leontes' only son, Mamillius, is announced, and Hermione appears to die of grief. The first three acts of *The Winter's Tale* thus enact a miniature tragedy (not unlike Shakespeare's tragedy of the jealous Othello) in which Leontes' actions result in the loss of wife, daughter, and son. His personal tragedy also affects his kingdom. The oracle proclaims: "the King shall live without an heir if that which is lost be not found" (3.2.132–33). A kingdom without an heir to the throne is a kingdom in danger.

But then something extraordinary happens. The character Time appears onstage, informing the audience that sixteen years have passed and that Perdita, abandoned on the seacoast of Bohemia, has survived. Suddenly, instead of the wintry world of Leontes' Sicilian court, the play bursts with the energies of a Bohemian summer. The Shepherd who rescued Perdita is about to hold a sheepshearing festival, and Florizel, King Polixenes' son, has fallen in love with Perdita. A series of extraordinary events returns the young couple to Leontes' court, where Perdita's true status as his child and heir is revealed. More wonders follow. Taken to see what they believe to be a statue of the long-dead Hermione, the King and his newly recovered daughter witness the seeming miracle of the statue's transformation into flesh and blood.

Shakespeare's chief source for this tale was Robert Greene's popular prose romance *Pandosto: The Triumph of Time,* first published in 1588. Greene provided Shakespeare with the story of a jealous king who loses queen and daughter, though eventually his daughter is restored to him. But the differences between Shakespeare's play and Greene's prose tale are as striking as the similarities. For example, Shakespeare carefully changed the names of most of the characters he borrowed from Greene. In *Pandosto*, the King's lost daughter is Fawnia, but Shakespeare names her Perdita, a word that in Latin means "lost one." In Shakespeare's hands, Perdita's lover ceases to be Dorastus and becomes, instead, Florizel, which suggests the young Prince's connection with the flowers of spring. Greene's protagonist, Pandosto, is transformed into Leontes, evoking the leonine or lionlike nature of his wrath. Shakespeare also reversed the kingdoms ruled by Greene's kings. In *Pandosto*, the protagonist is King of Bohemia and his childhood friend rules Sicilia. In *The Winter's Tale*, the reverse is true, and one reason may be the association of Sicilia with the myth of Proserpina, the beautiful daughter of Ceres abducted by Dis, the god of the underworld, as she was picking flowers. Her mother attempted to free Proserpina, but she was allowed to return to the upper world only six months of each year. During that period, spring and summer visit the earth, but winter reigns when Proserpina returns to Dis's kingdom. Similarly, Perdita's exile from Sicilia soon after her birth brings a wintry sixteen-year period of mourning to Leontes' kingdom before her return heralds the "rebirth" of her mother and the renewal of Leontes and his kingdom.

Shakespeare, however, made much larger changes in Greene's romance. For example, he enhanced the role of Leontes' son, who is barely mentioned by Greene; he added the characters of Paulina, Emilia, Antigonus, Autolycus, Clown, Time, and rustics such as Dorcas and Mopsa (in *Pandosto*, Mopsa was the name of the Old Shepherd's wife; in *The Winter's Tale*, that wife is long dead). The magnificent sheepshearing festival is Shakespeare's invention; nothing like it exists in *Pandosto*. Most important, Greene's romance ends on a tragic note. Although the King and his daughter are finally reunited, Pandosto's wife is never restored to him and, overcome with desire for his grown daughter, he attempts incest and later takes his own life.

Shakespeare thus reverses the trajectory of Greene's grim tale. For despair and suicide, he substitutes redemption and renewal. The play thus feels like a diptych of winter and summer, hinged by the appearance of Time. It is probably a mistake to account for this structure by using only one interpretive lens, for the play's elegant simplicity resonates with many narratives of renewal. Some have read the play in Christian terms, seeing Leontes as a sinner who, after a period of suffering and repentance, receives the gift of God's grace through the return of his daughter and the Christlike resurrection of his wife. The play loosely traces the liturgical calendar, moving from the hospitality associated with Christmas to the Lenten period of deprivation and repentance to the joyous celebration of Easter and the Maying festivals associated with Whitsuntide, which occurs seven weeks after Easter. Other critics have stressed the mythic qualities of the play—its resemblance, for example, to fertility rites in which the coming of spring and sexual fulfillment depend on the sacrifice of a figure, usually an old king, associated with winter. In *The Winter's Tale*, Leontes does not die, but he does mourn for sixteen years; and his servant Antigonus, who takes the babe to Bohemia and there names her Perdita, becomes Leontes' sacrificial substitute. Once he has deposited Perdita, Antigonus is mauled and eaten by a bear, an event preceded by one of the most famous stage directions in any of Shakespeare's plays: "*Exit, pursued by a bear*" (3.3.57). This event has caused scholars to wonder if a *real* bear from the nearby bearbaiting arenas could have been brought onstage at this point to heighten the terror of the scene before the storm passes and attention turns to the rescue of Perdita. As the Shepherd who finds the baby says to his son, who has witnessed the bear dining on Antigonus, "thou mett'st with things dying, I with things newborn" (3.3.103–04). Other critics stress the pattern of generational renewal informing the play as the sins of the father, Leontes, give way to the innocent goodness of Florizel and Perdita. In some productions, the actress playing Hermione also plays Perdita (although a double usually has to be employed in the statue scene when they are onstage together), deepening the sense that it is through their children that parents have a second life. More recently, environmental critics have stressed how contact with the natural world of Bohemia repairs the alienation from natural affection experienced in the sophisticated Sicilian court. Resonating with all these interpretive paradigms, *The Winter's Tale* capaciously embodies collective and ancient nightmares of loss and collective dreams of redemption and renewal.

In modern productions, the symbolic power of the play's diptych structure is often highlighted by contrasts in the costumes and sets used to distinguish Sicilia and Bohemia. Sicilia, for example, is often a snow kingdom, dominated by white clothing and metallic props; Bohemia, by contrast, evokes summer, the stage carpeted in green, the characters at the sheep-shearing festival a riot of variegated colors. When the Bohemian party comes to Sicilia, the winter landscape is literally overwritten with the colorful clothes associated with Whitsuntide.

The play, however, is not simply about the triumph of the young, the rebirth of a world of possibility. *The Winter's Tale,* as befits a tragicomedy, moves from sorrow to joy, but that joy is bittersweet. Whatever the importance of the younger generation to this old tale, the focus stays resolutely on the older generation. It is Leontes who sins and must repent, Leontes whose family is reconstituted. Crucially, that reconstitution is only partial and imperfect. Mamillius, the young son, dies, the ultimate sacrifice to Leontes' tyrannous actions; and in the play's last scene, the "statue" of Hermione has wrinkles, the mark of time on her body. Traduced while a fertile wife and mother, Hermione returns as a woman past childbearing. The ending of Shakespeare's tale induces wonder and joy, but it cannot make an old man young or erase all the consequences of rash deeds. Shakespeare's late plays achieve their rich emotional effects from the deep strains of melancholia that underwrite their measured celebrations of the return of love and hope to a chastened social order.

Nor, despite the archaic quality that permeates these plays, are they simple enactments of timeless patterns and narratives. The precipitating event of the play—the eruption of Leontes' jealousy—is a symptom of the faultlines in a particular patriarchal culture. Often said to be "irrational," this jealousy in actuality has its roots in the cultural practices that in Jacobean England made men the heads of families, lineages, and kingdoms, but at the same time made them crucially dependent on women's reproductive powers to generate legitimate heirs. As *The Winter's Tale* opens, Leontes asks Polixenes to extend his stay in Sicilia. Polixenes refuses, but when Hermione entreats him, he agrees. This event, and the sight of his pregnant wife conversing with his friend and holding him by the hand, triggers in Leontes so deep a suspicion of his wife's fidelity that he plans to have Polixenes killed and doubts the legitimacy of his son as well. In part, what disturbs Leontes is the unknowability of the biological origins of his children. Men theoretically had dominion over their wives, but as Leontes says, "No barricado for a belly" (1.2.203)—that is, no absolute defense of a woman's chastity but her own honor, and that lies in her control, not her husband's.

A deep ambivalence toward women and sexuality, moreover, surfaces earlier in the same scene when, reminiscing about his boyhood friendship with Leontes, Polixenes describes the two of them as twinned lambs who experienced a fall from paradise only when they felt sexual passion and had their first encounters with women. In this conversation, the two men echo a strand of early modern thought that viewed men's friendships with men as more valuable than what were seen as their more dangerous and unpredictable relations with women. Construed as physically imperfect and intellectually inferior to men, women were supposedly ruled by their passions and could in turn evoke dangerous and degrading emotions in men. Yet men were enjoined to marry these irrational creatures to procreate and to continue family lineage. Leontes' rage at Hermione seems to stem in part from his dependence on her to give him legitimate heirs.

Once his jealousy has been triggered, Leontes gives the rein to a deadly rage that finds its chief object in Hermione's pregnant body. This anger is played out in part through Leontes' increasing identification with his young son. In Mamillius, Leontes sees himself as he once was, a young boy not yet wearing either the breeches or the sharp phallic dagger associated with adult manhood (1.2.155–56). It is an image of innocence, but also of vulnerability. The name Mamillius, another of Shakespeare's brilliant inventions, suggests one source of that vulnerability: *mamilla* is the Latin word for the nipple on a breast, a diminutive form of *mamma,* the word for the breast itself. His name thus connects Mamillius to the lactating breast and to the world of women, who in early modern culture presided over childbirth and the early years of children's lives. Infants depended utterly on women, either wet nurses or mothers, to provide their earliest sustenance, breast milk. As was often true of women from the upper class, Hermione does not herself seem to have nursed Mamillius. As Leontes bitterly exclaims: "I am glad you did not nurse him" (2.1.57). Nonetheless, the young boy's name and his appearance in 2.1 with his pregnant mother and her waiting women clearly associate him with the feminine sphere of birth, lactation, and early childhood. In identifying with Mamillius, a boy so young his nurse's milk is scarcely out of him, Leontes seems to feel both the vulnerability of the infant dependent on the lactating body of woman and the vulnerability of the adult husband dependent on the pregnant body and the chastity of his wife for legitimate offspring. As if to deny these dependencies, Leontes banishes Mamillius from his mother's presence and Hermione to prison. Mamillius dies; Leontes appears to lose all that would link him to the future: wife, son, daughter.

The sexual politics of *The Winter's Tale*, though rooted in early modern social structures, remain strikingly relevant to the contemporary moment. How much should men control women and their bodies? How much power and autonomy is it acceptable for women to exercise? These questions are played out in our culture in debates about reproductive rights and glass ceilings, while the prevalence of rape and sexual violence against women suggests that the female body still remains a focal point for some of our culture's deepest and least resolved currents of anger and ambivalence.

*The Winter's Tale* shows that the end point of Leontes' suspicion and distrust is a profound isolation from all those around him, including his counselors. He becomes a dangerous tyrant whose anger and paranoia torture him and distort his speech. In the first three acts, Leontes' most characteristic action is to turn away from those who love or attempt to help him. He sends his wife to prison; casts out his infant daughter; refuses the good counsel of his courtiers; rages in misogynistic fury at Paulina, who brings Perdita to him from prison; and finally defies the oracle of Apollo. Lacking trust in his wife and in all those around him, Leontes condemns himself to deathlike isolation. As in Shakespeare's other late plays, much of the language of *The Winter's Tale* is difficult and dense. Normal word order is inverted; speeches begin and end in the middle of a line; figurative language is given elliptical expression. During his period of intense jealousy, Leontes' language becomes even more dense and compressed than is typical of the rest of the play. Looking at his son, he exclaims:

> Can thy dam—? May't be?—
> Affection, thy intention stabs the center;
> Thou dost make possible things not so held,
> Communicat'st with dreams—how can this be?—
> With what's unreal thou coactive art,
> And fellow'st nothing. Then 'tis very credent
> Thou mayst cojoin with something, and thou dost,
> And that beyond commission, and I find it,

> And that to the infection of my brains
> And hard'ning of my brows.
>
> (1.2.137–46)

In this difficult passage, Leontes wrestles with the knowledge that his "affection" (the passions of rage, jealousy, and suspicion released in him) wounds him and perhaps leads him to imagine things to be true that are not. On the other hand, his suspicions *may* be justified; he may already be a cuckold. In this horrible state of uncertainty, Leontes' speech verges on incoherence. He interrupts the flow of his own thoughts with questions and ejaculations; his mind darts from boy to mother to his own pain; he realizes he may be wrong, but returns, obsessively, to the coarse and shameful image of his forehead disfigured with the horns of a cuckold.

The inner disorder suggested by this language finds its outward manifestation in Leontes' increasingly tyrannical actions. In the early modern period, the ruler of a kingdom was often compared to the head of a family. Good order in the commonwealth had its foundation in a well-ordered domestic realm. In *The Winter's Tale*, Leontes oversteps his just authority in both domains, refusing to take counsel from his courtiers, defying the gods, and condemning his wife for adultery with no evidence but his own suspicions. Nowhere, however, does he more certainly exceed his patriarchal authority than when he orders Hermione to stand trial before the proper period of her lying-in has passed. In the Renaissance, childbirth was recognized as an event both important and dangerous. Women gave birth surrounded by other women, usually a hired midwife, as well as by neighbors and female family members. The laboring female body, opened to let the child pass into the world, was considered to be in a particularly vulnerable state, needing to be protected from the unhealthful air that might enter the open womb. Consequently, birthing took place in a closed chamber, and after birth had occurred, women lay in their chambers for an extended period, recovering strength and purging their bodies of the blood and other fluids associated with pregnancy. At the end of this period, often lasting a month but sometimes longer, the woman came out of her house and returned to her normal routines. This occasion was marked by a "churching" ceremony, a rite of purification and celebration in which thanks were given for the safe delivery of a child and the woman's body declared cleansed of the impurities of pregnancy and birth.

When Hermione is made to stand trial, the pathos of her dignified defense of herself is heightened by her weakened state. In many productions, she appears on stage unattended, almost unable to stand. Among the wrongs done her, she accuses Leontes of having "with immodest hatred / The childbed privilege denied, which 'longs / To women of all fashion. Lastly, hurried / Here to this place, i'th' open air, before / I have got strength of limit" (3.2.100–104). Leontes' fury against the maternal body extends to denying that body the privileges of the lying-in period and exposing it to the dangers of the open air of a public place. This is domestic tyranny of a hideous sort.

After such cruelty, what recovery? Bohemia seems to be the place of hope in the play, and that feeling is conveyed in part by the vast expansion of character and event in that pastoral locale. After the claustrophobic focus on Leontes, the action unfolds to encompass the tricks of a wily rogue, Autolycus (whose name links him to the Autolycus of classical mythology, a crafty thief and grandfather of Ulysses; Autolycus's own father, Mercury, was the god of thieves); the sports of a sheep-shearing festival; the courtship of Florizel and Perdita; and the intrigues that take many of these players back to Sicilia. The scene depicting the festival at the Shepherd's farm, 4.4, is one of the longest in Shakespeare's canon (820 lines), is entirely his own invention, and is a great feast of languages and events. It includes the singing of ballads, a dance of twelve satyrs, Perdita's lyrical catalog of the flowers appropriate to each stage of life, and the painful moment when Polixenes forbids his son's marriage.

In the early modern period, childbirth was largely the affair of women. In this picture from Jakob Rüff's *De conceptu et generatione hominis* (Concerning the conception and birth of man) (1580), several women attend to a woman in labor while, in the background, two men cast the child's horoscope.

As this last moment shows, although Bohemia is a place of healing, it is not a paradise. In Bohemia, "great creating nature" for a time replaces Apollo as the deity who presides over the action. The fertility of the earth and, by extension, the fertility of woman may here seem to be redeemed from the curse laid upon them by Leontes' suspicion of his wife; and Florizel's staunch commitment to Perdita in the face of mounting obstacles to their love augurs well. But Polixenes just as staunchly opposes their union, threatening to use his patriarchal power in a way that, as with Leontes, would separate him from his son and from the possibility of future lineage. Bohemia also contains the rogue Autolycus, picking the pockets of country bumpkins and hiding his identity by a series of disguises. Further, Bohemian life is marked by enormous disparities of wealth. The Shepherd is rich, in part because of the money he found with Perdita. For the sheep-shearing feast, Perdita can afford ingredients—raisins, rice, and spices, for example—that were exotic luxury goods, foodstuffs in excess of the subsistence diet of bread, beer, and cheese that many people ate. It is also possible that some of the Shepherd's wealth comes from the new profitability of raising sheep. Throughout the sixteenth and seventeenth centuries, land was increasingly enclosed—that is, fenced off for grazing sheep rather than available for communal use in raising food and feeding cattle. These enclosures were popularly blamed for perceived increases in rural poverty

In this late seventeenth-century woodcut from the Pepysian collection of early modern ballads, a peddler carries a huge pack and holds several rabbits, or conies, which suggests that he is also a cony-catcher—that is, a con man (like Autolycus), whose victims were popularly called "conies."

and for the creation of masterless men, poor folk who roamed the countryside without fixed places of residence and who were believed to feign sickness or deformity in order to enforce charity from those they met. Autolycus, pretending to have lost his clothes to a highwayman, is a comic version of such a masterless man, yet his presence in the play, juxtaposed to that of the rich Shepherd, is a reminder of the social tensions and economic stratifications that permeate the landscape with widespread enclosures and other changes in rural life.

Bohemia is also the locale of one of the great set pieces of the play—the debate between Polixenes and Perdita concerning the relative values of art and nature and the relationship between them. Today we find analogs to this debate in the controversy over genetically modified seeds and crops. Does the artifice of genetic modification improve nature in ways beneficial to many, or is it a dangerous distortion of it? The early modern period engaged in similar debates. Given the imperfections of the fallen world and humankind's weaknesses, could art be instrumental in calling into being a better world, or was it merely a temptation to pride or to competition with the divine creator? The refreshing thing about the handling of these issues in *The Winter's Tale* is that the play comes to no abstract resolution concerning them. Rather, it encases the debate between Polixenes and Perdita in multiple ironies, and it complexly connects this debate to the actions of characters who seemingly have no involvement with it. For Perdita, product of the pastoral landscape, art is a bad thing. She wants no grafted or hybrid flowers in her garden. Yet even as she speaks her condemnation of art, Perdita is reluctantly dressed as queen of the sheep-shearing feast, a bit of artifice that reveals a truth she herself cannot know: namely, that she is a queen's daughter. Polixenes, for his part, champions art, declaring that the practice of mixing wild and cultivated plants produces sturdy hybrids and that the art of grafting is itself a gift of nature. Yet when his son wishes to graft himself to a shepherd's daughter, Polixenes finds such a practice abhorrent.

Besides making the obvious point that people don't always act on their stated beliefs, this exchange shows the extreme pressure the play puts on the art-nature dichotomy. In Perdita's case, her "natural" condition as princess is revealed by two kinds of artifice: her dress as queen of the feast and the role Camillo creates for her as Florizel's Libyan princess when he devises a way for the two young lovers to return to Leontes' court. Camillo even goes so far as to provide lines for the two to speak. His goal is ameliorative: to satisfy the desires of the young (as well as his own deep longings to see his homeland again) and to heal the breach between the two dissevered kingdoms. The point seems to be not whether in some abstract sense "art" violates "nature," but how artfulness, defined broadly as the representation of the world through painting, statuary, plays, and song, can open new possibilities for imagining what nature is or could be.

This is not an inconsequential point, for in the badly flawed world depicted in *The Winter's Tale* art gradually emerges as one of the resources people can use, either badly or well, to affect the world around them: to correct old mistakes and to forge new realities. Its effects are determined and limited, of course, by the skill and intentions of the artist and by the receptiveness of the audience. Autolycus is a subversive con man who uses disguises and deceptions to fleece money from gulls. By contrast, in the play's second part, Paulina emerges as the chief representative of the ameliorative artist who uses her skills to make better the world around her. Once reviled by Leontes as a witch, Paulina becomes the King's spiritual guide in the last half of the play (her name linking her to the New Testament apostle St. Paul). This strikingly outspoken woman spends sixteen years preparing Leontes to be a fit spectator to the tableau of resurrection and renewal enacted in the last scene. When she had first brought the infant to Leontes from prison, Paulina had seemed to believe in the self-evident nature of truth. Laying the babe at Leontes' feet, she proclaimed that the "good goddess Nature" (2.3.103) had made it an exact copy of the father. Leontes had only to read what nature had written in the face of his child. But jealousy and rage at his wife bleared the King's vision. He would not or could not see himself in the female child he had fathered. So for sixteen years Paulina worked another way, fueling Leontes' remorse and artfully withholding both from him and from the theater audience the knowledge that Hermione lived. When the disguised Princess returns to Sicilia, Leontes gets a second chance. Looking at Perdita, he is finally able to see the unslandered image of his wife in the young girl before him. Having admired Perdita, Leontes says to Paulina, "I thought of her [Hermione] / Even in these looks I made" (5.1.226–27). When he can believe in the potential goodness of women, and specifically in the chastity of the young woman who is the simulacrum of his wife, then Leontes can help to create the reality in which Perdita is truly a princess and his wife a living being rather than the corpse into which his rage and distrust had transformed her.

The statue scene itself is one of the most moving and theatrically effective moments in any of Shakespeare's plays. Like Leontes, the untutored audience does not know that Hermione lives. Consequently, under Paulina's careful guidance, the spectators both onstage and off seem to participate in willing the statue into life. When Hermione descends from her pedestal, the audience can feel itself present at the miraculous resurrection of the dead. In theological terms, this scene touches on controversial matters. Protestants repudiated what they characterized as Catholic idolatry, which involved the veneration of images, including statues of the Virgin Mary. Protestants, by contrast, typically stressed the ear over the eye, words over images, faith over works. In the wake of the Reformation, more radical Protestants went so far as to smash stained-glass windows and the statues of saints that had for many centuries adorned Catholic churches. The final moments of *The Winter's Tale* gesture toward this repudiated world of images and their veneration. While Paulina insists that the audience awaken its faith, she does so in a scene that is visually organized to focus all eyes on a statue that might well evoke memories of prior Catholic practices. Characteristically, Shakespeare seems to have things two ways: drawing on the emotional power of Catholic rituals centered on the image, he simultaneously suggests that there is no statue on the stage at all, only a living woman roused to new vigor by the recovery of a long-lost daughter.

However ambiguous the theological implications of the final scene, it is a striking theatrical climax evoking wonder and awe and allowing the old tale to end happily, or mostly so. A penitent Leontes has been reunited with his wife and daughter, and amity has been restored between him and Polixenes. But such is the maturity of this play that the happy ending is a tempered one. The memory of things that were lost and can never be regained intrudes even on the celebration of the return of Perdita and Hermione. Paulina pointedly recalls her husband, Antigonus, lost in carrying Perdita to Bohemia; Hermione speaks to Perdita of the sixteen long years of their separation; Mamillius is gone forever. Moreover, the highly charged image of the pregnant female body is absent from this final scene. Perdita is not yet a wife; both Paulina and Hermione are probably too old for childbearing. For Perdita and Florizel, perhaps the greatest tests of faith and mutuality lie ahead, when Perdita's transformation from maid into wife and mother will present new occasions for the jealousy and distrust of patriarchal culture to resurface. The point of *The Winter's Tale* hardly seems to be that folly has no consequences or that earthly paradise is possible. Those claims would indeed make nature afraid. Rather, the play celebrates the true miracle of partial restorations, of moments of exquisite joy wrested by work, art, and good fortune from the pains of the imperfect world that men and women have made.

JEAN E. HOWARD

## SELECTED BIBLIOGRAPHY


Adelman, Janet. "Masculine Authority and the Maternal Body: The Return to Origins in the Romances." *Suffocating Mothers: Fantasies of Maternal Origin in Shakespeare's Plays, "Hamlet" to "The Tempest."* New York: Routledge, 1992. 193–238. Argues that the romances attempt to redress the loss of the idealized parents enacted in *Hamlet* and that *The Winter's Tale* dramatizes the positive restoration of the sexualized mother in the person of Hermione.

Egan, Robert. "'The Art Itself Is Nature': *The Winter's Tale.*" *Drama Within Drama: Shakespeare's Sense of His Art in "King Lear," "The Winter's Tale," and "The Tempest."* New York: Columbia UP, 1975. 56–89. Discusses the role of art in rectifying the disordered world of *The Winter's Tale.*

Frye, Northrop. "The Triumph of Time." *A Natural Perspective: The Development of Shakespearean Comedy and Romance.* New York: Columbia UP, 1965. 72–117. Discusses structures of action and conventions common across Shakespeare's comedies and romances.

Jensen, Phoebe. "Singing Psalms to Hornpipes: Festivity, Iconoclasm and Catholicism in *The Winter's Tale.*" *Religion and Revelry in Shakespeare's Festive World.* Cambridge: Cambridge UP, 2008. 194–233. Explores the play's relationship to Catholic and Protestant attitudes toward popular festivity.

Mowat, Barbara A. "Rogues, Shepherds, and the Counterfeit Distressed: Texts and Infracontexts of *The Winter's Tale* 4.3." *Shakespeare Studies* 22 (1994): 58–76. Examines the cultural contexts that help make sense of the figure of Autolycus, rogue and con man, in *The Winter's Tale.*

Newcomb, Lori H. "'If That Which Is Lost Be Not Found': Monumental Bodies, Spectacular Bodies in *The Winter's Tale.*" *Ovid and the Renaissance Body.* Ed. Goran V. Stanivukovic. Toronto: U of Toronto P, 2001. Analyzes the tension between the monumental (stasis and constraint) and the spectacular (metamorphosis and performative freedom) both in the text of *The Winter's Tale* and in its material history as book and as theater piece.

O'Connor, Marion. "'Imagine Me, Gentle Spectators': Iconomachy and *The Winter's Tale.*" *A Companion to Shakespeare's Works.* IV: *The Poems, Problem Comedies, Late Plays.* Ed. Richard Dutton and Jean E. Howard. Malden, MA: Blackwell, 2003. 365–88. Discusses the Renaissance theological debate about the value and truth of images as it bears on a number of early modern plays, including *The Winter's Tale*, in which statues are staged. Argues that Shakespeare insists on the collaboration of word and image, eschewing a total embrace of Reformation logocentrism or Catholic image-worship.

Paster, Gail Kern. "Quarreling with the Dug, or 'I Am Glad You Did Not Nurse Him.'" *The Body Embarrassed: Drama and the Disciplines of Shame in Early Modern England.* Ithaca, NY: Cornell UP, 1993. 215–80. Sets *The Winter's Tale* in an array of Shakespearean texts that anxiously explore early modern cultural practices surrounding reproduction and infant care, especially the practice of wet-nursing.

Ravelhofer, Barbara. "'Beasts of Recreacion': Henslowe's White Bears." *English Literary Renaissance* 32.2 (2002): 287–323. Explores the possibility that a real bear was used in performances of *The Winter's Tale* in Shakespeare's time.

Tigner, Amy. "*The Winter's Tale*: Gardens and the Marvels of Transformation." *English Literary Renaissance* 36.1 (2006): 114–34. Argues for the centrality of gardens to *The Winter's Tale* as they represent the body of women and mark the movement from suspicion to redemption. Discusses the possibility that the final scene in which Hermione's statue walks occurs in a garden setting.

### Film

*The Winter's Tale*. 1999. Dir. Robin Lough. UK. 170 min. A dark and moving Royal Shakespeare Company production with Anthony Sher as a Leontes truly made mad by jealousy and an impressively dignified Alexandra Gilbreath as Hermione. Imaginative staging of the bear and riveting statue scene as Hermione very slowly comes to life.

## TEXTUAL INTRODUCTION

The 1623 Folio text contains the only early version of *The Winter's Tale*, where it appears at the end of the comedies. The play dates probably from 1610, and the first recorded performance, noted by Simon Forman, took place on May 15, 1611, at the Globe Theatre. Forman pays attention to Autolycus but has nothing to say about the extraordinary restoration of Hermione in the last scene. The King's Men performed the play at court in Whitehall on November 5, 1611, and again at court during the Christmas season of 1612–13 in a group of plays that led up to the wedding of Princess Elizabeth, King James's only daughter, to Frederick, Elector Palatine of Germany, on February 14, 1613. The play's text includes a satyr dance in 4.4 in the long sheep-shearing scene, which seems indebted to a dance in Ben Jonson's *Masque of Oberon*, performed at court on January 1, 1611, in honor of Prince Henry. We cannot know, however, when or how this dance became part of *The Winter's Tale*.

Scholars generally agree that the scribe Ralph Crane probably created a transcript of the play, as he did for several of the King's Men plays, although we cannot be certain about what copy went to the printing house. The Folio text bears evidence of Crane's practice, such as typically indulging in extensive use of parentheses, hyphens, and apostrophes. Crane also lists all the characters at the beginning of the scene regardless of when they might appear. For clarity, this edition creates stage directions that indicate when the characters should enter the action. Beyond an initial stage direction, the printed text of *The Winter's Tale* never offers much more than simply noting entrances and exits of characters. The notable and famous exception, unlike anything else in the play, occurs in 3.3, where we find the stage direction that prompts immediate action from Antigonus: "*Exit, pursued by a bear.*" This single stage direction has caused consternation, amusement, puzzlement, much commentary by critics, and many problems for directors.

Curiously, in the Folio text a blank page precedes *The Winter's Tale*, and a blank page follows it, perhaps suggesting some uncertainty or a late addition of the play to the collection. Generally, the play lacks serious textual problems, a tribute possibly to Crane and the printer. Act and scene divisions are reliable, and this edition adheres to them. The text includes "The Names of the Actors" at the conclusion of the play, making *The Winter's Tale* one of only seven of the Folio texts that include such a list, and always at the end (four comedies, one history, and two tragedies). This practice contrasts with the usual modern editorial habit of listing the characters first.

DAVID M. BERGERON

## PERFORMANCE NOTE

*The Winter's Tale* takes greater risks with its audience than perhaps any other play by Shakespeare, repeatedly testing the capacities of its actors and the credulity of its audiences. Antigonus's "*Exit, pursued by a bear*" (3.3.57) is only one instance of the play seemingly going out of its way to expose a theater company's limitations. Actors are repeatedly tasked with representing things that are peculiarly resistant to representation, such as the personified abstraction "Time" and the statue of Hermione. In addition, productions must engage with the play's open inquiry into the role of nature and artifice in art, settling whether and how to legitimize Leontes' jealousy, to simulate or stylize the bear, to mask or accentuate Hermione's feigned inanimacy, to emphasize or underplay the fact that the text describes rather than depicts a scene that, by its own admission, was "a sight which was to be seen, cannot be spoken of" (5.2.39–40).

Productions must also address questions of characterization (Does Camillo's mingling of loyalty and treachery signify candor or cunning? Does "Clown" indicate the rustic's job description or his personality? Is Paulina a spiritual healer or a witch?) and genre (How capable of redemption should Leontes appear? Should the ghosts of Mamillius and Antigonus haunt the second half?). And they must decide how to identify and contrast Sicilia and Bohemia. Despite the comparative levity of the action in Bohemia, the love triangle that centers on Clown and the sudden aggression of Polixenes parallel tragic events in Sicilia, and productions sometimes emphasize those parallels by doubling roles or reprising bits of staging.

BRETT GAMBOA

# The Winter's Tale

## THE PERSONS OF THE PLAY[1]

LEONTES, King of Sicilia
HERMIONE, Queen to Leontes
MAMILLIUS, young Prince of Sicilia
PERDITA, daughter to Leontes and Hermione
CAMILLO, ANTIGONUS, CLEOMENES, DION } four lords of Sicilia
PAULINA, wife to Antigonus
EMILIA, a lady
JAILER
MARINER
LORDS and GENTLEMEN, LADIES, OFFICERS, and SERVANTS of Leontes' court

POLIXENES, King of Bohemia
FLORIZEL, Prince of Bohemia
SHEPHERD, reputed father of Perdita
CLOWN, his son
MOPSA, DORCAS } shepherdesses
AUTOLYCUS, a rogue
ARCHIDAMUS, a lord of Bohemia
Shepherds and Shepherdesses
Twelve Herdsmen disguised as Satyrs
TIME as Chorus

### 1.1

*Enter* CAMILLO *and* ARCHIDAMUS.

ARCHIDAMUS If you shall chance, Camillo, to visit Bohemia on the like occasion whereon my services are now on foot,[2] you shall see, as I have said, great difference betwixt our Bohemia and your Sicilia.

CAMILLO I think this coming summer the King of Sicilia means to pay Bohemia the visitation which he justly owes him.

ARCHIDAMUS Wherein our entertainment shall shame us, we will be justified in our loves;[3] for indeed—

CAMILLO Beseech you—

ARCHIDAMUS Verily, I speak it in the freedom of my knowledge. We cannot with such magnificence—in so rare—I know not what to say. We will give you sleepy drinks[4] that your

1.1 Location: Sicilia. The palace of Leontes.
1. TEXTUAL COMMENT *The Winter's Tale* is one of only seven plays in the Folio that contain a list of characters. As with the other plays, that list is placed at the end of the text. The Folio list overlooks several characters here included, and divides its characters by gender, as this edition does not. See Digital Edition TC 1.
2. *on the like . . . foot:* on an occasion similar to the one in which I am now engaged (that is, as attendant lord to a visiting king).
3. *Wherein . . . lover:* Insofar as our less elaborate hospitality will put us to shame, we will compensate by (the depth of) our love.
4. *sleepy drinks:* drinks to make you drowsy.

senses, unintelligent of our insufficience,[5] may, though they cannot praise us, as little accuse us.

CAMILLO You pay a great deal too dear for what's given freely.

ARCHIDAMUS Believe me, I speak as my understanding instructs me and as mine honesty puts it to utterance.

CAMILLO Sicilia cannot show himself over-kind to Bohemia. They were trained together in their childhoods, and there rooted betwixt them then such an affection which cannot choose but branch[6] now. Since their more mature dignities and royal necessities made separation of their society,° their encounters, though not personal, hath been royally attorneyed[7] with interchange of gifts, letters, loving embassies, that° they have seemed to be together though absent; shook hands as over a vast;° and embraced as it were from the ends of opposed winds.[8] The heavens continue their loves.

*forced them apart* / *so that* / *wide expanse*

ARCHIDAMUS I think there is not in the world either malice or matter to alter it. You have an unspeakable° comfort of° your young prince Mamillius. It° is a gentleman of the greatest promise that ever came into my note.

*inexpressible / in* / *(He)*

CAMILLO I very well agree with you in the hopes of him. It is a gallant child; one that, indeed, physics the subject,[9] makes old hearts fresh. They that went on crutches ere he was born desire yet their life° to see him a man.

*hope to live long enough*

ARCHIDAMUS Would they else be content to die?

CAMILLO Yes—if there were no other excuse why they should desire to live.

ARCHIDAMUS If the King had no son, they would desire to live on crutches till he had one. *Exeunt.*

## 1.2

*Enter* LEONTES, HERMIONE, MAMILLIUS, POLIXENES, [*and*] CAMILLO.[1]

POLIXENES Nine changes of the wat'ry star hath been
The shepherd's note[2] since we[3] have left our throne
Without a burden.° Time as long again
Would be filled up, my brother, with our thanks,
And yet we should for perpetuity
Go hence in debt.[4] And therefore, like a cipher,
Yet standing in rich place,[5] I multiply
With one "We thank you" many thousands more
That go before it.

*occupant*

LEONTES Stay° your thanks a while,
And pay them when you part.

*Postpone*

POLIXENES Sir, that's tomorrow.

5. Unaware of our inadequacy.
6. Flourish and spread (as a tree does when it puts forth branches); divide.
7. Performed by deputies.
8. *from . . . winds:* from opposite ends of the earth. Early modern atlases often showed the four "corners" of the earth as the source of the winds.
9. Restores the health of the King's subjects.

1.2 Location: Scene continues.
1. TEXTUAL COMMENT Though listed in the stage direction in F, Camillo has no part in this scene until line 208, when Leontes says, "What, Camillo there?" Camillo's first entrance may be marked by Leontes' exclamation, or he may be a silent observer for the first 208 lines. See Digital Edition TC 2.
2. *Nine . . . note:* The Shepherd has observed nine changes of the moon (that is, nine months). The moon is "the wat'ry star" because it governs the tides.
3. Both kings employ the royal "we," speaking of themselves in the plural.
4. *And yet . . . debt:* And even then we would depart forever in your debt.
5. *like . . . place:* like a zero ("cipher"), which is worthless in itself, but valuable when it follows another number.

I am questioned by my fears° of what may chance[6] *I am afraid*
Or breed upon° our absence, that may blow *develop because of*
No sneaping winds at home to make us say,
"This is put forth too truly."[7] Besides, I have stayed
To tire your royalty.

LEONTES We are tougher, brother,
Than you can put us to't.[8]

POLIXENES No longer stay.

LEONTES One sennight° longer. *week*

POLIXENES Very sooth,° tomorrow. *In truth (a mild oath)*

LEONTES We'll part the time° between's, then; and in that *split the diffference*
I'll no gainsaying.° *allow no contradiction*

POLIXENES Press me not, beseech you, so.
There is no tongue that moves, none, none i'th' world
So soon as yours could win me. So it should now,
Were there necessity in your request, although
'Twere needful I denied it. My affairs
Do even drag me homeward, which to hinder
Were in your love a whip to me,[9] my stay
To you a charge and trouble. To save both,
Farewell, our brother.

LEONTES Tongue-tied our queen? Speak you.

HERMIONE I had thought, sir, to have held my peace until
You had drawn oaths from him not to stay. You, sir,
Charge him too coldly. Tell him you are sure
All in Bohemia's well. This satisfaction
The bygone day proclaimed.[1] Say this to him,
He's beat from his best ward.[2]

LEONTES Well said, Hermione.

HERMIONE To tell° he longs to see his son were strong. *assert*
But let him say so, then, and let him go;
But let him swear so, and he shall not stay:
We'll thwack him hence with distaffs.[3]
[*to* POLIXENES] Yet of your royal presence I'll adventure° *risk*
The borrow° of a week. When at Bohemia *loan*
You take my lord, I'll give him my commission° *permission*
To let him there a month behind the gest
Prefixed for 's parting.[4] —Yet, good deed,° Leontes, *indeed*
I love thee not a jar° o'th' clock behind *tick*
What lady she her lord.[5] —You'll stay?

POLIXENES No, madam.

HERMIONE Nay, but you will?

POLIXENES I may not, verily.

HERMIONE Verily?
You put me off with limber° vows. But I, *weak*

6. Happen by chance.
7. *that may . . . too truly:* an obscure passage. Fearing the worst, Polixenes hopes that no biting ("sneaping") winds may blow (that is, no envious forces be active) at home to make him conclude that his worries were justified.
8. Than any test you put us to.
9. *which to . . . to me:* that is, to hinder me from going home, though lovingly done, would be a punishment ("whip") to me.
1. *This . . . proclaimed:* This good news was announced yesterday.
2. He's forced to relinquish his strongest position; a fencing metaphor.
3. Wooden sticks, usually about three feet long, which were used in spinning wool. Proverbially, they were female tools and symbols of female authority.
4. *To let . . . parting:* To remain there a month longer than the time ("gest") appointed in advance for his departure.
5. *I love . . . lord:* I love you no less than any noblewoman loves her husband.

Though you would seek t'unsphere the stars[6] with oaths,
Should yet say, "Sir, no going." Verily
You shall not go. A lady's "verily" is
As potent as a lord's. Will you go yet?
Force me to keep you as a prisoner,
Not like a guest; so you shall pay your fees
When you depart[7] and save your thanks. How say you?
My prisoner? Or my guest? By your dread "verily,"
One of them you shall be.

POLIXENES Your guest, then, madam;
To be your prisoner should import offending,° *mean I have offended you*
Which is for me less easy to commit
Than you to punish.

HERMIONE Not your jailer, then,
But your kind hostess. Come, I'll question you
Of my lord's tricks and yours when you were boys.
You were pretty lordings° then? *young lords*

POLIXENES We were, fair queen,
Two lads that thought there was no more behind° *in the future*
But such a day tomorrow as today,
And to be boy eternal.

HERMIONE Was not my lord
The verier wag° o'th' two? *greater mischief-maker*

POLIXENES We were as twinned° lambs that did frisk i'th' sun *identical*
And bleat the one at th'other. What we changed° *exchanged*
Was innocence for innocence. We knew not
The doctrine of ill-doing nor dreamed
That any did. Had we pursued that life,
And our weak spirits ne'er been higher reared
With stronger blood,° we should have answered heaven *With more mature passions*
Boldly, "Not guilty," the imposition cleared
Hereditary ours.[8]

HERMIONE By this we gather
You have tripped° since. *sinned*

POLIXENES O my most sacred lady,
Temptations have since then been born to's. For
In those unfledged[9] days was my wife a girl;
Your precious self had then not crossed the eyes
Of my young playfellow.

HERMIONE Grace to boot!° *Heaven help me*
Of this make no conclusion,[1] lest you say
Your queen and I are devils. Yet go on.
Th'offenses we have made you do we'll answer°— *answer for*
If you first sinned with us, and that with us
You did continue fault, and that you slipped not° *did not sin (have sex)*
With any but with us.

LEONTES Is he won° yet? *persuaded*

HERMIONE He'll stay, my lord.

6. To disorder the cosmos; alluding to the idea that the stars move in fixed orbits around the earth.
7. In early modern England, prisoners were required to pay fees to jailers both for provisions and upon their release.
8. Freed even of the charge of original sin. The doctrine of original sin held that everyone at birth was tainted by sin because the first humans, Adam and Eve, disobeyed God in the Garden of Eden. Here original sin is linked to the sexual desires that come with maturity.
9. Youthful. An unfledged, or young, bird is one as yet lacking the feathers necessary for flight.
1. Do not follow out this line of reasoning.

LEONTES At my request he would not.
Hermione, my dearest, thou never spok'st
To better purpose.
HERMIONE Never?
LEONTES Never, but once.
HERMIONE What, have I twice said well? When was't before?
I prithee tell me. Cram's° with praise and make's *Stuff us; overfeed us*
As fat as tame things. One good deed, dying tongueless,
Slaughters a thousand waiting upon that.[2]
Our praises are our wages. You may ride's
With one soft kiss a thousand furlongs ere
With spur we heat° an acre.[3] But to th' goal:° *race over / purpose*
My last good deed was to entreat his stay.
What was my first? It has an elder sister,
Or I mistake you. Oh, would her name were Grace![4]
But once before I spoke to th' purpose? When?
Nay, let me have't. I long.
LEONTES Why, that was when
Three crabbèd° months had soured themselves to death *bitter*
Ere I could make thee open thy white hand
And clap° thyself my love; then didst thou utter, *pledge*
"I am yours forever."
HERMIONE 'Tis grace indeed.
Why, lo you now, I have spoke to th' purpose twice:
The one for ever earned a royal husband;
Th'other for some while a friend.[5]
[HERMIONE *and* POLIXENES *stand apart, holding hands.*][6]
LEONTES [*aside*] Too hot, too hot.
To mingle friendship far is mingling bloods.[7]
I have *tremor cordis*[8] on me; my heart dances,
But not for joy, not joy. This entertainment° *hospitality*
May a free° face put on, derive a liberty *innocent*
From heartiness, from bounty, fertile bosom,° *generous affection*
And well become the agent[9]—'t may, I grant—
But to be paddling° palms and pinching fingers,[1] *caressing*
As now they are, and making practiced smiles
As in a looking glass; and then to sigh, as 'twere
The mort o'th' deer[2]—oh, that is entertainment
My bosom likes not, nor my brows.[3] —Mamillius,
Art thou my boy?

2. *One good . . . that:* If one virtuous act goes unremarked, then the thousand more that might have been inspired by it will not come to be.
3. *You may . . . acre:* that is, You'll go much farther with us if you will treat us kindly (with a pun on "ride" as meaning "enjoy us sexually").
4. Would that my first good act were virtuous (full of God's grace). Hermione may be countering Polixenes' earlier suggestion that she first caused Leontes to sin. With a possible allusion to the Three Graces (Aglaia, Euphrosyne, and Thalia) of classical mythology. Usually depicted nude and dancing in a circle, the three women represented the epitome of earthly beauty and harmony.
5. "Friend" could also mean "lover," a meaning that Leontes takes up in his next speech.
6. It is not certain when Hermione and Polixenes join hands, but by line 115 Leontes remarks that they are "paddling palms and pinching fingers."
7. Uniting in passion; having sexual intercourse. PERFORMANCE COMMENT Leontes' sudden extreme jealousy poses challenges for the actor playing the part. How will he motivate the sudden transformation? See Digital Edition PC 1.
8. A malady marked by an erratic heart rate.
9. And makes the actor of these deeds (Hermione) appear attractive.
1. Early modern texts often represent hands as erotic body parts. Moist palms were believed to be signs of sexual arousal; finger games may suggest sexual penetration.
2. *to sigh . . . deer:* to sigh as loudly as the horn blast that proclaims the death of a hunted deer.
3. Alluding to the proverbial notion that a cuckold sprouted horns from his brow.

MAMILLIUS Ay, my good lord.
LEONTES I'fecks!° *In faith (a mild oath)*
Why, that's my bawcock.° What, hast smutched° thy nose? *fine fellow / dirtied*
They say it is a copy out of mine. Come, captain,
We must be neat—not neat,[4] but cleanly, captain.
And yet the steer, the heifer, and the calf
Are all called "neat." —Still virginaling
Upon his palm?[5] —How now, you wanton° calf? *playful*
Art thou my calf?
MAMILLIUS Yes, if you will, my lord.
LEONTES Thou want'st a rough pash° and the shoots° that I have *shaggy head / horns*
To be full° like me. Yet they say we are *fully grown, fully horned*
Almost as like as eggs—women say so,
That will say anything. But were they false
As o'er-dyed blacks,[6] as wind, as waters, false
As dice are to be wished by one that fixes
No bourn° twixt his and mine, yet were it true *boundary; limit*
To say this boy were like me. Come, sir page,
Look on me with your welkin° eye. Sweet villain, *sky blue*
Most dear'st, my collop.[7] Can thy dam°—? May't be?— *mother*
Affection, thy intention stabs the center;[8]
Thou dost make possible things not so held,° *considered impossible*
Communicat'st with dreams—how can this be?—
With what's unreal thou coactive art,° *you collaborate*
And fellow'st° nothing. Then 'tis very credent° *are companion to / believable*
Thou mayst cojoin with something, and thou dost,
And that beyond commission,° and I find it, *what is permitted*
And that to the infection of my brains
And hard'ning of my brows.° *(with cuckold's horns)*
[POLIXENES *and* HERMIONE *step forward.*]
POLIXENES What means Sicilia?
HERMIONE He something seems° unsettled. *seems somewhat*
POLIXENES How, my lord?
LEONTES What cheer? How is't with you, best brother?
HERMIONE You look
As if you held a brow of much distraction.
Are you moved,° my lord? *angry*
LEONTES No, in good earnest.
How sometimes nature will betray its folly,
Its tenderness, and make itself a pastime° *source of amusement*
To harder bosoms! Looking on the lines
Of my boy's face, methoughts I did recoil° *go back*
Twenty-three years and saw myself unbreeched,[9]
In my green velvet coat, my dagger muzzled° *in its sheath; blunted*
Lest it should bite its master and so prove,
As ornaments oft do, too dangerous.

4. Punning on "neat" as meaning both "clean" and "cattle with horns."
5. Still caressing his hand as if playing the virginal, a legless keyboard instrument played on the lap; still acting chastely (like a virgin).
6. Referring to textiles dyed black. Such black cloth was made "false" or weakened by the harsh chemicals in the dye. With a possible reference to the dark skin of Africans, who were commonly thought to be licentious and thus sexually "false."
7. That is, my own flesh. (A "collop" is a portion of meat.)
8. *Affection . . . center:* Passion (probably the passion of jealousy), your intensity ("intention") pierces my heart, or to the core of my being.
9. Not yet old enough to wear men's clothing ("breeches"). Before about the age of six, both girls and boys in early modern England wore a dresslike garment. Giving a boy breeches was a sign of his passage out of childhood.

How like, methought, I then was to this kernel,
This squash,° this gentleman. —Mine honest friend, *unripe peapod*
Will you take eggs for money?[1]

MAMILLIUS No, my lord, I'll fight.

LEONTES You will? Why, happy man be 's dole.[2] My brother,
Are you so fond of your young prince as we
Do seem to be of ours?

POLIXENES If at home, sir,
He's all my exercise, my mirth, my matter;° *concern*
Now my sworn friend and then mine enemy;
My parasite, my soldier, statesman, all.
He makes a July's day short as December;
And with his varying childness° cures in me *youthful ways*
Thoughts that would thick my blood.[3]

LEONTES So stands this squire
Officed with me.[4] We two will walk, my lord,
And leave you to your graver steps. Hermione,
How thou lov'st us show in our brother's welcome.
Let what is dear in Sicily be cheap.
Next to thyself and my young rover, he's
Apparent° to my heart. *Heir apparent*

HERMIONE If you would seek us,
We are yours i'th' garden. Shall's attend you there?

LEONTES To your own bents° dispose you. You'll be found, *inclinations*
Be you beneath the sky. [*aside*] I am angling° now, *fishing; scheming*
Though you perceive me not how I give line.
Go to, go to!
How she holds up the neb, the bill, to him[5]
And arms her° with the boldness of a wife *herself*
To her allowing° husband. *approving*
[*Exeunt* POLIXENES *and* HERMIONE.]
Gone already!
Inch-thick, knee-deep, o'er head and ears a forked° one. *horned*
—Go play, boy, play. —Thy mother plays,° and I *dallies sexually*
Play° too, but so disgraced a part, whose issue[6] *Play a role*
Will hiss me to my grave. Contempt and clamor
Will be my knell.° —Go play, boy, play. —There have been, *death bell*
Or I am much deceived, cuckolds ere now,
And many a man there is, even at this present,
Now, while I speak this, holds his wife by th'arm,
That little thinks she has been sluiced[7] in's absence,
And his pond[8] fished by his next neighbor, by
Sir Smile, his neighbor.[9] Nay, there's comfort in't

1. *Will . . . money?*: A proverbial expression meaning "Will you accept a trifle in place of something valuable?"
2. *happy . . . dole*: proverbial for "May you have good luck!"
3. Ideas that would make me melancholy, a physical and emotional malady connected with a supposed excess of "thick blood."
4. *So . . . me:* So this young man performs the same duty for me.
5. *How . . . him:* How she holds up her face, her mouth to him (to be kissed).
6. Outcome, with puns on "issue" as also meaning "offspring" and "the exit an actor makes from a stage." Leontes' words imply that in playing the part of a cuckold, the result of his role will be disgrace; the illegitimate offspring produced by his wife will bring him disgrace; and his exit from the stage (at death) will be a disgraceful one.
7. Little thinks she has had sexual relations. A sluice was a trough or channel through which water could be directed. To be sluiced was to have water poured down one's "channel," here probably referring to the vagina.
8. Slang term for the sexual organs of his wife.
9. It is possible that "Sir Smile" is a reference to Polixenes.

Whiles other men have gates[1] and those gates opened,
As mine, against their will. Should all despair
That have revolted° wives, the tenth of mankind — *rebellious; unfaithful*
Would hang themselves. Physic° for't there's none. — *Medicine*
It is a bawdy planet that will strike
Where 'tis predominant;[2] and 'tis powerful, think it,
From east, west, north, and south; be it concluded,
No barricado for a belly.[3] Know't,
It will let in and out the enemy
With bag and baggage.[4] Many thousand on 's° — *of us*
Have the disease and feel't not. —How now, boy?

MAMILLIUS I am like you, they say.

LEONTES Why, that's some comfort.
—What, Camillo there?

CAMILLO [*coming forward*] Ay, my good lord.

LEONTES Go play, Mamillius. Thou'rt an honest man.
[*Exit* MAMILLIUS.]
Camillo, this great sir will yet stay longer.

CAMILLO You had much ado to make his anchor hold.
When you cast out, it still came home.° — *always failed to hold*

LEONTES Didst note it?

CAMILLO He would not stay at your petitions, made
His business more material.° — *important*

LEONTES Didst perceive it?
[*aside*] They're here with me[5] already, whisp'ring, rounding,° — *murmuring*
"Sicilia is a so-forth." 'Tis far gone
When I shall gust° it last. —How came't, Camillo, — *perceive; taste*
That he did stay?

CAMILLO At the good Queen's entreaty.

LEONTES "At the Queen's" be't. "Good" should be pertinent,
But so° it is, it is not. Was this taken° — *as / perceived*
By any understanding pate° but thine? — *head*
For thy conceit is soaking,° will draw in — *your wit is quick*
More than the common blocks.° Not noted, is't, — *dimwits*
But of° the finer natures, by some severals° — *by / individuals*
Of headpiece° extraordinary? Lower messes[6] — *intellect*
Perchance are to this business purblind?° Say. — *blind*

CAMILLO Business, my lord? I think most understand
Bohemia stays here longer.

LEONTES Ha?

CAMILLO Stays here longer.

LEONTES Ay, but why?

CAMILLO To satisfy your highness and the entreaties
Of our most gracious mistress.

LEONTES Satisfy?[7]
Th'entreaties of your mistress? Satisfy?
Let that suffice. I have trusted thee, Camillo,
With all the nearest things to my heart, as well

1. Another slang term for female genitalia. Leontes imagines the vulva as a gateway that ought to be entered only by a husband.
2. Alluding to the notion that planets control human actions and may exercise malign influences ("strike") when they are in certain "predominant" positions.
3. No means of defending a womb.
4. With full military (or sexual) equipment.
5. They know my secret.
6. Those of lower social status at the dining table. A "mess" refers to a group of four people who share meals together.
7. Punning on "satisfy" as meaning both "appease" and "give sexual pleasure to."

My chamber-counsels,° wherein, priestlike, thou — *secret matters*
Hast cleansed my bosom. I from thee departed
Thy penitent reformed. But we have been
Deceived in thy integrity, deceived
In that which seems so.

CAMILLO Be it forbid, my lord.

LEONTES To bide° upon't: thou art not honest; or — *dwell*
If thou inclin'st that way, thou art a coward,
Which hoxes° honesty behind, restraining — *disables; hamstrings*
From course required;[8] or else thou must be counted
A servant grafted in my serious trust,[9]
And therein negligent; or else a fool
That seest a game played home,° the rich stake drawn,° — *in earnest / won*
And tak'st it all for jest.

CAMILLO My gracious lord,
I may be negligent, foolish, and fearful.
In every one of these no man is free,° — *guiltless*
But that his negligence, his folly, fear,
Among the infinite doings of the world,
Sometime puts forth.° In your affairs, my lord, — *reveals itself*
If ever I were willful-negligent,
It was my folly; if industriously° — *deliberately*
I played the fool, it was my negligence,
Not weighing well the end. If ever fearful
To do a thing where I the issue° doubted, — *outcome*
Whereof the execution did cry out
Against the non-performance,[1] 'twas a fear
Which oft infects the wisest. These, my lord,
Are such allowed infirmities that honesty
Is never free of. But beseech your grace
Be plainer with me; let me know my trespass
By its own visage.° If I then deny it, — *face*
'Tis none of mine.

LEONTES Ha' not you seen, Camillo—
But that's past doubt; you have, or your eye-glass° — *the lens of your eye*
Is thicker than a cuckold's horn—or heard—
For, to a vision° so apparent, rumor — *sight*
Cannot be mute—or thought—for cogitation
Resides not in that man that does not think—
My wife is slippery? If thou wilt confess,
Or else be impudently negative,° — *shamelessly deny*
To have nor eyes, nor ears, nor thought, then say
My wife's a hobby-horse,[2] deserves a name
As rank° as any flax-wench[3] that puts to° — *indecent / has sexual relations*
Before her troth-plight.° Say't and justify't. — *betrothal*

CAMILLO I would not be a stander-by to hear
My sovereign mistress clouded so without

8. *restraining . . . required:* keeping (honesty) from the path it must take (to find out truth).
9. A servant who has grown into my confidence as a cutting is grafted onto a plant.
1. *Whereof . . . non-performance:* Even when the need to do the deed protested against its non-performance.
2. Whore. The image is of a woman who, like a horse, can be mounted. F has "Holy-Horse," an obscure phrase that nearly all modern editors emend to "hobby-horse."
3. A girl or woman, usually of low social status, who worked with flax, a fibrous plant used to make candlewicks, clothing, and linen.

My present° vengeance taken. 'Shrew° my heart, — *immediate / Curse*
You never spoke what did become you less
Than this, which to reiterate° were sin — *repeat*
As deep as that, though true.[4]

LEONTES Is whispering nothing?
Is leaning cheek to cheek? Is meeting noses?
Kissing with inside lip? Stopping the career° — *full gallop*
Of laughter with a sigh—a note° infallible — *sign*
Of breaking honesty?° Horsing foot on foot?[5] — *violating chastity*
Skulking in corners? Wishing clocks more swift?
Hours minutes? Noon midnight? And all eyes
Blind with the pin and web° but theirs, theirs only, — *cataract disease*
That would unseen be wicked? Is this nothing?
Why, then, the world and all that's in't is nothing,
The covering sky is nothing, Bohemia nothing,
My wife is nothing, nor nothing have these nothings[6]
If this be nothing.

CAMILLO Good my lord, be cured
Of this diseased opinion, and betimes,° — *quickly*
For 'tis most dangerous.

LEONTES Say it be, 'tis true.

CAMILLO No, no, my lord.

LEONTES It is. You lie, you lie.
I say thou liest, Camillo, and I hate thee,
Pronounce thee a gross lout, a mindless slave,
Or else a hovering° temporizer, that — *irresolute*
Canst with thine eyes at once see good and evil,
Inclining to them both. Were my wife's liver
Infected as her life,[7] she would not live
The running of one glass.° — *hourglass*

CAMILLO Who does infect her?

LEONTES Why he that wears her like her medal,[8] hanging
About his neck—Bohemia—who, if I
Had servants true about me that bare° eyes — *possessed*
To see alike mine honor as their profits,
Their own particular thrifts,° they would do that — *personal gain*
Which should undo° more doing.° Ay, and thou — *stop / sexual acts*
His cupbearer[9]—whom I from meaner form° — *lower rank or place*
Have benched and reared to worship,[1] who mayst see
Plainly as heaven sees earth and earth sees heaven
How I am galled°—mightst bespice a cup, — *sorely vexed*
To give mine enemy a lasting wink,[2]
Which draft to me were cordial.[3]

4. *sin . . . true:* that is, as grave as is the sin that you accuse your wife of, even if it were true (which it is not).
5. Mounting or rubbing one foot on another, a sexually titillating pastime.
6. Alluding to the proverbial notion that nothing can come of nothing. The word "nothing" appears many times in this play.
7. Were Hermione's liver as infected by disease as is her conduct. The liver was believed in Renaissance humoral psychology to be the seat of the passions.
8. As though she were a miniature portrait of herself. Ornate lockets ("medals") containing miniature portraits were popular love tokens among courtiers.
9. In a noble household, a male servant whose responsibilities included serving wine to his master.
1. Given authority and elevated to a dignified position. Referring to his "bench" or place at the dining table as a sign of his high rank.
2. To close my enemy's eyes forever.
3. Which drink would be medicinal to me.

CAMILLO Sir, my lord,
I could do this, and that with no rash° potion, — *quick-acting*
But with a lingering° dram that should not work — *slow-working*
Maliciously,° like poison. But I cannot — *Violently*
Believe this crack° to be in my dread mistress, — *flaw*
So sovereignly being honorable.
I have loved thee—

LEONTES Make that thy question,° and go rot. — *concern*
Dost think I am so muddy, so unsettled,
To appoint° myself in this vexation? — *put*
Sully the purity and whiteness of my sheets—
Which to preserve is sleep, which being spotted
Is goads,° thorns, nettles, tails of wasps— — *sharp sticks*
Give scandal to the blood o'th' prince, my son,
Who I do think is mine and love as mine,
Without ripe moving° to't? Would I do this? — *good reason*
Could man so blench?° — *stray (from sense)*

CAMILLO I must believe you, sir.
I do, and will fetch off° Bohemia for't— — *kill*
Provided that when he's removed your highness
Will take again your queen as yours at first,
Even for your son's sake, and thereby for sealing° — *silencing*
The injury of tongues in courts and kingdoms
Known and allied to yours.

LEONTES Thou dost advise me
Even so as I mine own course have set down.
I'll give no blemish to her honor, none.

CAMILLO My lord, go, then, and with a countenance as clear
As friendship wears at feasts, keep° with Bohemia — *associate*
And with your queen. I am his cupbearer.
If from me he have wholesome beverage,
Account me not your servant.

LEONTES This is all.
Do't, and thou hast the one half of my heart;
Do't not, thou splitt'st thine own.

CAMILLO I'll do't, my lord.

LEONTES I will seem friendly, as thou hast advised me.
*Exit.*

CAMILLO O miserable lady! But for me,
What case stand I in? I must be the poisoner
Of good Polixenes, and my ground to do't
Is the obedience to a master, one
Who in rebellion with himself will have
All that are his so too. To do this deed,
Promotion follows. If I could find example
Of thousands that had struck anointed kings
And flourished after, I'd not do't. But since
Nor° brass, nor stone, nor parchment bears not one,[4] — *Neither*
Let villainy itself forswear't.° I must — *swear not to do it*
Forsake the court. To do't or no is certain
To me a break-neck.° Happy° star reign now. — *death / Lucky*

4. *since . . . not one:* that is, since no form of historical record shows an example of a man who flourished after killing a king.

*Enter* POLIXENES.

Here comes Bohemia.

POLIXENES [*aside*] This is strange. Methinks
My favor here begins to warp. Not speak?
—Good day, Camillo.

CAMILLO Hail, most royal sir.

POLIXENES What is the news i'th' court?

CAMILLO None rare,° my lord. — *noteworthy*

POLIXENES The King hath on him such a countenance
As° he had lost some province and a region — *As if*
Loved as he loves himself. Even now I met him
With customary compliment, when he,
Wafting his eyes to th' contrary° and falling — *Shifting his gaze away*
A lip of much contempt,° speeds from me and — *sneering*
So leaves me to consider what is breeding
That changes thus his manners.

CAMILLO I dare not know, my lord.

POLIXENES How? "Dare not"? Do not? Do you know and dare not?
Be intelligent° to me—'tis thereabouts.[5] — *informative*
For to yourself what you do know you must,° — *(know)*
And cannot say you dare not. Good Camillo,
Your changed complexions are to me a mirror
Which shows me mine changed too; for I must be
A party in this alteration,° finding — *(of Leontes' manner)*
Myself thus altered with't.

CAMILLO There is a sickness
Which puts some of us in distemper, but
I cannot name the disease, and it is caught
Of you that yet are well.

POLIXENES How caught of me?
Make me not sighted like the basilisk.[6]
I have looked on thousands who have sped° the better — *fared*
By my regard, but killed none so. Camillo—
As you are certainly a gentleman, thereto
Clerk-like experienced,[7] which no less adorns
Our gentry° than our parents' noble names, — *status as gentlemen*
In whose success we are gentle[8]—I beseech you,
If you know aught which does behoove my knowledge
Thereof to be informed,[9] imprison't not
In ignorant concealment.[1]

CAMILLO I may not answer.

POLIXENES A sickness caught of me, and yet I well?
I must be answered. Dost thou hear, Camillo—,
I conjure thee, by all the parts° of man — *duties*
Which honor does acknowledge, whereof the least
Is not this suit of mine, that thou declare
What incidency° thou dost guess of harm — *event*
Is creeping toward me; how far off, how near,

5. That is, I'm more or less right (that you are afraid to tell me).
6. A mythical serpent whose glance was said to be fatal.
7. Also having the experience of an educated man.
8. *In whose . . . gentle:* By succession from whom we are made noble ("gentle").
9. *which . . . informed:* which it is necessary for me to know.
1. In concealment that keeps me ignorant; in concealment on the pretense that you are ignorant.

Which way to be prevented, if to be;
If not, how best to bear it.
CAMILLO Sir, I will tell you,
Since I am charged in honor and by him
That I think honorable. Therefore mark my counsel,
Which must be e'en as swiftly followed as
I mean to utter it; or both yourself and me
Cry lost, and so good night.° *good-bye forever*
POLIXENES On, good Camillo.
CAMILLO I am appointed him° to murder you. *by him*
POLIXENES By whom, Camillo?
CAMILLO By the King.
POLIXENES For what?
CAMILLO He thinks—nay, with all confidence he swears,
As he had seen't or been an instrument
To vice° you to't—that you have touched his queen *force*
Forbiddenly.
POLIXENES Oh, then my best blood turn
To an infected jelly and my name
Be yoked with his° that did betray the best.° *(Judas's) name / Christ*
Turn then my freshest reputation to
A savor° that may strike the dullest nostril *foul odor*
Where I arrive and my approach be shunned—
Nay, hated too—worse than the greatest infection
That e'er was heard or read.
CAMILLO Swear his thought over[2]
By each particular star in heaven and
By all their influences,[3] you may as well
Forbid the sea for to obey the moon
As or° by oath remove or counsel shake *either*
The fabric of his folly, whose foundation
Is piled upon his faith and will continue
The standing of his body.° *As long as he lives*
POLIXENES How should this grow?° *come to be*
CAMILLO I know not. But I am sure 'tis safer to
Avoid what's grown than question how 'tis born.
If therefore you dare trust my honesty
That lies enclosèd in this trunk,° which you *body*
Shall bear along impawned,[4] away tonight!
Your followers I will whisper to the business
And will by twos and threes at several posterns° *city gates*
Clear them o'th' city. For myself, I'll put
My fortunes to your service, which are here
By this discovery° lost. Be not uncertain, *revelation*
For by the honor of my parents, I
Have uttered truth; which if you seek to prove,
I dare not stand by, nor shall you be safer
Than one condemnèd by the King's own mouth,
Thereon his execution sworn.
POLIXENES I do believe thee.
I saw his heart in 's face. Give me thy hand;

2. You may swear that his allegations are false.
3. Substances that, according to contemporary astrological theories, were emitted by stars and helped to shape human destiny.
4. Shall carry with you as a pledge (of my faith).

Be pilot to me, and thy places° shall — *your position*
Still neighbor° mine. My ships are ready, and — *Always be near*
My people did expect my hence departure
Two days ago. This jealousy
Is for a precious creature. As she's rare,
Must it be great; and as his person's mighty,
Must it be violent; and as he does conceive
He is dishonored by a man which ever
Professed° to him, why, his revenges must — *Vowed love*
In that be made more bitter. Fear o'ershades me.
Good expedition° be my friend, and comfort — *speed (in leaving)*
The gracious Queen, part of his theme, but nothing
Of his ill-ta'en suspicion.[5] Come, Camillo,
I will respect thee as a father if
Thou bear'st my life off hence. Let us avoid.° — *be gone*

CAMILLO It is in mine authority to command
The keys of all the posterns. Please your highness
To take the urgent hour.° Come, sir, away. *Exeunt.* — *seize the moment*

## 2.1

*Enter* HERMIONE, MAMILLIUS, [*and*] LADIES.[1]

HERMIONE Take the boy to you; he so troubles me,
'Tis past enduring.

FIRST LADY Come, my gracious lord,
Shall I be your playfellow?

MAMILLIUS No, I'll none of you.

FIRST LADY Why, my sweet lord?

MAMILLIUS You'll kiss me hard and speak to me as if
I were a baby still. [*to* SECOND LADY] I love you better.

SECOND LADY And why so, my lord?

MAMILLIUS Not for° because — *Not*
Your brows° are blacker—yet black brows they say — *eyebrows*
Become° some women best, so° that there be not — *Suit / provided*
Too much hair there, but in a semicircle
Or a half-moon made with a pen.

SECOND LADY Who taught° this? — *taught you*

MAMILLIUS I learned it out of women's faces. Pray now,
What color are your eyebrows?

SECOND LADY Blue, my lord.

MAMILLIUS Nay, that's a mock. I have seen a lady's nose
That has been blue,[2] but not her eyebrows.

FIRST LADY Hark ye,
The Queen your mother rounds apace;° we shall — *grows round quickly*
Present our services to a fine new prince

5. *and comfort . . . suspicion:* and make easier the situation of the virtuous Queen, who is a part of Leontes' accusation (his proposition, or "theme"), but who is not guilty of his unjustified suspicion.

2.1 Location: Sicilia. The palace of Leontes.

1. TEXTUAL COMMENT Although the Folio text lists all the characters who appear in this scene as entering here, it makes more sense to have Leontes and Antigonus enter later (in this edition, between lines 33 and 34) and interrupt the conversation among Hermione, Mamillius, and the Ladies. See Digital Edition TC 3.

2. It is unclear whether Mamillius is making a joke here or possibly referring to noses made "blue" by the cold.

One of these days, and then you'd wanton° with us, *play*
If we would have you.
**SECOND LADY** She is spread of late
Into a goodly bulk: good time encounter her!° *good fortune be with her*
**HERMIONE** What wisdom stirs amongst you? Come, sir, now
I am for you again. Pray you sit by us
And tell's a tale.
**MAMILLIUS** Merry or sad shall't be?
**HERMIONE** As merry as you will.
**MAMILLIUS** A sad tale's best for winter. I have one
Of sprites and goblins.
**HERMIONE** Let's have that, good sir.
Come on, sit down; come on, and do your best
To fright me with your sprites. You're powerful at it.
**MAMILLIUS** There was a man—
**HERMIONE** Nay, come, sit down; then on.
**MAMILLIUS** Dwelt by a churchyard—I will tell it softly;
Yond crickets° shall not hear it. *(the other women)*
**HERMIONE** Come on, then, and give't me in mine ear.
[*Enter* LEONTES, ANTIGONUS, *and* LORDS.]
**LEONTES** Was he met there? His train?° Camillo with him? *retinue*
**LORD** Behind the tuft of pines I met them. Never
Saw I men scour° so on their way. I eyed them *hurry*
Even to their ships.
**LEONTES** How blest am I
In my just censure,° in my true opinion! *judgment*
Alack, for lesser knowledge!° How accursed *Would I knew less*
In being so blest! There may be in the cup
A spider steeped, and one may drink, depart,
And yet partake no venom, for his knowledge
Is not infected.[3] But if one present
Th'abhorred ingredient to his eye, make known
How he hath drunk, he cracks his gorge,° his sides *throat*
With violent hefts.° I have drunk and seen the spider. *retching*
Camillo was his help in this, his pander.[4]
There is a plot against my life, my crown.
All's true that is mistrusted.° That false villain *suspected*
Whom I employed was pre-employed by him.
He has discovered° my design, and I *revealed*
Remain a pinched° thing—yea, a very trick *tormented*
For them to play at will. How came the posterns
So easily open?
**LORD** By his great authority,
Which often hath no less prevailed than so
On your command.
**LEONTES** I know't too well.
[*to* HERMIONE] Give me the boy; I am glad you did not nurse him.[5]
Though he does bear some signs of me, yet you
Have too much blood in him.

3. Alluding to the belief that a spider consumed with food or drink would be poisonous only if its presence were known to the consumer.
4. A go-between; one who facilitates illicit sexual encounters.
5. Women who breast-fed infants were believed to shape an infant's character by substances transmitted in their milk.

HERMIONE What is this? Sport?
LEONTES Bear the boy hence; he shall not come about her.
Away with him, and let her sport herself
With that she's big with, [*to* HERMIONE] for 'tis Polixenes
Has made thee swell thus. [*Exit one with* MAMILLIUS.]
HERMIONE But I'd say he had not;
And I'll be sworn you would believe my saying,
Howe'er you lean to th' nayward.° *the contrary*
LEONTES You, my lords,
Look on her; mark her well. Be but about
To say she is a goodly lady, and
The justice of your hearts will thereto add,
"'Tis pity she's not honest,° honorable." *chaste*
Praise her but for this her without-door° form— *external*
Which on my faith deserves high speech—and straight° *immediately*
The shrug, the "hum," or "ha," these petty brands° *expressions; stigmas*
That calumny° doth use—oh, I am out!°— *slander / wrong*
That mercy does, for calumny will sear° *dry up; wither*
Virtue itself[6]—these shrugs, these "hum's" and "ha's,"
When you have said she's goodly, come between° *interrupt*
Ere you can say she's honest. But be't known
From him that has most cause to grieve it should be,
She's an adultress.
HERMIONE Should a villain say so,
The most replenished° villain in the world, *complete*
He were as much more° villain. You, my lord, *by so much more a*
Do but mistake.
LEONTES You have mistook,° my lady, *erred; improperly taken*
Polixenes for Leontes. O thou thing
Which I'll not call a creature of thy place[7]
Lest barbarism,° making me the precedent, *uncivilized rudeness*
Should a like° language use to all degrees° *the same / ranks*
And mannerly distinguishment° leave out *proper distinction*
Betwixt the prince and beggar. I have said
She's an adultress; I have said with whom.
More, she's a traitor; and Camillo is
A federary° with her, and one that knows *confederate*
What she should shame to know herself
But with her most vile principal,° that she's *partner*
A bed-swerver,° even as bad as those *adultress*
That vulgars give bold'st titles[8]—ay, and privy
To this their late° escape. *recent*
HERMIONE No, by my life,
Privy to none of this. How will this grieve you
When you shall come to clearer knowledge, that
You thus have published° me! Gentle my° lord, *proclaimed / My noble*
You scarce can right me thoroughly° then to say *fully do me justice*
You did mistake.
LEONTES No. If I mistake

6. On obscure passage. Leontes seems to mean that even mercy will use "hum's" and "ha's" to condemn Hermione because mercy's virtue has been dried up by calumny's force.

7. To whom I'll not give the title of your (high) social position.

8. That common people call by the coarsest names.

In those foundations which I build upon,
The center° is not big enough to bear *earth*
A schoolboy's top. —Away with her to prison.
He who shall speak for her is afar-off° guilty, *indirectly*
But that he speaks.° *Merely for speaking*

HERMIONE There's some ill planet reigns.
I must be patient till the heavens look
With an aspect more favorable.[9] Good my° lords, *My good*
I am not prone to weeping as our sex
Commonly are, the want° of which vain dew *lack*
Perchance shall dry your pities. But I have
That honorable grief lodged here which burns
Worse than tears drown. Beseech you all, my lords,
With thoughts so qualified° as your charities *tempered*
Shall best instruct you, measure me; and so
The King's will be performed.

LEONTES Shall I be heard?

HERMIONE Who is't that goes with me? Beseech your highness
My women may be with me, for you see
My plight requires it. —Do not weep, good fools;° *dear ones*
There is no cause. When you shall know your mistress
Has deserved prison, then abound in tears
As I come out. This action I now go on
Is for my better grace.[1] —Adieu, my lord.
I never wished to see you sorry; now
I trust I shall. My women, come, you have leave.° *permission*

LEONTES Go, do our bidding. Hence.

[*Exit* HERMIONE *with* LADIES.]

LORD Beseech your highness, call the Queen again.

ANTIGONUS Be certain what you do, sir, lest your justice
Prove violence, in the which three great ones suffer:
Yourself, your queen, your son.

LORD For her, my lord,
I dare my life lay down, and will do't, sir.
Please you t'accept it that the Queen is spotless
I'th' eyes of heaven, and to you—I mean
In this which you accuse her.

ANTIGONUS If it prove
She's otherwise, I'll keep my stables where
I lodge my wife;[2] I'll go in couples with her;[3]
Than when I feel and see her, no farther trust her.
For every inch of woman in the world—
Ay, every dram° of woman's flesh—is false *smallest piece*
If she be.

LEONTES Hold your peaces.

LORD Good my lord—

ANTIGONUS It is for you we speak, not for ourselves.
You are abused, and by some putter-on° *instigator*

9. Until the planets are aligned to have a more positive effect (on Hermione's fate).
1. *This action . . . grace:* This trial I am enduring is for my greater honor (when vindicated); *or* This suffering I am enduring is to refine and purge me, leading to greater virtue. In both cases, an affirmation of Hermione's confidence and her innocence.
2. *If it prove . . . wife:* an obscure passage. Antigonus probably means that if Hermione is unchaste, he will keep his horses in his wife's bedchamber since all women will have shown themselves no better than beasts.
3. *go . . . her:* have her tied to me (as hounds were leashed together for the hunt).

That will be damned for't. Would I knew the villain,
I would land-damn him.[4] Be she honor-flawed,
I have three daughters—the eldest is eleven;
The second and the third, nine and some five—
If this prove true, they'll pay for't. By mine honor,
I'll geld 'em all;[5] fourteen they shall not see
To bring false generations.° They are co-heirs, *illegitimate children*
And I had rather glib° myself than they *castrate*
Should not produce fair issue.° *legitimate offspring*

LEONTES Cease, no more.
You smell this business with a sense as cold
As is a dead man's nose. But I do see't and feel't,
As you feel doing thus; and see withal
The instruments that feel.[6]

ANTIGONUS If it be so,
We need no grave to bury honesty;° *chastity*
There's not a grain of it the face to sweeten° *to sweeten the face*
Of the whole dungy° earth. *foul*

LEONTES What? Lack I credit?

LORD I had rather you did lack than I, my lord,
Upon this ground;° and more it would content me *In this affair*
To have her honor true than your suspicion,
Be blamed for't how you might.

LEONTES Why, what need we
Commune with you of this, but rather follow
Our forceful instigation?° Our prerogative *impulse; motive*
Calls not your counsels,[7] but our natural goodness
Imparts this,° which if you—or° stupefied *this information / either*
Or seeming so in skill°—cannot or will not *cunningly*
Relish° a truth like us, inform yourselves *Appreciate*
We need no more of your advice. The matter—
The loss, the gain, the ordering on't°— *of it*
Is all properly ours.

ANTIGONUS And I wish, my liege,
You had only in your silent judgment tried it,
Without more overture.° *public disclosure*

LEONTES How could that be?
Either thou art most ignorant by age,
Or thou wert born a fool. Camillo's flight,
Added to their familiarity—
Which was as gross as ever touched conjecture,
That lacked sight only, naught for approbation
But only seeing;[8] all other circumstances
Made up to th' deed°—doth push on this proceeding.[9] *Pointed to the deed*
Yet, for a greater confirmation—
For in an act of this importance 'twere
Most piteous to be wild°—I have dispatched in post,° *rash / haste*

4. *land-damn:* a term of abuse whose exact meaning is unclear. It may be a dialect form of "lamback" or "lambaste," which means "thrash."
5. I'll make them all barren. Literally, I'll cut out their organs of generation.
6. Leontes here probably does some action (touching a courtier or rubbing his hands together) that shows how immediately or directly he feels Hermione's betrayal and sees as well the fingers ("instruments") with which he touches things, and with which Hermione and Polixenes touch each other.
7. *Our . . . counsels:* My privileges as King do not require that I seek your advice.
8. *as gross . . . seeing:* as obvious ("gross") as any suspicion ("conjecture") ever was that only lacked eyewitnesses ("sight" and "seeing") to confirm its truth.
9. Does urge on this course of action.

To sacred Delphos,[1] to Apollo's temple,
Cleomenes and Dion, whom you know
Of stuffed sufficiency.° Now from the oracle — *ample competence*
They will bring all, whose spiritual counsel had,° — *obtained*
Shall stop or spur me. Have I done well?

LORD Well done, my lord.

LEONTES Though I am satisfied and need no more
Than what I know, yet shall the oracle
Give rest to th' minds of others, such as he
Whose ignorant credulity will not
Come up to th' truth. So have we thought it good
From our free° person she should be confined, — *openly accessible*
Lest that the treachery of the two fled hence
Be left her to perform. Come, follow us.
We are to speak in public, for this business
Will raise° us all. — *rouse (to action)*

ANTIGONUS [*aside*] To laughter, as I take it,
If the good truth were known. *Exeunt.*

## 2.2

*Enter* PAULINA, *a Gentleman*[, *and Attendants*].

PAULINA The keeper of the prison, call to him.
Let him have knowledge who I am. [*Exit Gentleman.*]
Good lady,[1]
No court in Europe is too good for thee.
What dost thou then in prison?
[*Enter Gentleman with* JAILER.]
Now, good sir,
You know me, do you not?

JAILER For a worthy lady,
And one who much I honor.

PAULINA Pray you, then,
Conduct me to the Queen.

JAILER I may not, madam.
To the contrary I have express commandment.

PAULINA Here's ado,° — *Here's such a fuss*
To lock up honesty and honor from
Th'access of gentle° visitors. Is't lawful, pray you, — *noble; kind*
To see her women? Any of them? Emilia?

JAILER So please you, madam,
To put apart these your attendants, I
Shall bring Emilia forth.

PAULINA I pray now call her.
—Withdraw yourselves. [*Exeunt Gentleman and Attendants.*]

JAILER And, madam,
I must be present at your conference.

PAULINA Well, be't so, prithee. [*Exit* JAILER.]
Here's such ado to make no stain a stain
As passes coloring.[2]

1. Delos, often called Delphos by Renaissance writers, was the island where Apollo, the sun god, was born. It is here conflated with Delphi, the Greek mainland town where the oracle of Apollo could be consulted.

2.2 Location: Sicilia. A prison.

1. *Good lady*: Paulina is addressing Hermione here, even though she has not yet been admitted to her presence.

2. To make from no stain at all a stain that exceeds what the art of dyeing can do; to make of no sin a sin that surpasses all attempts to justify it.

[*Enter* JAILER *and* EMILIA.]
Dear gentlewoman,
How fares our gracious lady?
EMILIA As well as one so great and so forlorn
May hold together. On° her frights and griefs, *Because of*
Which never tender lady hath borne greater,
She is something° before her time delivered. *somewhat*
PAULINA A boy?
EMILIA A daughter and a goodly babe,
Lusty° and like° to live. The Queen receives *Vigorous / likely*
Much comfort in't; says, "My poor prisoner,
I am innocent as you."
PAULINA I dare be sworn.
These dangerous unsafe lunes° i'th' King, beshrew them. *fits of lunacy*
He must be told on't, and he shall. The office° *job*
Becomes a woman best. I'll take't upon me.
If I prove honey-mouthed, let my tongue blister[3]
And never to my red-looked° anger be *red-faced*
The trumpet[4] any more. Pray you, Emilia,
Commend° my best obedience to the Queen. *Send*
If she dares trust me with her little babe,
I'll show't the King, and undertake to be
Her advocate to th' loud'st. We do not know
How he may soften at the sight o'th' child.
The silence often of pure innocence
Persuades when speaking fails.
EMILIA Most worthy madam,
Your honor and your goodness is so evident
That your free° undertaking cannot miss *generous*
A thriving issue;[5] there is no lady living
So meet° for this great errand. Please your ladyship *suitable*
To visit the next room; I'll presently
Acquaint the Queen of your most noble offer,
Who but today hammered of° this design *mused upon*
But durst not tempt a minister of honor[6]
Lest she should be denied.
PAULINA Tell her, Emilia,
I'll use that tongue I have. If wit flow from't
As boldness from my bosom, let't not be doubted
I shall do good.
EMILIA Now be you blest for it!
I'll to the Queen. Please you come something° nearer. *somewhat*
JAILER Madam, if't please the Queen to send the babe,
I know not what° I shall incur to pass it,[7] *what risk*
Having no warrant.
PAULINA You need not fear it, sir.
This child was prisoner to the womb and is
By law and process of great nature thence
Freed and enfranchised, not a party to

3. Alluding to the proverb that deceitfulness causes blisters on the tongue.
4. In early modern warfare, a "trumpet" was a soldier who, bearing a trumpet, went before the red-coated herald who carried messages, often angry ones, to the enemy camp.
5. A successful outcome, with a pun on "issue" as "offspring."
6. But dared not risk asking a person of higher rank.
7. To let it pass (out of the prison).

The anger of the King, nor guilty of—
If any be—the trespass of the Queen.
JAILER I do believe it.
PAULINA Do not you fear. Upon mine honor, I
Will stand betwixt you and danger. *Exeunt.*

## 2.3

*Enter* LEONTES.

LEONTES Nor° night nor day, no rest. It is but weakness *Neither*
To bear the matter thus—mere weakness. If
The cause were not in being°—part o'th' cause, *alive*
She, th'adultress; for the harlot° King *lewd*
Is quite beyond mine arm, out of the blank° *target*
And level° of my brain, plot-proof. But she *aim*
I can hook to me. Say that she were gone,
Given to the fire,[1] a moiety° of my rest *portion*
Might come to me again. Who's there?
[*Enter* SERVANT.]
SERVANT My lord.
LEONTES How does the boy?
SERVANT He took good rest tonight.
'Tis hoped his sickness is discharged.
LEONTES To see his nobleness!
Conceiving° the dishonor of his mother, *Realizing*
He straight° declined, drooped, took it deeply, *immediately*
Fastened and fixed the shame on't° in himself, *of it*
Threw off his spirit, his appetite, his sleep,
And downright languished. Leave me solely.° Go, *alone*
See how he fares. [*Exit* SERVANT.]
Fie, fie, no thought of him!° *(Polixenes)*
The very thought of my revenges that way
Recoil upon me. In himself too mighty,
And in his parties,° his alliance.° Let him be *supporters / allies*
Until a time may serve. For present vengeance
Take it on her. Camillo and Polixenes
Laugh at me, make their pastime at my sorrow.
They should not laugh if I could reach them, nor
Shall she, within my power.
*Enter* PAULINA [*with the baby,* ANTIGONUS, LORDS, *and* SERVANT].
LORD You must not enter.
PAULINA Nay, rather, good my lords, be second to me.° *help me*
Fear you his tyrannous passion more, alas,
Than the Queen's life? A gracious innocent soul,
More free° than he is jealous. *innocent*
ANTIGONUS That's enough.
SERVANT Madam, he hath not slept tonight, commanded
None should come at him.
PAULINA Not so hot, good sir.
I come to bring him sleep. 'Tis such as you,
That creep like shadows by him and do sigh
At each his needless heavings—such as you

2.3 Location: Sicilia. The palace of Leontes.

1. Burned at the stake (for treason against the King).

Nourish the cause of his awaking.° I — *wakefulness*
Do come with words, as medicinal as true,
Honest as either, to purge him of that humor° — *mental disorder*
That presses him from sleep.

LEONTES What noise there, ho?

PAULINA No noise, my lord, but needful conference
About some gossips[2] for your highness.

LEONTES How?
Away with that audacious lady! Antigonus,
I charged thee that she should not come about me.
I knew she would.

ANTIGONUS I told her so, my lord,
On your displeasure's peril° and on mine, — *At the risk of your anger*
She should not visit you.

LEONTES What, canst not rule her?

PAULINA From all dishonesty he can. In this,
Unless he take the course that you have done—
Commit° me for committing honor—trust it, — *Imprison*
He shall not rule me.

ANTIGONUS La you now,° you hear. — *Observe this now*
When she will take the rein, I let her run,
But she'll not stumble.

PAULINA [*to* LEONTES] Good my liege, I come—
And I beseech you hear me, who professes
Myself your loyal servant, your physician,
Your most obedient counselor, yet that dares
Less appear so in comforting° your evils — *condoning*
Than such as most seem yours[3]—I say I come
From your good queen.

LEONTES Good queen?

PAULINA Good queen, my lord, good queen. I say good queen,
And would by combat make her good,[4] so were I
A man, the worst about° you. — *lowest in rank of*

LEONTES Force her hence.

PAULINA Let him that makes but trifles of his eyes
First hand° me. On mine own accord I'll off; — *touch*
But first I'll do my errand. The good Queen—
For she is good—hath brought you forth a daughter—
Here 'tis—commends it to your blessing.
[PAULINA *lays down the baby.*]

LEONTES Out!
A mankind° witch! Hence with her, out o'door— — *manlike*
A most intelligencing bawd.° — *spying go-between*

PAULINA Not so.
I am as ignorant in that as you
In so entitling me,° and no less honest — *In calling me that*
Than you are mad, which is enough, I'll warrant,
As this world goes, to pass for honest.

LEONTES Traitors!
Will you not push her out? [*to* ANTIGONUS] Give her the bastard,
Thou dotard; thou art woman-tired,[5] unroosted

2. Godparents or sponsors at a child's baptism.
3. Than those who (wrongly) seem most loyal.
4. Prove her to be innocent; alluding to the chivalric trials by combat in which knights would establish innocence or guilt by means of duels.
5. You are pecked at by women; a metaphor from falconry referring to tearing of flesh with the beak.

By thy Dame Partlet here.[6] Take up the bastard;
Take't up, I say; give't to thy crone.° *old woman*

PAULINA Forever
Unvenerable° be thy hands if thou *Unworthy of respect*
Tak'st up the Princess by that forcèd baseness[7]
Which he has put upon't.

LEONTES He dreads° his wife. *fears*

PAULINA So I would you did. Then 'twere past all doubt
You'd call your children yours.

LEONTES A nest of traitors!

ANTIGONUS I am none, by this good light.

PAULINA Nor I, nor any
But one that's here, and that's himself; for he
The sacred honor of himself, his queen's,
His hopeful son's, his babe's, betrays to slander,
Whose sting is sharper than the sword's; and will not—
For as the case now stands, it is a curse
He cannot be compelled to't—once remove
The root of his opinion, which is rotten
As ever oak or stone was sound.

LEONTES A callet° *scold; harlot*
Of boundless tongue, who late° hath beat her husband *recently*
And now baits° me. This brat is none of mine; *provokes*
It is the issue° of Polixenes. *offspring*
Hence with it, and together with the dam
Commit them to the fire!

PAULINA It is yours,
And might we lay th'old proverb to your charge,° *apply the proverb to you*
So like you 'tis the worse. Behold, my lords,
Although the print° be little, the whole matter *copy*
And copy of the father: eye, nose, lip,
The trick° of 's frown, his forehead, nay, the valley,[8] *distinctive character*
The pretty dimples of his chin and cheek, his smiles,
The very mold and frame of hand, nail, finger.
And thou, good goddess Nature, which hast made it
So like to him that got° it, if thou hast *begot*
The ordering of the mind too, 'mongst all colors
No yellow[9] in't, lest she suspect, as he does,
Her children not her husband's.

LEONTES A gross hag!
And, [*to* ANTIGONUS] lozel,° thou art worthy to be hanged *scoundrel*
That wilt not stay her tongue.

ANTIGONUS Hang all the husbands
That cannot do that feat, you'll leave yourself
Hardly one subject.

LEONTES Once more take her hence.

PAULINA A most unworthy and unnatural lord
Can do no more.

LEONTES I'll ha' thee burnt.

PAULINA I care not.

6. *unroosted . . . here:* expelled from your "roost" or "perch," the position of domestic authority assigned to men. "Partlet" is a traditional name for a hen.
7. Under that wrongful name of bastard.
8. Referring to an indentation in the lip or a cleft in the chin.
9. Proverbially, the color of jealousy.

It is an heretic that makes the fire,
Not she which burns in't.[1] I'll not call you tyrant;
But this most cruel usage of your queen—
Not able to produce more accusation
Than your own weak-hinged fancy—something savors
Of tyranny and will ignoble make you,
Yea, scandalous to the world.

LEONTES On your allegiance,
Out of the chamber with her! Were I a tyrant,
Where were her life? She durst not call me so,
If she did know me one. Away with her!

PAULINA —I pray you do not push me; I'll be gone.
—Look to your babe, my lord; 'tis yours. Jove° send her *(king of the gods)*
A better guiding spirit. —What needs these hands?[2]
You that are thus so tender o'er° his follies *gentle with*
Will never do him good, not one of you.
So, so. Farewell, we are gone. *Exit.*

LEONTES Thou, traitor, hast set on thy wife to this.
My child? Away with't! Even thou that hast
A heart so tender o'er it, take it hence
And see it instantly consumed with fire.
Even thou and none but thou. Take it up straight.° *at once*
Within this hour bring me word 'tis done,
And by good testimony,° or I'll seize thy life *with good evidence*
With what thou else call'st thine. If thou refuse,
And wilt encounter with my wrath, say so.
The bastard brains with these my proper° hands *own*
Shall I dash out. Go, take it to the fire,
For thou sett'st on° thy wife. *instructed; urged on*

ANTIGONUS I did not, sir.
These lords, my noble fellows, if they please,
Can clear me in't.

LORDS We can. My royal liege,
He is not guilty of her coming hither.

LEONTES You're liars all.

LORD Beseech your highness, give us better credit.° *think us more honorable*
We have always truly served you, and beseech
So to esteem of us. And on our knees we beg,
As recompense of our dear services
Past and to come, that you do change this purpose,
Which being so horrible, so bloody, must
Lead on to some foul issue. We all kneel.

LEONTES I am a feather for each wind that blows.
Shall I live on to see this bastard kneel
And call me father? Better burn it now
Than curse it then. But be it; let it live.
It shall not neither. You, sir, come you hither,
You that have been so tenderly officious
With Lady Margery,[3] your midwife there,

1. *It is . . . in't:* The heretic is the one who unjustly makes the fire (Leontes), not the woman who burns in it (Paulina or Hermione).
2. *What . . . hands?:* Why is it necessary for you to push me out (spoken to Leontes' attendant lords)?
3. A contemptuous name (like "Dame Partlet") for a disorderly woman. "Margery-prater" is a slang term for "hen."

To save this bastard's life—for 'tis a bastard
So sure as this beard's gray. What will you adventure° *risk*
To save this brat's life?
ANTIGONUS Anything, my lord,
That my ability may undergo
And nobleness impose—at least thus much:
I'll pawn the little blood which I have left[4]
To save the innocent—anything possible.
LEONTES It shall be possible. Swear by this sword
Thou wilt perform my bidding.
ANTIGONUS I will, my lord.
LEONTES Mark and perform it, seest thou? For the fail° *failure*
Of any point in't shall not only be
Death to thyself but to thy lewd-tongued wife,
Whom for this time we pardon. We enjoin thee,
As thou art liegeman° to us, that thou carry *loyal servant*
This female bastard hence and that thou bear it
To some remote and desert place quite out
Of our dominions; and that there thou leave it,
Without more mercy, to it° own protection *its*
And favor of the climate. As by strange fortune[5]
It came to us, I do in justice charge thee,
On thy soul's peril and thy body's torture,
That thou commend it strangely to some place[6]
Where chance may nurse° or end it. Take it up. *nurture; help*
ANTIGONUS I swear to do this, though a present death
Had been more merciful. Come on, poor babe;
Some powerful spirit instruct the kites° and ravens *birds of prey*
To be thy nurses. Wolves and bears, they say,
Casting their savageness aside, have done
Like° offices of pity. Sir, be prosperous *Similar*
In more than this deed does require;[7] and blessing
Against° this cruelty fight on thy side, *To counteract*
Poor thing, condemned to loss.° *Exit* [*with the baby*]. *ruin*
LEONTES No, I'll not rear
Another's issue.
*Enter a* SERVANT.
SERVANT Please your highness, posts° *messengers*
From those you sent to th'oracle are come
An hour since. Cleomenes and Dion,
Being well arrived from Delphos, are both landed,
Hasting to th' court.
LORD So please you, sir, their speed
Hath been beyond account.° *without precedent*
LEONTES Twenty-three days
They have been absent. 'Tis good speed, foretells
The great Apollo suddenly° will have *at once*
The truth of this appear. Prepare you, lords;
Summon a session° that we may arraign *trial*
Our most disloyal lady. For as she hath

4. Aging was thought to reduce the amount of blood in the body.
5. *As . . . fortune:* Since by some unusual chance; since by the act of a foreigner (Polixenes).
6. That you take it to some foreign land.
7. To a greater extent or in more ways than this action deserves.

Been publicly accused, so shall she have
A just and open trial. While she lives,
My heart will be a burden to me. Leave me
And think upon my bidding. *Exeunt.*

### 3.1

*Enter* CLEOMENES *and* DION.

CLEOMENES The climate's delicate, the air most sweet,
Fertile the isle,[1] the temple much surpassing
The common praise it bears.
DION I shall report,
For most it caught° me, the celestial habits°— *charmed / garments*
Methinks I so should term them—and the reverence
Of the grave wearers. Oh, the sacrifice!
How ceremonious, solemn, and unearthly
It was i'th' offering!
CLEOMENES But of all, the burst° *blast (of thunder)*
And the ear-deafening voice o'th' oracle,
Kin° to Jove's thunder, so surprised my sense, *Like*
That I was nothing.
DION If th'event° o'th' journey *outcome*
Prove as successful to the Queen—oh, be't so!—
As it hath been to us rare, pleasant, speedy,
The time is worth the use on't.[2]
CLEOMENES Great Apollo
Turn all to th' best! These proclamations,
So forcing faults upon Hermione,
I little like.
DION The violent carriage° of it *rash handling*
Will clear or end the business. When the oracle,
Thus by Apollo's great divine° sealed up, *priest*
Shall the contents discover,° something rare *reveal*
Even then will rush to knowledge. Go. —Fresh horses!
—And gracious be the issue.° *Exeunt.* *result; child*

### 3.2

*Enter* LEONTES, LORDS, [*and*] OFFICERS.[1]

LEONTES This sessions, to our great grief we pronounce,
Even pushes 'gainst our heart; the party tried,
The daughter of a king, our wife, and one
Of us° too much beloved. Let us be cleared *By us*
Of being tyrannous, since we so openly
Proceed in justice, which shall have due course
Even to the guilt or the purgation.° *acquittal*
Produce the prisoner.
OFFICER It is his highness' pleasure that the Queen

3.1 Location: A road in Sicilia.
1. The island of Delphos (Delos), Apollo's birthplace, here conflated with Delphi, where Apollo's oracle was located. See note to 2.1.184.
2. The time will have been well spent.
3.2 Location: Sicilia. A court of justice.

1. Textual Comment F includes all this scene's characters (except Paulina, who has no designated entry) in this opening stage direction; this edition has Paulina and Hermione arrive at line 10, announced by the Officer, and Cleomenes and Dion enter at line 121. See Digital Edition TC 4.

Appear in person here in court.

[*Enter* HERMIONE *as to her trial,* PAULINA, *and* LADIES.]

Silence![2]

LEONTES Read the indictment.

OFFICER [*reading*] "Hermione, queen to the worthy Leontes, King of Sicilia, thou art here accused and arraigned of high treason, in committing adultery with Polixenes, King of Bohemia, and conspiring with Camillo to take away the life of our sovereign lord the King, thy royal husband; the pretense° whereof being by circumstances partly laid open, thou, Hermione, contrary to the faith and allegiance of a true subject, didst counsel and aid them, for their better safety, to fly away by night." *purpose*

HERMIONE Since what I am to say must be but° that *only*
Which contradicts my accusation, and
The testimony on my part no other
But what comes from myself, it shall scarce boot° me *profit*
To say, "Not guilty." Mine integrity
Being counted falsehood, shall, as I express it,
Be so received. But thus: if powers divine
Behold our human actions—as they do—
I doubt not then but innocence shall make
False accusation blush and tyranny
Tremble at patience. You, my lord, best know,
Who least will seem to do so, my past life
Hath been as continent, as chaste, as true,
As I am now unhappy; which° is more *which unhappiness*
Than history can pattern,[3] though devised
And played to take° spectators. For behold me, *captivate*
A fellow of the royal bed, which owe° *who owns*
A moiety° of the throne, a great king's daughter, *portion*
The mother to a hopeful prince, here standing
To prate and talk for life and honor, fore° *before*
Who please to come and hear. For° life, I prize° it *As for / value*
As I weigh° grief, which I would spare.° For honor, *value / do without*
'Tis a derivative[4] from me to mine,° *(my children)*
And only that I stand° for. I appeal *fight*
To your own conscience, sir, before Polixenes
Came to your court, how I was in your grace,
How merited to be so; since he came,
With what encounter so uncurrent° I *conduct so unacceptable*
Have strained° t'appear thus.° If one jot beyond *transgressed / (on trial)*
The bound of honor, or in act or will
That way inclining, hardened be the hearts
Of all that hear me, and my nearest of kin
Cry "fie" upon my grave.

LEONTES I ne'er heard yet
That any of these bolder vices wanted
Less° impudence to gainsay° what they did *Were more lacking in / deny*
Than to perform it first.

HERMIONE That's true enough,
Though 'tis a saying, sir, not due° to me. *relevant*

2. TEXTUAL COMMENT In F, the word "Silence" is printed in italics and set as a stage direction. Here it is treated as an imperative and assigned to the Officer who announces the Queen's entrance. See Digital Edition TC 5.

3. Than story or drama can show a precedent for.

4. Something handed on.

LEONTES You will not own it.
HERMIONE More than mistress of
Which comes to me in name of fault, I must not
At all acknowledge.[5] For Polixenes,
With whom I am accused, I do confess
I loved him as in honor he required,° *was his due*
With such a kind of love as might become
A lady like me; with a love, even such,
So, and no other, as yourself commanded;
Which not to have done I think had been in me
Both disobedience and ingratitude
To you and toward your friend, whose love had spoke,
Even since it could speak, from an infant, freely
That it was yours. Now, for conspiracy,
I know not how it tastes, though it be dished° *served*
For me to try how; all I know of it
Is that Camillo was an honest man,
And why he left your court, the gods themselves,
Wotting° no more than I, are ignorant. *If they know*
LEONTES You knew of his departure, as you know
What you have underta'en to do in's absence.
HERMIONE Sir,
You speak a language that I understand not.
My life stands in the level of your dreams,[6]
Which I'll lay down.
LEONTES Your actions are my dreams.
You had a bastard by Polixenes,
And I but° dreamed it. As you were past all shame— *merely*
Those of your fact° are so—so past all truth, *(guilty) of your crime*
Which to deny concerns more than avails;[7] for as
Thy brat hath been cast out, like to itself,° *as it should be*
No father owning it—which is indeed
More criminal in thee than it—so thou
Shalt feel our justice, in whose easiest passage
Look for no less than death.[8]
HERMIONE Sir, spare your threats.
The bug° which you would fright me with I seek. *horrible object*
To me can life be no commodity.° *profit; comfort*
The crown and comfort of my life, your favor,
I do give° lost, for I do feel it gone *reckon*
But know not how it went. My second joy° *(Mamillius)*
And first fruits of my body, from his presence
I am barred, like one infectious. My third comfort,
Starred most unluckily,[9] is from my breast,
The innocent milk in it° most innocent mouth, *its*
Haled° out to murder. Myself on every post[1] *Dragged*
Proclaimed a strumpet; with immodest° hatred *excessive*

5. *More . . . acknowledge:* I must not answer for ("acknowledge") more than those faults that I actually possess (am "mistress of").
6. *in the . . . dreams:* as the target ("level") of your delusions; a metaphor from archery.
7. *Which . . . avails:* Your denial of the truth costs you more effort than it's worth.
8. *in whose . . . death:* in the mildest course of justice, you can expect death. The implication is that death may well be preceded by torture.
9. Born under most unlucky stars.
1. Alluding to the early modern practice of nailing proclamations to posts in public places.

The childbed privilege[2] denied, which 'longs° *belongs*
To women of all fashion.° Lastly, hurried *ranks*
Here to this place, i'th' open air, before
I have got strength of limit.[3] Now, my liege,
Tell me what blessings I have here alive,
That I should fear to die? Therefore proceed.
But yet hear this—mistake me not—no life,
I prize it not a straw, but for mine honor,
Which I would free°—if I shall be condemned *vindicate*
Upon surmises, all proofs sleeping else
But° what your jealousies awake, I tell you *except*
'Tis rigor° and not law. Your honors all, *severity; tyranny*
I do refer me° to the oracle. *appeal*
Apollo be my judge.

LORD This your request
Is altogether just. Therefore bring forth,
And in Apollo's name, his oracle. [*Exeunt* OFFICERS.]

HERMIONE The Emperor of Russia[4] was my father.
Oh, that he were alive and here beholding
His daughter's trial; that he did but see
The flatness° of my misery—yet with eyes *boundlessness*
Of pity, not revenge.

[*Enter* OFFICERS *with* CLEOMENES *and* DION.]

OFFICER You here shall swear upon this sword of justice,
That you, Cleomenes and Dion, have
Been both at Delphos, and from thence have brought
This sealed-up oracle, by the hand delivered
Of great Apollo's priest, and that since then
You have not dared to break the holy seal
Nor read the secrets in't.

CLEOMENES *and* DION All this we swear.

LEONTES Break up the seals and read.

OFFICER [*reads*] "Hermione is chaste, Polixenes blameless, Camillo a true subject, Leontes a jealous tyrant, his innocent babe truly begotten; and the King shall live without an heir if that which is lost be not found."

LORDS Now blessèd be the great Apollo.

HERMIONE Praisèd.

LEONTES Hast thou read truth?

OFFICER Ay, my lord, even so
As it is here set down.

LEONTES There is no truth at all i'th' oracle.
The sessions shall proceed. This is mere falsehood.

[*Enter* SERVANT.]

SERVANT My lord the King, the King!

LEONTES What is the business?

SERVANT O sir, I shall be hated to report it.
The Prince your son, with mere conceit° and fear *thought*

2. The right to enjoy a period of bedrest and seclusion after childbirth.

3. Before I have the strength that follows the customary period of confinement. Exposure to air outside the domestic space was considered unsafe for women weakened by childbirth.

4. To early modern theatergoers, Russia would have seemed a distant and exotic place, but the founding of the Muscovy Company in 1553 also showed London merchants' interest in trade with this region.

Of the Queen's speed,° is gone. *fortune*

LEONTES How? "Gone"?

SERVANT Is dead.

LEONTES Apollo's angry, and the heavens themselves
Do strike at my injustice.
[HERMIONE *swoons.*]
How now there?

PAULINA This news is mortal to the Queen. Look down
And see what death is doing.

LEONTES Take her hence.
Her heart is but o'ercharged;° she will recover. *overburdened (by emotion)*
I have too much believed mine own suspicion.
Beseech you, tenderly apply to her
Some remedies for life.
[*Exeunt* PAULINA *and* LADIES *with* HERMIONE.]
Apollo, pardon
My great profaneness 'gainst thine oracle.
I'll reconcile me to Polixenes,
New woo my queen, recall the good Camillo,
Whom I proclaim a man of truth, of mercy;
For being transported by my jealousies
To bloody thoughts and to revenge, I chose
Camillo for the minister to poison
My friend Polixenes, which had° been done *would have*
But that the good mind of Camillo tardied° *delayed*
My swift command, though I with death and with
Reward did threaten and encourage him,
Not doing it and being done.[5] He, most humane
And filled with honor, to my kingly guest
Unclasped my practice,° quit his fortunes here, *Revealed my plot*
Which you knew great, and to the hazard
Of all uncertainties himself commended,° *consigned himself*
No richer than his honor.[6] How he glisters
Through my rust,[7] and how his piety
Does my deeds make the blacker!
[*Enter* PAULINA.]

PAULINA Woe the while.
Oh, cut my lace,[8] lest my heart, cracking it,
Break too.

LORD What fit is this, good lady?

PAULINA What studied° torments, tyrant, hast for me? *expertly devised*
What wheels, racks, fires? What flaying, boiling
In leads or oils?[9] What old or newer torture
Must I receive, whose every word deserves
To taste of thy most worst? Thy tyranny,
Together working with thy jealousies—
Fancies too weak for boys, too green and idle° *immature and foolish*

5. *though . . . done:* that is, though I threatened him with death if he did not do it and encouraged him with the promise of reward if he did do it.
6. Possessing no fortune but his honor.
7. How he shines ("glisters") in comparison with my "rust" (i.e., my evil).
8. Paulina asks that someone cut the fabric that holds together the tight bodices characteristic of female dress in this period.
9. A list of early modern forms of torture. The wheel was a device to which a person was tied and his or her limbs broken, usually by beating. The rack typically consisted of a frame with a roller at each end; a person was attached to this frame and his or her limbs stretched by turning the rollers. To flay was to strip off someone's skin while he or she was still alive.

For girls of nine—oh, think what they have done,
And then run mad indeed, stark mad; for all
Thy bygone fooleries were but spices° of it. *slight tastes*
That thou betrayed'st Polixenes, 'twas nothing;
That did but show thee of° a fool, inconstant, *for*
And damnable° ingrateful. Nor was't much *damnably; cursedly*
Thou wouldst have poisoned good Camillo's honor,
To have him kill a king—poor° trespasses, *minor*
More monstrous standing by;[1] whereof I reckon
The casting forth to crows thy baby daughter
To be or° none or little, though a devil *either*
Would have shed water out of fire ere done't.[2]
Nor is't directly laid to thee the death
Of the young Prince, whose honorable thoughts—
Thoughts high for one so tender°—cleft the heart *young*
That could conceive a gross° and foolish sire *stupid*
Blemished his gracious dam.° This is not, no, *mother*
Laid to thy answer.[3] But the last—O lords,
When I have said,° cry woe!—the Queen, the Queen, *finished speaking*
The sweetest, dearest creature's dead; and vengeance for't
Not dropped down yet.

LORD The higher powers forbid.

PAULINA I say she's dead. I'll swear't. If word nor oath
Prevail not, go and see. If you can bring
Tincture° or luster in her lip, her eye, *Color*
Heat outwardly or breath within, I'll serve you
As I would do the gods. But, O thou tyrant,
Do not repent these things, for they are heavier
Than all thy woes° can stir.° Therefore betake thee *grief / remove*
To nothing but despair. A thousand knees,
Ten thousand years together, naked, fasting
Upon a barren mountain and still° winter *always*
In storm perpetual, could not move the gods
To look that way thou wert.° *in your direction*

LEONTES Go on, go on.
Thou canst not speak too much. I have deserved
All tongues to talk their bitt'rest.

LORD [*to* PAULINA] Say no more.
Howe'er the business goes, you have made fault
I'th' boldness of your speech.

PAULINA I am sorry for't.
All faults I make, when I shall come to know them,
I do repent. Alas, I have showed too much
The rashness of a woman. He is touched
To the noble heart. What's gone and what's past help
Should be past grief. [*to* LEONTES] Do not receive affliction
At my petition;° I beseech you, rather *Because of my injunction*
Let me be punished that have minded° you *reminded*
Of what you should forget. Now, good my liege,
Sir, royal sir, forgive a foolish woman.

1. In comparison with more monstrous ones near at hand.
2. A devil would have shed tears from his fiery eyes (or from hellfires) before he had done it.
3. *laid to thy answer:* presented as a charge you must answer.

The love I bore your queen—lo, fool again—
I'll speak of her no more, nor of your children;
I'll not remember you of my own lord,
Who is lost too. Take your patience to you,° *Be patient*
And I'll say nothing.

LEONTES Thou didst speak but well
When most the truth, which I receive much better
Than to be pitied of° thee. Prithee bring me *by*
To the dead bodies of my queen and son.
One grave shall be for both. Upon them shall
The causes of their death appear, unto
Our shame perpetual. Once a day I'll visit
The chapel where they lie, and tears shed there
Shall be my recreation.[4] So long as nature° *my body*
Will bear up with this exercise, so long
I daily vow to use it. Come, and lead me
To these sorrows. *Exeunt.*

## 3.3

*Enter* ANTIGONUS, *a* MARINER, [*with the*] *babe.*[1]

ANTIGONUS Thou art perfect,° then, our ship hath touched upon *certain*
The deserts of Bohemia?

MARINER Ay, my lord, and fear
We have landed in ill time. The skies look grimly
And threaten present blusters.° In my conscience° *impending storms / opinion*
The heavens with that we have in hand are angry
And frown upon's.

ANTIGONUS Their sacred wills be done. Go get aboard.
Look to thy bark.° I'll not be long before *ship*
I call upon thee.

MARINER Make your best haste, and go not
Too far i'th' land. 'Tis like to be loud° weather. *stormy*
Besides, this place is famous for the creatures
Of prey that keep° upon't. *live*

ANTIGONUS Go thou away.
I'll follow instantly.

MARINER I am glad at heart
To be so rid o'th' business. *Exit.*

ANTIGONUS Come, poor babe.
I have heard, but not believed, the spirits o'th' dead
May walk again. If such thing be, thy mother
Appeared to me last night, for ne'er was dream
So like a waking. To me comes a creature,
Sometimes her head on one side, some another;
I never saw a vessel° of like sorrow *person; receptacle*
So filled and so becoming.[2] In pure white robes
Like very sanctity she did approach

4. My spiritual renewal or re-creation.
3.3 Location: Bohemia. The seacoast. This play, as does Greene's *Pandosto,* credits Bohemia with a coast. Only for two brief periods in the late Middle Ages may Bohemia have controlled a small piece of territory on the Adriatic Sea, but it was otherwise landlocked.
1. Textual Comment The opening stage direction in the Folio text includes a "babe" (whom Antigonus is obviously carrying), the Shepherd, and Clown, even though the latter two do not appear until after Antigonus's exit, signaled by the striking stage direction: "*Exit, pursued by a bear*" (3.3.57). See Digital Edition TC 6.
2. So filled with sorrow and so beautiful.

My cabin where I lay; thrice bowed before me,
And, gasping to begin some speech, her eyes
Became two spouts; the fury spent, anon° *soon*
Did this break from her: "Good Antigonus,
Since fate, against thy better disposition,
Hath made thy person for the thrower-out
Of my poor babe, according to thine oath,
Places remote enough are in Bohemia;
There weep, and leave it crying; and, for° the babe *because*
Is counted lost for ever, Perdita[3]
I prithee call't. For this ungentle° business *unkind; ignoble*
Put on thee by my lord, thou ne'er shalt see
Thy wife Paulina more." And so with shrieks
She melted into air. Affrighted much,
I did in time collect myself and thought
This was so and no slumber. Dreams are toys,° *trifles*
Yet for this once—yea, superstitiously—
I will be squared° by this. I do believe *ruled*
Hermione hath suffered death and that
Apollo would, this being indeed the issue° *child*
Of King Polixenes, it should here be laid,
Either for life or death, upon the earth
Of its right father. Blossom, speed° thee well. *fare*
There lie, and there thy character.[4] There these,[5]
Which may, if fortune please, both breed thee, pretty,
And still rest thine.[6] [*Thunder.*] The storm begins, poor wretch,
That for thy mother's fault art thus exposed
To loss and what may follow. Weep I cannot,
But my heart bleeds; and most accursed am I
To be by oath enjoined to this. Farewell!
The day frowns more and more. Thou'rt like to have
A lullaby too rough. I never saw
The heavens so dim by day. A savage clamor!
Well may I get aboard. This is the chase.° *hunt*
I am gone for ever. *Exit, pursued by a bear.*[7]

[*Enter* SHEPHERD.]

SHEPHERD I would there were no age between ten and three-and-twenty, or that youth would sleep out the rest; for there is nothing in the between but getting wenches with child, wronging the ancientry,° stealing, fighting. Hark you now: would any but these boiled brains° of nineteen and two-and-twenty hunt this weather? They have scared away two of my best sheep, which I fear the wolf will sooner find than the master. If anywhere I have them, 'tis by the seaside, browsing of° ivy. Good luck, an't° be thy will. [*He sees the baby.*] What have we here? Mercy on 's, a bairn,° a very pretty bairn. A boy or a child,° I wonder? A pretty one, a very pretty one. Sure

*elderly people* (ancientry) · *lunatics* (boiled brains) · *on / if it* (of / an't) · *child* (bairn) · *girl* (child)

3. Latin for "lost one."
4. The written account of your history and parentage.
5. The gold and jewels with which the Shepherd grows rich and which are later used to identify the Princess. See 5.2.30–36.
6. *Which . . . thine:* Which may, if you are lucky, be sufficient to pay for your upbringing, and still leave you in possession of a fortune.
7. PERFORMANCE COMMENT One of the most famous stage directions in English drama. Did a real bear come on stage, perhaps from one of the bearbaiting arenas in Shakespeare's London, or a man in a bear costume? For the many staging possibilities, see Digital Edition PC 2.

some scape:[8] though I am not bookish,° yet I can read waiting-gentlewoman in the scape. This has been some stair-work, some trunk-work, some behind-door-work.[9] They were warmer that got° this than the poor thing is here. I'll take it up for pity; yet I'll tarry till my son come. He hallooed but even now. Whoa, ho, hoa!

*not familiar with books* · *begot*

*Enter* CLOWN.°

*rustic fellow*

CLOWN Hilloa, loa!

SHEPHERD What, art so near? If thou'lt see a thing to talk on° when thou art dead and rotten, come hither. What ail'st thou, man?

*about*

CLOWN I have seen two such sights, by sea and by land. But I am not to say it is a sea, for it is now the sky; betwixt the firmament and it you cannot thrust a bodkin's° point.

*needle's*

SHEPHERD Why, boy, how is it?

CLOWN I would you did but see how it chafes, how it rages, how it takes up the shore—but that's not to the point. Oh, the most piteous cry of the poor souls! Sometimes to see 'em, and not to see 'em; now the ship boring° the moon with her mainmast, and anon swallowed with yeast° and froth, as you'd thrust a cork into a hogshead.° And then for the land-service,[1] to see how the bear tore out his shoulder bone, how he cried to me for help and said his name was Antigonus, a nobleman. But to make an end of the ship, to see how the sea flapdragoned it![2] But first, how the poor souls roared, and the sea mocked them; and how the poor gentleman roared, and the bear mocked him, both roaring louder than the sea or weather.

*piercing* · *foam* · *cask of liquor*

SHEPHERD Name of mercy, when was this, boy?

CLOWN Now, now. I have not winked° since I saw these sights. The men are not yet cold under water, nor the bear half dined on the gentleman—he's at it now.

*blinked an eye*

SHEPHERD Would I had been by to have helped the old man.

CLOWN I would you had been by the ship side to have helped her; there your charity would have lacked footing.[3]

SHEPHERD Heavy° matters, heavy matters. But look thee here, boy. Now bless thyself: thou mett'st with things dying, I with things newborn. Here's a sight for thee. Look thee, a bearing-cloth[4] for a squire's child. Look thee here: take up, take up, boy. Open't. So, let's see; it was told me I should be rich by the fairies. This is some changeling.[5] Open't. What's within, boy?

*Sad*

CLOWN [*opening the box*] You're a made° old man. If the sins of your youth are forgiven you, you're well to live.° Gold, all gold![6]

*prosperous* · *well off; virtuous*

8. Sexual transgression. Early modern ballads and popular literature offer numerous accounts of female servants who abandon or kill children born out of wedlock.

9. Some secret sexual affair conducted on back stairs, in chests, or behind doors.

1. Punning on the military and culinary meanings of "service" to suggest both "combat on land" and "food to be served up on land."

2. Devoured it as if it were a flapdragon, a raisin floating on flaming brandy.

3. There you would not have had a secure place to stand, with a pun on "footing" as meaning "a foundation" (upon which a charity might be founded).

4. The blanket used to wrap an infant in preparation for baptism.

5. A child secretly substituted for another by fairies. The term could apply to the abducted child (usually beautiful) or to the one (often ugly or deformed) left in its place.

6. TEXTUAL COMMENT The Folio text reads "You're a mad olde man," but since nothing else suggests that the Shepherd is mad, editors usually emend to "made," as in the phrase "made man." See Digital Edition TC 7.

SHEPHERD This is fairy gold,[7] boy, and 'twill prove so. Up
with't; keep it close.° Home, home the next° way. We are *secret / nearest*
lucky, boy, and to be so still° requires nothing but secrecy. *always*
Let my sheep go. Come, good boy, the next way home.

CLOWN Go you the next way with your findings. I'll go see if
the bear be gone from the gentleman, and how much he
hath eaten. They are never curst° but when they are hungry. *vicious*
If there be any of him left, I'll bury it.

SHEPHERD That's a good deed. If thou mayst discern by that
which is left of him what he is,° fetch me to th' sight of him. *his identity or rank*

CLOWN Marry,[8] will I; and you shall help to put him i'th' ground.

SHEPHERD 'Tis a lucky day, boy, and we'll do good deeds
on't. *Exeunt.*

## 4.1

*Enter* TIME,[1] *the Chorus.*

TIME I, that please some, try° all; both joy and terror *test*
Of good and bad, that makes and unfolds error,
Now take upon me in the name° of Time *with the authority*
To use my wings. Impute it not a crime
To me or my swift passage that I slide
O'er sixteen years and leave the growth untried° *development unexamined*
Of that wide gap, since it is in my power
To o'erthrow law, and in one self-born° hour *selfsame*
To plant and o'erwhelm° custom. Let me pass *establish and overthrow*
The same I am, ere ancient'st order was,
Or what is now received.[2] I witness to
The times that brought them in, so shall I do
To th' freshest things now reigning and make stale
The glistering° of this present, as my tale *glittering shine*
Now seems to it.[3] Your patience this allowing,
I turn my glass,° and give my scene such growing *hourglass*
As° you had slept between. Leontes leaving— *As if*
Th'effects of his fond° jealousies so grieving *foolish*
That he shuts up himself—imagine me,
Gentle spectators, that I now may be
In fair Bohemia, and remember well
I mentioned a son o'th' King's, which Florizel
I now name to you; and with speed so pace° *proceed*
To speak of Perdita, now grown in grace
Equal with wond'ring.[4] What of her ensues
I list not° prophesy, but let Time's news *do not wish to*
Be known when 'tis brought forth: a shepherd's daughter
And what to her adheres,° which follows after, *pertains*

7. Riches left by fairies were unreliable. If not kept secret, they brought bad luck.
8. A mild oath derived from the name of the Virgin Mary.
4.1 Location: Bohemia. The seacoast.
1. PERFORMANCE COMMENT In early modern texts, Time was conventionally represented as an old bald man with wings, signifying how swiftly time passes. He often carried an hourglass and a scythe, symbol of the power of time to destroy life. A common saying was that Time was the revealer of Truth, or that Truth was the daughter of Time. Robert Greene's *Pandosto,* Shakespeare's chief source for *The Winter's Tale,* was subtitled *The Triumph of Time.* For ways this figure has been staged, see Digital Edition PC 3.
2. *Let me . . . received:* Let me remain as I have been from before the beginnings of civilization even to the time of present customs.
3. As my tale now seems stale in comparison with the present.
4. Now grown so gracious as to inspire admiration.

Is th'argument° of Time. Of this allow, *subject matter*
If ever you have spent time worse ere now;
If never, yet that Time himself doth say
He wishes earnestly you never may. *Exit.*

## 4.2

*Enter* POLIXENES *and* CAMILLO.

POLIXENES I pray thee, good Camillo, be no more importunate.° 'Tis a sickness denying° thee anything, a death to grant this. *ask no longer / to deny*

CAMILLO It is fifteen[1] years since I saw my country. Though I have, for the most part, been aired abroad,° I desire to lay my bones there. Besides, the penitent King, my master, hath sent for me, to whose feeling° sorrows I might be some allay°—or I o'erween° to think so—which is another spur to my departure. *breathed foreign air* *deeply felt* *relief / am bold enough*

POLIXENES As thou lov'st me, Camillo, wipe not out the rest of thy services by leaving me now. The need I have of thee thine own goodness hath made. Better not to have had thee than thus to want° thee. Thou, having made me businesses[2] which none without thee can sufficiently manage, must either stay to execute them thyself, or take away with thee the very services thou hast done, which if I have not enough considered°—as too much I cannot—to be more thankful to thee shall be my study, and my profit therein the heaping friendships.[3] Of that fatal° country Sicilia prithee speak no more, whose very naming punishes me with the remembrance of that penitent—as thou call'st him—and reconciled king my brother, whose loss of his most precious queen and children are even now to be afresh° lamented. Say to me, when sawest thou the Prince Florizel, my son? Kings are no less unhappy, their issue not being gracious,[4] than they are in losing them when they have approved° their virtues. *be without* *rewarded* *deadly* *newly* *demonstrated*

CAMILLO Sir, it is three days since I saw the Prince. What his happier affairs may be are to me unknown, but I have missingly noted° he is of late much retired from court and is less frequent to° his princely exercises than formerly he hath appeared. *noted by his absence* *less often engaged in*

POLIXENES I have considered so much, Camillo, and with some care, so far that I have eyes under my service° which look upon his removedness,° from whom I have this intelligence: that he is seldom from the house of a most homely° shepherd, a man, they say, that from very nothing, and beyond the imagination of his neighbors, is grown into an unspeakable estate.° *spies in my employ* *retirement (from court)* *simple* *untold wealth*

CAMILLO I have heard, sir, of such a man, who hath a daughter of most rare note;° the report of her is extended more than can be thought to begin° from such a cottage. *quality* *originate*

POLIXENES That's likewise part of my intelligence; but, I fear, the angle° that plucks our son thither. Thou shalt accompany *fishhook*

4.2 Location: Bohemia. The palace of Polixenes.
1. Although at 4.1.6, Time says that sixteen years have passed, the Folio reads "fifteene" here. This apparent error may be due to carelessness on Shakespeare's part or to a misreading of a Roman numeral by a compositor or scribe.
2. Performed services for me.
3. The accumulation of your kindnesses.
4. Their children not proving virtuous.

us to the place where we will, not appearing what we are, have some question with the shepherd, from whose simplicity I think it not uneasy° to get the cause of my son's resort *difficult* thither. Prithee, be my present partner in this business, and lay aside the thoughts of Sicilia.

CAMILLO I willingly obey your command.

POLIXENES My best Camillo! We must disguise ourselves.

*Exeunt.*

## 4.3

*Enter* AUTOLYCUS, *singing.*

AUTOLYCUS

When daffodils begin to peer,
With heigh, the doxy° over the dale, *beggar's wench*
Why, then comes in the sweet° o'the year, *sweetest part*
For the red blood reigns in the winter's pale.° *skin made pale by winter*

The white sheet bleaching on the hedge,[1]
With heigh, the sweet birds—oh, how they sing!—
Doth set my pugging° tooth on edge, *thieving*
For a quart of ale is a dish for a king.

The lark, that tirra-lirra chants,
With heigh, with heigh, the thrush and the jay,
Are summer songs for me and my aunts[2]
While we lie tumbling in the hay.

I have served Prince Florizel and in my time wore three-pile,[3] but now I am out of service.

[*Sings.*] But shall I go mourn for that, my dear?
The pale moon shines by night,
And when I wander here and there,
I then do most go right.

If tinkers[4] may have leave° to live, *permission*
And bear the sow-skin budget,[5]
Then my account I well may give,
And in the stocks avouch it.° *acknowledge (my crime)*

My traffic° is sheets; when the kite builds, look to lesser lin- *trade* en.[6] My father named me Autolycus,[7] who being, as I am, littered under Mercury,[8] was likewise a snapper-up of unconsidered trifles. With die and drab,° I purchased this *dice and whores* caparison,° and my revenue is the silly cheat.[9] Gallows and *garment* knock° are too powerful on the highway.[1] Beating and *beatings* hanging are terrors to me. For° the life to come, I sleep out *As for* the thought of it.

4.3 Location: A road in Bohemia.
1. It was common practice in the country to set clothes out to dry on hedges.
2. Another slang term for women who take beggars or vagabonds for lovers.
3. A rich velvet cloth with a thick nap or "pile."
4. Menders of metal pots and kettles. The term was also applied to itinerant beggars and thieves.
5. A pigskin bag in which a tinker carried his tools; hence, a sign of his trade.
6. The kite, a bird of prey, supposedly stole small pieces of linen to make its nest. Autolycus steals larger pieces of linen, probably sheets left to dry on hedges (4.3.5).
7. In classical mythology, a crafty thief and grandfather of Ulysses
8. Fathered by Mercury; born when the planet Mercury was ascendant. Mercury, the father of Autolycus, was god of thieves.
9. My income derives from petty swindles.
1. Autolycus fears the penalties meted out to highwaymen, implying he would rather be a petty thief.

*Enter* CLOWN.

A prize, a prize.

CLOWN Let me see. Every 'leven wether tods,[2] every tod yields pound and odd° shilling; fifteen hundred shorn, what comes the wool to?

*one*

AUTOLYCUS [*aside*] If the springe° hold, the cock's[3] mine.

*trap*

CLOWN I cannot do't without counters.[4] Let me see; what am I to buy for our sheep-shearing feast? Three pound of sugar, five pound of currants, rice—what will this sister of mine do with rice? But my father hath made her mistress of the feast, and she lays it on. She hath made me four-and-twenty nosegays for the shearers: three-man songmen[5] all, and very good ones, but they are most of them means° and basses—but one puritan amongst them, and he sings psalms to hornpipes.[6] I must have saffron to color the warden° pies; mace; dates, none—that's out of my note;° nutmegs, seven; a race° or two of ginger, but that I may beg; four pound of prunes; and as many of raisins o'th' sun.°

*tenors* / *winter pear* / *not on my list / root* / *sun-dried*

AUTOLYCUS [*groveling on the ground*] Oh, that ever I was born.

CLOWN I'th' name of me.

AUTOLYCUS Oh, help me, help me! Pluck but off these rags, and then death, death!

CLOWN Alack, poor soul; thou hast need of more rags to lay on thee rather than have these off.

AUTOLYCUS O sir, the loathsomeness of them offend me more than the stripes° I have received, which are mighty ones and millions.

*blows*

CLOWN Alas, poor man, a million of beating may come to a great matter.[7]

AUTOLYCUS I am robbed, sir, and beaten; my money and apparel ta'en from me, and these detestable things put upon me.

CLOWN What, by a horseman or a footman?

AUTOLYCUS A footman, sweet sir, a footman.

CLOWN Indeed, he should be a footman, by the garments he has left with thee. If this be a horseman's coat, it hath seen very hot service. Lend me thy hand; I'll help thee. Come, lend me thy hand.

AUTOLYCUS O good sir, tenderly. Oh!

CLOWN Alas, poor soul.

AUTOLYCUS O good sir; softly,° good sir. I fear, sir, my shoulder blade is out.

*gently*

CLOWN How now? Canst stand?

AUTOLYCUS [*picking Clown's pocket*] Softly, dear sir; good sir, softly. You ha' done me a charitable office.°

*service*

CLOWN Dost lack any money? I have a little money for thee.

AUTOLYCUS No, good sweet sir, no; I beseech you, sir. I have a kinsman not past three-quarters of a mile hence unto whom I was going. I shall there have money, or anything I want.

2. Every 11 rams will yield 28 pounds (a "tod") of wool. Clown and his father could expect to earn a substantial amount of money (almost 150 pounds) for their wool.
3. Woodcock, a bird easily caught and hence proverbial for its stupidity.
4. Disks used in calculating sums.
5. Men who sing three-part songs.
6. Shrill-sounding musical instruments often played at country dances but seldom used to accompany the singing of psalms. This may be a gentle satire of puritans, who were commonly accused both of being opposed to festivity and of hypocrisy.
7. A million blows can be a serious affair, with a pun on "matter" as "pus," caused by an infection from open wounds.

Offer me no money, I pray you; that kills° my heart. *touches*
CLOWN What manner of fellow was he that robbed you?
AUTOLYCUS A fellow, sir, that I have known to go about with
troll-madams.° I knew him once a servant of the Prince. I *whores*
cannot tell, good sir, for which of his virtues it was, but he
was certainly whipped out of the court.
CLOWN His vices you would say. There's no virtue whipped
out of the court. They cherish it to make it stay there; and
yet it will no more but abide.° *stay there only briefly*
AUTOLYCUS Vices I would say, sir. I know this man well; he
hath been since an ape-bearer,[8] then a process-server—a
bailiff[9]—then he compassed a motion° of the Prodigal Son,[1] *devised a puppet show*
and married a tinker's wife within a mile where my land and
living° lies; and, having flown over many knavish professions, *property*
he settled only in rogue.° Some call him Autolycus. *on the rogue's profession*
CLOWN Out upon him! Prig,° for my life, prig. He haunts *Thief*
wakes,° fairs, and bearbaitings. *festivals*
AUTOLYCUS Very true, sir. He, sir, he. That's the rogue that
put me into this apparel.
CLOWN Not a more cowardly rogue in all Bohemia. If you had
but looked big and spit at him, he'd have run.
AUTOLYCUS I must confess to you, sir, I am no fighter. I am
false of heart° that way, and that he knew, I warrant him. *without courage*
CLOWN How do you now?
AUTOLYCUS Sweet sir, much better than I was. I can stand
and walk. I will even take my leave of you, and pace softly
towards my kinsman's.
CLOWN Shall I bring thee° on the way? *escort you*
AUTOLYCUS No, good-faced sir, no, sweet sir.
CLOWN Then fare thee well. I must go buy spices for our
sheep-shearing. *Exit.*
AUTOLYCUS Prosper you, sweet sir. Your purse is not hot° *full*
enough to purchase your spice. I'll be with you at your
sheep-shearing, too. If I make not this cheat° bring out° *deception / lead to*
another and the shearers prove sheep, let me be unrolled[2]
and my name put in the book of virtue.
[*Sings.*] Jog on, jog on, the footpath way,
And merrily hent° the stile[3]-a. *grab (to leap over)*
A merry heart goes all the day,
Your sad tires in a mile-a. *Exit.*

## 4.4

*Enter* FLORIZEL, [disguised *as Doricles, and*] PERDITA.[1]

FLORIZEL These your unusual weeds° to each part of you *garments*
Does give a life—no shepherdess, but Flora° *goddess of flowers*
Peering in April's front.[2] This your sheep-shearing

8. One who carried about a trained monkey.
9. A process-server, or bailiff, is a person who serves legal summonses that order a person to be brought into court for litigation.
1. Alluding to the New Testament story in the Gospel of Luke (Luke 15:11–32) of a spendthrift son who squandered his money and was forgiven by his father.
2. Let my name be taken off the list (of thieves and vagabonds).
3. Steps by which people pass over a fence or hedge.

4.4 Location: The countryside in Bohemia where the Shepherd, Clown, and Perdita live.
1. TEXTUAL COMMENT Again, F lists in the initial stage direction all the major characters who appear in this very long scene. Florizel and Perdita seem, however, to have a private conversation before the Shepherd, Polixenes, and others enter at line 54 and Autolycus at line 213. See Digital Edition TC 8.
2. Peeping out in early April.

Is as a meeting of the petty gods,
And you the queen on't.° *of it*

PERDITA Sir, my gracious lord,
To chide at your extremes° it not becomes me— *extravagances*
Oh, pardon that I name them. Your high self,
The gracious mark o'th' land,[3] you have obscured
With a swain's wearing,° and me, poor lowly maid, *shepherd's costume*
Most goddess-like pranked up.° But that our feasts *adorned*
In every mess[4] have folly, and the feeders° *those who eat*
Digest it with a custom,[5] I should blush
To see you so attired; swoon, I think,
To show myself a glass.° *mirror*

FLORIZEL I bless the time
When my good falcon made her flight across
Thy father's ground.

PERDITA Now Jove afford you cause!
To me the difference° forges dread; your greatness *(in rank)*
Hath not been used to fear. Even now I tremble
To think your father by some accident
Should pass this way, as you did. Oh, the fates!
How would he look to see his work,° so noble, *offspring; writings*
Vilely bound up?[6] What would he say? Or how
Should I, in these my borrowed flaunts,° behold *rich garments*
The sternness of his presence?

FLORIZEL Apprehend
Nothing but jollity. The gods themselves,
Humbling their deities to love, have taken
The shapes of beasts upon them: Jupiter
Became a bull and bellowed; the green Neptune
A ram and bleated; and the fire-robed god,
Golden Apollo, a poor humble swain,
As I seem now.[7] Their transformations
Were never for a piece° of beauty rarer, *person*
Nor in a way so chaste,[8] since my desires
Run not before mine honor, nor my lusts
Burn hotter than my faith.

PERDITA Oh, but sir,
Your resolution cannot hold, when 'tis
Opposed, as it must be, by th' power of the King.
One of these two must be necessities,
Which then will speak that you must change this purpose,
Or I my life.[9]

FLORIZEL Thou dearest Perdita,
With these forced° thoughts I prithee darken not *unnatural; farfetched*
The mirth o'th' feast—or° I'll be thine, my fair, *either*
Or not my father's; for I cannot be
Mine own, nor anything to any, if

3. The one whose graces make him admired by all.
4. A group of four served at table together; see note to 1.2.225.
5. *Digest . . . custom:* Tolerate it because they have grown used to it.
6. Poorly dressed; poorly put between covers (a bookbinding metaphor).
7. In classical mythology, Jupiter transformed himself into a bull and abducted Europa; Neptune took on the shape of a ram to carry off Theopane; and the sun god Apollo disguised himself as a shepherd to court Alcestis.
8. Nor ever conducted with so chaste a purpose.
9. *you . . . life:* either you must change your intent, or I must change my life (that is, risk death).

I be not thine. To this I am most constant,
Though destiny say no. Be merry, gentle;
Strangle such thoughts as these with anything
That you behold the while. Your guests are coming;
Lift up your countenance as° it were the day — *as if*
Of celebration of that nuptial which
We two have sworn shall come.

PERDITA O Lady Fortune,
Stand you auspicious!° — *favorable*

FLORIZEL See, your guests approach.
Address° yourself to entertain them sprightly, — *Prepare*
And let's be red with mirth.

[*Enter* SHEPHERD, CLOWN, *with* POLIXENES *and* CAMILLO *disguised,* MOPSA, DORCAS, *Shepherds and Shepherdesses.*][1]

SHEPHERD Fie, daughter! When my old wife lived, upon
This day she was both pantler,° butler, cook, — *pantry maid*
Both dame° and servant, welcomed all, served all; — *mistress of the house*
Would sing her song and dance her turn; now here
At upper end o'th' table, now i'th' middle;
On his° shoulder and his,° her face afire — *one person's / another's*
With labor, and the thing she took to quench it
She would to each one sip. You are retired
As if you were a feasted one° and not — *guest*
The hostess of the meeting. Pray you bid
These unknown friends to 's welcome, for it is
A way to make us better friends, more known.
Come, quench your blushes and present yourself
That which you are, mistress o'th' feast. Come on,
And bid us welcome to your sheep-shearing,
As your good flock shall prosper.

PERDITA [*to* POLIXENES] Sir, welcome.
It is my father's will I should take on me
The hostess-ship o'th' day. [*to* CAMILLO] You're welcome, sir.
—Give me those flowers there, Dorcas. —Reverend sirs,
For you there's rosemary and rue; these keep° — *retain*
Seeming° and savor° all the winter long. — *Color / scent*
Grace and remembrance[2] be to you both,
And welcome to our shearing.

POLIXENES Shepherdess,
A fair one are you. Well you fit our ages
With flowers of winter.

PERDITA Sir, the year growing ancient,
Not yet on summer's death, nor on the birth
Of trembling winter, the fairest flowers o'th' season
Are our carnations and streaked gillyvors,[3]
Which some call nature's bastards; of that kind
Our rustic garden's barren, and I care not
To get slips° of them. — *cuttings*

1. PERFORMANCE COMMENT In Bohemia, many characters are introduced, some of whom were probably played by actors who performed different roles in the Sicilian scenes. This practice was known as "doubling." For examples of how it might work, see Digital Edition PC 4.

2. Grace ("repentance") and remembrance are qualities associated with rue and rosemary, respectively.

3. Gillyflowers, or multicolored carnations. Their variations in color were thought to result from crossbreeding with other flowers, which may be why Perdita calls them "nature's bastards."

POLIXENES Wherefore, gentle maiden,
Do you neglect them?
PERDITA For I have heard it said
There is an art[4] which in their piedness° shares *streaked color*
With great creating nature.
POLIXENES Say there be.
Yet nature is made better by no mean° *means*
But nature makes that mean. So over that art
Which you say adds to nature is an art
That nature makes. You see, sweet maid, we marry
A gentler scion to the wildest stock
And make conceive a bark of baser kind
By bud of nobler race.[5] This is an art
Which does mend nature—change it, rather—but
The art itself is nature.
PERDITA So it is.
POLIXENES Then make your garden rich in gillyvors,
And do not call them bastards.
PERDITA I'll not put
The dibble° in earth to set° one slip of them, *trowel / plant*
No more than, were I painted,° I would wish *wearing cosmetics*
This youth should say 'twere well and only therefore
Desire to breed by me. Here's flowers for you:
Hot[6] lavender, mints, savory, marjoram,
The marigold that goes to bed wi'th' sun
And with him rises weeping.[7] These are flowers
Of middle summer, and I think they are given
To men of middle age. You're very welcome.
CAMILLO I should leave grazing, were I of your flock,
And only live by gazing.
PERDITA Out, alas!
You'd be so lean that blasts of January
Would blow you through and through.
[*to* FLORIZEL] Now, my fair'st friend,
I would I had some flowers o'th' spring that might
Become your time of day— [*to* MOPSA] and yours,
[*to* DORCAS] and yours,
That wear upon your virgin branches yet
Your maidenheads growing. O Proserpina,[8]
For the flowers now that, frighted, thou lett'st fall
From Dis's wagon:° daffodils, *chariot*
That come before the swallow dares and take° *charm*
The winds of March with beauty; violets dim,° *with hanging heads*
But sweeter than the lids of Juno's eyes
Or Cytherea's breath;[9] pale primroses,

4. The art of crossbreeding or grafting.
5. *we marry . . . race:* we marry or graft a mother twig (scion) to a more lowly trunk (stock) so that this lowly tree sends forth new shoots (conceives) by union with the nobler graft (bud). This complicated metaphor implies that high-born and low-born people, as well as plants, can successfully unite.
6. Herbs were divided into "hot" and "cold" varieties based on their supposed temperatures.
7. The marigold, sometimes called "the spouse of the sun," supposedly closed at sunset and opened, filled with dew, in the morning when the sun came up.
8. In Ovid's *Metamorphoses,* Proserpina, the daughter of Ceres, is abducted by Dis, or Pluto, as she gathers flowers and is taken in his chariot ("wagon") to his underworld kingdom. At Ceres' request, Proserpina is allowed to return to earth for six months each year. Her sojourn on earth coincides with spring and summer, her return to the underworld with fall and winter.
9. Juno was queen of the gods; "Cytherea" was another name for Venus, the goddess of love.

That die unmarried ere they can behold
Bright Phoebus° in his strength—a malady *(the sun god)*
Most incident to maids;[1] bold oxlips and
The crown imperial;[2] lilies of all kinds,
The flower-de-luce[3] being one. Oh, these I lack
To make you garlands of and my sweet friend
To strew him o'er and o'er.

FLORIZEL What, like a corpse?

PERDITA No, like a bank for love to lie and play on.
Not like a corpse—or if, not to be buried,
But quick° and in mine arms. Come, take your flowers. *living*
Methinks I play as I have seen them do
In Whitsun pastorals.[4] Sure this robe of mine
Does change my disposition.

FLORIZEL What you do
Still° betters what is done. When you speak, sweet, *Always*
I'd have you do it ever. When you sing,
I'd have you buy and sell so, so give alms,
Pray so; and for the ordering° your affairs, *arranging of*
To sing them too. When you do dance, I wish you
A wave o'th' sea, that you might ever do
Nothing but that, move still, still so,
And own° no other function. Each your doing,° *have / Each thing you do*
So singular° in each particular, *distinctive*
Crowns what you are doing in the present deeds,
That all your acts are queens.

PERDITA O Doricles,[5]
Your praises are too large. But that your youth
And the true blood which peeps fairly through't
Do plainly give you out an unstained shepherd,
With wisdom I might fear, my Doricles,
You wooed me the false way.

FLORIZEL I think you have
As little skill° to fear as I have purpose *reason*
To put you to't. But come; our dance, I pray.
Your hand, my Perdita. So turtles[6] pair
That never mean to part.

PERDITA [*to* CAMILLO] I'll swear for 'em.

POLIXENES This is the prettiest lowborn lass that ever
Ran on the greensward.° Nothing she does or seems *grassy turf*
But smacks of something greater than herself,
Too noble for this place.

CAMILLO [*to* POLIXENES] He tells her something
That makes her blood look on't.° Good sooth, she is *makes her blush*
The queen of curds and cream.[7]

CLOWN Come on, strike up!

1. Alluding to the belief that women who died of a kind of anemia known as green sickness would be transformed into primroses. Green sickness was associated with virgins, and vigorous sexual activity was sometimes advocated as a cure.
2. A lily first imported into England from Turkey in the late sixteenth century.
3. Fleur-de-lis, the national flower of France.
4. English rural festivities traditionally held at Whitsuntide (Pentecost), the seventh Sunday after Easter. The festivities often included morris dances and Robin Hood plays, and were presided over by a festival king and queen.
5. The name Florizel has assumed.
6. Turtledoves, which proverbially mate for life.
7. Referring perhaps to a cream custard known as "white pot." In some May games, a woman was chosen as queen of white-pot cream.

DORCAS Mopsa must be your mistress. Marry, garlic to mend her kissing with.[8]

MOPSA Now in good time.

CLOWN Not a word, a word; we stand upon our manners.
Come, strike up!

*[Music.] Here a dance of Shepherds and Shepherdesses [including* PERDITA *and* FLORIZEL*].*

*[Exeunt Shepherds and Shepherdesses.]*

POLIXENES Pray, good shepherd, what fair swain is this
Which dances with your daughter?

SHEPHERD They call him Doricles, and boasts himself° (*he boasts*)
To have a worthy feeding;° but I have it (*good pasture land*)
Upon his own report, and I believe it:
He looks like sooth.° He says he loves my daughter; (*appears to be honest*)
I think so, too; for never gazed the moon
Upon the water as he'll stand and read,
As 'twere, my daughter's eyes. And, to be plain,
I think there is not half a kiss to choose
Who loves another° best. (*the other*)

POLIXENES She dances featly.° (*nimbly*)

SHEPHERD So she does anything, though I report it
That° should be silent. If young Doricles (*Who*)
Do light upon her,° she shall bring him that (*choose*)
Which he not dreams of.

*Enter* SERVANT.

SERVANT O master, if you did but hear the peddler at the door, you would never dance again after a tabor and pipe.[9] No, the bagpipe could not move you. He sings several° (*different*) tunes faster than you'll tell° (*count*) money. He utters them as he had eaten ballads[1] and all men's ears grew° (*listened intently*) to his tunes.

CLOWN He could never come better.° (*at a better time*) He shall come in. I love a ballad but even too well, if it be doleful matter merrily set down, or a very pleasant thing indeed and sung lamentably.

SERVANT He hath songs for man or woman of all sizes. No milliner[2] can so fit his customers with gloves. He has the prettiest love songs for maids, so without bawdry—which is strange—with such delicate burdens° (*refrains*) of "dildos" and fadings, "jump her and thump her."[3] And where some stretch-mouthed° (*obscene*) rascal would, as it were, mean mischief and break a foul gap into the matter,[4] he makes the maid to answer, "Whoop, do me no harm, good man"; puts him off, slights him, with "Whoop, do me no harm, good man."

POLIXENES This is a brave° (*fine*) fellow.

CLOWN Believe me, thou talkest of an admirable conceited° (*very witty*) fellow. Has he any unbraided° (*new; not shopworn*) wares?

8. To make her breath sweet (said ironically).
9. A small drum and fife used for morris dancing.
1. Alluding to the broadside ballads that were sung and sold by peddlers who traveled throughout the country.
2. One who sells fashionable articles of clothing such as hats and gloves.
3. Though the servant claims that the songs are without bawdiness, the refrains are in fact full of sexual puns that the servant may not understand. "Dildos" are artificial penises; "fadings" can mean "orgasms"; and "jump her and thump her" denotes sexual relations with a woman.
4. *break . . . matter:* interrupt the song with an indecent insertion.

SERVANT He hath ribbons of all the colors i'th' rainbow; points[5] more than all the lawyers in Bohemia can learnedly handle, though they come to him by th' gross; inkles, caddises, cambrics, lawns.[6] Why, he sings 'em over as they were gods or goddesses. You would think a smock° were a she-angel, he so chants to the sleeve-hand° and the work about the square on't.[7]

*woman's undergarment*
*wristband*

CLOWN Prithee bring him in, and let him approach singing.

PERDITA Forewarn him that he use no scurrilous words in 's tunes.

[*Exit* SERVANT.]

CLOWN You have of these° peddlers that have more in them than you'd think, sister.

*There are some*

PERDITA Ay, good brother, or go about° to think.

*intend*

*Enter* AUTOLYCUS, *singing.*

AUTOLYCUS Lawn as white as driven snow,
Cypress[8] black as e'er was crow,
Gloves as sweet° as damask roses, *perfumed*
Masks for faces and for noses;[9]
Bugle bracelet,[1] necklace amber,
Perfume for a lady's chamber:
Golden coifs° and stomachers[2] *caps*
For my lads to give their dears;
Pins and poking-sticks of steel,[3]
What maids lack from head to heel.
Come buy of me, come; come buy, come buy,
Buy, lads, or else your lasses cry. Come buy!

CLOWN If I were not in love with Mopsa, thou shouldst take no money of me; but being enthralled as I am, it will also be the bondage of certain ribbons and gloves.[4]

MOPSA I was promised them against° the feast, but they come not too late now.

*in time for*

DORCAS He hath promised you more than that, or there be liars.

MOPSA He hath paid° you all he promised you—maybe he has paid you more, which will shame you to give him again.[5]

*given; had sex with*

CLOWN Is there no manners left among maids? Will they wear their plackets where they should bear their faces?[6] Is there not milking time, when you are going to bed, or kiln-hole° to whistle of these secrets, but you must be tittle-tattling before all our guests? 'Tis well they are whispering. Clamor your tongues,[7] and not a word more.

*fireplace*

5. Laces for fastening garments, with a pun on "points" as meaning "legal arguments."
6. "Inkles" were linen tapes; "caddises" were worsted tapes used for garters; "cambrics" and "lawns" were heavy and sheer linens.
7. The stitching about the yoke of the garment.
8. A crepe material imported from Cyprus and used for mourning clothes.
9. Some English women wore masks to protect their skin from exposure to the sun. If women's noses were eaten away by syphilis, masks would also cover this deformity.
1. A bracelet of shiny black beads.
2. Embroidered bodices for dresses.
3. Metal rods used to iron the ruffs or stiff collars worn by both men and women. "Poking-stick" was also slang for "penis."
4. *but being . . . gloves:* because I am the prisoner of love, certain ribbons and gloves must also be put in bondage (bound up in a parcel).
5. "More" may mean a pregnancy that will result in an illegitimate child that Dorcas will give to Clown.
6. *Will . . . faces?:* that is, Will they reveal their most private affairs in public? (There is a pun on "placket," which refers to both an opening in a petticoat and female genitals.)
7. An obscure phrase. Clown clearly means they are to be quiet. To "clammer" is a term from bell ringing that means to make the jangling sound characteristic of bells before they grow silent.

MOPSA I have done. Come, you promised me a tawdry-lace[8] and a pair of sweet gloves.

CLOWN Have I not told thee how I was cozened by the way° and lost all my money?

*cheated on the road*

AUTOLYCUS And indeed, sir, there are cozeners abroad; therefore it behooves men to be wary.

CLOWN Fear not thou, man; thou shalt lose nothing here.

AUTOLYCUS I hope so, sir, for I have about me many parcels of charge.°

*valuable goods*

CLOWN What hast here? Ballads?

MOPSA Pray now, buy some. I love a ballad in print, alife,° for then we are sure they are true.

*on my life*

AUTOLYCUS Here's one to a very doleful tune, how a usurer's wife was brought to bed of twenty money-bags at a burden,° and how she longed to eat adders' heads and toads carbonadoed.°

*in one childbirth*

*cut and grilled*

MOPSA Is it true, think you?

AUTOLYCUS Very true, and but a month old.

DORCAS Bless me from marrying a usurer.

AUTOLYCUS Here's the midwife's name to't, one Mistress Tale-porter,[9] and five or six honest° wives that were present. Why should I carry lies abroad?

*truthful; chaste*

MOPSA Pray you now, buy it.

CLOWN Come on, lay it by, and let's first see more ballads. We'll buy the other things anon.

AUTOLYCUS Here's another ballad of a fish that appeared upon the coast on Wednesday the fourscore° of April, forty thousand fathom° above water, and sung this ballad against the hard hearts of maids. It was thought she was a woman and was turned into a cold fish, for she would not exchange flesh° with one that loved her. The ballad is very pitiful, and as true.

*eightieth day*

*measurement of six feet*

*have sex*

DORCAS Is it true too, think you?

AUTOLYCUS Five justices' hands at it,° and witnesses more than my pack will hold.

*signatures on it*

CLOWN Lay it by too. Another.

AUTOLYCUS This is a merry ballad, but a very pretty one.

MOPSA Let's have some merry ones.

AUTOLYCUS Why this is a passing° merry one and goes to the tune of "Two maids wooing a man." There's scarce a maid westward° but she sings it. 'Tis in request, I can tell you.

*very*

*in the West*

MOPSA We can both sing it; if thou'lt bear a part,[1] thou shalt hear. 'Tis in three parts.

DORCAS We had the tune on't° a month ago.

*of it*

AUTOLYCUS I can bear my part. You must know 'tis my occupation.° Have at it with you.

*job*

*Song.*

AUTOLYCUS Get you hence, for I must go
Where it fits not you to know.

DORCAS Whither?

8. A cheap, brightly colored scarf associated with St. Audrey's Fair. St. Audrey, founder of Ely Cathedral, died of a throat tumor that she believed was a punishment for wearing gay neckerchiefs in her youth.

9. The name punningly suggests one who reports gossip ("tales") as well as one who handles genitalia (slang meaning of "tail").

1. Sing a part in the song.

MOPSA Oh, whither?
DORCAS Whither?
MOPSA It becomes thy oath full well,
Thou to me thy secrets tell.
DORCAS Me, too; let me go thither.
MOPSA Or thou goest to th' grange° or mill. *farm*
DORCAS If to either thou dost ill.
AUTOLYCUS Neither.
DORCAS What, neither?
AUTOLYCUS Neither.
DORCAS Thou hast sworn my love to be.
MOPSA Thou hast sworn it more to me.
Then whither goest? Say, whither?

CLOWN We'll have this song out anon by ourselves. My father and the gentlemen are in sad° talk, and we'll not trouble them. Come, bring away thy pack after me. Wenches, I'll buy for you both. Peddler, let's have the first choice. Follow me, girls. [*Exit with* DORCAS *and* MOPSA.]

*serious*

AUTOLYCUS And you shall pay well for 'em.
*Song.* Will you buy any tape,
Or lace for your cape,
My dainty duck, my dear-a?
Any silk, any thread,
Any toys° for your head, *small ornaments*
Of the new'st and fin'st, fin'st wear-a?
Come to the peddler,
Money's a meddler,
That doth utter° all men's ware-a. *Exit.* *put on sale*

[*Enter* SERVANT.]

SERVANT Master, there is three carters,° three shepherds, three neatherds,° three swineherds that have made themselves all men of hair.[2] They call themselves saltiers,° and they have a dance which the wenches say is a gallimaufry of gambols,° because they are not in't. But they themselves are o'th' mind—if it be not too rough for some that know little but bowling°—it will please plentifully.

*drivers of carts* / *keepers of cows* / *jumpers* / *jumble of jumps* / *(a more sedate sport)*

SHEPHERD Away! We'll none on't. Here has been too much homely° foolery already. —I know, sir, we weary you.

*rough*

POLIXENES You weary those that° refresh us. Pray let's see these four threes° of herdsmen.

*who* / *trios*

SERVANT One three of them, by their own report, sir, hath danced before the King;[3] and not the worst of the three but jumps twelve foot and a half by th' square.°

*exactly*

SHEPHERD Leave your prating. Since these good men are pleased, let them come in; but quickly now.

SERVANT Why, they stay at door, sir.

[SERVANT *goes to door. Enter Dancers.*] *Here a dance of twelve satyrs.*

[*Exeunt Dancers.*]

2. Probably they are disguised in animal skins to resemble satyrs—mythical woodland figures, part man, part beast, having the pointed ears, legs, and short horns of a goat.

3. This may be a reference to a court performance of Ben Jonson's *Masque of Oberon*, which included a dance of twelve satyrs. It was performed on January 1, 1611, in honor of Prince Henry.

POLIXENES [*to* SHEPHERD] O father, you'll know more of that hereafter.
[*to* CAMILLO] Is it not too far gone? 'Tis time to part them.
He's simple and tells much. —How now, fair shepherd?
Your heart is full of something that does take
Your mind from feasting. Sooth, when I was young
And handed love,° as you do, I was wont *pledged love*
To load my she with knacks.° I would have ransacked *small gifts; trifles*
The peddler's silken treasury and have poured it
To her acceptance.° You have let him go *For her to choose*
And nothing marted with° him. If your lass *bought from*
Interpretation should abuse° and call this *Should misinterpret*
Your lack of love or bounty, you were straited° *hard-pressed*
For a reply, at least if you make a care
Of happy holding her.° *Of keeping her happy*
FLORIZEL Old sir, I know
She prizes not such trifles as these are.
The gifts she looks° from me are packed and locked *expects*
Up in my heart, which I have given already
But not delivered. [*to* PERDITA] Oh, hear me breathe my life° *make vows of eternal love*
Before this ancient sir, who, it should seem,
Hath sometime loved. I take thy hand, this hand
As soft as dove's down and as white as it,
Or Ethiopian's tooth, or the fanned snow that's bolted° *sifted*
By th' northern blasts twice o'er.
POLIXENES What follows this?
[*to* CAMILLO] How prettily th' young swain seems to wash
The hand was° fair before! [*to* FLORIZEL] I have put you out,° *that was / interrupted you*
But to your protestation. Let me hear
What you profess.
FLORIZEL Do, and be witness to't.
POLIXENES And this my neighbor too?
FLORIZEL And he, and more
Than he, and men, the earth, the heavens, and all.
That were I crowned the most imperial monarch,
Thereof most worthy; were I the fairest youth
That ever made eye swerve,° had force and knowledge *commanded attention*
More than was ever man's, I would not prize them
Without her love; for her, employ them all,
Commend them and condemn them to her service,
Or to their own perdition.[4]
POLIXENES Fairly offered.
CAMILLO This shows a sound affection.
SHEPHERD But, my daughter,
Say you the like to him?
PERDITA I cannot speak
So well, nothing so well; no, nor mean better.
By th' pattern of mine own thoughts I cut out
The purity of his.[5]
SHEPHERD Take hands, a bargain.
And, friends unknown, you shall bear witness to't.

4. *Commend . . . perdition:* Either dedicate my attributes to her service or sentence them to destruction.

5. *By . . . his:* By my pure thoughts I recognize the purity of his.

I give my daughter to him and will make
Her portion° equal his. *dowry*

FLORIZEL Oh, that must be
I'th' virtue of your daughter. One° being dead, *Someone*
I shall have more than you can dream of yet,
Enough then for your wonder. But come on,
Contract us fore these witnesses.[6]

SHEPHERD Come, your hand;
And, daughter, yours.

POLIXENES Soft,° swain, awhile, beseech you. *Go slowly*
Have you a father?

FLORIZEL I have. But what of him?

POLIXENES Knows he of this?

FLORIZEL He neither does nor shall.

POLIXENES Methinks a father
Is at the nuptial of his son a guest
That best becomes the table. Pray you once more,
Is not your father grown incapable
Of reasonable affairs? Is he not stupid
With age and altering rheums?° Can he speak, hear, *debilitating disease*
Know man from man? Dispute° his own estate?° *Discuss / condition*
Lies he not bedrid? And again does nothing
But what he did being childish?

FLORIZEL No, good sir,
He has his health and ampler strength indeed
Than most have of his age.

POLIXENES By my white beard,
You offer him, if this be so, a wrong
Something unfilial.° Reason my son[7] *Somewhat unbecoming a son*
Should choose himself a wife, but as good reason
The father, all whose joy is nothing else
But fair posterity, should hold some counsel
In such a business.

FLORIZEL I yield° all this; *grant*
But for some other reasons, my grave sir,
Which 'tis not fit you know, I not acquaint
My father of this business.

POLIXENES Let him know't.

FLORIZEL He shall not.

POLIXENES Prithee, let him.

FLORIZEL No, he must not.

SHEPHERD Let him, my son. He shall not need to grieve
At knowing of thy choice.

FLORIZEL Come, come, he must not.
Mark our contract.

POLIXENES [*removing his disguise*] Mark your divorce, young sir,
Whom son I dare not call. Thou art too base
To be acknowledged. Thou a scepter's heir
That thus affects° a sheephook? —Thou, old traitor, *desires*
I am sorry that by hanging thee I can

6. A pledge of marriage spoken before two witnesses was legally binding.

7. It is reasonable that my son.

But shorten thy life one week. —And thou, fresh piece
Of excellent witchcraft,[8] who of force° must know *of necessity*
The royal fool thou cop'st° with— *deal; have sex*

SHEPHERD Oh, my heart.

POLIXENES —I'll have thy beauty scratched with briars and made
More homely than thy state. —For thee, fond° boy, *foolish*
If I may ever know thou dost but sigh
That thou no more shalt see this knack°—as never *worthless thing*
I mean thou shalt—we'll bar thee from succession,
Not hold thee of our blood—no, not our kin—
Far than Deucalion off.[9] Mark thou my words.
Follow us to the court. [*to* SHEPHERD] Thou churl, for this time,
Though full of our displeasure, yet we free thee
From the dead° blow of it. [*to* PERDITA] And you, enchantment, *deadly*
Worthy enough a herdsman—yea, him° too, *(Florizel)*
That makes himself, but for our honor therein,
Unworthy thee[1]—if ever henceforth thou
These rural latches to his entrance open,
Or hoop° his body more with thy embraces, *encircle*
I will devise a death as cruel for thee
As thou art tender to't. *Exit.*

PERDITA Even here undone.
I was not much afeard, for once or twice
I was about to speak and tell him plainly
The selfsame sun that shines upon his court
Hides not his visage from our cottage, but
Looks on alike.° [*to* FLORIZEL] Will't please you, sir, be gone? *both alike*
I told you what would come of this. Beseech you,
Of your own state take care. This dream of mine
Being now awake, I'll queen it no inch farther,° *play the queen no further*
But milk my ewes and weep.

CAMILLO Why, how now, father?
Speak ere thou diest.

SHEPHERD I cannot speak nor think,
Nor dare to know that which I know. [*to* FLORIZEL] O sir,
You have undone a man of fourscore-three° *eighty-three*
That thought to fill his grave in quiet, yea,
To die upon the bed my father died,
To lie close by his honest bones. But now
Some hangman must put on my shroud and lay me
Where no priest shovels in dust.[2] [*to* PERDITA] O cursèd wretch,
That knew'st this was the Prince and wouldst adventure
To mingle faith° with him. Undone, undone! *exchange vows*
If I might die within this hour, I have lived
To die when I desire. *Exit.*

FLORIZEL [*to* PERDITA] Why look you so upon me?
I am but sorry, not afeard; delayed,

8. You beautiful young woman skilled in witchcraft.
9. Less linked in kinship than Deucalion, who according to classical mythology was, along with his wife, the only person to escape a flood sent by Zeus. He thus was the ancestor of humankind and the most distant relation one might have.
1. A difficult passage. Polixenes seems to mean that Florizel, by his actions, has made himself unworthy of even a shepherd's daughter.
2. As a criminal, he would be buried by the hangman without ritual. In regular funeral rites, the priest puts the first shovelful of dirt on the grave.

But nothing altered. What I was, I am,
More straining on for plucking back,[3] not following
My leash unwillingly.[4]

CAMILLO Gracious my lord,
You know your father's temper. At this time
He will allow no speech, which I do guess
You do not purpose° to him; and as hardly° *intend / unwillingly*
Will he endure your sight as yet, I fear;
Then till the fury of his highness settle,
Come not before him.

FLORIZEL I not purpose it.
I think—Camillo?[5]

CAMILLO Even he, my lord.

PERDITA [*to* FLORIZEL] How often have I told you 'twould be thus?
How often said my dignity would last
But° till 'twere known? *Only*

FLORIZEL It cannot fail but by
The violation of my faith, and then
Let nature crush the sides o'th' earth together
And mar the seeds° within. Lift up thy looks. *sources of life*
From my succession wipe me, father: I
Am heir to my affection.

CAMILLO Be advised.° *prudent*

FLORIZEL I am, and by my fancy.° If my reason *love*
Will thereto be obedient, I have reason;[6]
If not, my senses, better pleased with madness,
Do bid it° welcome. *(madness)*

CAMILLO This is desperate, sir.

FLORIZEL So call it. But it does fulfill my vow:
I needs must think it honesty. Camillo,
Not for Bohemia, nor the pomp that may
Be thereat gleaned; for all the sun sees, or
The close° earth wombs,° or the profound seas hides *secret / holds in her womb*
In unknown fathoms, will I break my oath
To this my fair beloved. Therefore, I pray you,
As you have ever been my father's honored friend,
When he shall miss me—as in faith I mean not
To see him any more—cast your good counsels
Upon his passion.° Let myself and fortune *anger*
Tug° for the time to come. This you may know, *Contend*
And so deliver:° I am put to sea *report*
With her who here I cannot hold on shore;
And most opportune to her need, I have
A vessel rides fast by,° but not prepared *anchored nearby*
For this design. What course I mean to hold
Shall nothing benefit your knowledge, nor
Concern me the reporting.[7]

3. More eager to go forward because of being pulled back.
4. Not following this course of action unwillingly.
5. Camillo may here have taken off his disguise or been recognized by Florizel even with it on.
6. If my reason will obey love, I will embrace reason.
7. *Shall . . . reporting:* Would not benefit you to know nor me to report.

CAMILLO O my lord,
I would your spirit were easier for advice° — *to advise*
Or stronger for your need.
FLORIZEL Hark, Perdita—
[*to* CAMILLO] I'll hear you by and by.
CAMILLO [*aside*] He's irremovable,° — *unyielding*
Resolved for flight. Now were I happy if
His going I could frame to serve my turn,
Save him from danger, do him love and honor,
Purchase the sight again of dear Sicilia
And that unhappy king, my master, whom
I so much thirst to see.
FLORIZEL Now, good Camillo,
I am so fraught with curious business° that — *matters requiring care*
I leave out ceremony.
CAMILLO Sir, I think
You have heard of my poor services, i'th' love
That I have borne your father?
FLORIZEL Very nobly
Have you deserved. It is my father's music
To speak your deeds, not little of his care
To have them recompensed as thought on.[8]
CAMILLO Well, my lord,
If you may please to think I love the King,
And through him what's nearest to him, which is
Your gracious self, embrace but my direction,° — *simply follow my advice*
If your more ponderous° and settled project — *weighty*
May suffer° alteration. On mine honor, — *permit*
I'll point you where you shall have such receiving
As shall become your highness, where you may
Enjoy your mistress, from the whom I see
There's no disjunction° to be made but by— — *separation*
As heavens forfend°—your ruin. Marry her, — *forbid*
And with my best endeavors in your absence,
Your discontenting° father strive to qualify° — *discontented / appease*
And bring him up to liking.° — *to giving approval*
FLORIZEL How, Camillo,
May this, almost a miracle, be done?—
That I may call thee something more than man,
And after that trust to thee.
CAMILLO Have you thought on° — *of*
A place whereto you'll go?
FLORIZEL Not any yet.
But as th'unthought-on accident is guilty
To what we wildly do,[9] so we profess
Ourselves to be the slaves of chance, and flies
Of every wind that blows.
CAMILLO Then list to me.
This follows, if you will not change your purpose
But undergo this flight: make for Sicilia,
And there present yourself and your fair princess,
For so I see she must be, fore Leontes;

8. *not little . . . thought on:* and no small matter among his affairs to reward your deeds as fully as he values them.

9. But as the unexpected event (Polixenes' discovery of our love) is responsible for our rash behavior now.

She shall be habited° as it becomes *dressed*
The partner of your bed. Methinks I see
Leontes opening his free° arms and weeping *generous*
His welcomes forth; asks thee there, "Son, forgiveness,"
As 'twere i'th' father's person,[1] kisses the hands
Of your fresh princess; o'er and o'er divides him
Twixt his unkindness and his kindness:[2] th'one
He chides° to hell and bids the other grow *rebukes*
Faster than thought or time.

FLORIZEL Worthy Camillo,
What color° for my visitation shall I *pretext*
Hold up before him?

CAMILLO Sent by the King your father
To greet him and to give him comforts. Sir,
The manner of your bearing towards him with
What you, as from your father, shall deliver°— *say*
Things known betwixt us three—I'll write you down,
The which shall point you forth° at every sitting *direct you*
What you must say, that he shall not perceive
But that you have your father's bosom° there *trust*
And speak his very heart.

FLORIZEL I am bound to you.
There is some sap° in this. *life*

CAMILLO A course more promising
Than a wild dedication of yourselves
To unpathed waters, undreamed shores, most certain
To miseries enough; no hope to help you,
But as you shake off one to take another;
Nothing so certain° as your anchors, who *(to detain you)*
Do their best office if they can but stay° you *keep*
Where you'll be loath to be. Besides, you know,
Prosperity's the very bond of love,
Whose fresh complexion and whose heart together
Affliction alters.° *changes for the worse*

PERDITA One of these is true.
I think affliction may subdue the cheek° *make one pale*
But not take in° the mind. *conquer*

CAMILLO Yea, say you so?
There shall not at your father's house these seven years[3]
Be born another such.

FLORIZEL My good Camillo,
She's as forward of her breeding as
She is i'th' rear our birth.[4]

CAMILLO I cannot say 'tis pity
She lacks instructions,° for she seems a mistress° *schooling / teacher*
To most that teach.

PERDITA Your pardon, sir; for this
I'll blush you thanks.

FLORIZEL My prettiest Perdita!

1. *As 'twere . . . person:* As if he were your father (granting you forgiveness), *or,* as if you stood in your father's place (and so could grant Leontes forgiveness for his great sin against Polixenes).
2. *divides . . . kindness:* divides his speech between his past unkindness to your father and the kindness he is eager to perform now.
3. Proverbial expression meaning "for a long time."
4. *She's . . . birth:* that is, She is as superior to her lowly upbringing as she is inferior to our noble birth.

But, oh, the thorns we stand upon! Camillo,
Preserver of my father, now of me,
The medicine of our house, how shall we do?
We are not furnished° like Bohemia's son, *dressed; equipped*
Nor shall appear in Sicilia—

CAMILLO My lord,
Fear none of this. I think you know my fortunes
Do all lie there. It shall be so my care
To have you royally appointed° as if *outfitted*
The scene you play were mine.° For instance, sir, *written by me*
That you may know you shall not want—one word.

[*They speak apart.*]

*Enter* AUTOLYCUS.

AUTOLYCUS Ha, ha, what a fool honesty is, and trust, his sworn brother, a very simple gentleman! I have sold all my trumpery; not a counterfeit stone, not a ribbon, glass, pomander,[5] brooch, table-book,° ballad, knife, tape, glove, shoe-tie, bracelet, horn-ring[6] to keep my pack from fasting.° They throng who should buy first, as if my trinkets had been hallowed° and brought a benediction to the buyer, by which means I saw whose purse was best in picture;° and what I saw, to my good use I remembered. My clown, who wants but something° to be a reasonable man, grew so in love with the wenches' song that he would not stir his pettitoes° till he had both tune and words, which so drew the rest of the herd to me that all their other senses stuck in ears.° You might have pinched a placket, it was senseless;° 'twas nothing to geld a codpiece[7] of a purse. I would have filed keys off that hung in chains. No hearing, no feeling, but my sir's song, and admiring the nothing° of it. So that in this time of lethargy I picked and cut most of their festival purses; and, had not the old man come in with a hubbub against his daughter and the King's son, and scared my choughs° from the chaff, I had not left a purse alive in the whole army.

*notebook*
*going empty*
*blessed; made sacred*
*looked best (to steal)*
*lacks only one thing*
*feet (pigs' toes)*
*were devoted to hearing*
*felt nothing*
*silliness*
*jackdaws (silly birds)*

[CAMILLO, FLORIZEL, *and* PERDITA *come forward.*]

CAMILLO Nay, but my letters by this means being there
So soon as you arrive shall clear that doubt.

FLORIZEL And those that you'll procure from King Leontes—

CAMILLO Shall satisfy your father.

PERDITA Happy be you!
All that you speak shows fair.

CAMILLO [*seeing* AUTOLYCUS] Who have we here?
We'll make an instrument of this, omit
Nothing° may give us aid. *Nothing that*

AUTOLYCUS [*aside*] If they have overheard me now, why, hanging.

CAMILLO How now, good fellow? Why shak'st thou so?
Fear not, man. Here's no harm intended to thee.

AUTOLYCUS I am a poor fellow, sir.

CAMILLO Why, be so still.° Here's nobody will steal that from thee. Yet, for the outside of thy poverty,° we must make an

*always*
*your ragged clothes*

5. A mixture of sweet-smelling substances made into a ball and carried about for ornament or to prevent infection.
6. A ring made from horn, which was said to possess magical qualities.
7. The baglike article of dress attached to the front of a man's hose and covering his genitals.

exchange. Therefore discase° thee instantly—thou must think there's a necessity in't—and change garments with this gentleman. Though the pennyworth° on his side be the worst, yet hold thee, there's some boot.° *undress* / *bargain* / *something more*

AUTOLYCUS I am a poor fellow, sir. [*aside*] I know ye well enough.

CAMILLO Nay, prithee dispatch;° the gentleman is half flayed[8] already. *hurry*

AUTOLYCUS Are you in earnest,[9] sir? [*aside*] I smell the trick on't.

FLORIZEL Dispatch, I prithee.

AUTOLYCUS Indeed I have had earnest, but I cannot with conscience take it.

CAMILLO Unbuckle, unbuckle.

[FLORIZEL *and* AUTOLYCUS *exchange garments.*]

Fortunate mistress, let my prophecy
Come home to ye;[1] you must retire yourself
Into some covert.° Take your sweetheart's hat *hiding place*
And pluck it o'er your brows, muffle your face,
Dismantle you, and, as you can, disliken° *disguise*
The truth of your own seeming,° that you may— *appearance*
For I do fear eyes over°—to shipboard *spies all about*
Get undescried.

PERDITA I see the play so lies
That I must bear a part.

CAMILLO No remedy.
Have you done there?

FLORIZEL Should I now meet my father,
He would not call me son.

CAMILLO Nay, you shall have no hat.
—Come, lady, come. —Farewell, my friend.

AUTOLYCUS Adieu, sir.

FLORIZEL O Perdita, what have we twain forgot!
Pray you, a word.

[*They talk apart.*]

CAMILLO [*aside*] What I do next shall be to tell the King
Of this escape and whither they are bound;
Wherein my hope is I shall so prevail
To force him after, in whose company
I shall review Sicilia, for whose sight
I have a woman's longing.[2]

FLORIZEL Fortune speed us.
Thus we set on, Camillo, to th' seaside.

CAMILLO The swifter speed, the better.

*Exeunt* [FLORIZEL, PERDITA, *and* CAMILLO].

AUTOLYCUS I understand the business; I hear it. To have an open ear, a quick eye, and a nimble hand is necessary for a cutpurse. A good nose is requisite also to smell out work for th'other senses. I see this is the time that the unjust man doth thrive. What an exchange had this been without boot!° What a boot[3] is here with this exchange! Sure the gods do *even without payment*

8. Half undressed (skinned).
9. Serious, with a pun on "earnest" as meaning both "sincere" and "an advance payment." See line 631.
1. Let my prophecy (that she be fortunate) be fulfilled.
2. Women were believed vulnerable to irrational and very intense cravings.
3. Benefit; shoe.

this year connive at° us, and we may do any thing extempore.° The Prince himself is about a piece of iniquity, stealing away from his father with his clog° at his heels. If I thought it were a piece of honesty to acquaint the King withal,° I would not do't. I hold it the more knavery to conceal it, and therein am I constant° to my profession.

*indulge / spontaneously; encumbrance (Perdita); with it; faithful*

*Enter* CLOWN *and* SHEPHERD.

Aside, aside! Here is more matter for a hot brain. Every lane's end, every shop, church, session,° hanging, yields a careful man work.

*court session*

CLOWN See, see, what a man you are now! There is no other way but to tell the King she's a changeling[4] and none of your flesh and blood.

SHEPHERD Nay, but hear me.

CLOWN Nay, but hear me.

SHEPHERD Go to,° then.

*Go ahead*

CLOWN She being none of your flesh and blood, your flesh and blood has not offended the King, and so your flesh and blood is not to be punished by him. Show those things you found about her, those secret things, all but what she has with her. This being done, let the law go whistle, I warrant you.

SHEPHERD I will tell the King all, every word, yea, and his son's pranks too, who, I may say, is no honest man, neither to his father nor to me, to go about to make me the King's brother-in-law.

CLOWN Indeed, brother-in-law was the farthest off° you could have been to him, and then your blood had been the dearer by I know how much an ounce.

*most remote relation*

AUTOLYCUS [*aside*] Very wisely, puppies.

SHEPHERD Well, let us to the King. There is that in this fardel° will make him scratch his beard.

*bundle*

AUTOLYCUS [*aside*] I know not what impediment this complaint may be to the flight of my master.°

*(Florizel)*

CLOWN Pray heartily he be at palace.

AUTOLYCUS [*aside*] Though I am not naturally honest, I am so sometimes by chance. Let me pocket up my peddler's excrement.°

*hair*

[*He takes off his false beard and steps forward.*]

How now, rustics, whither are you bound?

SHEPHERD To th' palace, an't° like your worship.

*if it*

AUTOLYCUS Your affairs there? What? With whom? The condition° of that fardel? The place of your dwelling? Your names? Your ages? Of what having,° breeding,° and anything that is fitting to be known, discover.°

*nature; property / upbringing; reveal*

CLOWN We are but plain° fellows, sir.

*simple; smooth*

AUTOLYCUS A lie! You are rough and hairy. Let me have no lying; it becomes none but tradesmen, and they often give us soldiers the lie;[5] but we pay them for it with stamped coin, not stabbing steel, therefore they do not give us the lie.[6]

4. A child left or abducted by fairies; see note to 3.3.107.
5. They call us soldiers liars; they cheat us soldiers.
6. *we pay . . . the lie:* since soldiers pay with good currency rather than by stabbing (the appropriate response to an insult), the tradesmen are prevented from perpetuating the quarrel.

CLOWN Your worship had like to have given us one° if you had not taken yourself with the manner.[7] *(the lie)*

SHEPHERD Are you a courtier, an't like you, sir?

AUTOLYCUS Whether it like me or no, I am a courtier. Seest thou not the air of the court in these enfoldings?° Hath not my gait in it the measure° of the court? Receives not thy nose court-odor from me? Reflect I not on thy baseness court-contempt? Think'st thou for that I insinuate° to toze° from thee thy business, I am therefore no courtier? I am courtier cap-à-pie° and one that will either push on or pluck back thy business there. Whereupon I command thee to open° thy affair. *(garments; stately walk; subtly work; tease out; from head to foot; reveal)*

SHEPHERD My business, sir, is to the King.

AUTOLYCUS What advocate hast thou to him?

SHEPHERD I know not, an't like you.

CLOWN Advocate's the court word for a pheasant.[8] Say you have none.

SHEPHERD None, sir. I have no pheasant, cock nor hen.

AUTOLYCUS [*aside*] How blessed are we that are not simple men!
Yet nature might have made me as these are,
Therefore I will not disdain.

CLOWN This cannot be but° a great courtier. *(anyone but)*

SHEPHERD His garments are rich, but he wears them not handsomely.

CLOWN He seems to be the more noble in being fantastical.° A great man, I'll warrant. I know by the picking on 's teeth.[9] *(eccentric)*

AUTOLYCUS The fardel there? What's i'th' fardel? Wherefore that box?

SHEPHERD Sir, there lies such secrets in this fardel and box which none must know but the King, and which he shall know within this hour, if I may come to th' speech of him.

AUTOLYCUS Age,° thou hast lost thy labor. *(Old man)*

SHEPHERD Why, sir?

AUTOLYCUS The King is not at the palace; he is gone aboard a new ship to purge melancholy and air himself. For if thou beest capable of° things serious, thou must know the King is full of grief. *(can understand)*

SHEPHERD So 'tis said, sir—about his son that should have married a shepherd's daughter.

AUTOLYCUS If that shepherd be not in handfast,° let him fly. The curses he shall have, the tortures he shall feel, will break the back of man, the heart of monster. *(arrested)*

CLOWN Think you so, sir?

AUTOLYCUS Not he alone shall suffer what wit can make heavy and vengeance bitter; but those that are germane° to him, though removed fifty times, shall all come under the hangman, which though it be great pity, yet it is necessary. An old sheep-whistling rogue,[1] a ram-tender, to offer to have *(related)*

7. If you had not stopped yourself in the middle.
8. Clown thinks "advocate" means "bribe" or "gift," of which a pheasant would be an example.
9. Ornate toothpicks were considered fashionable accessories.
1. An old rascal who whistles while he tends sheep.

his daughter come into grace!° Some say he shall be stoned, but that death is too soft for him, say I. Draw our throne into a sheepcote?° All deaths are too few, the sharpest too easy.

*favor (at court)*
*pen for sheep*

CLOWN Has the old man e'er a son, sir, do you hear, an't like you, sir?

AUTOLYCUS He has a son, who shall be flayed alive, then 'nointed over with honey, set on the head of a wasps' nest, then stand till he be three-quarters and a dram° dead, then recovered again with aqua vitae,° or some other hot infusion; then, raw as he is, and in the hottest day prognostication° proclaims, shall he be set against a brick wall, the sun looking with a southward eye upon him, where he is to behold him with flies blown° to death. But what talk we of these traitorly rascals, whose miseries are to be smiled at, their offenses being so capital? Tell me, for you seem to be honest plain men, what you have° to the King. Being something gently considered,[2] I'll bring you where he is aboard, tender° your persons to his presence, whisper him in your behalfs; and if it be in man, besides the King, to effect your suits, here is man shall do it.

*a tiny bit*
*brandy*
*almanac prediction*
*swollen*
*have to say*
*deliver*

CLOWN [*aside to* SHEPHERD] He seems to be of great authority; close° with him, give him gold. And though authority be a stubborn bear, yet he is oft led by the nose with gold. Show the inside of your purse to the outside of his hand, and no more ado. Remember "stoned" and "flayed alive."

*make a deal*

SHEPHERD An't please you, sir, to undertake the business for us, here is that° gold I have. I'll make it as much more, and leave this young man in pawn,° till I bring it you.

*what*
*as security*

AUTOLYCUS After I have done what I promised?

SHEPHERD Ay, sir.

AUTOLYCUS Well, give me the moiety.° Are you a party in this business?

*half*

CLOWN In some sort, sir. But though my case° be a pitiful one, I hope I shall not be flayed out of it.

*condition; skin*

AUTOLYCUS Oh, that's the case of the shepherd's son. Hang him, he'll be made an example.

CLOWN [*aside to* SHEPHERD] Comfort, good comfort. We must to the King and show our strange sights. He must know 'tis none of your daughter nor my sister. We are gone else.° —Sir, I will give you as much as this old man does when the business is performed, and remain, as he says, your pawn till it be brought you.

*otherwise lost*

AUTOLYCUS I will trust you. Walk before° toward the seaside; go on the right hand; I will but look upon the hedge[3] and follow you.

*ahead of me*

CLOWN We are blessed in this man. As I may say, even blessed.

SHEPHERD Let's before, as he bids us. He was provided to do us good. [*Exeunt* SHEPHERD *and* CLOWN.]

2. *Being . . . considered:* Since I am regarded as a gentleman (someone of high rank who does not labor with his hands and so is worthy of the attention of the King).

3. *look upon the hedge:* slang for "relieve myself."

AUTOLYCUS If I had a mind to be honest, I see Fortune would not suffer° me; she drops booties° in my mouth. I am courted now with a double occasion:° gold, and a means to do the Prince my master good, which who knows how that may turn back to my advancement? I will bring these two moles, these blind ones, aboard him;° if he think it fit to shore them[4] again, and that the complaint they have to the King concerns him nothing, let him call me rogue for being so far officious; for I am proof against° that title and what shame else belongs to't. To him will I present them. There may be matter in it. *Exit.*

*permit / prizes* — *opportunity* — *(his ship)* — *impervious to*

## 5.1

*Enter* LEONTES, CLEOMENES, DION, [*and*] PAULINA.

CLEOMENES Sir, you have done enough and have performed
A saint-like sorrow. No fault could you make
Which you have not redeemed, indeed, paid down
More penitence than done trespass.[1] At the last
Do as the heavens have done, forget your evil;
With them, forgive yourself.

LEONTES Whilst I remember
Her and her virtues, I cannot forget
My blemishes in them,° and so still think of    *in relation to them*
The wrong I did myself, which was so much
That heirless it hath made my kingdom and
Destroyed the sweet'st companion that e'er man
Bred his hopes out of. True?

PAULINA Too true, my lord.
If one by one you wedded all the world,
Or from the all that are took something good
To make a perfect woman, she you killed
Would be unparalleled.

LEONTES I think so. Killed?
She I killed? I did so, but thou strik'st me
Sorely to say I did. It is as bitter
Upon thy tongue as in my thought. Now, good now,°    *if you would*
Say so but seldom.

CLEOMENES Not at all,° good lady.    *Never (say these things)*
You might have spoken a thousand things that would
Have done the time more benefit and graced°    *showed*
Your kindness better.

PAULINA You are one of those
Would have him wed again.

DION If you would not so,
You pity not the state° nor the remembrance    *kingdom*
Of his most sovereign name,[2] consider little
What dangers by his highness' fail of issue°    *lack of offspring*
May drop upon his kingdom and devour
Incertain lookers-on.[3] What were more holy
Than to rejoice the former queen is well?°    *(in heaven)*

4. Put them ashore.

5.1 Location: Sicilia. The palace of Leontes.

1. *paid down . . . trespass:* performed more penance than your sin warranted.

2. *nor . . . name:* nor the perpetuation of his royal lineage (through a new child).

3. *and . . . lookers-on:* and destroy the confused bystanders.

What holier, than for royalty's repair,
For present comfort and for future good,
To bless the bed of majesty again
With a sweet fellow to't?

PAULINA
There is none worthy,
Respecting° her that's gone. Besides, the gods *In comparison to*
Will have fulfilled their secret purposes.
For has not the divine Apollo said—
Is't not the tenor of his oracle?—
That King Leontes shall not have an heir
Till his lost child be found? Which that it shall
Is all as monstrous° to our human reason *incredible*
As my Antigonus to break his grave
And come again to me, who, on my life,
Did perish with the infant. 'Tis your counsel
My lord should to the heavens be contrary,
Oppose against their wills.
[*to* LEONTES] Care not for° issue; *Do not worry about*
The crown will find an heir. Great Alexander
Left his to th' worthiest,[4] so his successor
Was like to be the best.

LEONTES
Good Paulina,
Who hast the memory of Hermione
I know in honor—oh, that ever I
Had squared me° to thy counsel! Then even now *conformed my actions*
I might have looked upon my queen's full eyes,
Have taken treasure from her lips.

PAULINA
And left them
More rich for what they yielded.

LEONTES
Thou speak'st truth.
No more such wives, therefore no wife. One worse
And better used° would make her sainted spirit *treated*
Again possess her° corpse, and on this stage, *(Hermione's)*
Where we offenders now appear, soul-vexed,° *with troubled soul*
And begin, "Why° to me?" *Why offer this insult*

PAULINA
Had she such power,
She had just cause.

LEONTES
She had, and would incense me
To murder her I married.

PAULINA
I should so.
Were I the ghost that walked, I'd bid you mark
Her eye and tell me for what dull part in't
You chose her. Then I'd shriek that even your ears
Should rift° to hear me; and the words that followed *split*
Should be, "Remember mine."° *(my eyes)*

LEONTES
Stars, stars,
And all eyes else° dead coals! Fear thou no wife; *all other eyes*
I'll have no wife, Paulina.

PAULINA
Will you swear
Never to marry but by my free leave?

4. Alexander the Great (356–323 B.C.E.), conqueror of Greece, Persia, and Egypt, died before his own son was born and reportedly urged his followers simply to choose the worthiest man as his successor.

LEONTES Never, Paulina, so be blest my spirit.
PAULINA Then good my lords, bear witness to his oath.
CLEOMENES You tempt° him over-much. *urge*
PAULINA Unless another,
As like Hermione as is her picture,
Affront° his eye. *Confront*
CLEOMENES Good madam, I have done.[5]
PAULINA Yet if my lord will marry—if you will, sir,
No remedy but you will—give me the office
To choose you a queen. She shall not be so young
As was your former, but she shall be such
As, walked your first queen's ghost,[6] it should take joy
To see her in your arms.
LEONTES My true Paulina,
We shall not marry till thou bidd'st us.
PAULINA That
Shall be when your first queen's again in breath.° *alive*
Never till then.

*Enter a* SERVANT.

SERVANT One that gives out himself° Prince Florizel, *claims to be*
Son of Polixenes, with his princess—she
The fairest I have yet beheld—desires access
To your high presence.
LEONTES What° with him? He comes not *Who comes*
Like to° his father's greatness. His approach, *As befits*
So out of circumstance° and sudden, tells us *informal*
'Tis not a visitation framed,° but forced *planned*
By need and accident. What train?° *retinue*
SERVANT But few,
And those but mean.° *of low rank*
LEONTES His princess, say you, with him?
SERVANT Ay, the most peerless piece of earth, I think,
That e'er the sun shone bright on.
PAULINA O Hermione,
As every present time doth boast itself
Above a better, gone, so must thy grave
Give way to what's seen now.[7] —Sir, you yourself
Have said and writ so, but your writing now
Is colder than that theme. She had not been
Nor was not to be equaled—thus your verse
Flowed with her beauty once; 'tis shrewdly° ebbed *grievously*
To say you have seen a better.
SERVANT Pardon, madam.
The one° I have almost forgot—your pardon— *(Hermione)*
The other, when she has obtained your eye,
Will have your tongue too. This is a creature,
Would she begin a sect, might quench the zeal
Of all professors else,[8] make proselytes° *converts*

5. Many editors emend this line to assign "I have done" to Paulina, rather than Cleomenes. As it stands, the line suggests Cleomenes' exasperation that Paulina will not listen to him. If given to Paulina, the line suggests that she knows she should stop berating the King.

6. *walked . . . ghost:* if Hermione appeared as a ghost.

7. *As every . . . seen now:* As each present time boasts itself to be superior to a time better than itself, but gone from view, so you, in your grave, must be superseded by what is now seen.

8. Of all those who professed other religions.

Of who° she but bid follow. — *Of those who*
PAULINA How? Not women?
SERVANT Women will love her that she is a woman
More worth° than any man; men, that she is — *worthy*
The rarest of all women.
LEONTES Go, Cleomenes,
Yourself, assisted with your honored friends,
Bring them to our embracement. Still 'tis strange,
He thus should steal upon us. *Exit* [CLEOMENES].
PAULINA Had our prince,
Jewel of children, seen this hour, he had paired
Well with this lord; there was not full a month° — *a full month*
Between their births.
LEONTES Prithee, no more; cease. Thou know'st
He dies to me again when talked of. Sure,
When I shall see this gentleman, thy speeches
Will bring me to consider that which may
Unfurnish me of reason.° — *Make me go mad*

*Enter* FLORIZEL, PERDITA, CLEOMENES, *and others.*

They are come.
—Your mother was most true to wedlock, Prince,
For she did print your royal father off,[9]
Conceiving you. Were I but twenty-one,
Your father's image is so hit° in you, — *exact*
His very air, that I should call you brother,
As I did him, and speak of something wildly
By us performed before. Most dearly welcome,
And your fair princess—goddess! Oh, alas,
I lost a couple that twixt heaven and earth
Might thus have stood begetting wonder as
You, gracious couple, do. And then I lost—
All mine own folly—the society,
Amity too, of your brave° father, whom, — *stouthearted*
Though bearing misery, I desire my life
Once more to look on him.[1]
FLORIZEL By his command
Have I here touched Sicilia and from him
Give you all greetings that a king at friend° — *in friendship*
Can send his brother; and but° infirmity, — *were it not that*
Which waits upon worn times,° hath something seized — *accompanies old age*
His wished ability,[2] he had himself
The lands and waters twixt your throne and his
Measured° to look upon you, whom he loves— — *Journeyed across*
He bade me say so—more than all the scepters,
And those that bear them, living.
LEONTES O my brother!
Good gentleman, the wrongs I have done thee stir
Afresh within me, and these thy offices,° — *greetings*
So rarely° kind, are as interpreters — *extraordinarily*
Of my behind-hand slackness.[3] Welcome hither,

9. *did print . . . off:* made an exact copy of Polixenes, as a printer produces a book.
1. *whom . . . on him:* whom, though I am suffering, I wish to live long enough to look on once more.
2. *hath . . . ability:* has somewhat deprived him of his desired strength.
3. *are . . . slackness:* are reminders of my slowness (in greeting you).

As is the spring to th'earth. And hath he too
Exposed this paragon to th' fearful usage—
At least ungentle—of the dreadful Neptune,° *(god of the sea)*
To greet a man not worth her pains, much less
Th'adventure° of her person? *risk*

FLORIZEL Good my lord,
She came from Libya.

LEONTES Where the warlike Smalus,[4]
That noble honored lord, is feared and loved?

FLORIZEL Most royal sir, from thence; from him whose daughter
His tears proclaimed his parting with her. Thence,
A prosperous south wind friendly, we have crossed
To execute the charge my father gave me
For visiting your highness. My best train
I have from your Sicilian shores dismissed,
Who for Bohemia bend° to signify *make their way*
Not only my success in Libya, sir,
But my arrival and my wife's in safety
Here where we are.

LEONTES The blessèd gods
Purge all infection from our air whilst you
Do climate° here. You have a holy father, *reside*
A graceful gentleman, against whose person,
So sacred as it is, I have done sin,
For which the heavens, taking angry note,
Have left me issueless; and your father's blessed,
As he from heaven merits it, with you,
Worthy his goodness. What might I have been,
Might I a son and daughter now have looked on,
Such goodly things as you?

*Enter a* LORD.

LORD Most noble sir,
That which I shall report will bear no credit
Were not the proof so nigh. Please you, great sir,
Bohemia greets you from himself by me;
Desires you to attach° his son, who has, *arrest*
His dignity and duty[5] both cast off,
Fled from his father, from his hopes, and with
A shepherd's daughter.

LEONTES Where's Bohemia? Speak.

LORD Here in your city; I now came from him.
I speak amazedly,° and it becomes° *confusedly / befits*
My marvel° and my message. To your court *astonishment*
Whiles he was hast'ning—in the chase, it seems,
Of this fair couple—meets he on the way
The father of this seeming° lady and *apparent; false*
Her brother, having both their country quitted
With this young prince.

FLORIZEL Camillo has betrayed me,
Whose honor and whose honesty till now
Endured all weathers.

4. *Smalus*: an obscure allusion; the name may be a misprint for "Synalus," a soldier from Carthage mentioned by Plutarch.

5. His royal status and his duty to his father.

LORD Lay't so to his charge.° *Accuse him directly*
He's with the King your father.
LEONTES Who, Camillo?
LORD Camillo, sir. I spake with him, who now
Has these poor men in question. Never saw I
Wretches so quake: they kneel, they kiss the earth,
Forswear° themselves as often as they speak. *Perjure*
Bohemia stops his ears and threatens them
With divers deaths in death.° *With diverse tortures*
PERDITA O my poor father!
The heaven sets spies upon us, will not have
Our contract celebrated.
LEONTES You are married?
FLORIZEL We are not, sir, nor are we like to be.
The stars, I see, will kiss the valleys first;
The odds for high and low's alike.[6]
LEONTES My lord,
Is this the daughter of a king?
FLORIZEL She is,
When once she is my wife.
LEONTES That "once," I see, by your good father's speed
Will come on very slowly. I am sorry,
Most sorry, you have broken from his liking,
Where you were tied in duty; and as sorry
Your choice is not so rich in worth° as beauty, *rank*
That you might well enjoy her.
FLORIZEL —Dear, look up.
Though Fortune, visible an enemy,
Should chase us with my father, power no jot
Hath she to change our loves.[7] —Beseech you, sir,
Remember since you owed no more to time
Than I do now.° With thought of such affections, *when you were my age*
Step forth mine advocate; at your request
My father will grant precious things as trifles.
LEONTES Would he do so, I'd beg your precious mistress,
Which he counts but a trifle.
PAULINA Sir, my liege,
Your eye hath too much youth in't. Not a month
Fore your queen died, she was more worth such gazes
Than what you look on now.
LEONTES I thought of her
Even in these looks I made. —But your petition
Is yet unanswered. I will to your father.
Your honor not o'erthrown by your desires,[8]
I am friend to them and you. Upon which errand
I now go toward him; therefore follow me,
And mark what way I make. Come, good my lord.
*Exeunt.*

6. *The odds . . . alike:* that is, Chance treats those of high and low rank identically.
7. *power . . . our loves:* even if Lady Fortune were to make herself apparent as our enemy and join my father in pursuit, she would remain powerless to change our love.
8. *Your honor . . . desires:* So long as you have not allowed passion to destroy your virtue.

## 5.2

*Enter* AUTOLYCUS *and a* GENTLEMAN.

AUTOLYCUS Beseech you, sir, were you present at this relation?° *when this was told*

FIRST GENTLEMAN I was by at the opening of the fardel, heard the old shepherd deliver the manner how he found it; whereupon, after a little amazedness, we were all commanded out of the chamber. Only this: methought I heard the shepherd say he found the child.

AUTOLYCUS I would most gladly know the issue° of it. *outcome*

FIRST GENTLEMAN I make a broken delivery° of the business, but the changes I perceived in the King and Camillo were very notes of admiration.[1] They seemed almost, with staring on one another, to tear the cases° of their eyes. There was speech in their dumbness, language in their very gesture. They looked as° they had heard of a world ransomed or one destroyed. A notable passion of wonder appeared in them, but the wisest beholder that knew no more but seeing could not say if th'importance were joy or sorrow. But in the extremity of the one,° it must needs be. *confused report* *burst the sockets* *as if* *of the one or the other*

*Enter another* GENTLEMAN.

Here comes a gentleman that happily° knows more. The news, Rogero? *perhaps*

SECOND GENTLEMAN Nothing but bonfires. The oracle is fulfilled; the King's daughter is found. Such a deal° of wonder is broken out within this hour that ballad-makers cannot be able to express it. *great quantity*

*Enter another* GENTLEMAN.

Here comes the Lady Paulina's steward. He can deliver you more. How goes it now, sir? This news which is called true is so like an old tale that the verity of it is in strong suspicion. Has the King found his heir?

THIRD GENTLEMAN Most true, if ever truth were pregnant by circumstance.° That which you hear you'll swear you see, there is such unity in the proofs. The mantle of Queen Hermione's; her jewel about the neck of it; the letters of Antigonus found with it, which they know to be his character;° the majesty of the creature in resemblance of the mother; the affection of° nobleness, which nature shows above her breeding;[2] and many other evidences, proclaim her with all certainty to be the King's daughter. Did you see the meeting of the two kings? *proven by evidence* *handwriting* *instinct toward*

SECOND GENTLEMAN No.

THIRD GENTLEMAN Then have you lost a sight which was to be seen, cannot be spoken of. There might you have beheld one joy crown another, so and in such manner that it seemed sorrow wept to take leave of them, for their joy waded in tears. There was casting up of eyes, holding up of hands, with countenance° of such distraction[3] that they were to be known by garment, not by favor.° Our *face* *features*

**5.2** Location: Scene continues.
1. Were the very marks of wonder.
2. *which . . . breeding*: which naturally shows in her in excess of her upbringing.
3. So altered by emotion.

King being ready to leap out of himself for joy of his found daughter, as if that joy were now become a loss, cries, "Oh, thy mother, thy mother!"; then asks Bohemia forgiveness, then embraces his son-in-law, then again worries he° his daughter with clipping° her. Now he thanks the old shepherd, which stands by like a weather-bitten conduit of[4] many kings' reigns. I never heard of such another encounter, which lames report to follow it[5] and undoes° description to do° it.

*he agitates / embracing / defies / express*

SECOND GENTLEMAN What, pray you, became of Antigonus that carried hence the child?

THIRD GENTLEMAN Like an old tale still, which will have matter to rehearse° though credit° be asleep and not an ear open: he was torn to pieces with a bear. This avouches° the shepherd's son, who has not only his innocence,° which seems much to justify him, but a handkerchief and rings of his° that Paulina knows.

*relate / belief / vows / simplemindedness / (of Antigonus)*

FIRST GENTLEMAN What became of his bark° and his followers?

*ship*

THIRD GENTLEMAN Wrecked the same instant of their master's death, and in the view of the shepherd; so that all the instruments which aided to expose the child were even then lost when it was found. But, oh, the noble combat that twixt joy and sorrow was fought in Paulina: she had one eye declined for the loss of her husband, another elevated that the oracle was fulfilled. She lifted the Princess from the earth, and so locks her in embracing as if she would pin her to her heart, that she might no more be in danger of losing.°

*of being lost*

FIRST GENTLEMAN The dignity of this act was worth the audi ence of kings and princes, for by such was it acted.

THIRD GENTLEMAN One of the prettiest touches of all, and that which angled for mine eyes—caught the water° though not the fish—was when at the relation of the Queen's death, with the manner how she came to't bravely confessed and lamented by the King, how attentiveness° wounded his daughter till from one sign of dolor° to another she did, with an "Alas," I would fain say bleed tears; for I am sure my heart wept blood. Who was most marble° there changed color. Some swooned, all sorrowed. If all the world could have seen't, the woe had been universal.

*(my tears) / intent listening / grief / unfeeling*

FIRST GENTLEMAN Are they returned to the court?

THIRD GENTLEMAN No. The Princess hearing of her mother's statue, which is in the keeping of Paulina, a piece many years in doing and now newly performed° by that rare Italian master, Giulio Romano,[6] who, had he himself eternity and could put breath into his work, would beguile° nature of her custom,° so perfectly he is her ape.° He so near to Hermione hath done Hermione that they say one would speak to her and stand in hope of answer. Thither

*completed / cheat / business / imitator*

4. *weather-bitten . . . of*: battered waterspout from.
5. Which makes any account of it seem deficient.
6. An Italian painter, a follower of Raphael, who died in 1546 and may have contributed to a well-known series of erotic drawings, *I modi*, illustrating sexual positions, or "postures."

with all greediness of affection are they gone, and there they intend to sup.

SECOND GENTLEMAN I thought she had some great matter there in hand, for she hath privately twice or thrice a day ever since the death of Hermione visited that removed° house. Shall we thither and with our company piece° the rejoicing?

*distant; hidden*
*join*

FIRST GENTLEMAN Who would be thence that has the benefit of access? Every wink of an eye some new grace will be born. Our absence makes us unthrifty to our knowledge.[7] Let's along. *Exeunt* [GENTLEMEN].

AUTOLYCUS Now, had I not the dash° of my former life in me, would preferment° drop on my head. I brought the old man and his son aboard the° Prince, told him I heard them talk of a fardel, and I know not what. But he at that time over-fond of the shepherd's daughter—so he then took her to be—who began to be much seasick and himself little better, extremity of weather continuing, this mystery remained undiscovered. But 'tis all one to me, for had I been the finder-out of this secret, it would not have relished° among my other discredits.

*stain; touch*
*royal favor*
*aboard the ship of the*
*appeared well*

*Enter* SHEPHERD *and* CLOWN.

Here come those I have done good to against my will, and already appearing in the blossoms of their fortune.

SHEPHERD Come, boy. I am past more children, but thy sons and daughters will be all gentlemen born.

CLOWN [*to* AUTOLYCUS] You are well met, sir. You denied to fight with me this other° day because I was no gentleman born. See you these clothes? Say you see them not and think me still no gentleman born. You were best say these robes are not gentlemen born. Give me the lie,[8] do, and try whether I am not now a gentleman born.

*the other*

AUTOLYCUS I know you are now, sir, a gentleman born.

CLOWN Ay, and have been so any time these four hours.

SHEPHERD And so have I, boy.

CLOWN So you have; but I was a gentleman born before my father, for the King's son took me by the hand and called me brother; and then the two kings called my father brother; and then the Prince my brother and the Princess my sister called my father, father. And so we wept, and there was the first gentleman-like tears that ever we shed.

SHEPHERD We may live, son, to shed many more.

CLOWN Ay, or else 'twere hard luck, being in so preposterous estate[9] as we are.

AUTOLYCUS I humbly beseech you, sir, to pardon me all the faults I have committed to your worship, and to give me your good report to the Prince my master.

7. Makes us squander an opportunity to add to our knowledge.
8. Insult me (so that I must respond like a gentleman, perhaps by offering to duel).
9. Clown probably means "prosperous," but "preposterous" is a nice blunder because preposterous means (1) contrary to nature or (2) putting last what should be first. By becoming gentlemen, the shepherds have inverted the social order and put "real" gentlemen behind "false" ones.

SHEPHERD Prithee, son, do, for we must be gentle° now we are gentlemen. *act nobly*
CLOWN Thou wilt amend thy life?
AUTOLYCUS Ay, an it like your good worship.
CLOWN Give me thy hand. I will swear to the Prince thou art as honest a true fellow as any is in Bohemia.
SHEPHERD You may say it, but not swear it.
CLOWN Not swear it now I am a gentleman? Let boors° and franklins° say it; I'll swear it. *peasants* *small farmers*
SHEPHERD How if it be false, son?
CLOWN If it be ne'er so false,° a true gentleman may swear it in the behalf of his friend. And I'll swear to the Prince thou art a tall fellow of thy hands° and that thou wilt not be drunk. But I know thou art no tall fellow of thy hands and that thou wilt be drunk, but I'll swear it, and I would thou wouldst be a tall fellow of thy hands. *Even if it is false* *brave man of action*
AUTOLYCUS I will prove so, sir, to my power.° *as well as I can*
CLOWN Ay, by any means prove a tall fellow. If I do not wonder how thou dar'st venture to be drunk, not being a tall fellow, trust me not. Hark, the kings and princes, our kindred, are going to see the Queen's picture.° Come, follow us. We'll be thy good masters. *Exeunt.* *likeness*

## 5.3

*Enter* LEONTES, POLIXENES, FLORIZEL, PERDITA, CAMILLO, PAULINA, HERMIONE (*like a statue*), LORDS, *etc.*[1]

LEONTES O grave and good Paulina, the great comfort
That I have had of thee!
PAULINA What,° sovereign sir, *Whatever*
I did not well, I meant well. All my services
You have paid home;° but that you have vouchsafed° *fully rewarded / vowed*
With your crowned brother and these your contracted
Heirs of your kingdoms my poor house to visit,
It is a surplus° of your grace which never *additional sign*
My life may last to answer.
LEONTES O Paulina,
We honor you with trouble,[2] but we came
To see the statue of our queen. Your gallery
Have we passed through, not without much content
In many singularities;° but we saw not *In seeing many rarities*
That which my daughter came to look upon,
The statue of her mother.
PAULINA As she lived peerless,
So her dead likeness I do well believe
Excels whatever yet you looked upon,
Or hand of man hath done; therefore I keep it
Lonely,° apart. But here it is. Prepare *Alone*
To see the life as lively mocked° as ever *realistically imitated*

5.3 Location: Sicilia. Paulina's house.
1. TEXTUAL COMMENT Hermione needs to enter here since the text gives her no other way to enter this scene, but the scene must be performed in a way that maintains for theatergoers the illusion that she is a statue. See Digital Edition TC 9.
2. *We honor you with trouble:* The honor we pay to you demands effort from you.

Still° sleep mocked death. Behold, and say 'tis well. *Quiet*
[PAULINA *reveals* HERMIONE, *standing like a statue.*][3]
I like your silence; it the more shows off
Your wonder. But yet speak; first you, my liege,
Comes it not something° near? *somewhat*

LEONTES Her natural posture.
—Chide me, dear stone, that I may say indeed
Thou art Hermione; or, rather, thou art she
In thy not chiding, for she was as tender
As infancy and grace. —But yet, Paulina,
Hermione was not so much wrinkled, nothing° *not at all*
So aged as this seems.

POLIXENES Oh, not by much.

PAULINA So much the more our carver's excellence,
Which lets go by some sixteen years and makes her
As° she lived now. *As if*

LEONTES As now she might have done,
So much to my good comfort as it is
Now piercing to my soul. Oh, thus she stood,
Even with such life of majesty—warm life,
As now it coldly stands—when first I wooed her.
I am ashamed. Does not the stone rebuke me
For being more stone° than it? O royal piece,° *hard / work of art*
There's magic in thy majesty, which has
My evils conjured° to remembrance, and *summoned*
From thy admiring° daughter took the spirits, *wondering*
Standing like stone with thee.

PERDITA And give me leave,
And do not say 'tis superstition that
I kneel and then implore her blessing.[4] Lady,
Dear Queen, that ended when I but began,
Give me that hand of yours to kiss.

PAULINA Oh, patience!
The statue is but newly fixed;° the color's *painted*
Not dry.

CAMILLO My lord, your sorrow was too sore° laid on, *painfully*
Which sixteen winters cannot blow away,
So many summers dry.° Scarce any joy *dry up*
Did ever so long live; no sorrow
But killed itself much sooner.

POLIXENES [*to* LEONTES] Dear my brother,
Let him that was the cause of this have power
To take off so much grief from you as he
Will piece up in himself.[5]

PAULINA Indeed, my lord,
If I had thought the sight of my poor image
Would thus have wrought you°—for the stone is mine— *made you distraught*
I'd not have showed it.

LEONTES Do not draw the curtain.

3. PERFORMANCE COMMENT The challenge for the actor playing Hermione is how to imitate a statue convincingly and for a considerable period of stage time. See Digital Edition PC 5.

4. A possible reference to the Catholic practice of kneeling before images of the Virgin Mary.

5. Will make a part of himself.

PAULINA No longer shall you gaze on't, lest your fancy
May think anon it moves.
LEONTES Let be, let be.
Would I were dead but that methinks already[6]—
What was he that did make it? See, my lord,
Would you not deem it breathed and that those veins
Did verily bear blood?
POLIXENES Masterly done.
The very life seems warm upon her lip.
LEONTES The fixure of her eye has motion in't,[7]
As° we are mocked with art. *In such a way that*
PAULINA I'll draw the curtain.
My lord's almost so far transported that
He'll think anon it lives.
LEONTES O sweet Paulina,
Make me to think so twenty years together.
No settled senses° of the world can match *calm state of mind*
The pleasure of that madness. Let 't alone.
PAULINA I am sorry, sir, I have thus far stirred you; but
I could afflict you farther.
LEONTES Do, Paulina.
For this affliction has a taste as sweet
As any cordial° comfort. Still methinks *restorative*
There is an air comes from her.° What fine chisel *she seems to breathe*
Could ever yet cut breath? Let no man mock me,
For I will kiss her.
PAULINA Good my lord, forbear.
The ruddiness upon her lip is wet.
You'll mar it if you kiss it, stain your own
With oily painting.° Shall I draw the curtain? *paint*
LEONTES No, not these twenty years.
PERDITA So long could I
Stand by, a looker-on.
PAULINA Either forbear,
Quit presently° the chapel, or resolve you *immediately*
For more amazement. If you can behold it,
I'll make the statue move indeed, descend,
And take you by the hand. But then you'll think—
Which I protest against—I am assisted
By wicked powers.
LEONTES What you can make her do,
I am content to look on; what to speak,
I am content to hear; for 'tis as easy
To make her speak as move.
PAULINA It is required
You do awake your faith. Then all stand still.
On! Those that think it is unlawful° business *unauthorized; illegal*
I am about, let them depart.

6. *Would . . . already:* May I die if I do not think it already moves.
7. TEXTUAL COMMENT Most editors emend to "fixture." This edition keeps the Folio's "fixure," meaning "fixed position," which seems to have been an intentional choice on Shakespeare's part. See Digital Edition TC 10.

LEONTES Proceed.
No foot shall stir.
PAULINA Music; awake her; strike!° *strike up!*
[*Music.*]
[*to* HERMIONE] 'Tis time. Descend. Be stone no more. Approach.
Strike all that look upon with marvel. Come,
I'll fill your grave up. Stir. Nay, come away.
Bequeath to death your numbness, for from him° *(death)*
Dear life redeems you. [*to* LEONTES] You perceive she stirs.
Start not. Her actions shall be holy as
You hear my spell is lawful. Do not shun her
Until you see her die again, for then
You kill her double.[8] Nay, present your hand.
When she was young, you wooed her; now, in age
Is she become the suitor?
LEONTES Oh, she's warm!
If this be magic, let it be an art
Lawful as eating.
POLIXENES She embraces him.
CAMILLO She hangs about his neck.
If she pertain to life,° let her speak too. *be truly alive*
POLIXENES Ay, and make it manifest where she has lived,
Or how stolen from the dead.
PAULINA That she is living,
Were it but told you, should be hooted at
Like an old tale. But it appears she lives,
Though yet she speak not. Mark a little while.
[*to* PERDITA] Please you to interpose, fair madam. Kneel
And pray your mother's blessing. [*to* HERMIONE] Turn, good lady:
Our Perdita is found.
HERMIONE You gods, look down,
And from your sacred vials pour your graces
Upon my daughter's head. Tell me, mine own,
Where hast thou been preserved? Where lived? How found
Thy father's court? For thou shalt hear that I,
Knowing by Paulina that the oracle
Gave hope thou wast in being,° have preserved *alive*
Myself to see the issue.° *outcome; child*
PAULINA There's time enough for that,
Lest they desire upon this push to trouble
Your joys with like relation.[9] —Go together,
You precious winners all. Your exultation
Partake° to every one. I, an old turtle,[1] *Spread your happiness*
Will wing me to some withered bough, and there
My mate, that's never to be found again,
Lament till I am lost.° *dead*
LEONTES Oh, peace, Paulina!
Thou shouldst a husband take by my consent,
As I by thine a wife. This is a match,

8. *You kill her double:* that is, If you were to shun her in this new life, you would kill her again.
9. Lest they (bystanders?) desire at this crucial moment to trouble your happiness with similar stories.
1. Turtledove, a symbol of faithful love.

And made between's by vows. Thou hast found mine,
But how is to be questioned, for I saw her,
As I thought, dead, and have in vain said many
A prayer upon her grave. I'll not seek far—
For him, I partly know his mind—to find thee
An honorable husband. Come, Camillo,
And take her by the hand, whose worth and honesty
Is richly noted, and here justified° *testified to*
By us, a pair of kings. Let's from this place.
[*to* HERMIONE] What? Look upon my brother. Both your pardons,
That e'er I put between your holy looks
My ill suspicion. This° your son-in-law, *This is*
And son unto the King, whom heavens directing
Is troth-plight° to your daughter. —Good Paulina, *betrothed*
Lead us from hence where we may leisurely
Each one demand and answer to his part
Performed in this wide gap of time since first
We were dissevered. Hastily lead away. *Exeunt.*

# The Tempest

*The Tempest* opens on a remote island of exile where Duke Prospero, deposed from power and thrust out of Milan by his wicked brother, has found shelter with his only daughter, Miranda. For the story that then unfolds, Shakespeare does not seem to have relied, as he often did, on a single dominant source, but rather to have drawn on motifs he had explored throughout his career. The play's preoccupation with loss and recovery and its air of wonder link *The Tempest* most closely to a succession of plays written toward the end of Shakespeare's professional life that modern editors generally call "romances" (*Pericles, The Winter's Tale, Cymbeline*), but it resonates as well with issues that long haunted his imagination: the painful necessity for a father to let his daughter go; the treacherous betrayal of a legitimate ruler; the murderous hatred of one brother for another; the perilous passage from civilized society to the wilderness and the dream of a return; the plight of a young woman, torn from her place in the social hierarchy; the dream of manipulating others by means of art; the threat of a radical loss of identity; the relationship between nature and nurture; the harnessing of magical powers. *The Tempest* is a kind of echo chamber of Shakespeare's lifelong preoccupations.

Though it is printed first among the plays in the First Folio (1623), *The Tempest* is probably one of the last that Shakespeare wrote. It can be dated fairly precisely: it uses material that was not available until late 1610, and there is a record of a performance before the king on Hallowmas Night, 1611. Since Shakespeare retired soon after to Stratford, *The Tempest* has seemed to many to be his valedictory to the theater. In this view, Prospero's strangely anxious and moving Epilogue—"Now my charms are all o'erthrown, / And what strength I have's mine own"—is the expression of the playwright's own professional leave-taking.

There are reasons to be skeptical: after finishing *The Tempest,* Shakespeare collaborated on at least two other plays, *Henry VIII* and *The Two Noble Kinsmen,* and it is risky to identify the author too closely with any of his characters, let alone an exiled, embittered, morally ambiguous wizard bent on recovering his lost dukedom. The wizard is in significant ways less like a playwright than an experimental scientist, one who creates and manipulates artificial situations in nature in order to observe the results.

Yet the echo-chamber effect is striking, and when Prospero and others speak of his powerful "art," it is difficult not to associate the skill of the great magician with the skill of the great playwright. Near the end of the play, the association is made explicit when Prospero uses his magic powers to produce what he terms "some vanity of mine art" (4.1.41), a betrothal masque performed by spirits whom he calls forth "to enact / My present fancies" (4.1.121–22). The masque, typically a lavish courtly performance with music and dancing, may have seemed particularly appropriate on the occasion of another early performance: *The Tempest* was one of fourteen plays provided as part of the elaborate festivities in honor of the betrothal and marriage of King James's daughter Elizabeth to Frederick, who as elector palatine ruled a territory in Germany. As Prospero's gift of the beautiful spectacle displays his magnificence and authority, so *The Tempest* and the other plays commanded by the king for his daughter's wedding would have enhanced his own prestige.

*The Tempest* opens with a spectacular storm that is indifferent to the ruler's authority: "What cares these roarers for the name of king?" (1.1.15–16), shouts the exasperated Boatswain at the aristocrats who are standing in his way. The Boatswain's outburst

Magical storm. From Olaus Magnus, *Historia de Gentibus Septentrionalibus* (1555 ed.).

seems unanswerable: like the implacable thunder in *King Lear,* the tempest marks the point at which exalted titles are revealed to be absurd pretensions, substanceless in the face of the elemental forces of nature and the desperate struggle for survival. But we soon learn that this tempest is not in fact natural and that it emphatically does hear and respond to human power, a power that is terrifying but, at least by its own account, benign: "The direful spectacle of the wreck," Prospero tells his daughter, "I have with such provision in mine art / So safely ordered" (1.2.26, 28–29) that no one on board has been harmed.

Shakespeare's contemporaries were fascinated by the figure of the magus, the great magician who by dint of deep learning, ascetic discipline, and patient skill could command the secret forces of the natural and supernatural world. Distinct from the village witch and "cunning man," figures engaged in local acts of healing and malice, and distinct, too, from alchemical experimenters bent on turning base metal into gold, the magus, cloaked in a robe covered with mysterious symbols, pronounced his occult charms, called forth spirits, and ranged in his imagination through the heavens and the earth, conjoining contemplative wisdom with action in the world. But there was a shiver of fear mingled with the popular admiration: when the person in Shakespeare's time most widely identified as a magus, the wizard John Dee, was away from his house, his library, one of the greatest private collections of books in England, was vandalized and plundered.

Book, costume, powerful language, the ability to enact the fancies of the brain: these are key elements of both magic and theater. "I have bedimmed / The noontide sun," Prospero declares (5.1.41–42), beginning an enumeration of extraordinary accomplishments that culminates with the revelation that "[g]raves at my command / Have waked their sleepers, oped, and let 'em forth / By my so potent art" (5.1.48–50).

For the playwright who conjured up the ghosts of Caesar and old Hamlet, the claim does not seem extravagant, but for a magician it amounts to an extremely dangerous confession. Necromancy—communing with the spirits of the dead—was the very essence of black magic, the hated practice from which Prospero is careful to distance himself throughout the play. Before his exile, the island had been the realm of the "damned witch Sycorax," who was banished there "[f]or mischiefs manifold and sorceries terrible" (1.2.263–64). The legitimacy of Prospero's power, including power over his slave Caliban, Sycorax's son, depends on his claims to moral authority, but for one disturbing moment it is difficult to see the difference between "foul witch" and princely magician. Small wonder that as soon as he has disclosed that he has trafficked with the dead, Prospero declares that he abjures his "rough magic" (5.1.50).

Prospero does not give an explicit reason for this abjuration, but it appears to be a key stage in the complex process that has led, before the time of the play, to his overthrow and will lead, after the play's events are over, to his return to power. This process in its entirety requires years to unfold, but the play depicts only a small, though crucially important, fragment of it. Together with his early *Comedy of Errors, The Tempest* is unusual among Shakespeare's plays in observing what literary critics of the age called the unities of time and place; unlike *Antony and Cleopatra,* for example, which ranges over a huge territory, or *The Winter's Tale,* which covers a huge span of time, the actions of *The Tempest* all take place in a single locale—the island—during the course of a single day. In a long scene of exposition just after the spectacular opening storm, Prospero tells Miranda that he is at a critical moment; everything depends on his seizing the opportunity that fortune has granted him. The whole play, then, is the spectacle of his timing—timing that might be cynically termed political opportunism or theatrical cunning but that Prospero himself associates with the working out of "Providence divine" (1.2.159). The opportunity he seizes has its tangled roots in what he calls "the dark backward and abysm of time" (1.2.50). Many years before, when he was Duke of Milan, Prospero's preoccupation with "secret studies" gave his ambitious and unscrupulous brother Antonio the opportunity to topple him from power. Now those same studies, perfected during his long exile, have enabled Prospero to cause Antonio and his shipmates, sailing back to Italy from Tunis, to be shipwrecked on his island, where they have fallen unwittingly under his control. His magic makes it possible not only to wrest back his dukedom but to avenge himself for the terrible wrong that his brother and his brother's principal ally, Alonso, the King of Naples, have done him: "They now are in my power" (3.3.91). Audiences in Shakespeare's time would have had an all too clear image of how horrendous the vengeance of enraged princes usually was. That Prospero restrains himself from the full exercise of his power to harm his enemies, that he breaks his magic staff and drowns his book, is his highest moral achievement, a triumphant display of self-mastery: "The rarer action is / In virtue than in vengeance" (5.1.27–28).

All of those who are shipwrecked on the island undergo the same shock of terror and unexpected survival, but their experiences, as they cross the yellow sands and make their way toward the interior of the island, differ markedly. The least affected are the mariners, including the feisty Boatswain; after their exhausting labors in the storm, they have sunk into a strange, uneasy sleep, only to be awakened in time to sail the miraculously restored ship back to Italy. The others are put through more complex trials; exposed to varying degrees of anxiety, temptation, grief, fear, and penitence, they are in effect subjects in a psychological experiment carefully conducted by Prospero, who attempts to instill in them moral self-control and work-discipline. The most generously treated is Ferdinand, the only son of the King of Naples, whom Prospero, in what is essentially a carefully planned dynastic alliance, has secretly chosen to be his son-in-law. As Ferdinand bewails what he assumes is his father's death by drowning, he hears strange, haunting music, including the remarkable song of death and metamorphosis, "Full fathom five thy father lies" (1.2.395). Ferdinand is the only one of the shipwrecked company, until the play's final scene, to encounter Prospero directly; the magician makes the experience menacing, humiliating, and frustrating, but this is the modest, salutary price the young man must pay to win the hand of the beautiful Miranda, who seems to him a goddess and who, for her part, has fallen in love with him at first sight.

Prospero directs the experience of the rest as well, but not in person; instead, they principally encounter his diligent servant, Ariel. Ariel is not human, although at a crucial moment he is able to imagine what he would feel "were I human" (5.1.20). He is, as the cast of characters describes him, an "airy spirit," capable of moving at

The conjurer. Engraving by Theodore de Bry after a drawing by John White. From Thomas Hariot, *A Brief and True Report of the New Found Land of Virginia* (1590).

immense speed, altering the weather, and producing vivid illusions. We learn that Ariel possesses an inherent moral "delicacy," a delicacy that in the past (that is, before the time depicted in the play) has brought him pain. For, as Prospero reminds him, he had been Sycorax's servant and was, for refusing "[t]o act her earthy and abhorred commands" (1.2.273), imprisoned by the witch for many years in a cloven pine. Prospero freed him from confinement and now demands in return a fixed term of service, which Ariel provides with a mixture of brilliant alacrity and grumbling. Prospero responds in turn with mingled affection and anger, alternating warm praises and dire threats. Although Prospero's "art," through which he commands Ariel and the lesser spirits, seems to foresee and control everything, this control is purchased through constant discipline.

And, for all his godlike powers, there are limits to what Prospero can do. He can make the loathed Antonio and the others know something of the bitterness of loss and isolation; he can produce in them irresistible drowsiness and startled awakenings; he can command Ariel to lay before them a splendid banquet and then make it suddenly vanish; he can drive them to desperation and madness. But in the case of his own brother and Alonso's similarly wicked brother Sebastian, Prospero cannot reshape their inner lives and effect a moral transformation. The most he can do with these deeply cynical men is to limit through continual vigilance any further harm they might do and to take back what is rightfully his. When, with an obvious effort, Prospero declares that he forgives his brother's "rankest fault" (5.1.132), Antonio is conspicuously silent.

But the higher moral purpose of Prospero's art is not all a failure. With Alonso, the project of provoking repentance by generating intense grief and fear succeeds admirably: Alonso not only gives up his power over the dukedom of Milan but begs Prospero's pardon for the wrong he committed in conspiring to overthrow him. (Both rulers, Alonso and Prospero, can look forward to a unification of their states in the next generation, through the marriage of Ferdinand and Miranda.) Moreover, Prospero's carefully contrived scenarios succeed in confirming the decency, loyalty, and goodness of Alonso's counselor, Gonzalo, who had years before provided the exiled Duke and his daughter with the means necessary for their survival.

It is Gonzalo's goodness that at the end of the play enables him to grasp the dynastic providence in the bewildering tangle of events—"Was Milan thrust from Milan that his issue / Should become kings of Naples?" (5.1.205–6)—and that earlier inspires him to sense the miraculous nature of their survival. Indifferent to the contemptuous mockery of Antonio and Sebastian, Gonzalo responds to shipwreck on the strange island by speculating on how he would govern it were he responsible for its "plantation":

> I'th' commonwealth I would by contraries
> Execute all things. For no kind of traffic
> Would I admit; no name of magistrate;
> Letters should not be known; riches, poverty,
> And use of service, none; contract, succession,
> Bourn, bound of land, tilth, vineyard, none;
> No use of metal, corn, or wine, or oil;
> No occupation, all men idle, all . . .
> (2.1.142–49)

Shakespeare adapted Gonzalo's utopian speculations from a passage in "Of Cannibals" (1580), a remarkably free-spirited essay by the French humanist Michel de Montaigne. The Brazilian Indians, Montaigne admiringly writes (in John Florio's 1603 translation), have "no kind of traffic, no knowledge of letters, no intelligence of numbers, no name of magistrate nor of politic superiority, no use of service, of riches or of poverty, no contracts, no successions . . . no occupation but idle, no respect of kindred but common, no apparel but natural, no manuring of lands, no use of wine, corn, or metal." For Montaigne, the European adventurers and colonists, confident in their cultural superiority, are the real barbarians, while the American natives, with their cannibalism and free love, live in accordance with nature.

The issues raised by Montaigne, and more generally by New World voyages, may have been particularly interesting to *The Tempest*'s early audiences as news reached London of the extraordinary adventures of the Virginia Company's colony at Jamestown. Shakespeare seems to have read a detailed account of these adventures in a letter written by the colony's secretary, William Strachey; although the letter was not printed until 1625, it was evidently circulating in manuscript in 1610. In 1609, a fleet carrying more than four hundred persons that had been sent out to reinforce the colony was struck by a hurricane near the Virginia coast. Two of the vessels reached their destination, but the third, the ship carrying the governor, Sir Thomas Gates, ran aground on an uninhabited island in the Bermudas. Remarkably enough, all of the passengers and crew survived; but their tribulations were not over. By forcing everyone to labor side by side in order to survive, the violence of the storm had weakened the governor's authority, and both the natural abundance and the isolation of the island where they were shipwrecked weakened it further. Gates ordered the company to build new ships in order to sail to Jamestown, but his command met with ominous grumblings and threats of mutiny. According to Strachey's letter, the main troublemaker directly challenged Gates's authority: "therefore let the Governour (said he) kiss, etc." In response, Gates had the troublemaker shot to death. New ships were built, and in an impressive feat of navigation the entire company reached Jamestown. The group found the settlement deeply demoralized: illness was rampant, food was scarce, and relations with the neighboring Indians, once amicable, had completely broken down. Only harsh military discipline kept the English colony from falling apart.

With the possible exception of some phrases from Strachey's description of the storm and a few scattered details, *The Tempest* does not directly use any of this vivid narrative. Prospero's island is evidently in the Mediterranean, and its immediate

*America.* Engraving by Theodor Galle after a drawing by Jan van der Straet (ca. 1580).

contemporary reference points are stories of dynastic intrigue, captivity, enslavement, and redemption associated with the perilous waters off the coast of North Africa. The New World is only mentioned as a far-off place, "the still-vexed Bermudas" (1.2.229), where the swift Ariel flies to fetch dew. Yet Shakespeare's play seems constantly to echo precisely the issues raised by the Bermuda shipwreck and its aftermath. What does it take to survive? How do men of different classes and moral character react during a state of emergency? What is the proper relation between theoretical understanding and practical experience or between knowledge and power? Is obedience to authority willing or forced? How can those in power protect themselves from the conspiracies of malcontents? Is it possible to detect a providential design in what looks at first like a succession of accidents? If there are natives to contend with, how should colonists establish friendly and profitable relations with them? What is to be done if relations turn sour? How can those who rule prevent an alliance between hostile natives and the poorer colonists, often disgruntled and themselves exploited? And—Montaigne's more radical questions—what is the justification of one person's rule over another? Who is the civilized man, and who is the barbarian?

The unregenerate nastiness of Antonio and Sebastian, conjoined with the goodness of Gonzalo, might seem indirectly to endorse Montaigne's critique of the Europeans and his praise of the cannibals, were it not for the disturbing presence in *The Tempest* of the character whose name is almost an anagram for "cannibal," Caliban. Caliban, whose god Setebos is mentioned in accounts of Magellan's voyages as a Patagonian deity, is anything but a noble savage. Shakespeare does not shrink from the darkest European fantasies about the Wild Man. Indeed, he exaggerates them: Caliban is deformed, lecherous, evil-smelling, treacherous, naive, drunken, lazy, rebellious, violent, and devil-worshipping. According to Prospero, he is not even human: "A devil, a born devil, on whose nature / Nurture can never stick" (4.1.188–89). When he first came to the island, Prospero recalls, he treated Caliban "with humane care" (1.2.346), lodging him in his own cell until the savage tried to rape Miranda. The arrival of the other Europeans brings out still worse qualities. Encountering the basest of the company, Alonso's jester, Trinculo, and drunken butler, Stefano, Caliban falls at their feet in brutish worship and then devises a conspiracy to murder Prospero in his sleep. Were the conspiracy to succeed, Caliban would get neither the girl for whom he lusts nor the freedom for which he shouts—he would become "King" Stefano's "foot-licker" (4.1.218)—but he would satisfy the enormous hatred he feels for Prospero.

Prospero's power, Caliban reasons, derives from his superior knowledge. "Remember / First to possess his books," he urges the louts, "for without them / He's but a sot as I am. . . . Burn but his books" (3.2.85–89). The strategy is a canny one, in recognizing an underlying link between literacy and authority, but the problem is not only that Stefano and Trinculo are hopeless fools but also that Prospero, like all Renaissance princes, has a diligent spy network: the invisible Ariel overhears the conspirators and warns his master of the approaching danger. Prospero's sudden recollection of the warning leads him to break off the betrothal masque with one of the most famous speeches in all of Shakespeare, "Our revels now are ended" (4.1.148ff). This brooding meditation on the theatrical insubstantiality of the entire world and the dreamlike nature of human existence has seemed to many readers and audiences the pinnacle of the play's visionary wisdom. But it does not subsume in its rich cadences the other voices in *The Tempest;* specifically, it does not silence the surprising power of Caliban's voice.

That voice has been amplified in the centuries that followed the first performances of *The Tempest,* as European colonialism saw its grand political, moral, and economic claims disputed and, after violent struggles, dismantled. During these struggles, many anticolonial writers and critics rewrote Shakespeare's play, casting Prospero as a smugly racist, sexist oppressor, Ariel as a native coopted and corrupted by his colonial master, and Caliban as a victimized hero. "Prospero invaded the islands," declared the Cuban writer Roberto Fernández Retamar, "killed our ancestors, enslaved Caliban, and taught him his language to make himself understood. What else can Caliban do but use that same language—today he has no other—to curse him, to wish that the 'red plague' would fall on him?"

Shakespeare, who wrote when the colonialist project was still in its early stages, could not have anticipated this afterlife, and some scholars have argued that the relevance to *The Tempest* of the New World voyages has been greatly exaggerated. But, as the Barbadian writer George Lamming puts it, "Caliban keeps answering back." Caliban enters the play cursing, grumbling, and, above all, disputing Prospero's authority: "This island's mine by Sycorax my mother, / Which thou tak'st from me" (1.2.331–32). By the close, his attempt to kill Prospero foiled and his body racked with cramps and bruises, Caliban declares that he will "be wise hereafter / And seek for grace" (5.1.296–97). Yet it is not his mumbled reformation but his vehement protests that leave an indelible mark on *The Tempest*. The play may depict Caliban, in Prospero's ugly term, as "filth," but it gives him a remarkable, unforgettable eloquence, the eloquence of bare life. To Miranda's taunting reminder that she taught him to speak, Caliban retorts, "You taught me language, and my profit on't / Is I know how to curse" (1.2.362–63). It is not only in cursing, however, that Caliban is gifted: in richly sensuous poetry, he speaks of the island's natural resources and of his dreams. Caliban can be beaten into submission, but the master cannot eradicate his slave's desires, his pleasures, and his inconsolable pain. And across the vast gulf that divides the triumphant prince and the defeated savage, there is a momentary, enigmatic glimpse of a hidden bond: "This thing of darkness," Prospero says of Caliban, "I / Acknowledge mine" (5.1.278–79). The words need only be a claim of ownership, but they seem to hint at a deeper, more disturbing link between father and monster, legitimate ruler and savage, judge and criminal. Perhaps the link is only an illusion, a trick of the imagination on a strange island, but as Prospero leaves the island, it is he who begs for pardon.

STEPHEN GREENBLATT

## SELECTED BIBLIOGRAPHY

Callaghan, Dympna. "Irish Memories in *The Tempest.*" *Shakespeare without Women: Representing Gender and Race on the Renaissance Stage.* London: Routledge, 2000. 97–138. Using the play's Irish echoes, considers how selective colonial recollection suppresses the cultural memory of the colonized.

Cartelli, Thomas. "Prospero in Africa: *The Tempest* as Colonialist Text and Pretext." *Repositioning Shakespeare: National Formations, Postcolonial Appropriations.* London: Routledge, 1999. 87–104. Argues that *The Tempest* can be made to operate both for and against the interests of modern Western ideology.

Greenblatt, Stephen. "Martial Law in the Land of Cockaigne." *Shakespearean Negotiations: The Circulation of Social Energy in Renaissance England.* Berkeley: U of California P, 1988. 129–63. Explores how the play apparently celebrates the restoration of patriarchal order yet also ironically scrutinizes the political manipulation of anxiety.

Hulme, Peter, and William H. Sherman, eds. *"The Tempest" and Its Travels.* Philadelphia: U of Pennsylvania P, 2000. Offers a range of critical and creative materials, situating the play amid the local and global contexts of its time and beyond.

Lupton, Julia. "Creature Caliban." *Shakespeare Quarterly* 51 (2000): 1–23. Asserts that at once Adamic and monstrous, Caliban is the embodiment of pure creaturely sentience.

Mowat, Barbara A. "Prospero's Book." *Shakespeare Quarterly* 52 (2001): 1–33. Posits that Prospero's particular magic book is likely to have been what Shakespeare's contemporaries called a "grimoire," a manual for the summoning of spirits.

Neill, Michael. "'Noises, / Sounds, and Sweet Airs': The Burden of Shakespeare's *Tempest.*" *Shakespeare Quarterly* 59.1 (Spring 2008): 36–59. Argues that, uniquely among the plays of its time, *The Tempest* is equipped with its own elaborate sound track, one in which violent, chaotic, and discordant noise is set against harmony.

Orgel, Stephen. *The Illusion of Power: Political Theater in the English Renaissance.* Berkeley: U of California P, 1975. Compares public and court theater practice, highlighting the masque's role in the allegorized expression of sovereign power.

Spiller, Elizabeth. "Shakespeare and the Making of Early Modern Science: Resituating Prospero's Art." *South Central Review* 26 (2009): 24–41. Discusses how *The Tempest* enables us to understand the role that art, poetry, and drama had on the early modern development of science.

Wilson, Richard. "Voyage to Tunis: New History and the Old World of *The Tempest.*" *Secret Shakespeare: Studies in Theatre, Religion, and Resistance.* Manchester: Manchester UP, 2004. 206–29. Asserts that Shakespeare's contemporaries would have understood *The Tempest* as a play about enslavement and redemption.

### Films

*Forbidden Planet.* 1956. Dir. Fred M. Wilcox. USA. 98 min. A science fiction cult classic in which Ariel is a robot and Caliban a monster of the id.

*The Tempest.* 1960. Dir. George Schaefer. USA. 76 min. A made-for-TV, one-camera film of a solid though short stage rendition, with Richard Burton standing out as Caliban.

*The Tempest.* 1979. Dir. Derek Jarman. UK. 95 min. Part Gothic, part punk; renders Juno's masque as a Broadway musical number.

*Tempest.* 1982. Dir. Paul Mazursky. USA. 140 min. A disenchanted New York architect escapes to a Greek island to reexamine his life.

*Prospero's Books.* 1991. Dir. Peter Greenaway. UK. 129 min. Surreal and baroque; focuses on the imagined contents of Prospero's library. John Gielgud stars.

# TEXTUAL INTRODUCTION

*The Tempest* was first printed in the First Folio of 1623 (F), where it appears as the opening play in the volume. This is the only surviving text with any claim to authority, and it seems to have been prepared with care: it is the basis of *The Norton Shakespeare* edition.

The text was evidently printed from copy supplied by Ralph Crane, the professional scribe who was responsible for the preparation of at least four other plays in the First Folio. We probably owe to Crane a number of the conspicuous features of the text, including the systematic divisions into acts and scenes, the detailed stage directions, and the list of characters at the end of the play. Crane may also have been responsible for the relatively heavy punctuation: surviving transcripts in his hand show a strong preference for colons, hyphens, and parentheses, and the frequency of each of these marks in *The Tempest* is roughly double that found in the Folio's non-Crane texts. Crane's habits may have been very different from those of Shakespeare, or indeed from the three or four printers who set the text and imposed their own conventions and quirks; but the 1623 printing is all we have to work with, and we have tried to make that text as accessible as possible to readers without sacrificing the Folio's stylistic cues and effects.

There are some confusions in the Folio's distinctions between verse and prose and, occasionally, in its line divisions: the layout of the songs is particularly muddled, and editors have tended to follow mid-seventeenth-century manuscripts for the structure of repeats and refrains. The modernization of spelling has, in places, forced us to choose between separate senses that Shakespeare might well have wanted to keep in play: for instance, when Ariel tells Prospero that his affections toward the courtiers would become tender "were I humàn" (5.1.20), the Folio spelling supports both "humane" and "human." And even though there are very few obvious errors in need of correction, there are some famous cruxes that require the intervention of editors: Does Ferdinand refer to "[s]o rare a wondered father and a wise" or ". . . a wife" (4.1.123)? Do his female acquaintances in 3.1.46 "put it to the foil" or the "soil"? When, where, and how does Juno descend at the beginning of the masque in 4.1? And what are the "scamels" that Caliban promises to fetch for Stefano and Trinculo (in 2.2.163, the only known use of this word in English)?

Full discussions of some of these problems can be found in the Textual Comments, and we also encourage readers to examine the original printings for themselves: comparing even a short passage in the Folio with the text in this or other modernized editions will immediately reveal how many choices editors make without their readers' knowledge. Modern eyes and ears will be especially struck by the different rhythms produced in the original syntax and may find that the play's many compound words convey a sense of compression or exoticism that is very much in keeping with the style and setting of the plot.

WILLIAM H. SHERMAN

## PERFORMANCE NOTE

*The Tempest* is conspicuously lacking in dramatic action. Very little happens in the play, and what does happen seems entirely at the discretion of Prospero, the agency of his counterparts effectively nullified by his magic. Directors therefore must engage audiences without legitimate conflict or dramatic uncertainty—a challenge amplified both by a protagonist who spends much of the play threatening his friends and by an adherence to the unity of time that blunts potential developmental arcs for the supporting cast. Directors typically respond to these challenges in two ways: by approaching the play as a kind of masque and appealing to audiences through a collection of striking visual and auditory effects; or, more commonly, by creating conflicts between characters based on subtextual cues and political topicality. Though Prospero can be portrayed as a benign scholar or disturbed magus, directors today frequently present him as a colonialist oppressor. Making Caliban a long-suffering hero, Ariel an unwilling captive, and Miranda the daughter to a domineering father, productions highlight Prospero's deficiencies and cloud the play's resolution.

Other productions locate the central conflict within Prospero, emphasizing his anxieties about authority, or his reluctance to forgive his enemies and relinquish power. Still others generate drama through contrasts between Prospero's love for Miranda and hate for Caliban; by suggesting that Ariel and Caliban represent contrasting aspects of Prospero's psyche; or by hinting that his affection for either, or even for Miranda, is attended by sexual frustration. Whatever the approach, directors and actors must determine whether Prospero will seem mild or severe; whether Caliban displays childlike innocence or mature hostility; whether Miranda is a pliable princess or a rebellious teen; and whether Ariel is male or female, ethereal or earthy, eager or reluctant to serve. Directors must also decide on the sources and manifestations of Prospero's Art, and on a degree of realism for spectacular effects (e.g., the shipwreck, the vanishing banquet, Juno's descent). Other considerations in performance include Caliban's deformity and costume; producing the near-constant soundscape called for in stage directions (e.g., thunder, solemn music and songs); managing the difficult drunken comedy of Stefano and Trinculo; and deciding on Sebastian and Antonio's ultimate state of reconciliation or estrangement.

Brett Gamboa

# The Tempest

## THE PERSONS OF THE PLAY

PROSPERO, the right Duke of Milan
MIRANDA, daughter to Prospero
ANTONIO, his brother, the usurping Duke of Milan

ALONSO, King of Naples
SEBASTIAN, his brother
FERDINAND, son to Alonso

GONZALO, an honest old councillor
ADRIAN and FRANCISCO, lords

ARIEL, an airy spirit
CALIBAN, a savage and deformed slave

TRINCULO, a jester
STEFANO, a drunken butler

MASTER of a ship
BOATSWAIN
MARINERS

SPIRITS *appearing as*
IRIS
CERES
JUNO
Nymphs
Reapers

*THE SCENE: An uninhabited island.*[1]

---

## 1.1

*A tempestuous noise of thunder and lightning heard. Enter a ship*[*'s*] MASTER *and a* BOATSWAIN.[2]

MASTER Boatswain!

BOATSWAIN Here, Master. What cheer?

MASTER Good,[3] speak to th' mariners. Fall to't yarely,° or we run ourselves aground. Bestir, bestir! *Exit.* — *promptly*

*Enter* MARINERS.

1. TEXTUAL COMMENT *The Tempest* is unusual among the plays gathered in the First Folio in having a specific setting. For more on the significance of the play's location, see Digital Edition TC 1.
1.1 Location: A ship at sea.

2. The Boatswain probably enters after the shipmaster calls him; the latter is perhaps on the upper stage.
3. Acknowledging the Boatswain's presence; or perhaps short for "good man."

**BOATSWAIN** Heigh, my hearts!° Cheerly, cheerly, my hearts! — *hearties*
Yare, yare! Take in the topsail.[4] Tend° to th' Master's whistle. — *Attend*
[*to the storm*] Blow till thou burst thy wind, if room enough![5]

*Enter* ALONSO, SEBASTIAN, ANTONIO, FERDINAND, GONZALO, *and others.*

**ALONSO** Good Boatswain, have care. Where's the Master? [*to the* MARINERS] Play the men!° — *Act like men*

**BOATSWAIN** I pray now, keep below.

**ANTONIO** Where is the Master, Boatswain?

**BOATSWAIN** Do you not hear him? You mar our labor. Keep your cabins: you do assist the storm!

**GONZALO** Nay, good,° be patient. — *good man*

**BOATSWAIN** When the sea is. Hence! What cares these roarers for the name of king?[6] To cabin! Silence! Trouble us not.

**GONZALO** Good, yet remember whom thou hast aboard.

**BOATSWAIN** None that I more love than myself. You are a councillor:[7] if you can command these elements to silence and
work the peace of the present,[8] we will not hand° a rope more. — *handle*
Use your authority! If you cannot, give thanks you have lived so long, and make yourself ready in your cabin for the mischance of the hour, if it so hap.° [*to the* MARINERS] Cheerly, — *happen*
good hearts! [*to* GONZALO] Out of our way, I say!

*Exit* [BOATSWAIN *with* MARINERS].

**GONZALO** I have great comfort from this fellow. Methinks he hath no drowning mark[9] upon him; his complexion is perfect gallows.[1] Stand fast, good Fate, to his hanging; make the rope of his destiny our cable,[2] for our own doth little advantage.° If he be not born to be hanged, our case is miserable. — *good*

*Exeunt* [GONZALO, ALONSO, SEBASTIAN, ANTONIO, *and* FERDINAND].

*Enter* BOATSWAIN.

**BOATSWAIN** Down with the topmast![3] Yare! Lower, lower! Bring her to try with main-course.[4] (*A cry within.*) A plague upon this howling! They are louder than the weather or our office.[5]

*Enter* SEBASTIAN, ANTONIO, *and* GONZALO.

Yet again? What do you here? Shall we give o'er° and drown? — *up*
Have you a mind to sink?

**SEBASTIAN** A pox o' your throat, you bawling, blasphemous, incharitable dog!

**BOATSWAIN** Work you, then.

**ANTONIO** Hang, cur! Hang, you whoreson insolent noise-maker! We are less afraid to be drowned than thou art.

**GONZALO** I'll warrant him from drowning,[6] though° the ship — *even if*
were no stronger than a nutshell and as leaky as an unstanched° — *a freely menstruating*
wench.

4. To reduce the surface area of the sail and thereby lessen the force of the wind pushing the ship toward the island.
5. Blow as hard as you like, as long as we have room between the ship and the rocks.
6. "Roarers," referring here to the waves, was also a term for riotous people.
7. Member of the King's council; also an adviser or persuader.
8. Of the present circumstances.
9. Birthmark whose position was held to portend death by drowning. "He that was born to be hanged will never be drowned" was proverbial.
1. His physiognomy, or appearance, shows that he will certainly be hanged.
2. Anchor cable (an anchor is actually useless in a storm).
3. To reduce the top weight of the ship and make it more stable.
4. Bring the ship close to the wind, sailing only with the mainsail.
5. Duties (in shouting orders).
6. I'll guarantee him against drowning.

BOATSWAIN Lay her a-hold, a-hold! Set her two courses![7] Off to sea again! Lay her off!

*Enter* MARINERS, *wet.*

MARINERS All lost! To prayers, to prayers! All lost!

[*Exeunt* MARINERS.]

BOATSWAIN What, must our mouths be cold?[8]

GONZALO The King and Prince at prayers! Let's assist them, for our case is as theirs.

SEBASTIAN I'm out of patience.

ANTONIO We are merely° cheated of our lives by drunkards. This wide-chopped° rascal—would thou mightst lie drowning the washing of ten tides![9]

*utterly* / *large-mouthed*

GONZALO He'll be hanged yet, though every drop of water swear against it and gape at widest to glut° him.

*its widest to swallow*

*A confused noise within.*[1]

MARINERS [*within*] Mercy on us! We split, we split! Farewell, my wife and children! Farewell, brother! We split, we split, we split!

[*Exit* BOATSWAIN.]

ANTONIO Let's all sink wi'th' King.

SEBASTIAN Let's take leave of him. *Exit* [*with* ANTONIO].

GONZALO Now would I give a thousand furlongs of sea for an acre of barren ground: long heath, brown furze,[2] anything. The wills above be done, but I would fain die a dry death.

*Exit.*

## 1.2

*Enter* PROSPERO *and* MIRANDA.

MIRANDA[1] If by your art,[2] my dearest father, you have
Put the wild waters in this roar, allay them.
The sky, it seems, would pour down stinking pitch
But that the sea, mounting to th' welkin's° cheek, — *sky's*
Dashes the fire out. Oh, I have suffered
With those that I saw suffer: a brave° vessel— — *splendid*
Who had, no doubt, some noble creature in her—
Dashed all to pieces! Oh, the cry did knock
Against my very heart! Poor souls, they perished.
Had I been any god of power, I would
Have sunk the sea within the earth or ere° — *before*
It should the good ship so have swallowed and
The fraughting souls[3] within her.

PROSPERO[4] Be collected.
No more amazement.° Tell your piteous° heart — *consternation / pitying*
There's no harm done.

MIRANDA Oh, woe the day!

7. Set the foresail in addition to the mainsail.
8. To be cold in the mouth—to be dead—was proverbial; may also suggest that the mariners warm their mouths with liquor (line 50).
9. Pirates were hanged on the shore at low-water mark and left there for the ebbing and flowing of three tides.
1. PERFORMANCE COMMENT How a production stages the capsizing of Alonso's vessel can powerfully affect the play's emotional undercurrents. A highly realistic storm might seem to confirm that the mariners have been lost at sea, heightening the sense of loss running through the play, while a more abstract or symbolic approach could emphasize Prospero's control. For more, see Digital Edition PC 1.
2. Heather and gorse—both shrubs that grow in poor soil.

1.2 Location: The rest of the play is set in various parts of Prospero's island.
1. "Miranda" in Latin means "admirable" or "wondering." Miranda uses the formal "you," contrasting with Prospero's more familiar "thou."
2. Skill; magic; learning; science. TEXTUAL COMMENT In the Folio, Miranda speaks of "Art" with a capital "A." For information on early modern practices of capitalization, and the special significance of "art" for *The Tempest*, see Digital Edition TC 2.
3. Souls constituting the freight; perhaps also suggesting "burdened."
4. "Prospero" in Italian and Spanish means "fortunate" or "prosperous."

PROSPERO No harm.
I have done nothing but in care of thee—
Of thee, my dear one, thee, my daughter—who
Art ignorant of what thou art, naught knowing
Of whence I am, nor that I am more better° *higher in rank*
Than Prospero, master of a full poor cell[5]
And thy no greater father.
MIRANDA More to know
Did never meddle with° my thoughts. *intrude upon*
PROSPERO 'Tis time
I should inform thee farther. Lend thy hand
And pluck my magic garment from me.—
[*She helps him remove the cloak, and he puts it aside.*]
—So,
Lie there, my art. —Wipe thou thine eyes; have comfort.
The direful spectacle of the wreck, which touched
The very virtue of compassion in thee,
I have with such provision° in mine art *foresight*
So safely ordered that there is no soul—
No, not so much perdition° as an hair *loss*
Betid° to any creature in the vessel *Happened*
Which° thou heard'st cry, which thou saw'st sink. Sit down, *Whom*
For thou must now know farther.
MIRANDA You have often
Begun to tell me what I am, but stopped
And left me to a bootless inquisition,° *profitless inquiry*
Concluding, "Stay: not yet."
PROSPERO The hour's now come;
The very minute bids thee ope° thine ear. *open*
Obey, and be attentive. Canst thou remember
A time before we came unto this cell?
I do not think thou canst, for then thou wast not
Out° three years old. *Fully*
MIRANDA Certainly, sir, I can.
PROSPERO By what? By any other house or person?
Of anything the image tell me that
Hath kept with thy remembrance.
MIRANDA 'Tis far off,
And rather like a dream than an assurance° *a certainty*
That my remembrance warrants.° Had I not *guarantees is true*
Four or five women once that tended me?
PROSPERO Thou hadst, and more, Miranda. But how is it
That this lives in thy mind? What seest thou else
In the dark backward° and abysm of time? *past*
If thou rememb'rest aught° ere thou cam'st here, *anything*
How thou cam'st here thou mayst.
MIRANDA But that I do not.
PROSPERO Twelve year since, Miranda, twelve year since,
Thy father was the Duke of Milan[6] and
A prince of power.
MIRANDA Sir, are not you my father?
PROSPERO Thy mother was a piece° of virtue,° and *perfect example / chastity*
She said thou wast my daughter, and thy father

5. Suggesting a hermit's or a poor man's dwelling. *full:* very.
6. Pronounced with stress on the first syllable.

Was Duke of Milan, and his only heir
And princess no worse issued.° — *no less nobly born*
MIRANDA O the heavens!
What foul play had we that we came from thence?
Or blessèd° was't we did? — *providential*
PROSPERO Both, both, my girl.
By foul play, as thou say'st, were we heaved thence,
But blessedly holp° hither. — *helped*
MIRANDA Oh, my heart bleeds
To think o'th' teen° that I have turned you to, — *sorrow; trouble*
Which is from° my remembrance! Please you, farther. — *out of*
PROSPERO My brother and thy uncle, called Antonio—
I pray thee mark me, that a brother should
Be so perfidious!—he whom next° thyself — *after*
Of all the world I loved, and to him put
The manage° of my state, as at that time — *control*
Through all the signories° it was the first — *lordships*
And Prospero the prime° duke, being so reputed — *foremost*
In dignity, and for the liberal arts[7]
Without a parallel. Those being all my study,
The government I cast upon my brother
And to my state grew stranger, being transported[8]
And rapt in secret studies. Thy false uncle—
Dost thou attend me?
MIRANDA Sir, most heedfully.
PROSPERO Being once perfected how to grant suits,[9]
How to deny them, who t'advance, and who
To trash for overtopping,[1] new created
The creatures° that were mine, I say, or changed 'em, — *dependents*
Or else new formed 'em;[2] having both the key° — *control*
Of officer and office, set all hearts i'th' state
To what tune pleased his ear, that° now he was — *so that*
The ivy which had hid my princely trunk
And sucked my verdure° out on't. Thou attend'st not. — *vitality; power*
MIRANDA O good sir, I do.
PROSPERO I pray thee, mark me.
I, thus neglecting worldly ends, all dedicated
To closeness° and the bettering of my mind — *seclusion*
With that which, but° by being so retired, — *merely*
O'er-prized all popular rate,[3] in my false brother
Awaked an evil nature; and my trust,
Like a good parent,[4] did beget of him
A falsehood in its contrary° as great — *inverse qualities*
As my trust was, which had indeed no limit,
A confidence sans° bound. He being thus lorded — *without*
Not only with what my revenue yielded,
But what my power might else exact, like one
Who, having into truth by telling of it,

7. As opposed to the "mechanical arts," the "liberal arts" encompassed the trivium (grammar, logic, and rhetoric) and the quadrivium (arithmetic, geometry, music, and astronomy).
8. Enraptured, with suggestions of "conveyed to another place." *grew stranger:* grew alienated from; became a foreigner to.
9. Having mastered the handling of formal requests.
1. For rising too high. *trash:* restrain, hold back (as by a leash).
2. *changed . . . 'em:* changed the duties and allegiance of existing officials, or created new ones.
3. Became too precious for the people to value or understand.
4. From the colloquial "Good parents breed bad children."

Made such a sinner of his memory
To credit his own lie,[5] he did believe
He was indeed the duke, out o'th'° substitution *as a consequence of the*
And executing° th'outward face° of royalty *portraying / image*
With all prerogative. Hence his ambition growing—
Dost thou hear?

MIRANDA Your tale, sir, would cure deafness.

PROSPERO To have no screen between this part he played
And him he played it for, he needs will be
Absolute Milan.[6] Me,° poor man, my library *As for me*
Was dukedom large enough. Of temporal royalties° *rule*
He thinks me now incapable; confederates,° *(he) plots*
So dry° he was for sway,° wi'th' King of Naples *thirsty / power*
To give him annual tribute, do him homage,
Subject his coronet to his crown,[7] and bend
The dukedom yet unbowed—alas, poor Milan!—
To most ignoble stooping.[8]

MIRANDA O the heavens!

PROSPERO Mark his condition° and th'event;° then tell me *treaty / outcome*
If this might be a brother.

MIRANDA I should sin
To think but° nobly of my grandmother. *anything but*
Good wombs have borne bad sons.[9]

PROSPERO Now the condition.
This King of Naples, being an enemy
To me inveterate, hearkens my brother's suit;
Which was that he, in lieu o'th' premises[1]
Of homage and I know not how much tribute,
Should presently extirpate me and mine
Out of the dukedom and confer fair Milan,
With all the honors, on my brother. Whereon,
A treacherous army levied, one midnight
Fated to th' purpose did Antonio open
The gates of Milan, and i'th' dead of darkness,
The ministers° for th' purpose hurried thence *agents*
Me and thy crying self.

MIRANDA Alack, for pity!
I, not remembering how I cried out then,
Will cry it o'er again; it is a hint° *an occasion*
That wrings mine eyes to't.

PROSPERO Hear a little further,
And then I'll bring thee to the present business
Which now's upon's, without the which this story
Were most impertinent.° *irrelevant*

MIRANDA Wherefore did they not
That hour destroy us?

PROSPERO Well demanded, wench:[2]
My tale provokes that question. Dear, they durst not,
So dear the love my people bore me, nor set

5. *like one . . . lie:* like someone who comes to believe his own repeatedly stated lie. *To:* So as to.
6. *To have . . . Milan:* He wanted to be the Duke of Milan in actual fact, rather than merely exercising power as the Duke's proxy. *screen:* partition, barrier.
7. Subject Antonio's coronet to Alonso's crown. *coronet:* a lesser crown indicating the wearer's inferiority to the sovereign.
8. *and bend . . . stooping:* by making Milan, previously free, a tributary subject of Naples.
9. Antonio's character need not imply that his mother was a bad parent (see line 94).
1. In return for the conditions agreed upon.
2. A young woman; also, term of endearment to wife, daughter, or sweetheart.

A mark so bloody on the business, but
With colors fairer painted their foul ends.
In few,° they hurried us aboard a bark,° *short / ship*
Bore us some leagues to sea, where they prepared
A rotten carcass of a butt,[3] not rigged,
Nor tackle, sail, nor mast—the very rats
Instinctively have quit it. There they hoist us
To cry to th' sea that roared to us; to sigh
To th' winds, whose pity, sighing back again,
Did us but loving wrong.[4]

MIRANDA Alack, what trouble
Was I then to you!

PROSPERO Oh, a cherubin
Thou wast that did preserve me. Thou didst smile,
Infusèd with a fortitude from heaven,
When I have decked° the sea with drops° full salt, *covered; adorned / tears*
Under my burden groaned,[5] which° raised in me *(Miranda's smile)*
An undergoing stomach° to bear up *A courage*
Against what should ensue.

MIRANDA How came we ashore?

PROSPERO By Providence divine.
Some food we had and some fresh water that
A noble Neapolitan, Gonzalo,
Out of his charity—who being then appointed
Master of this design—did give us, with
Rich garments, linens, stuffs, and necessaries,
Which since have steaded° much. So, of his gentleness,[6] *been useful*
Knowing I loved my books, he furnished me
From mine own library with volumes that
I prize above my dukedom.

MIRANDA Would I might
But ever see that man.

PROSPERO Now I arise.[7]
Sit still,° and hear the last of our sea-sorrow. *Continue to sit*
Here in this island we arrived, and here
Have I, thy schoolmaster, made thee more profit° *profit more*
Than other princes[8] can, that have more time
For vainer hours, and tutors not so careful.° *caring*

MIRANDA Heavens thank you for't. And now I pray you, sir,
For still 'tis beating in my mind, your reason
For raising this sea-storm?

PROSPERO Know thus far forth:
By accident most strange, bountiful Fortune,
Now my dear lady,[9] hath mine enemies
Brought to this shore; and by my prescience
I find my zenith[1] doth depend upon
A most auspicious star,[2] whose influence

3. Cask or tub: here, deprecatory for "boat."
4. The winds, responding sympathetically to our sighs, only blew us farther out to sea.
5. The secondary sense provides an image of giving birth.
6. Nobility; kindness.
7. Referring to the action of standing; or to Prospero's rising fortunes (as in lines 179–84). The former might visually reinforce the latter, especially if Prospero also resumes his magical powers by putting on his cloak.
8. *princes:* a generic plural for "princes and princesses."
9. Traditional characterization of Fortune as a woman changeable in her affections.
1. Highest point, as of a star in the sky.
2. Referring to the belief that celestial bodies had astrological influence on people and events.

If now I court not but omit,° my fortunes *disregard*
Will ever after droop. Here cease more questions.
Thou art inclined to sleep. 'Tis a good dullness,° *drowsiness*
And give it way. I know thou canst not choose.
[MIRANDA *sleeps*.]
[*to* ARIEL] Come away,° servant, come! I am ready now. *Come here*
Approach, my Ariel.[3] Come!
*Enter* ARIEL.
ARIEL All hail, great master; grave sir, hail! I come
To answer thy best pleasure, be't to fly,
To swim, to dive into the fire, to ride
On the curled clouds. To thy strong bidding task
Ariel and all his quality.° *cohorts; faculties*
PROSPERO Hast thou, spirit,
Performed to point° the tempest that I bade thee? *in detail*
ARIEL To every article.
I boarded the King's ship. Now on the beak,° *prow*
Now in the waist,° the deck,° in every cabin, *midship / poop*
I flamed amazement.[4] Sometimes I'd divide
And burn in many places;[5] on the topmast,
The yards, and bowsprit would I flame distinctly,
Then meet and join. Jove's lightning, the precursors
O'th' dreadful thunderclaps, more momentary
And sight-outrunning° were not. The fire and cracks *quicker than the eye*
Of sulfurous[6] roaring the most mighty Neptune
Seem to besiege and make his bold waves tremble,
Yea, his dread trident shake.
PROSPERO My brave spirit!
Who was so firm, so constant, that this coil° *turmoil*
Would not infect his reason?
ARIEL Not a soul
But felt a fever of the mad° and played *such as madmen feel*
Some tricks of desperation. All but mariners
Plunged in the foaming brine and quit the vessel,
Then all afire with me; the King's son Ferdinand,
With hair upstaring°—then like reeds, not hair— *standing on end*
Was the first man that leapt, cried, "Hell is empty,
And all the devils are here!"
PROSPERO Why, that's my spirit.
But was not this nigh shore?
ARIEL Close by, my master.
PROSPERO But are they, Ariel, safe?
ARIEL Not a hair perished.
On their sustaining[7] garments not a blemish,
But fresher than before; and, as thou bad'st° me, *commanded*
In troops° I have dispersed them 'bout the isle. *groups*
The King's son have I landed by himself,
Whom I left cooling of° the air with sighs *cooling*
In an odd angle° of the isle, and sitting, *corner*
His arms in this sad knot.[8]

3. Ariel's name, along with sounding like "airy," also means in Hebrew "lion of God." The name appears as that of a magical spirit in various occult texts.
4. I appeared as flames, causing terror.
5. The phosphorescent effect of St. Elmo's fire, caused in a thunderstorm by the charge of static electricity that builds up particularly around metal projections.
6. Sulfur was popularly associated with thunder and lightning.
7. Buoying up, and thus suggesting "life-giving."
8. Folded sadly, like this (folded arms implied sorrow).

PROSPERO Of the King's ship,
The mariners, say how thou hast disposed,
And all the rest o'th' fleet.

ARIEL Safely in harbor
Is the King's ship; in the deep nook where once
Thou called'st me up at midnight to fetch dew
From the still-vexed° Bermudas, there she's hid; *ever-stormy*
The mariners all under hatches stowed,
Who, with° a charm joined to° their suffered labor, *by virtue of / with*
I have left asleep; and for the rest o'th' fleet,
Which I dispersed, they all have met again
And are upon the Mediterranean float,° *billow; sea*
Bound sadly home for Naples,
Supposing that they saw the King's ship wrecked
And his great person perish.

PROSPERO Ariel, thy charge
Exactly is performed; but there's more work.
What is the time o'th' day?

ARIEL Past the mid-season.° *noon*

PROSPERO At least two glasses.° The time twixt six and now *hourglasses*
Must by us both be spent most preciously.

ARIEL Is there more toil? Since thou dost give me pains,° *tasks*
Let me remember° thee what thou hast promised, *remind*
Which is not yet performed me.

PROSPERO How now? Moody?
What is't thou canst demand?

ARIEL My liberty.

PROSPERO Before the time be out? No more.

ARIEL I prithee,
Remember I have done thee worthy service,
Told thee no lies, made no mistakings, served
Without or° grudge or grumblings. Thou did promise *either*
To bate° me a full year. *remit; excuse*

PROSPERO Dost thou forget
From what a torment I did free thee?

ARIEL No.

PROSPERO Thou dost, and think'st it much to tread the ooze
Of the salt deep,
To run upon the sharp wind of the north,
To do me business in the veins[9] o'th' earth
When it is baked° with frost. *dried and hardened*

ARIEL I do not, sir.

PROSPERO Thou liest, malignant thing![1] Hast thou forgot
The foul witch Sycorax, who with age and envy
Was grown into a hoop?° Hast thou forgot her? *bent over with age*

ARIEL No, sir.

PROSPERO Thou hast. Where was she born? Speak. Tell me.

ARIEL Sir, in Algiers.

PROSPERO Oh, was she so? I must
Once in a month recount what thou hast been,

9. Mineral veins or subterranean rivers.

1. PERFORMANCE COMMENT Prospero's threats to Ariel can disturb audiences by making the play's protagonist seem bullying and tyrannical. Some performances intensify the outbursts to affirm a despotic conception of the magician, while others moderate his anger, explaining his threats as needful attempts to maintain order. For more on how casting choices and other decisions affect the power dynamics between Prospero and Ariel, see Digital Edition PC 2.

Which thou forgett'st. This damned witch Sycorax,
For mischiefs manifold and sorceries terrible
To enter human hearing, from Algiers,
Thou know'st, was banished. For one thing she did
They would not take her life.[2] Is not this true?

ARIEL Ay, sir.

PROSPERO This blue-eyed[3] hag was hither brought with child
And here was left by th' sailors. Thou, my slave,
As thou report'st thyself, was then her servant;
And for° thou wast a spirit too delicate *because*
To act her earthy[4] and abhorred commands,
Refusing her grand hests,° she did confine thee, *commands*
By help of her more potent ministers,° *agents; slaves*
And in her most unmitigable rage,
Into a cloven pine; within which rift
Imprisoned thou didst painfully remain
A dozen years, within which space she died
And left thee there, where thou didst vent thy groans
As fast as millwheels strike.° Then was this island— *hit the water*
Save for the son that she did litter° here, *give birth to*
A freckled whelp, hag-born—not honored with
A human shape.

ARIEL Yes, Caliban her son.

PROSPERO Dull thing, I say so:[5] he, that Caliban
Whom now I keep in service. Thou best know'st
What torment I did find thee in: thy groans
Did make wolves howl, and penetrate° the breasts *arouse sympathy in*
Of ever-angry bears. It was a torment
To lay upon the damned, which Sycorax
Could not again undo. It was mine art,
When I arrived and heard thee, that made gape
The pine and let thee out.

ARIEL I thank thee, master.

PROSPERO If thou more murmur'st, I will rend an oak
And peg thee in his° knotty entrails till *its*
Thou hast howled away twelve winters.

ARIEL Pardon, master.
I will be correspondent° to command *compliant*
And do my spriting gently.° *graciously*

PROSPERO Do so, and after two days
I will discharge thee.[6]

ARIEL That's my noble master!
What shall I do? Say what, what shall I do?

PROSPERO Go make thyself like a nymph o'th' sea. Be subject
To no sight but thine and mine, invisible
To every eyeball else.[7] Go, take this shape° *appearance; disguise*
And hither come in't. Go! Hence with diligence.

*Exit* [ARIEL].

2. *For . . . life:* Only because she got pregnant. Capital sentences were commuted for pregnant women; ordinarily, condemned witches were either hanged or burned at the stake.
3. Textual Comment The description of Sycorax as "blew ey'd" has puzzled many readers, and editors have proposed a variety of emendations and interpretations. For more on this issue, see Digital Edition TC 3.
4. Difficult for Ariel, whose element is air; also, grossly material, coarse.
5. You dullard, that's just what I said.
6. Prospero reduces this to within two days at lines 419–20 and actually releases Ariel in about four hours' time.
7. *Be . . . else:* Ariel may wear a conventional costume, indicating his invisibility to other characters onstage.

[*to* MIRANDA] Awake, dear heart, awake! Thou hast slept well.
Awake.

MIRANDA The strangeness of your story put
Heaviness° in me. — *Sleepiness*

PROSPERO Shake it off. Come on;
We'll visit Caliban, my slave, who never
Yields us kind answer.

MIRANDA 'Tis a villain, sir,
I do not love to look on.

PROSPERO But, as 'tis,
We cannot miss° him. He does make our fire, — *avoid; do without*
Fetch in our wood, and serves in offices° — *capacities; duties*
That profit us. What ho! Slave! Caliban!
Thou earth, thou: speak!

CALIBAN (*within*) There's wood enough within.

PROSPERO Come forth, I say! There's other business for thee.
Come, thou tortoise! When?

*Enter* ARIEL *like a water nymph.*

—Fine apparition! My quaint[8] Ariel,
Hark in thine ear.

[*He whispers.*]

ARIEL My lord, it shall be done. *Exit.*

PROSPERO Thou poisonous slave, got° by the devil[9] himself — *begot*
Upon thy wicked dam,° come forth! — *harmful, foul mother*

*Enter* CALIBAN.[1]

CALIBAN As wicked dew as e'er my mother brushed[2]
With raven's feather from unwholesome fen° — *bog*
Drop on you both! A southwest[3] blow on ye
And blister you all o'er!

PROSPERO For this, be sure, tonight thou shalt have cramps,
Side-stitches that shall pen thy breath up; urchins[4]
Shall forth at vast of° night that they may work — *during the boundless*
All exercise on thee;[5] thou shalt be pinched
As thick as honeycomb,[6] each pinch more stinging
Than bees that made 'em.° — *(honeycomb cells)*

CALIBAN I must eat my dinner.
This island's mine by Sycorax my mother,
Which thou tak'st from me. When thou cam'st first
Thou strok'st me and made much of me; wouldst give me
Water with berries in't, and teach me how
To name the bigger light and how the less[7]
That burn by day and night. And then I loved thee
And showed thee all the qualities o'th' isle:
The fresh springs, brine-pits, barren place and fertile.
Cursèd be I that did so! All the charms° — *spells*

8. The term could simultaneously mean "ingenious," "curious in appearance," and "elegant."

9. Not merely an insult, but also an allusion to Caliban's birth from the devil (incubus) and witch.

1. PERFORMANCE COMMENT Caliban's costume and conduct in this first entrance often reveal whether a production has chosen to portray him as monstrous, or human, or both. Such choices help to determine whether the audience is moved more by Prospero's suffering or by Caliban's. For more on the complexities of the role, see Digital Edition PC 3.

2. Brushed up, collected. Dew was a common ingredient of magical potions.

3. A southerly wind was considered plague-bearing.

4. Hedgehogs; but here indicates spirits disguised as hedgehogs.

5. *that . . . thee:* in order that they may perform their habitual activity.

6. *thou . . . honeycomb:* The pinch marks will be as closely packed as, and of similar texture to, the cells of a honeycomb.

7. Recalls Genesis 1:16: "God then made two great lights: the greater light to rule the day, and the less light to rule the night."

Of Sycorax—toads, beetles, bats—light on you!
For I am all the subjects that you have,
Which first was mine own king; and here you sty me° *pen me up*
In this hard rock whiles you do keep from me
The rest o'th' island.

PROSPERO Thou most lying slave,
Whom stripes° may move, not kindness. I have used° thee, *lashes / treated*
Filth as thou art, with humane care, and lodged thee
In mine own cell till thou didst seek to violate
The honor of my child.

CALIBAN Oh ho, oh ho! Would't had been done!
Thou didst prevent me; I had peopled else
This isle with Calibans.

MIRANDA[8] Abhorrèd slave,
Which any print° of goodness wilt not take, *impression*
Being capable of° all ill. I pitied thee, *susceptible to*
Took pains to make thee speak, taught thee each hour
One thing or other. When thou didst not, savage,
Know thine own meaning but wouldst gabble like
A thing most brutish, I endowed thy purposes
With words that made them known. But thy vile race,° *hereditary nature*
Though thou didst learn, had that in't which good natures
Could not abide to be with; therefore wast thou
Deservedly confined into this rock,
Who hadst deserved more than a prison.

CALIBAN You taught me language, and my profit on't
Is I know how to curse. The red plague rid you[9]
For learning me your language!

PROSPERO Hag-seed,° hence! *Offspring of a hag*
Fetch us in fuel; and be quick, thou'rt best,
To answer other business.° Shrugg'st thou, malice? *perform other tasks*
If thou neglect'st or dost unwillingly
What I command, I'll rack thee with old[1] cramps,
Fill all thy bones with aches,[2] make thee roar,
That beasts shall tremble at thy din.

CALIBAN No, pray thee.
[*aside*] I must obey. His art is of such power
It would control my dam's god Setebos[3]
And make a vassal of him.

PROSPERO So, slave, hence. *Exit* CALIBAN.

*Enter* FERDINAND, *and* ARIEL, *invisible, playing and singing.*[4]

ARIEL [*sings*] Come unto these yellow sands,
And then take hands.
Curtsied when you have, and kissed,
The wild waves whist.[5]
Foot it featly° here and there, *Dance nimbly*

8. Textual Comment For roughly two and a half centuries, editors reassigned this speech to Prospero, finding it inappropriate for Miranda. For more, see Digital Edition TC 4.
9. The plague that gives red sores destroy, kill you.
1. As of aged people; long-accustomed.
2. As a noun, this was probably pronounced "aitches."
3. A name found in travel narratives as a god of the Patagonians.
4. This probably does not imply that Ferdinand enters first, even though such a staging is possible if Ferdinand is bewildered as to where this music is coming from. Ariel is invisible to all but Prospero and the audience. He is probably still dressed as a water nymph.
5. Become hushed and attentive.

And sweet sprites bear° — *spirits sing*
The burden.[6]

SPIRITS [*within, sing the*] (*burden dispersedly*) Hark, hark! Bow-wow!
The watch-dogs bark: bow-wow!

ARIEL Hark, hark. I hear
The strain of strutting Chanticleer
Cry cock-a-diddle-dow.

FERDINAND Where should this music be? I'th' air or th'earth?
It sounds no more; and sure it waits° upon — *attends*
Some god o'th' island. Sitting on a bank,
Weeping again the King my father's wreck,
This music crept by me upon the waters,
Allaying both their fury and my passion° — *grief*
With its sweet air.° Thence I have followed it, — *melody*
Or it hath drawn me rather; but 'tis gone.
No, it begins again.

ARIEL [*sings*] Full fathom five thy father lies;
Of his bones are coral made;
Those are pearls that were his eyes;
Nothing of him that doth fade,
But doth suffer a sea-change
Into something rich and strange.
Sea-nymphs hourly ring his knell.

SPIRITS [*within, sing the*] (*burden*) Ding dong.

ARIEL Hark, now I hear them.

SPIRITS [*within*] Ding dong, bell.

FERDINAND The ditty does remember[7] my drowned father.
This is no mortal° business, nor no sound — *human*
That the earth owes.° I hear it now above me. — *owns*

PROSPERO [*to* MIRANDA] The fringèd curtains of thine eye
advance° — *raise*
And say what thou seest yond.

MIRANDA What is't? A spirit?
Lord, how it looks about. Believe me, sir,
It carries a brave° form. But 'tis a spirit. — *splendid; gallant*

PROSPERO No, wench, it eats and sleeps and hath such senses
As we have—such. This gallant° which thou seest — *fine gentleman*
Was in the wreck; and but° he's something° stained — *except that / somewhat*
With grief—that's beauty's canker[8]—thou mightst call him
A goodly person. He hath lost his fellows
And strays about to find 'em.

MIRANDA I might call him
A thing divine, for nothing natural
I ever saw so noble.

PROSPERO [*aside*][9] It° goes on, I see, — *(My plan)*
As my soul prompts it. [*to* ARIEL] Spirit, fine spirit, I'll free thee
Within two days for this.

6. TEXTUAL COMMENT "Burden" is a technical term from Renaissance music meaning "refrain" or "undersong," but its other associations may lend extra significance to Ariel's use of the word in this song. For more, see Digital Edition TC 5.
7. Commemorate. *ditty*: the words of the song.
8. Cankerworm; caterpillar ("beauty" being seen as a flower); spreading sore.
9. Prospero's asides here and at lines 437, 449, and 492 may be either private utterances or addressed to Ariel. If the former, Ariel may nevertheless hear them; Prospero speaks to Ariel after all these instances. Their import may well be purposefully enigmatic.

FERDINAND Most sure, the goddess
On whom these airs attend![1] Vouchsafe° my prayer — *Grant*
May know if you remain° upon this island, — *dwell*
And that you will some good instruction give
How I may bear me° here. My prime request, — *conduct myself*
Which I do last pronounce, is—O you wonder![2]—
If you be maid[3] or no?

MIRANDA No wonder, sir,
But certainly a maid.

FERDINAND My language? Heavens!
I am the best[4] of them that speak this speech,
Were I but where 'tis spoken.

PROSPERO How? The best?
What wert thou if the King of Naples heard thee?

FERDINAND A single[5] thing, as I am now, that wonders
To hear thee speak of Naples. He does hear me,[6]
And that he does I weep. Myself am Naples,° — *King of Naples*
Who with mine eyes, never since at ebb,° beheld — *ceasing to flow*
The King my father wrecked.

MIRANDA Alack, for mercy!

FERDINAND Yes, faith, and all his lords, the Duke of Milan
And his brave son[7] being twain.

PROSPERO [*aside*] The Duke of Milan
And his more braver daughter could control[8] thee
If now 'twere fit to do't. At the first sight
They have changed eyes.[9] [*to* ARIEL] Delicate° Ariel, — *Graceful; artful*
I'll set thee free for this! [*to* FERDINAND] A word, good sir.
I fear you have done yourself some wrong.[1] A word.

MIRANDA Why speaks my father so ungently?° This — *discourteously*
Is the third man that e'er I saw, the first
That e'er I sighed for. Pity move my father
To be inclined my way.

FERDINAND Oh, if a virgin,
And your affection not gone forth,[2] I'll make you
The Queen of Naples.

PROSPERO Soft, sir! One word more.
[*aside*] They are both in either's powers. But this swift business
I must uneasy° make, lest too light[3] winning — *difficult*
Make the prize light. [*to* FERDINAND] One word more! I charge
thee
That thou attend me. Thou dost here usurp
The name thou ow'st° not, and hast put thyself — *own*
Upon this island as a spy to win it
From me, the lord on't.° — *of it*

1. *Most . . . attend:* Probably spoken aside, but possibly an invocation. *Most sure the goddess:* Echoes Aeneas's reaction to seeing Venus after his shipwreck, "o dea certe" (*Aeneid* I.328). *airs:* Ariel's melodies.
2. Miracle, punning on the meaning of Miranda's name.
3. Unmarried virgin; made (human).
4. Highest in rank, assuming he has succeeded his father.
5. Weak and helpless; solitary; one and the same.
6. "He" and "me" both refer to Ferdinand. Presuming his father to be dead, Ferdinand takes himself to be the new King of Naples (and as such, he hears himself speaking). Alternatively, Ferdinand thinks his father's spirit hears him.
7. The only instance in which Antonio is mentioned as having a son.
8. Challenge; take to task; exercise power over.
9. Exchanged loving glances; fallen in love at first sight.
1. Euphemistic for "told a lie about yourself."
2. Given over to someone else.
3. Easy; playing on the meanings of "little valued" and also "promiscuous" in line 451.

FERDINAND No, as I am a man.
MIRANDA There's nothing ill can dwell in such a temple.[4]
If the ill spirit have so fair a house,
Good things will strive to dwell with't.
PROSPERO [*to* FERDINAND] Follow me.
[*to* MIRANDA] Speak not you for him: he's a traitor. [*to* FERDINAND] Come!
I'll manacle thy neck and feet together.
Sea-water shalt thou drink; thy food shall be
The fresh-brook mussels,[5] withered roots, and husks
Wherein the acorn cradled. Follow!
FERDINAND No.
I will resist such entertainment° till *treatment*
Mine enemy has more power.

*He draws [his sword], and is charmed from moving.*

MIRANDA O dear father,
Make not too rash a trial of him, for
He's gentle and not fearful.[6]
PROSPERO What, I say,
My foot° my tutor? [*to* FERDINAND] Put thy sword up, traitor, *inferior*
Who mak'st a show but dar'st not strike, thy conscience
Is so possessed with guilt. Come from thy ward,° *defensive stance*
For I can here disarm thee with this stick° *magician's wand*
And make thy weapon drop.
MIRANDA Beseech you, father—
PROSPERO Hence! Hang not on my garments.
MIRANDA Sir, have pity.
I'll be his surety.
PROSPERO Silence! One word more
Shall make me chide thee, if not hate thee. What,
An advocate for an imposter? Hush!
Thou think'st there is no more such shapes° as he, *forms; men*
Having seen but him and Caliban. Foolish wench,
To° th' most of men this is a Caliban, *Compared to*
And they to him are angels.
MIRANDA My affections
Are then most humble. I have no ambition
To see a goodlier man.
PROSPERO [*to* FERDINAND] Come on, obey.
Thy nerves° are in their infancy again, *sinews*
And have no vigor in them.
FERDINAND So they are.
My spirits,° as in a dream, are all bound up. *mental powers*
My father's loss, the weakness which I feel,
The wreck of all my friends, nor this man's threats
To whom I am subdued, are but light to me,
Might I but through my prison once a day
Behold this maid. All corners else o'th' earth
Let liberty make use of; space enough
Have I in such a prison.

4. A common metaphor for the body; also, a conventional Renaissance notion that moral qualities were physically manifest.
5. Freshwater mussels are inedible.
6. He's noble and, therefore, not cowardly. Alternatively, not fearsome.

PROSPERO [*aside*] It works. [*to* FERDINAND] Come on!
[*to* ARIEL] Thou hast done well, fine Ariel. [*to* FERDINAND]
Follow me.
[*to* ARIEL] Hark what thou else shalt do me.
MIRANDA [*to* FERDINAND] Be of comfort;
My father's of a better nature, sir,
Than he appears by speech. This is unwonted° *unusual*
Which now came from him.
PROSPERO [*to* ARIEL] Thou shalt be as free
As mountain winds; but then° exactly do *until then*
All points of my command.
ARIEL To th' syllable.
PROSPERO [*to* FERDINAND] Come, follow. [*to* MIRANDA] Speak not
for him. *Exeunt.*

## 2.1

*Enter* ALONSO, SEBASTIAN, ANTONIO, GONZALO, ADRIAN, *and* FRANCISCO.

GONZALO Beseech you, sir, be merry. You have cause—
So have we all—of joy; for our escape
Is much beyond our loss. Our hint° of woe *occasion*
Is common: every day some sailor's wife,
The masters of some merchant, and the merchant[1]
Have just° our theme of woe. But for the miracle— *exactly*
I mean our preservation—few in millions
Can speak like us. Then wisely, good sir, weigh
Our sorrow with° our comfort. *against*
ALONSO Prithee, peace.[2]
SEBASTIAN [*to* ANTONIO] He receives comfort like cold porridge.° *broth*
ANTONIO [*to* SEBASTIAN] The visitor[3] will not give him o'er so.° *leave him alone*
SEBASTIAN Look, he's winding up the watch of his wit; by and by it will strike.
GONZALO [*to* ALONSO] Sir—
SEBASTIAN One. Tell.° *Keep count*
GONZALO When every grief is entertained° that's offered, comes to th'entertainer[4]— *harbored*
SEBASTIAN A dollar.[5]
GONZALO Dolor° comes to him, indeed. You have spoken truer than you purposed. *Sorrow*
SEBASTIAN You have taken it wiselier than I meant you should.
GONZALO [*to* ALONSO] Therefore, my lord—
ANTONIO Fie, what a spendthrift is he of his tongue!
ALONSO I prithee, spare.° *spare your words*
GONZALO Well, I have done. But yet—
SEBASTIAN He will be talking.
ANTONIO Which of he or Adrian, for a good wager, first begins to crow?[6]
SEBASTIAN The old cock.

2.1
1. The chief officers of some merchant ship and its owner.
2. Sebastian takes this as "pease," as in "pease porridge."
3. Antonio compares Gonzalo with one who visits and comforts the sick and distressed.
4. There comes to the person who accepts that grief.
5. *dollar:* English name for the German thaler.
6. Which of the two will first begin to speak ("crow")?

ANTONIO The cockerel.[7]
SEBASTIAN Done. The wager?
ANTONIO A laughter.[8]
SEBASTIAN A match.
ADRIAN Though this island seem to be desert°— *uninhabited*
ANTONIO Ha, ha, ha!
SEBASTIAN So, you're paid.[9]
ADRIAN Uninhabitable and almost inaccessible—
SEBASTIAN Yet—
ADRIAN Yet—
ANTONIO He could not miss't.
ADRIAN It must needs be of subtle, tender, and delicate[1] temperance.° *climate*
ANTONIO Temperance was a delicate wench.[2]
SEBASTIAN Ay, and a subtle, as he most learnedly delivered.[3]
ADRIAN The air breathes upon us here most sweetly.
SEBASTIAN As if it had lungs, and rotten ones.
ANTONIO Or as 'twere perfumed by a fen.° *bog*
GONZALO Here is everything advantageous to life.
ANTONIO True, save° means to live. *except*
SEBASTIAN Of that there's none, or little.
GONZALO How lush and lusty° the grass looks! How green! *tender and luxuriant*
ANTONIO The ground indeed is tawny.
SEBASTIAN With an eye[4] of green in't.
ANTONIO He misses not much.
SEBASTIAN No, he doth but mistake the truth totally.
GONZALO But the rarity[5] of it is, which is indeed almost beyond credit—
SEBASTIAN As many vouched° rarities are. *alleged; accepted*
GONZALO That our garments being, as they were, drenched in the sea, hold notwithstanding their freshness and gloss, being rather new-dyed than stained with salt water.
ANTONIO If but one of his pockets[6] could speak, would it not say he lies?
SEBASTIAN Ay, or very falsely pocket up his report.[7]
GONZALO Methinks our garments are now as fresh as when we put them on first in Africa, at the marriage of the King's fair daughter Claribel to the King of Tunis.
SEBASTIAN 'Twas a sweet marriage, and we prosper well in our return.
ADRIAN Tunis was never graced before with such a paragon to° their queen. *for*
GONZALO Not since widow Dido's[8] time.
ANTONIO Widow?[9] A pox o' that! How came that "widow" in? Widow Dido!

7. "The young cock crows as the old hears" was proverbial. "Old cock" refers to Gonzalo and "cockerel" to Adrian.
8. From the proverb "He laughs that wins."
9. Antonio's laugh is his prize.
1. Exquisite, but in Antonio's usage (line 43), "given to pleasure." *subtle:* fine, but in Sebastian's usage (line 44), "sexually expert" or "crafty."
2. Antonio takes "Temperance" to be the name of a girl.
3. "Learnedly delivered" was a popular phrase among puritans who wanted to appear pious.
4. A tinge. In Antonio's reply, an "eye of green" refers to Gonzalo's optimistic capacity to see green.
5. Exceptional quality; but in Sebastian's usage (line 58), "uncommon thing."
6. Seen as the garments' "mouth"; also implying that Gonzalo's pockets are stained.
7. The evidence of stained pockets would confute Gonzalo's words and reputation for honesty. *pocket up:* suppress, or keep silent; also, receive unprotestingly.
8. Queen of ancient Carthage, whose tragic love affair with Aeneas is related in Virgil's *Aeneid*.
9. Antonio picks on this designation for a woman abandoned by her lover as being either irrelevant or conspicuously prudish. Dido, however, was in fact a widow when she met Aeneas.

SEBASTIAN What if he had said "widower Aeneas" too? Good Lord, how you take° it! *fuss about*

ADRIAN "Widow Dido," said you? You make me study of° that: she was of Carthage, not of Tunis. *examine*

GONZALO This Tunis, sir, was Carthage.[1]

ADRIAN Carthage?

GONZALO I assure you, Carthage.

ANTONIO His word is more than the miraculous harp.[2]

SEBASTIAN He hath raised the wall, and houses too.

ANTONIO What impossible matter will he make easy next?

SEBASTIAN I think he will carry this island home in his pocket and give it his son for an apple.

ANTONIO And sowing the kernels° of it in the sea, bring forth more islands. *seeds*

GONZALO Ay.[3]

ANTONIO Why, in good time.

GONZALO [*to* ALONSO] Sir, we were talking, that our garments seem now as fresh as when we were at Tunis at the marriage of your daughter, who is now queen.

ANTONIO And the rarest that e'er came there.

SEBASTIAN Bate,[4] I beseech you, widow Dido.

ANTONIO Oh, widow Dido? Ay, widow Dido.

GONZALO Is not, sir, my doublet as fresh as the first day I wore it? I mean, in a sort.[5]

ANTONIO That "sort" was well fished for.

GONZALO When I wore it at your daughter's marriage.

ALONSO You cram these words into mine ears against  
The stomach of my sense.[6] Would I had never  
Married my daughter there; for coming thence  
My son is lost, and, in my rate,° she too, *consideration*  
Who is so far from Italy removed  
I ne'er again shall see her. O thou mine heir  
Of Naples and of Milan, what strange fish  
Hath made his meal on thee?

FRANCISCO Sir, he may live.  
I saw him beat the surges under him  
And ride upon their backs. He trod the water  
Whose enmity he flung aside, and breasted  
The surge, most swol'n, that met him. His bold head  
'Bove the contentious waves he kept, and oared  
Himself with his good arms in lusty° stroke *vigorous*  
To th' shore, that o'er his wave-worn basis bowed,[7]  
As° stooping to relieve him. I not° doubt *As if / do not*  
He came alive to land.

ALONSO No, no, he's gone.

SEBASTIAN Sir, you may thank yourself for this great loss,  
That would not bless our Europe with your daughter,  
But rather loose° her to an African, *lose; release*

1. The city of Tunis was actually built ten miles from the site of Carthage.
2. Referring to Amphion's harp, to the music of which the walls (but not the houses) of Thebes arose.
3. Affirming his belief that Tunis was Carthage; Antonio mocks the length of time this took.
4. Except (as a verb); don't mention.
5. Comparatively speaking; Antonio plays on "drawing lots."
6. *You . . . sense:* The image is of one being force-fed words against the appetite ("stomach") for hearing them.
7. *that . . . bowed:* that extended out and drooped over the foot of the cliff, which had been eroded by waves.

Where she, at least, is banished from your eye,
Who° hath cause to set the grief on't. *(Claribel)*

ALONSO Prithee, peace.

SEBASTIAN You were kneeled to and importuned otherwise[8]
By all of us; and the fair soul herself
Weighed, between loathness and obedience, at
Which end o'th' beam should bow.[9] We have lost your son,
I fear, forever. Milan and Naples have
More widows in them of this business' making
Than we bring men to comfort them. The fault's
Your own.

ALONSO So is the dearest o'th' loss.[1]

GONZALO My lord Sebastian,
The truth you speak doth lack some gentleness,
And time° to speak it in. You rub the sore[2] *(appropriate time)*
When you should bring the plaster.

SEBASTIAN Very well.

ANTONIO And most chirurgeonly.° *surgeonlike*

GONZALO [*to* ALONSO] It is foul weather in us all, good sir,
When you are cloudy.

SEBASTIAN Foul weather?

ANTONIO Very foul.

GONZALO Had I plantation[3] of this isle, my lord—

ANTONIO He'd sow't with nettle-seed.

SEBASTIAN Or docks, or mallows.[4]

GONZALO And were the king on't, what would I do?

SEBASTIAN Scape being drunk for want of wine.

GONZALO I'th' commonwealth I would by contraries
Execute all things.[5] For no kind of traffic° *commerce*
Would I admit; no name of magistrate;
Letters° should not be known; riches, poverty, *Writing; erudition*
And use of service,° none; contract, succession,[6] *servants*
Bourn,° bound of land, tilth,° vineyard, none; *Boundary / tillage*
No use of metal, corn,° or wine, or oil; *grain*
No occupation, all men idle, all;
And women too, but innocent and pure;[7]
No sovereignty—

SEBASTIAN Yet he would be king on't.

ANTONIO The latter end of his commonwealth forgets the beginning.

GONZALO —All things in common° nature should produce *for communal use*
Without sweat or endeavor. Treason, felony,
Sword, pike, knife, gun, or need of any engine° *weapon*
Would I not have; but nature should bring forth
Of it own kind, all foison,° all abundance, *plenty*
To feed my innocent people.

8. *otherwise:* to act differently.
9. *Weighed . . . bow:* Weighed loathness to marry against obedience to her father to find out which end of the scales' beam would sink.
1. That is, the most grievous, or costliest, part of the loss is also my own.
2. "To rub the sore" was proverbial. *plaster* (line 134): a soothing remedy.
3. Had I responsibility for colonization of the island; but also interpreted as "planting" by Antonio and Sebastian.
4. Cited as wild plants prone to grow on uncultivated land; but dock is a traditional soother of nettle stings, and mallow roots were used to make soothing ointment.
5. *I would . . . things:* I would advance the opposite to what would be usual. This speech is based on a passage in John Florio's translation of Montaigne's essay "Of Cannibals."
6. Inheritance of property.
7. Idleness proverbially begets lust.

SEBASTIAN No marrying[8] 'mong his subjects?
ANTONIO None, man, all idle: whores and knaves.
GONZALO I would with such perfection govern, sir,
T'excel the golden age.[9]
SEBASTIAN Save° his majesty! *God save*
ANTONIO Long live Gonzalo!
GONZALO And do you mark me, sir?
ALONSO Prithee, no more. Thou dost talk nothing to me.
GONZALO I do well believe your highness, and did it to minister occasion[1] to these gentlemen, who are of such sensible° *sensitive* and nimble lungs that they always use° *are accustomed* to laugh at nothing.
ANTONIO 'Twas you we laughed at.
GONZALO Who in this kind of merry fooling am nothing to you. So you may continue, and laugh at nothing still.
ANTONIO What a blow was there given!
SEBASTIAN An it had not fallen flatlong.[2]
GONZALO You are gentlemen of brave mettle;[3] you would lift the moon out of her sphere if she would continue in it five weeks without changing.[4]

*Enter* ARIEL [*invisible,*] *playing solemn music.*

SEBASTIAN We would so, and then go a-bat-fowling.[5]
ANTONIO Nay, good my lord, be not angry.
GONZALO No, I warrant you, I will not adventure my discretion so weakly.[6] Will you laugh me asleep, for I am very heavy?° *tired; serious*
ANTONIO Go sleep, and hear us.

[*All sleep, except* ALONSO, SEBASTIAN, *and* ANTONIO.]

ALONSO What, all so soon asleep? I wish mine eyes
Would, with themselves, shut up my thoughts. I find
They are inclined to do so.
SEBASTIAN Please you, sir,
Do not omit° the heavy offer° of it. *neglect / opportunity*
It seldom visits sorrow; when it doth,
It is a comforter.
ANTONIO We two, my lord,
Will guard your person while you take your rest,
And watch your safety.
ALONSO Thank you. Wondrous heavy.

[ALONSO *sleeps. Exit* ARIEL.]

SEBASTIAN What a strange drowsiness possesses them!
ANTONIO It is the quality o'th' climate.
SEBASTIAN Why
Doth it not then our eyelids sink? I find
Not myself disposed to sleep.
ANTONIO Nor I: my spirits are nimble.
They fell together all as by consent;° *consensus*
They dropped, as by a thunderstroke. What might,
Worthy Sebastian, oh, what might—? No more.

8. Seen as irrelevant to sexually innocent people; also a form of contract (line 146).
9. In classical mythology, the earliest of the ages—a time without strife, labor, or injustice, when abundant food grew without cultivation.
1. *minister occasion:* afford opportunity.
2. If it had not fallen on the flat, harmless side of the sword.
3. Courage; punning on "metal," as of a sword blade.
4. *you would . . . changing:* You would even steal the moon, if she were to stand still in her orbit ("sphere").
5. Trapping birds by using light to attract them and bats to strike them down; may also mean swindling and victimizing the simple.
6. I will not put my sound judgment at risk so foolishly.

And yet methinks I see it in thy face
What thou shouldst be. Th'occasion speaks° thee, and — *opportunity speaks to*
My strong imagination sees a crown
Dropping upon thy head.

SEBASTIAN What? Art thou waking?° — *awake*

ANTONIO Do you not hear me speak?

SEBASTIAN I do, and surely
It is a sleepy language, and thou speak'st
Out of thy sleep. What is it thou didst say?
This is a strange repose, to be asleep
With eyes wide open; standing, speaking, moving,
And yet so fast asleep.

ANTONIO Noble Sebastian,
Thou lett'st thy fortune sleep—die rather; wink'st° — *shut your eyes*
Whiles thou art waking.

SEBASTIAN Thou dost snore distinctly;° — *meaningfully*
There's meaning in thy snores.

ANTONIO I am more serious than my custom. You
Must be so too, if heed° me; which to do — *if you heed*
Trebles thee o'er.

SEBASTIAN Well, I am standing water.[7]

ANTONIO I'll teach you how to flow.

SEBASTIAN Do so. To ebb
Hereditary sloth[8] instructs me.

ANTONIO Oh!
If you but knew how you the purpose cherish
Whiles thus you mock it;[9] how in stripping it
You more invest° it. Ebbing° men, indeed, — *clothe / Declining*
Most often do so near the bottom run
By their own fear or sloth.

SEBASTIAN Prithee, say on.
The setting° of thine eye and cheek proclaim — *fixed look*
A matter° from thee; and a birth, indeed, — *Something important*
Which throes[1] thee much to yield.

ANTONIO Thus, sir:
[*indicating* GONZALO] Although this lord of weak
remembrance,° this, — *memory*
Who shall be of as little memory° — *as little remembered*
When he is earthed,° hath here almost persuaded— — *buried*
For he's a spirit of persuasion, only
Professes[2] to persuade—the King his son's alive,
'Tis as impossible that he's undrowned
As he that sleeps here swims.

SEBASTIAN I have no hope
That he's undrowned.

ANTONIO Oh, out of that no hope
What great hope have you! No hope that way° is — *(that he's not drowned)*
Another way so high a hope that even
Ambition cannot pierce a wink° beyond, — *catch a glimpse*

7. Between tides, and thus open to suggestion; also, associated with being slothful. *Trebles thee o'er:* Makes you three times as great.
8. Inherited laziness, or the slowness to attain prosperity arising from being born a younger brother.
9. *If . . . it:* If you only understood that your mockery reveals how great your aspirations really are; also, the hereditary position you mock is actually to your advantage. *cherish:* hold dear; cultivate.
1. Which puts in agony, as in childbirth.
2. *only / Professes:* his sole vocation is.

But doubt discovery there.[3] Will you grant with me
That Ferdinand is drowned?

**SEBASTIAN** He's gone.

**ANTONIO** Then tell me,
Who's the next heir of Naples?

**SEBASTIAN** Claribel.

**ANTONIO** She that is Queen of Tunis; she that dwells
Ten leagues beyond man's life;° she that from Naples — *lifetime journey*
Can have no note,° unless the sun were post°— — *information / messenger*
The man i'th' moon's too slow—till newborn chins
Be rough and razorable; she that from° whom — *returning from*
We all were sea-swallowed, though some cast again,[4]
And by that destiny to perform an act
Whereof what's past is prologue, what to come
In yours and my discharge.° — *performance*

**SEBASTIAN** What stuff is this? How say you?
'Tis true my brother's daughter's Queen of Tunis;
So is she heir of Naples, twixt which regions
There is some space.

**ANTONIO** A space whose ev'ry cubit° — *about 18 to 22 inches*
Seems to cry out, "How shall that Claribel
Measure us° back to Naples? Keep° in Tunis, — *(the cubits) / Stay*
And let Sebastian wake."° Say this were death — *(to his opportunity)*
That now hath seized them: why, they were no worse
Than now they are. There be that° can rule Naples — *those that*
As well as he that sleeps; lords that can prate
As amply and unnecessarily
As this Gonzalo; I myself could make
A chough of as deep chat.[5] Oh, that you bore
The mind that I do! What a sleep were this
For your advancement! Do you understand me?

**SEBASTIAN** Methinks I do.

**ANTONIO** And how does your content
Tender° your own good fortune? — *Regard; care for*

**SEBASTIAN** I remember
You did supplant your brother Prospero.

**ANTONIO** True:
And look how well my garments sit upon me,
Much feater° than before. My brother's servants — *more trimly*
Were then my fellows; now they are my men.

**SEBASTIAN** But for your conscience?

**ANTONIO** Ay, sir, where lies that? If 'twere a kibe,[6]
'Twould put me to° my slipper; but I feel not — *make me wear*
This deity in my bosom. Twenty consciences
That stand twixt me and Milan, candied[7] be they,
And melt ere they molest. Here lies your brother,
No better than the earth he lies upon
If he were that which now he's like—that's dead—
Whom I with this obedient steel,° three inches of it, — *sword*
Can lay to bed forever; whiles you, doing thus,

3. Doubt that there is anything to achieve beyond the high hope of the crown.
4. Regurgitated, cast ashore; also, possibly, theatrical role-playing.
5. *I . . . chat:* I could train a jackdaw (known for imitating speech) to speak as profoundly.
6. Chilblain; sore on the heel.
7. Turned to sugar; crystallized in sugar.

To the perpetual wink for aye° might put — *sleep forever*
This ancient morsel, this Sir Prudence, who
Should not upbraid our course. For all the rest,
They'll take suggestion° as a cat laps milk; — *prompting to evil*
They'll tell the clock° to any business that — *chime; agree*
We say befits the hour.

SEBASTIAN Thy case, dear friend,
Shall be my precedent. As thou gott'st Milan,
I'll come by Naples. Draw thy sword: one stroke
Shall free thee from the tribute which thou payest,
And I the King shall love thee.

ANTONIO Draw together;
And when I rear my hand, do you the like
To fall it on Gonzalo.

SEBASTIAN Oh, but one word.

*Enter* ARIEL, [*invisible,*] *with music and song.*

ARIEL My master through his art foresees the danger
That you his friend are in, and sends me forth—
For else° his project dies—to keep them[8] living. — *otherwise*

[*He*] *sings in Gonzalo's ear.*

While you here do snoring lie,
Open-eyed conspiracy
His time° doth take. — *opportunity*
If of life you keep a care,
Shake off slumber and beware.
Awake, awake!

ANTONIO Then let us both be sudden.

[ANTONIO *and* SEBASTIAN *draw their swords.*]

GONZALO [*waking*] Now, good angels preserve the King.

[*He wakes* ALONSO.]

ALONSO Why, how now? Ho! Awake! Why are you° drawn? — *your weapons*
Wherefore this ghastly° looking? — *fearful*

GONZALO What's the matter?

SEBASTIAN Whiles we stood here securing° your repose, — *guarding*
Even now we heard a hollow burst of bellowing,
Like bulls, or rather lions. Did't not wake you?
It struck mine ear most terribly.

ALONSO I heard nothing.

ANTONIO Oh, 'twas a din to fright a monster's ear,
To make an earthquake: sure it was the roar
Of a whole herd of lions.

ALONSO Heard you this, Gonzalo?

GONZALO Upon mine honor, sir, I heard a humming,
And that a strange one too, which did awake me.
I shaked you, sir, and cried.° As mine eyes opened, — *called out*
I saw their weapons drawn. There was a noise,
That's verily.° 'Tis best we stand upon our guard, — *the truth*
Or that we quit this place. Let's draw our weapons.

ALONSO Lead off this ground, and let's make further search
For my poor son.

GONZALO Heavens keep him from these beasts,
For he is sure i'th' island.

8. Gonzalo and Alonso.

ALONSO Lead away.
ARIEL[9] Prospero my lord shall know what I have done.
So, King, go safely on to seek thy son. *Exeunt.*

## 2.2

*Enter* CALIBAN *with a burden of wood.*

CALIBAN All the infections that the sun sucks up
From bogs, fens, flats,° on Prosper fall, and make him — *marshes*
By inchmeal° a disease! — *inch by inch*
*A noise of thunder heard.*[1]
His spirits hear me,
And yet I needs must curse. But they'll nor pinch,
Fright me with urchin-shows,[2] pitch me i'th' mire,
Nor lead me like a firebrand in the dark
Out of my way, unless he bid 'em. But
For every trifle are they set upon me;
Sometime like apes that mow° and chatter at me — *grimace*
And after bite me; then like hedgehogs, which
Lie tumbling in my barefoot way and mount
Their pricks at my footfall; sometime am I
All wound with° adders, who with cloven tongues — *entwined by*
Do hiss me into madness.
*Enter* TRINCULO.[3]
Lo, now, lo!
Here comes a spirit of his, and to torment me
For bringing wood in slowly. I'll fall flat.
Perchance he will not mind° me. — *notice*

TRINCULO Here's neither bush nor scrub to bear off° any weather at all, and another storm brewing: I hear it sing i'th' wind. Yond same black cloud, yond huge one, looks like a foul bombard[4] that would shed his liquor. If it should thunder as it did before, I know not where to hide my head. Yond same cloud cannot choose but fall by pailfuls. [*He sees* CALIBAN.] What have we here? A man or a fish? Dead or alive? A fish: he smells like a fish; a very ancient and fishlike smell; a kind of not-of-the-newest poor-john.[5] A strange fish. Were I in England now, as once I was, and had but this fish painted,[6] not a holiday fool there but would give a piece of silver. There would this monster make a man;[7] any strange beast there makes a man. When they will not give a doit° to relieve a lame beggar, they will lay out ten to see a dead Indian.[8] Legged like a man, and his fins like arms. Warm, o'my troth! I do now let loose my opinion, hold it no longer: this is no fish, but an islander that hath lately suffered by a thunderbolt. [*Thunder.*] Alas, the storm is come again. My best way is to creep under his gaberdine; there is no other shelter hereabout. Misery acquaints a man with strange bedfellows. I will here shroud° till the dregs[9] of the storm be past.

*ward off* — *small coin* — *take cover*

9. Ariel's following lines are spoken as the other characters depart; he probably exits in another direction.

2.2

1. Caliban takes this as a response to his curse; in F, the direction comes before Caliban speaks.
2. With the sight of hedgehoglike spirits.
3. Trinculo is probably dressed in traditional fool's motley (many-colored garment).
4. Large leather drinking vessel; stone-throwing military engine.
5. Dried hake, a poor person's staple.
6. On a sign to attract spectators.
7. Make a fortune for a man; become a man.
8. An allusion to exhibitions of American Indians in London.
9. Last drinks, as from the bottom of a "bombard" of wine.

*[He crawls under Caliban's cloak.]*

*Enter* STEFANO *singing.*

STEFANO I shall no more to sea, to sea,
Here shall I die ashore.

This is a very scurvy tune to sing at a man's funeral. Well, here's my comfort.

*[He] drinks [and] sings.*

The master, the swabber, the boatswain and I,
The gunner and his mate,
Loved Moll, Meg, and Marian, and Margery,
But none of us cared for Kate.
For she had a tongue with a tang,° *sting*
Would cry to a sailor, "Go hang!"
She loved not the savor of tar nor of pitch,
Yet a tailor might scratch her where'er she did itch.[1]
Then to sea, boys, and let her go hang!

This is a scurvy tune, too; but here's my comfort.

*[He] drinks.*

CALIBAN Do not torment me! Oh!

STEFANO What's the matter?° *What's going on?* Have we devils here? Do you put tricks upon 's with savages and men of Ind?° *India* Ha? I have not scaped drowning to be afeared now of your four legs; for it hath been said, "As proper a man as ever went on four legs[2] cannot make him give ground"; and it shall be said so again, while Stefano breathes at'° *at the* nostrils.

CALIBAN The spirit torments me! Oh!

STEFANO This is some monster of the isle with four legs who hath got, as I take it, an ague.° *a fit of fever* Where the devil should he learn our language? I will give him some relief if it be but for that. If I can recover° *cure* him and keep him tame and get to Naples with him, he's a present for any emperor that ever trod on neat's leather.° *cowhide; shoes*

CALIBAN Do not torment me, prithee! I'll bring my wood home faster.

STEFANO He's in his fit now, and does not talk after° *in the manner of* the wisest. He shall taste of my bottle. If he have never drunk wine afore, it will go near to° *almost* remove his fit. If I can recover him and keep him tame, I will not take too much for him.[3] He shall pay for him that hath° *gets* him, and that soundly.

CALIBAN Thou dost me yet but little hurt; thou wilt anon, I know it by thy trembling. Now Prosper works upon thee.

STEFANO Come on your ways.° *Come on* Open your mouth: here is that which will give language to you, cat.[4] Open your mouth: this will shake° *dislodge* your shaking, I can tell you, and that soundly. [CALIBAN *drinks.*] You cannot tell who's your friend. Open your chaps again.

TRINCULO I should know that voice. It should be—but he is drowned, and these are devils. Oh, defend me!

STEFANO Four legs and two voices: a most delicate° *exquisitely made* monster! His forward voice now is to speak well of his friend; his backward voice is to utter foul speeches and to detract. If all

1. Implying sexual desire and gratification. Tailors were often mocked for supposed lack of virility.
2. Comically varying "on two legs" (upright); also suggesting "on crutches."
3. No sum can be too high for him.
4. "Ale will make a cat speak" was proverbial.

the wine in my bottle will recover him,[5] I will help his ague. Come. [CALIBAN *drinks.*] Amen.° I will pour some in thy other mouth. *Enough*

TRINCULO Stefano!

STEFANO Doth thy other mouth call me? Mercy, mercy! This is a devil and no monster. I will leave him; I have no long spoon.[6]

TRINCULO Stefano? If thou beest Stefano, touch me and speak to me, for I am Trinculo—be not afeard—thy good friend Trinculo.

STEFANO If thou beest Trinculo, come forth: I'll pull thee by the lesser legs. If any be Trinculo's legs, these are they. [*He pulls him out.*] Thou art very° Trinculo indeed! How cam'st thou to be the siege° of this mooncalf?[7] Can he vent° Trinculos? *actual* / *excrement / defecate*

TRINCULO I took him to be killed with a thunderstroke. But art thou not drowned, Stefano? I hope now thou art not drowned. Is the storm overblown? I hid me under the dead mooncalf's gaberdine, for fear of the storm. And art thou living, Stefano? O Stefano, two Neapolitans scaped!

STEFANO Prithee, do not turn me about, my stomach is not constant.

CALIBAN [*aside*] These be fine things, an if° they be not sprites. That's a brave° god, and bears celestial liquor. I will kneel to him. *an if*=if / *an excellent; a fine*

STEFANO How didst thou scape? How cam'st thou hither? Swear by this bottle how thou cam'st hither. I escaped upon a butt of sack[8] which the sailors heaved o'erboard, by this bottle, which I made of the bark of a tree, with mine own hands, since I was cast ashore.

CALIBAN I'll swear upon that bottle to be thy true subject, for the liquor is not earthly.

STEFANO Here. Swear then how thou escaped'st.

TRINCULO Swum ashore, man, like a duck. I can swim like a duck, I'll be sworn.

STEFANO [*giving* TRINCULO *the bottle*] Here, kiss the Book.[9] Though thou canst swim like a duck, thou art made like a goose.[1]

TRINCULO O Stefano, hast any more of this?

STEFANO The whole butt, man. My cellar is in a rock by the seaside, where my wine is hid. [*to* CALIBAN] How now, mooncalf, how does thine ague?

CALIBAN Hast thou not dropped from heaven?

STEFANO Out o'th' moon I do assure thee. I was the man i'th' moon, when time was.° *once upon a time*

CALIBAN I have seen thee in her, and I do adore thee. My mistress° showed me thee, and thy dog, and thy bush.[2] *(Miranda)*

STEFANO [*giving the bottle to* CALIBAN] Come, swear to that: kiss the Book. I will furnish it anon with new contents. Swear.

5. If it takes all the wine in my bottle to cure him.
6. From the proverbial "He should have a long spoon that sups with the devil."
7. Deformed creature; miscarriage, owing to the supposed detrimental influence of the moon.
8. Cask of Spanish or Canary wine.
9. Confirming an oath by kissing the Bible; or the proverbial "Kiss the cup" ("Drink").
1. Probably alluding to Trinculo's outstretched neck with the bottle as a beak; also, a byword for giddiness and unsteadiness on the feet.
2. A dog and a thornbush were traditional attributes of the man in the moon; cf. *A Midsummer Night's Dream* 5.1.247–49.

TRINCULO By this good light,° this is a very shallow monster. I afeared of him? A very weak monster. The man i'th' moon? A most poor credulous monster. Well drawn,° monster, in good sooth. *sun* *drunk*

CALIBAN I'll show thee every fertile inch o'th' island, and I will kiss thy foot. I prithee, be my god.

TRINCULO By this light, a most perfidious and drunken monster! When 's god's asleep he'll rob his bottle.

CALIBAN I'll kiss thy foot. I'll swear myself thy subject.

STEFANO Come on, then: down and swear.

TRINCULO I shall laugh myself to death at this puppy-headed monster. A most scurvy monster. I could find in my heart to beat him—

STEFANO [*to* CALIBAN] Come, kiss.

TRINCULO —but that the poor monster's in drink.° An abominable monster. *drunk*

CALIBAN I'll show thee the best springs; I'll pluck thee berries;
I'll fish for thee, and get thee wood enough.
A plague upon the tyrant that I serve!
I'll bear him no more sticks but follow thee,
Thou wondrous man.

TRINCULO A most ridiculous monster, to make a wonder of a poor drunkard.

CALIBAN I prithee, let me bring thee where crabs° grow; *crab apples*
And I with my long nails will dig thee pig-nuts,° *edible tubers*
Show thee a jay's nest, and instruct thee how
To snare the nimble marmoset. I'll bring thee
To clust'ring filberts, and sometimes I'll get thee
Young scamels[3] from the rock. Wilt thou go with me?

STEFANO I prithee now lead the way without any more talking. Trinculo, the King and all our company else being drowned, we will inherit here. [*to* CALIBAN] Here, bear my bottle. —Fellow Trinculo, we'll fill him° by and by again. *it*

CALIBAN (*sings drunkenly*)[4] Farewell, master; farewell, farewell.

TRINCULO A howling monster, a drunken monster.

CALIBAN [*continuing to sing*] No more dams I'll make for° fish, *to trap*
Nor fetch in firing° *firewood*
At requiring,
Nor scrape trencher, nor wash dish,
'Ban, 'Ban, Ca-Caliban
Has a new master: get a new man.[5]
Freedom, high-day;° high-day, freedom; freedom, high-day, freedom! *holiday*

STEFANO O brave° monster, lead the way! *Exeunt.* *excellent; fine*

3. TEXTUAL COMMENT Shakespeare may have invented this exotic word, which appears nowhere else in the English language, but it seems more likely that "scamel" was the result of an error in transmission. For a survey of the many emendations editors have proposed, see Digital Edition TC 6.

4. This stage direction may be misplaced and may actually refer to the following song, "No more dams."

5. Addressed to the old master, Prospero.

## 3.1

*Enter* FERDINAND, *bearing a log.*

FERDINAND There be some sports are painful, and their labor
Delight in them sets off.[1] Some kinds of baseness
Are nobly undergone, and most poor matters
Point to rich ends. This my mean° task — *lowly*
Would be as heavy to me as odious, but° — *except that*
The mistress which I serve quickens° what's dead — *enlivens*
And makes my labors pleasures. Oh, she is
Ten times more gentle than her father's crabbed,
And he's composed of harshness. I must remove
Some thousands of these logs and pile them up,
Upon a sore° injunction. My sweet mistress — *harsh*
Weeps when she sees me work and says such baseness
Had never like executor. I forget;
But these sweet thoughts do even refresh my labors,
Most busil'est,[2] when I do it.° — *(labor)*

*Enter* MIRANDA, *and* PROSPERO [*unseen*].

MIRANDA Alas now, pray you,
Work not so hard. I would the lightning had
Burnt up those logs that you are enjoined to pile.
Pray set it down and rest you. When this burns
'Twill weep[3] for having wearied you. My father
Is hard at study. Pray now, rest yourself.
He's safe° for these three hours. — *We are safe from him*

FERDINAND O most dear mistress,
The sun will set before I shall discharge
What I must strive to do.

MIRANDA If you'll sit down
I'll bear your logs the while. Pray give me that:
I'll carry it to the pile.

FERDINAND No, precious creature,
I had rather crack my sinews, break my back,
Than you should such dishonor undergo
While I sit lazy by.

MIRANDA It would become me
As well as it does you; and I should do it
With much more ease, for my goodwill is to it,
And yours it is against.

PROSPERO [*aside*] Poor worm, thou art infected:[4]
This visitation[5] shows it.

MIRANDA You look wearily.

FERDINAND No, noble mistress, 'tis fresh morning with me
When you are by at night. I do beseech you,
Chiefly that I may set it in my prayers,
What is your name?

MIRANDA Miranda. —O my father,
I have broke your hest° to say so! — *disobeyed your command*

3.1
1. *their . . . off:* the greater effort invested amounts to more pleasure; the labor of painful activities ("sports") is offset by whatever delight we take in them.
2. Most busily (giving a double superlative).
3. By exuding drops of resin.
4. Afflicted with lovesickness. *worm:* an expression of tenderness; but a worm was often thought to carry disease.
5. Suggesting a pastoral or charitable visit to the sick; or may indicate a visit by the plague—here, lovesickness.

FERDINAND Admired[6] Miranda!
Indeed the top of admiration, worth
What's dearest to the world. Full many a lady
I have eyed with best regard, and many a time
Th' harmony of their tongues hath into bondage
Brought my too diligent° ear. For several virtues *attentive*
Have I liked several° women; never any *various*
With so full soul but some defect in her
Did quarrel with the noblest grace she owed° *owned*
And put it to the foil.[7] But you, O you,
So perfect and so peerless, are created
Of every creature's best.

MIRANDA I do not know
One of my sex; no woman's face remember
Save, from my glass,° mine own. Nor have I seen *mirror*
More that I may call men than you, good friend,
And my dear father. How features are abroad[8]
I am skilless° of; but by my modesty,° *ignorant / virginity*
The jewel in my dower,° I would not wish *dowry*
Any companion in the world but you,
Nor can imagination form a shape
Besides° yourself to like of. But I prattle *Other than*
Something° too wildly, and my father's precepts *Somewhat*
I therein do forget.

FERDINAND I am in my condition° *rank*
A prince, Miranda; I do think a king—
I would° not so!—and would no more endure *wish it were*
This wooden slavery[9] than to suffer
The flesh fly[1] blow my mouth. Hear my soul speak:
The very instant that I saw you did
My heart fly to your service, there resides
To make me slave to it, and for your sake
Am I this patient log-man.

MIRANDA Do you love me?

FERDINAND O heaven, O earth, bear witness to this sound,
And crown what I profess with kind event° *favorable outcome*
If I speak true! If hollowly,° invert *falsely*
What best is boded° me to mischief!° I, *foretold to / misfortune*
Beyond all limit of what° else i'th' world, *whatsoever*
Do love, prize, honor you.

MIRANDA I am a fool
To weep at what I am glad of.

PROSPERO [*aside*] Fair encounter
Of two most rare affections. Heavens rain grace
On that which breeds between 'em.

FERDINAND Wherefore weep you?

MIRANDA At mine unworthiness, that dare not offer
What I desire to give, and much less take
What I shall die to want.[2] But this is trifling,

6. Playing on the meaning of Miranda's name.
7. Foiled it, or made it ineffectual; challenged it, as in a fencing match (compare "quarrel" in line 45).
8. What people look like elsewhere.
9. The log as a symbol of Prospero's oppression.
1. Species of fly that deposits its eggs ("blows") in dead flesh.
2. *At . . . want:* Miranda is not at liberty to bestow her virginity or to obtain the consummation that she desires and lacks.

And all the more it seeks to hide itself
The bigger bulk it shows.[3] Hence, bashful cunning,° — *artful shyness*
And prompt me, plain and holy innocence!
I am your wife if you'll marry me;
If not, I'll die your maid.° To be your fellow° — *virgin; servant / equal*
You may deny me, but I'll be your servant
Whether you will or no.

FERDINAND My mistress,° dearest, — *sweetheart*
And I thus humble ever.

MIRANDA My husband, then?

FERDINAND Ay, with a heart as willing° — *desirous*
As bondage e'er of freedom. Here's my hand.[4]

MIRANDA And mine, with my heart in't. And now farewell
Till half an hour hence.

FERDINAND A thousand thousand!° — *(farewells)*

*Exeunt* [FERDINAND *and* MIRANDA, *separately*].

PROSPERO So glad of this as they I cannot be,
Who are surprised withal;° but my rejoicing — *overwhelmed by all*
At nothing can be more. I'll to my book,° — *book of magic*
For yet ere suppertime must I perform
Much business appertaining. *Exit.*

## 3.2

*Enter* CALIBAN, STEFANO, *and* TRINCULO.

STEFANO Tell not me. When the butt is out we will drink water, not a drop before. Therefore bear up and board 'em.[1] —Servant monster, drink to me!

TRINCULO "Servant monster"? The folly° of this island! They say there's but five upon this isle. We are three of them; if th'other two be brained° like us, the state totters. — *absurdity* / *have brains*

STEFANO Drink, servant monster, when I bid thee. Thy eyes are almost set° in thy head. — *fixed by drunkenness*

TRINCULO Where should they be set° else? He were a brave monster indeed if they were set in his tail. — *placed*

STEFANO My man-monster hath drowned his tongue in sack. For my part, the sea cannot drown me. I swam, ere I could recover the shore, five and thirty leagues,° off and on.[2] By this light, thou shalt be my lieutenant, monster, or my standard.[3] — *about 100 miles*

TRINCULO Your lieutenant, if you list;° he's no standard. — *wish*

STEFANO We'll not run, Monsieur Monster.

TRINCULO Nor go° neither, but you'll lie[4] like dogs and yet say nothing neither. — *walk*

STEFANO Mooncalf, speak once in thy life, if thou beest a good mooncalf.

CALIBAN How does thy honor? Let me lick thy shoe.
I'll not serve him; he is not valiant.

3. *all . . . shows:* an image of secret pregnancy.
4. *I am your wife* (line 83) . . . *hand:* Such an exchange could actually have constituted a marriage ceremony. In Shakespeare's time, weddings did not need to be witnessed and performed in a church to be valid (compare 4.1.14–19).

3.2

1. Force a way aboard, continuing the terminology of naval warfare; take onboard (drink). *bear up:* sail to the attack.
2. Tacking away from and toward the shore.
3. Standard-bearer; but in Trinculo's reply, "one who can stand up."
4. Lie (down); tell lies; excrete.

TRINCULO Thou liest, most ignorant monster; I am in case° to jostle a constable. Why, thou debauched fish thou, was there ever man a coward that hath drunk so much sack as I do today? Wilt thou tell a monstrous lie, being but half a fish and half a monster? *prepared*

CALIBAN Lo, how he mocks me. Wilt thou let him, my lord?

TRINCULO "Lord," quoth he? That a monster should be such a natural![5]

CALIBAN Lo, lo again! Bite him to death, I prithee.

STEFANO Trinculo, keep a good tongue in your head. If you prove a mutineer, the next tree!° The poor monster's my subject, and he shall not suffer indignity. *(for a gallows)*

CALIBAN I thank my noble lord. Wilt thou be pleased
To hearken once again to the suit I made to thee?

STEFANO Marry, will I. Kneel and repeat it. I will stand, and so shall Trinculo.

*Enter* ARIEL *invisible.*

CALIBAN As I told thee before, I am subject to a tyrant,
A sorcerer, that by his cunning hath
Cheated me of the island.

ARIEL Thou liest.

CALIBAN [*to* TRINCULO] Thou liest, thou jesting monkey, thou!
I would my valiant master would destroy thee.
I do not lie.

STEFANO Trinculo, if you trouble him any more in 's tale, by this hand, I will supplant° some of your teeth. *uproot*

TRINCULO Why, I said nothing.

STEFANO Mum, then, and no more. —Proceed.

CALIBAN I say by sorcery he got this isle;
From me he got it. If thy greatness will
Revenge it on him—for I know thou dar'st,
But this thing[6] dare not—

STEFANO That's most certain.

CALIBAN Thou shalt be lord of it, and I'll serve thee.

STEFANO How now shall this be compassed?° Canst thou bring me to the party?° *accomplished* / *person concerned*

CALIBAN Yea, yea, my lord. I'll yield him thee asleep,
Where thou mayst knock a nail into his head.[7]

ARIEL Thou liest; thou canst not.

CALIBAN What a pied ninny's° this! Thou scurvy patch!° *fool in motley / jester; idiot*
I do beseech thy greatness give him blows
And take his bottle from him. When that's gone,
He shall drink naught but brine, for I'll not show him
Where the quick freshes° are. *fast-flowing springs*

STEFANO Trinculo, run into no further danger. Interrupt the monster one word further and, by this hand, I'll turn my mercy out o'doors and make a stockfish of thee.[8]

TRINCULO Why, what did I? I did nothing. I'll go farther off.

STEFANO Didst thou not say he lied?

ARIEL Thou liest.

5. An idiot, punning on the idea that monsters were unnatural.
6. Trinculo; or perhaps Caliban himself.
7. As Jael murdered sleeping Sisera in Judges 4:21 and 5:26.
8. Proverbial allusion to the beating of dried fish before cooking it.

STEFANO Do I so?
[*He beats* TRINCULO.]
Take thou that! As you like this, give me the lie° another time. *call me a liar*

TRINCULO I did not give the lie! Out o'your wits, and hearing too? A pox o'your bottle. This can sack and drinking do. A murrain° on your monster, and the devil take your fingers! *plague*

CALIBAN Ha, ha, ha!

STEFANO Now forward with your tale. —Prithee stand further off.

CALIBAN Beat him enough. After a little time I'll beat him too.

STEFANO Stand farther. —Come, proceed.

CALIBAN Why, as I told thee, 'tis a custom with him
I'th' afternoon to sleep. There° thou mayst brain him, *Then*
Having first seized his books; or with a log
Batter his skull, or paunch° him with a stake, *disembowel*
Or cut his weasand° with thy knife. Remember *windpipe*
First to possess his books, for without them
He's but a sot° as I am, nor hath not *stupid fool*
One spirit to command—they all do hate him
As rootedly as I. Burn but his books.
He has brave utensils,[9] for so he calls them,
Which, when he has a house, he'll deck withal.
And that most deeply to consider is
The beauty of his daughter. He himself
Calls her a nonpareil.° I never saw a woman *one without equal*
But only Sycorax my dam and she;
But she as far surpasseth Sycorax
As great'st does least.

STEFANO Is it so brave° a lass? *excellent; fine*

CALIBAN Ay, lord. She will become thy bed, I warrant,
And bring thee forth brave brood.

STEFANO Monster, I will kill this man. His daughter and I will be king and queen—save° our graces—and Trinculo and thyself shall be viceroys. Dost thou like the plot, Trinculo? *God save*

TRINCULO Excellent.

STEFANO Give me thy hand. I am sorry I beat thee. But while thou liv'st, keep a good tongue in thy head.

CALIBAN Within this half hour will he be asleep.
Wilt thou destroy him then?

STEFANO Ay, on mine honor.

ARIEL [*aside*] This will I tell my master.

CALIBAN Thou mak'st me merry. I am full of pleasure;
Let us be jocund. Will you troll° the catch° *sing / round; song*
You taught me but whilere?° *a short time ago*

STEFANO At thy request, monster, I will do reason, any reason.° *anything reasonable*
Come on, Trinculo, let us sing.
(*Sings.*)[1] Flout 'em, and scout 'em
And scout° 'em, and flout 'em. *mock*
Thought is free.

CALIBAN That's not the tune.

9. Perhaps confusing implements for magic and household goods.

1. The stage direction suggests that the others cannot manage the catch and remain in bewildered silence. But Trinculo, and perhaps Caliban, may attempt to join in.

ARIEL *plays the tune on a tabor and pipe.*[2]

STEFANO What is this same?

TRINCULO This is the tune of our catch, played by the picture of Nobody.[3]

STEFANO If thou beest a man, show thyself in thy likeness. If thou beest a devil, take't as thou list.° *wish*

TRINCULO Oh, forgive me my sins!

STEFANO He that dies pays all debts.[4] I defy thee! Mercy upon us![5]

CALIBAN Art thou afeard?

STEFANO No, monster, not I.

CALIBAN Be not afeard: the isle is full of noises,
Sounds and sweet airs° that give delight and hurt not. *tunes*
Sometimes a thousand twangling instruments
Will hum about mine ears; and sometimes voices,
That, if I then had waked after long sleep,
Will make me sleep again; and then, in dreaming,
The clouds methought would open and show riches
Ready to drop upon me, that when I waked
I cried to dream again.

STEFANO This will prove a brave kingdom to me, where I shall have my music for nothing.[6]

CALIBAN When Prospero is destroyed.

STEFANO That shall be by and by:° I remember the story. *very soon*

[*Exit* ARIEL *playing music.*]

TRINCULO The sound is going away; let's follow it, and after do our work.

STEFANO Lead, monster, we'll follow. I would I could see this taborer: he lays it on.[7]

TRINCULO [*to* CALIBAN] Wilt come? I'll follow Stefano.

*Exeunt.*

## 3.3

*Enter* ALONSO, SEBASTIAN, ANTONIO, GONZALO, ADRIAN, *and* FRANCISCO.

GONZALO By'r lakin,[1] I can go no further, sir.
My old bones aches. Here's a maze trod indeed
Through forthrights and meanders.° By your patience, *direct and winding paths*
I needs must rest me.

ALONSO Old lord, I cannot blame thee,
Who am myself attached° with weariness *seized*
To th' dulling of my spirits. Sit down and rest.
Even° here I will put off my hope, and keep it *Exactly*
No longer for° my flatterer: he is drowned *as*
Whom thus we stray to find, and the sea mocks
Our frustrate° search on land. Well, let him go. *vain*

2. The tabor was a small drum slung on the left-hand side of the body; the tabor pipe was a long narrow pipe played with the left hand. The combination was associated with rustic dances and merrymaking.
3. "Nobody" was a character in a comedy who was depicted on the title page of the printed text. Large breeches up to his neck made him appear to have no trunk.
4. Varying the proverbial "Death pays all debts."
5. Stefano's defiance comically collapses.
6. James I spent large sums on court music, but not typically of the popular kind Ariel now plays.
7. He sets himself to his music vigorously. Stefano deserts Caliban in order to follow the music. Trinculo and Caliban in turn follow Stefano (line 145).

3.3

1. Ladykin: a colloquial form of reference to the Virgin Mary.

ANTONIO [*aside to* SEBASTIAN] I am right glad that he's so out of hope.
Do not, for° one repulse, forgo the purpose — *on account of*
That you resolved t'effect.
SEBASTIAN [*aside to* ANTONIO] The next advantage
Will we take throughly.° — *thoroughly*
ANTONIO [*aside to* SEBASTIAN] Let it be tonight;
For now they are oppressed with travail,° they — *journey; effort*
Will not nor cannot use such vigilance
As when they are fresh.
SEBASTIAN [*aside to* ANTONIO] I say tonight: no more.

*Solemn and strange music.* [*Enter*] PROSPERO *on the top,*[2] *invisible.*

ALONSO What harmony is this? My good friends, hark!
GONZALO Marvelous sweet music.

*Enter several strange shapes, bringing a banquet; and dance about it with gentle actions of salutations, and inviting the King etc. to eat, they depart.*

ALONSO Give us kind keepers,° heavens! What were these? — *guardian angels*
SEBASTIAN A living drollery.[3] Now I will believe
That there are unicorns; that in Arabia
There is one tree, the phoenix' throne, one phoenix[4]
At this hour reigning there.
ANTONIO I'll believe both;
And what does else want credit,° come to me, — *lack belief*
And I'll be sworn 'tis true. Travelers ne'er did lie,[5]
Though fools at home condemn 'em.
GONZALO If in Naples
I should report this now, would they believe me?
If I should say I saw such islanders—
For certes° these are people of the island— — *certainly*
Who, though they are of monstrous shape, yet note
Their manners are more gentle, kind, than of
Our human generation you shall find
Many, nay, almost any.
PROSPERO [*aside*] Honest lord,
Thou hast said well; for some of you there present
Are worse than devils.
ALONSO I cannot too much muse° — *marvel at*
Such shapes, such gesture, and such sound, expressing—
Although they want the use of tongue°—a kind — *language*
Of excellent dumb discourse.
PROSPERO [*aside*] Praise in departing.[6]
FRANCISCO They vanished strangely.
SEBASTIAN No matter, since
They have left their viands° behind; for we have stomachs.° — *food / good appetites*
Wilt please you taste of what is here?
ALONSO Not I.
GONZALO Faith, sir, you need not fear. When we were boys,

2. A small acting area above the upper stage.
3. A puppet show with live actors.
4. The unicorn and phoenix, a bird, were two mythological creatures that sometimes figured in travelers' tales. Only one phoenix was said to exist in the world at any one time.
5. Proverbially, "A traveler may lie with authority."
6. Reserve your praise until the end of the event.

Who would believe that there were mountaineers,° — *mountain dwellers*
Dewlapped like bulls, whose throats had hanging at 'em
Wallets° of flesh? Or that there were such men — *Pouches*
Whose heads stood in their breasts? Which now we find
Each putter-out of five for one[7] will bring us
Good warrant of.

ALONSO I will stand to and feed;° — *begin eating*
Although my last, no matter, since I feel
The best is past. Brother, my lord the duke,
Stand to and do as we.

*[ALONSO, SEBASTIAN, and ANTONIO approach the table.] Thunder and lightning.*
*Enter ARIEL, like a harpy;[8] claps his wings upon the table, and with a quaint device° the banquet vanishes.[9]* — *an ingenious mechanism*

ARIEL You are three men of sin, whom destiny—
That hath to° instrument this lower world — *as its*
And what is in't—the never-surfeited sea
Hath caused to belch up you, and on this island,
Where man doth not inhabit—you 'mongst men
Being most unfit to live. I have made you mad;
And even with suchlike valor[1] men hang and drown
Their proper selves.° — *Themselves*

*[ALONSO, SEBASTIAN, and ANTONIO draw their swords.][2]*

You fools, I and my fellows
Are ministers of fate. The elements
Of whom your swords are tempered[3] may as well
Wound the loud winds, or with bemocked-at stabs
Kill the still-closing[4] waters, as diminish
One dowl° that's in my plume.° My fellow ministers — *featherlet / plumage*
Are like° invulnerable. If you could hurt, — *similarly*
Your swords are now too massy° for your strengths — *heavy*
And will not be uplifted. But remember—
For that's my business to you—that you three
From Milan did supplant good Prospero;
Exposed unto the sea, which hath requit it,
Him and his innocent child; for which foul deed
The powers, delaying not forgetting,[5] have
Incensed the seas and shores—yea, all the creatures[6]—
Against your peace. Thee of thy son, Alonso,
They have bereft; and do pronounce by me

7. A traveler could profit from a voyage by laying down a sum with a broker before departing and undertaking to bring back evidence of having reached his destination; if successful, he was repaid fivefold.
8. A mythological monster with a vulture's wings and claws and a woman's face. Aeneas and his companions encountered these harpies, who stole their meals and threatened to punish them with slow starvation. *Thunder and lightning:* both spectacular and functional for disguising the mechanics of the "quaint device."
9. The simplest effective staging is by means of a rotating tabletop with the vessels of the banquet fixed to its surface. Leg-to-leg planks supporting the tabletop or a hanging cloth would conceal the vanished banquet. The harpy's wings would hide the mechanics from the audience, and clapping them would provide a visual distraction.
1. *suchlike valor:* fearlessness that comes from madness.
2. Ariel perhaps ascends beyond their reach here. Aeneas's companions, like Alonso here, similarly attempted to kill the harpies with swords.
3. Compounded and hardened. Metal was sometimes thought of as being compounded of earth and fire, here contrasted with winds and waters.
4. Self-healing, since they close immediately once parted.
5. Related to the proverb "God stays long but strikes at last."
6. Compare Genesis 1:21: "Then God created . . . everything living and moving."

Ling'ring perdition[7]—worse than any death
Can be at once—shall step by step attend
You and your ways; whose[8] wraths to guard you from,
Which here in this most desolate[9] isle else falls
Upon your heads, is nothing° but heart's sorrow — *there is no alternative*
And a clear life° ensuing. — *a life innocent of sin*

*He vanishes[1] in thunder; then, to soft music, enter the shapes again, and dance with mocks and mows,° and* [*then exeunt*], *carrying out the table.* — *grimaces*

PROSPERO [*aside*] Bravely the figure of this harpy hast thou
Performed, my Ariel; a grace it had, devouring.[2]
Of my instruction hast thou nothing bated° — *omitted*
In what thou hadst to say. So with good life[3]
And observation strange[4] my meaner ministers° — *lesser spirits*
Their several kinds° have done.° My high charms work, — *various roles / performed*
And these mine enemies are all knit up
In their distractions. They now are in my power;
And in these fits I leave them, while I visit
Young Ferdinand, whom they suppose is drowned,
And his and mine loved darling. [*Exit.*]

GONZALO I'th' name of something holy, sir, why stand you
In this strange stare?

ALONSO Oh, it is monstrous, monstrous!
Methought the billows spoke and told me of it,
The winds did sing it to me, and the thunder,
That deep and dreadful organ pipe, pronounced
The name of Prosper. It did bass my trespass.[5]
Therefore° my son i'th' ooze is bedded, and — *For that*
I'll seek him deeper than e'er plummet sounded,
And with him there lie mudded. [*Exit.*]

SEBASTIAN But one fiend at a time,
I'll fight their legions o'er!° — *from beginning to end*

ANTONIO I'll be thy second.

*Exeunt* [SEBASTIAN *and* ANTONIO].

GONZALO All three of them are desperate:° their great guilt, — *in despair; reckless*
Like poison given to work° a great time after, — *take effect*
Now gins to bite the spirits. I do beseech you
That are of suppler joints, follow them swiftly,
And hinder them from what this ecstasy° — *madness*
May now provoke them to.

ADRIAN Follow, I pray you. *Exeunt.*

## 4.1

*Enter* PROSPERO, FERDINAND, *and* MIRANDA.

PROSPERO [*to* FERDINAND] If I have too austerely punished you,
Your compensation makes amends, for I

7. Slow starvation; hell on earth of spiritual suffering. The phrase is first the object of "pronounce" and then the subject of "shall . . . attend."
8. Refers to "the powers" in line 74.
9. Joyless, wretched; barren, deserted.
1. Ariel is raised out of sight into the canopy.
2. In clapping his wings, Ariel has created the illusion of having devoured the banquet.
3. Convincingly; with vitality. *So:* In the same way.
4. Remarkable attention to the requirements of their parts, or instructions.
5. The thunder proclaimed my sin ("trespass") in a bass voice, or with a bass background; perhaps, wordplay on the "utter baseness" of trespass.

Have given you here a third[1] of mine own life—
Or that for which I live—who° once again *[whom]*
I tender° to thy hand. All thy vexations *[offer]*
Were but my trials of thy love, and thou
Hast strangely° stood the test. Here, afore heaven, *[wonderfully]*
I ratify this my rich gift. O Ferdinand,
Do not smile at me that I boast her off,° *[sing her praises]*
For thou shalt find she will outstrip all praise
And make it halt° behind her. *[limp]*

FERDINAND I do believe it against an oracle.[2]

PROSPERO Then, as my guest, and thine own acquisition
Worthily purchased,° take my daughter. But *[Gained by effort]*
If thou dost break her virgin-knot° before *[hymen]*
All sanctimonious° ceremonies may *[holy]*
With full and holy rite be ministered,
No sweet aspersion° shall the heavens let fall *[shower of grace]*
To make this contract grow; but barren hate,
Sour-eyed disdain, and discord shall bestrew
The union of your bed with weeds[3] so loathly
That you shall hate it both. Therefore take heed,
As Hymen's[4] lamps shall light you.

FERDINAND As I hope
For quiet days, fair issue,° and long life, *[children]*
With such love as 'tis now, the murkiest den,° *[cave]*
The most opportune place, the strong'st suggestion° *[temptation]*
Our worser genius can,[5] shall never melt
Mine honor into lust, to take away
The edge° of that day's celebration *[unblunted desire]*
When I shall think or° Phoebus' steeds are foundered,[6] *[either]*
Or night kept chained below.

PROSPERO Fairly spoke.
Sit then and talk with her: she is thine own.
—What,° Ariel! My industrious servant, Ariel! *[Now then]*

*Enter* ARIEL.

ARIEL What would my potent master? Here I am.

PROSPERO Thou and thy meaner° fellows your last service *[lesser]*
Did worthily perform, and I must use you
In such another trick. Go bring the rabble[7]
O'er whom I give thee pow'r here to this place.
Incite them to quick motion, for I must
Bestow upon the eyes of this young couple
Some vanity[8] of mine art. It is my promise,
And they expect it from me.

ARIEL Presently?° *[At once]*

PROSPERO Ay, with a twink.[9]

**4.1**

1. Miranda. The usual poetic conceit was a half; commentators variously conjecture the other third to be his dukedom, his books, or his late wife.
2. *I . . . oracle:* I would believe it even if an oracle said otherwise.
3. Weeds in place of the flowers traditionally strewn on the marriage bed; wordplay on both "marriage bed" and "seed-bed."
4. Classical god of marriage.
5. Is capable of. *worser genius:* evil spirit corresponding to a guardian angel.
6. Collapsed and made lame. *Phoebus' steeds:* the mythological horses that drew the chariot of the sun. Ferdinand anticipates that on his wedding day he will, in his impatience, think that the night will never come.
7. Troupe of lesser spirits. *trick:* theatrical device, or clever artifice.
8. Trifle; conceit; illusion; display.
9. In the twinkling of an eye.

ARIEL Before you can say "come" and "go,"
And breathe twice and cry "so, so,"
Each one tripping on his toe,
Will be here with mop and mow.[1]
Do you love me, master? No?

PROSPERO Dearly, my delicate Ariel. Do not approach
Till thou dost hear me call.

ARIEL Well; I conceive.° *Exit.* — *understand*

PROSPERO [*to* FERDINAND] Look thou be true;[2] do not give dalliance
Too much the rein.[3] The strongest oaths are straw
To th' fire i'th' blood. Be more abstemious,
Or else good night your vow.

FERDINAND I warrant you, sir,
The white cold virgin snow upon my heart
Abates the ardor of my liver.[4]

PROSPERO Well.
—Now come, my Ariel: bring a corollary° — *surplus*
Rather than want° a spirit. Appear, and pertly.° — *lack / briskly*

*Soft music.*

No tongue, all eyes! Be silent!

*Enter* IRIS.[5]

IRIS Ceres, most bounteous lady, thy rich leas[6]
Of wheat, rye, barley, vetches,[7] oats, and peas;
Thy turfy mountains where live nibbling sheep,
And flat meads° thatched with stover,[8] them to keep; — *meadows*
Thy banks with pionèd and twillèd[9] brims,
Which spongy° April at thy hest betrims[1] — *wet*
To make cold nymphs chaste crowns; and thy broom-groves,[2]
Whose shadow the dismissèd bachelor° loves, — *rejected suitor*
Being lass-lorn; thy poll-clipped vineyard,[3]
And thy sea-marge,° sterile and rocky-hard, — *seashore*
Where thou thyself dost air°—the queen o'th' sky,[4] — *take fresh air*
Whose wat'ry arch° and messenger am I, — *rainbow*
Bids thee leave these, and with her sovereign grace,
Here on this grass-plot,[5] in this very place
To come and sport. Her peacocks fly amain.[6]
Approach, rich Ceres, her to entertain.

*Enter* CERES.[7]

CERES Hail, many-colored messenger, that ne'er

1. With derisive and grimacing gestures.
2. Take care that you remain faithful to your promise. Prospero may have caught the lovers just indulging in dalliance.
3. To "give the rein" is to make a horse gallop.
4. *The . . . liver:* Virgin snow lies on his heart because he has remained chaste, never having given in to his ardent liver. The liver was held to be the seat of passion.
5. Goddess of the rainbow and messenger of Juno; her apparel is in the colors of the rainbow, and she wears "saffron wings" (line 78).
6. Arable land. Ceres was the Roman goddess of agriculture and generative nature.
7. Pealike plants grown for fodder.
8. Hay for winter fodder.
9. Reinforced with channels ("pioned") and with entwined branches ("twilled") to prevent riverbank erosion.
1. Adorns with flowers; recalls the colloquial "April showers bring forth May flowers."
2. Thickets of gorse, yellow-flowered shrubs. *cold:* chaste.
3. Vineyard with vines embracing, twined around, their supporting poles; pruned vineyard. "Vineyard" was pronounced as three syllables. *lass-lorn:* abandoned by the girl he wooed. *poll-clipped:* pruned short.
4. Juno, queen of the heavens and goddess of women, held to protect marriages and preside over childbirth.
5. Compare "this short-grassed green" (line 83) and "this green land" (line 130): a green carpet on the acting area is indicated.
6. In haste. Peacocks, sacred to Juno, drew her chariot.
7. Her part is probably played by Ariel (see line 167).

Dost disobey the wife of Jupiter;° *(Juno)*
Who with thy saffron wings upon my flowers
Diffusest honey-drops, refreshing showers,
And with each end of thy blue bow dost crown
My bosky[8] acres and my unshrubbed down,
Rich scarf[9] to my proud earth. Why hath thy queen
Summoned me hither to this short-grassed green?

IRIS A contract of true love to celebrate
And some donation freely to estate° *bestow*
On the blessed lovers.

CERES Tell me, heavenly bow,° *rainbow*
If Venus or her son,[1] as° thou dost know, *as far as*
Do now attend the Queen? Since they did plot
The means that dusky Dis[2] my daughter got,
Her and her blind boy's scandaled° company *scandalous; notorious*
I have forsworn.

IRIS Of her society
Be not afraid. I met her deity
Cutting the clouds towards Paphos,[3] and her son
Dove-drawn[4] with her. Here thought they to have done
Some wanton charm upon[5] this man and maid,
Whose vows are that no bed-right[6] shall be paid
Till Hymen's torch be lighted;[7] but in vain.
Mars's hot minion° is returned again; *lover; Venus*
Her waspish-headed[8] son has broke his arrows,
Swears he will shoot no more but play with sparrows,[9]
And be a boy right out.° *an ordinary boy*

JUNO *descends.*[1]

CERES Highest queen of state,
Great Juno comes; I know her by her gait.° *majestic bearing*

JUNO How does my bounteous sister? Go with me
To bless this twain that they may prosperous be
And honored in their issue.

[JUNO *and* CERES] *sing.*[2]

Honor, riches, marriage-blessing,
Long continuance and increasing,
Hourly joys be still° upon you, *always*
Juno sings her blessings on you.

CERES Earth's increase and foison° plenty, *abundance*
Barns and garners° never empty, *granaries*
Vines with clust'ring bunches growing,
Plants with goodly burden bowing;
Spring come to you at the farthest,

8. Covered with bushes and thickets.
9. Ornamental and hung across the body rather than around the neck.
1. Cupid, proverbially blind.
2. King of the underworld in classical mythology. Venus and her son Cupid made him fall in love with Ceres' daughter Proserpine, whom he abducted (Ovid, *Metamorphoses* 5.395ff).
3. City in Cyprus: associated with Venus.
4. Doves were sacred to Venus and drew her chariot.
5. *done . . . upon:* cast a lustful spell upon.
6. Right to consummate the marriage; also, suggesting a rite, as in line 17.
7. Until the wedding ceremony is performed.
8. Peevish, irritable, and with arrows like the wasp's sting.
9. Sparrows were associated with Venus because they were proverbially lustful.
1. TEXTUAL COMMENT Although most editors place "JUNO *descends*" at the point where Juno enters and speaks, in the Folio this stage direction appears around line 74. For possible explanations of the Folio's placement, and their implications for the way the scene is staged, see Digital Edition TC 7.
2. Ceres and Juno might be raised together in the flight apparatus and sing suspended above the stage. They would then vanish (line 138 stage direction) by being raised into the heavens.

In the very end of harvest.[3]
Scarcity and want shall shun you,
Ceres' blessing so is on you.

FERDINAND This is a most majestic vision, and
Harmonious charmingly.[4] May I be bold° — *Would I be right*
To think these spirits?

PROSPERO Spirits, which by mine art
I have from their confines[5] called to enact
My present fancies.

FERDINAND Let me live here ever!
So rare a wondered° father and a wise[6] — *endowed with wonders*
Makes this place paradise.

*JUNO and CERES whisper, and send IRIS on employment.*

PROSPERO Sweet° now, silence. — *Softly*
Juno and Ceres whisper seriously.
There's something else to do. Hush and be mute,
Or else our spell is marred.

IRIS You nymphs called naiads of the wind'ring[7] brooks,
With your sedged crowns° and ever-harmless looks, — *garlands of reeds*
Leave your crisp channels, and on this green land
Answer your summons; Juno does command.
Come, temperate nymphs, and help to celebrate
A contract of true love. Be not too late.

*Enter certain Nymphs.*

—You sunburned sicklemen° of August weary, — *harvesters*
Come hither from the furrow and be merry;
Make holiday; your rye-straw hats put on,
And these fresh nymphs encounter every one
In country footing.

*Enter certain Reapers, properly habited.[8] They join with the Nymphs in a graceful dance, towards the end whereof PROSPERO starts suddenly and speaks, after which, to a strange, hollow, and confused noise, they heavily vanish.[9]*

PROSPERO I had forgot that foul conspiracy
Of the beast Caliban and his confederates
Against my life. The minute of their plot
Is almost come. [*to the Spirits*] Well done. Avoid;° no more! — *Begone*

FERDINAND This is strange: your father's in some passion
That works° him strongly. — *agitates*

MIRANDA Never till this day
Saw I him touched with anger so distempered.° — *troubled; distracted*

PROSPERO You do look, my son, in a movèd sort,° — *disturbed manner*
As if you were dismayed. Be cheerful, sir.

3. Let spring return immediately after harvest, without any intervening winter. (In Greek mythology, winter was originally caused by Ceres abandoning the earth in search of Proserpine.)
4. Delightfully; magically; harmoniously.
5. Regions of dwelling. The word is accented on the second syllable.
6. Textual Comment Since the eighteenth century, some editors have changed "wise" to "wife," an emendation backed by disputed typographical evidence but with implications for the play's representation of women. For more on the long and vexed editorial history of this short word, see Digital Edition TC 8.
7. Perhaps a conflation of "wandering" and "winding." The naiads were mythical river nymphs.
8. Either appropriately or finely dressed.
9. Sorrowfully depart (probably not implying a trick of staging).

Our revels[1] now are ended. These our actors,
As I foretold you,° were all spirits and *told you before*
Are melted into air, into thin air;
And like the baseless fabric[2] of this vision,
The cloud-capped towers, the gorgeous palaces,
The solemn temples, the great globe[3] itself,
Yea, all which it inherit,[4] shall dissolve,
And, like this insubstantial pageant faded,
Leave not a rack° behind. We are such stuff *wisp of cloud*
As dreams are made on,° and our little life *of*
Is rounded[5] with a sleep. Sir, I am vexed.
Bear with my weakness: my old brain is troubled.
Be not disturbed with my infirmity.
If you be pleased, retire into my cell
And there repose. A turn or two I'll walk
To still my beating mind.

FERDINAND *and* MIRANDA We wish your peace. *Exeunt.*

PROSPERO Come with a thought.[6] I thank thee, Ariel. Come.

*Enter* ARIEL.

ARIEL Thy thoughts I cleave to. What's thy pleasure?

PROSPERO Spirit,
We must prepare to meet with Caliban.

ARIEL Ay, my commander. When I presented[7] Ceres
I thought to have told thee of it, but I feared
Lest I might anger thee.

PROSPERO Say again, where didst thou leave these varlets?° *ruffians*

ARIEL I told you, sir, they were red hot with drinking;
So full of valor that they smote the air
For breathing in their faces, beat the ground
For kissing of their feet; yet always bending° *aiming*
Towards their project. Then I beat my tabor,° *side drum*
At which like unbacked° colts they pricked their ears, *never-ridden*
Advanced° their eyelids, lifted up their noses *Opened*
As° they smelt music. So I charmed their ears *As if*
That calf-like they my lowing° followed through *mooing*
Toothed briars, sharp furzes, pricking gorse,° and thorns, *prickly shrubs*
Which entered their frail shins. At last I left them
I'th' filthy-mantled[8] pool beyond your cell,
There dancing up to th' chins, that° the foul lake *so that*
O'erstunk[9] their feet.

PROSPERO This was well done, my bird.° *chick; dear*
Thy shape invisible retain thou still.
The trumpery° in my house, go bring it hither *cheap goods*
For stale° to catch these thieves. *decoy; bait*

ARIEL I go, I go. *Exit.*

PROSPERO A devil, a born devil, on whose nature
Nurture can never stick; on whom my pains,
Humanely taken, all, all lost, quite lost;

1. Entertainment, in both festive and theatrical senses.
2. An edifice or substance without foundations; insubstantial, alluding to buildings in masque scenery.
3. World; also, with a passing allusion to the Globe theater.
4. All who come into possession of it.
5. Rounded off; surrounded; or, possibly, crowned.
6. Come as fast as thought, a colloquial simile.
7. Acted; produced the masque of; introduced while playing Iris.
8. Covered with filthy scum.
9. Made smelly; smelled worse than.

And, as with age his body uglier grows,
So his mind cankers.° I will plague them all, *festers*
Even to roaring.

*Enter* ARIEL, *laden with glistering apparel, etc.*

—Come, hang them on this line.[1]

*Enter* CALIBAN, STEFANO, *and* TRINCULO, *all wet.*

CALIBAN Pray you tread softly, that the blind mole may not
Hear a foot fall. We now are near his cell.

STEFANO Monster, your fairy, which you say is a harmless fairy, has done little better than played the jack° with us. *knave; will-o'-the-wisp*

TRINCULO Monster, I do smell° all horse-piss, at which my nose is in great indignation. *smell of*

STEFANO So is mine. Do you hear, monster? If I should take a displeasure against you, look you—

TRINCULO Thou wert but a lost monster.

CALIBAN Good my lord, give me thy favor still.
Be patient, for the prize I'll bring thee to
Shall hoodwink[2] this mischance. Therefore speak softly;
All's hushed as midnight yet.

TRINCULO Ay, but to lose our bottles in the pool!

STEFANO There is not only disgrace and dishonor in that, monster, but an infinite loss.

TRINCULO That's more to me than my wetting. Yet this is your harmless fairy, monster.

STEFANO I will fetch off[3] my bottle, though I be o'er ears° for my labor. *drowned*

CALIBAN Prithee, my king, be quiet. Seest thou here:
This is the mouth o'th' cell. No noise, and enter.
Do that good mischief which may make this island
Thine own forever, and I, thy Caliban,
For aye° thy foot-licker. *ever*

STEFANO Give me thy hand. I do begin to have bloody thoughts.

TRINCULO O King Stefano, O peer! O worthy Stefano, look what a wardrobe here is for thee.[4]

CALIBAN Let it alone, thou fool. It is but trash.

TRINCULO Oh ho, monster! We know what belongs to a frippery.° O King Stefano! *old-clothes shop*

STEFANO Put off that gown, Trinculo: by this hand, I'll have that gown.

TRINCULO Thy grace shall have it.

CALIBAN The dropsy[5] drown this fool! What do you mean
To dote thus on such luggage?° Let't alone *encumbrances*
And do the murder first. If he awake,
From toe to crown he'll fill our skins with pinches,
Make us° strange stuff. *Turn us into*

STEFANO Be you quiet, monster. Mistress line, is not this my jerkin?° Now is the jerkin under the line.[6] Now, jerkin, you *leather jacket*

1. Variant of lind, the lime tree or linden, probably indicating stage property tree.
2. Blind with a hood, as was done to pacify a hawk—hence, make harmless; also, put out of sight.
3. Recover; rescue; drink off.
4. Recalling "King Stephen was and a worthy peer, / His breeches cost him but a crown," a popular ballad about King Stephen, sung in part in *Othello* 2.3.77ff.
5. A disease characterized by the accumulation of fluid in connective tissue.
6. Below the lime tree; south of the equator; below the waist. Also, a possible allusion to the proverb "Thou hast stricken the ball under the line," meaning "You have cheated." Stefano has taken the jerkin from the lime tree.

are like to lose your hair and prove a bald jerkin.[7]

TRINCULO Do, do! We steal by line and level,[8] an't like° your grace. *if it please*

STEFANO I thank thee for that jest. Here's a garment for't. Wit shall not go unrewarded while I am king of this country. "Steal by line and level" is an excellent pass of pate.[9] There's another garment for't.

TRINCULO Monster, come, put some lime upon your fingers[1] and away with the rest.

CALIBAN I will have none on't. We shall lose our time
And all be turned to barnacles,[2] or to apes
With foreheads villainous° low. *wretchedly*

STEFANO Monster, lay to° your fingers. Help to bear this away, where my hogshead of wine is, or I'll turn you out of my kingdom. Go to, carry this. *apply*

TRINCULO And this.

STEFANO Ay, and this.

*A noise of hunters heard. Enter diverse° SPIRITS in shape of dogs and hounds, hunting them about, PROSPERO and ARIEL setting them on.* *various*

PROSPERO Hey, Mountain, hey!

ARIEL Silver! There it goes, Silver!

PROSPERO Fury, Fury! There, Tyrant, there! Hark, hark!

[*CALIBAN, STEFANO, and TRINCULO are chased off by SPIRITS.*]

[*to* ARIEL] Go, charge my goblins that they grind their joints
With dry convulsions, shorten up their sinews
With agèd cramps, and more pinch-spotted[3] make them
Than pard or cat o'mountain.[4]

ARIEL Hark, they roar!

PROSPERO Let them be hunted soundly.° At this hour *thoroughly*
Lies at my mercy all mine enemies.
Shortly shall all my labors end, and thou
Shalt have the air at freedom. For a little,
Follow and do me service. *Exeunt.*

## 5.1

*Enter* PROSPERO *in his magic robes, and* ARIEL.

PROSPERO Now does my project gather to a head:[1]
My charms crack not, my spirits obey, and time
Goes upright with his carriage.[2] How's the day?

ARIEL On the sixth hour; at which time, my lord,
You said our work should cease.

7. Baldness caused either through tropical disease or by sailors who customarily shaved the heads of passengers when they crossed the line of the equator for the first time. "Under the [waist]line" (line 234) could also be an allusion to baldness from syphilis.
8. An idiomatic expression for "properly, by the rules"—literally, "by plumb line and carpenter's level"; also, punning on "lime." *Do, do*: an expression of approval.
9. Thrust of wit (fencing term).
1. Be "lime-fingered," sticky-fingered (alluding to birdlime, a gluey substance used to catch birds).
2. Barnacle geese, also known as "tree geese" and supposed to begin life as barnacle shells.
3. Spotted with bruises from pinches. *agèd cramps:* the convulsions of old age.
4. Both terms are synonymous with "leopard"; the second is from Jeremiah 13:23: "May a man of Ind change his skin, and the cat of the mountain her spots?" (Bishops' Bible).

5.1
1. Draw to its fulfillment. "Project" suggests an alchemical projection or "experiment."
2. Because his carriage, or burden, is now light.

PROSPERO I did say so
When first I raised the tempest. Say, my spirit,
How fares the King and 's° followers? *and his*
ARIEL Confined together
In the same fashion as you gave in charge,
Just as you left them; all prisoners, sir,
In the line-grove which weather-fends[3] your cell:
They cannot budge till your release.° The King, *you release them*
His brother, and yours abide all three distracted,° *out of their wits*
And the remainder mourning over them,
Brimful of sorrow and dismay; but chiefly
Him that you termed, sir, the good old Lord Gonzalo:
His tears runs down his beard like winter's drops
From eaves of reeds.° Your charm so strongly works 'em *thatched roofs*
That if you now beheld them, your affections° *feelings*
Would become tender.
PROSPERO Dost thou think so, spirit?
ARIEL Mine would, sir, were I human.
PROSPERO And mine shall.
Hast thou, which art but air, a touch,° a feeling *sense*
Of their afflictions, and shall not myself—
One of their kind, that relish all as sharply
Passion as they[4]—be kindlier[5] moved than thou art?
Though with their high° wrongs I am struck to th' quick, *great*
Yet with my nobler reason 'gainst my fury
Do I take part.° The rarer action is *side*
In virtue than in vengeance. They being penitent,
The sole drift of my purpose doth extend
Not a frown further. Go, release them, Ariel.
My charms I'll break, their senses I'll restore,
And they shall be themselves.
ARIEL I'll fetch them, sir. *Exit.*
[PROSPERO *makes a circle on the stage.*][6]
PROSPERO[7] Ye elves of hills, brooks, standing lakes, and groves,
And ye that on the sands with printless foot
Do chase the ebbing Neptune, and do fly him
When he comes back; you demi-puppets[8] that
By moonshine do the green sour ringlets[9] make,
Whereof the ewe not bites; and you, whose pastime
Is to make midnight°-mushrooms, that rejoice *springing up overnight*
To hear the solemn curfew;[1] by whose aid—
Weak masters[2] though ye be—I have bedimmed
The noontide sun, called forth the mutinous winds,
And twixt the green sea and the azured vault° *the sky*
Set roaring war; to the dread rattling thunder

3. Which protects from the weather.
4. *that . . . they*: who feel as much strong emotion as they do.
5. More tenderly; more naturally.
6. The original text does not indicate when the circle is drawn. Other possibilities are at the beginning of the scene or before the entry at line 57.
7. Prospero's speech closely follows Ovid's *Metamorphoses* 7.265–77, in Arthur Golding's translation (1567); the speaker in Ovid is the sorceress Medea, who uses her witchcraft to vengeful ends.
8. Puppets; elves; quasi puppets.
9. Fairy rings: distinctive circles of grass supposed to be caused by dancing fairies but actually caused by mushrooms.
1. The bell rung at nightfall, indicating the time when spirits are abroad.
2. Ineffectual when acting independently; without supernatural power; subordinate spirits.

Have I given fire, and rifted° Jove's stout oak *split*
With his own bolt;° the strong-based promontory *lightning bolt*
Have I made shake, and by the spurs° plucked up *roots*
The pine and cedar. Graves at my command
Have waked their sleepers, oped, and let 'em forth
By my so potent art. But this rough[3] magic
I here abjure; and when I have required° *summoned*
Some heavenly music—which even now I do—
To work mine end upon their senses that° *the senses of whom*
This airy[4] charm is for, I'll break my staff,
Bury it certain° fathoms in the earth, *several*
And deeper than did ever plummet sound
I'll drown my book.

*Solemn music.*
*Here enters* ARIEL *before; then* ALONSO *with a frantic gesture, attended by* GONZALO; SEBASTIAN *and* ANTONIO *in like manner, attended by* ADRIAN *and* FRANCISCO. *They all enter the circle which* PROSPERO *had made, and there stand charmed; which* PROSPERO *observing, speaks.*[5]

A solemn air° and° the best comforter *song / which is*
To an unsettled fancy° cure thy brains, *imagination*
Now useless, boiled within thy skull. There stand,
For you are spell-stopped.
Holy Gonzalo, honorable man,
Mine eyes, e'en sociable° to the show° of thine, *sympathetic / appearance*
Fall fellowly drops. [*aside*] The charm dissolves apace
And, as the morning steals upon the night,
Melting the darkness, so their rising senses
Begin to chase the ignorant fumes[6] that mantle° *envelop*
Their clearer° reason. —O good Gonzalo, *growing clearer*
My true preserver and a loyal sir° *gentleman*
To him thou follow'st, I will pay° thy graces *requite*
Home° both in word and deed. Most cruelly *Fully*
Didst thou, Alonso, use me and my daughter.
Thy brother was a furtherer° in the act: *an accomplice*
Thou art pinched° for't now, Sebastian. Flesh and blood, *tortured; afflicted*
You, brother mine, that entertained ambition,
Expelled remorse and nature,[7] whom° with Sebastian— *who*
Whose inward pinches therefore are most strong—
Would here have killed your king, I do forgive thee,
Unnatural though thou art. [*aside*] Their understanding
Begins to swell,° and the approaching tide *(as does a tide)*
Will shortly fill the reasonable shore
That now lies foul and muddy. Not° one of them *There is not*
That yet looks on me or would know me. —Ariel,
Fetch me the hat and rapier[8] in my cell.
[ARIEL *exits and returns.*]
I will discase° me and myself present *undress*

3. Violent; discordant; crudely approximate.
4. Wrought by spirits of the air.
5. Prospero remains invisible and inaudible to Alonso and his party until he greets Alonso at line 106.
6. Fogs of ignorance; the image is of the sun ("rising senses") dissipating morning mist.
7. Pity and brotherly affection.
8. Elements of normal aristocratic dress.

As I was sometime Milan.[9] Quickly, spirit!
Thou shalt ere long be free.

ARIEL *sings and helps to attire him.*

ARIEL
Where the bee sucks, there suck I;
In a cowslip's bell I lie;
There I couch when owls do cry;
On the bat's back I do fly
After summer merrily.
Merrily, merrily shall I live now,
Under the blossom that hangs on the bough.

PROSPERO Why, that's my dainty Ariel! I shall miss
Thee, but yet thou shalt have freedom.—So, so, so.[1]
To the King's ship, invisible as thou art;
There shalt thou find the mariners asleep
Under the hatches. The Master and the Boatswain
Being awake, enforce them to this place,
And presently,° I prithee. *immediately*

ARIEL I drink the air before me and return
Or ere° your pulse twice beat. *Exit.* *Before*

GONZALO All torment, trouble, wonder, and amazement° *bewilderment*
Inhabits here. Some heavenly power guide us
Out of this fearful° country! *fearsome*

PROSPERO Behold, sir King,
The wrongèd Duke of Milan, Prospero.
For more assurance that a living prince
Does now speak to thee, I embrace thy body
And to thee and thy company I bid
A hearty welcome.

ALONSO Whe'er° thou beest he or no, *Whether*
Or some enchanted trifle[2] to abuse° me— *delude; maltreat*
As late I have been—I not know. Thy pulse
Beats as of flesh and blood; and since I saw thee,
Th'affliction of my mind amends, with which,
I fear, a madness held me. This must crave°— *requires, as explanation*
An if this be at all[3]—a most strange story.
Thy dukedom[4] I resign and do entreat
Thou pardon me my wrongs. But how should Prospero
Be living, and be here?

PROSPERO [*to* GONZALO] First, noble friend,
Let me embrace thine age,° whose honor cannot *old body*
Be measured or confined.

GONZALO Whether this be
Or be not, I'll not swear.

PROSPERO You do yet taste
Some subtleties[5] o'th' isle, that will not let you
Believe things certain. Welcome, my friends all.
[*aside to* SEBASTIAN *and* ANTONIO] But you, my brace° of *pair*
lords, were I so minded

9. Formerly, when Duke of Milan.
1. Prospero arranges his attire approvingly.
2. With a suggestion of the old sense of "trifle" as "deception."
3. If this is really happening.
4. Alonso's rights of homage and tribute from it.
5. *You . . . subtleties:* You still experience some of the illusions. "Subtleties" were also sweet confections shaped like castles, temples, beasts, allegorical figures, and the like, and arranged like a pageant.

I here could pluck his highness' frown upon you
And justify° you traitors. At this time — *prove*
I will tell no tales.

SEBASTIAN [*to* ANTONIO] The devil speaks in him!

PROSPERO No.
[*to* ANTONIO] For you, most wicked sir, whom to call brother
Would even infect my mouth, I do forgive
Thy rankest fault—all of them—and require
My dukedom of thee, which perforce° I know — *necessarily*
Thou must restore.

ALONSO If thou beest Prospero,
Give us particulars of thy preservation;
How thou hast met us here, whom three hours since
Were wrecked upon this shore, where I have lost—
How sharp the point of this remembrance is—
My dear son Ferdinand.

PROSPERO I am woe° for't, sir. — *I grieve*

ALONSO Irreparable is the loss, and patience
Says it is past her cure.

PROSPERO I rather think
You have not sought her help, of° whose soft grace° — *by / mercy*
For the like loss I have her sovereign aid
And rest myself content.

ALONSO You the like loss?

PROSPERO As great to me as late;° and supportable — *recent*
To make the dear loss[6] have I means much weaker
Than you may call to comfort you, for I
Have lost my daughter.[7]

ALONSO A daughter?
O heavens, that they were living both in Naples,
The King and Queen there! That they were, I wish
Myself were mudded in that oozy bed
Where my son lies. When did you lose your daughter?

PROSPERO In this last tempest. I perceive these lords
At this encounter do so much admire° — *wonder*
That they devour their reason[8] and scarce think
Their eyes do offices of truth,° their words — *function accurately*
Are natural breath. But, howsoe'er you have
Been jostled from your senses, know for certain
That I am Prospero, and that very duke
Which was thrust forth of Milan, who most strangely
Upon this shore where you were wrecked, was landed
To be the lord on't. No more yet of this,
For 'tis a chronicle of day by day,
Not a relation for a breakfast, nor
Befitting this first meeting. Welcome, sir;
This cell's my court. Here have I few attendants
And subjects none abroad.[9] Pray you look in.
My dukedom since you have given me again,

6. *supportable . . . loss:* in order to make the heartfelt loss bearable.

7. Prospero apparently means that Alonso still has a child, his daughter Claribel, to comfort him.

8. "Reason" has the additional sense of "discourse"; hence, the phrase is an extension of "swallow their words."

9. Elsewhere about the island; beyond the cell.

I will requite you with as good a thing;
At least bring forth a wonder to content ye
As much as me my dukedom.

*Here* PROSPERO *discovers*[1] FERDINAND *and* MIRANDA *playing at chess.*

MIRANDA Sweet lord, you play me false.° — *trick me*

FERDINAND No, my dearest love,
I would not for the world.

MIRANDA Yes, for a score of kingdoms you should wrangle,
And I would call it fair play.[2]

ALONSO If this prove
A vision of the island, one dear son
Shall I twice lose.

SEBASTIAN A most high miracle!

FERDINAND Though the seas threaten, they are merciful:
I have cursed them without cause.

[FERDINAND *kneels.*]

ALONSO Now all the blessings
Of a glad father compass thee about!° — *surround you*
Arise, and say how thou cam'st here.

MIRANDA Oh, wonder!
How many goodly creatures are there here!
How beauteous mankind is! Oh, brave new world
That has such people in't!

PROSPERO 'Tis new to thee.

ALONSO [*to* FERDINAND] What is this maid with whom thou wast at play?
Your eld'st° acquaintance cannot be three hours. — *longest*
Is she the goddess that hath severed us
And brought us thus together?

FERDINAND Sir, she is mortal;
But by immortal Providence she's mine.
I chose her when I could not ask my father
For his advice, nor thought I had one. She
Is daughter to this famous Duke of Milan—
Of whom so often I have heard renown
But never saw before—of whom I have
Received a second life; and second father
This lady makes him to me.

ALONSO I am hers.[3]
But oh, how oddly will it sound that I
Must ask my child° forgiveness! — *(Miranda)*

PROSPERO There, sir, stop.
Let us not burden our remembrances with
A heaviness° that's gone. — *sorrow*

GONZALO I have inly wept,
Or should have spoke ere this. Look down, you gods,
And on this couple drop a blessèd crown.
For it is you that have chalked forth° the way — *marked out*
Which brought us hither.

1. Reveals by drawing back a curtain hanging in front of the discovery space.
2. *for . . . play*: you could quarrel for twenty kingdoms, and I would still call it fair play.
3. I will be her second father: Alonso's assent to the betrothal.

ALONSO I say "Amen," Gonzalo.
GONZALO Was Milan° thrust from Milan that his issue — *the Duke of Milan*
Should become kings of Naples? Oh, rejoice
Beyond a common joy and set it down
With gold on lasting pillars:[4] in one voyage
Did Claribel her husband find at Tunis,
And Ferdinand her brother found a wife
Where he himself was lost; Prospero his dukedom
In a poor isle; and all of us ourselves
When no man was his own.[5]
ALONSO [*to* FERDINAND *and* MIRANDA] Give me your hands.
Let grief and sorrow still° embrace his heart — *always*
That° doth not wish you joy. — *Who*
GONZALO Be it so. Amen.

*Enter* ARIEL, *with the* MASTER *and* BOATSWAIN *amazedly following.*

Oh, look, sir, look, sir: here is more of us.
I prophesied if a gallows were on land
This fellow could not drown. [*to* BOATSWAIN] Now, blasphemy,° — *blasphemer*
That swear'st grace o'erboard, not an oath on shore?
Hast thou no mouth by land? What is the news?
BOATSWAIN The best news is that we have safely found
Our king and company; the next, our ship,
Which but three glasses° since we gave out° split, — *hourglasses / declared*
Is tight and yare[6] and bravely rigged as when
We first put out to sea.
ARIEL [*to* PROSPERO] Sir, all this service
Have I done since I went.
PROSPERO [*to* ARIEL] My tricksy° spirit! — *capricious; neat*
ALONSO These are not natural events; they strengthen° — *increase*
From strange to stranger. Say, how came you hither?
BOATSWAIN If I did think, sir, I were well awake,
I'd strive to tell you. We were dead of° sleep — *with*
And—how we know not—all clapped° under hatches, — *shut up*
Where but even now with strange and several° noises — *various*
Of roaring, shrieking, howling, jingling chains,
And more diversity of sounds, all horrible,
We were awaked; straightway at liberty,
Where we, in all our trim, freshly beheld
Our royal, good, and gallant ship, our Master
Cap'ring to eye° her. On° a trice, so please you, — *Dancing to see / In*
Even in a dream were we divided from them
And were brought moping° hither. — *dazed*
ARIEL [*to* PROSPERO] Was't well done?
PROSPERO [*to* ARIEL] Bravely, my diligence. Thou shalt be free.
ALONSO This is as strange a maze as e'er men trod,
And there is in this business more than nature
Was ever conduct° of. Some oracle — *conductor*
Must rectify our knowledge.
PROSPERO Sir, my liege,

4. Suggesting, perhaps, the triumphal arches commissioned to celebrate notable occasions.
5. When we all had lost our senses.
6. Is sound and ready to sail.

Do not infest° your mind with beating on[7]   *trouble*
The strangeness of this business. At picked leisure,
Which shall be shortly, single° I'll resolve you—   *in private*
Which to you shall seem probable°—of every   *plausible*
These happened accidents.° Till when, be cheerful   *occurrences*
And think of each thing well. [*to* ARIEL] Come hither, spirit.
Set Caliban and his companions free:
Untie the spell. [*Exit* ARIEL.]
[*to* ALONSO] How fares my gracious sir?
There are yet missing of your company
Some few odd lads that you remember not.

*Enter* ARIEL, *driving in* CALIBAN, STEFANO, *and* TRINCULO *in their stolen apparel.*

STEFANO Every man shift for all the rest, and let no man take care for himself;[8] for all is but fortune. *Coraggio*, bully monster,[9] *coraggio*!

TRINCULO If these° be true spies which I wear in my head, here's a goodly sight!   *these eyes*

CALIBAN O Setebos, these be brave spirits indeed!
How fine° my master is! I am afraid   *splendidly dressed*
He will chastise me.

SEBASTIAN Ha, ha! What things are these, my lord Antonio?
Will money buy 'em?

ANTONIO Very like.° One of them   *likely*
Is a plain° fish, and no doubt marketable.   *mere*

PROSPERO Mark but the badges[1] of these men, my lords;
Then say if they° be true. This misshapen knave,   *(the men); (the badges)*
His mother was a witch, and one so strong
That could control the moon, make flows and ebbs,
And deal in her command without her power.[2]
These three have robbed me, and this demi-devil[3]—
For he's a bastard one—had plotted with them
To take my life. Two of these fellows you
Must know and own;[4] this thing of darkness I
Acknowledge mine.

CALIBAN I shall be pinched to death.

ALONSO Is not this Stefano, my drunken butler?

SEBASTIAN He is drunk now. Where had he wine?

ALONSO And Trinculo is reeling-ripe.° Where should they   *drunk*
Find this grand liquor that hath gilded[5] 'em?
How cam'st thou in this pickle?[6]

TRINCULO I have been in such a pickle since I saw you last that I fear me will never out of my bones: I shall not fear flyblowing.[7]

SEBASTIAN Why, how now, Stefano?

STEFANO Oh, touch me not! I am not Stefano, but a cramp.

PROSPERO You'd be king o'the isle, sirrah?

7. With repeatedly worrying about.
8. Stefano drunkenly confuses the saying "Every man for himself."
9. Gallant monster. *Coraggio:* "Take courage" (Italian).
1. Livery. Servants often wore their master's emblem, but Prospero probably refers to the stolen apparel.
2. And wield her (the moon's) power without her authority, or beyond the reach of her might.
3. Being the offspring of Sycorax and the devil.
4. And acknowledge to be yours.
5. Probably alluding to the alchemical elixir ("liquor") known as *aurum potabile* (drinkable gold); hence, "gilded" (flushed).
6. Sorry plight; Trinculo takes up the literal sense of "preserving liquid," recalling both his drunkenness and his drenching in the lake.
7. Not fear being infested with flies, since he has been "pickled" (preserved).

STEFANO I should have been a sore° one then. — *an inept; severe; pained*
ALONSO [*indicating* CALIBAN] This is a strange thing as e'er
I looked on.
PROSPERO He is as disproportioned in his manners[8]
As in his shape. Go, sirrah, to my cell;
Take with you your companions. As you look
To have my pardon, trim° it handsomely. — *tidy; decorate*
CALIBAN Ay, that I will; and I'll be wise hereafter
And seek for grace. What a thrice-double ass
Was I to take this drunkard for a god
And worship this dull fool!
PROSPERO Go to, away.
ALONSO Hence, and bestow your luggage where you found it.
SEBASTIAN Or stole it rather.
[*Exeunt* CALIBAN, STEFANO, *and* TRINCULO.]
PROSPERO Sir, I invite your highness and your train
To my poor cell, where you shall take your rest
For this one night; which—part of it°—I'll waste° — *part of which / spend*
With such discourse as, I not doubt, shall make it
Go quick away: the story of my life
And the particular accidents° gone by — *events*
Since I came to this isle. And in the morn
I'll bring you to your ship, and so to Naples,
Where I have hope to see the nuptial
Of these our dear-belovèd solemnized,
And thence retire me to my Milan, where
Every third thought shall be my grave.
ALONSO I long
To hear the story of your life, which must
Take° the ear strangely. — *Captivate*
PROSPERO I'll deliver° all, — *relate*
And promise you calm seas, auspicious gales,
And sail so expeditious that shall° catch — *it will*
Your royal fleet far off. —My Ariel, chick,
That is thy charge. Then to the elements
Be free, and fare thou well. —Please you draw near.[9]
*Exeunt all* [*except* PROSPERO].[1]

## Epilogue

*Spoken by* PROSPERO.
Now my charms are all o'erthrown,
And what strength I have's mine own,
Which is most faint. Now 'tis true
I must be here confined by you,
Or sent to Naples. Let me not,
Since I have my dukedom got
And pardoned the deceiver, dwell
In this bare island° by your spell, — *(the stage)*

8. Behavior; moral character.
9. PERFORMANCE COMMENT Though most productions of *The Tempest* end happily, many questions remain unresolved. Are Antonio and Prospero truly reconciled, or do they remain suspicious of each other? What is Prospero's attitude toward abjuring his magical powers and leaving the island? Is Caliban left behind, content to be his own king, or is he miserable at the prospect of abandonment? Directors often explore such questions to suggest how the drama will continue when the play is done. For more, see Digital Edition PC 4.
1. The general exeunt is through Prospero's cell; Ariel departs in another direction.

But release me from my bands° — *fetters*
With the help of your good hands.° — *(applause)*
Gentle breath° of yours my sails — *Favorable comment*
Must fill or else my project fails,
Which was to please. Now I want° — *lack*
Spirits to enforce, art to enchant;
And my ending[1] is despair,
Unless I be relieved by prayer,
Which pierces so that it assaults
Mercy itself and frees all faults.
As you from crimes would pardoned be,
Let your indulgence[2] set me free. [*Exit.*]

**Epilogue**
1. Punning on the sense "death."
2. Approval; appeasement; remission for sin.

# Cardenio

Many readers have interpreted the end of *The Tempest* (1610–11), when the magician Prospero breaks his magic staff and drowns his book, as Shakespeare's own farewell to the theater. But in fact in the years that followed he collaborated on at least three plays with John Fletcher, the playwright Shakespeare seems to have chosen to succeed him as the principal dramatist of his company, the King's Men. One of these collaborations, *Henry VIII*, was included in the First Folio of 1623; another, *The Two Noble Kinsmen*, appeared in quarto in 1624. A third play left only a shadowy trace of its existence: two documents from the King's Treasurer's accounts for May and June 1613 record payments to John Heminges, then leader of the King's Men, for the presentation at court of a play called *Cardenna* or *Cardenno*. Heminges did not include this play in the First Folio he helped to edit, but many years later, on September 9, 1653, the London publisher Humphrey Moseley entered in the Stationers' Register a batch of plays including "The History of Cardenio, by Mr Fletcher and Shakespeare." For whatever reason, this play was either not printed at all or has been lost. *Cardenio,* then, is a ghost that has haunted those who long to read anything to which Shakespeare set his hand.

It is possible at least to conjure up the likely subject of the missing play. Cardenio is a character in Part One of Cervantes' *Don Quixote*. Cervantes' masterpiece, first published in Spanish in 1605, was translated into English remarkably quickly by the Dublin-born Catholic Thomas Shelton and, after some delay, was printed in London in 1612. Fletcher and Shakespeare must have read this translation almost immediately and set to work. Surprisingly, to Cervantes' modern readers, they evidently did not choose to dramatize the mad knight and his squire, but instead seized upon the story of a young man, Cardenio, whose false friend attempts to steal away the woman he loves.

Cardenio and Luscinda grow up together and fall in love. Before they can secure their fathers' consent to their marriage, Cardenio is compelled to leave home to serve in the court of a powerful nobleman with whose son, Don Fernando, he becomes close friends. Don Fernando, who has seduced the humbly born Dorotea with promises of marriage, now regrets his promise and, to escape Dorotea, goes home with Cardenio. There the irresponsible nobleman promptly falls in love with Luscinda. Having sent his friend Cardenio away on a pretext, Fernando asks Luscinda's parents for their daughter's hand, and, despite her protests, her parents, who are delighted by the socially advantageous match, agree. Luscinda desperately writes to Cardenio, who rushes home, arriving only in time to witness the marriage ceremony from behind a curtain. When he sees his beloved give her hand to the treacherous Fernando, Cardenio rushes away in despair. What he does not see then is that at the decisive moment, Luscinda swoons. A note is discovered in her bodice, declaring her intention to stab herself, whereupon Fernando storms off in a rage. Luscinda flees to a convent.

Unaware of these developments, Cardenio turns his back on civilization and, like Lear on the heath, wanders as a lunatic in the Sierra Morena. Meanwhile, learning that Fernando's marriage to Luscinda had been voided, the seduced and abandoned Dorotea decides (like Julia in *Two Gentlemen of Verona*) to go in search of him. Like Julia and any number of other Shakespearean heroines, she dresses herself as a boy, but the expedient does not in Dorotea's case provide safety. Fighting off an attempted rape, she pushes her assailant off a cliff. Then she too flees to the Sierra Morena.

Six months pass. Fernando discovers Luscinda in the convent and abducts her. Cardenio and Dorotea meet in the mountains; Cardenio's hopes (and his sanity) revive when Dorotea tells him that in her note Luscinda had declared that she could not marry Fernando since she was already pledged to Cardenio. They arrive with others at an inn, where a priest discovers a story among the innkeeper's possessions and proceeds to read it to the company. The story involves the newlywed Anselmo, who asks his best friend, Lothario, to attempt to seduce his wife in order to test her virtue. The wife and the friend fall in love and deceive the husband, and the love tangle ends for all in despair and death. In the wake of this storytelling interlude, Fernando and the abducted Luscinda arrive by chance at the same inn. When Dorotea reproaches Fernando for his treatment of her, he is ashamed and agrees to marry her, allowing Cardenio to have Luscinda. There is general rejoicing.

This characteristic Renaissance tragicomedy of male friendship and sexual betrayal was the kind of story that had gripped Shakespeare's imagination throughout his career, from the early *Two Gentlemen of Verona* to the late *Two Noble Kinsmen*. If this was the story that Shakespeare and Fletcher plucked from *Don Quixote*, it is not one that was immediately ripe for the plucking. The English playwrights had to disentangle it from the complex mesh in which Cervantes had interwoven it with the adventures of his chivalry-obsessed knight. The *Cardenio* plot only emerges in fits and starts, in the interstices of Quixote's encounters after he has arrived in the Sierra Morena and has decided to go mad for the love of Dulcinea. Nothing is delivered in straightforward narrative sequence, and the two English collaborators must have laughed or groaned as they tried to tease a coherent narrative out of Cervantes' deliberately mad tangle. The only hard evidence from the period that they succeeded in doing so is the title of the lost play: not *Don Quixote* but *Cardenio*.

No more information about this play survives from the seventeenth century, but in 1728 the talented but unreliable playwright, entrepreneur, and editor Lewis Theobald published a play based on the story of Cardenio called *Double Falsehood, or The Distrest Lovers,* which he claimed to have "revised and adapted" from one "written originally by W. Shakespeare." Theobald's play had been successfully produced at Drury Lane on December 13, 1727, and was repeatedly performed thereafter.

Theobald claimed to own several manuscripts of an original play by Shakespeare, and remarked that some of his contemporaries thought the style was Fletcher's, not Shakespeare's. When he himself came to edit Shakespeare's plays he did not include either *Double Falsehood* or the play on which he claimed to have based it; he simply edited the plays of the First Folio, not adding either *Pericles* or *The Two Noble Kinsmen*, though he believed they were partly by Shakespeare. And what of the documents Theobald claims to have found that led back to whatever it was that Shakespeare and Fletcher had written? In 1770 a newspaper stated that "the original manuscript" was "treasured up in the Museum of Covent Garden Playhouse"; fire destroyed the theater, including its library, in 1808.

Stephen Greenblatt

# The Two Noble Kinsmen

When Prospero proclaims near the end of *The Tempest* (1611), "But this rough magic / I here abjure" (5.1.50–51), audiences often think they are hearing Shakespeare's farewell to the theater. But the final passage Shakespeare wrote for the stage probably comes at the conclusion of *The Two Noble Kinsmen* (1613–14). Theseus, Duke of Athens, the play's highest-ranking character, attempts to grasp the paradoxical twists of fate he has witnessed:

Never Fortune
Did play a subtler game. The conquered triumphs;
The victor has the loss. Yet in the passage
The gods have been most equal. . . .
. . . . . . . . . . . . . . . . . . . . . . . . . . . . . . . . . . . . . . . . .
. . . Let us be thankful
For that which is, and with you [the gods] leave dispute
That are above our question.
(5.4.112–15, 134–36)

It is tempting to interpret Theseus's resigned disillusionment as Shakespeare's last word on things. The play's message is not easy to determine, however. Theseus's confidence in divine justice ("The gods have been most equal") underestimates the grimness that accompanies the pathos of the play. Chivalric military and sexual norms lend nobility to the action, but also generate the misery to which Theseus attempts to respond.

The problem of the work's tone is related to the question of authorship. Shakespeare wrote *The Two Noble Kinsmen* with John Fletcher (1579–1625), a younger contemporary who succeeded him as the leading dramatist of Shakespeare's acting company, the King's Men. Several of Shakespeare's very early and very late plays may have involved collaboration. In his final years, he worked with Fletcher on the lost *Cardenio* (1612–13; probably based on an episode from Part 1 of Cervantes' *Don Quixote*, 1605; translated 1612), on *Henry VIII* (1613), and on *The Two Noble Kinsmen*. For this last play, Shakespeare probably wrote most of the first and last acts plus a little more, while his colleague composed the rest. This division suggests that Shakespeare was the senior partner. The two dramatists differ in style, presentation, and outlook. The rhetorically knotty, ritualistic, near-tragic grandeur in Shakespeare's share contrasts with the syntactically simpler, dynamic, near-absurd deflation in Fletcher's. The play as a whole is, therefore, essentially neither Shakespearean nor Fletcherian. A product of collaboration, it is marked by both unity and dissonance.

*The Two Noble Kinsmen* is transitional between the more popular theater of Shakespeare's time and the more elite drama of Fletcher's. Typical in many ways of Shakespeare's last phase, it may be compared to other tragicomic romances written separately by Shakespeare and Fletcher in the preceding six or seven years. Among Shakespeare's leading works in this genre—*Pericles, The Winter's Tale, Cymbeline,* and *The Tempest*—one finds parallels to *The Two Noble Kinsmen*'s medieval source, pseudo-historical classical setting, spectacle and ceremony, innocence in the midst of corruption, striving for self-mastery, and transcendence of self-interest. Further similarities include insistence on death as a price of the survivors' happiness, successful supplication to the gods for aid, and consequent sense of a metaphysical presence that orders events in a manner beyond human control. Although limited to dry land, the work replicates even the trademark maritime imagery of Shakespearean romance, with its focus on peril: the dying Arcite "such a vessel 'tis that floats but for / The surge that next approaches" (5.4.83–84).

Yet *The Two Noble Kinsmen* feels different from other Shakespearean plays of the time. As the Prologue explains, "Chaucer—of all admired—the story gives" (line 13). The main plot is taken—with greater freedom by Shakespeare than by Fletcher—from *The Knight's Tale,* which immediately follows the General Prologue in *The Canterbury Tales* (late fourteenth century). Its subject is the mortal rivalry between Palamon and Arcite (two syllables, accented on the first), the two cousins referred to in the title, for the hand of Emilia. But the play's atypicality stems only partly from its resulting chivalric ethos and acts of courtesy, both emphasized more than in Chaucer. *The Two Noble Kinsmen* is set apart by the unusually somber resolution to its impossible dilemmas. Despite Theseus's assertions, the gods' behavior does not restore confidence in a benevolent Providence. Mars, whose intercession Arcite requests, and Venus, to whom Palamon prays, emblematize the chaos of human affairs. The play is also structurally distinctive. Shakespearean romance reveals the passage from suffering to serenity, the redemption of the older generation by the younger (and particularly by the virtuous daughter). But Shakespeare and Fletcher's play ignores the restorative workings of time. All relationships occur within a single generation, the young woman (Emilia) incites violence rather than reconciliation, and the work begins with a marriage and funeral—only to end the same way. This lack of movement may be connected to the play's well-defined five-act structure, a consequence of performance at the Blackfriars, an elite indoor theater that Shakespeare's company began using late in his career.

For these reasons, *The Two Noble Kinsmen* is sometimes viewed as an anti-romance. As such, it bears comparison both to Shakespeare's other collaborations with Fletcher and to several of Shakespeare's earlier plays, which are echoed particularly in Fletcher's scenes. Palamon and Arcite's initial resignation in prison recalls *Richard II;* their conflict over Emilia, *The Two Gentlemen of Verona;* Emilia's comparison of pictures, *Hamlet.* When Arcite asks for a sign before his decisive battle with Palamon, he correctly takes Mars's thunder as a promise of victory. But this reassurance is as duplicitous as the guarantee that "none of woman born / Shall harm Macbeth" (*Macbeth* 4.1.79–80), with the important difference that Macbeth is a mass murderer, whereas Arcite merely desires a woman his cousin saw first. The divine poetic justice often thought to be operating, however deviously, in *Macbeth* seems like a dirty trick in *The Two Noble Kinsmen.*

The subplot, mainly the work of Fletcher, dramatizes the unrequited love of the Jailer's Daughter for Palamon and has no known source. It borrows the morris dance before Theseus and Hippolyta in 3.5 not from Shakespeare but from a masque (an aristocratic theatrical event emphasizing song, dance, and spectacle) that Francis Beaumont composed for court performance in February 1613. (The morris dance itself is a rural folk form often performed on May Day by dancers in outlandish costumes who employ stock characters to partly mime traditional stories.) And the pastoral scenes of the second and third acts owe a more general debt to contemporary aristocratic dramatic forms. Otherwise, the Shakespearean legacy is pronounced. The Daughter's fall into madness when ignored by Palamon is modeled on Ophelia's in *Hamlet,* complete with attempted suicide. Her "Willow Song" (4.1.79–80) was earlier sung by Desdemona in *Othello.* The Doctor who prescribes her cure previously ministered to King Lear and, more unsuccessfully, to Lady Macbeth. When the Daughter joins the people whom "ruder tongues distinguish 'villager'" (3.5.107) in the morris dance, the allusion is to another play indebted to *The Knight's Tale:* in *A Midsummer Night's Dream,* "rude mechanicals" (artisans, 3.2.9) also perform before Theseus and Hippolyta at their wedding, and mismatched, frustrated lovers wander through the forest.

But *The Two Noble Kinsmen* is *A Midsummer Night's Dream* with a difference. *The Winter's Tale* might be understood as the tragic jealousy of *Othello* lightened by the pastoral experience of a romantic comedy, *As You Like It*. In *The Two Noble Kinsmen,* the comic tone of *A Midsummer Night's Dream* is darkened by the intervening experience of *Troilus and Cressida,* which also draws on Chaucer for a chivalric sensuality leading to violence and an indifference to the desires of the idealized woman. Indeed, Theseus's final words, quoted earlier, may recall Gloucester's metaphysical despair in *King Lear:*

> As flies to wanton boys are we to th' gods:
> They kill us for their sport.
> (Folio, 4.1.38–39)

A geographical, legendary legacy underlies this outlook. Although almost all of the play is set in and around Athens, the darker influence of Thebes is immediately felt. In the opening episode, greatly expanded from the source, three widowed queens beg Theseus to aid them against Thebes, thus introducing the military dimension of chivalric conduct. Theseus yields to Hippolyta's and Emilia's entreaties to defer his own pleasure (marriage to Hippolyta) to help dowagers in distress. His intervention pits him against Palamon and Arcite, who fight for their home city despite hating its ruler. This sequence implicitly invokes Thebes's history of intrafamilial violence: Cadmus sows the soil with serpent's teeth, from which armed men grow; these men slaughter each other and, with Cadmus, the survivors found Thebes. Later, Oedipus unwittingly murders his father. As the play opens, his two sons have killed each other in a battle for the throne that has also widowed the three queens.

The two cousins, imprisoned following Theseus's victory over Thebes, repeat this history. When Theseus catches them fighting over Emilia, he orders their deaths, only to reverse course at Hippolyta's and Emilia's request. He orders a chivalric combat in which each cousin is aided by three knights and all members of the losing side are to be executed. This plan unnecessarily increases the expected death toll, beyond what is found in Chaucer. It is thwarted by Arcite's accidental death, a death hard to see as providential but undeniably less brutal than Theseus's strategy. Earlier, Palamon laments "Mars's so scorned altar" and yearns for war "[t]o get the soldier work, that peace might purge / For her repletion" (1.2.20, 23–24). Arcite echoes this notion of war as a virtuous means of purging the excesses of peace in a prayer to Mars, who

> heal'st with blood
> The earth when it is sick, and cur'st the world
> O'th' pleurisy of people.
> (5.1.64–66)

Yet *The Two Noble Kinsmen* finds in war and chivalric combat less a cure for society than a loss of life.

A compulsive sexuality bears considerable blame for the resulting havoc. As Theseus says, "being sensually subdued, / We lose our human title" (1.1.232–33). Arcite and especially Palamon are willing to kill and die over a woman whom they know only by appearance, and that only from afar. Arcite seems partly motivated by competitive emulation, by a desire to spite Palamon. He tells his cousin that when he sees Emilia, he will "pitch between her arms to anger thee" (2.2.220). The kinsmen claim Emilia while in prison for life and without her knowing they exist, much less expressing interest in them. Her feelings don't matter. From this perspective, chivalric combat seems an appropriate mechanism for determining which cousin deserves her. Their stance is validated through the intervention of Theseus. Emilia doesn't have the choice of rejecting them both. When asked to choose, she is unable to decide between "[t]wo such young handsome men" (4.2.3). She, too, looks only to looks.

Palamon's prayer to Venus reveals a simultaneous approval and denigration of sexuality:

I knew a man
Of eighty winters—this I told them—who
A lass of fourteen brided. 'Twas thy power
To put life into dust: the agèd cramp
Had screwed his square foot round;
The gout had knit his fingers into knots;
Torturing convulsions from his globy eyes
Had almost drawn their spheres, that what was life
In him seemed torture. This anatomy
Had by his young fair fere [mate] a boy, and I
Believed it was his, for she swore it was—
And who would not believe her?

(5.1.107–18)

The power of love is exalted through repellent description. The reference to the "boy" anticipates imagery of sexuality and reproduction at the conclusion—"consummation," "miscarry," "conceives," "deliver" (5.3.94, 101, 137, 138)—that is associated with loss. The account ends with an apparently rhetorical but actually open question that undermines both Venus's sovereignty and female chastity. The very celebration of love thus raises anxieties about women's fidelity.

Heterosexual desire is rendered even more unappealing by representation of what it destroys. This positive alternative is same-sex attachment, whether understood as Renaissance ideal male friendship, girlish intimacy, or homoerotic attraction. In *Much Ado About Nothing,* a romantic comedy, rejection of heterosexual bonding is an immature foible to be overcome. Here, the movement from same-sex innocence to heterosexual experience is figured primarily as loss—comically in the Prologue, with its comparison of "[n]ew plays and maidenheads" (line 1), more grimly thereafter. Although temperamentally no military Amazon, Emilia prefers virginity and the company of females to marriage. She tells Theseus that if he does not grant her petition, she will not "be so hardy / Ever to take a husband" (1.1.204–05). In her sexual joking with her Woman, she says that "Men are mad things" (2.2.126) and praises the rose above all other flowers because "It is the very emblem of a maid" (2.2.137). Even after coming to admire the cousins, she still prays to Diana either that the more loving and deserving win her or that she be allowed to continue a virgin "in thy band" (5.1.162). When Theseus tells her, "[I]f you can love, end this difference" by choosing one of the kinsmen, she evasively replies, "I cannot, sir; they are both too excellent" (3.6.278, 287).

The beginning of *The Knight's Tale*, from *The Workes of Our Ancient and Learned English Poet, Geffrey Chaucer* (1602 edition).

This stance is explained by Emilia's recollection of her intimacy with Flavina, who died when each was eleven. Her account of two girls who "[l]oved for [simply because] we did" (1.3.61) culminates in this exchange:

The imprisoned Palamon and Arcite gazing at Emilia in the garden below. From a French translation of about 1455 of Giovanni Boccaccio's *Teseida* (the source of Chaucer's *Knight's Tale*), by René of Anjou.

EMILIA . . . the true love tween maid and maid may be
More than in sex individual.
HIPPOLYTA You're out of breath,
And this high-speeded pace is but to say
That you shall never, like the maid Flavina,
Love any that's called man.
EMILIA I am sure I shall not.
(1.3.81–85)

Female friendship thus stands against the monarch's commitment to enforced marriage. The play never repudiates this position.

Palamon and Arcite do so, however, choosing to kill and die—and hence to ruin their most precious possession, their love for each other—out of desire for Emilia. This resolution of the Renaissance debate over the claims of love and friendship has a paradoxical effect. The collapse of the cousins' attachment, which is not stressed in Chaucer, only highlights its value. Though they regret that life imprisonment precludes marriage and family, their thoughts quickly turn to each other. Arcite recommends "the enjoying of our griefs together" (2.2.60) and misogynistically notes the danger of freedom, which "might—like women— / Woo us to wander from" "the ways of honor" (lines 75–76, 73). "Were we at liberty, / A wife might part us lawfully," but in prison "[w]e are one another's wife, ever begetting / New births of love" (lines 88–89, 80–81).

But Palamon's first sight of Emilia undermines their resolution, though in surprising fashion. Talking to her Woman about the narcissus flower, Emilia reflects upon the myth of Narcissus, who fell in love with his own reflection in a pool and died pining for it: "That was a fair boy, certain, but a fool / To love himself. Were there not maids enough?" (2.2.120–21). The connection between Palamon and Narcissus is made explicit when Emilia remarks that Palamon shows

not a smile.
Yet these that we count errors may become him:
Narcissus was a sad boy, but a heavenly.
(4.2.30–32)

Palamon's suggested autoeroticism and preference for males over females is anticipated in Emilia's homosexual description of Arcite:

Just such another wanton Ganymede
Set Jove afire with, and enforced the god
Snatch up the goodly boy and set him by him. . . .
(4.2.15–17)

Similarly, as the cousins prepare to battle each other, Arcite admiringly remarks, "Defy me in these fair terms, and you show / More than a mistress to me" (3.6.25–26). And when Arcite is released from prison, Palamon imagines what would happen if the roles were reversed:

Were I at liberty, I would do things
Of such a virtuous greatness that this lady,
This blushing virgin, should take manhood to her
And seek to ravish me.
(2.2.259–62)

Even the thought of the woman he loves becomes a fantasy of homosexual rape.

If the play offers a balance between same-sex and other-sex bonding, it is in Theseus, whose friendship with Pirithous coexists with his impending marriage to Hippolyta. As noted earlier, however, Theseus's conduct is open to question. It is also suggested that marriage to Hippolyta will never measure up to friendship with Pirithous. Most important, the catastrophic experience of Emilia and the kinsmen outweighs Theseus's success with potentially antagonistic emotional and sexual attachments. Nonetheless, Theseus may be an idealized image of King James I, who combined marriage with homosexual behavior. In this interpretation, Arcite's death corresponds to that of James's oldest son, Prince Henry, in the fall of 1612. The concluding, bittersweet union of Emilia with Palamon parallels the marriage soon after of James's daughter Elizabeth with the Elector Palatine. The probable 1619–20 and 1625–26 revivals, as well as the First Quarto in 1634, may also have resonated with royal life. Yet evidence for the play's direct connection to the court is uncertain. Its members might not have been flattered by the comparisons. Such issues could not matter to subsequent audiences, however. Except for an adaptation in the late 1660s, *The Two Noble Kinsmen* probably remained unstaged until 1928. Since then, effective performances have tended to eschew realism for ritual. But a 1979 production provided an interesting alternative by employing an all-male cast to emphasize the work's homoerotic motifs.

Beginning with the late seventeenth-century adaptation, however, the most successful feature of the staging has been the Jailer's Daughter, who, though isolated and powerless, often emerges as the central figure. This prominence is consistent with the unusual number and importance of female roles in the work. The Daughter's mid-play soliloquies (2.4, 2.6, 3.2, 3.4), three of them probably—the fourth perhaps—by Fletcher, are marked by exclamations, questions, and a consequent intimacy with the audience denied the other characters. The Daughter's special stage position thus helps win sympathy for her. In Shakespeare, this position is characteristically reserved for a lower-class male character, a clown or fool, with whom the groundlings might identify. Here, Shakespeare's interest in folk culture meshes with Fletcher's fascination with strong women.

The Daughter is at the heart of a subplot that interacts with, and reflects on, the main action. Following the morris dancers' frank sexual talk in 2.3, she delivers her first soliloquy and frees Palamon from prison, hoping he will satisfy her sexual desire for him. Though the genders are reversed, the situation is the same in the main plot: the person in love knows little of the beloved, who is largely oblivious of the lover.

A joust celebrating the marriage of Henry IV of England to Joan of Navarre. From the Beauchamp Pageant (1485–90).

Her illness is cured amorally. On the Doctor's advice, and over the objections of her father (the Jailer), the Wooer pretends to be Palamon and has intercourse with her. Tricked into losing a virginity she was not trying to preserve, "she's well restored / And to be married shortly" (5.4.27–28) to the man who actually is right for her (earlier, he foils her attempted suicide). This outcome makes sense in light of Renaissance medicine, which believed hysteria was caused by a wandering womb that intercourse returned to its proper place. One might conclude, however, that all women really need is sex and that any man will do.

The Daughter thinks she is marrying one man only to end up with another. Similarly, as Emilia settles into her fate, fate forces her to resettle her affections. Neither woman is given a choice—which is just as well, since neither is capable of making distinctions. The generic names in the subplot—Daughter, Jailer, Wooer, Doctor, Brother, Friends—highlight a lack of individuality while pointing toward a similar absence in the main plot. The critical effort to discriminate between Palamon and Arcite inadvertently reaffirms what it seeks to deny: that it takes an effort to tell the cousins apart.

Even the Daughter's madness is much less destructive and arguably no more deviant than Palamon and Arcite's behavior. Yet the two noble kinsmen are taken seriously in a way she is not. Because she is a lower-class woman, she cannot expect her feelings to be reciprocated, even though she does more for Palamon than either cousin does for Emilia. It is unclear whether the play aims to call attention to this double standard. Her service to Palamon saves his life, however. Palamon meets the Jailer on his way to the executioner's block, acknowledges his gratitude to "[y]our gentle daughter" (5.4.24), and "*gives the* JAILER *a purse*" (5.4.32 SD) as part of the dowry for her marriage. His generosity infects the other knights slated to die with him:

FIRST KNIGHT Nay, let's be offerers all.
SECOND KNIGHT Is it a maid?
PALAMON Verily, I think so—
(5.4.32–33)

Ironically, "[*t*]*hey give their purses*" (5.4.35 SD) on a doubly false assumption—that they are doomed and that they are contributing to a virgin's dowry. But in another sense, the Daughter is bought off. Palamon speaks with greater accuracy than he knows in saying she is "more to me deserving / Than I can 'quite [requite] or speak of" (5.4.34–35).

Long before this, the Daughter's sequence of soliloquies has come to an end. In the second half of the play, having moved from one form of folly to another, she appears only in dialogue scenes and hence loses her unique contact with the audience. Yet even here, her vigor produces an immediacy that blends with the pathos of her predicament. She shares this pathos with the characters in the main plot, who watch uncomprehendingly as their ideals fail them when it matters most.

WALTER COHEN

## SELECTED BIBLIOGRAPHY


Bruster, Douglas. "The Jailer's Daughter and the Politics of Madwomen's Language." *Shakespeare Quarterly* 46 (1995): 277–300. Sees the Daughter as powerless and isolated but nonetheless central to the play, her unique language marked by class and gender, her madness constituting a form of resistance; more generally, her depiction is understood as the intersection of Shakespeare's interest in the folk and Fletcher's in strong women characters, and also as indicative of a transition to a less popular drama.

Clark, Sandra. "*The Two Noble Kinsmen*: Shakespeare's Final Phase: *The Two Noble Kinsmen* in Its Context." *Late Shakespeare: 1608–1613*. Ed. Andrew J. Power and Rory Loughnane. Cambridge: Cambridge UP, 2013. 124–38. Compares *Two Noble Kinsmen* to Shakespeare's other collaborations with Fletcher and to earlier Shakespeare plays, emphasizing the play's bleakness.

Crawforth, Hannah. "'Bride-habited, but maiden-hearted': Language and Gender in *The Two Noble Kinsmen*." *Women Making Shakespeare: Text, Reception, Performance*. Ed. Gordon McMullan, Lena Cowen Orlin, and Virginia Mason Vaughan. London: Bloomsbury, 2014. 25–34. Argues that the play's dualities of sameness and difference are embodied in its language through hyphenated coinages juxtaposing Latin and Germanic words, and the co-presence of contemporary and archaic meanings.

Gossett, Suzanne. "*The Two Noble Kinsmen* and *Henry VIII*: The Last Last Plays." *The Cambridge Companion to Shakespeare's Last Plays*. Ed. Catherine M. S. Alexander. Cambridge: Cambridge UP, 2009. 185–202. Reviews issues of authorship, collaboration, and publication and performance history, with emphasis on the darkness of tone.

Herman, Peter C. "'Is This Winning?': Prince Henry's Death and the Problem of Chivalry in *The Two Noble Kinsmen*." *South Atlantic Review* 62 (1997): 1–31. Discusses the death of King James's son and heir as a blow to chivalry, generating in the play a skepticism about its martial and erotic implications.

Masten, Jeffrey. *Textual Intercourse: Collaboration, Authorship, and Sexualities in Renaissance Drama*. Cambridge: Cambridge UP, 1997. 49–60. Emphasizes the homoerotic dimensions of the play, with parallels between the titular kinsmen and the two collaborative playwrights.

Potter, Lois, ed. *The Two Noble Kinsmen*. 3d ed. Walton-on-Thames, Surrey: Thomas Nelson, 1997. Outstanding scholarly edition with a lengthy critical introduction.

Sanders, Julie. "Mixed Messages: The Aesthetics of *The Two Noble Kinsmen*." *A Companion to Shakespeare's Works*. Ed. Richard Dutton and Jean Howard. Vol. 4: *The Poems, Problem Comedies, Late Plays*. Malden, MA: Blackwell, 2003. 445–61. Examines the play's innovative exploitation of five-act structure, partly to dramatize relations between court and country, and its more general relationship to elite theatrical and political events of the time.

Sprang, Felix C. H. "'Never Fortune did play a subtler game': The Creation of 'Medieval' Narratives in *Pericles* and *The Two Noble Kinsmen*." *European Journal of English Studies* 15 (2011): 115–28. Ties the play's conscious medievalism to the thematic emphasis on fate and formal turn to tragicomedy, seen, paradoxically, as a self-referentially modern genre.

Teramura, Misha. "The Anxiety of Auctoritas: Chaucer and *The Two Noble Kinsmen*." *Shakespeare Quarterly* 63 (2012): 544–76. Sees Chaucer's prestige as undermined from within by the play's challenge to heterosexuality; his relationship to the two playwrights is mirrored in the relationship of the older dramatist (Shakespeare) to the younger (Fletcher).

## TEXTUAL INTRODUCTION

*The Two Noble Kinsmen*, cowritten by William Shakespeare and John Fletcher in 1613–14, was not included in Shakespeare's First Folio (1623), but was printed in quarto in 1634. This is the only plausible base text, significantly predating the play's subsequent appearance in the Beaumont and Fletcher (Second) Folio (1679), its only other seventeenth-century printing. The 1634 Quarto (Q) was produced by the printer Thomas Cotes, who was also responsible for Shakespeare's Second Folio (1632), and it seems likely that the Quarto was partially designed to complement this publication. Cotes would also see a quarto of *Pericles* through his press in 1635; both volumes seem to have sold well, judging by the number of surviving copies. The practices of the Quarto's two compositors may cast light on important decisions in the printing of the Second Folio, a subject as yet little explored by critics.

Two key textual issues have dominated bibliographical scholarship on this play. The first is the collaborative nature of the text, which is reflected in certain internal inconsistencies, particularly regarding the use of verse and prose, which Shakespeare and Fletcher appear to treat quite differently (see Digital Edition TC 5). Scholars have tended to attribute to Shakespeare scenes 1.1–5, 3.1–2, 5.1, 5.3–5, and probably 2.1 and 4.3, while Fletcher is usually thought to have written 2.2–6, 3.3–6, 4.1–2, and 5.2. The handover from one playwright to another seems to explain certain peculiarities of the Quarto, such as the doubling of some entrances and exits (see Digital Edition TC 4). Scholars continue to apply stylometrics and computational analysis to the problem of how best to attribute authorship of its various scenes, and results vary around a reasonably clear core; what is beyond doubt, however, is that the play offers particularly interesting insight into the collaborative processes that characterize the latter phase of Shakespeare's career.

The second important textual consideration is the fact that Q contains nine marginal stage directions of a kind unseen elsewhere in early modern drama, and which afford an unprecedented glimpse into what went on backstage during a performance of one of Shakespeare's plays (see Digital Edition TC 3). In this edition, they have been assimilated into standard stage direction format. They stop after the end of the third act, when, we must imagine, the compositors learned they were not supposed to be setting these directions in this way and began incorporating them into the text. Some of these later directions name specific actors from the company of the King's Men ("*Curtis*," presumably Curtis Greville, at 4.2.70, and "*T. Tucke*," thought to be Thomas Tuckfield, at the start of 5.3). This supports the idea that the compositors worked from an annotated promptbook prepared by Edward Knight, bookkeeper to the company, for a revival of *The Two Noble Kinsmen* in 1625–26. Oddities in the formatting of these directions can largely be explained as attempts on the compositors' part to mimic the presentation of this hypothesized scribal copy. As such, the Quarto offers an unusual amount of information regarding early modern printing-house practice. For this reason, along with its implications for our understanding of life in the playhouses of Shakespeare's London and of the collaborative nature of his last plays, the text rewards detailed study.

HANNAH CRAWFORTH

## PERFORMANCE NOTE

*The Two Noble Kinsmen*—which is rarely staged—often inspires directors to adopt open artifice as a staging principle. Stylized acting, storybook sets, and elaborate presentations of ritual, pageantry, and divine intercession respond to the play's many elements of chivalric romance (courtly speeches, idealized heroes, abundant ceremony). Prioritizing unity of action over psychological depth, such staging also has the value of preempting objections to the play's thinly drawn characters while deepening the impact of comparatively realistic scenes, especially those featuring the Jailer's Daughter. Nevertheless the play is unusually malleable in production, capable of accommodating representations defined by sentimentality on the one hand, and emotional truth on the other. It is not uncommon for the protagonists to be distinguished by different styles of acting within the same production, Arcite typically playing the earthy foil to Palamon's starry-eyed dreamer. Depending on the production's approach, Palamon and Arcite can be perfect opposites or nearly indistinguishable from one another, and either kinsman can seem more deserving of the audience's sympathy or condemnation.

Much like Palamon and Arcite, Emilia and the Jailer's Daughter can complement or counteract each other. Some productions contrast Emilia's celibacy and inhibition with the unbridled sexuality of the Jailer's Daughter; others underscore the commonality whereby each, against her liking, marries a replacement for her intended. Some focus on the Daughter's misery at losing Palamon to one who had refused him; others show the women joyfully embracing their matches, unaware of the complications this presents to the generic outcome. Productions must clarify Emilia's initial reluctance to marry (whether because of commitment to chastity, same-sex desire, feminist rejection of patriarchy) and decide whether she marries eagerly or grudgingly. They must also decide whether the Daughter's sexual desire reflects experience or naïveté, and whether her marriage cures madness or feeds it. Other considerations include determining whether Arcite pursues Emilia out of sincere affection or competitive rivalry; whether the daughter's mad wanderings are scary or sweet; whether Theseus and Hippolyta's relationship is idealized or reflective of her subjugation; and whether to exploit the parallels among several robust homosocial—potentially homoerotic—relationships (Theseus/Perithous, Emilia/Flavina, Palamon/Arcite).

BRETT GAMBOA

# The Two Noble Kinsmen

[THE PERSONS OF THE PLAY

PROLOGUE

Hymen
BOY

THESEUS
HIPPOLYTA
EMILIA
PIRITHOUS
Artesius, officer
HERALD

Three QUEENS

PALAMON
ARCITE
VALERIUS
KNIGHTS, three seconding Palamon and three Arcite

JAILER
JAILER'S DAUGHTER
WOOER to Jailer's Daughter
JAILER'S BROTHER
Two FRIENDS to Jailer
Emilia's WOMAN
DOCTOR

Gerald, a SCHOOLMASTER
BAVIAN
NELL
Timothy, a TABORER
Four COUNTRYMEN
Four Countrywomen

GENTLEMEN
MESSENGERS
SERVANTS
Women, Nymphs, Attendants, Dancers, Executioner, Guard

EPILOGUE]

## Prologue

*Flourish.*° [*Enter* PROLOGUE.] — *Trumpet call*

PROLOGUE New plays and maidenheads are near akin:
Much followed° both, for both much money gi'en, — *pursued*
If they stand sound and well.[1] And a good play—
Whose modest scenes blush on his marriage day
And shake to lose his honor[2]—is like her
That after holy tie° and first night's stir — *marriage*
Yet still is modesty, and still retains
More of the maid to sight than husband's pains.[3]
We pray our play may be so.° For I am sure — *(modest)*
It has a noble breeder° and a pure, — *begetter*
A learnèd, and a poet never went° — *lived*
More famous yet twixt Po and silver Trent.[4]
Chaucer—of° all admired—the story gives; — *by*
There,° constant to eternity,° it lives. — *In his words / immortal*
If we let fall° the nobleness of this,° — *demean / (the poem)*
And the first sound this child° hear be a hiss, — *play*
How will it shake the bones of that good man,° — *(Chaucer)*
And make him cry from under ground: "Oh, fan
From me the witless chaff of such a writer
That blasts my bays and my famed works makes lighter
Than Robin Hood!"[5] This is the fear we bring;
For to say truth, it were an endless° thing — *never-ending; pointless*
And too ambitious to aspire to him,° — *(Chaucer)*
Weak as we are, and almost breathless swim
In this deep water. Do but you hold out
Your helping hands, and we shall tack about
And something do to save us:[6] you shall hear
Scenes, though below his art, may° yet appear — *that may*
Worth two hours' travail.[7] To his bones, sweet sleep;
Content° to you. If this play do not keep — *Contentment*
A little dull time from us,[8] we perceive
Our losses fall so thick we must needs leave.[9]

*Flourish.* [*Exit.*]

**Prologue**

1. *stand sound and well:* sexual wordplay about virility and lack of venereal disease.
2. *Whose . . . honor:* Whose previously unwatched scenes are "modest" and shy (they "blush") on opening night and "shake" with fear at the thought of being viewed (losing their virginity).
3. *still . . . pains:* still looks more like a virgin ("maid") than like a married woman who has experienced her husband's sexual exertions.
4. *a poet . . . Trent:* there has never been a more famous poet from Italy to England. The Po is a river in Italy, the Trent an English waterway.
5. *That . . . Hood:* Who disgraces my fame as a poet (garlands of bay or laurel were awarded to great poets, hence the name "poet laureate") and makes my renowned creations seem more trivial than a popular tale or ballad (such as that of Robin Hood).
6. *Do but . . . us:* Help us by applauding, and we will turn like a sailboat in the breeze produced by your clapping hands, thereby saving our reputation.
7. *two hours' travail:* the actors' labor ("travail") for two hours in performing the play (standard length was two to three hours); also, since Q reads "travel," the audience will take part in a two-hour imaginative journey while watching the play. "Travail" continues the metaphor of childbirth and rearing begun in line 10, which itself develops from the image of the loss of virginity on the marriage night.
8. *keep . . . us:* keep us amused.
9. Our losses will be so great that we will need to quit the theater. The "losses" refer to the decline in reputation from a poorly received play, and perhaps also to the burning of the Globe Theater on June 29, 1613, during a performance of *Henry VIII.*

## 1.1

*Enter Hymen,° with a torch burning; a* BOY *in a white robe before,° singing and strewing flowers; after Hymen, a Nymph, encompassed in her tresses, bearing a wheaten garland.*[1] *Then* THESEUS, *between two other Nymphs with wheaten chaplets° on their heads. Then* HIPPOLYTA,[2] *the bride, led by* PIRITHOUS, *and another [Nymph], holding a garland over her head, her tresses likewise hanging. After her,* EMILIA, *holding up her train[; Artesius, and Attendants].*

*god of marriage*
*ahead (of Hymen)*
*wreaths*

*The Song. Music.*

BOY [*sings*] Roses, their sharp spines being gone,
Not royal in their smells alone,
But in their hue.
Maiden pinks,° of odor faint, *low flowering plants*
Daisies, smell-less, yet most quaint,° *fine*
And sweet thyme° true. *(with pun on "time")*

Primrose, firstborn child of Ver,° *Spring*
Merry springtime's harbinger,
With harebells dim.° *dark hyacinths*
Oxlips,° in their cradles growing, *Flowering herbs*
Marigolds, on deathbeds blowing,° *flowering on graves*
Lark's-heels trim.° *Fine larkspur*
[*He*] *strews flowers.*

All dear Nature's children sweet
Lie fore bride and bridegroom's feet
Blessing their sense.° *Gratifying their senses*
Not an angle of the air,° *noisy, ravenous bird*
Bird melodious, or bird fair,
Is absent hence.

The crow, the sland'rous cuckoo,[3] nor
The boding° raven, nor chough hoar,[4] *ominous*
Nor chatt'ring pie,° *magpie*
May on our bridehouse° perch or sing, *wedding venue*
Or with them any discord bring,
But from it fly.

*Enter three* QUEENS *in black, with veils stained,° with imperial crowns. The* FIRST QUEEN *falls down at the foot of* THESEUS; *the* SECOND *falls down at the foot of Hippolyta; the* THIRD *before* EMILIA. *dyed black*

FIRST QUEEN [*to* THESEUS] For pity's sake and true gentility's,
Hear and respect° me. *attend to*

SECOND QUEEN [*to* HIPPOLYTA] For your mother's sake
And as you wish your womb may thrive with fair ones,
Hear and respect me.

THIRD QUEEN [*to* EMILIA] Now for the love of him whom Jove hath marked° *singled out for*
The honor of your bed and for the sake

1.1 Location: Athens, near the temple where Hippolyta and Theseus are to be married.
1. The young woman's hair hangs loose, indicating virginity; her garland signifies fertility.
2. According to legend, Hippolyta was queen of the Amazons before Theseus conquered her race of women warriors and brought her to Thebes as his captive and bride.
3. Because it yelled out "cuckold" (husband of an adulterous wife), impugning faithful wives.
4. A jackdaw—a small, rare, gray-headed ("hoar"), red-beaked, cliff-dwelling member of the crow family.

Of clear° virginity, be advocate — *unspotted*
For us and our distresses. This good deed
Shall raze you out o'th' book of trespasses
All you are set down there.[5]

THESEUS [*to* FIRST QUEEN] Sad lady, rise.

HIPPOLYTA [*to* SECOND QUEEN] Stand up.

EMILIA [*to* THIRD QUEEN] No knees to me.
What woman I may stead° that is distressed — *assist*
Does bind me to her.

[SECOND *and* THIRD QUEENS *rise.*]

THESEUS What's your request? [*to* FIRST QUEEN] Deliver° you for all. — *Speak*

FIRST QUEEN We are three queens, whose sovereigns fell before
The wrath of cruel Creon;[6] who° endured — *(the sovereigns)*
The beaks of ravens, talons of the kites,° — *birds of prey*
And pecks of crows in the foul fields° of Thebes. — *battlefields*
He will not suffer us to burn their bones,
To urn their ashes, nor to take th'offense
Of mortal loathsomeness from the blessed eye
Of holy Phoebus,° but infects the winds — *the sun*
With stench of our slain lords. O pity, Duke,
Thou purger of the earth;[7] draw thy feared sword
That does good turns to th' world; give us the bones
Of our dead kings, that we may chapel° them; — *entomb (in a chapel)*
And of° thy boundless goodness take some note — *in*
That for our crownèd heads we have no roof,
Save this° which is the lion's, and the bear's, — *(the sky)*
And vault° to every thing. — *ceiling*

THESEUS [*to* FIRST QUEEN] Pray you kneel not;
I was transported with° your speech and suffered — *moved by*
Your knees to wrong themselves.° I have heard the fortunes — *(by kneeling)*
Of your dead lords, which gives me such lamenting
As wakes my vengeance and revenge for 'em.
King Capaneus was your lord; the day
That he should° marry you, at such a season — *was about to*
As now it is with me, I met your groom.
By Mars's altar, you were that time fair!
Not Juno's mantle fairer than your tresses,
Nor in more bounty spread her;[8] your wheaten° wreath — *wedding (see 5.1.160)*
Was then nor° threshed nor blasted;° Fortune at you — *neither / withered*
Dimpled her cheek with smiles. Hercules our kinsman—
Then weaker than° your eyes—laid by his club; — *overwhelmed by*
He tumbled down upon his Nemean hide
And swore his sinews thawed.[9] O grief and time,
Fearful° consumers, you will all devour! — *Terrifying*

5. *Shall . . . there:* Will expunge your sins from the divine ledger.
6. Brother to Jocasta and, hence, both brother-in-law and uncle to Oedipus. Creon succeeded Oedipus's son Eteocles as king of Thebes following the siege known as the "Seven Against Thebes," in which both Eteocles and all the attackers, led by Eteocles' brother Polynices, were killed. Creon refused to bury any of the seven, including the husbands of the three Queens.
7. Like his cousin Hercules (see 1.1.66, 3.6.175), Theseus was known for ridding the world of monsters and evildoers.
8. Nor is Juno (goddess of marriage) more luxuriantly wrapped in her mantle than you were in your hanging tresses.
9. *He . . . thawed:* He (Hercules) flopped down on the hide of the Nemean lion (which he wore after killing it as one of his twelve labors) and swore his muscles were turned to liquid by your beauty. Most powerful of Greek mythological heroes, performer of "twelve strong labors" set for him by his cousin (3.6.175), Hercules was typically portrayed armed with a club.

FIRST QUEEN Oh, I hope some god,
Some god has put his mercy in your manhood,
Whereto he'll infuse power and press you forth,
Our undertaker.° *champion*

THESEUS Oh, no knees, none, widow;
Unto the helmeted Bellona° use them, *Roman goddess of war*
And pray for me, your soldier.
[FIRST QUEEN *rises.*]
Troubled I am.
[*He*] *turns away.*

SECOND QUEEN [*kneeling*] Honored Hippolyta,
Most dreaded Amazonian, that hast slain
The scythe-tusked boar;[1] that with thy arm, as strong
As it is white, wast near to° make the male *almost managed to*
To thy sex captive, but that this thy lord—
Born to uphold creation in that honor
First nature styled it in[2]—shrunk thee into
The bound thou wast o'er-flowing,[3] at once subduing
Thy force and thy affection. Soldieress,
That equally canst poise° sternness with pity, *balance*
Whom now I know hast much more power on° him *over*
Than ever he had on thee, who ow'st° his strength *owns*
And his love too, who is a servant for
The tenor of thy speech;[4] dear glass of° ladies, *mirror for*
Bid him that we, whom flaming war doth scorch,
Under the shadow of his sword may cool us;
Require him he° advance it o'er our heads. *Ask him to*
Speak't in a woman's key, like such a woman
As any of us three. Weep ere you fail.
Lend us a knee,[5]
But touch the ground for us no longer time
Than a dove's motion when the head's plucked off.
Tell him, if he i'th' blood-sized° field lay swollen, *blood-soaked*
Showing the sun his teeth, grinning at the moon,
What you would do.

HIPPOLYTA [*to* SECOND QUEEN] Poor lady, say no more.
I had as lief trace[6] this good action with you
As that° whereto I am going, and never yet *(marriage)*
Went I so willing way. My lord is taken° *affected*
Heart-deep with your distress. Let him consider:
I'll speak anon.° *soon*
[SECOND QUEEN *rises.*]

THIRD QUEEN [*kneeling to* EMILIA] Oh, my petition was
Set down in ice,[7] which by hot grief uncandied° *thawed*
Melts into drops; so sorrow wanting form
Is pressed with deeper matter.[8]

1. *Honored . . . boar:* Hippolyta is here confused with Atalanta, another Amazon, who participated with Meleager in the hunt for the Calydonian boar. See note to 3.5.14.
2. *Born . . . in:* Born to sustain the natural order of creation—the order of man over woman.
3. *shrunk . . . o'er-flowing:* returned you to the limits of your sex, which you had previously exceeded.
4. *who is . . . speech:* who (Theseus, not Hippolyta, who is referred to by the previous "Whom" and "who"), like a good lover, obeys your every spoken desire.
5. *Speak't . . . knee:* Don't speak like an Amazon. Use tears to avoid defeat. Join us in kneeling.
6. I would as willingly follow through.
7. *my . . . ice:* my former speech was cold and formal.
8. *so . . . matter:* so sorrow, lacking a way to express itself, is made yet more oppressive by its inarticulateness; or, perhaps, receives the stamp of "deeper" impulses.

EMILIA Pray stand up;
Your grief is written in your cheek.
THIRD QUEEN [*rising*] Oh, woe,
You cannot read it there. There,° through my tears, *In my eye*
Like wrinkled pebbles in a glassy stream
You may behold 'em.° Lady, lady, alack! *(my sorrows)*
He that will all the treasure know o'th' earth
Must know° the center too; he that will fish *dig deep throughout*
For my least minnow, let him lead° his line *weight with lead*
To catch one at my heart. Oh, pardon me;
Extremity, that sharpens sundry wits,
Makes me a fool.[9]
EMILIA Pray you say nothing, pray you:
Who cannot feel nor see the rain, being in't,
Knows neither wet nor dry. If that you were
The ground-piece of some painter,[1] I would buy you
T'instruct me 'gainst° a capital° grief, indeed *To prepare me for / deadly*
Such heart-pierced° demonstration. But, alas, *heartrending*
Being a natural sister of our sex[2]
Your sorrow beats so ardently° upon me *burningly*
That it shall make a counter-reflect 'gainst[3]
My brother's° heart and warm it to some pity, *brother-in-law's*
Though it were made of stone. Pray have good comfort.
THESEUS Forward to th' temple;° leave not out a jot *(for the wedding)*
O'th' sacred ceremony.
FIRST QUEEN Oh, this celebration
Will longer last and be more costly than
Your suppliants' war!° Remember that your fame *requested war*
Knolls° in the ear o'th' world: what you do quickly *Tolls like a bell*
Is not done rashly; your first thought is more
Than others' labored meditance,° your premeditating *careful meditation*
More than their actions. But, O Jove, your actions,
Soon as they move, as ospreys do the fish,[4]
Subdue before they touch. Think, dear Duke, think
What beds our slain kings have!
SECOND QUEEN What griefs our beds,
That our dear lords have none.
THIRD QUEEN None fit for th' dead.
Those that with cords, knives, drams' precipitance,° *poisons' suddenness*
Weary of this world's light, have to themselves
Been death's most horrid agents, human grace° *mercy*
Affords them dust and shadow—
FIRST QUEEN But our lords
Lie blist'ring fore the visitating° sun, *inspecting*
And were good kings, when living.
THESEUS It is true. And I will give you comfort,
To give° your dead lords graves; *By giving*
The which to do must make some work with Creon—

9. *Extremity . . . fool:* Extreme suffering, which makes some minds more clear, has made me speak inappropriately.
1. *If . . . painter:* If you were merely the subject (model; preliminary sketch?) of a painting.
2. Since you are actually a live woman (rather than a representation of a grieving wife).
3. That, like a mirror, I'll reflect your (sunlike) sorrow back toward.
4. According to popular legend, ospreys had the power to compel fish to rise to the surface and turn over, making themselves available for capture.

FIRST QUEEN And that work presents itself to th' doing.[5]
Now 'twill take form; the heats are gone tomorrow.[6]
Then, bootless° toil must recompense itself° *fruitless / itself only*
With its own sweat. Now he's secure,° *unaware of danger*
Nor dreams we stand before your puissance,° *power*
Rinsing° our holy begging in our eyes *(by crying)*
To make petition clear.° *pure; manifest*
SECOND QUEEN Now you may take him,
Drunk with his victory.
THIRD QUEEN And his army full
Of bread and sloth.
THESEUS Artesius—that best knowest
How to draw out,° fit to this enterprise, *select*
The prim'st° for this proceeding, and the number *best soldiers*
To carry° such a business—forth° and levy *conduct; win / go forth*
Our worthiest instruments, whilst we dispatch
This grand act of our life, this daring deed
Of fate[7] in wedlock.
FIRST QUEEN [*to* SECOND *and* THIRD QUEENS] Dowagers,° take° hands. *Widows / join*
Let us be widows to our woes; delay
Commends us to a famishing hope.[8]
ALL QUEENS Farewell.
SECOND QUEEN We come unseasonably,° but when could grief *at a bad time*
Cull forth,° as unpanged° judgment can, fitt'st time *Choose/ untormented*
For best solicitation?
THESEUS Why, good ladies,
This is a service, whereto I am going,
Greater than any war; it more imports me° *means more to me*
Than all the actions that I have foregone° *done to date*
Or futurely can cope.° *(with in battle)*
FIRST QUEEN The more proclaiming° *Clearly showing that*
Our suit shall be neglected when her arms,
Able to lock Jove from a synod,[9] shall
By warranting° moonlight corslet thee;[1] oh, when *authorizing*
Her twining cherries° shall their sweetness fall° *parting lips / let fall*
Upon thy taste-full° lips, what wilt thou think *savoring*
Of rotten kings or blubbered° queens? What care *tear-soaked*
For what thou feel'st not, what thou feel'st being able
To make Mars spurn his drum?° Oh, if thou couch *(battle signal)*
But one night with her, every hour in't will
Take hostage of thee° for a hundred,° and *Commit you / (more)*
Thou shalt remember nothing more than what
That banquet bids° thee to. *appetizer invites*
HIPPOLYTA Though much unlike
You should be so transported, as much sorry
I should be such a suitor;[2] yet I think
Did I not by th'abstaining of my joy—

5. And that work needs to be done as soon as possible.
6. While the plan, like molten metal, is still hot, it can be transformed into something—once it grows cold, it can no longer be shaped.
7. *this daring deed / Of fate:* this act (marriage) that challenges fate.
8. *Let . . . hope:* Let us mourn our misfortunes as we mourned our husbands (or, let us, widow-like, part from our woes), since by delaying the battle until his marriage is completed, Theseus consigns us to failure.
9. Able to keep Jupiter from a meeting of the gods.
1. Encircle you like a "corslet," close-fitting defensive armor. Theseus has traded arms (armor) for arms (embraces).
2. *Though . . . suitor:* Although it's highly unlikely you'd be so carried away by desire, and I'm just as sorry to inspire that and also request you to postpone the wedding.

Which breeds a deeper longing—cure their surfeit° *excess of grief*
That craves a present medicine,° I should pluck *an immediate relief*
All ladies' scandal° on me. [*She kneels.*] Therefore, sir, *reproach*
As I shall here make trial of my prayers—
Either presuming them to have some force,
Or sentencing for aye their vigor dumb[3]—
Prorogue° this business we are going about and hang *Delay*
Your shield afore your heart, about that neck *fight first (with care)*
Which is my fee,° and which I freely lend *property*
To do these poor queens service.

ALL QUEENS [*to* EMILIA] Oh, help now;
Our cause cries for your knee.

EMILIA [*kneeling to* THESEUS] If you grant not
My sister her petition—in that force,° *with that energy*
With that celerity° and nature which *speed*
She makes it in—from henceforth I'll not dare
To ask you anything, nor be so hardy° *bold*
Ever to take a husband.

THESEUS Pray, stand up.
I am entreating of myself to do
That which you kneel to have me.° [*They rise.*] —Pirithous, *have me do*
Lead on the bride; get you° and pray the gods *go*
For success and return; omit not anything
In the pretended° celebration. —Queens, *planned*
Follow your soldier.° [*to Artesius*] As before, hence, you, *Theseus*
And at the banks of Aulis[4] meet us with
The forces you can raise, where we shall find
The moiety of a number, for a business
More bigger-looked.[5] [*Exit Artesius.*]
[*to* HIPPOLYTA] Since that our theme is haste,
I stamp this kiss upon thy current lip;
Sweet, keep it as my token.[6] Set you forward,
For I will see you gone.
[*Procession moves toward the temple.*]
—Farewell, my beauteous sister. —Pirithous,
Keep the feast full;° bate° not an hour on't.° *fully / reduce / of it*

PIRITHOUS Sir,
I'll follow you at heels; the feast's solemnity° *ceremonial splendor*
Shall want° till your return. *be lacking*

THESEUS Cousin,° I charge you, *Friend*
Budge not from Athens. We shall be returning
Ere you can end this feast; of which, I pray you,
Make no abatement.° —Once more, farewell all. *reduction*
[*Exeunt all except* THESEUS *and* QUEENS.]

FIRST QUEEN Thus dost thou still make good the tongue o'th' world.[7]

SECOND QUEEN And earn'st a deity equal with Mars—

THIRD QUEEN If not above him, for

3. Or forever "sentencing" my prayers to silence, than which they are no more effectual.
4. Port where the Greek troops assembled before sailing for Troy.
5. *where . . . looked:* where we shall find part of an army already assembled for a larger campaign than this one (and for more dangerous "business" than marriage, line 196).
6. *I . . . token:* puns on coining and engraving. *stamp:* press (a kiss); make a coin by impressing an image on metal. *current:* flowing away (like a stream); red (currant); genuine, not counterfeit. *token:* memento (often of love); metal stamped and used as a coin.
7. In this way, you (Theseus) prove true everything the world says of you.

Thou, being but mortal, makest affections bend
To godlike honors;[8] they themselves, some say,
Groan under such a mast'ry.[9]

THESEUS As we are men,
Thus should we do; being sensually subdued,° *overcome by appetites*
We lose our human title.° Good cheer, ladies; *claim to humanity*
Now turn we toward your comforts. *Flourish. Exeunt.*

## 1.2

*Enter* PALAMON *and* ARCITE.

ARCITE Dear Palamon, dearer in love than blood° *a blood relation*
And our prime cousin,° yet unhardened in *nearest kin*
The crimes of nature[1] let us leave the city
Thebes—and the temptings° in't—before we further *temptations*
Sully our gloss of° youth. *Tarnish our pristine*
And here to keep in abstinence we shame
As in incontinence;[2] for not to swim
I'th' aid o'th' current° were almost to sink— *With the flow*
At least to frustrate striving[3]—and to follow
The common stream 'twould bring us to an eddy
Where we should turn° or drown; if labor through, *spin endlessly*
Our gain but life and weakness.[4]

PALAMON Your advice
Is cried up with example.[5] What strange ruins,° *ruined men*
Since first we went to school, may we perceive
Walking in Thebes! Scars and bare weeds° *tattered clothes*
The gain o'th' martialist,° who did propound *soldier*
To his bold ends[6] honor and golden ingots—
Which, though he won, he had not[7]—and, now, flirted° *(is) mocked*
By peace for whom he fought; who then shall offer
To Mars's so scorned altar? I do bleed
When such I meet and wish great Juno[8] would
Resume her ancient° fit of jealousy *former*
To get the soldier work, that peace might purge
For her repletion[9] and retain° anew *take into service*
Her° charitable heart, now hard and harsher *(Juno's); (peace's)*
Than strife or war could be.

ARCITE Are you not out?° *off the point*
Meet you no ruin but the soldier in
The cranks and turns° of Thebes? You did begin *winding streets*
As if you met decays of many kinds.
Perceive you none that do arouse your pity
But th'unconsidered° soldier? *neglected*

PALAMON Yes, I pity

8. *makest . . . honors:* subordinate your human passions to godlike deeds.
9. *they . . . mast'ry:* the gods themselves complain of such self-restraint; suffer because their passions master them.
1.2 Location: Thebes.
1. *unhardened . . . nature:* inexperienced in the natural vices of man.
2. *here . . . incontinence:* we incur as much shame here (in a corrupt city) by remaining innocent as we would elsewhere by debauching ourselves.
3. And at least renders our exertions (on behalf of goodness) pointless.
4. *if . . . weakness:* if we were to pass through such a whirlpool ("eddy"), we would gain only our lives in a weakened state.
5. Is borne out by numerous examples.
6. *propound . . . ends:* propose as recompense for his courage.
7. Which, though victorious in battle, he didn't receive.
8. Juno, whose jealousy led to the Trojan War, also hated Thebes.
9. *purge / For her repletion:* take medicine to alleviate her (peace's) overeating (the indulgent life of peacetime).

Decays where'er I find them, but such most
That, sweating in an honorable toil,
Are paid with ice° to cool 'em. *treated coldly*

ARCITE
'Tis not this
I did begin to speak of; this° is virtue *soldiers' merit*
Of no respect in Thebes. I spake of Thebes—
How dangerous, if we will keep our honors,
It is for our residing—where every evil
Hath a good color;° where ev'ry seeming good's *appearance*
A certain evil; where not to be e'en jump
As they are here were to be strangers and,
Such things to be, mere monsters.[1]

PALAMON
'Tis in our power—
Unless we fear that apes can tutor's°—to *that we're mere mimics*
Be masters of our manners. What need I
Affect another's gait, which is not catching° *infectious; attractive*
Where there is faith,[2] or to be fond° upon *to dote*
Another's way of speech, when by mine own
I may be reasonably conceived,° saved too, *understood*
Speaking it° truly? Why am I bound° *If I speak / (financially)*
By any generous° bond to follow him *noble*
Follows° his tailor, haply° so long until *Who heeds / at least*
The followed make pursuit?° Or let me know *(for unpaid bills)*
Why mine own barber is unblessed, with him
My poor chin too, for° 'tis not scissored just *since*
To such a favorite's glass?° What canon° is there *image / law; cannon*
That does command my rapier from my hip
To dangle't in my hand, or to go tiptoe
Before the street be foul?[3] Either I am
The fore-horse in the team or I am none
That draw i'th' sequent trace.[4] These poor slight sores
Need not a plantain;[5] that which rips my bosom
Almost to th' heart's—

ARCITE
Our uncle Creon—

PALAMON
He—
A most unbounded° tyrant—whose successes *unrestrained*
Makes heaven unfeared and villainy assured° *assured that*
Beyond its power there's nothing, almost puts
Faith in a fever,[6] and deifies alone
Voluble chance;° who only attributes *Variable fortune*
The faculties of other instruments
To his own nerves and act;[7] commands men service,
And what they win in't, boot° and glory; one *booty; gain*
That fears not to do harm; good, dares not.° Let *dares not to do good*
The blood of mine that's sib° to him be sucked *related*
From me with leeches;° let them break° and fall *medically purified / burst*
Off me with that° corruption. *(Creon's)*

1. *where . . . monsters:* where failure to conform exactly ("jump") makes you a foreigner and perfect conformity makes you a monster.
2. Self-reliance. Palamon's speech echoes familiar criticisms of the contrived, "effeminate" manners of courtiers and men of fashion, here contrasted with implicit religious norms ("faith"; "saved," line 48; "canon," line 55).
3. *go . . . foul:* tiptoe on a clean street (like a cowardly soldier).
4. *Either . . . trace:* I will not pull behind the lead ("fore-") horse (follow fashion).
5. Herb used for treating wounds.
6. *puts . . . fever:* undermines religion.
7. *attributes . . . act:* takes credit for others' successes.

ARCITE Clear-spirited° cousin, *Noble-spirited*
Let's leave his court, that we may nothing share
Of his loud° infamy. For our milk *well-known*
Will relish of the pasture,[8] and we must
Be vile or disobedient—not his kinsmen
In blood, unless in quality.[9]

PALAMON Nothing truer.
I think the echoes of his shames have deafed
The ear of heav'nly justice. Widows' cries
Descend again into their throats and have not
Due audience of° the gods. *Proper notice from*

*Enter* VALERIUS.

Valerius—

VALERIUS The King calls for you; yet be leaden-footed° *go slowly*
Till his great rage be off him. Phoebus, when
He broke his whipstock and exclaimed against
The horses of the sun,[1] but° whispered to° *merely / compared to*
The loudness of his fury.

PALAMON Small winds shake him.
But what's the matter?

VALERIUS Theseus—who, where he threats, appalls—hath sent
Deadly defiance to him° and pronounces *(Creon)*
Ruin to Thebes, who° is at hand to seal *(Theseus)*
The promise of his wrath.[2]

ARCITE Let him approach.
But that we fear the gods in him,° he brings not *justness of his cause*
A jot of terror to us. Yet what man
Thirds his own worth—the case is each of ours—
When that his action's dregged with mind assured
'Tis bad he goes about?[3]

PALAMON Leave that unreasoned.° *Forget that*
Our services stand now for Thebes, not Creon;
Yet° to be neutral to him were dishonor, *Still*
Rebellious° to oppose. Therefore we must *Treasonable*
With him stand to the mercy of° our fate, *submit to*
Who hath bounded our last minute.[4]

ARCITE So we must.
[*to* VALERIUS] Is't said this war's afoot, or it shall be
On fail of° some condition? *If Thebes rejects*

VALERIUS 'Tis in motion.
The intelligence of state° came in the instant *official announcement*
With the defier.° *herald of Theseus*

PALAMON Let's to the King—who, were he
A quarter carrier of that honor which
His enemy come in, the blood we venture
Should be as for our health,[5] which were not spent,° *wasted*
Rather laid out for purchase.° But, alas, *invested for profit*

8. Like cows whose milk absorbs the taste of whatever they eat.
9. *not . . . quality:* we ought not to act like his kinsmen unless we're willing to act like him; we're not his kinsmen unless we act like him.
1. After his son Phaëthon died driving the horses of the sun, Phoebus (the sun) vented his grief at the horses—hence the broken whip handle ("whipstock").
2. *seal . . . wrath:* turn anger to action.
3. *Yet . . . about:* Yet any man reduces his worth by two-thirds—as we do—when he knows the action he undertakes is unworthy.
4. *Who . . . minute:* Which has determined when we die.
5. *the blood . . . health:* our loss of blood in combat would be equivalent to a therapeutic bloodletting.

Our hands advanced before° our hearts, what will *beyond*
The fall o'th' stroke do damage?[6]

ARCITE
Let th'event,° *the outcome*
That never-erring arbitrator, tell us
When we know all ourselves[7]—and let us follow
The becking° of our chance. *Exeunt.* *calling*

## 1.3

*Enter* PIRITHOUS, HIPPOLYTA, *[and]* EMILIA.

PIRITHOUS No further.

HIPPOLYTA
Sir, farewell. Repeat my wishes
To our great lord, of whose success I dare not
Make any timorous question—yet I wish him
Excess and overflow of power, an't might be° *if possible*
To dure° ill-dealing fortune. Speed to him; *endure*
Store[1] never hurts good governors.

PIRITHOUS
Though I know
His ocean needs not my poor drops, yet they
Must yield their tribute there. [*to* EMILIA] My precious maid,
Those best affections° that the heavens infuse *inclinations*
In their best-tempered pieces° keep enthroned *greatest creations*
In your dear heart.

EMILIA
Thanks, sir. Remember me
To our all-royal brother, for whose speed° *success*
The great Bellona I'll solicit; and,
Since in our terrene state° petitions are not *earthly condition*
Without gifts understood, I'll offer to her
What I shall be advised she likes. Our hearts
Are in his army, in his tent.

HIPPOLYTA
In 's bosom.
We have been soldiers,° and we cannot weep *(as Amazons)*
When our friends don their helms,° or put to sea, *helmets*
Or tell of babes broached° on the lance, or women *speared*
That have sod° their infants in—and after ate them— *boiled*
The brine they wept at killing 'em.[2] Then, if
You stay to see of us such spinsters, we
Should hold you here for ever.[3]

PIRITHOUS
Peace be to you
As I pursue this war, which° shall be then *(peace)*
Beyond further requiring.° *Exit* PIRITHOUS. *In no need of prayer*

EMILIA
How his longing
Follows his friend! Since his depart,° his sports, *Theseus's departure*
Though craving° seriousness and skill, passed slightly *requiring*
His careless execution,[4] where nor° gain *neither*
Made him regard or loss consider, but
Playing one business in his hand, another
Directing in his head, his mind nurse equal
To these so-diff'ring twins.[5] Have you observed him
Since our great lord departed?

6. *what . . . damage:* what harm will "the fall o'th' stroke" do?
7. *tell . . . ourselves:* speak for itself.
1.3 Location: The outskirts of Athens.
1. Abundant resources (here, good men like Pirithous).
2. Miriam killed, cooked, and ate her son during the Roman siege of Jerusalem, adding her own tears for sauce.
3. *Then . . . for ever:* if you wait long enough for us to turn into spinners (housewives), you'll wait forever.
4. *passed . . . execution:* were pursued carelessly.
5. *his . . . twins:* his attention divided equally between sports and Theseus.

HIPPOLYTA
With much labor°— *diligence*
And I did love him for't. They two have cabined° *shared quarters*
In many as dangerous as poor a corner,
Peril and want contending;[6] they have skiffed° *sailed across*
Torrents whose roaring tyranny and power
I'th' least of these° was dreadful; and they have *At the weakest point*
Sought out together where Death's self was lodged;[7]
Yet fate hath brought them off. Their knot of love
Tied, weaved, entangled, with so true, so long,
And with a finger of so deep a cunning,° *skill*
May be outworn,° never undone. I think *worn out (in death)*
Theseus cannot be umpire to himself,
Cleaving his conscience into twain and doing
Each side like° justice, which[8] he loves best. *equal*

EMILIA
Doubtless
There is a best, and reason has no manners
To say it is not you. I was acquainted
Once with a time when I enjoyed a playfellow;
You were at wars when she the grave enriched,
Who made too proud the bed,° took leave o'th' moon[9]— *grave*
Which then looked pale at parting—when our count° *age*
Was each eleven.

HIPPOLYTA
'Twas Flavina.

EMILIA
Yes.
You talk of Pirithous' and Theseus' love;
Theirs has more ground,° is more maturely seasoned, *a stronger base*
More buckled° with strong judgment, and their needs *joined together*
The one of th'other may be said to water
Their intertangled roots of love; but I
And she I sigh and spoke of were things innocent,
Loved for° we did, and like the elements[1] *simply because*
That know not what, nor why, yet do effect° *create*
Rare issues° by their operance, our souls *Amazing results*
Did so to one another. What she liked
Was then of° me approved; what not, condemned— *by*
No more arraignment.° The flower that I would pluck *inquiry*
And put between my breasts—oh, then but beginning
To swell about the blossom—she would long° *desire*
Till she had such another and commit it
To the like innocent cradle where, phoenix-like,
They died in perfume.[2] On my head no toy° *trifle*
But was her pattern;° her affections—pretty, *model*
Though happily her careless wear—I followed
For my most serious decking.[3] Had mine ear
Stolen some new air° or at adventure° hummed one *tune / by chance*
From musical coinage,° why, it was a note *improvisation*
Whereon her spirits would sojourn—rather, dwell on—

6. Contending for which was the greater hardship.
7. *where . . . lodged:* the underworld, to rescue Proserpina, Roman fertility goddess abducted to the underworld by the god of the infernal region.
8. Pirithous or Hippolyta; or, Pirithous or Theseus.
9. Died. Diana (the moon goddess), who watched over virgins and Amazons; hence Emilia's (equivocal) patron.

1. Air, fire, earth, and water—constituents of all matter.
2. The phoenix died by being burned on aromatic wood, only to be reborn from its own ashes.
3. *her affections . . . decking:* whatever she wore—appealing, even though perhaps put on without thought—I'd imitate for my most serious clothing choices.

And sing it in her slumbers. This rehearsal—
Which, fury-innocent wots well, comes in
Like old emportment's bastard[4]—has this end:
That the true love tween maid and maid may be
More than in sex individual.[5]

HIPPOLYTA You're out of breath,
And this high-speeded pace is but to say
That you shall never, like the maid Flavina,[6]
Love any that's called man.

EMILIA I am sure I shall not.

HIPPOLYTA Now alack, weak sister,
I must no more believe thee in this point—
Though in't I know thou dost believe thyself—
Than I will trust a sickly appetite
That loathes even as it longs. But sure, my sister,
If I were ripe for your persuasion,° you *open to your views*
Have said enough to shake me from the arm
Of the all-noble Theseus, for whose fortunes
I will now in and kneel with great assurance
That we, more than his Pirithous, possess
The high throne in his heart.

EMILIA I am not
Against your faith, yet I continue mine. *Exeunt.*

*Two hearses ready with* PALAMON *and* ARCITE.
*The three* QUEENS, THESEUS, *and his lords ready.*[7]

## 1.4

*Cornetts. A battle struck within; then a retreat.*
*Flourish.*[1] *Then enter* THESEUS, *[as] victor[, followed*
*by* HERALD *and Attendants with two hearses,° bearing* *biers*
ARCITE *and* PALAMON]. *The three* QUEENS *meet him*
*and fall on their faces before him.*

FIRST QUEEN To thee no star be dark.° *unfavorable*

SECOND QUEEN Both heaven and earth
Friend thee forever.

THIRD QUEEN All the good that may
Be wished upon thy head, I cry "Amen" to't.

THESEUS Th'impartial gods, who from the mounted° heavens *high*
View us, their mortal herd, behold who err
And, in their time, chastise. Go and find out
The bones of your dead lords and honor them
With treble ceremony; rather than a gap
Should be in their dear° rites,° we would supply't. *valued / (also "rights")*
But those we will depute, which shall invest° *clothe*
You in your dignities, and even° each thing *rectify*
Our haste does leave imperfect. So adieu,

4. TEXTUAL COMMENT *This . . . bastard:* This narrative, which, as innocent passionate love well knows, is an illegitimate descendant (poor likeness) of my former passion (or, the former significance of the relationship). For the enigmatic phrase "fury-innocent," see Digital Edition TC 1.

5. *sex individual:* the different genders, male and female.

6. TEXTUAL COMMENT For inconsistent use of names here and elsewhere, see Digital Edition TC 2.

7. TEXTUAL COMMENT For the distinctiveness of this stage direction and others in the play, which refer to events offstage, see Digital Edition TC 3.

1.4 Location: The outskirts of Thebes.

1. Small horns sound offstage, signaling the start of battle, a retreat, and then a triumphal entrance.

And heaven's good eyes look on you. *Exeunt* QUEENS.
[*He notices the hearses.*] What are those?
HERALD Men of great quality,° as may be judged (rank)
By their appointment.° Some of Thebes have told's° (battle gear / told us)
They are sisters' children, nephews to the King.
THESEUS By th' helm of Mars, I saw them in the war,
Like to a pair of lions, smeared with prey,
Make lanes in troops aghast. I fixed my note° (attention)
Constantly on them, for they were a mark° (striking sight)
Worth a god's view. What prisoner was't that told me
When I inquired their names?
HERALD Wi' leave, they're called
Arcite and Palamon—
THESEUS 'Tis right; those, those.
They are not dead?
HERALD Nor in a state of life. Had they been taken
When their last hurts were given, 'twas possible
They might have been recovered;° yet they breathe (healed)
And have the name of men.
THESEUS Then like men use 'em.
The very lees of such, millions of rates,
Exceed the wine of others.[2] All our surgeons
Convent° in their behoof;° our richest balms, (Assemble / behalf)
Rather than niggard,° waste; their lives concern us (use stingily)
Much more than Thebes is worth. Rather than have 'em
Freed of this plight and in their morning° state, (former (healthy))
Sound and at liberty, I would 'em dead;
But forty-thousandfold we had rather have 'em
Prisoners to us than death. Bear 'em speedily
From our kind air—to them unkind[3]—and minister
What man to man may do, for our sake—more,° (even more)
Since I have known frights, fury, friends' behests,
Love's provocations, zeal, a mistress' task,
Desire of liberty, a fever, madness,
Hath set a mark which nature could not reach to
Without some imposition, sickness in will
O'er-wrestling strength in reason.[4] For our love
And great Apollo's° mercy, all our best (god of healing)
Their best skill tender. Lead into the city,
Where, having bound things scattered,° we will post° (reimposed order / hurry)
To Athens fore° our army. *Flourish. Exeunt.* (prior to)

## 1.5

*Music. Enter the* QUEENS *with the* [*Attendants bearing*] *hearses of their knights, in a funeral solemnity, etc.*

QUEENS [*sing*] Urns and odors bring away;
Vapors, sighs darken the day;
Our dole° more deadly looks than dying. (mourning; fate)

2. *The very . . . others:* The dregs of such men far exceed the best that others can offer.
3. Fresh air was thought dangerous to wounds.
4. *Since . . . reason:* Since compelling incentives can impel men to perform beyond their normal abilities, whereas otherwise weak will triumphs over strong reason. *mark:* target. *imposition:* powerful pressure.
1.5 Location: Scene continues.

Balms and gums[1] and heavy cheers,° — *sad countenances*
Sacred vials filled with tears,
And clamors through the wild air flying.

Come, all sad and solemn shows
That are quick-eyed pleasure's foes;
We convent naught else but woes.
We convent, etc.

THIRD QUEEN This funeral path brings° to your household's grave: — *leads*
Joy seize on you again; peace sleep with him.
SECOND QUEEN And this to yours.
FIRST QUEEN Yours this way. Heavens lend
A thousand differing ways to one sure end.° — *death*
THIRD QUEEN This world's a city full of straying streets,
And death's the marketplace where each one meets.
*Exeunt severally.*° — *separately*

## 2.1

*Enter* JAILER *and* WOOER.

JAILER I may depart with° little while I live; something I may — *may spare*
cast° to you, not much. Alas, the prison I keep, though it be — *give (as a dowry)*
for great ones, yet they seldom come; before one salmon,
you shall take a number of minnows. I am given out to be bet-
ter lined° than it can appear to me report° is a true speaker. I — *said to be richer / rumor*
would I were really that° I am delivered° to be. Marry,[1] what — *what / reported*
I have—be it what it will—I will assure upon° my daughter — *bequeath to*
at the day of my death.

WOOER Sir, I demand no more than your own offer, and I will
estate° your daughter in what I have promised— — *settle*

JAILER Well, we will talk more of this when the solemnity[2] is
passed. But have you a full promise of° her? — *from*
*Enter* [JAILER'S] DAUGHTER[, *carrying rushes*].° — *(as floor coverings)*
When that shall be seen, I tender my consent.

WOOER I have, sir. Here she comes.

JAILER [*to* JAILER'S DAUGHTER] Your friend and I have chanced
to name you here, upon the old business. But no more of
that now; so soon as the court hurry is over, we will have an
end of it. I'th' meantime, look tenderly° to the two prisoners. — *carefully*
I can tell you they are princes.

JAILER'S DAUGHTER These strewings° are for their chamber. — *rushes*
'Tis pity they are in prison, and 'twere pity they should be
out. I do think they have patience to make any adversity
ashamed; the prison itself is proud of 'em, and they have all
the world in their chamber.[3]

JAILER They are famed° to be a pair of absolute° men. — *reputed / perfect*

JAILER'S DAUGHTER By my troth, I think fame but stammers° — *underrates*
'em; they stand a grise° above the reach of report.° — *step / their reputation*

JAILER I heard them reported in the battle to be the only doers.° — *supreme achievers*

1. Aromatic substances used in mourning rituals.
2.1 Location: The palace garden in Athens, perhaps with the second, or higher, gallery above representing the window of the cell where Palamon and Arcite are being held.

1. To be sure (originally, by the Virgin Mary).
2. Theseus and Hippolyta's wedding.
3. They have everything they need in their prison cell, because they have each other. See 2.2.61–62.

JAILER'S DAUGHTER Nay, most likely, for they are noble suff'rers.[4] I marvel how they would have looked, had they been victors, that with such a constant nobility enforce a freedom out of bondage, making misery their mirth and affliction a toy° to jest at. *trifle*

JAILER Do they so?

JAILER'S DAUGHTER It seems to me they have no more sense of their captivity than I of ruling Athens. They eat well, look merrily, discourse of many things, but nothing of their own restraint° and disasters. Yet sometime a divided° sigh, martyred° as 'twere i'th' deliverance, will break from one of them—when the other presently° gives it so sweet a rebuke that I could wish myself a sigh to be so chid,° or at least a sigher to be comforted. *captivity / partial* *suppressed* *immediately* *chided*

WOOER I never saw 'em.

JAILER The Duke himself came privately in the night, and so did they;[5] what the reason of it is, I know not.

*Enter* PALAMON *and* ARCITE, *above.*

[*He points at* PALAMON *and* ARCITE.] Look, yonder they are; that's Arcite looks out.

JAILER'S DAUGHTER No, sir, no, that's Palamon. Arcite is the lower° of the twain; [*pointing at* ARCITE] you may perceive a part of him. *shorter*

JAILER Go to,° leave your pointing; they would not make us their object.[6] Out of their sight! *Come now*

JAILER'S DAUGHTER It is a holiday to look on them. Lord, the difference of° men! *between*

*Exeunt* [JAILER, WOOER, *and* JAILER'S DAUGHTER. PALAMON *and* ARCITE *remain*].[7]

## 2.2

PALAMON How do you, noble cousin?
ARCITE How do you, sir?
PALAMON Why, strong enough to laugh at misery
And bear the chance° of war yet; we are prisoners, *uncertainties*
I fear, forever, cousin.
ARCITE I believe it,
And to that destiny have patiently
Laid up my hour to come.° *Consigned my future*
PALAMON O cousin Arcite,
Where is Thebes now?[1] Where is our noble country?
Where are our friends and kindreds? Never more
Must we behold those comforts, never see
The hardy youths strive for° the games of honor— *in*
Hung with the painted favors° of their ladies, *love tokens*
Like tall ships under sail—then start amongst 'em

4. For they endure nobly what others do to them. To do and to suffer are antithetical.
5. Theseus brought them secretly at night.
6. They would not be so rude as to point at us; they don't want to look at us.
7. Textual Comment For the exits and nonexits here, as well as for the probable staging of the next scene on an upper stage and the possibility of Fletcher taking over from Shakespeare here, see Digital Edition TC 4.
2.2 Location: The prison in Athens, upper stage; as in 2.1, the garden is located on the main stage.
1. The kinsmen's view of Thebes in 1.2 is very different, perhaps because Shakespeare probably wrote the earlier scene and Fletcher this one, or perhaps because of their changed circumstances.

And, as an east° wind, leave 'em all behind us *(deadly)*
Like lazy clouds, whilst Palamon and Arcite,
Even in the wagging of a wanton leg,[2]
Outstripped the people's praises, won the garlands,
Ere they have time to wish 'em ours. Oh, never
Shall we two exercise, like twins of honor,
Our arms again, and feel our fiery horses
Like proud seas under us; our good swords now—
Better° the red-eyed god of war ne'er wore— *Better swords*
Ravished° our sides, like age must run to rust *Torn from*
And deck the temples of those gods° that hate us; *Juno; Minerva (Athena)*
These hands shall never draw 'em out like lightning
To blast° whole armies more. *annihilate*

ARCITE No, Palamon,
Those hopes are prisoners with us. Here we are,
And here the graces of our youths must wither
Like a too-timely° spring; here age must find us *Like buds in a premature*
And—which is heaviest,° Palamon—unmarried. *what is saddest*
The sweet embraces of a loving wife,
Loaden with kisses, armed with thousand cupids,
Shall never clasp our necks. No issue° know us; *children*
No figures° of ourselves shall we e'er see *images*
To glad our age, and like young eagles teach 'em
Boldly to gaze against bright arms[3] and say,
"Remember what your fathers were, and conquer!"
The fair-eyed maids shall weep our banishments,
And in their songs curse ever-blinded Fortune
Till she for shame see what a wrong she has done
To youth and nature. This is all our world;
We shall know nothing here but one another,
Hear nothing but the clock that tells° our woes. *enumerates*
The vine shall grow, but we shall never see it;
Summer shall come and with her all delights,
But dead-cold winter must inhabit here still.

PALAMON 'Tis too true, Arcite. To our Theban hounds
That shook the agèd forest with their echoes
No more now must we halloo; no more shake
Our pointed javelins whilst the angry swine° *the wild boar*
Flies like a Parthian[4] quiver from our rages,
Struck with our well-steeled darts. All valiant uses°— *activities*
The food and nourishment of noble minds—
In us two here shall perish; we shall die—
Which is the curse of honor—lastly,° *at last*
Children of grief and ignorance.° *Sad and unknown*

ARCITE Yet, cousin,
Even from the bottom of these miseries,
From all that Fortune can inflict upon us,
I see two comforts rising, two mere° blessings, *pure*
If the gods please: to hold here a brave patience,
And the enjoying of our griefs together.

2. *Even . . . leg*: Effortlessly; rapidly; playfully.
3. Eagles supposedly could gaze at the sun without being blinded.
4. During the era of ancient Rome's supremacy, the Parthians were renowned archers, famous for shooting behind them at their enemies as they pretended to flee.

Whilst Palamon is with me, let me perish
If I think this our prison.

PALAMON Certainly,
'Tis a main° goodness, cousin, that our fortunes — *great*
Were twined together. 'Tis most true, two souls
Put in two noble bodies, let 'em suffer
The gall of hazard,° so° they grow together — *bitterest luck / if*
Will never sink;° they must not, say° they could. — *succumb / even if*
A willing man dies sleeping,[5] and all's done.

ARCITE Shall we make worthy uses of this place
That all men hate so much?

PALAMON How, gentle cousin?

ARCITE Let's think this prison holy sanctuary,
To keep us from corruption of worse men.
We are young and yet desire the ways of honor
That liberty and common conversation,° — *worldly acquaintances*
The poison of pure spirits, might—like women—
Woo us to wander from. What worthy blessing
Can be,° but our imaginations — *Can there be*
May make it ours? And here being thus together,
We are an endless mine° to one another; — *resource*
We are one another's wife, ever begetting
New births of love; we are father, friends, acquaintance;
We are in one another families;
I am your heir and you are mine. This place
Is our inheritance; no hard oppressor
Dare take this from us; here, with a little patience,
We shall live long and loving. No surfeits° seek us; — *diseases from excess*
The hand of war hurts none here, nor the seas
Swallow their youth. Were we at liberty,
A wife might part us lawfully, or business;
Quarrels consume us; envy of ill men
Crave our acquaintance.[6] I might sicken, cousin,
Where you should never know it, and so perish
Without your noble hand to close mine eyes,
Or prayers to the gods. A thousand chances,
Were we from hence, would sever us.

PALAMON You have made me—
I thank you, cousin Arcite—almost wanton° — *frolicsome*
With my captivity. What a misery
It is to live abroad° and everywhere! — *out of captivity*
'Tis like a beast, methinks. I find the court here,
I am sure, a more content;° and all those pleasures — *greater happiness*
That woo the wills of men to vanity
I see through now, and am sufficient° — *in a position*
To tell the world 'tis but a gaudy shadow
That old Time, as he passes by, takes with him.
What had we been, old° in the court of Creon, — *grown old*
Where sin is justice, lust and ignorance
The virtues of the great ones? Cousin Arcite,
Had not the loving gods found this place for us,

5. A man resigned to his fate dies in peace, as if merely falling asleep.

6. *envy . . . acquaintance:* we might emulate the malice (or, our envy) of evil men.

We had died as they do—ill° old men, unwept— *wicked*
And had° their epitaphs, the people's curses. *had for*
Shall I say more?

ARCITE I would hear you still.

PALAMON Ye shall.
Is there record of any two that loved
Better than we do, Arcite?

ARCITE Sure there cannot.

PALAMON I do not think it possible our friendship
Should ever leave us.

ARCITE Till our deaths it cannot,

*Enter* EMILIA *and her* WOMAN [*below*°]. *(in the garden)*

And after death our spirits shall be led
To those that love eternally.° Speak on, sir. *(in Elysium)*

EMILIA [*to her* WOMAN] This garden has a world of pleasures in't.
What flower is this?

WOMAN 'Tis called "narcissus," madam.

EMILIA That was a fair boy, certain, but a fool
To love himself.[7] Were there not maids enough?

ARCITE [*to* PALAMON] Pray, forward.° *go on speaking*

PALAMON Yes.

EMILIA [*to her* WOMAN] Or were they all hard-hearted?

WOMAN They could not be to one so fair.

EMILIA Thou wouldst not.

WOMAN I think I should not, madam.

EMILIA That's a good wench.
But take heed to your kindness, though.

WOMAN Why, madam?

EMILIA Men are mad things.

ARCITE [*to* PALAMON] Will ye go forward, cousin?

EMILIA [*to her* WOMAN] Canst not thou work° such flowers in silk, wench? *embroider*

WOMAN Yes.

EMILIA I'll have a gown full of 'em, and of these.
This is a pretty color; will't not do
Rarely° upon a skirt, wench? *Beautifully*

WOMAN Dainty,° madam. *Very nicely*

ARCITE —Cousin, cousin! How do you, sir? Why, Palamon!

PALAMON Never till now I was in prison, Arcite.

ARCITE Why, what's the matter, man?

PALAMON [*gesturing to* EMILIA] Behold and wonder!
By heaven, she is a goddess.

ARCITE Ha!

PALAMON Do reverence.
She is a goddess, Arcite.

EMILIA [*to her* WOMAN] Of all flowers,
Methinks a rose is best.

WOMAN Why, gentle madam?

EMILIA It is the very emblem of a maid.
For, when the west wind courts her gently,
How modestly she blows° and paints the sun[8] *blooms*

7. Narcissus fell in love with his own reflection in a pool and drowned trying to embrace it. After his death, he was turned into a flower.

8. Tints the sunlight pink; the inside of a rose looks like an image of the sun.

With her chaste blushes! When the north° comes near her— *north wind*
Rude and impatient—then, like chastity,
She locks her beauties in her bud again
And leaves him to base briars.° *thorns*

WOMAN Yet, good madam,
Sometimes her modesty will blow° so far *open*
She falls for't.° A maid— *because of it*
If she have any honor—would be loath
To take example by her.

EMILIA Thou art wanton.

ARCITE [*to* PALAMON] She is wondrous fair.

PALAMON She is all the beauty extant.

EMILIA [*to her* WOMAN] The sun grows high; let's walk in.
Keep these flowers;
We'll see how near art can come near their colors.
I am wondrous merry-hearted; I could laugh now.

WOMAN I could lie down, I am sure.[9]

EMILIA And take one° with you? *(a rose); (a lover)*

WOMAN That's as we[1] bargain, madam—

EMILIA Well, agree,° then. *let's bargain*

*Exeunt* EMILIA *and* WOMAN.

PALAMON What think you of this beauty?

ARCITE 'Tis a rare one.

PALAMON Is't but a rare one?

ARCITE Yes, a matchless beauty.

PALAMON Might not a man well lose himself and love her?

ARCITE I cannot tell what you have done; I have,
Beshrew mine eyes° for't. Now I feel my shackles. *Curse me (an oath)*

PALAMON You love her, then?

ARCITE Who would not?

PALAMON And desire her?

ARCITE Before my liberty.

PALAMON I saw her first.

ARCITE That's nothing—

PALAMON But it shall be.

ARCITE I saw her too.

PALAMON Yes, but you must not love her.

ARCITE I will not, as you do, to worship her
As she is heavenly and a blessèd goddess;
I love her as a woman, to enjoy her.
So both may love.

PALAMON You shall not love at all.

ARCITE Not love at all? Who shall deny me?

PALAMON I that first saw her; I that took possession
First with mine eye of all those beauties
In her revealed to mankind. If thou[2] lov'st her,
Or entertain'st a hope to blast my wishes,
Thou art a traitor, Arcite, and a fellow
False as thy title to° her. Friendship, blood, *claim to possess*
And all the ties between us I disclaim,

9. "Laugh and lie down" was an Elizabethan card game; sexual allusion.
1. The Woman and her lover; or, the Woman and Emilia—with different implications.
2. The contemptuous "thou" replaces the more polite "you." Arcite follows suit at line 217.

If thou once think upon her.
ARCITE Yes, I love her,
And if the lives of all my name lay° on it, *my family depended*
I must do so; I love her with my soul.
If that will lose ye, farewell, Palamon.
I say again I love, and, in loving her, maintain[3]
I am as worthy and as free° a lover *noble*
And have as just a title to her beauty
As any Palamon or any living
That is a man's son.
PALAMON Have I called thee friend?
ARCITE Yes, and have found me so; why are you moved° thus? *incensed*
Let me deal coldly° with you. Am not I *dispassionately*
Part of your blood, part of your soul? You have told me
That I was Palamon and you were Arcite.
PALAMON Yes.
ARCITE Am not I liable to those affections,° *passions*
Those joys, griefs, angers, fears my friend shall suffer?
PALAMON Ye may be.
ARCITE Why, then, would you deal so cunningly,° *trickily*
So strangely,° so unlike a noble kinsman *unlike a friend*
To love alone? Speak truly: do you think me
Unworthy of her sight?° *to gaze at her*
PALAMON No, but unjust
If thou pursue that sight.
ARCITE Because another
First sees the enemy, shall I stand still,
And let mine honor down, and never charge?
PALAMON Yes, if he be but one.° *is alone*
ARCITE But say that one
Had rather combat me?
PALAMON Let that one say so,
And use thy freedom. Else, if thou pursuest her,
Be as that cursèd man that hates his country,
A branded villain.
ARCITE You are mad.
PALAMON I must be,
Till thou art worthy, Arcite—it concerns me;
And in this madness, if I hazard° thee *endanger*
And take thy life, I deal but truly.° *fairly*
ARCITE Fie, sir!
You play the child extremely. I will love her,
I must, I ought to do so, and I dare;
And all this justly.
PALAMON Oh, that now, that now
Thy false self and thy friend had but this fortune:
To be one hour at liberty and grasp
Our good swords in our hands! I would quickly teach thee
What 'twere to filch affection from another;
Thou art baser in it than a cutpurse.° *thief*

3. TEXTUAL COMMENT For attribution of scenes to Fletcher based on his more frequent use of hypermetric lines like this one, see Digital Edition TC 5.

Put but thy head out of this window more,
And—as I have a soul—I'll nail thy life to't.° *to the window frame*
ARCITE Thou dar'st not, fool; thou canst not; thou art feeble.
Put my head out? I'll throw my body out
And leap° the garden when I see her next *jump down to*
And pitch° between her arms to anger thee. *hurl myself*
*Enter* [JAILER].
PALAMON No more—the keeper's coming. I shall live
To knock thy brains out with my shackles.
ARCITE Do—
JAILER By your leave, gentlemen.
PALAMON Now, honest keeper—
JAILER Lord Arcite, you must presently° to th' Duke; *immediately*
The cause I know not yet.
ARCITE I am ready, keeper.
JAILER Prince Palamon, I must awhile bereave you
Of your fair cousin's company.
*Exeunt* ARCITE *and* [JAILER].
PALAMON And me too,
Even when you please, of life. Why is he sent for?
It may be he shall marry her; he's goodly,° *handsome*
And like enough the Duke hath taken notice
Both of his blood° and body. But his falsehood! *noble family*
Why should a friend be treacherous? If that
Get him a wife so noble and so fair,
Let honest men ne'er love again. Once more
I would but see this fair one. Blessèd garden,
And fruit and flowers more blessèd that still° blossom *perpetually*
As her bright eyes shine on ye! Would I were—
For all the fortune of my life hereafter—[4]
Yon little tree, yon blooming apricot!
How I would spread and fling my wanton arms
In at her window! I would bring her fruit
Fit for the gods to feed on; youth and pleasure
Still as° she tasted should be doubled on her; *Whenever*
And, if she be not heavenly, I would make her
So near the gods in nature they should fear her,
And then I am sure she would love me.
*Enter* [JAILER].
How now, keeper?
Where's Arcite?
JAILER Banished. Prince Pirithous
Obtained his liberty;[5] but never more,
Upon his oath and life, must he set foot
Upon this kingdom.
PALAMON He's a blessèd man.
He shall see Thebes again, and call to arms
The bold young men that, when he bids 'em charge,
Fall on like fire. Arcite shall have a fortune,° *chance*
If he dare make himself a worthy lover,
Yet in the field to strike a battle for her;

4. *For . . . hereafter*: And this is the only piece of good fortune I'd ever hope for.

5. The motives behind Pirithous's intercession are not explained.

And if he lose her then, he's a cold coward.
How bravely may he bear himself to win her,
If he be noble Arcite—thousand ways!
Were I at liberty, I would do things
Of such a virtuous greatness that this lady,
This blushing virgin, should take manhood to her
And seek to ravish me.

JAILER My lord, for you
I have this charge° to— *order*

PALAMON To discharge my life.

JAILER No, but from this place to remove your lordship;
The windows are too open.

PALAMON Devils take 'em
That are so envious° to me. Prithee, kill me— *spiteful*

JAILER And hang for't afterward?

PALAMON By this good light,
Had I a sword I would kill thee.

JAILER Why, my lord?

PALAMON Thou bring'st such pelting° scurvy news continually, *paltry*
Thou art not worthy life. I will not go.

JAILER Indeed you must, my lord.

PALAMON May I° see the garden? *Will I be able to*

JAILER No.

PALAMON Then I am resolved—I will not go.

JAILER I must constrain you, then; and—for° you are dangerous— *because*
I'll clap more irons on you.

PALAMON Do, good keeper!
I'll shake 'em so ye shall not sleep;
I'll make ye a new morris.[6] Must I go?

JAILER There is no remedy.

PALAMON Farewell, kind window;
May rude wind never hurt thee. —O my lady,
If ever thou hast felt what sorrow was,
Dream how I suffer. —Come; now bury me.[7]

*Exeunt* PALAMON *and* [JAILER].

## 2.3

*Enter* ARCITE.

ARCITE Banished the kingdom? 'Tis a benefit,
A mercy I must thank 'em for; but banished
The free enjoying of that face I die for—
Oh, 'twas a studied° punishment, a death *deliberate*
Beyond imagination, such a vengeance
That, were I old and wicked, all my sins
Could never pluck upon me. Palamon,
Thou hast the start° now; thou shalt stay and see *advantage*
Her bright eyes break° each morning 'gainst thy window *(like dawn)*
And let in life into thee; thou shalt feed
Upon the sweetness of a noble beauty
That nature ne'er exceeded nor ne'er shall.
Good gods! What happiness has Palamon!

6. Morris dancers wore bells on their clothes.
7. Palamon's new cell will be like a grave because he will be banished from Emilia.
2.3 Location: The countryside outside Athens.

Twenty to one, he'll come to speak to her
And, if she be as gentle as she's fair,
I know she's his; he has a tongue will tame
Tempests and make the wild rocks wanton.° Come what can come— *full of joy*
The worst is death—I will not leave the kingdom.
I know mine own° is but a heap of ruins, *(Thebes)*
And no redress there. If I go, he has her.
I am resolved another shape° shall make me, *a disguise*
Or end my fortunes. Either way I am happy:
I'll see her and be near her, or no more.° *or die*

*Enter four* COUNTRYMEN, *and one with a garland before them.* [ARCITE *stands aside.*]

FIRST COUNTRYMAN My masters, I'll be there, that's certain.
SECOND COUNTRYMAN And I'll be there.
THIRD COUNTRYMAN And I.
FOURTH COUNTRYMAN Why, then, have with ye,° boys. 'Tis but a chiding.[1] *I'll come too*
Let the plow play° today; I'll tickle't out *be idle*
Of the jades' tails tomorrow.[2]
FIRST COUNTRYMAN I am sure
To have my wife as jealous as a turkey[3]—
But that's all one. I'll go through—let her mumble.° *grumble*
SECOND COUNTRYMAN Clap her aboard tomorrow night, and stow her,[4]
And all's made up again.
THIRD COUNTRYMAN Ay, do but put
A fescue° in her fist, and you shall see her *teacher's pointer; penis*
Take a new lesson out° and be a good wench. *Learn a new lesson*
Do we all hold against the Maying?[5]
FOURTH COUNTRYMAN Hold? What should ail us?° *prevent us*
THIRD COUNTRYMAN Arcas will be there.
SECOND COUNTRYMAN And Sennois,
And Rycas—and three better lads ne'er danced
Under green tree—and ye know what wenches, ha?
But will the dainty dominie,° the schoolmaster, *fussy teacher*
Keep touch,° do you think? For he does all,[6] ye know. *Keep his word*
THIRD COUNTRYMAN He'll eat a hornbook[7] ere he fail. Go to—the matter's too far driven° between him and the tanner's daughter to let slip now; and she must° see the Duke, and she must dance too. *affair's gone too far* *really wants to*
FOURTH COUNTRYMAN Shall we be lusty?° *lively*
SECOND COUNTRYMAN All the boys in Athens blow wind i'th' breech on's.[8] [*He dances.*] And here I'll be, and there I'll be, for our town, and here again, and there again. Ha, boys, hey for the weavers![9]

1. The worst punishment I'll get (for not working) is a scolding.
2. *I'll . . . tomorrow:* I'll whip extra work out of the horses ("jades"—also women, hence sexual) tomorrow.
3. Thought to be jealously territorial.
4. Sexual metaphor: board her (like a ship) and fill up her cargo hold.
5. Are we still going to participate in the May Day celebrations (of fertility and the coming of spring)?
6. For he arranges everything.
7. A primer or tablet, protected by a translucent plate of horn, inscribed with the alphabet.
8. Will race to try—and fail—to keep up with us; will fart.
9. Hooray for the weavers (the profession to which the speaker apparently belongs).

FIRST COUNTRYMAN This° must be done i'th' woods. *(the Maying)*
FOURTH COUNTRYMAN Oh, pardon me.° *really?*
SECOND COUNTRYMAN By any° means. Our thing of learning° *all / Our teacher*
says so; where he himself will edify the Duke most parlously° *impressively (ironic)*
in our behalfs. He's excellent i'th' woods; bring him to th'
plains, his learning makes no cry.° *is ignored*
THIRD COUNTRYMAN We'll see the sports; then every man
to's tackle.° And, sweet companions, let's rehearse—by any *morris-dancing gear*
means—before the ladies see us, and do sweetly—and God
knows what may come on't.
FOURTH COUNTRYMAN Content; the sports once ended, we'll
perform. Away, boys—and hold!° *keep this promise*
[ARCITE *steps forward.*]
ARCITE By your leaves, honest friends; pray you—whither go you?
FOURTH COUNTRYMAN Whither? Why, what a° question's that! *what sort of a*
ARCITE Yes, 'tis a question to me that know not.
THIRD COUNTRYMAN To the games, my friend.
SECOND COUNTRYMAN [*to* ARCITE] Where were you bred, you
know it not?
ARCITE Not far, sir. Are there such games today?
FIRST COUNTRYMAN Yes, marry, are there, and such as you
never saw. The Duke himself will be in person there.
ARCITE What pastimes are they?
SECOND COUNTRYMAN Wrestling and running. [*aside to the others*]
'Tis a pretty fellow.
THIRD COUNTRYMAN [*to* ARCITE] Thou wilt not go along?
ARCITE Not yet, sir.
FOURTH COUNTRYMAN Well, sir—take your own time. Come,
boys—
FIRST COUNTRYMAN [*aside to the others*] My mind misgives
me. This fellow has a vengeance trick o'th' hip[1]—mark how
his body's made for't.
SECOND COUNTRYMAN [*aside*] I'll be hanged, though, if he dare
venture. Hang him, plum porridge![2] He wrestle? He roast
eggs![3] Come, let's be gone, lads.
*Exeunt four* [COUNTRYMEN].
ARCITE This is an offered° opportunity *unsought*
I durst not° wish for. Well I could have wrestled[4]— *would not have dared*
The best men called it excellent—and run
Swifter than wind upon a field of corn,° *wheat*
Curling the wealthy° ears, never° flew. I'll venture *abundant / ever*
And in some poor disguise be there; who knows
Whether my brows may not be girt with garlands,
And happiness prefer° me to a place *good fortune promote*
Where I may ever dwell in sight of her? *Exit* ARCITE.

## 2.4

*Enter* JAILER'S DAUGHTER, *alone.*
JAILER'S DAUGHTER Why should I love this gentleman? 'Tis odds° *Chances are*
He never will affect° me. I am base, *love*

1. *My . . . hip:* I fear that this man may be a skillful wrestler.
2. Contemptuous, suggesting that Arcite is out of shape. Plum porridge was a heavy dessert of stewed dried fruits eaten at Christmas.
3. He'd be a better cook than wrestler (?); he probably can't cook an egg (?).
4. I knew how to wrestle.
2.4 Location: The prison in Athens.

My father the mean° keeper of his prison, *lowly*
And he a prince. To marry him is hopeless;
To be his whore[1] is witless. Out upon't!° *(expressing abhorrence)*
What pushes° are we wenches driven to *extremities*
When fifteen° once has found us? First I saw him; *(the age)*
I, seeing, thought he was a goodly man;
He has as much to please a woman in him,
If he please to bestow it so, as ever
These eyes yet looked on. Next I pitied him—
And so would any young wench, o' my conscience,
That ever dreamed, or vowed her maidenhead° *virginity*
To a young handsome man. Then I loved him—
Extremely loved him, infinitely loved him!
And yet he had a cousin, fair as he, too;
But in my heart was Palamon and there,
Lord, what a coil he keeps!° To hear him *turmoil he makes*
Sing in an evening, what a heaven it is!
And yet his songs are sad ones. Fairer spoken
Was never gentleman. When I come in
To bring him water in a morning, first
He bows his noble body, then salutes° me thus: *greets*
"Fair gentle maid, good morrow; may thy goodness
Get thee a happy husband." Once he kissed me:
I loved my lips the better ten days after—
Would he would do so every day! He grieves much—
And me as much to see his misery.
What should I do to make him know I love him?
For I would fain° enjoy him.° Say I ventured *eagerly / (sexually)*
To set him free—what says the law then? Thus much
For law or kindred! I will do it—
And this night, or tomorrow, he shall love me. *Exit.*

## 2.5

*Enter* THESEUS, HIPPOLYTA, PIRITHOUS, EMILIA, ARCITE [*disguised as a countryman*] *with a garland,* [*and Attendants*]. *A short flourish of cornetts and shouts within.*[1]

THESEUS You have done worthily; I have not seen,
Since Hercules, a man of tougher sinews.° *muscles*
Whate'er you are, you run the best, and wrestle,° *wrestle the best*
That these times can allow.° *show*
ARCITE I am proud to please you.
THESEUS What country bred you?
ARCITE This—but far off, prince.
THESEUS Are you a gentleman?
ARCITE My father said so,
And to those gentle uses gave me life.[2]
THESEUS Are you his heir?
ARCITE His youngest, sir.
THESEUS Your father

1. To engage in premarital sex, not prostitution.
2.5 Location: Athens, near the site of the athletic games.
1. TEXTUAL COMMENT For the misnumbering of this—and other—scenes, and the relationship of these errors to the Jailer's Daughter's soliloquies, see Digital Edition TC 6.
2. And raised me for those genteel pursuits.

Sure is a happy sire, then.[3] What proves you?° *(a gentleman)*
ARCITE A little of all noble qualities.° *accomplishments*
I could have kept° a hawk, and well have hallooed *I knew how to keep*
To a deep° cry of dogs; I dare not praise *loud*
My feat in horsemanship—yet they that knew me
Would say it was my best piece;° last, and greatest, *attribute*
I would° be thought a soldier. *used to*
THESEUS You are perfect.° *perfectly well-rounded*
PIRITHOUS Upon my soul, a proper° man. *handsome*
EMILIA He is so.
PIRITHOUS [*to* HIPPOLYTA] How do you like him, lady?
HIPPOLYTA I admire° him. *am amazed at*
I have not seen so young a man so noble—
If he say true—of his sort.° *rank*
EMILIA Believe° *Be sure*
His mother was a wondrous handsome woman—
His face, methinks, goes that way.° *demonstrates that*
HIPPOLYTA But his body
And fiery mind illustrate° a brave father. *indicate; copy*
PIRITHOUS Mark how his virtue,° like a hidden sun, *excellence*
Breaks through his baser garments.
HIPPOLYTA He's well got,° sure. *well-born*
THESEUS [*to* ARCITE] What made you seek this place, sir?
ARCITE Noble Theseus,
To purchase name° and do my ablest service *get a reputation*
To such a well-found° wonder as thy worth— *well-deserved*
For only in thy court, of all the world,
Dwells fair-eyed honor.
PIRITHOUS All his words are worthy.
THESEUS Sir, we are much indebted to your travel,° *journey; effort*
Nor shall you lose your wish. —Pirithous,
Dispose of° this fair gentleman. *Place*
PIRITHOUS Thanks, Theseus.
[*to* ARCITE] Whate'er you are, you're mine, and I shall give you
To a most noble service—to this lady,
This bright young virgin [*gesturing to* EMILIA]; pray observe° her goodness. *respect*
You have honored her fair birthday with your virtues,
And, as your due, you're hers—kiss her fair hand, sir.
ARCITE Sir, you're a noble giver. [*to* EMILIA] Dearest beauty,
Thus let me seal my vowed faith. [*He kisses her hand.*] When your servant—
Your most unworthy creature—but offends you,
Command him die; he shall.
EMILIA [*to* ARCITE] That were too cruel.
If you deserve well, sir, I shall soon see't.
You're mine, and somewhat better than your rank° I'll use you. *position*
PIRITHOUS [*to* ARCITE] I'll see you furnished,° and because you say *equipped*
You are a horseman, I must needs entreat you
This afternoon to ride—but 'tis a rough one.° *(horse)*
ARCITE I like him better, prince: I shall not then

3. Since even his younger (and presumably lesser) son is so accomplished.

Freeze in my saddle.
THESEUS [*to* HIPPOLYTA] Sweet, you must be ready—
And you, Emilia, and [*to* PIRITHOUS] you, friend, and all—
Tomorrow, by the sun,° to do observance° *by sunrise / honor*
To flow'ry May in Dian's wood. [*to* ARCITE] Wait well, sir,
Upon your mistress. —Emily, I hope
He shall not go afoot.
EMILIA That were a shame, sir,
While I have horses. [*to* ARCITE] Take your choice, and what
You want° at any time, let me but know it. *lack*
If you serve faithfully, I dare assure you
You'll find a loving mistress.
ARCITE If I do not,
Let me find that° my father ever hated; *that which*
Disgrace and blows.
THESEUS Go, lead the way; you have won it.[4]
It shall be so: you shall receive all dues
Fit for the honor you have won—'twere wrong else.
[*aside to* EMILIA] Sister, beshrew my heart, you have a servant
That—if I were a woman—would be master.
But you are wise—
EMILIA I hope too wise for that, sir.
*Flourish. Exeunt.*

## 2.6

*Enter* JAILER'S DAUGHTER, *alone.*

JAILER'S DAUGHTER Let all the dukes and all the devils roar;
He is at liberty! I have ventured° for him, *taken a risk*
And out I have brought him. To a little wood
A mile hence I have sent him—where a cedar
Higher than all the rest spreads like a plane° *plane tree*
Fast° by a brook—and there he shall keep close° *Close / shall hide*
Till I provide him files and food, for yet
His iron bracelets° are not off. O Love,° *shackles / Cupid*
What a stouthearted child thou art! My father
Durst better have endured cold iron than done it.[1]
I love him beyond love and beyond reason,
Or wit,° or safety. I have made him know it; *sense*
I care not; I am desperate. If the law
Find me and then condemn me for't, some wenches,
Some honest-hearted maids, will sing my dirge,
And tell to memory my death was noble,
Dying almost a martyr. That way he takes,
I purpose, is my way too. Sure he cannot
Be so unmanly as to leave me here;
If he do, maids will not so easily
Trust men again. And yet he has not thanked me
For what I have done; no, not so much as kissed me,
And that, methinks, is not so well; nor scarcely
Could I persuade him to become a free man,

4. Won the honor of leading the procession.
2.6 Location: Near the prison in Athens.
1. *My . . . it:* My father would sooner have been run through (or decapitated, or chained up) than have freed a prisoner.

He made such scruples of the wrong he did
To me and to my father. Yet I hope,
When he considers more, this love of mine
Will take more root within him. Let him do
What he will with me, so he use me kindly,[2]
For use me° so he shall—or I'll proclaim him, *(sexually)*
And to his face, no man.° I'll presently *(sexually)*
Provide him necessaries and pack my clothes up,
And where there is a path of ground I'll venture,
So he° be with me; by him like a shadow *As long as he'll*
I'll ever dwell. Within this hour the hubbub
Will be all o'er the prison; I am then
Kissing the man they look for. Farewell, father—
Get° many more such prisoners, and such daughters, *Catch; beget*
And shortly you may keep yourself.[3] Now to him! [*Exit.*]

## 3.1

*Cornetts in sundry° places; noise and hallooing as people a-Maying.*[1] *various (offstage)*
*Enter* ARCITE, *alone.*

ARCITE The Duke has lost Hippolyta; each took° *went to*
A several laund.° This is a solemn rite *A different clearing*
They owe bloomed May, and the Athenians pay° it *observe*
To th' heart of° ceremony. O Queen Emilia, *With the utmost*
Fresher than May, sweeter
Than her gold buttons° on the boughs, or all *buds*
Th'enameled knacks° o'th' mead° or garden; yea, *flowers / meadow*
We challenge too the bank of any nymph
That makes the stream seem flowers.[2] Thou—O jewel
O'th' wood, o'th' world—hast likewise blessed a place° *path through the woods*
With thy sole° presence. In thy rumination *mere; solo*
That I, poor man, might eftsoons come between
And chop on some cold thought![3] Thrice blessèd chance
To drop on° such a mistress; expectation *run into*
Most guiltless on't.° Tell me, O Lady Fortune— *unexpectedly*
Next, after Emily, my sovereign—how far
I may be proud. She takes strong note of me,
Hath made me near her, and this beauteous morn—
The prim'st° of all the year—presents me with *best*
A brace° of horses; two such steeds might well *pair*
Be by a pair of kings backed,° in a field *ridden*
That their crowns' titles tried.[4] Alas, alas,
Poor cousin Palamon, poor prisoner, thou
So little dream'st upon my fortune that
Thou think'st thyself the happier thing, to be
So near Emilia; me thou deem'st at Thebes,

2. Provided that he treat me gently; naturally; nobly, in a manner befitting a man of his kind.
3. You yourself may use the jail, since everyone else will either have escaped or been freed.
3.1 Location: All of act 3 takes place in a forest near Athens.
1. May Day celebrations included feasts, hunting, music, entertainments (such as the morris dance of 3.5.140), and dancing around the maypole. See note to 2.3.35.
2. *We . . . flowers:* Emilia surpasses in beauty even a nymph's flowered riverbank, whose reflection makes the river itself seem covered with flowers.
3. *That . . . thought:* Would that I, "poor man," might suddenly come upon you and seize some chaste thought.
4. *in . . . tried:* on a battlefield where they were fighting for each other's kingdoms.

And therein wretched, although free. But if
Thou knew'st my mistress breathed on me, and that
I eared her language,° lived in her eye—O coz, *listened to her*
What passion would enclose° thee! *rage would possess*

*Enter* PALAMON *as out of a bush, with his shackles.*
*[He] bends*° *his fist at* ARCITE. *shakes*

PALAMON Traitor kinsman,
Thou shouldst perceive my passion if these signs
Of prisonment[5] were off me and this hand
But owner of a sword! By all oaths in one,
I—and the justice of my love—would make thee
A confessed traitor. O thou most perfidious
That ever gently looked,° the void'st of honor *seemed gentlemanly*
That e'er bore gentle token,° falsest cousin *wore noble emblems*
That ever blood made kin: call'st thou her thine?
I'll prove it in my shackles—with these hands,
Void of appointment°—that thou liest and art *Devoid of weapons*
A very thief in love, a chaffy° lord *worthless*
Not worth the name of villain. Had I a sword,
And these house-clogs° away— *fetters*

ARCITE Dear cousin Palamon—

PALAMON Cozener° Arcite, give me language such *Cheater (punning)*
As thou hast showed me feat.[6]

ARCITE Not finding in
The circuit of my breast any gross stuff
To form me like your blazon holds me to
This gentleness of answer;[7] 'tis your passion
That thus mistakes, the which, to you being enemy,
Cannot to me be kind.[8] Honor and honesty
I cherish and depend on, howsoe'er
You skip° them in me—and with them, fair coz, *ignore*
I'll maintain my proceedings. Pray be pleased
To show in generous° terms your griefs,° since that *genteel / grievances*
Your question's° with your equal, who professes *dispute is*
To clear his own way[9] with the mind and sword
Of a true gentleman—

PALAMON That thou durst,° Arcite! *You wouldn't dare*

ARCITE My coz, my coz, you have been well advertised° *informed*
How much I dare; you've seen me use my sword
Against th'advice° of fear. Sure, of° another *the warning / by*
You would not hear me doubted, but your silence
Should break out, though i'th' sanctuary![1]

PALAMON Sir,
I have seen you move in such a place° which well *battle; tournament*
Might justify your manhood; you were called
A good knight and a bold. But the whole week's not fair

5. *signs / Of prisonment:* shackles.
6. *give . . . feat:* use words that accord better with your (perfidious) actions.
7. *Not . . . answer:* Since I find nothing in me that fits your description of me, I answer gently. *blazon:* (description of a) coat of arms.
8. *'tis . . . kind:* your anger ("passion") is your enemy (distorts your judgment) and thus to me cannot be kind (because you are my kinsman—"kind" also means "kin"—and friend, and hence we share all enemies).
9. To justify; to make his own way.
1. *your . . . sanctuary:* you would speak to defend me even if you were hiding in a safe place (or in a church).

If any day it rain. Their valiant temper° *attitude*
Men lose when they incline to treachery,
And then they fight like compelled bears—would fly
Were they not tied.[2]

ARCITE Kinsman, you might as well
Speak this and act it in your glass° as to *mirror*
His ear which now disdains you.

PALAMON Come up to me;
Quit° me of these cold gyves;° give me a sword— *Free / chains*
Though it be rusty—and the charity
Of one meal lend me. Come before me then,
A good sword in thy hand, and do but say
That Emily is thine—I will forgive
The trespass° thou hast done me, yea, my life *wrong*
If then thou carry't,° and brave souls in shades° *beat me / Hades*
That have died manly, which will seek of me
Some news from earth, they shall get none but this:
That thou art brave and noble.

ARCITE Be content;
Again betake you to° your hawthorn house. *go back into*
With counsel of the night[3] I will be here
With wholesome viands;° these impediments° *food / shackles*
Will I file off; you shall have garments, and
Perfumes to kill the smell o'th' prison. After,
When you shall stretch yourself and say but, "Arcite,
I am in plight,"° there shall be at your choice *I am ready*
Both sword and armor.

PALAMON O you heavens, dares any
So noble bear a guilty business?° None, *act shamefully*
But only Arcite; therefore none but Arcite
In this kind is so bold.

ARCITE Sweet Palamon—

PALAMON I do embrace you and your offer; for
Your offer do't I only, sir; your person
Without hypocrisy I may not wish
More than my sword's edge on't—[4]

*Wind° horns off.° Cornetts.* *Sound / (offstage)*

ARCITE You hear the horns;
Enter your musit,° lest this match between's *gap in a thicket*
Be crossed ere met.° Give me your hand. Farewell! *prevented before begun*
I'll bring you every needful thing. I pray you
Take comfort and be strong.

PALAMON Pray hold your promise,
And do the deed with a bent brow.° Most certain *stern countenance*
You love me not; be rough with me, and pour
This oil° out of your language. By this air, *smoothness; flattery*
I could for each word give a cuff, my stomach° *anger*
Not reconciled by reason—

ARCITE Plainly spoken.
Yet pardon me hard language. When I spur

2. In bearbaiting competitions (a popular pastime with connections to the theater), bears were tied to a stake.

3. With darkness to assist (and hide) me.

4. *for . . . on't:* I embrace you (physically) and your offer (metaphorically) only because of the nobility of that offer; as for your "person" (your body) itself: I want to run my sword through it. Claiming to want to do anything else would be hypocritical.

My horse, I chide him not; content and anger
In me have but one face.° *the same expression*
*Wind horns.*
Hark, sir, they call
The scattered to the banquet; you must guess
I have an office° there. *assigned duty*

PALAMON Sir, your attendance
Cannot please heaven, and I know your office
Unjustly is achieved.° *Was earned unfairly*

ARCITE 'Tis a good title.° *It was won justly*
I am persuaded this question—sick between's—
By bleeding must be cured.[5] I am a suitor° *I beg*
That to your sword you will bequeath this plea° *lawsuit*
And talk of it no more.

PALAMON But this one word:
You are going now to gaze upon my mistress—
For note you, mine she is—

ARCITE Nay, then—

PALAMON Nay, pray you—
You talk of feeding me to breed me strength;° *strengthen me*
You are going now to look upon a sun
That strengthens what it looks on—there
You have a vantage° o'er me. But enjoy't till *advantage*
I may enforce my remedy. Farewell. *Exeunt.*

## 3.2

*Enter* JAILER'S DAUGHTER, *alone.*

JAILER'S DAUGHTER He has mistook the brake° I meant, is gone *thicket*
After[1] his fancy. 'Tis now well-nigh morning;
No matter—would it were perpetual night
And darkness lord o'th' world. —Hark, 'tis a wolf!
In me hath grief slain fear and, but for one thing,
I care for nothing—and that's Palamon.
I reck° not if the wolves would jaw° me, so° *care / gnaw / if*
He had this file. What if I hallooed for him?
I cannot halloo. If I whooped, what then?
If he not answered I should call a wolf
And do him but that service.[2] I have heard
Strange howls this livelong night; why, may't not be
They have made prey of him? He has no weapons;
He cannot run—the jangling of his gyves
Might call fell° things to listen, who have in them *fiercely fatal*
A sense to know a man unarmed and can
Smell where resistance is. I'll set it down° *record it as fact*
He's torn to pieces; they howled many together,
And then they feed on him. So much for that!
Be bold to ring the bell,° how stand I then? *ring his death knell*
All's chared° when he is gone. No, no, I lie— *My work is all done*
My father's to be hanged for his escape;
Myself to beg,° if I prized life so much *I'd be reduced to beggary*
As to deny my act—but that I would not,

5. *I am . . . cured:* I am convinced that the dispute between us (here, imagined as a sick person) can only be settled (cured) by a bloodletting.

3.2 Location: Scene continues.
1. *is gone / After:* is led by (only).
2. I would at least serve him by calling a wolf to attack him or herself (ironic).

Should I try death by dozens.[3] I am moped;° *dazed*
Food took I none these two days;
Sipped some water. I have not closed mine eyes,
Save when my lids scoured off their brine.[4] Alas,
Dissolve, my life! Let not my sense unsettle,° *reason come unhinged*
Lest I should drown, or stab, or hang myself.
O state of nature,° fail together° in me, *life / entirely; all at once*
Since thy best props° are warped. So, which way now? *supports*
The best way is the next° way to a grave; *nearest*
Each errant step beside[5] is torment. Lo,
The moon is down, the crickets chirp, the screech owl
Calls in the dawn; all offices are done
Save what I fail in.[6] But the point is this:
An end,° and that is all. *Exit.* *A death*

## 3.3

*Enter* ARCITE *with meat, wine, and files.*

ARCITE I should be near the place. Ho! Cousin Palamon!

*Enter* PALAMON.

PALAMON Arcite?

ARCITE The same. I have brought you food and files.
Come forth and fear not; here's no Theseus.

PALAMON Nor none so honest, Arcite.

ARCITE That's no matter;
We'll argue that hereafter. Come, take courage;
You shall not die thus beastly.° Here, sir, drink— *like an animal*
I know you are faint—then I'll talk further with you.

PALAMON Arcite, thou mightst now poison me.

ARCITE I might.
But I must° fear you first. Sit down and, good now,° *should need to / please*
No more of these vain parleys;° let us not, *pointless comments*
Having our ancient[1] reputation with us,
Make talk for[2] fools and cowards. [*He raises his glass.*] To your health—

PALAMON Do.° *You drink first*

ARCITE Pray, sit down, then, and let me entreat you,
By all the honesty and honor in you,
No mention of this woman; 'twill disturb us.
We shall have time enough.

PALAMON Well, sir, I'll pledge you.° *drink your health in reply*

[*He drinks.*]

ARCITE Drink a good hearty draught; it breeds good blood,° man! *makes you strong*
Do not you feel it thaw you?

PALAMON Stay—I'll tell you
After a draught or two more.

ARCITE Spare it not;
The Duke has more, coz. Eat now.

PALAMON Yes.

[*He eats.*]

3. Even if I had to die dozens of times (ways).
4. Except when I blinked to clear my eyes of tears.
5. Each step that wanders from the direct path to the grave.
6. *all . . . in:* all tasks are done, except the one I've failed to complete (either giving the file to Palamon or killing herself).

3.3 Location: Scene continues.
1. Of long standing; former (now reestablished through escape).
2. Talk as though we were; make ourselves the talk of.

ARCITE I am glad
You have so good a stomach.° *an appetite; an anger*
PALAMON I am gladder
I have so good meat° to't. *(to feed my anger)*
ARCITE Is't not mad° lodging *strange; maddening*
Here in the wild woods,[3] cousin?
PALAMON Yes, for them
That have wild° consciences. *uncivilized*
ARCITE How tastes your victuals?
Your hunger needs no sauce, I see.
PALAMON Not much.
But if it did, yours is too tart,[4] sweet cousin.
[*He lifts a piece of meat.*] What is this?
ARCITE Venison.
PALAMON 'Tis a lusty° meat. *hearty*
Give me more wine. Here, Arcite, to the wenches
We have known in our days! The Lord Steward's daughter—
Do you remember her?
ARCITE After you,[5] coz.
PALAMON She loved a black-haired man—
ARCITE She did so. Well, sir?
PALAMON And I have heard some call him Arcite. And—
ARCITE Out with't, faith.
PALAMON She met him in an arbor.
What did she there, coz? Play o'th' virginals?[6]
ARCITE Something° she did, sir. *To some extent*
PALAMON Made her groan° a month for't—or two, or three, or ten. *(in pregnancy)*
ARCITE The Marshal's sister
Had her share too, as I remember, cousin,
Else there be tales° abroad. You'll pledge her? *false rumors*
PALAMON Yes.
ARCITE A pretty brown° wench 'tis. There was a time *brunette*
When young men went a-hunting, and a wood,
And a broad beech—and thereby hangs a tale. [*He sighs.*] Heigh-ho!
PALAMON For Emily, upon my life! Fool,
Away with this strained mirth. I say again—
That sigh was breathed for Emily! Base cousin,
Dar'st thou break[7] first?
ARCITE You are wide.° *wide of the mark*
PALAMON By heaven and earth, there's nothing in thee honest.
ARCITE Then I'll leave you; you are a beast° now. *behaving savagely*
PALAMON As thou mak'st me, traitor.
ARCITE There's all things needful: files, and shirts, and perfumes.
I'll come again some two hours hence and bring
That that shall quiet° all— *silence*
PALAMON A sword and armor.
ARCITE Fear° me not. You are now too foul;° farewell. *Doubt / beastly*
Get off your trinkets;° you shall want naught. *shackles*

3. *woods:* Pun on "wode" (mad).
4. Your insolence ("sauce," line 25) is too bitter ("tart").
5. Finish your toast first, before I propose mine.
6. Small keyboard instrument; (sexual).
7. Break our agreement (not to refer to Emilia).

PALAMON Sirrah°— *(an insult)*
ARCITE I'll hear no more. *Exit.*
PALAMON If he keep touch,° he dies for't.
*Exit.* *keeps his promise*

## 3.4

*Enter* JAILER'S DAUGHTER.

JAILER'S DAUGHTER I am very cold, and all the stars are out, too—
The little stars and all, that look like aglets.° *shiny ornaments*
The sun has seen my folly. Palamon!
Alas, no—he's in heaven. Where am I now?
Yonder's the sea, and there's a ship—how't tumbles!
And there's a rock lies watching under water;
Now, now, it° beats upon it; now, now, now! *(the ship)*
There's a leak sprung, a sound° one; how they cry! *large*
Run[1] her before the wind, you'll lose all else;
Up with a course° or two, and tack° about, boys! *lower sail / turn*
Good night, good night; you're gone. I am very hungry.
Would I could find a fine frog—he would tell me
News from all parts o'th' world; then would I make
A carrack° of a cockleshell and sail *cargo ship*
By east and northeast to the king of pygmies,
For he tells fortunes rarely.° Now, my father *wonderfully*
Twenty to one is trussed up in a trice° *to be hanged quickly*
Tomorrow morning; I'll say never a word.
(*Sings.*) For I'll cut my green coat a foot above my knee,
And I'll clip my yellow locks an inch below mine eye.
Hey nonny, nonny, nonny.
He's buy° me a white cut,[2] forth for to ride, *He shall buy*
And I'll go seek him through the world that is so wide.
Hey nonny, nonny, nonny.
Oh, for a prick now, like a nightingale to put my breast
Against.[3] I shall sleep like a top° else. *Exit.* *soundly*

## 3.5

*Enter* [*Gerald*] *a* SCHOOLMASTER, *four* COUNTRYMEN, [BAVIAN,][1] [NELL, *and four other Countrywomen,*] *with a* TABORER.° *Player of a small drum*

SCHOOLMASTER Fie, fie, what tediosity and disinsanity[2] is here among ye! Have my rudiments° been labored so long with ye, milked unto ye, and—by a figure°—even the very plum broth and marrow[3] of my understanding laid upon ye, and do you still cry "Where?" and "How?" and "Wherefore?" You most coarse-frieze capacities, ye jean judgments[4]—have I said, "Thus let be," and "There let be," and "Then let be,"

*lessons; rehearsals*
*figure of speech*

3.4 Location: Scene continues.
1. TEXTUAL COMMENT For the emendation to "Run" here and what it suggests about the printing of the play, see Digital Edition TC 7.
2. Horse (called a "cut" because it was a gelding or had a cropped tail).
3. *Oh . . . Against:* Nightingales supposedly pricked themselves to stay awake at night. "Prick" also carries a sexual meaning; compare the sexual punning here with that in Ophelia's "mad" speeches in *Hamlet*.

3.5 Location: Scene continues.
1. *Bavian:* a countryman dressed as a baboon for the morris dance, a rural folk dance of north English origin, performed in costume. The dancer who took the part of the fool always dressed as an ape or a baboon.
2. What tedium and insanity (pedantic).
3. "Plum broth" (hearty stew of dried fruits and suet) and "marrow" both suggest essence or fortifying sustenance.
4. *You . . . judgments:* You people of rudimentary intellects. "Frieze" and "jean" were coarse fabrics worn by laborers.

and no man understand me? *Proh deum! Medius fidius!*[5] Ye
are all dunces. For why? Here stand I; here the Duke comes;
there are you close° in the thicket; the Duke appears; I meet    *hidden*
him, and unto him I utter learned things and many figures;
he hears, and nods, and hums,° and then cries "Rare!" and I    *murmurs approval*
go forward.° At length, I fling my cap up—mark there! Then    *continue*
do you, as once did Meleager and the boar,[6] break comely
out° before him; like true lovers,[7] cast yourselves in a body    *appear decorously*
decently;[8] and sweetly, by a figure, trace° and turn, boys.    *follow the steps*

FIRST COUNTRYMAN And sweetly we will do it, Master Gerald.

SECOND COUNTRYMAN Draw up the company. Where's the taborer?

[TABORER *steps forward.*]

THIRD COUNTRYMAN Why, Timothy!

TABORER Here, my mad boys, have at ye!°    *go ahead; I'm ready*

SCHOOLMASTER But, I say, where's their women?

[NELL *and other Countrywomen step forward.*]

FOURTH COUNTRYMAN Here's Friz and Maudlin.

SECOND COUNTRYMAN And little Luce with the white legs,
and bouncing° Barbary.    *robust*

FIRST COUNTRYMAN And freckled Nell, that never failed her
master.°    *(with sexual overtone)*

SCHOOLMASTER Where be your ribbons,[9] maids? Swim° with    *Dance gracefully*
your bodies,
And carry it° sweetly and deliverly,°    *move / nimbly*
And now and then a favor° and a frisk.°    *kiss; bow / leap*

NELL Let us alone,° sir.    *Leave it to us*

SCHOOLMASTER Where's the rest o'th' music?°    *musicians*

THIRD COUNTRYMAN Dispersed° as you commanded.    *Placed here and there*

SCHOOLMASTER Couple,° then,    *Pair up*
And see what's wanting.° [*They assemble for the dance.*]    *who's missing*
Where's the Bavian?

[BAVIAN *steps forward.*]

—My friend, carry your tail without offense°    *sexual offense*
Or scandal to the ladies, and be sure
You tumble with audacity and manhood,°    *bravery*
And when you bark,[1] do it with judgment.

BAVIAN Yes, sir.

SCHOOLMASTER *Quo usque tandem!*[2] Here is a woman wanting.

FOURTH COUNTRYMAN We may go whistle; all the fat's i'th' fire.[3]

SCHOOLMASTER We have, as learnèd authors utter, washed a
tile;°    *worked in vain*
We have been *fatuus*,° and labored vainly.    *foolish (Latin)*

SECOND COUNTRYMAN This is that scornful piece,° that scurvy    *person*
hilding°    *worthless woman*
That gave her promise faithfully she would be here—

5. O God, heaven help me (mangled Latin).
6. Meleager was a Greek warrior who killed the great Calydonian boar and brought its head to the Amazon warrior Atalanta.
7. Like loving subjects of Theseus; in couples, as lovers do.
8. Position yourselves appropriately for the dance.
9. Morris dancers carried ribbons or streamers as props.
1. Baboons were considered half man, half dog.
2. How much longer (must I wait)? (Latin, as throughout the scene.) Expression of impatience that opens the ancient Roman writer Cicero's first oration against Catiline, but here indicates the Schoolmaster's pomposity.
3. We may as well give up, since all our work has produced nothing. Both phrases were proverbial, although the second has a different meaning today.

Cicely, the sempster's° daughter. *seamstress's*
The next gloves that I give her shall be dogskin!° *cheap leather*
Nay, an° she fail me once—you can tell, Arcas,° *if / one of the countrymen*
She swore by wine and bread she would not break.° *(her solemn oath)*

SCHOOLMASTER An eel and woman—
A learnèd poet says—unless by th' tail
And with thy teeth thou hold, will either° fail. *both*
In manners this was false position.[4]

FIRST COUNTRYMAN A fire ill take her;° does she flinch now? *A pox infect her*

THIRD COUNTRYMAN What shall we determine,° sir? *decide to do*

SCHOOLMASTER Nothing—our business is become a nullity,
Yea, and a woeful and a piteous nullity.

FOURTH COUNTRYMAN Now when the credit of our town lay on it,
Now to be frampold, now to piss o'th' nettle![5]
Go thy ways—I'll remember thee; I'll fit thee°— *get even with you*

*Enter* JAILER'S DAUGHTER.

JAILER'S DAUGHTER [*sings*] The George Alow[6] came from the South,
From the coast of Barbary-a;
And there he met with brave gallants of war,° *warships*
By one, by two, by three-a.
"Well hailed, well hailed, you jolly gallants,
And whither now are you bound-a?
Oh, let me have your company
Till I come to the sound-a."
There was three fools fell out about an owlet—
[*Sings.*] The one he said it was an owl,
The other he said nay,
The third he said it was a hawk,
And her bells were cut away.[7]

THIRD COUNTRYMAN There's a dainty° madwoman, master— *fine* comes i'th' nick°—as mad as a March hare. If we can get her *(of time)* dance, we are made again.° I warrant her, she'll do the rarest *all will be well* gambols.° *finest capers*

FIRST COUNTRYMAN A madwoman? We are made, boys!

SCHOOLMASTER And are you mad, good woman?

JAILER'S DAUGHTER I would be sorry else. Give me your hand.

SCHOOLMASTER Why?

JAILER'S DAUGHTER I can tell your fortune.
You are a fool. Tell ten. —I have posed him.[8] Buzz!° *Silence*
—Friend, you must eat no white bread; if you do,
Your teeth will bleed extremely.[9] Shall we dance, ho?
I know you, you're a tinker.° Sirrah tinker, *mender of kettles*

4. A false (pro)position is a logical fallacy. The Schoolmaster compares Cicely's flawed manners to faulty logic.
5. Now to be temperamental, to lose her temper.
6. Probably taken from "The George Alow and the Sweepstake," a ballad published in 1611. The George Alow was a ship.
7. Hawks used for falconry wore bells in order to make them easier to catch.
8. *Tell . . . him:* Count to ten (a common test for insanity or idiocy)—I have stumped ("posed") him. The Jailer's Daughter tests the Schoolmaster for idiocy and fails him.
9. *Your . . . extremely:* Perhaps drawing on the popular belief that a woman's pregnancy causes the man's toothache.

Stop no more holes° but what you should. *(sexual)*
SCHOOLMASTER *Dii boni!*° A tinker, damsel? *Good gods*
JAILER'S DAUGHTER Or a conjurer.° Raise me a devil° now, and let him play *Chi passa* o'th' bells and bones.[1] *magician / (sexual)*
SCHOOLMASTER Go, take her and fluently persuade her to a peace.° *Et opus exegi, quod nec Jovis ira, nec ignis.*[2] Strike up! And lead her in. *to do what we want*
[TABORER *plays.*]
SECOND COUNTRYMAN Come, lass, let's trip it.° *let's dance*
JAILER'S DAUGHTER I'll lead— [*She dances.*]
THIRD COUNTRYMAN Do, do!
SCHOOLMASTER Persuasively, and cunningly.° Away, boys! (*Wind horns.*) I hear the horns. Give me some meditation°—and mark° your cue. *skillfully* / *time to think / don't forget*
*Exeunt all but* SCHOOLMASTER.
Pallas,° inspire me. *goddess of wisdom*
*Enter* THESEUS, PIRITHOUS, HIPPOLYTA, EMILIA, ARCITE, *and train.*
THESEUS This way the stag took.
SCHOOLMASTER Stay, and edify.° *be edified*
THESEUS What have we here?
PIRITHOUS Some country sport, upon my life, sir.
THESEUS [*to* SCHOOLMASTER] Well, sir, go forward, we will "edify."
*Chair and stools* [*brought*] *out.*
Ladies, sit down; we'll stay it.° *stay to watch*
[THESEUS, HIPPOLYTA *and* EMILIA *sit.*]
SCHOOLMASTER Thou doughty Duke, all hail! All hail, sweet ladies!
THESEUS This is a cold° beginning— *(punning on "hail")*
SCHOOLMASTER If you but favor,[3] our country pastime made is.
We are a few of those collected here
That ruder tongues distinguish° "villager." *call*
And—to say verity, and not to fable—
We are a merry rout, or else a rabble,
Or company, or—by a figure°—chorus, *figure of speech*
That fore thy dignity will dance a morris.
And I that am the rectifier° of all, *director; connector*
By title *pedagogus*°—that let fall *teacher*
The birch upon the breeches of the small ones,
And humble with a ferula° the tall ones— *cane (to whip students)*
Do here present this machine or this frame.[4]
And dainty Duke—whose doughty dismal° fame *awe-inspiring*
From Dis to Daedalus,[5] from post to pillar,
Is blown abroad—help me, thy poor well-willer,° *well-wisher*

1. *Chi passa* (Italian: who passes) were the first words of a common dance tune. Bones were used as percussion instruments, along with bells.
2. "And I have created a work that neither Jove's anger nor fire [can destroy]." Slightly misquoted from Ovid's *Metamorphoses* 15.871.
3. Approve. Compare Quince's speech to Theseus in *A Midsummer Night's Dream* 5.1.126–50.
4. Both "machine" and "frame" mean "structure" or "production."
5. Dis was god of the underworld; Daedalus was creator of the Cretan labyrinth and inventor of wings for human flight. Theseus triumphed over both the underworld and the labyrinth. Daedalus is invoked for the sake of alliteration and, because of his association with flight and hence the heavens, for contrast to Dis.

And with thy twinkling eyes, look right and straight
Upon this mighty "Moor" of mickle° weight. *much*
"Is" now comes in[6]—which, being glued together,
Makes "Morris," and the cause that we came hither:
The body of our sport, of no small study.[7]
I first appear—though rude, and raw, and muddy—
To speak before thy noble grace this tenor,[8]
At whose great feet I offer up my penner;° *pen case*
The next,° the Lord of May and Lady bright; *next to appear*
The Chambermaid and Servingman, by night
That seek out silent hanging;[9] then mine Host,
And his fat Spouse, that welcomes to their cost
The gallèd° traveler and with a beck'ning *saddle-sore*
Informs the tapster° to inflame the reck'ning;° *bartender / overcharge*
Then the beest-eating Clown,[1] and next the fool,
The Bavian with long tail and eke long tool,° *penis*
*Cum multis aliis*° that make a dance. *With many others (Latin)*
Say "Ay," and all shall presently° advance. *at once*

THESEUS Ay, ay, by any means, dear *Domine*.° *Teacher*

PIRITHOUS Produce.° *Lead them out*

SCHOOLMASTER *Intrate filii!*[2] Come forth and foot it.

[SCHOOLMASTER *knocks. Enter the dance.*]
*Music; dance.*

[*Sings.*] Ladies, if we have been merry
And have pleased thee with a derry,
And a derry and a down,° *(song refrain words)*
Say the Schoolmaster's no clown.
Duke, if we have pleased thee too,
And have done as good boys should do,
Give us but a tree or twain
For a maypole, and again
Ere another year run out,
We'll make thee laugh and all this rout.° *company*

THESEUS Take twenty,° *Domine*. [*to* HIPPOLYTA] How does my sweetheart? *(trees)*

HIPPOLYTA Never so pleased, sir.

EMILIA 'Twas an excellent dance,
And for a preface° I never heard a better. *as for the prologue*

THESEUS —Schoolmaster, I thank you. —One° see 'em all rewarded. *Someone*

PIRITHOUS And here's something to paint your pole withal.

[*He gives* SCHOOLMASTER *money.*]

THESEUS Now to our sports again.

SCHOOLMASTER [*sings*] May the stag thou hunt'st stand long,° *give a good chase*
And thy dogs be swift and strong;

6. The Schoolmaster displays the word "morris" from two placards, possibly held by the dancers. In Q the word is split into two syllables, "Morr" (here emended to "Moor") and "Is," perhaps an old spelling of "Ice." They may have been spelled out, or perhaps pictograms were used, with the first placard depicting a Moor and the second the allegorical figure Winter.

7. The main part in our entertainment, carefully prepared.

8. Argument; tenner (ten-syllable line).

9. Curtain behind which they can make love.

1. Clown or country shepherd (see line 144) who likes "beest," the thick milk produced by a cow for the first few days after calving.

2. Come in, my sons (children). The masculine *filii* is especially appropriate, since the women's parts were played by boy actors.

May they kill him without lets,° — *obstacles*
And the ladies eat his dowsets.° — *testicles (a delicacy)*
*Wind horns.* [*Exeunt* THESEUS *and party.*]
—Come, we are all made.
*Dii deaeque omnes*;° ye have danced rarely, wenches. — *Gods and goddesses all*
*Exeunt.*

## 3.6

*Enter* PALAMON *from the bush.*

PALAMON About this hour my cousin gave his faith° — *word*
To visit me again, and with him bring
Two swords and two good armors;° if he fail, — *suits of armor*
He's neither man nor soldier. When he left me
I did not think a week could have restored
My lost strength to me, I was grown so low
And crestfall'n with my wants. I thank thee, Arcite:
Thou art yet a fair foe; and I feel myself,
With this refreshing, able once again
To outdure° danger. To delay it longer — *endure; outlast*
Would make the world think—when it comes to hearing°— — *when word gets out*
That I lay fatting like a swine to fight,
And not a soldier.[1] Therefore this blessed morning
Shall be the last, and that sword he refuses,° — *(in choosing first)*
If it but hold,° I kill him with; 'tis justice. — *Unless it breaks*
So, love and fortune for me!
*Enter* ARCITE *with armors and swords.*
—Oh, good morrow.
ARCITE Good morrow, noble kinsman.
PALAMON I have put you
To too much pains, sir.
ARCITE That too much, fair cousin,
Is but a debt to honor, and my duty.
PALAMON Would you were so in all, sir; I could wish ye
As kind a kinsman as you force me find
A beneficial foe, that my embraces
Might thank ye, not my blows.
ARCITE I shall think either,
Well done, a noble recompense.
PALAMON Then I shall quit° you. — *repay*
ARCITE Defy me in these fair terms, and you show° — *show yourself to be*
More than a mistress to me. No more anger,
As you love anything that's honorable!
We were not bred to talk, man. When we are armed
And both upon our guards, then let our fury,
Like meeting of two tides, fly strongly from us,
And then to whom the birthright° of this beauty — *rightful possession*
Truly pertains°—without upbraidings, scorns, — *belongs*
Despisings of our persons, and such poutings
Fitter for girls and schoolboys—will be seen,
And quickly, yours or mine. Will't please you arm, sir?

3.6 Location: Scene continues.
1. *fatting . . . soldier:* being fattened like a swine for the slaughter, rather than preparing myself like a warrior for the fight.

Or, if you feel yourself not fitting° yet *ready*
And furnished with your old strength, I'll stay,° cousin, *wait*
And every day discourse you into health,
As I am spared.° Your person I am friends with, *In my spare time*
And I could wish I had not said I loved her,
Though I had died.[2] But loving such a lady,
And justifying° my love, I must not fly from't. *affirming*

PALAMON Arcite, thou art so brave an enemy
That no man but thy cousin's fit to kill thee.
I am well and lusty.° Choose your arms. *eager to do battle*

ARCITE Choose you, sir.

PALAMON Wilt thou exceed in all,[3] or dost thou do it
To make me spare thee?

ARCITE If you think so, cousin,
You are deceived—for, as I am a soldier,
I will not spare you.

PALAMON That's well said.

ARCITE You'll find it.° *find it so*

PALAMON Then, as I am an honest man, and love
With all the justice of affection,[4]
I'll pay thee soundly.° [*He chooses his armor.*] This I'll take. *punish you properly*

ARCITE [*taking the other set of armor*] That's mine then.
I'll arm you first.

PALAMON Do. [ARCITE *helps him into his armor.*]
Pray thee tell me, cousin,
Where gott'st thou this good armor?

ARCITE 'Tis the Duke's—
And, to say true, I stole it. Do I pinch you?

PALAMON No.

ARCITE Isn't not too heavy?

PALAMON I have worn a lighter,
But I shall make it serve.

ARCITE I'll buckle't close.° *tightly*

PALAMON By any means.

ARCITE You care not for a grand guard?[5]

PALAMON No, no—we'll use no horses. I perceive
You would fain be at that fight.° *rather fight mounted*

ARCITE I am indifferent.

PALAMON Faith, so am I. Good cousin, thrust the buckle
Through far enough.

ARCITE I warrant you.° *Trust me*

PALAMON My casque,° now. *helmet*

ARCITE Will you fight bare-armed?

PALAMON We shall be the nimbler.

ARCITE But use your gauntlets, though; those are o'th' least.° *too small*
Prithee take mine, good cousin.

PALAMON Thank you, Arcite.
How do I look? Am I fall'n much away?° *much thinner*

ARCITE Faith, very little; love has used you kindly.

PALAMON I'll warrant thee—I'll strike home.

2. Although it would have killed me to keep silent.
3. Will you always outdo me in courtesy (as here, by letting me choose my arms first)?
4. Palamon's love of Emilia is just; Palamon will deal justly (honorably) with Arcite because he loves him.
5. Chestplate for fighting on horseback.

ARCITE Do, and spare not;
I'll give you cause, sweet cousin.
PALAMON Now to you, sir.
[*He helps* ARCITE *into his armor.*]
Methinks this armor's very like that, Arcite,
Thou wor'st that day the three kings fell—but lighter.
ARCITE That was a very good one. And that day,
I well remember, you outdid me, cousin;
I never saw such valor. When you charged
Upon the left wing of the enemy,
I spurred hard to come up,° and under me *keep up with you*
I had a right good horse—
PALAMON You had indeed—
A bright bay, I remember.
ARCITE Yes, but all
Was vainly labored in me; you outwent me,
Nor could my wishes reach you.[6] Yet a little
I did by imitation.
PALAMON More by virtue;° *valor*
You are modest, cousin.
ARCITE When I saw you charge first,
Methought I heard a dreadful clap of thunder
Break from the troop.
PALAMON But still before that flew
The lightning of your valor. [ARCITE *starts to move away.*]
Stay a little,
Is not this piece too strait?° *tight*
ARCITE No, no, 'tis well.
PALAMON I would have nothing hurt thee but my sword;
A bruise would be dishonor.
ARCITE Now I am perfect.° *ready*
PALAMON Stand off,° then. *Step back*
ARCITE Take my sword; I hold° it better. *consider*
PALAMON I thank ye, no; keep it, your life lies° on it.[7] *depends*
Here's one—if it but hold,° I ask no more *holds together*
For all my hopes: my cause and honor guard me.
ARCITE And me my love.
*They bow several ways,*[8] *then advance and stand.*
Is there aught else to say?
PALAMON This only, and no more: thou art mine aunt's son,
And that blood we desire to shed is mutual—
In me, thine, and in thee, mine. My sword
Is in my hand, and if thou kill'st me,
The gods and I forgive thee. If there be
A place prepared for those that sleep in honor,
I wish his weary soul that falls may win it.
Fight bravely, cousin; give me thy noble hand.
ARCITE Here, Palamon. This hand shall never more
Come near thee with such friendship.
PALAMON I commend thee.° *(to God)*

6. My wishes to keep up with you were not answered.
7. TEXTUAL COMMENT For the effect of decisions about punctuation on the characterization of Palamon and consequent stage action, see Digital Edition TC 8.
8. They make ceremonial bows in various directions, as if they were jousting in a tournament.

ARCITE If I fall, curse me and say I was a coward,
For none but such dare die in these just trials.° *(disagreeing with Palamon)*
Once more, farewell, my cousin.
PALAMON Farewell, Arcite.
*[They] fight. Horns within; they stand.*
ARCITE Lo, cousin, lo; our folly has undone us!
PALAMON Why?
ARCITE This is the Duke, a-hunting as I told you;
If we be found, we are wretched. Oh, retire,
For honor's sake; and safely, presently,
Into your bush again. Sir, we shall find
Too many° hours to die in; gentle cousin, *More than enough*
If you be seen, you perish instantly
For breaking prison, and I—if you reveal me—
For my contempt.[9] Then all the world will scorn us
And say we had a noble difference,
But base disposers of it.° *settled it ignobly*
PALAMON No, no, cousin,
I will no more be hidden, nor put off
This great adventure° to a second trial. *undertaking*
I know your cunning, and I know your cause;° *motive (for delay)*
He that faints° now, shame take him! Put thyself *is fainthearted*
Upon thy present guard°— *At once on guard*
ARCITE You are not mad?
PALAMON —Or° I will make th'advantage of this hour *Either I'm mad or*
Mine own, and what to come shall threaten me
I fear less than my fortune.° Know, weak cousin, *(in this fight)*
I love Emilia, and in that I'll bury
Thee and all crosses else.° *all other obstacles*
ARCITE Then come what can come,
Thou shalt know, Palamon, I dare as well
Die as discourse or sleep. Only this fears° me: *frightens*
The law will have the honor of our ends.[1]
Have at thy life!
PALAMON Look to thine own° well, Arcite. *(own life)*
*[They] fight again. Horns.*
*Enter* THESEUS, HIPPOLYTA, EMILIA, PIRITHOUS, *and train.*
THESEUS What ignorant and mad malicious° traitors *evil-minded*
Are you, that, 'gainst the tenor° of my laws *purport*
Are making battle, thus like knights appointed,° *armed*
Without my leave and officers of arms?[2]
By Castor,[3] both shall die!
PALAMON Hold° thy word, Theseus. *Keep*
We are certainly both traitors, both despisers° *disobedient*
Of thee and of thy goodness. I am Palamon,
That cannot love thee, he that broke thy prison—
Think well what that deserves—and this is Arcite:
A bolder traitor never trod thy ground;
A falser ne'er seemed friend. This is the man

9. For my disobedience to Theseus's order that I be banished.
1. We will die by execution rather than combat.
2. Overseers of chivalric combat.
3. Common Roman oath. Castor and Pollux, twins, were sons of Jupiter.

Was begged° and banished; this is he condemns thee *petitioned for*
And what thou dar'st do; and in this disguise,
Against thy own edict, follows thy sister,° *sister-in-law*
That fortunate bright° star, the fair Emilia— *luck-bringing*
Whose servant,° if there be a right in seeing *courtly lover*
And first bequeathing of the soul to, justly
I am—and, which is more, dares think her his.
This treachery, like a most trusty lover,
I called him now to answer. If thou beest
As thou art spoken°—great and virtuous, *reported to be*
The true decider of all injuries—
Say, "Fight again," and thou shalt see me, Theseus,
Do such a justice thou thyself wilt envy.
Then take my life; I'll woo thee to't.° *urge; persuade*

PIRITHOUS O heaven,
What more than man is this!

THESEUS I have sworn—

ARCITE We seek not
Thy breath of mercy, Theseus. 'Tis to me
A thing as soon to die as thee to say it,
And no more moved. Where this man calls me traitor,
Let me say thus much: if in love be treason
In service of so excellent a beauty
As I love most and in that faith will perish,
As I have brought my life here to confirm it,
As I have served her truest, worthiest,
As I dare kill this cousin that denies it,
So let me be most traitor, and ye please me.
For° scorning thy edict, Duke, [*indicating* EMILIA] ask that lady *As for*
Why she is fair, and why her eyes command me
Stay here to love her; and if she say "traitor,"
I am a villain fit to lie unburied.

PALAMON Thou shalt have pity of° us both, O Theseus, *on*
If unto neither thou show mercy. Stop,
As thou art just, thy noble ear against us;
As thou art valiant—for thy cousin's° soul, *(Hercules')*
Whose twelve strong labors crown his memory—
Let's° die together at one instant, Duke. *Allow us*
Only a little let him fall before me,
That I may tell my soul he shall not have her.

THESEUS I grant your wish, for, to say true, your cousin
Has ten times more offended, for I gave him
More mercy than you found, sir, your offenses
Being no more than his. None here speak for 'em,
For, ere the sun set, both shall sleep forever.

HIPPOLYTA Alas, the pity! —Now or never, sister,
Speak not° to be denied. That face of yours *Speak so as not*
Will bear the curses else° of after ages *otherwise*
For these lost cousins.

EMILIA In my face, dear sister,
I find no anger to 'em, nor no ruin;
The misadventure of their own eyes kill° 'em. *kills*
Yet that° I will be woman and have pity, *to show that*
My knees shall grow to th' ground but° I'll get mercy. *unless*
Help me, dear sister, in a deed so virtuous

The powers of all women will be with us.
[EMILIA *and* HIPPOLYTA *kneel*.]
—Most royal brother—
HIPPOLYTA Sir, by our tie of marriage—
EMILIA By your own spotless honor—
HIPPOLYTA By that faith,
That fair hand, and that honest heart you gave me—
EMILIA By that you would have pity in another;[4]
By your own virtues infinite—
HIPPOLYTA By valor;
By all the chaste° nights I have ever pleased you— *faithful only to you*
THESEUS These are strange conjurings.° *incantations*
PIRITHOUS Nay, then I'll in too.
[*He kneels*.] By all our friendship, sir; by all our dangers;
By all you love most—wars and [*indicating* HIPPOLYTA] this sweet lady—
EMILIA By that° you would have trembled to deny *(chivalric aid)*
A blushing maid—
HIPPOLYTA By your own eyes; by strength,
In which you swore I went beyond° all women, *I excelled*
Almost all men, and yet I yielded, Theseus—
PIRITHOUS To crown all this, by your most noble soul,
Which cannot want° due mercy, I beg first. *lack*
HIPPOLYTA Next hear my prayers.
EMILIA Last let me entreat, sir.
PIRITHOUS For mercy.
HIPPOLYTA Mercy.
EMILIA Mercy on these princes.
THESEUS Ye make my faith reel.[5]
[EMILIA, HIPPOLYTA, *and* PIRITHOUS *rise*.]
Say I felt
Compassion to 'em both, how would you place° it? *have me bestow*
EMILIA Upon their lives—but with their banishments.
THESEUS You are a right° woman, sister; you have pity, *typical*
But want the understanding where to use it.
If you desire their lives, invent a way
Safer than banishment. Can these two live,
And have the agony of love about 'em,
And not kill one another? Every day
They'd fight about you; hourly bring your honor
In public question with their swords.[6] Be wise, then,
And here forget 'em. It concerns your credit° *reputation*
And my oath equally; I have said they die—
Better they fall by th' law than one another.
Bow not my honor.[7]
EMILIA O my noble brother,
That oath was rashly° made, and in your anger; *impulsively*
Your reason will not hold° it. If such vows *sustain*
Stand for express will,° all the world must perish. *steadfast resolve*
Besides, I have another oath 'gainst yours,

4. By whatever you would expect someone else to pity.
5. You make my constancy to my own oath (to kill the kinsmen) waver.
6. *They'd . . . swords:* They'd fight publicly over you, thus compromising your honor.
7. Don't force me to lower my standards of honor.

Of more authority, I am sure more love,
Not made in passion, neither, but good heed.° *thoughtfulness*
THESEUS What is it, sister?
PIRITHOUS Urge it home, brave lady.
EMILIA That you would ne'er deny me anything
Fit for my modest suit, and your free granting—
I tie you to your word now. If ye fail in't,
Think how you maim your honor—
For now° I am set a-begging, sir, I am deaf *now that*
To all but your compassion—how their lives
Might breed the ruin of my name, opinion.° *my reputation*
Shall anything that loves me perish for° me? *because of*
That were a cruel wisdom. Do men prune
The straight young boughs that blush with thousand blossoms
Because they may be° rotten? O Duke Theseus, *become*
The goodly mothers that have groaned for these° *(in childbirth)*
And all the longing maids that ever loved,
If your vow stand,° shall curse me and my beauty, *holds*
And in their funeral songs for these two cousins
Despise my cruelty and cry woe worth° me, *befall*
Till I am nothing but the scorn of women.
For heaven's sake, save their lives and banish 'em.
THESEUS On what conditions?
EMILIA Swear 'em° never more *Have them swear*
To make me their contention, or to know me,° *think of me*
To tread upon thy dukedom, and to be—
Wherever they shall travel—ever strangers
To one another.
PALAMON I'll be cut a-pieces
Before I take this oath. Forget I love her?
O all ye gods, despise me then! Thy banishment
I not mislike, so we may fairly carry
Our swords and cause along; else never trifle,
But take our lives, Duke. I must love, and will,
And for that love must, and dare, kill this cousin
On any piece° the earth has. *spot of ground*
THESEUS Will you, Arcite,
Take these conditions?
PALAMON He's a villain, then.
PIRITHOUS These are men—
ARCITE No, never, Duke! 'Tis worse to me than begging
To take° my life so basely. Though I think *save*
I never shall enjoy her, yet I'll preserve
The honor of affection and die for her,
Make death a devil.° *Even horribly*
THESEUS What may be done? For now I feel compassion.
PIRITHOUS Let it not fail° again, sir. *diminish*
THESEUS Say, Emilia,
If one of them were dead, as one must, are you
Content to take th'other to your husband?
They cannot both enjoy you. They are princes
As goodly as your own eyes and as noble
As ever fame yet spoke of; look upon 'em,
And, if you can love, end this difference—

I give consent. Are you content too, princes?
PALAMON *and* ARCITE With all our souls.
THESEUS He that she refuses
Must die, then.
PALAMON *and* ARCITE Any death thou canst invent, Duke.
PALAMON If I fall from that mouth,° I fall with favor, *(because of her decision)*
And lovers yet unborn shall bless my ashes.
ARCITE If she refuse me, yet my grave will wed me
And soldiers sing my epitaph.
THESEUS [*to* EMILIA] Make choice, then.
EMILIA I cannot, sir; they are both too excellent;
For° me, a hair shall never fall of° these men. *On account of / from*
HIPPOLYTA What will become of 'em?
THESEUS Thus I ordain it,
And by mine honor once again it stands,
Or both shall die. You shall both to your country,
And each within this month, accompanied
With three fair knights, appear again in this place,
In which I'll plant° a pyramid; and whether,° *fix / whichever*
Before us that are here, can force his cousin,
By fair and knightly strength, to touch the pillar,
He shall enjoy her; the other lose his head,
And all his friends. Nor shall he grudge to fall,[8]
Nor think he dies with interest in° this lady. *a rightful claim to*
Will this content ye?
PALAMON Yes. Here, cousin Arcite,
I am friends again till that hour.
ARCITE I embrace ye.
THESEUS Are you content, sister?
EMILIA Yes, I must, sir,
Else both miscarry.° *perish*
THESEUS [*to* PALAMON *and* ARCITE] Come, shake hands again,
then,
And take heed—as you are gentlemen—this quarrel
Sleep till the hour prefixed, and hold your course.° *keep your resolve*
PALAMON We dare not fail thee, Theseus.
THESEUS Come, I'll give ye
Now usage like to princes and to friends.
When ye return, who wins, I'll settle here;° *set up in Athens*
Who loses, yet I'll weep upon his bier. *Exeunt.*

## 4.1

*Enter* JAILER *and* FIRST FRIEND.

JAILER Heard you no more? Was nothing said of me
Concerning the escape of Palamon?
Good sir, remember!
FIRST FRIEND Nothing that I heard,
For I came home before the business
Was fully ended. Yet I might perceive,
Ere I departed, a great likelihood
Of both their pardons. For Hippolyta

8. And all his friends will die with him; nor should he consider his execution unjust.

4.1 Location: The prison in Athens.

And fair-eyed Emily, upon their knees,
Begged with such handsome pity that the Duke
Methought stood staggering° whether he should follow — *wavering as to*
His rash oath or the sweet compassion
Of those two ladies; and, to second them,
That truly noble prince, Pirithous—
Half his own heart[1]—set in too, that° I hope — *so that*
All shall be well. Neither heard I one question
Of your name, or his scape.

*Enter* SECOND FRIEND.

JAILER Pray heaven it hold° so— — *continue*

SECOND FRIEND Be of good comfort, man; I bring you news,
Good news!

JAILER They are welcome.

SECOND FRIEND Palamon has cleared you,
And got your pardon, and discovered° how, — *exposed*
And by whose means, he escaped—which was your daughter's—
Whose pardon is procured too, and the prisoner,
Not to be held ungrateful to her goodness,
Has given a sum of money to her marriage—
A large one, I'll assure you.

JAILER Ye are a good man
And ever bring good news.

FIRST FRIEND How was it ended?

SECOND FRIEND Why, as it should be. They that ne'er begged
But they prevailed° had their suits fairly granted: — *Without prevailing*
The prisoners have their lives.

FIRST FRIEND I knew 'twould be so.

SECOND FRIEND But there be new conditions, which you'll hear of
At better time.

JAILER I hope they are good—

SECOND FRIEND They are honorable;
How good they'll prove, I know not.

*Enter* WOOER.

FIRST FRIEND 'Twill be known.

WOOER [*to* JAILER] Alas, sir, where's your daughter?

JAILER Why do you ask?

WOOER O sir, when did you see her?

SECOND FRIEND [*aside*] How he looks!

JAILER This morning.

WOOER Was she well? Was she in health?
Sir, when did she sleep?

FIRST FRIEND [*aside*] These are strange questions.

JAILER I do not think she was very well, for now
You make me mind° her. But this very day — *remind me of*
I asked her questions, and she answered me
So far from what she was,° so childishly, — *her usual manner*
So sillily, as if she were a fool,
An innocent, and I was very angry.
But what of her, sir?

WOOER Nothing but my pity.[2]
But you must know it, and as good by me
As by another that less loves her—

1. Hippolyta is (has) the other half.

2. My pity for you and her makes me speak.

JAILER Well, sir?
FIRST FRIEND Not right?° *in her right mind*
SECOND FRIEND Not well?
WOOER No, sir, not well.
'Tis too true—she is mad.
FIRST FRIEND It cannot be.
WOOER Believe—you'll find it so.
JAILER I half suspected
What you told me. The gods comfort her!
Either this was her love to Palamon,
Or fear of my miscarrying[3] on his scape,
Or both—
WOOER 'Tis likely.
JAILER But why all this haste, sir?
WOOER I'll tell you quickly. As I late was angling° *fishing*
In the great lake that lies behind the palace,
From the far shore, thickset with reeds and sedges,
As patiently I was attending sport,° *awaiting a fish*
I heard a voice—a shrill one—and, attentive,
I gave my ear—when I might well perceive
'Twas one that sung and, by the smallness° of it, *high pitch*
A boy or woman. I then left my angle° *fishing rod*
To his own skill,° came near, but yet perceived not *To fish by itself*
Who made the sound, the rushes and the reeds
Had so encompassed it.° I laid me down *overgrown the place*
And listened to the words she sung—for then,
Through a small glade cut by the fishermen,
I saw it was your daughter.
JAILER Pray, go on, sir.
WOOER She sung much, but no sense; only I heard her
Repeat this often: "Palamon is gone,
Is gone to th' wood to gather mulberries—
I'll find him out tomorrow."
FIRST FRIEND Pretty soul!
WOOER "His shackles will betray him; he'll be taken,
And what shall I do then? I'll bring a bevy,° *company*
A hundred black-eyed maids that love as I do—
With chaplets° on their heads of daffadillies, *wreaths*
With cherry lips, and cheeks of damask roses—
And all we'll dance an antic° fore the Duke *a grotesque dance*
And beg his pardon."[4] [*to the* JAILER] Then she talked of you, sir—
That you must lose your head tomorrow morning,
And she must gather flowers to bury you,
And see the house made handsome.° Then she sung *neat*
Nothing but "Willow, willow, willow"[5] and, between,
Ever was "Palamon, fair Palamon"
And "Palamon was a tall° young man." The place *valiant*
Was knee-deep° where she sat; her careless tresses *(in rushes)*
A wreath of bullrush rounded;° about her stuck *encircled*
Thousand freshwater flowers of several° colors, *various*
That° methought she appeared like the fair nymph *Such that*

3. My being punished because of.
4. Beg Duke Theseus to pardon Palamon.
5. Refrain of a popular song, also sung by Desdemona in *Othello* 4.3.

That feeds the lake with waters, or as Iris[6]
Newly dropped down from heaven. Rings she made
Of rushes that grew by,[7] and to 'em spoke
The prettiest posies:[8] "Thus our true love's tied,"
"This you may lose, not me," and many a one.
And then she wept, and sung again, and sighed,
And with the same breath smiled and kissed her hand.

SECOND FRIEND Alas, what pity it is!

WOOER I made in to° her; *approached*
She saw me and straight sought the flood.° I saved her *at once jumped in*
And set her safe to land, when presently
She slipped away and to the city made
With such a cry and swiftness that, believe me,
She left me far behind her. Three or four
I saw from far off cross° her—[*to the* JAILER] one of 'em *intercept*
I knew to be your brother—where she stayed° *stopped*
And fell, scarce to be got away. I left them with her
And hither came to tell you.

*Enter* JAILER'S BROTHER, JAILER'S DAUGHTER, *and others.*

Here they are.

JAILER'S DAUGHTER [*sings*] May you never more enjoy the light,° etc. *(unknown song)*
—Is not this a fine song?

JAILER'S BROTHER Oh, a very fine one.

JAILER'S DAUGHTER I can sing twenty more.

JAILER'S BROTHER I think you can.

JAILER'S DAUGHTER Yes, truly can I—I can sing "The Broom"
And "Bonny Robin."[9] Are not you a tailor?

JAILER'S BROTHER Yes.

JAILER'S DAUGHTER Where's my wedding gown?

JAILER'S BROTHER I'll bring it tomorrow.

JAILER'S DAUGHTER Do, very rarely;° I must be abroad else° *early / or I'll be out*
To call the maids and pay the minstrels—
For I must lose my maidenhead by cocklight;° *before dawn*
'Twill never thrive else.[1]
[*Sings.*] O fair, O sweet, etc.[2]

JAILER'S BROTHER [*aside to* JAILER] You must e'en take it patiently.

JAILER 'Tis true,

JAILER'S DAUGHTER [*to* JAILER *and others*] Good e'en,° good men. Pray, did you ever hear *(evening)*
Of one young Palamon?

JAILER Yes, wench, we know him.

JAILER'S DAUGHTER Is't not a fine young gentleman?

JAILER 'Tis, love.

JAILER'S BROTHER [*aside to* JAILER] By no mean cross her—she is then distempered

6. Goddess of the rainbow and Juno's messenger.
7. *Rings . . . by:* sometimes used as wedding rings in rural (or mock) wedding ceremonies.
8. Mottoes and aphorisms, sometimes engraved on the inside of rings.
9. "The Broom" and "Bonny Robin" were popular songs (Ophelia sings a line of the latter in *Hamlet* 4.5). "Robin" could mean "penis."
1. Otherwise things (or possibly the marriage) won't prosper for me.
2. A song adapted from the seventh of Sir Philip Sidney's *Certain Sonnets* (1598).

Far worse than now she shows.[3]

FIRST FRIEND [*to* JAILER'S DAUGHTER] Yes, he's a fine man.

JAILER'S DAUGHTER Oh, is he so? You have a sister?

FIRST FRIEND Yes.

JAILER'S DAUGHTER But she shall never have him—tell her so—
For° a trick that I know. You'd best look to her— *Because of*
For if she see him once she's gone, she's done
And undone[4] in an hour. All the young maids
Of our town are in love with him, but I laugh at 'em
And let 'em all alone. Is't not a wise course?

FIRST FRIEND Yes.

JAILER'S DAUGHTER There is at least two hundred now with child by him;
There must be four!° Yet I keep close[5] for all this, *four hundred*
Close as a cockle.° And all these° must be boys— *clam / (the offspring)*
He has the trick on't°—and at ten years old *of producing boys*
They must be all gelt for musicians,[6]
And sing the wars of Theseus.

SECOND FRIEND [*aside*] This is strange.

JAILER'S BROTHER [*aside*] As ever you heard—but say nothing.

FIRST FRIEND [*aside*] No.

JAILER'S DAUGHTER They come from all parts of the dukedom to him.
I'll warrant ye, he had not so few last night
As twenty to dispatch; he'll tickle't up° *do the (sexual) job*
In two hours, if his hand be in.° *if he's in good shape*

JAILER She's lost
Past all cure.

JAILER'S BROTHER Heaven forbid, man.

JAILER'S DAUGHTER [*to* JAILER] Come hither; you are a wise man.

FIRST FRIEND [*aside to* SECOND FRIEND] Does she know him?° *recognize her father*

SECOND FRIEND [*to* FIRST FRIEND] No, would she did.

JAILER'S DAUGHTER [*to* JAILER] You are master of a ship?

JAILER Yes.

JAILER'S DAUGHTER Where's your compass?

JAILER Here.

JAILER'S DAUGHTER Set it to th' north.
And now direct your course to th' wood, where Palamon
Lies longing for me. For the tackling,° *rigging*
Let me alone.° Come, weigh,° my hearts, cheerily! *I'll do it / lift anchor*

ALL Ugh, ugh, ugh![7]
'Tis up!° The wind's fair! Top the bowline![8] *(the anchor)*
Out with the mainsail! —Where's your whistle, master?

JAILER'S BROTHER Let's get her in.° *inside (an aside)*

JAILER Up to the top,° boy. *top of the mast*

JAILER'S BROTHER Where's the pilot?

FIRST FRIEND Here—

JAILER'S DAUGHTER What kenn'st thou?° *What do you see*

3. *By . . . shows:* Don't contradict her in any way, or she'll become far more deranged than she is now.
4. *She's done / And undone*: she will fall in love with him and lose her virginity.
5. Keep my mouth (and thighs) closed.
6. They must all be castrated so that their voices do not deepen and they can become singers (of higher parts). Castrati, castrated male singers, became popular in sixteenth-century Italy.
7. Grunts of exertion; possibly the sound of the wind in the sails.
8. *Top the bowline*: Tighten the sail-steadying rope.

SECOND FRIEND A fair wood.

JAILER'S DAUGHTER Bear for° it, master. *Steer toward*

Tack about!

[*Sings*.] When Cynthia° with her borrowed light, etc.[9] *the moon*

*Exeunt*.

## 4.2

*Enter* EMILIA *alone, with two pictures*.° *(of Palamon and Arcite)*

EMILIA Yet I may bind those wounds up that must open
And bleed to death for my sake else;° I'll choose *otherwise*
And end their strife. Two such young handsome men
Shall never fall for° me; their weeping mothers, *die because of*
Following the dead cold ashes of their sons,
Shall never curse my cruelty. [*She looks at one picture*.]
Good heaven,
What a sweet face has Arcite! If wise Nature—
With all her best endowments, all those beauties
She sows into the births of noble bodies—
Were here a mortal woman, and had in her
The coy° denials of young maids, yet doubtless *modest*
She would run mad for this man. What an eye,
Of what a fiery sparkle and quick° sweetness, *lively*
Has this young prince! Here° Love himself sits smiling— *In his eye*
Just such another wanton Ganymede
Set Jove afire with, and enforced the god
Snatch up the goodly boy and set him by him,
A shining constellation.[1] What a brow,
Of what a spacious majesty, he carries,
Arched like the great-eyed Juno's but far sweeter,
Smoother than Pelops' shoulder!° Fame and honor *(made of ivory)*
Methinks from hence,° as from a promontory *his brow*
Pointed° in heaven, should clap their wings and sing *Reaching its peak*
To all the underworld° the loves and fights *lower world, of humanity*
Of gods and such men near 'em.° [*She looks at the other picture*.] Palamon *men most like gods*
Is but his foil;[2] to him a mere dull shadow;
He's swarth and meager;° of an eye as heavy° *dark and thin / sad*
As if he had lost his mother; a still temper°— *lethargic disposition*
No stirring in him, no alacrity;
Of all this° sprightly sharpness, not a smile.° *(Arcite's) / trace*
Yet these° that we count errors may become him: *these qualities*
Narcissus was a sad° boy, but a heavenly.° *serious / beautiful*
Oh, who can find the bent of woman's fancy?[3]
I am a fool; my reason is lost in me;
I have no choice[4]—and I have lied so lewdly° *wickedly*
That women ought to beat me. On my knees
I ask thy pardon, Palamon: thou art alone° *uniquely*

9. Line from an unknown song.
**4.2** Location: Theseus's palace in Athens.
1. With "Just such another [smile], wanton Ganymede / Set Jove afire." Ganymede was a beautiful youth whom Jupiter became enamored of and carried off to be his cupbearer on Mt. Olympus. In the end, Ganymede was transformed into the constellation Aquarius.
2. Piece of thin, reflective metal in which a jewel was set, enhancing the jewel's brilliance (setting it off by contrast).
3. Who can discern which way a woman's affections will tend?
4. I am incapable of choosing.

And only beautiful, and these the eyes,
These the bright lamps of beauty, that command
And threaten love—and what young maid dare cross° 'em? *oppose*
What a bold gravity, and yet inviting,
Has this brown manly face! O Love, this only,
From this hour, is complexion![5] [*She puts down Arcite's picture.*] —Lie there, Arcite;
Thou art a changeling to him, a mere gypsy,[6]
[*She turns back to Palamon's picture.*] And this the noble body. —I am sotted,° *made stupid*
Utterly lost. My virgin's faith[7] has fled me.
For if my brother but even now had asked me
Whether I loved, I had run mad for Arcite;
Now, if my sister, more for Palamon.
Stand both together.° Now, come ask me, brother; *(comparing portraits)*
Alas, I know not. Ask me now, sweet sister;
I may go look.° What a mere child is Fancy, *seek further*
That having two fair gauds° of equal sweetness *toys*
Cannot distinguish,° but must cry for both. *choose*

*Enter* GENTLEMAN.

EMILIA How now, sir?
GENTLEMAN From the noble Duke your brother,
Madam, I bring you news: the knights are come.
EMILIA To end the quarrel?
GENTLEMAN Yes.
EMILIA Would I might end first!
—What sins have I committed, chaste Diana,[8]
That my unspotted youth must now be soiled° *defiled*
With blood of princes, and my chastity
Be made the altar where the lives of lovers—
Two greater and two better never yet
Made mothers joy—must be the sacrifice
To my unhappy beauty?

*Enter* THESEUS, HIPPOLYTA, PIRITHOUS, *and Attendants.*

THESEUS Bring 'em in
Quickly, by any means; I long to see 'em.
[*to* EMILIA] Your two contending lovers are returned,
And with them their fair knights. Now, my fair sister,
You must love one of them.
EMILIA I had rather both,
So° neither for my sake should fall untimely.° *So that / prematurely*
THESEUS —Who saw 'em?
PIRITHOUS I, awhile.
GENTLEMAN And I.

*Enter* MESSENGER.

THESEUS
—From whence come you, sir?

5. *this only . . . complexion:* the only "complexion" I'll appreciate from now on is a dark one.
6. A changeling was an ugly or deformed child left by fairies in exchange for one they stole. Gypsies were also thought to steal children; otherwise the meaning is unclear, since the word generally referred to a swarthy person and Palamon has the dark complexion. Perhaps if a dark complexion is "fair," Arcite's fair skin will be considered the "gypsy" one.
7. My prior oath (1.3.85) to remain a virgin.
8. Virgin goddess of the moon and of the Amazons. See 1.3.52 and note.

MESSENGER From the knights.
THESEUS Pray, speak,
You that have seen them, what they are.
MESSENGER I will, sir,
And truly what I think. Six braver spirits
Than these they have brought—if we judge by the outside—
I never saw nor read of.[9] He that stands
In the first place with Arcite, by his seeming° *appearance*
Should be a stout° man, by his face a prince— *brave*
His very looks so say° him. His complexion, *declare*
Nearer a brown than black, stern, and yet noble—
Which shows him hardy, fearless, proud° of dangers. *scornful*
The circles of his eyes show fire within him,
And as a heated° lion, so he looks. *an angry*
His hair hangs long behind him, black and shining,
Like ravens' wings. His shoulders, broad and strong,
Armed long and round,[1] and on his thigh a sword,
Hung by a curious baldric, when he frowns,
To seal his will with.[2] Better,° o'my conscience, *A better sword*
Was never soldier's friend.
THESEUS Thou hast well described him—
PIRITHOUS Yet a great deal short,
Methinks, of him that's first with Palamon.
THESEUS Pray, speak° him, friend. *describe*
PIRITHOUS I guess he is a prince too,
And, if it may be, greater; for his show° *appearance*
Has all the ornament of honor in't.
He's somewhat bigger than the knight he° spoke of, *(the messenger)*
But of a face far sweeter. His complexion
Is as a ripe grape, ruddy. He has felt
Without doubt what he fights for,° and so apter *(love)*
To make this cause his own. In 's face appears
All the fair hopes of° what he undertakes, *confidence about*
And when he's angry, then a settled° valor— *steady*
Not tainted with extremes—runs through his body
And guides his arm to brave things. Fear he cannot;
He shows no such soft temper. His head's yellow,
Hard-haired,[3] and curled, thick-twined like ivy tods,° *bushy branches of ivy*
Not to undo with° thunder. In his face *Not to be destroyed by*
The livery of the warlike maid[4] appears,
Pure red and white, for yet no beard has blessed him;
And in his rolling° eyes sits Victory, *passionate*
As if she ever° meant to court his valor. *(Victory) always*
His nose stands high, a character° of honor. *distinguishing mark*
His red lips, after fights, are fit for ladies.
EMILIA [*aside*] Must these men die too?
PIRITHOUS When he speaks, his tongue

9. *nor read of:* possibly a joke on the playwright's part; the following descriptions closely follow Chaucer's *Knight's Tale* 2129–78.
1. With long, well-muscled arms.
2. *Hung . . . with:* Hung from an artfully crafted ("curious") sword belt ("baldric"), which he uses to carry out his will when he is angry.
3. Perhaps influenced by Thomas Speght's 1602 edition of Chaucer's *Knight's Tale*, where King Emetrius's hair "was of yron" (was made of iron) instead of "yronne" (curled).
4. *The . . . maid:* His allegiance to Bellona, goddess of war (or possibly to Athena, also associated with warlike powers).

Sounds like a trumpet. All his lineaments° — *body parts*
Are as a man would wish 'em—strong and clean;° — *perfectly shaped*
He wears a well-steeled° ax, the staff° of gold; — *well-honed / handle*
His age some five-and-twenty.

MESSENGER There's another—
A little man, but of a tough soul, seeming
As great° as any; fairer promises — *noble*
In such a body yet I never looked on.

PIRITHOUS Oh, he that's freckle-faced?

MESSENGER The same, my lord.
Are they° not sweet ones? — *(the freckles)*

PIRITHOUS Yes, they are well.

MESSENGER Methinks,
Being so few and well disposed,° they show — *arranged*
Great and fine art in nature. He's white-haired°— — *blond*
Not wanton white,° but such a manly color — *effeminately fair*
Next to an auburn; tough and nimble set,° — *lithe*
Which shows an active soul. His arms are brawny,
Lined with strong sinews; to the shoulder piece
Gently they swell—like women new-conceived°— — *starting pregnancy*
Which speaks him prone to labor, never fainting
Under the weight of arms; stout-hearted, still°— — *when motionless*
But when he stirs, a tiger. He's gray-eyed,[5]
Which yields compassion where he conquers; sharp
To spy advantages, and where he finds 'em,
He's swift to make 'em his. He does no wrongs,
Nor takes none.° He's round-faced, and when he smiles, — *tolerates any*
He shows° a lover; when he frowns, a soldier. — *looks like*
About his head he wears the winner's oak[6]
And in it stuck the favor of his lady.
His age, some six-and-thirty. In his hand
He bears a charging-staff,° embossed with silver. — *lance*

THESEUS Are they all thus?

PIRITHOUS They are all the sons of honor.

THESEUS Now as I have a soul I long to see 'em.
[*to* HIPPOLYTA] Lady, you shall see men fight now.

HIPPOLYTA I wish it,
But not the cause, my lord. They would show
Bravely about the titles of two kingdoms;[7]
'Tis pity love should be so tyrannous.
—O my soft-hearted sister, what think you?
Weep not till they weep blood, wench: it must be.

THESEUS You have steeled 'em° with your beauty. — *made them determined*
[*to* PIRITHOUS] Honored friend,
To you I give the field;° pray, order it — *charge of the combat*
Fitting° the persons that must use it. — *So it is fit for*

PIRITHOUS Yes, sir.

THESEUS Come, I'll go visit 'em. I cannot stay:° — *wait*
Their fame° has fired me so. —Till they appear, — *This account of them*
Good friend, be royal.° — *treat them royally*

5. With eyes of blue or blue-gray. Eyes of this color supposedly implied compassion.
6. Valiant soldiers received a wreath of oak leaves, particularly if they saved their friends in battle.
7. *They . . . kingdoms:* It would be more appropriate if they were fighting for each other's kingdoms.

PIRITHOUS There shall want° no bravery.° *lack / splendor*

EMILIA Poor wench,° go weep; for whosoever wins
Loses a noble cousin for thy sins. *Exeunt.* *(addressing herself)*

## 4.3

*Enter* JAILER, WOOER, [*and*] DOCTOR.[1]

DOCTOR Her distraction is more at some time of the moon than at other some,° is it not? *at others*

JAILER She is continually in a harmless distemper;° sleeps little; altogether without appetite, save often drinking; dreaming of another world and a better; and what broken piece of matter soe'er she's about, the name Palamon lards it,[2] that she farces° every business withal,° fits it to every question. *state of confusion* / *stuffs / with it*

*Enter* JAILER'S DAUGHTER.

Look where she comes; you shall perceive her behavior.

JAILER'S DAUGHTER I have forgot it quite. The burden on't° was "Down-a, down-a," and penned by no worse man than Geraldo, Emilia's schoolmaster. He's as fantastical,° too, as ever he may go upon's legs°—for in the next world will Dido see Palamon, and then will she be out of love with Aeneas.[3] *refrain of the song* / *fanciful* / *as any man*

DOCTOR What stuff's here? Poor soul—

JAILER E'en thus all day long.

JAILER'S DAUGHTER Now for this charm that I told you of: you must bring a piece of silver on the tip of your tongue, or no ferry;[4] then if it be your chance to come where the blessed spirits are—there's a sight now! We maids that have our livers perished,[5] cracked to pieces with love, we shall come there and do nothing all day long but pick flowers with Proserpine.[6] Then will I make Palamon a nosegay;° then let him mark° me; then— *flower bouquet* / *notice*

DOCTOR How prettily she's amiss! Note her a little further.

JAILER'S DAUGHTER Faith, I'll tell you, sometime we go to barley-break[7]—we of the blessed. Alas, 'tis a sore life they have i'th' other place°—such burning, frying, boiling, hissing, howling, chattering, cursing—oh, they have shrewd measure,° take heed! If one be mad, or hang or drown themselves, thither they go—Jupiter bless us!—and there shall we be put in a cauldron of lead and usurers' grease[8] amongst a whole million of cutpurses, and there boil like a gammon° of bacon that will never be enough.° *(hell)* / *harsh retribution* / *side* / *cooked enough*

DOCTOR How her brain coins!° *invents*

4.3 Location: The prison.

1. TEXTUAL COMMENT For the problem of whether this scene should be in prose or verse, see Digital Edition TC 9.

2. Whatever disjointed piece of business she tries to do (or discuss), Palamon's name is inserted into it (like a piece of fat into lean meat in order to make it cook better).

3. Presumably the Schoolmaster has written a song about Dido and her lover, Aeneas, who abandons her in Virgil's *Aeneid*. The Jailer's Daughter imagines a new ending in which Dido falls in love with Palamon rather than Aeneas in the afterworld.

4. Charon demanded payment for ferrying dead souls across the river Styx to the underworld. Hence the custom of placing a coin on the tongues of the dead.

5. Shrivel up from unrequited love. The liver was supposed to be the seat of the passions.

6. One day while she was picking flowers, Proserpine was spotted by Pluto, who carried her off to the underworld to be his queen. Her mother, Demeter, got Zeus to allow her to spend six months on earth each year.

7. A game played with male-female couples: one couple assigned to a place in the field called "hell" attempted to entrap the other couples.

8. The traditional punishment for avarice was boiling in oil (here, imagined as the sweat, "grease," given off by usurers).

JAILER'S DAUGHTER Lords and courtiers that have got maids with child—they are in this place; they shall stand in fire up to the navel and in ice up to th' heart, and there th'offending part burns and the deceiving part freezes—in truth a very grievous punishment, as one would think, for such a trifle. Believe me, one would marry a leprous witch to be rid on't, I'll assure you.

DOCTOR How she continues this fancy! 'Tis not an engraft madness but a most thick and profound melancholy.[9]

JAILER'S DAUGHTER To hear there a proud° lady and a proud city wife° howl together! I were a beast an° I'd call it good sport. One cries, "Oh, this smoke!"; another, "This fire!" One cries, "Oh, that ever I did it behind the arras!"° and then howls; th'other curses a suing fellow and her garden house.[1]

*an aristocratic*
*merchant's wife / if*
*wall hanging*

(*Sings.*) I will be true, my stars, my fate°— *(unknown song)*

*Exit* JAILER'S DAUGHTER.

JAILER What think you of her, sir?

DOCTOR I think she has a perturbed mind, which I cannot minister to.

JAILER Alas, what then?

DOCTOR Understand you she ever affected° any man ere she beheld Palamon? *loved*

JAILER I was once, sir, in great hope she had fixed her liking on this gentleman [*gesturing to* WOOER], my friend.

WOOER I did think so too, and would account I had a great penn'orth° on't to give half my state that both she and I at this present stood unfeignedly on the same terms.[2] *bargain*

DOCTOR That intemp'rate surfeit of her eye hath distempered the other senses;[3] they may return and settle again to execute their preordained faculties, but they are now in a most extravagant vagary.° This you must do: confine her to a place where the light may rather seem to steal in than be permitted; take upon you [*gesturing to* WOOER]—young sir, her friend—the name of Palamon; say you come to eat with her and to commune of love. This will catch her attention, for this her mind beats upon;° other objects that are inserted tween her mind and eye become the pranks and friskins° of her madness. Sing to her such green songs[4] of love as she says Palamon hath sung in prison. Come to her stuck in° as sweet flowers as the season is mistress of, and thereto make an addition of some other compounded odors° which are grateful° to the sense. All this shall become° Palamon, for Palamon can sing, and Palamon is sweet and ev'ry good thing. Desire to eat with her, crave her, drink to her, and, still among,[5] intermingle your petition of grace and acceptance into her favor. Learn what maids have been her companions

*errant wandering*
*is obsessed with*
*tricks and frolics (tools)*
*decorated with*
*blended perfumes*
*pleasant / befit*

9. It is not a rooted ("an engraft") madness, but a deep depression (what today might be called love sickness).
1. *a suing . . . garden house:* a persuasive wooer who lured the lamenting woman into a house in a garden, a site notorious for amorous trysts.
2. *to give . . . same terms:* if I could give half my property so that she and I were as we were before her madness.
3. Her excessive gazing at Palamon has thrown her other senses off.
4. Songs typical of youth.
5. Among these pastimes.

and play-feres,° and let them repair to her with "Palamon" in *playmates*
their mouths and appear with tokens, as if they suggested° *interceded*
for him. It is a falsehood° she is in, which is with falsehoods *delusion*
to be combated. This may bring° her to eat, to sleep, and *induce*
reduce what's now out of square° in her into their former *disordered*
law and regiment.° I have seen it approved[6]—how many *rule*
times I know not—but to make the number more I have
great hope in this. I will between the passages° of this proj- *stages*
ect come in with my appliance.[7] Let us put it in execution
and hasten the success,° which, doubt not, will bring forth *outcome*
comfort. *Exeunt.*

## 5.1

*Flourish. Enter* THESEUS, PIRITHOUS, HIPPOLYTA, [*and*] *Attendants.*

THESEUS Now let 'em enter, and before the gods
Tender their holy prayers. Let the temples
Burn bright with sacred fires and the altars
In hallowed clouds commend° their swelling incense *deliver*
To those above us. Let no due° be wanting— *proper ritual*
They have a noble work in hand will° honor *that will*
The very powers that love 'em.

*Flourish of cornetts. Enter* PALAMON *and* ARCITE *and their* KNIGHTS.

PIRITHOUS Sir, they enter.
THESEUS You valiant and strong-hearted enemies,
You royal german° foes, that this day come *closely related*
To blow that nearness° out that flames between ye: *close kinship*
Lay by your anger for an hour and, dove-like,
Before the holy altars of your helpers,
The all-feared gods, bow down your stubborn bodies.
Your ire° is more than mortal; so° your help be, *anger / so may*
And—as the gods regard° ye—fight with justice. *are watching*
I'll leave you to your prayers, and betwixt ye
I part my wishes.° *divide my hopes*
PIRITHOUS Honor crown the worthiest.

*Exeunt* THESEUS *and his train* [*and* PIRITHOUS].

PALAMON The glass° is running now that cannot finish *hourglass*
Till one of us expire. Think you but thus:
That were there aught in me which strove to show° *to expose itself as*
Mine enemy in this business, were't one eye
Against another, arm oppressed by arm,
I would destroy th'offender, coz—I would,
Though parcel° of myself. Then from this gather *it were a piece*
How I should tender° you. *treat*
ARCITE I am in labor
To push your name, your ancient love, our kindred° *kinship*
Out of my memory, and i'th' selfsame place

6. I have seen this type of treatment successfully carried out.
7. My final mode of treatment (see 5.2).
5.1 Location: The forest. A single altar is probably visible upstage, perhaps on the inner stage, for this scene (at least from line 34) and the next two. Here, it is dedicated to Mars. Q treats these first three scenes as a single one. This makes sense if there are three altars onstage, rather than, as assumed here, only one, which successively represents three different altars, presumably in different locations.

To seat something I would confound.° So hoist we *destroy*
The sails that must these vessels port, even where° *bring to port, wherever*
The heavenly limiter° pleases. *(of life)*

PALAMON You speak well.
Before I turn,° let me embrace thee, cousin—
[*They embrace.*] *turn away*
This I shall never do again.

ARCITE One farewell.

PALAMON Why, let it be so. Farewell, coz.

*Exeunt* PALAMON *and his* KNIGHTS.

ARCITE Farewell, sir.
—Knights, kinsmen, lovers—yea, my sacrifices[1]—
True worshippers of Mars, whose spirit in you
Expels the seeds of fear and th'apprehension
Which still is farther off it[2]—go with me
Before the god of our profession.° There *god we worship*
Require° of him the hearts of lions and *Request*
The breath° of tigers; yea, the fierceness too; *endurance*
Yea, the speed also—to go on,° I mean— *go forward*
Else° wish we to be snails. You know my prize *Otherwise (in retreat)*
Must be dragged out of blood; force and great feat
Must put my garland on, where she sticks
The queen of flowers.[3] Our intercession, then,
Must be to him° that makes the camp a cistern *(Mars)*
Brimmed with the blood of men. Give me your aid,
And bend your spirits toward him.

*They [prostrate themselves before the altar and then] kneel [to address Mars].*

Thou mighty one, that with thy power hast turned
Green Neptune° into purple,[4] whose approach *god of the sea*
Comets prewarn,° whose havoc in vast field *forecast*
Unearthèd° skulls proclaim, whose breath blows down *As yet unburied*
The teeming Ceres' foison,[5] who dost pluck° *pull down*
With hand armipotent[6] from forth blue clouds
The masoned° turrets, that both mak'st and break'st *stone*
The stony girths° of cities; me thy pupil, *walls*
Youngest follower of thy drum, instruct this day
With military skill, that to thy laud° *praise*
I may advance my streamer° and by thee *banner*
Be styled° the lord o'th' day; give me, great Mars, *named*
Some token of thy pleasure.

*Here they fall on their faces as formerly, and there is heard clanging of armor, with a short thunder, as the burst of a battle, whereupon they all rise and bow to the altar.*

O great corrector of enormous° times, *disordered*
Shaker of o'er-rank° states; thou grand decider *overripe*

1. The three knights may literally become human sacrifices from Arcite to Mars if Arcite loses the battle.
2. *th'apprehension . . . it:* the anticipation of a daunting situation, which always is more distant from fear itself.
3. *Must put . . . flowers:* Will win for my head (where Emilia already resides) the victor's laurels, of which she, as the most beautiful of flowers, is part.
4. Red with blood.
5. *whose breath . . . foison:* whose breath (wind) destroys the plenty of the fields produced by Ceres, goddess of agriculture.
6. *armipotent:* powerful in arms. TEXTUAL COMMENT For Shakespeare's use of archaic Chaucerian language, see Digital Edition TC 10.

Of dusty and old titles, that heal'st with blood° *through bloodletting*
The earth when it is sick, and cur'st the world
O'th' pleurisy° of people: I do take *excess*
Thy signs auspiciously, and in thy name
To my design march boldly. —Let us go.

*Exeunt* [ARCITE *and his* KNIGHTS].

*Enter* PALAMON *and his* KNIGHTS, *with the former observance.*° *same rituals as Arcite*

PALAMON Our stars must glister° with new fire or be *fortunes must glisten*
Today extinct.° Our argument is love, *extinguished*
Which, if the goddess of it grant, she gives
Victory too. Then blend your spirits with mine,
You whose free nobleness° do make my cause *generous nobility*
Your personal hazard; to the goddess Venus
Commend° we our proceeding and implore *Commit*
Her power unto our party.

*Here they kneel as formerly* [*to address Venus*].

Hail, sovereign queen of secrets,[7] who hast power
To call the fiercest tyrant from his rage
And weep unto a girl;[8] that hast the might,
Even with an eye-glance, to choke° Mars' drum *silence*
And turn th'alarm° to whispers; that canst make *call to arms*
A cripple flourish with° his crutch and cure him *brandish*
Before Apollo;[9] that mayst force the king
To be his subject's vassal and induce
Stale gravity° to dance! The polled° bachelor— *old men / bald*
Whose youth, like wanton boys through bonfires,
Have skipped° thy flame—at seventy thou canst catch, *Has escaped*
And make him, to the scorn° of his hoarse throat, *(by listeners)*
Abuse young lays of love.[1] What godlike power
Hast thou not power upon? To Phoebus° thou *the sun*
Add'st flames hotter than his; the heavenly fires
Did scorch his mortal son,[2] thine him; the huntress,
All moist and cold, some say, began to throw
Her bow away and sigh.[3] Take to thy grace
Me, thy vowed soldier—who do bear thy yoke
As 'twere a wreath of roses, yet is° heavier *though the yoke is*
Than lead itself, stings more than nettles.
I have never been foul-mouthed against thy law;
Ne'er revealed secret, for I knew none—would not,
Had I kenned° all that were. I never practiced *known*
Upon[4] man's wife, nor would the libels° read *(against love)*
Of liberal° wits. I never at great feasts *licentious*
Sought to betray° a beauty, but have blushed *expose the affairs of*
At simpering sirs that did. I have been harsh
To large confessors[5] and have hotly asked them
If they had mothers; I had one—a woman—

7. As the speech later indicates, beginning at line 99, secrecy and discretion were essential components of the chivalric love code.
8. Make him weep for a girl (or, weep so much that he becomes like a girl).
9. Even more quickly than Apollo, the god of medicine.
1. Botch young lovers' love songs.
2. See note to 1.2.85–87.
3. *the huntress . . . sigh:* Diana, notwithstanding her vow of chastity, fell in love with the shepherd Endymion. *cold:* chaste.
4. *practiced / Upon:* wooed.
5. To those who boast of their love conquests.

And women 'twere they wronged. I knew a man
Of eighty winters—this I told them—who
A lass of fourteen brided.° 'Twas thy° power — *wedded / Venus's*
To put life into dust: the agèd cramp° — *cramp of old age*
Had screwed° his square foot round; — *twisted*
The gout had knit his fingers into knots;
Torturing convulsions from his globy eyes° — *swollen sockets*
Had almost drawn their spheres,° that° what was life — *eyeballs / so that*
In him seemed torture. This anatomy° — *skeleton*
Had by his young fair fere° a boy, and I — *mate*
Believed it was his, for she swore it was—
And who would not believe her? Brief,° I am, — *In short*
To those that prate and have done,[6] no companion;
To those that boast and have not,° a defier; — *have done nothing*
To those that would and cannot, a rejoicer.
Yea, him I do not love that tells close offices° — *secret matters*
The foulest way, nor names concealments[7] in
The boldest language. Such a one I am,
And vow that lover never yet made sigh
Truer than I. O, then, most soft sweet goddess,
Give me the victory of this question,° which — *conflict*
Is true love's merit,° and bless me with a sign — *just deserts*
Of thy great pleasure.
*Here music is heard; doves° are seen to flutter. They fall again upon their faces, then [rise to] their knees.* — *(sacred to Venus)*
O thou that from eleven to ninety reign'st
In mortal bosoms, whose chase° is this world — *hunting ground*
And we in herds thy game, I give thee thanks
For this fair token which, being laid unto° — *added to*
Mine innocent true heart, arms in assurance
My body to this business. [*to his* KNIGHTS] Let us rise
And bow before the goddess.
*They bow.*
Time comes on.° — *It's time (for combat)*
*Exeunt* [PALAMON *and his* KNIGHTS].

*Still° music of recorders. Enter* EMILIA *in white, her hair about her shoulders, [wearing] a wheaten wreath, [with] one [Woman] in white holding up her train, her hair stuck with flowers, [and] one [Woman] before her carrying a silver hind,[8] in which is conveyed incense and sweet odors, which being set up on the altar, her maids standing aloof, she sets fire to it. Then they curtsey and kneel.* — *Soft*

EMILIA O sacred, shadowy, cold, and constant queen;[9]
Abandoner of revels; mute, contemplative,
Sweet, solitary, white, as chaste and pure
As wind-fanned° snow; who to thy female knights — *wind-blown*
Allow'st no more blood° than will make a blush, — *sexual desire*
Which is their order's robe: I here thy priest
Am humbled fore thine altar. Oh, vouchsafe,
With that thy rare green eye, which never yet

6. To those who talk of deeds they have actually done.
7. Nor exposes what should remain hidden.
8. Female deer associated with virginity and hence linked to Diana.
9. *shadowy*: as goddess of the moon, Diana was associated with the night. See 1.3.52, 4.2.58, and 5.1.92–94, notes to these lines.

Beheld thing maculate,° look on thy virgin; *tainted*
And, sacred silver mistress, lend thine ear—
Which ne'er heard scurrile° term, into whose port° *scurrilous / opening*
Ne'er entered wanton° sound—to my petition, *lewd*
Seasoned with holy fear.° This is my last *pious awe*
Of vestal office.[1] I am bride-habited,° *dressed as a bride*
But maiden-hearted; a husband I have 'pointed,° *have been assigned*
But do not know him. Out of two, I should
Choose one and pray for his success, but I
Am guiltless of election.[2] Of mine eyes,
Were I to lose one, they are equal precious;
I could doom neither—that which perished should
Go to't unsentenced.[3] Therefore, most modest queen,
He of the two pretenders° that best loves me *suitors*
And has the truest title in't,° let him *claim to me*
Take off my wheaten garland,° or else grant *Deflower me (see 1.1.64)*
The file and quality I hold I may
Continue in thy band.[4]

*Here the hind vanishes under the altar, and in the place ascends a rose tree, having one rose° up on it.* *(symbol of virginity)*

See what our general of ebbs and flows[5]
Out from the bowels of her holy altar
With sacred act advances: but one rose!
If well inspired,[6] this battle shall confound° *destroy*
Both these brave knights and I, a virgin flower,
Must grow alone, unplucked.

*Here is heard a sudden twang of instruments, the rose falls from the tree*[*, and the tree descends*].

The flower is fall'n; the tree descends. O mistress,
Thou here dischargest me. I shall be gathered[7]—
I think so—but I know not thine own will:
Unclasp thy mystery!° [*to her Women*] I hope she's pleased; *Reveal your meaning*
Her signs were gracious. *They curtsey and exeunt.*

## 5.2

*Enter* DOCTOR, JAILER, *and* WOOER *in* [*the*] *habit of*° *Palamon.* *dressed as*

DOCTOR Has this advice I told you done any good upon her?
WOOER Oh, very much! The maids that kept her company
Have half persuaded her that I am Palamon.
Within this half-hour she came smiling to me,
And asked me what I would eat and when I would kiss her.
I told her "Presently!"° and kissed her twice. *at once*
DOCTOR 'Twas well done; twenty times had been far better,
For there° the cure lies mainly. *(in kissing)*
WOOER Then she told me

1. *my . . . office:* my last duty as your virginal devotee.
2. Am not guilty of having made a choice (and hence of having betrayed my vows).
3. *of mine . . . unsentenced:* In "my eyes" the two noble kinsmen "are equal precious," and hence it is impossible for me to condemn either. Or, I couldn't prefer to "lose one" of my eyes over the other, since "they are equal precious"; I feel the same way about the two men as I do about my eyes.
4. *grant . . . band:* grant that I may continue to hold the rank and condition (of virginity) as one of your devotees.
5. Our ruler of the moon and, hence, of tides.
6. If this is a true omen.
7. I shall be married; I shall lose my virginity.
5.2 Location: The prison.

She would watch° with me tonight, for well she knew — *stay up*
What hour my fit° would take me. — *urgent inclination*

DOCTOR Let her do so—
And when your fit comes, fit her home,[1]
And presently.

WOOER She would have me sing.

DOCTOR You did so?

WOOER No.

DOCTOR 'Twas very ill done then;
You should observe° her ev'ry way. — *accommodate*

WOOER Alas,
I have no voice, sir, to confirm° her that way. — *persuade*

DOCTOR That's all one,° if ye make a noise. — *That doesn't matter*
If she entreat° again, do anything— — *beg*
Lie with her if she ask you.

JAILER Whoa there, Doctor!

DOCTOR Yes, in the way of cure.

JAILER But first, by your leave,
I'th' way of honesty.° — *(after marriage)*

DOCTOR That's but a niceness.° — *an excessive scruple*
Ne'er cast your child away for honesty;[2]
Cure her first this way; then if she will° be honest,° — *wants to / chaste*
She has the path° before her. — *(of marriage)*

JAILER Thank ye, Doctor.

DOCTOR Pray bring her in and let's see how she is.

JAILER I will, and tell her her Palamon stays° for her. — *waits*
But, Doctor, methinks you are i'th' wrong still. *Exit* JAILER.

DOCTOR Go, go!
You fathers are fine fools: her honesty?
An we should give her physic till we find that[3]—

WOOER Why, do you think she is not honest, sir?

DOCTOR How old is she?

WOOER She's eighteen.

DOCTOR She may be,
But that's all one; 'tis nothing to our purpose.° — *it makes no difference*
Whate'er her father says, if you perceive
Her mood inclining that way that I spoke of,
*Videlicet,*° the way of flesh—you have me? — *Namely*

WOOER Yes, very well, sir.

DOCTOR Please her appetite,
And do it home;° it cures her, *ipso facto,*[4] — *completely*
The melancholy humor° that infects her. — *mood (medical)*

WOOER I am of your mind, Doctor.

*Enter* JAILER [*and*] JAILER'S DAUGHTER, *mad.*

DOCTOR You'll find it so. She comes; pray, humor her.

JAILER [*to* JAILER'S DAUGHTER] Come, your love Palamon stays for you, child,
And has done this long hour, to visit you.

JAILER'S DAUGHTER I thank him for his gentle patience;

1. Fully serve her needs (have sex with her).
2. A paradox: don't lose your daughter (to her madness) in order to keep her (chaste).
3. If we were to treat her until we could be sure of her virginity (the obvious continuation of the unfinished thought being, we'd be treating her forever).
4. By the very act (*ipso facto*) of having sex, she'll be cured. The Doctor assumes, correctly in the event, that the Daughter suffers from hysteria, thought to be caused by a wandering womb and cured by intercourse.

He's a kind gentleman, and I am much bound° to him. *obliged*
Did you ne'er see the horse he gave me?
JAILER Yes.
JAILER'S DAUGHTER How do you like him?
JAILER He's a very fair° one. *beautiful*
JAILER'S DAUGHTER You never saw him dance?
JAILER No.
JAILER'S DAUGHTER I have, often.
He dances very finely, very comely—
And for a jig, come cut and long tail to him,[5]
He turns ye like a top.
JAILER That's fine indeed.
JAILER'S DAUGHTER He'll dance the morris twenty mile an hour,
And that will founder the best hobbyhorse[6]—
If I have any skill°—in all the parish; *judgment*
And gallops to the tune of "Light o' Love."[7]
What think you of this horse?
JAILER Having these virtues,
I think he might be brought° to play at tennis. *taught*
JAILER'S DAUGHTER Alas, that's nothing.
JAILER Can he write and read too?
JAILER'S DAUGHTER A very fair hand, and casts himself th'accounts[8]
Of all his hay and provender—that ostler
Must rise betimes that cozens° him. You know *get up early to cheat*
The chestnut mare the Duke has?
JAILER Very well.
JAILER'S DAUGHTER She is horribly in love with him, poor beast!
But he is like his master—coy° and scornful. *aloof*
JAILER What dowry has she?
JAILER'S DAUGHTER Some two hundred bottles° *bales of hay*
And twenty strike° of oats; but he'll ne'er have her. *bushels*
He lisps in 's neighing, able to entice a miller's mare.[9]
He'll be the death of her.
DOCTOR What stuff she utters!
JAILER [*to* JAILER'S DAUGHTER] Make curtsey—here your love comes.
WOOER [*approaching* JAILER'S DAUGHTER] Pretty soul,
How do ye? [*She curtsies.*] That's a fine maid; there's a curtsey!
JAILER'S DAUGHTER Yours to command i'th' way of honesty.
—How far is't now to th'end o'th' world, my masters?
DOCTOR Why, a day's journey, wench.
JAILER'S DAUGHTER Will you go with me?
WOOER What shall we do there, wench?
JAILER'S DAUGHTER Why, play at stool-ball;[1]
What is there else to do?
WOOER I am content
If we shall keep our wedding° there. *As long as we marry*

5. *He . . . him:* He dances finely no matter what horse he is compared with. *cut:* a horse with a docked tail (see note to 3.4.22). There is sexual wordplay throughout this scene.
6. That will lame ("founder") the best morris dancer. *hobbyhorse:* one extremely agile morris dancer was dressed as a horse and imitated its movements.
7. Popular ballad, also referred to in *Much Ado About Nothing* 3.4.39 and *The Two Gentlemen of Verona* 1.2.83. The title means "inconstant in love."
8. He has beautiful penmanship and reckons his own expenses.
9. *He . . . mare:* He's such a smooth talker he could seduce even a miller's mare—a workhorse renowned for its steadfast, circular plodding and, hence, least likely to be distracted.
1. A game, somewhat like cricket, played with ball and bat by women or by men and women together.

JAILER'S DAUGHTER 'Tis true—
For there, I will assure you, we shall find
Some blind priest for the purpose that will venture
To marry us; for here they are nice° and foolish. *too scrupulous*
Besides, my father must be hanged tomorrow,
And that would be a blot i'th' business.
Are not you Palamon?
WOOER Do not you know me?
JAILER'S DAUGHTER Yes, but you care not for me; I have nothing
But this poor petticoat and two coarse smocks.° *undergarments*
WOOER That's all one—I will have you.
JAILER'S DAUGHTER Will you surely?
WOOER Yes, by this fair hand, will I.
[*He takes her hand.*]
JAILER'S DAUGHTER We'll to bed, then.
WOOER E'en when you will.° *Whenever you like*
[*He kisses her.*]
JAILER'S DAUGHTER [*She rubs off the kiss.*] O sir, you would fain be nibbling!
WOOER Why do you rub my kiss off?
JAILER'S DAUGHTER 'Tis a sweet one,
And will perfume me finely against° the wedding. *in preparation for*
[*She gestures to the* DOCTOR.] Is not this your cousin, Arcite?
DOCTOR Yes, sweetheart,
And I am glad my cousin Palamon
Has made so fair a choice.
JAILER'S DAUGHTER Do you think he'll have me?
DOCTOR Yes, without doubt.
JAILER'S DAUGHTER [*to* JAILER] Do you think so too?
JAILER Yes.
JAILER'S DAUGHTER We shall have many children.
[*to* DOCTOR] Lord, how you're grown!
My Palamon, I hope, will grow too,[2] finely,
Now he's at liberty. Alas, poor chicken,
He was kept down with hard meat° and ill lodging— *coarse food*
But I'll kiss him up again.
*Enter a* MESSENGER.
MESSENGER What do you here? You'll lose the noblest sight
That e'er was seen!
JAILER Are they i'th' field?
MESSENGER They are.
You bear a charge° there too. *have a duty*
JAILER I'll away straight;
[*to* DOCTOR] I must e'en leave you here.
DOCTOR Nay, we'll go with you—
I will not lose the sight.
JAILER [*gesturing to* JAILER'S DAUGHTER] How did you like her?
DOCTOR I'll warrant you, within these three or four days
I'll make her right again. [*to* WOOER] You must not from her,
But still preserve° her in this way. *keep treating*
WOOER I will.
DOCTOR Let's get her in.

2. Get fat; have an erection.

WOOER [*to* JAILER'S DAUGHTER] Come, sweet—we'll go to dinner,
And then we'll play at cards.
JAILER'S DAUGHTER And shall we kiss too?
WOOER A hundred times.
JAILER'S DAUGHTER And twenty?
WOOER Ay, and twenty.
DAUGHTER And then we'll sleep together.
DOCTOR [*aside to* WOOER] Take her offer.
WOOER [*to* JAILER'S DAUGHTER] Yes, marry, will we.
JAILER'S DAUGHTER But you shall not hurt me.
WOOER I will not, sweet.
JAILER'S DAUGHTER If you do, love, I'll cry. *Exeunt.*

## 5.3

*Flourish. Enter* THESEUS, HIPPOLYTA, EMILIA, PIRITHOUS, *and some Attendants.*

EMILIA [*hanging back, aside to* PIRITHOUS] I'll no step further.
PIRITHOUS Will you lose this sight?
EMILIA I had rather see a wren hawk at° a fly — *attack in midair*
Than this decision. Ev'ry blow that falls
Threats a brave life; each stroke laments
The place whereon it falls and sounds more like
A bell° than blade. I will stay here: — *death knell*
It is enough my hearing shall be punished
With what shall happen, gainst the which there is
No deafing, but to hear, not taint mine eye[1]
With dread sights it may shun.
PIRITHOUS [*calling ahead to* THESEUS] Sir, my good lord,
Your sister will no further.
THESEUS Oh, she must.
She shall see deeds of honor in their kind,° — *true nature*
Which sometime show well penciled.° Nature now — *even when just drawn*
Shall make and act° the story, the belief — *invent and perform*
Both sealed with eye and ear.[2] —You must be present:
You are the victor's meed,° the prize and garland, — *reward*
To crown the question's title.[3]
EMILIA Pardon me,
If I were there, I'd wink°— — *keep my eyes closed*
THESEUS You must be there:
This trial is, as 'twere, i'th' night, and you
The only star to shine.
EMILIA I am extinct.° — *extinguished*
There is but envy° in that light which shows — *malice*
The one the other.[4] Darkness—which ever was
The dam° of horror, who does stand accursed — *mother*
Of many mortal millions—may even now,
By casting her black mantle over both
That° neither could find other, get herself — *So that*

5.3 Location: The forest, near the tournament field.
1. *there . . . eye:* there is no way to block out the noise in order not to hear, but I will not upset my sight ("taint mine eye").
2. *the belief . . . ear:* the story will be rendered credible by all that is seen and heard.
3. To crown the rightful victor in the dispute.
4. *shows . . . other:* reveals Palamon to Arcite, and vice versa.

Some part of a good name, and many a murder
Set off whereto° she's guilty. *Atone for of which*

HIPPOLYTA You must go.

EMILIA In faith, I will not.

THESEUS Why, the knights must kindle
Their valor at your eye. Know of this war
You are the treasure, and must needs be by° *nearby*
To give the service pay.° *reward the winner*

EMILIA Sir, pardon me—
The title of a kingdom may be tried
Out of itself.° *Outside the kingdom*

THESEUS Well, well, then—at your pleasure.
Those that remain with you could wish their office
To any of their enemies.

HIPPOLYTA Farewell, sister.
I am like to know your husband fore yourself
By some small start of time. He whom the gods
Do of the two know° best, I pray them he *know to be*
Be made your lot.

*Exeunt* [*all except* EMILIA].

EMILIA [*comparing the kinsmen's portraits*] Arcite is gently
visaged,° yet his eye *has a gentle expression*
Is like an engine bent[5] or a sharp weapon
In a soft sheath; mercy and manly courage
Are bedfellows in his visage. Palamon
Has a most menacing aspect; his brow
Is graved° and seems to bury what it frowns on— *furrowed*
Yet sometime 'tis not so, but alters to° *according to*
The quality° of his thoughts. Long time his eye *nature*
Will dwell upon his object. Melancholy
Becomes° him nobly. So does Arcite's mirth, *Suits*
But Palamon's sadness is a kind of mirth,
So mingled as if mirth did make him sad
And sadness merry. Those darker humors° that *moods*
Stick misbecomingly° on others, on him *Seem misplaced*
Live in fair dwelling.[6]

*Cornetts. Trumpets sound as to a charge.*

Hark how yon spurs to spirit° do incite *bravery*
The princes to their proof!° Arcite may win me— *to prove themselves*
And yet may Palamon wound Arcite to
The spoiling of his figure.° Oh, what pity *(so as to disfigure him)*
Enough for such a chance?[7] If I were by,
I might do hurt, for they would glance their eyes
Toward my seat, and in that motion might
Omit a ward or forfeit an offense
Which craved that very time.[8] It is much better
I am not there. Oh, better never born
Than minister to such harm!

*Cornetts. A great cry and noise within crying,*
*"A Palamon!"*[9]

5. Is like a weapon, such as a bow, ready to be released.
6. *on him . . . dwelling:* suit him well.
7. Would be sufficient for such a (sad) turn of events.
8. *might . . . time:* might miss the perfect moment for a defensive parry or an offensive move.
9. War cry supporting Palamon.

*Enter* SERVANT.

What is the chance?° *Who won*

SERVANT The cry's "A Palamon!"

EMILIA Then he has won. 'Twas ever likely—
He looked all grace and success, and he is
Doubtless the prim'st° of men. I prithee, run *most perfect*
And tell me how it goes.

*Shout, and cornetts; crying, "A Palamon!"*

SERVANT Still "Palamon!"

EMILIA Run and inquire. [*Exit* SERVANT.]
[*to Arcite's portrait*] Poor servant,° thou hast lost. *lover (Arcite)*
Upon my right side still I° wore thy picture, *I always*
Palamon's on the left; why so, I know not—
I had no end° in't—else chance would have it so. *purpose*
On the sinister side the heart lies: Palamon
Had the best boding chance.[1]

*Another cry and shout within, and cornetts.*

This burst of clamor
Is sure th'end o'th' combat.

*Enter* SERVANT.

SERVANT They said that Palamon had Arcite's body
Within an inch o'th' pyramid, that the cry
Was general "A Palamon!" But anon
Th'assistants° made a brave redemption,° and *knights / rescue*
The two bold titlers° at this instant are *fighters for the title*
Hand-to-hand at it.

EMILIA Were they° metamorphosed *I wish they were*
Both into one! Oh, why? There were no woman
Worth so composed a man.[2] Their single share,
Their nobleness peculiar to them, gives
The prejudice of disparity—value's shortness—
To any lady breathing.[3]

*Cornetts. Cry within: "Arcite! Arcite!"*

More exulting?
"Palamon" still?

SERVANT Nay, now the sound is "Arcite!"

EMILIA I prithee, lay attention to the cry;
Set both thine ears to th' business.

*Cornetts. A great shout and cry: "Arcite! Victory!"*

SERVANT The cry is
"Arcite!" and "Victory!" Hark! "Arcite! Victory!"
The combat's consummation° is proclaimed *conclusion*
By the wind instruments.

EMILIA Half-sights saw° *Mere glimpses showed*
That Arcite was no babe. God's lid,° his richness *By God's eyelid*
And costliness of spirit looked through him; it could
No more be hid in him than fire in flax,° *straw*
Than humble banks can go to law with° waters *can battle*
That drift° winds force to raging. I did think *driving*

1. *On . . . chance:* The location of Palamon's picture—on Emilia's left ("sinister") side, where her heart is—portended victory, since the contest is about love.
2. *There . . . man:* No woman could be worthy of this composite man made up of both Palamon and Arcite.
3. *Their single . . . breathing:* No woman could have as much nobility as either one of them. *their single share:* each one's value.

Good Palamon would miscarry—yet I knew not
Why I did think so. Our reasons are not prophets
When oft our fancies are. They are coming off.° *leaving the field*
Alas, poor Palamon!
*Cornetts. Enter* THESEUS, HIPPOLYTA, PIRITHOUS,
ARCITE *as victor, and Attendants.*
THESEUS Lo, where our sister is in expectation,
Yet quaking and unsettled. —Fairest Emily,
The gods by their divine arbitrament° *arbitration*
Have given you this knight [*indicating* ARCITE]—he is a
good one
As ever struck at head. Give me your hands:
[*joining their hands*] Receive you her, you him; be plighted
with
A love that grows as you decay.
ARCITE Emily,
To buy you I have lost what's dearest to me,
Save what is bought°—and yet I purchase cheaply, *(Emilia)*
As I do rate your value.
THESEUS O loved sister,
He speaks now of as brave a knight as e'er
Did spur a noble steed. Surely the gods
Would have him die a bachelor, lest his race
Should show i'th' world too godlike. His behavior
So charmed me that methought Alcides° was *Hercules*
To him a sow of lead.[4] If I could praise
Each part of him to th'all I have spoke,[5] your Arcite
Did° not lose by't. For he that was thus good *Would*
Encountered yet his better. I have heard
Two emulous Philomels[6] beat the ear o'th' night
With their contentious throats—now one the higher,
Anon the other, then again the first,
And by and by out-breasted—that the sense[7]
Could not be judge between 'em. So it fared
Good space° between these kinsmen, till heavens did *For a good while*
Make hardly° one the winner. [*to* ARCITE] Wear the garland *Barely make*
With joy that you have won. —For the subdued,° *losers*
Give them our present° justice, since I know *immediate*
Their lives but pinch° 'em. Let it here be done. *torment*
The scene's not for our seeing; go we hence,
Right joyful, with some sorrow. [*to* ARCITE] Arm° your prize; *Give your arm to*
I know you will not lose her. —Hippolyta,
I see one eye of yours conceives a tear,
The which it will deliver.
*Flourish.*
EMILIA Is this winning?
O all you heavenly powers, where is your mercy?
But that your wills have said it must be so—
And charge me live to comfort this unfriended,° *deprived of his friend*

4. *To . . . lead:* Compared to him, like an ingot.
5. *to . . . spoke:* in the same way I have praised Palamon as a whole.
6. Two rival nightingales. In Greek mythology, Philomela was raped by her sister's husband, who cut out her tongue so she couldn't accuse him. By weaving the story into cloth, she nonetheless informed her sister, who fed her husband their son. The gods turned the sister into a nightingale and Philomela into a swallow.
7. *And . . . sense:* And in turn outsung, so that the sense of hearing.

This miserable prince, that cuts away
A life more worthy from him than all women—
I should and would die too.

HIPPOLYTA Infinite pity,
That four such eyes should be so fixed on one° *one woman*
That two must needs be blind for't.[8]

THESEUS So it is. *Exeunt.*

## 5.4

*Enter* PALAMON *and his* KNIGHTS, *pinioned,* JAILER, *Executioner, and Guard* [*bringing in a block*].

PALAMON There's many a man alive that hath outlived
The love o'th' people; yea, i'th' selfsame state
Stands many a father with his child—some comfort
We have by so considering. We expire,
And not without men's pity; to live still,
Have their good wishes.[1] We prevent° *avoid*
The loathsome misery of age, beguile° *cheat*
The gout and rheum° that in lag° hours attend° *coughing / final / wait*
For gray approachers.° We come toward the gods *(to death)*
Young and unwappered,° not halting under° crimes *untired / weighed down by*
Many and stale°—that sure shall please the gods *of long duration*
Sooner than such,° to give us nectar with 'em, *(sinful old men)*
For we are more clear° spirits. [*to his* KNIGHTS] My dear kinsmen, *innocent*
Whose lives for this poor comfort are laid down,
You have sold 'em° too, too cheap. *(your lives)*

FIRST KNIGHT What ending could be
Of more content? O'er us the victors have
Fortune, whose title° is as momentary *claim*
As to us death is certain. A grain of honor
They not o'er-weigh us.[2]

SECOND KNIGHT Let us bid farewell,
And with our patience anger tottering° Fortune, *unstable*
Who at her certain'st reels.[3]

THIRD KNIGHT Come, who begins?

PALAMON E'en he that led you to this banquet shall
Taste to you all.[4] [*to* JAILER] Aha, my friend, my friend,
Your gentle daughter gave me freedom once;
You'll see't done° now for ever. Pray, how does she? *see me set free*
I heard she was not well; her kind of ill° *illness*
Gave me some sorrow.

JAILER Sir, she's well restored,
And to be married shortly.

PALAMON By my short life,
I am most glad on't. 'Tis the latest° thing *last*

8. That two eyes must be blinded (in death); that two men could be so blind as to fight to the death for one woman.
**5.4** Location: Scene continues.
1. *We expire . . . wishes:* Even though we are to die, we have men's good wishes that we might go on living.
2. *A grain . . . us:* They have no more honor than we do.
3. Who, when she seems most certain, suddenly changes direction.
4. Taste (death) first, like the servant at a state banquet who was required to taste the food before the king and guests to make sure it wasn't poisoned.

I shall be glad of—prithee, tell her so.
Commend me to her, and to piece her portion° *increase her dowry*
Tender her this.
*[He gives the* JAILER *a purse.]*
FIRST KNIGHT Nay, let's be offerers all.
SECOND KNIGHT Is it a maid?° *virgin*
PALAMON Verily, I think so—
A right good creature, more to me° deserving *from me*
Than I can 'quite° or speak of. *requite*
ALL KNIGHTS Commend us to her.
*They give their purses.*
JAILER The gods requite you all and make her thankful.
PALAMON Adieu—and let my life be now as short
As my leave-taking.
*[He] lies on the block.*
FIRST KNIGHT Lead, courageous cousin.
FIRST *and* SECOND KNIGHTS We'll follow cheerfully—
*A great noise within, crying, "Run! Save! Hold!"*
*Enter in haste a* MESSENGER.
MESSENGER Hold, hold! Oh, hold, hold, hold!
*Enter* PIRITHOUS *in haste.*
PIRITHOUS Hold, ho! It is a cursèd haste you made
If you have done° so quickly. —Noble Palamon, *finished*
The gods will show their glory in a life
That thou art yet to lead.
PALAMON Can that be,
When Venus, I have said, is false? How do things fare?
PIRITHOUS Arise, great sir, and give the tidings ear
That are most rarely sweet and bitter.
PALAMON *[rising from the block]* What
Hath waked us from our dream?
PIRITHOUS List,° then. Your cousin, *Listen*
Mounted upon a steed that Emily
Did first bestow on him, a black one, owing° *owning*
Not a hair-worth of white—which some will say
Weakens his price, and many will not buy
His goodness with this note,[5] which superstition
Here finds allowance°—on this horse is Arcite *gains support*
Trotting the stones of Athens, which the calkins
Did rather tell than trample,[6] for the horse
Would make his length° a mile if't pleased his rider *length of stride*
To put pride in him.° As he thus went counting *let him show his spirit*
The flinty pavement, dancing as 'twere to th' music
His own hoofs made—for, as they say, from iron
Came music's origin[7]—what envious flint,° *cobblestone*
Cold as old Saturn[8] and, like him, possessed
With fire malevolent, darted a spark,

5. *Weakens . . . note:* Makes him less valuable, because dark horses were considered vicious or ill-omened, and "many will not buy" such a horse, despite his good qualities, because of this feature.
6. *which . . . trample:* the horse's gait was so long and light that its feet seemed more to count ("tell") the cobbles one by one than to trample them. *calkins:* turned-down edges of a horseshoe.
7. Pythagoras is supposed to have discovered music when walking through a blacksmith's forge.
8. According to Chaucer's *Knight's Tale,* Saturn, father of Jupiter, was responsible for the reversal of fortune described here, because he had promised Venus that Palamon would win Emilia. Shakespeare and Fletcher limit Saturn's responsibility to a simile.

Or what fierce sulfur else to this end made,[9]
I comment not. The hot horse, hot as fire,
Took toy° at this and fell to what disorder — *a capricious dislike*
His power could give his will, bounds, comes on end,° — *bucks and rears*
Forgets school-doing°—being therein trained — *school training*
And of kind *manège*.° Pig-like he whines — *well disciplined*
At the sharp rowel,° which he frets at rather — *spur*
Than any jot obeys, seeks all foul means
Of boist'rous and rough jadery° to disseat — *behavior like a nag*
His lord, that kept it bravely.° When naught served— — *who kept his seat well*
When neither curb° would crack, girth break, nor diff'ring° plunges — *jaw restraint / / various*
Disroot his rider whence he grew,° but that — *was fixed*
He kept him tween his legs—on his hind hoofs,
On end he stands,
That Arcite's legs, being higher than his head,
Seemed with strange art to hang. His victor's wreath
Even then fell off his head, and presently
Backward the jade comes o'er, and his full poise° — *weight*
Becomes the rider's load. Yet is he living,
But such a vessel 'tis that floats but for
The surge that next approaches.[1] He much desires
To have some speech with you.

*Enter* THESEUS, HIPPOLYTA, EMILIA, [*and*] ARCITE, *in a chair* [*carried by Attendants*].

Lo, he appears.

PALAMON Oh, miserable end of our alliance!
The gods are mighty. Arcite, if thy heart—
Thy worthy, manly heart—be yet unbroken,
Give me thy last words. I am Palamon,
One that yet loves thee dying.

ARCITE Take Emilia,
And with her all the world's joy. Reach° thy hand— — *Give me*
Farewell. I have told° my last hour. I was false, — *counted*
Yet never treacherous.[2] Forgive me, cousin.
One kiss from fair Emilia. [EMILIA *kisses him.*] 'Tis done.
Take her. I die. [*He dies.*]

PALAMON Thy brave soul seek Elysium!

EMILIA I'll close thine eyes, prince; blessed souls be with thee.
Thou art a right good man, and while I live,
This day I give to tears.

PALAMON And I to honor.

THESEUS In this place first you fought; e'en very here
I sundered you.° Acknowledge to the gods — *separated your fight*
Our thanks that you are living.
His part is played and, though it were too short,
He did it well. Your day is lengthened, and
The blissful dew of heaven does arrose° you. — *sprinkle*
The powerful Venus well hath graced her altar
And given you your love. Our master Mars

9. Or some spark of hellfire made for this purpose.
1. *But such . . . approaches:* But he can live only until the next onslaught (like a boat that can stay afloat only until the next wave hits).
2. *I was . . . treacherous:* I was "false" to our friendship (because Palamon did see Emilia first) but "never treacherous" in vying for Emilia's love.

Hast vouched° his oracle and to Arcite gave *made good on*
The grace of the contention.° So the deities *victory in the battle*
Have showed due justice.
[*to the Attendants, indicating Arcite's corpse*]
Bear this hence.

PALAMON O cousin,
That we should things desire which do cost us
The loss of our desire! That naught could buy
Dear love but loss of dear love!
[*Arcite's corpse is carried out.*]

THESEUS Never Fortune
Did play a subtler game. The conquered triumphs;
The victor has the loss. Yet in the passage° *proceedings*
The gods have been most equal.° —Palamon, *impartial*
Your kinsman hath confessed the right o'th' lady° *the right to Emilia*
Did lie in you,° for you first saw her and *Was yours*
Even then proclaimed your fancy. He restored her
As your stolen jewel and desired your spirit
To send him hence forgiven. The gods my justice
Take from my hand, and they themselves become
The executioners.° Lead your lady off, *executors of justice*
And call your lovers from the stage of death,° *friends from the scaffold*
Whom I adopt my friends. A day or two
Let us look sadly and give grace unto
The funeral of Arcite, in whose end° *after which*
The visages of bridegrooms we'll put on
And smile with Palamon—for whom an hour,
But one hour since, I was as dearly sorry
As glad of Arcite, and am now as glad
As for him sorry. O you heavenly charmers,° *gods who enchant us*
What things you make of us! For what we lack,
We laugh;° for what we have, are sorry, still *enjoy contemplating*
Are children in some kind. Let us be thankful
For that which is, and with you leave dispute
That are above our question.[3] Let's go off,
And bear us like° the time. *Flourish. Exeunt.* *act in accordance with*

## Epilogue

[*Enter* EPILOGUE.]

EPILOGUE I would now ask ye how ye like the play,
But, as it is with schoolboys, cannot say;° *speak*
I am cruel fearful.° Pray yet stay awhile[1] *horribly afraid*
And let me look upon ye. No man smile?
Then it goes hard, I see. He that has
Loved a young handsome wench, then, show his face—
'Tis strange if none be here—and if he will,
Against his conscience° let him hiss and kill *actual feelings*
Our market.° 'Tis in vain, I see, to stay° ye; *Our prospects / prevent*
Have at the worst can come,° then! Now, what say ye? *Do your worst*
And yet mistake me not. I am not bold;
We have no such cause.° If the tale we have told, *reason to invite criticism*

3. *with . . . question:* cease to dispute with you, who are beyond our questioning.

**Epilogue**
1. Don't hiss or applaud yet.

For 'tis no other, any way content° ye— *please*
For to that honest purpose it was meant ye°— *intended for you*
We have our end,° and ye shall have ere long, *achieved our aim*
I dare say, many a better, to prolong
Your old loves to us.° We and all our might° *(the actors) / all we can do*
Rest at your service. Gentlemen, good night! *Flourish.* [*Exit.*]

# POEMS

# Venus and Adonis

When Shakespeare wrote the narrative poem *Venus and Adonis,* he was already an up-and-coming playwright; but he called his poem "the first heir of my invention" because, in 1593, it was his earliest work to see print. While plays were considered the property of the theater company and found their way to the printing house erratically if at all, an author could publish nondramatic works like *Venus and Adonis* and *The Rape of Lucrece* without impediment. It was customary to dedicate such published poems to aristocrats who might provide financial support or other forms of patronage. Shakespeare dedicated *Venus and Adonis* to Henry Wriothesley, Earl of Southampton, a handsome nineteen-year-old aristocrat with sophisticated literary tastes, who was soon to come into a substantial fortune. But despite the conventionally flattering language of the dedication, Shakespeare intended to appeal to a larger audience than merely the patron to whom the poem was nominally addressed. Indeed, *Venus and Adonis* was exceedingly popular in Shakespeare's lifetime, apparently the most popular poem of the period. It went through at least nine editions during his lifetime—sixteen before 1640—and Shakespeare's contemporaries quote passages from it more often than they quote from any other Shakespearean play or poem.

Part of the attraction of the poem for Shakespeare's contemporaries was its apparently effortless deployment of an elaborate poetic form. The poem's *ababcc* stanza, a quatrain followed by a couplet, was popular among many Elizabethan poets—George Gascoigne, Thomas Lodge, Edmund Spenser, and Philip Sidney, among others—but Shakespeare's virtuosity was so widely recognized that it has henceforth been known in English not by its Italian name, *sesta rima,* but as the "Venus and Adonis stanza." A sort of abbreviated sonnet, this stanza, in Shakespeare's hands, tends often to proffer a snatch of narrative in the quatrain, followed by a summarizing or reflective couplet, thus alternating between advancing the plot and commenting, pithily and wittily, upon the action.

Yet the key to the extraordinary success of *Venus and Adonis* was probably not merely its formal beauty but its witty, profound, and, by the standards of its time, explicit treatment of a sexual encounter. *Venus and Adonis* is an "erotic epyllion," a narrative poem of a type that had become popular in the 1580s and grew even more so in the 1590s, partly because of the success of Shakespeare's poem and of Christopher Marlowe's roughly contemporaneous *Hero and Leander.* Like Marlowe and most of the other writers of epyllia, Shakespeare found his story in Ovid's *Metamorphoses,* a poem in fifteen books that retells, in beautiful Latin, more than two hundred pagan myths of transformation. Since Elizabethan schoolboys were required to memorize long passages from the *Metamorphoses,* many of Shakespeare's readers knew Ovid in the original; others read him in a popular 1567 English translation by Arthur Golding. Shakespeare would have been aware that the cult of Adonis was widespread in antiquity, a cult that involved rites of fertility and seasonal renewal and was associated with the adoration of a mother goddess variously identified as Venus, Aphrodite, Astoreth, Isis, or Cybele. In the Old Testament, the Israelites are periodically chastised for abandoning their male divinity for the worship of this heathen goddess; her cult thus seems, at least for the Jews of antiquity, to have constituted an alluring alternative to patriarchal monotheism. For Christian interpreters, the myth of the mutilated, transformed Adonis resembles the story of Christ closely enough to be read, on the one hand, as a pagan analogue to Christ's death and resurrection and, on the

Cupid taking aim. From George Wither, *A Collection of Emblems* (1635). The motto reads: "Be wary, whosoe're thou be, / For from Love's arrows, none are free."

other hand, as a demonstration of the superior power of the Judeo-Christian God, who, unlike Venus, can confer true immortality.

While Shakespeare acquired his plot from a classical source, he learned how to treat that plot from a medieval and Renaissance tradition of erotic poetry, deriving from the Italian poet Petrarch and developed in English by such poets as Thomas Wyatt, Philip Sidney, and Edmund Spenser. In *Venus and Adonis,* Shakespeare reconceives his mythological protagonists so that his poem might in some respects more closely approximate a Petrarchan norm. When Ovid's Venus is dazzled by Adonis, she resolves to appeal to him by feigning an interest in his favorite sport. By donning hunting gear and resolutely chasing rabbits, she successfully captures the gorgeous huntsman, her true quarry. Shakespeare's Venus declares herself in a much more forthright fashion, but his Adonis, unlike Ovid's, remains unresponsive to her charms. Thus *Venus and Adonis* reproduces a dynamic that Petrarch and his followers had made familiar by the late sixteenth century, in which a yearning lover pleads endlessly with a chilly love object.

The enduring fascination of this scenario for Renaissance poets lay in their recognition that "An oven that is stopped, or river stayed, / Burneth more hotly, swelleth with more rage" (lines 331–32). In Petrarchan poetry, little of consequence seems to happen, but the apparent lack of momentum is actually a prime stimulus to creativity. Frustration hones techniques of erotic persuasion; it energizes lament and interestingly complicates the poet-lover's state of mind. The sophisticated pleasure of intense self-awareness replaces the straightforward, even mindless pleasure of the sex act itself. In *Venus and Adonis,* Shakespeare's concentration on psychological detail produces an extraordinary slowing down and drawing out of the action. Ovid spends about eighty-five lines on Adonis, beginning with a brisk description of his birth and ending with an equally succinct account of his metamorphosis into an anemone flower. Shakespeare manages to devote almost twelve hundred lines to the last twenty-four hours of Adonis's life.

In some important respects, however, the story of Venus and Adonis encourages Shakespeare to play with the tradition he has inherited from Ovid and Petrarch. Most of the classical stories in the *Metamorphoses* involve male gods—Jupiter, Neptune,

Apollo, or Pluto—courting or raping beautiful young women or boys. In Petrarchan poetry, although the pleading lover is no rapist, he does take the rhetorical intiative: his beloved is generally passive and silent. In the case of Venus and Adonis, though, the powerful deity is female and the vulnerable beloved is male.

Shakespeare's revisions of the story exaggerate the effects of this gender switch. He attributes some conventionally "masculine" traits to his heroine and some conventionally "feminine" ones to his hero. His Venus is experienced, immensely strong, and apparently quite a bit larger than the Adonis whom she effortlessly tucks under one arm. Shakespeare's Adonis is dimpled, tender, coy, and virginal. At the same time, a female, even one as formidable as Venus, is imagined to be incapable of rape, so Venus cannot simply overpower her beloved as Apollo or Jove might do. Anatomical constraints force her to play a quite different but also conventionally masculine part: the pleading, unsatisfied role conventionally assigned to the male lover in Petrarchan poetry.

Since in Renaissance erotic poetry the positions of actively desiring, verbally fluent male and passive, unwilling female are ordinarily strictly demarcated, the sexual transpositions in the Venus and Adonis story have immediate consequences for Shakespeare's use of poetic conventions. Obviously they give those conventions a fresh twist. In Shakespeare's hands, such novelty is often comic: the aggressive, rhetorically hyperbolic Venus and the fastidious Adonis are funny, because now as then they violate conventional notions of appropriate gender-specific behavior. Some of these reversals are obvious to a modern reader, since our courtship rituals retain vestiges of the assumption that males are naturally dominant and inclined to take the sexual initiative. Other reversals are more specific to the poetic tradition in which Shakespeare wrote. In traditional love poetry, for instance, the enamored man "blazons," or elaborately describes, the features of the woman he desires, dwelling on the incomparable beauty of her eyes, hair, lips, hands, voice, gestures, and so forth. But in *Venus and Adonis,* Venus is compelled to blazon her own charms, because Adonis will not do it for her.

> "Mine eyes are gray and bright and quick in turning.
> My beauty as the spring doth yearly grow;
> My flesh is soft and plump, my marrow burning;
> . . . . . . . . . . . . . . . . . . . . . . . . . . . . . . . . . . . . . . . .
> Bid me discourse, I will enchant thine ear,
> Or like a fairy trip upon the green,
> Or like a nymph, with long disheveled hair,
> Dance on the sands, and yet no footing seen."
> (lines 140–48)

While in the conventional love situation the blazon is a man's cry of yearning for an exquisite object, here it becomes a woman's calculated, but unsuccessful, advertising campaign.

Shakespeare also dwells on the comic quality of Venus's divine attributes, such as the miraculous weightlessness of her robust body. At one point, Venus describes herself as a kind of giant balloon: "Witness this primrose bank whereon I lie: / These forceless flowers like sturdy trees support me" (lines 151–52). Her physical strength contrasts vividly with her quintessentially feminine body: when Venus "locks her lily fingers one in one" (line 228), she turns out to have a grip of steel. Shakespeare's interest in such apparent incongruities foreshadowed his much more elaborate exploration of the effects of transvestism and sexual reversal in such plays as *As You Like It, Twelfth Night, All's Well That Ends Well, Macbeth,* and *Antony and Cleopatra.* The humor of *Venus and Adonis* is two-edged, however, for it implicitly mocks not merely the aberrant protagonists but the standards from which they deviate. In what sense are particular traits or behaviors "naturally" masculine or feminine if actual males and females do not possess them?

Two horses mating. From Antonio Tempesta, *Horses of Different Lands.*

The upending of gender stereotypes in *Venus and Adonis* is only one of the strategies of reversal that structure the imagery of the poem. Again and again, its metaphors and similes insist on the similarity of what seems different, the difference in what seems the same. Hunting is and is not like sexual pursuit; killing is and is not like loving; female sexual desire is and is not like maternal nurture; the boar, savagely rooting in Adonis's groin, is and is not like Venus; Adonis is and is not like the sun god or the flower into which he eventually transforms. Many of these comparisons or implied comparisons are traditional ones; Shakespeare's virtuosity is evident not as much in the originality of his individual conceits as in their extraordinary profusion and in the surprising way in which apparently incompatible images are tellingly juxtaposed.

The handling of imagery corresponds with the poem's abrupt reversals of mood and with the unpredictable, accidental quality of the story. The frank comedy of the beginning swerves into tragedy, or at least pathos, at the close, as the immortal goddess confronts the death of her reluctant beloved. Over the course of the poem, our estimation of both characters undergoes dizzying shifts. Venus—goddess, whore, cradle robber, and queen—is funny, scary, eloquent, and pitiable by turns. Adonis's sexual diffidence at first seems as ridiculous to the reader as it does to Venus; but he suddenly seems less absurd when he replies, gravely even if rather too sanctimoniously, to Venus's importunities.

Venus's frank joy in the pleasures of sex suggests an uninhibited pagan universe, in which gods, animals, and human beings all are ruled by the same laws of generation and sensual enjoyment. Shakespeare's lavish attention to the forest setting in which the poem takes place suggests his keen appreciation of the sensuous possibilities of a purely natural world. The bodies of animals—Adonis's splendid courser, inflamed by lust; the ferocious boar, bursting through the thorniest thickets; the zigzagging hunted hare—all are accorded blazons of their own, as if they, not merely the human lovers, were full participants in the story of love and death. At such moments, the poem seems enthusiastically to endorse the original religious significance of the Venus and Adonis story, which linked human lives with the rhythms of a natural environment.

The boar attacking Adonis. From Henry Peacham, *Minerva Britanna* (1612).

But Shakespeare's poem hardly evokes a sexual utopia. Even though the pagan setting of the poem presumably frees the characters from the sexually abstemious culture of Christianity, the heroine and hero still disagree vehemently about the value of sexual indulgence. Chastity has its attractions even apart from whatever supernatural reinforcement Christian faith might lend to it—especially, as Adonis notes, for those who are not yet fully adult. The immortal Venus thinks of experience as an endless series of pleasurable present-tense moments; the mortal Adonis wants to conceive of his life in terms of narrative development, building slowly and coherently to a future maturity. His untimely death suggests the risks of thinking of one's life in this fashion; he seems unwisely to have forgone present satisfaction in the hope of a reward that will never materialize.

On the other hand, why should Adonis, the victim of a sexual attack, enjoy caresses he has neither invited nor encouraged? Just as Shakespeare's reversal of gender stereotypes calls into question the adequacy of those stereotypes, so Adonis's recoil from Venus calls into question the naturalness of reproductive sexuality. Venus, the goddess of love, is supposed to be the apex of heterosexual desirability, both source and goal of every man's desire. Adonis, however, does not desire her even when she presses herself upon him. The congress of male and female thus seems simultaneously natural—what Adonis's palfrey, or riding horse, and a passing mare know without tutelage—and optional, a possibility that some males, at any rate, may be willing to do without.

Shakespeare writes almost entirely from Venus's perspective: the boy, not the woman, is the sex object in *Venus and Adonis*. In an age lacking our comparatively rigid conception of sexual orientation, lovely androgynous boys were assumed to be attractive to adult men and women alike. Shakespeare returned to the subject of the adolescent boy's ambiguous, half-conscious sexiness in his transvestite comedies, and to the adult man's reluctance to commit himself to exclusively heterosexual alliances in those plays as well as in *The Merchant of Venice*. *Venus and Adonis* can thus be read both as a narrative of frustrated heterosexual desire and, perhaps, as a parable of desire for a beautiful boy by a male poet—a scenario also sketched in many of Shakespeare's sonnets.

What is the meaning of sexuality? *Venus and Adonis* suggests a wide variety of possibilities: it is both a joke and a cosmic principle, a function of stern reproductive necessity and of sheer animal exuberance, a link with the animal world and an escape from it, a necessity and an option, a reminder of mortality and an intimation of immortality, a celebration of personal uniqueness and a threat to the formation of an individual identity. The shifting perspectives of the poem exploit the ambivalence with which Shakespeare's culture, as well as our own, treats sexual matters as simultaneously comical and deeply serious. The language of *Venus and Adonis* is especially good at capturing the confusing, contradictory array of sensations produced by another person's unfamiliar body close to one's own, a sensation at once grand, comic, oppressive, arousing, and repellant. The sweating, reeking, melting, and liquefying that at first seem specific to Venus's courtship of Adonis appear, by the end of the poem, to represent a principle of mortal existence and moral evaluation, as one thing merges unsteadily, unexpectedly, into another.

Biographical critics have found in *Venus and Adonis* ample grounds for speculation.

Does the sexual dynamic of this poem reflect Shakespeare's experience with the older Anne Hathaway, hauling him into some bosky nook outside Stratford? Or, alternatively, does it register an infatuation with the poem's dedicatee, Henry Wriothesley, the gorgeous youth to whom, some speculate, the early sonnets are devoted in both senses of the word? Given the scanty biographical data that have come down to us, it is impossible to know. What is clear is that *Venus and Adonis* inaugurates many of the distinctive features of Shakespeare's later work: a fascination, and capacity to sympathize, with sexually assertive women and self-contained, immature young men; an erotic energy that is both exuberant and hard to pin down; a complex moral sensibility capable of apprehending contradictory ethical imperatives at the same time; and an uncanny ability to combine comic, tragic, pathetic, and sensuous effects in a single work, even in a single poetic moment.

KATHARINE EISAMAN MAUS

## SELECTED BIBLIOGRAPHY

Bate, Jonathan. "Sexual Poetry." *Shakespeare and Ovid.* Oxford: Oxford UP, 1993. 48–65. Examines Shakespeare's adaptation of Ovid's story of transgressive desire.

Belsey, Catherine. "Love as Trompe l'Oeil: Taxonomies of Desire in *Venus and Adonis.*" *Shakespeare Quarterly* 46 (1995): 257–76. Argues that the poem reflects cultural changes in the understanding of love and lust, and the relationship between them.

Erne, Lukas, and Tamsin Badcoe. "Shakespeare and the Popularity of Poetry Books in Print, 1583–1622." *Review of English Studies* 65 (2014): 33–57. Presents a comprehensive statistical comparison of printed editions of Shakespeare's poetry with his contemporaries', demonstrating the remarkable and unparalleled popularity of *Venus and Adonis.*

Hughes, Ted. "Conception and Gestation of the Equation's Tragic Myth." *Shakespeare and the Goddess of Complete Being.* London: Faber and Faber, 1992. 49–92. Sees *Venus and Adonis* as Shakespeare's version of an ancient myth, filtered through Roman Catholicism, of goddess and sacrificed consort.

Hulse, Clark. *Metamorphic Verse: The Elizabethan Minor Epic.* Princeton, NJ: Princeton UP, 1981. 141–75. Looks at *Venus and Adonis* in relation to its sources and immediate predecessors.

Kahn, Coppélia. "Self as Eros in *Venus and Adonis.*" *Man's Estate: Masculine Identity in Shakespeare.* Berkeley: U of California P, 1981. 21–46. Analyzes Adonis as a narcissist.

Keach, William. "Venus and Adonis." *Elizabethan Erotic Narratives: Irony and Pathos in the Ovidian Poetry of Shakespeare, Marlowe, and Their Contemporaries.* New Brunswick, NJ: Rutgers UP, 1977. 52–84. Considers the poem among others of its genre.

Kolin, Philip C. *Venus and Adonis: Critical Essays.* New York: Garland, 1997. A collection of articles.

Menon, Madhavi. "Spurning Teleology in *Venus and Adonis.*" *GLQ: A Journal of Lesbian and Gay Studies* 11 (2005): 491–519. Looks at the failure of end-directed activity in sexuality and narrative.

Rambuss, Richard. "What It Feels Like for a Boy: Shakespeare's *Venus and Adonis.*" *A Companion to Shakespeare's Works,* vol. 4: *Poems, Problem Comedies, Late Plays.* Ed. Richard Dutton and Jean Howard. Malden, MA: Blackwell, 2003. Examines *Venus and Adonis* as a "proto-gay" poem.

## TEXTUAL INTRODUCTION

*Venus and Adonis* was entered in the Stationers' Register on April 18, 1593. This entry records the first reference to a printed work by William Shakespeare, but it does not mention the author by name. Instead, it enters the work to the printer, Richard Field. Since Field was from Stratford-upon-Avon, he was a likely choice for Shakespeare to turn to for his first publication. Yet Field had established a reputation for producing well-set books with literary cachet—most notably, Sir John Harington's elaborately printed translation of Ariosto's *Orlando Furioso* in 1591.

*Venus and Adonis* was published later in 1593 as a quarto and includes prefatory material designed to advertise it as an important literary work. In addition to a floral border at the top, the title page includes a Latin epigraph from Ovid, Shakespeare's favorite poet (*Amores*, Elegy 1.15.35–36), while the next page adds a prose dedicatory epistle, addressed to Henry Wriothesley, Earl of Southampton, and signed "William Shakespeare." *Venus* is thus the first work to be publicly signed by this author, and one of only two works extant to do so (the other is the dedicatory epistle to *The Rape of Lucrece*, also addressed to Southampton). *Venus* shows Shakespeare in the process of trying to secure patronage from a wealthy young aristocrat.

Accordingly, the handsome book of twenty-eight leaves is carefully printed throughout. Unfortunately, it survives in only a single copy, held in the Bodleian Library, Oxford. This copy is missing the final or H leaf, which likely was left blank anyway. Since no other copies of the 1593 edition exist, there are no known press variants. We also do not know whether the book was printed from Shakespeare's autograph copy or from a copy prepared by a scribe; attempts to base a judgment on spelling have proved inconclusive. In any case, Shakespeare may have read copy in Field's shop, as the book includes very few typographical errors. However, the compositor occasionally misplaced a letter, as in "Bnt" at line 393 (for 'But") or in "aud" at line 301 (for "and"). He especially had difficulty preserving the layout of Shakespeare's six-line stanza (a sixain, rhyming *ababcc*), which indented the concluding couplet: on more than half the pages, he tried to save space by varying the indentation, sometimes within the couplet itself. He also resorted to two other devices that could save space: the use of a tilde (a mark printed above a letter to indicate omission of another letter) and an ampersand (&).

Because of the careful printing of the text, editors have had to make very few interventions. As recorded in the list of variants, some subsequently printed quartos (nine editions were published in Shakespeare's lifetime) began silently correcting a few errors, while over the centuries editors have made a few changes of their own. Yet no substantial textual cruxes exist; this is unusual for a work of Shakespeare.

PATRICK CHENEY

### TEXTUAL BIBLIOGRAPHY

Burrow, Colin, ed. *The Complete Sonnets and Poems*. The Oxford Shakespeare. Oxford World's Classics. Oxford: Oxford UP, 2002.

Duncan-Jones, Katherine, and H. R. Woudhuysen, eds. *Shakespeare's Poems*. The Arden Shakespeare. London: Thomson Learning, 2007.

Roe, John, ed. *The Poems: Venus and Adonis, The Rape of Lucrece, The Phoenix and the Turtle, The Passionate Pilgrim, A Lover's Complaint*. The New Cambridge Shakespeare. Updated Edition. Cambridge: Cambridge UP, 2006.

# Venus and Adonis

*Vilia miretur vulgus: mihi flauus Apollo*
*Pocula Castalia plena ministret aqua.*[1]

To the Right Honorable, Henry Wriothesley,
Earl of Southampton and Baron of Titchfield[2]

Right Honorable,
I know not how I shall offend in dedicating my unpolished lines to your lordship, nor how the world will censure° me for choosing so strong a prop to support so weak a burden. Only if your honor seem but pleased, I account myself highly praised, and vow to take advantage of all idle hours, till I have honored you with some graver labor. But if the first heir[3] of my invention prove deformed, I shall be sorry it had so noble a godfather; and never after ear° so barren a land, for fear it yield me still° so bad a harvest. I leave it to your honorable survey, and your honor to your heart's content, which I wish may always answer your own wish and the world's hopeful expectation. *judge* *cultivate / always*

Your honor's in all duty,
William Shakespeare

---

Even as the sun with purple-colored face
Had ta'en his last leave of the weeping morn,[1]
Rose-cheeked Adonis hied him° to the chase: *hurried*
Hunting he loved, but love he laughed to scorn.
Sick-thoughted° Venus makes amain° unto him, *Lovesick / speedily*
And like a bold-faced suitor gins to woo him.

"Thrice fairer than myself," thus she began,
"The field's chief flower, sweet above compare,
Stain to all nymphs,° more lovely than a man, *Eclipsing all women*
More white and red than doves or roses are:
Nature that made thee with herself at strife
Saith that the world hath ending with thy life.[2]

"Vouchsafe, thou wonder, to alight thy steed,
And rein his proud head to the saddle bow.

**Dedication**
1. "Let vile people admire vile things; may fair-haired Apollo serve me goblets filled with Castalian water" (Ovid, *Amores,* Elegy 1.15.35–36). Apollo is the god of poetry; the Castalian spring is sacred to the Muses.
2. Prominent courtier, nineteen years old at the time of *Venus and Adonis*'s publication. Shakespeare also dedicated *The Rape of Lucrece* to him.
3. *Venus and Adonis* was Shakespeare's first published work.

**Poem**
1. Aurora, goddess of the dawn, weeps tears of dew when forsaken each morning by her lover, the sun.
2. *Nature . . . life*: Nature, who strove to surpass herself in making you, says that if you die, the world will end.

If thou wilt deign this favor, for thy meed° *reward*
A thousand honey secrets shalt thou know.
Here come and sit, where never serpent hisses,
And being set, I'll smother thee with kisses;

"And yet not cloy thy lips with loathed satiety,
But rather famish them amid their plenty,
Making them red and pale with fresh variety:
Ten kisses short as one, one long as twenty.
A summer's day will seem an hour but short,
Being wasted° in such time-beguiling sport." *spent*

With this she seizeth on his sweating palm,
The precedent of pith and livelihood,[3]
And trembling in her passion, calls it balm,
Earth's sovereign° salve, to do a goddess good. *potent*
Being so enraged, desire doth lend her force
Courageously to pluck him from his horse.

Over one arm the lusty courser's rein;
Under her other was the tender boy,
Who blushed and pouted in a dull disdain,
With leaden appetite, unapt to toy:[4]
She red and hot, as coals of glowing fire;
He red for shame, but frosty in desire.

The studded bridle on a ragged bough
Nimbly she fastens (oh, how quick is love!);
The steed is stallèd° up, and even now *fastened*
To tie the rider she begins to prove.° *try*
Backward she pushed him, as she would be thrust,
And governed him in strength, though not in lust.

So soon was she along° as he was down, *alongside him*
Each leaning on their elbows and their hips.
Now doth she stroke his cheek, now doth he frown,
And gins to chide, but soon she stops his lips,
And kissing speaks, with lustful language broken,° *interrupted*
"If thou wilt chide, thy lips shall never open."

He burns with bashful shame; she with her tears
Doth quench the maiden burning of his cheeks.
Then with her windy sighs and golden hairs
To fan and blow them dry again she seeks.
He saith she is immodest, blames her miss;° *misbehavior*
What follows more, she murders with a kiss.

Even as an empty eagle, sharp by fast,° *hungry from fasting*
Tires° with her beak on feathers, flesh, and bone, *Tears*
Shaking her wings, devouring all in haste,
Till either gorge° be stuffed, or prey be gone: *stomach*
Even so she kissed his brow, his cheek, his chin,
And where she ends she doth anew begin.

3. The evidence of strength and liveliness.

4. Uninterested in sex play.

Forced to content,° but never to obey,° — *acquiesce / respond*
Panting he lies, and breatheth in her face.
She feedeth on the steam, as on a prey,
And calls it heavenly moisture, air of grace,
    Wishing her cheeks were gardens full of flowers,
    So they were dewed with such distilling° showers. — *gently dropping*

Look how a bird lies tangled in a net,
So fastened in her arms Adonis lies.
Pure shame and awed° resistance made him fret, — *overpowered*
Which bred more beauty in his angry eyes:
    Rain added to a river that is rank° — *full*
    Perforce will force it overflow the bank.

Still she entreats, and prettily entreats,
For to a pretty ear she tunes her tale.
Still is he sullen, still he lours° and frets, — *frowns*
Twixt crimson shame and anger ashy pale.
    Being red, she loves him best, and being white,
    Her best is bettered with a more delight.

Look how he can, she cannot choose but love,
And by her fair immortal hand she swears
From his soft bosom never to remove
Till he take truce° with her contending tears, — *come to terms*
    Which long have rained, making her cheeks all wet:
    And one sweet kiss shall pay this countless debt.

Upon this promise did he raise his chin,
Like a dive-dapper[5] peering through a wave,
Who, being looked on, ducks as quickly in:
So offers he to give what she did crave;
    But when her lips were ready for his pay,
    He winks,° and turns his lips another way. — *shuts his eyes*

Never did passenger° in summer's heat — *traveler*
More thirst for drink than she for this good turn.
Her help she sees, but help she cannot get;
She bathes in water, yet her fire must burn.
    "Oh, pity," gan she cry, "flint-hearted boy,
    'Tis but a kiss I beg; why art thou coy?

"I have been wooed as I entreat thee now,
Even by the stern and direful god of war,° — *Mars*
Whose sinewy neck in battle ne'er did bow,
Who conquers where he comes in every jar;° — *conflict*
    Yet hath he been my captive and my slave,
    And begged for that which thou unasked shalt have.

"Over my altars hath he hung his lance,
His battered shield, his uncontrollèd° crest, — *unvanquished*
And for my sake hath learned to sport and dance,

5. Grebe (small English waterbird).

To toy, to wanton, dally, smile, and jest,
Scorning his churlish drum and ensign red,
Making my arms° his field, his tent my bed. *(a pun)*

"Thus he that overruled I over-swayed,
Leading him prisoner in a red-rose chain.
Strong-tempered steel his stronger strength obeyed;
Yet was he servile to my coy disdain.
Oh, be not proud, nor brag not of thy might,
For mast'ring her that foiled° the god of fight. *conquered*

"Touch but my lips with those fair lips of thine—
Though mine be not so fair, yet are they red—
The kiss shall be thine own as well as mine.
What see'st thou in the ground? Hold up thy head.
Look in mine eyeballs; there thy beauty lies.° *lies reflected*
Then why not lips on lips, since eyes in eyes?

"Art thou ashamed to kiss? Then wink again,
And I will wink; so shall the day seem night.
Love keeps his revels where there are but twain;
Be bold to play; our sport is not in sight.° *unobserved*
These blue-veined violets whereon we lean
Never can blab, nor know not[6] what we mean.

"The tender spring° upon thy tempting lip *growth of new beard*
Shows thee unripe; yet mayst thou well be tasted.
Make use of time, let not advantage slip;
Beauty within itself should not be wasted:
Fair flowers that are not gathered in their prime
Rot and consume themselves in little time.

"Were I hard-favored,° foul, or wrinkled old, *ugly*
Ill-nurtured, crooked, churlish, harsh in voice,
O'er-worn,° despisèd, rheumatic, and cold, *Worn out*
Thick-sighted,° barren, lean, and lacking juice, *Partly blind*
Then mightst thou pause, for then I were not for thee;
But having no defects, why dost abhor me?

"Thou canst not see one wrinkle in my brow;
Mine eyes are gray[7] and bright and quick in turning.
My beauty as the spring doth yearly grow;° *rejuvenate*
My flesh is soft and plump, my marrow° burning; *vital spirits*
My smooth moist hand, were it with thy hand felt,
Would in thy palm dissolve, or seem to melt.

"Bid me discourse, I will enchant thine ear,
Or like a fairy trip upon the green,
Or like a nymph, with long disheveled hair,
Dance on the sands, and yet no footing° seen. *footprint*
Love is a spirit all compact° of fire, *made up*
Not gross° to sink, but light, and will aspire.° *heavy / rise*

6. The double negative ("nor . . . not") was acceptable in Elizabethan English.

7. Considered the best eye color by medieval and Renaissance love poets.

"Witness this primrose bank whereon I lie:
These forceless flowers like sturdy trees support me.
Two strengthless doves[8] will draw me through the sky
From morn till night, even where I list° to sport me. *wherever I wish*
Is love so light, sweet boy, and may it be
That thou should think it heavy unto thee?

"Is thine own heart to thine own face affected?° *attracted*
Can thy right hand seize love upon thy left?° *by clasping the left*
Then woo thyself, be of thyself rejected,
Steal thine own freedom,° and complain on theft. *Capture your affections*
Narcissus[9] so himself himself forsook,
And died to kiss his shadow in the brook.

"Torches are made to light, jewels to wear,
Dainties to taste, fresh beauty for the use,
Herbs for their smell, and sappy plants to bear.
Things growing to themselves° are growth's abuse; *only for themselves*
Seeds spring from seeds, and beauty breedeth beauty:
Thou wast begot; to get° it is thy duty. *beget*

"Upon the earth's increase why shouldst thou feed,
Unless the earth with thy increase be fed?
By law of nature thou art bound to breed,
That thine° may live when thou thyself art dead: *(your children)*
And so in spite of death thou dost survive,
In that thy likeness still is left alive."

By this° the lovesick queen began to sweat, *By this time*
For where they lay the shadow had forsook them,
And Titan,° tired in the midday heat, *sun god*
With burning eye did hotly overlook them,
Wishing Adonis had his team° to guide, *(of sun horses)*
So he° were like him° and by Venus' side. *(Titan) / (Adonis)*

And now Adonis with a lazy sprite° *dull spirit*
And with a heavy, dark, disliking eye,
His louring brows o'erwhelming° his fair sight, *overhanging*
Like misty vapors when they blot the sky,
Souring his cheeks,° cries, "Fie, no more of love! *Frowning*
The sun doth burn my face; I must remove."° *leave*

"Ay me," quoth Venus, "young, and so unkind,° *unnatural*
What bare° excuses mak'st thou to be gone? *poor*
I'll sigh celestial breath, whose gentle wind
Shall cool the heat of this descending sun.
I'll make a shadow for thee of my hairs;
If they burn too, I'll quench them with my tears.

"The sun that shines from heaven shines but warm,° *merely warms me*
And, lo, I lie between that sun and thee;

8. Traditionally, Venus's chariot was drawn by swans or doves; see lines 1190–92.
9. In classical mythology, a young man who fell in love with his own image reflected in the water; after he pined to death, he was turned into a flower.

The heat I have from thence doth little harm;
Thine eye darts forth the fire that burneth me.
    And were I not immortal, life were done,° *destroyed*
    Between this heavenly and earthly sun.

"Art thou obdurate, flinty, hard as steel?
Nay, more than flint, for stone at rain relenteth.° *wears away*
Art thou a woman's son, and canst not feel
What 'tis to love, how want of love° tormenteth? *being denied love*
    Oh, had thy mother borne so hard a mind,
    She had not brought forth thee, but died unkind.[1]

"What am I, that thou shouldst contemn° me this? *deny; scorn*
Or what great danger dwells upon my suit?
What were thy lips the worse for one poor kiss?
Speak, fair, but speak fair words, or else be mute.
    Give me one kiss, I'll give it thee again,
    And one for int'rest, if thou wilt have twain.

"Fie, lifeless picture, cold and senseless° stone, *insensible*
Well-painted idol, image dull and dead,
Statue contenting but the eye alone,
Thing like a man, but of no woman bred:
    Thou art no man, though of a man's complexion,° *appearance*
    For men will kiss even by their own direction."° *inclination*

This said, impatience chokes her pleading tongue
And swelling passion doth provoke a pause;
Red cheeks and fiery eyes blaze forth° her wrong: *display; flame out*
Being judge in love, she cannot right her cause.[2]
    And now she weeps, and now she fain° would speak, *gladly*
    And now her sobs do her intendments° break. *intended words*

Sometime she shakes her head, and then his hand;
Now gazeth she on him, now on the ground;
Sometime her arms enfold him like a band:° *fetter*
She would, he will not in her arms be bound.
    And when from thence he struggles to be gone,
    She locks her lily fingers one in one.

"Fondling,"° she saith, "since I have hemmed thee here *Foolish one; beloved*
Within the circuit of this ivory pale,° *fence*
I'll be a park, and thou shalt be my deer:
Feed where thou wilt, on mountain or in dale;
    Graze on my lips, and if those hills be dry,
    Stray lower, where the pleasant fountains lie.

"Within this limit is relief[3] enough,
Sweet bottom-grass[4] and high delightful plain,
Round rising hillocks, brakes obscure and rough,° *dark, shaggy thickets*
To shelter thee from tempest and from rain:

1. Without fulfilling her nature.
2. *Being . . . cause*: Although (or because) she is love's arbiter, she cannot win her own case.
3. Pasture; variety of landscape; sexual gratification.
4. Valley grass (pubic hair); Venus's body-landscape is intentionally suggestive throughout.

Then be my deer, since I am such a park;
No dog shall rouse thee,° though a thousand bark." *drive you from cover*

At this Adonis smiles as in disdain,
That in each cheek appears a pretty dimple.
Love made those hollows; if° himself were slain, *so that if*
He might be buried in a tomb so simple,
Foreknowing well, if there he came to lie,
Why, there love lived, and there he could not die.

These lovely caves, these round enchanting pits,
Opened their mouths to swallow Venus' liking:° *to engulf her desire*
Being mad before, how doth she now for wits?[5]
Struck dead at first, what needs a second striking?
Poor Queen of Love, in thine own law forlorn,° *condemned to suffer*
To love a cheek that smiles at thee in scorn.

Now which way shall she turn? What shall she say?
Her words are done, her woes the more increasing;
The time is spent, her object will away,
And from her twining arms doth urge releasing.
"Pity," she cries, "some favor, some remorse."° *compassion*
Away he springs, and hasteth to his horse.

But lo, from forth a copse° that neighbors by, *thicket*
A breeding jennet,° lusty, young, and proud, *mare in heat*
Adonis' trampling courser doth espy;
And forth she rushes, snorts, and neighs aloud.
The strong-necked steed, being tied unto a tree,
Breaketh his rein, and to her straight goes he.

Imperiously he leaps, he neighs, he bounds,
And now his woven girths he breaks asunder.
The bearing[6] earth with his hard hoof he wounds,
Whose hollow womb resounds like heaven's thunder.
The iron bit he crusheth tween his teeth,
Controlling what he was controllèd with.

His ears up pricked, his braided hanging mane
Upon his compassed crest° now stand on end; *arched neck*
His nostrils drink the air, and forth again,
As from a furnace, vapors doth he send.
His eye, which scornfully glisters like fire,
Shows his hot courage° and his high desire. *lust*

Sometime he trots, as if he told° the steps, *counted*
With gentle majesty and modest pride.
Anon he rears upright, curvets[7] and leaps,
As who° should say, "Lo, thus my strength is tried.° *one who / tested*
And this I do to captivate the eye
Of the fair breeder that is standing by."

5. *how . . . wits:* how does she keep her sanity now?
6. Supporting; suffering; generative.
7. Bounds on his hind legs with raised forelegs.

What recketh he° his rider's angry stir,° *cares he about / noise*
His flattering° "Holla" or his "Stand, I say"? *cajoling*
What cares he now for curb° or pricking spur, *bit*
For rich caparisons,° or trappings gay? *saddle blankets*
He sees his love, and nothing else he sees,
For nothing else with his proud sight agrees.

Look when° a painter would surpass the life *Just as*
In limning out° a well-proportioned steed, *depicting*
His art with nature's workmanship at strife,
As if the dead the living should exceed:
So did this horse excel a common one
In shape, in courage, color, pace, and bone.° *frame*

Round-hoofed, short-jointed, fetlocks shag and long,[8]
Broad breast, full eye, small head, and nostril wide,
High crest, short ears, straight legs, and passing° strong, *extremely*
Thin mane, thick tail, broad buttock, tender hide:
Look what° a horse should have, he did not lack, *Whatever*
Save a proud rider on so proud a back.

Sometime he scuds° far off and there he stares; *darts*
Anon he starts at stirring of a feather.
To bid the wind a base[9] he now prepares,
And where° he run or fly they know not whether:° *whether / which*
For through his mane and tail the high wind sings,
Fanning the hairs, who wave like feathered wings.

He looks upon his love and neighs unto her;
She answers him, as if she knew his mind.
Being proud, as females are, to see him woo her,
She puts on outward strangeness,° seems unkind, *reserve*
Spurns at° his love, and scorns the heat he feels, *Repels; kicks*
Beating his kind° embracements with her heels. *amorous; natural*

Then like a melancholy malcontent
He vails° his tail that, like a falling plume, *lowers*
Cool shadow to his melting buttock lent;
He stamps, and bites the poor flies in his fume.° *anger*
His love, perceiving how he was enraged,
Grew kinder, and his fury was assuaged.

His testy° master goeth about° to take him, *angry / tries*
When lo, the unbacked breeder,[1] full of fear,
Jealous of catching,° swiftly doth forsake him— *Fearful of being caught*
With her the horse, and left Adonis there.
As they were mad, unto the wood they hie them,
Outstripping crows that strive to overfly them.

All swoll'n with chafing,° down Adonis sits, *anger*
Banning° his boist'rous and unruly beast. *Cursing*

8. *short-jointed . . . long:* with short pasterns (the bone just above the horse's hoof) and shaggy joints above the hooves.

9. To dare the wind to run (from a children's game, prisoner's base).

1. Mare without mount (rider or stallion).

And now the happy season once more fits° *is suited*
That lovesick Love by pleading may be blest:
For lovers say the heart hath treble wrong
When it is barred the aidance of the tongue.

An oven that is stopped, or river stayed,° *dammed*
Burneth more hotly, swelleth with more rage:
So of concealèd sorrow may be said,
Free vent of words love's fire doth assuage.
But when the heart's attorney° once is mute, *pleader (the tongue)*
The client breaks,[2] as desperate in his suit.

He sees her coming and begins to glow,
Even as a dying coal revives with wind;
And with his bonnet° hides his angry brow, *hat*
Looks on the dull earth with disturbèd mind,
Taking no notice that she is so nigh,
For all askance he holds her in his eye.

Oh, what a sight it was wistly° to view *intently*
How she came stealing to the wayward boy,
To note the fighting conflict of her hue:
How white and red each other did destroy.
But now her cheek was pale, and by and by
It flashed forth fire, as lightning from the sky.

Now was she just before him as he sat,
And like a lowly lover down she kneels;
With one fair hand she heaveth up his hat,
Her other tender hand his fair cheek feels.
His tend'rer cheek receives her soft hand's print,
As apt as new-fall'n snow takes any dint.° *dent*

Oh, what a war of looks was then between them,
Her eyes petitioners to his eyes suing.
His eyes saw her eyes as they had not seen them;
Her eyes wooed still, his eyes disdained the wooing.
And all this dumb play had his° acts made plain *its*
With tears, which chorus-like her eyes did rain.[3]

Full gently now she takes him by the hand,
A lily prisoned in a jail of snow,
Or ivory in an alabaster band:
So white a friend engirts° so white a foe. *encircles*
This beauteous combat, willful and unwilling,
Showed° like two silver doves that sit a-billing. *Looked*

Once more the engine of her thoughts began:
"O fairest mover on this mortal round,° *earth*
Would thou wert as I am, and I a man.
My heart all whole as thine, thy heart my wound,° *suffering my wound*

2. Breaks apart; goes bankrupt.
3. Venus's tears interpret her mute gestures as the chorus in a play explains a dumb show.

For one sweet look thy help I would assure thee,
Though nothing but my body's bane° would cure thee." *destruction*

"Give me my hand," saith he, "why dost thou feel it?"
"Give me my heart," saith she, "and thou shalt have it.
Oh, give it me, lest thy hard heart do steel it,[4]
And being steeled, soft sighs can never grave° it. *engrave*
Then love's deep groans I never shall regard,
Because Adonis' heart hath made mine hard."

"For shame," he cries, "let go, and let me go;
My day's delight is past, my horse is gone,
And 'tis your fault I am bereft him so.
I pray you, hence, and leave me here alone,
For all my mind, my thought, my busy care,
Is how to get my palfrey° from the mare." *riding horse*

Thus she replies: "Thy palfrey, as he should,
Welcomes the warm approach of sweet desire.
Affection° is a coal that must be cooled, *Passion*
Else, suffered,° it will set the heart on fire. *allowed to persist*
The sea hath bounds, but deep desire hath none.
Therefore, no marvel though thy horse be gone.

"How like a jade° he stood, tied to the tree, *nag*
Servilely mastered with a leathern rein.
But when he saw his love, his youth's fair fee,° *reward*
He held such petty bondage in disdain,
Throwing the base thong from his bending crest,
Enfranchising° his mouth, his back, his breast. *Setting free*

"Who sees his true-love in her naked bed,
Teaching the sheets a whiter hue than white,
But when his glutton eye so full hath fed,
His other agents° aim at like delight? *faculties*
Who is so faint that dares not be so bold
To touch the fire, the weather being cold?

"Let me excuse thy courser, gentle boy,
And learn of him, I heartily beseech thee,
To take advantage on° presented joy. *of*
Though I were dumb, yet his proceedings teach thee.
Oh, learn to love; the lesson is but plain,
And once made perfect,° never lost again." *learned by heart*

"I know not love," quoth he, "nor will not know it,
Unless it be a boar, and then I chase it.
'Tis much to borrow, and I will not owe it.
My love to love is love but to disgrace it,[5]
For I have heard it is a life in death,
That laughs and weeps, and all but with a breath.

4. *steel it*: turn my heart to steel; steal my heart.
5. *My . . . it:* My only interest in love is in discrediting it.

"Who wears a garment shapeless and unfinished?
Who plucks the bud before one leaf put forth?
If springing° things be any jot diminished, *immature*
They wither in their prime, prove nothing worth.
The colt that's backed° and burdened being young *ridden*
Loseth his pride, and never waxeth strong.

"You hurt my hand with wringing; let us part,
And leave this idle° theme, this bootless° chat. *useless / pointless*
Remove your siege from my unyielding heart;
To love's alarms° it will not ope the gate. *assaults*
Dismiss your vows, your feignèd tears, your flatt'ry,
For where a heart is hard they make no batt'ry."° *breach*

"What, canst thou talk," quoth she, "hast thou a tongue?
Oh, would thou hadst not, or I had no hearing.
Thy mermaid's voice[6] hath done me double wrong;
I had my load before, now pressed° with bearing: *oppressed*
Melodious discord, heavenly tune harsh sounding,
Ears' deep sweet music, and heart's deep sore wounding.

"Had I no eyes but ears, my ears would love
That inward beauty and invisible;
Or were I deaf, thy outward parts would move
Each part in me that were but sensible.° *perceiving*
Though neither eyes nor ears, to hear nor see,
Yet should I be in love by touching thee.

"Say that the sense of feeling were bereft me,
And that I could not see, nor hear, nor touch,
And nothing but the very smell were left me,
Yet would my love to thee be still as much;
For from the stillatory[7] of thy face excelling° *incomparable*
Comes breath perfumed, that breedeth love by smelling.

"But oh, what banquet wert thou to the taste,
Being nurse and feeder of the other four.° *(senses)*
Would they not wish the feast might ever last,
And bid Suspicion° double-lock the door, *Wariness*
Lest Jealousy, that sour unwelcome guest,
Should by his stealing in disturb the feast?"

Once more the ruby-colored portal° opened, *threshold (mouth)*
Which to his speech did honey passage yield,
Like a red morn that ever yet betokened
Wrack° to the seaman, tempest to the field, *Shipwreck*
Sorrow to shepherds, woe unto the birds,
Gusts and foul flaws° to herdmen and to herds. *winds*

This ill presage advisedly she marketh,[8]
Even as the wind is hushed before it raineth,

6. Which, irresistible in song, was supposed to lure sailors onto rocks.
7. Apparatus used to distill perfume.
8. *This . . . marketh*: She notices this bad omen carefully.

Or as the wolf doth grin° before he barketh, *show his teeth*
Or as the berry breaks before it staineth,
Or like the deadly bullet of a gun,
His meaning struck her ere his words begun.

And at his look she flatly falleth down,
For looks kill love, and love by looks reviveth.
A smile recures° the wounding of a frown, *cures*
But blessed bankrupt that by loss so thriveth.[9]
The silly° boy, believing she is dead, *naive*
Claps her pale cheek, till clapping makes it red.

And all amazed,° brake° off his late intent, *perplexed / broke*
For sharply he did think to reprehend her,
Which cunning love did wittily prevent.
Fair fall[1] the wit that can so well defend her,
For on the grass she lies as she were slain,
Till his breath breatheth life in her again.

He wrings her nose, he strikes her on the cheeks,
He bends her fingers, holds her pulses hard,° *takes her pulse*
He chafes her lips: a thousand ways he seeks
To mend the hurt that his unkindness marred.° *caused to injure her*
He kisses her, and she by her good will° *consent*
Will never rise, so he will kiss her still.° *keep kissing her*

The night of sorrow now is turned to day.
Her two blue windows° faintly she upheaveth, *(her eyes)*
Like the fair sun when in his fresh array
He cheers the morn and all the earth relieveth.
And as the bright sun glorifies the sky,
So is her face illumined with her eye,

Whose beams upon his hairless face are fixed,
As if from thence they borrowed all their shine.
Were never four such lamps together mixed,
Had not his clouded with his brows' repine.° *discontent*
But hers, which through the crystal tears gave light,
Shone like the moon in water seen by night.

"Oh, where am I," quoth she, "in earth or heaven,
Or in the ocean drenched,° or in the fire? *submerged*
What hour is this? Or° morn or weary even?° *Either / evening*
Do I delight to die or life desire?
But° now I lived, and life was death's annoy;° *Just / deathly pain*
But now I died, and death was lively° joy. *living*

"Oh, thou didst kill me; kill me once again.
Thy eyes' shrewd° tutor, that hard heart of thine, *stern*
Hath taught them scornful tricks and such disdain
That they have murdered this poor heart of mine;

9. Textual Comment "Loss" is "love" in the First Quarto. For the rationale behind the emendation to "loss," see Digital Edition TC 1.
1. Good luck befall (with wordplay on "fall down").

And these mine eyes, true leaders° to their queen, *guides*
But for thy piteous° lips no more had seen. *pitying*

"Long may they kiss each other for this cure.
Oh, never let their crimson liveries wear;° *wear out*
And as they last, their verdure[2] still endure,
To drive infection from the dangerous year,
That the stargazers, having writ on death,° *predicted plague*
May say the plague is banished by thy breath.

"Pure lips, sweet seals in my soft lips imprinted,
What bargains may I make, still to be sealing?° *kissing; making deals*
To sell myself I can be well contented,
So° thou wilt buy, and pay, and use good dealing, *If*
Which purchase if thou make, for fear of slips,° *fraud*
Set thy seal manual° on my wax-red lips. *identifying stamp*

"A thousand kisses buys my heart from me,
And pay them at thy leisure, one by one.
What is ten hundred touches° unto thee? *(of the lips)*
Are they not quickly told,° and quickly gone? *counted*
Say for non-payment that the debt should double,
Is twenty hundred kisses such a trouble?"

"Fair queen," quoth he, "if any love you owe me,
Measure my strangeness° with my unripe years. *Explain my coldness*
Before I know myself, seek not to know me;
No fisher but the ungrown fry forbears.[3]
The mellow plum doth fall, the green sticks fast,
Or being early plucked, is sour to taste.

"Look, the world's comforter° with weary gait *(the sun)*
His day's hot task hath ended in the West.
The owl (night's herald) shrieks: 'tis very late.
The sheep are gone to fold, birds to their nest,
And coal-black clouds, that shadow heaven's light,
Do summon us to part, and bid good night.

"Now let me say good night, and so say you;
If you will say so, you shall have a kiss."
"Good night," quoth she, and ere he says adieu
The honey° fee of parting tendered° is. *sweet / given*
Her arms do lend his neck a sweet embrace,
Incorporate° then they seem: face grows to face. *United in one body*

Till breathless he disjoined, and backward drew
The heavenly moisture, that sweet coral mouth,
Whose precious taste her thirsty lips well knew,
Whereon they surfeit, yet complain on drouth.
He with her plenty pressed, she faint with dearth,
Their lips together glued, fall to the earth.

2. Literally, greenness; here, freshness. The lips ward off disease as fresh parsley was believed to do.

3. *No . . . forbears*: Every fisherman spares the young fish.

Now quick desire hath caught the yielding prey,
And glutton-like she feeds, yet never filleth.
Her lips are conquerors, his lips obey,
Paying what ransom the insulter° willeth: *conqueror*
Whose vulture° thought doth pitch the price so high *ravenous*
That she will draw his lips' rich treasure dry.

And having felt the sweetness of the spoil,
With blindfold fury she begins to forage.
Her face doth reek° and smoke; her blood doth boil; *steam*
And careless° lust stirs up a desperate courage, *reckless*
Planting° oblivion, beating reason back, *Implanting*
Forgetting shame's pure blush and honor's wrack.° *ruin*

Hot, faint, and weary, with her hard embracing,
Like a wild bird being tamed with too much handling,
Or as the fleet-foot roe that's tired with chasing,
Or like the froward° infant stilled with dandling, *fretful*
He now obeys, and now no more resisteth,
While she takes all she can, not all she listeth.° *desires*

What wax so frozen but dissolves with temp'ring,° *fingering*
And yields at last to every light impression?
Things out of° hope are compassed° oft with vent'ring, *beyond / accomplished*
Chiefly in love, whose leave exceeds commission.[4]
Affection faints° not like a pale-faced coward, *Passion relents*
But then woos best when most his choice is froward.

When he did frown, oh, had she then gave over,
Such nectar from his lips she had not sucked.
Foul° words and frowns must not repel a lover. *Harsh*
What though the rose have prickles? Yet 'tis plucked.
Were beauty under twenty locks kept fast,
Yet love breaks through, and picks them all at last.

For pity now she can no more detain him;
The poor fool° prays her that he may depart. *(term of affection)*
She is resolved no longer to restrain him,
Bids him farewell, and look well to° her heart, *take good care of*
The which by Cupid's bow she doth protest
He carries thence encagèd in his breast.

"Sweet boy," she says, "this night I'll waste in sorrow,
For my sick heart commands mine eyes to watch.
Tell me, love's master, shall we meet tomorrow?
Say, shall we, shall we, wilt thou make the match?"
He tells her no; tomorrow he intends
To hunt the boar with certain of his friends.

"The boar," quoth she, whereat a sudden pale,
Like lawn° being spread upon the blushing rose, *fine linen*
Usurps her cheek; she trembles at his tale,

4. *whose . . . commission*: which is permitted to do extraordinary things.

And on his neck her yoking arms she throws.
She sinketh down, still hanging by his neck;
He on her belly falls, she on her back.

Now is she in the very lists[5] of love,
Her champion mounted for the hot encounter.
All is imaginary she doth prove:[6]
He will not manage her,° although he mount her, *ride her (like a horse)*
That worse than Tantalus is her annoy,[7]
To clip Elysium[8] and to lack her joy.

Even so poor birds, deceived with painted grapes,
Do surfeit by the eye and pine the maw.[9]
Even so she languisheth in her mishaps,
As° those poor birds that helpless° berries saw. *Like / unusable*
The warm effects° which she in him finds missing *outward signs*
She seeks to kindle with continual kissing.

But all in vain, good queen, it will not be;
She hath assayed° as much as may be proved.° *attempted / tried*
Her pleading hath deserved a greater fee:[1]
She's Love, she loves, and yet she is not loved.
"Fie, fie," he says, "you crush me; let me go;
You have no reason to withhold me so."

"Thou hadst been gone," quoth she, "sweet boy, ere this,
But that thou told'st me thou wouldst hunt the boar.
Oh, be advised, thou know'st not what it is,
With javelin's point a churlish swine to gore,
Whose tushes° never sheathed he whetteth still,° *tusks / continually*
Like to a mortal° butcher bent° to kill. *deadly / intending*

"On his bow-back° he hath a battle[2] set *arched back*
Of bristly pikes that ever threat his foes;
His eyes like glowworms shine when he doth fret;
His snout digs sepulchers where'er he goes.
Being moved,° he strikes whate'er is in his way, *angered*
And whom he strikes his crooked tushes slay.

"His brawny sides with hairy bristles armed
Are better proof° than thy spear's point can enter. *armor*
His short thick neck cannot be easily harmed:
Being ireful,° on the lion he will venture. *angry*
The thorny brambles and embracing bushes,
As° fearful of him, part, through whom° he rushes. *As if / which*

"Alas, he naught esteems that face of thine,
To which love's eyes pays tributary gazes;

5. Enclosed tournament arena.
6. *All . . . prove*: The hot encounter is only imaginary, she finds.
7. Torment. In classical mythology, Tantalus was punished by eternal hunger and thirst; food and water were always visible but receded at his approach.
8. In classical mythology, the abode of the blessed dead. *clip*: embrace.
9. Starve the stomach. The ancient Greek artist Zeuxis painted grapes so realistic that birds pecked at them.
1. *Her . . . fee:* A legal metaphor: Venus, acting as an attorney, deserves a better payment.
2. Row of armed soldiers.

Nor thy soft hands, sweet lips, and crystal eyne,° *eyes (archaic)*
Whose full perfection all the world amazes.
But having thee at vantage°—wondrous dread!— *his mercy*
Would root° these beauties as he roots the mead.° *root up / meadow*

"Oh, let him keep° his loathsome cabin° still; *stay in / lair*
Beauty hath naught to do with such foul fiends.
Come not within his danger by thy will;
They that thrive well take counsel of their friends.
When thou didst name the boar, not to dissemble,[3]
I feared thy fortune, and my joints did tremble.

"Didst thou not mark my face? Was it not white?
Sawest thou not signs of fear lurk in mine eye?
Grew I not faint, and fell I not downright?
Within my bosom, whereon thou dost lie,
My boding heart pants, beats, and takes no rest,
But like an earthquake shakes thee on my breast.

"For where Love reigns, disturbing Jealousy° *Apprehension*
Doth call himself Affection's sentinel;
Gives false alarms, suggesteth mutiny,° *incites rebellion*
And in a peaceful hour doth cry, 'Kill, kill!'° *(a battle cry)*
Distemp'ring° gentle Love in his desire, *Quenching*
As air and water do abate the fire.

"This sour informer, this bate-breeding° spy, *conflict-breeding*
This canker° that eats up love's tender spring,° *cankerworm / sprout*
This carry-tale,° dissentious° Jealousy, *tale-bearer / quarrelsome*
That sometime true news, sometime false doth bring,
Knocks at my heart and whispers in mine ear,
That if I love thee, I thy death should fear.

"And more than so, presenteth to mine eye
The picture of an angry chafing boar,
Under whose sharp fangs on his back doth lie
An image like thyself, all stained with gore,
Whose blood upon the fresh flowers being shed
Doth make them droop with grief, and hang the head.

"What should I do, seeing thee so indeed,
That tremble at th'imagination?
The thought of it doth make my faint heart bleed,
And fear doth teach it divination:
I prophesy thy death, my living sorrow,
If thou encounter with the boar tomorrow.

"But if thou needs wilt° hunt, be ruled by me: *must*
Uncouple° at the timorous flying° hare, *Unleash the dogs / fleeing*
Or at the fox, which lives by subtlety,
Or at the roe, which no encounter dare.
Pursue these fearful° creatures o'er the downs, *timid*
And on thy well-breathed horse keep with thy hounds.

3. *not to dissemble*: to tell the truth.

"And when thou hast on foot the purblind° hare, *dim-sighted*
Mark the poor wretch, to overshoot° his troubles, *run past*
How he outruns the wind, and with what care
He cranks and crosses° with a thousand doubles. *twists and turns*
The many musits° through the which he goes *hedge gaps*
Are like a labyrinth to amaze° his foes. *confuse*

"Sometime he runs among a flock of sheep
To make the cunning hounds mistake their smell;
And sometime where earth-delving conies° keep, *rabbits*
To stop the loud pursuers in their yell;
And sometime sorteth° with a herd of deer: *consorts*
Danger deviseth shifts;° wit waits on fear. *tricks*

"For there his smell with others being mingled,
The hot scent-snuffing hounds are driven to doubt,
Ceasing their clamorous cry till they have singled
With much ado the cold fault° cleanly out. *lost scent*
Then do they spend their mouths;° Echo replies, *give tongue*
As if another chase were in the skies.

"By this poor Wat,° far off upon a hill, *(name for a hare)*
Stands on his hinder legs with list'ning ear,
To hearken if his foes pursue him still.
Anon their loud alarums° he doth hear, *calls to battle*
And now his grief may be comparèd well
To one sore sick that hears the passing bell.[4]

"Then shalt thou see the dew-bedabbled wretch
Turn, and return, indenting° with the way. *zigzagging*
Each envious° briar his weary legs do scratch; *malicious*
Each shadow makes him stop, each murmur stay,
For misery is trodden on by many,
And being low, never relieved by any.

"Lie quietly, and hear a little more;
Nay, do not struggle, for thou shalt not rise.
To make thee hate the hunting of the boar,
Unlike myself thou hear'st me moralize,[5]
Applying° this to that, and so to so, *Showing the pertinence of*
For love can comment upon every woe.

"Where did I leave?"° "No matter where," quoth he. *leave off*
"Leave me, and then the story aptly ends.
The night is spent." "Why, what of that?" quoth she.
"I am," quoth he, "expected of° my friends; *by*
And now 'tis dark, and going I shall fall."
"In night," quoth she, "desire sees best of all.

"But if thou fall, oh, then imagine this,
The earth, in love with thee, thy footing trips,
And all is but to rob thee of a kiss.

4. Bell tolled for one who has just died.
5. *Unlike . . . moralize:* Although I (the goddess of love) do not usually make moral points, I do so now.

Rich preys° make true° men thieves: so do thy lips *spoils / honest*
Make modest Dian[6] cloudy and forlorn,
Lest she should steal a kiss and die forsworn.[7]

"Now of this dark night I perceive the reason:
Cynthia for shame obscures her silver shine,
Till forging° Nature be condemned of treason, *counterfeiting*
For stealing molds from heaven that were divine,
Wherein she framed thee in high heaven's despite,° *defiance*
To shame the sun by day, and her by night.

"And therefore hath she bribed the Destinies
To cross the curious° workmanship of Nature, *elaborate*
To mingle beauty with infirmities,
And pure perfection with impure defeature,° *disfigurement*
Making it subject to the tyranny
Of mad mischances, and much misery.

"As burning fevers, agues pale and faint,
Life-poisoning pestilence, and frenzies wood,° *insane fits*
The marrow-eating sickness,[8] whose attaint° *infection*
Disorder breeds by heating of the blood,
Surfeits, impostumes,° grief, and damned despair *abscesses*
Swear Nature's death for framing° thee so fair. *making*

"And not the least of all these maladies
But in one minute's fight brings beauty under.
Both favor, savor,° hue, and qualities, *beauty; smell*
Whereat th'impartial gazer late did wonder,
Are on the sudden wasted,° thawed, and done, *wasted away*
As mountain snow melts with the midday sun.

"Therefore, despite of fruitless° chastity, *defying barren*
Love-lacking vestals° and self-loving nuns, *virgins*
That on the earth would breed a scarcity
And barren dearth of daughters and of sons,
Be prodigal: the lamp that burns by night
Dries up his oil to lend the world his light.

"What is thy body but a swallowing grave,
Seeming to bury that posterity
Which by the rights of time thou needs must have,
If thou destroy them not in dark obscurity?
If so, the world will hold thee in disdain,
Sith° in thy pride so fair a hope is slain. *Since*

"So in thyself thyself art made away,° *destroyed*
A mischief° worse than civil homebred strife, *An evil*
Or theirs whose desperate hands themselves do slay,
Or butcher-sire, that reaves° his son of life. *robs*
Foul cank'ring rust the hidden treasure frets,° *eats away*
But gold that's put to use more gold begets."

6. Goddess of the moon, hunting, and virginity, also called "Cynthia" (line 728); "cloudy" because covered with clouds and because made sorrowful by her love of Adonis.
7. Die having violated her oath of chastity.
8. Syphilis, which attacks the bones.

"Nay, then," quoth Adon, "you will fall again
Into your idle° over-handled theme. — *unprofitable*
The kiss I gave you is bestowed in vain,
And all in vain you strive against the stream.
    For by this black-faced night, desire's foul nurse,
    Your treatise° makes me like you worse and worse. — *discussion; plea*

"If love have lent you twenty thousand tongues,
And every tongue more moving than your own,
Bewitching like the wanton mermaid's songs,
Yet from mine ear the tempting tune is blown.
    For know my heart stands armèd in mine ear,
    And will not let a false sound enter there,

"Lest the deceiving harmony should run
Into the quiet closure° of my breast; — *enclosure*
And then my little heart were quite undone,
In his bedchamber to be barred of rest.
    No, lady, no; my heart longs not to groan,
    But soundly sleeps, while now it sleeps alone.

"What have you urged that I cannot reprove?
The path is smooth that leadeth on to danger.
I hate not love, but your device° in love, — *tactics*
That lends embracements unto every stranger.
    You do it for increase.° Oh, strange excuse, — *procreation; reproduction*
    When reason is the bawd° to lust's abuse! — *pimp*

"Call it not love, for Love to heaven is fled,
Since sweating Lust on earth usurped his name,
Under whose simple° semblance he hath fed — *innocent*
Upon fresh beauty, blotting it with blame,
    Which the hot tyrant stains and soon bereaves,
    As caterpillars do the tender leaves.

"Love comforteth like sunshine after rain;
But Lust's effect is tempest after sun;
Love's gentle spring doth always fresh remain;
Lust's winter comes ere summer half be done.
    Love surfeits not; Lust like a glutton dies;
    Love is all truth; Lust full of forgèd lies.

"More I could tell, but more I dare not say:
The text is old, the orator too green.
Therefore, in sadness° now I will away. — *truly*
My face is full of shame, my heart of teen;° — *grief*
    Mine ears that to your wanton talk attended
    Do burn themselves for having so offended."

With this he breaketh from the sweet embrace
Of those fair arms, which bound him to her breast,
And homeward through the dark laund° runs apace; — *glade*
Leaves Love upon her back, deeply distressed.
    Look how a bright star shooteth from the sky:
    So glides he in the night from Venus' eye,

Which after him she darts, as one on shore
Gazing upon a late embarkèd friend,
Till the wild waves will have him seen no more,
Whose ridges with the meeting clouds contend:
So did the merciless and pitchy night
Fold in the object that did feed her sight.

Whereat amazed,° as one that unaware *shocked*
Hath dropped a precious jewel in the flood,
Or 'stonished,° as night wand'rers often are, *confused*
Their light blown out in some mistrustful° wood: *anxiety-producing*
Even so, confounded in the dark she lay,
Having lost the fair discovery of her way.[9]

And now she beats her heart, whereat it groans,
That all the neighbor caves, as seeming troubled,
Make verbal repetition of her moans:
Passion° on passion deeply is redoubled. *Lamentation*
"Ay me," she cries, and twenty times, "woe, woe,"
And twenty echoes twenty times cry so.

She, marking them, begins a wailing note,
And sings extemporally a woeful ditty,
How love makes young men thrall° and old men dote, *enslaved*
How love is wise in folly, foolish witty.
Her heavy° anthem still concludes in woe, *sorrowful*
And still the choir of echoes answer so.

Her song was tedious and outwore the night,
For lovers' hours are long, though seeming short.
If pleased themselves, others, they think, delight
In suchlike circumstance, with suchlike sport:
Their copious stories, oftentimes begun,
End without audience, and are never done.

For who hath she to spend the night withal,° *with*
But idle sounds resembling parasites?° *flattering hangers-on*
Like shrill-tongued tapsters° answering every call, *tavern keepers*
Soothing the humor of fantastic wits.[1]
She says "'tis so"; they answer all "'tis so,"
And would say after her, if she said "no."

Lo, here the gentle lark, weary of rest,
From his moist cabinet° mounts up on high, *nest*
And wakes the morning,° from whose silver breast *(Aurora)*
The sun ariseth in his majesty,
Who doth the world so gloriously behold,
That cedar tops and hills seem burnished gold.

Venus salutes him with this fair good morrow:
"O thou clear° god and patron of all light, *bright*
From whom each lamp and shining star doth borrow

9. *the fair . . . way:* a clear view of her path; a beautiful guide.

1. *Soothing . . . wits:* Catering to the moods of erratic people.

The beauteous influence[2] that makes him bright,
    There lives a son° that sucked an earthly mother *(Adonis)*
    May° lend thee light, as thou dost lend to other." *Who may*

This said, she hasteth to a myrtle grove,
Musing° the morning is so much o'erworn,° *Wondering / spent*
And yet she hears no tidings of her love.
She hearkens for his hounds and for his horn.
    Anon° she hears them chant it lustily,° *Soon / sing out heartily*
    And all in haste she coasteth° to the cry. *rushes*

And as she runs, the bushes in the way,
Some catch her by the neck, some kiss her face,
Some twined about her thigh to make her stay.
She wildly breaketh from their strict° embrace, *restricting*
    Like a milch° doe, whose swelling dugs° do ache, *milk / udders*
    Hasting to feed her fawn, hid in some brake.° *thicket*

By this° she hears the hounds are at a bay,[3] *By now*
Whereat she starts, like one that spies an adder
Wreathed up in fatal folds just in his way,
The fear whereof doth make him shake and shudder.
    Even so the timorous yelping of the hounds
    Appalls her senses and her spirit confounds.

For now she knows it is no gentle chase,
But the blunt° boar, rough bear, or lion proud, *rude*
Because the cry remaineth in one place,
Where fearfully the dogs exclaim aloud.
    Finding their enemy to be so cursed,° *vicious*
    They all strain court'sy[4] who shall cope° him first. *contend with*

This dismal cry rings sadly in her ear,
Through which it enters to surprise° her heart, *assault*
Who, overcome by doubt and bloodless fear,
With cold-pale weakness numbs each feeling part:° *sense organ*
    Like soldiers when their captain once doth yield,
    They basely fly and dare not stay° the field. *remain in*

Thus stands she in a trembling ecstasy,° *stupor*
Till, cheering up her senses all dismayed,
She tells them 'tis a causeless fantasy
And childish error that they are afraid;
    Bids them leave quaking; bids them fear no more.
    And with that word she spied the hunted boar,

Whose frothy mouth bepainted all with red,
Like milk and blood being mingled both together,
A second fear through all her sinews spread,
Which madly hurries her she knows not whither.
    This way she runs, and now she will no further,
    But back retires, to rate° the boar for murther.° *berate / murder*

2. The ethereal stream that in Renaissance astrology was supposed to flow from stars and planets.

3. Stopped by the quarry, which is making a stand.

4. Politely defer to one another.

A thousand spleens° bear her a thousand ways; *impulses*
She treads the path that she untreads again.
Her more than haste is mated° with delays, *counteracted*
Like the proceedings of a drunken brain:
Full of respects,° yet naught at all respecting, *considerations*
In hand with all things, naught at all effecting.[5]

Here kenneled in a brake, she finds a hound,
And asks the weary caitiff° for his master; *wretch*
And there another licking of his wound,
'Gainst venomed sores the only sovereign plaster;° *effective remedy*
And here she meets another sadly scowling,
To whom she speaks, and he replies with howling.

When he hath ceased his ill-resounding noise,
Another flap-mouthed mourner, black and grim,
Against the welkin° volleys out his voice. *sky*
Another and another answer him,
Clapping their proud tails to the ground below,
Shaking their scratched ears, bleeding as they go.

Look how the world's poor people are amazed
At apparitions, signs, and prodigies,° *strange occurrences*
Whereon with fearful eyes they long have gazed,
Infusing them with° dreadful prophecies. *Reading into them*
So she at these sad signs draws up her breath,
And sighing it again, exclaims on° Death: *berates*

"Hard-favored tyrant, ugly, meager, lean,
Hateful divorce of love," thus chides she Death,
"Grim-grinning° ghost, earth's worm, what dost thou mean *(like a skull)*
To stifle beauty and to steal his breath,
Who, when he lived, his breath and beauty set
Gloss on the rose, smell to the violet?

"If he be dead—oh, no, it cannot be,
Seeing his beauty, thou shouldst strike at it—
Oh, yes, it may: thou hast no eyes to see,[6]
But hatefully at random dost thou hit.
Thy mark° is feeble age, but thy false dart *target*
Mistakes that aim and cleaves an infant's heart.

"Hadst thou but bid beware, then he° had spoke, *(Adonis)*
And hearing him, thy power had lost his° power. *its*
The Destinies will curse thee for this stroke:
They bid thee crop a weed; thou pluck'st a flower.
Love's golden arrow at him should have fled,° *flown*
And not Death's ebon° dart to strike him dead. *black*

"Dost thou drink tears, that thou provok'st such weeping?
What may a heavy groan advantage° thee? *benefit*
Why hast thou cast into eternal sleeping

5. *In . . . effecting:* Full of notions, yet actually attending to nothing.

6. Death's eye sockets are empty, like a skull's.

Those eyes that taught all other eyes to see?
 Now Nature cares not for thy mortal vigor,[7]
 Since her best work is ruined with thy rigor."

Here overcome as one full of despair
She veiled° her eyelids, who, like sluices, stopped *lowered*
The crystal tide that from her two cheeks fair
In the sweet channel of her bosom dropped;
 But through the floodgates breaks the silver rain
 And with his strong course opens them again.

Oh, how her eyes and tears did lend and borrow.° *(by reflection)*
Her eye seen in the tears, tears in her eye:
Both crystals, where they viewed each other's sorrow—
Sorrow that friendly° sighs sought still to dry; *consoling; like-minded*
 But like a stormy day, now wind, now rain,
 Sighs dry her cheeks, tears make them wet again.

Variable passions throng her constant woe,
As striving who should best become° her grief. *fit*
All entertained,° each passion labors so *permitted to enter*
That every present sorrow seemeth chief;
 But none is best. Then join they all together,
 Like many clouds consulting° for foul weather. *gathering*

By this far off she hears some huntsman hallow;° *(hunting call)*
A nurse's song ne'er pleased her babe so well.
The dire imagination° she did follow *train of thought*
This sound of hope doth labor to expel.
 For now reviving joy bids her rejoice,
 And flatters her it is Adonis' voice.

Whereat her tears began to turn their tide,° *to ebb*
Being prisoned in her eye, like pearls in glass;
Yet sometimes falls an orient° drop beside, *a glistening*
Which her cheek melts, as° scorning it should pass *as if*
 To wash the foul° face of the sluttish ground, *dirty*
 Who is but drunken when she seemeth drowned.

O hard-believing love, how strange it seems
Not to believe, and yet too credulous!
Thy weal° and woe are both of them extremes; *prosperity*
Despair and hope makes thee ridiculous:
 The one doth flatter thee in thoughts unlikely;
 In likely thoughts the other kills thee quickly.

Now she unweaves the web that she hath wrought:
Adonis lives, and Death is not to blame;
It was not she that called him all to naught.[8]
Now she adds honors to his hateful name:
 She clepes° him king of graves, and grave for kings, *calls (archaic)*
 Imperious supreme° of all mortal things. *Imperial ruler*

7. *Nature . . . vigor:* Nature does not heed your lethal power.

8. *She . . . naught:* she who called Death everything bad.

"No, no," quoth she, "sweet Death, I did but jest.
Yet pardon me: I felt a kind of fear
Whenas I met the boar, that bloody beast,
Which knows no pity but is still severe.
  Then, gentle shadow—truth I must confess—
  I railed on thee, fearing my love's decease.

"'Tis not my fault; the boar provoked my tongue.
Be wreaked° on him, invisible commander. — *revenged*
'Tis he, foul creature, that hath done thee wrong.
I did but act;° he's author of thy slander. — *(as an agent)*
  Grief hath two tongues,° and never woman yet — *is doubly loud*
  Could rule them both without ten women's wit."

Thus, hoping that Adonis is alive,
Her rash suspect° she doth extenuate, — *suspicion*
And that his beauty may the better thrive,
With Death she humbly doth insinuate:° — *curry favor*
  Tells him of trophies, statues, tombs; and stories[9]
  His victories, his triumphs, and his glories.

"O Jove," quoth she, "how much a fool was I
To be of such a weak and silly mind
To wail his death who lives and must not die
Till mutual° overthrow of mortal kind? — *universal*
  For he being dead, with him is beauty slain,
  And beauty dead, black chaos comes again.

"Fie, fie, fond° love, thou art as full of fear — *foolish; affectionate*
As one with treasure laden, hemmed with thieves.
Trifles unwitnessed with eye or ear
Thy coward heart with false bethinking° grieves." — *imagination*
  Even at this word she hears a merry horn,
  Whereat she leaps° that was but late° forlorn. — *(for joy) / lately*

As falcons to the lure, away she flies.
The grass stoops not, she treads on it so light,
And in her haste unfortunately spies
The foul boar's conquest on her fair delight,
  Which seen, her eyes, as murdered with the view,[1]
  Like stars ashamed of° day, themselves withdrew.° — *put to shame by / shut*

Or as the snail, whose tender horns being hit,
Shrinks backward in his shelly cave with pain,
And there, all smothered up, in shade doth sit,
Long after fearing to creep forth again:
  So at his bloody view her eyes are fled
  Into the deep-dark cabins of her head,

9. TEXTUAL COMMENT Although the First Quarto prints a comma after "stories," editors consider it a verb meaning "to tell about." In this edition, a semicolon after "tombs" clarifies the grammar of the sentence. For a fuller explanation, see Digital Edition TC 2.

1. TEXTUAL COMMENT The First Quarto prints "are murdered," not "as murdered." This edition, though not all modern editions, accepts an emendation from the Third Quarto that clarifies the simile-within-the-simile. For a longer discussion of the textual crux, see Digital Edition TC 3.

Where they resign their office and their light
To the disposing of her troubled brain,
Who bids them still consort with° ugly night, *always accompany*
And never wound the heart with looks again;
Who,° like a king perplexèd° in his throne, *(the heart) / troubled*
By their suggestion° gives a deadly groan, *(the eyes') incitement*

Whereat each tributary subject[2] quakes,
As when the wind imprisoned in the ground,
Struggling for passage, earth's foundation shakes,[3]
Which with cold terror doth men's minds confound.
This mutiny each part doth so surprise° *assail*
That from their dark beds once more leap her eyes;

And, being opened, threw unwilling light
Upon the wide wound that the boar had trenched
In his soft flank, whose wonted° lily white *usual*
With purple tears, that his wound wept, was drenched.
No flower was nigh, no grass, herb, leaf, or weed
But stole his blood and seemed with him to bleed.

This solemn sympathy poor Venus noteth;
Over one shoulder doth she hang her head.
Dumbly° she passions,° frantically she doteth: *Mutely / suffers*
She thinks he could not die; he is not dead.
Her voice is stopped, her joints forget to bow;° *cannot bend*
Her eyes are mad that they have wept till° now. *before*

Upon his hurt she looks so steadfastly
That her sight, dazzling,° makes the wound seem three; *blurring*
And then she reprehends her mangling eye
That makes more gashes where no breach should be:
His face seems twain; each several limb is doubled;
For oft the eye mistakes, the brain being troubled.

"My tongue cannot express my grief for one,
And yet," quoth she, "behold two Adons dead.
My sighs are blown away, my salt tears gone;
Mine eyes are turned to fire, my heart to lead.
Heavy heart's lead, melt at mine eyes' red fire:
So shall I die by drops of hot desire.

"Alas, poor world, what treasure hast thou lost?
What face remains alive that's worth the viewing?
Whose tongue is music now? What canst thou boast
Of things long since, or anything ensuing?
The flowers are sweet, their colors fresh and trim,
But true sweet beauty lived and died with him.

"Bonnet nor veil henceforth no creature wear,° *(to preserve complexion)*
Nor sun nor wind will ever strive to kiss you.
Having no fair° to lose, you need not fear. *beauty*
The sun doth scorn you, and the wind doth hiss you.

2. Each inferior organ of Venus's body.

3. Sixteenth-century explanation of earthquakes.

But when Adonis lived, sun and sharp air
Lurked like two thieves to rob him of his fair.

"And therefore would he put his bonnet on,
Under whose brim the gaudy sun would peep.
The wind would blow it off, and, being gone,
Play with his locks. Then would Adonis weep,
And straight° in pity of his tender years — *immediately*
They both would strive who first should dry his tears.

"To see his face, the lion walked along
Behind some hedge, because he would not fear° him; — *frighten*
To recreate° himself° when he hath sung, — *entertain / (Adonis)*
The tiger would be tame and gently hear him.
If he had spoke, the wolf would leave his prey
And never fright the silly° lamb that day. — *innocent*

"When he beheld his shadow in the brook,
The fishes spread on it their golden gills.
When he was by, the birds such pleasure took
That some would sing, some other in their bills
Would bring him mulberries and ripe-red cherries:
He fed them with his sight, they him with berries.

"But this foul, grim, and urchin-snouted° boar, — *hedgehog-snouted*
Whose downward eye still looketh for a grave,
Ne'er saw the beauteous livery[4] that he wore.
Witness the entertainment° that he gave. — *reception*
If he did see his face, why then I know
He thought to kiss him, and hath killed him so.

"'Tis true, 'tis true, thus was Adonis slain.
He ran upon the boar with his sharp spear,
Who did not whet his teeth at him again,° — *in return*
But by a kiss thought to persuade him° there. — *win him over*
And, nuzzling in his flank, the loving swine
Sheathed unaware the tusk in his soft groin.

"Had I been toothed like him, I must confess,
With kissing him I should have killed him first.
But he is dead, and never did he bless
My youth with his: the more am I accursed."
With this, she falleth in the place she stood
And stains her face with his congealèd blood.

She looks upon his lips, and they are pale;
She takes him by the hand, and that is cold;
She whispers in his ears a heavy tale,
As if they heard the woeful words she told.
She lifts the coffer-lids° that close his eyes, — *treasure-chest lids*
Where, lo, two lamps burned out in darkness lies:

4. His appearance (literally, garment).

Two glasses where herself herself beheld
A thousand times, and now no more reflect,
Their virtue° lost wherein they late excelled, *power*
And every beauty robbed of his° effect. *its*
"Wonder of time," quoth she, "this is my spite,° *torment*
That, thou being dead, the day should yet be light.

"Since thou art dead, lo, here I prophesy:
Sorrow on love hereafter shall attend;
It° shall be waited on with jealousy, *(Love)*
Find sweet beginning but unsavory end;
Ne'er settled equally, but high or low,[5]
That all love's pleasure shall not match his woe.

"It shall be fickle, false, and full of fraud,
Bud, and be blasted,° in a breathing while;° *blighted / moment*
The bottom poison, and the top o'er-strawed° *strewn over*
With sweets that shall the truest sight beguile.
The strongest body shall it make most weak,
Strike the wise dumb,° and teach the fool to speak. *mute*

"It shall be sparing° and too full of riot,° *miserly / excess*
Teaching decrepit age to tread the measures;[6]
The staring° ruffian shall it keep in quiet, *glaring*
Pluck down the rich, enrich the poor with treasures;
It shall be raging mad and silly mild,
Make the young old, the old become a child.

"It shall suspect where is no cause of fear;
It shall not fear where it should most mistrust;
It shall be merciful and too severe,
And most deceiving when it seems most just;° *honest*
Perverse it shall be where it shows most toward,[7]
Put fear to valor, courage to the coward.

"It shall be cause of war and dire events,
And set dissension twixt the son and sire;
Subject and servile to all discontents,[8]
As dry combustious matter is to fire.
Sith° in his prime death doth my love destroy, *Since*
They that love best their loves shall not enjoy."

By this the boy that by her side lay killed
Was melted like a vapor from her sight;
And in his blood that on the ground lay spilled
A purple flower sprung up, checkered with white,° *(the anemone)*
Resembling well his pale cheeks and the blood
Which in round drops upon their whiteness stood.

She bows her head the new-sprung flower to smell,
Comparing it to her Adonis' breath,

5. *Ne'er . . . low:* Love shall involve extremes of happiness and grief rather than equanimity; lovers shall come from different social stations.
6. To dance (inappropriately).
7. *Perverse . . . toward:* It shall be stubborn where it seems most compliant.
8. *Subject . . . discontents:* Cause and slave of all discontentedness.

And says within her bosom it shall dwell,
Since he himself is reft° from her by death. *torn*
She crops the stalk, and in the breach appears
Green-dropping sap, which she compares to tears.

"Poor flower," quoth she, "this was thy father's guise,° *habit*
Sweet issue° of a more sweet-smelling sire, *offspring; emission*
For every little grief to wet his eyes.
To grow unto himself° was his desire, *mature independently*
And so 'tis thine; but know it is as good
To wither in my breast as in his blood.

"Here was thy father's bed, here in my breast.
Thou art the next of blood,° and 'tis thy right. *heir (with wordplay)*
Lo, in this hollow cradle take thy rest;
My throbbing heart shall rock thee day and night.
There shall not be one minute in an hour
Wherein I will not kiss my sweet love's flower."

Thus weary of the world, away she hies,
And yokes her silver doves, by whose swift aid
Their mistress, mounted through the empty skies
In her light chariot, quickly is conveyed,
Holding their course to Paphos,[9] where their queen
Means to immure° herself and not be seen. *confine*

9. Venus's abode in Cyprus.

# The Rape of Lucrece

In the dedication to *Venus and Adonis* in 1593, Shakespeare promised his patron the Earl of Southampton a "graver labor"; a year later, *The Rape of Lucrece* delivered on his pledge. Like most nondramatic poems of the period, in other words, this one was dedicated to a wealthy individual whom Shakespeare hoped would reward his efforts, and may reflect Shakespeare's awareness of that person's tastes. Perhaps not surprisingly, then, the two poems have much in common: their classical inspiration; their lush, highly rhetorical narrative verse; their interest in the dynamic of a one-sided sexual passion. Yet whereas *Venus and Adonis*, despite its sad end, remains playful even in its pathos, *The Rape of Lucrece* retells a politically and psychologically complex story of rape and revolution. It is written in rhyme royal, a seven-line iambic-pentameter stanza with the rhyme scheme *ababbcc*, a verse form reserved since the time of Chaucer for elevated, tragic subjects. Shakespeare's contemporary Gabriel Harvey captures the difference between the two poems when he comments that *Venus and Adonis* appeals to "the younger sort," while *The Rape of Lucrece*, like *Hamlet*, pleases "the wiser sort." Certainly both poems were remarkably popular: *The Rape of Lucrece* was reprinted at least six times during Shakespeare's lifetime.

Slightly different versions of the tale of Tarquin and Lucretia were available in Livy's history of Rome and in Ovid's *Fasti*, both commonly read in Elizabethan grammar schools. In 509 B.C.E., Rome's king was Tarquin the Proud, a good military leader but an oppressive ruler over his own subjects. Sextus Tarquinius, the king's son, raped Lucretia, the wife of Collatinus, one of his aristocratic retainers. Lucretia committed suicide after revealing the crime to her male relatives and exhorting them to revenge her. After her corpse was exhibited in the Roman Forum, a wholesale revolt against the Tarquins erupted, led by the king's nephew Lucius Junius Brutus. The royal family was defeated and exiled, and Rome became a republic, ruled by a Senate and administered by one or more elected "consuls," of which Lucius Junius Brutus was the first.

For a Renaissance as well as for its original Roman audience, the story of Tarquin and Lucretia displayed vividly the complicated relationship between civic and domestic order, between public and private realms, between sexual and political violence. In the patriarchal society of ancient Rome, political or public agency was vested exclusively in men, especially elite men, while women resided in households governed by their male kin. A man like Collatinus, then, was simultaneously subject to his ruler, in the civic sphere, and the lord over his own family, in the domestic sphere. This conception would have been familiar to Shakespeare and his readers, for while ancient Roman and sixteenth-century English society differed in many respects, some of the same assumptions still prevailed about politics, gender, and the relationship between monarchical and husbandly authority. When he rapes Lucretia, then, Tarquin is not merely perpetrating an act of brutal violence against her; he is refusing to respect her husband Collatinus's exclusive rights over her body. This double sense of rape, both as a crime against the victim of sexual assault and, just as important, as an outrage against the property rights of her male relatives, pervades the poem and helps explain the conduct of the principal characters.

As a political fable, the story of Tarquin suggested the limits of sovereign authority and the circumstances in which subjects were permitted, even obliged, to challenge the authority of their sovereign. In the late sixteenth century, when monarchies in

*Lucretia.* Raphael.

western Europe were strengthening their power at the expense of parliaments and the higher aristocracy, the story could be cited as a precedent for resisting tyranny. Purely as a sexual melodrama, too, the story had wide appeal. Again and again, Renaissance painters portrayed Tarquin stealing into Lucretia's bed, Lucretia stabbing herself, and Lucius Junius Brutus exhorting over her body in the marketplace, often incorporating all three scenes into the same picture. Lucretia became a focus of especially fierce debate. On the one hand, she seemed a model of wifely duty, a woman to whom marital fidelity was not merely a matter of social respectability but a fundamental life principle. On the other hand, suicide by the sword—the traditional last, defiant gesture of heroic Roman men—could seem improperly self-assertive in a woman. Moreover, some Christian writers considered Lucretia's suicide not merely indecorous but sinful. In *The City of God*, Augustine argued that since virtues are properties of the will and not the body, Lucretia was innocent of unchastity. But ironically, her sexual blamelessness rendered her suicide completely inexcusable; Augustine considered her a murderess who had taken her own life out of misplaced pride. By Shakespeare's time, therefore, Lucretia could be held up, variously, as a model of female propriety and as an example of pagan willfulness, as a woman who breaks from the usual constraints upon her sex even while she seems most strenuously to endorse them.

Adapting the story to his own purposes, Shakespeare makes interesting changes of detail and emphasis. As Ovid and Livy recount it, the story of violation, suicide, and revolution is full of turbulent physical action and unexpected revelations—and in Livy especially, the political consequences of the rape receive much more attention than the sexual assault itself. Shakespeare's version downplays—though it does not eliminate—the political aspects of the story, and it contains most of the feverish momentum of the original story in the prefatory "Argument": "The same night he treacherously stealeth into her chamber, violently ravished her, and early in the morning speedeth away. Lucrece, in this lamentable plight, hastily dispatcheth messengers. . . ." The poem itself, by contrast, concentrates not upon moments of violence or haste but upon what precedes and follows those moments: what Tarquin thinks as he stealthily makes his way to Lucrece's bedchamber, how Lucrece occupies herself between the time she sends off her messenger and Collatine's return.

Like *Venus and Adonis, The Rape of Lucrece* eschews eventfulness for elaborate psychological analysis, attempting to capture in verse the uneven surge and flow of troubled, self-divided consciousnesses. In Shakespeare's hands, the story of Tarquin and Lucrece becomes a story about how first the perpetrator of a crime, and then its victim, make choices that lead to violence. Everything in the poem is the consequence of a decision, not an accident of fate, and nothing seems inevitable. The poem teases the reader with alternative possibilities. What if Collatine had kept his marital happiness to himself? What if Tarquin's conscience had overcome his lust? What if Lucrece's beauty had blinded Tarquin permanently instead of temporarily? What if Collatine had arrived to save Lucrece at the last moment? What if Lucrece had resolved to kill Tarquin rather than herself? The poem is constantly suggesting that the characters would be better off doing something else; and, interestingly, the characters themselves at times seem lucidly aware of that fact. Tarquin tells himself that his assault will desecrate the very virtue he admires in Lucrece, destroy his own self-respect, and bring dishonor upon himself and his family. Then he rapes Lucrece. Lucrece argues to herself what her husband and father will tell her later: that she cannot incur guilt by a sexual act to which she has not consented, and that therefore she need not take her own life. Then she commits suicide.

In both cases, the characters' stubborn refusal to acknowledge the obvious seems to follow from their tendency to conceive of themselves in terms of a few crucial metaphors. In Tarquin's case, the metaphors are military: "Affection is my captain, and he leadeth; / . . . My heart shall never countermand mine eye" (lines 271, 276). Such images attract Tarquin because they portray a rash, grossly disorderly act in terms of strict discipline. Even as he overturns the proper subordination of passion to reason, he elaborates a clear, if perverse, hierarchy of priorities. Moreover, by casting himself as a warrior and Lucrece as an enemy territory, Tarquin minimizes the blame that attaches to rape, an act conventionally associated with (and often excused in) soldiers pillaging an enemy town.

Of course, as Lucrece reminds him, she is not his foe, and Tarquin's actions violate not only her bodily integrity but her husband's trust in a friend and superior. Her pleas show how tendentious are Tarquin's interpretations of the metaphors he attaches to himself. Eventually, the rape that Tarquin tries to think of as an orderly military maneuver leads not only to his psychological fragmentation and self-torment but to literal exile, an exile Lucrece describes as already having occurred metaphorically.

After the rape and Tarquin's departure, the narrative focus shifts to Lucrece. Although she knows that she is not intentionally guilty of breaking her marital vows, she nonetheless construes herself as culpable. Like her violator, Lucrece thinks of herself and her body in symbolic terms, although in her case the governing metaphors are fortress, house, mansion, temple, tree. By emphasizing the protective function of the body, these metaphors make it easy for Lucrece to think of herself as irreparably damaged once her body has been assaulted by Tarquin's lust:

> Ay me, the bark pilled from the lofty pine,
> His leaves will wither and his sap decay;
> So must my soul, her bark being pilled away.
> (lines 1167–69)

Once Tarquin sacks and batters Lucrece's fortress, she suffers regardless of her innocence, like the inhabitant of a plundered town. While she is able to distinguish between her body and her soul, she desperately attempts to resolve the inconsistency between them by declaring herself irredeemably contaminated. In doing so, she endorses—indeed, almost celebrates—a literally fatal ambivalence in the definition of female chastity. For despite Augustine's objections, female chastity ordinarily refers to a physical condition as well as to a mental attitude in cultures that value female bodily "purity." This ambivalence still haunts many rape survivors today: they often blame themselves for their own victimization, and in some societies they are shamed and punished as if they, as well as their rapists, had committed a crime.

Comprehensible though Lucrece's suicide may be, however, it is ironically fraught with the very contradictions she seeks to avoid. She "revenges" herself upon Tarquin by completing the assault he began, plunging the phallic blade into what Shakespeare calls the "sheath" of her breast (the Latin word for sheath is *vagina*). She insists that she is acting in Collatine's interests even while she ignores his clearly stated wishes. She proves her innocence by demanding of herself that she pay the penalty for guilt. She validates her version of the rape story by silencing herself more effectively than Tarquin had with the bedclothes.

*Tarquin and Lucretia.* Titian.

Although the ways Tarquin and Lucrece think about their respective situations may be highly problematic, their trains of thought are definitely not arbitrary. Both protagonists derive their figures of speech from the same medieval and Renaissance poetic tradition Shakespeare had already drawn upon in *Venus and Adonis*. The configuration of characters—the warrior-lover desperately pursuing his passion, the beautiful woman whose chastity makes her irresistibly desirable—is likewise conventional. Shakespeare suggests the importance of this poetic mentality for *The Rape of Lucrece* by anachronistically importing the language of chivalry into a poem about ancient Rome: Tarquin agonizes about the consequences of his transgression for his family's coat of arms, and Lucrece accuses him of breaking "knighthood, gentry, and sweet friendship's oath" (line 569). This is closer to the world of Thomas Malory's Arthurian romances, Thomas Wyatt's sonnets, Philip Sidney's *Arcadia,* or Edmund Spenser's *Faerie Queene* than it is to the world of Livy or Ovid.

In fact, it is possible to see *The Rape of Lucrece*, like *Venus and Adonis*, as attempting to renovate a rhetoric of sexual passion that had begun to seem trite by Shakespeare's time. But the two poems employ almost exactly opposite strategies of renewal. *Venus and Adonis* surprises the reader by turning conventional expectations of gendered behavior upside down, assigning the aggressive, desiring role to the woman and casting the male as an uncorrupted fortress of virtue. *The Rape of Lucrece*, on the other hand, pushes the conventional language of love poetry in a relentlessly literal direction, making it disturbingly interesting by unleashing the latent ferocity and misogyny of a courtly love aesthetic. Lovers in the poetry of Spenser and Sidney, Petrarch and Wyatt, think of themselves as soldiers of desire, but they are so awed by their mistresses that aggressive thoughts are quenched by a mere glance from their imperious beloveds. Shakespeare's Tarquin, in contrast, more consistent and less exquisitely sensitive, uses the implicitly coercive rhetoric of love poetry as a pretext for violence.

Given the poem's intense interest in the use and misuse of language, it is not surprising that *The Rape of Lucrece* is also attentive to the relationship of rhetoric to other forms of representation. This persistent concern culminates in a long passage in which Lucrece contemplates a tapestry of Troy. In multiple ways, the tapestry is relevant to her own case, for the Trojan War was the consequence of a rape, and after the city's destruction, Trojan refugees were supposed to have founded Rome. After Lucrece's suicide, the account of her rape will provide the pretext for another founding, that of the Roman Republic. Eventually, her story will be displayed by artists in the same way that the legend of Troy is illustrated here—a series of chronologically distinct episodes represented simultaneously on the same panel. As Lucrece gazes at the painter's vast panorama of violation and suffering, the poet emphasizes both the vivid realism of the depiction and the artificial means by which that realism is produced: "Here one man's hand leaned on another's head, / His nose being shadowed by his neighbor's ear" (lines 1415–16). Portraying people according to the laws of perspective makes them look "natural," but it also reduces them to a collection of

From Jost Amman, *Icones Livianae* (1572). This picture shows both the rape of Lucretia, in the left background, and her suicide, in the right foreground.

grotesquely amputated shapes. Like *Venus and Adonis, The Rape of Lucrece* invokes nature as a category of value and then subverts it; but whereas the earlier poem undermines "nature" by suggesting that its supposed precepts are inadequate, the later poem undermines "nature" by suggesting that its effect is achieved only by extraordinary artifice. Shakespeare will consider the issue again in such plays as *A Midsummer Night's Dream, The Winter's Tale, The Tempest*, and, of course, *Hamlet*.

KATHARINE EISAMAN MAUS

## SELECTED BIBLIOGRAPHY

Arkin, Samuel. "'That map which deep impression bears': Lucrece and the Anatomy of Shakespeare's Sympathy." *Shakespeare Quarterly* 64 (2013): 349–71. Looks at sympathy, witnessing, and consent within the poem and in the experience of reading it.

Belsey, Catherine. "Tarquin Dispossessed: Expropriation and Consent in *The Rape of Lucrece.*" *Shakespeare Quarterly* 52 (2001): 45–70. Examines Lucrece as property and as person.

Donaldson, Ian. *The Rapes of Lucretia: A Myth and Its Transformations*. Oxford: Oxford UP, 1982. Discusses Shakespeare's poem alongside other literary and artistic treatments of the story.

Fineman, Joel. "Shakespeare's Will: The Temporality of Rape." *Representations* 20 (Fall 1987): 25–76. Features an ingenious discussion of the "let" as both hindering Tarquin and spurring him to action.

Hadfield, Andrew. "Tarquin's Everlasting Banishment: Republicanism and Constitutionalism in *The Rape of Lucrece* and *Titus Andronicus*." *Parergon: Journal of the Australian and New Zealand Association for Medieval and Renaissance Studies* 19 (2002): 77–104. Discusses the political issues in the poem.

Hehmeyer, Jeffrey Paxton. "Heralding the Commonplace: Authorship, Voice, and the Commonplace in Shakespeare's *Rape of Lucrece*." *Shakespeare Quarterly* 64 (2013): 139–64. Looks at aphorism and originality in the voices of the poet and of the raped woman.

Kahn, Coppélia. "The Rape in Shakespeare's *Lucrece*." *Shakespeare Studies* 9 (1976): 45–72. Presents a feminist account of rape and patriarchy in the poem.

Maus, Katharine Eisaman. "Taking Tropes Seriously: Language and Violence in Shakespeare's *Rape of Lucrece*." *Shakespeare Quarterly* 37 (1986): 66–82. Analyzes *The Rape of Lucrece* as a literalization of Petrarchan metaphors.

Vickers, Nancy. "The Blazon of Sweet Beauty's Best: Shakespeare's *Lucrece*." *Shakespeare and the Question of Theory*. Ed. Patricia Parker and Geoffrey Hartman. New York: Methuen, 1985. 95–115. Explores the sexual politics of the blazon, or detailed description of Lucrece's body.

## TEXTUAL INTRODUCTION

*The Rape of Lucrece* was entered in the Stationers' Register on May 9, 1594, to John Harrison, Senior, and was printed by Shakespeare's fellow Stratfordian Richard Field.

*Lucrece* was published as a quarto probably in summer 1594. Like *Venus and Adonis*, the book includes prefatory material designed to advertise it as an important literary work. The title page prints the title simply as *Lucrece*, with the longer version reserved for the running heads: *The Rape of Lucrece*. The title page includes a floral border at the top and a printer's device (an anchor) in the middle, both used in *Venus and Adonis*, although Field's device is larger in *Lucrece* because, unlike *Venus*, the title page does not require room for a Latin tag. Like *Venus*, nonetheless, the next page adds a prose dedicatory epistle, again addressed to Henry Wriothesley, Earl of Southampton, and signed "William Shakespeare." New to the design of the book is a prose "Argument," which details the historical background leading up to the poem's action. Like *Venus*, then, *Lucrece* presents Shakespeare as securing patronage from a wealthy young aristocrat in an attempt to make a significant contribution to English poetry.

The book is thus another handsome one under Shakespeare's name. It is carefully printed and includes forty-eight leaves, collated as A2 B-M4 N2. The book survives in ten copies and a fragment, none of which includes the final leaf (sig. N2), which most likely would have been blank. The extant copies exist in two states: uncorrected (Qu) and corrected (Qc). The press corrections were made to the inner forme of signatures B and H and the outer formes of C, D, I, K, and M, affecting readings in the following lines: 24, 31, 50, 125, 126, 162, 396, 1118, 1182, 1335, 1350, and 1832 (see the list of Textual Variants for details). Outer I is unique in that it survives in two corrected states. Nothing in any of the corrections confirms that Shakespeare made them himself. In two cases (lines 31 and 1350), some modern editors have chosen to retain the uncorrected reading because it seems to make more sense. The corrected copy of Q1 found in the Folger Shakespeare Library is the base text for this edition.

Three textual cruxes exist. First, at lines 129–30 the syntax is extremely complex and the punctuation evidently in error, as the compositor was perhaps thrown off by Shakespeare's unusual use of a stanza with five feminine rhyme-endings: "revolving . . . obtaining . . . resolving . . . abstaining . . . gaining" (cf. lines 428–34 for seven feminine rhyme-endings, as well as *VA* 409–12). The confusing punctuation exists in both states of the Quarto, but it prompted correction in later quartos. The question becomes just how to group the various clauses. Q1 includes a period at the end of line 129, and no punctuation at the end of line 130, so that the first five lines of the stanza read (in modern spelling):

> As one of which doth Tarquin lie revolving
> The sundry dangers of his will's obtaining;
> Yet ever to obtain his will resolving.
> Though weak-built hopes persuade him to abstaining
> Despair to gain doth traffic oft for gaining . . .

Most modern editors agree that the lines contain at least one error in punctuation, but they do not always parse the lines identically. They agree on missing punctuation at the end of line 130 after "abstaining," but disagree about what the punctuation should be, and about the punctuation after "resolving" in line 129. Retaining a period after "resolving," but inserting a comma after "abstaining," adopted in this edition, ensures that line 129 completes the thought of the first two lines, and gives the next two lines their own thought: although Tarquin's weak hopes persuade him to abstain from raping Lucrece, his strong despair overtakes that hope.

In the second crux, at line 639, the text prints the phrase "rash relier," apparently meaning a headstrong dependent. This has prompted editorial speculation—for instance, Q6 first prints "rash reply"—but the *OED* lists Shakespeare's usage of "relier" as its only example, and it has accordingly been retained here.

A third crux occurs at line 1544, where the compositor printed "beguild" in the difficult phrase "armèd to beguild," which could mean either "beguiled" or "be-gilded," suggesting that Tarquin comes to Lucrece either armed to beguile or armed to gloss over his true intent. The spelling "beguild" has been adopted for the present text to retain this double meaning.

A final feature of the 1594 Quarto is worth mentioning: a number of lines or sets of lines begin with double opening inverted commas (") to mark off "sentences" or *sententiae*, pithy moral maxims (lines 87–88, 460, 528, 530, 560, 831–32, 853, 867–68, 1109–18, 1125, 1127, 1216, 1687). The present edition does not retain these markings, in part because the original Quarto does not identify the *sententiae* in a clear and consistent manner and in part because of a design feature for *The Norton Shakespeare* as a whole (*Venus and Adonis*, for instance, does not print the markings, even though it, too, includes *sententiae*).

As with *Venus*, editors have been unable to determine whether the book was printed from Shakespeare's autograph copy or from a copy prepared by a scribe. Nevertheless, editors have found more spellings in *Lucrece* than in *Venus* that appear to be characteristically Shakespearean, especially "bedred" for "bedrid" (line 975) and "on" for "one" (line 1680).

As with *Venus*, the compositor confronted a layout problem, made more challenging because of *Lucrece*'s seven-line rhyme royal stanza (rhyming *ababbcc*), for which the last two lines of each stanza were indented. To remain within his margins, he resorted to various devices: running the lines over, relying on tildes (a mark printed above a letter to indicate omission of another letter), and using ampersands (&).

Because of the generally careful printing of the text, editors have made only a few interventions. As recorded in the list of variants, some subsequently printed editions (six were published in Shakespeare's lifetime) began silently correcting a few errors. For a work of William Shakespeare, *Lucrece* is in a relatively pristine state.

PATRICK CHENEY

# The Rape of Lucrece

To the Right Honorable Henry Wriothesley,
Earl of Southampton and Baron of Titchfield[1]

The love I dedicate to your lordship is without end, whereof this pamphlet° without beginning[2] is but a superfluous moiety.° The warrant° I have of your honorable disposition, not the worth of my untutored lines, makes it assured of acceptance. What I have done is yours; what I have to do is yours; being part in all I have, devoted yours. Were my worth greater, my duty would show greater; meantime, as it is, it is bound to your Lordship, to whom I wish long life still° lengthened with all happiness.

*short work / part*
*assurance*
*continually*

Your lordship's in all duty,
William Shakespeare

---

## THE ARGUMENT°

*plot*

Lucius Tarquinius, for his excessive pride surnamed Superbus,° after he had caused his own father-in-law Servius Tullius to be cruelly murdered and, contrary to the Roman laws and customs, not requiring[3] or staying for the people's suffrages,° had possessed himself of the kingdom, went, accompanied with his sons and other noblemen of Rome, to besiege Ardea.[4] During which siege, the principal men of the army meeting one evening at the tent of Sextus Tarquinius, the King's son, in their discourses after supper everyone commended the virtues of his own wife, among whom Collatinus extolled the incomparable chastity of his wife Lucretia. In that pleasant humor° they all posted° to Rome, and intending by their secret and sudden arrival to make trial of that which every one had before avouched, only Collatinus finds his wife (though it were late in the night) spinning amongst her maids; the other ladies were all found dancing and reveling, or in several disports.° Whereupon the noblemen yielded Collatinus the victory, and his wife the fame. At that time Sextus Tarquinius, being enflamed with Lucrece' beauty, yet smothering his passions for the present, departed with the rest back to the camp. From whence he shortly after privily° withdrew himself, and was (according to his estate°) royally entertained and lodged by Lucrece at Collatium.[5] The same night he treacherously stealeth into her chamber, violently ravished her, and early in the morning speedeth away. Lucrece, in

*"the Proud"*
*approval*
*merry mood / hurried*
*diversions*
*secretly*
*rank*

**Dedication and Argument**

1. Prominent courtier, twenty years old at the time of the publication of *The Rape of Lucrece*. Shakespeare also dedicated *Venus and Adonis* to him.
2. *The Rape of Lucrece* begins *in medias res* (in the middle of the story), as the Latin poet Horace recommends in *The Art of Poetry*.
3. Not asking for.
4. City twenty-five miles south of Rome.
5. Town ten miles east of Rome; the ancestral home of Collatinus's family.

this lamentable plight, hastily dispatcheth messengers, one to Rome for her father, another to the camp for Collatine. They came, the one accompanied with Junius Brutus, the other with Publius Valerius; and finding Lucrece attired in mourning habit, demanded the cause of her sorrow. She, first taking an oath of them for her revenge, revealed the actor° (doer) and whole manner of his dealing, and withal° (moreover) suddenly stabbed herself. Which done, with one consent they all vowed to root out the whole hated family of the Tarquins; and bearing the dead body to Rome, Brutus acquainted the people with the doer and manner of the vile deed, with a bitter invective against the tyranny of the King. Wherewith the people were so moved that, with one consent and a general acclamation, the Tarquins were all exiled, and the state government changed from kings to consuls.[6]

---

From the besiegèd Ardea all in post,° *haste*
Borne by the trustless wings of false desire,
Lust-breathèd° Tarquin leaves the Roman host, *Lust-inspired*
And to Collatium bears the lightless° fire, *smoldering*
Which, in pale embers hid, lurks to aspire° *rise up*
And girdle with embracing flames the waist
Of Collatine's fair love, Lucrece the chaste.

Haply° that name of "chaste" unhapp'ly° set *Perhaps / unfortunately*
This bateless° edge on his keen appetite, *unbluntable*
When Collatine unwisely did not let° *forbear*
To praise the clear unmatchèd red and white, *(Lucrece's face)*
Which triumphed in that sky of his delight,°
Where mortal stars° as bright as heaven's beauties *(her eyes)*
With pure aspects[1] did him peculiar° duties. *exclusive*

For he, the night before in Tarquin's tent,
Unlocked the treasure of his happy state:
What priceless wealth the heavens had him lent
In the possession of his beauteous mate,
Reck'ning his fortune at such high proud rate
That kings might be espousèd to more fame,
But° king nor peer to such a peerless dame.[2] *But neither*

Oh, happiness enjoyed but of° a few, *only by*
And if possessed as soon decayed and done
As is the morning's silver melting dew[3]
Against the golden splendor of the sun,
An expired date° canceled ere well begun. *time limit*
Honor and beauty in the owner's arms
Are weakly fortressed from a world of harms.

6. Chief magistrates, elected for one-year terms.

**Poem**

1. Looks; astral influences.

2. TEXTUAL COMMENT In line 21, the Second Quarto substitutes "prince" for "peer," but this is probably a mistake and the First Quarto reading is retained here. For a fuller discussion, see Digital Edition TC 1.

3. TEXTUAL COMMENT Some copies of the First Quarto have "morning silver dew," corrected to "mornings" (i.e., "morning's," turning the word into a possessive). This edition chooses "morning's" for reasons explained in Digital Edition TC 2.

Beauty itself doth of° itself persuade *by*
The eyes of men without an orator.
What needeth then apology be made[4]
To set forth that which is so singular?° *unique*
Or why is Collatine the publisher° *publicizer*
Of that rich jewel he should keep unknown
From thievish ears, because it is his own?

Perchance his boast of Lucrece' sov'reignty° *superiority*
Suggested° this proud issue° of a king; *Tempted / offspring*
For by our ears our hearts oft tainted be.
Perchance that envy of so rich a thing,
Braving compare,° disdainfully did sting *Defying comparison*
His high-pitched thoughts that meaner° men should vaunt° *inferior* *boast*
That golden hap° which their superiors want.° *luck / lack*

But some untimely thought did instigate
His all-too-timeless° speed, if none of those. *untimely; rapid*
His honor, his affairs, his friends, his state,° *rank*
Neglected all, with swift intent he goes
To quench the coal which in his liver° glows. *(seat of lust)*
O rash false heat, wrapped in repentant cold,
Thy hasty spring still blasts° and ne'er grows old. *is always frostbitten*

When at Collatium this false lord arrived,
Well was he welcomed by the Roman dame,
Within whose face Beauty and Virtue strived
Which of them both should underprop her fame.
When Virtue bragged, Beauty would blush for shame;
When Beauty boasted blushes, in despite° *defiance*
Virtue would stain° that o'er with silver white. *dye*

But Beauty, in that white entitlèd° *claiming title*
From Venus' doves, doth challenge that fair field.[5]
Then Virtue claims from Beauty Beauty's red,
Which Virtue gave the golden age to gild[6]
Their silver cheeks, and called it then their shield,
Teaching them thus to use it in the fight:
When shame assailed, the red should fence° the white. *defend*

This heraldry in Lucrece' face was seen,
Argued° by Beauty's red and Virtue's white. *Demonstrated; disputed*
Of either's color was the other queen,
Proving from world's minority° their right. *earliest age*
Yet their ambition makes them still to fight,
The sovereignty of either being so great
That oft they interchange each other's seat.

4. TEXTUAL COMMENT Here is another press variant: the word "apology" was corrected to "apologies." But the Norton editor believes the correction was made in error and retains the original reading; for reasoning, see Digital Edition TC 3.

5. Territory; battlefield; surface on which a coat of arms is displayed. *Venus' doves:* white turtledoves draw the chariot of Venus, the love goddess.

6. Coat with gold; cover with red (as in a blush). *the golden age:* a mythical, ideal era of innocence and plenty.

This silent war of lilies and of roses,
Which Tarquin viewed in her fair face's field,
In their pure ranks his traitor eye encloses,
Where, lest between them both it should be killed,
The coward-captive vanquishèd doth yield
To those two armies that would let him go,
Rather than triumph in° so false a foe. *over*

Now thinks he that her husband's shallow tongue,
The niggard prodigal that praised her so,
In that high task hath done her beauty wrong,
Which far exceeds his barren skill to show.° *describe*
Therefore that praise which Collatine doth owe° *fail to render*
Enchanted Tarquin answers° with surmise, *compensates for*
In silent wonder of still-gazing eyes.

This earthly saint adorèd by this devil
Little suspecteth the false worshipper:
For unstained thoughts do seldom dream on evil;
Birds never limed° no secret bushes fear. *trapped*
So, guiltless, she securely° gives good cheer[7] *unsuspectingly*
And reverent welcome to her princely guest,
Whose inward ill no outward harm expressed.

For that he colored° with his high estate, *disguised*
Hiding base sin in pleats° of majesty, *folds*
That° nothing in him seemed inordinate,° *So that / out of order*
Save sometime too much wonder of his eye,
Which, having all, all could not satisfy,
But, poorly rich, so wanteth in his store° *plenty*
That, cloyed with much, he pineth still for more.

But she that never coped with stranger° eyes *strangers'*
Could pick no meaning from their parling° looks, *persuasive*
Nor read the subtle shining secrecies
Writ in the glassy margins[8] of such books.
She touched no unknown baits, nor feared no hooks,
Nor could she moralize° his wanton sight° *interpret / looking*
More than his eyes were opened to the light.[9]

He stories to her ears her husband's fame,
Won in the fields of fruitful Italy,
And decks with praises Collatine's high name,
Made glorious by his manly chivalry,
With bruisèd arms° and wreaths of victory. *dented weapons*
Her joy with heaved-up hand she doth express,
And wordless so greets heaven for his success.

Far from the purpose of his coming thither,
He makes excuses for his being there.

7. Hospitable entertainment.
8. Where summaries and interpretive remarks were often placed. *glassy*: shiny.
9. *opened to the light*: made obvious.

No cloudy show of stormy blust'ring weather
Doth yet in his fair welkin° once appear, *sky (face)*
Till sable° night, mother of dread and fear, *black*
Upon the world dim darkness doth display,
And in her vaulty prison stows the day.

For then is Tarquin brought unto his bed,
Intending° weariness with heavy sprite.° *Pretending / spirit*
For after supper long he questionèd° *conversed*
With modest Lucrece and wore out the night.
Now leaden slumber with life's strength doth fight,
And everyone to rest themselves betake,[1]
Save thieves, and cares, and troubled minds that wake.

As one of which doth Tarquin lie revolving° *considering*
The sundry dangers of his will's obtaining;° *gratifying his desire*
Yet ever to obtain his will resolving.[2]
Though weak-built hopes[3] persuade him to abstaining,
Despair to gain doth traffic oft for gaining,[4]
And when great treasure is the meed° proposed, *prize*
Though death be adjunct,[5] there's no death supposed.° *thought of*

Those that much covet are with gain so fond° *infatuated*
That what° they have not—that which they possess— *That for what*
They scatter and unloose it from their bond,° *ownership*
And so by hoping more they have but less;
Or gaining more, the profit° of excess *advantage*
Is but to surfeit, and such griefs[6] sustain
That they° prove bankrupt in this poor-rich gain. *(the covetous)*

The aim of all is but to nurse the life
With honor, wealth, and ease in waning age;
And in this aim there is such thwarting strife
That one for all or all for one we gage°— *risk*
As° life for honor, in fell° battle's rage, *For instance / cruel*
Honor for wealth, and oft that wealth doth cost
The death of all, and altogether lost.

So that, in vent'ring ill,[7] we leave to be
The things we are for that which we expect;
And this ambitious foul infirmity,
In having° much, torments us with defect *While we have*
Of that we have; so then we do neglect
The thing we have, and all for want of wit° *lack of sense*
Make something nothing by augmenting it.

1. TEXTUAL COMMENT Lines 125–26 exist in two slightly different states, and editors disagree on which one to choose; *The Norton Shakespeare* prints the version that is closer to modern usage. For a discussion of the options, see Digital Edition TC 4.
2. TEXTUAL COMMENT In the Quarto the punctuation of lines 129–30 seems to be erroneous, but modern editors disagree about what the proper punctuation ought to be. For a discussion of the problem and its possible solutions, see Digital Edition TC 5.
3. The fact that his hopes are flimsy.
4. *Despair . . . gaining:* Despair of gaining her (rightfully) often encourages him to gain her (by any means possible).
5. Be joined with it.
6. That is, the ills that accompany excess.
7. In taking serious risks; in undertaking evil deeds.

Such hazard now must doting Tarquin make,
Pawning his honor to obtain his lust,
And for himself himself he must forsake.
Then where is truth if there be no self-trust?° *truth to oneself*
When shall he think to find a stranger just,
When he himself himself confounds, betrays
To sland'rous tongues and wretched hateful days?

Now stole upon the time the dead of night,
When heavy sleep had closed up mortal eyes.
No comfortable star did lend his° light, *its*
No noise but owls' and wolves' death-boding cries.
Now serves the season that they may surprise
The silly° lambs. Pure thoughts are dead and still, *innocent*
While lust and murder wakes to stain° and kill. *defile*

And now this lustful lord leaped from his bed,
Throwing his mantle rudely o'er his arm,
Is madly tossed between desire and dread:
Th'one sweetly flatters, th'other feareth harm;
But honest fear, bewitched with lust's foul charm,
Doth too too oft betake him to retire,° *retreat*
Beaten away by brainsick rude desire.

His falchion° on a flint he softly smiteth, *curved sword*
That from the cold stone sparks of fire do fly,
Whereat a waxen torch forthwith he lighteth,
Which must be lodestar° to his lustful eye, *guiding light*
And to the flame thus speaks advisedly:° *deliberately*
"As from this cold flint I enforced this fire,
So Lucrece must I force to my desire."

Here, pale with fear, he doth premeditate
The dangers of his loathsome enterprise,
And in his inward mind he doth debate
What following sorrow may on this arise.
Then, looking scornfully, he doth despise
His naked armor of still-slaughtered lust,[8]
And justly thus controls° his thoughts unjust. *rebukes; restrains*

"Fair torch, burn out thy light, and lend it not
To darken her whose light excelleth thine;
And die, unhallowed thoughts, before you blot
With your uncleanness that which is divine.
Offer pure incense to so pure a shrine.
Let fair humanity abhor the deed
That spots and stains love's modest snow-white weed.° *attire (chastity)*

"Oh, shame to knighthood and to shining arms!
Oh, foul dishonor to my household's grave!° *ancestral tomb*
Oh, impious act including° all foul harms— *encompassing*

8. *His . . . lust:* His ineffective defense against his lust, always quenched in the moment of fulfillment; his not-yet-erect penis.

A martial man to be soft fancy's° slave! *love's*
True valor still a true respect[9] should have;
Then my digression° is so vile, so base, *error*
That it will live engraven in my face.

"Yea, though I die the scandal will survive
And be an eyesore in my golden coat.° *(of arms)*
Some loathsome dash[1] the herald will contrive
To cipher me how fondly° I did dote, *To show how foolishly*
That my posterity, shamed with the note,° *stigma*
Shall curse my bones and hold it for no sin
To wish that I their father had not been.

"What win I if I gain the thing I seek?
A dream, a breath, a froth of fleeting joy.
Who buys a minute's mirth to wail a week,
Or sells eternity to get a toy?° *trifle*
For one sweet grape who will the vine destroy?
Or what fond beggar, but to touch the crown,
Would with the scepter straight be strucken down?

"If Collatinus dream of my intent,
Will he not wake, and in a desp'rate rage
Post hither this vile purpose to prevent?
This siege that hath engirt° his marriage, *surrounded*
This blur° to youth, this sorrow to the sage, *blot*
This dying virtue, this surviving shame,
Whose crime will bear an ever-during° blame. *everlasting*

"Oh, what excuse can my invention° make *ingenuity*
When thou shalt charge me with so black a deed?
Will not my tongue be mute, my frail joints shake,
Mine eyes forgo their light,° my false heart bleed? *power of vision*
The guilt being great, the fear doth still exceed,
And extreme fear can neither fight nor fly,
But coward-like with trembling terror die.

"Had Collatinus killed my son or sire,
Or lain in ambush to betray my life,
Or were he not my dear friend, this desire
Might have excuse to work upon his wife,
As in revenge or quittal° of such strife. *requital*
But as he is my kinsman,° my dear friend, *(Collatine was a cousin.)*
The shame and fault finds no excuse nor end.

"Shameful it is—ay, if the fact° be known, *deed*
Hateful it is. There is no hate in loving.
I'll beg her love, but she is not her own.
The worst is but denial and reproving.
My will is strong, past reason's weak removing.

9. A suitable awareness of virtue.
1. Bar in a coat of arms, indicating a dishonorable action by an ancestor.

Who fears a sentence° or an old man's saw° *maxim / proverb*
Shall by a painted cloth be kept in awe."[2]

Thus graceless holds he disputation
Tween frozen conscience and hot-burning will,
And with good thoughts makes dispensation,° *dispenses*
Urging the worser sense for vantage still,
Which in a moment doth confound and kill
All pure effects,° and doth so far proceed *tendencies*
That what is vile shows like a virtuous deed.

Quoth he, "She took me kindly by the hand,
And gazed for tidings in my eager eyes,
Fearing some hard news from the warlike band
Where her belovèd Collatinus lies.
Oh, how her fear did make her color rise!
First red as roses that on lawn° we lay, *fine linen*
Then white as lawn, the roses took away.

"And how her hand, in my hand being locked,
Forced it to tremble with her loyal fear,
Which struck her sad, and then it faster rocked,
Until her husband's welfare she did hear,
Whereat she smilèd with so sweet a cheer° *an expression*
That had Narcissus[2] seen her as she stood
Self-love had never drowned him in the flood.

"Why hunt I then for color° or excuses? *pretext*
All orators are dumb when beauty pleadeth.
Poor wretches have remorse in poor abuses.° *regret minor lapses*
Love thrives not in the heart that shadows° dreadeth; *illusory scruples*
Affection° is my captain, and he leadeth; *Passion*
And when his gaudy banner is displayed,
The coward fights and will not be dismayed.

"Then childish fear avaunt,° debating die, *be gone*
Respect° and reason wait on° wrinkled age! *Circumspection / attend*
My heart shall never countermand mine eye.
Sad° pause and deep regard beseems the sage; *Serious*
My part is youth and beats these from the stage.[4]
Desire my pilot is, beauty my prize.° *pirate's booty*
Then who fears sinking where such treasure lies?"

As corn° o'ergrown by weeds, so heedful fear *grain*
Is almost choked by unresisted lust.
Away he steals with open list'ning ear,
Full of foul hope and full of fond° mistrust, *foolish; passionate*
Both which, as servitors° to the unjust, *servants*
So cross him with their opposite persuasion
That now he vows a league, and now invasion.

2. *Shall . . . awe:* Will be awed by a tapestry (often depicting morally significant narratives, as in lines 1366ff).
3. In classical mythology, a youth who fell in love with his reflection in a pool; in some versions of the tale, he drowned attempting to kiss the image.
4. Like the Vice character in medieval morality plays.

Within his thought her heavenly image sits,
And in the selfsame seat sits Collatine.
That eye which looks on her confounds his wits,
That eye which him beholds, as° more divine, *because it is*
Unto a view so false will not incline,
But with a pure appeal seeks° to the heart, *applies*
Which once corrupted takes the worser part;

And therein heartens up his servile powers,[5]
Who, flattered by their leader's jocund show,
Stuff up his lust as minutes fill up hours;
And as their captain, so their pride doth grow,
Paying more slavish tribute than they owe.[6]
By reprobate desire thus madly led,
The Roman lord marcheth to Lucrece' bed.

The locks between her chamber and his will,
Each one by him enforced, retires his ward;° *withdraws its bolt*
But as they open they all rate° his ill, *berate (by squeaking)*
Which drives the creeping thief to some regard.° *caution*
The threshold grates the door to have him heard;
Night-wand'ring weasels[7] shriek to see him there:
They fright him, yet he still pursues his fear.° *that which makes him fear*

As each unwilling portal yields him way,
Through little vents and crannies of the place
The wind wars with his torch to make him stay,
And blows the smoke of it into his face,
Extinguishing his conduct° in this case. *guide; behavior*
But his hot heart, which fond desire doth scorch,
Puffs forth another wind that fires the torch.

And being lighted, by the light he spies
Lucretia's glove wherein her needle sticks.
He takes it from the rushes where it lies
And, gripping it, the needle his finger pricks,
As who should say, "This glove to wanton tricks
Is not inured. Return again in haste.
Thou seest our mistress' ornaments are chaste."

But all these poor forbiddings could not stay him;
He in the worst sense consters° their denial. *construes*
The doors, the wind, the glove that did delay him
He takes for accidental things of trial;° *tests of resolve*
Or as those bars which stop the hourly dial,[8]
Who with a ling'ring stay his course doth let° *hinder; permit*
Till every minute pays the hour his debt.

"So, so," quoth he, "these lets attend the time,
Like little frosts that sometime threat the spring

5. Appetites or passions, imagined as servants of the heart, the seat of conscience.
6. That is, debasing themselves by collaborating and encouraging the corrupted heart.
7. Weasels were kept to catch vermin.
8. The marks on a clock face, where the hands pause before jerking forward.

To add a more rejoicing to the prime,° *spring*
And give the sneapèd° birds more cause to sing. *pinched with cold*
Pain pays the income° of each precious thing. *is the price*
Huge rocks, high winds, strong pirates, shelves,° and sands *reefs*
The merchant fears, ere rich at home he lands."

Now is he come unto the chamber door
That shuts him from the heaven of his thought,
Which with a yielding latch, and with no more,
Hath barred him from the blessèd thing he sought.
So from° himself impiety hath wrought° *unlike / made him*
That for his prey to pray he doth begin,
As if the heavens should countenance his sin.

But in the midst of his unfruitful prayer,
Having solicited th'eternal power
That his foul thoughts might compass° his fair fair,[9] *obtain; embrace*
And they would stand auspicious to the hour,
Even there he starts.° Quoth he, "I must deflower; *is startled*
The powers to whom I pray abhor this fact.° *deed*
How can they then assist me in the act?

"Then love and fortune be my gods, my guide.
My will is backed with resolution.
Thoughts are but dreams till their effects be tried.
The blackest sin is cleared with absolution.
Against love's fire, fear's frost hath dissolution.
The eye of heaven is out,° and misty night *extinguished*
Covers the shame that follows sweet delight."

This said, his guilty hand plucked up the latch,
And with his knee the door he opens wide.
The dove sleeps fast that this night-owl will catch.
Thus treason works ere traitors be espied.
Who sees the lurking serpent steps aside,
But she, sound sleeping, fearing no such thing,
Lies at the mercy of his mortal° sting. *lethal*

Into the chamber wickedly he stalks,° *steals*
And gazeth on her yet unstainèd bed.
The curtains being close,° about he walks, *shut*
Rolling his greedy eyeballs in his head.
By their high treason is his heart misled,
Which gives the watchword to his hand full soon
To draw the cloud° that hides the silver moon. *(the bed curtain)*

Look as° the fair and fiery-pointed sun, *See how*
Rushing from forth a cloud, bereaves our sight;
Even so, the curtain drawn, his eyes begun
To wink,° being blinded with a greater light. *close*
Whether it is that she reflects so bright
That dazzleth them, or else some shame supposed,
But blind they are and keep themselves enclosed.

9. *his fair fair:* his virtuous and beautiful one.

Oh, had they in that darksome prison died,
Then had they seen the period° of their ill. *end*
Then Collatine again by Lucrece' side
In his clear° bed might have reposèd still. *undefiled*
But they must ope, this blessèd league° to kill, *marriage*
And holy-thoughted Lucrece to their sight
Must sell her joy, her life, her world's delight.

Her lily hand her rosy cheek lies under,
Coz'ning° the pillow of a lawful kiss, *Cheating*
Who, therefore angry, seems to part in sunder,° *in two*
Swelling on either side to want his bliss;[1]
Between whose hills her head entombèd is,
Where like a virtuous monument she lies
To be admired of lewd unhallowed eyes.

Without the bed her other fair hand was
On the green coverlet, whose perfect white
Showed like an April daisy on the grass,
With pearly sweat resembling dew of night.
Her eyes like marigolds[2] had sheathed their light,
And canopied in darkness sweetly lay
Till they might open to adorn the day.

Her hair like golden threads played with her breath—
Oh, modest wantons, wanton modesty!—
Showing life's triumph in the map° of death, *image*
And death's dim look in life's mortality.
Each° in her sleep themselves so beautify, *(life and death)*
As if between them twain there were no strife,
But that life lived in death, and death in life.

Her breasts like ivory globes circled with blue,
A pair of maiden[3] worlds unconquerèd,
Save of their lord no bearing yoke they knew,
And him by oath they truly honorèd.
These worlds in Tarquin new ambition bred,
Who like a foul usurper went about
From this fair throne to heave the owner out.

What could he see but mightily he noted?
What did he note but strongly he desired?
What he beheld, on that he firmly doted,
And in his will° his willful eye he tired.[4] *lust*
With more than admiration he admired
Her azure veins, her alabaster skin,
Her coral lips, her snow-white dimpled chin.

As the grim lion fawneth° o'er his prey, *shows delight*
Sharp hunger by the conquest satisfied,

1. Because it is denied its pleasure (of her lips touching its surface).
2. The pot marigold folds up its flowers at day's end.
3. Used of an unconquered citadel.
4. Wearied; fed greedily (as a hawk tears flesh with its beak).

So o'er this sleeping soul doth Tarquin stay,
His rage of lust by gazing qualified,° *mollified*
Slaked, not suppressed, for standing by her side.
His eye, which late this mutiny restrains,
Unto a greater uproar tempts his veins;

And they, like straggling slaves° for pillage fighting, *lowborn soldiers*
Obdurate vassals fell° exploits effecting, *fierce*
In bloody death and ravishment delighting,
Nor° children's tears nor mothers' groans respecting, *Neither*
Swell in their pride, the onset still° expecting. *at any moment*
Anon his beating heart, alarum° striking, *signal to attack*
Gives the hot charge, and bids them do their liking.

His drumming heart cheers up his burning eye;
His eye commends° the leading to his hand. *entrusts*
His hand, as proud of such a dignity,
Smoking with pride, marched on to make his stand
On her bare breast, the heart of all her land,
Whose ranks of blue veins, as his hand did scale,° *climb*
Left their round turrets destitute and pale.

They must'ring° to the quiet cabinet° *gathering / room (heart)*
Where their dear governess° and lady lies, *ruler*
Do tell her she is dreadfully beset,
And fright her with confusion of their cries.
She much amazed breaks ope her locked-up eyes,
Who, peeping forth this tumult to behold,
Are by his flaming torch dimmed and controlled.° *overwhelmed*

Imagine her as one in dead of night
From forth dull sleep by dreadful fancy waking,
That thinks she hath beheld some ghastly sprite,
Whose grim aspect sets every joint a-shaking.
What terror 'tis! But she in worser taking,° *plight*
From sleep disturbèd, heedfully doth view
The sight which makes supposèd terror true.

Wrapped and confounded in a thousand fears,
Like to a new-killed bird she trembling lies.
She dares not look, yet winking° there appears *shutting her eyes*
Quick-shifting antics,° ugly in her eyes. *grotesque shapes*
Such shadows are the weak brain's forgeries,
Who, angry that the eyes fly from their lights,
In darkness daunts them with more dreadful sights.

His hand that yet remains upon her breast—
Rude ram° to batter such an ivory wall— *battering ram*
May feel her heart, poor citizen, distressed,
Wounding itself to death, rise up and fall,
Beating her bulk,° that his hand shakes withal.° *chest / as well*
This moves in him more rage and lesser pity,
To make the breach and enter this sweet city.

First like a trumpet doth his tongue begin<br>
To sound a parley[5] to his heartless° foe, *terrified*<br>
Who o'er the white sheet peers her whiter chin,<br>
The reason of this rash alarm to know,<br>
Which he by dumb demeanor° seeks to show. *mute gesture*<br>
But she with vehement prayers urgeth still<br>
Under what color° he commits this ill. *pretext*

Thus he replies: "The color in thy face,<br>
That even for anger makes the lily pale<br>
And the red rose blush at her own disgrace,<br>
Shall plead for me and tell my loving tale.<br>
Under that color° am I come to scale *pretext; hue; flag*<br>
Thy never-conquered fort. The fault is thine,<br>
For those thine eyes betray thee unto mine.

"Thus I forestall thee, if thou mean to chide:<br>
Thy beauty hath ensnared thee to this night,<br>
Where thou with patience must my will abide,<br>
My will that marks thee for my earth's° delight, *earthly; bodily*<br>
Which I to conquer sought with all my might.<br>
But as reproof and reason beat it° dead, *(my lust)*<br>
By thy bright beauty was it newly bred.

"I see what crosses° my attempt will bring; *misfortunes*<br>
I know what thorns the growing rose defends;<br>
I think° the honey guarded with a sting: *know*<br>
All this beforehand counsel° comprehends. *wisdom*<br>
But Will is deaf, and hears no heedful friends.<br>
Only he hath an eye to gaze on beauty,<br>
And dotes on what he looks, 'gainst law or duty.

"I have debated even in my soul,<br>
What wrong, what shame, what sorrow I shall breed;<br>
But nothing can affection's° course control, *passion's*<br>
Or stop the headlong fury of his speed.<br>
I know repentant tears ensue° the deed, *follow*<br>
Reproach, disdain, and deadly enmity,<br>
Yet strive I to embrace mine infamy."

This said, he shakes aloft his Roman blade,<br>
Which like a falcon tow'ring in the skies<br>
Coucheth the fowl° below with his wings' shade, *Makes the prey crouch*<br>
Whose crookèd beak threats, if he° mount he dies. *(the fowl)*<br>
So under his insulting° falchion lies *triumphantly exulting*<br>
Harmless Lucretia, marking what he tells<br>
With trembling fear, as fowl hear falcons' bells.[6]

"Lucrece," quoth he, "this night I must enjoy thee.<br>
If thou deny, then force must work my way,<br>
For in thy bed I purpose to destroy thee.<br>
That done, some worthless slave of thine I'll slay

5. A call to a negotiation.

6. Hunting falcons had bells attached to their legs.

To kill thine honor with thy life's decay;[7]
And in thy dead arms do I mean to place him,
Swearing I slew him, seeing thee embrace him.

"So thy surviving husband shall remain
The scornful mark of every open eye;° *observer*
Thy kinsmen hang their heads at this disdain;
Thy issue blurred with nameless bastardy;[8]
And thou, the author of their obloquy,
Shalt have thy trespass cited up in rhymes° *described in ballads*
And sung by children in succeeding times.

"But if thou yield, I rest thy secret friend:
The fault unknown is as a thought unacted.
A little harm done to a great good end
For lawful policy remains enacted.[9]
The poisonous simple° sometime is compacted° *ingredient / mixed*
In a pure° compound; being so applied, *benign*
His venom in effect is purified.

"Then for thy husband and thy children's sake
Tender my suit;° bequeath not to their lot *Regard my plea*
The shame that from them no device[1] can take,
The blemish that will never be forgot,
Worse than a slavish wipe or birth-hour's blot.[2]
For marks descried in men's nativity
Are nature's faults, not their own infamy."

Here with a cockatrice'[3] dead-killing eye,
He rouseth up himself, and makes a pause,
While she, the picture of pure piety,
Like a white hind° under the gripe's° sharp claws, *doe / griffin's*
Pleads in a wilderness where are no laws
To the rough beast that knows no gentle right,° *law of gentility*
Nor aught° obeys but his foul appetite. *anything*

But when a black-faced cloud the world doth threat,
In his dim mist th'aspiring mountains hiding,
From earth's dark womb some gentle gust doth get,
Which blow these pitchy vapors from their biding,° *place*
Hind'ring their present° fall by this dividing, *immediate*
So his unhallowed haste her words delays,
And moody Pluto winks while Orpheus plays.[4]

Yet, foul night-waking cat, he doth but dally
While in his holdfast foot the weak mouse panteth;
Her sad behavior feeds his vulture folly,° *ravenous insanity*
A swallowing gulf° that even in plenty wanteth. *whirlpool; belly*

7. *To kill . . . decay:* To destroy your reputation along with your life.
8. *Thy . . . bastardy:* Your children suspected of being bastards whose father's name is unknown.
9. *For . . . enacted:* Is allowed as proper statesmanship.
1. Ingenuity; heraldic emblem.
2. A slave's brand or birthmark.
3. Legendary monster whose glance was deadly.
4. When Orpheus, a legendary musician and poet, attempted to regain his dead wife from the underworld, he charmed Pluto, god of the underworld, by playing on the lyre.

His ear her prayers admits, but his heart granteth
No penetrable entrance to her plaining:° *lament*
Tears harden lust, though marble wear with raining.

Her pity-pleading eyes are sadly fixed
In the remorseless wrinkles of his face.
Her modest eloquence with sighs is mixed,
Which to her oratory adds more grace.
She puts the period often from his° place, *its*
And midst the sentence so her accent breaks,
That twice she doth begin ere once she speaks.

She conjures him by high almighty Jove,
By knighthood, gentry,° and sweet friendship's oath, *noble birth*
By her untimely tears, her husband's love,
By holy human law, and common troth,[5]
By heaven and earth and all the power of both,
That to his borrowed° bed he make retire, *(guest)*
And stoop[6] to honor, not to foul desire.

Quoth she, "Reward not hospitality
With such black payment as thou hast pretended;° *offered*
Mud not the fountain that gave drink to thee;
Mar not the thing that cannot be amended;
End thy ill aim before thy shoot be ended.
He is no woodman° that doth bend his bow *sportsman*
To strike a poor unseasonable° doe. *out-of-season*

"My husband is thy friend; for his sake spare me.
Thyself art mighty; for thine own sake leave me.
Myself a weakling; do not then ensnare me.
Thou look'st not like deceit; do not deceive me.
My sighs like whirlwinds labor hence to heave thee.
If ever man were moved with woman's moans,
Be movèd with my tears, my sighs, my groans.

"All which together, like a troubled ocean,
Beat at thy rocky and wreck-threat'ning heart
To soften it with their continual motion,
For stones dissolved to water do convert.
Oh, if no harder than a stone thou art,
Melt at my tears and be compassionate.
Soft pity enters at an iron gate.

"In Tarquin's likeness I did entertain thee.
Hast thou put on his shape to do him shame?
To all the host of heaven I complain me.
Thou wrong'st his honor, wound'st his princely name.
Thou art not what thou seem'st, and if the same,
Thou seem'st not what thou art, a god, a king:
For kings like gods should govern everything.

5. *common troth:* the good faith that binds communities together.

6. Swoop down to a lure (in falconry); lie down; subject himself.

"How will thy shame be seeded° in thine age *ripened*
When thus thy vices bud before thy spring?
If in thy hope° thou dar'st do such outrage, *If not yet in power*
What dar'st thou not when once thou art a king?
Oh, be remembered, no outrageous thing
From vassal actors° can be wiped away: *lowborn criminals*
Then kings' misdeeds cannot be hid in clay.° *(even after death)*

"This deed will make thee only loved for° fear; *obeyed out of*
But happy monarchs still° are feared for love. *always*
With foul offenders thou perforce must bear,
When they in thee the like offenses prove;
If but for fear of this, thy will remove.
For princes are the glass,° the school, the book, *mirror*
Where subjects' eyes do learn, do read, do look.

"And wilt thou be the school where lust shall learn?
Must he in thee read lectures of such shame?
Wilt thou be glass wherein it shall discern
Authority for sin, warrant for blame,
To privilege° dishonor in thy name? *justify*
Thou back'st° reproach against long-living laud,° *support / praise*
And mak'st fair reputation but a bawd.

"Hast thou command?° By him° that gave it thee, *authority / (God)*
From a pure heart command thy rebel will.
Draw not thy sword to guard iniquity,
For it was lent thee all that brood° to kill. *kind of thing*
Thy princely office how canst thou fulfill
When, patterned° by thy fault, foul Sin may say *given a precedent*
He learned to sin, and thou didst teach the way?

"Think but how vile a spectacle it were
To view thy present trespass in another.
Men's faults do seldom to themselves appear;
Their own transgressions partially they smother.° *hide (from themselves)*
This guilt would seem death-worthy in thy brother.
Oh, how are they wrapped in with infamies,
That from their own misdeeds askance° their eyes! *turn away*

"To thee, to thee, my heaved-up hands appeal,
Not to seducing lust, thy rash relier.[7]
I sue for exiled majesty's repeal;° *recall from exile*
Let him return, and flatt'ring thoughts retire.
His true respect° will prison false desire, *judgment*
And wipe the dim mist from thy doting eyne,° *eyes (archaic)*
That thou shalt see thy state, and pity mine."

"Have done," quoth he; "my uncontrollèd tide
Turns not, but swells the higher by this let.° *restraint*
Small lights are soon blown out; huge fires abide,

7. *thy rash relier:* on which you rashly rely. TEXTUAL COMMENT Since the word "relier" had never been used before and Shakespeare did not use it again, some people have believed that there is a misprint here; but most modern editors retain the First Quarto reading. For a fuller discussion of the textual problem, see Digital Edition TC 6.

And with the wind in greater fury fret.
The petty streams, that pay a daily debt
To their salt sovereign,° with their fresh falls' haste *(the sea)*
Add to his flow, but alter not his taste."

"Thou art," quoth she, "a sea, a sovereign king,
And lo, there falls into thy boundless flood
Black lust, dishonor, shame, misgoverning,
Who seek to stain the ocean of thy blood.° *disposition; birthright*
If all these petty ills shall change thy good,
Thy sea within a puddle's womb is hearsed,° *enclosed*
And not the puddle in thy sea dispersed.

"So shall these slaves° be king, and thou their slave; *(lust, dishonor, etc.)*
Thou nobly base, they basely dignified;
Thou their fair life, and they thy fouler grave;
Thou loathèd in their shame, they in thy pride.
The lesser thing should not the greater hide:
The cedar stoops not to the base shrub's foot,
But low shrubs wither at the cedar's root.

"So let thy thoughts, low vassals to thy state—"
"No more," quoth he. "By heaven, I will not hear thee.
Yield to my love. If not, enforcèd hate
Instead of love's coy° touch shall rudely tear thee. *gentle*
That done, despitefully° I mean to bear thee *maliciously*
Unto the base bed of some rascal groom° *servant*
To be thy partner in this shameful doom."

This said, he sets his foot upon the light,
For light and lust are deadly enemies.
Shame folded up in blind concealing night,
When most unseen, then most doth tyrannize.
The wolf hath seized his prey, the poor lamb cries,
Till with her own white fleece° her voice controlled,° *(bedclothes) / overpowered*
Entombs her outcry in her lips' sweet fold.° *crevice; sheep pen*

For with the nightly linen that she wears
He pens her piteous clamors in her head,
Cooling his hot face in the chastest tears
That ever modest eyes with sorrow shed.
Oh, that prone° lust should stain so pure a bed![8] *eager; face-down*
The spots whereof could weeping purify,° *if weeping could purify*
Her tears should drop on them perpetually.

But she hath lost a dearer thing than life,
And he hath won what he would lose again.
This forcèd league° doth force a further strife; *joining together*
This momentary joy breeds months of pain;
This hot desire converts to cold disdain:

8. Textual Comment The Fourth Quarto (1600) emended "prone" to "proud," and the Sixth (1616) emended it to "fowle," but modern editors accept the original reading. For discussion of these choices, see Digital Edition TC 7.

Pure chastity is rifled of her store,
And lust, the thief, far poorer than before.

Look° as the full-fed hound or gorgèd hawk, *Just*
Unapt for tender° smell or speedy flight, *delicate*
Make slow pursuit, or altogether balk° *turn from*
The prey wherein by nature they delight,
So surfeit-taking Tarquin fares° this night: *behaves; feeds*
His taste delicious, in digestion souring,
Devours his will that lived by foul devouring.

Oh, deeper sin than bottomless conceit° *unlimited fantasy*
Can comprehend in still imagination!
Drunken desire must vomit his receipt° *what he swallowed*
Ere he can see his own abomination.
While lust is in his pride, no exclamation
Can curb his heat or rein his rash desire,
Till like a jade° self-will himself doth tire. *recalcitrant horse*

And then with lank and lean discolored cheek,
With heavy eye, knit brow, and strengthless pace,
Feeble desire all recreant,[9] poor, and meek,
Like to a bankrupt beggar wails his case.
The flesh being proud, desire doth fight with grace,
For there it revels, and when that decays,° *subsides*
The guilty rebel for remission° prays. *pardon*

So fares it with this faultful lord of Rome,
Who this accomplishment so hotly chased,
For now against himself he sounds° this doom,° *pronounces / sentence*
That through the length of times he stands disgraced.
Besides, his soul's fair temple is defaced,
To whose weak ruins muster troops of cares,
To ask the spotted princess° how she fares. *(the defiled soul)*

She says her subjects with foul insurrection
Have battered down her consecrated wall,
And by their mortal° fault brought in subjection *deadly*
Her immortality, and made her thrall
To living death and pain perpetual,
Which° in her prescience she controllèd still, *(the soul's subjects)*
But her foresight could not forestall their will.

E'en in this thought through the dark night he stealeth,
A captive victor that hath lost in gain;
Bearing away the wound that nothing healeth,
The scar that will, despite of cure, remain,
Leaving his spoil° perplexed in greater pain. *prey*
She bears the load of lust he left behind,
And he the burden of a guilty mind.

He like a thievish dog creeps sadly thence;
She like a wearied lamb lies panting there.

9. Cowardly; faithless; exhausted.

He scowls and hates himself for his offense;
She, desperate, with her nails her flesh doth tear.
He faintly flies, sweating with guilty fear;
She stays, exclaiming on° the direful night. *denouncing*
He runs and chides his vanished loathed delight.

He thence departs, a heavy convertite;° *sad penitent*
She there remains, a hopeless castaway.
He in his speed looks for the morning light;
She prays she never may behold the day.
"For day," quoth she, "night's scapes° doth open lay, *sins*
And my true eyes have never practiced how
To cloak offenses with a cunning brow.

"They think not but that° every eye can see *only think*
The same disgrace which they themselves behold;
And therefore would they still in darkness be,
To have their unseen sin remain untold.
For they their guilt with weeping will unfold
And grave,° like water that doth eat in steel,[1] *engrave*
Upon my cheeks what helpless shame I feel."

Here she exclaims against repose and rest,
And bids her eyes hereafter still° be blind. *always*
She wakes her heart by beating on her breast,
And bids it leap from thence where it may find
Some purer chest to close° so pure a mind. *enclose*
Frantic with grief, thus breathes she forth her spite° *reproach*
Against the unseen secrecy of night:

"O comfort-killing Night, image of hell,
Dim register° and notary of shame, *recorder*
Black stage for tragedies and murders fell,
Vast sin-concealing chaos, nurse of blame!
Blind muffled bawd, dark harbor for defame,° *infamy*
Grim cave of death, whisp'ring conspirator,
With close-tongued treason and the ravisher!

"O hateful, vaporous, and foggy Night!
Since thou art guilty of my cureless crime,
Muster thy mists to meet the eastern light;
Make war against proportioned° course of time; *orderly*
Or if thou wilt permit the sun to climb
His wonted height, yet ere he go to bed,
Knit poisonous clouds about his golden head.

"With rotten damps° ravish the morning air; *vapors*
Let their exhaled unwholesome breaths make sick
The life of purity, the supreme fair,° *(the sun)*
Ere he arrive his weary noontide prick;° *mark on a clock*
And let thy musty vapors march so thick

1. *water . . . steel*: aqua fortis (literally, "strong water"), nitric acid.

That in their smoky ranks his smothered light
May set at noon and make perpetual night.

"Were Tarquin Night, as he is but Night's child,
The silver-shining queen[2] he would distain;° *stain*
Her twinkling handmaids° too—by him defiled— *(the stars)*
Through Night's black bosom should not peep again.
So should I have copartners in my pain,
And fellowship in woe doth woe assuage,
As palmers'° chat makes short their pilgrimage. *pilgrims'*

"Where now I have no one to blush with me,
To cross their arms[3] and hang their heads with mine,
To mask their brows and hide their infamy;
But I alone, alone must sit and pine,
Seasoning the earth with showers of silver brine,
Mingling my talk with tears, my grief with groans,
Poor wasting monuments° of lasting moans. *short-lived tokens*

"O Night, thou furnace of foul-reeking smoke!
Let not the jealous° day behold that face, *suspicious*
Which underneath thy black all-hiding cloak
Immodestly lies martyred with disgrace.
Keep still possession of thy gloomy place,
That all the faults which in thy reign are made
May likewise be sepulchered° in thy shade. *entombed*

"Make me not object° to the telltale day; *manifest*
The light will show charactered° in my brow *written*
The story of sweet chastity's decay,
The impious breach of holy wedlock vow.
Yea, the illiterate, that know not how
To cipher° what is writ in learnèd books, *decipher*
Will quote° my loathsome trespass in my looks. *note*

"The nurse to still her child will tell my story,
And fright her crying babe with Tarquin's name.
The orator to deck his oratory
Will couple my reproach to Tarquin's shame.
Feast-finding minstrels,[4] tuning my defame,
Will tie the hearers to attend° each line, *listen to*
How Tarquin wrongèd me, I Collatine.

"Let my good name, that senseless° reputation, *intangible*
For Collatine's dear love be kept unspotted.
If that be made a theme for disputation,
The branches of another root are rotted,[5]
And undeserved reproach to him allotted,
That is as clear from this attaint° of mine *stain*
As I ere this was pure to Collatine.

2. The moon, symbol of chastity.
3. This is a conventional gesture of melancholy.
4. Minstrels were paid to perform at banquets.
5. That is, Collatine's reputation is also destroyed.

"Oh, unseen shame, invisible disgrace!
Oh, unfelt sore, crest-wounding[6] private scar!
Reproach° is stamped in Collatinus' face, *Reproof; dishonor*
And Tarquin's eye may read the mot° afar, *motto*
How he in peace is wounded, not in war.
Alas, how many bear such shameful blows,
Which not themselves but he that gives them knows.

"If, Collatine, thine honor lay in me,
From me by strong assault it is bereft;
My honey lost, and I, a drone-like bee,
Have no perfection of my summer left,[7]
But robbed and ransacked by injurious theft.
In thy weak hive a wandering wasp hath crept,
And sucked the honey which thy chaste bee kept.

"Yet am I guilty of thy honor's wrack;° *ruin*
Yet for thy honor did I entertain him.
Coming from thee I could not put him back,
For it had been dishonor to disdain him.
Besides, of weariness he did complain him,
And talked of virtue—oh, unlooked-for evil,
When virtue is profaned in such a devil!

"Why should the worm intrude the maiden bud,
Or hateful cuckoos hatch in sparrows' nests,
Or toads infect fair founts with venom° mud, *venomous*
Or tyrant folly° lurk in gentle breasts, *cruel lewdness*
Or kings be breakers of their own behests?° *commands*
But no perfection is so absolute
That some impurity doth not pollute.

"The agèd man that coffers up his gold
Is plagued with cramps and gouts and painful fits,
And scarce hath eyes his treasure to behold;
But like still-pining Tantalus[8] he sits,
And useless barns° the harvest of his wits, *hoards*
Having no other pleasure of his gain,
But torment that it cannot cure his pain.

"So then he hath it when he cannot use it,
And leaves it to be mastered° by his young,° *possessed / children*
Who in their pride do presently° abuse it. *immediately*
Their father was too weak and they too strong
To hold their cursèd-blessèd fortune long.
The sweets we wish for turn to loathèd sours,
Even in the moment that we call them ours.

"Unruly blasts wait on the tender spring;
Unwholesome weeds take root with precious flowers;

6. Damaging the coat of arms, hence family honor (cf. lines 204–10).
7. *Have . . . left:* Have nothing left of what I made in the summer; have none of the purity of my prime remaining.
8. A mythological figure who was punished in Hades by eternal hunger and thirst; food and water were always visible but receded at his approach.

The adder hisses where the sweet birds sing:
What virtue breeds, iniquity devours.
We have no good that we can say is ours,
But ill-annexèd Opportunity[9]
Or° kills his life or else his quality. *Either*

"O Opportunity, thy guilt is great!
'Tis thou that execut'st the traitor's treason;
Thou sets the wolf where he the lamb may get;
Whoever plots the sin, thou point'st° the season. *appoint*
'Tis thou that spurn'st at° right, at law, at reason; *rejects*
And in thy shady cell, where none may spy him,
Sits Sin to seize the souls that wander by him.

"Thou makest the vestal[1] violate her oath;
Thou blowest the fire when temperance is thawed;
Thou smotherest honesty, thou murd'rest troth,
Thou foul abettor, thou notorious bawd;° *pimp*
Thou plantest scandal and displacest laud.° *praise*
Thou ravisher, thou traitor, thou false thief,
Thy honey turns to gall, thy joy to grief.

"Thy secret pleasure turns to open shame;
Thy private feasting to a public fast,
Thy smoothing° titles to a ragged name, *flattering*
Thy sugared tongue to bitter wormwood taste;
Thy violent vanities can never last.
How comes it then, vile Opportunity,
Being so bad, such numbers seek for thee?

"When wilt thou be the humble suppliant's friend,
And bring him where his suit may be obtained?
When wilt thou sort° an hour great strifes to end, *select*
Or free that soul which wretchedness hath chained?
Give physic° to the sick, ease to the pained? *medicine*
The poor, lame, blind, halt,° creep, cry out for thee, *limp*
But they ne'er meet with Opportunity.

"The patient dies while the physician sleeps;
The orphan pines while the oppressor feeds;
Justice is feasting while the widow weeps;
Advice° is sporting while infection breeds. *(medical advice)*
Thou grant'st no time for charitable deeds:
Wrath, envy, treason, rape, and murder's rages,
Thy heinous hours wait on them as their pages.

"When Truth and Virtue have to do with thee,
A thousand crosses° keep them from thy aid. *impediments*
They buy° thy help, but Sin ne'er gives a fee; *(must pay for)*
He gratis comes, and thou art well apaid° *satisfied*
As well to hear as grant what he hath said.

9. *ill-annexèd Opportunity:* bad circumstances joined to or following from the good.

1. The priestess of Vesta, Roman goddess of the hearth and household; vestals were sworn to lifelong virginity.

My Collatine would else have come to me
When Tarquin did, but he was stayed by thee.

"Guilty thou art of murder and of theft,
Guilty of perjury and subornation,[2]
Guilty of treason, forgery, and shift,° *fraud*
Guilty of incest, that abomination:
An accessory by thine inclination° *nature*
To all sins past and all that are to come,
From the creation to the general doom.° *Judgment Day*

"Misshapen Time, copesmate° of ugly Night, *comrade*
Swift subtle post,° carrier of grisly care, *messenger*
Eater of youth, false slave to false delight,
Base watch° of woes, sin's packhorse, virtue's snare, *town crier; announcer*
Thou nursest all, and murd'rest all that are.
Oh, hear me then, injurious shifting° Time: *changing; traitorous*
Be guilty of my death, since° of my crime. *as you are*

"Why hath thy servant Opportunity
Betrayed the hours thou gav'st me to repose,
Canceled my fortunes, and enchainèd me
To endless date° of never-ending woes? *duration*
Time's office is to fine° the hate of foes, *end; punish*
To eat up errors by opinion° bred, *rumor*
Not spend the dowry of a lawful bed.

"Time's glory is to calm contending kings,
To unmask falsehood and bring truth to light,
To stamp the seal of time in agèd things,
To wake the morn and sentinel° the night, *guard*
To wrong the wronger till he render right,
To ruinate proud buildings with thy hours,
And smear with dust their glitt'ring golden towers;

"To fill with wormholes stately monuments,
To feed oblivion with decay of things,
To blot old books and alter their contents,
To pluck the quills from ancient ravens' wings,
To dry the old oak's sap and cherish springs,[3]
To spoil antiquities of hammered steel,
And turn the giddy round of Fortune's wheel;

"To show the beldam° daughters of her daughter, *old woman*
To make the child a man, the man a child,
To slay the tiger that doth live by slaughter,
To tame the unicorn and lion wild,
To mock the subtle in themselves beguiled,[4]
To cheer the plowman with increaseful crops,
And waste huge stones with little water drops.

2. Bribing others to give false testimony.
3. Textual Comment The phrase "cherish springs," meaning "nourish the shoots of trees," has sometimes been emended, but the contrast with "dry the old oak's sap" is consistent with the double focus, in the following lines, on Time as both a destroyer and a nurturer. For a fuller discussion, see Digital Edition TC 8.
4. *the subtle . . . beguiled:* the cunning, taken in by their own schemes.

"Why work'st thou mischief in thy pilgrimage,
Unless thou couldst return to make amends?
One poor retiring[5] minute in an age
Would purchase thee a thousand thousand friends,
Lending him wit that to bad debtors lends.
  Oh, this dread night, wouldst thou one hour come back,
  I could prevent this storm, and shun thy wrack!

"Thou ceaseless lackey° to eternity, *eternal servant*
With some mischance cross Tarquin in his flight.
Devise extremes beyond extremity
To make him curse this cursèd crimeful night.
Let ghastly shadows his lewd eyes affright,
  And the dire thought of his committed evil
  Shape every bush a hideous shapeless devil.

"Disturb his hours of rest with restless trances;° *dreams; seizures*
Afflict him in his bed with bedrid° groans; *bedridden*
Let there bechance him pitiful mischances
To make him moan, but pity not his moans.
Stone him with hardened hearts harder than stones,
  And let mild women to him lose their mildness,
  Wilder to him than tigers in their wildness.

"Let him have time to tear his curlèd hair,
Let him have time against himself to rave,
Let him have time of Time's help to despair,
Let him have time to live a loathèd slave,
Let him have time a beggar's orts° to crave, *scraps*
  And time to see one that by alms doth live
  Disdain to him disdainèd scraps to give.

"Let him have time to see his friends his foes,
And merry fools to mock at him resort;° *gather*
Let him have time to mark how slow time goes
In time of sorrow, and how swift and short
His time of folly and his time of sport;
  And ever let his unrecalling crime[6]
  Have time to wail th'abusing of his time.

"O Time, thou tutor both to good and bad,
Teach me to curse him that thou taught'st this ill;
At his own shadow let the thief run mad,
Himself himself seek every hour to kill;
Such wretched hands such wretched blood should spill.
  For who so base would such an office have
  As sland'rous deathsman° to so base a slave? *detested executioner*

"The baser is he, coming from a king,
To shame his hope with deeds degenerate.
The mightier man, the mightier is the thing
That makes him honored or begets him hate,

5. Returning (thus permitting people to do things differently).

6. Crime that cannot be undone.

For greatest scandal waits on greatest state.[7]
The moon being clouded presently° is missed, *immediately*
But little stars may hide them when they list.° *wish*

"The crow may bathe his coal-black wings in mire,
And unperceived fly with the filth away;
But if the like the snow-white swan desire,
The stain upon his silver down will stay.
Poor grooms° are sightless° night, kings glorious day; *servants / dark*
Gnats are unnoted wheresoe'er they fly,
But eagles gazed upon with every eye.

"Out, idle words, servants to shallow fools,
Unprofitable sounds, weak arbitrators!
Busy your selves in skill-contending schools;° *(of rhetoric)*
Debate where leisure serves with dull debaters;
To trembling clients be you mediators.
For me, I force° not argument a straw, *value*
Since that my case is past the help of law.

"In vain I rail at Opportunity,
At Time, at Tarquin, and uncheerful Night;
In vain I cavil with° mine infamy; *object to*
In vain I spurn at my confirmed despite.° *irreparable injury*
This helpless° smoke of words doth me no right. *unhelpful; weak*
The remedy indeed to do me good
Is to let forth my foul defilèd blood.

"Poor hand, why quiver'st thou at this decree?
Honor thyself to rid me of this shame.
For if I die, my honor lives in thee;
But if I live, thou liv'st in my defame.° *infamy*
Since thou couldst not defend thy loyal dame,
And wast afeard to scratch her wicked foe,
Kill both thyself and her for yielding so."

This said, from her betumbled couch she starteth,
To find some desp'rate instrument of death.
But this, no slaughterhouse, no tool imparteth° *furnishes*
To make more vent° for passage of her breath, *a bigger hole*
Which thronging through her lips so vanisheth
As smoke from Etna° that in air consumes, *(a volcanic mountain)*
Or that which from dischargèd cannon fumes.

"In vain," quoth she, "I live, and seek in vain
Some happy mean to end a hapless life.
I feared by Tarquin's falchion to be slain,
Yet for the selfsame purpose seek a knife.
But when I feared, I was a loyal wife;
So am I now—oh, no, that cannot be:
Of that true type° hath Tarquin rifled me. *pattern of virtue*

7. *waits on greatest state:* attends those of highest rank.

"Oh, that is gone for which I sought to live,
And therefore now I need not fear to die.
To clear this spot by death, at least I give
A badge of fame to slander's livery,° *servant's uniform*
A dying life to living infamy.
  Poor helpless help, the treasure stol'n away,
  To burn the guiltless casket where it lay.

"Well, well, dear Collatine, thou shalt not know
The stainèd taste of violated troth.
I will not wrong thy true affection so,
To flatter thee with an infringèd oath.
This bastard graft[8] shall never come to growth:
  He shall not boast who did thy stock pollute
  That thou art doting father of his fruit.

"Nor shall he smile at thee in secret thought,
Nor laugh with his companions at thy state.
But thou shalt know thy int'rest° was not bought *property*
Basely with gold, but stol'n from forth thy gate.
For me, I am the mistress of my fate,
  And with my trespass never will dispense° *dispense with = excuse*
  Till life to death acquit° my forced offense. *atone for*

"I will not poison thee with my attaint,° *contamination*
Nor fold° my fault in cleanly coined excuses. *envelop*
My sable ground[9] of sin I will not paint
To hide the truth of this false night's abuses.
My tongue shall utter all; mine eyes, like sluices,
  As from a mountain spring that feeds a dale,
  Shall gush pure streams to purge my impure tale."

By this, lamenting Philomel[1] had ended
The well-tuned warble of her nightly sorrow,
And solemn night with slow sad gait descended
To ugly hell, when lo, the blushing morrow
Lends light to all fair eyes that light will borrow.
  But cloudy° Lucrece shames° herself to see, *melancholy / is ashamed*
  And therefore still in night would cloistered be.

Revealing day through every cranny spies,
And seems to point her out where she sits weeping,
To whom she sobbing speaks, "O eye of eyes,
Why pry'st thou through my window? Leave thy peeping;
Mock with thy tickling beams eyes that are sleeping;
  Brand not my forehead with thy piercing light,
  For day hath naught to do° what's done by night." *nothing to do with*

Thus cavils she with everything she sees:
True grief is fond° and testy as a child *foolish*

8. Lucrece assumes that Tarquin has made her pregnant. Her image is from the grafting of plants, in which two different kinds of plants are artificially forced to grow as one; a "bastard slip" is an unwanted shoot.

9. Black background (a heraldic term).

1. The nightingale. In classical mythology, Philomel was raped by King Tereus, her sister's husband, and with her sister took vengeance on him. All three were changed into birds (see Ovid, *Metamorphoses* 6).

Who, wayward once,° his mood with naught agrees. *once out of sorts*
Old woes, not infant sorrows, bear them mild:° *bear themselves mildly*
Continuance tames the one; the other wild,
Like an unpracticed swimmer plunging still° *constantly*
With too much labor drowns for want of skill.

So she, deep drenchèd in a sea of care,
Holds disputation with each thing she views,
And to herself all sorrow doth compare.
No object but her passion's strength renews,
And as one shifts,° another straight° ensues. *moves / immediately*
Sometime her grief is dumb° and hath no words; *mute*
Sometime 'tis mad and too much talk affords.

The little birds that tune their morning's joy
Make her moans mad with their sweet melody,
For mirth doth search° the bottom of annoy;° *probe / vexation*
Sad souls are slain° in merry company; *overcome with distress*
Grief best is pleased with grief's society:
True sorrow then is feelingly sufficed° *properly contented*
When with like semblance it is sympathized.° *matched*

'Tis double death to drown in ken° of shore; *sight*
He ten times pines° that pines beholding food; *starves*
To see the salve doth make the wound ache more;
Great grief grieves most at that would do it good;
Deep woes roll forward like a gentle flood
Who, being stopped, the bounding° banks o'erflows: *confining*
Grief dallied° with nor° law nor limit knows. *trifled / neither*

"You mocking birds," quoth she, "your tunes entomb
Within your hollow-swelling feathered breasts,
And in my hearing be you mute and dumb:
My restless discord loves no stops nor rests;
A woeful hostess brooks° not merry guests. *tolerates*
Relish° your nimble notes to pleasing ears; *Warble; make pleasing*
Distress likes dumps° when time is kept with tears. *sad songs*

"Come, Philomel, that sing'st of ravishment:
Make thy sad grove in my disheveled hair.
As the dank earth weeps at thy languishment,° *lamentation*
So I at each sad strain will strain a tear,
And with deep groans the diapason° bear: *harmony*
For burden-wise,[2] I'll hum on Tarquin still,
While thou on Tereus descants better skill.[3]

"And whiles against a thorn[4] thou bear'st thy part,
To keep thy sharp woes waking, wretched I,
To imitate thee well, against my heart
Will fix a sharp knife to affright mine eye,
Who° if it wink° shall thereon fall and die. *(I) / (my eye) close*

2. Like a bass line; playing on "burden" as sorrow, weight.
3. Sing the treble part more skillfully.
4. The nightingale was imagined to press against a thorn to keep itself awake during the night.

These means, as frets° upon an instrument, *(punning on "vexation")*
Shall tune our heartstrings to true languishment.

"And for,° poor bird, thou sing'st not in the day, **because**
As shaming any eye should thee behold,
Some dark deep desert seated from the way,[5]
That knows not parching heat nor freezing cold,
Will we find out, and there we will unfold
To creatures stern sad tunes to change their kinds:° **natures**
Since men prove beasts, let beasts bear gentle minds."

As the poor frighted deer that stands at gaze,
Wildly determining which way to fly,
Or one encompassed with a winding maze
That cannot tread the way out readily,
So with herself is she in mutiny,
To live or die which of the twain were better
When life is shamed and death reproach's debtor.° **will incur reproach**

"To kill myself," quoth she, "alack, what were it,
But with my body my poor soul's pollution?[6]
They that lose half with greater patience bear it
Than they whose whole is swallowed in confusion.° **ruin**
That mother tries a merciless conclusion° **experiment**
Who, having two sweet babes, when death takes one
Will slay the other, and be nurse to none.

"My body or my soul, which was the dearer
When the one pure, the other made divine?
Whose love of either to myself was nearer
When both were kept for heaven and Collatine?
Ay me, the bark pilled° from the lofty pine, **peeled**
His leaves will wither and his sap decay:
So must my soul, her bark being pilled away.

"Her house is sacked, her quiet interrupted,
Her mansion battered by the enemy,
Her sacred temple spotted, spoiled, corrupted,
Grossly engirt with daring° infamy. **unrestrained**
Then let it not be called impiety,
If in this blemished fort° I make some hole, *(my body)*
Through which I may convey° this troubled soul. **steal away**

"Yet die I will not till my Collatine
Have heard the cause of my untimely death,
That he may vow in that sad hour of mine
Revenge on him that made me stop my breath.
My stained blood to Tarquin I'll bequeath,
Which by him tainted shall for him be spent,
And as his due writ° in my testament.° **written / last will**

5. *Some . . . way:* Some uninhabited place located far from the road.

6. *with . . . pollution:* to pollute my poor soul, as my body has already been polluted.

"My honor I'll bequeath unto the knife
That wounds my body so dishonorèd.
'Tis honor to deprive° dishonored life; *take away*
The one° will live, the other° being dead. *(honor) / (life)*
So of shame's ashes shall my fame be bred,[7]
For in my death I murder shameful scorn;
My shame so dead, mine honor is new born.

"Dear lord of that dear jewel° I have lost, *(chastity)*
What legacy shall I bequeath to thee?
My resolution, love, shall be thy boast,
By whose example thou revenged mayst be.
How Tarquin must be used, read it in me:
Myself, thy friend, will kill myself, thy foe,
And for my sake serve° thou false Tarquin so. *treat*

"This brief abridgement of my will I make:
My soul and body to the skies and ground.
My resolution, husband, do thou take;
Mine honor be the knife's that makes my wound;
My shame be his that did my fame confound,
And all my fame that lives disbursèd be° *that remains be paid out*
To those that live and think no shame of me.

"Thou, Collatine, shalt oversee° this will. *execute*
How was I overseen° that thou shalt see it? *deluded*
My blood shall wash the slander of mine ill;
My life's foul deed my life's fair end shall free it.
Faint not, faint heart, but stoutly say, 'So be it.'
Yield to my hand; my hand shall conquer thee:
Thou dead, both die, and both shall victors be."

This plot of death when sadly she had laid
And wiped the brinish° pearl from her bright eyes, *salty*
With untuned° tongue she hoarsely calls her maid, *inharmonious*
Whose swift obedience to her mistress hies,° *hastens*
For fleet-winged duty with thought's feathers flies.
Poor Lucrece' cheeks unto her maid seem so
As winter meads° when sun doth melt their snow. *meadows*

Her mistress she doth give demure good-morrow,
With soft slow tongue, true mark of modesty,
And sorts° a sad look to her lady's sorrow, *suits*
For why° her face wore sorrow's livery,° *Because / attire*
But durst not ask of her audaciously
Why her two suns° were cloud-eclipsèd so, *(her eyes)*
Nor why her fair cheeks over-washed with woe.

But as the earth doth weep, the sun being set,
Each flower moistened like a melting eye:
Even so the maid with swelling drops gan° wet *began to*

7. *So . . . bred:* My honor will be like the mythological phoenix, consumed in fire only to be reborn from the ashes.

Her circled° eyne, enforced° by sympathy *roun*
Of those fair suns set in her mistress' sky,
Who in a salt-waved ocean quench their light,
Which makes the maid weep like the dewy night.

A pretty while° these pretty creatures stand, *fair amount of time*
Like ivory conduits coral cisterns filling:
One justly weeps, the other takes in hand° *acknowledges*
No cause but company of her drops spilling.
Their gentle sex to weep are often willing,
Grieving themselves to guess at° others' smarts,° *conjecture / pains*
And then they drown their eyes or break their hearts.

For men have marble, women waxen minds,
And therefore are they formed as marble will.
The weak oppressed, th'impression of strange kinds° *alien natures*
Is formed in them by force, by fraud, or skill.
Then call them not the authors of their ill,
No more than wax shall be accounted evil
Wherein is stamped the semblance of a devil.

Their smoothness, like a goodly champaign plain,° *open field*
Lays open° all the little worms that creep; *Reveals*
In men, as in a rough-grown grove, remain
Cave-keeping° evils that obscurely° sleep. *Concealed / unseen*
Through crystal walls each little mote° will peep. *speck*
Though men can cover crimes with bold stern looks,
Poor women's faces are their own faults' books.

No man° inveigh against the withered flower, *Let no man*
But chide rough winter that the flower hath killed;
Not that devoured, but that which doth devour,
Is worthy blame. Oh, let it not be held
Poor women's faults that they are so fulfilled
With men's abuses: those proud lords, to blame,
Make weak-made women tenants to their shame.

The precedent° whereof in Lucrece view, *proof*
Assailed by night with circumstances strong
Of present° death, and shame that might ensue *immediate*
By that her death, to do her husband wrong.
Such danger to resistance did belong
That dying fear through all her body spread;
And who cannot abuse a body dead?

By this,° mild patience bid fair Lucrece speak *this time*
To the poor counterfeit of her complaining.° *(the weeping maid)*
"My girl," quoth she, "on what occasion break
Those tears from thee that down thy cheeks are raining?
If thou dost weep for grief of my sustaining,° *borne by me*
Know, gentle wench, it small avails° my mood: *little helps*
If tears could help, mine own would do me good.

"But tell me, girl, when went"—and there she stayed
Till after a deep groan—"Tarquin from hence?"

"Madam, ere I was up," replied the maid,
"The more to blame my sluggard negligence.
Yet with the fault I thus far can dispense:° *excuse*
Myself was stirring ere the break of day,
And ere I rose was Tarquin gone away.

"But, lady, if your maid may be so bold,
She would request to know your heaviness."° *sorrow*
"Oh, peace," quoth Lucrece, "if it should be told,
The repetition cannot make it less,
For more it is than I can well express,
And that deep torture may be called a hell
When more is felt than one hath power to tell.

"Go get me hither paper, ink, and pen;
Yet save that labor, for I have them here.
What should I say? One of my husband's men
Bid thou be ready by and by to bear
A letter to my lord, my love, my dear.
Bid him with speed prepare to carry it;
The cause craves° haste, and it will soon be writ." *requires*

Her maid is gone, and she prepares to write,
First hovering o'er the paper with her quill.
Conceit° and grief an eager combat fight: *Imagination*
What wit° sets down is blotted straight with will.° *thought / passion*
This is too curious-good,° this blunt and ill: *elaborate*
Much like a press° of people at a door *crowd*
Throng her inventions, which shall go before.° *first*

At last she thus begins: "Thou worthy lord
Of that unworthy wife that greeteth thee,
Health to thy person! Next, vouchsafe t'afford
(If ever, love, thy Lucrece thou wilt see)
Some present° speed to come and visit me. *immediate*
So I commend me,° from our house in grief; *ask to be remembered*
My woes are tedious, though my words are brief."

Here folds she up the tenor° of her woe, *gist*
Her certain sorrow writ uncertainly.
By this short schedule° Collatine may know *summary*
Her grief, but not her grief's true quality.
She dares not thereof make discovery,° *revelation*
Lest he should hold it her own gross abuse,° *trespass*
Ere she with blood had stained her stained excuse.

Besides, the life and feeling of her passion
She hoards, to spend when he is by to hear her,
When sighs and groans and tears may grace the fashion° *appearance; fashioning*
Of her disgrace, the better so to clear her
From that suspicion which the world might bear her.
To shun this blot, she would not blot the letter
With words, till action might become° them better. *suit*

To see sad sights moves more than hear them told,
For then the eye interprets to the ear

The heavy motion° that it doth behold, *sad action*
When every part a part of woe doth bear.
'Tis but a part of sorrow that we hear:
    Deep sounds make lesser noise than shallow fords,
    And sorrow ebbs, being blown with wind of words.

Her letter now is sealed, and on it writ
"At Ardea to my lord with more than haste."
The post attends,° and she delivers it, *messenger waits*
Charging the sour-faced groom to hie as fast
As lagging fowls before the northern blast.
    Speed more than speed° but dull and slow she deems: *Even unusual speed*
    Extremity still urgeth such extremes.

The homely villain° curtsies to her low, *unpolished menial*
And blushing on her with a steadfast eye
Receives the scroll without or° yea or no, *either*
And forth with bashful innocence doth hie.
But they whose guilt within their bosoms lie
    Imagine every eye beholds their blame:
    For Lucrece thought he blushed to see her shame,

When, silly groom,° God wot,° it was defect *simple servant / knows*
Of spirit, life, and bold audacity.
Such harmless creatures have a true respect
To talk in deeds,[8] while others saucily
Promise more speed, but do it leisurely.
    Even so, this pattern of the worn-out age° *old-fashioned model*
    Pawned° honest looks, but laid no words to gage.° *Offered / as a pledge*

His kindled duty[9] kindled her mistrust,
That two red fires in both their faces blazed.
She thought he blushed as knowing Tarquin's lust,
And blushing with him, wistly° on him gazed. *attentively*
Her earnest eye did make him more amazed:° *bewildered*
    The more she saw the blood his cheeks replenish,
    The more she thought he spied in her some blemish.

But long she thinks° till he return again, *she thinks it long*
And yet the duteous vassal scarce is gone.
The weary time she cannot entertain,° *while away*
For now 'tis stale to sigh, to weep, and groan.
So woe hath wearied woe, moan tired moan,
    That she her plaints a little while doth stay,
    Pausing for means to mourn some newer way.

At last she calls to mind where hangs a piece
Of skillful painting made for° Priam's Troy, *representing*
Before the which is drawn the power° of Greece, *army*
For Helen's rape the city to destroy,
Threat'ning cloud-kissing Ilion° with annoy,° *high-built Troy / injury*

8. *have . . . deeds:* rightly express their deference by their actions (rather than merely by their words).

9. His blushing bow; his ardent loyalty.

Which the conceited° painter drew so proud — *ingenious*
As heaven (it seemed) to kiss the turrets bowed.

A thousand lamentable objects there,
In scorn of° nature, art gave lifeless life; — *Defying*
Many a dry drop seemed a weeping tear,
Shed for the slaughtered husband by the wife.
The red blood reeked° to show the painter's strife,[1] — *smoked*
And dying eyes gleamed forth their ashy lights,
Like dying coals burnt out in tedious nights.

There might you see the laboring pioneer° — *trench digger*
Begrimed with sweat and smearèd all with dust;
And from the tow'rs of Troy there would appear
The very eyes of men through loopholes thrust,
Gazing upon the Greeks with little lust.° — *pleasure*
Such sweet observance° in this work was had — *verisimilitude*
That one might see those far-off eyes look sad.

In great commanders grace and majesty
You might behold, triumphing in their faces;
In youth, quick°-bearing and dexterity; — *lively*
And here and there the painter interlaces
Pale cowards marching on with trembling paces,
Which heartless° peasants did so well resemble — *dejected*
That one would swear he saw them quake and tremble.

In Ajax and Ulysses, oh, what art
Of physiognomy might one behold!
The face of either ciphered° either's heart; — *represented*
Their face their manners most expressly told.
In Ajax' eyes blunt° rage and rigor rolled, — *rude*
But the mild glance that sly Ulysses lent
Showed deep regard° and smiling government.° — *judgment / self-control*

There pleading° might you see grave Nestor stand, — *persuading*
As 'twere encouraging the Greeks to fight,
Making such sober action with his hand
That it beguiled attention, charmed the sight.
In speech it seemed his beard, all silver-white,
Wagged up and down, and from his lips did fly
Thin winding breath, which purled° up to the sky. — *curled*

About him were a press of gaping faces,
Which seemed to swallow up his sound advice,
All jointly list'ning, but with several graces,° — *various attitudes*
As if some mermaid did their ears entice:
Some high, some low, the painter was so nice.° — *skillful; subtle*
The scalps of many, almost hid behind,
To jump up higher seemed to mock the mind.° — *(by artistic illusion)*

Here one man's hand leaned on another's head,
His nose being shadowed by his neighbor's ear;

1. Conflict between Trojans and Greeks; conflict between nature and art.

Here one being thronged bears° back, all boll'n° and red; *crowded pushes / swollen*
Another, smothered, seems to pelt° and swear; *scold*
And in their rage such signs of rage they bear
As, but for loss of° Nestor's golden words, *That except they might miss*
It seemed they would debate with angry swords.

For much imaginary° work was there: *creative*
Conceit deceitful, so compact,° so kind,° *efficient / natural*
That for Achilles' image stood his spear,
Gripped in an armèd hand; himself behind
Was left unseen, save to the eye of mind:
A hand, a foot, a face, a leg, a head
Stood for the whole to be imaginèd.

And from the walls of strong-besiegèd Troy,
When their brave hope, bold Hector, marched to field,
Stood many Trojan mothers, sharing joy
To see their youthful sons bright weapons wield;
And to their hope they such odd action° yield *contrary gestures*
That through their light joy seemèd to appear,
Like bright things stained, a kind of heavy fear.

And from the strand° of Dardan where they fought, *shore*
To Simois'° reedy banks the red blood ran, *Trojan river*
Whose waves to imitate the battle sought
With swelling ridges; and their ranks began
To break upon the gallèd° shore, and then *eroded; injured*
Retire again, till meeting greater ranks
They join, and shoot their foam at Simois' banks.

To this well-painted piece is Lucrece come,
To find a face where all distress is stelled.° *engraved*
Many she sees where cares have carvèd some,
But none where all distress and dolor dwelled,
Till she despairing Hecuba° beheld, *Queen of Troy*
Staring on Priam's° wounds with her old eyes, *King of Troy*
Which bleeding under Pyrrhus' proud foot lies.

In her the painter had anatomized° *laid open*
Time's ruin, beauty's wrack, and grim care's reign.
Her cheeks with chops° and wrinkles were disguised:° *cracks / disfigured*
Of what she was no semblance did remain.
Her blue blood changed to black in every vein,
Wanting° the spring that those shrunk pipes had fed, *Lacking*
Showed life imprisoned in a body dead.

On this sad shadow Lucrece spends her eyes,
And shapes her sorrow to the beldam's° woes, *old woman's*
Who nothing wants to answer her[2] but cries
And bitter words to ban° her cruel foes. *curse*
The painter was no god to lend her those,
And therefore Lucrece swears he did her wrong
To give her so much grief, and not a tongue.

2. *Who . . . her:* Who lacks nothing to resemble her.

"Poor instrument," quoth she, "without a sound,
I'll tune° thy woes with my lamenting tongue, *sing*
And drop sweet balm in Priam's painted wound,
And rail on Pyrrhus that hath done him wrong,
And with my tears quench Troy that burns so long,
And with my knife scratch out the angry eyes
Of all the Greeks that are thine enemies.

"Show me the strumpet° that began this stir,° *(Helen) / dispute*
That with my nails her beauty I may tear.
Thy heat of lust, fond Paris, did incur
This load of wrath that burning Troy doth bear:
Thy eye kindled the fire that burneth here,
And here in Troy, for trespass of thine eye,
The sire, the son, the dame, and daughter die.

"Why should the private pleasure of someone
Become the public plague of many moe?° *more*
Let sin, alone° committed, light alone *by one person*
Upon his head that hath transgressèd so;
Let guiltless souls be freed from guilty woe.
For one's offense why should so many fall,
To plague a private sin in general?° *collectively*

"Lo, here weeps Hecuba, here Priam dies,
Here manly Hector faints, here Troilus sounds,° *swoons*
Here friend by friend in bloody channel° lies, *gutter*
And friend to friend gives unadvisèd° wounds, *unintended*
And one man's lust these many lives confounds.
Had doting Priam checked his son's desire,
Troy had been bright with fame, and not with fire."

Here feelingly she weeps Troy's painted woes;
For sorrow, like a heavy hanging bell,
Once set on ringing, with his° own weight goes; *its*
Then little strength rings out the doleful knell.
So Lucrece set a-work, sad tales doth tell
To penciled pensiveness and colored sorrow;
She lends them words, and she their looks doth borrow.

She throws her eyes about the painting round,
And who she finds forlorn she doth lament.
At last she sees a wretched image bound,
That piteous looks to Phrygian shepherds lent.[3]
His face, though full of cares, yet showed content.
Onward to Troy with the blunt swains° he goes, *rough rustics*
So mild that patience° seemed to scorn his woes. *his patience*

In him the painter labored with his skill
To hide deceit and give the harmless show° *appearance*
An humble gait, calm looks, eyes wailing still,° *weeping continually*
A brow unbent that seemed to welcome woe,
Cheeks neither red nor pale, but mingled so

3. *That . . . lent:* That made Phrygian shepherds look on in pity (Phrygia was the area around Troy).

That blushing red no guilty instance° gave, *sign*
Nor ashy pale the fear that false hearts have.

But like a constant and confirmèd devil
He entertained° a show so seeming just, *maintained*
And therein so ensconced° his secret evil *concealed*
That jealousy° itself could not mistrust° *suspicion / suspect*
False creeping craft and perjury should thrust
Into so bright a day such black-faced storms,
Or blot with hell-born sin such saintlike forms.

The well-skilled workman this mild image drew
For perjured Sinon,[4] whose enchanting° story *deluding*
The credulous old Priam after slew;
Whose words like wildfire[5] burnt the shining glory
Of rich-built Ilion, that the skies were sorry,
And little stars shot from their fixed places
When their glass° fell, wherein they viewed their faces. *mirror (Troy)*

This picture she advisedly° perused, *carefully*
And chid° the painter for his wondrous skill, *scolded*
Saying, some shape° in Sinon's was abused: *(other person's shape)*
So fair a form lodged not a mind so ill.
And still on him she gazed, and gazing still,
Such signs of truth in his plain° face she spied *open*
That she concludes the picture was belied.° *shown to be false*

"It cannot be," quoth she, "that so much guile"—
She would have said "can lurk in such a look."
But Tarquin's shape came in her mind the while,
And from her tongue "can lurk" from "cannot" took.
"It cannot be" she in that sense forsook,
And turned it thus: "It cannot be, I find,
But such a face should bear a wicked mind.

"For even as subtle Sinon here is painted,
So sober sad, so weary, and so mild,
As if with grief or travail° he had fainted, *effort*
To me came Tarquin armèd to beguild[6]
With outward honesty, but yet defiled
With inward vice. As Priam him did cherish,
So did I Tarquin, so my Troy did perish.

"Look, look, how list'ning Priam wets his eyes
To see those borrowed° tears that Sinon sheds. *inauthentic*
Priam, why art thou old and yet not wise?
For every tear he falls° a Trojan bleeds: *(Sinon) lets fall*
His eye drops fire, no water thence proceeds.

4. Sinon was a Greek who pretended to have fled from his own people; once "rescued" and brought to Troy, he persuaded the Trojans to receive the wooden horse into their city.

5. A mixture of sulfur, tar, and other combustible substances, used to set fires during battle.

6. TEXTUAL COMMENT "Beguild" means "trick," but also "cover with gold" (that is, Tarquin's magnificence is all on the surface). The difficulty of the line led some eighteenth- and nineteenth-century editors to emend it, but most modern editors retain the original wording. For a fuller discussion, see Digital Edition TC 9.

Those round clear pearls of his that move thy pity
Are balls of quenchless fire to burn thy city.

"Such devils steal effects° from lightless hell, *illusions*
For Sinon in his fire doth quake with cold,
And in that cold hot-burning fire doth dwell.
These contraries such unity do hold
Only to flatter° fools and make them bold; *encourage*
So Priam's trust false Sinon's tears doth flatter
That he finds means to burn his Troy with water."

Here, all enraged, such passion her assails
That patience is quite beaten from her breast.
She tears the senseless° Sinon with her nails, *unfeeling*
Comparing him to that unhappy° guest *misfortune-bringing*
Whose deed hath made herself herself detest.
At last she smilingly with this gives o'er:
"Fool, fool," quoth she, "his wounds will not be sore."

Thus ebbs and flows the current of her sorrow,
And time doth weary time with her complaining.
She looks for night, and then she longs for morrow,
And both she thinks too long with her remaining.
Short time seems long in sorrow's sharp sustaining:° *painful enduring*
Though woe be heavy, yet it seldom sleeps,
And they that watch° see time how slow it creeps. *remain awake*

Which all this time hath overslipped her thought
That she with painted images hath spent,
Being from the feeling of her own grief brought
By deep surmise° of others' detriment,° *contemplation / suffering*
Losing her woes in shows of discontent.° *pictures of sorrow*
It easeth some, though none it ever cured,
To think their dolor others have endured.

But now the mindful° messenger come back *dutiful*
Brings home his lord and other company,
Who finds his Lucrece clad in mourning black,
And round about her tear-distainèd° eye *tear-stained*
Blue circles streamed, like rainbows in the sky:
These water-galls° in her dim element° *rainbow fragments / sky*
Foretell new storms to° those already spent. *in addition to*

Which when her sad-beholding husband saw,
Amazedly in her sad face he stares:
Her eyes, though sod° in tears, looked red and raw, *sodden*
Her lively color killed with deadly cares.
He hath no power to ask her how she fares.
Both stood like old acquaintance in a trance,
Met far from home, wond'ring each other's chance.° *fortune*

At last he takes her by the bloodless hand,
And thus begins: "What uncouth° ill event *strange*
Hath thee befall'n, that thou dost trembling stand?
Sweet love, what spite° hath thy fair color spent? *harm*

Why art thou thus attired in discontent?[7]
Unmask,° dear dear, this moody heaviness, *Disclose*
And tell thy grief, that we may give redress."

Three times with sighs she gives her sorrow fire,[8]
Ere once she can discharge one word of woe.
At length addressed° to answer his desire, *ready*
She modestly prepares to let them know
Her honor is ta'en prisoner by the foe,
While Collatine and his consorted° lords *accompanying*
With sad attention long to hear her words.

And now this pale swan in her wat'ry nest
Begins the sad dirge of her certain ending:[9]
"Few words," quoth she, "shall fit the trespass best,
Where no excuse can give the fault amending.
In me more woes than words are now depending,° *weighing; belonging*
And my laments would be drawn out too long
To tell them all with one poor tired tongue.

"Then be this all the task it hath to say:
Dear husband, in the interest° of thy bed *claiming possession*
A stranger came, and on that pillow lay
Where thou wast wont to rest thy weary head;
And what wrong else may be imaginèd
By foul enforcement might be done to me,
From that, alas, thy Lucrece is not free.

"For in the dreadful dead of dark midnight,
With shining falchion in my chamber came
A creeping creature with a flaming light,
And softly cried, 'Awake, thou Roman dame,
And entertain° my love, else lasting shame *receive*
On thee and thine this night I will inflict,
If thou my love's desire do contradict.

"'For some hard-favored° groom of thine,' quoth he, *ugly*
'Unless thou yoke thy liking to my will,
I'll murder straight,° and then I'll slaughter thee, *immediately*
And swear I found you where you did fulfill
The loathsome act of lust, and so did kill
The lechers in their deed: this act will be
My fame, and thy perpetual infamy.'

"With this I did begin to start and cry,
And then against my heart he set his sword,
Swearing, unless I took all patiently,
I should not live to speak another word.
So should my shame still rest upon record,
And never be forgot in mighty Rome
Th'adulterate° death of Lucrece and her groom. *adulterous*

7. In black; see line 1585.
8. As sixteenth-century gunners lighted firearms with matches.
9. Swans were supposed to sing only when they were on the point of death.

"Mine enemy was strong, my poor self weak,
And far the weaker with so strong a fear.
My bloody judge forbade my tongue to speak;
No rightful plea might plead for justice there.
His scarlet lust came° evidence to swear — *gave*
That my poor beauty had purloined his eyes,
And when the judge is robbed, the prisoner dies.

"Oh, teach me how to make mine own excuse,
Or at the least this refuge let me find:
Though my gross blood be stained with this abuse,
Immaculate and spotless is my mind.
That was not forced, that never was inclined
To accessory yieldings,[1] but still pure
Doth in her poisoned closet yet endure."

Lo, here the hopeless merchant° of this loss, — *owner (Collatine)*
With head declined° and voice dammed up with woe, — *bent*
With sad-set eyes and wreathèd arms across,[2]
From lips new waxen° pale begins to blow — *newly grown*
The grief away that stops his answer so.
But, wretched as he is, he strives in vain:
What he breathes out, his breath drinks up again.

As through an arch° the violent roaring tide — *(under a bridge)*
Outruns the eye that doth behold his° haste, — *its (the tide's)*
Yet in the eddy boundeth in his pride
Back to the strait that forced him on so fast,
In rage sent out, recalled in rage being past:
Even so his° sighs; his sorrows make a saw,[3] — *(Collatine's)*
To push grief on, and back the same grief draw.

Which speechless woe of his poor she attendeth,° — *poor Lucrece notes*
And his untimely frenzy° thus awaketh: — *delirium*
"Dear lord, thy sorrow to my sorrow lendeth
Another power;° no flood by raining slaketh. — *Greater strength*
My woe too sensible° thy passion maketh — *acutely felt*
More feeling painful. Let it then suffice
To drown one woe, one pair of weeping eyes.

"And for my sake, when I might charm thee so,[4]
For she that was thy Lucrece, now attend me:
Be suddenly revengèd on my foe—
Thine, mine, his own. Suppose thou dost defend me
From what is past; the help that thou shalt lend me
Comes all too late, yet let the traitor die:
For sparing° justice feeds° iniquity. — *lenient / encourages*

"But ere I name him, you fair lords," quoth she,
Speaking to those that came with Collatine,

1. To yielding that would make me an accessory to the crime.
2. See line 793 and note.
3. Go back and forth (inhaling and exhaling), like a saw cutting wood.
4. *when . . . so:* as I used to be when I charmed you (before the rape).

"Shall plight° your honorable faiths to me, *pledge*
With swift pursuit to venge this wrong of mine.
For 'tis a meritorious fair design° *intention*
To chase injustice with revengeful arms:
Knights, by their oaths, should right poor ladies' harms."

At this request, with noble disposition° *purpose*
Each present lord began to promise aid,
As bound in knighthood to her imposition,° *imposed task*
Longing to hear the hateful foe bewrayed.° *revealed*
But she that yet her sad task hath not said,° *completed*
The protestation stops. "Oh, speak," quoth she,
"How may this forcèd stain be wiped from me?

"What is the quality of my offense,
Being constrained with dreadful circumstance?
May my pure mind with the foul act dispense,
My low-declinèd honor to advance?° *raise*
May any terms acquit me from this chance?° *mishap*
The poisoned fountain clears itself again,
And why not I from this compellèd stain?"

With this they all at once began to say
Her body's stain her mind untainted clears,
While with a joyless smile she turns away
The face, that map which deep impression bears
Of hard misfortune, carved in it with tears.
"No, no," quoth she, "no dame hereafter living
By my excuse shall claim excuses giving."

Here with a sigh as if her heart would break,
She throws forth Tarquin's name. "He, he," she says,
But more than "he" her poor tongue could not speak,
Till after many accents° and delays, *sighs*
Untimely breathings, sick and short assays,° *attempts*
She utters this: "He, he, fair lords, 'tis he
That guides this hand to give this wound to me."

Even here she sheathèd in her harmless° breast *innocent*
A harmful knife, that thence her soul unsheathed.
That blow did bail° it from the deep unrest *liberate*
Of that polluted prison where it breathed.
Her contrite sighs unto the clouds bequeathed
Her wingèd sprite,° and through her wounds doth fly *spirit*
Life's lasting date[5] from canceled destiny.

Stone-still, astonished° with this deadly deed, *stunned*
Stood Collatine and all his lordly crew,
Till Lucrece' father that beholds her bleed
Himself on her self-slaughtered body threw;

5. *lasting date*: eternal duration. The line is difficult, and could mean that Lucrece's immortal soul separates from her earthly life and body (canceled destiny), or that Lucrece, by taking her fate into her own hands (canceling her destiny), makes her fame eternal.

And from the purple fountain Brutus[6] drew
The murd'rous knife, and as it left the place,
Her blood in poor revenge held it in chase;

And bubbling from her breast, it doth divide
In two slow rivers, that the crimson blood
Circles her body in on every side,
Who like a late-sacked° island vastly° stood *just-looted / devastated*
Bare and unpeopled in this fearful° flood. *fearsome*
Some of her blood still pure and red remained,
And some looked black, and that false Tarquin stained.

About the mourning and congealèd face
Of that black blood, a wat'ry rigol° goes, *circle*
Which seems to weep upon the tainted place;
And ever since, as pitying Lucrece' woes,
Corrupted blood some watery token shows,
And blood untainted still doth red abide,
Blushing at that which is so putrefied.

"Daughter, dear daughter," old Lucretius cries,
"That life was mine which thou hast here deprived.
If in the child the father's image lies,
Where shall I live now Lucrece is unlived?° *slain*
Thou wast not to this end from me derived.
If children predecease progenitors,
We are their offspring, and they none of ours.

"Poor broken glass,° I often did behold *mirror*
In thy sweet semblance my old age new born;
But now that fair fresh mirror, dim and old,
Shows me a bare-boned death° by time outworn. *skull*
Oh, from thy cheeks my image thou hast torn,
And shivered all the beauty of my glass,
That I no more can see what once I was.

"O Time, cease thou thy course and last no longer,
If they surcease° to be that should survive. *cease*
Shall rotten death make conquest of the stronger,
And leave the falt'ring feeble souls alive?
The old bees die, the young possess their hive.
Then live, sweet Lucrece, live again and see
Thy father die, and not thy father thee."

By this starts Collatine as from a dream,
And bids Lucretius give his sorrow place;° *precedence*
And then in key-cold° Lucrece' bleeding stream *cold as metal*
He falls, and bathes the pale fear in his face,
And counterfeits to die with her a space,
Till manly shame bids him possess his breath,
And live to be revengèd on her death.

6. Lucius Junius Brutus. Tarquin the Proud, the rapist's father, had killed Brutus's brother, but Brutus, whose name means "stupid," escaped royal suspicion by pretending to be mentally retarded. After Lucrece's rape, he led the coup that overthrew the Tarquins and established republican government in Rome.

The deep vexation of his inward soul
Hath served a dumb arrest° upon his tongue, *silent injunction*
Who, mad that sorrow should his use control,° *prevent*
Or keep him from heart-easing words so long,
Begins to talk; but through his lips do throng
    Weak words, so thick come in his poor heart's aid
    That no man could distinguish what he said.

Yet sometime "Tarquin" was pronouncèd plain,
But through his teeth, as if the name he tore.
This windy tempest, till it blow up rain,
Held back his sorrow's tide to make it more.
At last it rains, and busy winds give o'er.
    Then son° and father weep with equal strife *son-in-law*
    Who should weep most, for daughter or for wife.

The one doth call her his, the other his,
Yet neither may possess the claim they lay.
The father says, "She's mine"; "Oh, mine she is,"
Replies her husband: "do not take away
My sorrow's interest.° Let no mourner say *title of possession*
    He weeps for her, for she was only mine,
    And only must be wailed by Collatine."

"Oh," quoth Lucretius, "I did give that life
Which she too early and too late hath spilled."
"Woe, woe," quoth Collatine, "she was my wife.
I owed° her, and 'tis mine that she hath killed." *owned*
"My daughter" and "my wife" with clamors filled
    The dispersèd air, who, holding Lucrece' life,[7]
    Answered° their cries, "my daughter" and "my wife." *Echoed*

Brutus, who plucked the knife from Lucrece' side,
Seeing such emulation° in their woe, *competition*
Began to clothe his wit in state° and pride, *dignity*
Burying in Lucrece' wound his folly's show.° *pretended stupidity*
He with the Romans was esteemèd so
    As silly jeering idiots° are with kings, *court jesters*
    For sportive words and utt'ring foolish things.

But now he throws that shallow habit° by, *foolish appearance*
Wherein deep policy° did him disguise, *shrewdness*
And armed his long-hid wits advisedly,° *prudently*
To check the tears in Collatinus' eyes.
"Thou wrongèd lord of Rome," quoth he, "arise.
    Let my unsounded° self, supposed a fool, *of unknown depth*
    Now set thy long-experienced wit to school.

"Why, Collatine, is woe the cure for woe?
Do wounds help wounds, or grief help grievous deeds?
Is it revenge to give thyself a blow
For his foul act by whom thy fair wife bleeds?
Such childish humor° from weak minds proceeds. *silly behavior*

7. See lines 1727ff.

Thy wretched wife mistook the matter so
To slay herself, that should have slain her foe.

"Courageous Roman, do not steep thy heart
In such relenting dew of lamentations,
But kneel with me and help to bear thy part
To rouse our Roman gods with invocations,
That they will suffer° these abominations, *allow*
Since Rome herself in them doth stand disgraced,
By our strong arms from forth her fair streets chased.° *to be chased*

"Now by the Capitol[8] that we adore,
And by this chaste blood so unjustly stained,
By heaven's fair sun that breeds the fat° earth's store,° *fertile / plenty*
By all our country° rights in Rome maintained, *civic*
And by chaste Lucrece' soul that late complained
Her wrongs to us, and by this bloody knife,
We will revenge the death of this true wife."

This said, he struck his hand upon his breast,
And kissed the fatal knife to end his vow,
And to his protestation urged the rest,
Who, wond'ring at him, did his words allow.° *approve*
Then jointly to the ground their knees they bow,
And that deep vow which Brutus made before
He doth again repeat, and that they swore.

When they had sworn to this advisèd doom,° *considered judgment*
They did conclude to bear dead Lucrece thence,
To show her bleeding body thorough° Rome, *throughout*
And so to publish° Tarquin's foul offense, *publicize*
Which, being done with speedy diligence,
The Romans plausibly° did give consent *with applause*
To Tarquins' everlasting banishment.

8. The Capitol was the religious and political center of ancient Rome.

# The Passionate Pilgrim

*The Passionate Pilgrim*, a collection of love poetry, appeared under Shakespeare's name in 1599, apparently without his approval and to his dismay. Of its twenty poems, five are lifted from Shakespeare's other works—*Love's Labor's Lost* and the sonnets—and hence also appear elsewhere in this volume; four can clearly be assigned to other writers; and eleven remain unattributed. Numbers 4, 6, and 9—all sonnets—are noteworthy for their focus on the theme of *Venus and Adonis*, to which they may be a response. By 1599, Shakespeare's name had considerable cachet. *The Passionate Pilgrim* very possibly seeks to exploit that cachet, interweaving a few pieces by Shakespeare with other poems so as to produce a thematically resonant sequence that obscures the homoeroticism of some of the sonnets and in effect becomes a testament to poetic artifice. In the present volume, this collection is placed chronologically not by year of publication but according to the date by which Shakespeare is likely to have composed the five poems in it that are his. (See the Textual Introductions to *Love's Labor's Lost* and the sonnets.)

WALTER COHEN

## SELECTED BIBLIOGRAPHY

Bednarz, James P. "*The Passionate Pilgrim* and 'The Phoenix and Turtle.'" *The Cambridge Companion to Shakespeare's Poetry*. Ed. Patrick Cheney. New York: Cambridge UP, 2007. 108–24. Locates these works in the context of late Elizabethan poetic publication and literary and theatrical competition.

Roberts, Sasha. *Reading Shakespeare's Poems in Early Modern England*. Houndmills, Basingstoke: Palgrave Macmillan, 2003. 154–58, 177–90. Emphasizes the various interpretive contexts generated by different collections, seeing *The Passionate Pilgrim* as suppressing the homoeroticism of Shakespeare's sonnets, contributing to misogynistic literature, and celebrating erotic poetry.

Schoenfeldt, Michael. *The Cambridge Introduction to Shakespeare's Poetry*. Cambridge: Cambridge UP, 2010. 122–43. Focuses on the simple but elusive language of "The Phoenix and Turtle" and the "fantasies of Shakespearean authorship" in the various poems.

## TEXTUAL INTRODUCTION

*The Passionate Pilgrim* survives in three early modern editions, all octavos: O1 (undated and without title page, but probably printed in 1599, though possibly in 1598); O2 (1599); and O3 (1612). Scholars believed that the current O2 was the first edition until 1939, when Joseph Quincy Adams determined that a fragment in the Folger Library was in fact the first edition: not simply does the 1612 edition call itself "The Third Edition," suggesting that an edition before O2 existed, but the Folger copy includes substantial textual variants from O2. In other words, the earliest surviving text for *The Passionate Pilgrim* is drastically abbreviated, presenting textual editors with a rare conundrum in Shakespeare studies, especially for those basing a modern text on a single extant copy. Consequently, the present text follows O2 and records variants to it from O1 and other editions and copies of individual poems available.

The O1 fragment consists of eleven leaves, none of which includes a signature or page number. Since the title page is not among the extant leaves, we lack bibliographical information such as the title of the work, its date, its printer, and its publisher. Scholars believe that the original text consisted of twenty-eight leaves, with the collation formula A=C8, D4 (meaning that the first three gatherings of pages, labeled A, B, and C, each have eight leaves of paper, and the fourth gathering, D, four leaves). Only signatures A3–A7 and C2–C7 remain extant, printing eight of the twenty poems that survive in O2, numbered by modern editions Poems 1, 2, 3, 4, 5, 16, 17, 18. Scholars speculate that O1 was printed by T. Judson for William Jaggard.

The title page to O2 supplies the bibliographical information missing in O1:

> THE | PASSIONATE | PILGRIME. | *By W. Shakespeare.* | [Ornament] | *AT LONDON* | Printed for W. Iaggard, and are | to be sold by W. Leake, at the Grey- | hound in Paules Churchyard. | 1599.

Since Leake owned copyright to *Venus and Adonis*, Jaggard was almost certainly trying to capitalize on the enormous success of Shakespeare's narrative poem, along with that of *The Rape of Lucrece*, and thus on Shakespeare's standing as an important Elizabethan poet. Even so, as a book *The Passionate Pilgrim* is rare among Elizabethan examples because it prints individual poems on rectos alone, as if Jaggard lacked material to make a complete book; toward the end, however, he abandoned this plan when space suddenly became constricted, so he printed poems on both rectos and versos (i.e., on both sides of each leaf). O2 consists of thirty-two leaves, collates A–D8, and is extant in only two copies: in the collections of Trinity College, Cambridge, and the Huntington Library, San Marino, California.

A second title page appears on signature C3r, reading "SONNETS | To sundry notes of Musicke," effectively dividing the book into two parts, Poems 1–14 and Poems 15–20. Some scholars speculate that Jaggard inserted the second title page to appease Shakespeare's wrath at being identified as the author of the entire book, while others think that the second title page was inserted simply to pad out the volume.

Modern scholarship has determined that only five of the twenty poems were written by Shakespeare. Poems 1 and 2 are variations on Sonnets 138 and 144. Poems 3, 5, and 16 are songs and sonnets from *Love's Labor's Lost*, first published in 1598. Poems 8 and 20 are now assigned to Richard Barnfield, and Poem 11 to Bartholomew Griffin. Poem 19 combines two poems: part of Marlowe's "The Passionate Shepherd to His Love" and a stanza of Sir Walter Ralegh's "The Nymph's Reply," here set off with a subtitle, "Love's Answer." (The full texts of both poems appeared the next year, 1600, in *England's Helicon*.) The final eleven poems remain anonymous; cases have sometimes been made for Shakespeare's authorship of some of them, but modern editors reject the attributions. Curiously, then, Jaggard's attempt to present "W. Shakespeare" as "The Passionate Pilgrim"—an allusion to Romeo and Juliet's use of the pilgrim metaphor in their love-sonnet—falsifies the record and caused immediate (and long-lasting) indignation, including by Shakespeare.

A third edition of *The Passionate Pilgrim* was published in 1612. O3 is important especially because it exists with two different title pages: one with Shakespeare's name on it, and one without. The one with Shakespeare's name on it reads,

> THE | PASSIONATE | PILGRIME. | OR | *Certaine Amorous Sonnets,* | *betweene* Venus *and* Adonis, | *newly corrected and aug-* | *mented.* | *By W. Shakespere.* | The third Edition. | Where-unto is newly ad- | ded two Loue-Epistles, the first | from *Paris* to *Hellen*, and | *Hellens* answere backe | againe to *Paris*. | Printed by W. Iaggard. | 1612.

The reference to the sonnets about Venus and Adonis singles out a group of four poems on this topic (Poems 4, 6, 9, 11), likely trying to draw in readers of Shakespeare's narrative poem, while the two new "Loue-Epistles" were two of nine written by Thomas Heywood. We know this because Heywood in a postscript to his 1612 *Apology for Actors* accused Jaggard of printing his own poems dishonestly, and added that he knew Shakespeare to be "much offended with M. Jaggard (that altogether unknowne to him) presumed to make so bold with his name." Scholars speculate that Heywood's accusation led Jaggard to produce a new title page to the 1612 octavo, deleting Shakespeare's name.

The text of *The Passionate Pilgrim* presents few editorial problems. In a few cases, O1 provides a preferred reading (see Textual Variants), while occasionally later emendations are adopted. The major change between O1 and O2 occurs in Poem 18, where O2 prints O1's lines 13–24 after the current line 36. The present edition adopts O1 as preferable.

While *The Passionate Pilgrim* is a poorly designed book, it consolidates Shakespeare's standing, at the midpoint of his career, as a major English poet. Jaggard has been accused of many things, including bad judgment and dishonesty, but because he was the first to publish Shakespeare's collected plays (the First Folio), he qualifies as the first publisher of collected editions of Shakespeare's poems and plays.

PATRICK CHENEY

# The Passionate Pilgrim

## 1[1]

When my love swears that she is made of truth,
I do believe her (though I know she lies),
That° she might think me some untutored youth, *So that*
Unskillful in the world's false forgeries.
Thus vainly° thinking that she thinks me young, *in vain; with vanity*
Although I know my years be past the best,
I, smiling, credit° her false-speaking tongue, *(pretend to) believe*
Outfacing faults in love with love's ill rest.
But wherefore says my love that she is young?
And wherefore say not I that I am old?
Oh, love's best habit is° a soothing tongue, *love is best dressed in*
And age, in love, loves not to have years told.° *counted*
    Therefore I'll lie° with love, and love with me, *tell lies; lie down*
    Since that our faults in love thus smothered be.

## 2[1]

Two loves I have, of comfort and despair,
That like two spirits do suggest° me still: *entice*
My better angel is a man (right fair)
My worser spirit a woman (colored ill).° *darkly*
To win me soon to hell, my female evil
Tempteth my better angel from my side,
And would corrupt my saint to be a devil,
Wooing his purity with her fair pride.
And whether that my angel be turned fiend,
Suspect I may, yet not directly tell:
For being both to me, both to each, friend,[2]
I guess one angel in another's hell.[3]
    The truth I shall not know, but live in doubt,
    Till my bad angel fire my good one out.[4]

## 3[1]

Did not the heavenly rhetoric of thine eye,
'Gainst whom the world could not hold argument,
Persuade my heart to this false perjury?
Vows for thee broke deserve not punishment.
A woman I forswore; but I will prove,
Thou being a goddess, I forswore not thee:
My vow was earthly, thou a heavenly love;

1

1. Textual Comment This is another version of Sonnet 138. For the differences, see Digital Edition TC 1 and appendix of comparative scenes.

2

1. Textual Comment This is another version of Sonnet 144. For the differences, see Digital Edition TC 2 and appendix of comparative scenes.

2. The two are both my lovers, and both are lovers to each other.

3. Each torments the other; they are in the "hell," or middle den, of a (sexual) game called barley-break; the man occupies the sex organ ("hell") of the woman.

4. Until my bad angel expels my good one, who has become an animal to be smoked out of a burrow; until my bad angel infects my good one with venereal disease; until bad money ("angel" = gold coin) drives out good.

3

1. Textual Comment This is another version of a sonnet that appears in *Love's Labor's Lost* at 4.3.55–68. For the differences, see Digital Edition TC 3.

Thy grace° being gained cures all disgrace in me. *favor*
My vow was breath, and breath a vapor is;
Then thou, fair sun, that on this earth doth shine,
Exhale° this vapor vow; in thee it is. *Draw up*
If broken, then it is no fault of mine.
If by me broke, what fool is not so wise
To break an oath to win a paradise?

**4**

Sweet Cytherea,[1] sitting by a brook
With young Adonis, lovely, fresh, and green,° *young; inexperienced*
Did court the lad with many a lovely° look— *amorous*
Such looks as none could look but beauty's queen.
She told him stories to delight his ear;
She showed him favors to allure his eye.
To win his heart, she touched him here and there:
Touches so soft still° conquer chastity. *always*
But whether unripe years did want conceit,° *lack understanding*
Or he refused to take her figured° proffer, *implied*
The tender nibbler would not touch the bait,
But smile and jest at every gentle offer.
Then fell she on her back, fair queen, and toward;° *ready*
He rose and ran away, ah, fool too froward.° *obstinate*

**5[1]**

If love make me forsworn, how shall I swear to love?
Oh, never faith could hold, if not to beauty vowed.
Though to myself forsworn, to thee I'll constant prove;
Those thoughts to me like oaks,[2] to thee like osiers° bowed. *willows*
Study his bias leaves,° and make his book thine eyes, *goes off course*
Where all those pleasures live that art can comprehend.
If knowledge be the mark,° to know thee shall suffice: *aim*
Well-learnèd is that tongue that well can thee commend;
All ignorant that soul that sees thee without wonder,
Which is to me some praise, that I thy parts° admire. *qualities*
Thine eye Jove's lightning seems, thy voice his dreadful thunder,
Which (not to anger bent) is music and sweet fire.
Celestial as thou art, oh, do not love that wrong
To sing heaven's praise with such an earthly tongue.[3]

**6**

Scarce had the sun dried up the dewy morn,
And scarce the herd gone to the hedge for shade,
When Cytherea (all in love forlorn)
A longing tarriance° for Adonis made *waiting*
Under an osier growing by a brook,

**4**
1. Sonnets 4, 6, 9, and 11 all treat the unsuccessful wooing of the beautiful but unresponsive young man Adonis by Venus ("Cytherea"), the goddess of love.
**5**
1. TEXTUAL COMMENT This is another version of a sonnet—composed, however, in hexameters—that appears in *Love's Labor's Lost* at 4.2.98–111. For the differences, see Digital Edition TC 4.
2. Those resolutions that seemed to me to be as strong as oaks.
3. *do . . . tongue:* possibly a misprint of the *Love's Labor's Lost* version. As printed, the lines might be stretched to mean: do not love those that do wrong by singing (or: do not love [me] if it is "wrong / To sing") "heaven's praise with such an earthly tongue." But since it is not wrong, *do* love me.

A brook where Adon used to cool his spleen.° *hot temper*
Hot was the day; she hotter, that did look
For his approach that often there had been.
Anon he comes and throws his mantle by,
And stood stark naked on the brook's green brim.
The sun looked on the world with glorious eye,
Yet not so wistly° as this queen on him. *eagerly; longingly*
He, spying her, bounced in whereas he stood.[1]
"O Jove," quoth she, "why was not I a flood?"° *body of water*

## 7

Fair is my love, but not so fair as fickle;
Mild as a dove, but neither true nor trusty;° *trustworthy*
Brighter than glass, and yet as glass is, brittle;
Softer than wax, and yet as iron rusty:° *corrupt (morally)*
A lily pale, with damask° dye to grace her, *red*
None fairer, nor none falser to deface her.[1]

Her lips to mine how often hath she joined,
Between each kiss her oaths of true love swearing.
How many tales to please me hath she coined,° *invented*
Dreading my love, the loss whereof still fearing.[2]
Yet in the midst of all her pure protestings
Her faith, her oaths, her tears, and all were jestings.

She burned with love as straw with fire flameth;
She burned out love as soon as straw out burneth;
She framed° the love, and yet she foiled° the framing; *built / ruined*
She bade love last, and yet she fell a-turning.° *(to another lover)*
Was this a lover, or a lecher, whether?° *which of the two*
Bad in the best, though excellent in neither.[3]

## 8[1]

If music and sweet poetry agree,
As they must needs (the sister and the brother),
Then must the love be great twixt thee and me,
Because thou lov'st the one,° and I the other.° *(music) / (poetry)*
Dowland[2] to thee is dear, whose heavenly touch
Upon the lute doth ravish human sense;
Spenser[3] to me, whose deep conceit° is such *understanding*
As passing all conceit° needs no defense. *esteem*
Thou lov'st to hear the sweet melodious sound
That Phoebus'[4] lute (the queen of music) makes;
And I in deep delight am chiefly drowned,
When as° himself to singing he betakes. *When*
One god is god of both (as poets feign),
One knight° loves both, and both in thee remain. *(the reference is unknown)*

6
1. Jumped in from where he stood.

7
1. Nor is anyone more false, to her discredit; with a possible reference to cosmetics in "falser" and "deface."
2. Continually being anxious about losing my love, and upset at that prospect.
3. Bad in romance, but not outstanding merely as a sexual partner either.

8
1. From *Poems in Diverse Humors*, an appendix that Richard Barnfield added to his *Encomion of Lady Pecunia* (1598).
2. John Dowland (1563?–1626), composer, singer, instrumentalist.
3. Poet Edmund Spenser (1552–1599), author of *The Faerie Queene* (1590, 1596).
4. Apollo's. Here, Apollo is god of music, in line 12 ("singing") god of poetry, and in line 13 "god of both."

## 9

Fair was the morn, when the fair queen of love,° *(Venus)*
. . . . . . . . . . . . . . . . . . . . . . . . . . . . . . . .[1]
Paler for sorrow than her milk-white dove,
For Adon's sake, a youngster proud and wild,
Her stand she takes upon a steep-up hill.
Anon° Adonis comes with horn and hounds; *Soon*
She, silly° queen, with more than love's good will, *foolish*
Forbade the boy he should not pass those grounds.° *cross those valleys*
"Once," quoth she, "did I see a fair sweet youth
Here in these brakes,° deep wounded with° a boar, *thickets / by*
Deep in the thigh, a spectacle of ruth.° *pity*
See in my thigh," quoth she, "here was the sore."
She showèd hers; he saw more wounds than one,° *(sexual)*
And blushing fled, and left her all alone.

## 10

Sweet rose, fair flower, untimely plucked, soon vaded,° *faded; departed*
Plucked in the bud, and vaded in the spring;
Bright orient pearl, alack too timely shaded,[1]
Fair creature killed too soon by death's sharp sting,
Like a green plum that hangs upon a tree,
And falls (through wind) before the fall should be.

I weep for thee, and yet no cause I have;
For why° thou left'st me nothing in thy will. *Because*
And yet thou left'st me more than I did crave;
For why I cravèd nothing of thee still.[2]
Oh, yes, dear friend, I pardon crave of thee:[3]
Thy discontent° thou didst bequeath to me. *sadness*

## 11[1]

Venus with Adonis sitting by her
Under a myrtle shade began to woo him.
She told the youngling how god Mars did try her,
And as he fell to her, she fell to him.
"Even thus," quoth she, "the warlike god embraced me."
And then she clipped° Adonis in her arms; *embraced*
"Even thus," quoth she, "the warlike god unlaced me,"
As if the boy should use like° loving charms. *similar*
"Even thus," quoth she, "he seizèd on my lips,"
And with her lips on his did act the seizure.
And as she fetchèd breath, away he skips,
And would not take her meaning nor her pleasure.[2]
Ah, that I had my lady at this bay,° *cornered in this way*
To kiss and clip me till I run away.

**9**
1. A line is missing here in the original edition.

**10**
1. Darkened too soon. "Orient" pearls were valued as more lustrous than their European counterparts, with overtones of the sun rising in the East and setting in the West.
2. "Nothing" (lines 8, 10) evokes the tangibility of absence caused by death. But "nothing" also may denote female sexual organs. In line 8, it would go with "will" (testament; lust) to suggest that the dead woman's desire (formerly) made her sexually available to the speaker. In line 10, the speaker would be saying that he always ("still") desired her.
3. This line seems to contradict the previous one by claiming that the speaker did, after all, "crave" something—"pardon."

**11**
1. From *Fidessa*, a sonnet sequence by Bartholomew Griffin (published 1596).
2. *take . . . pleasure:* understand "her meaning" or agree to (accept) the "pleasure" she wanted and offered.

## 12

Crabbèd° age and youth cannot live together: *Ill-tempered*
Youth is full of pleasance, age is full of care;
Youth like summer morn, age like winter weather;
Youth like summer brave,° age like winter bare. *well dressed*
Youth is full of sport, age's breath is short;
Youth is nimble, age is lame;
Youth is hot and bold, age is weak and cold;
Youth is wild, and age is tame.
Age, I do abhor thee; youth, I do adore thee.
Oh, my love, my love is young.
Age, I do defy thee. O sweet shepherd, hie thee,° *hurry up*
For methinks thou stays° too long. *delays*

## 13

Beauty is but a vain and doubtful good,
A shining gloss that vadeth° suddenly, *fades*
A flower that dies when first it gins° to bud, *begins*
A brittle glass that's broken presently,° *immediately*
A doubtful good, a gloss, a glass, a flower,
Lost, vaded, broken, dead within an hour.

And as goods lost are seld° or never found, *seldom*
As vaded gloss no rubbing will refresh,
As flowers dead lie withered on the ground,
As broken glass no cement can redress,° *repair*
So beauty blemished once, for ever lost,° *is forever lost*
In spite of physic,° painting,° pain,° and cost. *medicine / make-up / labor*

## 14

Good night, good rest, ah, neither be my share.
She bade good night that kept my rest away,
And daffed° me to a cabin hanged° with care, *dismissed / room adorned*
To descant on the doubts° of my decay. *expand upon the fears*
"Farewell," quoth she, "and come again tomorrow."
Fare° well I could not, for I supped with sorrow. *Do; eat*

Yet at my parting sweetly did she smile,
In scorn or friendship, nil I conster whether:[1]
'T may be she joyed to jest at my exile;
'T may be again to make me wander thither.
Wander—a word for shadows like myself,
As take the pain but cannot pluck the pelf.° *reward*

Lord, how mine eyes throw gazes to the East!
My heart doth charge the watch;[2] the morning rise° *break of day*
Doth cite° each moving° sense from idle rest, *summon / living*
Not daring trust the office of mine eyes.[3]
While Philomela° sits and sings, I sit and mark,° *the nightingale / listen*
And wish her lays were tunèd like the lark.[4]

**14**
1. I will not guess which of the two.
2. Perhaps: My heart orders those on night watch to watch for morning.
3. Since daybreak doesn't trust my eyes to be alert, it rouses all my senses.
4. And wish her (nighttime) songs were the songs of the (morning) lark.

For she doth welcome daylight with her ditty,° *song*
And drives away dark dreaming night:
The night so packed,° I post° unto my pretty. *sent off / hurry*
Heart hath his hope, and eyes their wishèd sight;
Sorrow changed to solace, and solace mixed with sorrow;
For why° she sighed and bade me come tomorrow. *Because*

Were I with her, the night would post too soon,
But now are minutes added to the hours.
To spite me now, each minute seems a moon;° *night; month*
Yet not for me, shine sun[5] to succor flowers.
Pack night, peep day; good day, of night now borrow;
Short night tonight, and length thyself tomorrow.[6]

## Sonnets to Sundry Notes of Music

### 15

It was a lording's° daughter, the fairest one of three, *lord's*
That likèd of her master,° as well as well might be, *tutor*
Till looking on an Englishman, the fairest that eye could see,
Her fancy fell a-turning.° *(to another lover)*
Long was the combat doubtful,° that love with love did fight *uncertain*
To leave the master loveless, or kill the gallant knight;
To put in practice either, alas it was a spite° *would be a vexation*
Unto the silly° damsel. *helpless*
But one must be refused; more mickle° was the pain, *great*
That nothing could be used° to turn them both to gain, *done*
For of the two the trusty knight was wounded with disdain,
Alas, she could not help it.
Thus art° with arms contending was victor of the day, *learning*
Which by a gift of learning did bear the maid away.
Then, lullaby, the learnèd man hath got the lady gay,
For now my song is ended.

### 16[1]

On a day (alack the day)
Love, whose month was ever May,
Spied a blossom passing° fair, *surpassingly*
Playing in the wanton° air. *playful*
Through the velvet leaves the wind
All unseen gan passage find,° *began to find passage*
That° the lover, sick to death, *So that*
Wished himself the heaven's breath.
"Air," quoth he, "thy cheeks may blow;
Air, would I might triumph so.
But (alas) my hand hath sworn
Ne'er to pluck thee from thy thorn;[2]

5. Let the sun shine, not for my sake, but.
6. The speaker is asking night to shorten now and to lengthen tomorrow, when he's with his mistress.

16
1. TEXTUAL COMMENT This poem is another version of lines that appear in *Love's Labor's Lost* at 4.3.96–115. For the differences, see Digital Edition TC 5.
2. TEXTUAL COMMENT For the editorial emendation of the printed version both here and in *Love's Labor's Lost*, see Digital Edition TC 6.

Vow (alack) for youth unmeet,° *inappropriate*
Youth, so apt to pluck a sweet.
Thou for whom Jove would swear
Juno but an Ethiop[3] were,
And deny himself for° Jove, *to be*
Turning mortal for thy love.

## 17

My flocks feed not, my ewes breed not,
My rams speed° not, all is amiss. *thrive*
Love is dying, faith's defying,[1]
Heart's denying, causer of this.
All my merry jigs° are quite forgot; *dances; sports*
All my lady's love is lost (God wot°). *knows*
Where her faith was firmly fixed in love,
There a "nay" is placed without remove.° *immovably*
One silly cross° wrought all my loss. *foolish mishap*
O frowning Fortune, cursèd fickle dame,
For now I see inconstancy
More in women than in men remain.

In black mourn I, all fears scorn I;
Love hath forlorn me, living in thrall.° *enslaved (to love)*
Heart is bleeding, all help needing.
Oh, cruel speeding,° fraughted° with gall.° *fortune / laden / rancor*
My shepherd's pipe can sound no deal;° *not at all*
My wether's[2] bell rings doleful knell;
My curtal dog[3] that wont to° have played, *formerly liked to*
Plays not at all, but seems afraid.
With sighs so deep, procures° to weep, *is able*
In howling wise,° to see my doleful plight. *fashion*
How sighs resound through heartless ground,
Like a thousand vanquished men in bloody fight.

Clear wells spring not, sweet birds sing not,
Green plants bring not forth their dye,
Herds stand weeping, flocks all sleeping,
Nymphs back° peeping fearfully. *back up*
All our pleasure known to us poor swains,° *shepherds*
All our merry meetings on the plains,
All our evening sport from us is fled,
All our love is lost, for love is dead.
Farewell, sweet love, thy like ne'er was
For a sweet content, the cause all my woe.
Poor Corydon[4] must live alone:
Other help for him I see that there is none.

3. Black African (used here in racist fashion to signify ugliness).

17
1. Faith's rejection; "de-fying" means de-faithing.
2. A male sheep castrated while still immature. The "bellwether" is the lead sheep of the flock.
3. Dog with a cut tail.
4. Conventional name for a shepherd (from one of Virgil's *Eclogues*, ca. 39–38 B.C.E., a collection of pastoral poems).

## 18

Whenas° thine eye hath chose the dame, *When*
And stalled° the deer° that thou shouldst strike, *trapped / (pun on "dear")*
Let reason rule things worthy blame,
As well as fancy, partial might.[1]
Take counsel of some wiser head,
Neither too young, nor yet unwed.

And when thou com'st thy tale to tell,
Smooth not thy tongue with filèd° talk, *rehearsed; scheming*
Lest she some subtle practice° smell— *deception*
A cripple soon can find a halt[2]—
But plainly say thou lov'st her well,
And set her person forth to sale.[3]

And to her will° frame all thy ways;° *desire / habits*
Spare not to spend, and chiefly there
Where thy desert may merit praise
By ringing in thy lady's ear.[4]
The strongest castle, tower, and town,
The golden bullet° beats it down. *words; money*

Serve always with assurèd trust,° *reliability*
And in thy suit be humble true;
Unless thy lady prove unjust,° *unfaithful*
Press never thou to choose a new.[5]
When time° shall serve, be thou not slack *occasion*
To proffer, though she put thee back.[6]

What though° her frowning brows be bent, *Although*
Her cloudy looks will calm ere night,
And then too late she will repent
That thus dissembled her delight,[7]
And twice desire,° ere it be day, *(sexual gratification)*
That which with scorn she put away.° *rejected*

What though she strive to try her strength
And ban° and brawl,° and say thee "nay," *curse / shout*
Her feeble force will yield at length,
When craft° hath taught her thus to say, *craftiness*
"Had women been so strong as men,
In faith, you had not had it then."

The wiles and guiles that women work,° *employ*
Dissembled with an outward show;
The tricks and toys° that in them lurk, *whims*

**18**

1. Let reason as well as desire ("fancy"), which is biased and by itself inadequate, govern your potentially blameworthy love affairs.
2. Those practiced in deceit can easily sense deception. *find a halt:* detect a limp.
3. Like a salesman, start praising her qualities. One of the manuscript versions of this poem has "& set thy body forth to sell."
4. Don't be stingy about spending your money in ways that will draw your lady's attention to your merit.
5. Don't make attempts to choose someone else (?).
6. Even if she resists you. The "proffer," at first an offer, becomes outright rape here and in the following stanzas.
7. She who in this way concealed her desire.

The cock that treads them[8] shall not know.
Have you not heard it said full oft,
"A woman's 'nay' doth stand for naught"?[9]

Think women still to strive with men
To sin, and never for to saint.[1]
There is no heaven: be holy then
When time with age shall them attaint.[2]
Were kisses all the joys in bed,
One woman would another wed.

But soft, enough; too much I fear,
Lest that my mistress hear my song.
She will not stick to round me on the ear,[3]
To teach my tongue to be so long.
Yet will she blush, here be it said,
To hear her secrets so bewrayed.° *revealed*

### 19[1]

Live with me and be my love,
And we will all the pleasures prove° *try*
That hills and valleys, dales and fields,
And all the craggy mountains yield.

There will we sit upon the rocks,
And see the shepherds feed their flocks,
By shallow rivers, by whose falls
Melodious birds sing madrigals.

There will I make thee a bed of roses,
With a thousand fragrant posies,° *flower bunches*
A cap of flowers and a kirtle° *gown or skirt*
Embroidered all with leaves of myrtle.

A belt of straw and ivy buds,
With coral clasps and amber studs,
And if these pleasures may thee move,
Then live with me, and be my love.

### Love's Answer

If that the world and love were young,
And truth in every shepherd's tongue,
These pretty pleasures might me move
To live with thee and be thy love.

8. The man who copulates with them.
9. Nothing; (sexual) naughtiness; female sexual organ.
1. Expect women always to engage (compete) with men in sin but not in saintliness, or chastity.
2. There is no thought of heaven (purity) in women seeking sexual pleasure. Let them be holy when they're old and unattractive.
3. She won't refrain from scolding me (boxing me) on the ear.

19

1. Part of a poem by Christopher Marlowe (1564–1593), with a reply by Walter Ralegh (1552–1618). See the Textual Introduction.

## 20

As it fell upon a day,
In the merry month of May,
Sitting in a pleasant shade,
Which a grove of myrtles made,
Beasts did leap, and birds did sing,
Trees did grow, and plants did spring.
Every thing did banish moan,
Save the nightingale alone.
She (poor bird) as all forlorn,
Leaned her breast up-till a thorn,
And there sung the dolful'st ditty,
That to hear it was great pity.
"Fie, fie, fie," now would she cry;
"Tereu, Tereu,"[1] by and by:
That to hear her so complain
Scarce I could from tears refrain,
For her griefs so lively shown
Made me think upon mine own.
Ah, thought I, thou mourn'st in vain,
None takes pity on thy pain:
Senseless trees, they cannot hear thee;
Ruthless bears, they will not cheer thee.
King Pandion,[2] he is dead;
All thy friends are lapped° in lead. *wrapped up*
All thy fellow birds do sing,
Careless of thy sorrowing.
Whilst as fickle Fortune smiled,
Thou and I were both beguiled.
Everyone that flatters thee
Is no friend in misery.
Words are easy, like the wind;
Faithful friends are hard to find.
Every man will be thy friend,
Whilst thou hast wherewith to spend;
But if store of crowns be scant,
No man will supply thy want.
If that one be prodigal,
"Bountiful" they will him call,
And with suchlike flattering:
"Pity but he were° a king." *It's a pity he's not*
If he be addict to vice,
Quickly him they will entice;
If to women he be bent,° *inclined*
They have° at commandment;° *(women) / on demand*
But if Fortune once do frown,
Then farewell his great renown:
They that fawned on him before
Use his company no more.

**20**

1 The nightingale's sound, from Tereus, who, in Ovid's *Metamorphoses* (by 8 C.E.), rapes Philomela (hence, a name for a nightingale) and cuts out her tongue.

2. Father of Philomela and legendary king of Athens.

He that is thy friend indeed,
He will help thee in thy need.
If thou sorrow, he will weep;
If thou wake, he cannot sleep.
Thus of every grief in heart
He with thee doth bear a part.
These are certain signs to know
Faithful friend from flatt'ring foe.

# The Phoenix and Turtle

"The Phoenix and Turtle" was one of several poems—others were by George Chapman, Ben Jonson, and John Marston—appended to Robert Chester's *Love's Martyr* (1601). An abstruse philosophical composition, "The Phoenix and Turtle" may represent Shakespeare's effort to refashion himself as a different kind of poet from the one who appeared two years earlier in unauthorized form in *The Passionate Pilgrim*. Literary innovation here may also have an element of poetic competition with his three fellow contributors to Chester's volume, all of whom were dramatists as well. With two of them, Jonson and Marston, Shakespeare was then probably engaged in the satirical Poets' War, a battle of rival playwrights.

"The Phoenix and Turtle" is composed in trochaic tetrameter with the final (unstressed) syllable dropped—an otherwise atypical meter in the period that, however, Shakespeare employs in his plays for incantations and epitaphs. The poem can be divided into either two or three parts, depending on whether one goes by rhyme scheme or poetic speaker (see Digital Edition TC 1). A tripartite division may ultimately derive from Plato. The first five quatrains, or "requiem" (line 16), may be indebted to Chaucer's late fourteenth-century *Parliament of Fowls* and, behind it, to the elegy on a dead parrot of the classical Latin poet Ovid. In a language of elaborate circumlocution, these lines merely call the birds together to mourn the deaths of two remarkably constant lovers—the proverbially faithful turtledove (here, male) and the legendary phoenix (here, female). Supposedly, only one phoenix was alive at any given moment, and the bird died only to be reborn from its own ashes. Neither of the two birds is named yet, however.

The "anthem" (line 21), which constitutes the next eight stanzas, is presumably intoned by the birds. In a reversal of the procedure of the opening twenty lines, this combination of burial hymn, possibly with Catholic overtones, and epithalamion (marriage celebration) turns to a deceptively simple vocabulary that conceals dense argumentation. As marriage poem, it invokes the work of Shakespeare's older contemporary, Edmund Spenser. Behind the emphasis on the paradoxical unity of two separate beings lies the mystery of the Christian Trinity as understood in Scholastic theology—medieval Europe's assimilation beginning in the twelfth century of the recently translated writings of Aristotle. The ideal love of the two birds ultimately defies the efforts at comprehension by Reason, which cannot understand how

> love in twain,
> Had the essence but in one,
> Two distincts, division none:
> (lines 25–27)

or how

> the self was not the same:
> Single nature's double name,
> Neither two nor one was called.
> (lines 38–40)

In other words, the rationalist vocabulary of this section ultimately undermines its own legitimacy. Perhaps the lines vindicate the more mystical understanding of ideal love that Renaissance thought derived from Plato, whose doctrines Aristotle had sought to answer. In any case, the heterosexual love praised in this self-contradictory fashion parallels the celebration of homoerotic love in the sonnets to the young man: "Let me confess that we two must be twain, / Although our undivided loves are one" (36.1–2).

Following the anthem, Reason delivers the final section of the poem, the *Threnos,* or mourning song. These lines retain the straightforwardly abstract diction of the anthem and the trochaic-tetrameter meter of all that has preceded, but they abandon quatrains (rhyming *abba*) for tercets (rhyming *aaa*). Like the three-part structure, this particular rhyme scheme perhaps alludes to the Trinity. Similarly, the division of the poem into two rhyme schemes may be an effort to replicate formally the rationally incomprehensible unity of the phoenix and turtle. The last five stanzas emphasize the finality of the death of the couple, which apparently excludes both rebirth (even on the part of the immortal phoenix) and "posterity"—the latter as a result of a "married chastity" (lines 59, 61) that has the same (lack of) consequences as the love for the young man in the sonnets. The result is the diminution of life: the only authentic or perhaps ideal "[t]ruth and beauty buried be" (line 64). Here, the poem is of a piece with Shakespearean tragedy in its refusal to find transcendence in death. In this sense, the poem reenacts English literary history, moving from Shakespeare's two most important predecessors, Chaucer and Spenser, to Shakespeare himself.

"The Phoenix and Turtle" raises all sorts of interpretive problems. Since the *Threnos* is spoken by Reason, who has been defeated by the phoenix and turtle, should the concluding stanzas be seen not as authorial statement but as the position of a fallible character who lets fly a crow of triumph at the couple's death? Moreover, the concluding summons of all "[t]hat are either true or fair" (line 66) sits oddly with the immediately preceding insistence that genuine truth and beauty no longer exist: perhaps now they exist only separately. And why does Shakespeare, through Reason, insist on the lack of offspring and, apparently rejecting a central feature of the legend, on the mortality of the phoenix? This last question is only emphasized by the circumstances of publication. All of the poems with which "The Phoenix and Turtle" were printed are on the subject of the phoenix and turtle, and all but Shakespeare's deny the finality of the phoenix's death. "The Phoenix and Turtle" alone forgoes the possibility of exploiting the standard treatment of the phoenix as the intersection of the temporal and the timeless.

The title page of the volume advertises Chester's long poem as "[a]llegorically shadowing the truth of Love, in the constant Fate of the Phoenix and Turtle." This claim, the abstract language of "The Phoenix and Turtle," and the avowed purpose of the volume—to honor Sir John Salusbury of Lleweni, knighted by the Queen in June 1601—have all encouraged a search in Shakespeare's poem for allegorical meaning (beyond the praise of ideal human union through a tale of two birds). The marriage of phoenix and turtle has been seen as the joining of the literal and the metaphorical in poetry, so that the poem self-referentially becomes a metaphor for metaphor itself. Historical readings have found candidates for the parts of the turtle and the phoenix in Salusbury and his wife, as well as in the Earl of Essex, Salusbury, or the English people in relation to Queen Elizabeth. Although none of these theories is convincing, in part because of a failure to explain what real "tragic scene" is being allegorically represented by the couple's deaths (line 52), all testify to the poem's ability to hint at hidden meanings. The most plausible of these possibilities links Salusbury to Elizabeth—and, in more broadly political and religious terms, Catholic Wales to Protestant England. In the aftermath of the Reformation, funeral rites and prayers turned from intercession to commemoration. Recourse to the classical tradition perhaps offered a secular form of intercession, in which the poem itself, represented as the "urn" (line 65), promises a different kind of immortality. In any case, "The Phoenix and Turtle" labors to construct an ideal image of love while simultaneously circumscribing the real utility of that ideal. Marriage and funeral, celebration and dirge, ideal affirmation and pragmatic denial—the poem is a characteristically Shakespearean venture in having it both ways.

WALTER COHEN

## SELECTED BIBLIOGRAPHY

Bednarz, James P. "*The Passionate Pilgrim* and 'The Phoenix and Turtle.'" *The Cambridge Companion to Shakespeare's Poetry.* Ed. Patrick Cheney. New York: Cambridge UP, 2007. 108–24. Locates these works in the context of late Elizabethan poetic publication and literary and theatrical competition.

———. *Shakespeare and the Truth of Love: The Mystery of "The Phoenix and Turtle."* London: Palgrave Macmillan, 2012. Rejects topical readings in favor of seeing the poem as a mythmaking, metaphysical work drawing on the mystery of the Trinity to investigate the intersubjective nature of love.

Cheney, Patrick. "The Voice of the Author in 'The Phoenix and Turtle': Chaucer, Shakespeare, Spenser." *Shakespeare and the Middle Ages.* Ed. Curtis Perry and John Watkins. Oxford: Oxford UP, 2009. 103–25. Traces the poem's three-part structure back to Plato and especially to Chaucer's *Parliament of Fowls*, and sees a movement in it from Spenserian romance epic through Chaucerian complaint to Shakespearean tragedy.

Davies, H. Neville. "*The Phoenix and Turtle:* Requiem and Rite." *Review of English Studies* 46 (1995): 525–30. Ties the poem's funeral rite to the Elizabethan Book of Common Prayer.

Enterline, Lynn. "'The Phoenix and the Turtle,' Renaissance Elegies and the Language of Grief." *Early Modern English Poetry: A Critical Companion.* Ed. Patrick Cheney, Andrew Hadfield, and Garrett A. Sullivan, Jr. New York: Oxford UP, 2007. 147–59. Locates the poem in the post-Reformation transition from intercession to commemoration in mourning the dead, with the return to the classical tradition, especially Ovid, self-referentially converting the poem itself into a secular afterlife.

Kerrigan, John. "Reading 'The Phoenix and Turtle.'" *The Oxford Handbook of Shakespeare's Poetry.* Ed. Jonathan F. S. Post. Oxford: Oxford UP, 2013. 540–59. Offers a detailed commentary on the poem attentive to its multiple possible meanings, seeing it as a post-Reformation funeral ritual with Catholic and heraldic elements, and with connections to Elizabeth.

———. "Shakespeare, Elegy, and Epitaph 1557–1640." *The Oxford Handbook of Shakespeare's Poetry.* Ed. Jonathan F. S. Post. Oxford: Oxford UP, 2013. 225–44. Links "The Phoenix and Turtle" to the elegies attributed to Shakespeare, to the volume in which the poem appeared, to the period's competition—in poetry and in stone—in constructing memorials, and to the relationship between Catholic Wales and Protestant England.

Klause, John. "'The Phoenix and Turtle' in Its Time." *In the Company of Shakespeare.* Ed. Thomas Moisan and Douglas Bruster. Madison, NJ: Fairleigh Dickinson UP, 2002. 206–30. Reads "The Phoenix and Turtle" as an ironic critique of Salusbury as well as of the other poets who contributed to the collection, and as a covert defense of Catholicism.

Schoenfeldt, Michael. *The Cambridge Introduction to Shakespeare's Poetry.* Cambridge: Cambridge UP, 2010. 122–29. Focuses on the simple but elusive language of "The Phoenix and Turtle."

Steel, Karl. "*The Phoenix and the Turtle*: 'Number There in Love Was Slain.'" *Shakesqueer: A Queer Companion to the Complete Works of Shakespeare.* Ed. Madhavi Menon. Durham, NC: Duke UP, 2011. 271–77. Ties the undermining of Reason to the multiple possible relationships the poem imagines between the phoenix and the turtle.

## TEXTUAL INTRODUCTION

"The Phoenix and Turtle" was printed in 1601 as part of Robert Chester's *Love's Martyr: or, Rosalin's Complaint*, a voluminous work not entered in the Stationers' Register. Like *Venus and Adonis* and *The Rape of Lucrece*, Chester's book was printed by Richard Field, although in this case the publisher was Edward Blount. The Quarto volume of ninety-eight leaves is a curious amalgamation, including Chester's own long narrative poem but also what the title page to the book advertises as "some new compositions, of several modern writers whose names are subscribed to their several works, upon the first subject: viz. the *Phoenix and Turtle*." The "modern writers," who appear in a section of their own marked by the heading "Diverse Poetical Essays," contribute fourteen poems, the first two by a "Vatum Chorus" (Chorus of Poets), with several signed by authors' names: John Marston, George Chapman, Ben Jonson, "Ignoto," and William Shakespeare (the fifth poem in the collaborative sequence). Only three copies of the first edition of *Love's Martyr* are extant, with only two of them complete (the Folger and Huntington copies; a third copy, in the National Library of Wales, is imperfect). In 1611, a reissue was printed, with only one copy extant (in the British Library, London).

Shakespeare's poem appears on signatures Z3v–4v but is curiously printed in two parts. On Z3v–4r, there is no title ("The Phoenix and Turtle" is a modern invention), just the first part of the poem (lines 1–52, or the first thirteen stanzas, all rhyming *abba*). Then, at the top of Z4v, a heading appears, *Threnos* (Mourning song), followed by the second part of the poem (lines 53–67, or the last five stanzas, rhyming *aaa*). Beneath this second part, the name "William Shake-speare" appears. Some scholars want to read the sixty-seven-line poem as two poems, although all recent editors print it as a single composition, signed, like *Venus* and *Lucrece*, by the author.

Shakespeare's poem has no textual cruxes or substantive variants. The syntax of a single line has produced some division among editors. For line 39, the Quarto reads "Single Natures double name," which most editors modernize as "Single Nature's double name"; but some editors read the line differently, as "Single natures, double name," making this elliptical poem even more elliptical here. Although this remains an intriguing intervention, it is not adopted for the present edition, which suggests that the "double name" is that of "[s]ingle nature."

Patrick Cheney

# The Phoenix and Turtle[1]

Let the bird of loudest lay[2]
On the sole Arabian tree,[3]
Herald sad and trumpet be:
To whose sound chaste wings° obey. *virtuous birds*

But thou, shrieking harbinger,° *(the screech owl)*
Foul precurrer of the fiend,[4]
Augur of the fever's end,° *Prophet of death or cure*
To this troop[5] come thou not near.

From this session° interdict° *(of a court) / forbid*
Every fowl of tyrant wing,° *bird of prey*
Save the eagle, feathered king:
Keep the obsequy° so strict. *funeral rite*

Let the priest in surplice white,[6]
That defunctive music can,[7]
Be the death-divining swan,
Lest the requiem lack his right.° *its due; its rite*

And thou, treble-dated° crow, *long-lived*
That thy sable gender mak'st
With the breath thou giv'st and tak'st,[8]
'Mongst our mourners shalt thou go.

Here the anthem doth commence:
Love and constancy is dead,
Phoenix and the Turtle fled
In a mutual flame from hence.

1. *Phoenix:* a legendary, self-resurrecting bird believed to live in cycles of several centuries, dying in flames and being reborn from its own ashes—here, regarded as female. *Turtle:* turtledove, symbol of constancy—here, regarded as male. TEXTUAL COMMENT For the two main ways of understanding the structure of the poem, see Digital Edition TC 1.
2. Song. It is unclear which bird this refers to—possibly the phoenix, unless one reads "Death is now the Phoenix' nest" (line 56) not as part of a cycle but as a final resting place. Alternatively, it might be some other bird (the rooster?) known for its loud voice.
3. Supposedly, a unique tree on which sits the phoenix, which is similarly unique: only one exists at any given time.
4. Precursor of the devil: screech owls were thought to foretell death.
5. The mourning birds called forth by "the bird of loudest lay" (line 1).
6. The swan. A "surplice" is a loose clerical outer garment.
7. That is skilled in funereal music. Swans were thought to sing beautifully just before (their own) death (hence, the phrase "swan song").
8. *That . . . tak'st:* crows were believed to conceive by billing (kissing)—hence, "With the breath." *giv'st and tak'st:* Job 1:21: "The Lord giveth and the Lord taketh away." Also used in the Anglican funeral rite. *sable gender:* black offspring.

So they loved as° love in twain, *that*
Had the essence but in one,
Two distincts, division none:
Number there in love was slain.[9]

Hearts remote,° yet not asunder; *separate*
Distance and no space was seen
Twixt this Turtle and his queen:
But in them it were a wonder.[1]

So° between them love did shine *So much*
That the Turtle saw his right° *due; possession; nature*
Flaming in the Phoenix' sight;° *eyes; appearance*
Either was the other's mine.° *self; wealth*

Property was thus appalled
That the self was not the same:[2]
Single nature's double name,[3]
Neither two nor one was called.

Reason in itself confounded° *thoroughly destroyed*
Saw division grow together;
To themselves yet either neither,[4]
Simple were so well compounded,[5]

That it cried, "How true a twain
Seemeth this concordant one!
Love hath reason, reason none,
If what parts can so remain."[6]

Whereupon it made this threne[7]
To the Phoenix and the Dove,
Co-supremes° and stars of love, *Joint rulers*
As chorus to their tragic scene.

*Threnos*

Beauty, truth, and rarity,
Grace in all simplicity,
Here enclosed, in cinders lie.

9. The stanza toys with the commonplace paradox of lovers' simultaneous unity and separateness, ending with the hyperbolic claim that being neither one nor two, the love of the phoenix and the turtle killed the very notion of "number" (line 28).
1. It would have seemed extraordinary in any creatures but them.
2. The notion of an essential self was thus weakened by the fact that the self was not identical to itself.
3. An indivisible essence with two separate names. Textual Comment For the different possible meanings of the line, depending on how one punctuates it, see Digital Edition TC 2.
4. Saw separate entities paradoxically become one, but each one was neither single nor united. *division*: things divided.
5. Single elements were so perfectly combined (appearing to remain "simple" rather than "compounded").
6. Love represents a higher reason than reason itself because of this embodiment of the paradox of unity of separate elements.
7. Reason made this threnody (a mourning song or epitaph).

Death is now the Phoenix' nest,[8]
And the Turtle's loyal breast
To eternity doth rest.[9]

Leaving no posterity,
'Twas not their infirmity:° *sterility*
It was married chastity.

Truth may seem, but cannot be;
Beauty brag but 'tis not she:[1]
Truth and beauty buried be.

To this urn let those repair° *go*
That are either true or fair:
For these dead birds sigh a prayer.

8. The phoenix's nest, ordinarily a site of regeneration, is finally a place of death; alternatively, the regenerative qualities of the phoenix's nest will overcome death.

9. Rests eternally; endures forever.

1. Any appearances of fidelity or beauty will only be illusions.

# The Sonnets

Shakespeare's plays often seem indifferent to high-cultural rules of construction. His sonnets (composed from about 1592 to 1604, possibly revised thereafter, and published in 1609) are the opposite: they belong to an international tradition inspired by the fourteenth-century Italian poet Petrarch. The very strictness of sonnet structure provides the basis for originality. The form's fixed length of fourteen lines, rigorous rhyme scheme, and relatively unvarying metrical structure encourage a logical approach to the standard topic of the Renaissance sonnet—love and its emotions (desire, jealousy, etc.). In Shakespeare, the conflict between passionate feelings and an intellect often skeptical of those feelings becomes a central theme of the poems. And that skepticism is conveyed through a linguistic virtuosity marked by metaphors and puns (only a fraction of which are identified in the notes) that work both with and against the larger structure of the sonnet.

Thematically, the sonnets are equally distinctive. The typical object of love—the unapproachable lady—is replaced by a daring representation of homoerotic and adulterous passions. Almost the entire sequence can be divided along these lines. Sonnets 1–126 recount the speaker's initially idealized but sometimes painful love for a femininely beautiful, well-born male youth; 127–152 discuss his unidealized, ultimately bitter affair with a darkly attractive, unaristocratic "mistress"—where this term invokes, ironically, courtly love rather than the derogatory modern meaning. The two love relationships are complicated by a lovers' triangle (40–42, 133–134, 144) and a poetic rival for the youth's affections (78–80, 82–86). These topics provide the occasion for meditation upon time, nature, mortality, economics, perhaps class and race, and, not least, artistic immortality.

The poems may be approached by locating their formal specificity within the sonnet tradition. The Petrarchan version ends in "feminine rhyme"—a stressed syllable followed by an unstressed one, both of which must rhyme with one or more other line endings. English offers possibilities ("mother-brother," "wonder-thunder"); but in Shakespeare and most other English Renaissance sonneteers, feminine rhyme is rare. The tendency is to stick to ten-syllable iambic pentameter lines and hence to conclude on a stressed syllable, usually a monosyllabic word. This preference may indicate a conventional difference between the treatment of rhymed and unrhymed poetry. In the second half of his career, Shakespeare frequently resorted to feminine endings in blank verse but not in rhyme. Yet the aversion to feminine rhyme is also rooted in the English language, where the erosion of word endings increased the percentage of monosyllabic words and reduced the opportunities of rhyme, especially of polysyllabic rhyme. Feminine rhyme can sound sing-song or comical—hence, its use in limericks.

Shakespeare does, however, occasionally rhyme polysyllabic words on their secondary stress:

> Not marble nor the gilded monuments
> Of princes shall outlive this powerful rhyme,
> But you shall shine more bright in these contents
> Than unswept stone besmeared with sluttish time.
> (55.1–4)

Here, Shakespeare is after the durability, the immortality of his art. Subsequent rhyme words in the sonnet include "overturn," "masonry," "memory," "enmity," and "posterity" (lines 5, 6, 8, 9, 11). The rhymes' stately sound effects reinforce the sonnet's semantic thrust.

The structure of English also helps explain Shakespeare's rhyme scheme. The Petrarchan sonnet is divided into two frequently contrasting units, an octave (eight lines) and a sestet (six lines), by its rhymes—*abbaabba* (rarely varied) *cdcdcd* (often varied), where each letter represents a line and a repeated letter indicates a rhyme. The Petrarchan mode reached England by the early sixteenth century in the works of Thomas Wyatt and Henry Howard, Earl of Surrey, the latter of whom pioneered the modified rhyme scheme later taken over by Shakespeare (*abab cdcd efef gg*). Because English is a relatively rhyme-poor language, there are more rhyme sounds in the Shakespearean sonnet—seven rather than Petrarch's four or five. Thus, Shakespeare never has to find more than two words that rhyme on a given sound, whereas Petrarch needs up to four.

The Shakespearean rhyme scheme divides the sonnet into three quatrains (four-line groupings) and a couplet. This organization offers greater conceptual range than does Petrarch's. The quatrains can operate in parallel, represent steps in an argument, or contradict each other. They may be grouped into larger units of eight-and-four lines or eight-and-six (if the couplet is included) that are set against each other. In turn, the epigrammatic concluding couplet, whose conceptual tendencies contrast with the more experiential approach of at least the first two quatrains, can summarize, generalize, draw appropriate inferences, contribute a new thought, or even reverse the preceding argument.

Sonnet structure often guides Shakespeare's pervasive use of imagery and metaphor. In Sonnet 73, each quatrain pursues a different metaphor as part of a single argument:

> That time of year thou mayst in me behold
> When yellow leaves, or none, or few do hang
> Upon those boughs which shake against the cold,
> Bare ruined choirs where late the sweet birds sang.
> In me thou seest the twilight of such day
> As after sunset fadeth in the west,
> Which by and by black night doth take away,
> Death's second self that seals up all in rest.
> In me thou seest the glowing of such fire
> That on the ashes of his youth doth lie,
> As the deathbed whereon it must expire,
> Consumed with that which it was nourished by.
>     This thou perceiv'st, which makes thy love more strong,
>     To love that well which thou must leave ere long.

The evocation of fall in the opening quatrain nostalgically communicates the sadness of aging. Enjambment supports the imagistic pattern: it causes meaning to "hang" in the balance at the end of the line, just as "yellow leaves . . . do hang / Upon those boughs." The "yellow leaves" are also leaves of a book, "bare ruined choirs," or quires (manuscript gatherings). Similarly, the birds' former song, together with the primary meaning of "choirs" (the part of a church where the choir sings), may refer to the speaker's own voice and hence to a lost poetic creativity. In short, aging is compared to the annual movement toward colder seasons and to the decline of artistic inspiration. In the second quatrain, duration constricts: "That time of year" is replaced by "the twilight of such day." Although, like autumn, sunset is a natural process, it is not organic. Emphasis accordingly shifts away from bodily degeneration. These lines also look forward, unlike the first quatrain. Twilight is taken away by "black night . . . , / Death's second self that seals up all in rest." Nighttime rest brings comfort, but night is compared with death, and the syntax, at odds with the literal meaning, suggests that it is death rather than night "that seals up all in [eternal] rest."

The third quatrain opens like the second, with "In me thou seest," a phrase also partly anticipated in the poem's opening line. This repetition reinforces the parallelism among the quatrains: the poem proceeds less by narrative progression than by thematic variation. This quatrain, highlighting the transition from aging to mortality, narrows time further, to the "glowing" fire (line 9), thereby abandoning the previous temporal model for a spatial metaphor. Only ashes remain from the fire's and the speaker's "youth" (line 10); they are also the fire's and the speaker's "deathbed" (line 11). Although the fire of old age no longer rages, it is still "glowing." The present thus continues the past. Furthermore, the metaphorical relationship becomes reciprocal. The dying fire is a metaphor for aging, but aging is a metaphor for the dying fire.

The fire is "[c]onsumed with that which it was nourished by"; it is "consumed" (or choked) by—and along with—the ashes that, as fuel, previously "nourished" it. Normally, the fire consumes the fuel, not the other way around. Both "consumed" and "nourished" metaphorically explain the already metaphorical fire, which their allusions to eating connect to humanity. The speaker's fiery passion for the youth he addresses nourished him when he was young but consumes him now. The line structurally enacts this tacit rejection of temporal decline. It is an example of chiasmus, in which the elements of the first half ("Consumed . . . that") are repeated in reverse order in the second ("which . . . nourished"), thus producing an *abba* semantic pattern. Accordingly, this quatrain does not echo the earlier "cold" or "night" metaphorically responsible for the approach of death. Life and death have the same source.

All three quatrains use cyclical metaphors of life, death, and rebirth. But the cycle remains incomplete. Autumn does not lead to spring or night to day. The "long-lived phoenix" (19.4), the self-resurrecting bird that dies in flames and is reborn from the ashes, doesn't appear. Perhaps these suppressed allusions to cyclical patterns raise, then frustrate expectations, denying the consolation of the future. The concluding couplet, which abandons metaphor for a new idea, suggests this interpretation. Recognizing the speaker's passion makes the youth's "love more strong" (line 13). The youth, therefore, loves "well" what he "must leave ere long" (line 14)—explicitly, the speaker; implicitly, his own life, partly because what he "must leave" recalls the earlier "yellow leaves." The destructive power of time is only partly counteracted by love.

Sonnet 73 suggests how conformity to sonnet convention can enable a thoughtful interplay among time, love, death, and art. But Sonnet 81 offers a radical disjunction of syntax and rhyme scheme: almost any two consecutive lines can produce a complete sentence, depending on how you punctuate:

> And toungs to be, your beeing shall rehearse,
> When all the breathers of this world are dead,
> You still shall liue (such vertue hath my Pen).
> (81.11–13)

This three-line sequence, presented as it appears in the first edition, the Quarto of 1609, runs over the end of a quatrain but nonetheless produces two possible sentences (lines 11–12 or 12–13). The unorthodox move is the implicit equation of the speaker with his social superior, the youth. The poet's literary prowess promises enduring renown for both writer and subject matter. Or does it? If you take lines 11 and 12 together, as modern editions do, the emphasis falls on "dead." But if you connect lines 12 and 13, "liue" and "my Pen" are emphasized. The poem thus promises both death and immortality, just as "rehearse" (line 11) predicts a future where the youth is still spoken about and re-hearsed.

The relationship between formal and thematic innovation can also be approached by considering the sonnets as a sequence. English enthusiasm for such sequences was triggered by the posthumous printing of Philip Sidney's *Astrophel and Stella* (1591). Sonnets also circulated in manuscript, since print was often considered undignified by (would-be) gentlemen or courtier-poets. The vogue for sonnet sequences responded to poets' ambitions as well as to the gender politics of the late Elizabethan court. Middle-class writers sought financial assistance for their work by praising their aristocratic patrons. Expressions of love may be less indications of deep feeling than competitive strategies of advancement. Shakespeare's "rival poet" sonnets seem to convert this competition into a literary theme. It is thus often hard to determine where sentiment ends and calculation begins.

Further, given uncertainties about Shakespeare's role in the publication of the sonnets, their ordering may or may not represent the poet's final intent. (See the Textual Introduction.) It is also easy to overstate the internal organization of the sonnets as we have them. The division of the sequence into two main groups is arguably unwarranted. Most of the poems are not explicitly about either the youth or the mistress, not even designating the sex of the person discussed. Only their relative position in the collection has produced the standard simplification adopted here. Furthermore, the sequence as a whole is relatively uninterested in plot. The poems to the mistress in particular show little organization or process, combining occasional affection with frequent disgust. Perhaps, in 1609, they had not yet been placed in a particular order; perhaps they were intended for a separate collection. But the first 126 sonnets, too, evince only intermittent interest in linear movement, anticipating both the desire and the anguish of the subsequent poems.

Nonetheless, many of the sonnets *are* ordered in pairs or longer groups. The lovers' triangle and rival poet sonnets, noted above, are examples. Others are identified in the notes. More important, the two main sections of the sequence are thematically compelling. For the two centuries ending a generation ago, the homoerotic attachment to the youth, now routine in critical discussion, provoked revulsion or denial. Sonnet 20 was—and still is—the center of the debate:

> A woman's face with Nature's own hand painted
> Hast thou, the master-mistress of my passion;
> A woman's gentle heart, but not acquainted
> With shifting change as is false women's fashion;
> An eye more bright than theirs, less false in rolling,
> Gilding the object whereupon it gazeth;
> A man in hue, all hues in his controlling,
> Which steals men's eyes and women's souls amazeth.
> And for a woman wert thou first created,
> Till Nature as she wrought thee fell a-doting,
> And by addition me of thee defeated
> By adding one thing to my purpose nothing.
>    But since she pricked thee out for women's pleasure,
>    Mine be thy love, and thy love's use their treasure.

Nature originally intended the youth to be female (the octave). But she fell in love with her creation and hence made him a man, a change that benefited her but forced the speaker to limit himself to love without sexual consummation (the sestet). The poem plays with gender boundaries—"master-mistress," "A woman's face," "one thing" (a penis), "A man in hue" (further sexualized if "hue" was pronounced like "you"; lines 2, 1, 12, 7). "Acquainted" and "controlling" pun on "cunt"; "nothing" and "treasure" also refer to the female sexual organ (lines 3, 7, 12, 14). As someone "pricked . . . out for women's pleasure" (line 13), the youth can both give and receive women's pleasure (be "pricked"). Moreover, this is the only sonnet in which all the rhymes have feminine endings—a thematically resonant stylistic joke. Finally, the poem's misogynistic complaint about "false" women (lines 4, 5) is consistent with its homoeroticism. Women are resented because the speaker prefers the youth, and because they can enjoy "love's use," while he gets only "love" (line 14)—where "love" carries both its

Renaissance meaning of "friendship" and its modern sense of romantic and sexual desire.

Sonnet 20 looks forward to poems that express erotic love for the youth, apparently without sexual fulfillment. But it also looks back to the opening seventeen sonnets, in which the speaker urges the youth to marry and produce an heir. The speaker solicits the youth's love for someone else, since the point is procreation and, therefore, immortality comparable to the artistic immortality promised later in the sequence. The exhortation cuts against both the love sonnet's conventional aspirations and the speaker's unconventional aim of winning the youth. But this is because the multiple possible meanings of "love" in Sonnet 20 generally characterize the poems to the youth.

"Thy beauty's form in table of my heart" (24.2). Here a man is holding a "table" (tablet) in front of his heart while another man engraves the first man's portrait on it. From Geffrey Whitney, *A Choice of Emblems* (1586).

How the case for marriage is argued in the early sonnets is instructive. Shakespeare's reversal of the metaphorical relationship in Sonnet 73, it will be recalled, removes any fixed point of reference. A comparable reversal also marks economic imagery of the initial sonnets, and beyond. As in Sonnet 20 (line 14), that imagery frequently turns on usury. Long denounced, Renaissance English usury was beginning its conversion into the respectable financial category of interest. Shakespeare shared the prevailing dislike of making money out of money. The speaker condemns his mistress for her affair with the young man, represented as collecting a debt:

> The statute of thy beauty thou wilt take—
> Thou usurer that putt'st forth all to use.
> (134.9–10)

She will "take" the "statute of" her "beauty"—what's owed to her financially (sexually)—because, like a "usurer," she employs "all" her wealth (her body) for profit (where "use" means "engage in usury" and "engage in sexual activity"). Elsewhere, ambivalently, the youth is criticized as, paradoxically, both "unthrifty" and a "niggard" (4.1, 5):

> Profitless usurer, why dost thou use
> So great a sum of sums, yet canst not live?
> (4.7–8)

Here, "use" antithetically means "use up" and "lend at interest." Literally, how can the youth lend vast "sums" for profit and be poor? Metaphorically, he acts in a "profitless" manner in wasting his personal endowments. Hence, he cannot "live" on in his children. By implication, a usurer is valueless.

But the lines also imagine the opposite. A profitless usurer implies a profitable one. This good usurer predominates elsewhere:

> That use is not forbidden usury
> Which happies those that pay the willing loan.
> (6.5–6)

Is all, or just unallowable, usury "forbidden"? Keeping one's "treasure" to oneself merits only "thriftless praise"; "beauty's use" deserves "much more praise" if a child results (2.6–9). At least "an unthrift" allows the world to enjoy his wealth; "beauty's waste" is indefensible—"kept unused the user so destroys it" (9.9–12). And Sonnet 20 ends, as we've seen, with the speaker getting the youth's love, whereas the "treasure" women enjoy is merely the "use" (metaphorically, children) of that love. He obtains the principal, they the interest. These passages activate metaphorical meanings of "use" to promote marriage and family. In so doing, they connect the proper use of beauty with usury, which is understood as the economic equivalent of human reproduction, the early sonnets' highest ideal. Neofeudal celebration of traditional lineage smuggles in economic behavior destructive of tradition. Usury becomes potentially noble. Through metaphor, Shakespeare entertains ideas that were less accessible as bald statements.

The poems to the speaker's mistress are also unconventional—in depicting sordid adultery with an unfaithful woman marked by passionate desire and recrimination. Even serene sonnets in this section undermine convention:

> My mistress' eyes are nothing like the sun;
> . . . . . . . . . . . . . . . . . . . . . . . . . . . . . . . .
> And yet, by heaven, I think my love as rare
> As any she belied with false compare.
> (130.1, 13–14)

The target is standard Petrarchan praise and, more generally, falsely idealizing rhetoric:

> When my love swears that she is made of truth,
> I do believe her though I know she lies,
> . . . . . . . . . . . . . . . . . . . . . . . . . . . . . . . .
> Therefore I lie with her, and she with me,
> And in our faults by lies we flattered be.
> (138.1–2, 13–14)

In Sonnet 130, true love requires the speaker to reject "false compare." In Sonnet 138, love paradoxically requires the speaker to "credit . . . false-speaking," to suppress "simple truth" (lines 7–8), and to embrace "lies." The sequence ends, however, with the disabused deployment of the same rhetoric against speaker and woman alike:

> For I have sworn thee fair—more perjured eye,
> To swear against the truth so foul a lie.
> (152.13–14)

This couplet recalls the opening poem on the mistress:

> In the old age black was not counted fair,
> . . . . . . . . . . . . . . . . . . . . . . . . . . . . . . . .
> But now is black beauty's successive heir.
> (127.1, 3)

Black is the color of the woman's eyes, eyebrows, breasts, hair (127.9–10, 132.3, 130.3–4), and skin:

> Then I will swear beauty herself is black,
> And all they foul that thy complexion lack.
> (132.13–14)

This anticonventional praise of blackness echoes the biblical Song of Songs as well as sixteenth-century Continental and English poetry, including Sidney's. The praise is often inseparable from misogynistic denunciation of cosmetics' artificial beauty (127.4–12). Black hair and eyes gained prestige in the 1590s through a shift in fashion. Thus, the speaker's views accord with broader social change.

The mistress's color may or may not be racialized, since dark skin might merely distinguish her from falsely idealized women or aristocratic ladies who avoided the sun. Nonetheless, *Titus Andronicus*, *Othello*, *Antony and Cleopatra*, and *The Tempest* feature actual or threatened interracial coupling. The mistress's blackness and promiscuity may thus provoke desire and fear of exotic female sexuality. Blackness accordingly moves from paradox to cliché: "In nothing art thou black save in thy deeds" (131.13); "For I have sworn thee fair, and thought thee bright, / Who art as black as hell, as dark as night" (147.13–14). Like usury, then, blackness oscillates between convention and innovation. Such is the case with the sonnets generally.

Finally, the intense emotion associated with the "I" of the sonnets, the psychological complexity with which that emotion is scrutinized, the unconventional subject matter, the sense that one is overhearing snatches of conversation, the first-person speaker, that speaker's self-conscious identification with Shakespeare (135 and 136)—all encourage biographical interpretation. For two centuries, such interpretation has proven risky to undertake—or to avoid. Scholars have failed to discover the real people whom Shakespeare presumably discusses but does not name. (See the Textual Introduction.) This outcome led mid-twentieth-century critics to focus on formal concerns. But the resulting advances often entailed evading the biographical material that the poems seem to provide. Shakespeare's sonnets, like his plays, combine verbal artistry and conceptual unorthodoxy with psychological exploration. Their special fascination, however, is that the soul they examine may be Shakespeare's own.

Walter Cohen

## SELECTED BIBLIOGRAPHY

Booth, Stephen, ed. *Shakespeare's Sonnets*. New Haven, CT: Yale UP, 1977. Provides the 1609 Quarto of the sonnets and a modernized version, with a commentary detailing multiple overlapping structures within individual sonnets, structures that expand possible meaning without cohering into a unified whole.

Dubrow, Heather. *Echoes of Desire: English Petrarchism and Its Counterdiscourses*. Ithaca, NY: Cornell UP, 1995. 119–34. Argues that Shakespeare's sonnets both follow many Petrarchan conventions and, especially beginning with Sonnet 127, challenge those conventions as well.

Empson, William. *Some Versions of Pastoral*. London: Chatto & Windus, 1935. 89–101. Shows, in a classic close reading, that the ironies of Sonnet 94 result in complex, multiple meanings that center on the speaker advocating a hypocritical, but dangerous, Machiavellianism on the part of the youth.

Flesch, William. "Personal Identity and Vicarious Experience in Shakespeare's Sonnets." *A Companion to Shakespeare's Sonnets*. Ed. Michael Schoenfeldt. Malden, MA: Blackwell, 2007. 383–401. Investigates the poems' account of the limitations of one's access to another's subjectivity through discussion of the sonnets' elusive descriptions of the youth, appeals to the youth's vanity, and emphasis on our vicarious interest in others.

Gregerson, Linda. "Open Voicing: Wyatt and Shakespeare." *The Oxford Handbook of Shakespeare's Poetry*. Ed. Jonathan F. S. Post. Oxford: Oxford UP, 2013. 151–67. Traces to Wyatt's lyrics a discontinuous subjectivity that produces psychological complexity and is then taken up by Shakespeare in his sonnets and plays.

Halpern, Richard. *Shakespeare's Perfume: Sodomy and Sublimity in the Sonnets, Wilde, Freud, and Lacan*. Philadelphia: U of Pennsylvania P, 2002. 11–31. Links sodomy, aesthetics, sublimation, and the sublime.

Kalas, Rayna. *Frame, Glass, Verse: The Technology of Poetic Invention in the English Renaissance*. Ithaca, NY: Cornell UP, 2007. 166–98. Finds in the sonnets a craft of poetic production tied to contemporary production in glass—the mirror, window, and hourglass—and thereby also to matters of property and social status.

Schoenfeldt, Michael. "The Sonnets." *The Cambridge Companion to Shakespeare's Poetry.* Ed. Patrick Cheney. Cambridge: Cambridge UP, 2007. 125–43. Presents an overview of the sonnets, emphasizing erotic and emotional desire, its frustration, and the limited resources (progeny, poetry) for mitigating the ravages of time.

Trevor, Douglas. "Shakespeare's Love Objects." *A Companion to Shakespeare's Sonnets.* Ed. Michael Schoenfeldt. Malden, MA: Blackwell, 2007. 225–41. Proposes that Shakespeare rejects transcendence and places his faith less in the objects of his love than in his poetic creation.

Vendler, Helen. *The Art of Shakespeare's Sonnets.* Cambridge: Belknap P, 1997. Offers a detailed sonnet-by-sonnet interpretation, focusing on formal considerations, together with the 1609 Quarto and a modernized version of the text, as well as a CD-ROM of Vendler reading the poems.

## TEXTUAL INTRODUCTION

On May 20, 1609, the publisher Thomas Thorpe entered "Shakespeares sonnetts" in the Stationers' Register. The Quarto (Q) was printed in the same year by George Eld, the only edition until John Benson's *Poems* (1640). Along with 154 sonnets, Q includes the separately titled "A Lover's Complaint," also identified as "by William Shakespeare." Thirteen surviving copies preserve two states, some identifying John Wright and others William Aspley as bookseller.

The size and prominence of "SHAKE-SPEARES SONNETS" on the title page suggest the value Thorpe placed on the writer's name as advertising copy, but it is not clear if Q was printed with Shakespeare's consent or knowledge. Shakespeare provided dedicatory epistles for *Venus and Adonis* and *The Rape of Lucrece* but not for the sonnets. Thorpe set his own initials to a stylized dedication on the second leaf, visually reminiscent of a monument inscription: "TO.THE.ONLIE.BEGETTER.OF.THESE.INSVING. SONNETS. M$^{r}$. W. H."

The present edition emends Thorpe's dedication, accepting scholarly arguments that the "only begetter" is meant to be Shakespeare and "M$^{r}$. W. H." in Q is a misprint for "M$^{r}$. W. S." (or "SH."). Error is assumed on the grounds that the unexpected letter "H" obscures a straightforward message (Foster, "Master W. H., R.I.P."; see Digital Edition TC 1). A compositor setting type from Thorpe's manuscript epigraph could plausibly have mistaken a malformed "S" for an "h" in secretary hand or a "sh" with indistinct long "s" for "H"—or he could simply have picked up the wrong piece of type. This error could have gone uncorrected in an edition that shows only cursory signs of proofreading. The *H/S* error has a precedent: "*Hyn.*" for "*Syn.*" (the character Sindefy) goes uncorrected in Eld's print shop in the first edition of *Eastward Ho,* published by Aspley and Thorpe in 1605 (sig. C1r).

Efforts to make sense of "M$^{r}$. W. H." have rested on insecure premises. Although poems as author's progeny is a standard trope, most current interpretations associate "the only begetter" with the young man of Sonnets 1–126. Often, they gloss over the unlikeliness of a complimentary address to a nobleman (the earls of Pembroke and Southampton being leading contenders) omitting "the right honorable . . . Earl of . . ." and substituting "M[aster]," a form of respectful address appropriate to no rank higher than gentleman or esquire. Indeed, in 1610 and 1616 Thorpe addressed dedications to the Earl of Pembroke using his titles and elaborately deferential language. In contrast, when respectful admirers praised Shakespeare in poems accompanying the 1623 First Folio, "Master" was the address term they chose.

Questions remain about the extent of Thorpe's or an intermediary's editorial intervention. We cannot be sure if the manuscript he acquired consisted of a single sequence in the Quarto's order, nor do we know whether Shakespeare capped his sonnets with "A Lover's Complaint" or Thorpe filled out a short volume with the narrative poem. The authorship of "A Lover's Complaint" remains in doubt.

Date and time span of composition are uncertain. External evidence establishes that some sonnets were extant in the 1590s. In 1599, Sonnets 138 and 144 were printed in *The Passionate Pilgrim*. In 1598, Francis Meres's *Palladis Tamia* mentioned Shakespeare's "sugared Sonnets among his private friends," suggesting that some had circulated in manuscript. However, while over twenty existing manuscripts include Shakespeare sonnets or excerpts, these generally date ca. 1620–60 and derive from the 1609 Quarto or the 1640 edition. Research comparing linguistic elements like rare vocabulary with phases of Shakespeare's corpus provides a speculative chronology for composition and possible revision of discrete sonnet groupings (Jackson, "Vocabulary"). The final "mistress" grouping, 127–154, is likely the earliest written (ca. 1592–95); the concluding group to the youth (104–126) probably latest (ca. 1598–1604). The mid-1590s (ca. 1594–96) is the likeliest period for other "young man" sonnets (1–103), with the "marriage" subgroup (1–17) sometimes dated earlier and the "rival poet" sonnets (78–80, 82–86) later.

Scribal copy almost certainly served as the copy-text, placing Q at least two removes from an authorial manuscript. A recurring error in Q ("their" printed for "thy") evidently derives from the manuscript copy. Not replicated elsewhere in Shakespeare's canon, it is not attributable to his handwriting; nor to compositor idiosyncrasy, given MacDonald P. Jackson's demonstration ("Punctuation") that at least two compositors worked on Q, both setting "their" for "thy." Jackson identified distinctive spelling and punctuation patterns for each compositor. For example, Compositor B preferred "O" rather than "Oh" spellings in interjections and punctuated 53 percent of third quatrain endings with full stops, while Compositor A used "Oh" exclusively and closed quatrain 3 with heavier punctuation (70 percent full stop).

This modernized edition preserves only the more significant of Q's features. While Elizabethan spellings may suggest puns unavailable in modern spelling, Q reflects compositorial rather than authorial spelling. In contrast to Q's heavy line-end punctuation, Hand D of *Sir Thomas More* (possibly Shakespeare's) exhibits virtually no line-end punctuation but moderate mid-line punctuation, usually commas marking caesuras or intonation shifts. Some mid-line commas in Q may serve these functions but do not invariably produce credible readings. On the principle that some Shakespeare sonnets tend to reflection and longer sentence or utterance units, while others are strongly dramatic or dialogic, this edition introduces more short sentences in the latter (e.g., 58.9–12).

Q is attuned to prosody, using apostrophe for poetic elision. Its use of capitals and italics is not systematic. In 135 and 136, these devices cue punning on the name "Will," but capital letters only sometimes signal personification, and this edition uses capitals only for sustained personification. Finally, Q's readings are retained in some cases where editorial tradition has favored emendation (e.g., "steeled" 24.1, "worth" 25.9, "there" 31.8, "loss" 34.12, "by" 54.14). In other cases, this edition reinterprets Q by repunctuating (e.g., 6.9, 16.12, 51.11, 131.9, 142.7).

LYNNE MAGNUSSON

## TEXTUAL BIBLIOGRAPHY

Foster, Donald W. "Master W. H., R.I.P." *PMLA* 102 (1987): 42–54.

Jackson, MacDonald P. "Punctuation and the Compositors of Shakespeare's *Sonnets*, 1609." *Library* 5th ser. 30 (1975): 1–24.

———. "Vocabulary and Chronology: The Case of Shakespeare's Sonnets." *Review of English Studies* n.s. 52 (2001): 59–75.

# Sonnets

**TO.THE.ONLY.BEGETTER.OF.**
**THESE.ENSUING.SONNETS.**
**M$^{r}$. W. [S.][1] ALL.HAPPINESS.**
**AND.THAT.ETERNITY.**
**PROMISED.**
**BY.**
**OUR.EVER-LIVING.POET.[2]**
**WISHETH.**
**THE.WELL-WISHING.**
**ADVENTURER.°IN.** *(as in a sea voyage)*
**SETTING.**
**FORTH.**

T. T.[3]

**1**

From fairest creatures° we desire increase,° *living things / offspring*
That° thereby beauty's rose[1] might never die, *So that*
But as the riper should by time decease
His tender heir[2] might bear his memory.° *(in his look)*
But thou, contracted° to thine own bright eyes, *engaged; reduced*
Feed'st thy light's flame with self-substantial fuel,[3]
Making a famine where abundance lies,
Thyself thy foe, to thy sweet self too cruel.
Thou, that art now the world's fresh° ornament *young*
And only herald to the gaudy° spring, *ornate*
Within thine own bud buriest thy content° *offspring; happiness*
And, tender churl,° mak'st waste in niggarding.° *young old miser / (paradox)*
 Pity the world,° or else this glutton be, *Have a child*
 To eat the world's due, by the grave and thee.[4]

**2**

When forty winters shall besiege thy brow
And dig deep trenches° in thy beauty's field, *wrinkles*
Thy youth's proud livery,° so gazed on now, *uniform; appearance*

**Dedication**

1. Textual Comment The identity of the Quarto's W. H. has generated much speculation. For the interpretation of the initials as a misprint for "W. S." or "W. SH." (William Shakespeare), see the Textual Introduction and Digital Edition TC 1.
2. Textual Comment Perhaps God, literally "ever-living," who promises eternity to Shakespeare (if "W. H." refers to Shakespeare); or perhaps Shakespeare, who promises "eternity" to the young man. See Digital Edition TC 1.
3. Thomas Thorpe, the printer, is the "well-wishing adventurer."

**Sonnet 1**

1. In Q, "rose," unlike most other nouns, is always capitalized (35.2; 54.3, 6, 11; 67.8; 95.2; 98.10; 99.8; 109.14; and 130.5, 6). Here, in Q, it is also italicized. These printing conventions, combined with the placement of the word near the beginning of the first sonnet and its frequent repetition thereafter, suggest that "rose" is the poet's name for the object of his desire, on the model of, for instance, Stella in Sidney's influential sonnet sequence *Astrophel and Stella* (published 1591). The rose had long been associated with female genitalia, most notably in the thirteenth-century French narrative poem *The Romance of the Rose,* by Guillaume de Lorris and Jean de Meun. In Shakespeare's case, however, the object of desire is male. He is most frequently referred to as "youth," almost never as "boy" or "man." Shakespeare's "mistress" is later contrasted with "roses" (130.5, 6).
2. The rose's (that is, the youth's) young child.
3. Are consuming yourself like a candle.
4. *or else . . . thee:* otherwise you'll be a glutton by causing your posterity, which is due to the world, to be consumed both by the grave and within yourself.

Will be a tattered weed° of small worth held. *clothing; plant*
Then being asked where all thy beauty lies,
Where all the treasure of thy lusty days,
To say within thine own deep-sunken eyes
Were an all-eating shame and thriftless praise.[1]
How much more praise deserved thy beauty's use[2]
If thou couldst answer, "This fair child of mine
Shall sum my count and make my old excuse,"[3]
Proving his beauty by succession thine.° *inherited from you*
This were° to be new made when thou art old *would be*
And see thy blood warm when thou feel'st it cold.

## 3

Look in thy glass,° and tell the face thou viewest, *mirror; hourglass (?)*
Now is the time that face should form another,
Whose° fresh repair,° if now thou not renewest, *(the face's) / state; (pun on "pair")*
Thou dost beguile° the world, unbless° some mother. *swindle / leave childless*
For where is she so fair whose uneared° womb *unplowed; unheired*
Disdains the tillage of thy husbandry?[1]
Or who is he so fond will be the tomb
Of his self-love to stop posterity?[2]
Thou art thy mother's glass, and she in thee
Calls back the lovely April of her prime;
So thou through windows of thine age[3] shalt see,
Despite of wrinkles, this thy golden time.° *youth*
But if thou live remembered not to be,[4]
Die single, and thine image dies with thee.

## 4

Unthrifty loveliness, why dost thou spend
Upon thyself thy beauty's legacy?[1]
Nature's bequest gives nothing but doth lend,
And being frank she lends to those are free.[2]
Then, beauteous niggard, why dost thou abuse
The bounteous largesse given thee to give?
Profitless usurer, why dost thou use° *lend for profit; spend*
So great a sum of sums, yet canst not live?[3]
For having traffic° with thyself alone, *(commercial); (sexual)*
Thou of thyself thy sweet self dost deceive.° *defraud (of offspring)*
Then how, when nature calls thee to be gone—
What acceptable audit canst thou leave?
Thy unused[4] beauty must be tombed with thee,
Which usèd lives th'executor to be.

**Sonnet 2**
1. Would be an all-consuming shame and praise that brings no profit.
2. How much more would the use (employment; investment or usurious lending) of your beauty merit.
3. Shall make my accounts balance and defend (or absolve) me in my age.

**Sonnet 3**
1. Cultivation; acting as a husband.
2. *who . . . posterity:* who is so foolish that he will selfishly deny posterity a child?
3. Eyes weakened by old age; your children.
4. But if you live to be forgotten.

**Sonnet 4**
1. *legacy:* both from your parents and to your children.
2. And being generous, she lends to those who (also) are generous.
3. Make a living; live on in your children.
4. Not put to use; not interest-bearing.

## 5

Those hours that with gentle work did frame° *form*
The lovely gaze° where every eye° doth dwell *face / (pun on "I"?)*
Will play the tyrants to the very same
And that unfair which fairly doth excel.[1]
For never-resting time leads summer on
To hideous winter and confounds him° there, *destroys summer*
Sap checked with frost and lusty leaves quite gone,
Beauty o'er-snowed and bareness everywhere.
Then were not summer's distillation left
A liquid prisoner pent in walls of glass,
Beauty's effect with beauty were bereft,[2]
Nor° it nor no remembrance what it was. *Neither*
  But flowers distilled, though they with winter meet,
  Lose[3] but their show; their substance still lives sweet.

## 6[1]

Then let not winter's ragged° hand deface[2] *rough*
In thee thy summer ere thou be distilled.° *(in children)*
Make sweet some vial;° treasure° thou some place *womb / enrich*
With beauty's treasure ere it be self-killed.
That use° is not forbidden usury *lending for profit*
Which happies those that pay the willing loan:[3]
That's for thyself° to breed another thee, *So you would do*
Or ten times happier, be it ten for one.° *1,000 percent interest*
Ten times thyself were happier than thou art:
If ten of thine ten times refigured° thee, *copied*
Then what could death do if thou shouldst depart,
Leaving thee living in posterity?
  Be not self-willed,[4] for thou art much too fair
  To be death's conquest and make worms thine heir.

## 7

Lo, in the orient° when the gracious light° *East / sun*
Lifts up his burning head, each under° eye *earthly*
Doth homage to his new-appearing sight,
Serving with looks his sacred majesty;
And having climbed the steep-up heavenly hill,
Resembling strong youth in his middle age,° *noon*
Yet mortal looks adore his beauty still,
Attending on his golden pilgrimage.
But when from highmost pitch with weary car° *sun god's chariot*
Like feeble age he reeleth from the day,
The eyes, fore duteous, now converted° are *turned away*
From his low tract° and look another way. *path*

**Sonnet 5**
1. Will make unattractive that which now excels in beauty.
2. *Then . . . bereft:* Then if there were no perfume distilled from flowers bottled in glass vials, both beauty and its effect would be lost. *pent:* (with pun on "penned").
3. Q has "Leese," thus allowing a pun on "lease." See 13.5.

**Sonnet 6**
1. This sonnet links with 5.
2. Disfigure; de-face, through death.
3. Which makes happy those who willingly lend, or who willingly repay the loan with interest (in the form of children).
4. Stubborn; leaving everything in a will to yourself alone.

So thou, thyself outgoing in thy noon,[1]
Unlooked on diest unless thou get° a son.° *beget / (sun)*

## 8

Music to hear,[1] why hear'st thou music sadly?
Sweets° with sweets war not, joy delights in joy. *Sweet things*
Why lov'st thou that which thou receiv'st not gladly,
Or else receiv'st with pleasure thine annoy?° *pun on "ennui" (boredom)*
If the true concord of well-tunèd sounds,
By unions° married, do offend thine ear, *harmony*
They do but sweetly chide thee, who confounds° *destroys*
In singleness the parts[2] that thou shouldst bear.
Mark how one string, sweet husband to another,
Strikes each in each° by mutual ordering, *Resonates*
Resembling sire and child and happy mother,
Who all in one one pleasing note do sing;
Whose speechless° song (being many, seeming one) *The strings' wordless*
Sings this to thee: "Thou single wilt prove none."[3]

## 9

Is it for fear to wet a widow's eye
That thou consum'st thyself in single life?
Ah, if thou issueless° shalt hap to die, *childless*
The world will wail thee like a makeless° wife. *widowed*
The world will be thy widow and still° weep *continually*
That thou no form of thee hast left behind,
When every private° widow well may keep, *individual*
By children's eyes, her husband's shape in mind.
Look what° an unthrift in the world doth spend *Whatever*
Shifts but his° place, for still the world enjoys it; *its*
But beauty's waste hath in the world an end,
And kept unused the user° so destroys it. *spender; lender*
No love toward others in that bosom sits
That on himself such murd'rous shame commits.

## 10

For° shame deny that thou bear'st love to any, *Out of*
Who for thyself art so unprovident.° *not foreseeing the future*
Grant, if thou wilt, thou art beloved of many,
But that thou none lov'st is most evident.
For thou art so possessed with murd'rous hate
That 'gainst thyself thou stick'st not to conspire,° *don't balk at conspiring*
Seeking that beauteous roof° to ruinate *house (family); head*
Which to repair should be thy chief desire.
Oh, change thy thought, that I may change my mind!° *judgment*
Shall hate be fairer lodged than gentle love?
Be as thy presence° is, gracious and kind, *appearance*
Or to thyself at least kind-hearted prove.
Make thee another self for love of me,
That beauty still may live in thine or thee.

**Sonnet 7**
1. Declining from the high point of your youth; going out (like a light).

**Sonnet 8**
1. You whose voice is music.
2. Musical parts; roles as husband and father; children.
3. Without an heir, death will render you nothing (alluding to the proverb "One is no number").

## 11

As fast as thou shalt wane, so fast thou grow'st
In one of thine from that which thou departest,[1]
And that fresh blood which youngly thou bestow'st
Thou mayst call thine when thou from youth convertest.° *turn away*
Herein lives wisdom, beauty, and increase;° *offspring*
Without this, folly, age, and cold decay.
If all were minded so, the times should cease,
And threescore year would make the world away.
Let those whom Nature hath not made for store°— *breeding*
Harsh,° featureless,° and rude°—barrenly perish. *Rough / ugly / unrefined*
Look whom she best endowed she gave the more,[2]
Which bounteous gift thou shouldst in bounty° cherish. *by using bountifully*
  She carved thee for her seal,° and meant thereby *stamp of authority*
  Thou shouldst print more, not let that copy die.

## 12

When I do count the clock° that tells the time, *hours as they strike*
And see the brave° day sunk in hideous night; *fine*
When I behold the violet° past prime *(the flower)*
And sable curls° ensilvered o'er with white; *black hair*
When lofty trees I see barren of leaves,
Which erst° from heat did canopy the herd, *once*
And summer's green, all girded up in sheaves,
Borne on the bier with white and bristly beard;[1]
Then of thy beauty do I question make
That thou among the wastes of time must go,
Since sweets° and beauties do themselves forsake *sweet things*
And die as fast as they see others grow;
  And nothing 'gainst Time's scythe can make defense
  Save breed, to brave him° when he takes thee hence. *children, to defy time*

## 13

Oh, that you were yourself! But, love, you are
No longer yours than you yourself here live.
Against° this coming end you should prepare *For*
And your sweet semblance to some other give.
So should that beauty which you hold in lease
Find no determination.° Then you were° *Never end / would be*
Yourself again after your self's decease,
When your sweet issue your sweet form should bear.
Who lets so fair a house fall to decay,
Which husbandry[1] in honor might uphold
Against the stormy gusts of winter's day
And barren rage of death's eternal cold?
  Oh, none but unthrifts!° Dear my love, you know *spendthrifts*
  You had a father; let your son say so.

**Sonnet 11**
1. *As . . . departest:* As you decline with age, so you become youthful through your child.
2. Nature gave extra reproductive abilities to whomever nature made best-looking. "Best endowed" and "more" allude to Matthew 25:29, the paradoxical parable of the talents: "For unto every man that hath, it shall be given."

**Sonnet 12**
1. *And . . . beard:* And sheaves of mature ("bearded") grain carried away on the harvest cart; old man borne on a funeral bier.

**Sonnet 13**
1. Stewardship; being a husband.

### 14

Not from the stars do I my judgment pluck,
And yet methinks I have astronomy,° *astrological knowledge*
But not to tell of good or evil luck,
Of plagues, of dearths, or seasons' quality;
Nor can I fortune to brief minutes° tell, *precisely*
Pointing to each his thunder, rain, and wind,
Or say with princes if it shall go well
By oft predict° that I in heaven find; *numerous signs*
But from thine eyes my knowledge I derive,
And, constant stars,° in them I read such art *the eyes; (astrological)*
As[1] truth and beauty shall together thrive
If from thyself to store thou wouldst convert[2]—
Or else, of thee this I prognosticate:
Thy end is truth's and beauty's doom and date.° *final judgment and end*

### 15

When I consider every thing that grows
Holds° in perfection but a little moment, *Remains*
That this huge stage presenteth naught but shows
Whereon the stars in secret influence° comment; *(astrologically)*
When I perceive that men as plants increase,
Cheerèd and checked even by the selfsame sky,
Vaunt° in their youthful sap,° at height decrease, *Gloat / strength*
And wear their brave state out of memory;[1]
Then the conceit° of this inconstant stay° *imagination / (on earth)*
Sets you most rich in youth before my sight,
Where wasteful Time debateth° with Decay *competes*
To change your day of youth to sullied night;
And all in war with Time for love of you,
As he takes from you, I engraft you new.[2]

### 16[1]

But wherefore do not you a mightier way
Make war upon this bloody tyrant Time,
And fortify yourself in your decay
With means more blessèd than my barren rhyme?
Now stand you on the top of happy hours,° *in your prime*
And many maiden gardens, yet unset,° *unplanted*
With virtuous wish would bear your living flowers,
Much liker° than your painted counterfeit.° *more like you / portrait*
So should the lines of life that life repair,[2]
Which this time's pencil or my pupil pen[3]
Neither in inward worth nor outward fair° *beauty*
Can make° you. —Live yourself° in eyes of men! *do for / as yourself*

**Sonnet 14**
1. *such art / As:* such predictions as that.
2. If you would provide for the future.

**Sonnet 15**
1. Wear their splendid clothing until they are forgotten (with a sense of "wearing out").
2. *And . . . new:* And I, in competition with time because I love you, restore you to life with (re-plant you via; rejuvenate you by grafting you to) my verse.

**Sonnet 16**
1. This sonnet links with 15.
2. *So . . . repair:* So ought (or would) your appearance (or facial wrinkles, lineage, descendants, palm's life-lines)—in short, living lines, unlike those of poet or painter—restore your life. Or vice versa: "So should" your life restore "the lines of life."
3. *this . . . pen:* today's painters ("pencil" means "paintbrush") nor I, who imitate painting in my verse. TEXTUAL COMMENT For the significance of the punctuation of this line and of line 12, see Digital Edition TC 2.

To give away yourself keeps yourself still,° *(as children)*
And you must live, drawn by your own sweet skill.

### 17

Who will believe my verse in time to come
If it were filled with your most high deserts?
Though yet, heaven knows, it is but as a tomb
Which hides your life and shows not half your parts.° *attributes*
If I could write the beauty of your eyes
And in fresh numbers° number all your graces, *lively verses*
The age to come would say, "This poet lies:
Such heavenly touches ne'er touched earthly faces."
So should my papers, yellowed with their age,
Be scorned, like old men of less truth than tongue,
And your true rights° be termed a poet's rage° *praises / hyperbole*
And stretchèd meter° of an antique song. *overwrought poetry*
But were some child of yours alive that time,
You should live twice—in it and in my rhyme.

### 18

Shall I compare thee to a summer's day?
Thou art more lovely and more temperate.
Rough winds do shake the darling buds of May,
And summer's lease° hath all too short a date. *fixed span of time*
Sometime too hot the eye of heaven shines
And often is his° gold complexion dimmed, *its*
And every fair from fair[1] sometime declines,
By chance or nature's changing course untrimmed.° *rendered ordinary*
But thy eternal summer shall not fade
Nor lose possession of that fair° thou ow'st,° *beauty / own*
Nor shall Death brag thou wand'rest in his shade,
When in eternal lines to time thou grow'st.[2]
So long as men can breathe or eyes can see,
So long lives this, and this gives life to thee.

### 19

Devouring Time, blunt thou the lion's paws,
And make the earth devour° her own sweet brood. *(in death)*
Pluck the keen teeth from the fierce tiger's jaws,
And burn the long-lived phoenix[1] in her blood.° *alive*
Make glad and sorry seasons as thou fleet'st,
And do whate'er thou wilt, swift-footed Time,
To the wide world and all her fading sweets.° *sweet things*
But I forbid thee one most heinous crime:
Oh, carve not with thy hours my love's fair brow,
Nor draw no lines there with thine antique° pen; *old*
Him in thy course untainted do allow
For° beauty's pattern to succeeding men. *As*
Yet do thy worst, old Time. Despite thy wrong,
My love shall in my verse ever live young.

**Sonnet 18**
1. Lovely thing from loveliness.
2. When in immortal poetry you become engrafted to time.

**Sonnet 19**
1. Legendary, self-resurrecting bird believed to live in cycles of several centuries, dying in flames and being reborn from the ashes. See also 73.9–12.

## 20[1]

A woman's face with Nature's own hand° painted *(without cosmetics)*
Hast thou, the master-mistress of my passion;[2]
A woman's gentle heart, but not acquainted° *(pun on "quaint," "cunt")*
With shifting change as is false women's fashion;
An eye more bright than theirs, less false in rolling,° *wandering (sexually)*
Gilding the object whereupon it gazeth;
A man in hue, all hues in his controlling,[3]
Which steals men's eyes and women's souls amazeth.° *overwhelms*
And for° a woman wert thou first created, *to be; to be with*
Till Nature as she wrought thee fell a-doting,° *behaved foolishly*
And by addition me of thee defeated° *cheated me of you*
By adding one thing to my purpose nothing.[4]
  But since she pricked° thee out for women's pleasure,[5] *chose; (sexual)*
  Mine be thy love, and thy love's use their treasure.[6]

## 21

So is it not with me as with that muse° *poet*
Stirred by a painted° beauty to his verse, *(with cosmetics)*
Who° heaven itself for ornament° doth use *(the poet) / poetic imagery*
And every fair with his fair doth rehearse,[1]
Making a couplement of proud compare[2]
With sun and moon, with earth and sea's rich gems,
With April's firstborn flowers and all things rare
That heaven's air in this huge rondure hems.° *globe surrounds*
Oh, let me true in love but truly write,
And then, believe me, my love is as fair
As any mother's child, though not so bright
As those gold candles° fixed in heaven's air. *(the stars)*
  Let them say more that like of hearsay° well; *clichés*
  I will not praise that purpose not° to sell. *since I don't intend*

## 22

My glass° shall not persuade me I am old *mirror*
So long as youth and thou are of one date,° *While you're young*
But when in thee time's furrows I behold,
Then look I° death my days should expiate.° *I expect / conclude*
For all that beauty that doth cover thee
Is but the seemly° raiment of my heart, *fitting*
Which in thy breast doth live as thine in me:
How can I then be elder than thou art?
O therefore, love, be of thyself so wary
As I not for myself but for thee will,[1]

**Sonnet 20**

1. The only sonnet in exclusively feminine rhyme.
2. *master . . . passion:* The hyphenated words designate the youth's feminine looks and position as patron and (homoerotic) sexual mistress. Hence, object or controller of my love or passionate poetry.
3. A man whose looks enable him to attract and dominate all others; a man whose looks encompass all other appearances (both male and female). "Hue" may pun on "you" with possible sexual connotations. "Hues" may pun on "use"; see line 14 and note 6. "Controlling" puns on "cunt."
4. *one . . . nothing:* something (a penis) of no use to me; "thing" meant male sexual organ; "nothing" meant female sexual organ.
5. To give women pleasure; to have the pleasure women have.
6. I'll have the main part of your love (the capital or principal), while women get just the "use" (interest; pleasure; children) of it (or: while you use women sexually).

**Sonnet 21**

1. And compares every beautiful thing with his beloved.
2. Making a link in proud comparison.

**Sonnet 22**

1. *be . . . will:* care for yourself as much as I do for myself, which I do not for myself but for you.

Bearing thy heart, which I will keep so chary° *cautiously*
As tender nurse her babe from faring ill.
Presume not on[2] thy heart when mine is slain.
Thou gav'st me thine not to give back again.

## 23

As an unperfect actor on the stage
Who with his fear is put besides° his part, *forgets*
Or° some fierce thing replete with too much rage *Or like*
Whose strength's abundance weakens his own heart,
So I, for fear of trust,° forget to say *lack of confidence*
The perfect ceremony of love's rite,[1]
And in mine own love's strength seem to decay,
O'ercharged with burden of mine own love's might.
Oh, let my books be then the eloquence
And dumb presagers° of my speaking breast, *mute presenters*
Who plead for love and look for recompense
More than that tongue that more hath more expressed.[2]
Oh, learn to read what silent love hath writ!
To hear with eyes belongs to love's fine wit.

## 24

Mine eye hath played the painter[1] and hath steeled[2]
Thy beauty's form in table° of my heart; *the painted tablet*
My body is the frame wherein 'tis held,° *(pun on "healed"?)*
And perspective it is best painter's art.[3]
For through° the painter must you see his skill *by means of; by looking in*
To find where your true image pictured lies,° *rests; fibs*
Which in my bosom's shop° is hanging still, *heart's workshop*
That hath his windows glazèd with thine eyes.[4]
Now see what good turns eyes for eyes have done:
Mine eyes have drawn thy shape, and thine for me
Are windows to my breast, wherethrough the sun
Delights to peep, to gaze therein on thee.
Yet eyes this cunning want° to grace their art: *lack this talent*
They draw but what they see, know not the heart.° *(of the youth)*

## 25

Let those who are in favor with their stars
Of public honor and proud titles boast,
Whilst I, whom fortune of such triumph bars,
Unlooked for joy in that I honor most.[1]
Great princes' favorites their fair leaves spread

2. Do not expect to get back.

**Sonnet 23**

1. Q reads "right," suggesting love's due as well as ritual. Lines 5–6 pick up the comparison to "an unperfect actor" (lines 1–2); lines 7–8 to "some fierce thing" (lines 3–4).
2. More than that (rival) speaker who has more extravagantly and more often spoken.

**Sonnet 24**

1. The running conceit is of the speaker and addressee looking into each other's eyes, seeing both the other and himself reflected.
2. Engraved. Editors often emend Q's "steeld" to "stell'd" ("fixed, placed") for a better fit with "painter."
3. *perspective . . . art:* seen from the proper angle (through my painter's eyes), your form is an excellent work of art. A "perspective" was a distorted painting that looked right only if viewed from the correct angle. The meter of the line is similarly distorted.
4. The addressee looks into the speaker's eyes ("windows"), which seem fitted with glass ("glazèd") by the reflection there of the addressee's own eyes. The eyes are the heart's ("his" [its], referring to "bosom's shop," line 7) windows, through which the addressee can therefore see his own image in the speaker's heart.

**Sonnet 25**

1. Unexpectedly (or privately) take pleasure in what I most esteem (the youth).

But as the marigold at the sun's eye,[2]
And in themselves their pride lies° burièd, — *will lie*
For at a frown they in their glory die.
The painful warrior famousèd for worth,[3]
After a thousand victories once foiled,
Is from the book of honor razèd° quite — *deleted*
And all the rest forgot for which he toiled.
Then happy I, that love and am beloved
Where I may not remove nor be removed.

## 26

Lord of my love, to whom in vassalage° — *feudal allegiance*
Thy merit hath my duty strongly knit,
To thee I send this written embassage° — *missive*
To witness duty, not to show my wit;
Duty so great, which wit so poor as mine
May make seem bare, in wanting° words to show it, — *lacking*
But that I hope some good conceit° of thine — *opinion; ingenuity*
In thy soul's thought (all naked)[1] will bestow° it, — *provide a place for*
Till whatsoever star that guides my moving° — *actions*
Points on me graciously with fair aspect° — *astrological influence*
And puts apparel on my tattered loving
To show me worthy of thy[2] sweet respect.
Then may I dare to boast how I do love thee;
Till then, not show my head where thou mayst prove° me. — *test*

## 27

Weary with toil, I haste me to my bed,
The dear repose for limbs with travel° tired, — *work; journeying*
But then begins a journey in my head
To work my mind, when body's work's expired.
For then my thoughts (from far where I abide)
Intend a zealous pilgrimage to thee,
And keep my drooping eyelids open wide,
Looking on darkness which the blind do see;
Save that my soul's imaginary sight
Presents thy shadow° to my sightless view, — *picture*
Which like a jewel hung in ghastly night
Makes black night beauteous and her old face new.
Lo thus, by day my limbs, by night my mind,
For° thee, and for myself, no quiet find. — *Because of*

## 28[1]

How can I then return in happy plight° — *condition*
That am debarred the benefit of rest,
When day's oppression is not eased by night,
But day by night and night by day oppressed?
And each (though enemies to either's° reign) — *each other's*

2. Only at the princes' pleasure or whim.
3. TEXTUAL COMMENT For the retention here of Q's uncharacteristic absence of rhyme between lines 9 and 11, see Digital Edition TC 3.

**Sonnet 26**
1. Refers to his "bare"-seeming "duty."
2. TEXTUAL COMMENT For the emendation of Q's "their" to "thy" here and elsewhere, based on Elizabethan handwriting, see Digital Edition TC 4.

**Sonnet 28**
1. This sonnet links with 27.

Do in consent shake hands to torture me,
The one by toil, the other to complain[2]
How far I toil, still farther off from thee.
I tell the day, to please him, thou art bright
And dost him grace when clouds do blot the heaven;[3]
So flatter I the swart°-complexioned night, *dark*
When sparkling stars twire not thou gild'st the even.[4]
But day doth daily draw my sorrows longer,
And night doth nightly make grief's length seem stronger.

## 29

When in disgrace with fortune and men's eyes,
I all alone beweep my outcast state,
And trouble deaf heaven with my bootless° cries, *fruitless*
And look upon myself and curse my fate;
Wishing me like to one more rich in hope,
Featured like him, like him with friends possessed,[1]
Desiring this man's art° and that man's scope,° *skill / range*
With what I most enjoy° contented least; *like; own*
Yet in these thoughts myself almost despising,
Haply[2] I think on thee, and then my state° *mood; fortunes*
Like to the lark at break of day arising
From sullen earth sings hymns at heaven's gate.
For thy sweet love remembered such wealth brings
That then I scorn to change my state with kings.

## 30

When to the sessions° of sweet silent thought *court sittings*
I summon° up remembrance of things past, *(play on court summons)*
I sigh° the lack of many a thing I sought *mourn*
And with old woes new wail my dear time's waste.[1]
Then can I drown an eye, unused to flow,
For precious friends hid in death's dateless° night, *endless*
And weep afresh love's long-since-canceled° woe, *repaid (with sorrow)*
And moan th'expense° of many a vanished sight. *passing*
Then can I grieve at grievances foregone,° *bygone*
And heavily° from woe to woe tell° o'er *sadly / say; count*
The sad account° of fore-bemoanèd moan, *story; finances*
Which I new pay as if not paid before.
But if the while I think on thee, dear friend,
All losses are restored and sorrows end.

## 31

Thy bosom is endearèd with° all hearts *loved by; enriched by*
Which I by lacking have supposèd dead,
And there reigns love, and all love's loving parts,
And all those friends which I thought burièd.
How many a holy and obsequious° tear *dutifully mourning*

2. *one:* day. *other:* night, making me "complain."
3. And confer beauty on him as a substitute for the sun.
4. By saying that when stars aren't twinkling, you brighten the evening.

**Sonnet 29**

1. *Wishing . . . possessed:* Three people he wants to be like—"like to one" with better prospects, better looking "like him," and having friends "like him."
2. By chance; also, pun on "happily."

**Sonnet 30**

1. *my . . . waste:* the frittering or wasting away of my precious time.

Hath dear religious° love stol'n from mine eye — *devoted*
As interest of° the dead, which° now appear — *due payment to / who*
But things removed° that hidden in there lie! — *absent*
Thou art the grave where buried love doth live,
Hung with the trophies° of my lovers[1] gone, — *memorials*
Who all their parts° of me to thee did give: — *shares*
That due of many[2] now is thine alone.
Their images I loved I view in thee,
And thou, all they,[3] hast all the all of me.

## 32

If thou survive my well-contented day[1]
When that churl death my bones with dust shall cover,
And shalt by fortune° once more resurvey — *chance*
These poor rude° lines of thy deceasèd lover, — *rough*
Compare them with the bett'ring° of the time, — *progress; better art*
And though they be outstripped by every pen,
Reserve° them for my love,° not for their rhyme, — *keep / out of love for me*
Exceeded by the height of happier men.[2]
Oh, then vouchsafe me but this loving thought:
"Had my friend's muse grown with this growing age,
A dearer birth° than this his love had brought — *worthier poem*
To march in ranks of better equipage;° — *poems*
But since he died and poets better prove,° — *have improved*
Theirs for their style I'll read, his for his love."

## 33

Full many a glorious morning have I seen
Flatter the mountain tops with sovereign eye,° — *sunlight*
Kissing with golden face the meadows green,
Gilding pale streams with heavenly alchemy,
Anon° permit the basest° clouds to ride — *(But) soon / darkest*
With ugly rack° on his celestial face — *cloudy mask*
And from the forlorn world his visage hide,
Stealing unseen to west° with this disgrace. — *to the west*
Even so my sun one early morn did shine
With all triumphant splendor on my brow,
But, out alack,° he was but one hour mine: — *alas*
The region° cloud hath masked him from me now. — *high*
Yet him for this my love no whit disdaineth;
Suns° of the world may stain,° when heaven's sun staineth. — *(pun on "sons") / darken*

## 34[1]

Why didst thou promise such a beauteous day
And make me travel forth without my cloak,
To let base clouds o'ertake me in my way,
Hiding thy brav'ry° in their rotten smoke?° — *finery / noxious mists*
'Tis not enough that through the cloud thou break

**Sonnet 31**
1. Paramours; friends.
2. That love which was owed to many.
3. And you, who are made up of all of them.

**Sonnet 32**
1. Day of my death (possibly also: my span of life), which I shall willingly accept.
2. *Exceeded . . . men:* Which is surpassed by poets more fortunate in their talent.

**Sonnet 34**
1. This sonnet links with 33.

To dry the rain on my storm-beaten face,
For no man well of such a salve can speak
That heals the wound and cures not the disgrace.[2]
Nor can thy shame° give physic to° my grief: *remorse / cure*
Though thou repent, yet I have still the loss;
Th' offender's sorrow lends but weak relief
To him that bears the strong offense's loss.
    Ah, but those tears are pearl which thy love sheds,
    And they are rich and ransom° all ill deeds. *atone for*

## 35

No more be grieved at that which thou hast done.
Roses have thorns, and silver fountains mud;
Clouds and eclipses stain° both moon and sun, *darken*
And loathsome canker° lives in sweetest bud. *(worm)*
All men make faults, and even I in this,
Authorizing thy trespass with compare,[1]
Myself corrupting salving thy amiss,[2]
Excusing thy sins more than thy sins are;[3]
For to thy sensual fault I bring in sense[4]—
Thy adverse party° is thy advocate°— *plaintiff / defender*
And 'gainst myself a lawful plea commence.
Such civil war is in my love and hate
    That I an accessory needs must be
    To that sweet thief which sourly° robs from me. *cruelly; bitterly*

## 36

Let me confess that we two must be twain,[1]
Although our undivided loves are one;
So shall those blots° that do with me remain *flaws; sources of shame*
Without thy help by me be borne alone.
In our two loves there is but one respect,° *mutual affection*
Though in our lives a separable spite,[2]
Which, though it alter not love's sole° effect, *single-minded*
Yet doth it steal sweet hours from love's delight.
I may not evermore acknowledge thee
Lest my bewailèd guilt° should do thee shame, *(the poet's, or youth's)*
Nor thou with public kindness honor me
Unless thou take° that honor from thy name.° *lose / family name*
    But do not so. I love thee in such sort° *such a way*
    As thou being mine, mine is thy good report.[3]

## 37

As a decrepit father takes delight
To see his active child do deeds of youth,
So I, made lame by fortune's dearest° spite, *direst*
Take all my comfort of° thy worth and truth. *in*

2. Disfigurement; dishonor done the poet by the youth's neglect.

**Sonnet 35**

1. Justifying your offense with comparisons.
2. Corrupting myself in minimizing your transgression.
3. Excusing you (overindulgently) from worse sins than the ones you've committed.
4. I use reason to defend your sensual offense.

**Sonnet 36**

1. Separated; but also, paradoxically, two of a kind or bound together.
2. Separation that causes vexation; vexation that causes separation.
3. *mine . . . report:* your good reputation is also mine. This couplet also ends Sonnet 96.

For whether beauty, birth, or wealth, or wit,
Or any of these all, or all, or more,
Entitled in their parts,[1] do crownèd sit,
I make my love engrafted to this store.[2]
So then I am not lame, poor, nor despised
Whilst that this shadow° doth such substance give *idea*
That I in thy abundance am sufficed,
And by a part of all thy glory live.
  Look what° is best, that best I wish in thee. *Whatever*
  This° wish I have—then ten times happy me! *When this*

## 38

How can my muse want subject to invent° *lack subject matter*
While thou dost breathe, that pour'st into my verse
Thine own sweet argument,° too excellent *theme*
For every vulgar paper to rehearse?[1]
Oh, give thyself the thanks if aught in me
Worthy perusal stand against thy sight.[2]
For who's so dumb that cannot write to thee
When thou thyself dost give invention light?
Be thou the tenth muse—ten times more in worth
Than those old nine which rhymers invocate—
And he that calls on thee, let him bring forth
Eternal numbers° to outlive long° date. *verses / a distant*
  If my slight muse do please these curious° days, *finicky*
  The pain° be mine, but thine shall be the praise. *pains; effort*

## 39

Oh,[1] how thy worth with manners° may I sing *modesty*
When thou art all the better part of me?
What can mine own praise to mine own self bring,
And what is't but mine own when I praise thee?
Even for° this, let us divided live, *Because of*
And our dear love lose name of single one,° *the reputation of unity*
That by this separation I may give
That due to thee which thou deserv'st alone.
O[2] absence, what a torment wouldst thou prove,
Were it not° thy sour leisure gave sweet leave *not that*
To entertain° the time with thoughts of love *enliven*
(Which time and thoughts so sweetly doth deceive)
  And that thou° teachest how to make one twain, *(absence)*
  By praising him here° who doth hence remain. *in this poem*

**Sonnet 37**
1. Enrolled among your good qualities.
2. I engraft my love onto this abundance (of good qualities).

**Sonnet 38**
1. Every ordinary, commonplace piece of writing to set forth.
2. *if . . . sight:* if you see anything in my writing worth reading.

**Sonnet 39**
1. TEXTUAL COMMENT For the spellings "Oh" and "O" in this edition and their possible meanings, see Digital Edition TC 5.
2. TEXTUAL COMMENT For the same spellings in Q, see Digital Edition TC 6.

## 40[1]

Take all my loves, my love, yea, take them all!
What hast thou then more than thou hadst before?
No love, my love, that thou mayst true love call:
All mine was thine before thou hadst this more.
Then if for my love thou my love receivest,[2]
I cannot blame thee, for my love thou usest.[3]
But yet be blamed, if thou this self[4] deceivest
By willful taste of what thyself° refusest. *your better nature*
I do forgive thy robb'ry, gentle thief,
Although thou steal thee all my poverty;° *what little I own*
And yet love knows it is a greater grief
To bear love's wrong than hate's known injury.
Lascivious grace,° in whom all ill well shows, *Charming one*
Kill me with spites,° yet we must not be foes. *offenses*

## 41

Those pretty° wrongs that liberty° commits *minor / licentiousness*
When I am sometime absent from thy heart,
Thy beauty and thy years full well befits,
For still° temptation follows where thou art. *continually*
Gentle° thou art, and therefore to be won; *Tender; upper-class*
Beauteous thou art, therefore to be assailed;
And when a woman woos, what woman's son
Will sourly leave her till he have prevailed?° *(sexually)*
Ay me, but yet thou mightst my seat° forbear, *(sexual) place*
And chide thy beauty and thy straying youth,
Who lead thee in their riot° even there *depraved conduct*
Where thou art forced to break a twofold truth:
Hers—by thy beauty tempting her to thee;
Thine—by thy beauty being false to me.

## 42

That thou hast her it is not all my grief,
And yet it may be said I loved her dearly;
That she hath thee is of my wailing chief,° *chief reason*
A loss in love that touches me more nearly.
Loving offenders, thus I will excuse ye:
Thou dost love her because thou know'st I love her,
And for my sake even so doth she abuse° me, *mistreat*
Suff'ring my friend for my sake to approve her.[1]
If I lose thee, my loss is my love's gain,
And, losing° her, my friend hath found that loss; *I losing*
Both find each other, and I lose both twain,
And both for my sake lay on me this cross.° *affliction*
But here's the joy: my friend and I are one.
Sweet flattery!° Then she loves but me alone. *Pleasing delusion*

**Sonnet 40**
1. Sonnets 40–42 concern a situation that may be identical to the love triangle described in 133–134 and 144.
2. Then if for/in place of love of me you host/take my beloved.
3. *for . . . usest:* because you use my beloved (sexually).
4. The poet (often emended, perhaps rightly, to "thyself").

**Sonnet 42**
1. To put her to the test (sexually).

## 43

When most I wink,° then do mine eyes best see, — *shut my eyes*
For all the day they view things unrespected,° — *unheeded; unworthy*
But when I sleep, in dreams they look on thee,
And, darkly bright, are bright in dark directed.[1]
Then thou, whose shadow shadows doth make bright[2]—
How would thy shadow's form° form happy show° — *substance / sight*
To the clear day, with thy much clearer light,
When to unseeing eyes[3] thy shade shines so!
How would (I say) mine eyes be blessèd made
By looking on thee in the living day,
When in dead night thy fair imperfect shade° — *incorporeal shadow*
Through heavy sleep on sightless eyes doth stay!° — *remain*
All days are nights to see till I see thee,
And nights bright days when dreams do show thee me.° — *to me*

## 44

If the dull° substance of my flesh were thought, — *heavy*
Injurious distance should not stop my way,
For then despite of space I would be brought,
From limits° far remote, where° thou dost stay. — *places / to where*
No matter then, although my foot did stand
Upon the farthest earth removed from thee,
For nimble thought can jump both sea and land
As soon as think the place where he° would be. — *(thought)*
But ah, thought kills me that I am not thought,
To leap large lengths of miles when thou art gone,
But that, so much of earth and water wrought,[1]
I must attend time's leisure[2] with my moan,
Receiving naught by elements so slow
But heavy tears, badges of either's woe.[3]

## 45[1]

The other two,[2] slight° air and purging fire, — *light*
Are both with thee, wherever I abide,
The first my thought, the other my desire:
These present-absent[3] with swift motion slide.
For when these quicker° elements are gone — *livelier*
In tender embassy of love to thee,
My life, being made of four, with two alone
Sinks down to death, oppressed with melancholy,
Until life's composition° be recured° — *mix of elements / restored*
By those swift messengers returned from thee,
Who even but now come back again assured
Of thy fair health, recounting it to me.
This told, I joy; but then, no longer glad,
I send them back again and straight° grow sad. — *at once*

**Sonnet 43**
1. (My eyes) seeing in the dark turn toward your bright eyes in the dark.
2. Whose image lightens darkness.
3. Because closed in sleep.

**Sonnet 44**
1. Being compounded of so much earth and water (the heavy elements).
2. I must wait humbly (as if on a great man) for time to reunite us.
3. Emblems of the grief of each of the poet's elements (earth because heavy [sad], water because wet).

**Sonnet 45**
1. This sonnet links with 44.
2. Of the poet's four elements. See 44.11.
3. Now present, now absent; constantly coming and going.

## 46

Mine eye and heart are at a mortal° war — *lethal*
How to divide the conquest of thy sight.[1]
Mine eye my° heart thy picture's sight would bar, — *to my*
My heart mine° eye the freedom° of that right. — *to my / free enjoyment*
My heart doth plead that thou in him° dost lie — *(the heart)*
(A closet° never pierced with crystal eyes), — *room*
But the defendant° doth that plea deny — *the eyes*
And says in him thy fair appearance lies.
To 'cide° this title is impanelèd° — *decide / enrolled*
A quest° of thoughts, all tenants to the heart, — *jury*
And by their verdict is determinèd
The clear eye's moiety° and the dear heart's part, — *share*
As thus: mine eye's due is thy outward part,
And my heart's right, thy inward love of heart.° — *the love from your heart*

## 47[1]

Betwixt mine eye and heart a league is took,° — *truce is made*
And each doth good turns now unto the other.
When that mine eye is famished for a look,
Or heart in love with sighs himself doth smother,[2]
With my love's picture then my eye doth feast
And to the painted banquet bids my heart;
Another time mine eye is my heart's guest,
And in his thoughts of love doth share a part.
So either by thy picture or my love,
Thyself, away, art present still° with me, — *always*
For thou no farther than my thoughts canst move,
And I am still with them, and they with thee;
Or if they sleep, thy picture in my sight
Awakes my heart, to heart's and eye's delight.

## 48

How careful was I when I took my way° — *set off*
Each trifle under truest bars° to thrust, — *strongest barriers*
That to my use° it might unusèd stay° — *benefit / remain safe*
From hands of falsehood, in sure wards° of trust! — *certain guards*
But thou, to° whom my jewels trifles are, — *compared to*
Most worthy comfort, now my greatest grief,[1]
Thou best of dearest, and mine only care,
Art left the prey of every vulgar thief.
Thee have I not locked up in any chest,
Save where thou art not, though I feel thou art,
Within the gentle closure of my breast,
From whence at pleasure thou mayst come and part;° — *go*
And even thence thou wilt be stol'n, I fear,
For truth° proves thievish for a prize so dear. — *even honesty*

## 49

Against° that time (if ever that time come) — *In preparation for*
When I shall see thee frown on my defects,

**Sonnet 46**
1. The spoils of the sight of you (possibly in a painting; see 47.5–14).

**Sonnet 47**
1. This sonnet links with 46.
2. Or when my loving heart smothers itself with sighs.

**Sonnet 48**
1. Because absent and in danger of being stolen.

Whenas thy love hath cast his utmost sum,[1]
Called to that audit by advised respects;° *judicious reasons*
Against that time when thou shalt strangely° pass *as a stranger*
And scarcely greet me with that sun, thine eye,
When love converted from the thing it was
Shall reasons find of settled gravity;[2]
Against that time do I ensconce me° here *secure myself*
Within the knowledge of mine own desert,[3]
And this my hand against myself uprear° *testify against myself*
To guard the lawful reasons on thy part.° *defend your case*
To leave poor me, thou hast the strength of laws,
Since why to love° I can allege no cause. *why you should love*

## 50

How heavy° do I journey on the way *wearily*
When what I seek, my weary travel's end,
Doth teach that ease and that repose to say,[1]
"Thus far the miles are measured from thy friend."
The beast that bears me, tired with my woe,
Plods dully on to bear° that weight in me, *while bearing*
As if by some instinct the wretch did know
His rider loved not speed being made[2] from thee.
The bloody spur cannot provoke him on
That sometimes anger thrusts into his hide,
Which heavily he answers with a groan
More sharp to me than spurring to his side,
For that same groan doth put this in my mind:
My grief lies onward and my joy behind.

## 51[1]

Thus can my love excuse the slow offense° *offense of slowness*
Of my dull bearer when from thee I speed:
"From where thou art why should I haste me thence?
Till I return, of posting° is no need." *riding quickly*
Oh, what excuse will my poor beast then find
When swift extremity° can seem but slow? *extreme (return) speed*
Then should I spur, though mounted on the wind;
In wingèd speed no motion shall I know![2]
Then can no horse with my desire keep pace.
Therefore desire (of perfect'st love being made)
Shall neigh (no dull flesh in his fiery race!);[3]
But love, for love,° thus shall excuse my jade:° *on love's behalf / horse*
"Since from thee going he went willful slow,
Towards thee I'll run, and give him leave to go."° *walk*

**Sonnet 49**
1. When your love has calculated the bottom line.
2. Shall find reasons for a dignified reserve; shall find reasons of well-established seriousness (for leaving me).
3. My (lack of?) worthiness to be loved.

**Sonnet 50**
1. Teach the comforts at the end of the road to remind me that.
2. *speed being made:* hastening away; haste, when and because it is.

**Sonnet 51**
1. This sonnet links with 50.
2. I will feel no motion when desire carries me back through the air. See line 11 and Sonnets 44–45 for the association of fire and air with desire and thought, and of earth and water with dull, slow flesh.
3. TEXTUAL COMMENT For the retention of Q's wording but not its punctuation of this line, see Digital Edition TC 7.

## 52

So am I as the rich° whose blessèd key *rich man*
Can bring him to his sweet up-lockèd treasure,
The which he will not ev'ry hour survey
For° blunting the fine point of seldom° pleasure. *To avoid / occasional*
Therefore are feasts° so solemn° and so rare, *feast days / dignified*
Since, seldom coming, in the long year set
Like stones of worth they thinly placèd are,
Or captain° jewels in the carcanet.° *chief / jeweled collar*
So is the time that keeps you as° my chest,° *like / jewel case*
Or as the wardrobe,° which the robe doth hide *room for costly clothes*
To make some special instant special blest
By new unfolding his imprisoned pride.
    Blessèd are you whose worthiness gives scope,
    Being had, to triumph; being lacked, to hope.[1]

## 53

What is your substance, whereof are you made,
That millions of strange shadows on you tend,° *attend*
Since everyone hath, every one, one shade,[1]
And you, but one, can every shadow lend?[2]
Describe° Adonis, and the counterfeit° *Draw / likeness*
Is poorly imitated after you.° *Is a poor imitation of you*
On Helen's cheek all art of beauty set,
And you in Grecian tires are painted new.[3]
Speak of the spring and foison° of the year: *harvest time*
The one doth shadow of your beauty show,
The other as your bounty doth appear,
And you° in every blessèd shape we know.° *you are / recognize*
    In all external grace you have some part,
    But you like none, none you,° for constant heart.° *like you / (pun on "art")*

## 54

Oh, how much more doth beauty beauteous seem
By° that sweet ornament which truth doth give! *Because of*
The rose looks fair, but fairer we it deem
For that sweet odor which doth in it live.
The canker blooms[1] have full as deep a dye
As the perfumèd tincture° of the roses, *color*
Hang on such thorns, and play as wantonly° *flatter as playfully*
When summer's breath their maskèd buds discloses;
But, for° their virtue only is° their show, *since / lies wholly in*
They live unwooed, and unrespected° fade, *unappreciated*
Die to themselves.° Sweet roses do not so; *alone; without influence*
Of their sweet deaths are sweetest odors made.
    And so of you, beauteous and lovely youth:
    When that° shall vade, by verse distills your truth.[2] *beauty*

**Sonnet 52**
1. *gives . . . hope:* allows me to exult when with you and to hope when not with you.

**Sonnet 53**
1. Since each person has an individual shadow.
2. Can cast all shadows (are visible in every beautiful image).
3. *On . . . new:* If one were to use every art to reproduce the beauty of Helen of Troy (or use artful cosmetics on Helen's cheek), it would look like you in Grecian headgear.

**Sonnet 54**
1. Dog roses (having little scent)—hence, run-of-the-mill people, but also with the connotation of the cankerworm that destroys the rose.
2. *vade . . . truth:* "vade" is a variant of "fade" but also means "depart," from the Latin *vadere.* By my verse your truth is distilled. See Sonnet 5 for distilling.

## 55

Not marble nor the gilded monuments
Of princes shall outlive this powerful rhyme,
But you shall shine more bright in these contents
Than unswept stone besmeared with sluttish° time. *slovenly*
When wasteful war shall statues overturn
And broils° root out the work of masonry, *battles*
Nor Mars his° sword nor war's quick fire shall burn *Neither Mars's*
The living record of your memory.
'Gainst death and all oblivious enmity
Shall you pace forth. Your praise shall still find room
Even in the eyes of all posterity
That wear this world out to the ending doom.[1]
  So till the judgment that yourself arise,
  You live in this, and dwell in lovers' eyes.

## 56

Sweet love,° renew thy force. Be it not said *(the feeling, not the lover)*
Thy edge should blunter be than appetite,
Which, but° today, by feeding is allayed, *only for*
Tomorrow sharpened in his former might.
So, love, be thou. Although today thou fill
Thy hungry eyes even till they wink° with fullness, *close (to sleep)*
Tomorrow see again and do not kill
The spirit of love with a perpetual dullness.
Let this sad int'rim like the ocean be
Which parts the shore° where two, contracted new,° *shores / newly betrothed*
Come daily to the banks, that when they see
Return of love,° more blessed may be the view— *the other lover*
  Or call it winter, which, being full of care,
  Makes summer's welcome thrice more wished, more rare.° *valuable*

## 57

Being your slave, what should I do but tend° *wait*
Upon the hours and times of your desire?
I have no precious time at all to spend
Nor services to do till you require.° *(my services)*
Nor dare I chide the world-without-end° hour *endless*
Whilst I, my sovereign,° watch the clock for you, *you (directly addressed)*
Nor think the bitterness of absence sour
When you have bid your servant once adieu.
Nor dare I question with my jealous thought
Where you may be, or your affairs suppose,° *speculate on*
But like a sad slave stay and think of naught
Save, where you are, how happy you make those.° *(who are with you)*
  So true a fool is love that in your will,[1]
  Though you do anything, he thinks no ill.

**Sonnet 55**
1. Doomsday: in Christianity, the Day of Judgment, when dead bodies are supposed to "arise" (line 13) from the grave and be united with their souls.

**Sonnet 57**
1. Desire (including sexual desire); capitalized in Q, perhaps punning on Shakespeare's first name—Will, nickname for William. See 135–136, 143.

## 58[1]

That° god forbid that made me first your slave — *May that*
I should in thought control your times of pleasure,
Or at your hand th'account of hours to crave,[2]
Being your vassal° bound to stay° your leisure. — *slave (and) / wait upon*
Oh, let me suffer, being at your beck,
Th'imprisoned absence of your liberty,[3]
And patience, tame to sufferance, bide each check[4]
Without accusing you of injury.
Be where you list.° Your charter° is so strong — *wish / freedom*
That you yourself may privilege° your time — *allocate*
To what you will. To you it doth belong
Yourself to pardon of self-doing° crime. — *committed by you*
I am to wait, though waiting so be hell,
Not blame your pleasure, be it ill or well.

## 59

If there be nothing new, but that which is
Hath been before, how are our brains beguiled,° — *cheated*
Which, laboring for° invention, bear amiss — *working at; giving birth to*
The second burden of a former child?[1]
Oh, that record° could with a backward look — *if only written memory*
Even of five hundred courses of the sun
Show me your image in some antique book,
Since mind at first in character was done,[2]
That I might see what the old world could say
To this composèd wonder of your frame:[3]
Whether we are mended,° or whe'er better they, — *improved*
Or whether revolution be the same.[4]
Oh, sure I am the wits° of former days — *clever writers*
To subjects worse have given admiring praise.

## 60

Like as the waves make towards the pebbled shore,
So do our minutes hasten to their end,
Each changing place with that which goes before;
In sequent toil all forwards do contend.[1]
Nativity,° once in the main of light,° — *A newborn / in the world*
Crawls to maturity, wherewith being crowned,
Crookèd° eclipses 'gainst his glory fight, — *Pernicious*
And Time that gave doth now his gift confound.° — *ruin*
Time doth transfix the flourish[2] set on youth
And delves the parallels° in beauty's brow, — *carves the wrinkles*
Feeds on the rarities of nature's truth,[3]
And nothing stands but for his scythe to mow.
And yet to times in hope° my verse shall stand, — *future days*
Praising thy worth, despite his° cruel hand. — *(Time's)*

**Sonnet 58**
1. This sonnet links with 57.
2. Or seek an account of how you pass your time.
3. The imprisoned feeling caused by your licentiousness when you're away.
4. And (let me) patiently, acquiescent in suffering, endure each setback.

**Sonnet 59**
1. *bear . . . child:* mistakenly give birth for a second time to a (brain-)child that has already been born.
2. Since writing was invented.
3. To the wonderful composition of your form (perhaps referring to the sonnet itself as well).
4. Whether the revolving of the ages makes no difference.

**Sonnet 60**
1. Toiling one after the other, all seek to move forward.
2. Time pierces and destroys the ornament (beauty).
3. On the most precious products of nature's perfection.

## 61

Is it thy will thy image should keep open
My heavy eyelids to the weary night?
Dost thou desire my slumbers should be broken,
While shadows° like to thee do mock my sight? *visions*
Is it thy spirit that thou send'st from thee
So far from home into my deeds to pry,
To find out shames and idle hours in me,° *my leisure-time misdeeds*
The scope and tenor of thy jealousy?[1]
Oh no, thy love, though much, is not so great;
It is my love that keeps mine eye awake,
Mine own true love that doth my rest defeat
To play the watchman ever for thy sake.
For thee watch I,° whilst thou dost wake elsewhere, *I remain awake*
From me far off, with others all too near.

## 62

Sin of self-love possesseth all mine eye,
And all my soul, and all my every part;
And for this sin there is no remedy,
It is so grounded inward in my heart.
Methinks no face so gracious is as mine,
No shape so true,° no truth of such account, *perfect*
And for myself mine own worth do define
As° I all other° in all worths surmount. *As if / others*
But when my glass° shows me myself indeed, *mirror*
Beated and chopped with tanned antiquity,
Mine own self-love quite contrary I read:
Self so self-loving were iniquity.
'Tis thee (my self)° that for° myself I praise, *you, my other self / as*
Painting my age with beauty of thy days.

## 63

Against° my love shall be as I am now, *Preparing for when*
With Time's injurious hand crushed and o'erworn,
When hours have drained his blood and filled his brow
With lines and wrinkles, when his youthful morn
Hath traveled° on to age's steepy[1] night *progressed; toiled*
And all those beauties whereof now he's king
Are vanishing, or vanished out of sight,
Stealing away the treasure of his spring—
For such a time do I now fortify
Against confounding° age's cruel knife, *devastating*
That he° shall never cut from memory *(age)*
My sweet love's beauty, though° my lover's life. *though he will sever*
His beauty shall in these black lines be seen,
And they shall live, and he in them still green.° *perpetually youthful*

**Sonnet 61**
1. (Which are) the object and intent of your distrust (that is, the "shames and idle hours," line 7).

**Sonnet 63**
1. Precipitous (like the path of the setting sun).

## 64

When I have seen by Time's fell° hand defaced — *fierce*
The rich proud cost° of outworn buried age, — *expense*
When sometime° lofty towers I see down razed — *once*
And brass eternal slave to mortal rage;[1]
When I have seen the hungry ocean gain
Advantage on the kingdom of the shore
And the firm soil win of° the wat'ry main, — *win ground from*
Increasing store with loss, and loss with store;[2]
When I have seen such interchange of state,
Or state[3] itself confounded to decay,° — *reduced to ruins*
Ruin hath taught me thus to ruminate
That Time will come and take my love away.
  This thought is as a death, which° cannot choose — *(thought)*
  But weep to have° that which it fears to lose. — *at having*

## 65

Since° brass, nor stone, nor earth, nor boundless sea, — *Since there is neither*
But sad mortality o'ersways their power,
How with this rage shall beauty hold a plea,[1]
Whose action is no stronger than a flower?
Oh, how shall summer's honey breath hold out
Against the wrackful° siege of batt'ring days, — *damaging*
When rocks impregnable are not so stout,
Nor gates of steel so strong, but Time decays?° — *decays them*
Oh, fearful meditation; where, alack,
Shall Time's best jewel° from Time's chest[2] lie hid? — *(the beloved)*
Or what strong hand can hold his° swift foot back, — *(Time's)*
Or who his spoil° of beauty can forbid? — *destruction*
  Oh, none, unless this miracle have might,
  That in black ink my love may still shine bright.

## 66

Tired with all these,° for restful death I cry: — *(the ensuing wrongs)*
As to behold desert a beggar born,
And needy nothing trimmed in jollity,[1]
And purest faith unhappily forsworn,° — *betrayed; perjured*
And gilded honor shamefully misplaced,
And maiden virtue rudely strumpeted,
And right perfection wrongfully disgraced,
And strength by limping sway° disablèd, — *feeble leaders*
And art made tongue-tied° by authority, — *learning silenced*
And folly (doctor-like) controlling skill,[2]
And simple truth miscalled simplicity,° — *naïveté*
And captive good attending° captain ill. — *serving*
  Tired with all these, from these would I be gone,
  Save that to die I leave my love alone.

**Sonnet 64**
1. And eternal brass forever succumbs to death's violence.
2. Adding to the stock of one by loss of the other, and vice versa.
3. *state* (line 9): condition; sovereign territory. *state* (line 10): pomp.

**Sonnet 65**
1. How can beauty make a (legal) case against such a power to destroy?
2. (Miser's) treasure chest; coffin.

**Sonnet 66**
1. *As . . . jollity:* For example, to see merit (a worthy person) born in poverty (and hence without prospects) / And talentless (or impoverished) worthlessness adorned with finery.
2. And folly, feigning erudition, dominating true wisdom or ability. Before modern medicine, doctors were often portrayed as fools or con artists.

## 67

Ah, wherefore with infection[1] should he live
And with his presence grace impiety,
That° sin by him advantage should achieve — *So that*
And lace° itself with his society? — *decorate*
Why should false painting imitate his cheek
And steal dead seeing of[2] his living hue?
Why should poor° beauty indirectly seek — *lesser; aged*
Roses of shadow,° since his rose is true? — *Cosmetic beauty*
Why should he live, now Nature bankrupt is,
Beggared° of blood to blush° through lively veins, — *Bereft / flow red*
For she hath no exchequer° now but his — *treasury*
And, proud of many, lives upon his gains?[3]
  Oh, him she stores,° to show what wealth she had — *keeps*
  In days long since, before these last so bad.

## 68[1]

Thus is his cheek the map° of days outworn — *image*
When beauty lived and died as flowers do now,
Before these bastard signs of fair° were borne° — *cosmetics / worn; born*
Or durst inhabit on a living brow;
Before the golden tresses of the dead,
The right of sepulchers,[2] were shorn away
To live a second life on second head;
Ere beauty's dead fleece made another gay.
In him those holy antique hours° are seen — *good old days*
Without all ornament, itself and true,
Making no summer of another's green,
Robbing no old to dress his beauty new;
  And him as for a map doth Nature store,° — *keep*
  To show false Art what beauty was of yore.

## 69

Those parts of thee that the world's eye doth view
Want° nothing that the thought of hearts can mend;° — *Lack / imagine better*
All tongues (the voice of souls) give thee that due,
Utt'ring bare truth, even so as foes commend.[1]
Thy outward thus with outward praise is crowned,
But those same tongues that give thee so thine own° — *your due*
In other accents° do this praise confound° — *words / undermine*
By seeing farther than the eye hath shown.
They look into the beauty of thy mind,
And that in guess they measure by thy deeds.
Then, churls, their thoughts (although their eyes were kind)
To thy fair flower add the rank smell of weeds.
  But why thy odor matcheth not thy show,° — *appearance*
  The soil is this, that thou dost common grow.[2]

**Sonnet 67**
1. The world's ills (as in 66).
2. *dead seeing of*: an inanimate outward resemblance from.
3. Though (falsely, nostalgically) taking pride in her abundance (of lesser or former beauties), lives off the interest he earns (from his endowment of true beauty).

**Sonnet 68**
1. This sonnet links with 67.
2. Properly belonging to tombs (wigs were made from the hair of corpses).

**Sonnet 69**
1. Uttering minimal truth, in the way that enemies praise.
2. The ground (reason; also, stain) is this: you are becoming low (promiscuous).

## 70[1]

That thou art blamed shall not be thy defect,
For slander's mark° was ever yet the fair. *target*
The ornament of beauty is suspect,° *suspicion*
A crow that flies in heaven's sweetest air.
So° thou be good, slander doth but approve *So long as*
Thy worth the greater, being wooed of time,[2]
For canker vice[3] the sweetest buds doth love,
And thou present'st a pure unstainèd prime.° *youth*
Thou hast passed by the ambush of young days
Either not assailed or victor being charged;° *defeating an attack*
Yet this thy praise cannot be so° thy praise *enough*
To tie up envy, evermore enlarged.° *forever at large; growing*
If some suspect° of ill masked not thy show,° *suspicion / appearance*
Then thou alone kingdoms of hearts shouldst owe.° *own*

## 71[1]

No longer mourn for me when I am dead
Than you shall hear the surly sullen bell
Give warning to the world that I am fled
From this vile world with vilest[2] worms to dwell.
Nay, if you read this line, remember not
The hand that writ it, for I love you so
That I in your sweet thoughts would be forgot
If thinking on me then should make you woe.
Oh, if, I say, you look upon this verse
When I, perhaps, compounded am° with clay, *am mixed*
Do not so much as my poor name rehearse,° *repeat; rebury*
But let your love even with my life decay,
Lest the wise world should look into your moan
And mock you with me° after I am gone. *for loving me*

## 72

Oh, lest the world should task you to recite
What merit lived in me that you should love,
After my death, dear love, forget me quite,
For you in me can nothing worthy prove°— *provide evidence of*
Unless you would devise some virtuous lie
To do more for me than mine own desert,
And hang more praise upon deceasèd I
Than niggard truth would willingly impart.
Oh, lest your true love may seem false in this,
That you for love speak well of me untrue,° *untruthfully*
My° name be buried where my body is *Let my*
And live no more to shame nor me nor you;
For I am shamed by that which I bring forth,[1]
And so should you,° to love things nothing worth. *you be*

**Sonnet 70**
1. This sonnet links with 69.
2. *slander . . . time:* the gossip merely proves that because you're so popular ("wooed of time"), you're worth even more.
3. Slander, like a cankerworm.

**Sonnet 71**
1. The first of four linked sonnets.
2. Q's "vildest" is an archaic form of "vilest" that may also carry the connotation of "most reviled."

**Sonnet 72**
1. Presumably alluding to the writer's poems or to his profession as actor and playwright.

## 73

That time of year thou mayst in me behold
When yellow leaves, or none, or few do hang
Upon those boughs which shake against the cold,
Bare ruined choirs where late the sweet birds sang.[1]
In me thou seest the twilight of such day
As after sunset fadeth in the west,
Which by and by black night doth take away,
Death's second self that seals up all in rest.
In me thou seest the glowing of such fire
That° on the ashes of his youth[2] doth lie, *As*
As the deathbed whereon it must expire,
Consumed with that which it was nourished by.[3]
  This thou perceiv'st, which makes thy love more strong,
  To love that° well which thou must leave ere long. *(the speaker); (life)*

## 74

But be contented when that fell arrest° *fearful death*
Without all bail shall carry me away.
My life hath in this line° some interest,° *verse / legal claim*
Which for memorial still with thee shall stay.
When thou reviewest° this, thou dost review *reread*
The very part° was consecrate° to thee: *part of me that / devoted*
The earth can have but earth, which is his° due; *its*
My spirit is thine, the better part of me.
So then thou hast but lost the dregs of life,
The prey of worms, my body being dead,
The coward conquest of a wretch's knife,[1]
Too base of° thee to be rememberèd. *by*
  The worth of that° is that which it contains, *(the body)*
  And that is this,° and this with thee remains. *the spirit (his poetry)*

## 75

So are you to my thoughts as food to life
Or as sweet seasoned° showers are to the ground, *spring*
And for the peace of you° I hold such strife *you provide*
As twixt a miser and his wealth is found:
Now proud as an enjoyer, and anon° *soon; immediately*
Doubting the filching age[1] will steal his treasure;
Now counting° best to be with you alone, *estimating*
Then bettered° that the world may see my pleasure; *better contented*
Sometime all full with feasting on your sight
And by and by clean° starvèd for a look; *wholly*
Possessing or pursuing no delight
Save what is had° or must° from you be took. *(already) / (later)*
  Thus do I pine and surfeit day by day,
  Or° gluttoning on all, or all away.° *Either / having nothing*

**Sonnet 73**

1. *choirs:* the area in a church where the choir ("sweet birds") sings; gatherings of manuscript "leaves" (line 2), or quires ("quiers" in Q).
2. Perhaps referring to the phoenix, a legendary self-resurrecting bird believed to live in cycles of several centuries, dying in flames and being reborn from the ashes. See also 19.4 and Shakespeare's "The Phoenix and Turtle."
3. Ironically, the fire is choked ("consumed") by (along with) the ashes, which are the residue of the fuel that the fire previously fed upon ("was nourished by").

**Sonnet 74**

1. The cowardly conquest of a wretch such as Death (who was thought to carry a scythe).

**Sonnet 75**

1. Fearing that these dishonest times.

## 76

Why is my verse so barren of new pride,° *adornments*
So far from variation or quick° change? *lively*
Why with the time° do I not glance aside *following the fashion*
To new-found methods and to compounds[1] strange?
Why write I still all one, ever the same,
And keep invention in a noted weed,[2]
That every word doth almost tell my name,
Showing their birth, and where° they did proceed? *whence*
Oh, know, sweet love, I always write of you,
And you and love are still my argument.° *always my topic*
So all my best is dressing old words new,
Spending again what is already spent,
  For as the sun is daily new and old,
  So is my love still telling what is told.

## 77[1]

Thy glass° will show thee how thy beauties wear,[2] *mirror*
Thy dial° how thy precious minutes waste, *sundial*
The vacant leaves thy mind's imprint° will bear, *written ideas*
And of this book this learning° mayst thou taste: *(what you write)*
The wrinkles which thy glass will truly show
Of mouthèd° graves will give thee memory;° *gaping / remind you*
Thou by thy dial's shady stealth° mayst know *stealing shadow*
Time's thievish progress to eternity.
Look what° thy memory cannot contain *Whatever*
Commit to these waste blanks,° and thou shalt find *empty pages*
Those children nursed,° delivered from thy brain, *preserved*
To take a new acquaintance of thy mind.° *strike you afresh*
  These offices,° so oft as thou wilt look, *functions*
  Shall profit thee and much enrich thy book.

## 78[1]

So oft have I invoked thee for my muse
And found such fair assistance in my verse
As every alien pen hath got my use,[2]
And under thee° their poesy disperse. *with you as patron*
Thine eyes, that taught the dumb on high° to sing *aloud*
And heavy ignorance aloft to fly,
Have added feathers to the learned's wing[3]
And given grace° a double majesty. *excellence*
Yet be most proud of that which I compile,° *write*
Whose influence° is thine and born of thee. *power to move*
In others' works thou dost but mend° the style, *improve*
And arts° with thy sweet graces gracèd be. *(their) artistry*
  But thou art all my art, and dost advance
  As high as learning my rude ignorance.

**Sonnet 76**
1. *compounds:* stylistic or formal mixtures; compound words; elaborate medicines (with "methods," which also refers to both literary and medical treatments).
2. And keep literary creativity in such familiar clothing.
**Sonnet 77**
1. This sonnet is presented as accompanying the gift of a notebook.
2. Last; wear away; "were" (Q's spelling).
**Sonnet 78**
1. This sonnet begins the rival poet sequence (78–80, 82–86).
2. That every other poet imitates me.
3. Have improved the poetic "flights" of even accomplished poets.

## 79

Whilst I alone did call upon thy aid,
My verse alone had all thy gentle grace;
But now my gracious numbers are decayed,
And my sick muse doth give another place.° — *way to another poet*
I grant, sweet love, thy lovely argument[1]
Deserves the travail° of a worthier pen, — *labor*
Yet what of thee thy poet° doth invent — *(the writer or his rival)*
He robs thee of and pays it thee again.
He lends thee virtue, and he stole that word
From thy behavior; beauty doth he give
And found it in thy cheek: he can afford° — *extend*
No praise to thee but what in thee doth live.
  Then thank him not for that which he doth say,
  Since what he owes thee thou thyself dost pay.

## 80

Oh, how I faint° when I of you do write, — *get discouraged*
Knowing a better spirit° doth use your name — *(the rival poet)*
And, in the praise thereof, spends all his might
To make me tongue-tied speaking of your fame.
But since your worth, wide as the ocean is,
The humble as° the proudest sail doth bear, — *as well as*
My saucy bark,° inferior far to his, — *impudent boat*
On your broad main° doth willfully appear. — *waters*
Your shallowest help will hold me up afloat
Whilst he upon your soundless° deep doth ride, — *bottomless*
Or, being wrecked, I am a worthless boat,
He of tall building° and of goodly pride.° — *strong build / magnificence*
  Then if he thrive and I be cast away,
  The worst was this: my love was my decay.

## 81[1]

Or° I shall live your epitaph to make, — *Either*
Or you survive when I in earth am rotten;
From hence° your memory death cannot take, — *the world; my poetry*
Although in me each part° will be forgotten. — *each of my attributes*
Your name from hence° immortal life shall have, — *henceforth; my poetry*
Though I, once gone, to all the world must die;
The earth can yield me but a common grave,
When you entombèd in men's eyes shall lie.
Your monument shall be my gentle verse,
Which eyes not yet created shall o'er-read,
And tongues to be° your being shall rehearse° — *future tongues / recite*
When all the breathers of this world are dead.
  You still shall live—such virtue° hath my pen— — *power*
  Where breath most breathes, even in° the mouths of men. — *right in*

**Sonnet 79**
1. The subject of your loveliness.

**Sonnet 81**
1. Except for lines 2–3 and 10–11, any two consecutive lines in this sonnet form a complete sentence.

## 82

I grant thou wert not married to my muse,
And therefore mayst without attaint o'erlook° (*dishonor read*)
The dedicated[1] words which writers° use (*other writers*)
Of their fair subject, blessing[2] every book.
Thou art as fair in knowledge as in hue,° (*appearance*)
Finding thy worth a limit° past my praise, (*region*)
And therefore art enforced to seek anew
Some fresher stamp of the time-bettering days.[3]
And do so, love! Yet when they have devised
What strainèd touches rhetoric can lend,
Thou, truly fair, wert truly sympathized[4]
In true plain words by thy true-telling friend,
  And their gross painting° might be better used (*cosmetics; flattery*)
  Where cheeks need blood. In thee, it is abused.° (*used wrongly*)

## 83

I never saw that you did painting° need, (*cosmetics; exaggeration*)
And therefore to your fair° no painting set. (*beauty*)
I found—or thought I found—you did exceed
The barren tender° of a poet's debt; (*payment*)
And therefore have I slept in your report,[1]
That° you yourself, being extant, well might show (*So that*)
How far a modern° quill doth come too short, (*trite; fashionable*)
Speaking of worth, what worth[2] in you doth grow.
This silence for° my sin you did impute, (*to be*)
Which shall be most my glory, being dumb,
For I impair not beauty, being mute,
When others would give life and bring a tomb.[3]
  There lives more life in one of your fair eyes
  Than both your poets can in praise devise.

## 84

Who is it that says most which[1] can say more
Than this rich praise—that you alone are you;
In whose confine immurèd is the store
Which should example where your equal grew?[2]
Lean penury within that pen doth dwell
That to his subject lends not some small glory;
But he that writes of you, if he can tell
That you are you, so dignifies his story.
Let him but copy what in you is writ,
Not making worse what nature made so clear,° (*purely excellent*)
And such a counterpart shall fame° his wit, (*copy will make famous*)
Making his style admirèd everywhere.
  You to your beauteous blessings add a curse,[3]
  Being fond on praise, which makes your praises worse.[4]

**Sonnet 82**
1. Devoted; referring to a prefatory dedication.
2. Either the writers or the youth is "blessing," just as either the poet or the youth is "finding" (line 6).
3. Some more recent imprint (commendation) of these culturally progressive times.
4. Would be accurately represented.

**Sonnet 83**
1. Neglected to sing your praises.
2. In speaking of value of the worth that.
3. When others who try to make you live in their writings only end up burying you.

**Sonnet 84**
1. *Who . . . which:* What hyperbolical enthusiast.
2. *In . . . grew:* Within whom is contained the stock that would be needed to produce your equal?
3. Personality flaw; vexation (for those who would praise you).
4. Being (too) fond of praise, which makes the praise seem like flattery; being (too) fond of the sort of praise that detracts from you (because you're better than it).

## 85

My tongue-tied muse in manners holds her still,° *tactfully says nothing*
While comments of° your praise, richly compiled, *commentaries in*
Reserve their character° with golden quill *Hoard up your features*
And precious phrase by all the muses filed.° *polished*
I think good thoughts, whilst other° write good words, *others*
And like unlettered clerk still cry "Amen"
To every hymn[1] that able spirit affords° *offers*
In polished form of well-refinèd pen.
Hearing you praised, I say, "'Tis so, 'tis true,"
And to the most° of praise add something more— *highest*
But that is in my thought,° whose love to you, *unspoken*
Though words come hindmost, holds his rank before.° *before all others*
Then others for the breath of words respect,° *hold in esteem*
Me for my dumb thoughts, speaking in effect.° *in reality*

## 86

Was it the proud full sail of his° great verse, *(a rival poet's)*
Bound for the prize° of all-too-precious you, *pirate's spoils*
That did my ripe thoughts in my brain inhearse,° *bury*
Making their tomb the womb wherein they grew?
Was it his spirit, by spirits taught to write
Above a mortal pitch,° that struck me dead? *height*
No, neither he, nor his compeers[1] by night
Giving him aid, my verse astonishèd.° *made silent*
He, nor that affable familiar ghost° *spirit*
Which nightly gulls° him with intelligence,° *fools / ideas*
As victors of my silence cannot boast:
I was not sick of any fear from thence.
But when your countenance filled up[2] his line,
Then lacked I matter. That enfeebled mine.

## 87

Farewell! Thou art too dear° for my possessing, *costly*
And like° enough thou know'st thy estimate.° *it is likely / value*
The charter of thy worth gives thee releasing;[1]
My bonds in thee are all determinate.° *terminated*
For how do I hold thee but by thy granting,
And for that riches where is my deserving?
The cause° of° this fair gift in me is wanting, *reason; legal case / for*
And so my patent back again is swerving.[2]
Thyself thou gav'st, thy own worth then not knowing,
Or me, to whom thou gav'st it, else mistaking;° *overestimating*
So thy great gift, upon misprision growing,° *based on error*
Comes home again on better judgment making.[3]
Thus have I had thee as a dream doth flatter:° *creates an illusion*
In sleep a king, but waking no such matter.

**Sonnet 85**
1. *like . . . hymn:* like an illiterate parish clerk reflexively approve ("cry 'Amen'" after) every poem ("hymn") of praise.

**Sonnet 86**
1. Colleagues (the "spirits" in line 5).
2. Your features gave the entire subject-matter to; your approval made up for any lack in.

**Sonnet 87**
1. The privilege you derive from your worth releases you from love's bonds.
2. My rights of possession revert to you.
3. *on . . . making:* when you realize your error.

## 88

When thou shalt be disposed to set me light° — *value me little*
And place my merit in the eye of scorn,
Upon thy side against myself I'll fight
And prove thee virtuous, though thou art forsworn.
With mine own weakness being best acquainted,
Upon thy part° I can set down a story — *On your behalf*
Of faults concealed wherein I am attainted° — *charged; tainted*
That° thou, in losing me, shall win much glory; — *So that*
And I by this will be a gainer too,
For, bending all my loving thoughts on thee,
The injuries that to myself I do,
Doing thee vantage,° double vantage me.[1] — *advantage*
  Such is my love, to thee I so belong,
  That for thy right myself will bear° all wrong. — *suffer; reveal (bare)*

## 89

Say that thou didst forsake me for some fault,
And I will comment° upon that offense. — *elaborate*
Speak of my lameness, and I straight will halt,[1]
Against thy reasons making no defense.
Thou canst not, love, disgrace me half so ill,
To set a form upon desirèd change,[2]
As I'll myself disgrace, knowing thy will.
I will acquaintance strangle and look strange,[3]
Be absent from thy walks,° and in my tongue, — *familiar places*
Thy sweet belovèd name no more shall dwell,
Lest I, too much profane, should do it wrong
And haply° of our old acquaintance tell. — *by chance*
  For thee, against myself I'll vow debate,° — *combat*
  For I must ne'er love him whom thou dost hate.

## 90[1]

Then hate me when thou wilt—if ever, now!
Now, while the world is bent my deeds to cross,° — *foil*
Join with the spite of fortune, make me bow,
And do not drop in for an after-loss.[2]
Ah, do not, when my heart hath scaped this sorrow,
Come in the rearward of a conquered woe;[3]
Give not a windy night a rainy morrow
To linger out a purposed overthrow.[4]
If thou wilt leave me, do not leave me last,
When other petty griefs have done their spite,
But in the onset come. So shall I taste
At first the very worst of fortune's might,
  And other strains° of woe, which now seem woe, — *types; burdens*
  Compared with loss of thee, will not seem so.

**Sonnet 88**

1. "Double" because the speaker is now being honest and because he takes pleasure in benefiting his beloved; but perhaps "double" also means "duplicitous."

**Sonnet 89**

1. Talk of my disability (perhaps alluding to the lame meter of line 2), and I at once will limp (stop objecting).
2. To lend justification to the change you seek.
3. I will end our familiarity and act like a stranger.

**Sonnet 90**

1. This sonnet links with 89.
2. Do not fall upon me to inflict a later disaster.
3. Assault me again after I have overcome my present grief.
4. *To . . . overthrow:* By protracting or delaying your intended assault.

## 91

Some glory in their birth, some in their skill,
Some in their wealth, some in their body's force,
Some in their garments (though new-fangled ill),° *fashionably ugly*
Some in their hawks and hounds, some in their horse;° *horses*
And every humor hath his° adjunct pleasure *temperament has its*
Wherein it finds a joy above the rest.
But these particulars are not my measure;° *(of joy)*
All these I better° in one general best. *exceed*
Thy love is better than high birth to me,
Richer than wealth, prouder than garments' cost,
Of more delight than hawks or horses be;
And having thee, of all men's pride[1] I boast—
Wretched in this alone, that thou mayst take
All this away, and me most wretched make.

## 92[1]

But do thy worst to steal thyself away,
For term of° life thou art assurèd mine, *the duration of my*
And life no longer than thy love will stay,
For it depends upon that love of thine.
Then need I not to fear the worst of wrongs,
When in the least of them[2] my life hath end;
I see a better state° to me belongs *condition; situation*
Than that which on thy humor° doth depend. *mood*
Thou canst not vex me with inconstant mind,
Since that my life on thy revolt doth lie.[3]
Oh, what a happy title[4] do I find:
Happy to have thy love, happy to die!
But what's so blessèd fair that fears no blot?
Thou mayst be false, and yet I know it not.

## 93[1]

So shall I live supposing thou art true,
Like a deceivèd husband; so love's face° *appearance*
May still seem love to me, though altered new—
Thy looks with me, thy heart in other place.
For there can live no hatred in thine eye;
Therefore in that I cannot know thy change.
In many's looks, the false heart's history
Is writ in moods and frowns and wrinkles strange,[2]
But heaven in thy creation did decree
That in thy face sweet love should ever dwell;
Whate'er thy thoughts or thy heart's workings be,
Thy looks should nothing thence but sweetness tell.
How like Eve's apple doth thy beauty grow,
If thy sweet virtue answer not thy show.[3]

**Sonnet 91**
1. Of everything in which others take pride.

**Sonnet 92**
1. This sonnet links with 91.
2. In the slightest sign of your displeasure.
3. Since change in your affections would kill me.
4. What a claim to be considered happy.

**Sonnet 93**
1. This sonnet links with 92.
2. In signs of anger and frowns and displeased expressions.
3. Does not correspond to your looks.

## 94

They that have power to hurt and will do none,
That do not do the thing they most do show,[1]
Who, moving others, are themselves as stone,
Unmovèd, cold,° and to temptation slow— *composed*
They rightly° do inherit heaven's graces *truly*
And husband nature's riches from expense;[2]
They are the lords and owners of their faces,
Others but stewards° of their excellence. *hired managers*
The summer's flower is to the summer sweet,
Though to itself it only live and die,[3]
But if that flower with base infection meet,
The basest weed outbraves his dignity:[4]
For sweetest things turn sourest by their deeds;
Lilies that fester smell far worse than weeds.[5]

## 95

How sweet and lovely dost thou make the shame
Which, like a canker° in the fragrant rose, *cankerworm*
Doth spot the beauty of thy budding name!° *fame*
Oh, in what sweets dost thou thy sins enclose!
That tongue that tells the story of thy days,
Making lascivious comments on thy sport,° *amorous adventures*
Cannot dispraise but in a kind of praise:
Naming thy name blesses° an ill report. *makes positive*
Oh, what a mansion have those vices got
Which for their habitation chose out thee,
Where beauty's veil doth cover every blot
And all things turns to fair that eyes can see!
Take heed, dear heart, of this large privilege;
The hardest knife ill used doth lose his° edge. *its*

## 96

Some say thy fault is youth, some wantonness;° *promiscuity; frivolity*
Some say thy grace is youth and gentle sport.[1]
Both grace and faults are loved of more and less;° *by people of all ranks*
Thou mak'st faults graces that to thee resort.
As on the finger of a thronèd queen
The basest jewel will be well esteemed,
So are those errors that in thee are seen
To truths translated° and for true things deemed. *converted*
How many lambs might the stern° wolf betray *vicious*
If like° a lamb he could his looks translate? *into*
How many gazers mightst thou lead away
If thou wouldst use the strength of all thy state?° *power*
But do not so. I love thee in such sort
As, thou being mine, mine is thy good report.[2]

**Sonnet 94**
1. *they most do show:* that their appearance implies.
2. And protect nature's rich endowment from waste.
3. *is . . . die:* emits its sweetness to others even though it lives and dies only for itself and in apparent isolation (unpollinated: compare 54.5–11).
4. Exceeds the flower in magnificence.
5. This line also occurs in *Edward III,* a play printed anonymously in 1596 and probably written in part by Shakespeare.

**Sonnet 96**
1. Gentlemanly conduct (including sexual license).
2. See 36.13–14 and note 3 for the same couplet. *such sort*: such a way.

## 97

How like a winter hath my absence been
From thee, the° pleasure of the fleeting year! *(who are) the*
What freezings have I felt, what dark days seen,
What old December's bareness everywhere!
And yet this time removed° was summer's time, *away*
The teeming autumn big° with rich increase, *pregnant*
Bearing the wanton burden of the prime° *harvest of wanton spring*
Like widowed wombs after their lords' decease.
Yet this abundant issue seemed[1] to me
But hope of orphans and unfathered fruit,
For summer and his° pleasures wait° on thee, *its / attend*
And, thou away, the very birds are mute;
  Or if they sing, 'tis with so dull a cheer,° *such a dismal mood*
  That leaves look pale, dreading the winter's near.

## 98

From you have I been absent in the spring
When proud-pied° April, dressed in all his trim,° *multicolored / finery*
Hath put a spirit of youth in everything,
That° heavy Saturn[1] laughed and leapt with him. *So that*
Yet nor the lays° of birds nor the sweet smell *not the songs*
Of different flowers° in odor and in hue *flowers differing*
Could make me any summer's story tell,° *speak (write) happily*
Or from their proud lap° pluck them where they grew. *(the ground)*
Nor did I wonder at the lily's white,
Nor praise the deep vermilion in the rose;
They were but sweet, but figures° of delight, *merely emblems*
Drawn after you, you pattern of all those.
  Yet seemed it winter still, and, you away,
  As with your shadow I with these did play.[2]

## 99[1]

The forward° violet thus did I chide: *early*
"Sweet thief, whence didst thou steal thy sweet° that smells *perfume*
If not from my love's breath? The purple pride° *beauty*
Which on thy soft cheek for complexion dwells
In my love's veins thou hast too grossly° dyed."[2] *obviously*
The lily I condemnèd for thy hand,[3]
And buds of marjoram[4] had stol'n thy hair.
The roses fearfully on thorns did stand,
One blushing shame, another white despair;
A third, nor red, nor white, had stol'n of both,° *(making it pink)*
And to° his robb'ry had annexed thy breath, *in addition to*
But for his theft in pride of all his growth
A vengeful canker° ate him up to death. *cankerworm*
  More flowers I noted, yet I none could see,
  But sweet° or color it had stol'n from thee. *perfume*

**Sonnet 97.**
1. Offspring seemed in prospect.

**Sonnet 98**
1. The planet Saturn was regarded as cold and slow, exerting a melancholy influence.
2. As if with your image I played with these flowers.

**Sonnet 99**
1. This sonnet has an extra opening line.
2. The violet has been dyed purple in "my love's veins," with a play on "died": the blood of the dead beloved nourishes the flower.
3. For stealing whiteness from your (the beloved's) hand.
4. The herb, sweet of scent and auburn in color.

## 100

Where art thou, Muse, that thou forgett'st so long
To speak of that which gives thee all thy might?
Spend'st thou thy fury[1] on some worthless song,
Dark'ning° thy power to lend base subjects light? *Debasing*
Return, forgetful Muse, and straight° redeem *immediately*
In gentle numbers° time so idly spent. *noble poetry*
Sing to the ear that doth thy lays° esteem *songs*
And gives thy pen both skill and argument.° *substance*
Rise, resty° Muse, my love's sweet face survey *lazy*
If° Time have any wrinkle graven there; *To see if*
If any, be a satire to° decay *satirist of*
And make Time's spoils despisèd everywhere.
    Give my love fame faster than Time wastes life;
    So° thou prevent'st° his scythe and crooked knife. *Thereby / impede*

## 101[1]

O truant Muse, what shall be thy amends
For thy neglect of truth in beauty dyed?
Both truth and beauty on my love depends;
So dost thou too, and therein° dignified. *therein are you*
Make answer, Muse. Wilt thou not haply° say, *perhaps*
"Truth needs no color with his color fixed,[2]
Beauty no pencil beauty's truth to lay,[3]
But best is best if never intermixed"?° *(with cosmetics)*
Because he needs no praise, wilt thou be dumb?
Excuse not silence so, for't lies in thee
To make him much outlive a gilded tomb
And to be praised of° ages yet to be. *by*
    Then do thy office,° Muse. I teach thee how *duty*
    To make him seem long° hence as he shows° now. *a long time / appears*

## 102

My love is strengthened though more weak in seeming;° *appearance*
I love not less, though less the show appear.
That love is merchandized[1] whose rich esteeming° *appraisal*
The owner's tongue doth publish everywhere.
Our love was new, and then but in the spring° *just beginning*
When I was wont to greet it with my lays,
As Philomel[2] in summer's front° doth sing *beginning*
And stops her pipe in growth of riper days—
Not that the summer is less pleasant now
Than when her mournful hymns did hush the night,
But that wild music burdens[3] every bough,
And sweets grown common lose their dear delight.
    Therefore, like her, I sometime hold my tongue,
    Because I would not dull° you with my song. *overfeed*

**Sonnet 100**
1. Inspiration (the "poet's rage" of 17.11).

**Sonnet 101**
1. This sonnet links with 100.
2. Truth needs no artificial color to be added to his natural coloring.
3. True beauty needs no cosmetics brush.

**Sonnet 102**
1. (Debased by being) turned into merchandise for sale.
2. Nightingale; with ambiguous hints of the myth of Philomela, whose brother-in-law raped her and ripped out her tongue to ensure her silence. See Book 6 of Ovid's *Metamorphoses*.
3. Loads; provides a musical refrain (probably from many other poets) on.

## 103

Alack, what poverty my muse brings forth,
That, having such a scope to show her pride,[1]
The argument all bare° is of more worth *subject in itself*
Than when it hath my added praise beside.
Oh, blame me not if I no more can write.
Look in your glass,° and there appears a face *mirror*
That overgoes my blunt invention[2] quite,
Dulling° my lines and doing me disgrace. *Deadening (by contrast)*
Were it not sinful then, striving to mend,° *improve*
To mar the subject that before was well?
For to no other pass° my verses tend *end*
Than of your graces and your gifts to tell;
And more—much more than in my verse can sit—
Your own glass shows you when you look in it.

## 104

To me, fair friend, you never can be old,
For as you were when first your eye I eyed,
Such seems your beauty still. Three winters cold
Have from the forests shook three summers' pride;° *splendor*
Three beauteous springs to yellow autumn turned
In process° of the seasons have I seen; *the progress*
Three April perfumes in three hot Junes burned
Since first I saw you fresh, which yet° are green. *who still*
Ah, yet doth beauty, like a dial hand,
Steal from his figure, and no pace perceived;[1]
So your sweet hue,° which methinks still doth stand,[2] *appearance*
Hath motion,° and mine eye may be deceived. *changes*
For fear of which, hear this, thou age unbred:° *future age*
Ere you were born was beauty's summer dead.

## 105

Let not my love be called idolatry,
Nor my belovèd as an idol show,[1]
Since all alike my songs and praises be
To one,° of one, still° such, and ever so. *the beloved / continually*
Kind is my love[2] today, tomorrow kind,
Still constant in a wondrous excellence.
Therefore my verse, to constancy confined,
One thing expressing, leaves out[3] difference.° *diversity (of theme)*
"Fair, kind, and true" is all my argument;
"Fair, kind, and true," varying to other words—
And in this change is my invention spent[4]—
Three themes in one, which wondrous° scope affords. *(with pun on "one")*
"Fair," "kind," and "true" have often lived alone,° *separately*
Which three, till now, never kept seat° in one. *dwelt permanently*

**Sonnet 103**
1. Considering that she has such opportunity (in you) to display her skill (her pride in you).
2. That surpasses my dull powers of invention.

**Sonnet 104**
1. *doth . . . perceived:* beauty imperceptibly "steals" (departs stealthily from; robs from) the youthful appearance ("figure") of the beloved as the hand of the watch ("dial") stealthily progresses ("steals") away from the number ("figure") on the watch face.
2. Is unchanged or motionless (in contrast with "pace," line 10, and "motion," line 12).

**Sonnet 105**
1. Seem like an idol; seem idle.
2. The youth; the speaker's feelings.
3. Omits; perhaps "leaves" of paper, referring to "verse," line 7. See 73.2.
4. And in varying the words alone my inventiveness is expended.

## 106

When in the chronicle of wasted° time — *past*
I see descriptions of the fairest wights,° — *people*
And beauty making beautiful old rhyme
In praise of ladies dead and lovely knights,
Then in the blazon[1] of sweet beauty's best—
Of hand, of foot, of lip, of eye, of brow—
I see their antique pen would have expressed
Even such a beauty as you master° now. — *possess*
So all their praises are but prophecies
Of this our time, all you prefiguring;
And for° they looked but with divining° eyes, — *as / prophetic*
They had not skill enough your worth to sing;
For we,° which now behold these present days, — *even we*
Have eyes to wonder, but lack tongues to praise.

## 107

Not mine own fears, nor the prophetic soul
Of the wide world,° dreaming on° things to come, — *people / predicting*
Can yet the lease° of my true love° control, — *allotted term / affection*
Supposed as forfeit to a confined doom.[1]
The mortal moon hath her eclipse endured,[2]
And the sad augurs mock their own presage;[3]
Incertainties now crown themselves assured,[4]
And peace proclaims olives of endless age.[5]
Now with the drops[6] of this most balmy time,
My love looks fresh, and Death to me subscribes,° — *submits*
Since spite of him° I'll live in this poor rhyme, — *(death)*
While he insults° o'er dull and speechless tribes.[7] — *prevails*
And thou in this shalt find thy monument,
When tyrants' crests and tombs of brass are spent.° — *ruined*

## 108

What's in the brain that ink may character° — *express*
Which hath not figured° to thee my true spirit? — *shown*
What's new to speak, what now to register,° — *record*
That may express my love or thy dear merit?
Nothing, sweet boy. But yet, like prayers divine,
I must each day say o'er° the very same— — *repeat*
Counting no old thing old, thou mine, I thine,
Even as when first I hallowed thy fair name—
So that eternal love in love's fresh case° — *covering*
Weighs not° the dust and injury of age, — *Overlooks*
Nor gives to necessary° wrinkles place,° — *inevitable / priority*
But makes antiquity for aye his page,[1]

**Sonnet 106**
1. Poetic catalog of virtues.

**Sonnet 107**
1. Wrongly imagined as limited to a finite term.
2. Survived. Referring to an eclipse of the moon or perhaps to an event in the life (or 1603 death) of Queen Elizabeth (often known as Diana, the moon goddess).
3. And prophets of doom now ridicule their own prophecies.
4. Desired but doubtful possibilities now celebrate their realization—possibly alluding to the accession of James I in 1603.
5. And peace declares the olive branches that symbolize it to be everlasting. Perhaps a reference to the peace treaty with Spain signed by James.
6. Soothing drops of dew, rain, or balm. Balm was used in the coronation ceremony.
7. Over those legions of dead who have no poetic legacy.

**Sonnet 108**
1. But makes (old) age forever the (youthful) servant to love; perhaps referring to the pages of poetry written when the "sweet boy" (line 5) was still young.

Finding the first conceit of love there bred[2]
Where time and outward form would° show it dead. — *want to*

### 109

Oh, never say that I was false of heart,
Though absence seemed my flame to qualify;° — *reduce*
As easy might I from myself depart
As from my soul, which in thy breast doth lie.
That is my home of love. If I have ranged,
Like him that travels, I return again,
Just to the time,° not with the time exchanged,[1] — *Punctually*
So that myself bring water for my stain.[2]
Never believe, though in my nature reigned
All frailties that besiege all kinds of blood,° — *disposition*
That it could so preposterously be stained
To leave for° nothing all thy sum of good: — *exchange for*
For nothing this wide universe I call,
Save thou, my rose; in it thou art my all.

### 110

Alas, 'tis true, I have gone here and there,
And made myself a motley to the view;[1]
Gored° mine own thoughts, sold cheap what is most dear, — *Injured*
Made old offenses of affections new.[2]
Most true it is that I have looked on truth° — *fidelity*
Askance and strangely.° But by all above, — *coldly*
These blenches° gave my heart another youth, — *alterations*
And worse essays° proved thee my best of love. — *experiments*
Now all is done. Have what shall have no end.[3]
Mine appetite I never more will grind[4]
On newer proof, to try° an older friend, — *test*
A god in love, to whom I am confined.
Then give me welcome, next my heaven the best,° — *next best to heaven*
Even to thy pure and most most loving breast.

### 111

Oh, for my sake do you with[1] Fortune chide,
The guilty goddess of my harmful deeds,
That did not better for my life provide
Than public means, which public manners breeds.[2]
Thence comes it that my name receives a brand,° — *stigma*
And almost thence my nature is subdued
To what it works in, like the dyer's hand.
Pity me then, and wish I were renewed,° — *cured*

2. Recovering the first feeling (poetic expression) of love generated in that place (the beloved; the past; the poem).

**Sonnet 109**

1. Not changed by the times (or passage of time).
2. *water for my stain:* tears to cleanse the stain of my absence.

**Sonnet 110**

1. Referring to the multicolored outfit of the fool, clown, or jester—onstage and off—and hence probably to Shakespeare's theatrical career, including acting. *motley to the view*: clown to the world.
2. Repeated the traditional misbehavior of infidelity (or offended old friends) in (my treatment of) new attachments.
3. *Have . . . end:* Take that (my love) which will not expire.
4. *grind:* sharpen with new experience.

**Sonnet 111**

1. Q has "wish," which gives a more problematic array of alternative meanings.
2. Probably: Than employment as an actor, which requires one to curry favor with the public.

Whilst, like a willing patient, I will drink
Potions of eisel° 'gainst my strong infection; *medicinal vinegar*
No° bitterness that I will bitter think, *There is no*
Nor double penance to correct correction.° *correct me twice over*
  Pity me then, dear friend, and I assure ye
  Even that your pity is enough to cure me.

## 112[1]

Your love and pity doth th'impression fill° *eliminates the scar*
Which vulgar° scandal stamped upon my brow; *public*
For what care I who calls me well or ill,
So you o'er-green my bad, my good allow?[2]
You are my all the world, and I must strive
To know my shames and praises from your tongue;
None else to me, nor I to none alive,
That my steeled sense or changes right or wrong.[3]
In so profound abysm I throw all care
Of others' voices that my adder's sense° *deaf ears*
To critic and to flatterer stoppèd are.
Mark how with my neglect I do dispense:[4]
  You are so strongly in my purpose bred[5]
  That all the world besides methinks are dead.

## 113

Since I left you, mine eye is in my mind,[1]
And that which governs me to go about° *And my real sight*
Doth part his° function, and is partly blind, *Divides its (the eye's)*
Seems seeing, but effectually is out.° *blind*
For it no form delivers to the heart
Of bird, of flower, or shape which it doth latch;° *catch sight of*
Of his quick objects° hath the mind no part, *the eye's fleeting sights*
Nor his own vision holds[2] what it doth catch.
For if it see the rud'st or gentlest° sight— *coarsest or noblest*
The most sweet favor[3] or deformed'st creature,
The mountain or the sea, the day or night,
The crow or dove—it shapes them to your feature.[4]
  Incapable of more, replete with you,
  My most true mind thus makes mine eye untrue.

## 114[1]

Or whether doth my mind, being crowned with you,[2]
Drink up the monarch's plague, this flattery?
Or whether shall I say mine eye saith true,
And that your love taught it this alchemy,[3]
To make of monsters and things indigest° *chaotic*

**Sonnet 112**
1. This sonnet links with 111.
2. So long as you allow new growth to cover what is bad in me, and give credit for what is good.
3. *None . . . wrong:* No one else is alive to me, or I to them, who can change my hardened disposition rightly or wrongly.
4. How I excuse my neglect (of "others' voices," line 10).
5. Nurtured in all my plans.

**Sonnet 113**
1. I see with my mind's eye.
2. Nor does the eye's vision hold on to.
3. Face; perhaps Q's "sweet-favor" means "sweet-favored" or "good-looking."
4. It makes them look like you.

**Sonnet 114**
1. This sonnet links with 113.
2. Being made a king by having you. "Or whether" (lines 1, 3) introduces alternatives.
3. And that love of you taught my eye how thus to transform things.

Such cherubins° as your sweet self resemble, *angels*
Creating every° bad a perfect best *from every*
As fast as objects to his beams assemble?[4]
Oh, 'tis the first! 'Tis flatt'ry in my seeing,
And my great° mind most kingly drinks it up. *pompous*
Mine eye well knows what with his gust is 'greeing[5]
And to his palate doth prepare the cup.
If it be poisoned, 'tis the lesser sin
That mine eye loves it and doth first begin.[6]

## 115

Those lines that I before have writ do lie,
Even those that said I could not love you dearer;
Yet then my judgment knew no reason why
My most full flame should afterwards burn clearer.
But reckoning time,[1] whose millioned accidents
Creep in twixt vows° and change decrees of kings, *(and their performance)*
Tan° sacred beauty, blunt the sharp'st intents, *Darken*
Divert strong minds to th' course of alt'ring things—
Alas, why, fearing of time's tyranny,
Might I not then say,[2] "Now I love you best,"
When I was certain o'er° incertainty, *beyond*
Crowning° the present, doubting of the rest? *Exalting*
Love is a babe. Then might I not say so,[3]
To give° full growth to that which still doth grow. *Thereby giving*

## 116

Let me not to the marriage of true minds
Admit impediments.° Love is not love *legal barriers to marriage*
Which alters when it alteration finds
Or bends with the remover to remove.[1]
Oh no, it is an ever-fixèd mark,[2]
That looks on tempests and is never shaken;
It is the star to every wand'ring bark,
Whose worth's unknown, although his height be taken.[3]
Love's not Time's fool,° though rosy lips and cheeks *plaything*
Within his bending sickle's compass[4] come;
Love alters not with his° brief hours and weeks, *its*
But bears it out even to the edge of doom.[5]
If this be error and upon° me proved, *against*
I never writ, nor no man ever loved.

4. As fast as objects come before its gaze. (The eye was thought to emit beams of light.)
5. What pleases the mind's appetite.
6. And drinks first (like a king's taster).

**Sonnet 115**

1. But taking time into account; but time, which settles accounts.
2. Was I not then right to have said.
3. Thus I shouldn't say, "Now I love you best" (line 10).

**Sonnet 116**

1. Or abandons the relationship when the loved one is unfaithful or has departed or died, or when time ("the remover") alters things for the worse.
2. An unmoving sea mark, such as a lighthouse or a beacon, that provides a constant reference point for sailors.
3. *Whose . . . taken:* The star's (great) intrinsic value cannot be assessed, although navigators at sea can measure height above the horizon.
4. Within range of time's curved (and hostile) scythe. "Compass" also recalls the imagery of the second quatrain. *his:* (Time's).
5. But endures until the eve of doomsday.

### 117

Accuse me thus: that I have scanted° all *neglected*
Wherein I should your great deserts repay;
Forgot upon your dearest love to call,
Whereto all bonds do tie me day by day;
That I have frequent° been with unknown minds° *friendly / strangers*
And given to time your own dear-purchased right;[1]
That I have hoisted sail to all the winds
Which should° transport me farthest from your sight. *were likely to*
Book both my willfulness and errors down,
And on just proof surmise accumulate.[2]
Bring me within the level° of your frown, *aim*
But shoot not at me in your wakened hate,
    Since my appeal says I did strive to prove[3]
    The constancy and virtue of your love.

### 118

Like° as to make our appetites more keen *Just*
With eager° compounds we our palate urge,° *sharp / stimulate*
As to prevent° our maladies unseen *forestall*
We sicken to shun sickness when we purge;[1]
Even so, being full of your ne'er-cloying sweetness,
To bitter sauces did I frame° my feeding, *adjust*
And, sick of welfare,[2] found a kind of meetness° *suitability*
To be diseased ere that there was true needing.
Thus policy° in love, t'anticipate *strategy*
The ills that were not, grew to faults assured,
And brought to[3] medicine a healthful state
Which, rank of goodness, would by ill be cured.[4]
    But thence I learn and find the lesson true:
    Drugs poison him that so° fell sick of you. *thus; so badly*

### 119

What potions have I drunk of siren[1] tears
Distilled from limbecks° foul as hell within, *stills*
Applying° fears to hopes, and hopes to fears, *(as a medicine)*
Still° losing when I saw myself° to win? *Always / expected*
What wretched errors hath my heart committed
Whilst it hath thought itself so blessèd never?° *more blessed than ever*
How have mine eyes out of their spheres been fitted[2]
In the distraction° of this madding° fever? *delirium / fit-inducing*
Oh, benefit of ill! Now I find true
That better is by evil still made better,
And ruined love, when it is built anew,
Grows fairer than at first, more strong, far greater.
    So I return rebuked to my content,
    And gain by ills thrice more than I have spent.

**Sonnet 117**
1. And wasted idly what should have been your right (rite) because acquired by your great worth and affection (because acquired at your great cost).
2. And pile suspicion on top of your proof.
3. Since my defense is that I was trying to test.

**Sonnet 118**
1. We sicken ourselves with medicine that causes vomiting or bowel movements so as to prevent greater illness.
2. Made ill by good food.
3. Treated with; brought to the need of.
4. Overfull with goodness (health, the beloved), sought to be cured by disease (evil).

**Sonnet 119**
1. Deceitfully and dangerously alluring. Sirens were mythological creatures, part bird, part woman, said to lure sailors to their death with their songs.
2. Been driven convulsively out of their sockets.

## 120

That you were once unkind befriends me now,
And, for° that sorrow which I then did feel, — *because of*
Needs must I under my transgression bow,
Unless my nerves° were brass or hammered steel. — *sinews*
For if you were by my unkindness shaken
As I by yours, you've passed a hell of time,
And I, a tyrant, have no leisure taken
To weigh° how once I suffered in° your crime. — *contemplate / from*
Oh, that our night of woe[1] might have remembered° — *reminded*
My deepest sense how hard true sorrow hits,
And soon to you, as you to me then, tendered° — *offered*
The humble salve, which wounded bosoms fits![2]
　　But that your trespass° now becomes a fee:° — *offense / payment*
　　Mine ransoms° yours, and yours must ransom me. — *absolves*

## 121

'Tis better to be vile than vile esteemed° — *reputed vile*
When not to be receives reproach of being,° — *being vile*
And the just pleasure lost, which is so deemed
Not by our feeling but by others' seeing.[1]
For why should others' false adulterate° eyes — *corrupted*
Give salutation to my sportive blood?[2]
Or on my frailties why are frailer spies,
Which in their wills[3] count bad what I think good?
No, I am that I am,[4] and they that level° — *aim*
At my abuses reckon up their own.
I may be straight though they themselves be bevel;° — *crooked*
By their rank° thoughts my deeds must not be shown°— — *foul / measured*
　　Unless this general evil they maintain:
　　All men are bad and in their badness reign.° — *thrive*

## 122

Thy gift, thy tables,° are° within my brain — *notebook / are already*
Full charactered° with lasting memory, — *written*
Which shall above that idle rank[1] remain
Beyond all date, even to eternity—
Or at the least so long as brain and heart
Have faculty° by nature to subsist; — *power*
Till each to razed° oblivion yield his part — *demolished*
Of thee, thy record never can be missed.° — *lost*
That poor retention[2] could not so much hold,
Nor need I tallies thy dear love to score.[3]
Therefore to give them° from me was I bold, — *(the "tables")*
To trust those tables° that receive thee more. — *memory*
　　To keep an adjunct° to remember thee — *aid*
　　Were to import° forgetfulness in me. — *imply*

**Sonnet 120**
1. Our earlier time of suffering (caused by the youth's unfaithfulness).
2. The salve of apology that is just the thing for an injured heart.

**Sonnet 121**
1. *And . . . seeing:* And we are denied the appropriate, innocent pleasure, which is considered sinful not by us but by others.
2. Greet me as a fellow sinner owing to my sexual behavior.
3. *Or . . . wills:* Why should my failings be pried into by even more culpable people, who willfully (who licentiously; who in Will Shakespeare).
4. God's words, Exodus 3:14.

**Sonnet 122**
1. Trivial status (of the "tables" as opposed to "memory").
2. That inadequate container (the "tables").
3. Nor do I need the notched sticks used in calculating sums (to which the "tables" are contemptuously compared) to reckon up your precious love.

## 123

No! Time, thou shalt not boast that I do change.
Thy pyramids built up with newer might[1]
To me are nothing° novel, nothing strange. *in no way*
They are but dressings of a former sight.[2]
Our dates° are brief, and therefore we admire *lives*
What thou dost foist upon us that is old,
And rather make them born to our desire[3]
Than think that we before have heard them told.° *described*
Thy registers° and thee I both defy, *records*
Not wond'ring at the present nor the past,
For thy records and what we see doth lie,
Made more or less by thy continual haste.[4]
This I do vow and this shall ever be:
I will be true despite thy scythe and thee.

## 124

If my dear love° were but the child of state,[1] *(for you)*
It might for fortune's bastard be unfathered,[2]
As subject to time's love or to time's hate,
Weeds among weeds, or flowers with flowers gathered.[3]
No, it was builded far from accident;° *chance*
It suffers° not in smiling pomp, nor falls *changes*
Under the blow of thrallèd° discontent, *captive*
Whereto th'inviting time our fashion calls.[4]
It fears not policy,° that heretic, *expediency*
Which works on leases of short-numbered hours,° *short-term contracts*
But all alone stands hugely politic,° *prudent*
That it nor° grows with heat° nor drowns with showers. *neither / prosperity*
To this I witness call the fools of time,
Which die for goodness, who have lived for crime.[5]

## 125

Were't aught to me I bore the canopy,[1]
With my extern° the outward honoring, *exterior action*
Or laid great bases for eternity,[2]
Which proves more short than waste° or ruining? *decay*
Have I not seen dwellers on form and favor[3]
Lose all, and more, by paying too much rent,° *overdoing homage*
For compound sweet forgoing simple savor,[4]
Pitiful thrivers, in their gazing spent?[5]

**Sonnet 123**
1. Grand buildings constructed by more modern means. Possibly referring to structures erected in Rome in 1586 or in London in 1603 (for James's coronation), but retaining a sense of almost timeless Egyptian antiquity.
2. Replicas of what's been seen before.
3. And consider them made just for us.
4. Raised and destroyed by time's swift passage; made to seem more or less majestic by virtue of newness or antiquity and the tastes of the times.

**Sonnet 124**
1. Were simply the result of circumstances (or of your high position).
2. It might be disinherited as a passing fancy, a product of fortune (chance, wealth).
3. *As . . . gathered:* Regarded as useless or valuable as time and fortune decide.
4. To which ("pomp" and "discontent") we are driven by the latest trend ("fashion").
5. *To . . . crime:* I call as witness those playthings of time who, having lived wicked lives, reform or repent at death.

**Sonnet 125**
1. Would I care if I enhanced my status by carrying a ceremonial canopy for a royal person?
2. Laid foundations for eternal monuments.
3. Seen those who depend (linger) on ceremony and appearance.
4. For obsequious praise (or fleeting worldly concerns) giving up plain candor (or true values).
5. Pitiful in their empty achievements, ruined by love of show.

No, let me be obsequious° in thy heart, *dutiful*
And take thou my oblation,° poor but free,° *offering / freely given*
Which is not mixed with seconds,[6] knows no art,° *artifice*
But mutual render°—only me for thee. *exchange*
    Hence, thou suborned informer![7] A true soul,
    When most impeached,° stands least in thy control. *accused*

## 126[1]

O thou, my lovely boy, who in thy power
Dost hold Time's fickle glass,[2] his sickle hour;° *reaping time*
Who hast by waning grown,[3] and therein show'st
Thy lover's withering as thy sweet self grow'st—
If Nature, sovereign mistress over wrack,° *decay*
As thou goest onwards still° will pluck thee back, *constantly*
She keeps thee to this purpose: that her skill
May Time disgrace and wretched minute° kill. *life's miserable brevity*
Yet fear her, O thou minion° of her pleasure! *darling*
She may detain, but not still° keep, her treasure. *always*
Her audit,° though delayed, answered° must be, *debt (to time) / paid*
And her quietus° is to render° thee. *settlement / relinquish*
(                                        )
(                                        )

## 127[1]

In the old age° black was not counted fair,[2] *old days*
Or if it were, it bore not beauty's name;° *reputation*
But now is black beauty's successive heir,° *heir by succession*
And beauty slandered with a bastard shame.[3]
For since each hand hath put on° nature's power, *usurped*
Fairing° the foul with art's false borrowed face, *Beautifying*
Sweet beauty hath no name, no holy bower,
But is profaned, if not lives in disgrace.
Therefore my mistress' eyes are raven black,
Her brows so suited,[4] and they mourners seem
At such who, not born fair, no beauty lack,
Sland'ring creation with a false esteem.[5]
    Yet so° they mourn, becoming of° their woe, *in such a way / adorning*
    That every tongue says beauty should look so.

6. The second-rate.
7. Paid spy: jealousy or the detractor whose charges the poem answers.

**Sonnet 126**

1. TEXTUAL COMMENT This "sonnet" or envoi, of six couplets, concludes the part of the sequence apparently addressed to the youth and formally signals a change in tone and subject matter in the remaining sonnets. For the distinctive form of this poem, the only one in the sequence with twelve lines, see Digital Edition TC 8.
2. Hourglass from which the sands of life run out; mirror showing decay.
3. Become more beautiful with age. As the sand in the top half of an hourglass wanes, the sand in the bottom part grows.

**Sonnet 127**

1. Sonnets 127–152 have been traditionally known as the "dark lady" group, although their subject matter is not uniform and their object is only once called "dark" (147.14) and never a "lady." She is referred to as the poet's "mistress" (127.9; 130.1, 8, 12), however, and is often described as "black" (127.1, 3, 9; 130.4; 131.12, 13; 132.3, 13; 147.14). The celebration of black beauty goes back to the biblical Song of Songs 1:4: "I am blacke . . . but comelie." See the Introduction.
2. Beautiful; light-colored.
3. And (fair) beauty accused of illegitimacy (by use of cosmetics).
4. Her brow dressed (or matched) in an eyebrow black like her eyes (and for the same reason).
5. *At . . . esteem:* Because of those who, not being fair, make up for it with cosmetics, so that even natural beauty is presumed artificial.

## 128

How oft, when thou, my music, music play'st
Upon that blessèd wood whose motion° sounds — *mechanism*
With thy sweet fingers when thou gently sway'st° — *govern*
The wiry concord that mine ear confounds,° — *amazes (with delight)*
Do I envy those jacks[1] that nimble leap
To kiss the tender inward of thy hand,
Whilst my poor lips, which should that harvest reap,
At the wood's boldness by thee blushing stand!
To be so tickled they would change their state
And situation with those dancing chips,
O'er whom thy fingers walk with gentle gait,
Making dead wood more blest than living lips.
  Since saucy° jacks so happy are in this, — *impudent*
  Give them thy fingers, me thy lips to kiss.

## 129

Th'expense of spirit in a waste of shame
Is lust in action;[1] and till action, lust
Is perjured, murd'rous, bloody, full of blame,
Savage, extreme, rude,° cruel, not to trust;° — *harsh / be trusted*
Enjoyed no sooner but despisèd straight;° — *immediately*
Past reason° hunted, and no sooner had, — *Madly*
Past reason hated, as a swallowed bait
On purpose laid to make the taker mad;
Mad in pursuit and in possession so;° — *(mad)*
Had, having, and in quest to have, extreme;
A bliss in proof, and proved,[2] a very woe;
Before, a joy proposed; behind, a dream.
  All this the world well knows, yet none knows well
  To shun the heaven that leads men to this hell.

## 130

My mistress' eyes are nothing like the sun;
Coral is far more red than her lips' red;
If snow be white, why then her breasts are dun;° — *grayish brown*
If hairs be wires,[1] black wires grow on her head.
I have seen roses damasked,° red and white, — *dappled*
But no such roses see I in her cheeks;
And in some perfumes is there more delight
Than in the breath that from my mistress reeks.° — *issues; smells*
I love to hear her speak, yet well I know
That music hath a far more pleasing sound.
I grant I never saw a goddess go;° — *walk*
My mistress when she walks treads on the ground.
  And yet, by heaven, I think my love as rare
  As any she belied with false compare.[2]

**Sonnet 128**
1. Keys of the virginal, a harpsichord-like instrument; fellows.

**Sonnet 129**
1. *Th'expense . . . action:* The expenditure of vital energy (including semen) in a shameful waste (waist) is consummated lust.
2. *in proof:* while being experienced. *proved:* having been experienced.

**Sonnet 130**
1. Elizabethan poets often compared women's hair to golden wires.
2. As any woman misrepresented by falsely flattering comparison. (Despite the apparent contrast signaled by "yet," line 13, the speaker continues the poem's ironic repudiation of the hyperbole conventional in love poetry, calling his beloved "as rare," not "more rare," and hence no more attractive than any woman overpraised for her beauty.)

## 131

Thou art as tyrannous, so as thou art,[1]
As those whose beauties proudly make them cruel;
For well thou know'st to my dear° doting heart — *fond(ly)*
Thou art the fairest and most precious jewel.
Yet, in good faith, some say that thee behold,
Thy face hath not the power to make love groan;
To say they err I dare not be so bold,
Although I swear it to myself alone.
And, to be sure,° that is not false I swear: — *for proof; surely*
A thousand groans, but thinking on° thy face, — *just thinking about*
One on another's neck° do witness bear — *In quick succession*
Thy black° is fairest in my judgment's place.[2] — *dark appearance*
In nothing art thou black° save in thy deeds, — *ugly*
And thence this slander,[3] as I think, proceeds.

## 132

Thine eyes I love, and they, as° pitying me— — *as if*
Knowing thy heart torment° me with disdain— — *to torment*
Have put on black, and loving mourners be,
Looking with pretty ruth° upon my pain. — *pity*
And truly not the morning sun of heaven
Better becomes° the gray cheeks° of the east, — *beautifies / clouds*
Nor that full star that ushers in the even° — *(Venus, the evening star)*
Doth° half that glory to the sober west — *Imparts*
As those two mourning° eyes become thy face. — *(pun on "morning")*
Oh, let it then as well beseem° thy heart — *become*
To mourn for me, since mourning doth thee grace,
And suit thy pity like in every part.[1]
Then will I swear beauty herself is black,
And all they foul° that thy complexion lack. — *ugly*

## 133

Beshrew° that heart that makes my heart to groan — *Curse (a mild term)*
For that deep wound it gives my friend and me.
Is't not enough to torture me alone,
But slave to slavery° my sweet'st friend must be? — *utterly enslaved*
Me from myself thy cruel eye hath taken,
And my next self thou harder hast engrossed;[1]
Of him, myself, and thee I am forsaken,
A torment thrice threefold thus to be crossed.° — *afflicted*
Prison° my heart in thy steel bosom's ward,° — *Imprison / cell*
But then my friend's heart let my poor heart bail.
Whoe'er keeps° me, let my heart be his guard;[2] — *guards*
Thou canst not then use rigor° in my jail. — *severity*
And yet thou wilt, for I, being pent° in thee, — *locked up*
Perforce am thine, and° all that is in me. — *as is*

**Sonnet 131**
1. As cruel as you are dark (hence, not conventionally beautiful).
2. In my opinion.
3. See line 6 for "this slander."

**Sonnet 132**
1. And dress (or soot, blacken, playing on "suit") your pity similarly, in heart as well as eyes.

**Sonnet 133**
1. And my second self, or closest friend, you have even more cruelly monopolized.
2. My friend's prison.

## 134[1]

So now° I have confessed that he is thine — *now that*
And I myself am mortgaged to thy will,° — *intent; sexual desire*
Myself I'll forfeit, so that other mine[2]
Thou wilt restore to be my comfort still.
But thou wilt not, nor he will not° be free, — *doesn't want to*
For thou art covetous, and he is kind.
He learned but surety-like° to write° for me — *as guarantor / sign*
Under that bond° that him as fast[3] doth bind. — *(of infatuation)*
The statute[4] of thy beauty thou wilt take—
Thou usurer that putt'st forth all to use°— — *at interest; for sex*
And sue a friend came° debtor for my sake; — *who became*
So him I lose through my unkind abuse.[5]
  Him have I lost, thou hast both him and me;
  He pays the whole,° and yet am I not free. — *(pun on "hole")*

## 135[1]

Whoever hath her wish, thou hast thy Will,
And Will to boot,° and Will in overplus. — *in addition*
More than enough am I that vex thee still,° — *always (by wooing)*
To thy sweet will making addition° thus. — *increasing your pleasure*
Wilt thou, whose will is large and spacious,
Not once vouchsafe to hide my will in thine?° — *(sexual)*
Shall will in others° seem right gracious, — *others' wills*
And in my will no fair acceptance shine?[2]
The sea, all water, yet receives rain still,
And in abundance addeth to his° store; — *its*
So° thou, being rich in Will, add° to thy Will — *Similarly / should add*
One will of mine° to make thy large Will more. — *the poet; (sexual)*
  Let "no," unkind, no fair beseechers kill;[3]
  Think all but one,° and me in that one Will. — *one suitor*

## 136[1]

If thy soul check° thee that I come so near,[2] — *chide*
Swear to thy blind soul that I was thy Will,[3]
And will, thy soul knows, is admitted there.
Thus far for love my love-suit, sweet, fulfill.° — *grant*
Will will fulfill the treasure° of thy love; — *fill up the treasury*
Ay, fill it full with wills, and my will one.° — *one of them*
In things of great receipt° with ease we prove — *volume*
Among a number one is reckoned none.[4]
Then in the number let me pass untold,° — *uncounted*
Though in thy store's account° I one must be; — *tally (of lovers)*
For nothing hold me, so it please thee hold

**Sonnet 134**
1. This sonnet links with 133.
2. So long as my other self.
3. As firmly as myself.
4. The total guaranteed by the bond.
5. Through your ill treatment of me; perhaps: through my ill treatment of the youth.

**Sonnet 135**
1. This sonnet, as well as 136, 143, and "A Lover's Complaint," lines 126–33, puns elaborately on different senses of "will": wishes, sexual desire, futurity, testament, the name "Will" (applied to one or more persons, including Shakespeare, and capitalized and sometimes italicized in Q), and the male and female sexual organs. See also 57.13 and note 1.
2. And my will not be greeted with a kind reception.
3. Do not ungenerously say "no," an act that would kill your honorable (or good-looking) suitors.

**Sonnet 136**
1. This sonnet links with 135.
2. I am so forthright; I am so physically close.
3. See Sonnet 135, note 1.
4. Proverbially, one is no number.

That nothing me a something sweet to thee.[5]
Make but my name thy love,[6] and love that still,° *always*
And then thou lovest me, for my name is Will.° *(the speaker); lust*

## 137

Thou blind fool love, what dost thou to mine eyes,
That they behold and see not what they see?
They know what beauty is, see where it lies,
Yet what the best is take the worst to be.[1]
If eyes corrupt° by over-partial° looks *corrupted / overly doting*
Be anchored in the bay where all men ride,[2]
Why of eyes' falsehood hast thou forgèd hooks
Whereto the judgment of my heart is tied?
Why should my heart think that° a several plot° *that place / private land*
Which my heart knows the wide world's common place?[3]
Or° mine eyes, seeing this, say this is not, *Or why should*
To put fair truth upon so foul a face?
In things right true my heart and eyes have erred,
And to this false plague[4] are they now transferred.

## 138[1]

When my love swears that she is made of truth,
I do believe her though I know she lies,
That° she might think me some untutored youth, *So that*
Unlearnèd in the world's false subtleties.
Thus vainly° thinking that she thinks me young, *in vain; with vanity*
Although she knows my days are past the best,
Simply I credit[2] her false-speaking tongue.
On both sides thus is simple truth suppressed.
But wherefore says she not she is unjust?° *unfaithful*
And wherefore say not I that I am old?
Oh, love's best habit is in seeming trust,[3]
And age in love loves not to have years told.° *counted*
Therefore I lie° with her, and she with me, *tell lies; lie down*
And in our faults by lies we flattered be.

## 139

Oh, call° not me to justify° the wrong *ask / approve*
That thy unkindness° lays upon my heart. *infidelity*
Wound me not with thine eye,[1] but with thy tongue;
Use power with power,[2] and slay me not by art.° *by deceit*
Tell me thou lov'st elsewhere; but in my sight,
Dear heart, forbear to glance thine eye aside.
What° need'st thou wound with cunning, when thy might *Why*

5. *For . . . thee:* Think me worthless so long as, my darling, you treasure worthless me (sexually).
6. Love only my name, "Will"; that is, act on your desire.

**Sonnet 137**
1. Yet take the worst to be the best.
2. Harbor for general use (suggesting a promiscuous woman).
3. *the wide . . . place:* common land, open to all (also, the mistress's vagina).
4. This plague of false perception; this deceitful woman.

**Sonnet 138**
1. TEXTUAL COMMENT Another version of this sonnet appears as Poem 1 in *The Passionate Pilgrim.* For the differences between the two versions, see Textual Comment 1 to that work.
2. Naively (foolishly; giving the appearance of folly) I (pretend to) believe.
3. Love is best dressed in (also, love's best behavior is) apparent fidelity.

**Sonnet 139**
1. By looking elsewhere, at other men (see line 6).
2. Use power frankly; fairly.

Is more than my o'erpressed defense can bide?° — *endure*
Let me excuse thee: "Ah, my love well knows
Her pretty looks have been mine enemies,
And therefore from my face she turns my foes,° — *her looks*
That they elsewhere might dart their injuries."
Yet do not so; but since I am near slain,
Kill me outright with looks, and rid° my pain. — *put an end to*

## 140

Be wise as thou art cruel; do not press
My tongue-tied patience with too much disdain,
Lest sorrow lend me words, and words express
The manner of my pity-wanting[1] pain.
If I might teach thee wit,° better it were, — *wisdom*
Though not to love, yet, love, to tell me so—
As testy sick men when their deaths be near
No news but health from their physicians know.° — *learn*
For if I should despair I should grow mad,
And in my madness might speak ill of thee;
Now this ill-wresting world[2] is grown so bad
Mad slanderers by mad ears believèd be.
That I may not be so, nor thou belied,° — *maligned*
Bear thine eyes straight,[3] though thy proud heart go wide.° — *astray*

## 141

In faith, I do not love thee with mine eyes,
For they in thee a thousand errors note,
But 'tis my heart that loves what they despise,
Who in despite of view° is pleased to dote; — *despite what it sees*
Nor are mine ears with thy tongue's tune delighted,
Nor tender feeling to base touches prone,[1]
Nor taste, nor smell, desire to be invited
To any sensual feast with thee alone;
But my five wits[2] nor my five senses can
Dissuade one foolish heart from serving thee,
Who leaves unswayed the likeness of a man,[3]
Thy proud heart's slave and vassal wretch to be.
Only my plague thus far° I count my gain, — *to this extent*
That she that makes me sin awards me pain.[4]

## 142[1]

Love is my sin, and thy dear virtue hate,
Hate of my sin, grounded on sinful loving.[2]
Oh, but with mine, compare thou thine own state,
And thou shalt find it° merits not reproving; — *(my state)*

**Sonnet 140**
1. Unpitied; desiring pity; pitiable.
2. Now this world, which tends to interpret in the worst light.
3. Keep looking only at me (see 139).

**Sonnet 141**
1. Nor is my keen sense of touch susceptible to "base" sexual contact.
2. Mental faculties (common sense, imagination, fancy, judgment, memory).
3. Which (the heart, serving you) leaves without a commander (the five wits or senses) what is therefore the mere semblance of a man.
4. By making me sin, she causes me to suffer punitive penance, which will reduce my sufferings after death (or she just makes me suffer).

**Sonnet 142**
1. This sonnet links with 141.
2. *Love . . . loving:* My only sin is love, and your most valuable virtue is hatred, hatred of my sin in loving you (but also, your most valuable virtue is the haughty rejection of my wooing) based on (your) immoral sexual affairs.

Or if it do, not from those lips of thine,
That have profaned their scarlet ornaments,[3]
And sealed false bonds of love as oft as mine
Robbed others' beds' revenues of their rents.[4]
Be it lawful° I love thee as thou lov'st those — *Let it be lawful that*
Whom thine eyes woo as mine importune thee.
Root pity in thy heart, that, when it grows,
Thy pity may deserve to pitied be.° — *make you pitiable*
  If thou dost seek to have what thou dost hide,° — *(pity)*
  By self-example mayst thou be denied.

## 143

Lo, as a careful° housewife runs to catch — *busy*
One of her feathered creatures broke° away, — *that has broken*
Sets down her babe, and makes all swift dispatch° — *hurries*
In pursuit of the thing she would have stay,
Whilst her neglected child holds her in chase,° — *pursues her*
Cries to catch her whose busy care is bent
To follow that which flies before her face,
Not prizing° her poor infant's discontent; — *regarding*
So runn'st thou after that which flies from thee,
Whilst I, thy babe, chase thee afar behind.
But if thou catch thy hope, turn back to me
And play the mother's part: kiss me, be kind.
  So will I pray that thou mayst have thy Will,[1]
  If thou turn back and my loud crying still.° — *quiet*

## 144[1]

Two loves I have, of comfort and despair,
Which like two spirits do suggest° me still: — *entice*
The better angel is a man right fair,
The worser spirit a woman colored ill.° — *darkly*
To win me soon to hell my female evil
Tempteth my better angel from my side,
And would corrupt my saint to be a devil,
Wooing his purity with her foul pride.
And whether that my angel be turned fiend
Suspect I may, yet not directly tell;
But being both from me, both to each friend,[2]
I guess one angel in another's hell.[3]
  Yet this shall I ne'er know, but live in doubt,
  Till my bad angel fire my good one out.[4]

3. Lips, which are scarlet, like a cardinal's robe.

4. And kissed others' lips as often as I have stolen the sexual and emotional intimacy ("rents" paid by a tenant) from others' marriages by committing adultery, thus reducing the possibility that these marriages will result in children ("revenues," estates that yield income). Q has a comma after "mine" that, if retained, would mean that the mistress is guilty both of kissing others' lips as often as those of the poet and of robbing "others' beds' revenues." "Sealed" with a kiss: comparing the mistress's lips to the red wax used to seal official documents.

**Sonnet 143**

1. A pun; see Sonnet 135, note 1.

**Sonnet 144**

1. TEXTUAL COMMENT Another version of this sonnet appears as Poem 2 in *The Passionate Pilgrim*. For the differences between the two versions, see Digital Edition TC 2 to that work.

2. Both away from me and lovers to one another.

3. Each torments the other; they are in the "hell," or middle den, of a (sexual) game called barley-break; the man occupies the sex organ ("hell") of the woman.

4. Until my bad angel expels my good one, who has become an animal to be smoked out of a burrow; until my bad angel infects my good one with venereal disease; until bad money ("angel" = gold coin) drives out good.

## 145[1]

Those lips that love's own hand did make
Breathed forth the sound that said "I hate"
To me that languished for her sake;
But when she saw my woeful state,
Straight in her heart did mercy come,
Chiding that tongue that, ever sweet,
Was used in giving gentle doom,° *mild judgment*
And taught it thus anew to greet:
"I hate" she altered with an end
That followed it as gentle day
Doth follow night, who, like a fiend,
From heaven to hell is flown away.
"I hate" from hate away she threw,[2]
And saved my life, saying "not you."

## 146

Poor soul, the center of my sinful earth,
Shamed by these rebel powers that thee array,[1]
Why dost thou pine within and suffer dearth,
Painting thy outward walls so costly gay?
Why so large cost, having so short a lease,
Dost thou upon thy fading mansion° spend? *(the body)*
Shall worms, inheritors of this excess,
Eat up thy charge?° Is this thy body's end? *expense*
Then, soul, live thou upon thy servant's° loss, *(the body's)*
And let that pine to aggravate thy store.[2]
Buy terms divine° in selling hours of dross;° *eternal life / waste*
Within be fed, without be rich no more.
So shalt thou feed on death, that feeds on men,
And death once dead, there's no more dying then.

## 147

My love is as a fever, longing still° *continually*
For that which longer nurseth° the disease, *nourishes*
Feeding on that which doth preserve° the ill, *prolong*
Th'uncertain° sickly appetite to please. *capricious*
My reason, the physician to my love,
Angry that his prescriptions are not kept,
Hath left me, and I desperate now approve
Desire is death, which physic did except.[1]
Past cure I am, now reason is past care,[2]
And frantic mad with ever more° unrest. *constant*
My thoughts and my discourse as madmen's are,

**Sonnet 145**

1. Unlike the other sonnets, which are in iambic pentameter, 145 is composed of eight-syllable (iambic tetrameter) lines.

2. She converted the normal meaning of the phrase "I hate" away from "hate." A pun on "hate away" and "(Anne) Hathaway," Shakespeare's wife, is possible.

**Sonnet 146**

1. This rebellious body in which you are clothed. TEXTUAL COMMENT At the beginning of the line, Q repeats "My sinful earth" from the previous line. There is no way of discovering with certainty what Shakespeare wrote. For the emendation adopted here, see Digital Edition TC 9.

2. And let the body dwindle to add to your wealth.

**Sonnet 147**

1. *now . . . except:* now discover that desire, which medicine rejected (or, possibly, which rejected medicine), is fatal.

2. Medical care: inverting the proverb "Past cure, past care" (don't worry about what you can't control). In the proverb, you don't care because you can't cure; here, because you don't care, you can't cure.

At random from° the truth, vainly° expressed, *unconnected to / idly*
For I have sworn thee fair, and thought thee bright,
Who art as black as hell, as dark as night.

### 148

Oh, me! What eyes hath love put in my head,
Which have no correspondence with true sight?
Or if they have, where is my judgment fled,
That censures falsely[1] what they see aright?
If that be fair whereon my false eyes dote,
What means the world to say it is not so?
If it be not, then love doth well denote[2]
Love's eye is not so true as all men's "no."[3]
How can it? Oh, how can love's eye be true,
That is so vexed with watching° and with tears? *staying awake*
No marvel then though I° mistake my view; *that I (eye)*
The sun itself sees not till heaven clears.
O cunning love, with tears thou keep'st me blind,
Lest eyes, well seeing, thy foul faults should find.

### 149

Canst thou, O cruel, say I love thee not
When I against myself with thee partake?° *take sides*
Do I not think on thee when I forgot
Am of myself—all, tyrant,[1] for thy sake?
Who hateth thee that I do call my friend?
On whom frown'st thou that I do fawn upon?
Nay, if thou lour'st° on me, do I not spend° *scowl / wreak*
Revenge upon myself with present moan?° *instant anguish*
What merit do I in myself respect° *value; note*
That is so proud thy service to despise,[2]
When all my best° doth worship thy defect,° *best qualities / flaws*
Commanded by the motion of thine eyes?
But, love, hate on, for now I know thy mind:
Those that can see thou lov'st, and I am blind.[3]

### 150

Oh, from what power hast thou this powerful might
With insufficiency° my heart to sway, *By your flaws*
To make me give the lie to my true sight
And swear that brightness doth not grace the day?[1]
Whence hast thou this becoming of things ill,[2]
That in the very refuse of thy deeds° *your basest behavior*
There is such strength and warrantise° of skill *guarantee*
That in my mind thy worst all best exceeds?

**Sonnet 148**
1. That judges inaccurately (dishonestly). "False" (line 5) has similar meanings.
2. Then my self-delusion in love proves that.
3. Not so true as all other men's denial, suggesting a pun on "eye/ay" (yes).

**Sonnet 149**
1. *when . . . all, tyrant:* when I neglect myself—doing all of this, you tyrant.
2. So proud as to scorn to serve you.
3. You love those who see you accurately and thus admire you, but I am blinded (by love and, thus, from your point of view, unworthy of being loved). The first clause may have the opposite sense, however: you love those who see your defects well enough not to love you.

**Sonnet 150**
1. *To . . . day:* The speaker is so blindly in love that he finds beauty only in the blackness he associates with his mistress.
2. This capacity to render the ugly attractive.

Who taught thee how to make me love thee more,
The more I hear and see just cause of hate?
Oh, though I love what others do abhor,° *(pun on "whore")*
With others thou shouldst not abhor my state.
If thy unworthiness raised° love in me, *(sexual)*
More worthy I to be beloved of thee.[3]

## 151

Love is too young° to know what conscience is; *(Cupid being a boy)*
Yet who knows not conscience[1] is born of love?
Then, gentle cheater, urge° not my amiss,° *stress / fault*
Lest guilty of my faults thy sweet self prove.
For, thou betraying me, I do betray
My nobler part° to my gross body's treason. *(the soul)*
My soul doth tell my body that he° may *(the body)*
Triumph in love; flesh stays no farther reason,[2]
But, rising at thy name, doth point out thee
As his triumphant prize. Proud of this pride,[3]
He is contented thy poor drudge to be—
To stand° in thy affairs, fall by thy side. *assist; be erect*
No want of conscience hold it that I call
Her "love," for whose dear love I rise and fall.

## 152

In loving thee thou know'st I am forsworn,[1]
But thou art twice forsworn, to me love swearing:° *in swearing love to me*
In act thy bed-vow° broke, and new faith torn *to husband (or lover)*
In vowing new hate after new love bearing.[2]
But why of two oaths' breach do I accuse thee,
When I break twenty? I am perjured most,
For all my vows are oaths but to misuse° thee; *deceive*
And all my honest faith in thee is lost.
For I have sworn deep oaths of thy deep kindness—
Oaths of thy love, thy truth, thy constancy—
And to enlighten thee gave eyes to blindness,[3]
Or made them swear against the thing they see.
For I have sworn thee fair—more perjured eye,° *(punning on "I")*
To swear against the truth so foul a lie.

3. Love me owing to my generosity; perhaps: love me because my bad judgment makes me a suitable match.

**Sonnet 151**

1. Moral sense; carnal knowledge.
2. Flesh, specifically the sexual organ, needs no further encouragement.
3. Swelling with pride (and lust).

**Sonnet 152**

1. Forsworn presumably in breaking loving vows—perhaps to his wife, to the youth to whom he promised unswerving devotion in earlier sonnets, or to both.
2. *new faith . . . bearing:* the "new faith" followed by "new hate" may be addressed either to the speaker's young friend or to the speaker himself.
3. And to make you fair (give you insight), I looked blindly on your failings (pretended to see what I couldn't).

## 153[1]

Cupid[2] laid by his brand° and fell asleep. *torch; (phallic)*
A maid of Dian's[3] this advantage found,° *seized*
And his love-kindling fire did quickly steep
In a cold valley-fountain of that ground,
Which borrowed from this holy fire of Love
A dateless° lively heat still° to endure, *An endless / always*
And grew a seething bath, which yet men prove
Against strange maladies a sovereign cure.[4]
But at my mistress' eye Love's brand new fired,° *being newly lit*
The boy for trial° needs would touch my breast. *to test it*
I, sick withal,° the help of bath desired, *from it*
And thither hied, a sad distempered° guest, *seriously ill*
    But found no cure. The bath for my help lies
    Where Cupid got new fire: my mistress' eyes.

## 154[1]

The little love-god, lying once asleep,
Laid by his side his heart-inflaming brand,° *torch*
Whilst many nymphs that vowed chaste life to keep
Came tripping by; but in her maiden hand,
The fairest votary° took up that fire *religious adherent*
Which many legions of true hearts° had warmed, *lovers*
And so the general° of hot desire *commander (Cupid)*
Was, sleeping, by a virgin hand disarmed.
This brand she quenchèd in a cool well by,° *close by*
Which from Love's fire took heat perpetual,
Growing a bath and healthful remedy
For men diseased. But I, my mistress' thrall,° *slave*
    Came there for cure, and this° by that I prove: *the following*
    Love's fire heats water, water cools not love.

**Sonnet 153**
1. This and the following sonnet derive indirectly from classical fifth-century Greek epigrams.
2. God of love (especially erotic desire), a boy, son of Venus, goddess of love—associated with the speaker's mistress rather than with the male youth.
3. Diana, goddess of chastity.
4. *And grew . . . cure:* And became a boiling-hot medicinal bath (used, among other purposes, for the treatment of venereal disease), which men still find to be an outstanding remedy for foreign illnesses (venereal diseases were associated with foreigners). There may be an allusion here and in Sonnet 154 to the town of Bath, which became a famous health spa in the eighteenth century.

**Sonnet 154**
1. This sonnet varies the topic of 153.

# A Lover's Complaint

Shakespeare's sonnets first appeared in print in the Quarto of 1609, but they did not appear alone. In that volume, they were followed by "A Lover's Complaint," a poem probably from the first years of the seventeenth century and possibly by Shakespeare. (See the Textual Introduction). In complaint poetry, a woman laments her (usually) sexual ruin amid doleful reflections on life. Between 1593 and 1596, six poets published works consisting of a sonnet sequence, a brief intermediate piece usually based on ancient Greek form or subject matter (Cupid, for example), and a concluding complaint. The sonnets section of one such work, Richard Barnfield's *Cynthia* (1595), from which Shakespeare probably borrowed, is addressed to an attractive male youth. Another poet anticipates Shakespeare's sequence in dividing his sonnets into two main groups. It would be wrong to overstate the homogeneity of this mini-tradition. Nonetheless, the 1609 Quarto—a sonnet sequence plausibly divided into two parts, the first concerning a beautiful male youth and the second a woman; two concluding sonnets on Cupid; and a poetic complaint—is less miscellaneous collection than multigeneric form.

That form is characterized by its links between the sonnets and the complaint. The voyeuristic poems dealing with the affair between the male youth and the speaker's mistress anticipate "A Lover's Complaint." In a conventional pastoral landscape, the "Complaint's" narrator overhears a young woman tell an old man of her seduction and abandonment by an attractive young man. The "double voice" (line 3) the narrator hears—explicitly, an echo—also anticipates the young woman's extended quotation of the young man inside her own tale, the young man's duplicitous method of wooing (using poetry and theater), and even the uncertain veracity of the woman, the old man, and the narrator. Except for the old man, the characters resemble the three central figures in the sonnet sequence.

Yet in "A Lover's Complaint," but only ambiguously if at all in the sonnets, the male youth seduces the woman, and both seemingly get to speak for themselves. The first-person voice—the only one heard in the sonnets—is denied even the concluding comment promised by the opening frame. Instead, the betrayed woman closes the poem, whose ornamental, archaic diction, partly modeled on the works of Shakespeare's older contemporary Edmund Spenser, contrasts with the sonnets' mixture of down-to-earth colloquialism and metaphorical density. Again, though written (like the sonnets) in rhymed iambic pentameter, "A Lover's Complaint" has a different form—rime royal, a seven-line stanza rhyming *ababbcc* used extensively by Chaucer, occasionally by Spenser, and by Shakespeare himself in *The Rape of Lucrece*. As in *Lucrece*, enjambment is more common than in the sonnets, perhaps owing to the greater emphasis on narrative in "A Lover's Complaint." Finally, the woman's voice, rather than the first person, is employed as elsewhere in complaint poetry to ventriloquize the male poet's views. But here, the self-referential turn emphasizes not the memorializing but the destructive power of poetry.

Walter Cohen

## SELECTED BIBLIOGRAPHY

Cheney, Patrick. "'Deep-Brained Sonnets' and 'Tragic Shows': Shakespeare's Late Ovidian Art in *A Lover's Complaint.*" *Critical Essays on Shakespeare's "A Lover's Complaint."* Ed. Shirley Sharon-Zisser. Aldershot, Hampshire: Ashgate, 2006. 55–77. Reads the poem as a self-referential attempt to reconcile competing literary traditions (lyrical-tragic vs. pastoral-epic) and views of nationhood (liberty vs. monarchy), in which the female protagonist is both agent and victim of the seductiveness of art.

Rowe, Katherine. "A Lover's Complaint." *The Cambridge Companion to Shakespeare's Poetry.* Ed. Patrick Cheney. Cambridge: Cambridge UP, 2007. 144–60. Places the poem in relation to the tradition of complaint poetry, to treatment of the emotions, and to the use of ostentatiously artificial language.

## TEXTUAL INTRODUCTION

"A Louers complaint. | *BY* | WILLIAM SHAKE-SPEARE" follows the "FINIS." of Shakespeare's sonnets in the 1609 Quarto, filling out the last eleven pages of the brief volume (sigs. K1–L2). Neither publisher Thomas Thorpe's entry of the sonnets in the Stationers' Register on May 20, 1609, nor the Quarto's title page and dedication of "INSVING.SONNETS" mentions this complaint poem, written in the seven-line rime royal stanza that is also used in *The Rape of Lucrece.* Despite the Quarto's attribution of the poem to Shakespeare, its authorship has been widely debated. It was questioned in the first half of the twentieth century as awkward in expression (e.g., "sawn" as past participle of "see" to fit the rhyme at line 91) and un-Shakespearean in vocabulary. New arguments in the 1960s, however, turned the tide back in favor of Shakespeare's authorship: even the high proportion of "non-Shakespearean" vocabulary, for instance, was reconceived in quantitative studies as positive evidence when set in comparison with rates of new vocabulary in other Shakespearean works (Jackson 169–83). Positive critical evaluations, often claiming the complaint poem as an integral coda to the sonnets, suggested an emerging consensus about the poem's authenticity over the next few decades, but the authorship debate has since been rekindled, especially in response to Brian Vickers's proposal of John Davies of Hereford as a candidate. Some recent approaches emphasize recognizable collocation and phrasal patterns, rhetorical figures, metrical characteristics (including stress profiles and syntactic breaks), and distinctive spellings, and the poem has also become a testing ground for computer-assisted stylometric analysis synthesizing complex variables. Definitive conclusions do, however, remain elusive.

LYNNE MAGNUSSON

### TEXTUAL BIBLIOGRAPHY

Jackson, MacDonald P. *Determining the Shakespeare Canon:* Arden of Faversham *and* A Lover's Complaint. Oxford: Oxford UP, 2014.

Vickers, Brian. *Shakespeare, "A Lover's Complaint," and John Davies of Hereford.* Cambridge: Cambridge UP, 2007.

# A Lover's Complaint

From off a hill whose concave womb reworded° *hollow side echoed*
A plaintful story from a sist'ring° vale, *nearby*
My spirits t'attend° this double voice accorded,° *hear / agreed*
And down I laid to list° the sad-tuned tale; *listen to*
Ere long espied a fickle° maid full pale, *disturbed*
Tearing of papers, breaking rings a-twain,° *in two*
Storming her world with sorrow's wind and rain.

Upon her head a plaited hive° of straw, *hat*
Which fortified° her visage from the sun, *protected*
Whereon the thought° might think sometime it saw *imagination*
The carcass° of a beauty spent and done. *dead remainder*
Time had not scythèd all that youth begun,
Nor youth all quit,° but spite° of heaven's fell° rage, *gone / in spite / fierce*
Some beauty peeped through lattice of seared° age. *withered*

Oft did she heave her napkin to her eyne,[1]
Which on it had conceited characters,° *imaginative designs*
Laund'ring the silken figures in the brine
That seasoned° woe had pelleted in tears, *experienced; salted*
And often reading° what contents it bears; *(the "figures," line 17)*
As often shrieking undistinguished° woe *inarticulate*
In clamors of all size, both high and low.

Sometimes her leveled eyes their carriage ride[2]
As° they did batt'ry to the spheres° intend; *As if / planets*
Sometime diverted, their poor balls° are tied *eyeballs; cannonballs*
To th'orbèd° earth; sometimes they do extend *spherical*
Their view right on;° anon their gazes° lend *straight / the eyes*
To every place at once and nowhere fixed,
The mind and sight distractedly commixed.° *confused*

Her hair, nor° loose nor tied in formal plait, *neither*
Proclaimed in her a careless hand of pride;[3]
For some, untucked, descended her sheaved hat,° *fell from her straw hat*
Hanging her pale and pinèd cheek beside;
Some in her threaden fillet° still did bide *headband*
And, true to bondage, would not break from thence,
Though slackly braided in loose negligence.

A thousand favors° from a maund° she drew, *love tokens / basket*
Of amber, crystal, and of beaded jet,° *beads of black stone*

1. Often did she raise her handkerchief to her eyes.
2. Sometimes her eyes, aimed (like a cannon), glare (are mounted on a swivel).
3. A hand careless of pride; a hand proud in its carelessness (knowing that she could attract with no effort).

Which one by one she in a river threw,
Upon whose weeping margin she was set,° *seated*
Like usury applying wet to wet,[4]
Or monarch's hands that lets not bounty fall
Where want cries some, but where excess begs all.[5]

Of folded schedules° had she many a one, *letters*
Which she perused, sighed, tore, and gave the flood;
Cracked many a ring of posied gold and bone,[6]
Bidding them find their sepulchers in mud;
Found yet more letters, sadly penned in blood,
With sleided silk feat and affectedly
Enswathed[7] and sealed to curious° secrecy. *careful*

These often bathed she in her fluxive° eyes, *flowing*
And often kissed, and often gave to tear,
Cried, "O false blood, thou register° of lies, *record*
What unapprovèd° witness dost thou bear! *unreliable*
Ink would have seemed more black and damnèd here!"
This said, in top of rage the lines she rents,° *rips*
Big° discontent so breaking their contents. *Powerful*

A reverend man that grazed his cattle nigh
(Sometime a blusterer that the ruffle knew[8]
Of court, of city, and had let go by
The swiftest hours observèd as they flew[9])
Towards this afflicted fancy fastly[1] drew
And, privileged by age, desires to know
In brief the grounds and motives of her woe.

So slides he down upon his grainèd bat[2]
And, comely° distant, sits he by her side, *politely*
When he again desires her, being sat,
Her grievance with his hearing to divide.° *share*
If that from him there may be aught° applied *anything*
Which may her suffering ecstasy° assuage, *grief*
'Tis promised in the charity of age.

"Father," she says, "though in me you behold
The injury of many a blasting° hour, *disfiguring*
Let it not tell your judgment I am old:
Not age, but sorrow, over me hath power.
I might as yet have been a spreading° flower, *blooming*
Fresh to myself, if I had self-applied
Love to myself, and to no love beside.

4. Like usury making wealth wealthier (by adding tears to the stream).
5. *Or . . . all:* Or like the monarch who, rather than give a little to the truly needy, gives a great deal to those who already have plenty.
6. A ring of gold and ivory inscribed with messages (of love).
7. *With . . . / Enswathed:* Delicately and affectionately wrapped in strands of separated ("sleided") silk.
8. Once a loudmouthed man of the world who was accustomed to the busier life.
9. *had . . . flew:* was past the prime of life, but had learned from experience.
1. Toward this person afflicted by love rapidly (close by).
2. So he comes down the bank with the help of his forked herdsman's staff.

"But woe is me, too early I attended
A youthful suit—it was° to gain my grace°— *was designed / favor*
Oh, one by nature's outwards° so commended *external appearance*
That maidens' eyes stuck over all° his face. *were glued to*
Love lacked a dwelling and made him her place,
And when in his fair parts she did abide,
She was new lodged and newly deified.

"His browny locks did hang in crooked curls,
And every light occasion° of the wind *chance stirring*
Upon his lips their silken parcels° hurls. *(of hair)*
What's sweet to do, to do will aptly find:[3]
Each eye that saw him did enchant the mind,
For on his visage was in little° drawn *miniature*
What largeness thinks in paradise was sawn.[4]

"Small show of man was yet upon his chin:
His phoenix° down began but to appear, *singularly lovely*
Like unshorn velvet, on that termless skin[5]
Whose bare out-bragged the web[6] it seemed to wear;
Yet showed his visage by that cost more dear,[7]
And nice affections° wavering stood in doubt *discriminating tastes*
If best were as it was, or best without.° *(shaven)*

"His qualities° were beauteous as his form, *skills; manners*
For maiden-tongued° he was and thereof free;° *modest of speech / fluent*
Yet if men moved° him, was he such a storm *angered*
As oft twixt May and April is to see
When winds breathe sweet, unruly though they be.
His rudeness so with his authorized youth
Did livery falseness in a pride of truth.[8]

"Well could he ride, and often men would say,
'That horse his mettle from his rider takes:
Proud of subjection, noble by the sway,° *control*
What rounds, what bounds, what course,° what stop he makes!' *gallop*
And controversy hence a question takes:
Whether the horse by him became his deed,
Or he his manage by th' well-doing steed.[9]

"But quickly on this side the verdict went:
His real habitude° gave life and grace *royal manner (or attire)*
To appertainings° and to ornament— *external outfits*
Accomplished in himself, not in his case;° *mere appearance; clothes*
All aids, themselves made fairer by their place,

3. Ways are easily found to do pleasant things (look, love).
4. What one would imagine seeing on a larger scale in paradise.
5. Like velvet with its nap unclipped, on that indescribable (invulnerable to time) skin.
6. Whose naked surface showed more beautiful than the down covering.
7. Yet his face looked more precious (attractive) because of its rich clothing.
8. *His . . . truth:* His roughness, sanctioned by his "youth," employed falseness in truth's uniform.
9. *Whether . . . steed:* Whether he performed so well because of his horsemanship or because his grace in horsemanship (French: *manège*) was a result of the horse's skill.

Came for additions;[1] yet their purposed trim
Pieced not[2] his grace, but were all graced by him.

"So on the tip of his subduing tongue
All kind of arguments and question deep,
All replication prompt,° and reason strong *quick reply*
For his advantage still did wake and sleep.[3]
To make the weeper laugh, the laugher weep,
He had the dialect and different skill,[4]
Catching all passions in his craft of will,[5]

"That° he did in the general bosom° reign *So that / all hearts*
Of young, of old, and sexes both° enchanted *both sexes*
To dwell with him in thoughts, or to remain
In personal duty, following where he haunted.° *often went*
Consents,[6] bewitched, ere he desire° have granted, *before he asks*
And dialogued for him what° he would say, *anticipated what words*
Asked their own wills and made their wills obey.

"Many there were that did his picture get
To serve their eyes, and in it put their mind,
Like fools that in th'imagination set
The goodly objects° which abroad° they find *sights / traveling*
Of lands and mansions, theirs in thought assigned,
And laboring in more pleasures to bestow them[7]
Than the true gouty landlord which doth owe° them. *own*

"So many have, that never touched his hand,
Sweetly supposed them mistress of his heart.
My woeful self, that did in freedom stand
And was my own fee-simple[8] (not in part),
What with his art in youth and youth in art
Threw my affections in his charmèd° power, *magical; songlike*
Reserved the stalk and gave him all my flower.

"Yet did I not, as some my equals° did, *young girls of my rank*
Demand of him; nor, being desired, yielded.° *yielded sexual favors*
Finding my self in honor so forbid,
With safest distance I mine honor° shielded. *chastity*
Experience° for me many bulwarks builded *(of "my equals")*
Of proofs new bleeding, which remained the foil[9]
Of this false jewel and his amorous spoil.

"But ah, who ever shunned by precedent
The destined ill she must herself assay?° *try out*

1. Attempted to increase his worth.
2. *their . . . not:* their anticipated decorative effect did not increase (or: mend—continuation of the stanza's ostensibly denied emphasis on external garments).
3. *For . . . sleep:* (Like servants) adjusted their waking and sleeping hours for the benefit of their master.
4. The manner of speech and versatile skill.
5. His faculty of persuasion. Here and in the next stanza, there are suggestions of other senses of "will," including the author's name. See Sonnets 135 and 136.
6. (Sexually) consenting people.
7. *theirs . . . them:* imagining the "lands and mansions" their own, they try harder to use them pleasurably.
8. And had absolute control of myself (as of land in freehold).
9. *Of . . . foil:* Fresh examples of seduction, which remained the defense (or sword—picking up the military, specifically fencing, imagery of "distance," "shielded," "bulwarks," "bleeding," lines 151–53). But "foil" as the dark material in which gems are set to make them look more brilliant also works with "false jewel" in the following line, to suggest that the young man's sexual escapades made him more attractive.

Or forced examples 'gainst her own content
To put the bypast perils in her way?[1]
Counsel may stop awhile what will not stay,° *stop for good*
For when we rage,° advice is often seen *(with lust)*
By blunting° us to make our wits more keen. *repressing*

"Nor gives it satisfaction to our blood° *sexuality*
That we must curb it upon others' proof°— *experience*
To be forbid° the sweets that seems so good *forbidden*
For fear of harms that preach in our behoof.° *for our benefit*
O appetite, from judgment stand aloof!
The one a palate hath that needs will taste,
Though reason weep and cry, 'It is thy last!'

"For further I could say, 'This man's untrue';[2]
And knew the patterns° of his foul beguiling, *instances*
Heard where his plants in others' orchards° grew, *(wombs)*
Saw how deceits were gilded in his smiling,
Knew vows were ever brokers° to defiling, *go-betweens*
Thought characters and words merely but art,[3]
And bastards of his foul adulterate heart.

"And long upon these terms I held my city,° *chastity*
Till thus he gan° besiege me: 'Gentle maid, *began to*
Have of my suffering youth some feeling pity,
And be not of my holy vows afraid.
That's° to ye sworn to none was ever said: *What is*
For feasts of love I have been called unto,
Till now, did° ne'er invite nor never woo. *(I) did*

"'All my offenses that abroad° you see° *in the world / learn of*
Are errors of the blood,° none of the mind. *sexual passion*
Love made them not; with acture they may be,[4]
Where neither party is nor true nor kind.° *faithful or loving*
They sought their shame that so° their shame did find, *who in this way*
And so much less of shame in me remains
By how much of me their reproach contains.[5]

"'Among the many that mine eyes have seen,
Not° one whose flame my heart so much as warmèd *There is not*
Or my affection put to th' smallest teen° *pain*
Or any of my leisures° ever charmèd. *hours of leisure*
Harm have I done to them but ne'er was harmèd;
Kept hearts in liveries,° but mine own was free *in uniform (service)*
And reigned commanding in his monarchy.

"'Look here what tributes wounded fancies° sent me *lovers*
Of pallid pearls and rubies red as blood,
Figuring° that they their passions likewise lent me *Showing*

1. *Or . . . way:* Or reminded herself, to counter her present inclinations, of bygone dangers. *forced:* urged.
2. I am able to say more about this man's perfidy.
3. Written and spoken words were merely instruments of skill (in seduction).
4. *with . . . be:* by a mere physical act they may be performed.
5. *By . . . contains:* The more they name me in their reproaches (thus revealing that they are unchaste and, hence, by this logic, to blame).

Of grief and blushes, aptly understood
In bloodless white and the encrimsoned mood°— *form (of rubies)*
Effects of terror and dear modesty,
Encamped in hearts, but fighting outwardly.[6]

"'And lo, behold these talents° of their hair *riches*
With twisted metal amorously impleached[7]
I have received from many a several fair° *a different beauty*
(Their kind acceptance weepingly beseeched),
With th'annexions° of fair gems enriched *additions*
And deep-brained sonnets that did amplify° *expound; increase*
Each stone's dear° nature, worth, and quality. *precious*

"'The diamond? Why, 'twas beautiful and hard,
Whereto his invised[8] properties did tend;
The deep green em'rald, in whose fresh regard
Weak sights their sickly radiance do amend;[9]
The heaven-hued sapphire and the opal blend[1]
With objects manifold: each several° stone, *distinct*
With wit well blazoned,° smiled or made some moan. *described*

"'Lo, all these trophies of affections° hot, *passions*
Of pensive° and subdued desires the tender,° *saddened / gifts*
Nature hath charged me that I hoard them not,
But yield them up where I myself must render:
That is to you, my origin and ender;° *alpha and omega; all*
For these of force must your oblations be,[2]
Since I their altar, you enpatron me.[3]

"'Oh, then, advance of yours that phraseless° hand *beyond description*
Whose white weighs down the airy scale of praise.[4]
Take all these similes[5] to your own command,
Hallowed with sighs that burning° lungs did raise. *(with love)*
What me, your minister, for you obeys,
Works under you,[6] and to your audit° comes *account*
Their distract parcels° in combinèd sums. *component parts*

"'Lo, this device was sent me from a nun,
Or sister sanctified of holiest note,° *reputation*
Which late her noble suit° in court did shun, *attendance; suitors*
Whose rarest havings° made the blossoms° dote; *qualities / young nobles*
For she was sought by spirits of richest coat,° *coat of arms*
But kept cold distance and did thence remove
To spend her living° in eternal love.° *life / (of God)*

6. *Effects . . . outwardly:* White ("terror") and red (blushing "modesty") fighting on their faces.
7. With metal clasps lovingly intertwined.
8. Its unseen—referring to the diamond but also, perhaps, to the equally "beautiful and hard" young man.
9. *in . . . amend:* which, when looked at, can heal weak vision.
1. Blended: many-colored; accompanying other "objects" (line 216).
2. For these necessarily must be offerings at your altar.
3. Since I am the altar (on which they were offered), you must necessarily be the patron saint of the altar (me).
4. Whose white exceeds any measure of praise.
5. These emblematic gifts and the sonnets that explain them.
6. *What . . . under you:* Whatever pays homage to me, your agent, serves you.

"'But oh, my sweet, what labor is't to leave
The thing we have not, mast'ring what not strives,° *does not resist*
Planing° the place which did no form[7] receive, *Smoothing*
Playing patient sports in unconstrainèd gyves?[8]
She that her fame so to herself contrives[9]
The scars of battle scapeth° by the flight, *escapes*
And makes her absence valiant, not her might.[1]

"'Oh, pardon me in that my boast is true!
The accident which brought me to her eye
Upon the moment° did her force° subdue, *Immediately / resolve*
And now she would the cagèd cloister fly:
Religious° love put out religion's eye. *Devoted (sexual)*
Not to be tempted would she be immured,° *walled up*
And now, to tempt, all liberty procured.

"'How mighty then you are, oh, hear me tell!
The broken bosoms° that to me belong *hearts*
Have emptied all their fountains in my well,
And mine I pour° your ocean all among: *pour into*
I strong o'er them, and you o'er me being strong,
Must for your victory us all congest,° *gather*
As compound° love, to physic° your cold breast. *medicinal / treat*

"'My parts° had power to charm a sacred nun, *attributes; limbs; roles*
Who, disciplined, ay, dieted in° grace, *sustained by*
Believed her eyes when they t'assail begun,[2]
All vows and consecrations giving place.° *yielding*
O most potential love! Vow, bond, nor space
In thee hath neither sting, knot, nor confine,[3]
For thou art all, and all things else are thine.

"'When thou impressest,[4] what are precepts worth
Of stale example? When thou wilt inflame,
How coldly those impediments stand forth
Of wealth, of filial fear, law, kindred, fame!° *reputation*
Love's arms are° peace, 'gainst rule, 'gainst sense, 'gainst shame; *Love's power compels*
And° sweetens in the suff'ring pangs it bears *And love*
The aloes° of all forces, shocks, and fears. *bitterness*

"'Now all these hearts that do on mine depend,
Feeling it break, with bleeding groans they pine,[5]
And, supplicant,° their sighs to you extend *as supplicants*
To leave° the batt'ry that you make 'gainst mine, *cease*
Lending soft audience to my sweet design[6]

7. No impression (of love, on the heart).
8. Pretending to patiently endure shackles ("gyves") that have not been forced upon one and that can be removed (or that do not constrain). (The entire sentence is ironic.)
9. She who thus contrives for herself the reputation of disinterest in love.
1. And achieves a reputation for valor by avoiding the temptation of love, not by strongly resisting it.
2. When my attributes ("parts") began to assail her heart.
3. *potential . . . confine:* powerful love: a "vow" has no force ("sting"), a "bond" does not tie ("knot"), and "space" does not restrain ("confine").
4. When you draft someone into your (military) service; make an impression on the heart.
5. Because each sigh supposedly robbed the heart of a drop of blood.
6. Looking favorably on my good intentions.

And credent° soul to that strong bonded oath — *trustful*
That shall prefer and undertake° my troth.' — *advance and guarantee*

"This said, his wat'ry eyes he did dismount,° — *lower (military)*
Whose sights till then were leveled° on my face. — *aimed*
Each cheek, a river running from a fount,
With brinish current downward flowed apace.
Oh, how the channel° to the stream° gave grace, — *cheeks / tears*
Who, glazed with crystal, 'gat the glowing roses
That flame through water which their hue encloses.[7]

"O father, what a hell of witchcraft lies
In the small orb of one particular° tear! — *single*
But, with the inundation of the eyes,
What rocky heart to° water will not wear?° — *eroded by / wear away*
What breast so cold that is not warmèd here?
Or cleft° effect—cold modesty, hot wrath°— — *divided / passion*
Both fire from hence and chill extincture hath?[8]

"For lo, his passion,° but an art of craft, — *passionate speech*
Even there resolved° my reason into tears. — *dissolved*
There my white stole of chastity I daffed,° — *took off*
Shook off my sober guards and civil° fears; — *respectable; sober*
Appear to him as he to me appears—
All melting, though our drops this diff'rence bore:
His poisoned me, and mine did him restore.

"In him a plenitude of subtle matter,° — *raw material; cunning*
Applied to cautels,° all strange forms receives[9]— — *tricky devices*
Of burning blushes, or of weeping water,
Or swooning paleness; and he takes and leaves° — *uses this and shuns that*
In either's aptness° as it best deceives: — *As each is appropriate*
To blush at speeches rank,° to weep at woes, — *offensive*
Or to turn white and swoon at tragic shows;

"That not a heart which in his level° came — *range (of fire)*
Could scape the hail of his all-hurting aim,
Showing fair nature is° both kind and tame; — *Pretending his nature is*
And, veiled in them,° did win whom he would maim. — *(kindness and tameness)*
Against the thing he sought he would exclaim:
When he most burned in heart-wished luxury,° — *lust*
He preached pure maid° and praised cold chastity. — *virginal purity*

"Thus, merely with the garment of a grace[1]
The naked and concealèd fiend° he covered, — *devil*
That th'unexperient° gave the tempter place,° — *inexperienced / entry*
Which° like a cherubin above them hovered.° — *(The tempter) / (ironic)*
Who, young and simple, would not be so lovered?[2]

7. *Who . . . encloses:* The stream (of tears) is seen as a kind of glass covering ("crystal") over the cheeks ("roses"), to which it imparts a passionate color that shines through the "water," like a jewel enclosed in glass. *Who:* (the stream).
8. *Both . . . hath:* Tears heat up "cold modesty" and extinguish "hot" passion (as the following stanza elaborates).
9. *all . . . receives:* is shaped into novel forms.
1. With (merely) external appeal; also part of the religious language of the stanza, while looking back to earlier uses of "grace" with a variety of meanings.
2. Would not desire such a lover.

Ay me, I fell, and yet do question make° — *wonder*
What I should do again for such a sake.° — *person; pleasure*

"Oh, that infected° moisture of his eye! — *tainted*
Oh, that false fire which in his cheek so glowed!
Oh, that forced thunder from° his heart did fly! — *that from*
Oh, that sad breath his spongy lungs bestowed!° — *emitted*
Oh, all that borrowed motion, seeming owed,[3]
Would yet again betray the fore-betrayed
And new pervert a reconcilèd° maid." — *penitent*

3. That emotion apparently his own.

# APPENDICES

# Attributed Poems

None of the attributed poems is incontrovertibly by Shakespeare, though the case is much better for some than for others. (See the Textual Introduction.) "A song, 'Shall I die?'"—probably not by Shakespeare—is noteworthy mainly as a virtuoso display of rhyming: there are usually eight pairs of rhyme words in each eight-line stanza, with the rhymes occurring as often as every three syllables and on occasion every two syllables ("Being set, lips met," line 31). Several of the other poems are, like the last part of "The Phoenix and Turtle," elegies—compositions in memory of the dead, though sometimes written while the subject was still alive. The first of the two epitaphs on the usurer John Combe reveals a conventional hostility to usury. The second, however, deploys the complex, sometimes positive, metaphorical relationship between usury and breeding characteristic of the early sonnets. Combe

did gather [wealth from usury]
To make the poor his issue [heirs]; he, their father,
. . . [made] record of his tilth and seeds.
(lines 3–5)

Urging marriage and a family, Sonnet 3 speaks of "the tillage of thy husbandry" (line 6). And Sonnet 6 argues:

That use is not forbidden usury
Which happies those that pay the willing loan:
That's for thyself to breed another thee,
Or ten times happier, be it ten for one.
(lines 5–8)

Thus, in the sonnets, the language of usury helps clarify paternity, whereas in the second epitaph the language of paternity helps clarify usury. In both, however, the two terms are mutually illuminating. The last line quoted from Sonnet 6 is also reminiscent of the opening of the first epitaph: "Ten in the hundred here lies engraved; / A hundred to ten his soul is ne'er saved." Both refer to the highest legal interest rate—ten in a hundred, or 10 percent. But where the sonnet converts the allusion into a positive image, the elegy reverses the interest rate to denote the long odds against the usurer's salvation.

Similarly, "Verses on the Stanley Tomb at Tong" closely parallels the language of some of Shakespeare's sonnets concerned with the destructive power of time. The "register" and the "sky-aspiring pyramids" (East end 3, West end 2) also appear in Sonnet 123 ("pyramids built up," "registers," lines 2, 9). Closer still is the connection to Sonnet 55: "Not marble nor the gilded monuments / Of princes shall outlive this powerful rhyme" (lines 1–2). Stanley's "fame is more perpetual than these stones" (East 4); "Not monumental stone preserves our fame" (West 1). Stanley's "memory," however, "[s]hall outlive marble and defacers' hands" as well as "time's consumption" (West 3, 4, 5), just as "memory" need not worry that "war shall statues overturn" and is not dependent on "unswept stone besmeared with sluttish time" in Sonnet 55 (lines 8, 5, 4). Although the guarantee of immortality seems to rest on Stanley's life rather than the "powerful rhyme" of the sonnet (line 2), the end is the same: Stanley "is not dead; he doth but sleep" (East 2), while in the sonnet, "'[g]ainst death and all oblivious enmity / Shall you pace forth" (lines 9–10). Ultimately, poetic fame in the sonnet lasts only "till the judgment that yourself arise" (on Judgment Day, line 13); analogously, "Stanley for whom this stands shall stand in heaven" (West 6). The pun on the name in this concluding line ("Stanley/stands/stand") is similar to the sign of the author's hand left in "Upon a Pair of Gloves that Master Sent to his Mistress," where "[t]he will is all" recalls Shakespeare's emphatic references to his first name in Sonnets 135 and 136.

"Upon a Pair of Gloves" seems to reveal the poet intruding himself into a composition ostensibly from Alexander Aspinall to his (future?) wife; the "Epitaph on Himself" is strikingly impersonal. The lack of specificity may in this case be a poetic signature, however. By 1616, perhaps only Shakespeare could have written about Shakespeare without reference to his theatrical or literary career. This modesty coincides with an open threat: "cursed be he that moves my bones" (line 4). The apparently conventional warning was designed to forestall the very real danger of his body being dug up to make room for fresh corpses; in this case, it proved successful.

Walter Cohen

## SELECTED BIBLIOGRAPHY

Kerrigan, John. "Shakespeare, Elegy, and Epitaph 1557–1640." *The Oxford Handbook of Shakespeare's Poetry.* Ed. Jonathan F. S. Post. Oxford: Oxford UP, 2013. 225–44. Links "The Phoenix and Turtle" to the elegies attributed to Shakespeare, to the volume in which the poem appeared, to the period's competition—in poetry and in stone—in constructing memorials, and to the relationship between Catholic Wales and Protestant England.

Schoenfeldt, Michael. *The Cambridge Introduction to Shakespeare's Poetry.* Cambridge: Cambridge UP, 2010. 135–43. Focuses on the "fantasies of Shakespearean authorship" in the attributed poems.

## TEXTUAL INTRODUCTION

The present edition prints nine poems attributed to William Shakespeare in the seventeenth century. None of them can be confirmed as written by the author. Nonetheless, scholars have made compelling cases for the funeral verse (Poems 3, 4, 5, 6, 7, 9), with circumstantial evidence supporting attribution for the epitaph on Elias James (Poem 5), that on the Stanley tomb at Tong (Poem 3), and especially the second of the two poems on John Combe (Poem 7).

James was a brewer whose establishment was located near Shakespeare's accommodation in Puddle Dock Hill, London, and Combe was a noted usurer in Stratford-upon-Avon, while Shakespeare himself is known to have had links with the Stanley family. It is also not impossible that he wrote the epitaph upon himself (Poem 9); it has become hard to think about this wry poem as being written by someone other than the Bard. Of course, Shakespeare was a friend and rival of Ben Jonson, even if the capping of verses here (Poem 4) feels apocryphal. The gift poem to Alexander Aspinall (Poem 2), a schoolmaster in Stratford, is a smaller matter, however charming, while the verse on James I (Poem 8)—by the leading playwright of the King's Men—feels appropriately weighty. The longest of the poems, "A Song, 'Shall I Die?'" (Poem 1), is now believed by few to have been written by Shakespeare.

The texts for the nine attributed poems come from a variety of sources: manuscripts, books, engravings, funeral monuments themselves. "A Song, 'Shall I die?'" exists in two manuscripts: one at Yale University and one in the Bodleian Library (dating to the 1630s). Since only the latter attributes the poem to Shakespeare, it is used here as control text; its readings also tend to be preferred, although, as the list of variants indicates, in a few cases recent editors have found the Yale version preferable. Consensus continues to build denying Shakespeare's authorship.

Only one contemporary attribution exists for "Upon a Pair of Gloves"—in a manuscript miscellany compiled around 1629 by Sir Francis Fane and now in the Shakespeare Birth Place Trust Records Office, Stratford. This manuscript also includes an inscription of "Epitaph on Himself" and a version of the first epitaph on Combe. Aspinall was married to Anne Shaw, the widow of Ralph Shaw; the Shaws were neighbors of the Shakespeares, and in 1616 their son July (or Julianus) was a witness of Shakespeare's will. It was conventional to write a poem and include it with the gift of a pair of gloves, and the poem is so slight that it does not secure authorship one way or another, even though critics have been attracted to the word "will" in line 2 as a personal signature.

The text for the "Verses on the Stanley Tomb at Tong" come directly from the inscription at St. Bartholomew Church, so there are no textual variants. The tomb, as well as its inscription, is undated. A manuscript dating to the 1630s is the first to assign authorship to Shakespeare, although Milton in his 1630 memorial poem to Shakespeare (first published in the 1632 Folio) shows evidence that he understood the poem to be by Shakespeare. The link between Shakespeare and the Stanley family—especially Ferdinando Stanley, Lord Strange, patron of Lord Strange's Men—has been reasonably well established. Of all the nine poems, this one feels the most like William Shakespeare. It includes several verbal echoes of such freestanding poems as the sonnets and *The Rape of Lucrece*.

"On Ben Jonson" comes from a manuscript in the Bodleian Library compiled by Nicholas Burghe, perhaps in the mid-seventeenth century.

"An Epitaph on Elias James" is first printed by John Stow in his 1633 *Survey of London*, where it was unattributed. Originally, however, it appeared in the church of St. Andrews by the Wardrobe, London, at the lower end of the south aisle, but the church was destroyed by the Great Fire in 1666. A manuscript version in the Bodleian Library attributes the epitaph to Shakespeare, the same manuscript that attributes to him "A Song, 'Shall I die?'" James worked close to the Blackfriars Theatre; the church where he is buried is opposite to the Blackfriars Gate-House, which Shakespeare owned. Scholars are uncertain whether Shakespeare wrote the epitaph.

The two epitaphs on John Combe are not created equal. Shakespeare almost certainly knew the Stratford moneylender, who died on July 10, 1614: in 1602, Combe and his uncle sold Old Stratford land to Shakespeare; and in his will of 1616 the author left Combe's brother Thomas his sword. The epitaph on the tomb in Holy Trinity Church has disappeared, but in 1673 Robert Dobyns transcribed it in a manuscript preserved at the Folger Library. Despite the connection with Combe, scholars do not think Shakespeare wrote "An Extemporary Epitaph on John Combe, a Noted Usurer." The case is stronger for "Another Epitaph on John Combe," which is attributed to Shakespeare in a manuscript in the Bodleian Library.

"Upon the King" has a complicated transmission history that is still being tracked, but the four-line verse appears beneath a picture of James I in the 1616 edition of his own *Works*, from which the text for the present edition comes. The poem was attributed to Shakespeare in two manuscripts, now in the Folger Library, dating to ca. 1633–34 and ca. 1650, respectively, perhaps simply because he was the leading writer for the King's Men. While the dating of the poem is widely disputed, it may have been written around 1611, making Shakespeare's authorship possible.

Shakespeare's "Epitaph on Himself" comes from the inscription on his grave in Holy Trinity Church, Stratford.

PATRICK CHENEY

# Attributed Poems

## 1
## A song, "Shall I die?"[1]

[1]

Shall I die? Shall I fly
Lovers' baits and deceits, sorrow breeding?
Shall I tend?° Shall I send? *wait passively*
Shall I shew,° and not rue my proceeding?° *appear / (as in a lawsuit)*
In all duty her beauty
Binds me her servant forever.
If she scorn, I mourn,
I retire to despair, joining° never. *(sexually; militarily)*

[2]

Yet I must vent my lust
And explain inward pain by my love breeding.[2]
If she smiles, she exiles
All my moan; if she frown, all my hope's deceiving.
Suspicious doubt,° oh, keep out, *fear (of rejection)*
For thou art my tormentor.
Fly away, pack away;
I will love, for hope bids me venture.

[3]

'Twere abuse to accuse
My fair love, ere I prove° her affection. *test*
Therefore, try! Her reply
Gives thee joy or annoy or affliction.[3]
Yet howe'er, I will bear
Her pleasure with patience, for beauty
Sure will not seem to blot
Her deserts; wronging him doth her duty.[4]

[4]

In a dream it did seem
(But alas, dreams do pass as do shadows)
I did walk, I did talk
With my love, with my dove, through fair meadows.
Still° we passed till at last *Continually*
We sat to repose us for pleasure.
Being set, lips met,
Arms twined, and did bind my heart's treasure.

1

1. Textual Comment For differences between the two manuscript versions of this poem (lines 4, 8, 10, 15, 54), see Digital Edition TC 1.
2. Yet I must give expression to my lust by explaining (in poetry) the pain caused by my love.
3. "Affliction" may also suggest a sexually transmitted disease.
4. *for beauty . . . duty*: for true beauty will not allow her reputation to appear tarnished; wronging him serves her well.

[5]

Gentle wind sport did find
Wantonly° to make fly her gold tresses. *Capriciously*
As they shook, I did look,
But her fair° did impair all my senses. *beauty*
As amazed, I gazed
On more than a mortal complexion.
You that love can prove[5]
Such force in beauty's inflection.° *bending*

[6]

Next° her hair, forehead fair, *Next to*
Smooth and high; next doth lie, without wrinkle,
Her fair brows;° under those, *forehead*
Star-like eyes win love's prize when they twinkle.
In her cheeks who° seeks *whoever*
Shall find there displayed beauty's banner.° *(a blush)*
Oh, admiring desiring
Breeds, as I look still upon her.

[7]

Thin lips red, fancy's[6] fed
With all sweets when he meets, and is granted
There to trade,[7] and is made
Happy, sure, to endure still undaunted.
Pretty chin doth win
Of all that's called commendations;[8]
Fairest neck, no speck.
All her parts merit high admirations.

[8]

Pretty bare, past compare,
Parts, those plots which besots still asunder.[9]
It is meet naught but sweet
Should come near that so rare 'tis a wonder.[1]
No mishap, no scape° *transgression*
Inferior to nature's perfection.
No blot, no spot:
She's beauty's queen in election.

[9]

Whilst I dreamt, I exempt
From all care, seemed to share pleasure's plenty.
But awake, care take,
For I find to my mind pleasures scanty.
Therefore I will try
To compass° my heart's chief contenting. *accomplish*
To delay, some say,
In such a case causeth repenting.

5. You who are in love are able to test.
6. Affection is; imagination is.
7. *granted / There to trade*: allowed to kiss there.
8. Wins praise from all people.
9. *Pretty . . . asunder*: Incomparably pretty "bare" skin and breasts (exposed above a low neckline), those nipples ("plots") that, always separated, (always) cause infatuation.
1. It is proper that nothing but good should come near that which is so wonderfully valuable.

## 2
## Upon a Pair of Gloves That Master Sent to His Mistress

The gift is small,
The will is all:[1]
Alexander Aspinall[2]

## 3
## Verses on the Stanley Tomb at Tong

[East end]
Ask who lies here, but do not weep.
He is not dead; he doth but sleep.
This stony register° is for his bones; *record*
His fame is more perpetual than these stones,
And his own goodness, with himself being gone,
Shall live when earthly monument is none.

[West end]
Not monumental stone preserves our fame,
Nor sky-aspiring pyramids our name.
The memory of him for whom this stands
Shall outlive marble and defacers' hands.
When all to time's consumption shall be given,
Stanley for whom this stands shall stand in heaven.

## 4
## On Ben Jonson[1]

Master Ben Jonson and Master William Shakespeare, being merry at a tavern, Master Jonson having begun this for his epitaph:
Here lies Ben Jonson
That was once one,° *alive*
he gives it to Master Shakespeare to make up who presently writes:
Who while he lived was a slow thing,[2]
And now, being dead, is no thing.

## 5
## An Epitaph on Elias James

When God was pleased, the world unwilling yet,[1]
Elias James to nature paid his debt,
And here reposeth. As he lived, he died,
The saying strongly in him verified:
"Such life, such death."° Then, a known truth to tell, *One dies as one lives*
He lived a godly life, and died as well.

2
1. With a characteristic pun on the poet's name: the goodwill behind the gift is all-encompassing; it's the thought that counts.
2. Stratford schoolmaster from 1582 to 1624.
4
1. One of the best known of Shakespeare's fellow playwrights (1572–1637).
2. Jonson was a notoriously slow writer.
5
1. Though the world was still unwilling.

## 6
## An Extemporary Epitaph on John Combe, a Noted Usurer

Ten in the hundred[1] here lies engraved;
A hundred to ten° his soul is ne'er saved. *(odds)*
If anyone ask who lies in this tomb,
"O ho!" quoth the devil, "'tis my John-a-Combe."

## 7
## Another Epitaph on John Combe

Howe'er he livèd judge not,
John Combe shall never be forgot
While poor hath memory, for he did gather[1]
To make the poor his issue;° he, their father, *offspring; heirs*
As record of his tilth and seeds[2]
Did crown° him in his latter deeds. *honor; praise*

## 8
## Upon the King

Crowns have their compass,° length of days their date,° *boundaries / limit*
Triumphs their tombs, felicity her fate:
Of more than earth, can earth make none partaker,[1]
But knowledge makes the King most like his maker.

## 9
## Epitaph on Himself

Good friend, for Jesus' sake forbear
To dig the dust enclosèd here.
Blessed be the man that spares these stones,
And cursed be he that moves my bones.

6
1. *Ten . . . hundred*: a slang term for "usurer," suggesting one who lends money at 10 percent interest.
7
1. Accumulate wealth (through usury).
2. Tillage and planting (offspring).
8
1. No earthly power (not even a king) has power over the afterlife.

# Early Modern Map Culture

In the early modern period, maps were often considered rare and precious objects, and seeing a map could be an important and life-changing event. This was so for Richard Hakluyt, whose book *The Principal Navigations, Voyages, Traffics and Discoveries of the English Nation* (1598–1600) was the first major collection of narratives describing England's overseas trading ventures. Hakluyt tells how, as a boy still at school in London, he visited his uncle's law chambers and saw a book of cosmography lying open there. Perceiving his nephew's interest in the maps, the uncle turned to a modern map and "pointed with his wand to all the knowen Seas, Gulfs, Bayes, Straights, Capes, Rivers, Empires, Kingdomes, Dukedomes, and Territories of ech part, with declaration also of their speciall commodities and particular wants, which by the benefit of traffike, and entercourse of merchants, are plentifully supplied. From the Mappe he brought me to the Bible, and turning to the 107 Psalme, directed mee to the 23 and 24 verses, where I read, that they which go downe to the sea in ships, and occupy [work] by the great waters, they see the works of the Lord, and his woonders in the deepe." This event, Hakluyt records, made so deep an impression on him that he vowed he would devote his life to the study of this kind of knowledge. *The Principal Navigations* was the result, a book that mixes a concern with the profit to be made from trade and from geographical knowledge with praise for the Christian god who made the "great waters" and, in Hakluyt's view, looked with special favor on the English merchants and sailors who voyaged over them.

In the early modern period, access to maps was far less easy than it is today. Before the advent of printing in the late fifteenth century, maps were drawn and decorated by hand. Because they were rare and expensive, these medieval maps were for the most part owned by the wealthy and the powerful. Sometimes adorned with pictures of fabulous sea monsters and exotic creatures, maps often revealed the Christian worldview of those who composed them. Jerusalem appeared squarely in the middle of many maps (called T and O maps), with Asia, Africa, and Europe, representing the rest of the known world, arranged symmetrically around the Holy City. Because they had not yet been discovered by Europeans, North and South America were not depicted.

Mapping practices changed markedly during the late fifteenth and sixteenth centuries both because of the advent of print and also because European nations such as Portugal and Spain began sending ships on long sea voyages to open new trade routes to the East and, eventually, to the Americas. During this period, monarchs competed to have the best cartographers supply them with accurate maps of their realms and especially of lands in Africa, Asia, or the Americas, where they hoped to trade or plant settlements. Such knowledge was precious and jealously guarded. The value of such maps and the secrecy that surrounded them are indicated by a story in Hakluyt's *Principal Navigations*. An English ship had captured a Portuguese vessel in the Azores, and a map was discovered among the ship's valuable cargo, which included spices, silks, carpets, porcelain, and other exotic commercial objects. The map was "inclosed in a case of sweete Cedar wood, and lapped up almost an hundred fold in fine calicut-cloth, as though it had been some incomparable jewell." The value of the map and an explanation for the careful way in which it was packed lay in the particular information it afforded the English about Portuguese trading routes. More than beautiful objects, maps like this one were crucial to the international race to find safe sea routes to the most profitable trading centers in the East.

In the sixteenth century, books of maps began to be printed, making them more affordable for ordinary people, though some of these books, published as big folio volumes, remained too dear for any but wealthy patrons to buy. Yet maps were increasingly a part of daily life, and printing made many of them more accessible. Playgoers in Shakespeare's audiences must have understood in general the value and uses of maps, for they appear as props in a number of his plays. Most famously, at the beginning of *King Lear*, the old king has a map brought onstage showing the extent of his kingdom. He then points on the map to the three separate parts into which he intends to divide his realm to share among his daughters. The map, often unfurled with a flourish on a table or held up for view by members of Lear's retinue, signals the crucial relationship of the land to the monarch. He is his domains, and the map signifies his possession of them. To divide the kingdom, in essence to tear apart the map, would have been judged foolish and destructive by early modern political theorists. Similarly, in *1 Henry IV*, when rebels against the sitting monarch, Henry IV, plot to overthrow him, they bring a map onstage in order to decide what part of the kingdom will be given to each rebel leader. Their proposed dismemberment of the realm signifies the danger they pose. Treasonously, they would rend in pieces the body of the commonwealth.

Maps, of course, had other uses besides signifying royal domains. In some instances, they were used pragmatically to help people find their way from one place to another. A very common kind of map, a portolan chart, depicted in minute detail the coastline of a particular body of water. Used by sailors, these maps frequently were made by people native to the region they described. Many world or regional maps, because they were beautifully decorated and embellished with vivid colors, were used for decorative purposes. John Dee, a learned adviser to Queen Elizabeth and a great book collector, wrote that some people used maps "to beautifie their Halls, Parlers, Chambers, Galeries, Studies, or Libraries." He also spoke of more scholarly uses for these objects. They could, for example, be useful aids in the study of history or geography, enabling people to locate "thinges past, as battels fought, earthquakes, heavenly fyringes, and such occurents in histories mentioned." Today we make similar use of maps, like those included in this volume, when, in reading Shakespeare's plays, we resort to a map to find out where the Battle of Agincourt took place or where Othello sailed when he left Venice for Cyprus.

The print edition of *The Norton Shakespeare* includes five maps; the Digital Edition seven. Four of these maps, found in both editions, are modern ones drawn specifically to show the location of places important to Shakespeare's plays. They depict the British Isles and western France, London, and the Mediterranean world, in addition to a map of England showing the typical routes the Chamberlain's Men followed when they went on tour outside of London. The print and digital editions also both contain a period map of the Christian Holy Lands at the eastern tip of the Mediterranean Sea. This map was included in what was known as the Bishops' Bible, first printed in London in 1568. Put together under the leadership of the Archbishop of Canterbury, Matthew Parker, working with a committee of Anglican bishops, the 1568 edition featured beautiful typography and illustrations. The text continued to undergo revisions, and twenty editions of it were published between 1568 and 1602.

This last map shows places mentioned in the first four Gospels (Matthew, Mark, Luke, and John), which collectively tell of the life and deeds of Jesus. It indicates, for example, the location of Bethlehem, where he was born; Nazareth, where he spent his youth; and Cana of Galilee, where he turned water into wine at a marriage. It suggests that, to the English reader, this particular territory was overwritten by and completely intertwined with Christian history. Yet in the Mediterranean Sea, on the left of the map, several large ships are visible, reminders of another fact about this region: it was a vigorous trading arena where European Christian merchants did business with local merchants—Christian, Jew, and Muslim—and with traders bringing luxury goods by overland routes from the East. A number of Shakespeare's plays are set in this complex eastern Mediterranean region where several religious traditions laid claim to territory and many commercial powers competed for preeminence. *Pericles*, for example, has a hero who is the ruler of Tyre, a city on the upper right side of the map. In the course of his wanderings, Pericles visits many cities along the eastern coasts of the Mediterranean. The conclusion of the play, in which the hero is reunited both with his long-lost daughter and with the wife he believes dead, has seemed to many critics to share in a sense of Christian miracle, despite its ostensibly pagan setting. *The Comedy of Errors* and parts of *Othello* and of *Antony and Cleopatra* are also set in the Eastern Mediterranean. One of Shakespeare's earliest plays, *The Comedy of Errors,* is an urban comedy in which the protagonists are merchants deeply involved in commercial transactions. It is also the first play in which Shakespeare mentions the Americas, which he does in an extended joke in which he compares parts of a serving woman's body to the countries on a map including Ireland, France, and the Americas. In *Othello,* the eastern Mediterranean island of Cyprus is represented as a tense Christian outpost defending Venetian interests against the Muslim Turks. In *Antony and Cleopatra,* Egypt figures as the site of Eastern luxury and also of imperial conquest, an extension of the Roman Empire. Clearly, this region was to Shakespeare and his audiences one of the most complex and highly charged areas of the world: a site of religious, commercial, and imperial significance.

Two other maps occur only in the Digital Edition, where their colors and their details can be appreciated. The first is a map of London that appeared in a 1574 edition of a famous German atlas, *Civitates Orbis Terrarum* (*Cities of the World*), compiled by George Braun with engravings by Franz Hogenberg. This remarkable atlas includes maps and information on cities throughout Europe, Asia, and North Africa; the first of its six volumes appeared in 1572, the last in 1617. Being included in the volume indicated a city's status as a recognized metropolitan center. In a charming touch, Braun added to his city maps pictures of figures in local dress. At the bottom of the map of London, for example, there are four figures who appear to represent the city's prosperous citizens. In the center, a man in a long robe holds the hand of a soberly dressed matron. On either side of them are younger and more ornately dressed figures. The young man sports a long sword and a short cloak, the woman a dress with elaborate skirts. In the atlas, the map is colored, and the clothes of the two young people echo one another in shades of green and red.

At the time the map was made, London was a rapidly expanding metropolis. In 1550, it contained about 55,000 people; by 1600, it would contain nearly 200,000. The map shows the densely populated old walled city north of the Thames River, in the middle of which was Eastcheap, the commercial district where, in Shakespeare's plays about the reign of Henry IV, Falstaff holds court in a tavern. The map also shows that by 1570 London was spreading westward beyond the wall toward Westminster Palace. This medieval structure, which appears on the extreme left side of the map, was where English monarchs resided when in London and where, at the end of *2 Henry IV*, the king dies in the fabled Jerusalem Chamber of the Westminster complex. On the far right of the map, one can see the Tower of London, where Edward IV's young sons were imprisoned by Richard III, an event depicted in Shakespeare's *The Tragedy of King Richard the Third*. The map also indicates the centrality of the Thames to London's commercial life. It shows the river full of boats; some of those on the east side of London Bridge are large oceangoing vessels with several masts. South of the river, where many of the most famous London theaters, including Shakespeare's Globe, were to be constructed in the 1590s, there are relatively few buildings. By 1600, this would change, as Southwark, as it was known, came to be an increasingly busy entertainment, residential, and commercial district.

The final map, of Great Britain and Ireland, comes from a 1612 edition of John Speed's *The Theatre of the Empire of Great Britain,* an innovative atlas containing individual maps of counties and towns in England and Wales, as well as larger maps that include Scotland and Ireland. Speed was by trade a tailor who increasingly devoted his time to the study of history and cartography. Befriended by the antiquarian scholar William Camden, he eventually won patronage from Sir Fulke Greville, who gave him a pension that allowed him to devote himself full-time to his scholarly endeavors. *The Theatre* was one product of this newfound freedom. The map included here, one of his most ambitious, shows the entire British Isles, nominated by Speed as "The Kingdome of Great Britaine and Ireland," though at this time Ireland was far from under the control of the English crown and Scotland was still an independent kingdom. James I, a Scot by birth, had unsuccessfully tried to forge a formal union between England and Scotland. This problem of the relationship of the parts of the British Isles to one another, and England's assertion of power over the others, is treated in *Henry V*, in which officers from Wales, Ireland, and Scotland are sharply delineated yet all depicted as loyal subjects of the English king.

One striking aspect of Speed's map is the balance it strikes between the two capital cities, London on the left, prominently featuring the Thames and London Bridge, and Edinburgh on the right. This would have pleased James, whose interest in his native country Shakespeare played to in his writing of *Macbeth*, which is based on material from Scottish history. Speed's map acknowledges the claims of the monarch to the territory it depicts. In the upper left corner, the British lion and the Scottish unicorn support a roundel topped with a crown. When James became king of England in 1603, he created this merged symbol of Scottish-English unity. The motto of the Royal Order of the Garter, "*Honi soit qui mal y pense*" (Shamed be he who thinks ill of it), is inscribed around the circumference. In the bottom left corner of the map, another locus of authority is established. Two cherubs, one holding a compass, the other a globe, sit beneath a banner on which is inscribed "Performed by John Speed." If the territory is the monarch's, the craft that depicts it belongs to the tailor turned cartographer.

Today, maps are readily available from shops or on the Internet, but in early modern England they were rare and valuable objects that could generate great excitement in those who owned or beheld them. Along with other precious items, maps were sometimes put on display in libraries and sitting rooms, but they had functions beyond the ornamental. They helped to explain and order the world, indicating who claimed certain domains, showing where the familiar stories of the Bible or of English history occurred, helping merchants find their way to distant markets. As John Dee, the early modern map enthusiast concluded, "Some, for one purpose: and some, for an other, liketh, loveth, getteth, and useth, Mappes, Chartes, and Geographicall Globes."

Jean E. Howard

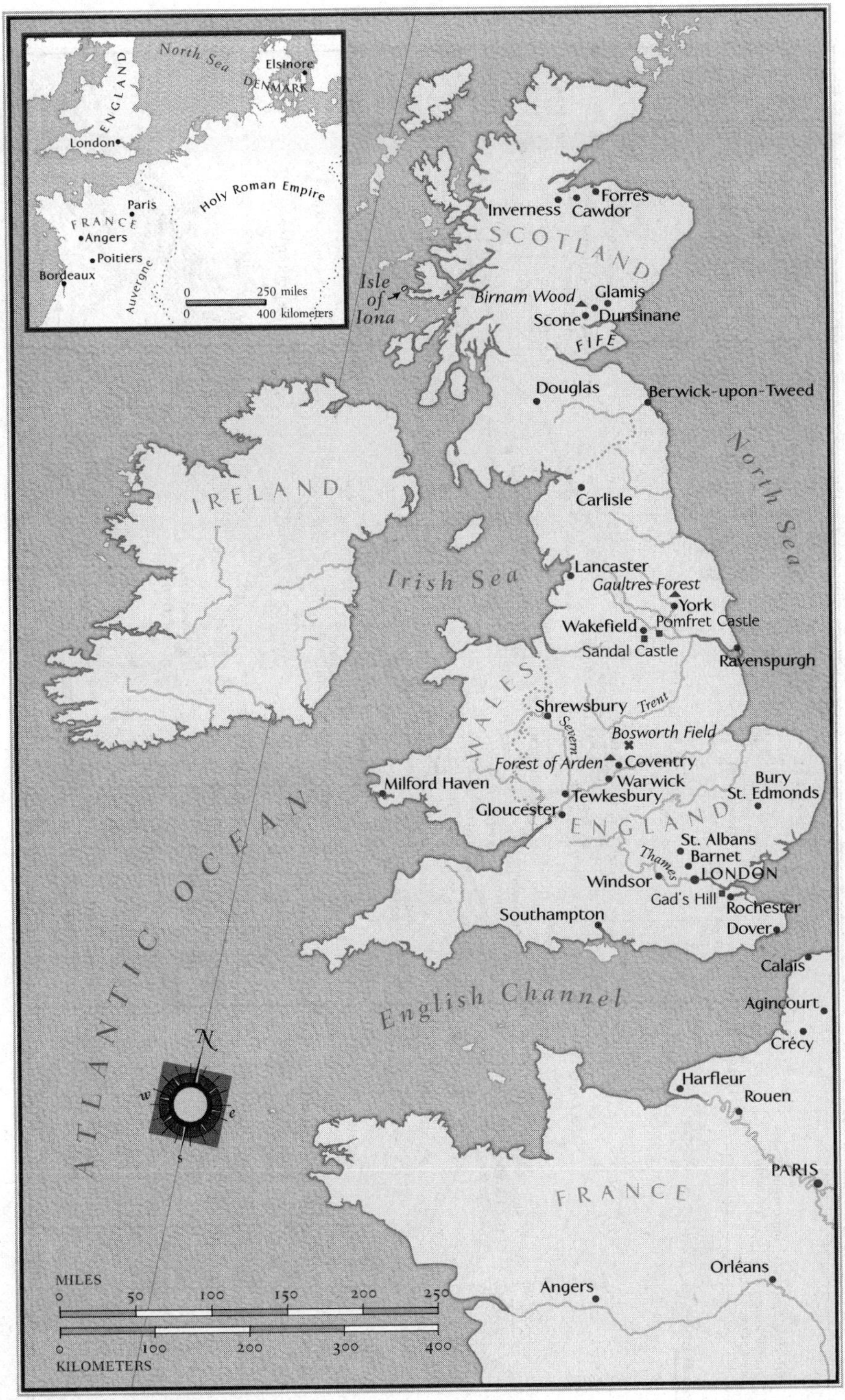


**Ireland, Scotland, Wales, England, and Western France: Places Important to Shakespeare's Plays**

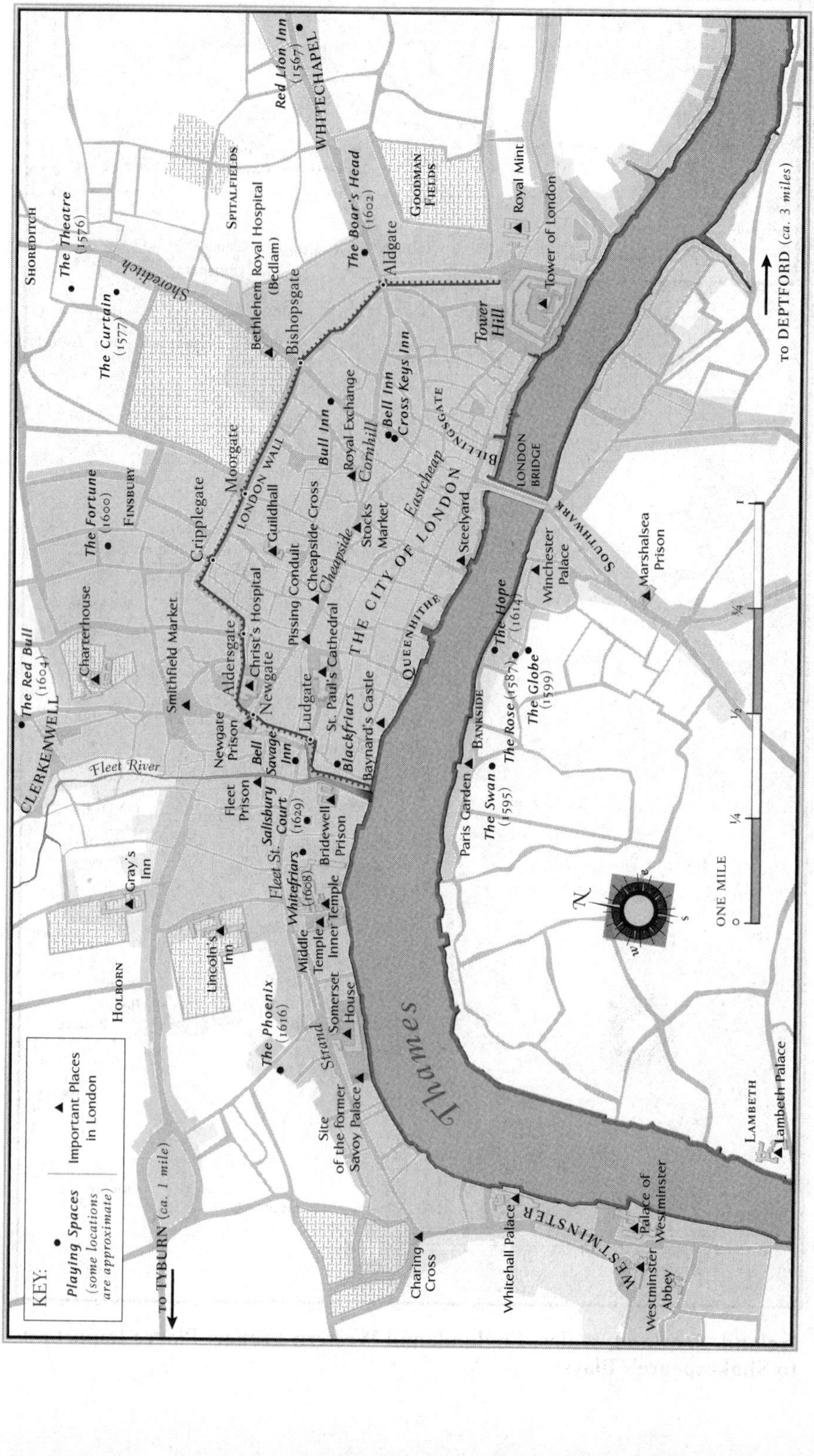


**London: Places Important to Shakespeare's Plays and London Playgoing**

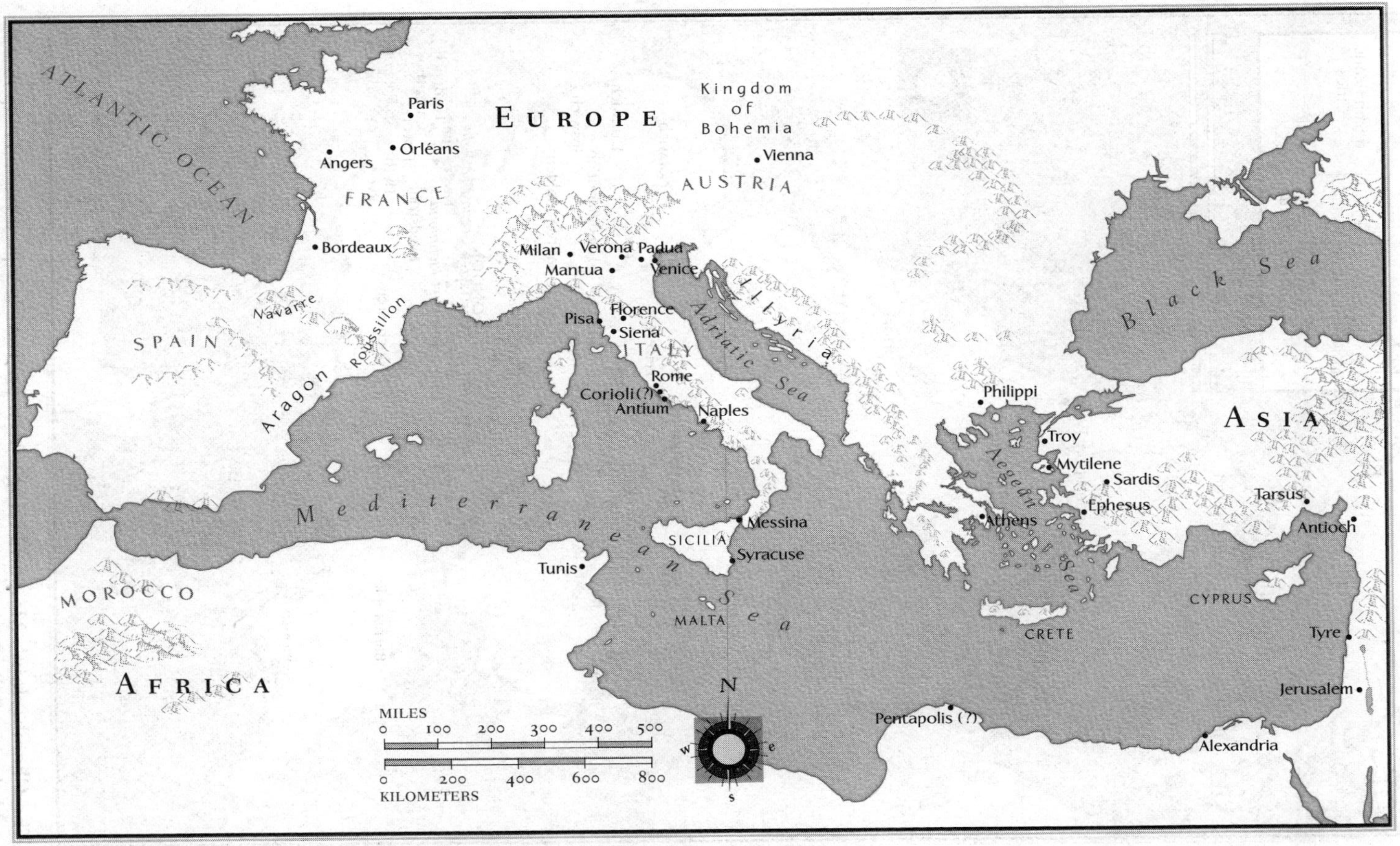


The Mediterranean World: Places Important to Shakespeare's Plays

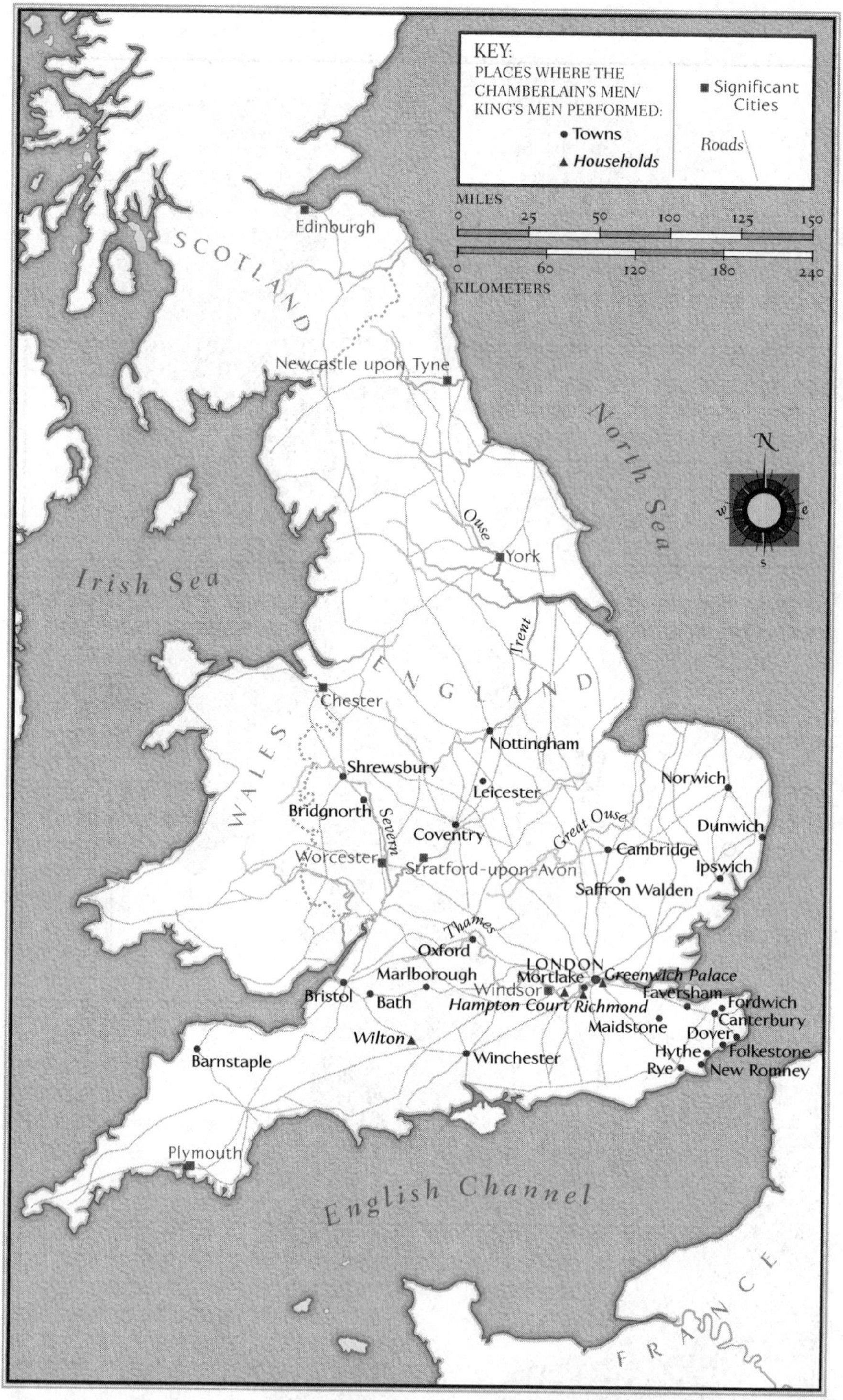


**The Chamberlain's Men and King's Men on Tour** (adapted from a map first published by Sally-Beth MacLean in "Tour Routes: 'Provincial Wanderings' or 'Traditional Circuits'?" *Medieval and Renaissance Drama in England* 6 [1992]: 1–14).

Map of the Holy Land, from the Bishops' Bible, printed in London, 1568

# Documents

The documents in this section provide some early perspectives on Shakespeare's reputation and the works included in this volume. A much more extensive selection of documents can be found in the Digital Edition of *The Norton Shakespeare*, which offers a broad range of contemporary testimony about Shakespeare's character, his art, and the social and institutional conditions under which his art was produced. The first digital section, "Shakespeare and His Works," contains traces of Shakespeare's life and career, evidence of his reputation in the literary community, and a variety of reactions to his plays and poems. The second section, "The Theater Scene," takes a wider view of Shakespeare's professional world with playhouse documents that offer a behind-the-scenes glimpse of companies acquiring scripts and properties, actors rehearsing their parts, and new theaters being constructed, while government documents show dramatic patronage, regulation, and censorship in action.

MISHA TERAMURA

## Francis Meres on Shakespeare (1598)

[Francis Meres (1565–1647) was educated at Cambridge and was active in London literary circles in 1597–98, after which he became a rector and schoolmaster in the country. The descriptions of Shakespeare are taken from a section on poetry in *Palladis Tamia. Wits Treasury*, a work largely consisting of translated classical quotations and *exempla*. Unlike the main body of the work, the subsections on poetry, painting, and music include comparisons of English artists to figures of antiquity. Meres goes on after the extract below to list Shakespeare among the best English writers of lyric, tragedy, comedy, and love poetry. The text is modernized from the first edition of *Palladis Tamia* (London, 1598).]

As the Greek tongue is made famous and eloquent by Homer, Hesiod, Euripides, Aeschylus, Sophocles, Pindarus, Phocylides, and Aristophanes, and the Latin tongue by Virgil, Ovid, Horace, Silius Italicus, Lucanus, Lucretius, Ausonius, and Claudianus, so the English tongue is mightily enriched and gorgeously invested in rare ornaments and resplendent habiliments[1] by Sir Philip Sidney, Spenser, Daniel, Drayton, Warner, Shakespeare, Marlowe, and Chapman. . . .

As the soul of Euphorbus was thought to live in Pythagoras, so the sweet witty soul of Ovid lives in mellifluous and honey-tongued Shakespeare. Witness his *Venus and Adonis*, his *Lucrece*, his sugared sonnets among his private friends, etc.

As Plautus and Seneca are accounted the best for comedy and tragedy among the Latins, so Shakespeare among the English is the most excellent in both kinds for the stage. For comedy, witness his *Gentlemen of Verona*, his *Errors*, his *Love Labor's Lost*, his *Love Labor's Won*,[2] his *Midsummer's Night Dream*, and his *Merchant of Venice*; for tragedy, his *Richard the 2*, *Richard the 3*, *Henry the 4*, *King John*, *Titus Andronicus*, and his *Romeo and Juliet*.

1. Sumptuous clothing.
2. Either the play has not survived, or it is now known by a different name. However, this title is recorded elsewhere, in a bookseller's jottings of 1603, where it again appears following *Lover's Labor's Lost*.

As Epius Stolo said that the Muses would speak with Plautus' tongue if they would speak Latin, so I say that the Muses would speak with Shakespeare's fine-filed phrase if they would speak English.

## *Parnassus* Plays on Shakespeare (1599–1601)

[The three *Parnassus* plays, *The Pilgrimage to Parnassus* and *The Return from Parnassus, Parts 1* and 2, were performed at Christmastime, probably in 1598, 1599, and 1601, by students of St. John's College, Cambridge. The references to Shakespeare and other contemporary writers are frequently ironic or equivocal. In the excerpts from *The Return, Part 1*, Ingenioso is an aspiring poet and Gullio a fop. In the second excerpt, Ingenioso is presenting the verses requested in the previous excerpt, having begun with examples in the vein or style of Chaucer and Spenser. Ingenioso returns in *Part* 2 to discuss the merits of contemporary poets with Judicio (a critic). The text is modernized from J. B. Leishman's edition of 1949 (London: Nicholson and Watson).]

### *The Return from Parnassus, Part 1*

#### ACT 3, SCENE 1

GULLIO Suppose also that thou wert my mistress, as sometime wooden statues represent the goddesses. Thus I would look amorously, thus I would pace, thus I would salute thee.

INGENIOSO [*aside*] It will be my luck to die no other death than by hearing of his follies. I fear this speech that's a-coming will breed a deadly disease in my ears.

GULLIO Pardon, fair lady, though sick-thoughted Gullio makes amain unto thee and like a bold-faced suitor 'gins to woo thee.[1]

INGENIOSO [*aside*] We shall have nothing but pure Shakespeare and shreds of poetry that he hath gathered at the theaters.

GULLIO Pardon me, *moi mitressa*, ast am a gentleman, the moon in comparison of thy bright hue[2] a mere slut, Antony's Cleopatra a black-browed milkmaid, Helen a dowdy.[3]

INGENIOSO [*aside*] Mark *Romeo and Juliet*—oh, monstrous theft! I think he will run through a whole book of Samuel Daniel's.[4]

GULLIO "Thrice fairer than myself," thus I began,
"The gods' fair riches, sweet above compare,
Stain to all nymphs, [m]ore lovely tha[n] a man,
More white and red than doves and roses are,
Nature, that made thee, with herself at strife,
Saith that the world hath ending with thy life."[5]

INGENIOSO Sweet Master Shakespeare.

GULLIO As I am a scholar,
These arms of mine are long and strong withal.
Thus elms by vines are compassed ere they fall.

1. *sick-thoughted . . . thee:* compare *Venus and Adonis*, lines 5–6. Of the numerous quotations and allusions, only those referring to Shakespeare are identified. *amain:* speedily.
2. *hue:* hue is. *ast:* as I.
3. *Antony's . . . dowdy:* compare *Romeo and Juliet* 2.2.37.
4. Probably Samuel Daniel's sonnet sequence *Delia*.
5. *Thrice . . . life:* Compare *Venus and Adonis*, lines 7–12. The corrections in the text are based on Shakespeare's poem; other slight errors or misquotations are left uncorrected. *had strife:* Shakespeare has "at strife."

INGENIOSO Faith, gentleman, your reading is wonderful in our English poets.

GULLIO Sweet mistress, I vouchsafe to take some of their words and apply them to mine own matters by a scholastical imitation. Report thou upon thy credit, is not my vein in courting gallant and honorable?

INGENIOSO Admirable sans compare. Never was so mellifluous a wit joined to so pure a phrase, such comely gesture, such gentleman-like behavior.

GULLIO But stay. It's very true, good wits have bad memories. I had almost forgotten the chief point I called thee out for: New Year's Day approacheth, and whereas other gallants bestow jewels upon their mistresses (as I have done whilom[6]), I now count it base to do as the common people do. I will bestow upon them the precious stones of my wit, a diamond of invention that shall be above all value and esteem. Therefore, sithens I am employed in some weighty affairs of the court, I will have thee, Ingenioso, to make them, and when thou hast done, I will peruse, polish, and correct them.

INGENIOSO My pen is your bounden vassal[7] to command. But what vein would it please you to have them in?

GULLIO Not in a vain vein—pretty, i'faith. Make me them in two or three divers veins, in Chaucer's, Gower's, and Spenser's. And Master Shakespeare's. Marry, I think I shall entertain[8] those verses which run like these:

"Even as the sun with purple-colored face
Had ta'en his last leave on the weeping morn,"[9] etc.

O sweet Master Shakespeare! I'll have his picture in my study at the court.

INGENIOSO [*aside*] Take heed, my masters. He'll kill you with tediousness ere I can rid him of the stage.

GULLIO Come, let us in.

## ACT 4, SCENE 1

GULLIO You scholars are simple fellows, men that never came where ladies grow. I that have spent my life among them knows best what becometh my pen and their ladyships' ears. Let me hear Master Shakespeare's vein.

INGENIOSO "Fair Venus, queen of beauty and of love,
Thy red doth stain the blushing of the morn,
Thy snowy neck shameth the milk-white dove,
Thy presence doth this naked world adorn,
Gazing on thee, all other nymphs I scorn.
Whene'er thou die'st, slow shine that Saturday.
Beauty and grace must sleep with thee for aye."

GULLIO No more. I am one that can judge, according to the proverb, *bovem ex unguibus*.[1] Ay marry, sir, these have some life in them. Let this duncified world esteem of Spenser and Chaucer. I'll worship sweet Master Shakespeare and to honor him will lay his *Venus and Adonis* under my pillow, as we read of one[2]—I do not well remember his name, but I am sure he was a king—slept with Homer under his bed's head. Well, I'll bestow a French crown[3] in the fair writing of them out, and then I'll instruct thee about the delivery of them. Meanwhile, I'll have thee make an elegant description of my mistress. Liken the worst part of her to Cynthia. Make also a familiar dialogue betwixt her and myself. I'll now in and correct these verses. *Exit.*

6. Formerly.
7. Obedient servant.
8. Accept; prefer.
9. *Even . . . morn*: compare *Venus and Adonis*, lines 1–2.

1. The bull by his hoof: Gullio's corruption of the phrase *leonem ex unguibus estimare* (to know the lion by his claws).
2. Alexander the Great.
3. A gold coin.

**Ingenioso** Why, who could endure this post put into a satin suit, this haberdasher of lies, this Braggadocio, this lady-monger, this mere rapier and dagger,[4] this cringer, this foretop,[5] but a man that's ordained to misery? Well, Madam Pecunia,[6] once more for thy sake will I wait on this trunk, and with soothing him up, in time will leave him a greater fool than I found him. *Exit.*

### *The Return from Parnassus, Part 2*

#### ACT 1, SCENE 2

**Ingenioso** Benjamin Jonson.

**Judicio** The wittiest fellow of a bricklayer in England.

**Ingenioso** A mere empiric, one that gets what he hath by observation, and makes only Nature privy to what he endites;[7] so slow an inventor that he were better betake himself to his old trade of bricklaying; a bold whoreson, as confident now in making of a book as he was in times past in laying of a brick.
William Shakespeare.

**Judicio** Who loves not Adon's love, or Lucrece's rape?
His sweeter verse contains heart-robbing lines,
Could but a graver subject him content,
Without love's foolish lazy languishment.

## Simon Forman on *Cymbeline* and *The Winter's Tale* (1611)

[Simon Forman (1552–1611) was a largely self-educated physician and astrologer who rose from humble beginnings to establish a successful London practice. A large parcel of his manuscripts, including scientific and autobiographical material as well as the diary from which this account of the plays is taken, has survived, making his life one of the best-documented Elizabethan lives. These manuscripts provide detailed information about Forman's many sidelines, such as the manufacture of talismans, alchemy, and necromancy, as well as about his sex life. *Cymbeline* and *The Winter's Tale* were two of four plays described in Forman's "Book of Plays"; the others were *Macbeth* and a non-Shakespearean play based on the life of Richard II. The text is modernized from E. K. Chambers, *William Shakespeare: A Study of Facts and Problems*, 2 vols. (Oxford: Clarendon, 1930), vol. 2.]

### *The Book of Plays and Notes thereof, per Forman for Common Policy*[1]

#### Of *Cymbeline, King of England*.

Remember also the story of *Cymbeline, King of England*, in Lucius' time, how Lucius came from Octavius Caesar for tribute and, being denied, after sent Lucius with a great army of soldiers, who landed at Milford Haven, and after were vanquished by Cymbeline, and Lucius taken prisoner, and all by means of 3 outlaws, of the which 2 of them were the sons of Cymbeline, stolen from him when they were but 2 years old by an old man whom Cymbeline banished, and he kept them as his own sons 20 years with him in a cave; and how [one] of them slew Cloten

4. That is, the dueling weapons worn by gentlemen at court. *Braggadocio:* braggart.
5. This sycophant; this fop.
6. A personification of money.
7. Writes.

1. *Common Policy:* practical use. Forman's title for his notes on plays is not printed in Chambers, but is interpolated here from G. Blakemore Evans's transcription in *The Riverside Shakespeare*.

(that was the Queen's son) going to Milford Haven to seek the love of Innogen, the King's daughter, whom he had banished also for loving his daughter;[2] and how the Italian that came from her love conveyed himself into a chest, and said it was a chest of plate sent from her love and others to be presented to the King, and in the deepest of the night, she being asleep, he opened the chest and came forth of it, and viewed her in her bed and the marks of her body, and took away her bracelet, and after accused her of adultery to her love, etc., and in th'end how he came with the Romans into England and was taken prisoner, and after revealed to Innogen, who had turned herself into man's apparel and fled to meet her love at Milford Haven, and chanced to fall on the cave in the woods where her 2 brothers were, and how, by eating a sleeping dram, they thought she had been dead and laid her in the woods, and the body of Cloten by her in her love's apparel that he left behind him, and how she was found by Lucius, etc.

In *The Winter's Tale* at the Globe, 1611, the 15 of May, ☿ [Wednesday].

Observe there how Leontes, the King of Sicilia, was overcome with jealousy of his wife with the King of Bohemia, his friend, that came to see him, and how he contrived his death, and would have had his cupbearer to have poisoned [him], who gave the King of Bohemia warning thereof and fled with him to Bohemia.

Remember also how he sent to the Oracle of Apollo and the answer of Apollo that she was guiltless and that the King was jealous, etc., and how, except the child was found again that was lost, the King should die without issue, for the child was carried into Bohemia and there laid in a forest and brought up by a shepherd; and the King of Bohemia his son married that wench, and how they fled into Sicilia to Leontes; and the shepherd, having showed the letter of the nobleman by whom Leontes sent a was [away?] that child, and the jewels found about her, she was known to be Leontes' daughter and was then 16 years old.

Remember also the rogue[3] that came in all tattered like colt-pixie,[4] and how he feigned him sick and to have been robbed of all that he had, and how he cozened the poor man of all his money, and after came to the sheep-shear[5] with a pedlar's pack, and there cozened them again of all their money, and how he changed apparel with the King of Bohemia his son, and then how he turned courtier, etc. Beware of trusting feigned beggars or fawning fellows.

## Front Matter from the First Folio of Shakespeare's Plays (1623)

After Shakespeare's death in 1616, his friends and colleagues John Heminges and Henry Condell organized this first publication of his collected (thirty-six) plays. Eighteen of the plays had not appeared in print before, and for these the First Folio is the sole surviving source. Only *Pericles, The Two Noble Kinsmen, Sir Thomas More,* and *Edward III* are not included in the volume. Reproduced below in reduced facsimile are the title page (which includes Droeshout's famous portrait of Shakespeare), Heminges and Condell's prefatory address "To the great Variety of Readers," the book's table of contents, and the first page of text from *The Tempest*. Following the facsimile images is a commendatory poem by Shakespeare's great contemporary Ben Jonson (1572–1637), which was also published in the First Folio's front matter.

2. Morgan/Berlarius is not banished in the version of the play that comes down to us.
3. Autolycus.
4. A mischievous sprite or fairy.
5. Sheepshearing.

Mr. WILLIAM
SHAKESPEARES
COMEDIES,
HISTORIES, &
TRAGEDIES.

Publiſhed according to the True Originall Copies.

Martin Droeshout sculpsit London.

LONDON
Printed by Iſaac Iaggard, and Ed. Blount. 1623.

## *To the great Variety of Readers.*

FRom the moſt able, to him that can but ſpell: There you are number'd. We had rather you were weighd. Eſpecially, when the fate of all Bookes depends vpon your capacities : and not of your heads alone, but of your purſes. Well ! It is now publique, & you wil ſtand for your priuiledges wee know : to read, and cenſure. Do ſo, but buy it firſt. That doth beſt commend a Booke, the Stationer ſaies. Then, how odde ſoeuer your braines be, or your wiſedomes, make your licence the ſame, and ſpare not. Iudge your ſixe-pen'orth, your ſhillings worth, your fiue ſhillings worth at a time, or higher, ſo you riſe to the iuſt rates, and welcome. But, what euer you do, Buy. Cenſure will not driue a Trade, or make the Iacke go. And though you be a Magiſtrate of wit, and ſit on the Stage at *Black-Friers*, or the *Cock-pit*, to arraigne Playes dailie, know, theſe Playes haue had their triall alreadie, and ſtood out all Appeales; and do now come forth quitted rather by a Decree of Court, then any purchas'd Letters of commendation.

It had bene a thing, we confeſſe, worthie to haue bene wiſhed, that the Author himſelfe had liu'd to haue ſet forth, and ouerſeen his owne writings; But ſince it hath bin ordain'd otherwiſe, and he by death departed from that right, we pray you do not envie his Friends, the office of their care, and paine, to haue collected & publiſh'd them; and ſo to haue publiſh'd them, as where (before) you were abus'd with diuerſe ſtolne, and ſurreptitious copies, maimed, and deformed by the frauds and ſtealthes of iniurious impoſtors, that expos'd them: euen thoſe, are now offer'd to your view cur'd, and perfect of their limbes; and all the reſt, abſolute in their numbers, as he conceiued thẽ. Who, as he was a happie imitator of Nature, was a moſt gentle expreſſer of it. His mind and hand went together: And what he thought, he vttered with that eaſineſſe, that wee haue ſcarſe receiued from him a blot in his papers. But it is not our prouince, who onely gather his works, and giue them you, to praiſe him. It is yours that reade him. And there we hope, to your diuers capacities, you will finde enough, both to draw, and hold you: for his wit can no more lie hid, then it could be loſt. Reade him, therefore; and againe, and againe: And if then you doe not like him, ſurely you are in ſome manifeſt danger, not to vnderſtand him. And ſo we leaue you to other of his Friends, whom if you need, can bee your guides: if you neede them not, you can leade your ſelues, and others. And ſuch Readers we wiſh him.

*A 3* *Iohn Heminge.*
*Henrie Condell.*

Line 8. *Stationer*: bookseller.
Line 13. *Iacke*: machine.
Lines 13–14. *And though . . . dailie*: addressed in particular to men of fashion who occupied seats onstage so they could be seen while watching the play.
Lines 15–17. *these Playes . . . commendation:* The legal puns that began with "Magistrate of wit" (fashionable playgoer) in line 13 continue here. The "purchas'd Letters of commendation" refer to escaping the consequences of a crime by means of bribery or other undue influence; Shakespeare's plays, by contrast, have been acquitted after a proper and rigorous trial (approved by theater audiences and not insinuated into the public favor by some outside influence).
Line 27. *absolute in their numbers*: correct in their versification. *thẽ*: them.
Line 28. *a happie*: an apt; a successful.

# A CATALOGVE

of the ſeuerall Comedies, Hiſtories, and Tragedies contained in this Volume.

## COMEDIES.



## HISTORIES.



## TRAGEDIES.



*Troilus and Cressida*, despite its absence from the "Catalogue," was in fact printed in the First Folio. Due to negotiations over printing rights, it was included only at the last minute and placed between the histories and tragedies.

# THE TEMPEST.

## *Actus primus, Scena prima.*

*A tempeſtuous noiſe of Thunder and Lightning heard: Enter a Ship-maſter, and a Boteſwaine.*

*Maſter.*

Bote-ſwaine.

*Botes.* Heere Maſter: What cheere?

*Maſt.* Good: Speake to th'Mariners: fall too't, yarely, or we run our ſelues a ground, beſtirre, beſtirre. *Exit.*

*Enter Mariners.*

*Botes.* Heigh my hearts, cheerely, cheerely my harts: yare, yare: Take in the toppe-ſale: Tend to th'Maſters whiſtle: Blow till thou burſt thy winde, if roome enough.

*Enter Alonſo, Sebaſtian, Anthonio, Ferdinando, Gonzalo, and others.*

*Alon.* Good Boteſwaine haue care: where's the Maſter? Play the men.

*Botes.* I pray now keepe below.

*Anth.* Where is the Maſter, Boſon?

*Botes.* Do you not heare him? you marre our labour, Keepe your Cabines: you do aſsiſt the ſtorme.

*Gonz.* Nay, good be patient.

*Botes.* When the Sea is: hence, what cares theſe roarers for the name of King? to Cabine; ſilence: trouble vs not.

*Gon.* Good, yet remember whom thou haſt aboord.

*Botes.* None that I more loue then my ſelfe. You are a Counſellor, if you can command theſe Elements to ſilence, and worke the peace of the preſent, wee will not hand a rope more, vſe your authoritie: If you cannot, giue thankes you haue liu'd ſo long, and make your ſelfe readie in your Cabine for the miſchance of the houre, if it ſo hap. Cheerely good hearts: out of our way I ſay. *Exit.*

*Gon.* I haue great comfort from this fellow: methinks he hath no drowning marke vpon him, his complexion is perfect Gallowes: ſtand faſt good Fate to his hanging, make the rope of his deſtiny our cable, for our owne doth little aduantage: If he be not borne to bee hang'd, our caſe is miſerable. *Exit.*

*Enter Boteſwaine.*

*Botes.* Downe with the top-Maſt: yare, lower, lower, bring her to Try with Maine-courſe. A plague——

*A cry within. Enter Sebaſtian, Anthonio & Gonzalo.*

vpon this howling: they are lowder then the weather, or our office: yet againe? What do you heere? Shal we giue ore and drowne, haue you a minde to ſinke?

*Sebas.* A poxe o'your throat, you bawling, blaſphemous incharitable Dog.

*Botes.* Worke you then.

*Anth.* Hang cur, hang, you whoreſon inſolent Noyſemaker, we are leſſe afraid to be drownde, then thou art.

*Gonz.* I'le warrant him for drowning, though the Ship were no ſtronger then a Nutt-ſhell, and as leaky as an vnſtanched wench.

*Botes.* Lay her a hold, a hold, ſet her two courſes off to Sea againe, lay her off.

*Enter Mariners wet.*

*Mari.* All loſt, to prayers, to prayers, all loſt.

*Botes.* What muſt our mouths be cold?

*Gonz.* The King, and Prince, at prayers, let's aſſiſt them, for our caſe is as theirs.

*Sebas.* I'am out of patience.

*An.* We are meerly cheated of our liues by drunkards,
This wide-chopt-raſcall, would thou mightſt lye drowning the waſhing of ten Tides.

*Gonz.* Hee'l be hang'd yet,
Though euery drop of water ſweare againſt it,
And gape at widſt to glut him. *A confuſed noyſe within.*
Mercy on vs.
We ſplit, we ſplit, Farewell my wife, and children,
Farewell brother: we ſplit, we ſplit, we ſplit.

*Anth.* Let's all ſinke with' King

*Seb.* Let's take leaue of him. *Exit.*

*Gonz.* Now would I giue a thouſand furlongs of Sea, for an Acre of barren ground: Long heath, Browne firrs, any thing; the wills aboue be done, but I would faine dye a dry death. *Exit.*

## Scena Secunda.

*Enter Proſpero and Miranda.*

*Mira.* If by your Art (my deereſt father) you haue
Put the wild waters in this Rore; alay them:
The skye it ſeemes would powre down ſtinking pitch,
But that the Sea, mounting to th' welkins cheeke,
Daſhes the fire out. Oh! I haue ſuffered
With thoſe that I ſaw ſuffer: A braue veſſell

A (Who

# To the memory of my beloved, The AUTHOR
# Mr. William Shakespeare: And
# what he hath left us.*

To draw no envy, Shakespeare, on thy name,
Am I thus ample to° thy book and fame, *copious in praising*
While I confess thy writings to be such
As neither man nor muse can praise too much:
'Tis true, and all men's suffrage.° But these ways *agreement*
Were not the paths I meant° unto thy praise, *(to take)*
For seeliest[1] ignorance on these may light,
Which, when it sounds, at best, but° echoes right; *merely*
Or blind affection, which doth ne'er advance
The truth, but gropes, and urgeth all by chance;
Or crafty malice might pretend this praise,
And think° to ruin, where it seemed to raise. *intend*
These are as° some infamous bawd or whore *as though*
Should praise a matron: what could hurt her more?
But thou art proof against° them, and indeed *impervious to*
Above th' ill fortune of them, or the need.
I therefore will begin. Soul of the age!
The applause, delight, the wonder of our stage!
My Shakespeare, rise! I will not lodge thee by
Chaucer or Spenser, or bid Beaumont lie
A little further to make thee a room;[2]
Thou art a monument without a tomb
And art alive still while thy book doth live,
And we have wits to read and praise to give.
That I not mix thee so, my brain excuses,
I mean with great but disproportioned° muses. *not comparable*
For if I thought my judgment were of years° *mature*
I should commit° thee surely with thy peers, *compare*
And tell how far thou didst our Lyly outshine,
Or sporting Kyd, or Marlowe's mighty line.[3]
And though thou hadst small Latin and less Greek,[4]
From thence to honor thee I would not seek° *lack*

* By Ben Jonson.

1. Silliest; blindest (falcons' eyelids were "seeled," or stitched shut, while they were being tamed).

2. Geoffrey Chaucer, Edmund Spenser, and Francis Beaumont were all buried near each other in Westminster Abbey (known today as the "Poets' Corner"), while Shakespeare was buried in Stratford-upon-Avon. An earlier elegy for Shakespeare had begun: "Renownèd Spenser, lie a thought more nigh / To learned Chaucer, and, rare Beaumont, lie / A little nearer Spenser to make room / For Shakespeare . . ."

3. John Lyly, Thomas Kyd, and Christopher Marlowe were all celebrated Elizabethan playwrights. *sporting:* gamesome; frolicking (like a young goat, or "kid").

4. The underrating of Shakespeare's Latin was likely influenced by Jonson's pride in his own impressive classical learning.

For names, but call forth thund'ring Aeschylus,
  Euripides, and Sophocles to us,
Pacuvius, Accius, him of Cordova dead,[5]
  To life again, to hear thy buskin tread
And shake a stage; or, when thy socks were on,[6]
  Leave thee alone for the comparison
Of all that insolent Greece or haughty Rome
  Sent forth, or since did from their ashes come.
Triumph, my Britain; thou hast one to show
  To whom all scenes° of Europe homage owe. — *stages*
He was not of an age, but for all time!
  And all the Muses still were in their prime
When like Apollo° he came forth to warm — *god of poetry*
  Our ears, or like a Mercury° to charm! — *god of eloquence*
Nature herself was proud of his designs,
  And joyed to wear the dressing of his lines,
Which were so richly spun and woven so fit
  As, since, she will vouchsafe° no other wit. — *grant*
The merry Greek, tart Aristophanes,
  Neat Terence, witty Plautus[7] now not please,
But antiquated and deserted lie,
  As they were not of Nature's family.
Yet must I not give Nature all; thy art,
  My gentle Shakespeare, must enjoy a part.
For though the poet's matter° nature be, — *raw material*
  His art doth give the fashion.° And that he° — *form / that he=he*
Who casts° to write a living line must sweat — *intends*
  (Such as thine are) and strike the second heat
Upon the Muses' anvil, turn the same,
  And himself with it, that he thinks to frame,
Or for the laurel he may gain a scorn;[8]
  For a good poet's made as well as born,
And such wert thou. Look how the father's face
  Lives in his issue;° even so, the race — *offspring*
Of Shakespeare's mind and manners brightly shines
  In his well-turnèd and true-filèd° lines, — *truly polished*
In each of which he seems to shake a lance,[9]
  As brandished at the eyes of ignorance.
Sweet swan of Avon, what a sight it were
  To see thee in our waters yet appear,
And make those flights upon the banks of Thames
  That so did take° Eliza and our James![1] — *transport*
But stay; I see thee in the hemisphere
  Advanced and made a constellation there.[2]

5. While the Latin tragedians Marcus Pacuvius and Lucius Accius were known to Jonson only by reputation, Seneca the Younger ("him of Cordova") was a major influence on Renaissance revenge tragedies.
6. The boots ("buskins") and shoes ("socks") worn by classical actors were symbolic of tragedy and comedy, respectively.
7. Aristophanes was a Greek writer of satirical comedies; Terence and Plautus were Roman comic dramatists.
8. Or else, instead of the laurel (the symbol of poetic accomplishment), he may gain derision.
9. Punning on Shakespeare's name.
1. Queen Elizabeth and King James.
2. It was a commonplace in classical literature that those who lived glorious lives became constellations after death.

Shine forth, thou star of poets, and with rage
Or influence,[3] chide or cheer the drooping° stage, *dejected*
Which, since thy flight from hence, hath mourned like night,
And despairs day, but for thy volume's light.

BEN: JONSON.

3. Stars and planets were thought to affect human affairs. "Rage" suggests poetic inspiration.

# Timeline

Dates for plays by Shakespeare and others are conjectural dates of composition, based on current understanding of the evidence. Works of poetry and prose are listed by date of publication.

| TEXT | CONTEXT |
| --- | --- |
| | **1558** Queen Mary I, a Roman Catholic, dies; her sister, Elizabeth, raised Protestant, is proclaimed queen. |
| | **1559** Church of England is reestablished under the authority of the sovereign with the passage of the Act of Uniformity and the Act of Supremacy. |
| **1562** *The Tragedy of Gorboduc*, by Thomas Norton and Thomas Sackville; the first English play in blank verse. | **1563** The Church of England adopts the Thirty-nine Articles of Religion, detailing its points of doctrine and clarifying its differences both from Roman Catholicism and from more radical forms of Protestantism. |
| | **1564** William Shakespeare is born in Stratford to John and Mary Arden Shakespeare; he is christened a few days later, on April 26. |
| | **1565** John Shakespeare is made an alderman of Stratford. |
| | **1567** Mary Queen of Scots is imprisoned on suspicion of the murder of her husband, Lord Darnley. Their infant son, Charles James, is crowned James VI of Scotland. John Brayne builds the first English professional theater in the garden of a farmhouse called the Red Lion on the outskirts of London. |
| | **1568** John Shakespeare is elected Bailiff of Stratford, the town's highest office. Performances in Stratford by the Queen's Players and the Earl of Worcester's men. |
| | **1572** An act is passed that severely punishes vagrants and wanderers, including actors not affiliated with a patron. Performances in Stratford by the Earl of Leicester's men. |

| TEXT | CONTEXT |
|---|---|
| | **1574** The Earl of Warwick's and Earl of Worcester's men perform in Stratford. |
| | **1576** James Burbage, father of Richard, later the leading actor in Shakespeare's company, builds The Theatre in Shoreditch, a suburb of London. |
| **1577** First edition of Holinshed's *Chronicles*. | **1577** The Curtain Theater opens in Shoreditch. |
| | **1577–80** Sir Francis Drake circumnavigates the globe. |
| | **1578** Mary Shakespeare pawns her lands, suggesting that the family is in financial distress.<br>Lord Strange's Men and Lord Essex's Men perform at Stratford. |
| **1579** Sir Thomas North's English translation of Plutarch's *Lives*. | **1580** A Jesuit mission is established in England with the aim of reconverting the nation to Roman Catholicism.<br>Francis Drake returns from circumnavigation of globe. |
| | **1582** Shakespeare marries Anne Hathaway. |
| | **1583** The birth of Shakespeare's older daughter, Susanna. |
| | **1584** Sir Walter Ralegh establishes the first English colony in the New World at Roanoke Island in modern North Carolina; the colony fails. |
| | **1585** The birth of Shakespeare's twin son and daughter, Hamnet and Judith.<br>John Shakespeare is fined for not going to church. |
| | **1586** Sir Philip Sidney dies from battle wounds. |
| **1587** Thomas Kyd, *The Spanish Tragedy*; Christopher Marlowe, *Tamburlaine*. | **1587** Mary Queen of Scots is executed for treason against Elizabeth I.<br>Francis Drake, leading a daring raid at Cádiz, destroys many Spanish naval vessels and materiel.<br>John Shakespeare loses his position as an alderman.<br>Philip Henslowe builds the Rose theater at Bank-side, on the Thames. |
| | **1588** The Spanish Armada attempts an invasion of England but is defeated. |

| TEXT | CONTEXT |
|---|---|
| **1589** Robert Greene, *Friar Bacon and Friar Bungay.*<br>Thomas Kyd(?), *Hamlet* (not extant; perhaps a source for Shakespeare's *Hamlet*).<br>Christopher Marlowe, *The Jew of Malta.*<br>Anonymous, *The True Chronicle History of King Leir, and His Three Daughters.* | **1589** Shakespeare is possibly affiliated with Strange's men, Pembroke's men, or both between this time and 1594. |
| **1590** Edmund Spenser, *The Faerie Queene* (1st edition, Books 1–3).<br>Sir Philip Sidney, *Arcadia.* | **1590** James VI of Scotland marries Anne of Denmark. James believes that witches raised a magical storm in an attempt to sink the ship carrying him home with his bride.<br>Witch trials in Scotland. |
| **1591–92** *Two Gentlemen of Verona.*<br>*2 and 3 Henry VI.*<br>*The Taming of the Shrew.*<br>*I Henry VI.* | **1592** The theatrical entrepreneur and financial manager of the Admiral's Men, Philip Henslowe, begins a diary—an important source for theater historians—recording his business transactions; continued until 1604. |
| **1592–93** *Titus Andronicus.*<br>*Richard III.*<br>*Edward III.*<br>*Venus and Adonis.* | From June 1592 to June 1594, London theaters are frequently shut down because of the plague; acting companies tour the provinces. |
| **1594** *The Rape of Lucrece.*<br>*The Comedy of Errors.* | **1594** Roderigo Lopez, a Christian physician of Portuguese Jewish descent, is executed on slight evidence for having plotted to poison Elizabeth I.<br>The birth of James VI's first son, Henry. |
| **1594–96** *Love's Labor's Lost.*<br>*Richard II.*<br>*Romeo and Juliet.*<br>*A Midsummer Night's Dream.*<br>*King John.* | **1595** Shakespeare lives in St. Helen's Parish, Bishopsgate, London.<br>Shakespeare apparently becomes a sharer in (provides capital for) the newly formed Lord Chamberlain's Men.<br>The Swan Theater is built in Bankside.<br>Hugh O'Neill, Earl of Tyrone, rebels against English rule in Ireland.<br>Walter Ralegh explores Guiana, on the north coast of South America. |
| **1596** Edmund Spenser, *The Faerie Queene* (2nd edition, with Books 4–6).<br><br>**1596–97** *I Henry IV.*<br>*The Merchant of Venice.* | **1596** John Shakespeare is granted a coat of arms; hence the title of "gentleman."<br>William Shakespeare's son Hamnet dies.<br>James Burbage buys a medieval hall in the former Blackfriars monastery and transforms it into an indoor theater. |
| | **1597** The landlord refuses to renew the lease on the land under The Theatre in Shoreditch. |

| TEXT | CONTEXT |
| --- | --- |
| **1598** *2 Henry IV.*<br>*Much Ado About Nothing.*<br>George Chapman begins to publish his translation of Homer.<br>Ben Jonson, *Every Man in His Humor,* which lists Shakespeare as one of the actors. | **1598** Unable to renew the lease, the Chamberlain's Men move from The Theatre to the nearby Curtain Theater.<br>The Edict of Nantes ends the French civil wars, granting toleration to Protestants.<br>Materials from the demolished Theatre in Shoreditch are transported across the Thames to be used in building the Globe Theater, which opens in the following year. |
| **1599** *The Merry Wives of Windsor.*<br>*Henry V.*<br>*As You Like It.*<br>*Julius Caesar.*<br>*The Passionate Pilgrim*, attributed entirely to Shakespeare.<br>Michael Drayton and several collaborators, who object to Shakespeare's depiction of Oldcastle-Falstaff in the *Henry IV* plays, write *The First Part of the True and Honorable History of the Life of Sir John Oldcastle, the Good Lord Cobham.* | **1599** The Queen's favorite, Robert Devereux, Earl of Essex, leads an expedition to Ireland in March, but returning home without royal permission in September, is rebuked by the Queen and imprisoned.<br>Satires and other offensive books are prohibited by ecclesiastical order.<br>Extant copies are gathered and burned.<br>Two notorious satirists, Thomas Nashe and Gabriel Harvey, are forbidden to publish. |
| **1600–1601** *Hamlet.*<br>*Twelfth Night.* | **1600** The Earl of Essex is suspended from some of his offices and confined to house arrest.<br>The birth of James VI's second son, Charles.<br>The founding of the East India Company.<br>Edward Alleyn and Philip Henslowe build the Fortune Theater for the Lord Admiral's Men. |
| **1601** "The Phoenix and Turtle" published in Robert Chester's *Love's Martyr.*<br>In the "War of the Theaters," Ben Jonson, John Marston, and Thomas Dekker write a series of satiric plays mocking one another. | **1601** The Earl of Essex leads a rebellion against the principal adviser to Elizabeth I and possibly against the Queen herself. The previous afternoon, hoping to enlist support, some of the rebels pay for a performance of *Richard II.* Implicated in the uprising, which is quickly quelled, Shakespeare's patron, the Earl of Southampton, is imprisoned. The Earl of Essex is convicted of treason and beheaded, along with several of his chief supporters.<br>Shakespeare's father dies. |
| **1601–02** *Troilus and Cressida.* | **1602** Shakespeare makes substantial real-estate purchases in Stratford.<br>The opening of the Bodleian Library in Oxford. |

| TEXT | CONTEXT |
|---|---|
| **1601–03** *Othello.* | |
| **1603** John Florio's translation of Montaigne's *Essays.*<br>Ben Jonson, *Sejanus*, which lists Shakespeare as one of the actors. | **1603** Queen Elizabeth dies; she is succeeded by her cousin, James VI of Scotland (now James I of England). |
| **1603–04** *Sir Thomas More* (revised version). | Plague closes the London theaters from mid-1603 to April 1604.<br>Hugh O'Neill surrenders in Ireland. |
| **1604** *Measure for Measure.* | **1604** The conclusion of a peace with Spain makes travel across the Atlantic safer, encouraging plans for English colonies in the Americas. |
| **1605** *The History of King Lear.* | **1605** The discovery of the Gunpowder Plot by some radical Catholics to blow up the Houses of Parliament during its opening ceremonies, when the royal family, Lords, and Commons are assembled in one place.<br>The Red Bull Theater built. |
| **1606–07** *Timon of Athens.*<br>*All's Well That Ends Well.*<br>*Macbeth.*<br>*Antony and Cleopatra.*<br>Middleton(?), *The Revenger's Tragedy.* | **1606** The London and Plymouth Companies receive charters to colonize Virginia.<br>Parliament passes "An Act to Restrain Abuses of Players," prohibiting oaths or blasphemy onstage. |
| **1607–08** *Pericles.* | **1607** An English colony is established in Jamestown, Virginia.<br>Shakespeare's daughter Susanna marries John Hall.<br>Shakespeare's brother Edmund (described as a player) dies. |
| **1608** *Coriolanus.* | |
| **1609** *Shakespeare's Sonnets.* | |
| **1610** *Cymbeline.*<br>Ben Jonson, *The Alchemist.* | **1610** Henry is made Prince of Wales.<br>Shakespeare probably returns to Stratford and settles there.<br>The King's Men begin using Blackfriars Theater as a second, indoor venue. |

| TEXT | CONTEXT |
|---|---|
| **1611** *The Winter's Tale.*<br>*The Tempest.*<br>Francis Beaumont and John Fletcher, *A King and No King.*<br>Publication of the Authorized (King James) Bible. | **1611** Plantation of Ulster in Ireland, a colony of English and Scottish Protestants settled on land confiscated from Irish rebels. |
| **1612–13** *Cardenio,* with John Fletcher (not extant).<br>*Henry VIII,* with John Fletcher.<br>John Webster, *The White Devil.* | **1612** Prince Henry dies. |
| **1613–14** *The Two Noble Kinsmen,* with John Fletcher. | **1613** Princess Elizabeth marries Frederick V, Elector Palatine.<br>The Globe Theater burns down during a performance of *Henry VIII.* |
| **1614** Ben Jonson, *Bartholomew Fair.*<br>John Webster, *The Duchess of Malfi.* | **1614** Philip Henslowe and Jacob Meade build the Hope Theater, used both for play performances and as a bearbaiting arena.<br>The Globe Theater reopens. |
| **1616** Ben Jonson publishes his *Works,* including the first collection of plays by a commercial English dramatist. | **1616** William Harvey describes the circulation of the blood.<br>Shakespeare's daughter Judith marries.<br>Shakespeare dies on April 23. |
| **1623** Members of the King's Men publish the First Folio of Shakespeare's plays. | |

# Glossary

## STAGE TERMS

**"above"** The gallery on the upper level of the stage's back wall (see *frons scenae*). In open-air theaters, such as the Globe, this space may have included the lords' rooms. The central section of the gallery was sometimes used by the players for short scenes. Indoor theaters such as Blackfriars featured a curtained alcove for musicians above the stage.

**"aloft"** See *"above."*

**amphitheater** An open-air theater, such as the Globe.

**arras** See *curtain.*

**cellarage** See *trap.*

**chorus** In the works of Shakespeare and other Elizabethan playwrights, a single individual (not, as in Greek tragedy, a group) who speaks before the play (and sometimes before each act or, in *Pericles*, at other times), describing events not shown on stage as well as commenting on the action witnessed by the audience.

**curtain** Curtains, or arras (hanging tapestries), probably covered a part of the stage's back wall (see *frons scenae*), thus concealing the discovery space, and may also have been draped around the edge of the stage to conceal the open area underneath.

**discovery space** A central opening or alcove concealed behind a curtain in the center of the stage's back wall (see *frons scenae*). The curtain could be drawn aside to "discover" tableaux such as Portia's caskets, the body of Polonius, or the statue of Hermione. Shakespeare appears to have used this stage device only sparingly.

**doubling** The common practice of having one actor play multiple roles, so that a play with a large cast of characters might be performed by a relatively small company.

**dumb shows** Mimed scenes performed before a play or as part of the play itself, summarizing or foreshadowing the plot. Dumb shows were popular in early Elizabethan drama; although they already seemed old-fashioned in Shakespeare's time, they were employed by writers up to the 1640s.

**epilogue** A brief speech or poem addressed to the audience by an actor after the play. In some cases, as in *2 Henry IV,* the epilogue could be combined with, or could merge into, the jig.

***frons scenae*** The wall at the back of the stage, behind which lay the players' tiring house. The *frons scenae* of the Globe featured two doors flanking the central discovery space, with a gallery "above."

**gallery** Covered seating area surrounding the open yard of the public amphitheater. There were three levels of galleries at the Globe; admission to these seats cost an extra penny (in addition to the basic admission fee of one penny to the yard), and seating in the higher galleries another penny yet.

**gatherers** Persons employed by the playing company to take money at the entrances to the theater.

**groundlings** Audience members who paid the minimum price of admission (one penny) to stand in the yard of the open-air theaters; also referred to as "understanders." "Groundling" is an unusual word, possibly coined by Shakespeare; it is unclear whether it was in common usage at the time.

**heavens** The canopied roof over the stage in the open-air theaters, protecting the players and their costumes from rain. The "heavens" may have been brightly decorated with sun, moon, and stars, and perhaps the signs of the zodiac.

**jig** A song-and-dance performance by the clown and other members of the company at the conclusion of a play. These performances were frequently bawdy and were officially banned in 1612.

**lords' rooms** Partitioned sections of the gallery above the stage, or just to the left and right of the stage, where the most prestigious and expensive seats in the public playhouses were located. These rooms did not provide the best view of the action on the stage below. They were designed to make their privileged occupants conspicuous to the rest of the audience.

**open-air theaters** Unroofed public playhouses in the suburbs of London, such as The Theatre, the Rose, and the Globe.

**part** The character played by an actor. In Shakespeare's theater, actors were given a roll of paper called a "part" containing all of the speeches and all of the cues belonging to their character. The term "role," synonymous with "part," is derived from such rolls of paper.

**patrons** Important nobles and members of the royal family under whose protection the theatrical companies of London operated; players not in the service of patrons were punishable as vagabonds. The companies were referred to as their patrons' "Men" or "Servants." Thus the company to which Shakespeare belonged for most of his career was first known as the Lord Chamberlain's Servants, then became the King's Men in 1603, when James I became their patron.

**pillars** The "heavens" were supported by two tall painted pillars or posts near the front of the stage. These occasionally played a role in stage action, allowing a character to "hide" while remaining in full view of the audience.

**pit** The area in front of the stage in indoor theaters such as Blackfriars; unlike an open-air playhouse's yard, the pit was designed for a seated audience.

**posts** See *pillars*.

**proscenium** The arch that divides the stage, scenery, and backstage area from the auditorium in many theaters built in and after the eighteenth century. It also separates actors and audiences, potentially creating the so-called fourth wall. The stages on which Shakespeare's plays were first performed had no proscenium.

**repertory** The stock of plays a company had ready for performance at a given time. Companies generally performed a different play each day, often more than a dozen plays in a month and more than thirty in the course of the season.

**role** See *part*.

**sharers** Senior actors holding shares in a joint-stock theatrical company; they paid for costumes, hired hands, and new plays, and they shared profits and losses equally. Shakespeare was not only a longtime "sharer" of the Lord Chamberlain's Men but, from 1599, a "housekeeper," the holder of a one-eighth share in the Globe playhouse.

**tiring house** The players' dressing (attiring) room, a structure located at the back of the stage and connected to the stage by two or more doors in the *frons scenae.*

**trap** A trapdoor near the front of the stage that allowed access to the cellarage beneath and was frequently associated with hell's mouth. Another trapdoor in the heavens opened for the descent of gods to the stage below.

**"within"** The tiring house, from which offstage sound effects such as shouts, drums, and trumpets were produced.

**yard** The central space in open-air theaters such as the Globe, into which the stage projected and in which audience members stood. Admission to the yard in the public theaters cost a penny, the cheapest admission available.

## TEXTUAL TERMS

**aside** See *stage direction.*

**autograph** Text written in the author's own hand. With the possible exception of a few pages of the collaborative play *Sir Thomas More,* no dramatic works or poems written in Shakespeare's hand are known to survive.

**"bad quartos"** A polemical term for a group of Shakespeare quartos that are different from and often demonstrably inferior to other versions of the plays in question as they are found in later quartos or in the First Folio. Some of these texts are very short; others include notable distortions of language. Explanations for the "bad quartos" (or, more neutrally, "short quartos") include the possibility that they were Shakespeare's early drafts, abbreviated scripts prepared for performance under circumstances such as touring, or "memorial reconstructions."

**base text** The early text upon which a modern edition is based, also known as a "control text."

**canonical** Of an author, the writings generally accepted as authentic. In the case of Shakespeare's dramatic works, only two plays that are not among the thirty-six plays contained in the First Folio, *Pericles* and *The Two Noble Kinsmen,* have won widespread acceptance into the Shakespearean canon, but recent scholarship suggests that he wrote parts of a number of others, including *Edward III* and *Sir Thomas More.*

**casting off** The practice of dividing up a manuscript to anticipate the number of pages needed to contain it in print. Errors in casting off sometimes led compositors to crowd lines, abbreviate spellings, and print verse as prose. If on the contrary a compositor found he had too much space remaining, he might leave spaces around stage directions, add ornaments, or break prose up into short "verse" lines.

**catchword** A word printed below the text at the bottom of a page, matching the first word on the following page. The catchword enabled the printer to keep the pages in their proper sequence. Where the catchword fails to match the word at the top of the next page, there is reason to suspect that something has been lost or misplaced.

**collaboration** The practice of two or more writers working together to create a play (or other literature). More than half of the plays in Shakespeare's period were collaborative. Shakespeare collaborated with John Fletcher on *Henry VIII*, *The Two Noble Kinsmen,* and the missing *Cardenio*; with George Wilkins on *Pericles;* and with Thomas Middleton on *Timon of Athens.* Shakespeare plays that probably have sections composed by others include *Titus Andronicus*, *1 Henry VI*, and *Macbeth*; in turn, Shakespeare seems to have contributed a section to *Sir Thomas More.*

**compositor** A person employed in a print shop to set type. To speed the printing process, most of Shakespeare's plays were set by more than one compositor. Compositors were expected to adjust spelling and provide punctuation and can often be identified by their different habits and preferences (e.g., *been/beene* or *O/Oh* and speech prefixes such as *Que./Queene*). They invariably introduced errors into the texts—for instance, by selecting the wrong letter from the type case or by setting the correct letter upside down.

**conflation** A version of a play created by combining readings from more than one substantive text. Since the early eighteenth century, for example, most versions of *King Lear* and of several other plays by Shakespeare have been conflations of quarto and First Folio texts.

**deus ex machina** Literally, "god from a machine," the term can refer to any plot device introduced to resolve a seemingly insurmountable problem.

**dramatis personae (or The Persons of the Play)** A list of the characters that appear in the play. In the First Folio such lists, called "The Names of the Actors," were printed at the end of some but not all of the plays. In 1709 the editor Nicholas Rowe first provided lists of dramatis personae for all of Shakespeare's dramatic works.

**emendation** A correction made in a text by an editor where he or she believes on the basis of evidence and/or inference that it has been corrupted in transmission and needs to be altered for coherence or sense.

**exeunt / exit** See *stage direction.*

**fair copy** A transcript of the "foul papers" made either by a scribe or by the playwright.

**folio** A bookmaking format in which each large sheet of paper is folded once, making two leaves (a leaf is part of a folded sheet of paper with a page on each side). This format produced large volumes, generally handsome and expensive. The First Folio of Shakespeare's plays was printed in 1623.

**forme** A body of type secured in a chase, or wooden frame, ready for printing. The forme would be placed into the press and inked and a sheet of paper lowered onto it for imprinting.

**foul papers** A term for a playwright's working draft of a play, which is presumed to have contained "false starts," blotted-out passages, ghost characters, and revisions. To judge by apparent errors in the printed texts, several of Shakespeare's plays appear to have been printed from foul papers rather than fair copy; however, no clearcut instance of his foul papers survives, though certain pages in the manuscript of *Sir Thomas More* may represent this stage of the writing process.

**ghost characters** Characters named in a stage direction who have no lines during the ensuing action. They may represent a "false start" as the author composed the play, and may not have actually appeared onstage in performance.

**licensing** By an order of 1581, new plays could not be performed until they had received a license from the Master of the Revels. A separate license, granted by the Court of High Commission, was required for publication, though in practice plays were often printed without license. From 1610, the Master of the Revels had the authority to license plays for publication as well as for performance.

**manent / manet** See *stage direction.*

**massed entry** The grouping of all characters who will appear at any point in a scene into a single opening direction. Playwrights such as Ben Jonson preferred this style because of its conformity with classical practice, and it was followed by certain scribes. Modern editors write entry directions to show the point in the scene at which each character enters.

**memorial reconstruction** The theory that some texts may have been reconstructed from memory by one or more actors, either because a promptbook had been destroyed or because it was not available—for example, while touring. It has been proposed that memorial reconstruction might explain the existence of "bad" or inferior quartos of some of Shakespeare's plays, though this is no longer universally accepted.

**octavo** A bookmaking format in which each large sheet of paper is folded three times, making eight leaves (sixteen pages front and back). Only one of Shakespeare's plays, *3 Henry VI* (1595), was published in octavo format.

**playbook** See *promptbook.*

**press variants** Minor textual variations among pages in books of the same edition, resulting from corrections made in the course of printing or from damaged or slipped type.

**promptbook** A manuscript of a play (either foul papers or fair copy) annotated and adapted for performance by the theatrical company. The promptbook incorporated stage directions, notes on properties and special effects, and revisions, sometimes including those required by the Master of the Revels. Promptbooks may be identifiable by the replacement of characters' names with actors' names.

**quarto** A bookmaking format in which each large sheet of paper is folded twice, making four leaves (eight pages front and back). Quarto volumes were smaller and less expensive than books printed in the folio format.

**recto** Literally, the right-hand page; in a quarto volume, each signature consisted of four leaves each of which had a recto and a verso; the pages were then numbered 1r[ecto], 1v[erso], 2r, 2v, 3r, 3v, 4r, 4v.

**scribal copy** A transcript of a play produced by a professional scribe (or "scrivener"). Scribes tended to employ their own preferred spellings, abbreviations, and punctuation and could be responsible for introducing a variety of errors.

**signature** A section of an early book consisting of one group of folded pages (e.g., in a quarto, four leaves or eight pages). Early modern printers indicated each signature by a letter (e.g., A) to assist them in keeping track of the parts of the book to bind together.

**single-text editing** Editing a work by staying as close as possible to a single early authoritative base text, emending only where necessary for sense and without either conflating by incorporating words or passages from other cognate texts or by reconstructing passages from source materials or other forms of inference.

**speech prefix (SP)** The indication of the identity of the speaker of the following line or lines. Early editions of Shakespeare's plays often use different prefixes at different points to designate the same person. On occasion, the name of the actor who was to play the role appears in place of the name of the character.

**stage direction (SD)** The part of the text that is not spoken by any character but that indicates actions to be performed onstage. Stage directions in the earliest editions of Shakespeare's plays are sparse; some necessary directions, most notably exits, are missing, and others may appear earlier or later than the plot requires. Directions for action (e.g., "Pray you, undo this button") may be implied in the dialogue but are not necessarily followed in a given production. By convention, the most basic stage directions were written in Latin. "Exit" indicates the departure of a single actor from the stage, "exeunt" the departure of more than one. "Manet" indicates that a single actor remains onstage, "manent" that more than one remains. Lines accompanied by the stage direction "aside" are spoken so as not to be heard by the others onstage. This stage direction appeared in some early editions of Shakespeare plays, but other means were also used to indicate such speech (such as placing the words within parentheses), and sometimes no indication was provided.

**Stationers' Register** The account books of the Company of Stationers (the guild of printers, publishers, and booksellers that controlled the London book trade), recording the fees paid by publishers to secure their rights to certain texts, as well as the transfer of these rights between publishers. The Stationers' Register thus provides a valuable if incomplete record of publication in England.

**substantive text** The text of an edition based upon access to a manuscript, as opposed to a derivative text based only on an earlier edition.

**typecase** The compartmentalized box in which movable type (metal letters, punctuation, etc.) was stored; capital, or "upper-case," letters were traditionally stored at the top of the typecase, "lower-case" letters at the bottom. Compositors drew individual type from the typecase for placing into a "compositor's stick" that held one line of type; from there the type would be transferred to a chase and secured to create a forme. Mistakes in sorting used type back into the typecase may account for some textual errors.

**variorum editions** Comprehensive editions of a work or works in which the various views of previous editors and commentators are compiled.

**verso** See *recto*

# Essential Reference Books


Bate, Jonathan, and Russell Jackson, eds. *Shakespeare: An Illustrated Stage History.* New York: Oxford UP, 1996.

Bullough, Geoffrey, ed. *Narrative and Dramatic Sources of Shakespeare.* 8 vols. New York: Columbia UP, 1957–75.

Chambers, E. K. *The Elizabethan Stage.* 4 vols. Oxford: Clarendon, 1923.

———. *William Shakespeare: A Study of Facts and Problems.* 2 vols. Oxford: Clarendon, 1930.

Crystal, David. *Pronouncing Shakespeare: The Globe Experiment.* Cambridge: Cambridge UP, 2005.

Dent, R. W. *Shakespeare's Proverbial Language: An Index.* Berkeley: U of California P, 1981.

Dessen, Alan C., and Leslie Thomson. *A Dictionary of Stage Directions in English Drama, 1580–1642.* New York: Cambridge UP, 1999.

Dobson, E. J. *English Pronunciation, 1500–1700.* 2nd ed. 2 vols. Oxford: Clarendon, 1968.

Dobson, Michael, and Stanley Wells, eds. *The Oxford Companion to Shakespeare.* Oxford: Oxford UP, 2001.

Duffin, Ross W. *Shakespeare's Songbook.* New York: Norton, 2004.

Foakes, R. A. *Illustrations of the English Stage, 1580–1642.* Stanford: Stanford UP, 1985.

Greenblatt, Stephen, and Peter G. Platt, eds. *Shakespeare's Montaigne: The Florio Translation of the Essays, a Selection.* New York: New York Review Books, 2014.

Greg, W. W., ed. *Dramatic Documents from the Elizabethan Playhouses: Stage Plots: Actors' Parts: Prompt Books.* 2 vols. Oxford: Clarendon, 1931.

Gurr, Andrew. *Playgoing in Shakespeare's London.* 3rd ed. New York: Cambridge UP, 2004.

———. *The Shakespearean Stage, 1574–1642.* 4th ed. New York: Cambridge UP, 2009.

Henslowe, Philip. *Henslowe's Diary.* Ed. R. A. Foakes. 2nd ed. New York: Cambridge UP, 2002.

Hosley, Richard, ed. *Shakespeare's Holinshed: An Edition of Holinshed's Chronicles, 1587.* New York: Putnam, 1968.

Murphy, Andrew. *Shakespeare in Print: A History and Chronology of Shakespeare Publishing.* New York: Cambridge UP, 2003.

*Oxford Dictionary of National Biography.* Oxford: Oxford UP, 2004. www.oxforddnb.com/

*Oxford English Dictionary.* Oxford: Clarendon, 1989. www.oed.com/

Partridge, A. C. *Orthography in Shakespeare and Elizabethan Drama.* London: E. Arnold, 1964.

Partridge, Eric. *Shakespeare's Bawdy: A Literary and Psychological Essay and a Comprehensive Glossary.* 3rd ed. New York: Routledge, 2001.

Schoenbaum, Samuel. *William Shakespeare: A Documentary Life.* New York: Oxford UP, 1975.

Spevack, Marvin. *A Complete and Systematic Concordance to the Works of Shakespeare.* 9 vols. Hildesheim: George Olms, 1968–80.

Stern, Tiffany. *Documents of Performance in Early Modern England.* Cambridge: Cambridge UP, 2009

Tilley, Morris Palmer. *A Dictionary of the Proverbs in England in the Sixteenth and Seventeenth Centuries.* Ann Arbor: U of Michigan P, 1950.

Wells, Stanley. *A Dictionary of Shakespeare.* 2nd ed. New York: Oxford UP, 2005.

———. *Re-Editing Shakespeare for the Modern Reader.* New York: Oxford UP, 1984.

Wickham, Glynne. *Early English Stages, 1300 to 1660.* 4 vols. New York: Routledge, 2002.

Williams, Gordon. *A Dictionary of Sexual Language and Imagery in Shakespearean and Stuart Literature.* 3 vols. London: Athlone, 1994.

For a much fuller bibliography, including critical and historical works bearing on the study of Shakespeare, see the Digital Edition of *The Norton Shakespeare.*

# ILLUSTRATION ACKNOWLEDGMENTS

**General Introduction:** **3** By permission of The Folger Shakespeare Library; **9** Spencer Collection, The New York Public Library, Astor, Lenox, and Tilden Foundations / Art Resource, NY; **13** By permission of The Huntington Library, San Marino, CA; **15** By permission of The Folger Shakespeare Library; **17** By permission of the National Museum of Wales; **20** Woburn Abbey, Bedfordshire, UK / Bridgeman Images; **23** By permission of The Huntington Library, San Marino, CA; **24** By permission of the Houghton Library, Harvard University; **26** Library of Congress, Rare Book and Special Collections Division; **27** © British Library Board / Robana / Art Resource, NY; **28** By permission of the Trustees of Dulwich Picture Gallery; **29** © Fitzwilliam Museum Cambridge / Art Resource, NY; **30** Bodleian Library, University of Oxford, 4 G.17 Art; **33** © British Library Board / Robana / Art Resource, NY; **35** Erich Lessing / Art Resource, NY; **37** By permission of the Pepys Library, Magdalene College, Cambridge; **38** By permission of the Huntington Library, San Marino, CA; **43** liszt collection / Alamy; **46** Library of Congress, Prints and Photographs Division; **47** Tate, London / Art Resource, NY; **57** By permission of the Trustees of Dulwich Picture Gallery; **58** By permission of the Huntington Library, San Marino, CA.

**General Textual Introduction:** **79** By permission of the Folger Shakespeare Library; **80** By permission of the Folger Shakespeare Library; **81** By permission of the Folger Shakespeare Library; **82** The British Library; **83** *The Norton Facsimile of the First Folio of Shakespeare*; **86** By permission of the British Library; **89 top** *The Norton Facsimile of the First Folio of Shakespeare*; **89 bottom** *The Norton Facsimile of the First Folio of Shakespeare*; **90** Oxford University Press.

**The Theater in Shakespeare's Time:** **95** By permission of the British Library; **96** © Museum of London; **98** Museum of London Archaeology / Getty Images; **102–03** London Metropolitan Archives, City of London; **108** © British Library Board / Robana / Art Resource, NY; **109** © Dulwich Picture Gallery, London UK / Bridgeman Images; **111** *The Norton Facsimile of the First Folio of Shakespeare*; **112** Dulwich College MSS 1, Article 138; **113** University Library, Utrecht, MS 842, f.132; **114** Courtesy of the International Shakespeare Globe Center Ltd. Photo: John Tramper; **115** Courtesy of the International Shakespeare Globe Center Ltd. Photo: Richard Kalina; **116** Photographic Survey, The Courtauld Institute of Art, London. Private collection; **117** MOLA / Getty Images.

**Shakespearean Romance:** **125** By permission of the Fine Arts Museums of San Francisco; **130** Scala / Art Resource, NY; **131** Alinar / Art Resource, NY; **133** Library of Congress, Geography, and Map Division, Washington D.C.; **134** F&A Archive The Art Archive at Art Resource, NY.

**Pericles:** **140** © British Library Board / Robana / Art Resource, NY; **142** HIP / Art Resource, NY.

**Cymbeline:** **210 and 212** © The Trustees of the British Museum / Art Resource, NY **214** Duke University Libraries.

**The Winter's Tale:** **304** (1656), Jan van Bronckhorst, Royal Palace Amsterdam; **309** By permission of the Folger Shakespeare Library; **310** By permission of the Pepys Library, Magdalene College, Cambridge.

**The Tempest:** **388** Reproduced by permission of The Huntington Library, San Marino, CA; **390** Courtesy of The John Carter Brown Library at Brown University; **392** Private Collection, The Stapleton Collection / Bridgeman Images.

**The Two Noble Kinsmen:** **454** Österreichische Nationalbibliothek, Vienna; **455** © British Library Board / Robana / Art Resource, NY.

**Venus and Adonis:** **540** By permission of the Houghton Library, Harvard University; **542** © The Trustees of the British Museum / Art Resource, NY; **543** By permission of the Folger Shakespeare Library.

**The Rape of Lucrece:** **576** Image copyright © The Metropolitan Museum of Art. Image source: Art Resource, NY; **578** © Fitzwilliam Museum, Cambridge / Art Resource, NY. **579** Rare Books and Manuscripts Division, The New York Public Library, Astor, Lenox and Tilden Foundations / Art Resource, NY.

**The Sonnets:** **651** By permission of the Folger Shakespeare Library.

**Maps:** The Holy Land–National Library of Scotland; London, 1574 (*digital only*)—HIP / Art Resource NY; "The Kingdome of Great Britain and Ireland" (*digital only*)—HIP / Art Resource, NY.

# Index of Poems: Titles and First Lines

# The House of Lancaster

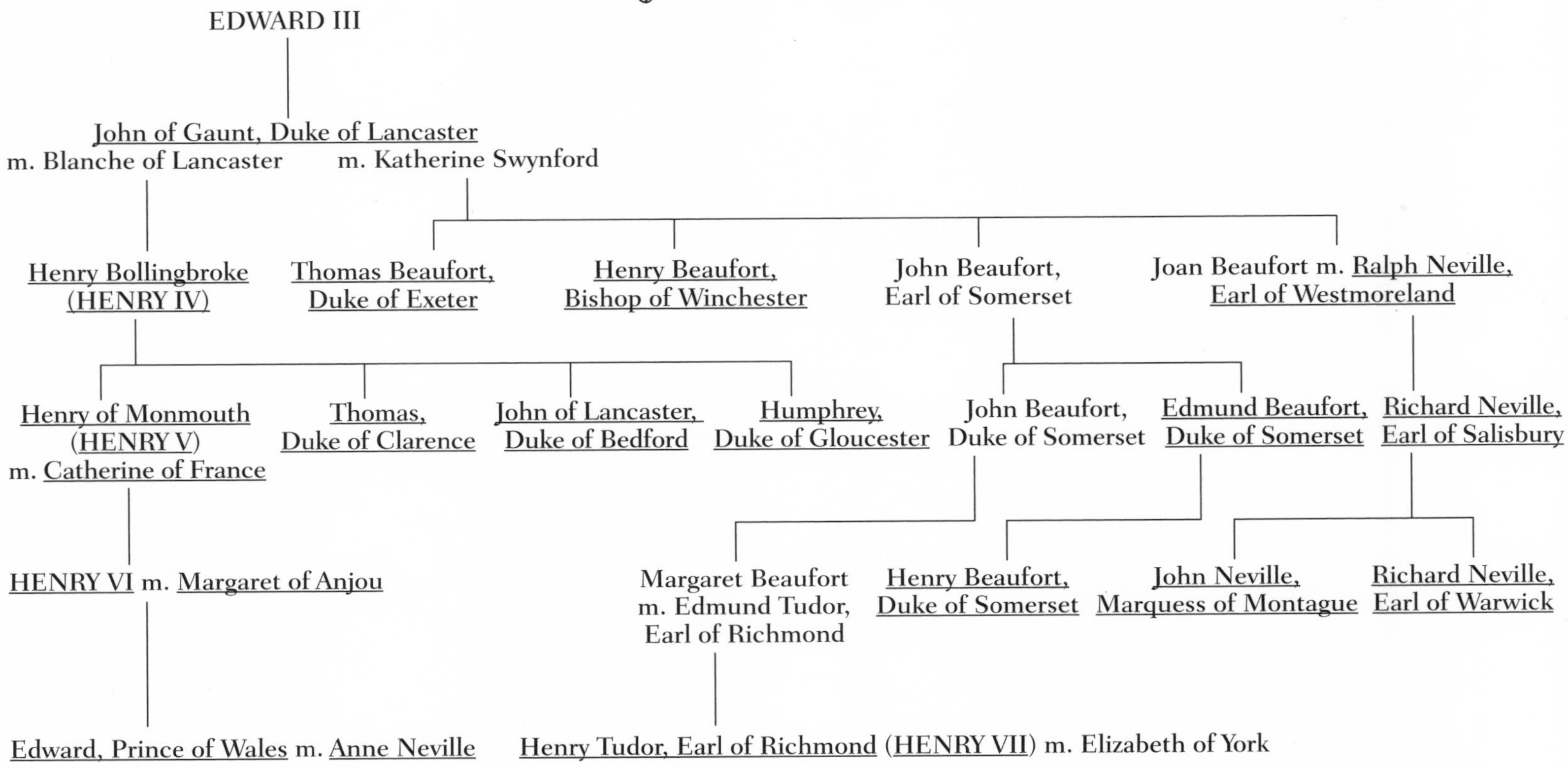

EDWARD III
John of Gaunt, Duke of Lancaster
m. Blanche of Lancaster
m. Katherine Swynford
Henry Bollingbroke (HENRY IV)
Thomas Beaufort, Duke of Exeter
Henry Beaufort, Bishop of Winchester
John Beaufort, Earl of Somerset
Joan Beaufort m. Ralph Neville, Earl of Westmoreland
Henry of Monmouth (HENRY V) m. Catherine of France
Thomas, Duke of Clarence
John of Lancaster, Duke of Bedford
Humphrey, Duke of Gloucester
John Beaufort, Duke of Somerset
Edmund Beaufort, Duke of Somerset
Richard Neville, Earl of Salisbury
HENRY VI m. Margaret of Anjou
Margaret Beaufort m. Edmund Tudor, Earl of Richmond
Henry Beaufort, Duke of Somerset
John Neville, Marquess of Montague
Richard Neville, Earl of Warwick
Edward, Prince of Wales m. Anne Neville
Henry Tudor, Earl of Richmond (HENRY VII) m. Elizabeth of York

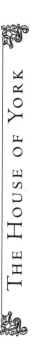

# The House of York

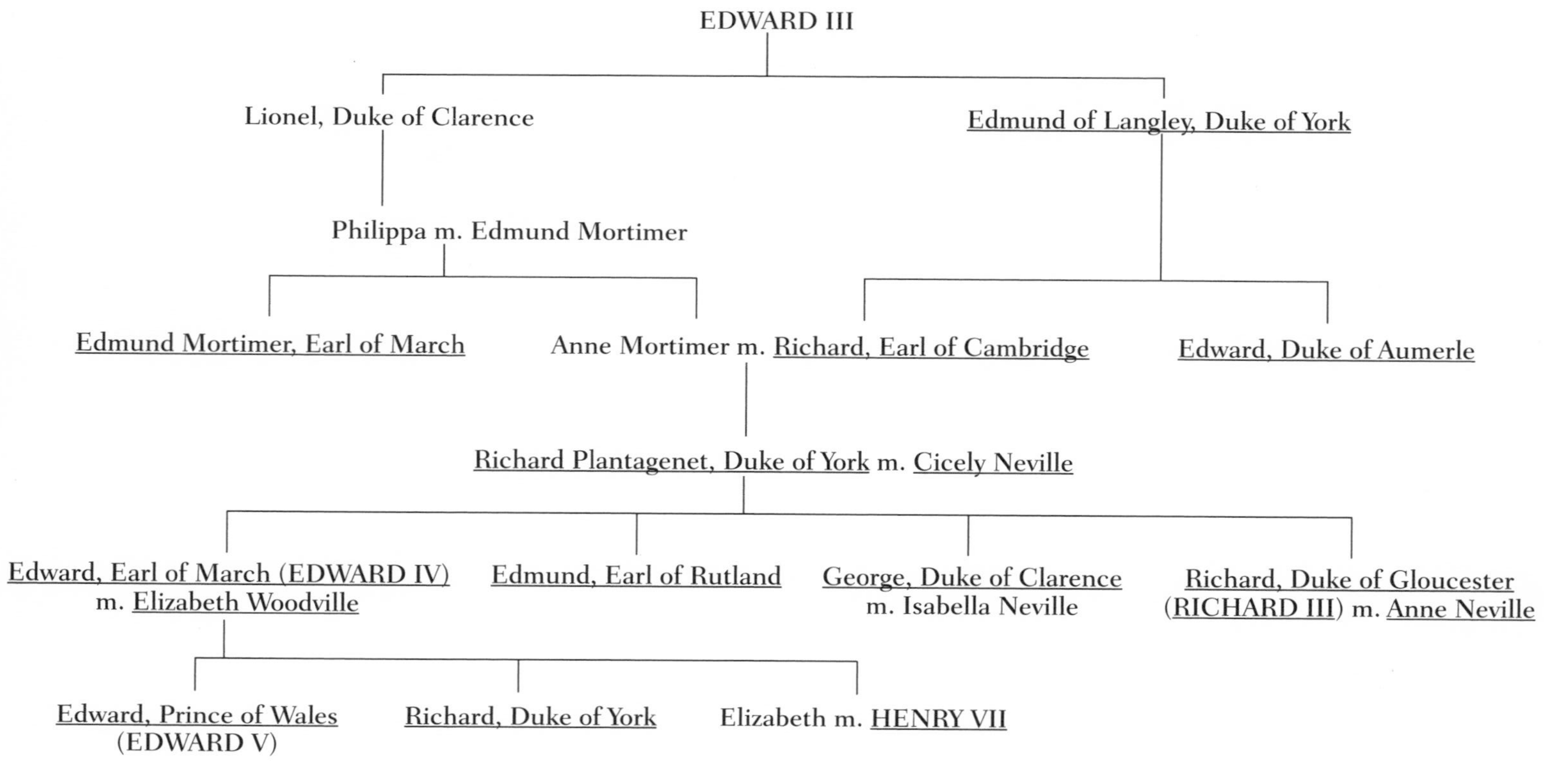